ROMAN PRIVATE LAW

IN THE TIMES OF CICERO AND OF THE ANTONINES

by

HENRY JOHN ROBY

M.A., Hon. LL.D. Cantab., Hon. LL.D. Edinb.,
Honorary Fellow of St John's College, Cambridge

Volume I

THE LAWBOOK EXCHANGE, LTD.

UNION, NEW JERSEY

2000

ISBN 1-58477-074-0

Printed in the United States of America
on Acid-Free Paper

The Lawbook Exchange, Ltd.
965 Jefferson Avenue
Union, New Jersey 07083-8605

Please see catalogue at rear of this volume
or our website http://www.lawbookexchange.com
for a selection of our other reprints.

Library of Congress Cataloging-in-Publication Data

Roby, Henry John, 1830-1915.
Roman private law in the times of Cicero and of the Antonines / by Henry John Roby.
v. ; cm.
Originally published: Cambridge: Cambridge University Press, 1902.
Includes bibliographical references and index.
ISBN 1-58477-074-0 (cloth : alk. paper)
1. Roman law—History. I. Title.

KJA147 .R63 2000
340.5'4'09—dc21 99-059270

ROMAN PRIVATE LAW

IN THE TIMES OF CICERO AND OF THE ANTONINES

In two Volumes,
Vol. I

Introduction.
Book I. Citizenship and *Status*.
Book II. Family.
Book III. Inheritance.
Essay on *Cretio*.
Book IV. Property.
Essay on *Recipere*.

London: C. J. CLAY AND SONS,
CAMBRIDGE UNIVERSITY PRESS WAREHOUSE,
AVE MARIA LANE,
AND
STEVENS AND SONS, LTD,
119 AND 120, CHANCERY LANE.

Glasgow: 50, WELLINGTON STREET.
Leipzig: F. A. BROCKHAUS.
New York: THE MACMILLAN COMPANY.
Bombay and Calcutta: MACMILLAN AND CO., LTD.

ROMAN PRIVATE LAW

IN THE TIMES OF CICERO AND OF THE ANTONINES

by

HENRY JOHN ROBY

M.A., Hon. LL.D. Cantab., Hon. LL.D. Edinb.,
Honorary Fellow of St John's College, Cambridge

Volume I

Cambridge:
at the University Press
1902

Cambridge:
PRINTED BY J. & C. F. CLAY,
AT THE UNIVERSITY PRESS.

PREFACE.

ROMAN law has formed and to a large extent still forms the substance of much of the law of modern Europe, and indeed of the civilised world generally. Its authentic source is the legislation of Justinian, Roman Emperor at Constantinople from A.D. 527 to 565. The principal part of this legislation was (1) the Digest, *i.e.* a selection of extracts from the writings of the Roman Jurists, nearly all of the period of about A.D. 100 to 230; (2) the Code, *i.e.* a selection of laws and decisions of the Emperors, the earliest constitution being one of Hadrian's, and only about a score being earlier than Severus, many being from Justinian himself; (3) the Institutes, *i.e.* an elementary treatise, largely founded on Gaius' Institutes. These three books, Digest, Code (revised edition), Institutes, were published in the years A.D. 533 and 534. A number of laws were issued by Justinian during the remainder of his life, but principally before A.D. 545 when his great minister Tribonian died. These are called Novels (*Novellae Constitutiones*). Some few contain important modifications of Private Law.

It is the law as consolidated and enacted by Justinian which (with or without adaptation to modern times and particular countries) forms the subject of most treatises on Roman Law. But this was not the law known and practised in the times with which students of Classical Rome are chiefly concerned, times distant from Justinian three to six centuries. To the law as altered by Justinian I make little reference in the following pages. My aim is to exhibit a summary of classical Roman Private Law as it stood long before Constantinople existed, when Rome was still the capital of the world. But the task has difficulties which greatly impede its due execution. A good deal of detail is necessary in order to make the scope and limitations of law properly intelligible: and in order to find material for a detailed account we have to come to a later period than one would otherwise have been disposed to select. It is not until the middle of the second century of our era that we can find a single lawbook on which to base the narrative, and for adequate detail we have to resort to Justinian's compilations. For law in the Roman Republic before Cicero we have no trustworthy source of information: for the time of Cicero himself we have hardly anything beyond scattered allusions in his writings and a few speeches in private suits. For the early empire we have only meagre references in general histories. It was the discovery of Gaius' Institutes, 80 years ago, which first made it fairly practicable to give a connected account of Roman private law within or approaching to the classical period.

But though Gaius affords a trustworthy basis, he does not carry us far. Partly from the small scale of the work itself and partly from its imperfect preservation we have many gaps, some only of which are supplied by the scanty relics which we have received directly of other ante-Justinian lawyers. Justinian's Digest gives ample extracts, except on some parts of procedure, from the books of the great jurists of the times of Hadrian and the Antonines: but, before any use is made of them for such a purpose as mine, one has to ask how far they represent the law of Rome in the second or third century after Christ, as well as that of Byzantium in the sixth. It is not only that they omit much that would be interesting to a classical student or historian, though (what seems often forgotten) mere omission may alter substantially the import of what is left. But the truth is, Julian, Gaius, Papinian, Ulpian, Paul and others have sometimes no doubt written what appears in the Digest under their names, but sometimes also they have written what was different or even contrary: indeed often, perhaps usually, what they wrote was an account of the law with qualifications and doubts and suggestions, which Tribonian and his colleagues have omitted, abridged, twisted and altered[1]. I have given specimens of this treatment in my *Introduction to Justinian's Digest* by a comparison of some extracts from the lawyers which we happen to have received from other sources with the same passages as they appear, edited under Justinian's authority, in the Digest. Recent discussion in Germany has been busy with this question and often with good fruit. On the other hand it seems to me often very inconsistent. While with one eye it detects Tribonian's interpolations everywhere, with the other it attempts to trace the opinions of the individual lawyers and the history of doctrines and procedure, as if we had in the Digest the jurisprudence of two hundred and fifty years adequately represented and faithfully exhibited. Such an exhibition was as far as possible from being in Tribonian's intentions or compatible with his method of work[2]. Needless to say, I have tried to bear in mind the real state of the case. For it is impossible to avoid drawing largely[3] of the waters of the Digest, however suspicious one may justly feel of their being tainted. Justinian's great work in consolidating and amending Roman law was absolutely necessary, if it was to take the place it has taken in the usage of European nations, but his books are full of pitfalls for the student of earlier law. *Incedo per ignes suppositos cineri doloso.*

The alterations made by Justinian in the extracts forming the Digest and in the earlier constitutions of the Code may perhaps be classed under three heads; omission of antiquated law, decision of disputed points, independent improvement[4]. The Byzantine Emperor was not a man to refrain from proclaiming his own merits, and therefore on many matters under each of these heads, we have information given us in his Constitutions and Institutes which, in order to explain and glorify his amendments, shews the main lines and some of the details of

[1] *E.g.* compare *Collat.* xii 7 with D. ix 2 fr 27; Gai. i 98 sqq. with D. i 2; ii 86 sqq. with D. xli 1 fr 10; and Vat. 77—80, 83 with D. vii 2 fr 1, 3.

[2] See my *Introduction to Justinian's Digest*, chapp. iv, v.

[3] *Expertus loquor.* My first draft was made almost entirely from ante-Justinian sources.

[4] Cf. Const. *Deo auctore* §§ 2, 7, 8; *Tanta* §§ 10, 15; *Cordi* §§ 1, 4.

the earlier law. This is probably the case with the principal matters under the third head, though minor improvements may have been silently introduced. As regards the second head we may console ourselves with the belief that in taking law from the Digest we are getting the view, though perhaps not unmodified, of *some* leading jurists of Antonine times. The first head raises more serious difficulty. What was practically obsolete in Justinian's time, or required little beyond a stroke of the pen to remove, was omitted by Tribonian or his colleagues with little or no notice. The abolition or obsolescence of both the statutable and the formular procedure, of *mancipatio* and *in jure cessio*, of *conventio in manum*, of *cretio*, of the different modes of bequest, of the distinction between *legatum* and *fideicommissum*, of *litterarum obligatio*, of *sponsores* and *fiducia*, of *cognitores*, of the *lex Cincia* and *lex Julia* and *Poppaea, etc.* must have removed or obscured a multitude of distinctions and niceties which it is impossible now rightly to reproduce. Whenever any of these matters come in, one is bound to exercise circumspection and reserve. Gaius' *Institutes*, Ulpian's *Rules*, Paul's *Opinions*[1] (so far as they have come to us independently of the Digest), the Vatican *Fragments*, and other minor relics of Antonine law are then our only pure or relatively pure[2] source of information and warning against Byzantine alterations. But the information to be obtained from these survivals is often very meagre[3], and on some matters fails us altogether, so that, whether we like it or not, for the great mass of the detail the Digest is our only resort.

By careful examination of the language of Justinian and of the Digest-jurists, Lenel, Gradenwitz, A. Pernice, Eisele and others have shewn the high probability, if not certainty, of interpolation in many extracts from the jurists. In the course of time probably still more will be done in this direction. Meantime I have usually avoided relying on clearly questionable

1 These books I have referred to simply by the authors' names.

2 Even Ulpian's *Regulae* and Paul's *Sententiae* in the form known to us are only abridgments of the originals.

3 *E.g.* the law of obligations forms only one-sixth of Gaius' Institutes, and even this is very unequally distributed.

extracts, and have sometimes thought it better to omit a point altogether than to run the risk of giving Justinian's amendments instead of Antonine law.

The principal matter then of this book is the private law of Rome, shorn no doubt of some refinements and special details, and containing, I fear, some Byzantine modifications, but substantially as it stood at the time of its highest development, or at least of the development best known to us; *i.e.* towards and after the close of the second century of our era: or, to speak more precisely, in the period from Marcus Aurelius, emperor from A.D. 161, under whom Gaius' Institutes were principally written, to (say) the murder of Ulpian A.D. 228 or the death of Paul perhaps a few years later. Of the books quoted in the Digest few indeed were written after the death of Caracalla in A.D. 217, to whose reign are referred the above-named books of Ulpian and Paul. The law was altered in some points during the period I have described, especially by Marcus Aurelius and Sept. Severus, but, after that, probably remained much the same until Diocletian. I have occasionally made use of constitutions and extracts later than Ulpian and Paul, when they seemed to be only declaratory.

A good deal of this law, one fondly believes (the belief is doubly hazardous when the statements rest only on the Digest), applies also to the time of Cicero, whose earliest preserved speech was made in 81 B.C., and who was killed in 43 B.C. But in the course of two and a half or three centuries the law as a whole must have come to assume a different aspect from that which was familiar to him[1]. Many doctrines which in his time were probably unsettled and tentative were developed and fixed by the discussions of the Jurists, the action of the Praetors and the rescripts of the emperors. Legislation such as the *leges Juliae* of various subject-matter, the *lex Papia Poppaea*, *lex Aelia Sentia*, and numerous *Senatus consulta*, especially under Hadrian and the Antonines had much indirect

[1] There is about the same distance of time between Coke's Institutes (1628) and our own day; but I do not imagine the law and legal procedure at Rome were nearly so much changed in this period as English law and practice have been by statute and the development of equity.

influence as well as direct effect. In Cicero's time the character and authority of the Courts were still fluctuating: law was still struggling amid religious ceremonies and sanctions, old practices, political prejudices, and personal favour and caprice[1]: equity had not yet won complete victory over the rigid forms and meagre conceptions of early law. If this is true of the last century of the republic, it is still more true of the times before. I admire the enterprise and ingenuity with which some learned German writers have by a combination of isolated facts and statements (some, I fear, from the age, character and purpose of their authors—lay historians, grammarians, anecdote-mongers—little fitted to bear such weight of inference) endeavoured to fix what was in growth or flux, and to determine out of many possibilities what was the law in early periods[2]. But for my own part I have neither the ability to see in the dark or make bricks without straw, nor yet that happy temperament, which seems often to accompany a fine gift of conjectural inference and makes the enthusiast pleased with the superstructure in proportion to the insufficiency of foundation. All that appears to me possible, at least in a book of this character and size, is to add to the summary of Antonine law such references to Cicero and some other writers, as may shew or suggest the existence of particular doctrines or institutes in previous times, especially towards the close of the republic and beginning of the Empire. I exclude as a rule matters of constitutional and criminal law and procedure; I refer but little to the times before Cicero[3], as I refer little to times after

[1] Cf. *e.g.* Cic. *Flac.* 3 § 6.

[2] Notwithstanding Moritz Voigt's great learning and elaborate industry I regard his 'Law of the XII Tables' as a house of cards. And what is to be said of a reconstructor of ancient law who can imagine that *actio noxiae nocitae* ('action for past harm') and *noxiae nocendae* ('for future harm') are Latin phrases? Or that a Roman could take a wife with a formula '*Hunc* (!) *ego hominem ex jure Quiritium uxorem meam esse aio*'? (*Die* XII *Tafeln* ii pp. 329, 700).

[3] I cannot but give some quotations from Plautus, but a comic playwriter, working on Greek originals, is scarcely a trustworthy authority for Roman law. See however Bekker's thoughtful discussion in *ZRG.* xxvi pp. 99—108.

the Antonines; and I omit or pass lightly over things which do not allow of simple statement but only of bottomless controversy. I have gladly discussed at some length the four speeches of Cicero which turn on private law, documents of special value and interest for my purpose, because they exhibit Roman law in life and action instead of in abstract exposition. Some other appendices deal with points where fuller treatment was required than a note could well contain. That on *litterarum obligatio* sets forth a simpler view than has been generally taken[1]. That on *nexum* gives the result of the facts and statements known to us with the minimum of imaginative hypothesis. Two others deal with certain passages of Cicero which have been misunderstood by some interpreters and throw light on general questions.

My account even of Antonine law does not profess to be exhaustive, and the degree and amount of detail which should be given cannot but be somewhat arbitrary. Persons used to German *Pandekten* (and who that takes an interest in Roman law has not occasion to use them and cause to be grateful?) may miss the collection of principles and practice common to many parts of the law which forms the General Part[2] of such books. The truth is, I have been unwilling to add to the inherent difficulties of my task by entering on an analysis which can hardly, I think, be successfully performed, and is alien to the practice of the Roman lawyers. They were not philosophers but thoughtful examiners of particular cases. They argued from concrete to concrete; they rested on analogy, not on abstractions; their method was that of Type, not of Definitions. The Digest and Code are not scientific treatises on law, but ordered collections of decisions, with more or less reasoning,

[1] Of this essay and those on Cicero's four speeches I distributed some copies privately in Jan. 1902. I have made some few corrections since.

[2] Alf. Pernice's *Labeo*, which was to give a 'System of Roman law in the first century of the Empire under the Claudian and Flavian houses' (Pref. to vol. i 1872), has not yet arrived at the end of the General part. Am I wrong in thinking that this heroic attempt has failed from the insufficiency of the material for such a task and its unsuitableness for Pernice's analytical treatment? (Since writing this I regret to see that Pernice died in Sept. 1901.)

on the acts and position, real or assumed, of certain classes of persons in family or business relations. Such generalizations as we find are but little removed from particular facts, are applicable to very limited spheres, are often inconsistent, and may be subject to many exceptions. A German Pandektist writes under the control of two special considerations; first, that Justinian's compilations are, or were till recently, in his country to a large extent binding law; and secondly, that he has to deal with modern society and to adjust Paul and Ulpian to scientific methods and present needs. In England[1] at the present day Roman law is interesting but not practical; instructive and suggestive but not obligatory; if it appear at all in the Courts, it wears a cloistered and apologetic air; it is foreign, historical, antiquarian. And such a description being still more applicable to the law of the Antonines than it is to that of Justinian, I have felt myself neither entitled nor tempted either to pour the old wine into new bottles and import modern abstractions into the Roman forum, or to omit matters of law or procedure which are alien from modern usage, but may serve to shew the mode in which the Roman jurists applied their stock of remedies to the wrongs and perplexities of private life. For instance, the acts and position of slaves gave occasion for much subtle and rational treatment which a student of legal history cannot ignore. I have too sometimes preserved language and illustrations which exhibit the difference of that world from ours, or perhaps an interesting similarity.

But further I may point out that the use of the Digest for my purpose is under different conditions from its use, for the purposes of law, by anyone writing in a country where Justinian's collections are received as law. The jurists whose works were pillaged by Tribonian did not write as members of a commission, engaged in a common task and adjusting their language and conceptions to a prearranged scheme. Most, if

[1] In Scotland Roman law has more significance, as an English reader of *Rob Roy* is reminded by such words as Baillie Jarvie's "Ye'll mind it's a bail *judicio sisti*, not *judicatum solvi*; for there's muckle difference" (Chap. xxii). In cases respecting easements, Roman law is occasionally referred to by English judges, as if entitled to some (moral) authority.

not all, had indeed some official place or recognition, but they ought not to be regarded as what Justinian made them, joint contributors to an imperial authoritative law-book, but as each writing his own book in his own way and expressing only his own view of the practical law in a somewhat conversational style. Unfortunately we have only fragments of their books, and these fragments selected for a different purpose from that of the authors; and their language, even apart from possible alteration by the compilers, seems to me hardly adapted, as it was not intended, to bear the pressure often used to make it support or refute modern theories.

I may here repeat what I have said on another occasion[1] respecting the retention or translation into English of Roman legal terms. I quite admit that sometimes the nature of the argument makes it necessary, or at least convenient, to retain them, and that for some expressions it is not easy to find a tolerable English equivalent. But except in these two cases, I see no ground for a pedantic retention, which makes the subject difficult for a student to comprehend, and is repulsive in point of style. No doubt the sphere of conception denoted by *heres* differs from that denoted by *heir* (even in popular language), just as a Roman *rex* differed from an English 'king' and a Roman *liber* from a modern 'book.' But the question really is whether the analogy is sufficient to form a basis for raising the new conception, and whether the conception when raised is kept purer from misleading admixture by using in English discourse a Latin term. I can understand the reluctance a precise writer may feel to translate ἀρετή by 'virtue' or *delictum* by 'tort.' But it seems to be overlooked that here comes in a psychological difficulty. The student does not in either case leave the English word out of account. He can hardly dispense with the associations which vivify and clothe the bald conception. What he does is to start with the English notion and gradually correct it, strip off some constituents and engraft others; and this he does whether the author uses ἀρετή or 'virtue,' *delictum* or 'tort,' *heres* or 'heir.' The difference is only this: if 'virtue'

[1] *Academy*, 29 May, 1886.

is used, he is, as it were, on the ground at once and can begin his building or modifying; if ἀρετή is used, he first translates into 'virtue' and then proceeds as before. In a comparison of the law or philosophy of one country or system with that of another it may be convenient to use throughout their respective technical terms, but in an ordinary treatise on Roman law I cannot see what is gained by talking of *aditio hereditatis, servus legatus, legatum, exceptio quod metus causa, etc.*; and accordingly I have preferred, as I am writing for English students, to use English words where I can do so without misleading my readers.

So much depends on Gaius' Institutes in such inquiries as mine, that it may be well to recount briefly the history of our knowledge of them[1]. The book was probably written at the end of Antoninus Pius' and beginning of Marcus Aurelius' reign. Nothing is known of the author's life or position, not even his full name[2]. He appears not to have been a jurisconsult, but was perhaps a professor of law at Rome, or, as some have thought, in Asia, and certainly an able expositor. He speaks of himself as belonging to the Sabinian School of Jurists[3]. A considerable number of extracts from his writings (one as late as A.D. 178) are found in the Digest and have often seemed specially suitable for my use in this book[4]. The manuscript of the Institutes was first discovered by Niebuhr in the Chapter Library of Verona in 1816[5]. It is written in uncial characters, probably of the fifth century, with many contractions, and it is a palimpsest, *i.e.* the parchment has been scraped to enable a treatise of St Jerome's to be written on it; and Gaius is difficult to decipher under the later writing. Indeed, about a fourth of the MS. has had two writings over

1 See Studemund's Preface to his and Krüger's edition; and Krüger's *Geschichte* § 30.

2 For examination and refutation of recent attempts to identify him with Gaius Cassius Longinus see Herzen in *ZRG.* xxxiii p. 211.

3 See below, p. 15, and more fully in my *Introduction to Justinian's Digest*, chap. ix.

4 *E.g.* fr 72—81 *ad legem Falcidiam* (D. xxxv 2).

5 Niebuhr's interesting account of his discovery will be found in Savigny's *Verm. Schr.* iii 155 sq.

Gaius. The first printed edition by Göschen appeared in 1820. Some additional readings were got by Bluhme in 1822–3 and were used in Göschen's second edition (1824). Wilhelm Studemund in 1866–68 made a fresh copy of the MS. containing much that had not been previously read, and he published a kind of *facsimile* in 1874, and in conjunction with Paul Krüger a very careful and convenient edition in 1877[1]. In 1878 and 1883 Studemund re-examined the MS. and thus obtained additions and corrections of some importance, which were published in subsequent editions of his and P. Krüger's book. The editors note the fact (full of warning for other cases also) that few of the many supplements produced by ingenious conjecture of P. E. Huschke, of themselves and others were confirmed, and that many were disproved by the re-examination. The MS. looks to me now in a very hopeless state, due in some degree to Bluhme's, perhaps also to Studemund's, application of chemicals to revive the earlier writing. At any rate he must have wonderful sight and skill, who can now read what Studemund (*'oculatissumus ille'*) failed to make out. Previously to Niebuhr's discovery, one leaf containing iv 134—144, not palimpsest, had been separated from the MS., and was read and published in 1732 and again in 1816. Excepting this single leaf and a few fragments in the Digest, an Epitome[2], made probably in the fifth century, was all that was known of the Institutes, but we now see how largely the book was used as the (avowed) basis of Justinian's Institutes (cf. Just. *Praef.* § 6). In reading modern treatises it is well to bear in mind the dates 1874 when Studemund's new readings were first fully[3] published, and 1884 when the

[1] A very complete and handy edition of Studemund's text with the various readings and conjectures of editors of Gaius up to date was made by E. Dubois and published in 1881 (Paris).

[2] Some passages of the Epitome are quoted by Krüger in the notes to Gaius, where Gaius' own text is mutilated. The whole Epitome is in the Bonn *Corpus Jur. Antejustin.* vol. i Pt. 2.

[3] A few of the new readings were made known by Studemund in an address to a conference of Philologists at Wurzburg in 1868, the address being published in 1869. Krüger also gave some in his *Krit. Versuche*, pp. 13, 84, 113 sq. (1870).

results of his re-examination were issued. A good many theories have been founded on, or supported by, supposed words of Gaius which were not his at all[1]. With the exception of naïve etymologies[2] and a few casual remarks I have embodied in this book all Gaius' Institutes, sometimes closely translated.

I have written throughout from the original sources. Any special obligations to modern writers I have gladly acknowledged in their place. But I cannot omit here to record my deep sense of the most skilful and unwearied labours of Theodor Mommsen and his allies and scholars in ascertaining the texts of law-books, authors and inscriptions. Lenel's important work on the Edict (*Edictum perpetuum*, 1883) has been constantly in my hands. Intelligent discussion and full references to modern writers will be found (amongst other books) in Vangerow's and Windscheid's *Pandekten*, Muirhead's *Historical Introduction to the Private Law of Rome*, Paul F. Girard's *Manuel de Droit Romain* ed. 2 (1898), and Ed. Cuq's *Institutions Juridiques des Romains* (1891 and 1902, just finished).

I have of course used Krüger and Studemund's edition of Gaius (1891)[3] and Mommsen and Krüger's editions of other ante-Justinian texts and of the Digest and Code; and followed their numbering. Bruns' *Fontes Juris* (sixth edition by Mommsen and Gradenwitz, 1893) is frequently referred to and contains almost all the inscriptions to which I have here called attention[4]. The second part of that book gives most of the passages bearing on law which are found in Cato, Varro, Festus, Servius and other

1 Cf. *e.g.* Gai. ii 58; iii 201.

2 The practice of drawing inferences of law from etymology is not confined to the old Roman lawyers, and is not purged of its mischief by the etymology's being, as it sometimes is, probably right. The actual meaning of a word is determined by its use, not by its origin.

3 The edition of 1900 reached my hands only lately. The Autun MS. of a commentary on Gaius there printed seems by general agreement to be of very small value.

4 A handy book, containing most of the ante-Justinian matter in the above-named books and Justinian's Institutes as well, has been edited by P. F. Girard (*Textes de Droit Romain*, 2nd ed. 1895). Useful notices are prefixed to the several documents.

writers of the kind, including the worthless Pseudo-Asconius. For Cicero I have usually followed Müller and Friedrich's texts or the critical so-called second edition of Orelli by Baiter, Halm and Jordan. By *ZGR.* I mean the *Zeitschrift für geschichtliche Rechtswissenschaft* edited by Savigny and others (15 vols. 1815—1850), and by *ZRG.* the *Zeitschrift für Rechtsgeschichte* by Rudorff and others (13 vols. 1861—1879), and its avowed and most useful successor *Zeitschrift der Savigny-Stiftung für Rechtsgeschichte* by Bruns, A. Pernice and others (at present 22 vols. 1880—1901). For this last I adopt the numbering continuous with its predecessor, so that *ZRG.* xiv = Sav. Stift. i and *ZRG.* xxxiii = Sav. Stift. xx, *etc.* Justinian's Institutes I have usually quoted by *Just.* (simply), and the Digest by D. The separate extracts in the Digest and the constitutions in the Code I have denoted by *fr.* (for 'fragment'), not as in my book on Justinian by *l*, the former term being alone suitable to a book which tries to go behind Justinian's legislation.

I shall be grateful to anyone who criticizes this book, or amends my statements, either publicly or privately. Considering the nature of the materials, I cannot hope for more than a comparative success—by giving students an account fuller than is found in histories of Roman law, and free, so far as may be, from Byzantine alterations, which naturally and properly shape and colour dogmatic treatises on the Civil Law. It is only in executing the task that one becomes thoroughly aware of the difficulties, but it is perhaps pardonable at my age not to defer the publication of a work, which might indeed well occupy still longer time, but could never be made by its author insusceptible of improvement. *Quod facere volueram juvenis, senex quo potui modo feci.*

H. J. R.

Lancrigg, GRASMERE,
Sept. 1902.

CONTENTS OF VOLUME I.

Dates of some important or relevant events, p. xxix.

INTRODUCTION.

A. Arrangement of Matter, p. 1.

B. Sources of Law: Gaius' account, p. 5:

Further details: 1. Statutes; 2. Senate's decrees, p. 7; 3. Imperial *decreta, edicta, rescripta, mandata*, p. 8; 4. Prætor's edict, p. 10; 5. *Responsa prudentium*, p. 14. Principal lawyers, p. 15.

C. Applicability of Roman law, p. 16.

BOOK I. CITIZENSHIP AND *STATUS* GENERALLY.

CHAP. I. CLASSIFICATION OF PERSONS:

A. Freemen: Romans, Latins, Foreigners, *Dediticii*, p. 18.

B. Slaves, p. 19.

CHAP. II. ACQUISITION OF CITIZENSHIP:

A. By Birth: rules and exceptions, p. 21. Period of gestation, p. 22.

B. By Grant:

1. to Italians, p. 22; 2. to foreign communities, p. 23; 3. to individuals, p. 24; 4. to Roman world, p. 24.

C. By Manumission: i. Form:

1. *censu*, p. 25; 2. *vindicta*, p. 25; 3. *testamento*, p. 26; *statuliber*, p. 27.

ii. Effect and requirements of valid manumission:

1. effect; 2. who can manumit? 3. *suis nummis emi*, pp. 28, 29; 4. *lex Aelia Sentia*: (*a*) age of parties, (*b*) intent to defraud creditors, (*c*) slaves' conduct, pp. 30—32; 5. *lex Fufia Caninia*, p. 33; 6. *lex Julia*, p. 34.

D. Without manumission:

1. reward for detection of master's murder, p. 35;
2. failure of promised manumission, p. 35;
3. to preserve freedoms left by will, p. 35.

CHAP. III. GRADUAL ACQUISITION OF CITIZENSHIP:

A. Informal manumission, p. 36: *Latini Juniani*, p. 38.

B. Acquisition of *jus Quiritium* by Latins, *etc.*:

1. under *lex Aelia Sentia*: *causae probatio*, p. 38;
2. under senate's decree: *erroris probatio*, p. 39;
3. by formal manumission, p. 39; 4. by three children, p. 40;
5. by certain occupations, p. 40; 6. by Emperor's grant, p. 40.

CHAP. IV. LOSS OF CITIZENSHIP: *capitis deminutio*, p. 41:

A. Consequent on loss of freedom: 1. capture by enemy, p. 41;
2. non-enrolment, p. 43; 3. sale for slaves, p. 43;
4. cohabiting with slave, p. 43; 5. capital punishment, p. 44;
6. illegal domicile, p. 44; 7. ungrateful freedmen, p. 44.

B. Retaining freedom:

1. becoming citizens of other communities, p. 44;
2. interdictions from water and fire, p. 44.

CHAP. V. SUITS ABOUT FREEDOM:

A. Claim of freedom, p. 47; B. Claim of freebirth, p. 49;
C. Limitation of time for suit, p. 50.

BOOK II. FAMILY.

CHAP. I. OF THE HOUSEHOLD PROPER, p. 52.

CHAP. II. SLAVES: their position and *peculium*, p. 53.

CHAP. III. CHILDREN: *patria potestas*, p. 57:

A. Come under power: 1. by birth, p. 57;
2. by adoption, p. 58:
(*a*) adoption proper, p. 60, (*b*) arrogation, p. 60;
3. by grant, p. 62.

B. 1. interdict *de liberis exhibendis*, p. 63; 2. other procedure, p. 64.

C. Position of children *in potestate*, p. 64.

D. *Castrense peculium*, p. 66.

CHAP. IV. WIVES *in manu*:

1. by use, p. 68; 2. by spelt-loaf, p. 69; 3. by copurchase, p. 70.

CHAP. V. MEMBERS OF HOUSEHOLD FOR TECHNICAL REASONS:

A. Women in hand, p. 71:

1. *tutelae evitandae causa*, p. 72; 2. *testamenti faciendi causa*, p. 73.

B. Persons in handtake (*in mancipio*), p. 73:

1. in process of emancipation, p. 74; 2. in process of adoption, p. 75;
3. position of persons in handtake, p. 76.

CHAP. VI. REMOVAL OF FATHERLY POWER, p. 77.

CHAP. VII. AGNATI, p. 79; COGNATI, p. 80; GENS, p. 80:
Capitis deminutio minima, p. 80.

CHAP. VIII. ALIMONY, p. 81.

CHAP. IX. PATRON AND FREEDMAN:

A. Position of freedman, p. 82; B. Who was patron? p. 82;

C. Patron's rights: 1. inheritance, p. 83; 2. *alimenta*, p. 84; 3. *obsequium*, p. 84; 4. *operae*, p. 85.

D. Praetor's control, p. 89.

E. Loss and non-acquisition of such rights, p. 90.

F. Trial of *Status*, p. 92.

CHAP. X. GUARDIAN AND WARD, p. 92:

A. Appointment of Guardians:
1. by will, p. 93; 2. by statute, p. 95; 3. by praetor, *etc.*, p. 97.

B. Qualification and functions, p. 100:
1. of guardians for women, p. 101;
2. of guardians for *impuberes*, p. 103.

C. Administration (for *impuberes*), p. 103.

D. Alienation of land forbidden, p. 108.

E. Actions (against guardians of *impuberes*):
1. *tutelae judicium*, p. 109; 2. *jud. rationibus distrahendis*, p. 111.

F. Liability of sureties and magistrates, p. 112.

G. Liability of pro-guardians; of false guardians, p. 114.

H. Excuses from guardianship, p. 115.
Potioris nominatio, p. 118.

J. Removal of guardians, p. 119.

CHAP. XI. CARETAKERS:

1. for madmen and spendthrifts, p. 121;
2. for deaf, dumb, *etc.*, p. 122; 3. in addition to guardian, p. 122;
4. for minors, p. 123; 5. special cases, p. 126.

CHAP. XII. HUSBAND AND WIFE:

A. Conditions of lawful marriage, p. 127:
1. *conubium*, p. 128; 2. age, p. 131; 3. consent, p. 131.
Betrothal, p. 132.

B. Dissolution of marriage, p. 133;
Marriage with freedwomen, p. 135.

C. Dowry, p. 136: I. nature of husband's liability, p. 137.

II. Establishment of Dowry, p. 139.

III. Content of Dowry:

1. conveyance of land, p. 141; 2. grant of usufruct, p. 142;
3. money, p. 143; 4. *Dos aestimata*, p. 143; 5. promise, p. 144;
6. formal release, p. 144; 7. relinquishment of legacy, *etc.*, p. 145;
8. legacy, p. 145.

IV. *Pacta dotalia*, p. 145.
Restoration during marriage, p. 147.

V. Fate of dowry on dissolution of marriage:

i. on wife's death, p. 148; ii. on husband's death, p. 149;
iii. on divorce, p. 150:

1. retentions, (*a*) *propter liberos*, p. 150;

(*b*) *propter mores*, p. 150; (*c*) *propter impensas*, p. 150;
(*d*) *propter res donatas*, p. 151; (*e*) *propter res amotas*, p. 152; (*f*) for ransom of *affines*, p. 152.

2. Apportionment of last year's profits, p. 152.
3. (*a*) *judicium rei uxoriae*, p. 153; (*b*) *ex stipulatu*, p. 156.

VI. 1. *Judicium de moribus mulieris*, p. 157;
2. *judicium rerum amotarum*, p. 158.

D. Gifts between husband and wife, p. 159:
1. What is invalid gift? p. 160;
Valid gifts: 2. between betrothed, p. 160;
3. gifts not to take effect during marriage:
(*a*) *donationis causa*, p. 161, (*b*) relaxation of rule, p. 162;
4. gifts which do not enrich or impoverish, p. 162;
5. petty gifts and customary presents, p. 163.

Recovery of invalid gifts, p. 164.

Gifts between families of husband and wife, p. 165.

CHAP. XIII. ACKNOWLEDGMENT OF CHILDREN, p. 166.

CHAP. XIV. 1. *Concubinatus*, p. 168; 2. *Contubernium*, p. 169.

Book III. Inheritance.

Chap. I. *Hereditas vacans*, p. 171.

Chap. II. Inheritance by will:

A. Will-making:

1. what is a will? p. 173;
2. who can make a will? p. 174;
3. how a will is made, p. 175;
4. codicils, p. 181;
5. opening a will, p. 184;
6. *SC. Silanianum*, p. 185.

B. Contents of will:

1. appointment of heir, p. 187;
2. own heirs, p. 188; postumous, p. 191;
3. who else can be heirs, p. 193;
4. appointment of slaves as heirs, p. 195;
5. conditional appointment of heirs, p. 198;
6. distribution among heirs, p. 200;
7. substitution, p. 202; pupillar wills, p. 203.

C. How wills are broken or invalidated:

1. *Agnatione*, p. 207; 2. by adoption of child, p. 208;
3. by later will, p. 208; 4. by heir's not entering, p. 209;
5. by tearing, *etc.*, p. 209; 6. *Capitis deminutione*, p. 210.

D. Plaint of unduteous will, p. 211.

E. Soldiers' wills, p. 216.

Chap. III. Intestate succession (to freeborn citizens):

A. By civil law under xii tables, p. 218.
Stemma agnationis, p. 222.

B. *SC. Tertullianum*, p. 223.

C. *SC. Orfitianum*, p. 225.

D. Uncertain survivorship, p. 226.

Chap. IV. Acquisition of inheritance:

A. *Usucapio pro herede*, p. 227.

B. Transfer of inheritance, p. 228.

C. Entry, p. 229; *Cretio*, p. 231;
Pro herede gestio, p. 232; meddling with estate, p. 233;
Entry at father's or master's order, p. 234.

CHAP. V. *BONORUM POSSESSIO*:

A. Character and protection:
1. general character, p. 236; 2. *Agnitio*, p. 238;
3. *interdictum quorum bonorum*, p. 239;
4. *interdictum quod legatorum*, p. 240.

B. *Bonorum possessio contra tabulas*:
i. by children:
1. children under power, p. 241; 2. emancipated, p. 242;
3. given in adoption, p. 243; 4. father adopted, p. 243;
5. acceptance of testator's judgment, p. 244;
6. condition of grant, p. 244; 7. effect of disherison, p. 245.
8. adjustments by praetor:
(*a*) joining of children, p. 246;
contribution, (*b*) *Collatio bonorum*, p. 247;
(*c*) *Collatio dotis*, p. 249;
(*d*) saving of legacies to children and parents, p. 250.
ii. *Bon. poss.* by *manumissor*, p. 254.

C. *Bonor. poss. secundum tabulas*, p. 255.

D. *Bonor. poss. ab intestato* (deceased being freeborn):
Defects of old law, p. 258.
Praetorian order: 1. *Liberi*, p. 259; 2. *Legitimi*, p. 261;
3. *Cognati*, p. 261; *Stemma cognationis*, p. 262;
4. *Vir et uxor*, p. 264; 5. *Cognati manumissoris*, p. 264.
Time for deliberation, p. 264.

E. *Missio ventris in possessionem*, p. 266.

F. *Carbonianum edictum*, p. 268.

CHAP. VI. SUCCESSION TO ROMAN FREEDMEN, *etc.* DECEASED:

A. General view:
1. right of patron in estate of (*a*) freedman, p. 270, (*b*) of freedwoman, p. 271;
2. right of patron's son, *etc.*, p. 271;
3. right of patron's daughter, *etc.*, p. 271;
4. right of patroness, p. 272; 5. right of patroness' son, p. 273;
6. effect of *SC. Orfitianum*, p. 274.

B. Patron's claim to *bon. poss. contra tabulas* (further details), p. 273.

C. Patron's claim to succession *ab intestato*:
i. by civil law, p. 276;
ii. by praetorian grant, p. 277.

D. Succession to Latin freedmen, *etc.*, p. 279.

CHAP. VII. A. *HEREDITATIS PETITIO*, p. 281.

SC. Juventianum, p. 283.

B. *Familiae erciscundae judicium*, p. 287.

CHAP. VIII. LEGACY, p. 293.

A. How legacies are made:

1. *per vindicationem*, p. 294; 2. *per damnationem*, p. 295;
3. *sinendi modo*, p. 297; 4. *per praeceptionem*, p. 298.

B. Who is liable to pay legacies?

1. general, p. 299; 2. substitute, p. 300; 3. special case, p. 301;
4. legacies to heirs, p. 301; 5. when inheritance is sold, p. 302;
6. *omissa causa testamenti*, p. 302.

C. What legacies are invalid:

1. preceding appointment of heir, p. 303;
2. *post mortem heredis*, p. 304; 3. *poenae causa*, p. 304;
4. parts of buildings, p. 304; 5. want of *testamenti factio*, p. 305;
6. to person *in potestate heredis*, p. 305;
7. to father or master of heir, p. 306;
8. to uncertain person, p. 306; 9. to alien postumous child, p. 307;
10. to towns, p. 307;
(11. Not vitiated by mistake in description, p. 307; or 12. in reason, p. 308.)
13. by insolvent testator or to incapable person, p. 308.

D. Renouncement of legacy, p. 308.

E. Repetition of legacy, p. 309.

F. Ademption and transference of legacy, p. 310.

G. Vesting of legacy (*dies cedit*), p. 312.

H. Fulfilment of conditions of legacy or freedom:

1. joint or disjoint, p. 315; 2. several conditions, p. 315;
3. consent of heir, p. 316; 4. fulfilment hindered, p. 316;
5. impossible condition, p. 317; 6. disgraceful condition, p. 317;
7. in restraint of marriage, p. 317; 8. *Muciana cautio*, p. 318;
9. conditions of freedom, viz.:
   (*a*) to perform services, p. 319,
   (*b*) to give or perform something, p. 319,
   (*c*) to give accounts, p. 321;
   (*d*) an impossible condition, p. 322;
10. *legatum sub modo*, p. 322.

J. Place and time of payment, p. 322.

K. Contents of legacy, p. 324:

1. a share of estate, p. 325; 2. a specific thing, p. 326;
3. generic thing, p. 329; 4. option, p. 329.

L. Special legacies:

1. usufruct, p. 330; 2. *reditus*, p. 331;
3. annuity, p. 331; 4. *alimenta*, p. 331;
5. *nomen*, p. 332; 6. release, p. 333;
7. debt, p. 333; 8. dowry, p. 335;
9. *peculium*, p. 337; 10. *instrumentum*, p. 339;
11. *fundus instructus*, p. 339; 12. house, *etc.* and contents, p. 340;
13. *uxoris causa parata*, p. 340; 14. *suppellex*, p. 341;
15. *aurum, argentum*, p. 341; 16. *ornamenta*, p. 342;
17. *mundus muliebris*, p. 342; 18. *vestis*, p. 342;
19. *penus*, p. 342; 20. wine, p. 343;
21. various expressions, p. 344; 22. 'my own' slaves, *etc.*, p. 344.

M. Restrictions on amount of legacies:

lex Furia, p. 344; *lex Voconia*, p. 345;
lex Falcidia, p. 345.

N. Protection of legatees, p. 354.

CHAP. IX. TRUSTS (*FIDEICOMMISSA*):

A. 1. history and effect, p. 356; 2. terms of creation, p. 357;
3. what will bear a trust, p. 358; 4. execution of trust, p. 360;
5. invalid trusts, p. 361; 6. family trusts, p. 361;
7. dying *sine liberis*, p. 363;
8. trusts for freedom to slaves, p. 363;
9. partial failure, p. 364;
10. *SC. Rubrianum, Dasumianum, Vitrasianum, Articuleianum, Juncianum*, p. 365;
11. extraordinary favour to trusts for freedom, p. 366.

B. Differences between direct disposition and trusts, p. 366.

C. Transference by heir at law to heir by trust:

SC. Trebellianum, p. 370; *Pegasianum*, p. 371.
Voluntary transference, p. 372.
Transference under compulsion, p. 376.

CHAP. X. A. RESTRICTIONS ON CAPACITY OF CHILDLESS PERSONS.

Lex Julia et Papia Poppaea, p. 379.

B. *Caduca*, p. 383.

C. Forfeiture of legacies and inheritance, p. 384.

CHAP. XI. CONNEXION OF *SACRA* WITH DECEASED'S ESTATE, p. 387.

CHAP. XII. OF BURIALS AND GRAVES:

1. whose duty, p. 390; 2. charge, p. 391;
3. effect on ground, p. 391;
4. family and hereditary tomb, p. 393;
5. violation of tombs, p. 394.

APPENDIX TO BOOK III CHAP. IV C.

Cretio in Ciceron. *Att.* xi 12; xiii 46, p. 396.

BOOK IV. PROPERTY.

CHAP. I. WHAT THINGS ARE NOT PRIVATE PROPERTY?

1. *res sacrae, religiosae, sanctae*, p. 408;
2. things public, p. 409;
3. protection of use of public and sacred places:
   (*a*) general, p. 410, (*b*) sea shore, p. 410,
   (*c*) public rivers, p. 411, (*d*) roads, p. 411,
   (*e*) places, p. 412, (*f*) sacred places, p. 412.

CHAP. II. DISTINCTIONS OF THINGS AND OF RIGHTS, p. 413.

CHAP. III. A. OWNERSHIP. Restrictions on same, p. 414.

B. Original acquisition:
1. by occupation, p. 415: (*a*) of animals, p. 416,
   (*b*) jewels and things abandoned, p. 416,
   (*c*) treasure trove, p. 417;
2. by alluvion, p. 417; 3. of fruits, p. 418;
4. by capture from enemy, p. 419.

C. Derivative acquisition:
1. by combination, p. 419; 2. by specification, p. 421;
3. by adjudication, p. 422; 4. by will (see Book III).

D. Voluntary transference *inter vivos*, p. 423:
(*a*) mancipation, p. 423, (*b*) *in jure cessio*, p. 425,
(*c*) *traditio*, p. 426,
(*d*) effect of informal transfer, p. 427.
Ownership *ex jure Quiritium* and *in bonis*, p. 428,
(*e*) provincial lands, p. 429.

E. Restrictions on alienation:
1. by women, p. 430; 2. by wards, p. 431.

F. Alienation by non-owners, p. 432.

G. Acquisition: i. through persons *in potestate, etc.*:
1. children and slaves, p. 432;
2. women in hand and persons in handtake, p. 434;
3. slaves in usufruct, p. 435;
4. persons *bona fide* possessed, p. 436;
ii. acquisition through persons not *in potestate*, p. 437.

H. Actions to ascertain property:
1. *rei vindicatio*, p. 438; 2. *Publiciana in rem actio*, p. 443;
3. *ad exhibendum*, p. 447; 4. *finium regundorum*, p. 449.

CHAP. IV. A. POSSESSION:
1. different kinds, p. 451;
2. conditions of possession through others, p. 455;
3. acquisition of possession, p. 456; 4. loss of possession, p. 458.

B. Protection of possession:
1. *interdictum uti possidetis*, p. 460; 2. *int. utrubi*, p. 461;
3. *int. de vi*, p. 462; 4. *int. de vi armata*, p. 465;
5. *precarium*, p. 466.

C. Usucapion:
i. general, p. 467: requires
1. civil possession, p. 468; 2. for certain period, p. 469;
3. uninterrupted, p. 470; 4. honestly acquired, p. 471;
5. what things are incapable of usucapion, p. 474.
ii. special cases, p. 477:
1. *pro herede*, p. 227; 2. *usureceptio ex fiducia*, p. 477;
3. *usureceptio ex praediatura*, p. 478;
praedibus praediisque cavere, p. 479.

D. Prescription, p. 483.

CHAP. V. SERVITUDES, p. 484. Personal:
1. *Ususfructus* (*a*) character, p. 484, (*b*) rights, p. 484,
(*c*) bond, p. 487, (*d*) special usufructs, p. 487,
(*e*) creation, p. 489, (*f*) extinction, p. 490,
(*g*) transfer, p. 491, (*h*) acquisition through others, p. 493,
(*j*) division and account, p. 494, (*k*) action, p. 495;
2. *fructus*, p. 496; 3. *operae*, p. 496; 4. *usus*, p. 496;
5. *habitatio*, p. 497.

CHAP. VI. SERVITUDES (continued). Predial:
1. character, p. 497; 2. principal easements, p. 498;
3. nature, p. 500; 4. creation, p. 501; 5. loss, p. 503
6. actions, p. 503.

CHAP. VII. PROTECTION OF EASEMENTS and the like:

1. *interdictum de itinere, etc.*, p. 505; 2. *int. de aqua*, p. 506;
3. *int. de rivis*, p. 507; 4. *int. de cloacis*, p. 508;
5. *int. de arboribus caedendis*, p. 508;
6. *int. de glande legenda*, p. 509.

CHAP. VIII. PROTECTION AGAINST NEIGHBOURS, *etc.*:

1. *damni infecti*, p. 509;
2. *aquae pluviae arcendae*, p. 515;
3. *operis novi nuntiatio*, p. 517;
4. *interdictum quod vi aut clam*, p. 520.

CHAP. IX. GIFT:

A. *inter vivos:*

1. nature, p. 525; 2. *lex Cincia*, p. 526;
3. validity, p. 527; 4. donor's position, p. 529;
5. gift by delegation, p. 529; 6. gift for purpose, p. 529;
7. miscellaneous, p. 530.

B. *Mortis causa donatio*, p. 530.
Mortis causa capere, p. 532.

C. *Pollicitatio*, p. 533.

APPENDIX TO BOOK IV CHAP. VI.

Recipere (of servitudes), p. 534.

CORRIGENDA IN VOL. I.

p. 153, line 4 from bottom, *for* Book II *read* Book III (p. 323).
p. 442, line 7 from bottom, *read* 'The old *legis actio* was used before the praetor when the suit was to come before the Centumviri.'
p. 501, line 3 from bottom, *for* § 109 *read* § 179.

In references to Book VI the number of the chapters is often wrongly stated, *e.g.*

p. 48, line 3 from bottom, *for* chap. iv *read* chap. vi.
p. 282, last line, *for* chap. vi J *read* chap. viii H.
p. 442, last line, *for* chap. iv A *read* chap. vi A.
p. 443, line 8 from top, *for* chap. vi J *read* chap. viii H.
p. 443, line 11 from top, *for* chap. vii B *read* chap. ix B.
p. 482, lines 7 and 9 from top, *for* chap. xiii *read* chap. xv.
p. 520, last line, *for* chap. xiv *read* chap. xvi.

DATES OF SOME RELEVANT OR IMPORTANT EVENTS.

A.U.C.	B.C.	
1	753	Rome founded.
245	509	The first Consuls.
260	494	1st Secession of Plebs.
303–4	451–0	*Decemviri leg. scrib.*
		XII. tables.
305	449	2nd Secession of Plebs.
		Leges Valeriae Horatiae.
311	443	Censorship established (A.U.C. 319 Mommsen).
387	367	*Leges Liciniae Sextiae.*
388	366	First Praetor.
390	364	Rome taken by Gauls.
442	312	App. Claudius *censor.*
450	304	Cn. Flavius publishes forms of oral pleading.
467	287	3rd Secession of Plebs.
		Lex Hortensia.
490	264	1st Punic war begins.
cir. 512	242	*Praetor peregrinus.*
513	241	*Sicilia,* first province.
		End of 1st Punic war.
523	231	*Sardinia* a province.
527	227	First provincial Praetors.
536	218	2nd Punic war begins.
538	216	Battle of Cannae.
550	204	*Lex Cincia.*
553	201	2nd Punic war ends.
557	197	*Hispania,* two provinces.
570	184	Cato *censor.*
		Plautus dies (an old man).
585	169	*Lex Voconia.*
after 587	167	*Illyricum* a province.
595	159	Terentius dies (his first play 588).
605	149	3rd Punic war begins.
		M'. Manilius, *cos.*
608	146	Carthage destroyed.
		Africa, Macedonia, Achaia made provinces.
621	133	Tib. Gracchus killed.
		P. Mucius Scaevola, *cos.*

	A.U.C.	B.C.	
	621	133	*Asia* a province.
	631	123	C. Gracchus killed.
	634	120	*Gallia Narbonensis* a province.
	637	117	Q. Mucius Scaevola (augur) *cos.*
	639	115	M. Aemilius Scaurus *cos.*
	649	105	P. Rutilius Rufus *cos.*
	652–3	102–1	Marius defeats Teutones and Cimbri.
	652	102	Cilicia treated as province (organised U.C. 687).
	659	95	L. Licinius Crassus, Q. Mucius Scaevola *pontifex* } *coss.*
	663–6	91–88	Social war.
	672	82	Sulla dictator. *Leges Corneliae.*
	673	81	Cicero's speech *pro Quinctio.*
			Gallia Cisalpina a province.
	675	79	Sulla retires.
	680	74	*Bithynia, Cyrene* provinces.
	687	67	*Creta* a province.
	688	66	C. Aquilius *praetor.*
	690	64	*Syria* a province.
	691	63	M. Tullius Cicero *cos.*
	694	60	JUL. CAESAR, Pompeius, Crassus *tresviri.*
	695	59	C. Julius Caesar *cos.*
	702	52	Milo kills Clodius.
	703	51	Ser. Sulpicius *cos.*
	705	49	Caesar crosses Rubico.
	706	48	Battle of Pharsalus.
	709	45	*Lex Julia municipalis.*
	710	44	Jul. Caesar killed.
			Lex Ursonensis.
	711	43	Octavius, Antonius, Lepidus *tresviri.*
			Cicero killed (aged 63).
			Ser. Sulpicius dies.
before	712	42	*Lex Rubria.*
	712	42	Battle of Philippi.
	714	40	*Lex Falcidia.*
	715	39	Alfenus Varus *cos. suff.*
	723	31	Battle of Actium.
	724	30	*Aegyptus* a province.
	725	29	CAESAR OCTAVIANUS receives *trib. pot.* and *imperium* for life.
	727	27	Octavianus called Augustus.
	731	23	*Trib. pot.* part of Augustus' title.
	736	18	*Leges Juliae de adulteriis,* and *de marit. ordin.* passed by Senate.

A.U.C.	B.C.	
751–4	3–1 A.D.	Birth of Christ.
757	4	*Lex Aelia Sentia.*
758	5	C. Ateius Capito *cos.*
761	8	*Lex Fufia Caninia.*
762	9	*Lex Papia Poppaea.*
763	10	*SC. Silanianum.*
767	14	TIBERIUS *imp.*
772	19	*Lex Junia* (*Norbana*) (placed by some before *lex Aelia Sentia*, e.g. U.C. 728).
780	27	*Lex Junia Vellaea.*
783	30	C. Cassius Longinus *cos. suff.*
786	33	M. Cocceius Nerva dies.
790	37	CALIGULA *imp.*
794	41	CLAUDIUS *imp.*
799	46	*SC. Velleianum.*
807	54	NERO *imp.*
809	57	*SC. Trebellianum.*
817	64	Burning of Rome.
818	65	Conspiracy of Piso.
821	68	GALBA *imp.*
		VITELLIUS *imp.*
		VESPASIANUS *imp.*
823	70	Destruction of Jerusalem.
cir. 823	cir. 70	*SC. Pegasianum.*
832	79	TITUS *imp.*
834	81	DOMITIANUS *imp.*
834–7	81–4	*Lex Salpensana.*
		Lex Malacitana.
848	95	Quintilianus dies, aged cir. 60.
849	96	NERVA *imp.*
851	98	TRAJANUS *imp.*
856	103	*SC. Rubrianum* (D. XL 5 fr 26 § 7).
859	106	L. Minicius Natalis *cos.*
866	113	C. Plinius (the younger) dies, aged 51.
870	117	HADRIANUS *imp.*
872	127	*SC. Juncianum* (D. XL 5 fr 28 § 4).
882	129	P. Juventius Celsus *cos.*
		SC. Juventianum.
temp. Hadrian.		*SC. Tertullianum.*
891	138	ANTONINUS PIUS *imp.*
		M. Vindius Verus, Pactumeius Clemens *coss.*
914	161	M. AURELIUS, L. VERUS *impp.*
922	169	VERUS dies.
930	177	COMMODUS *co-imp.*

A.U.C.	A.D.	
931	178	*SC. Orfitianum.*
933	180	COMMODUS alone *imp.*
945	192	PERTINAX *imp.*
946	193	DIDIUS JULIANUS *imp.*
		SEPTIMIUS SEVERUS *imp.*
948	195	*SC. ne tutores praedia distrahant.*
951	198	CARACALLA *co-imp.*
959	206	*SC. de donationibus inter virum et uxorem.*
965	212	Severus dies. CARACALLA, GETA *impp.*
		Geta killed.
		Papinianus killed.
970	217	MACRINUS *imp.*
971	218	ELAGABALUS *imp.*
975	222	ALEXANDER SEVERUS *imp.*
981	228	Ulpianus killed.
988	235	MAXIMINUS *imp.*
991	238	GORDIANUS I *imp.*
		GORDIANUS II *imp.*
		GORDIANUS III *imp.*
997	244	PHILIPPUS *imp.* (till 249).

(*Of other Emperors only a few are here selected.*)

A.D.	
284–305	DIOCLETIANUS *imp.*
307–337	CONSTANTINUS *imp.*
330	Constantinople, seat of Government.
364	Empire divided.
	VALENTINIANUS I *imp.* West.
	VALENS *imp.* East.
392	THEODOSIUS over whole Empire.
395	HONORIUS *imp.* West.
	ARCADIUS *imp.* East.
410	Alarich, Chief of West Goths in Rome.
439	*Codex Theodosianus* in force.
493	Theodorich, Chief of East Goths in Italy.
527	JUSTINIANUS *imp.*
528	Code ordered.
529	Code published.
530	Digest ordered.
533	Digest, Institutes, published.
	New course of study.
534	Revision of Code.
545	Tribonian dies.
565	Justinian dies.

INTRODUCTION.

De quibus causis scriptis legibus non utimur, id custodiri oportet quod moribus et consuetudine inductum est, et, si qua in re hoc deficeret, tunc quod proximum et consequens ei est; si nec id quidem appareat, tum jus quo urbs Roma utitur servari oportet (Julian D. i 3 fr 32).

Non omnium, quae a majoribus constituta sunt, ratio reddi potest (*Id.* fr 20).

Non possunt omnes articuli singillatim aut legibus aut senatusconsultis comprehendi; sed, cum in aliqua causa sententia eorum manifesta est, is qui jurisdictioni praeest ad similia procedere atque ita jus dicere debet (*Id.* fr 12).

Incivile est nisi tota lege perspecta, una aliqua particula ejus proposita, judicare vel respondere (Celsus D. i 3 fr 24).

A. Arrangement of matter.

All law aims at assuring and regulating control over things or control over persons. The arrangements for making laws, levying contributions for the public service, and appointing and controlling the administrators are the subject of public law. The punishment of individuals for acts deemed to be offences against the nation as a whole is matter for criminal law. Private law deals with the acts and position of individuals so far as they control or affect individuals only.

The State does not lend its assistance to maintain and enforce control over things or persons for individual interests, except to persons duly qualified and on the observance of certain formalities. The standard of due qualification in Roman law is a freeman and citizen of full age, of sane mind, and independent of his father or other ascendants. Each of these points requires legal definition. Who are free and citizens, how one becomes such, what is full age, what are the conditions of dependence or independence on his family superiors, all require decision and explanation. If a person does not possess all the attributes of a fully qualified citizen, he may yet possess some, and the State may allow him control over things or over persons, or subject him to such control, in degrees varying with his approach to or distance from the standard. Besides the freeman there is the freewoman, sometimes in the heart of the family, and her position and claims have to be defined and regulated. Insufficient age or want of mental capacity requires control and safeguarding. Slaves, their passage into freedom, and their subsequent position, are an allied matter. Two sections of private law therefore are concerned with Citizenship and the Family, forming together the law of Persons.

Apart from such control of things or persons as may arise directly from these relations, the action of persons themselves, purposely or accidentally, gives rise to the appropriation of things and the establishment in some persons of control over others' services. What are the requisites of property, and the conditions of its acquisition and transference, temporarily or permanently, from one person to another, is another section of law, and naturally falls into two great divisions, transference between the living, and succession to property vacant by death. Control over other free persons' services, called by the Romans Obligation, forms another section which is of great variety and stands in a closer and more necessary relation to the law-courts than control over things. That may be exercised to some extent by a possessor without others' aid; but obligation is a claim on the personal action of other free and independent persons, and has no legal basis or substance, whatever may be the case in custom or morality or religion, except so far as the law lends its help; and hence obligation and action (or suit) are terms often used indifferently for the same right. Lastly the courts, the procedure, and the formalities, through which the law is put in force both for these and for other claims, make another section.

The important sections of the law are then Citizenship, Family, Property, Succession on death, Obligation and Procedure. None of these sections can however be treated or understood independently of others; and the order of importance in an old Roman's eyes is perhaps not that most suitable for a student. With the person of a Roman citizen were intimately connected Family and Inheritance[1], *familia* being (sometimes) used to comprehend the persons and things as a whole belonging to a *paterfamilias,* and Inheritance being the devolution of the headship of the family to one or more successors, with the chattels (slaves, animals, things) and the rights and liabilities belonging. These three sections (Books I, II, III) deal primarily with the Roman citizen in his family, the other three (Books IV, V, VI) principally with his business relations to the world.

Courts of Justice are provided for the enforcement of all kinds of legal rights, and suits (or actions) will exhibit a corresponding variety. But there is one primary distinction. A suit may either be directed to a thing or matter and therefore be unlimited[2] as regards persons, or it may be particular to a person. The former are *actiones in rem*; the latter *actiones in personam.* In the former class a suitor alleges that some thing (an inheritance, a farm, a slave, a cup, *etc.*) or some right (personal freedom, an easement, an usufruct) is his; and his suit is therefore directed against any one who detains his thing, or being in possession impedes the exercise of his right. It is not exhausted by action against one; it may be brought against numbers of persons in succession and yet relate to the same matter; his right exists before contact with others, and the particular opponent is only ascertained by the fact of possession. In the latter class of suits, a suitor alleges that a particular

[1] Ulpian's *Rules,* so far as we have them, are entirely on these three sections except one chapter on Acquisition. My order differs from Gaius mainly in putting Inheritance before Property.

[2] This is a frequent use of *in rem* in the lawyers, *e.g.* D. ii 14 fr 7 § 8; vii 9 fr 5 pr; xiii 5 fr 5 § 2; xlii 5 fr 12 pr; xliv 4 fr 2 § 1, *etc.*

person has either voluntarily (or sometimes involuntarily) come under a special obligation to him to do or to refrain from doing something: he has perhaps promised and has not performed: or he has acted or received on my behalf and has not paid or otherwise satisfied me; or he has injured and has not remedied or compensated for the injury: his action or negligence, or the action or negligence of others for whom he is by law responsible, has created for me a new claim for satisfaction or redress, personal to me and personal to him. My suit is against him or his representative only and on this account only. It aims at payment or performance of what has been promised or at pecuniary compensation for the injury or neglect; not at the establishment or recognition of any previously existing right, or (except incidentally) at the restoration of any particular thing.

The distinction between these two classes of suits leads to differences in some legal forms and procedure. The language of the suitor in the first class is that the thing or right is his; and that the court should compel its restoration and protect its enjoyment. The language of the second class is that the opponent is bound to give or do or be answerable for something, and the court should compel him. The former declares *rem suam esse*; the latter that *Titium i.e.* his adversary *dare facere praestare oportere.* What is ours already may be relieved from others' interference, but cannot be made ours more than it is; it cannot be conveyed or made over (*dari*) to us so as to become ours. The former class of suits were called *vindicationes,* they were suits *in rem*; the latter (*in personam*) are said indeed to have been sometimes embraced under the name of *condictiones,* but normally and usually are described by the name of the particular cause of the suit (*e.g. ex empto, furti*); and *condictio* is then, as it was originally, restricted to one class of personal suits (Gai. iv 1—5; D. xliv 2 fr 14 § 2; 7 fr 25 pr).

Suits being the mode adopted in civilised society for obtaining protection for rights, the complainant must apply to the court on some particular occurrence and justify his application by stating or proving his title to sue. The statements of law under the several sections of a treatise on the law are thus in effect discussions of the title to sue; some relating mainly to the qualification to sue at all, as that of citizenship[1] and of family, others dealing with specific subject-matter, either with rights against all the world, or with claims on a particular person or persons. Actions *in rem* and Interdicts, as regards their content or scope or application, will be described mainly under the head of Property; actions *in personam* mainly in connexion with Obligations. Actions connected with Dowry, Guardianship, Inheritance, will be briefly given in the sections treating those subjects. The formalities and incidents of judicial proceeding, whether by action proper or interdict, come in the book on Procedure.

B. Sources of law.

Gaius gives the following account:

'The Roman people, like all others which are governed by 'Statutes and Customs, is partly under law peculiar to itself, 'partly under law common to it with the world generally[2]. The

[1] Cf. Cic. *Top.* 2 § 9 *Jus civile est aequitas constituta iis qui ejusdem civitatis sunt ad res suas optinendas.*

[2] Cf. Cic. *Off.* iii 5 § 23 *Neque vero hoc solum natura, id est jure gentium, sed etiam legibus populorum, quibus in singulis civitatibus res publica continetur, eodem modo constitutum est, ut non liceat sui commodi causa nocere alteri*; *ib.* 17 § 69 *Itaque majores aliud jus gentium, aliud jus civile esse voluerunt; quod civile non idem continuo gentium, quod autem gentium idem civile esse debet.* That is to say, Roman law contains some rules and doctrines which may or may not be found elsewhere, others which being less conventional and the natural product of human reason are prevalent in other or all nations just as much as in Rome. The following are named as belonging to *jus gentium*: verbal contracts and release by question and answer (Gai. iii 93; D. xlvi 4 fr 8 § 4), sale, lease, partnership, deposit, loans of money (D. ii 14 fr 7 pr), obligation by payment of money down (Gai. iii 132), acquisition by delivery (Vat. 47 a), by alluvion (D. xli 1 fr 7 § 1), by capture in war (D. xli 1 fr 5 § 7), rights over slaves (Gai. i 52), requirement of guardians for minors (Gai. i 189), descent of intestate property to children (Quint. vii 1 46), prohibition, as incest, of connexion of ascendants and descendants (D. xxiii 2 fr 68), rights of natural self-defence (Sall. *Jug.* 22 § 4), of safe conduct for embassies (*ib.* 35 § 7), exemption of divine property from usucapion (Cic. *H. R.* 14 § 42), free

'peculiar law is that which it has established for itself, and is 'called civil law (*jus civile, i.e.* the law of the citizens) as if 'peculiar to the particular community. The law established by 'natural reason among all men is equally observed by all peoples, 'and is called the law of the world (*jus gentium*).

'The laws of the Roman people consist of statutes, commons' 'resolutions, senate's decrees, emperors' constitutions, edicts of 'certain magistrates, and answers of skilled lawyers[1].

1. 'Statute (*lex*) is that which is ordered and established by 'the people, comprising patricians and commons.

'Commons' resolutions (*plebiscita*) are that which is ordered 'and established by the commons. By Commons are meant all 'citizens except the patricians. In former days the patricians 'used to declare that they were not bound by the resolutions of 'the Commons, because they had not authorised them. The '*lex Hortensia* (287 B.C.) afterwards was passed, and enacted 'that the Commons' resolutions should bind the whole people; 'and in this way they were put on a level with Statutes.

2. 'A senate's decree (*senatus consultum*) is what is ordered 'and established by the senate, and that takes the place of a 'statute (*legis vicem optinet*, cf. § 83), although this position has 'been questioned.

3. 'A constitution of the emperor (*constitutio principis*) 'is what the emperor has established by decree or by edict 'or by letter[2]. No doubt has ever been entertained that it

use of sea shore (D. xviii 1 fr 51), tenure on sufferance (*precarium* D. xliii 26 fr 1 § 2). See Nettleship *Contrib. Lat. Lex.* p. 505 sq. (referred to by Mommsen *Staatsr.* iii 604).

[1] Papinian (D. i fr 7) agrees well with Gaius: *Jus civile est quod ex legibus, plebis scitis, senatus consultis, decretis principum, auctoritate prudentium venit. Jus praetorium est quod praetores introduxerunt adjuvandi vel supplendi vel corrigendi juris civilis gratia propter utilitatem publicam. Quod et honorarium dicitur.* Cicero has a somewhat fuller list of the sources of law: *Jus civile id est quod in legibus, senatusconsultis, rebus judicatis, jurisperitorum auctoritate, edictis magistratuum, more, aequitate consistit* (*Top.* 5 § 28). *More* and *aequitate* are not really additional sources: they require recognition by legal authority.

[2] As regards the form of imperial constitutions Bruns (*Kl. Schrift.* i pp. 49, 80, 81) says that down to the time of Diocletian they were all letters addressed to private persons or officials. They followed the style of

'takes the place of a statute, seeing that the Emperor himself 'receives the imperial power by means of a statute.

4. 'Edicts are issued by magistrates of the Roman people, 'but the largest body of law (*amplissimum jus*) is in the edicts 'of the city praetors and the foreign praetors, whose jurisdiction 'in the provinces is exercised by their Governors; and in the 'edicts of the curule aediles, whose jurisdiction in the provinces 'of the Roman people is exercised by quaestors. The provinces 'of Caesar have no quaestors, and consequently in these provinces 'this edict is not published (*proponitur*).

5. 'Answers of skilled lawyers (*responsa prudentium*) are 'the conclusions and opinions of those who have been licensed to 'lay down the law. If the opinions of all these agree, their 'opinion takes the place of a statute; if they differ, the judge 'may follow which he will. There is a rescript of Hadrian to 'that effect.' (Gai. i 1—7.)

6. 'Custom' (*mores*), mentioned by Gaius in the commencement, is defined by Ulpian as 'the tacit consent of the people, 'which consent has become rooted by long habit' (Ulp. i § 4; cf. D. i 3 fr 32—36).

Some fuller notice of these matters is required:

1. The legislative power continued to be exercised by the popular assembly at least in form till and in Tiberius' reign, and instances of *leges* are mentioned still later (Tac. *A.* xi 13; D. xlvii 21 fr 3 § 1).

2. Senates' decrees practically took the place of statutes: they were sometimes introduced by a speech from the Emperor which defined the scope of the legislation (*e.g.* D. v 3 fr 20 § 6; fr 40 pr). Several made important changes in private law, *e.g.* in Claudian's time the *SC. Vellaeanum*, in Nero's the *SC. Trebellianum* and one on legacies; in Vespasian's the *Pegasianum* and

letters such as Cicero's and Pliny's: they commenced with the names of the Emperor and of the person addressed, and they closed with the date and place and an ordinary greeting such as *vale*, *opto te valere*, *etc.* Only date, place and greeting were written by the hand of the Emperor (as in other letters by private persons) and this formed the imperial *subscriptio*. He did not add his own name.

Macedonianum; in Trajan's the *Rubrianum*; in Hadrian's the *Juventianum, Tertullianum* and *Juncianum*; in M. Aurelius' the *Orfitianum, etc.*

3. The Emperor's power which at first worked to a large extent under the forms of the old constitution came gradually more and more to the front. In matters of private law, as distinguished from administrative acts, it appeared chiefly in decrees and rescripts. The *decreta* were judicial decisions given either in original suits or on appeals. *Rescripta* were answers to questions of law submitted to him either by magistrates or private persons, and would differ from the answers of a leading jurisconsult (by whom no doubt they were often composed)[1] not so much in their general character as in the authority they bore. The Emperor was acting not as legislator, but as interpreter of existing laws and practices, though being irresponsible he might easily overstep the bounds of interpretation proper. How far rescripts had general application beyond the particular occasion which gave rise to them, must often have been very doubtful (cf. D. xxxiii 8 fr 6 § 4; xxviii 5 fr 9 § 2), but in theory they were general, so that they were held to override any local byelaws inconsistent with them (D. xlvii 12 fr 3 § 5). It appears very probable that those intended to be of wide application were published[2] on the wall of some public building at Rome, and the document registered; and that books were compiled of such rescripts, which the jurists consulted. Rescripts are mentioned, but have not come down, of the Emperors before Trajan, who we are told had objections to making rescripts general; none are found by or after Constantine. (Mommsen *ZRG.* xxv 262 sqq; Hist. Aug. *Macrin.* 13; *Decret. Gord. ad Scaptoparenos*, Bruns[6] p. 248; Plin. *Ep. Traj.* 65 *ad fin.*). Where the rescript was clearly personal, granting an indulgence or awarding a penalty on an individual's merits or assisting the petitioner in an unprecedented manner, the jurists held that no general application should be given to it (D. i 4 fr 1 § 2): and, if events

[1] Cf. F. Hofmann *Krit. Stud.* p. 21.

[2] *Propositum* is the term used: and this is meant by the letters *pp.* with a date following, as often seen at the end of rescripts, *e.g.* Cod. ii. 18 fr 1—16.

occurred which appeared not to have been anticipated, they held that the letter of the rescript should give way to equitable considerations (D. xxviii 6 fr 43 pr). A rescript of M. Aurelius is given (in D. xxxvii 14 fr 17), which expressly on further consideration alters the law laid down in an earlier one. The difficulty of access to such documents, or doubt as to their general application, perhaps appears in Gaius' expression (in ii 221) *quae sententia dicitur divi Hadriani constitutione confirmata esse.* (A similar expression is used of a senate's decree i 32 b[1].) See Wlassak *Krit. Stud.* p. 114.

The *Edicta* of the Emperor would approach nearest to a law, but they appear not to have been frequent. Augustus by edict forbad disinheriting of a *filius familias* serving in the army (D. xxviii 2 fr 26); Claudius offered Roman citizenship to Latins who should have done service in the corn supply (infr. p. 40), and freedom to infirm slaves abandoned by their master (D. xl 8 fr 2); M. Aurelius gave a privileged position to creditors who had advanced money for the restoration of buildings (D. xlii 5 fr 24 § 1), *etc.*; but no large change in private law was introduced by this means till after the Antonine times.

In Justinian's code only 23 constitutions are earlier than Sept. Severus. Constitutions of Ant. Pius and M. Aurelius are rarely found in the Code, because they had been often commented on or quoted by the later lawyers and thus embodied more or less in the Digest. It should be borne in mind that both the constitutions quoted in the Digest and those given in the Code may contain, and no doubt do contain, more or less often, alterations by Justinian. (See the passages referred to in Preface.)

Gaius does not mention the Emperor's *mandata*, *i.e.* instructions to provincial governors. We have an extract from Trajan's *mandata* whereby he granted the right to soldiers to

[1] In Cicero's time even *leges* were not very accessible: *Legum custodiam nullam habemus. Itaque eae leges sunt, quas apparitores nostri volunt; a librariis petimus, publicis litteris consignatam memoriam publicam nullam habemus* (*Legg.* iii. 20 § 46). Proposed laws were put up in public: Cicero speaks of sending several copyists to make him a copy of Rullus' bill for distributing land (*Agrar.* ii 5 § 13).

make a valid will without regard to form (D. xxix 1 fr 1): and the marriage of civil and military officers with the women of the province in which they were serving was prohibited by *mandata* (D. xxiii 2 fr 38, 63, *etc.*). But *mandata* usually gave administrative directions and not alterations of private law (*e.g.* D. i 18 fr 3; xlvii 11 fr 6 pr; tit. 22 fr 1 pr, *etc.*).

The law referred to by Gaius conferring the imperial power on the Emperor is apparently preserved to us in part by an inscription relating to Vespasian (Bruns No. 53). It gives him 'the right to do whatever he shall think to be conformable to 'the service of the state and to the greatness of things divine, 'human, public and private, in as ample a manner as it was had 'by Augustus, Tiberius, and Claudius Caesar, any law or senate's 'decree notwithstanding.' And such right was in effect confirmed by the oath of assent and obedience taken by soldiers, magistrates and senate (Tac. *An.* i 7; iv 11).

Whatever deference may have been shewn either in legislation or administration to old constitutional theories and practices especially during the first century *p. Chr.*, the emperor's power was really limited only by his own sense of what was prudent, and ultimately rested on the adhesion of the army[1]. In cases of peaceful succession the alterations in law would usually be allowed to continue[2] after the death of the emperor who made or sanctioned them. I doubt whether the annulment of the acts of a deceased emperor would have much or any effect on those points of general private law which had been settled by an imperial constitution.

4. Of the edicts of the praetors that of the city praetor was the most important. The praetor was partly administrator of the old and recognised law of the citizens (*jus civile*), partly in virtue of his *imperium* an original authority in matters of executive justice[3]. By his decrees or his public notices (*edicta*)

[1] Cf. Tac. *An.* xiii 4 *Nero curiam ingressus et de auctoritate patrum et consensu militum praefatus* (quoted by Gibbon *Decline and Fall* ch. iii).

[2] On the whole subject see Mommsen *Staatsr.* ii 867 foll. ed. 2; Madvig *Verf.* i 535, 546, *etc.*; Wlassak *Krit. Stud.* § 9, *etc.*; A. Pernice *ZRG* xix 294 foll.

[3] Cf. Cic. *Verr.* ii 1 42 § 109 *Qui plurimum tribuunt edicto praetoris, edictum legem annuam dicunt esse.* See my *Introd. to Digest* p. clxiv sqq.

he gave or refused, or declared his intention in certain cases of giving or refusing, the power of the state to applicants, according as he held to be required by equitable considerations and not to be directly contrary to the civil law. In this way, for instance, the praetor admitted to inheritance many who had no claim by the old law, and he did it, not by making them heirs (*praetor heredes facere non potest* Gai. iii 32), but by giving them possession of the inheritance and protecting them therein against all inferior claims: he gave creditors the protection and eventual distribution of the estates of absent or recalcitrant debtors; he ordered security to be given to meet future or contingent claims; he recognised rights of action for which the existing laws had made no provision, or where the letter did not cover the spirit or intention[1]; and he cancelled acts and proceedings where youth, ignorance, mistake, fraud, intimidation, or other influence had produced an inequitable result. This large power was checked formally by the veto of an equal or superior magistrate, and practically by public opinion; the office of praetor being held only for a year, any misuse of the power by an individual soon came to an end. But on the whole the plan appears to have worked well, giving a flexibility to the law which is unattainable by statute, and meeting the new cases, which arose as the community developed, by continual and gradual adaptation.

It was the practice of the praetor not only to issue edicts or orders for particular occasions, but to announce beforehand at the commencement of his year of office the general rules on which he would proceed in exercising his quasi-legislative and official jurisdiction[2]. Such a general advertisement, as

[1] Rights of action resting on the civil law are said *ipso jure competere*; those added by the praetor *a praetore dari* (Gai. iv 112, 113, also in ii 255). But the latter phrase is also applicable to civil actions (cf. D. xxxvi 1 fr 1 §2 with *ib.* fr 41 pr), as the praetor had a discretion in giving or refusing them.

[2] Cf. Cic. *Fin.* ii 22 § 74 *Quid enim, Torquate* (praetor 49 B.C.), ... *jam cum magistratum inieris et in contionem ascenderis? est enim tibi edicendum quae sis observaturus in jure dicendo et fortasse etiam, si tibi erit visum, aliquid de majoribus tuis et de te ipso dices more majorum*, etc. In *Off.* iii 20 § 80 he speaks of a common edict authorised by *collegium praetorium* summoned by the *tribuni plebis* in 84 B.C. (see Essay on *pro Quinct.* App. to vol. II).

distinguished from particular orders, was called *edictum perpetuum*, *i.e.* the standing notice or edict. To a great extent these rules would be taken from the edict of his predecessors, but some parts might be recast, and additions or omissions be made, according as the praetor recognised the importance of further development of the law or found previous rules to have failed in practice, or new circumstances to require authoritative and general regulation. The bulk however would be traditional (*tralaticium*), and be regarded as confirmed by use, and thus to be almost as much removed from the caprice of an individual praetor as a statute or time-honoured custom. The praetor's issue of his standing edict did not exhaust his power in any way, but it is obvious that the very purpose of such a general notification would be frustrated, if the praetor disregarded it in practice and refused to grant actions in circumstances for which he had publicly promised them. Verres' colleague Piso put his veto on many of Verres' decrees made contrary to his Sicilian edict (Cic. *Verr.* II i 46 § 119); and a plebiscite was afterwards carried by Cornelius (*trib. pl.* A.D. 67) directing the praetors *ex edictis suis perpetuis jus dicere* (Ascon. *in Corn.* p. 58). Cicero dwells on this point in commenting on Verres' conduct (Cic. *Verr.* II i capp. 40—48).

Such edicts were issued not only by the city praetor, but also by the praetor who had charge of foreigners' suits, and by the provincial governors each for his own province. Cicero gives us some information respecting his own edict as proconsul of Cilicia. He drew it up in Rome, but added at the request of the tax farmers some clauses, apparently taken from his predecessor's edict. With two matters he dealt specifically, one being provincial and comprising the money affairs of the several towns, borrowed money, interest, written instruments of debt, and the tax farmers; the other being of a more general character, but requiring the announcement of rules to guide suitors in making their applications and conducting the business, such as grants of possession of inheritances, the seizure and sale of bankrupts' estates and appointment of managers for the same. On all other matters of law he announced that he should follow in his decrees the edicts of the city praetor. He introduced a clause allowing want of equity to be pleaded against the enforcement of any obligation, and allowed the suits of Greeks with one another to be decided according to their own laws; these two clauses being taken from the edict of Q. Mucius Scaevola (the Pontifex) for the province of Asia: and he added directions to prevent unnecessary expenditure by the provincials on himself and his suite (Cic. *Att.* vi 1 § 15; *Fam.* iii 8 § 4). Something of this kind was probably done by other proconsuls: and we can see from this the traditional and eclectic character of the particular edict, and the general authority accorded to the city edict[1].

Under Hadrian's authority this mass of general rules of praetorian action (*jus praetorium, jus honorarium* 'official law'), at least as contained in the edict of the city praetor, was no doubt to some extent rearranged amended and supplemented, but, at any rate, settled by the lawyer Julian, and confirmed by a Senate's decree, as a permanent part of Roman law (const. *Tanta* § 18; const. δέδωκεν § 18). The edict of the Curule Aediles referring to sales of slaves and beasts was appended by Julian to his revision of the Edict. The edict of the foreign praetor is referred to in the *lex Rubria* 25 (B.C. 49—42; given in Bruns' *Fontes*) and by Gaius in the passage quoted above. Gaius commented on *Edictum provinciale*, which may have been the ordinary part of provincial Governors' edicts, as revised by Julian; it apparently resembled the city edict.

The edict of the city praetor thus settled is what is commonly referred to in the Digest, and is the only one of which we have any substantial knowledge. It consisted apparently of a series of declarations of claims which the praetor would (or would not) recognize, accompanied by blank model *formulae* for the trial of such claims as he approved. There were *formulae* also for actions of the *jus civile.* At the end came forms of interdicts, of defensive pleas, and of recognizances (*praetoriae stipulationes*). On some matters fuller directions were given (see those *de inspiciendo ventre* D. xxv 4 fr 1 § 10;

[1] Cf. Cic. *Legg.* i 5 § 17 where Cicero makes Atticus say: *Non ergo a praetoris edicto ut plerique nunc neque a duodecim tabulis ut superiores, sed penitus ex intima philosophia hauriendam juris disciplinam putas.*

and those for taking possession of a debtor's estate, Cic. *Quinct.* 27 §84). Some idea of the form and nature of the Edict may be got from Otto Lenel's skilful collection and arrangement of the bits found in the Digest (Bruns' *Fontes* Part I. cap. VI). See also Wlassak's *Edict und Klageform.*

The Edict was written on a white board (*album*; cf. *lex Rubr.* 20; Gai. iv 46; D. ii 1 fr 9) and exposed in public, presumably in the forum.

It was taken as a text for the exposition of law, probably by many lawyers. Ulpian wrote commentaries on it (including the Curule Aediles' edict) in 83 books, Paul in 88. From a fourth to a fifth of the whole Digest is taken from Ulpian's commentary.

5. As regards the 'answers of skilled lawyers'[1] our only information (beyond this passage of Gaius) is from Pomponius (D. i 2 fr 2 §49), who tells us that whereas before Augustus' time lawyers were consulted and their answers written by themselves to the judge, or declared before witnesses who produced the affidavit before the Court, Augustus licensed (certain) lawyers to give such answers under his authority. Sabinus is the only lawyer of whom we are actually informed (*ib.* §48) that he received this licence. But, either as licensees dealing with an individual case or in consequence of the general recognition of their knowledge and ability, the lawyers whose writings have been excerpted in order to compose Justinian's Digest may be regarded as practically a large source of law, though in theory what they gave was only interpretation of the laws or application of their principles to similar or analogous cases. (Legal validity was actually given in later times to the writings of some great Jurists, especially

[1] The ordinary duties of a practising lawyer are summed up by Cicero in speaking of Servius Sulpicius: *Servius hic nobiscum hanc urbanam militiam respondendi, scribendi, cavendi secutus est*: consultations, writing (treatises?), drawing stipulations, conditions of mancipation, wills, *etc.* (*Muren.* 9 § 19). In *Orat.* i 48 § 212 he speaks of *respondendum agendum* and *cavendum*, where *agendum* means advise on the conduct of an action, *e.g.* the formula to choose, the plea to make, *etc.* The statement of a litigant's case before the judge was for an orator, not for a jurisconsult.

by a law of Theodosius and Valentinian in 426 A.D. See my *Introd. Digest,* Chap. VI.)

The most distinguished jurists referred to or quoted in the Digest are the following (the usual title being italicised).

(1) Of Cicero's time: Q. *Mucius* Scaevola (pontifex), C. *Aquilius* Gallus, *Servius* Sulpicius Rufus, P. *Alfenus* Varus, C. *Trebatius* Testa, A. *Ofilius* and Q. Aelius *Tubero.* Only from Mucius and Alfenus are actual extracts given, and those are few.

(2) Of the early Empire: M. Antistius *Labeo,* C. Ateius *Capito,* Masurius *Sabinus,* M. Cocceius *Nerva,* Sempronius *Proculus,* C. *Cassius* Longinus. Extracts from Labeo and Proculus and possibly Sabinus appear, but are not numerous.

(3) From Trajan to Ant. Pius: *Neratius* Priscus, Titius *Aristo, Javolenus* Priscus, P. Juventius *Celsus* (the younger), P. Salvius *Julianus,* Sex. *Pomponius, Gaius.*

(4) Later (to cir. 235 A.D.): L. Ulpius *Marcellus,* Q. Cervidius *Scaevola,* Aemilius *Papinianus,* Domitius *Ulpianus* and Julius *Paulus.* More than one half of Justinian's Digest is taken from the writings of the last two lawyers, not on account of any pre-eminence as lawyers over some of their predecessors[1], but because they were the latest of the great jurists who wrote systematically on all parts of the law. After *Modestinus* (who wrote partly in Greek and died after A.D. 244), the development of law appears to have taken place chiefly through Imperial constitutions.

Pomponius speaks of two schools of Jurists, starting from Labeo and Capito, each of whom had their following (*sectas*); Labeo's chief 'successors' being Nerva, Proculus, Pegasus, Celsus and Neratius; Capito's being Sabinus, Cassius, Javolen, and Julian. Labeo's school was often called *Proculiani,* Capito's *Sabiniani.* Gaius belonged to the latter, and often mentions the opposing opinions. In later Jurists we hear nothing of these schools. It is difficult to trace any clear principle lying at

[1] The list prefixed to the Digest by its compilers is headed by Julian and Papinian without regard to their proper chronological place,—a distinction due, no doubt, to Julian's being the editor of the edict, and Papinian's being regarded by Justinian as the greatest of jurists.

the root of the division. Whether the succession was merely intellectual or, as has been not improbably suggested, referred to the occupancy of professorial or other posts is not known. (D. i 2 fr 2 §§ 47—53.) See my *Introduction to Justinian's Digest*, Chap. IX.

C. Applicability of Roman law.

Roman (private) law was a personal, not a territorial, law. It controlled and was applicable to, not all persons within a certain district but, all Roman citizens, wherever they were. Originally law made by and for the citizens of Rome, it always had its chief seat in Rome and within a mile outside the walls. After the second Punic war, praefects were sent to the Campanian towns to administer Roman as well as other law. In the provinces the Governors administered it, though not to the exclusion of the Roman praetor. Further the Roman dominion was a complex of communities; and those which did not possess the citizenship of Rome, whether formally autonomous like the Latins, or federated peoples, or simply permitted to remain autonomous, maintained their own administration of justice, when neither party to a suit was a Roman citizen. If one was a Roman citizen, the Roman law usually applied. But the autonomy was sometimes broken by arbitrary interference on the part of Roman officials. Foreigners at Rome were apparently readily admitted to the Roman Courts, as is shown by the establishment of a *praetor qui inter peregrinos jus dicat* (cir. 241 B.C.), and by the use of fictions (Gai. iv 37: cf. Mommsen *Abriss d. röm. Staatsr.* p. 241; Wlassak *Pr. G.* § 27).

BOOK I.

CITIZENSHIP AND *STATUS* GENERALLY.

O jura praeclara atque divinitus jam inde a principio Romani nominis a majoribus nostris comparata, ne quis nostrum plus quam unius civitatis esse possit (dissimilitudo enim civitatum varietatem juris habeat necesse est), ne quis invitus civitate mutetur neve in civitate maneat invitus. Illud vero sine ulla dubitatione maxime nostrum fundavit imperium, quod princeps ille creator hujus urbis, Romulus, foedere Sabino docuit etiam hostibus recipiendis augeri hanc civitatem oportere. Cujus auctoritate et exemplo numquam est intermissa a majoribus nostris largitio et communicatio civitatis (Cic. *Balb.* 13 § 31).

Quod attinet ad jus civile, servi pro nullis habentur; quod ad jus naturale attinet, omnes homines aequales sunt (Ulp. D. L 17 fr 32).

Cum servus manumittitur, hodie incipit statum habere (D. iv 5 fr 3 § 1, 4).

CHAPTER I.

CLASSIFICATION OF PERSONS.

The Roman world of mankind consisted of freemen and slaves. Freemen were of two classes, either born free (*ingenui*), or made free by release from lawful (*justa*) slavery. This last class were called *libertini* (Gaius), or *liberti* (Ulpian)[1], the former term being properly applicable when the class is spoken of, the latter when the relation of the particular persons as freedmen to their patrons is denoted (cf. D. xl 14 fr 6). Some freedmen may have been born free in another country, made or acquired as slaves by Romans and afterwards freed, but they were not *ingenui* in the view of the Romans, because they had been slaves in Roman territory. A freeborn Roman, though captured and enslaved by others, resumed his original rights and position on return to Roman territory. He did not become *libertinus*, the slavery not being *justa*.

A. Freemen were either Roman citizens or Latins or foreigners, or *dediticii*.

1. Roman citizens whether *ingenui* or *libertini* had full control over their children, could make a valid will, take under a valid will, be appointed guardians by will, be witnesses to a will; they could hold and deal with all kinds of property; and some special forms of acquiring and conveying property, *e.g.* *mancipatio, in jure cessio, usucapio* were peculiar to them, except

[1] The son of a *libertinus* is *ingenuus*, if born of a lawful marriage after his parent's emancipation. Suetonius (*Claud.* 24) speaks of a time when *libertinus* meant, not a freedman, but a freedman's son. This is not supported by other writers or by usage (Mommsen *Staatsr.* iii p. 422).

so far as *commercium* (which included mancipation) had been granted to Latins or foreigners (Ulp. xix 4).

2. Latins meant originally inhabitants of Latium, and was afterwards applied to members of Latin colonies, who were often Roman citizens originally. They had rights of inter-marriage and commercial dealings with Romans, only when specially granted by treaty or Roman statute. Certain Latin colonies, Ariminum and eleven others, had rights of mancipation and inheritance with Romans. But the Latins spoken of in imperial times are chiefly slaves imperfectly emancipated but protected by a law (*lex Junia*) to be mentioned later (Cic. *Caecin.* 35 §§ 101, 102; Gai. i 22, 79; iii 56).

3. Foreigners (*peregrini*) may be shortly defined as freemen who were not either Roman citizens or Latins (though the original Latins were foreigners Gai. i 79). They were not regarded by the Romans as having such full rights over their children as Romans had (Gai. i 55), but certain rights of inter-marriage with Romans were recognized, with the effect that the children became in some cases Roman citizens or Latins (see below). Business was transacted with them according to what the Romans called the law of the world (*jus gentium*): rights of verbal contract, and of tort, *e.g.* theft and Aquilian damage, are expressly named as recognized (Gai. iii 93; iv 37), and in some cases mancipation (Ulp. xix 4). They could not take under a Roman will: and to this disability Gaius attributes the origin of trusts (*fidei commissa*), which were however forbidden for this purpose by or before Hadrian (Gai. ii 285). Provision was made at Rome for suits between Romans and foreigners, and between foreigners with each other (Gai. i 6; iv 38, 105).

4. *Dediticii* are foreigners who had fought against the Romans and surrendered (cf. Liv. vii 31 § 9). They occupied the lowest place in the rank of freemen (Gai. i 14). To them were assimilated by the *lex Aelia Sentia* such freedmen as had been slaves and incurred disgrace. (See below, p. 32.)

B. Slaves were human beings without any legal rights, held and treated as articles of property, like intelligent animals. The contrast between their natural and legal position was constantly coming to the fore, and furnished matter for innumerable legal discussions and decisions. Persons became slaves principally by capture in war, or by birth from a slave mother. Some other special cases are given below (p. 43). Cf. D. i 5 fr 5.

CHAPTER II.

ACQUISITION OF CITIZENSHIP.

Roman citizenship was acquired by birth, by grant, by manumission, and under certain statutable provisions, especially some in favour of Latins.

A. CITIZENSHIP BY BIRTH.

Citizenship was primarily acquired by being the child of a Roman father by a lawful marriage (*justis nuptiis, justo matrimonio*)[1]. As regards nationality, if the mother was not Roman, she must be a citizen of a place or class recognized for intermarriage as on an equality with Rome. With slaves there could be no *conubium* (Ulp. v 2—5).

If there is *conubium* the child follows the condition of the father at the time of its conception: if there is not *conubium*, the law of the world (*jus gentium*) comes into exclusive force, and the child follows the condition of the mother at the time of the child's birth[2] (Gai. i 76—78, 89; Ulp. v 8—10; D. i 5 fr 19). An exception in favour of a child's freedom is mentioned below.

[1] *Conubium* between patricians and plebeians was effected by the *lex Canuleia* B.C. 445. Liv. iv 6; cf. *ib.* 3 § 11.

[2] This legal doctrine is applied with some humour in Cic. *Nat. D.* iii 18 § 45 to the question of the divinity of mythological heroes. *Quorum patres di, non erunt in deorum numero? Quid quorum matres? Opinor etiam magis. Ut enim jure civili qui est matre libera liber est, item jure naturae qui dea matre est, deus sit necesse est.*

In accordance with this law of the world, if the mother is a Roman citizen and the marriage or connexion is irregular, her child is Roman likewise. And this rule holds whether the father be a Latin or foreigner or *dediticius* or a slave. It is only by special statute that any other result comes. A *lex Minicia* directed that the child of a Roman woman and a foreigner (where there was no *conubium*) should be foreign; and a senate's decree under Hadrian made him the lawful child of his father. The same decree expressly sanctioned the rule, that the child follows the mother's condition where there is no *conubium*, in the case of marriages between a Roman wife and a Latin husband, and between Latins and foreigners, whether husbands or wives. The sanction appears to have been given to allay doubts which had been felt in consequence of the *lex Aelia Sentia* being thought to have created *conubium* between those who married in accordance with its provisions (Gai. i 77—82, 30; Ulp. iii 3; v 8).

Some cases of exception created by statute are mentioned. By the senate's decree under Claudius, confirming agreements to that effect between the woman and the master, a Roman woman cohabiting with a slave with the consent of the slave's owner gave birth to slave children. Hadrian restored the normal rule in this case also. Again by some law (not named in our text of Gaius) if a freeman cohabited with another's slave, believing her to be free, the children if male were free, if female were slave. Vespasian restored the rule, so that all followed the condition of the mother. Gaius adds that another clause of the same law remained in force by which the children of a free-woman who cohabited with one whom she knew to be the slave of another, were, contrary to the law of the world, slave (Gai. i 84, 85).

As illustrations of the rule that a child begotten in a lawful marriage (*justae nuptiae*) is of the condition of the father, whatever that of the mother be, Gaius gives three examples. A Roman wife, pregnant by a lawful marriage, suffers interdiction from fire and water. This makes her a foreigner, but her child though born afterwards is Roman. A like woman becomes a slave by the Claudian senate's decree for cohabiting with a slave against the express prohibition of the slave's owner. Still, if the child was the fruit of a previous lawful connexion, it is Roman. A foreign woman marries a foreigner according to the laws of the foreigners: if she herself becomes a Roman citizen, her child is still born a foreigner, unless (under the Hadrian senate's decree) the father also have a grant of Roman citizenship. But in all these cases, if the child was the fruit of an irregular connexion (*vulgo conceptus*), the status depends on the position of the mother at birth, and the child therefore is in the first case a foreigner, in the second a slave, in the third a Roman (Gai. i 89—92; Ulp. v 8, 9).

Paul, dealing with freedom not citizenship, makes the child to be free whether the mother be free at birth or at conception or only at an intermediate period; and (by Antonine rescripts) even though she be not actually free during gestation, provided there was a trust for her freedom and improper delay in giving effect to it (*Sent.* ii 24 §§ 1—4; cf. D. i 5 fr 5, 22; xxxviii 16 fr 1 § 1). Otherwise a child born of a *statulibera* is the heir's slave (D. xl 7 fr 16).

As regards the period of gestation recognized by the law, the XII tables declared that a child born in, but not after, ten months from the death of his father, was legitimate (*justus*). Hadrian is said to have allowed one born in the eleventh month to be legitimate (Gell. iii 16 § 12)[1]. On the other hand a child born in the seventh month was held (on the authority of Harpocrates) to be perfect, and accordingly one born on the 182nd day after the emancipation of his mother was decided by Ant. Pius to have been duly conceived in freedom (D. i 5 fr 12; xxxviii 16 fr 3 §§ 11, 12).

B. CITIZENSHIP BY GRANT[2].

1. Whole communities were from early days admitted to

[1] Pliny (*H. N.* vii § 40) gives a story on the authority of Masurius (Sabinus) that the praetor L. Papirius, holding the period of gestation to be uncertain, decided in favour of the possible legitimacy of a child alleged by his mother to be born in thirteen months.

[2] The 2nd and 3rd classes are referred to by Pliny (*Paneg.* 37) in speaking of the exemption from the 5 per cent. tax on inheritance which was at first restricted to the older citizens: *Haec mansuetudo legis veteribus civibus*

Roman citizenship[1]. On the conclusion of the Social war Roman citizenship was given by the *lex Julia* (B.C. 90) to all such *municipia* within Italy south of the Po as assented to the grant, and by the *lex Plautia Papiria* B.C. 89 to all members of communities in alliance with Rome who were then domiciled in Italy or within sixty days had declared their acceptance before the praetor (Cic. *Balb.* 8 § 21; *Arch.* 4 § 7). In B.C. 49 Julius Caesar gave citizenship to the transpadane Italians[2]. The emperor Claudius confirmed as Roman citizens the population of some districts adjoining Trento who had long acted as citizens (*Edict. de Anaunis*, Bruns No. 94, p. 240^b).

2. Some foreign communities obtained, either from the Roman people or the Senate or the Emperor, what was called the *jus Latii*[3] (*i.e.* the right of Latin colonists; Ascon. *in Pison.* p. 3 Kiessling). This was of two kinds, the greater and the less (*majus aut minus Latium*). By the greater all who held a magistracy or public office (*honorem*) and all members of the local council (*decuriones*) obtain Roman citizenship. In those communities which had the lesser right, only the holders of magistracy or public office obtain Roman citizenship. Gaius speaks of the children in both cases attaining citizenship along with their fathers (Gai. i 95, 96). In the Spanish borough of Salpensa, though possessing only the lesser right, parents, wives, and children born of a statutable marriage, and grandchildren through a son, if in the power of their parents, get citizenship

servabatur; novi, seu per Latium in civitatem seu beneficio principis venissent, nisi simul cognationis jura impetrassent, alienissimi habebantur quibus conjunctissimi fuerant. Kinship (*cognatio*) rested on descent from a lawful marriage, and that presumed *conubium*; which there was not between Roman and this kind of Latin (cf. Huschke *Gaius* p. 19).

[1] Cf. Cic. *Balb.* 13 § 31 *Et ex Latio multi ut Tusculani, ut Lanuvini, et ex ceteris regionibus gentes universae in civitatem sunt receptae, ut Sabinorum, Volscorum, Hernicorum.*

[2] See on these and other grants Madvig *Verwaltung* i §§ 2, 3; Mommsen *Staatsrecht* iii 662.

[3] Asconius mentions this right as given to the Transpadani by Cn. Pompeius Strabo (father of Pomp. Magnus). Cicero refers to it in speaking (B.C. 51) of a citizen of Como whom Marcellus had beaten; *Marcellus foede de Comensi: etsi ille magistratum non gesserat erat tamen Transpadanus* (*Att.* v 11 § 2, cf. Appian *B. Civ.* ii 26).

along with the magistrate, *etc.* himself (*lex munic. Salp.* 21). The *majus Latium* is only known to us through Gaius (Mommsen *Staatsr.* iii p. 640).

3. Individuals also sometimes obtained Roman citizenship (*jus Quiritium*) from a victorious general (cf. Cic. *Balb.* 8 § 19; 21 § 48; *Arch.* 10 §§ 24, 25), later from the emperor (Ulp. iii 2)[1]. Special instances of this are the grants to veterans on their discharge; if they were foreigners, they obtained citizenship for themselves their children and descendants[2], and the right of intermarriage (*conubium*) with their wives if they had one, if not, with such wife as they next married. If they were already Roman citizens, the grant is of intermarriage with foreigners and consequent Roman citizenship for the children (Gai. i 5, 7). Many bronze tablets exist, ranging from Claudius to Diocletian which were given to soldiers in evidence of such a grant. (Corp. I. R. iii 843—919; Eph. Epig. ii, iv, v; specimens in Bruns[6], p. 252 sqq.)

4. Caracalla in 212 A.D. granted Roman citizenship to all persons in the Roman world, *in orbe Romano qui sunt* (D. i 5 fr 17; Dion Cass. lxxvii 9), *i.e.* to all free persons at that time. Whether further limitations should be made on the generality of the expression, *e.g.* whether all Junian Latins, whether *dediticii, etc.* were included, is doubtful. The notices are very meagre. It is stated that this grant was dictated by financial considerations, in order to increase the number of persons liable to the death-duty of 5 per cent. (*vicesima*) or, as Caracalla made it, 10 per cent. (*decima*) on inheritances (Dion Cass. l.c.).

C. Citizenship by manumission.

Slaves had no civic position: they belonged to the family,

[1] Suetonius says of Augustus (cap. 40) *Magni existimans sincerum atque ab omni colluvione peregrini ac servilis sanguinis incorruptum servare populum, et civitatem Romanam parcissime dedit et manumittendi modum terminavit* (cf. *lex Fuf. Canin.* p. 33).

[2] *Liberis posterisque* is omitted in some grants: others have *ipsis filiisque, etc.* (Bruns p. 253). *Caligula negabat jure civitatem Romanam usurpasse eos quorum majores sibi posterisque eam impetrassent, nisi si filii essent, neque enim intellegi debere posteros ultra hunc gradum* (Suet. *Cal.* 38).

not to the State. But their manumission was a matter of State concern (xl 5 fr 53), for they thereby became citizens[1].

i. Manumission in due form took place in three ways only, *censu, vindicta, testamento*[2], *i.e.* by official inclusion in the list of citizens, or by an act of the slave's master before one of the higher magistrates, or by the dying declaration of the head of the family, to whom the XII tables had given quasi-legislative authority over his own estate.

1. *Censu* 'by entry in the censor's roll of citizens,' the slave declaring his property (*censum profiteri*) as one of the citizens at the bidding of his master. It was a disputed question, as early as Cicero's time at least, whether the freedom dated from the entry on the roll or from the formal conclusion of the *lustrum* (Cic. *Orat.* i 40 § 183; Ulp. i 9; Dosith. 17). This proceeding took place only at Rome, but a somewhat similar declaration was used in the provinces (Dosith. l.c.).

2. *Vindicta* 'by rod,' *i.e.* by symbolical action of the master before the consul, praetor, proconsul (after leaving Rome) or Caesar's lieutenant or praefect of Egypt. A formal sitting in Court was not required: it could be done as the praetor, *etc.* was passing along the streets to the bath or theatre or for a ride or was staying in a country house (Gai. i 20; Ulp. i 7; D. xl 2 fr 7, 8, 17, 18, 21). A praetor could manumit his own slaves *apud se*, his own authority being sufficient, and he could as father or guardian authorize his son or ward to manumit in the same way. But he could not manumit before his own colleague or any one who had only equal *imperium* to himself. The actual presence of the master was held not to be necessary, if he authorised his son to act[3] (fr 1, 5, 18, 22, cf. 15 § 3; xl 1 fr 14). The details of the ceremony are variously and

[1] Cf. Plin. *Ep.* viii 16 *Servis respublica quaedam et quasi civitas domus est.* The ordinary plea in excuse of non-appearance in court, that the person was absent on public service (*reipublicae causa*), had no application in the case of a slave (D. ii 11 fr 7).

[2] This enumeration is found in Cic. *Top.* 2 § 10 *Si neque censu nec vindicta nec testamento liber factus est, non est liber.*

[3] Mitteis (*ZRG.* xxxiv p. 202), with reason, takes all passages speaking of rod-manumission by a son with consent of his father to have originally referred only to formless manumission and to have been interpolated.

incompletely reported[1]. The freedom took effect at once. Doubts of either master or slave as to ownership did not prevent the freedom, if he really was master (D. xl 2 fr 4 § 1).

3. *Testamento* 'by last will of the master' (Ulp. i 9). This was done in such words as *Stichus* (or *Stichus servus meus*) *liber esto*, or *liber sit* or *Stichum liberum esse jubeo.* If no time or condition was added, the freedom took effect if a necessary heir existed (even though abstaining from the inheritance), or if any of the heirs entered, or if they passed over the will and obtained possession of the estate. The heir's obtaining subsequent reinstatement (*in integrum restitutus*) does not affect the freedom once gained. Where the freedom is postponed till a certain time, or made dependent on a condition, the freedom takes

[1] The usual theory is that it was a feigned suit (like *in jure cessio*) at least originally (see Unterholzner *ZRG.* ii p. 139 sq. and others). This is supported by Boethius (*ad* Cic. *Top.* 2 § 10), who says the lictor put a rod (*vindicta*, explained by *virgula*) on the head of the slave and claimed him into freedom (*in libertatem vindicabat*, see below p. 46. Cf. Gai. iv 16; Cic. *Att.* vii 2 *ad fin.*; Liv. xli 9, which however is corrupt and not clearly intelligible). Persius (v 175) speaks of *festuca, lictor quam jactat.* Hermogenian (D. xl 2 fr 23) says the ceremony in his time (4th century?) was done entirely by lictors, the master saying nothing, and the customary formula being taken as said. According to the earlier Jurists it is the master who imposes the rod and declares the slave to be free (*e.g.* D. xl 12 fr 12 § 2, *etc.*; Karlowa *RG.* ii 132 sq.). In Festus' description (abridged by Paul, p. 158) nothing is said of the rod; the master holding the head or one of the limbs of the slave said *hunc hominem liberum esse volo*, and then gives him a turn and *e manu hominem liberum mittit.* Persius (v 78) also speaks of the turn; *verterit hunc dominus, momento turbinis exit Marcus Dama*, 'by the force of the whirl the slave comes out free.' So also Appian *B. Civ.* iv 135, Sen. *Ep.* i 8 § 7, Quint. *Decl.* 342. The scholiast on Persius (v 76, 88) speaks of a blow given to the slave on the head by the praetor; so also Claudian (*Cons. Hon.* iv 615) and other late writers in Rein *Privatrecht* p. 571. Acro on Hor. *Sat.* ii 7, 76 is uncertain whether the slave was struck with the rod or it was placed on him: Horace himself speaks of *vindicta imposita.* Plautus speaks of slaves going to the praetor that he may free them (*Pseudol.* 358), no doubt referring to the formal declaration after the ceremony. He refers to the rod *Mil.* 961 *Ingenua, an festucā facta e serva liberast.*

Cicero refers metaphorically to this mode of manumission in writing to Quintus his brother: *Te item ab eo vindico et libero*, 'I declare you free from all obligations to him' (iii 1. 3 § 9).

effect on the arrival of the time or occurrence of the condition. No application to the heir or action by him was necessary. The testator can take away the freedom by the same will or by codicil confirmed by the will, but the taking away must be in like words to the giving. A slave in order to be set free by will must be testator's slave in full right, both at the time of making the will and at the time of death. This rule is as old as Servius. (Gai. ii 267; Ulp. i 22, 23; ii 7, 12; D. xl 4 fr 23, 25, 32, 35; tit. 5 fr 55 § 1; Cod. vii 2 fr 3).

Slaves directed to be set free by a damnatory form or by words of trust are not strictly set free by will, but wait for the heir or other trustee to free them *vindicta*.

A slave manumitted by will, if the manumission is only to take place after a certain time or on the occurrence of a condition, was called a *statuliber* 'free by appointment[1].' Before the will was made effective by an heir's entry, the prospect of freedom might be extinguished by usucapion or otherwise. But after an heir has entered, the slave's position is assured, and cannot be affected by his being sold or bequeathed or adjudicated or gained by usucapion or noxally surrendered or in any other way alienated or pledged. He carries his title to freedom with him (*cum sua causa alienatur*). When the condition is fulfilled or the time limited comes, he is free (Ulp. ii 1—6; Festus s. v. *statuliber*; D. xl 7 fr 1, 2 § 1, 6 § 3). If the heir or other interested person puts hindrances in the way of the condition being fulfilled, the condition is treated as fulfilled. If the condition is one requiring performance on the slave's part, his readiness to perform was held to be sufficient (*Hoc jure utimur in statulibero ut sufficiat per eum non stare quo minus condicioni pareat, ib.* fr 3 § 10; tit. 4 fr 55 pr; see Book III chap. viii H 9). In the interim a *statuliber* is just like any other slave: his position was not altered, but there was a tendency to protect him and facilitate his freedom. The position, if not the name, was recognised by the XII tables (Ulp. ii 4; D. xl 7 fr 29 pr, 33).

Slaves under a trust for manumission are meantime in the

[1] Cf. Plaut. *Curcul.* i 1. 5 *status condictus dies cum hoste*, 'a day appointed and agreed with the enemy.'

position of a *statuliber* and protected in the same way (D. xl 5 fr 24 § 21; fr 51 § 3). See below Book III chap. ix 8.

A slave, bequeathed and directed to be free on payment to the legatee, derives his freedom from testator, and the bequest is thereby extinguished. Q. Mucius, Aquilius Gallus, and Labeo held him to be *statuliber*; Servius and Ofilius denied this, regarding him as in the interim the slave of the legatee. Ulpian (in D.) agrees with the former (D. xl 7 fr 39 pr).

ii. Effect and requirements of valid manumission.

1. A slave manumitted became, as a rule the freedman of the manumitter. If manumitted by will, he was called *orcinus libertus*, freedman of Orcus (who was taken as representing the dead), and the rights of patron were exercised by deceased's children or such as he assigned them to (see Ch. ix). If the manumission was completely regular, the freedman became at once a Roman citizen; an informal manumission (if valid) made the slave only a Latin.

2. For valid manumission the manumitter must have full ownership and full power of disposal. If the slave is his only *in bonis* (see Book IV chap. iii c 5), he becomes a Latin; if only *ex jure Quiritium*, the manumission would have no effect on the slave's position, but would probably destroy his own right, and the equitable owner would become by accretion full owner (cf. Vangerow *Lat. Jun.* p. 44). A partial owner by manumitting forfeits his share, which then accrues to his partner, if the manumission was by will[1] or rod; if it was informal, most lawyers held that it had no effect. If the usufruct is out in another, the bare owner by formal manumission destroys his own right; and the slave becomes ownerless, but still subject to the right of the usufructuary (Ulp. i 16, 18, 19; Paul iv. 12 § 1; Dosith. 9—11). A husband if solvent can, while the marriage subsists, free a dowry-slave and become his patron

[1] In cases of trust, rescripts of Severus and Caracalla decided that the other partner should be compelled to sell his share to a partner wishing to emancipate a slave. Some lawyers held this earlier (Cod. vii 7 fr 1 § 1 *a*).

(D. xxxviii 16 fr 3 § 2; xl 1 fr 21). If a slave is bequeathed and the heir manumits him, he becomes free only if the legatee renounce; or, where the bequest was conditional, only if the condition fail (Vat. 84; D. xli 1 fr 11). The vendor or promiser of a slave can free him, as until delivery he remains owner, though liable on his contract (*ib.* fr 18). A woman unless she has the *jus trium liberorum* (see Book II chap. X B), and wards require their guardian's authority for manumission besides the approval required by the Aelian Sentian law (Ulp. i 17; D. xxvi 8 fr 9 § 1). Deaf and dumb persons could free a slave informally only; they could however attach to the sale of a slave a condition for his being freed (Paul iv 12 § 2). A son in his father's power could not free a slave belonging to his *peculium*, unless by order of his father, in which case the slave became the father's freedman (D. xxxvii 14 fr 13).

3. A letter of M. Aurelius and his brother authorised or regulated the purchase by slaves of their freedom. An arrangement would be made by a slave with some third party to purchase him from his master, with money supplied by the slave, and then manumit him. It did not matter whence the money came, whether from the slave's *peculium*[1] (belonging in law to the vendor) or not: it might be from some chance gain, or from the kindness of a friend giving it or advancing it or guarantying it, or even money of the purchaser's own, provided it was merely an advance, and the purchaser bought by an arrangement made with the slave and not on his own account. Neither the age of the vendor nor that of the purchaser was regarded: an *impubes* could act as purchaser, for he was not, in freeing the slave, alienating anything really his own. A slave so self-purchased was said *suis nummis emi*, although, as Ulpian says, he could have no money legally his own; the whole purchase was fictitious (*imaginaria*) and winked at by the law. If the nominal purchaser did not

[1] Application of money from the *peculium* to purchase a slave's freedom was no doubt often made before this constitution of Hadrian. Cf. Sen. *Ep.* 80 § 4 *Peculium suum, quod comparaverunt ventre fraudato, pro capite numerant.* A slave might make agreements for this purpose with his master, cf. D. xxxiii 8 fr 8 § 5.

manumit him after receiving payment in full, the slave could himself *consistere cum domino, i.e.* himself bring his plaint against his master into the court of the city praefect or, in the provinces, of the Governor[1]. If he failed to prove his case, he was liable to be sent to the mines, unless his master preferred to have him given back to him, but no severer punishment was allowed. If he proved his case, the purchaser was compelled to set him free, his freedom dating from the purchase; for M. Aurelius' constitution directed not that he should be pronounced free, but that his liberty should be restored to him (D. xl 1 fr 4, 5; v 1 fr 67).

4. The *lex Aelia Sentia* A.D. 4 (cf. Dion Cass. lv 13) enacted various provisions in restraint of inconsiderate manumission[2]:

(*a*) No slave less than 30 years[3] old should become a Roman citizen unless manumitted by rod for lawful cause shewn and approved. Lawful cause usually was near relationship or association, *e.g.* if a person manumitted his (natural) son or daughter or brother or sister or father or mother or a foster brother or teacher (*educator, paedagogus*) or school

[1] Papinian held that though a mandate given by a slave to a third person to buy and free him was in itself null, yet it might be regarded as creating for his master an action against the purchaser to compel his manumission (D. xvii 1 fr 54).

[2] Cf. Suet. *Aug.* 40 *Augustus servos non contentus multis difficultatibus a libertate et multo pluribus a libertate justa removisse, cum aut de numero et de conditione ac differentia eorum qui manumitterentur curiose cavisset, hoc quoque adjecit ne vinctus umquam tortusve quis ullo libertatis genere civitatem adipisceretur.*

[3] A person is not under 20 (or 30) years of age on completion (at midnight) of the 365th day of the 20th (or 30th) year from his birth. The last day is treated as indivisible. A person born any hour on 1 Jan. A.D. 4 was not under 20 years of age a moment after the midnight which completes the 31 Dec. A.D. 24; but not over 20 until after midnight of 1 Jan. A.D. 25 (D. xl 1 fr 1). This mode of reckoning applies also to usucapion (D. xli 3 fr 6, 7), to age for will capacity (D. xxviii 1 fr 5), and to the age of a child (*anniculus*) required for obtaining citizenship under the *lex Aelia Sentia* (D. L 16 fr 134). Savigny suggests that it would apply generally where a right has to be acquired; but that a right (*e.g.* of bringing suit) is not lost until the 365th day has been completed (D. xliv 7 fr 6; *Syst.* iv § 188). But see Windscheid *Pand.* § 103.

attendant (*capsarius*) or nurse or (especially in the case of women manumitters) a nursling; or one intended to be his procurator (provided he was at least 18 years old), or a female slave intended to be the manumitter's wife, provided in accordance with a decree of the senate that he made oath to marry her within six months. Further the manumitter must have more slaves than the one manumitted. Other lawful causes are that the manumitter has been appointed heir on condition of his manumitting a slave, or has received a gift or price expressly for the manumission, or that he is fulfilling the trust for which the slave has been given him; or that the slave has aided him in battle or against robbers or plots or in sickness. The cause, whatever it be, must be approved[1] by a special bench, composed in Rome of five senators and five Roman knights of full age (*puberes*); in the provinces of twenty Recoverers, all Roman citizens. The time for this procedure was in Rome on certain fixed days; in the provinces on the last day of the assize. In default of such approval, a slave manumitted by rod remained a slave (of Caesar, according to Ulpian's text), manumitted by will, became a Latin. And even for informal manumission so as to make him a Latin, the consent of the bench was required by a master under 20 years of age[1]. Such a master could not stipulate that his debtor should manumit a slave; nor by will could he manumit any, although if *pubes* he could make a will, appoint an heir, and leave legacies. An attempted manumission by will made the slave only a Latin (Gai. i 18—20, 38—41; Ulp. i 12—13*a*; D. xlv 1 fr 66; xl 2 fr 11—16, 20). A master under the age of puberty requires his guardian's authority as well as the approval of the bench, and the slave does not carry away his *peculium* (*ib.* fr 24).

The only exception to the requirement of 30 years of age for the slave was where he was appointed heir and free by a

[1] See note 3, p. 30. A like rule is laid down in the charter of Salpensa cap. 28. A burgher under 20 years of age frees his slave (who becomes a Latin, Salpensa being a Latin colony) before the *duoviri*, but has to get approval of his action by the same number of town councillors (*decuriones*) as is required for making a borough-decree.

master who was insolvent and could have no other heir under the will. If the master also appointed a substitute, the substitute was preferred (Gai. i 21; D. xxviii 5 fr 58).

(*b*) Another provision of the law refused freedom to all slaves manumitted with intent to defraud creditors or patron (Gai. i 47; Ulp. i 15). There was a breach of the law if the manumitter was not solvent at the time (both of death and heir's entry) or would cease to be solvent if the freedoms took effect. Fraudulent purpose was required as well as insufficient means, otherwise the freedoms are not revoked (Cod. vii 11 fr 1; D. xl 9 fr 10; cf. Just. i 6 § 3). If several were manumitted and testator's means allowed of some becoming free, those first named had the preference, unless they were too valuable, in which case later ones got the benefit (D. xl 9 fr 18, 24). This part of the law was extended by a senate's decree on Hadrian's authority to the wills of foreigners (Gai. i 47); and to trusts for inheritance and freedoms (D. xxviii 5 fr 84 § 1). Entry on the inheritance by a wealthy heir did not mend the original fault; nor was it mended, if the slave himself (though not from his *peculium*) or another for him pays his value (D. xl 9 fr 5 pr, 18, 91). A slave in (particular) pledge could not be freed unless the owner were solvent or the debt were paid (*ib.* fr 29, cf. Cod. vii 8 fr 1—5). A slave freed was in the position of a *statuliber*, till the creditor or creditors decided on enforcing their rights (D. xl 7 fr 1).

(*c*) Further the law provided that slaves who had suffered disgrace by being put in chains by their masters or had been branded, or put to the question by torture for some harmful act (*ob noxam*) and been convicted thereof, or had been given over to fight as gladiators or with wild beasts, or had been sent into a gladiatorial school or into prison, and afterwards manumitted formally or informally by the same master or another, whether under or over 30 years, should not become Roman citizens or even Latins but be classed with *peregrini dediticii*. They could not take under a will and, according to the better opinion, could not make a will, though this was not clearly expressed in the statute. Their estate passed on death to their patrons, according as they would have been Roman citizens or Latins but for their fault. They were not allowed to reside in, or within a hundred miles of, Rome: if they did, they and their estates were to be sold, on the terms of their not so residing and not being manumitted. If manumitted, they became slaves of the Roman people. And no statute or senate's decree or imperial constitution opened for these *dediticii* any way to citizenship. Ulpian accounts for their not being able to make a will by the consideration that being foreigners they could not make a will as Romans, and yet were not of any particular foreign community so as to make a will according to the laws of that state. (Gai. i 13—15; 25—27; iii 74—76; Ulp. i 11; xx 14.)

Such a bar to full freedom was so serious, that it was allowed only where the chaining was the intelligent act of an absolute owner. If it was done by a part owner or by a madman or by one under the age of puberty or by an heir charged with a trust for manumission, it did not prejudice the slave's claims to lawful freedom (*justa libertas*). Nor of course, if when tortured he confessed to no fault. Nor if he be in pledge, can either creditor or debtor chain him without the other's consent. On the other hand it is not necessary that the master should act personally: if he order the chaining or approve the act of his procurator or other agent in so punishing the slave, it is enough, though the liberty is not prejudiced, if he was willing to condone the conduct before he heard of his being put in chains. Imprisonment did not convey the same disgrace as chains (Paul iv 12 §§ 2—8; D. L 16 fr 216).

On similar grounds of policy, slaves were debarred from freedom by the praefect or governor on account of some criminal offence; and a constitution of Hadrian refused freedom to one manumitted in order to avoid a criminal charge. By the Fabian law a slave punished by his master for kidnapping could not be set free for ten years from the time of his master's death. Nor could a slave be freed who had been sold with the condition not to be freed, or had been forbidden freedom by his master's will (D. xl 1 fr 8 § 3, 9, 12).

5. The *lex Fufia Caninia* passed in the reign of Augustus (Suet. *Aug.* 40) put a limit to the number of slaves who might be freed by will. The limit was in proportion to the number

of slaves owned by testator. Anyone might free one or two; above two he might free one half of his slaves not exceeding five; above five, one third of his slaves not exceeding ten; above ten he was limited to freeing one fourth not exceeding twenty-five; above twenty-five, one-fifth; nor in any case might he free more than one hundred. If the number allowed was exceeded, all manumissions in excess were void; whenever there was no ascertainable order for manumission, all were void (Gai. i 42—46; Ulp. i 24, 25; Paul iv 14 § 4). The like rules applied, if a master being sick tried to evade the law by not making any will, but at the point of death writing to free slaves in excess of the number allowed (Gai. *Epit.* i. 3); or if he bequeathed a slave with a request to the legatee to free him in like excess (D. xxxv 1 fr 37). Manumissions by codicils, whenever made, ranked after those contained in the will itself. Slaves who had run away were counted in the full number of testator's slaves for the purpose of calculating the limit. The law required that slaves, who were to be freed, should be named (*libertates nominatim dentur*), *i.e.* identified by name or trade, *etc.* (Paul iv 14; Ulp. i 25; D. xl 4 fr 24). This law did not in any way interfere with manumissions *inter vivos* whether formal or informal, so that, if there were no other obstruction, a man might, whilst alive and well, free all his slaves (Gai. i 44; *Epit.* i § 4).

6. The *lex Julia de adulteriis* provided that no woman should free or alienate any of her slaves within sixty days from her divorce (unless the divorce was friendly) or repudiation, the object being to prevent slaves from being withdrawn from examination which might prove her adultery. Her father and mother were also forbidden to manumit any slaves belonging to them but assigned for their daughter's service. The lawyers extended the application of the statute so as to invalidate manumissions made after sixty days, where the inquiry was not finished and the slaves were supposed to be cognisant of or concerned in the offence; and also any manumissions or alienations made before divorce but clearly shown to have been made in contemplation of it. A slave actually manumitted before the sixty days is in the position of a *statuliber* (D. xl 9 fr 12—14).

D. Freedom (and citizenship) by statute without manumission.

(1) One who exposed the murder of his master received freedom as a reward and became *orcinus libertus*, unless the praetor in conferring freedom assigned him to some one as patron (D. xxxviii 16 fr 3 § 4; xl 8 fr 5).

(2) One who was sold (or given, Cod. iv 57 fr 1) on condition of being manumitted within a certain time or during the life of the purchaser, and was not duly manumitted became, by a constitution of M. Aurelius, free at the expiration of the time or at the death of the purchaser, as the case might be, unless the vendor, being alive when the manumission should take place, no longer desired effect to be given to the condition (*ib.* fr 1, 3, 4). Such a slave became freedman of the purchaser, who however had no right to impose services (D. xxxvii 14 fr 8 § 1; xxxviii 1 fr 13 pr; tit. 16 fr 3 § 3). So also when a master received money to free a slave of his own and did not do so (D. xl 12 fr 38 § 1).

(3) One to whom freedom was due under a trust, but those charged with the trust, though summoned by the praetor did not appear, was pronounced by the praetor to be as if freed directly (*SC. Rubrianum* A.D. 103). The like enactment was made by the *SC. Dasumianum*, where the parties charged were lawfully absent (D. xl 5 fr 26 § 7; 36 pr. See also *SC. Juncianum* A.D. 127, *ib.* fr 28 § 4, and Book III chap. ix).

(4) A rescript of M. Aurelius (quoted in Just. iii 11) facilitated the freedom of slaves, whenever, a testator having given freedoms either directly or by way of trust, no heir whether under the will or *ab intestato* was willing to enter on account of the debts, and the estate was thus in danger of being sold and the freedoms being defeated. M. Aurelius directed that if any one of the slaves thus in danger of losing his freedom should undertake to give security for the discharge of the debts in full with interest, the estate should be assigned (*bona addicentur*) to him, and the other slaves as well as himself should become free at once, or, if the will postponed the freedom of the others, then they should become free according

as the will prescribed. Those who were to be freed under trust became his freedmen; those to whom freedom was given directly would be *orcini liberti,* unless in his application to the praetor he made the condition that they should become his freedmen and they consented thereto. The benefit of this constitution was extended also to cases of intestacy where trust freedoms were given by codicils, and to cases where the slaves to be freed were not the testator's. According to a rescript of Gordian (Cod. vii 2 fr 6 and recital in fr 15) not only one of the slaves but an outsider was permitted to make an application under this rescript; a slave in pledge was not. The assignee of the estate was put in the same position as a *bonorum possessor,* and would have right to the tombs (*jura sepulcrorum*). If the estate should be assigned to more than one slave, they will hold in common and be patrons in common, with a right to the suit *fam. ercisc.* (D. xl 5 fr 2—4; Cod. vi 27 fr 1).

CHAPTER III.

GRADUAL ACQUISITION OF CITIZENSHIP.

A. In the ways described Roman citizenship was obtained at once; but there were not a few cases in which a slave became a citizen, only after passing through an intermediate condition in which he was assimilated to a Latin colonist. Informal manumission[1], *i.e.* manumission by a living owner without observance of the ceremony of the rod was apparently common enough, partly perhaps from the difficulty, especially in the provinces, of finding a competent magistrate ready and present to sanction the act[2]. If a master simply by word of mouth in

[1] Cf. Tac. *An.* xiii 27 *Quin et manumittendi duas species institutas ut relinqueretur paenitentiae aut novo beneficio locus. Quos vindicta patronus non liberaverit, velut vinclo servitutis attineri. Dispiceret quisque merita, tardeque concederet quod datum non amitteretur.*

[2] Pliny writing to his wife's grandfather, a man of advanced age, tells him that a friend Caelestinus Tiro is passing through Ticinum (now

ordinary intercourse (*inter amicos*) declared a slave to be henceforth free, or addressed a letter to him with the like declaration, there was no legal change in the slave's condition, but practical recognition was given to the master's declared will. The slave remained a slave in the eye of the law, his acquisitions, however made, vested in his master exactly as a slave's *peculium*, and remained his master's on the quasi-slave's death: he could sue and be sued only through him. But the praetor protected him against otherwise being treated as a slave (*e.g. per vim duci, servire, etc.*). He was described as being or abiding in freedom (*esse, morari in libertate*) by his master's will and being released from actual servitude. The act of the master must be entirely voluntary: it is vitiated by any compulsion whether by individuals or by popular acclamation (Gai. iii 56; Dosith. 4, 5, 7, cf. D. xl 9 fr 17 pr; xli 2 fr 38 pr).

The like condition of imperfect freedom was the result of other acts showing the owner's intention[1]. Slaves who by the deceased's or his heir's direction preceded his funeral wearing a cap (*pileati*) or even standing on the litter and fanning the corpse; slave women given by their owners in marriage and furnished with a deed of dowry; slaves whose masters handed over to them or destroyed the documents shewing them to be slaves; or who were addressed in the court proceedings (*apud acta*) by their masters with the name of sons, took the same position. So also women who had been prostituted in violation of the conditions of sale, slaves who had been abandoned on account of grave sickness (by edict of Claudius), or had been freed by will or rod but expressly declared only to be Latins; or been freed by a master under the age of twenty (above p. 31), or by one who had not ownership *ex jure Quiritium*; and even a *statuliber* manumitted by an outsider before the condition of

Pavia) to the province of Baetica as proconsul, and adds *confido facile me impetraturum ut ex itinere deflectat ad te, si voles vindicta liberare, quos proxime inter amicos manumisisti* (*Ep.* vii 16). In *Ep.* 32 (cf. also 23) he says *quod scribis, oblata occasione proconsulis plurimos manumissos, unice laetor.* A proconsul had jurisdiction for this purpose immediately after leaving Rome. For an allusion to the long journey sometimes necessary to obtain full manumission see D. xii 4 fr 5 § 4.

[1] Cf. Quintil. *Dec.* 340, 342.

freedom occurred. There were, according to Justinian's somewhat boastful rhetoric, innumerable other cases (Cod. vii 6, cf. vi 4 fr 4 § 2).

Such half-emancipated slaves obtained through the *lex Junia* (passed probably in Augustus' reign[1] before the *lex Aelia Sentia*) legal *status*; they were made freemen with the rights of Latin colonists, but with an important modification. They had no power of making a will, nor except by way of trust could they take either inheritance or legacy under a will, or be appointed guardians by a will, but they were competent to take part as witnesses, balance-holder, or purchaser of the family for another's will. Such freedmen were often called to distinguish them from the older Latins, *Latini Juniani* (Gai. i 22; Dosith. 6; Ulp. i 10, xi 16, xx 8, xxii 3, 8). For some modification of the rights of patrons to their estate by the *SC. Largianum* and for succession to Latins generally, see Book III chap. vi D.

Manumission by a foreigner had the same effect as informal manumission by a Roman before the *lex Junia*; the slave did not become a Latin, but was protected in freedom by the praetor unless some foreign law provided otherwise (Dosith. 12).

B. Several modes were provided for Latins and foreigners to become full Roman citizens (*ex jure Quiritium*). They were due to a desire of the legislator to encourage either marriage or certain occupations useful to the State.

1. The *lex Aelia Sentia* (Gai. i 29, 80; *lex Junia* Ulp. iii 3) dealt with the case of slaves manumitted under 30 years of age without the justification and approval required by that law. A senate's decree in the consulship of Pegasus and Pusio (*i.e.* in Vespasian's time) extended the provisions to persons above that age who had been manumitted and become (Junian) Latins. Under these provisions any Latin who had married a Roman or Latin wife, whether she was a Latin colonist or one

[1] It used to be referred to A.D. 19 on account of the title *Junia Norbana* given it by Just. i 5 § 3; Mommsen is inclined to put it at end of Republic (*Staatsr.* iii 626): Ducaillaud and Schneider put it in B.C. 25 (*ZRG.* xviii 249; cf. also vols. xx and xxi). Girard (*Dr. R.* p. 120) puts it between A.U.C. 710 and 727.

of the same position as her husband, and had a child by her at least a year old (*anniculus*) could apply to the Praetor (or provincial Govèrnor), with a declaration made by him in the presence of seven Roman citizens of full age that he had married her in order to acquire children (*liberorum quaerendorum causa*), and if the praetor, before whom the case had been proved (*causa probata*), pronounced the fact to be so, he, his wife and the child (if not already Roman citizens, see chap. ii A) all became Roman citizens and the child was under his father's power. If the husband died before he had proved his case, the widow was allowed to do so (Gai. i 29—32; Ulp. iii 3; D. L 16 fr 134).

2. A senate's decree (perhaps that in the consulship of Pegasus and Pusio) extended this privilege and procedure to the case of Latins and foreigners with whom there was no *conubium*, married under a mistake of their legal *status* and having a child of any age (Gai. i 67, 73 mutilated). The cases mentioned are:

(*a*) a Roman man married to a Latin, foreign or dediticious woman believing her to be Roman (Gai. i 67);

(*b*) a Roman woman married to a foreign or dediticious man believing him to be Roman or Latin (*ib.* 68);

(*c*) a Latin man married to a foreign woman believing her to be Roman or Latin (*ib.* 69);

(*d*) a Latin woman married to a foreign man believing him to be Latin (*ib.* 69);

(*e*) a Roman man married to a Latin woman believing himself to be Latin; or married to a foreign woman believing himself to be foreign (*ib.* 71);

(*f*) a foreign man married to a Roman woman believing her to be foreign. This last case was inferred from an expression in a rescript of Antoninus Pius (*ib.* 74, 75).

But a dediticious person did not become a Roman citizen even by this application, though his wife or her husband (as the case might be) and the child did, but the child did not come under his father's power.

3. Latins of more than 30 years of age became Roman citizens by the master's repeating (*iteratione*) the manumission

either by rod, census or will, provided the master was owner *ex jure Quiritium*, whether he had the slave *in bonis* also or not. But if he was bare Quiritary owner, he had no right to the inheritance of his freedman: that passed by grant of possession to the equitable owner (Gai. i 35; Ulp. iii 4). This was probably enacted by the *lex Junia*. The *SC. Pegasianum* gave him the right of obtaining on application citizenship for his children (Ulp. i 1).

4. A senate's decree gave Roman citizenship to Latin women who had three children by irregular intercourse. (So Ulp. iii 1, but text doubtful.)

5. Certain occupations gave Latins the *jus Quiritium*, viz.,

(*a*) by the *lex Visellia* (probably A.D. 24, Mommsen *Staatsr.* iii 424) military service in the fire-brigade (*inter vigiles*) at Rome for six years. A senate's decree is said to have reduced the period to three years (Gai. i 32 *b*; Ulp. iii 5);

(*b*) by an edict of Claudius[1], building a seagoing vessel capable of carrying not less than ten thousand bushels (*modii*) of corn and carrying corn in her or in a substitute to Rome for six years (Gai. i 33; Ulp. iii 6);

(*c*) by a constitution of Nero (probably), having a property of 200000 sesterces or more, and spending not less than half on the erection of a house in Rome (Gai. i 33; Ulp. iii 1);

(*d*) by a constitution of Trajan, carrying on a bakery in Rome, for not less than 100 bushels (*modios*) of corn daily (Gai. i 34; Ulp. iii 1).

6. Grant of citizenship from the Emperor was sometimes obtained[2]. Trajan laid down that if a Latin obtained this without the knowledge or consent of his patron, he was a citizen in other respects and his children were citizens also, but his patron could claim his estate on death. If he made a will, he must

[1] Cf. Suet. *Claud.* 18, 19 *Naves mercaturae causa fabricantibus magna commoda constituit pro conditione cujusque; civi vacationem legis Papiae Poppaeae, Latino jus Quiritium, feminis jus* IIII. *liberorum; quae constituta hodieque servantur.*

[2] Cf. Plin. *Ep. Traj.* 6 (=22) *Ago gratias, domine, quod et jus Quiritium libertis necessariae mihi feminae et civitatem Romanam Harpocrati iatraliptae meo sine mora indulsisti; ib.* 11 (=6); 104 (=105) where the subjects are spoken of as Latins.

appoint his patron heir, and could appoint a substitute only if the patron declined. Hadrian however allowed him to gain full citizenship, if he proved his case under the Aelian Sentian law or the senate's decree (Ulp. iii 2; Gai. iii 72, 73).

CHAPTER IV.

LOSS OF CITIZENSHIP.

The various rights, which belonged to a Roman as freeman, citizen, and member of a family, were regarded collectively as forming his *caput* ('head,' 'life,' 'personality'), and any loss of such rights was a 'lessening, impairing, of the *caput*.' The words *deminutio* and *diminutio* are both used[1]. It is by Gaius paralleled, in some cases of obligation, to death (Gai. iii 101); after incurring such loss the person was differently situated; and rights and obligations which were suitable to his former position were incompatible with his new one, or at least required renewal.

The Romans made three degrees of such 'head-lessening' or 'head-abatement,' according as it was the loss of freedom, of citizenship, of family membership; *maxima*, *media* or *minor*, and *minima capitis deminutio*. The last will be dealt with in Book II.

A. Roman citizenship is lost usually in consequence of the loss of freedom (*maxima capitis deminutio*) but sometimes without. Thus the following citizens become slaves:

1. Those captured by the enemy. Capture by pirates or brigands, or by the opposite party in civil war, has no such effect, but actual capture by the public enemy or surrender to

[1] Rarely in lay writers, *e.g.* Liv. xxii 60 § 15 of Romans captured by Hannibal; Caes. *Civ.* ii 32 § 9 of Domitius surrendered to Caesar; Hor. *Od.* iii 5, 42 *capitis minor* of Regulus captive to Carthaginians. See my *De usufructu* p. 165 sqq.

them makes a man, if brought within their territory, their slave; and so also capture, when there is no war, by any people who were in no relation of friendship or treaty with the Romans. But if such a captive returned to his own or to a friendly country with no intention of going back again to the enemy[1], he resumed his rights and *status* as before captivity. This reverter was called the *jus postliminii* 'the law of recrossing the threshold.' If he died in captivity, he was deemed to have died when captured; if he returned, he was deemed never to have been a captive and slave. One who deserted or surrendered himself to the enemy had no right of reverter (D. xlix 15 fr 5, 16—18, 19 §§ 2, 4, 21 § 1). See also Book V chap. viii.

A freeman captured by the enemy and redeemed by payment of a ransom did not become the slave of his ransomer, but was held by him as it were in pledge until the ransom was repaid; meanwhile his position was in suspense. He was deemed to be in the power (*in potestate*) of his redeemer, and therefore incapable of being witness to his will. Nor could he be enrolled in the army. His redeemer could be forced by an interdict (*de libero exhibendo*) to set him free if the price was tendered. His death while still in his redeemer's power put an end to the pledge, so that he was held to die in his old *status*, and his children would be *sui heredes*, though some held

[1] M. Regulus captured by the enemy (B.C. 255) was held not entitled to *postliminium* because he had sworn to return to Carthage (B.C. 250) D. xlix 15 fr 5 § 3. So also the captives sent by Hannibal after the battle of Cannae as negotiators to Rome (Gell. vi 18). A person sold into slavery either by his father or by the Roman people or formally given up by the *pater patratus* was not entitled to *postliminium*.

The case of Mancinus who was surrendered to the Numantines B.C. 136 and not received by them was much discussed by the lawyers Brutus and Q. Mucius Scaevola. Some maintained (so Cicero) that he did not lose his Roman *status* unless received by the other nation; Q. Mucius and others that the surrender was effectual of itself. And this opinion appears to have prevailed, for a law was passed to give Mancinus citizenship (Cic. *Caecin.* 33 § 98; *Orat.* i 40 §§ 181, 182; D. xlix 15 fr 4; L 7 fr 18). Cicero argues that the non-acceptance made the surrender void, as a gift not accepted goes for nothing (*Top.* 8 § 37).

that they must repay the ransom. Children of a woman so held in pledge were not themselves bound; and children born in captivity and returning with their father were held to be lawful children; if the father did not return, they were spurious (D. xxviii 1 fr 20 § 1; xxxviii 16 fr 1 § 4; xliii 29 fr 3 § 3; xlix 15 fr 15, 25; 16 fr 8; Cod. viii 50 fr 1 §§ 1, 2; *etc.*). A freeborn captive woman, purchased from the enemy and retained as a wife by the redeemer, is held to be consequently freed from the pledge, and loses no *status* by being (with her child) manumitted by her redeemer in ignorance of her being freeborn (xlix 15 fr 21 pr).

2. Those who not being enrolled in the census were directed by the censor to be sold as slaves (Gai. i 160; Cic. *Caecin.* 34 § 99[1]).

3. Those who, being above 20 years old and knowing themselves to be free, allowed themselves to be sold as slaves in order to get the price (D. i 5 fr 5 § 1). If manumitted they become *libertini* (fr 21). The children of such a slave-woman, born during her slavery, were not allowed to claim freedom (D. xl 13 fr 3).

4. By a senate's decree under Claudius (but cf. Suet. *Vesp.* 11) a freeborn woman, Roman or Latin, knowing herself to be free and yet cohabiting with another's slave, notwithstanding notice (*denuntiatio*) by the slave's master, becomes a slave; but the lawyers held that a formal adjudication by the Governor (or Praetor at Rome?) was required to make her his slave. The notice might be given on the master's or father's order by his procurator or son or slave or by a ward's guardian. If the slave is part of the *peculium* of a son under power, and the woman persists in cohabitation notwithstanding the son's notice, she becomes the father's slave without any question as to his consent. If the slave is part of a camp-*peculium*, the son becomes owner of the woman himself. If the slave's owner

[1] Cicero in this speech, arguing against involuntary loss of citizenship mentions another case: *Populus cum eum vendit qui miles factus non est,* (cf. Liv. *Epit.* 55; Val. M. vi 3 §§ 3, 4) *non adimit ei libertatem, sed judicat non esse eum liberum qui ut liber sit adire periculum nolit.* Cf. D. xlix 16 fr 4 § 10.

permits the cohabitation, the woman becomes his freedwoman. A freedwoman acting in the same way becomes a slave of the slave's master, if his patron knows of her action, if not, she becomes her patron's slave without the possibility of ever being made by him a Roman citizen. But cohabitation with a slave of her patron does not affect her *status*. A daughter under power, so acting without the knowledge or consent of her father, cannot impair his position, and therefore retains her *status*, but if she acts by her father's order or if she persist after his death, she becomes a slave. Neither a mother cohabiting with her son's slave nor a patroness cohabiting with her freedman's slave loses her *status*, notwithstanding notice by the owner. When there are several joint-owners of a slave, the one who first gives notice will become the owner of the freewoman reduced to slavery. A freeborn woman cohabiting with a slave belonging to a borough becomes a slave, without any notice, if she acts knowingly, or persists notwithstanding knowledge. Persistence brings on the penalty also, if a freewoman at first supposed herself to be a slave (Gai. i 160; Paul ii 21 A; Tac. *A.* xii 53). A freeborn man did not become a slave by cohabiting with another's slave after notice by the owner (Cod. vii 16 fr 3).

5. Those who are condemned to capital punishment are *servi poenae*, slaves not to some person but to their punishment. Such are persons condemned to fight with beasts or sent into the mines. Unless pardoned and restored, they cease to be citizens and free, and their property is confiscated (D. xlviii 19 fr 8 §§4, 11; fr 17 pr). If a married woman becomes *serva poenae*, her dowry passes to her husband at once, unless she is condemned for treason, public violence, parricide, poisoning or assassination, in which case it passes to the fisc subject to the husband's rights (D. xlviii 20 fr 4, 5).

6. Those who had a domicile in Rome contrary to a statute (unnamed), lost freedom and citizenship (Gai. i 160 mutilated).

7. By a constitution of Commodus freedmen who had struck and deserted their patrons in poverty and ill health were reduced into their patron's service or even sold as slaves (D. xxv 3 fr 6 § 1).

B. Citizenship is lost but freedom retained. This is *minor*, or *media, capitis deminutio,* and took place in two cases:

1. When a colony was sent by the Roman people into Latin districts those who, at the bidding of their parent, gave in their names to be colonists, ceased to be in their parent's power, because they became citizens of another community (*civitas*) (Cic. *Caecin.* 33 § 98; Gai. i 131).

2. The second case is the result of punishment. It occurred when in olden times a man was prohibited the use of water and fire[1]; for which in imperial times deportation into an island came to be substituted. Such a sentence required the approval of the Emperor or of the City praefect (Gai. i 161; D. xlviii 19 fr 2 § 1). Such a person is sometimes compared to a dead man (D. xxxvii 4 fr 1 § 8): he lost his property (which went to the fisc, subject however to any charges) and all rights belonging to the *jus civile,* and hence his freedmen, and even his kinships and affinities: his will was invalidated: he could not manumit a slave, make a will or take a legacy or trust, but he retained his freedom[2] and the *jus gentium,* and could deal with any property acquired since his condemnation, sell, buy, let, hire, lend on interest, *etc.* If his father had imposed on him a trust to restore at his death the inheritance to his sons or to such of them as he should appoint, he retained the right to appoint, and the trust would only take effect at his natural death. If there was a trust conditioned on his dying without children, the condition would be fulfilled, if he left

[1] Cicero frequently argues that loss of Roman citizenship is not a punishment, but is consequent on acquisition of another citizenship in order to avoid punishment. *Exilium non supplicium est, sed perfugium portusque supplicii. Nam qui volunt poenam aliquam subterfugere aut calamitatem, eo solum vertunt, hoc est, sedem ac locum mutant. Nam cum ex nostro jure duarum civitatum nemo esse posset, tum amittitur haec civitas denique, cum is qui profugit receptus est in exilium, hoc est, in aliam civitatem* (Cic. *Caecin.* 34; so also *Dom.* 30 § 78; *Balb.* 11 § 27; 13 § 3). The right of withdrawal from punishment was given by the *lex Porcia* (Sall. *Cat.* 51).

Pliny (*Ep.* iv 11) tells us that *quibus aqua et igni interdictum est* lost the right of wearing a toga.

[2] The contrary statement in D. L 13 fr 5 § 3 is generally discredited.

only children conceived since his deportation. His children born before were not otherwise affected than by losing his inheritance and rights over freedmen (D. xxxviii 10 fr 4 § 11; xxxi fr 77 § 4; xxxvi 1 fr 18 § 5; xlviii 19 fr 17, 26; tit. 22 fr 3, 6 pr, 15; xxviii 1 fr 8 § 1). Banishment (*relegatio*) had no effect on citizenship (xlviii 22 fr 14, 17).

Deserters to the enemy, and persons judged by the senate or people to be enemies, may be classed with those coming under the last paragraph (D. iv 5 fr 5 § 1).

CHAPTER V.

SUITS ABOUT FREEDOM (*CAUSAE LIBERALES*).

A. The case of persons being held in slavery who were really freemen[1], and of others passing as freemen who were really slaves, must have not unfrequently occurred in the ancient world (cf. D. xli 3 fr 44 pr). There was no distinction of colour or other visible indications to act as a *prima facie* warning, and, if there had been originally, the practice of manumission would have removed it. The court[2] was open for both claims, viz. for claiming into freedom one who was in a state of slavery, and for claiming into slavery one who was in possession of freedom. But a slave could not conduct his own case in court. He required a freeman to act as claimant (*adsertor*)[3] for him, and

[1] In Pliny's letters to Trajan (*Ep.* 65, 66=71, 72) the case is mentioned of freeborn children being exposed and then brought up by others and treated as slaves (called θρεπτοί, *i.e. alumni*). Trajan decides: *nec adsertionem denegandam iis qui ex ejusmodi causa in libertatem vindicabuntur puto neque ipsam libertatem redimendam pretio alimentorum.*

[2] In Cicero's time the court was the *decemviri stlitibus judicandis* (*Caecin.* 33 § 97).

[3] Cf. Ascon. *in Corn.* p. 56 Kiessling: *Cum quendam civem idem Metellus servum suum esse contendens vi arripuisset ac verberibus affecisset, Curio assertorem ei comparavit. Dein cum appareret, eum exitum judicii illius futurum ut liber is judicaretur quem Metellus verberibus affectum esse negare*

whoever undertook it could not abandon the case in the midst, on pain of being proceeded against *extra ordinem*: if he did, it was open to another to assume the position (Paul v 1 § 5). If an apparent slave claims his freedom, the *adsertor* has the position of plaintiff and the apparent master is defendant: if an apparent freeman is claimed into slavery, he is defendant and the claimant is plaintiff. Should there be any doubt as to which of the two parties is the real claimant, the judge tries that point first, and if the person in question is shewn to be without fraud (*sine dolo malo*) in the actual enjoyment of freedom, he is defendant, and the proof of the case lies with the other. If more than one person claim to be owners, or one to be owner and another fructuary, they ought, as the senate decreed, to be sent before the same judge, and each be able to put forward his claim (D. xl 12 fr 7 § 5—fr 9 pr). Any one believing himself to be free and bearing himself as such (not a runaway) is held to be without fraud in the possession of freedom, although he may turn out to be a slave. Such a case is that of one who has been always brought up as free, or has been made free by a will which proves to be invalid, or has been manumitted with the rod by one who was not his owner (fr 10—fr 12 § 3)[1].

The claim of freedom may be maintained, if the person himself be unwilling to do so and even against his will, by a

non poterat, inter Metellum et Curionem facta pactio est ut neque arbitrium de libertate perageretur, rediret tamen ille in libertatem de quo agebatur. The same word is used of one who claimed an apparent freeman as a slave. So of Claudius in claiming Verginia (Liv. iii 44 § 8; 45 § 3 etc.). The form in either case appears to have been laying the hand on the person: *Virgini manum injecit, serva sua natam servamque appellans, sequique se jubebat* (*ib.* § 6). Hence the ordinary phrase *adserere aliquem manu causa liberali* 'on the ground of freedom.' Plaut. *Curc.* 490; *Poen.* 964, *etc.*; Ter. *Ad.* 40; Cic. *Flacc.* 17 § 40 *Huic eidem nuper tres equites Romani cum in causa liberali eum qui asserebatur cognatum suum esse diceret, non crediderunt.* For *asserere* we often have *vindicare*, *e.g.* Liv. iii 45 § 11. So Cicero metaphorically, *P. Scipio ex dominatu Ti. Gracchi privatus in libertatem rem publicam vindicavit* (*Brut.* 58 § 212).

[1] Justinian did away with the necessity of an *adsertor* and the Digest has probably been altered accordingly (Cod. vii 17 fr 1; cf. Gradenwitz *Interpol.* p. 100; *ZRG.* xxvii 120).

parent or son, or kinsmen, or if none such be found, by mother or daughter or sister or other kinswomen; all being naturally pained and wronged by a kinsman being in slavery (fr 1—3).

By a rescript of Hadrian no person is allowed to claim freedom, who being more than 20 years old and free has allowed himself to be sold into slavery in order to get a share of the price (see above p. 43), unless the purchaser bought him, knowing that he was a freeman. Such a purchaser deserves no indulgence (fr 7 pr—§ 2; cf. xl 13 fr 2 pr).

When once the suit for freedom is arranged, *i.e.* issue joined, the person whose *status* is in question is treated as a freeman (*liberi loco habetur*)[1], so that actions are granted him against others and even against the person claiming to be his master; and joinder of issue in these has the regular effect of preventing rights of actions being lost by lapse of time: but the prosecution of the actions has to await the result of the claims for freedom, and then drop if he is proved a slave. So actions against him are admissible, and he is called on like any other defendant to give security for his appearance in court to meet them. If however he is eventually shewn to be a slave, any acquisitions made by him are deemed to have passed to his master. And even for the purposes of possession, though his master has by joinder of issue ceased to possess him, he is held capable of possessing through the litigant just as through a fugitive slave (D. xl 12 fr 24, 25 § 2).

If a master succeeds in proving his opponent to be a slave, he is not obliged to accept damages instead, but can lead off the slave if he chooses (*ib.* fr 36). And he can recover by a special action on the case damages for loss, wrongfully (*dolo*) occasioned him by one whom he believed to be his slave but who now succeeds in proving his freedom. If the loss was caused by fault only, the master must sue under the *lex Aquilia* (fr 12 §6; 13 pr).

1 This corresponds to the rule laid down in the XII tables. *Postulant ut lege ab ipso lata vindicias* (Appius) *det secundum libertatem*, cf. Liv. iii 44 § 12; cf. *ib.* § 5; cap. 56 § 4. (For *vindicias dare secundum quem* see Book VI chap. iv; and Gai. iv 14, 16.) Whether this rule applied to cases of persons not hitherto in the enjoyment of liberty is very doubtful. Cf. Maschke *Freiheitsprocess* p. 30 sqq.; Schlossman *ZRG.* xxvi 228.

The precise form of the suit is not clear. In the times of the *legis actio* the suit was conducted like other suits *in rem*, and the deposit (*sacramentum*)[1] to be made by an *adsertor* was put at only 50 asses, so that the claim of freedom might not be unduly burthened (Gai. i 14; cf. Cic. *Caecin.* 33 §97; Liv. iii 44). And in formulary times too the *petitio in servitutem* appears to be a vindication. Whether the like applies to the *petitio in libertatem* or whether the suit took the form of a *praejudicium* is doubtful (see Lenel *EP.* §§ 178, 179). A suit for liberty could be brought again[2] (three times, apparently) if unsuccessful at first (Cod. vii 17 fr 1 pr).

B. A judicial process was also instituted to determine a claim to be freeborn. This was by a *praejudicium*, when any (supposed) patron claimed services or respect, or when he was summoned into court by his supposed freedman, or even when there was no such special cause. The process could be set in motion by either party (cf. D. xxii 3 fr 14). The question was not prejudged by the fact of the person having been manumitted or enrolled in the list of Crown slaves (*fiscalis familia*), or having in fear stated in court (*apud acta praesidis*) that he was a slave (Paul v 1 §§2—4; D. xl 14 fr 6). If the freebirth was established, anything acquired by the person even by gift from the supposed patron since his manumission had to be given up: other acquisitions he retained (D. *ib.* fr 3). If he had not been manumitted, he could take only what he had brought with him into the master's household (D. xl 12 fr 32).

If it was found that there had been collusion between the master and his slave to establish his free birth, a senate's decree under Domitian made the falsely declared freeman to become the slave of the person who exposed the collusion (D. xl 16 fr 1).

[1] The deposit is probably referred to by Martial i 52: *Si de servitio gravi querentur, adsertor venias satisque praestes.*

[2] Cicero speaks of such a suit being brought over again whenever desired: *Si decemviri sacramentum in libertatem injustum judicassent, tamen quotienscumque vellet quis, hoc in genere solo rem judicatam referri posse voluerunt* (*Dom.* 29 §78).

C. No suit could be brought for establishing *status* as freeborn after five years from manumission, or for shewing that such a decree was obtained by collusion after five years from the judgment, unless it be desirable to defer the reopening of the question till the person has come to the age of puberty. This latter was ruled by M. Aurelius. And if the decision was arrived at without a lawful (*justus*) opponent, the decree is not to be treated as a judgment. A patron, ignorant of the decision of the question, was not precluded by the lapse of five years from raising the question (D. xl 14 fr 4, 5; tit. 16 fr 2, 3).

Nerva by an edict forbad any question against the *status* of one who was dead being raised after five years from the death. Nor within the five years could it be raised, if it would affect one dead more than five years. And Hadrian decided that the *status* of one living could not be questioned if it would affect that of one dead more than five years. M. Aurelius decided that any suit commenced for contesting a decision in favour of a person's being freeborn was at once extinguished by his death. Questions in favour of a dead person's *status* (*e.g.* to shew that the mother of a living slave was a freewoman) were not limited in practice to five years (D. xl 15 fr 1, 4).

BOOK II.

FAMILY.

Jure proprio familiam dicimus plures personas quae sunt sub unius potestate aut natura aut jure subjectae. Communi jure (universae cognationis), familiam dicimus omnium adgnatorum; nam etsi patre familias mortuo singuli singulas familias habent, tamen omnes qui sub unius potestate fuerunt recte ejusdem familiae appellabuntur, qui ex eadem domo et gente proditi sunt (Ulp. D. L 16 fr 195).

Mulier familiae suae et caput et finis est (*ib.*).

Feminarum liberos in familia earum non esse palam est, quia qui nascuntur patris familiam sequuntur (Gaius *ap.* D. L 16 fr 196).

Servus juris civilis communionem non habet in totum, ne praetoris quidem edicti (Ulp. D. xxviii 1 fr 20 § 7).

Servile caput nullum jus habet (Paul D. iv 5 fr 3 § 1).

Libertinus nullo modo patri heres fieri potest, qui nec patrem habuisse videtur, cum servilis cognatio nulla sit (Ulp. *Reg.* xii 3).

In adoptionem datus aut emancipatus, quascunque cognationes adfinitatesque habuit, retinet; adgnationis jura perdit. Sed in eam familiam, ad quam per adoptionem venit, nemo est illi cognatus praeter patrem eosve quibus adgnascitur: adfinis autem ei omnino in ea familia nemo est (Modestin D. xxxviii 10 fr 4 § 10).

CHAPTER I.

OF THE HOUSEHOLD PROPER.

Roman citizens were members of a household (*familia*), as well as members of the State or community. They might be heads of households (*patres familiarum*), or subordinate members. The term *paterfamilias* was applied to any one who was not in a subordinate position, whether he was father with children or bachelor. Similarly any woman who was not as daughter in the power of a living father (or grandfather, *etc.*) was called *materfamilias*[1], though originally that term was applied only to a legally married woman in the power of her husband or his father or other ascendant (Cic. *Top.* iii § 14 quoted below). A person in the power of his or her father or other ascendant was called *filius familias, filia familias* (D. i 6 § 4).

A Roman household might contain four classes of subordinates: slaves, children (both *in potestate*), women in hand (*in manu*) and persons in handtake (*in mancipio*)[2]. As regards legal position they might be reduced to two classes, *servi* and *liberi*, the slave and the free, the latter being the children; for women in hand rank as daughters, and persons in handtake are *servorum loco*. All these were in the power of the head of the family, who was *dominus* (owner or master) to the slaves, and *pater* to the free. Slaves when emancipated still remained in connexion with their former master, called in relation to them *patronus*, and with their master's children (Gai. i 19, 52, 55, 97, 114, 123). Women not in the hand of their husband, though legally married, were not members of his family, but of their own father's or were independent.

1 Festus *s.v.* p. 125 excludes from the title widows and childless.

2 Compare the words of the *lex Cincia* 204 B.C. (ap. Vat. 300) *Excipiuntur et ii qui in potestate eorum vel manu mancipiove, item quorum in potestate manu mancipiove erunt.*

CHAPTER II.

SLAVES.

(*a*) Slaves had no independent legal existence as persons. *Qui in potestate nostra est nihil suum habere potest* (Gai. ii 87); *in personam servilem nulla cadit obligatio* (D. L 17 fr 22); *cum servo nulla actio est* (*ib.* fr 107); *cum servis nullum est conubium* (Ulp. v 5); *cognatio servilis nulla est* (Ulp. xii 3). In the eye of theoretical law they were mere chattels, objects, not subjects, of property or other rights, with no more appeal to the courts of justice and no more legally recognised kinship among themselves than any other animal. Their master, as owner, had over them the power of life and death, had the property in anything which they acquired, was entitled to sue for injuries to them, and was liable for injuries done by them to others. Such was their condition according to the ordinary law of the ancient world (*jure gentium*), but it was modified in both respects by Roman law and practice. The power over the person was controlled by public opinion[1], and by natural feeling towards members of the same household, and eventually by a constitution of Antoninus Pius, who directed that one who killed[2] his own slave should be punished as if he had killed another's slave; and by rescripts in particular cases, that, if a master treated his slaves with intolerable cruelty or starved them, he should be compelled to sell them so that they should never return under his power. 'To give such protection to slaves,' said the emperor, 'was required by the interests of masters, whose power over their slaves should be preserved in full. The obedience of slaves should be secured not only by power but by

[1] See the Stoic Seneca *Clem.* i 18 *Et in mancipio cogitandum est non quantum illud impune possit pati sed quantum tibi permittat aequi bonique natura. Servis ad statuam licet confugere; cum in servum omnia liceant, est aliquid quod in hominem licere commune jus animantium vetet*: and the whole of *Ep.* 47.

[2] Hadrian is said to have forbidden masters to kill their slaves and to have ordered them to send slaves before a tribunal (Spart. *Hadr.* 18); on which see Mommsen *Strafr.* p. 617.

moderate rule, sufficient supplies, and lawful tasks' (Gai. i 52, 53; *Consult.* iii 3; D. i 6 fr 1, 2). A *lex Petronia* (perhaps A.D. 19) and several senate's decrees relating to it took away from masters the right to send a slave to fight wild beasts, without bringing him before a court and the court's approving the punishment (D. xlviii 8 fr 11 § 2). The city praefect had the duty of hearing the complaints of slaves who were treated cruelly or indecently by their masters (D. i 12 fr 1 § 8)[1].

(*b*) Slaves who committed punishable offences, not of a grave character, were excused if they had acted in obedience to their masters or to the master's guardian or caretaker (D. L 17 fr 157 pr). But his master's order did not excuse a slave who killed a man or committed theft or violence (D. xliv 7 fr 20).

Slaves were liable to be put to the question (*i.e.* torture) to give evidence in criminal cases, but rarely in civil matters (see Book VI chap. xi). They could not be examined against their owner (whether owner wholly or partly) or former owner, unless they had been purchased merely to prevent such examination. And manumission with that object did not prevent the question. Of other persons' slaves only one can be examined against the same person, and that only with the consent of the owner, or on the applicant's readiness to pay the value as estimated by the slave's owner, or at least the depreciation caused by the torture (Paul v 16 §§ 2—9).

In cases of civil damage a slave was liable to be surrendered (*noxae dedi*) to the injured person, just like an animal which had committed *pauperies* (see Book V chap. vii C).

(*c*) Legal property a slave had none, but a master usually allowed (express permission was not necessary) a slave to accumulate gifts or savings and to act in regard of this accumulation as an independent person. It was called his *peculium*[2] ('petty stock'), though legally the property of his

[1] Cf. Sen. *Ben.* iii 22 § 3 *Atqui de injuriis dominorum in servos qui audiat positus est, qui et saevitiam et libidinem et in praebendis ad victum necessariis avaritiam compescat.*

[2] Proculus is reported to have mentioned that in the civil wars people put aside a stock of money; and that rustics referring to this used to say

master. He entered into all kinds of business transactions, ostensibly and in ordinary parlance for himself, but in the eye of the law for the master's account, who could repudiate each separate transaction if he had not ordered it or benefited by it. The slave could not validly alienate any thing belonging to his *peculium*, unless his master had granted him unrestricted management (*libera peculi administratio*), in which case he could make a loan of money, sell and pledge, pay debts, accept payments, take and tender an oath, novate obligations, settle, on business considerations, claims against others for theft, *etc.* but even then could not make a present or undertake a gratuitous obligation for some one else. This was in accordance with the general maxim *melior condicio nostra per servos fieri potest, deterior fieri non potest* (D. L 17 fr 133. Cf. Mandry *Familiengüterrecht* § 63). The *peculium* might contain anything moveable or immoveable, land, money, slaves (called *vicarii*), credits and investments (*nomina*), rights of action for torts, inheritances or legacies, *etc.* It included his own dress, except such as being intended for special occasions was regarded as only lent him for use. He sued and was sued only in the name of his master, who to the extent of the *peculium* was always answerable to outsiders for his slave's debts, and answerable in full if he had ordered the matter, or, apart from the *peculium*, had reaped the benefit (see Book V chap. vii). A slave could neither give nor take a valid *vadimonium*; and if it appeared in the course of a suit by a procurator that he was suing for a slave, the judge would direct a nonsuit (D. ii 11 fr 13; v 1 fr 44 § 1; vi 1 fr 41 § 1; xii 1 fr 11 § 2; tit. 2 fr 20; xiv 6 fr 3 § 3; xv 1 fr 3 § 8; 7 § 3, 21 § 3, 25, 41, 46; xx 3 fr 1 § 2; xlvii 2 fr 52 § 26). A slave was by the same natural, though strictly abusive, language said to buy from and sell to his master; and anything due on a balance to his master was regarded as *ipso facto* diminishing the *peculium*, which indeed existed only so long as his master chose. *Peculium definit Tubero* (a lawyer of Cicero's time), *quod servus domini permissu separatum a rationibus dominicus habet, deducto*

pecunium sine peculio fragilem esse 'that money was little to be trusted without a private hoard' (D. xxxii fr 79 § 1). For the use of *peculium* for *parapherna* see chap. xii.

inde si quid domino debetur (D. xv 1 fr 5 § 4). Delivery or other definite action was required, as in dealings among freemen, in order to transfer anything from the master's ordinary property to the slave's *peculium*; but nothing more than the master's will was required to absorb the *peculium* into his own (ordinary) property (*ib.* fr 8). A ward could not, even with his guardian's authority, establish a slave's *peculium* (fr 3 § 3). For the application of money from the *peculium* to purchase a slave's freedom see Book I chap. ii C ii 3.

(*d*) The *peculium* did not pass with the slave on alienation either *inter vivos* or by will, unless expressly granted by the master (D. xviii 1 fr 29; xxxiii 8 fr 24; but cf. Paul iii 6 § 34)[1]. Neither if he were set free by will did it accompany him unless so declared; but if he were freed by a living master, either by rod or informally, it was held to be given him if not expressly taken away. To make it his own however he required usucapion, and to collect debts he required a transfer of his master's rights of action (Vat. 261; D. xv 1 fr 53; Cod. vii 23). For as everything acquired by a slave passed at once to his master, all actions to which the master was entitled on the slave's (or his own) account remained with him notwithstanding the slave's alienation or manumission or death. Consequently a slave after manumission and bequest of his *peculium* could not sue on a purchase made before manumission but not perfected by delivery (D. xxi 3 fr 1 § 4; xxix 2 fr 79; xliv 7 fr 56). On the other hand a slave when set free could not be sued for a loan or other debt or contract made previously, but he was liable for torts committed against others than his former master. A rescript of Severus decided that no previous theft or injury towards his former master would ground an action against him now, though in some cases, *e.g.* theft, he might practically become liable by handling the stolen object after manumission (Paul ii 13 § 9; D. iii 5 fr 16; iv 4 fr 11 pr; xliv 7 fr 14; xlvii 2 fr 17 § 1).

[1] Varro (*RR.* ii 10 § 5) says *In servorum emptione solet accedere peculium aut excipi*, 'His *peculium* generally accompanies a slave when sold or else is expressly reserved.' But from this statement of what generally occurred it must not be inferred that the purchaser had a right to the *peculium* if nothing was said. Cf. D. xxi 2 fr 3.

(*e*) Equitable ownership (*in bonis*) is sufficient to give legal power over slaves; a merely legal master (*ex jure Quiritium*) has it not (Gai. i 54).

(*f*) In rare cases only, *e.g.* (by a rescript of M. Aurelius and Commodus) where the master was charged with suppressing a will granting freedom to a slave, or with not manumitting him when he had purchased him with the slave's own money, was a slave capable of bringing his master into court (D. xlviii 10 fr 7; i 12 fr 1 § 1; cf. v 1 fr 53, 67: see above Book I chap. ii c ii 3). A slave, to whom an heir was directed to restore the inheritance, was allowed to apply to the praetor to compel the heir to enter and restore, not only if freedom was actually given him by the will but also if there was a trust for it (D. xxxvi 1 fr 23 § 1).

CHAPTER III.

CHILDREN.

A. Children come under their father's power either by birth or adoption or special grant. If however their father is himself under another's power, they are not under his power but with him under their grandfather or other male ascendant, and fall under their own father's power only on his becoming head of the family by the death of the grandfather, *etc.* Nor, if he is emancipated, do his children (whether born or conceived) accompany him, unless the grandfather, *etc.* emancipates them also (D. i 6 fr 4, 5; xlviii 5 fr 22; Just. i 12 § 9).

The right of *patria potestas* was deemed to be peculiar to the Romans, and was so stated in an edict of Hadrian. Gaius however records the fact, that the Galatians considered themselves to have the same power (Gai. i 55).

No woman has children in her power (*ib.* 104).

1. BY BIRTH children come under the power of their father only if their father is a Roman citizen and has begotten

them in a lawful marriage. The conditions of a lawful marriage were the *conubium* of the parties, the consent of themselves and, if they were not *sui juris*, of their family superior, and the age of puberty. See below chap. xi. Insanity of either father or mother before or after conception does not prevent the child of married persons being in the father's power, though it is a bar to marriage (D. i 6 fr 8).

A child born of a man's wife is deemed to have been begotten by him unless the time of his absence or infirmity disprove it (D. i 6 fr 6). *Pater is est quem nuptiae demonstrant* (D. ii 4 fr 5).

The child of a Roman by a female slave follows its mother's *status* and is not in his power, even though before giving birth to it she be manumitted and become a Roman citizen along with her child (Gai. i 87, 88).

2. BY ADOPTION persons come into the family of a Roman, and are under his power just as if they were his lawful natural children. No woman can adopt, for a woman is not the head of a family. Any male of the age of puberty and independent can adopt another male or female as his child (Gai. i 103, 104; Ulp. viii). If the person adopted is independent, his consent is required; if he is in the power of his father, or other superior, the consent or at least the tacit acquiescence of both are required (D. i 7 fr 5)[1].

Adoption breaks all relation with the former family according to the civil law, and the former relation is not resumed if the adopted person is emancipated by his adoptive father[2]; but he is in the same position as if emancipated by his natural father.

[1] Justinian in the Institutes (i 11 *fin.*) says Cato mentions adoption (and consequent freedom) of slaves by their master. Nothing more is known of this, but Gellius (v 19) refers to Masurius Sabinus who speaks of it as obsolete, and as an argument against permitting the adoption of freedmen. (On this see below, p. 62.)

[2] It is however resumed, if the natural father takes him back by arrogation or adoption. Papinian uses strong language: *In omni fere jure sic observari convenit ut veri patris adoptivus filius numquam intellegatur, ne imagine naturae veritas adumbretur, videlicet quod non translatus sed redditus videretur* (D. xxviii 2 fr 23 pr).

In the adoptive family he (or she) is brother (or sister) to the adoptive father's other children, but is not of kin to the father's wife or mother; *adoptio non jus sanguinis sed jus adgnationis adfert* (Gai. ii 137; D. fr 12, 23). If my son is emancipated and adopts a child, this child is not my grandchild (fr 26).

A person may be adopted not as a child but as a grandchild, either as if child of a specified son, or generally, even if the adopter has no son at all. The consent (*auctoritas*) of any such specified son is required, if the adopted child is to fall into his power on the death of the adopter. And if the relation of consanguinity is to exist between the adopted grandchild and other of the son's children, it must be clearly so stated in the formula of adoption (fr 11, 37, 43, 44).

An adopted child may be emancipated or given in adoption to another; and in both cases the relation created by the first adoption is wholly extinguished for all purposes, except in some cases as a bar to marriage; nor can he be readopted by the same person. Any child of an adopted son is deemed to be adoptive also (fr 13, 14, 27, 37 § 1; Gai. i 105; ii 136). Temporary adoption was not valid; *nec enim*, says Labeo, *moribus nostris convenit filium temporalem habere* (D. fr 34).

There were two procedures for adoption[1]: (*a*) one was for

[1] The so-called adoption by will appears to be really appointment of heir with direction to bear testator's name. Any actual entry under the fatherly power could not exist after death, and it was only on death that the will took effect. The lawyers make no mention of such an adoption, but Gaius in D. xxxvi 1 fr 65 §§ 9, 10 mentions among conditions of inheritance that of bearing testator's name. Cf. Cic. *Off.* iii 18 § 74 *Basilus M. Satrium sororis filium nomen suum ferre voluit eumque fecit heredem.* Dolabella was made partial heir by a woman's will and bidden to change his name (Cic. *Att.* vii 8 § 3). But L. Crassus is said to have 'adopted' by will his daughter's son (Cic. *Brut.* 58 § 112): Atticus was thus adopted by his mother's brother (Nep. *Att.* 5); Octavius by Julius Caesar who *in ima cera Octavium etiam in familiam nomenque adoptavit* (Suet. *Jul.* 83). Of Augustus' will it is said *Tiberium et Liviam heredes habuit; Livia in familiam Juliam nomenque Augustae adsumebatur* (Tac. *A.* i 8). Suetonius speaks of Galba's adoption by a woman: *adoptatus a noverca sua Livi nomen et Ocellae cognomen assumpsit mutato praenomine* (*Galb.* 4). The adoption of Octavius Caesar was confirmed by a proceeding in the *comitia curiata* (App. *Civ.* iii 18 § 94), but from such a record in the case of Caesar we can scarcely argue to ordinary practice. (For Mommsen's view see *Staatsr.* iii p. 39 ed. 2.)

the adoption of persons male or female still under their father's (or grandfather's, *etc.*) power, and retained the general name *adoptio*; (*b*) the other was for the adoption of persons *sui juris*, and was called frequently *adrogatio.*

(*a*) Adoption ordinarily so called, was made under the executive authority (*imperio*) of the consul or praetor or provincial governor even outside his own province, these officers being competent to preside over statutable proceedings (*apud quos legis actio est*). There was no requirement of age in the person adopted, but the adopter must be older and (according to the Digest) eighteen years older. The father or other superior gives the child in adoption, the form consisting of mancipation, followed by a claim in court (see below chap. V B 2; Gai. i 102, 134; D. fr 36 § 1, 40 § 1)[1]. There could be no property passing under such adoption of a person who was in the power of another.

(*b*) Adrogation was effected only at Rome, and *per populum, i.e.* it required the solemnity of a bill (*rogatio*) passed by the *comitia curiata* under the authority of the pontifices (*arbitris pontificibus*). The form of this bill is given by Gellius (v 19 § 6). *Velitis jubeatis* (*Quirites*) *uti L. Valerius L. Titio tam jure legeque filius siet, quam si ex eo patre matreque familias ejus natus esset, utique ei vitae necisque in eum potestas siet, uti patri endo filio est* (*i.e.* 'as a father has in the case of a son'). *Haec ita uti dixi, ita vos Quirites rogo.* The consents of the intended father and son are also formally demanded. Cicero gives for the latter the form, *Auctorne es ut in te P. Fonteius* (intended father) *vitae necisque potestatem habeat, ut in filio* (*Dom.* 29 § 77). The consent of a caretaker was not required until the time of Claudius (D. i 7 fr 8). In imperial times the authority of the emperor was eventually (by Diocletian? cf. Cod. viii 47 fr 2 § 1) substituted for that of the people. Gaius and Ulpian still

[1] An obscure *SC. Afinianum* apparently gave an adoptive child, being one of three sons of his natural father, a claim to a fourth of his adopter's intestate estate, even though emancipated (Just. iii 1 § 14; Theophil. *ad eundem*). Schrader (ad Just. *l.c.*) suggests that Ant. Pius followed this decree in giving a fourth to an *impubes* arrogator. (This *SC.* is by some MSS. and modern authors called *Sabinianum*.)

preserve the description *per populum*, for which Justinian gives *per principem* (cf. Gai. i 98, *etc.* with D. fr 2). The formula was however at least partly retained (cf. fr 44 from Proculus).

The circumstances of the two parties were inquired into[1] both lest the motives for having natural children should be discouraged, and lest the interests financial and other of the person arrogated should be betrayed and injured. The arrogator ought as a rule to be sixty years of age or infirm, to be childless, be older (eighteen years in fr 40) than the person arrogated, and not, except for good cause, to arrogate more than one person or to arrogate another's freedman. If he is guardian or caretaker, he must not arrogate his ward or charge, before the time for giving accounts (25 years old) is passed. Great caution was exercised in allowing arrogation of any one under the age of puberty, guardians being held incompetent to authorize the subjection of their ward to the power of another. The arrogator had at one time to take an oath (framed by Q. Mucius); later he had to enter into a covenant with a slave of the community; that if the child died before puberty he would restore all the child's estate to those to whom it would have come if he had not been arrogated (*e.g.* substitutes, legatees, *etc.*, freedoms being also protected); and that if he without good cause emancipated him or though retaining disinherited him, the child was entitled to get from him or his heirs not only all his own (former) property, and anything acquired through him by the arrogator, but also one fourth of the arrogator's estate. This fourth, introduced by Ant. Pius in a letter to the Pontifices, was sometimes called *quarta divi Pii* (fr 15 § 2—fr 22, 40; Just. i 11 § 3; D. x 2 fr 2 § 1; cf. Cod. viii 47 fr 2).

[1] Cicero in pleading before the chief Priests argues against the validity of Clodius' arrogation: *Quod est, pontifices, jus adoptionis? Nempe ut is adoptet qui neque procreare jam liberos possit, et cum potuerit sit expertus. Quae deinde causa cuique sit adoptionis, quae ratio generum ac dignitatis, quae sacrorum, quaeri a pontificum collegio solet. Quid est horum in ista adoptione quaesitum? Adoptat annos viginti natus, etiam minor, senatorem. Liberorumne causa? At procreare potest; habet uxorem, suscipit ex ea liberos; exheredabit igitur pater filium. Quid sacra Clodiae gentis? cur intereunt quod in te est? quae omnis notio pontificum cum adoptarere esse debuit* (*Dom.* 13 § 34 foll.).

The effect of arrogation was that all the estate of the person arrogated, whether corporal or incorporal, passed at once to the arrogator, except such rights as were lost altogether by the alteration of *status* (*capitis deminutio*) arising from mancipation. Debts due to him passed also to the arrogator who could sue, *e.g.* for theft of the child's property committed before arrogation (D. xlvii 2 fr 41 § 1). Debts due by him were lost in strict law, and an action *de peculio* for previously contracted debts was not, according to Sabinus and Cassius, granted against the arrogator: but eventually an action (*utilis*) was allowed to enforce them, the loss of *status* being cancelled; and if he was not defended by his new father, the creditors were permitted by the praetor to seize and sell all such property as would have been his if the adoption had not taken place. Any debts, due to and from him as heir to some one else, passed to the arrogator, who in fact became heir and responsible in his place. Any children in his power born or unborn pass into the power of the arrogator (Gai. i 107; iii 83, 84; iv 38, 80; D. i 7 fr 15 pr; xv 1 fr 42). The arrogation of a freedman was discouraged (*admittenda non est*), but if it took place, the freedman concealing his *status*, the consequences were strictly limited to his being regarded as freeborn in his new family only. His patron preserved his rights, and he himself was not eligible for marriage in a senatorial family (D. ii 4 fr 10 § 2; xxiii 2 fr 32; xxxvii 12 fr 1 § 2; xxxviii 2 fr 49).

The better opinion was that women could not be arrogated, at least in Gaius and Ulpian's times (Gai. i 101; Ulp. viii 5; cf. D. i 7 fr 21; Cod. vii 47 fr 8).

The official position being independent of position in the family, a praetor might without other authority (*apud se*) validly give his sons in adoption and even, if *filius familias*, be given in adoption himself (D. fr 3, 4). Nor was a senator affected in his public position by being adopted by a plebeian (fr 35).

3. BY GRANT, children who have not sprung from what the Romans deemed a lawful marriage were sometimes put under the power of their father, if he was a Roman citizen. This

was usually the case where Latins or foreigners, by application to the court constituted under the Aelian Sentian statute, obtained citizenship for themselves and their family on the ground of marriage in accordance with that statute, or of marriage under misapprehension of their wife or husband's condition. When a foreigner is granted citizenship by the emperor[1], his children are put in his power only if he applies for this, and if after inquiry, specially careful in the case of children under the age of puberty or absent, it appear to be for the interest of the children. The grant of the greater or lesser Latinity to a whole community carries with it the Roman power over children (Gai. i 87, 93—95).

B. *INTERDICTA DE LIBERIS EXHIBENDIS ET DUCENDIS.*

1. The right of a father to the custody of a child in his power was supported by an interdict *de liberis exhibendis* and a consequent interdict *de liberis ducendis* (D. xliii 30), the former being to compel the production in court of a child by the person with whom he is (*si apud te est*) and the latter to allow the father to lead him away, when produced.

Both interdicts are peremptory and admit of few pleas. But, if the child is with his mother, rescripts of Ant. Pius, M. Aurelius and Severus allowed this to be pleaded, and if it was expedient for the child to remain, the father's claim was refused. And the like held in favour of the husband, if the father was claiming to withdraw his married daughter. Apparently the father's right was to be recognised, but persuasion used to induce him not harshly to exercise it. Whether the praetor overruled him if contumacious, we are not told (cf. Glück's *Pand.* xxvi. 257). If a judgment has been given (though wrongfully) that the child was not in the power of the claimant, the plea 'matter decided' was in place and the merits not inquired into (fr 1).

[1] Cf. Plin. *Ep. Traj.* 11 (=6) *Proxima infirmitas mea, domine, obligavit me Postumio Marino medico. Rogo ergo ut propinquis ejus des civitatem, Chrysippo uxorique Chrysippi, item liberis ejusdem Chrysippi, Epigono et Mithridati, ita ut sint in patris potestate utque iis in libertos servetur jus patronorum.*

In the case of the second interdict, if there is no one to act as defendant, the interdict drops, and the praetor inquires by himself. The child is not admitted as defendant, for if his own will is the cause of his not returning to his father he is *apud se* not *apud alium*; the interdict does not apply. If the child is under age of puberty, the comparative characters of plaintiff and defendant have to be considered, so that a child may not be taken away from the custody of a worthy man, but the case be deferred till he come of age, and that on the other hand if the claim be just and the defendant a rogue, no time be lost in the decision (cf. fr 3, 5).

Females and boys[1] should be put in the custody of a woman of known respectability until the case is decided (cf. fr 3 § 6).

A procurator was not allowed to apply for this interdict, unless specially commissioned by the father, or where the father was prevented by illness, *etc.* (D. iii 3 fr 40 pr).

2. Besides these interdicts the lawyers held that the ordinary action for recovery of property (*vindicatio*) could be applied to a child under power, if the terms of the claim were modified to suit the case. Thus instead of claiming '*L. Titium meum esse*' he would say '*L. Titium filium meum esse*' or '*L. Titium in potestate mea ex jure Quiritium esse.*' But the ordinary form of suit was by interdict as above, or special inquiry by the praetor himself (*cognitio*), or by a preliminary issue (*praejudicium*) when the question of fatherly power arose in connexion with another suit (D. vi 1 fr 1 § 2; cf. xxii 3 fr 8).

C. The position of children under power was in some respects similar to that of slaves, in other respects very different. Fatherly power (*patria potestas*) included in the case of children, as of slaves, the power of punishment even to death[2].

[1] *Praetextatum, eumque qui proxime praetextati aetatem accedet*, *i.e.* boys under the age of puberty or somewhat over. See Savigny *Syst.* iii p. 62.

[2] The power of the father to expose a newborn child is alluded to in the comic poets, *e.g.* Ter. *Haut.* 650; *Hec.* 400; Plaut. *Cas.* 41, *etc.* and implied in the (frequent) use of *tollere*, Ter. *Andr.* 464, and *suscipere*, *e.g.* Cic. *Att.* xi 9 § 3 *Haec die natali meo scripsi, quo utinam susceptus non*

Such exercise of the power of putting to death is occasionally recorded (*e.g.* Sall. *Cat.* 39); and of banishment (Sen. *Clem.* i 15; cf. Cic. *Off.* iii 31 § 112; Mommsen *Strafrecht* p. 18 foll.). The power is explicitly given in case of a daughter's adultery (*Coll.* iv 7—12). In cases of theft by a child from his father, the father's power rendered the grant of an action unnecessary and incongruous (D. xlvii 2 fr 17 pr). But if a father in extreme poverty sold his children, it was held that their freedom was not thereby legally destroyed, and, though he could let out their services, if he pledged or mortgaged them, the creditor with knowledge was liable to deportation (Paul v 1 § 1; cf. D. xxi 2 fr 39 § 3). In fact the attempt in practice to treat a child as a chattel was quite alien to the temper of the law in the period with which we are concerned. Surrender of a son for a noxal offence was recognised even in Antonine times, but the holder would be compelled to manumit him when he had received through him the equivalent of the damage (Papin. ap. Coll. iii 3). Support of parents by children and of children by parents was recognised and enforceable by law (D. xxv 3 fr 5), see below, p. 81.

As regards other obligations sons could enter into them both actively and (if *puberes*) passively, and could sue and be sued, but whatever they acquired became at once their father's property, and no action of theirs unless authorised by him diminished his property. Hence execution on their property was impossible, for they had none in law (Gai. ii 87); and execution on the person for a contract or judgment debt is nowhere mentioned in the case of a son under power. If their father allowed them a *peculium*, he was liable *de peculio* just as on account of a slave; but even if they had free administration, they could not make a gift or a cash loan. But the son, being capable of obligation during the continuance of the power, became after emancipation liable for obligations incurred before, and therein differed essentially from a slave. His liability was however restricted to his financial ability (*in id quod facere potest*; D. v 1 fr 57; xiv 6 fr 3 § 2; xv 1 fr 44; tit. 5 fr 2 pr, 5 pr;

essem, cf. Plin. *Ep. Traj.* 66. In the Digest exposing a child is spoken of as equivalent to killing him (D. xxv 3 fr 4).

xliv 7 fr 39; xlv 1 fr 141 § 2; xvii 2 fr 58 § 2). A son under power could sue in his own name only *injuriarum*, *quod vi aut clam*, *commodati*, *depositi* and in (some) actions *in factum* (D. xliv 7 fr 9, 13), but where his father was absent, he was allowed sometimes to sue both for torts and eventually on contracts, apparently in the name of his father, by an *actio utilis* (D. v 1 fr 18 § 1; ii 4 fr 12). Other persons under power (daughter, wife in hand, person in handtake) were not capable of passive obligation (Gai. iii 104. Cf. Mandry *Familiengüt.* §§ 26, 38, 45, *etc.*; Karlowa *RG.* ii p. 91).

As regards the ordinary *peculium* children stood on the same footing as slaves[1], but by a constitution of Claudius a son's *peculium* was excepted when the fisc took the father's estate for debt (D. iv 4 fr 3 § 4).

If a son under power was elected a *decurio* (member of the borough council) with the father's consent (which was assumed if he was present and did not oppose it) the father was treated as guarantor of the son in all his public work (D. L 1 fr 2).

As regards anything acquired in military service a son was allowed special privilege, as follows:

D. *Castrense peculium.*

1. Amongst other favours shewn to soldiers was this of *filii familias* being treated as if they were not under the power of their father in what concerned anything acquired through their military service, which they would not otherwise have had. The *castrense peculium* included not only a soldier's payments as soldier but anything given or left him for the purchase of what he required for the campaign, and any acquisitions from comrades whose acquaintance he owed to the service. Land given him by his father on entrance into service did not become part of his camp-*peculium*, but land bought with his earnings or coming to him otherwise in connexion with the service did. Profits from such property, and inheritances or legacies to slaves included in it went to the same account. Over this he

[1] Cf. Suet. *Tib.* 15: Tiberius was adopted by Augustus; *nec quicquam postea pro patre familias egit aut jus quod amiserat ex ulla parte retinuit. Nam neque donavit neque manumisit, ne hereditatem quidem aut legata percepit ulla aliter quam ut peculio referret accepta.*

had full control, as if he were *paterfamilias*: he could with this enter into legal obligations with his father or others and they with him: his slaves' acquisitions passed to him, and he could manumit them, and they became (by a rescript of Hadrian, D. xxxviii 2 fr 22) his freedmen. His father could not be sued *de peculio* on any such engagements, but if the soldier had another ordinary *peculium*, that came under the ordinary law. If the soldier *filius familias* made a will, whether during service or after his discharge, it affected his camp-*peculium* only; but though a soldier might die partly testate, partly intestate, a non-soldier could not, and thus if his father had died without his knowledge and he had become independent, his will made after discharge was held to cover all his property (D. xlix 17 fr 4 § 1, 6, 8, 11, 15 §§ 1—3, 16 § 1, 17 § 1, 19 § 2; xxix 1 fr 11 § 2, 13 § 1; Cod. iii 36 fr 4; xii 36 fr 1).

If the soldier-son made his father heir, the father took as any other heir; but if the son died without leaving a will which took effect, the father was held to resume his ancient right to this *peculium* as if it had been his all along, though the right was suspended during the time of the son's control. Any alienation of property or manumission of slaves belonging to this *peculium*, if made by the father during the son's life, had no present effect. Indeed the father's manumission by rod of a slave belonging to his son's camp-*peculium* was quite ineffectual, but manumission by will or legacy, if the son died intestate before the will took effect, was valid. If the father is made by his son heir to his camp-*peculium*, and without acting on this title by will takes the property as by a father's right, he will be liable for the legacies left by the son (D. fr 2, 9, 17 § 1, 18 § 1, 19 § 4; cf. xli 1 § 33). Dowry given or promised to a soldier did not become part of the camp-*peculium* (D. xlix 17 fr 16 pr).

The institution of camp-*peculium* is due to imperial constitutions beginning with Augustus and carried on by Nerva and Trajan. Hadrian was the first to allow soldiers to deal with it by will after their discharge (Just. ii 12 pr).

CHAPTER IV.

WIVES IN HAND.

Women come into hand (*in manum conveniunt*)[1] in three ways; by use, by the spelt loaf, by copurchase (*usu, farreo, coemptione* Gai. i 110)[2], all requiring the authority of their father (or grandfather, *etc.*) or of their guardians (Paul *ap. Collat.* iv 2 § 3; 7). A woman in the hand of her husband had the legal position of daughter (Gai. i 115 *a*). All her property passed as a whole without separate delivery of the items to her husband (Gai. ii 98)[3].

1. By use a woman comes into the hand of her husband if she has remained his wife for a whole year without interruption, just as a moveable becomes a man's property by uninterrupted possession for the same period. So the woman *velut annua possessione usucapiebatur*. The XII. tables provided that, if she desired to prevent this result, she should absent herself for three nights (*trinoctium*) every year, and thereby break the

[1] Cicero confines the term *materfamilias* to women who had been married and come into the hand of their husbands (or husbands' fathers). Treating of a case where a legacy had been charged on the husband (as heir) in favour of his wife, provided she were *materfamilias* to him, he says: *Si ea in manum non convenerat, nihil debetur. Genus enim est uxor; ejus duae formae; una matrum familias, eae sunt quae in manum convenerunt; altera earum quae tantummodo uxores habentur* (*Top.* 3 § 14). So Gell. xviii 6 § 7 *Tradiderunt matrem familias appellatam esse eam solam quae in mariti manu mancipioque, aut in ejus, in cujus maritus manu mancipioque esset.*

[2] In the speech *pro Flacco* 34 § 84 Cicero recognizes only two modes, at least as there applicable (in a marriage of plebeians). '*In manum*' *inquit* '*convenerat.*' *Quaero usu an coemptione? Usu non potuit; nihil enim potest de tutela legitima nisi omnium tutorum auctoritate deminui. Coemptione? Omnibus ergo auctoribus; in quibus Flaccum fuisse non dices* (on *usu non potuit* cf. Cic. *Att.* i 5 § 6 quoted Book III chap. iv A). Confarreation is supposed to have been peculiar to patricians.

[3] Other cases of this wholesale transfer of property (*per universitatem*) are the becoming heir, obtaining *bonorum possessio* of one deceased, purchase of an insolvent estate, and adoption (Gai. ii 98).

use. The three nights must be a period of three complete consecutive nights of twelve hours each[1], and the absence must be for this purpose (*usurpandi, i.e. interrumpendi causa*, cf. D. xli 3 fr 2). It must not be a mere absence of the body by chance or some other cause, but there must be an adverse act of the mind as well. By Gaius' time this marriage by use had ceased, partly by statutes, partly by desuetude (Gai. i 110, 111; Q. Mucius ap. Gell. iii 2 §§ 12, 13; cf. Karlowa *RG.* ii 163).

2. The proceeding by spelt loaf was a sacrifice to Jupiter of the spelt (*Jovi Farreo*)[2]. A loaf of spelt was used, ten witnesses were present, and various things were done with fixed traditional words (*certis et sollemnibus*)[3]. Gaius gives no further description, but by his time the proceeding took place only in connexion with certain great priesthoods. The greater Flamens (*i.e.* of Jove, Mars and Quirinus) and the Kings of sacred rites were elected only from persons who had been born from a marriage with the spelt loaf; and they must themselves so marry in order to hold their office (Gai. i 112; Ulp. ix). In the time of Augustus a relaxation[4] of the economic incidents of such a marriage was made in the case of the *Flaminica Dialis*:

[1] *E.g.* if a woman entered her husband's house as his wife on the 1st Jan. and left it for the purpose of preventing *manus* on 29 Dec. following, she would not have been absent three complete nights before the commencement of the 1st Jan. of the following year, *i.e.* midnight between 31 Dec. and 1 Jan. See Gell. *l.c.*; D. xli 3 fr 6; Savigny *Syst.* iv p. 369.

[2] Dionys. Hal. ii 25 speaks of this marriage: ἐκάλουν τοὺς ἱεροὺς καὶ νομίμους οἱ παλαιοὶ γάμους Ῥωμαικῇ προσηγορίᾳ περιλαμβάνοντες 'φαρραχείους' ἐπὶ τῆς κοινωνίας τοῦ φαρρὸς ὃ καλοῦμεν ἡμεῖς ζέαν.

[3] Servius (ad Verg. *Georg.* i 31) speaks of it as a union *per fruges et molam salsam* and says the children are called *patrimi* and *matrimi.* He makes the *Pontifex Maximus* and the *Flamen Dialis* to be the officiating persons.

[4] The MS. of Gaius is mutilated, but he appears to refer this relaxation to the consulship of Fabius Maximus and Aelius Tubero B.C. 11. Tacitus (*Ann.* iv 16) makes the passing of a *lex* for this object to take place in A.D. 23, the cause being the rarity of confarreation, owing to neglect both by men and women and the difficulties of the ceremony. For the election of a Flamen Dialis three patricians born of a confarreated marriage had to be named, of whom one was elected.

she was to be in her husband's hand only so far as the sacred rites were concerned (Gai. i 136). A mode of dissolution of such a marriage, called *diffarreatio*, is mentioned by Festus *s.v.*

3. The most usual form by which a woman passed on marriage into the hand of her husband was copurchase (*coemptio*)[1]. This consisted partly of an adaptation of the ordinary form of mancipation, partly of some other ceremonies. Ulpian in his *Institutes* (according to Boeth. ad Cic. *Top.* iii 14) says that there was mutual questioning[2]. The man asks the woman whether she wills to be mother of the household (*materfamilias*) to him. She answers that she so wills. The woman asks, whether the man wills to be father of the household to her. He answers that he so wills. The mancipation was conducted as usual with five Roman citizens of the age of puberty as witnesses and a balance-holder, the purchaser being the husband, who used a formula couched in different words from those used in the mancipation of a slave or of a child. The woman (in this form of marriage, as in the other two) did not pass into a servile condition under her husband; she came into his hand, not into handtake; she was *loco filiae*, not *loco servi*. But she experienced a change of civic position (*capitis deminutio*), and as a consequence all her property passed to her husband in the same way and with the same limitations as in the case of a man's being arrogated. If she had been in her father's power, she by copurchase ceased to be so[3] (Gai. i 113, 123; ii 98; iii 83, 84; iv 38, 80).

[1] An advocate, says an interlocutor in Cicero, need not know the words of the marriage service: *neque illud est mirandum qui quibus verbis coemptio fiat nesciat, eundem ejus mulieris quae coemptionem fecerit causam posse defendere* (*Orat.* i 56 § 237). In the speech *pro Murena* (12 § 27) Cicero laughs at the lawyers for thinking that all women who made a copurchase were called *Caia*, just because some writer of precedents had used that name. Cf. Quintil. *Inst.* i 7 § 28.

[2] Servius and Isidore (see extracts in Bruns) speak of husband and wife purchasing one another. This seems to be a misunderstanding of Ulpian's words *sese in coemendo invicem interrogabant* and is hardly compatible with the distinctly subordinate position taken by a wife in hand.

[3] She consequently lost all right to her father's (intestate) inheritance. So in the *laudatio Juniae*, Bruns, no. 104 v 16, it is said a woman *omnium fore expertem, quod emancupata esset Cluvio.*

Marriage by copurchase was analogous to acquisition of ownership by mancipation, as marriage by use was analogous to usucapion.

The last mention that we have of *conventio in manum* appears to be in some extracts from Papinian's and Paul's comments on the *lex Julia de adulteriis* (*Collat.* iv 2 § 3; 7). In course of time a freer marriage, resting on consent publicly evidenced, without change in the woman's civic or pecuniary condition, became more usual than any of those forms of marriage which put her in the hand of her husband. For this see chap. xi A.

CHAPTER V.

MEMBERS OF HOUSEHOLD FOR TECHNICAL REASONS.

Included technically in the family are two classes of persons who owe their existence, usually transitory, to the legal forms requisite for breaking or modifying the family connexion. These are (A) women in hand for other purposes than marriage; and (B) persons in handtake (*in mancipio*).

A. WOMEN IN HAND. Copurchase having the effect of breaking the woman's connexion with her former family came to be applied to purposes where marriage was not intended, viz. for getting rid of an inconvenient guardian (*tutelae evitandae causa*)[1] and for becoming capable of making a will. In both

[1] Cicero in scoffing at the depraved ingenuity of lawyers (*Muren.* 12 § 27) says: *Mulieres omnes propter infirmitatem consilii majores in tutorum potestate esse voluerunt; hi invenerunt genera tutorum quae potestate mulierum continerentur. Sacra interire alii noluerunt; horum ingenio senes ad coemptiones faciendas interimendorum sacrorum causa reperti sunt.* The first sentence refers to Gaius' *tutelae evitandae causa*; the second gives a third use of copurchase in trust, doubtless obsolete in Gaius' time, and obscure to us. Savigny (*Verm. Schr.* i p. 190) suggests that the obligation to perform the sacred rites of a family passed with the woman's property as a whole to the copurchaser, an old man being selected for this purpose, who then retransferred the property not as a whole but by single items to

cases the copurchase was done under a trust (*fiduciae causa*), that is to say it was accompanied by declarations stating the object of the proceeding and thus distinguishing it from matrimonial copurchase or ordinary mancipation, and ensuring by the trust-obligation[1] thereby created the loyalty of the agents.

1. The ceremony for a change of guardian consisted first of a copurchase under the authority of her guardians: then the copurchaser, who might be her husband (if she was not already in hand to him) or another, having the woman in hand remancipates her (copurchase being reckoned as a first mancipation) to the person she chooses for her guardian; he then manumits her by rod (*vindicta*), and thus being technically her patron becomes her guardian—called fiduciary guardian. The mancipations and manumission were done with the same words as the mancipation and manumission of slaves, and consequently brought the woman temporarily into the legal position of a slave, and thus broke the agnatic bond. Each of these operations, copurchase, mancipation, and manumission, involved theoretically a change of civic position (*capitis deminutio*), and a transfer and loss of property and rights as in one arrogated. It is however reasonable to suppose that the Romans did not allow the practical object to be frustrated by the usual incidents of the forms applied, and that the woman emerged from the series of formalities (probably continuously and quickly performed) with her property and rights belonging to her (Gai. i 115, 118, 123, 162).

the woman. The old man retained the obligation of the *sacra* and was doubtless rewarded for the burden. The obligation died with him. Mommsen (*St.R.* iii M. 1 p. 21 ed. 2) and others suppose an actual marriage, which seems to me improbable. Plautus (*Bac.* 976) and Curius (ap. Cic. *Fam.* vii 29) speak of *senes coemptionales* with contempt. On the pontifical rules for dealing with this obligation see Cic. *Legg.* ii 19—21, and below, Book III chap. xi.

[1] It is uncertain in what precise relation the declaration of trust stood to the legal act of mancipation, *etc.*, or what form it took. An *actio fiduciae* is spoken of in connexion with pledge (see Book V chap. iv c): and the Baetic inscription (*ib.*) has, besides *fidi fiduciae causa* in the record of mancipation, a regular *pactum conventum* added. See Karlowa *RG.* ii 565 sqq.; Ihering *Geist* ii 2, p. 530 sqq.

2. The second application of copurchase was to enable a woman to make a will[1]. The series of ceremonies was the same, except that there was not necessarily a change of guardian. The agnatic bond being broken, she obtained the free disposal of her property, either with her guardian's authority if she had one, or in some cases by herself (see below). Until the time of Hadrian, only certain persons were able to make a will without undergoing copurchase. These excepted persons were probably the Vestal Virgins, the *Flaminica Dialis*, and (under the Papian law) freeborn women with three children. A senate's decree under Hadrian made the indulgence general (Gai. i 115 *a*, 136, 145, ii 112).

A woman in the hand of a copurchaser who was not her husband could compel him to remancipate her, but her husband, except by first divorcing him, she could not compel, any more than a daughter could compel her father (Gai. i 137, 190).

B. Persons in handtake. The class of persons in handtake (*in mancipio*) is mainly the creation of technical law. All persons in the power of their father (whether by birth or adoption) can be mancipated by him just like slaves: after such mancipation a freeman is in handtake of the person to whom he has been mancipated[2]. Possibly in very early times the

[1] The incapacity to make a will (without copurchase) seems to me to be absolute, and not merely, as some have supposed, inability to make a will without her guardian's authority. Gaius' words (*tunc enim non aliter feminae testamenti faciendi jus habebant quam si, etc.*) are clear and are supported by Cic. *Top.* 4 § 18 *Si ea mulier testamentum fecit quae se capite numquam diminuit, non videtur ex edicto praetoris secundum eas tabulas possessio dari, i.e.* the will is not merely an ineffective will, but absolutely no will, just like (as Cicero's argument proceeds) a will made by a slave or an exile or a boy. A woman goes through the copurchase in this case, not to get a compliant guardian, but to break the family bond. She might have no desire to change her guardians, but they could not enable her to dispose of her property by will: they could however authorise the copurchase which set her and them free.

[2] Cf. Cic. *Caecin.* 34 § 98 *Si pater vendidit eum quem in suam potestatem susceperat, ex potestate dimittit,* Cicero's argument being that any further consequences, *e.g.* loss of citizenship, are due to the purchaser's holding

mancipation of a child may have been a real sale, and in the time with which we are concerned noxal surrender of a child involved mancipation; but otherwise it was a mere bit of procedure adapted to a practical result very different from what theory would have implied. The object of the procedure was (1) emancipation from the father's power or (2) adoption by another.

1. The XII. tables declared that if a father gave his son thrice for sale, the son should be free from the father; *si pater filium ter venum duit, a patre filius liber esto.* What was thus apparently intended as a check upon a father who treated his children as if they were slaves, was applied by means of a series of fictitious sales to emancipate a child, and was taken literally. A son had to be mancipated thrice, a daughter or grandchild (not being expressly named in the statute) only once. The business was thus managed in the case of a son. The father mancipates him to some one who takes him with the same formula as would be used in buying a slave (see below Book IV, Gai. i 119), and then as if dealing with a slave sets him free with the rod. The son reverts into his father's power. The father again mancipates him to some one, usually the same person, but it may be to another, who again sets him free by the rod, and he falls into his father's power again. Mancipation by the father again takes place, and by this third mancipation he ceases to be in his father's power, and is in handtake to the last purchaser. Two courses are now open. The last purchaser can either manumit him at once, and thereby make him his freedman, and as patron be entitled to succeed to half of his estate on his death. Or else, as the matter was generally arranged, he remancipates him to his father, who now holds

him captive and treating him as a slave. Apparently Cicero is referring to a real sale. Cf. Liv. xli 8 § 10 where we find the Samnites and Paeligni complaining (B.C. 177) of their countrymen becoming Roman citizens and leaving their homes. The law allowed this only to such as left a stock behind them, but the law was evaded: *Ne stirpem domi relinquerent, liberos suos quibusquibus Romanis, in eam conditionem ut manumitterentur, mancipio dabant, libertinique cives essent.* See Mommsen *Staatsr.* iii p. 630 ed. 2.

On the general subject of sale of children in the ancient world see Mitteis *Reichsrecht* p. 358 sqq.

him in handtake, sets him free, and thus has a patron's rights to the exclusion of all claim on the part of the last purchaser. Such an arrangement is made in trust, and the purchaser is on that account called a fiduciary father. The several mancipations could be done on the same day or with an interval, and before the same or different witnesses. The son is throughout treated as a slave, formally sold and formally manumitted (Gai. i 132; Paul ii. 25 § 2[1]. The Epitome of Gaius (i 6 § 3) adds that each mancipation was accompanied with the transfer of one or two coins as symbol of price). A son could not be emancipated without his consent; nor could services be stipulated for from him as from a slave. The ceremony could be performed on a holiday (*die feriato*) as well as on other days, and before such municipal magistrates as have *legis actio* (Paul ii 25 §§ 3—5; D. xxxvii 12 fr 4). The mancipations made by a copurchaser to enable a woman to change her guardian or make a will had the same character and effect (Gai. i 118).

2. A like series of fictitious sales by mancipation was applied in the case of ordinary adoption before the praetor[2]. The three sales remove the power of the natural father. The son is in handtake to the last purchaser. Again two courses are open. Either he is remancipated to his father, and then the person who adopts him claims him in court as his son, and on the father making no counterclaim the praetor assigns him to the adopter. Or the father, having by the third mancipation parted with his power, has nothing more to do; the adopter at once claims the son as his own from the last purchaser, whose acquiescence and the praetor's decision complete the business. Gaius says it is more convenient to take the former course but gives no explanation. Probably the reason was a desire to dispense, as far as possible, with outsiders, and

[1] The presence of the praetor would be necessary for manumission in Rome, though not mentioned in the case of sons by Gaius and Ulpian (in the present state of the texts).

[2] Cf. Suet. *Aug.* 64 *Augustus nepotes ex Agrippa et Julia Gaium et Lucium adoptavit domi per assem et libram emptos a patre Agrippa* where *domi* means that it was done by his own power without resort to the praetor (cf. p. 60).

to secure to the natural father his rights to the last[1]. It will be seen that adoption combines the two favourite conveyancing methods of the early Romans, formal sale by mancipation and surrender in court (*in jure cessio,* Gai. i 134).

3. Position of persons in handtake. The Roman lawyers seem often to have carried on the discussion of principles and the logical application of them, regardless of the frequency or probability of occurrence of the cases supposed. To this habit, I imagine, we owe their analysis of the position of persons in handtake, though, as Gaius says, it is usually a mere matter of form done in a moment (*plerumque hoc fit dicis gratia uno momento* i 141). Persons in handtake are not *servi* but *servorum loco*; it is a *liberum caput* which is mancipated and manumitted. Like slaves they acquire, not for themselves, but for their (temporary) master, and they cannot be bound by stipulation, but they are protected against any contumelious treatment by the liability of their master to a suit for insult (*injuriarum*) by their natural father or the copurchaser or other mancipant. Their status in the eye of the law is changed, they have ceased to be in the circle of agnates, and they are released from their position only as a slave is set free, by the rod, by the census, or by will. Registration in the census made them free, even without the consent of their (temporary) master, unless there was a trust for remancipation to the natural father, or the mancipation was for the purpose of a noxal surrender (*i.e.* for theft), so that there was a pecuniary interest in his retention (*hunc actor pro pecunia habet*). By will they could take neither inheritance nor legacy from their temporary master unless expressly directed to be free. The *lex Aelia Sentia* however was held not to apply to persons in handtake: there was no limitation of the number of such persons who might be freed, and no inquiry into the age of manumitter or manumittee, or whether the manumitter had a patron or creditor, whose claims might be injured by the

[1] Karlowa (*RG.* ii 244) points out that it might be important that the real father should appear in the final procedure as ceding his right to the adopter.

manumission (Gai. i 123, 138—141, 162, 163; ii 90; iii 104; iv 79; on iv 80 see Lenel *EP*. p. 339).

The natural father had after the first and second mancipations a reserve of power, so that a child begotten by a person in handtake, though born after the third mancipation, is in the power of his grandfather and can be either emancipated or given in adoption by him. The case of a child begotten by one still in handtake after the third mancipation was different. According to Labeo he is in handtake when born, like his father, but the practice was, says Gaius, to consider his position in suspense until the father is either set free or die. If he be set free, the child falls into his father's power: if the father die, the child is independent (Gai. i 135).

The above-named repeated mancipations were required in the case of a son only. For a daughter or a grandchild one mancipation was sufficient to remove the father's power. Hence the above-named procedure for a son after the third mancipation applies to others after one mancipation (Gai. i 132, 134, 135 *a*).

CHAPTER VI.

REMOVAL OF FATHERLY POWER.

The principal modes in which persons are released from their father's power in his lifetime are emancipation, adoption, copurchase.

1. Emancipation[1] is described above. A father who had

[1] The word *emancipare* is used not only of freeing persons under power but of giving up control so that another gets it, stress being laid not on the fact of conveyance by mancipation, real or metaphorical, but on the resulting abandonment to another. So Cic. *Fin.* i 7 § 24 *Filium in adoptionem D. Silano emancipaverat*; *Sen.* 11 § 38 *Ita senectus honesta est, si se ipsa defendit, si jus suum retinet, si nemini emancipata est*; *Phil.* ii 21 § 51 *Iste venditum atque emancipatum tribunatum consiliis vestris opposuit*, whence Horace *Epod.* ix 11 says of Antony's soldiers *Romanus eheu!*

in his power not only sons but grandsons could free sons and retain their children, or retain sons and free one or more of the children, or he could free both sons and grandchildren. And the like with great-grandchildren, *etc.* (Gai. ap. D. i 7 fr 28).

On emancipation of a child things contained in his *peculium* were treated as given to him if they were not taken away. But he required usucapion to perfect the gift. Debts he could not sue for, unless he was made by his father attorney (*cognitor*) for his own interest, or had the debtors delegated to him. But payment to him without dissent on the part of his father was a good discharge for the debtor (Vat. 260). No services could be imposed on him as on a freedman: his duty was affection (*pietas*, D. xxxvii 15 fr 10). As regards his father's claim to inheritance see Book III. As stated above, p. 65, he could be sued for contracts and delicts made or incurred before emancipation.

A son (of whatever age) had no power to compel his father to emancipate him (D. i 7 fr 31).

2. By adoption described above a child was released from the power of one in order to come under the power of another. All rights gained by adoption were lost by emancipation from the adoptive father (D. xxxvii 3 fr 3 § 2).

3. By copurchase a woman passed from the power of her father into the hand of her husband or other copurchaser (Gai. i 136).

4. Loss of fatherly power followed loss of citizenship either on the sons' part or their father's. A foreigner could not be in the power of a Roman, nor have a Roman in his power. The cases of interdiction from the use of water and fire and of capture by the enemy are particularly mentioned. In the case of captives, if they returned, the relation was revived; if they died, it was in Gaius' time a moot question whether the fatherly power ceased at the time of capture or at the time of death

emancipatus feminae (sc. Cleopatrae); Plaut. *Bac.* 92 *mulier, tibi me emancupo, tuos sum.* So of conveyance of property; *cuidam de parte finium cum vicino litiganti* (Otho) *adhibitus arbiter, totum agrum redemit emancipavitque* (Suet. *Oth.* 4). Cf. Plin. *Ep. Traj.* 4; Fest. p. 77; *Corp. Inscr. Lat.* xi no. 3003=Bruns[6], no. 116, 15; Quintil. vi 3 § 44.

(Gai. i 128, 129, cf. Ulp. x 4). The former view is given in the Digest; see above, p. 42.

A further case is that of sons becoming members of Latin colonies at their father's bidding (*jussu parentis, ib.* 131).

5. Males left their father's power if 'inaugurated' as flamens of Jove; females if 'taken[1]' as Vestal Virgins (*ib.* 130), or married to a *flamen Jovis* and passing into his hand (Tac. *An.* iv 16).

6. By the death of the father all the children become *sui juris*; but grandchildren become independent only if their own father is also dead or has already passed from his father's power in some other way. If their father is alive and becomes independent by their grandfather's death, they fall under his power (Gai. i 127; Ulp. x).

CHAPTER VII.

AGNATES and *CAPITIS DEMINUTIO MINIMA.*

1. Outside the family proper were the *agnati, i.e.* persons related to the head of the family through males. Such are brother and sister by the same father (whether the mother be the same or not), brothers' children and descendants through males, father's brother and his children and descendants through males[2]. Those related by adoption or brought under power by *causae probatio* (Book I chap. iii B) are as much agnates as those related by blood; and all agnates are also cognate to the same persons. In fact agnates are such as have been, or if born, *etc.* would have been, members of the same family at one time.

[1] Cf. Gell. i 12 § 9 *Virgo Vestalis simul est capta atque in atrium Vestae deducta et pontificibus tradita est, eo statim tempore sine emancipatione ac sine capitis minutione e patris potestate exit et jus testamenti faciendi apiscitur.* § 13 *Capi autem virgo propterea dici videtur, quia pontificis maximi manu prensa, ab eo parente in cujus potestate est veluti bello capta abducitur.*

[2] See the *stemma agnationis*, Book III chap. iii.

Cognates[1] are all who are agnates and also all related through women. A mother's brother and sister and their descendants, a sister's children and descendants are cognates but not agnates, *i.e.* they are kin by blood but not members of the same Roman family (Gai. i 156; Paul *ap. Collat.* xvi 3 §§ 13, 14; D. xxxviii 16 fr 2; L 16 fr 195 § 2).

Outside the agnates stood in the old civil law the clan (*gens*) or clansmen (*gentiles*), with common sacrificial and burial rites or places, as if of common descent. But this had ceased to be regarded in the times of the Classical Jurists; and their claims to intestate inheritance and guardianship were superseded by the praetor (Gai. iii 17; Ulp. *ap. Collat.* xvi 4 § 2). See below in Book III chap. iii.

2. The loss of the agnatic or family connexion was *capitis deminutio minima*[2]. This is in some respects not well described as a loss: it is a change, *statûs mutatio*, and occurs when a person is adopted, or a woman makes a copurchase, or free persons are mancipated, or are manumitted after mancipation; and this change of *status* takes place *toties quoties* (Gai. i 159—162)[3].

The effect of this loss or change of *status* was to break the agnatic connexion (for the person himself, not for his descendants), and to destroy all such rights as the old civil

1 *Cognatio* was recognised in many parts of the law, but never beyond the seventh degree, and there only in a second cousin's child (*sobrino sobrinave natus, nata*). All to and in the sixth degree were recognised by the praetor in granting *bonorum possessio* (D. xxxviii 8 fr 1 § 3), by the *lex Furia* excepting from restrictions on amount of legacies (Vat. 301; Gai. ii 225), *lex Julia* restricting calling witnesses in criminal cases (D. xxii 5 fr 4), *lex Papia Poppaea* excepting from disabilities in taking under wills (Vat. 215, 216), and the speech of Severus on excuses from guardianship (Vat. 158). All to and in the fifth degree were recognised by the *lex Cincia* on gifts (Vat. 298, 299), *lex Acilia repetundarum* disqualifying relatives to be judges (Bruns, no. 10 v 22), *lex Cornelia* disqualifying for judges in suits for insult (D. xlvii 10 fr 5 pr), and the *lex Julia* as given in *Collat.* ix 2 § 3. Only four degrees are named in *lex Pompeia de parricidiis* (D. xlviii 9 fr 1). See Bruns *Kr. Schr.* ii p. 310. A complete list of cognates is given in D. xlviii 10 fr 10. See Book III chap. v.

2 For *capitis dem. minor* and *maxima* see Book I chap. iv.

3 See my n. on *de Usufructu* fr 25 § 2.

law attached to membership of a family and other rights created under its sanction (Gai. i 158, 163; D. xxxviii 16 fr 4, 11; tit. 17 fr 1 § 8). These are

(*a*) Rights of intestate inheritance, and guardianship resting on the XII. tables (*legitima hereditas, legitima tutela*, Ulp. xxvii 5; xi 7; D. iv 5 fr 7 pr). And a will already made is broken (Gai. ii 145).

(*b*) Usufructs (Vat. 60—64).

(*c*) Services which a freedman is bound by oath to perform for his patron (Gai. iii 83; D. xxxviii 1 fr 7).

(*d*) Suits in which issue has been joined in a statutable trial (Gai. iii 83, text mutilated).

(*e*) Partnership; which however could be reestablished at once by consent (Gai. iii 153; D. xvii 2 fr 58 § 2).

(*f*) The right of an *adstipulator* to sue (Gai. iii 114; see also D. xlvi 3 fr 38 pr).

(*g*) Liability to creditors: this however was practically restored by the action of the praetor (Gai. iii 84; iv 38). See above under arrogation.

Liability for insult or other delicts follows the offender notwithstanding the change (*cum capite ambulat*, D. iv 5 fr 7 § 1).

The public position of a person (magistrate, senator, judge) is not affected by *capitis dem. minima* (D. iv 5 fr 5 § 2).

CHAPTER VIII.

ALIMONY.

A reciprocal obligation upon parents to support their children and on children to support (*alere, exhibere*) their parents was recognised. There are several constitutions of the Antonines to this effect. Application was made to the consul and he appointed a judge to inquire summarily into the circumstances, whether the relation was as stated, and whether the one was unable to support himself and the other was able to support him. Not only children under power but those who were emancipated or otherwise independent were both liable to give, and able to claim, support. Fathers and other ascendants and, according to the better opinion, mothers and their ascendants, had a claim. The like duty is imposed on mothers and their children not born in lawful marriage. Sons are not bound to pay their father's debts; nor are a son's heirs liable to support his father, unless in extreme need. A daughter's children have no claim on her father. A judgment that alimony is to be paid does not prejudge the question of parentage (so M. Aurelius decided). If the decision is not obeyed, a distress will issue, to compel obedience (D. xxv 3 fr 5 pr—§ 18, fr 8; Cod. v 25).

CHAPTER IX.

PATRON AND FREEDMAN.

A. Position of freedman. A slave on being set free assumed the name (*nomen* and *praenomen*, cf. D. xxxi fr 88 § 6) of his master, to whom he did not cease to belong. The relation of patron and freedman was in fact a continuance as regards the family in a modified form of the relation of master and slave. But his business relations with the world generally, including his patron, were now on a different footing: he could act and was responsible for himself. His children born after manumission were freeborn, and did not stand in any such quasi-servile relation to their father's patron.

B. Who was patron? On the patron's death the position of patron (*patronatus*) passed to his agnatic descendants, *i.e.* children, sons' children, *etc.* of the nearest degree, *i.e.* to all of the same degree collectively, division not being allowed (D. x 2 fr 41). The same were patrons of persons freed by will (*orcini liberti* D. xxvi 4 fr 3 § 3). But, by a senate's decree made in the time of Claudius (41—47 A.D.), any patron who had in his power two or more children born in lawful marriage, might assign one or more of his freedmen or freedwomen to such of his children as he chose, who would then be patron or patrons in full right of the freedmen or freedwomen assigned; but if such assignees died without leaving children, the patronage should revert to their brothers and sisters. 'Children' throughout the decree was taken to include grandsons, granddaughters, *etc.*

The assignment might be made in any words or by signs or writing, by will or codicils or in the lifetime of the patron. It might refer to slaves made free by will as well as to those who were freed already. It could be conditional or deferred for a time, and, until the condition occurred or the time came, the rights of all the patron's children remained unaffected; and therefore, if the freedman died meanwhile, all the children and not the assignee only, were entitled to the inheritance or possession of his estate. If the assignee brought a capital charge against the freedman, he could not, but his brothers could, apply for possession of the freedman's estate against the will. They could apply also, if the assignee neglected to do so. If there were two joint patrons, the assignment by one did not affect more than his own share. An assignment might be revoked by a simple act of will. Disherison of a son did not affect the assignment of a freedman to him, unless that effect was intended. Modestin thought that assignment might be made to an emancipated son, if the patron, in accordance with the words of the senate's decree, had two or more still in his power. Julian is said to have held with others that the assignment dropt, if the assignee was emancipated afterwards. The emancipated children of an assignee were held to have some claim to benefit by the assignment in preference to the assignor's other sons though unemancipated, but what benefit is not stated. A patron's son had no right of assignment (D. xxxviii 2 fr 3 § 9; tit. 4 fr 1 pr—§ 6; fr 3; fr 7—10, 12, 13 pr; Just. iii 8 § 2).

C. PATRON'S RIGHTS. A patron's rights consisted in a claim (1) to the whole or part of his deceased freedman's estate; (2) to support in case of need; (3) to due respect; and (4) to services.

1. On the patron's claim to *hereditas* and *bonorum possessio* see Book III chap. vi. A freedman was not allowed to defeat

this claim by gifts to others in his lifetime (*Actio Fabia et Calvisiana*, Book V chap. viii 8).

2. *Alimenta.* 'Alimony.' A patron in need had a right to be supported by his freedman or freedwoman (Paul ii 32). The amount of monthly support was determined by an arbiter, having regard to the freedman's means. Sometimes after inquiry a patron's children also, and even (if he himself and his children are not alive) his father and mother, could claim support from well-to-do freedmen (D. xxiv 3 fr 5 §§ 19, 20, 24—26; fr 9). A mother's freedman could also be compelled to support her children (*ib.* fr 5 § 21). The question, whether a person is the patron's freedman or not, can be tried as a preliminary issue (*ib.* fr 5 § 18).

3. *Obsequium.* Freedmen were bound to show respect to their patron and his children, and that in several ways. They were punishable for abusive language, while they had no action against him for the like or for slight blows or correction. They could not bring any action at all against him or his parents or his children without the permission of the praetor, who would grant the patron an action for breach. All actions imputing disgraceful conduct (*famosae*) such as, for taking money to bring or not bring suits against others, for *injuriarum, de servo corrupto,* interdicts *unde vi* or *quod vi aut clam,* and actions and pleas of fraud or intimidation were not admissible in that shape: an action or plea stating the facts without imputation (*in factum*) was substituted, at least in some cases (D. iv 3 fr 11; xliii 16 fr 1 § 43; xlvii 10 fr 7 § 2). A plea of fraud could not be used by a freedman himself even against his patron's heirs (D. xliv 4 fr 4 § 16). Nor if he tendered an oath to his freedman could the freedman call upon him to take the oath of good faith (*de calumnia*). Such respect was personal to the patron, whether suing for himself or for others, but was not required towards his representative. Further, in any action against a patron, condemnation could be obtained only so far as the patron's means allowed (Gai. iv 46, 183, 187; D. ii 4 fr 4 § 1; fr 10 §§ 5, 12, 13; xxxvii 15 fr 2, 5—7). The city praefect (or in the provinces the governor) was specially charged with the control of freedmen, and could, if any were accused by their patron (or if

there were more than one patron, then by all) of persistent want of respect or of graver conduct, visit them with personal chastisement, or forfeiture of part of their estate to their patron, or banishment; or even labour in the mines (D. i 12 fr 1 § 2; xxxvii 14 fr 1, 7 § 1; xl 9 fr 30 § 4)[1]. A constitution of Commodus directed that freedmen who had used grave violence to their patrons, or abandoned them in poverty or sickness, should be reduced into their patron's power, or even sold as slaves and the purchase money given to their patron (D. xxv 3 fr 6 § 1). Theft by a freedman from his patron (being punishable otherwise) did not give rise to an action *furti* (D. xlvii 2 fr 90). The freedman of a civic community or other corporation was not prevented from suing the individual members (D. ii 4 fr 10 § 4).

4. *Operae.* The services which a slave was in the habit of performing or might perform to his master often survived the change in their relation. It was held that a freedman was under a natural duty to perform (*edere, dare, praestare*) services to his patron (*natura operas patrono libertus debet*, D. xii 6 fr 26 § 12). Services were of two kinds, dutiful (*officiales*) and industrial (*fabriles*). The former were of a personal and domestic character, such as to accompany him on journeys, to manage his lawsuits, to guard his house, *etc.*, and were regarded as performable only to the patron or his children: they would naturally vary according to the wants of the patron and the capacity of the freedman. But a freedman might, like any one else, have special qualifications, *e.g.* as a doctor, architect, pantomime actor, painter, book-keeper, copyist, or might practise some handicraft. Such industrial services were obviously in no way special to the relation between freedman and patron. Other persons could do them, others could receive them, they could be let for hire, they had a money value, and, if paid when not due, could be the subject of a condiction. The

[1] A discussion took place in the senate A.D. 56 on the conduct of freedmen, and it was urged that they should be liable to be brought back into slavery: *quid enim aliud laeso patrono concessum est quam ut vicesimum ultra lapidem in oram Campaniae libertum releget* (Tac. *An.* xiii 26 where the mention of Campania is probably ironical). Claudius it is said *ingratos et de quibus patroni quererentur revocavit in servitutem* (Suet. *Claud.* 25).

patron could require their being rendered gratuitously not only to himself but to his friends: he need not always be ill himself in order to make use of the services of his freedman who was a doctor. And if the freedman gave up the practice of such special craft, the patron might then require other services. But all services must be reasonable, regard being had to the age, health, and habits both of freedman and patron; and compatible with the freedman's plan of life and his dignity. They must be so regulated as to allow of the freedman's attending to his personal wants (*corporis cura*); and as the service is to be performed at his own cost, he must, unless the patron supply him, have time to work for his own living (D. xxxviii 1 fr 6, 9, 16, 17, 27, 38, 50).

In order to give legal sanction to the freedman's natural duty the following practice was resorted to. Services were promised on oath by the slave (even if *impubes*) before manumission: this oath did not bind legally, though doubts on this point existed at one time, but was intended to induce the repetition of the oath immediately after manumission. This second oath gave rise (as no other oath did) to a civil obligation[1], which could be extinguished by formal release and was lost by *capitis deminutio* (Gai. iii 83, 96; *Epit.* ii 9 § 4; D. xxxviii 1 fr 7 pr; xl 12 fr 44; xlvi 4 fr 13 pr). Instead of an oath, a stipulation was often made after manumission.

The oath or stipulation generally covered gifts as well as services, *donum, munus, operas se praestaturum.* By *donum* was meant any gift; by *munus* a gift on some special occasion such as births or marriages[2]. A service was a day's work and

[1] Cicero (*Fam.* vii 2 *ad fin.*) refers apparently to a refusal of a freedman to repeat the oath made before manumission. He is speaking of some freedmen of his own who had committed theft etc. and had deserted his son. *Itaque usurpavi vetus illud Drusi ut ferunt praetoris in eo qui eadem liber non juraret, me istos liberos non addixisse, praesertim cum adesset nemo a quo recte vindicarentur*, *i.e.* he cancelled their (inchoate ?) manumission.

[2] *Labeo ait, munus esse donum cum causa; ut puta natalicium, nuptalicium* (D. L 16 fr 194). *Munus proprie est quod necessarie obimus lege more imperioque ejus qui jubendi habet potestatem. Dona autem proprie sunt quae nulla necessitate juris (aut) officii sed sponte praestantur: quae si non praestantur, nulla reprehensio est, et si praestantur, plerumque laus est* (*ib.* fr 214).

was regarded as a whole, not divisible. If division had to be made (as between co-heirs, *etc.*) it was done either by dividing the number of days, or by dividing the money value. The obligation of services imposed by the patron and undertaken by the freedman was ascertained in number and character, no doubt often by agreement between master and slave before manumission; and the gifts were probably also ascertained, perhaps by custom. But this is not enough to ground an action against the freedman. The general promise of so many services requires to be supplemented by a declaration or notice given by the patron of the particular work required and the days when it is to be performed. It is implied that the convenience of the patron will decide this, and hence the insertion of such words as *cum poposcero* in the oath or stipulation is unnecessary. Until this notice (*indictio*) is given, the service of whatever kind[1] is not legally due; and suit cannot be brought until the time for performing the service is over, without its being performed (*semper praeterita opera quae jam dari non possit petitur*). Nor is the service due if the freedman is too ill to perform it or is hindered by the patron. It must be performed at the place where the patron is, the time and expense of getting there being at the patron's cost: but the freedman is not bound to follow him all about the world (D. xxxviii 1 fr 1, 7 § 3, fr 8, 15, 20—22 pr; xlv 1 fr 54 § 1, 73 pr; L 16 fr 53 pr, 214). There was an interdict to compel the production of a freedman, to whom his patron desired to give notice of services (Gai. iv 162).

It was contrary to the Aelian Sentian statute for the patron to impose upon his freedman a rent (*merces*) instead of services, thus converting a personal relation of gratitude and respect into a purely commercial claim. But if he could not use them in kind, *e.g.* the services of a doctor or actor, he might let them without coming under the statute. And such an arrangement

[1] Leist (in Glück's *Pand.* § 1622, Part v, § 158, p. 226) misunderstands fr 24 as if it distinguished between *op. fabriles* and others due to a patron: whereas Julian is treating of stipulations for services certain in general and contrasts them with stipulations for services to be rendered by freedman to patron.

might always be made by agreement with the freedman. Or the patron could give the freedman the alternative of either performing services or paying a sum in lieu of each (D. xxxvii 14 fr 6 § 1; xxxviii 1 fr 25; xl 9 fr 32 §§ 1, 2).

Services may be promised expressly to a patron's children as well as to himself (*patrono liberisque*) and can then be claimed by the children (grandchildren, *etc.*) after his death, whether emancipated or not, and whether made heirs by their father or not. Even posthumous children are included. Children given in adoption are included, only if made heirs by their father. If the promise is made simply *patrono*, children can claim only if heirs (directly, not through a slave). Children claim services equally, whatever be their share in their father's inheritance (D. xxxviii 1 fr 5, fr 7 §§ 6—8, fr 22 § 1; cf. L 16 fr 70). Industrial services pass to the heir and can be sued for (*i.e.* the value of past services) even by outsiders just as repayment of a loan may be sued for[1]. Dutiful services do not pass to the heir, and an outsider cannot continue the suit, even if begun and issue joined by the patron: whereas children (expressly included in the freedman's promise) can bring, and, unless expressly disinherited, can continue such a suit (D. xxxviii 1 fr 4, 6, 29[2]). A transfer of an inheritance under a trust does not carry with it the action for freedman's services (D. xxxvi 1 fr 57 pr). Sureties are liable in case of delay on the part of the freedman, but such delay cannot exist on their own part, for they are incapable of performing the services (D. xxxviii 1 fr 44). Assignment of the patron's right to one child does not exclude his brothers from a claim to services promised previously; nor is a grandson of one patron excluded by the son of another from services promised to the joint owners who manumitted the slave (fr 51).

If services are promised to the patron or Titius, the freedman is discharged by performing them to Titius, only if they

[1] *Perinde enim operae a libertis ac pecunia credita petitur* (Pomp. ap. D. xxxviii 1 fr 4). Just as money lent is spent by the borrower, so services (*i.e.* so many days' work) may be spent by the freedman for his own purposes and the creditor or patron or heir has a strict suit for the amount or value.

[2] I refer this fragment to *operae officiales*. Others omit *non*. Lenel (*Paling.* ii 795) retains *non*.

are industrial services, and he performs such as he would perform to his patron (fr 10 § 1—fr 12, 23 pr; xii 6 fr 26 § 12).

D. PRAETOR'S CONTROL. The praetor included suits against freedmen in his edict in order to exercise control over the demands, often oppressive[1] (as Servius declared), made by patrons upon their freedmen. The Praetor Rutilius was the first to declare in his edict that he would grant actions only for services and to give effect to bargains made by the patron for admission to partnership in the freedman's property if there were default of due respect (*obsequium*). On this analogy subsequent praetors admitted patrons to possession of a certain share of their deceased freedman's estate contrary to the will (see Book III chap. vi). But the bargain of a partnership was held as invalid *ipso jure*, presumably because contrary to the reasonable terms and voluntary character of Partnership (D. xxxviii 1 fr 2, 36, tit. 2 fr 1; xliv 5 fr 1 § 7; cf. xvii 2 fr 3 § 3). And if a patron, after manumission without any previous bargain, got the freedman to make a promise, which the patron could hold over him *in terrorem* and enforce as a penalty for any conduct of the freedman which displeased him (thus avoiding the necessity of proving the freedman's ill-conduct), the praetor granted a plea to prevent the execution of such a burden on his liberty (*exceptio onerandae libertatis causa*). Sureties and *expromissor*, if any, could take advantage of this plea. When the promise was made, not immediately on manumission, but after an interval, there being then no real compulsion on the freedman to make it, doubts were entertained whether the plea should be granted; but it was allowed if after due hearing it appeared that the freedman had been intimidated or overawed by the patron (D. xliv 5 fr 1 §§ 5, 6, 8; fr 2 § 2). If however the patron had delegated the freedman under this promise to his creditor, or the freedman had delegated his debtor to the patron, the plea was not good against creditor or patron, but the freedman had a condiction against the patron to recover the amount (xliv 5 fr 1 §§ 10, 11). A stipulation

[1] *Libertis majores nostri non multo secus ac servis imperabant* (Cic. *Q. Fr.* i 1.4 § 13).

for the freedman to refund what had come into his hands, when as slave he managed his master's business, or to pay his patron the price agreed for his liberty, or a sum in settlement of all claims for services and other patron's rights, was not open to any such objection (*ib.* fr 1 § 4, 2 § 2; xxxviii 1 fr 41; cf. L 16 fr 53).

An oath against lawful marriage was (by the *lex Julia*) not enforceable on either freedman or freedwoman, nor (by the *lex Aelia Sentia*) was an oath enforceable on a freedwoman not to marry within a certain time or only to marry a fellow-freedman or relative of the patron or with the patron's consent; but a prohibition to marry while her children were still *impuberes* was not unlawful (D. xxxvii 14 fr 6 § 4; xxxviii 16 fr 3 § 5; xl 9 fr 31). A freedwoman married to her patron could not, without his consent, leave him and marry another (D. xxiii 2 fr 45 pr §§ 4, 5), but this did not apply to one whom he had freed in compliance with a trust (*ib.* fr 50).

E. Loss and non-acquisition of patron's rights.

1. Under the *lex Julia et Papia Poppaea* a freedman (not being a stage-player or one who let himself out to fight with wild beasts) who had, or had had, two or more natural children in his power, or one child if five years old, was released from all obligations to his patron for services or gifts, whether the obligation rested on oath or stipulation. Even if suit has been already commenced, the freedman is discharged, but not if he has been actually condemned: nor if the patron has got him to promise a creditor instead of himself[1]; for the delegation being equivalent to payment, the creditor is entitled to keep what he has received. If the freedman has got some one to promise in his place, such an *expromissor* is not freed; but sureties are freed along with the freedman himself (D. xxxviii 1 fr 37). No action for services lies against a freedwoman who is more than 50 years old, or is wife or concubine to her patron, or has married with the consent of her patron,

[1] If the freedman promised the patron and afterwards was delegated to a creditor *in id quod patrono promisit*, Paul held that the law possibly freed him, for the words of the law dealt not with what he owed, but with what he promised to the patron (D. xxxviii 1 fr 37 § 4).

or one who has attained a position which makes service to a male patron unsuitable. A patroness, though consenting to her marriage, can still claim a freedwoman's services (*ib.* fr 34, 35, 46, 48 § 2).

2. A patron lost all rights as patron if he suffered *capitis deminutio*, except that *minima cap. dem.* did not entitle the freedman to summon him into court without the praetor's permission (Gai. iii 51; D. ii 4 fr 10 §§ 2, 6). He lost all rights to duties imposed as a condition of manumission, if he failed to support his freedman in need. This was by the *lex Aelia Sentia* and a constitution of Caracalla (D. xxxviii 2 fr 33; xxxvii 14 fr 5 § 1). By the same law he forfeited his rights as patron, if he compelled his freedman or freedwoman to take an oath not to marry (see above), and in this case the permission of the praetor was not required to summon his patron into court (D. ii 4 fr 8 § 2). Or if he required his freedman to pay him money instead of performing services, or resold to his freedman his rights[1], or remitted them either while alive or by will, the rights ceased (cf. D. xxv 3 fr 5 § 22; xxxviii 2 fr 37; Cod. vi 3 fr 4; tit. 4 fr 4 §§ 1—9 which contains other cases, possibly belonging to later times). For loss of rights to inheritance or other succession see Book III chap. vi B.

3. The full position and privileges of a patron did not always come to the master of the slave set free. Thus where the master was not acting of his own free will, he had no claim to what was regarded as compensation for freeing his slave. One to whom the inheritance of a deceased is assigned under the constitution of M. Aurelius has no right of imposing services on the slaves thereby freed (D. xxxviii 1 fr 13 § 1): nor has the nominal purchaser of a slave, who buys his freedom with his own money (D. xxv 3 fr 5 § 22; Cod. vi 3 fr 8): nor anyone who has bought a slave with the condition of setting him free, and has when the time came broken faith, the slave becoming free by the constitution of M. Aurelius (D. ii 4 fr 10 pr; xxxviii

[1] D. xxxvii 14 fr 20 speaking of the patron's option between succession to his freedman's inheritance or suit for obligation imposed in view of freedom appears to refer to some such bargain. See Leist, Glück's *Pand.* Pt. v, p. 442 note.

1 fr 13 pr; cf. xl 9 fr 30 pr). Nor (by constitutions of Hadrian and others) did manumission in compliance with a trust give the manumitter (at least if not a son of testator) any claim over the person of the freedman but only over his inheritance (Vat. 225; D. xxx fr 95; xxxviii 1 fr 7 § 4; tit. 2 fr 29 pr); and one who endeavoured to shirk a trust did not have even this (D. xxvi 3 fr 1 § 3). A freedman however having full knowledge of the want of liability and yet promising services to his manumitter by trust was held to be bound (D. xxxviii 1 fr 47).

4. If a freedman received from the emperor the right of golden rings, the patron loses his claim over his person but not over his inheritance (Vat. 226; D. xxxviii 2 fr 3 pr). He was regarded as *ingenuus* (D. xl 10 fr 5, 6). If he was *natalibus suis restitutus*, *i.e.* granted the *status* of a freeborn person, the patron lost all rights. Usually the patron's consent was obtained for such a grant (D. xl 11 fr 2).

The charter of Salpensa in giving Roman citizenship to the (Latin) officials and their families, expressly preserves to them the rights over all such freedmen of their own or their father's as were not also made Roman citizens (cap. 23; Bruns[6] p. 143).

F. The question whether an alleged freedman was so, could be tried at either party's instance by a *praejudicium* (see Book I chap. v) and the result was decisive as to his *status*. But an oath of the patron, declaring the freedman to be his, entitled the patron to be exempt from summons and gave him other claims, but did not affect the right of succession (D. ii 4 fr 8 § 1; xxxvii 14 fr 14).

CHAPTER X.

GUARDIAN AND WARD.

Guardianship is said to have been defined by Servius Sulpicius as 'Force and power (*vis ac potestas*) given and allowed by the civil law over a free person to protect one who on account of age is unable of his own will to defend himself'

(D. xxvi I fr I pr). Probably Servius added to 'age' 'or on account of sex.'

All males under the age of puberty and all females of whatever age, married or not, required a guardian, if they were not under fatherly power or in hand or handtake.

A. APPOINTMENT OF GUARDIANS. Guardians are variously classified[1], but the most important division is according as they are appointed by will, or by a magistrate such as the praetor, or become such by statute.

1. Guardians appointed (*dati*) by will (under authority of XII tables[2]).

By will or codicils a father could appoint a guardian or guardians for his children under his power, and for grandchildren, provided that their father is no longer under his power: otherwise on the grandfather's death they naturally fall into their father's power. He can appoint guardians also for postumous children or grandchildren, provided that they would, if born during his life, be in his power. A wife or daughter in law in his hand being regarded as child and grandchild respectively, he can appoint guardians for them also. The regular words of appointment were: 'I give L. Titius as guardian to my children[3]'; but a good appointment is also made by the words 'Titius shall be (*esto*) guardian to my children' or 'to my wife.' It was necessary that the person should be ascertained and that the appointment should be direct, not by way of trust; but it might be conditional, or to or from a certain time. But a guardian was not appointed merely for a particular piece of business, though eventually it

[1] Gaius (i 188) tells us that Q. Mucius made five kinds of guardians, Serv. Sulpicius three, Labeo two. Ulpian (xi 2) divides into *legitimi* (including testamentary and Atilian), *senatus consultis constituti* and *moribus introducti*, e.g. *ad litem datus*.

[2] Ulpian gives the words of the statute in this form: *uti legassit super pecunia tutelaque suae rei ita jus esto* (other authorities vary), 'as he has directed concerning the stock and guard of his estate, so shall the law be.' The words appear to be general, and 'legacy' and 'guardianship' to be later specifications.

[3] *Liberi* includes grandchildren; *filii* does not, but does include *filiae*. *Postumi* includes grandchildren (D. xxvi 2 fr 6, 16 pr).

was allowed to appoint a guardian for *e.g.* 'my African estate' or 'for my Syrian estate[1],' *etc.* Persons who were not *sui juris* could be appointed by will as guardians, and even a slave of testator or another, of course with freedom, which would be assumed to have been intended, if necessary. Only Roman citizens or persons recognised as on equality with them could be appointed by will: the Junian Latins were expressly excluded. Whether a guardian could be appointed before the heir was disputed: the Sabinians said no; the Proculians yes, because nothing was taken out of the inheritance by an appointment of guardian. The question of validity may perhaps (so says Gaius) arise respecting an appointment 'after the death of the heir.'

The person appointed could abdicate, *i.e.* declare that he would not be guardian, and thereupon he ceased to be so. Surrender in court was not required or applicable. Nor did he lose his guardianship by *capitis deminutio.* The appointment dates from the will's becoming operative by the entry of any one heir (Gai. i 144—149; ii 231, 234, 240, 289; Ulp. xi 14—17; D. L 17 fr 73 § 1; xxvi 2 fr 9, 10 § 4, 12—15, 20).

Guardians not validly appointed were sometimes confirmed by the praetor. Such are a guardian appointed by a father by a will which proves invalid, or appointed by a patron, or by an outsider to the family for an *impubes* whom he has made heir and who has no other property. So also a guardian appointed by a mother's or uncle's will was confirmed after due inquiry (D. xxvi 3, fr 2—5; xxxi fr 69 § 2; Cod. v 28, fr 1, 4; tit. 29, fr 1, 2).

Practice allowed a wife in hand to be given by her husband the choice of her guardian[2]. The words were: 'I give my wife Titia the choice of a guardian.' The wife then could choose a guardian for all matters or for one or two, and could change

[1] Paul (Vat. 229) says, *Hoc modo scribere potest: 'Lucio Titio filio meo et si mihi vivo mortuove nati (ali) erunt, tutores do Lucium Aurelium et Gaium Optatum, a quibus peto ut tutelam liberorum meorum gerant ita ut ea quae in Asia reliquero, Aurelius, ea autem quae in Italia, Optatus administret.'*

[2] '*Tutoris optio*' was granted by senate's decree to Fecenia Hispala (a *meretrix*) *quasi ei vir testamento dedisset* (Liv. xxxix 19).

her guardian as often as she liked. The testator might however confine her to one or two exercises of choice, *e.g.* by inserting the words *dumtaxat semel* or *dumtaxat bis*, 'once only,' or 'twice only.'

Guardians appointed by will by name were called *dativi*; those chosen by a wife *optivi* (Gai. i 150—154).

2. Statutable guardians (*legitimi*[1]), and others connected therewith.

(*a*) If no guardian was appointed by will, or if a guardian was appointed but died before the ward reached puberty, the agnate in the nearest degree became guardian. Such were brothers, brothers' sons, father's brother, father's brothers' sons. If there were more agnates than one, equally near, all became guardians. If a statutable guardian dies or suffers *cap. dem.*, his son, not his heir, succeeds. A statutable guardian cannot abdicate. The agnatic guardianship of women was abolished by a *lex Claudia* (Gai. i 155—158; Ulp. xi 3, 4, 17; D. xxvi 1 fr 16; tit. 4 fr 3 § 9, fr 6—9).

The fact that a testamentary guardian was excused or removed or was appointed only on a condition or from a time which had not arrived, did not give any title to an agnate to become guardian (D. xxvi 2 fr 11).

In early times the *gens* was entitled to guardianship (as well as to inheritance) if there were no agnates. This is alluded to

[1] Mommsen in a careful essay in *ZRG.* xxv p. 267 sqq. shews that *legitimus* is a technical word only in connexion with *heres*, *hereditas*, *tutor*, *tutela* and *judicium*; *lege agere* and *legis actio* are similarly technical in their ordinary use: but *legitima* applied to *actio* is not, any more than when applied to *civis*, *matrimonium*, *nuptiae*, *uxor*, *filius*, *liberi*, *tempus*, *aetas*, *horae*, *modus*, *usurae*, *spatium*, *latitudo*, *numerus*, *pars*, *jus*. In these combinations it means 'conformable to the lawful order,' whether or not any special statute was in the mind of the user. It may be opposed to what is unlawful, or often to what rests on the magistrate's discretion. In the technical use it refers, not exactly to the statute of the XII tables, but to what that symbolized, the most ancient legal constitution of the Roman community. As compared with this, even testamentary succession and regulations by later statutes (cf. D. xxxviii 16 fr 11) were exceptional; and still more praetorian succession, praetorian suits and praetorian appointments. I have usually translated it by 'statutable.'

in Cic. *Balb.* 25 § 56, and in the *laudatio Turiae,* v 20 (Bruns, p. 283), probably about 750 U.C.

(*b*) Freedwomen and, if under the age of puberty, freedmen, were in the guardianship of their patrons, or, on their patron's death, of his male children, *etc.* This was not enacted by the XII tables, but inferred from the analogy of the agnate's claim, the right of guardianship being deemed to accompany the right of inheritance, and to pass to the manumitter's children in the same order. On one of several patrons dying or suffering loss of *status* (*capit. dem.*), the guardianship did not pass to the son of deceased as long as the other patrons remained. Nor did it pass to a grandson if a son remained. The removal or excuse of a patron from guardianship did not let in succession (Gai. i 165; D. xxvi 4 fr 3 pr, §§ 4—8). If the manumitter had only the property of the slave *in bonis,* and the owner *ex jure Quiritium* had not joined, the freed persons become Latins, and by the *lex Junia* the former has title only to the inheritance, the latter is guardian (Gai. i 167: cf. Ulp. xi 10, 19). The right of guardianship belonged to one who manumitted in compliance with a trust, or with a condition made at his purchase of the slave (D. fr 3 §§ 1, 2). An *orcinus libertus* has testator's children for guardians (fr 3 § 3).

(*c*) In the place of a statutable guardian is a parent (father, grandfather, *etc.*) who has mancipated a daughter, or son's daughter, *etc.* to another on condition of her being remancipated to him, and has then manumitted her (Gai. i 172, 175). The same is the case when a parent has thus mancipated and manumitted a son or son's son if under the age of puberty (D. xxvi 4 fr 3 § 10), but this case is apparently omitted by Gaius.

Connected with statutable guardians are two others, *fiduciarii* and *cessicii.*

(*d*) A right of guardianship analogous to that of patrons was recognized to belong to one who, not being the parent, had manumitted a freeborn person after mancipation to him by the person's parent or copurchaser. Such guardians are called *fiduciarii,* and were often selected by the woman (see above, chap. v). If the manumitter was the father, grandfather, *etc.*

he himself was reckoned as a statutable guardian; but his sons, becoming guardians on his death, were in the place of fiduciary guardians (Gai. i 166 *a*, 175, 195 *a*).

(*e*) Agnates and patrons and fiduciary guardians were permitted to divest themselves, at least for a time, of the guardianship of a woman, but only by surrendering it in court to another who was called a guardian by surrender (*cessicius*). A son under power could not surrender as he was not capable of a *legis actio*. The guardianship of males, ceasing at the age of their puberty, was held not to be sufficiently burdensome to justify such a concession, which also ceased to be operative in the case of agnatic guardianship of women by the *lex Claudia* named above. And there were doubts whether fiduciary guardians who were not fathers (and as such entitled to at least as much respect as patrons), but outsiders who had voluntarily accepted the position (of receivers by mancipation or copurchase), should be allowed to surrender their charge.

Such a guardianship by surrender lasted only so long as both surrenderor and surrenderee were alive and suffered no loss of civic *status*. If either of these events happened to the surrenderee, the guardianship reverted to the old statutable guardian: if it happened to the surrenderor, the guardianship passed at once to the next in succession to him (Gai. i 168—172; Ulp. xi 3—8; Sin. schol. 18 § 49).

3. Guardians appointed by the praetor or by governors of provinces[1], *etc.*

(*a*) By a senate's decree a woman was allowed to apply to the praetor (or in the provinces to the governor) for a guardian (*tutorem petere*) in place of one who was absent. The length of absence was not important. On a guardian being appointed (*datus*) in this way, the absentee ceased to be guardian. Such an application was not as a rule allowed, when the guardian was patron or patron's son or a father who had become a statutable guardian by manumitting a daughter or other female descendant from handtake (Gai. i 173—175; Ulp. xi 22).

[1] In D. L 17 fr 77 *tutoris datio* is named among acts which do not admit of conditions or limitation of time. It is generally taken to refer to appointments by the praetor, cf. Cujac. *ad loc.* (iv. 1693); Keller *Pand.* § 427.

But in some cases guardians were allowed to be appointed in place of statutable guardians: (1) by a senate's decree, when the patron was absent, and a woman required authority to enter on an inheritance: (2) when a woman who had to marry under the *lex Julia de maritandis ordinibus* required the establishment of a dowry, and her original patron's son was under the age of puberty and consequently incapable of giving authority: this law authorised application to the city praetor, and a senate's decree authorised like applications in the provinces to the governors: (3) by a senate's decree also, when the statutable guardian was mad or dumb. But in these cases the appointment is merely temporary, and does not involve the removal of the patron or patron's son from their guardianship.

The senate's decree also authorized the appointment of a guardian in place of any one who was removed as suspect (Chap. X. J) or excused for some lawful reason. In such cases the former guardian loses his charge altogether.

In early times, if proceedings under the statute (*lege agere*) took place between the woman or ward and the guardian, as the guardian could not give his authority when he himself was a party, a guardian was by custom (*moribus*) appointed by the city praetor for authorizing the suit. But after proceedings under the statute were taken away, some lawyers thought that this kind of guardian was obsolete, others (followed by Ulpian) that it could be resorted to in a statutable trial. Such a guardian was called *praetorius*. A caretaker appears to have been substituted in later times (Gai. i 176—184; Ulp. xi 20, 21, 23, 24; Just. i 21 § 3).

(*b*) If there was no guardian at all, by the *lex Atilia* a guardian was appointed (*datus*) at Rome by the praetor and majority of the tribunes[1] and called *tutor Atilianus*. A Latin was ineligible. Such a guardian was appointed in the provinces under the *lex Julia et Titia* by the governor[2]. The case arises

[1] Cf. Liv. xxxix 9 *sub fin. Illa post patroni mortem, quia in nullius manu erat, tutore a tribunis et praetore petito quum testamentum faceret, unum Aebutium instituit heredem.* This was in 186 B.C.

[2] The charter of the borough of Salpensa (cap. 29) authorizes the appointment by the *duoviri juri dicundo* of a guardian for any burgher who

when a guardian has been appointed by will under a condition or only from a certain day; or when, though the appointment was absolute, no heir has yet entered, so as to make the will operative; or when a guardian has been captured by the enemy. The guardian appointed under these statutes ceases when the emergency ceases (Gai. i 185—187; Ulp. xi 18; Sin. Schol. 17 and 20). Application for a guardian has also to be made under these statutes by a freedwoman who has been manumitted by a woman; or when her patron or his son has been adopted; or there was no son left in the family on the patron's death (Gai. i 195—195 *c*). According to Justinian's *Institutes* (i 20 § 3) this jurisdiction was transferred by Claudius to the consuls and by M. Aurelius to a special praetor for guardianship (*praetor tutelaris*), because these statutes gave no power to compel guardians to undertake the office or to give security.

Application for the appointment of a guardian for a person under the age of puberty could be made by relatives or friends. A rescript of Severus made it the duty of a mother to apply, and, if those thereon appointed were excused or rejected, to apply again, the penalty for neglect being the loss of all right to the estate of her children if they died intestate. A similar duty was held to be incumbent on freedmen of the father, and they were liable to punishment if they neglected it (D. xxvi 6 fr 2 pr—§ 2; xxxviii 17 fr 2 §§ 23—43). Creditors and legatees had to urge such application on the relatives, and only if these did not apply were they authorized to apply themselves (D. xxvi 6 fr 2 § 3).

The right of appointment was not a matter of ordinary jurisdiction or executive power: it belonged only to those to whom it was expressly (*nominatim*) given by statute or senate's

has none or none certain: the applicant is to propose a person for the office, and the *duoviri* after hearing the case may in their discretion appoint him. If application is made on behalf of one who is in wardship or there is only one magistrate, then the magistrate has to hear the case, and may on the decree of the decurions, two-thirds of them being present, appoint the person nominated, who is to be as fully guardian as if he were a Roman citizen next agnate to the ward, but the existing guardian is not displaced.

decree, or the emperor (D. xxvi 1 fr 6 § 2). Municipal magistrates (or, in default of such, a majority of the decurions) had the power of appointment within their own borough or district, but could appoint only their own citizens (D. xxvi 5 fr 3, 19).

B. Qualification and functions of guardians.

Only males could become guardians: even the mother was not qualified. Only *puberes* could act as guardians, even though the function had devolved on them by statute. Dumb or deaf persons could not be appointed (D. xxvi 1 fr 1 §§ 2, 3; fr 9, 16; tit. 2 fr 26; Gai. i 195).

A guardian being a creation of the civil law had a formal function and importance irrespective of any practical counsel or management of affairs which might also belong to him. The interposition of his authority was essential to the validity of his ward's acts, so far as they were part of the civil law, or if the ward was *impubes,* involved loss or liability. The authority was to be given by the guardian in person at the time of the act's being done, on its completion. He gave it orally; usually but not necessarily in reply to a question (perhaps *auctorne es? auctor sum*); it must not be coupled with any condition; subsequent declaration, or declaration by letter went for nothing. If there are several guardians, all must give their authority to each matter, except that, if they were appointed by will, one sufficed (provided he has not been forbidden to act). If a suit lay between two persons under the same guardian, probably one declaration of authority sufficed for both. No guardian could authorise a matter in which he was himself a party, but the acceptance by the ward of an inheritance which was in debt to the guardian could be authorized by him: he was only incidentally concerned. Not so the transference to a guardian by the ward as heir in trust of an inheritance. No contract could be made between guardian and ward without the authority of another guardian. Nor (by rescript of Severus and Antoninus) could a guardian buy any of the ward's things through another person or secretly (Ulp. xi 24, 26; D. xxvi 8 fr 1, 3, 4, 8, 9 §§ 5, 6; fr 15; xxix 2 fr 25 § 4; xxxvi 1 fr 1 § 13; Cod. v 59 fr 5 pr).

1. As regards a grown-up woman a guardian did not manage her affairs: he only interposed his authority. This authority was required[1] if she sued by statute (*lege agit*), which phrase would include conveyance by surrender in court; or if she sued in a statutable trial (cf. Book VI chap. x); or if she performed any business belonging to the civil law (*e.g.* constitute a usufruct or other servitude, manumit a slave, make a will, give a formal release (*acceptilatio*), accept an inheritance, contract a *manus*-marriage, establish a dowry[2]); or if she alienate mancipable property; or if she put herself under an obligation[3]; or if she permit her freedwoman to cohabitate with another's slave (cf. Book I chap. iv 4). But she is capable without her guardian's authority of alienating non-mancipable things[4], and consequently can make a cash loan on her own behalf, and can receive anything due whether mancipable or not; and give a good discharge for money[5] or other non-mancipable thing owed her (Ulp. xi 27; Gai. ii 80, 81, 83, 85; Vat. 45; D. L 17 fr 77).

[1] Cato (according to Livy) speaking B.C. 195 says *Majores nostri nullam ne privatam quidem rem agere feminas sine tutore auctore voluerunt* (Liv. xxxiv 2 § 11). Cf. Cic. *Mur.* 12 § 27.

[2] Cf. Cic. *Caecin.* 25 § 73 *Iste vester testis nunquam auderet judicare deberi viro dotem quam mulier nullo auctore dixisset*; *Flac.* 34 § 84; 35 § 86 where the authority of all her guardians is stated to be necessary for a woman to come into hand either by use or copurchase or to declare a dowry.

[3] Cf. Cic. *Caecin.* 25 § 72 *Hoc dici non potest 'judica quod mulier sine tutore auctore promiserit deberi.'*

[4] If a woman sold land without her guardian's authority (according to Sabinus, Cassius and Labeo) the purchaser neither acquires the property, nor is in a way to acquire it by usucapion; for his possession is not *bona fide*. But she can alienate the possession without guardian's authority, that being *res nec mancipi*, and hence the purchaser can acquire the fruits. Julian however on the ground of an unknown *Rutiliana constitutio* held that if the woman received the price of the land, and did not tender it back before the two years expired, the purchaser gained by usucapion (Vat. 1). By Julian's time the guardian's authority as regards women had become a mere form. See Scheurl *Beitr.* ii 1 § 10. Karlowa (*RG.* ii 404) suggests that Julian was applying to this case the analogy of the *constitutio quae de redemptis lata est* (D. xlix 15 fr 12 § 8), and that the author of the 'constitution' was P. Rutilius *tr. pleb.* mentioned in Cic. *Orat.* i 40 § 181.

[5] Cf. Cic. *Top.* 11 § 46, quoted Book IV chap. iii D.

As a rule women were under guardianship all their lives. But the Vestal Virgins were, from respect to their office, made by the XII tables free from guardianship. By the *lex Julia* and *Papia Poppaea* freeborn women who had three children, and freedwomen who had four, were also freed even from statutable guardianship (Gai. i 145, 194; Ulp. xxix 3).

Gaius criticises the guardianship of women, which seemed to him without adequate justification. They managed their own business affairs; the guardian interposed his authority for form's sake only, and was often compelled by the praetor to give it against his will. A woman (above the age of puberty) had no action *tutelae* against her guardian as an *impubes* had; and the ordinary explanation, that women's levity of mind required the safeguard and control of a guardian, seems in these circumstances more specious than real. But this criticism does not apply to the statutable guardianship belonging to patrons and to parents who have emancipated their children. For they could not be compelled to authorise the making of a will or alienation of mancipable property or undertaking of obligations: and in fact it was in order that their right to the inheritance of their daughters or freedwomen dying intestate might not be destroyed, or the inheritance itself be impaired or laden with debt, that they were made guardians (Gai. i 190—192).

The guardianship of grown-up women became obsolete[1] and is not mentioned in Justinian's Digest. Something of the kind was, says Gaius, generally found among foreigners, *e.g.* in Bithynia a woman's contracts required the authority of her husband or of a grown-up son (Gai. i 193).

2. The guardianship of *impuberes* had a more solid basis in natural reason, and was found not only at Rome, but, as Gaius says, in all communities. Imperfect age requires the guidance of an older person. At Rome the guardianship of boys expired at the age of puberty. What this age was, the lawyers were not agreed[2]. The Sabinians held that it was shewn by the

[1] The last certain mention is said to be Vat. 325, of the date of 294 A.D., cf. Girard *Manuel* p. 216.

[2] Quintilian gives the question *pubertas annis an corporis habitu aestimetur* as arguable before the *centumviri* (*Inst.* iv 2 § 5).

growth of the body and defined to be when the particular person was considered able to beget a child. The Proculians held that it should be reckoned generally at fourteen years complete. Priscus held that the age of fourteen and the bodily growth were both requisite. *Spadones* were by all lawyers held to be *puberes* and freed from guardianship at the age of fourteen (Gai. i 196; Ulp. xi 28). Girls were held to be *puberes* and capable of marriage at the age of twelve years complete (Just. i 22 pr), but, as before said, they do not thereby cease to be under guardianship.

Adoption of a ward or deportation or capture by the enemy or loss of freedom put an end to his being under guardianship at least for the time. Statutable guardianships are ended by any loss of civic status (Ulp. xi 9; cf. Just. i 22 § 4).

C. Administration by guardians of *impuberes*.

Unless he has a valid excuse a guardian must take up the administration of his ward's affairs as soon as he knows of his appointment. He has to act with absolute good faith and the same care that a sensible man is expected to use in his own affairs (D. xxvi 7 fr 1 pr, 33 pr, but cf. xxvii 3 fr 1 pr). He should make an inventory of the assets, deposit (in a temple? with a banker?) any sums of money suitable for purchasing land, and in due time make such purchases, or put out money at interest to solvent persons, sell anything likely to spoil by time[1], pay (without necessarily waiting for judgment), or resist (if advisable) demands upon his ward, bring actions, novate obligations, enter into stipulations, *etc.* on his ward's behalf. Where a stipulation has to be made, the ward or ward's slave should make it: if the ward is too young and has no slave, or if the ward is absent, the guardian must make it himself, and the ward was then allowed an analogous (*utilis*) action on it.

[1] At one time there was a stringent law directing guardians to sell gold, silver, jewels, robes and other valuable moveables, city slaves, houses, baths, warehouses and everything within the towns, and reduce all into money except land and country slaves. Constantine repealed it as being contrary to the interest of many minors (Cod. v 37 fr 22 pr). The *lex* referred to was probably some constitution later than the *Oratio Severi* (below p. 108). Cf. Glück, *Pand.* xxxii p. 477.

A like action was allowed the ward, when his guardian had made a *constitutum* for him. If suit is brought against the ward and he is absent or unable to speak, the guardian defends the action, but judgment is executed against the ward (as rescripts of Ant. Pius and others declared), and neither the guardian nor any sureties that he may have given are liable. If the ward is not an infant, he defends himself with the guardian's authority. A guardian bringing a suit on behalf of his ward was not always required to give security even in Gaius' time, and later (in Ulpian's time?) the practice was not to require it. He must pay to the estate anything due from him, and treat himself with the same strictness with which he would treat his own debtors. Any debt due to himself he can pay from the estate (D. xxvi 7 fr 1 § 2; fr 7 pr — § 3; fr 9 pr — § 6, fr 10, 22, 23; tit. 9 fr 7; Cod. v 51 fr 13 § 2; D. xiv 5 fr 5 § 9).

His duty including care of the ward himself as well as of his estate, he must find him a proper abode, the mother, if still a widow, having the preference, arrange for his maintenance, and engage and pay proper teachers on a scale suited to the ward's rank and estate. Such matters were constantly submitted to the praetor to decide, but it was not always necessary to do so, where circumstances made it undesirable to expose the amount of the ward's estate. The ward cannot refuse to allow such payments made for him by his guardian, 'as if he had lived on air' (*quasi vento vixerit*). The guardian had also to maintain the slaves and freedmen and sometimes, if expedient for the ward, even outsiders and the ward's mother and sisters, if in absolute need. He should make customary presents to parents and relatives. But dowry for his ward's sister by a different father, and marriage gifts for his ward's mother or sister are outside his duty (D. xxvi 7 fr 12 § 3; 13 § 2; xxvii 2 fr 1—3; Cod. v 37 fr 3; tit. 49 fr 1; tit. 50 fr 2 § 2). In general gifts made by a guardian are not good against the ward (D. xxvi 7 fr 22).

A guardian can made no profit of his charge, but has a right to repayment of expenses *bona fide* incurred thereon, unless the person who appointed him fixed a certain remuneration (D. xxvi 7 fr 33 § 3; 58 pr *ad fin.*). A legacy left him, directly or by way of trust, to recoup any loss he might incur by acting as guardian, is good, but a direction by testator that a guardian should not be liable to account is bad, as against public policy (fr 5 § 7).

As a rule, a guardian is liable for interest on any moneys of the ward which he has not duly put out to interest or deposited with a view to the purchase of land. The ordinary rate of interest in such a case (*pupillares usurae*) varies according to the custom of the district, 5 per cent. or 4 per cent. or less. But he is usually ordered by the praetor to pay statutable interest (*legitimae usurae, i.e.* 12 per cent.), if he has applied any of the ward's moneys whether principal or interest to his own use, or has delayed in depositing it, after an order from the praetor, or has himself received statutable interest from the ward's debtors, or, while he had moneys of the ward's, has denied having any for the ward's support, or has made it necessary for his ward to borrow at statutable interest. The proof of any application of ward's money to the guardian's use must be strict: mere non-investment or non-deposition is, as Severus declared, not sufficient. Nor is a guardian who was in debt to the ward's father, and has not paid it off to himself, liable for a higher rate of interest than that agreed upon with the father. Two months is allowed the guardian in the ordinary course for getting in moneys due to the ward and investing the proceeds: only after that (unless he has used them in his own concerns) is he chargeable with interest (D. xxvi 7 fr 7 §§ 3—15). If he has delayed for six months from the knowledge of his appointment to invest the moneys which he has found lying idle, he is liable for principal and interest: otherwise he is liable for bad investments, whether in land or on loan, only in case of gross negligence[1]. If he stipulates on loans in his own name, he is in theory liable to make good any losses, and to transfer all good investments, but the better view was that the ward must either take all or decline all. And this view applied also to investments made in the ward's name (D. xxvi 7 fr 1 § 1; 7 §§ 1, 2; 15, 16). Interest is reckoned up to the time not

[1] Cf. Quintil. vii 4 § 35 *In quo judicio (tutelae) solet quaeri an alia de re quam de calculis cognosci oporteat, an fidem praestare debeat tantum, non etiam consilium et eventum.*

merely when the guardianship is ended but when the actual transfer to the ward is effected (fr 7 § 15).

Where a single guardian was from his age or health or rank or from the distance of some of his ward's affairs unable to manage matters himself, the praetor made an order appointing a manager (*actor*) to do it, but the guardian was responsible for him. And this course was necessarily adopted, if the ward was absent or an infant so as to be unable to appoint a procurator, for a guardian was not competent to appoint a procurator for the ward until after he had himself joined issue (D. xxvi 7 fr 24 pr; Cod. ii 12 fr 11).

It was desirable, especially for the conduct of suits on behalf of the ward, that the guardianship should be in the hands of one man. If a testator appoint several guardians without directing which should have the administration, the praetor will direct them to meet and choose one by a majority; or if any one of them offer to give the others security for the safekeeping of the ward's estate, and the others are not also willing to do the same, the praetor would appoint such a one, if otherwise suitable, to administer. The selection either by testator or praetor of one guardian does not relieve the others (sometimes called 'honorary guardians') from liability; they have to watch his conduct and his solvency, see that the ward's money is duly deposited, observe generally anything tending to justify suspicion, and if necessary apply for his removal (D. xxvi 2 fr 17; tit. 7 fr 3 §§ 1, 2, 6, 7). If the other guardians have not sufficient confidence in the one selected, all will be allowed to act; and if they desire it, they can have the work divided either by the character of the business or by territories; *e.g.* one acting for Rome and another for the provinces, or one acting for Italy and another for Africa, *etc.* (D. xxvi 7 fr 3 §§ 4, 8, fr 4; cf. fr 51). Where all are acting in common, they are equally responsible, but by imperial constitutions suit must be brought first against the one who acted in the particular matter. If all have so acted, and one is sued for the whole amount, he can, by the plea of fraud or by the judge's own motion, obtain division. And where the administration is divided, any one who is sued for a matter not belonging to his sphere can meet it with a like plea; or if he has been condemned and has paid in such a matter, or has paid in full where another was equally concerned, he can obtain from the judge at the time a surrender of the ward's actions against his fellow-guardians: and if from delay or otherwise he does not obtain that, he can by constitutions of Ant. Pius and others bring an analogous action against them (D. xxvii 3 fr 1 §§ 10—13, § 18; xlvi 3, fr 76; Cod. v 38 fr 2; 58 fr 2; cf. the later Cod. v 51 fr 6; tit. 52 fr 2). If the guardians are guilty of a fraud in common, none, if sued, can claim either surrender or analogous action, and compromise by one does not help the others: but full payment by one (in this case as in cases of loan, deposit, mandate, *etc.*) satisfies the debt and clears all. The same result occurs where all the guardians have neglected to act: probably however they can obtain division of the suit. If any guardian is insolvent and his sureties cannot pay, his fellow-guardians are then liable for his share; and, if they have been nominated by a magistrate, the magistrates are liable after them. A guardian who has not acted at all is liable to suit (*utilis*) only if the ward has suffered from his neglect; and generally he is called on only after the property of the guardians who have acted is exhausted. But one who has committed the administration to another or has taken security from his fellow-guardians for the safekeeping of the ward's estate is held to have acted, and cannot claim postponement of his liability under the imperial constitutions (D. xxvi 7 fr 38; 46 § 6 arg.; 55 pr §§ 2, 3; xxvii 3 fr 1 § 14; fr 15; Cod. v fr 55 § 2).

All division of work affects the guardians only among themselves in relation to their ward: outsiders can sue any of them for debts due from their ward so far as they have acted, and may set off such a debt against any suit brought in his name (D. xxvi 7 fr 36). A guardian suing outsiders on matters not within his sphere will be stopped by the praetor (*ib.* fr 4). Payment even to an honorary guardian of a debt due to a ward is good, unless he be charged as suspect or is interdicted by the praetor from all administration (D. xxvi 7 fr 46 § 5; xlvi 3 fr 14 § 1).

Wards are bound to outsiders by acts done with their

guardian's authority and (by rescripts of Trajan and Hadrian) by acts of their guardian within his competence on their account. They cannot therefore vindicate a thing lawfully sold by him. And if they have been enriched by the guardian's act, the guardian's fraud can be pleaded against the ward's suit (D. xxvi 7 fr 12 § 1; xliv 4 fr 4 §§ 23, 24 *a*; cf. xv 1 fr 21 § 1). If a ward is possessor of an estate which has to be given up to a successful claimant, and anything has been lost through fraud or fault of the guardian, the ward is liable for the damages at the sum assessed by plaintiff's oath, provided the guardian is solvent; if he is not solvent, the ward must cede to the plaintiff his actions against the guardian (D. xxvi 7 fr 61; tit. 8 fr 1).

D. ALIENATION OF WARDS' LAND PROHIBITED.

A senate's decree under Severus A.D. 195 prohibited guardians and caretakers from selling any country land or suburban land[1] of their wards, unless the parent had provided for it by his will or codicils. Sales made contrary to the decree were null. If the land was owned in common by the ward and another, or was mortgaged and the co-owner demanded division, or the creditor insisted on his right, this decree was not to interfere. If there was so much debt on the estate that it could be paid no other way, application was to be made to the praetor to decide what land could be sold or mortgaged. If the praetor was deceived, right was reserved to the ward to proceed accordingly (D. xxvii 9 fr 1. pr—§ 2; Cod. v 70 fr 2; 72 fr 1).

The prohibition was held to extend to any alienation of long leases (*emphyteusis*) or mines or usufructs or the grant of a usufruct, or any land *bona fide* purchased though not the ward's own. Nor without the praetor's authority could the guardian either perform a promise given by the ward to alienate lands, or repudiate land bequeathed, or mortgage land even for part of the purchase money (D. *ib.* fr 1 § 4, fr 2, fr 3 §§ 4—6, fr 5 pr—§§ 5, 8). But a sale or alienation begun by the

[1] *i.e.* agricultural land as opposed to buildings and building plots, cf. D. L 16 fr 198 and the use in servitudes.

father, or promised by him, was not within the decree, nor any alienation under judicial process (fr 3 §§ 1—3; fr 5 §§ 6, 7).

The praetor was bound to make strict inquiry, whether it was really necessary to sell the land, and whether it was not better to raise the money required on mortgage: he must consult the friends of the ward and assign counsel to plead the ward's case: he must take care that no more money was raised than was necessary, and must see to its due application. If land was held in common, the demand of the co-owner to divide must be waited for. The guardian must follow strictly the praetor's order and not sell if authorised to mortgage, or *vice versa*. The praetor could authorise sale of provincial land, if the guardianship business was managed from Rome. The praetor had no jurisdiction to authorise sale except to pay urgent debt (D. *ib.* fr 5 §§ 9—14; fr 7 § 3).

If the praetor was misled into ordering a sale, *etc.* the ward had not merely an action against the guardian but against others and, according to the better opinion, could vindicate the land. If the guardian had by mistake sold land without authority from the praetor, and paid debts of the ward's father, the ward in bringing suit would be met by a plea of fraud, and have in return for the land to repay the price, with interest to the creditor from the time of the sale (*ib.* fr 5 § 15, fr 13).

E. Actions by ward against guardian, and *vice versâ*.

There were two special actions which a ward could bring against his guardian, *judicium tutelae*, and *jud. rationibus distrahendis*. Neither could be brought till the guardianship was ended: ordinary actions such as for theft, Aquilian damage, or a condiction (*cond. furtiva*) could in strict law be brought during the guardian's administration, but were not granted by the praetor to the ward so long as the guardian continued in office (D. xxvii 2 fr 9 § 7, fr 10).

1. The former, or 'guardianship' action was general in character, comprising all the guardian's acts and omissions, and enforcing his liability for fraud, fault, and care, during the guardianship. He is bound to give full account of his administration; and, if necessary, the judge will take evidence from

the slaves and put them to the question (D. xxvii 3 fr 1 pr § 3; 4 pr). The guardianship is ended by the ward's arriving at puberty or by his or the guardian's death. If a time or condition was fixed by will for its commencement or end, and another guardian by statute or praetorian appointment fills up the time till puberty, both guardians are liable in their turn to this action. If the guardian is captured by the enemy, the action may be brought against his sureties or the defender or caretaker of the estate at once, though, if he returns, his guardianship and personal liability will revive (fr 7 § 1; 9 § 2). Any administrative acts by the guardian after the period of guardianship are dealt with by this suit, only if they are closely connected with his previous administration so as to be practically inseparable. Where the guardian was himself under power for part of the time, the action is brought against the father *de peculio*: the son was liable for acts done since he became *sui juris* in full, for previous acts only so far as his means allowed, irrespectively whether his *peculium* was taken away or not (D. xxvi 7 fr 37 §§ 1, 2; xxvii 3 fr 11). If a guardian fraudulently omitted to make an inventory, he is liable for the amount of the ward's interest, and the value is fixed by the ward's oath (D. xxvi 7 fr 7 pr). The action is *bonae fidei*, and condemnation involved infamy (Gai. iv 62, 182). It is called an *arbitrium* (Cod. v 51 rubr.; cf. D. xlvi 6 fr 12). The ward has priority over ordinary creditors for anything recoverable by this action from his guardian or guardian's heirs (D. xlii 5 fr 19 sqq.; xxvi 3 fr 22).

A counter action is granted to the guardian against the ward to enforce repayment of any expenditure he may have rightly made from his own pocket on the ward's account. He is entitled to interest at 4 per cent. or other the usual rate of the district: if he had to borrow, then he got the same rate he had to pay or forego, or from which his lending relieved his ward. It was not requisite that his expenditure should have been successful, provided the business was honestly and carefully done. He can also enforce liberation from an obligation incurred or from pledge of his own property on behalf of his ward. If he has neglected to get in a debt due to the ward and had to pay the amount himself, he is entitled to a transfer of the ward's actions. The action may be used to get a set-off to the direct action or it may be brought independently, but only when the guardianship is at an end (D. xxvii 4 fr 1 §§ 1, 8, fr 3 §§ 1, 7, fr 6; xliv 7 fr 5 § 1; xlvi 3 fr 95 § 10).

Both these actions can be brought without limitation of time by and against heirs and other successors, not only on their predecessors' account but on their own, if they have continued the administration or have neglected to do what was necessary (D. xxvii 3 fr 1, §§ 16, 17: tit. 7 fr 1). But, by a rescript of Severus and Caracalla, an action did not lie against the heirs of a guardian for negligence, unless either it was gross, or the suit had been begun against the guardian himself, or they had sought personal gain at the expense of the ward (Cod. v 54 fr 1). A speech (introducing a SC.?) of Severus made the damages for a guardian's fraud twice the amount of what he sought to defraud his ward (Paul ii 30). Actions against all the guardians or their heirs were sent before the same judge (Cod. v 51 fr 5).

2. The action *rationibus distrahendis* 'for separation of accounts[1]' came from the XII tables and applied only to those who during their administration had carried something off from the ward's estate. By their position as guardians they were justified in handling anything of their ward's, and hence the action of theft was thought unsuitable[2]. The damages for arbitration were, according to the better opinion, twice the value of the thing (not twice the ward's interest), one value being for penalty. It could not be brought after the regular *jud. tutelae* had been brought, nor could that be brought after this, except for different matters. Where there was an actual

[1] The *judicium tutelae* often mentioned by Cicero appears to correspond rather with this than with the (probably later) *actio tutelae*. In *Orat.* i 36 §§ 166, 167 he calls it *turpe tutelae judicium* and refers it to the XII tables. In *Rosc. Com.* 6 § 16 *judicium tutelae* is put with *fiduciae* and *societatis*, and the three are called *judicia summae existimationis et paene dicam capitis*, 'issues involving a man's highest reputation and indeed almost his life': the ground of the action is said to be *pupillum fraudare*. In *Caecin.* 3 § 7 similar language is used and the ground is said to be *delictum*.

[2] It may be noted that in the order of the Edict Guardianship was immediately followed by Theft.

interception of the ward's money or property with thievish intention, the action of theft would lie as well as this. If by a *condictio furtiva* the ward was recouped, this action would not lie.

The action *rat. distr.* is perpetual and can be brought by the ward's heirs, but only for something abstracted during the ward's life: being penal, it did not lie against heirs. Payment of the double value by one guardian did not apparently clear the others (D. xxvi 7 fr 55 § 1; xxvii 3 fr 1 §§ 19—24; fr 2).

F. Liability of sureties and magistrates to wards.

1. Statutable guardians and guardians appointed by the praetor or others are usually required to give sureties for the safekeeping of the ward's estate (*rem pupilli salvam fore*). Guardians appointed by will are not required to do so, testator's choice being taken as a sufficient guaranty of their honesty and carefulness. Nor is a patron, if of honourable position, usually required, especially if the estate is small: he has an interest himself in the preservation of the estate. Where a guardian was appointed by an invalid will or by a mother's will, and was confirmed by the praetor, security was not required (Gai. i 199, 200; D. xxvi 2 fr 17; tit. 3 fr 2, 3; tit. 4 fr 5 § 1; cf. Cod. v 42 fr 3). If the ward was present and old enough to speak, though not to understand the business, it was the practice to allow a stipulation made by him for this purpose to be good. If he was absent or an infant, his slave must stipulate for him, one being bought for the purpose if necessary: or else a slave of the community or some one specially appointed by the praetor has to stipulate. In the last two cases the ward is granted an analogous action on the stipulation made by deputy; in the others, having made the stipulation himself he has the regular action (D. xlvi 6 fr 2, 6). The content of the stipulation and the time to bring suit upon it is the same as in the regular guardianship action: there is a breach of the stipulation whenever that is not given or done which it is the duty of the guardian to give or do (*ib.* fr 1, 9, 11). For acts done without necessity by a guardian, after the ward has attained puberty, sureties are not liable (D. xxvi 7 fr 46 § 4). Sureties are liable

for interest at the same rates as the guardian, and can make the same counter-claims (D. xxvii 7 fr 3, 5). Whether there is one guardian or more, each surety is in strict law liable for the whole, if there is breach of duty by any guardian. Usually the amount to be paid will be divided among the solvent sureties: the ward however is not compellable to divide his claim, but may sue one and cede to him his actions against the others. Others than the ward are compellable to divide their claim against the sureties. If the guardians have divided the administration, A's sureties are not liable on a matter within B's province. No liability attaches to the surety of a guardian who has not acted at all (D. xxvi 7 fr 51; xxvii 7 fr 6, 7; xlvi 6 fr 4 § 3, fr 12).

If persons are named as sureties by the guardians in person and allow their names to be entered in the court proceedings, they are liable as if on a stipulation. And the same liability attaches when persons have declared in court that the guardians are fit persons for the office: such are called *adfirmatores* (D. xxvii 7 fr 4 § 3).

If a son under power is appointed guardian and the father refuses to be surety for him, the father should (according to a rescript of Hadrian) be appointed guardian along with him (D. xxvii 1 fr 15 § 17).

2. Where guardians were appointed by inferior magistrates and proved unable to meet the ward's claims, the magistrates were liable for the deficiency. The same was the case, when the magistrates had through favour or bribery given a false report to the praetor or governor on the solvency of persons to be by him appointed guardians: or when the magistrates had been required by the praetor or governor to get good sureties for a guardian and had not done so. Or again, if they ought to appoint a guardian and had failed to do so, they are liable for any loss to the ward which occurred before he obtained a guardian. Where the person appointed was good at the time, and sureties were duly taken, but they all afterwards proved insolvent, the magistrates were not liable if they proved that they were solvent when taken. But any private agreement among the magistrates that one of them should bear the

risk, did not remove their liability if he failed; it only postponed their liability to his. (So a rescript of Hadrian.) The magistrates were liable only for an equal share, unless they had acted fraudulently, in which case the ward could sue any one of them for the full amount. Interest (by a rescript of Severus and Antoninus) could be charged against them as against guardians. Magistrates' heirs were not liable unless, as a rescript of Ant. Pius decided, the magistrates had been guilty of gross negligence in taking clearly insufficient sureties or none at all (D. xxvii 8; Cod. v 75 fr 1—4).

This right of action was established by a senate's decree under Trajan (D. *ib.* fr 2; Cod. *ib.* fr 5). The action was called Subsidiary (D. *ib.* fr 1 pr).

G. Liability of pro-guardians and false guardians.

1. One who did the business of an *impubes*, either believing himself to be his guardian or feigning himself to be so, was liable to a similar action to that of a guardian. This action was called *pro-tutelae actio*, and could be brought before the ward attained puberty. But if the ward had passed the age of puberty or was not even born, guardianship was impossible, and there was no base for this action, but only for *negotiorum gestio*. If a slave acted as guardian, a rescript of Severus gave an analogous action against the slave's master. The person so acting was liable for omissions, if they were such as another would not have made, and liable even if he gave up acting as soon as he found he was not guardian, unless he informed the ward's friends so that they might apply for a guardian to be appointed. One who acted as guardian and was really guardian, but did not know it, was liable *pro-tutelae*, not *tutelae*, because he had not the *animus* of a guardian.

The *pro-guardian* was liable for want of good faith and care in the same way as a guardian, and for like interest of money. He could bring a counter action (D. xxvii 5).

2. When a person not really guardian (*falsus tutor*) professed to give authority to the act of a girl or a boy under the age of puberty, the other party to the business, if ignorant of his not being guardian, could by a special part of the praetor's

edict apply for a cancel of the proceeding. If this other party was also a ward, it is the ignorance of his guardian that is material. If the pretended guardian acted fraudulently in taking this position, he was liable to a suit *in factum* for damages to cover the whole interest of the aggrieved party, including his expenses in applying for the cancel. The action lies for heirs, but not against heirs: and is noxal if the pretended guardian was under power. If there were more than one pretended guardian, they are liable until the plaintiff has been fully satisfied (D. xxvii 6 fr 1, 6—9). A like action lay against one who gave pretended authority to the act of a woman, if she was not independent (*ib.* fr 11 § 2).

H. Excuses from guardianship.

The post of guardian (or caretaker) was regarded as part of a citizen's duty, and could not be declined except on recognised grounds. Anyone without authorisation declining to act does so at his own risk (*suo periculo cessat*); and forfeits anything left him by the will. The regulation of this matter is largely due to M. Aurelius and Severus (cf. Vat. 125, 147, 155, 158, *etc.*; D. xxvii 1 fr 1 § 4, *etc.*).

No freedman (unless freed under a trust) was excused from guardianship to his patron's children or to such descendants as might possibly become patrons. The same applies to the children, but not to further descendants of a patroness (Vat. 152, 224, 225). No excuse was allowed to persons who had promised the ward's father to take the office or had actually meddled with his affairs (Vat. 153, 154).

Recognised excuses were

1. Natural children whether lawful (*justi*) or not, and whether emancipated or given in adoption or not, provided they are either alive or have died in war[1] in their country's service. For excuse from a guardianship at Rome three (at the time of appointment) were required, in the towns of Italy four, in the provinces five. This privilege was allowed to Junian Latins as well as to Roman citizens. A child *en ventre*

[1] In the Digest (xxvii 1 fr 18) this is limited to death in battle, and apparently Ulpian's text is altered.

sa mère did not count. If a son was dead leaving children, whether one or more, they count in the father's place. But grandchildren by a daughter do not count, unless (by a constitution of M. Aurelius A.D. 168) the father was a veteran soldier (Vat. 169, 191—199; D. xxvii 1 fr 2 §§ 3—8). The *jus liberorum* granted by the emperor does not avail for this (Vat. 170).

2. Three burdens of the kind (whether as guardian or caretaker) held at the time of appointment, either by himself or any one in the same legal family, and involving one man's responsibility. Guardianship to more than one brother or sister counts only as one, if the estate is undivided. Any guardianship, taken when it could have been declined, does not count in the three (Vat. 125—128, 186—190). If the new appointment or one of the three already held is within six months of expiration, it does not count (D. fr 17 pr). Two burdens and two children do not form sufficient excuse under either of these heads (D. fr 15 § 11; Cod. v 69; cf. Vat. 245).

3. Magistracy at Rome. Moreover a senator was excused from any guardianship of *impuberes* more than 200 miles from Rome (knights were appointed instead); and from guardianship of persons of rank inferior to senators. A senator's freedman (but not more than one) managing his affairs was excused from all guardianship (Vat. 131—133, 146, 147; D. fr 15 § 2).

4. Military service while it lasts. Veterans and *primipilares* who have served their full time or at least 20 years and had honourable discharge are freed entirely from guardianship, except to children (not grandchildren) of soldiers in the same regiment or of veterans, from which guardianship they are freed only for one year from their discharge (Vat. 140, 141, 145; D. fr 8 pr), but they are not required to hold more than one at a time (Cod. v 65 fr 2).

Those who have served five years but less than twenty have a proportionate freedom from guardianship (D. fr 8 § 3).

5. Profession as philosophers, grammarians, rhetoricians or doctors. This by an epistle of Ant. Pius excused from guardianship as from all military service and public office. This immunity was limited to ten doctors, five grammarians, five rhetoricians in the largest cities, *i.e.* the capitals: to seven

doctors, four of each of the others, in the cities which had law sessions; five doctors, three of each of the others, in smaller cities. No limit was put to philosophers, as they were rare. In order to have this immunity, the local council must vote a professor into the prescribed number, and he must (unless of extraordinary knowledge) exercise his profession in his own country or in Rome, which may be regarded as the common country of all. Teachers of law were not excused except in Rome, and students of law there were also excused. Land-surveyors (*geometrae*) were not excused (Vat. 149, 150, 204; D. fr 6 §§ 1—11; fr 22).

6. Madness, deafness, dumbness, blindness (Vat. 238; Cod. v 68). Age under 25 years unless experienced in affairs, or over 70 years complete at time of appointment (Just. i 25 § 13, cf. Vat. 223: D. fr 2 § 1). Ill health such as to incapacitate him for managing his own affairs: but the praetor's inspection is required. Rheumatism, epilepsy, *etc.* are also good excuses. Such excuses may be good for resigning a guardianship already held as well as for refusing a new appointment. Or they may justify only temporary relief, a caretaker being appointed meanwhile (Vat. 129, 130, cf. 183 *a*; D. fr 10 § 8—fr 12 pr).

7. Poverty, and sometimes low station and rusticity; but ignorance of letters is no excuse, if the person has experience in business (Vat. 185, 240, 243; D. fr 6 § 19).

8. Non-possession of a domicile in Rome if the guardianship lies in a province, or non-possession of a domicile in the particular province (Vat. 203; cf. 173; D. fr 19, 46 § 2; Cod. v 62 fr 11 pr).

9. Capital quarrel with the ward's father, or the father's having contested his status as a freeman. Mere non-acquaintance with the father is no excuse (Paul ii 27 § 1; Just. i 25 §§ 9—12; D. fr 15 § 14).

10. Any one having to be absent from Rome on public business was relieved from his guardianship during his absence, and was not obliged to accept any new guardianship for a year from his return by direct route (D. fr 10 §§ 2, 3).

11. Members of the Guild of Bakers at Rome to the number of one hundred, actually exercising their craft, were

exempted from guardianship even of the children of their fellows. This was by Hadrian's rescript as interpreted by Severus and Caracalla. So also men carrying on business *in foro suario*, if they help the corn supply with two-thirds of their estate. The Guilds of Smiths have similar immunity unless their funds should increase so as to make them compellable to undertake other public tasks (Vat. 233—237; D. fr 17 § 2).

12. The people of Ilium on account of the dignity of the city and its being the origin of Rome were given by senate's decrees and imperial constitutions the fullest immunities: and thus were exempt from guardianship of all except their own citizens (D. fr 17 § 1).

There are some other special exceptions of particular offices.

By a constitution of M. Aurelius any one living in Rome or within 100 miles who thinks he has an excuse must within 50 days give notice to the person seeking him as guardian, and come to the praetor if there are sittings either on the tribunal or the level (= in court or chambers) and state the excuse: if there are no sittings, he must make a duly-witnessed petition. Meanwhile he must not meddle with the ward's business. The rule about time and distance was applied to other places where appointments were made. Any one residing more than 100 miles off has 30 days, and one more day for every 20 miles, not being less in all than 50 days. The time may be extended in case of illness or perils on the journey. This time is only for appearance before the appointing magistrate: four months are allowed for the whole matter. If the appointment was invalid, no obligation attaches in any way (Vat. 155, 156; D. xxvii 1 fr 13, 37). Appeal from an appointment as guardian was not allowed until an excuse had been rejected (D. *ib.* fr 13 pr; xlix 4 fr 1 § 1).

One who had no sufficient excuse might yet within this period name, *i.e.* propose to the praetor, another person as better qualified (*potior*) than himself. Severus excluded from this privilege all persons who were colleagues of the father or the ward in the same *decuria* or corporation (*corpus*), and all within the same degrees of kinship or affinity as are within the exceptions of Julian and Papian law (Book III chap. x); and prescribed that others might name only persons within these classes. The person proposed must be more nearly connected and be substantial and honourable. Neighbourhood was no ground of greater qualification (Vat. 158). Any one so nominating must attend all the sittings of the court until the appointment or otherwise of the person nominated or until he has got a letter to the magistrates ordering him to appear. Within ten days after he has delivered this letter to the magistrates he must apply for an answer and bring it to the praetor. Two days and one for every twenty miles are allowed for taking it to the local magistrate, and the like for bringing the reply. After the reply is brought, his attendance at the sittings is required. A special form is prescribed for making the nomination, and the petitioner has to give five copies if the application be in court, four copies if it be in chambers (*de plano* Vat. 157, 161—167; 206—219).

This privilege of nominating is open to freedmen as well as that of excusing themselves (except to guardianship of patron's children, as above-named Vat. 160).

Freeborn persons were excused from being guardians to freedmen, by an oration of M. Aurelius (D. fr 1 § 4; Cod. v 62 fr 3). A Junian Latin had the same right of excuse as Roman citizens (Vat. 193).

J. Removal of guardians.

Any guardian however appointed could be removed from office by the praetor or provincial governor or a proconsular legate or one to whom the praetor has delegated his jurisdiction. Any one could apply for the removal of a guardian (*suspectum postulare*[1]), or, as it was then called, make him suspect (*suspectum facere*). Not however *impuberes* themselves, except on the advice of their friends. Women nearly connected, *e.g.* mother, grandmother, nurse, or (by a rescript of Severus) sister, or even others, could apply. The ground of such an impeachment was fraud, or wild or corrupt or injurious action during the guardianship; if the guardian kept out of the way so that the ward

[1] The phrases *suspecti accusatio*, *suspecti crimen* or *cognitio* are also found (where *suspecti* is masculine).

did not get proper supplies, or if inconsiderately he kept the ward from accepting his father's inheritance, or shewed hostility to the ward or his parent, or for any other just cause, he might be removed, and the removal brought infamy (*famosus erit*). For want of supplies the ward was sent into possession by rescript of Severus and Caracalla. Mere ignorance, laziness, rusticity or stupidity, was also reason for removal, but without any slur on the man's character. Poverty was no reason in itself. The praetor ought to signify in his decree the cause of removal, and if no cause was given, the guardian's reputation was not affected (D. xxvi 10 fr 1, 3 §§ 5, 12, 14, 17, 18; fr 4 §§ 1, 2; Just. i 26 §§ 4, 9, *etc.*).

Any cause of this kind arising in connexion with the ward or his estate before the guardianship commenced was not basis for the charge. But one who had written in the will himself as guardian to the testator's child is suspect on that account. And if the guardianship was over, the matter could be dealt with in the ordinary guardianship action and was no basis for removing him from being caretaker, or from a second guardianship of the same ward. Nor could a guardian who had taken no share in the administration be removed as suspect (D. *ib.* fr 3 §§ 5—7; fr 4 § 4; Paul iii 6 § 15). A guardian, whether during his guardianship or since, can impeach a fellow-guardian if continuing (fr 3 pr). If process has not been finished before the guardianship ends, it drops (fr 11). Offer by a guardian to give security does not justify his continuing in office, if his removal be otherwise desirable (fr 5, 6).

If the guardian was related to the ward by kinship or affinity, or was patron of the ward's father, it was held better not to remove him from the guardianship but to add a caretaker (fr 9). Freedmen will be acting rightly in applying for removal of guardians mismanaging their patrons' or patrons' children's estates, but are not allowed to apply for removal of their patron himself from a guardianship (fr 3 § 1).

This impeachment of guardians is based on the XII tables (fr 1 § 2).

CHAPTER XI.

CARETAKERS (*CURATORES*).

1. The XII tables placed under the care of their agnates madmen (*furiosi*)[1] and such spendthrifts (*prodigi*)[2] as had been formally prohibited from dealing with their estates. Such formal prohibition was made by the praetor *extra ordinem* (see Book VI chap. XV). Agnates however were ousted when such persons were made heirs by a will, and freedmen have no agnates[3]: so that, while in the case of freeborn children being disinherited or of their father's dying intestate, agnates were entitled to act as caretakers, in other cases the praetor (or in the provinces the governor) appointed such caretakers as were required. And further, if the agnate entitled was not a suitable person, the praetor appointed a caretaker to supersede him in the practical management of the estate (Ulp. xii 1—3; D. xxvii 10 fr 1 pr 13). If there were more agnates than one entitled, the praetor usually decreed that one only should act (D. xxvi 7 fr 3 pr; cf. xxvii 10 fr 7 § 3). Persons under the age of puberty had guardians, and therefore required no caretakers; and if a minor was insane, and had a general caretaker on that account, no other was required (D. xxvi 1 fr 3 pr § 1).

Furiosus nullum negotium gerere potest, quia non intellegit quid agat (Gai. iii 106). Hence the caretaker of a madman or

1 Cicero refers to this: *Lex: Si furiosus escit, adgnatum gentiliumque in eo pecuniaque ejus potestas esto* (*Inv.* ii 50 § 148. So also *ad Heren.* ii 13 § 23). He distinguishes *furere* from *insanire*, the latter being apparently excitement and want of judgment, while *furor* is mental alienation (*Tusc. D.* iii 4, 5), cf. *mente est captus atque ad agnatos et gentiles est deducendus* (Varr. *R. R.* i 2 § 8); *Interdicto huic omne adimat jus Praetor et ad sanos abeat tutela propinquos* (Hor. *Sat.* ii 3. 217), where *interdicto* and *tutela* are used improperly.

2 This treatment of spendthrifts is sometimes said to have arisen from custom (*moribus* Paul iii 4). An instance of the praetor's interference in this way is given in Val. Max. iii 5 § 2. Cf. Cic. *Sen.* 7 § 22.

3 Hence Horace (only son of a freedman) says *insanire putas sollemnia me neque rides nec medici credis nec curatoris egere a praetore dati* (*Ep.* i 1 101; cf. Pernice *Lab.* i p. 235).

spendthrift represented him in suits, could make a valid pledge of his ward's property, and could alienate any of it, except country lands (see above, chap. x D), if his ward was thereby advantaged. He could tender oaths for him, and suit by him put the matter in issue and gave rise to the plea of matter decided. He could authorise the madman's slave or son freely to manage their *peculium*. All alienations were made in the name of the ward. The caretaker could not manumit a slave or give away or dedicate anything (D. xxvii 10 fr 7 § 1, fr 10—12, 17; xii 2 fr 17 § 2; xv 1 fr 24; xl 1 fr 13; cf. Gai. iv 99, 101). He conducted his ward's business, and was subject to and protected by an action *negotiorum gestorum* (D. iii 5 fr 5 § 5). Caretakers appointed by the consul, praetor, or provincial governor, were usually not required to give security for the safe-keeping of the ward's estate; others were (Gai. i 199, 200). A caretaker could enforce his claims against his ward by a counter-action (D. xxvii 4 fr 1 § 2). Whether, on sanity being temporarily recovered, a caretaker's office was thereby ended, was a matter much disputed (Cod. v 70 fr 6 pr). A son might be appointed a caretaker to his father, though this was doubted before Ant. Pius (D xxv 5 fr 12; xxvii 10 fr 1 § 1).

2. Deaf and dumb had caretakers, probably for the purpose of stipulations and suits (D. xxvi 5 fr 8 § 3; cf. Just. i 23 § 4); and so others who were physically disabled (D. xxvii 10 fr 2; cf. xlii 5 fr 19 § 1 sqq.).

3. There were some cases in which one under the age of puberty, who had a guardian, required another adviser, viz. (*a*) when he desired to sue his guardian or his guardian to sue him (*curator in litem datus*). In such a case the ward must be present and apply for the appointment (an infant is therefore unable to have one): if the suit is against the ward, the praetor will compel him to apply (D. xxvi 1 fr 3 § 2, fr 4; xxvii 3 fr 9 § 4; Cod. v 44). (*b*) Another case is when a ward's guardian is absent in the service of the State (D. xxvi 5 fr 15); and (*c*) when a ward's estate is so widely distributed or has received so large an addition that the guardian requires assistance (D. xxvi 7 fr 3 § 4; fr 9 § 9).

Similar is the case of a woman who requires assistance in

taking accounts from her pupillar guardian (Cod. v 3 fr 7); or is about to marry or even has married and requires advice in constituting or increasing or changing her dowry (D. xxvi 5 fr 7). Whether in the latter case the caretaker is additional to the guardian sometimes nominated for this purpose (Gai. i 178), the caretaker giving advice, and the guardian giving only formal authority (cf. Vat. 110), or 'the caretaker's consent' has been substituted by Justinian for 'the guardian's authority' in the original texts, is not clear (D. xxiii 3 fr 60: *auctoritas* in fr 61 pr could hardly be used of a caretaker, cf. D. i 7 fr 8)[1].

4. A more frequent use of caretakers was to advise and control youths (*adulescentes, adulti*), often called minors[2] (*i.e. minores xxv annis*), after puberty when guardianship ceased, until the age of 25 years, when they were regarded as no longer needing such assistance in managing their own affairs. But the history of this institute is imperfectly known to us. According to the old Roman law every male above the age of puberty, and not mad or spendthrift as above named, was fully capable of all legal acts and responsible for his doings. Neither custom nor statute invalidated business done by him in due form without advice or contrary to advice, or established any distinction in private affairs between a boy and a fully grown man. The first interference of which we know was a *lex Plaetoria*[3] (probably passed about 200 B.C.) which appears to

[1] Cf. Bechmann *Dotalrecht* ii p. 20 sq.; Czyhlarz *Dot.* p. 166 sqq.; Pernice *Labeo* i p. 230.

[2] *Pupillus* was not properly applied to one above the age of puberty. Cf. Cic. *Caecin.* 19 § 54 *Testamento si recitatus heres esset 'pupillus' Cornelius, isque jam annos xx haberet vobis interpretibus* (*i.e.* on a strict literal interpretation) *omitteret hereditatem.* Pompon. D. L 16 fr 239 pr *Pupillus est qui, cum impubes est, desiit in patris potestate esse aut morte aut emancipatione.* But it is sometimes used improperly in the lawyers, *e.g.* D. xxiii 2 fr 20 (a rescript of Severus and Caracalla).

[3] This law (called *Laetoria*, except in the *lex Jul. municipalis* 112) is no doubt that meant by Plaut. *Pseudol.* 303 *Perii: annorum lex me perdit quinavicenaria: metuont credere omnes* (the date of this play was 191 B.C.), cf. *Rud.* 1382. It is twice spoken of by Cicero, *Nat. D.* iii 30 § 74 *Inde judicium publicum rei privatae lege Laetoria; Off.* iii 15 § 61 *iste dolus malus erat vindicatus ut (in) tutela duodecim tabulis, circumscriptio adulescentium lege Laetoria.* Priscian (viii 21 quoting Suetonius as using

have enacted some penalty against any one who 'got round' (*circumscripsit*) youths under the age of 25 years. A condemnation under this law or on the ground of acting contrary to it made a man infamous[1]. And the praetor granted a special plea, if a suit was brought on a transaction with a minor within its scope[2]. The next step was the promise in the praetor's edict of subjecting any business transaction with one under the age of 25 to revision: and, if he found sufficient cause, he annulled the transaction (see Book V chap. viii A). The effect of these measures singly and together was to deter persons from doing business with a minor on account of the risk and uncertainty incident thereto, and thus in effect to disqualify minors and injure their material interests. To meet this difficulty the analogy of madmen and spendthrifts was followed, and for particular emergencies caretakers were appointed. According to a statement of Capitolinus[3] (not however a very satisfactory authority) M. Aurelius directed or sanctioned the appointment of caretakers for all minors, without any special

stipulari passively) says: *Laetoria quae vetat minorem annis viginti quinque stipulari* (see also xviii 149), where if *stipulari* is not used actively, it can at most be taken generally 'to enter into a stipulation.' On this law see Savigny *Verm. Schr.* ii p. 321 sq.; Huschke *ZRG.* xiii 311 sqq. The law appears to be mentioned (*Laetoriae*) in a recently found fragment, Krüger *Jus Antiq.* ii p. 300; and in a papyrus fragment *ZRG.* xxxv 170.

1 In an enumeration, given by the *lex Julia municipalis*, of the disqualifications for being a decurion in boroughs, which largely coincides with the disqualifications for suing contained in the edict (see Book VI chap. ii B), we find § 112 *queive lege Plaetoria ob eamve rem quod adversus eam legem fecit fecerit condemnatus est erit.*

2 D. xliv 1 fr 7 § 1 *exceptio competit fidejussori si...pro minore viginti quinque annis circumscripto.* Compare also xix 1 fr 13 § 28 *Et si quis minorem viginti quinque annis circumvenerit, huic hactenus dabimus actionem ex empto.*

3 Hist. Aug. *M. Aurel.* 10 *De curatoribus vero cum ante non nisi ex lege Laetoria vel propter lasciviam vel propter dementiam darentur, ita statuit ut omnes adulti curatores acciperent non redditis causis.* This is generally interpreted to mean that before this Emperor there were caretakers appointed under the *lex Laetoria*, as well as those for prodigals and madmen. I am inclined to suspect the writer made a blunder in his legal history and took the appointment of these to be due to the *lex Laetoria* instead of the XII tables (using *vel...vel* for *either...or*, not *or...or*).

ground being required. Other authorities also speak of the appointment of caretakers for minors as a matter of course (Ulp. xii 4; Epit. Gai. i 8; cf. Gai. 197, 198; D. iv 4 fr 1 § 3). Women as well as men had caretakers (Just. i 23 pr; cf. D. xxiii 2 fr 20; Cod. v 39 fr 1, *etc.*).

M. Aurelius' decree was not however equivalent in law to prolonging the incapacity of a child beyond puberty to the age of 25 years. A youth who was *pubes* still remained capable of dealing with his property, of obliging and being obliged (D. xlv 1 fr 101)[1], and even the appointment of a caretaker was made by the praetor (or provincial governor) on the youth's own application or with his knowledge and consent on the application of his late guardian or of his friends; and thus even in later times some minors had no guardians (D. xxvi 6 fr 2 §§ 4, 5; iv 4 fr 7 § 2). The caretaker had no formal authority to give as a guardian had; it was his experience and judgment that were required, so that the praetor might be willing to give effect to the minor's acts and to refuse him reinstatement when he had acted under proper and honest advice. Persons dealing with the minor would naturally require the consent of the caretaker, and in this way the position of a caretaker in managing the youth's business became very similar to that of a guardian in managing that of a child. But his actual presence was not necessary. He was, like a guardian, liable for fraud, fault and care (*diligentia*), and could enforce claims by a counter-action. But he was subject only to the ordinary action *negotiorum gestorum*, which might be brought either during or at the close of the caretaking (D. xxvi 7 fr 33 pr; xxvii 4 fr 1 § 2). He was responsible (by a rescript of M. Aurelius and Commodus) for all business of the minor after the cessation of guardianship, even though begun before, but did not bear the

[1] It is not likely that the *lex Plaetoria* contained any such specific disqualification as is stated in the passage of Suetonius quoted above (pp. 123, 124). The effect of the law is probably what the writer meant. In the constitution of Diocletian (Cod. ii 21 fr 3) which is often quoted as contrary to D. xlv 1 fr 101, I understand *contractum servari non oportet* to mean not that the contract is a nullity but that it ought not to be enforced. The matter is much discussed, see *e.g.* Puchta *Inst.* § 202 n. aa; Ihering *Ges. Aufs.* ii p. 383 sq., *etc.*

risk of such previous investments as he rightly deemed not good and had not accepted (D. xxvi 7 fr 33 § 1, fr 35, 44 pr). If there were more caretakers than one, one only was sufficient for any particular piece of business, and though not obliged to give account to his fellow-caretaker, he was liable to removal if he did not make him aware of his proceedings and did not act in good faith (D. xxvi 7 fr 3 pr, fr 19). He could be removed on the like grounds as a guardian, and had the like excuses for serving, but being always appointed by the praetor (or governor), and therefore presumably fit, was not usually required to give security for his faithful administration (D. xxvi 10 fr 3 § 2; xxvii 1 *passim*; Gai. i 200). If a father named in his will a caretaker, he was usually appointed by the praetor without inquiry; if the mother named one, inquiry was made into his fitness (D. xxvi 3 fr 2 § 1; cf. fr 6; Just. i 23 § 1). By rescript of Severus and Caracalla a guardian could not be compelled to act as caretaker to the ward, when he became *pubes*, unless he was freedman to the ward's father; but any guardian so acting was liable only to an action *negotiorum gestorum* (D. xxvii fr 3 fr 13; Vat. 200; Cod. v 62 fr 5). A caretaker's heirs and the appointing magistrates are liable as in the case of guardians (D. xxvi 7 fr 46 § 1; xxvii 8 fr 1 § 5).

Actions were brought by or against the minor with the consent of his caretaker, or by or against the caretaker himself. Where a caretaker has lent the ward's money or bought land with it in his own name, the ward was granted an analogous action to recover the loan or vindicate the land (D. xxvi 7 fr 1 §§ 3, 4; tit. 9 fr 2).

The plea given by the *lex Plaetoria* remained in force: whether the penal action did is doubtful.

5. Caretakers were often appointed for dealing with property which had not at the time a capable owner, *e.g.* when a person has been taken captive by the enemy (D. iv 6 fr 15 pr); or an insolvent has surrendered his estate to his creditors (D. xlii 7 fr 5); or a creditor is in possession of a debtor's estate and a right of action is in danger of being lost (*ib.* 5 fr 14); or the estate of a deceased senator or other distinguished person requires liquidation (D. xxvii 10 fr 5); or the heirs are

deliberating whether to accept an inheritance (*ib.* fr 3); or when it is claimed by a widow for her unborn child (*ventris nomine, ib.* fr 8).

CHAPTER XII.

HUSBAND AND WIFE.

A. Conditions of lawful Marriage.

As has been already mentioned, lawful marriage (*justae nuptiae*), with the consequences to the children of full citizenship and submission to the control of the head of the family, might take place with different consequences to the wife. In the old strict form she passed completely with all her property into the hand of her husband, and occupied in his family the position of a daughter. She ceased altogether to belong to her father's family and connexions. This was the result of *conventio in manum* whether produced by confarreation or copurchase or unbroken use. Beside this, from early times there grew up another form of marriage in which the wife was not separated from her birth-family, and in the matter of property remained as she was, except so far as either by herself or her relatives or friends a dowry was conveyed or secured to the husband as her contribution to the expenses of the household. Legally she remained outside her husband's family, being either *sui juris* or under her father's (or other ascendant's) control. She was *uxor*, but still either *filia familias* or (according to post-Ciceronian usage) *materfamilias*, according as she was dependent or independent of her father. But marriage in either form was a union of man and woman for the purpose of having children as members of a family in the Roman Commonwealth[1]. They must therefore be duly qualified persons, of sufficient age, acting

[1] The 'purpose of acquirement of children' was part of the formula for a marriage. So Plaut. *Capt.* 889 *Liberorum quaerundorum causa ei, credo, uxor datast.* Enn. *Cresph.* 350 ed. Müller *ducit me uxorem liberorum sibi quaesendum gratia*; D. L 16 fr 220 § 3; Val. Max. vii 7 § 4 (containing a decision of Augustus) *quia non creandorum liberorum causa conjugium*

with the consent of themselves and their legal superiors. That is, there must be *conubium, pubertas, consensus.*

1. *Conubium* or the right of intermarriage is necessary to give the children the rights of Roman citizens, and to bring the relations of the parties as regards property under the Roman law. Both parties must be Roman citizens or citizens of some community which the Romans recognize for this purpose (Ulp. v 4). See Book I. No man could have two wives at the same time, nor any woman have two husbands (Gai. i 63).

Further the parties must not be closely akin. Marriage of parents or grandparents with their children or grandchildren is forbidden as wicked (*nefariae*). Nor is it allowed between near collaterals, *e.g.* brother with sister of the whole or half-blood; but the marriage of brothers' children with brothers' or sisters' children, *i.e.* first cousins, was allowed, though at one time forbidden[1]. The marriage of uncle or aunt with niece or nephew or more distant collaterals of this class, *e.g.* great niece, *etc.*, is likewise forbidden (uncles and aunts being deemed to be

intercesserat. So also in the *lex Junia* ap. Ulp. iii 3; Varro ap. Macrob. *Sat.* i 16 § 18; and the censor's formula given below; cf. Savigny, *Verm. Schr.* i p. 84. Hence *quaerere, quaesitus* of getting a child, *e.g.* D. xxxvii 4 fr 3 § 8; xxxviii 17 fr 1 § 2 *liberi vulgo quaesiti, etc.*

The definition of marriage given by Modestin (D. xxiii 2 fr 1) 'the union of man and woman as partners in their whole life and sharers in divine and human rights' is by some thought to be an echo of Greek philosophy. But Aristotle (*ap.* Stob. *Ecl.* ii 7 p. 322) gives a very good definition πολιτεία πρώτη σύνοδος ἀνδρὸς καὶ γυναικὸς κατὰ νόμον ἐπὶ τέκνων γενέσει καὶ βίου κοινωνίᾳ; cf. Voigt *Jus Nat.* ii p. 850. The definition in Just. i 9 § 1 is incomplete: *viri et mulieris conjunctio, individuam consuetudinem vitae continens.*

[1] The senator Vitellius in advocating the marriage of Claudius with Agrippina says, '*Conjugia sobrinarum* (second cousins) *diu ignorata tempore addito percrebuisse*' (Tac. *An.* xii 6). And this is confirmed by a recently discovered fragment of Livy's Book xx (*Hermes* iv 372) *i.e.* before the second Punic War; *P. Celius* (Cloelius?) *patricius primus adversus veterem morem intra septimum cognationis gradum duxit uxorem* (he married his *sobrina, i.e.* sixth degree). Ulpian v 6 speaks of a time when first cousins (*consobrini*) were not allowed to marry: *inter cognatos ex transverso gradu olim quidem usque ad quartum gradum matrimonia contrahi non poterant.* The first recorded instance of marriage of first cousins appears to be in 171 B.C. (Liv. xlii 34 § 3). It is spoken of as quite honourable in Cic. *Clu.* 5 § 12.

in parentis loco D. xxiii 2 fr 39 pr; Just. i 10 § 5). The Emperor Claudius however married his brother's daughter (Agrippina), and therefore an exception was made in favour of such a marriage, but not extended to sister's daughter (but cf. fr 57 *a*). Nor is marriage allowed with one who is or has been mother-in-law[1], or daughter-in-law, or step-mother, or step-daughter, or step-son's wife, or more distant degrees of the like affinity: and the corresponding affinities bar a woman's marriage (*e.g.* with father-in-law, *etc.*)[2]. A step-son of one parent is not forbidden to marry a step-daughter of the other, although they may have a common brother by their step-parents' marriage. As regards relatives by adoption, marriage of parents with children or grandchildren is forbidden even after the adoption is dissolved; a brother and sister cannot be married so long as they are in the same family, but an adoptive sister's daughter or adoptive father's sister by a different father are not of kin, as adoption creates kinship only in the lines of agnation. If it is desired to adopt a son-in-law or daughter-in-law, the daughter in the first case, the son in the second, should first be emancipated (Gai. i 59—63; Ulp. v 5, 6; D. xxiii 2 fr 12 § 4, 14 § 4, 17, 34 § 2, 53—56). Near kinship by blood or affinity, though arisen in slavery, is a bar to the marriage of freed persons (D. *ib.* fr 8, 14 §§ 2, 3).

Marriages forbidden by public morals (*moribus, jure gentium*) were deemed incestuous. Such are the marriages of parents with children, or even with step-daughters or step-mothers or daughters-in-law, and marriages of brothers with sisters. In these cases both parties, in other cases usually only the man, could be prosecuted criminally (*Collat.* vi 13; D. xxiii 2 fr 39 pr —§ 5; xlviii 5 fr 39 § 2). The marriage was null and the children were regarded as having no father and being *vulgo concepti* or *spurii* (Gai. i 64; Ulp. v 7). To use the words in Justinian's Institutes, *si adversus ea quae diximus aliqui coierint nec vir nec uxor nec nuptiae nec matrimonium nec dos*

1 In Cic. *pro Cluentio* 5 § 14 we have an instance of this in the marriage of Sassia: *Nubit genero socrus nullis auspicibus, nullis auctoribus, funestis ominibus omnium.*

2 Marriage with a wife's sister or brother's wife was held lawful until Constantine's law of A.D. 355 (Cod. Theod. iii 12).

intellegitur (Just. i 10 § 12; cf. D. xii 7 fr 5). Where the marriage was between collaterals or *affines* and celebrated openly, the possibility of mistake was allowed for and the punishment less severe (D. xxiii 2 fr 68).

Other bars to marriage were created by statute. The *lex Julia* or *Papia* forbad the betrothal or marriage knowingly of a senator or senator's children or descendants (through males) with freed persons[1] or with any whose father (natural or adoptive) or mother had been stage-players, or with any prostitute. All freeborn men were forbidden to marry either bawds or any women manumitted by a pandar or bawd, or one caught in adultery, or condemned in a public *i.e.* criminal trial (not being a trial merely for *calumnia* or prevarication), or one condemned by the senate, or a stage-player. Such marriages were null (Ulp. xiii; D. xxiii 2 fr 42 § 1, 44; Cod. v 4 fr 28 pr). A speech of M. Aurelius, followed by a senate's decree, nullified the marriage of a senator's daughter to a freedman. The connexion of this with the previous enactment is obscure (D. fr 16). Severus and Antoninus allowed criminal prosecution of any freedman who dared to marry his patroness, or the daughter or wife or granddaughter or great-granddaughter of his patron (Cod. v 4 fr 3; Paul ii 19 § 9). But exception was made for a senator's daughter or a patroness of disreputable life (D. fr 3, 47).

A senate's decree under M. Aurelius and Commodus prohibited any guardian from marrying his ward (unless betrothed or definitely intended for him by her father), lest he should thereby evade or restrict his liability to account for the management of her property. On this ground a guardian's heir as well as his son and grandson were debarred from the marriage, and, if the guardian was under power, the father was debarred also. The prohibition applied to caretakers also, and lasted until the ward was 26 years old. Sons given in adoption, and adopted sons, unless emancipated, are within the prohibition. Such

[1] A more general prohibition appears to have been in force in earlier times, as has been inferred from the special concession to the freedwoman *meretrix* who revealed the Bacchanalian mysteries: *uti ei ingenuo nubere liceret neu quid ei qui eum duxisset ob id fraudi ignominiaeve esset* (*SC.* ap. Liv. xxxix 19).

marriages are null: a guardian or caretaker contracting them is *infamis*, and liable to accusation for adultery. A guardian is not prohibited from giving his daughter in marriage to his ward, nor, if the ward has grown up and died leaving a daughter before the account was rendered, was the guardian or caretaker debarred from giving this daughter in marriage to his own son (D. fr 36, 59, 60, 64 §§ 1, 2, 66, 67; xlviii 5 fr 7; Cod. v 62 fr 4; cf. Vat. 102, 201).

An official, civil or military, in a province (not being his own country) was forbidden by the imperial *mandata* to marry any woman there born or domiciled[1], or to consent to his son's so marrying. But he is not prevented from marrying one long betrothed to him, or from betrothal, the woman however having the right of declining the marriage after the period of office has expired, on simply giving back the earnest money received. Nor is he prevented from giving his daughters in marriage to persons in his province. If an official married contrary to the *mandata* and the marriage continued after leaving office, it was held to have become lawful, and the children subsequently born were legitimate (D. fr 38, 57, 65). The marriage of soldiers during service appears to have been prohibited in Trajan's time (Epist. Traj., ap. Bruns, p. 381).

Mad persons could not contract marriage, but madness supervening did not dissolve a marriage (Paul ii 19 § 7). Their children were allowed to marry, though some doubts were entertained in the case of sons, because a constitution of M. Aurelius, allowing it to sons of persons out of their mind (*mente capti, dementes*), did not name madmen (*furiosi*) (Cod. v 4 fr 25 pr—§ 2).

2. The minimum age required was that of puberty, *i.e.* fourteen or thereabouts in men, twelve in women. If a woman is married before that age the marriage does not become legitimate until then (Gai. i 196; Ulp. v 10; D. xxiii 2 fr 4). Marriage with a *spado* was not invalid, with one castrated was (D. xxiii 3 fr 39 § 1; cf. xxviii 2 fr 6).

3. The consent of both parties is required if they are *sui juris*. If they are not, the consent of their father, or other

1 This prohibition did not extend to concubines (D. xxvi 7 fr 5).

family-superior, is also requisite, and if the grandfather is head of the family, the father's consent is also requisite to the marriage of his son. If the father or grandfather is mad, the consent of the other is sufficient. Parental consent may be given after the marriage. If the father is taken by the enemy, or his whereabouts not known, after three years the marriage can take place, and even before that time if the match is one which he would be sure to approve (Ulp. v 2; Vat. 102; xxiii 2 fr 9—11, xlix 15 fr 12 § 3). The *lex Julia* directed provincial governors to compel those who had children in their power to consent to their marriage and give dowries, if they unreasonably abstained from consenting (D. xxiii 2 fr 19). Even a soldier requires his father's consent (D. xxiii 2 fr 35).

The distinctive mark of marriage was the wife's being led into the house of her husband. There she was received with an offer of water and fire[1]. This could be done in the absence of the husband, and required only a message or letter from him. The marriage however rested on consent, not on marital intercourse. *Nuptias non concubitus sed consensus facit* (D. xxiii 2 fr 5; xxiv 1 fr 66; xxxv 1 fr 15). Declarations by witnesses were sometimes made to facilitate proof, but were not essential (D. xx 1 fr 4).

Betrothal.

It was not unusual for betrothal (*sponsalia*)[2] to take place

[1] Cf. Fest. p. 2 *Aqua et igni tam interdici solet damnatis quam accipiuntur nuptae, videlicet quia hae duae res humanam vitam maxime continent.*

[2] In Plautus cases of betrothal are common, *e.g.* *Aul.* 255 *Quid nunc? etiam mi despondes filiam.* E. *Illis legibus cum illa dote quam tibi dixi.* M. *Sponden' ergo?* E. *Spondeo.* *Trin.* 500 *nunc tuam sororem filio posco meo.* L. *quando ita vis, di bene vortant, spondeo.* *Poen.* 1156. So Cic. *Att.* i 3 *Tulliolam C. Pisoni LF. Frugi despondimus.* Whether it meant in all cases more than unceremonial consent to marriage is not clear. Cicero uses it metaphorically in *Att.* i 16 § 8 *Desponsam Pisoni jam Syriam ademi.*

There was no action at Rome for breach, so far as we know. In early times, preceding the grant of citizenship to all Latium by the *lex Julia*, the practice in Latium, according to Servius Sulpicius, was that one who intended marriage stipulated with the father for the giving of his daughter in

before the actual marriage, and in early days such an agreement for a future marriage was made by stipulation and answer (*sponsio*). Bare consent was sufficient in the Antonine lawyers' time. *Conubium* and consents of parents were required as for marriage, but a daughter under power was taken to have her father's consent and he to have hers, if there was no open dissent. Indeed she could dissent only if her father chose for betrothal a person of unworthy and disgraceful character. The parties should be of an intelligent age. A betrothal can be broken by either party, the technical words being *condicione tua non utor* 'I make no use of the match with you.' A father can break the betrothal of a daughter under his power, and guardians can do so with the daughter's consent (D. xxiii 1; xxiv 2 fr 2 § 2).

A rescript of Severus and Caracalla made a betrothed woman liable to accusation of adultery by her intended husband (D. xlviii 5 fr 14 § 3).

B. Dissolution of marriage.

Marriage was dissolved by death, slavery, or captivity of either of the parties (D. xxiv 2 fr 1). Nor if a captive returned home did the marriage revive as of course; it required a fresh consent. In the Digest it is laid down that a wife could not marry again, so long as it was certain that her husband was alive, without incurring penalties, nor, if he was not known to be dead, until five years from the date of his capture (D. *ib.* fr 6). It is generally supposed that this passage of Julian has been largely interpolated (Glück's *Pand.* xxvi p. 224 sq.; Gradenwitz, *Interp.* p. 10). Deportation did not dissolve marriage, if the other party did not choose (D. xlviii 20 fr 5 § 1; Cod. v 17 fr 1; D. xxiv 1 fr 13 pr is interpolated). For the time within which a widow might not remarry see Book VI chap. iii. If

marriage, and the father stipulated for the man's marrying her. Hence came the terms *sponsalia* for the contract, *sponsus*, *sponsa* for the parties. If the woman was not given or not taken, the stipulator had an action *ex sponsu*, and the judge, if he found no good cause for the breach of promise, gave damages estimated at the amount of the interest of the plaintiff in the fulfilment of the contract (Gell. iv 4). Varro (*L. L.* vi 69—72) as well as Ulpian (D. xxiii 1 fr 2) both speak of it as an old practice, but without reference to Latium.

she gave birth to a child, she might remarry at once (D. iii 2 fr 11 § 2).

A marriage could also be dissolved by the voluntary action of either or both of the parties[1]. A dissolution by mutual consent was called *divortium bona gratia*, one-sided action was *repudium*, but *divortium* was also used. When the wife was in the hand of her husband, we know little of the forms or conditions of divorce. A marriage formed by *confarreatio* was apparently dissolved by a form of the same character, *diffareatio*, but the Flamen and Flaminia were not allowed a divorce. The dissolution of a marriage by copurchase involved a further use of mancipation, in order to break the filial connexion of the wife with her husband (Gai. i 137 *a*). Of any special form for dissolving a marriage formed by use we know nothing. The information which we have appears to relate principally to divorce from free marriage.

A declaration of divorce might be made personally to the other party or communicated through one who is in the divorcee's power or in whose power he or she is. The traditional words, approved still in Gaius' time, were *tuas res tibi habeto*, 'keep thy affairs to thyself,' or *tuas res tibi agito* 'manage thy affairs for thyself[2].' These, with other phrases,

[1] A. Gellius (iv 3, xvii 21 § 44) tells us that the first divorce in Rome was A.U.C. 523 (or 519, or, according to the consuls named, 527) by Sp. Carvilius Ruga who divorced a wife whom he loved because she was barren, and he had taken an oath before the censors that he would have a wife *liberûm quaesundûm gratia.* Possibly this was not the first divorce of any kind, but the first on grounds independent of the wife's conduct. Plutarch (*Rom.* 22) speaks of Romulus having enacted that a wife should not divorce her husband, but a husband might divorce his wife for applying drugs to his children, or getting false keys or committing adultery; and that if he divorced her for any other reason, part of his property should be his wife's and part sacred to Ceres. Compare Dionys. *Ant. Rom.* ii 25. The accuracy of these statements and the time to which they may really refer is uncertain. Cf. Karlowa *RG.* ii 185 sqq.

[2] Cic. *Phil.* ii 28 § 69 *Frugi factus est Antonius; mimulam suam suas res sibi habere jussit; ex duodecim tabulis clavis ademit, exegit.* Of this practice in accordance with the XII tables we know no more. '*Exegit*,' 'drove out' (cf. Pl. *Merc.* 810, 816) refers to another coarser way of giving intimation of divorce, as in Mart. xi 104 *Uxor vade foras aut moribus utere*

are found in earlier times. The *lex Julia de adulteriis* declared no divorce (of Roman citizens) to be good unless made in the presence of seven Roman citizens of full age, besides the declarant's freedman[1] who was directed to make or deliver the declaration (D. xxiv 2 fr 2, 8, 9; xxxviii 11 fr 1 § 1).

A declaration of divorce, if made in heat and repented of, counts for nothing, unless the other party, though knowing of the change of declarant's mind, accepts the divorce. In such a case the acceptor becomes the party really responsible for the divorce. If however the dowry has been given back, or either party has married another, any renewal of conjugal relations counts as another marriage and requires fresh consents of the parents (D. xxiv 2 fr 3, 7; xxiii 2 fr 8, 33). Among causes for agreed divorce are mentioned barrenness, old age, ill-health, service in the army, sacerdotal office (D. xxiv 1 fr 60—62).

If either husband or wife was under power, the father (or other ascendant) could of himself give a notice of divorce to the other party: but if the married persons did not themselves wish for a divorce, a constitution of M. Aurelius made the notice ineffectual, and the marriage continued notwithstanding (Cod. v 17 fr 5; cf. D. xxiv 1 fr 32 § 19).

Bargains or penal stipulations against divorce, or for a different penalty from what the general law contained, were not held valid (Cod. viii 38 fr 2; D. xlv 1 fr 19).

Marriage of a man with his freedwoman had special incidents. A slave set free for the purpose could marry no one else, unless her patron renounced her marriage. A freedwoman married to her patron was by the *lex Julia* debarred from divorcing him against his will: that is to say she could not

nostris. Both are used in Titin. ap. Non. iv 306 *Aliquis nuntiet geminae, ut res suas procuret, facessat aedibus.* The former is in Plaut. *Amph.* 928; Mart. x 41, 2. A general expression is used in Cic. *Att.* i 13 § 3 *Uxori Caesar nuntium remisit.* In *Or.* i 40 § 183 he speaks of a case where a man left his wife pregnant in Spain, and, without sending her a message of divorce (*nec nuntium remisit*), married in Rome and died intestate, leaving a son by each marriage. The question was whether marriage could be dissolved *ipso facto* by a new marriage or only *certis quibusdam verbis.*

[1] Cf. Juv. vi 146 '*Collige sarcinulas*' *dicet libertus* '*et exi.*'

marry again until the patron in some way signified his assent to the dissolution of the marriage, or acted as if it were dissolved. The prohibition was held good even if the husband were captured by the enemy; and even when her husband was not sole patron. A patron's son married to his father's freedwoman had the like rights, unless she had been assigned to a different son as patron. A patron who set a slavewoman free under a trust, or had purchased her, but not with his own money (see Book I chap. ii C ii 3), or had established his right as patron merely by oath, had not these rights (D. xxiii 2 fr 45, 46, 48, 50, 51; xxiv 2 fr 11).

C. Dowry (*dos*).

Relations touching property between husband and wife were concerned principally with two matters, Dowry and Gift. Of neither, in the strict sense of the terms, could there be any question in the case of marriage *cum conventione in manum.* When an independent woman passed into her husband's hand, her property passed as a whole to her husband[1], and she became in law his daughter, and had from thenceforth no property of her own, was entirely subject to his control and had only claims to inheritance along with his children. What

[1] Cicero in his speech against Flaccus (35 § 87) says *doti Valeria pecuniam omnem suam dixerat*: from 34 § 84 we learn that *Valeria in manum convenerat.* There is an interesting passage quoted from Cato by Gellius (xvii 6). In advocating the *lex Voconia* Cato said *Principio vobis mulier magnam dotem adtulit, tum magnam pecuniam recipit, quam in viri potestatem non committit; eam pecuniam viro mutuam dat, postea, ubi irata facta est, servum recepticium sectari atque flagitare virum jubet.* I do not understand this to be a recital of an actual case (*vobis* is not natural for that): if it were, I should take *principio* and *tum* to denote rhetorical, not historical order. 'She has begun to give a large dowry; she proceeds etc.' But it is more likely that Cato (possibly with particular cases in his mind) is describing with imaginative rhetoric the change in the position of dowry from the good old times. At first Roman husbands got a big dowry with their wives; then the wife keeps back a big sum so as not to put it into her husband's power; she lends the money to her husband; and afterwards in a fit of temper sends a slave belonging to her reserved property to pursue and dun him. Karlowa takes it to refer to a marriage *cum conventione in manum* (*RG.* ii 191). I think the latter part (*tum* etc.) at any rate does not.

rights and liabilities were not transferable to her husband were lost to her also. When a woman, under her father's power (*filia familias*), passed into the hand of her husband, no property passed with her, unless her father or a friend gave some to her husband as a contribution to the expenses of the married couple. It is reasonable to suppose that some conditions would be made for the case of the husband's death or of divorce. It is possible that like conditions were also made on the marriage of an independent woman with property. A. Gellius (iv 3) tells us that the tradition was that for about 500 years from the foundation of Rome there were no actions or bonds for a wife's property (*nullas rei uxoriae neque actiones neque cautiones*) in the city or in Latium, and accounts for it by the non-occurrence of divorces. Servius Sulpicius is quoted to the same effect. His contemporary, Cicero (*Top.* 4 § 23), says that a woman's property when coming into hand became the husband's as dowry (*dotis nomine*). Whether he meant that the rules of dowry applied in that case, or merely that the wife's property was then a contribution to the expenses of the marriage, as dowry was in other cases, is not apparent[1]. Gaius speaking of the passing of the property (ii 98; iii 83, 84) says nothing about dowry. The doctrine of Dowry given to us by the Roman jurists, as well as that of Gift between husband and wife, obviously relates to the marriage of Romans *sine conventione in manum*, *i.e.* to what is often called 'free' marriage. The origin of this doctrine is not known.

I. NATURE OF DOWRY.

Dowry (*dos*) was property given or secured to the husband by or on behalf of the wife, either before or after the marriage, for the purposes of the marriage. It presumes a lawful marriage, *neque enim dos sine matrimonio esse potest:* if given before, it still takes effect as dowry only on marriage, and is intended to be for the whole period of the marriage (Paul ii 21 B § 1; D. xxiii 3 fr 1, 3, 37). It may be given as such by the father or other ascendant of the wife, or at least from

[1] Cf. Bechmann, *Dotalrecht* i pp. 40, 102 sqq.; Czyhlarz, *Dotalrecht*, p. 13; Schilling's *Bemerkungen* pp. 176, 177.

his property, and is then called *dos profecticia* (*i.e. quae a patre profecta est,* Vat. 108). It is for this purpose immaterial whether the wife is emancipated or not. Or it may be given by the wife herself or by some third person, and is then called *dos adventicia.* The former is restored to the giver if alive, on the wife's death, subject to deductions in case there are children of the marriage: the latter remains with the husband unless the giver has stipulated for its return to him. In that case it is called *dos recepticia.* If the husband die before the wife, or if they are divorced, the dowry is returned in all cases, subject to certain deductions, as stated below (Ulp. vi 3—6; D. xxiii 3 fr 5).

The things forming the dowry become the property of the husband[1], subject to the contingent right of the wife or donor to reconveyance or repayment. If it consist in Italic land, he has no power of alienation. If it consist in slaves, he can manumit them and become their patron, but, unless the wife consent to the manumission, he will have to make up the loss to the wife. As owner he can vindicate anything belonging to the dowry, and, if it be stolen, can (and his wife cannot) bring an action *furti* and a condiction (*furtiva*) against the thief. But none the less it is and is called the wife's dowry (*e.g. dos sua quam apud maritum habet* Vat. 28, *dos quam maritus a socero petit, intellegitur filiae adquiri* D. xliv 4 fr 4 § 22), and he is responsible for its due preservation and return in certain contingencies (Gai. ii 63; D. xxiii 3 fr 7 § 3, 9 pr § 1, 46 pr, 61, 75; xxv 2 fr 24, xxxviii 16 fr 3 § 2). If the husband is not *sui juris,* his father or other ascendant is the legal owner and responsible: but for brevity's sake I usually speak of the husband only.

The husband after acceptance of a dowry is answerable for fraud and for fault, including excessive cruelty to slaves, and for want of such care as he shews in dealing with his own property (D. xxiii 3 fr 17 pr, 24 § 5). He has a right to all fruits gathered or separated during the marriage, subject to the

[1] This does not prevent the land *etc.* being spoken of sometimes as the wife's; *e.g.* Cic. *Caecin.* 4 § 11 *Fulcinius curavit ut in eo fundo dos collocaretur....Huic fundo uxoris continentia quaedam praedia mercatur.* Again § 15.

usual obligation in the case of cattle to keep up the herd; and has a right to all gains from the services of slaves belonging to the dowry, and to the produce of stone and chalk quarries, sand pits, gold and silver mines, and coppices. But other accretions not included in fruits belong to the dowry, and come eventually into capital account, *e.g.* slaves' offspring, inheritances and legacies left to slaves, timber, marble not previously worked (except such as grows again[1]) and treasure trove, except the finder's share (D. fr 7 pr § 1, fr 10 §§ 1—3, 32: tit. 5 fr 18; xxiv 3 fr 7 §§ 12—15; fr 8 pr). The *peculium* of a dowry slave may thus be partly the husband's (so far as derived from his property or the slave's services) and partly belong to the dowry (D. xv 1 fr 19 § 1). In case of eviction, the husband can claim against wife's father, or wife, only if there has been fraud, or the conveyance has been in execution of a promise which therefore has not been fulfilled. Against the wife the action would not be *doli* but *actio in factum*, in order to spare the wife's reputation (Cod. v 12 fr 1). Whether the wife's father, if he had given the dowry, had sufficient interest to sue his *auctor* was answered affirmatively, with some doubt however, especially if his daughter was not in his power (D. xxi 2 fr 71).

II. Establishment of dowry.

A dowry may be established in various ways and may consist in property transferred or bequeathed, in rights established, in promises made, in the extinguishment of debts, or in any other emolument. Ulpian says *dos aut datur aut dicitur aut promittitur*, 'handed over or declared or promised,' following apparently the *lex Julia* (on marriage) which spoke of a guardian being appointed *ad dotem dandam dicendam promittendam*[2] (Ulp. vi 1; xi 20; Gai. i 178); but this is probably not meant as an exhaustive enumeration.

[1] The Digest adds *quales sunt in Gallia, sunt et in Asia.* Cf. Plin. *N.H.* xxxvi 125.

[2] Cf. Cic. *Flac.* 35 § 87 '*Doti*' *inquit* '*Valeria pecuniam omnem suam dixerat.*' *Si in tutela Flacci fuit, quaecumque sine hoc auctore est dicta dos, nulla est.* *Caecin.* 25 § 73 *Nemo auderet judicare deberi viro dotem quam mulier nullo auctore dixisset.* The presence of a caretaker was not sufficient (Vat. 110).

Dotis dictio[1] was an old form whereby a one-sided statement (*e.g. ille fundus tibi doti erit*, cf. D. xxiii 3 fr 25, 44, 57) fulfilled the purpose usually filled by promise in reply to stipulation. The only persons competent to make such a declaration were the woman herself (not being under power) who was about to marry, her debtor acting at her order, and her father or father's father. As such an act belonged to the civil law, the woman required the authority of her guardian (Ulp. vi 2; xi 27; Vat. 99). The declaration was perhaps made at the time of betrothal, the competent persons being just those whose consent to betrothal and marriage was indispensable. (The woman's debtor is only an instrument.) Other modes of establishing a dowry were open to all who had the power of valid alienation or of obligatory promise. The declaration (*dotis dictio*) would create only a valid obligation, and would require in some cases to be supplemented by mancipation or other appropriate conveyance (cf. D. L 16 fr 125; Gai. iii 95 *a* and *Epit.*). A mere statement in a deed is not enough to establish a dowry any more than a statement, not followed by payment, makes a valid loan (Cod. v 15 fr 1).

Nothing counted as dowry or part of dowry, unless and until the marriage which it was to serve took place. This was understood as a condition, whether expressed or not at the time of conveyance or in the stipulation. If the marriage be renounced before celebration, the stipulation dropped (D. xxiii 3 fr 10 §§4, 5, fr 21—23). As a rule the husband acquired no property in anything transferred before the marriage, unless the intention of the conveyance was that he should, and in that case the property could be recovered by a condiction, if the marriage did not ensue (fr 7 § 3, fr 8). If a giver, other than the woman herself, died before the marriage, the gift failed in strict law, but from the favour shewn to marriage the heir was compelled to assent (fr 9 § 1). If the things transferred were not the giver's own, or were not duly transferred, usucapion ran as a rule only from the date of marriage (D. fr 7 § 3—fr 9 pr, cf. D. xli 9 fr 1, 2; Vat. 111).

[1] Cf. Bechmann ii p. 88 sqq.; Czyhlarz p. 113 sqq.

A dowry given for one marriage cannot be applied to another even with the same person, unless there be a fresh consent on the part of the giver, which however may usually be presumed (D. xxiii 3 fr 30, 63; cf. xxii 4 fr 26 § 5). A mere temporary quarrel, not carried out to a divorce, did not interfere with the position of the dowry (D. xxiii 3, fr 64).

It was regarded as a duty of a father to give his daughter a dowry, and possibly this was enacted by the *lex Julia.* A constitution of Severus and Antoninus imposed on governors of provinces the duty of compelling persons who had children in their power to place them in marriage and give them dowries (D. xxiii. 2 fr 19; cf. Cod. v 11 fr 7 § 2).

III. Content of dowry.

The incidents of different modes of constituting a dowry were as follows:—

1. If Italian land was given in dowry, the *lex Julia* (*de adulteriis*) forbad any alienation by the husband without the wife's consent, and any mortgaging even with her consent. (The latter would be an intercession, and thus forbidden by the *SC. Vellaeanum.*) The jurists applied the prohibition to betrothed persons before marriage also. Where land was bought with money of the dowry, or bequeathed to a slave belonging to the dowry, or in any other way became object of dowry, the prohibition applied. The husband could not impose servitudes on it, or give up servitudes belonging to it. The inalienability attached to the land in the hands of the husband's heir, or the crown (*fiscus*), and attached so long as the wife had an action for recovering dowry, but did not prevent its acquisition by a neighbour on the ground of apprehended damage (*damni infecti*); nor did it prevent usucapion by an outsider, if begun before it was given in dowry. Otherwise it could be claimed back by the wife after dissolution of marriage, and apparently by the husband before such dissolution. All land whether open or covered with buildings came under the statute (Gai. ii 63; Paul ii 21 B § 2; D. xxiii 5 fr 1—6, 13 pr, 16; Cod. v 13 § 15). Gaius speaks of the application to provincial land as being doubtful (cf. Sin. schol. 5).

2. A usufruct in land was not infrequently granted as dowry, and its repayment was variously effected. Several cases may occur. (*a*) The woman, having a usufruct in land of the husband's, grants it him by way of dowry. It then merges in the ownership, and if a divorce ensue, he would have to re-create it in favour of his wife. If she die while married the usufruct remains merged.

(*b*) A father having a usufruct in his son-in-law's land grants it him as dowry for his daughter. If she die in marriage, he can claim its re-constitution in his own right. If there be a divorce it would have to be re-constituted for the wife.

(*c*) The woman grants the husband by way of dowry a usufruct in land of her own. Suppose he loses it by non-use. The wife is then undowered, but as she benefits by its merger in her ownership, she cannot recover anything by action against him. But if she has parted with the ownership, and the usufruct lost by her husband's non-use then falls in, she has an action against the husband for the value. Again, if the husband does not lose the usufruct by non-use, he will retain it notwithstanding the wife's death: but if a divorce occurs, he must cede it to her if she still has the propriety, and if she has it no longer, she can still compel him to give up the usufruct, so as either to free her from an obligation to the purchaser of the propriety, or to enable her to get the value from him (according as she has sold him land or bare propriety). At the least she can thus gratify her feelings by depriving her unfriendly husband of it. In any case the fruits for the year of divorce will be apportioned.

If the woman grant her husband the usufruct of some land by way of dowry, and afterwards during marriage sell him the propriety, she can on a divorce recover from him the value of the usufruct, but if before joinder of issue he dies, the usufruct remains merged in the propriety, and his heirs are not bound to repay what has thus been naturally extinguished. If she had sold him not merely the propriety but the whole land, she has nothing more to get, having in the price received back her dowry (D. xxiii 3 fr 78 pr — § 3; xxiv 3 fr 57).

(*d*) Another case is where an outsider grants by way of dowry a usufruct in some land of his, and a divorce takes place. The husband cannot cede the usufruct, except to the owner of the propriety, and such a cession is of no good to the wife. The only thing to be done is for him to let or sell to her for a nominal sum (*nummo uno*) the practical enjoyment of the usufruct. Of course its duration is only for the husband's life (D. xxiii 3 fr 66).

3. If the dowry consisted in money or other fungibles paid over, they are at the risk of the husband and he is bound to restore the like quantity and quality (fr 42).

4. A similar case was where other things than money or fungibles were transferred by way of dowry, and the husband undertook to restore, not the actual things but their value (*dos aestimata*), and in that case they were alienable at his will: he took all produce and accessions and bore all risk just as if they had been purchased by him. Before the marriage they were at the wife's risk, and if it does not take place, he has to return, not their value but whatever he may have received or thereby obtained. After the marriage, whatever happens to them, unless they are evicted, he is responsible for the agreed value, and cannot even deduct for wear and tear of dress, valued as part of the dowry for his wife's use. If they are evicted without any fault on his part, he is no longer responsible for their value, and can sue his wife as on a purchase; and she has no defence, unless she has acted in good faith, or the dowry has been given by her father and she is not his heir. If she has promised double the value in case of eviction (which she need not do) and the husband recovers this amount, it is treated as so much added to her dowry. If too low a value has been placed on the dowry-components by the wife's mistake, the husband has the option either to give up the thing itself or to be liable for the just value, though, if it perish, the value is taken as first arranged, unless indeed the woman is a minor and obtains reinstatement (Vat. 94, 105; D. xxiii 3 fr 10 pr, § 5, 12 § 1, 16, 52; xxiv 3 fr 49 § 1; Cod. v 12 fr 1, 5; 13 § 9 *a*). If the things themselves have to be restored, a value fixed in case of non-restoration does not make the dowry a *dos aestimata* (D. xxiii 3 fr 69 § 7).

5. If a dowry is constituted not by actual transference, but by promise either of the wife or her father, it is at the wife's risk: the husband cannot (though Julian thought otherwise) be held responsible for not taking legal measures to compel fulfilment of the promise. Nor can he be unduly pressed to sue an outsider, who has promised the dowry as a gift. If however an outsider, being a debtor to the wife or her father, has promised at their bidding, the husband is bound to get in the dowry with due speed; and, if he fail to do so and the debtor become insolvent, the husband is responsible for the amount. So he is, if he accept the promise as dowry, when he knows that the promiser is insolvent, or if by novation or formal release he take the risk or obligation of the dowry on himself (D. xxiii 3 fr 33, 35, 41 § 3, 49; cf. fr 71). A dowry constituted by the wife's father *mortis causa* is subject to revocation by him on regaining his health, but is otherwise valid. A wife cannot so constitute a dowry; for what is due only on her death cannot contribute to bear the burdens of marriage (D. fr 76). A promise by the wife's father to give on a day certain a dowry of undefined nature or amount is good, the means of the promiser and rank of the husband affording a measure of the amount. If it is expressly left to the discretion of the promiser (*arbitratu soceri*), still it must be a reasonable discretion, *arbitrium boni viri* (Cod. v 11 fr 3; cf. D. xxxi fr 1 § 1).

Neither emancipation of the woman nor death of the father affects a promise given by the latter; he or his heirs are liable (D. xxiii 3 fr 44 pr). Nor if a supposed debtor has made a promise for the purpose of a dowry at the order of the woman or another, and finds he was not really a debtor, can he resist the husband's suit by a plea of fraud: it is not the husband's fault, and he is not concerned with the ground of the promiser's engagement, who must look for his remedy to the person who gave him the order (D. xii 4 fr 9 § 1).

A promise by the woman of all her estate (*omnia bona*) as dowry carried the assets less the debts: the husband's own means would not be liable to her creditors' suits (D. xxiii 3 fr 72 pr).

6. Another mode of constituting a dowry was by formal

release (*acceptilatione*) of a debt due from the husband. This could be done by any creditor, whether the woman herself or her father or an outsider. In such a case the claim by the wife or other to recovery of the dowry would be satisfied by a revival of the obligation or payment of the debt, according as the debt was conditional or absolute (D. xxiii 3 fr 41 § 2, 43; cf. xii 4 fr 10). The payment would be made at the usual dates for dowry. A similar effect was produced by a declaration (*dictio*) by the woman or her father, as the case might be, that the debt owed by the husband should form the dowry (*quod mihi debes, doti erit*). Whether in this case the debt was absolutely extinguished, or the debtor only provided with a peremptory plea of 'bargain agreed,' seems not to be clear (D. fr 44, 77; cf. fr 12 § 2, 58 § 1).

7. In some cases, it appears, the woman or her father arranged with the husband, who had a claim to an inheritance or legacy after them or as a substitute, not to take it up, in order that he might succeed to it *dotis causa*. Such an acquisition would not form a profecticious dowry, but land so coming to the husband would be counted as dowry land (D. xxiii 3 fr 5 § 5; tit. 5 fr 14 § 14).

8. Where a bequest is made by way of dowry and the husband is the legatee, Proculus held that it was for the husband to sue, Gaius that it was for the wife, Julian that both could sue. In any case, being dowry it would be claimed by the wife on divorce. If there has been a previous promise of dowry made to the husband, the legacy gives him no fresh right; he can sue on the promise; but if the legacy is in form to the wife, she can sue on the legacy, and if she can show the testator's intention to be to duplicate the dowry, the heir will have to satisfy both the husband's and wife's suits (D. xxiii 3 fr 29, 48 § 1; xxx fr 69 § 2; xxxv 1 fr 71 § 3).

IV. Modification of general law by agreement.

Beside the general law of dowry special agreements were frequent (*pacta dotalia*), but must not contradict the general principles of dowry (Paul *ap. Consult.* iv 3). Hence they could not provide for the husband's not getting the profits of the dowry, nor for the husband's never suing for the promised dowry. For in both cases there would be in fact no dowry as a help to the husband to bear the burdens of the marriage. Nor could an agreement for the husband to pay the annual proceeds to the wife be enforced, for that would be an invalid gift (D. xxiii 4 fr 4 pr, 12 § 1 ad fin., 22). Public policy required that no private agreement made before or during marriage should impair the woman's responsibility for conduct (*de moribus*), or either's responsibility for making away with the other's property (*rerum amotarum*), or the husband's responsibility for fault as well as for fraud in dealing with the dowry, or should make gifts between them lawful, or alter the law which made necessary expenses a diminution *ipso facto* of the dowry (D. fr 5, 20 pr). Otherwise the giver of a dowry can before marriage make such terms with the husband in reference to the dowry as he chooses (*legem quam velit dicere potest*). If it be only promised, he can bargain for its not being exacted from himself or certain of his heirs. Both before and after marriage agreements may be made for the wife, who has promised a dowry, maintaining herself and not paying over the dowry during marriage, or for her paying the husband a certain amount and being supported by him, or for the time or mode of repaying the dowry, when the marriage is at an end, or for the conversion of the dowry or part of it from money into land[1] or land into money or the like. But no such agreement for the time of repayment of the dowry can make the position of the woman worse by postponing the date (D. fr 7, 10, 12 § 1, 14—17, 20 §§ 1, 2, 21; xxiii 3 fr 25, 26).

All agreements respecting the repayment of the dowry bind only those who are parties (and their heirs), whether they have to pay or to recover the dowry, and the benefit is as a rule confined to them, but the wife or the donor's son was sometimes allowed after the donor's death to sue *utiliter* on the donor's contingent stipulation in their favour for the return of the dowry (D. xxiii 4 fr 9, 23; xxiv 3 fr 45). If a woman providing her own dowry, bargain for its repayment to her mother, if she

[1] Cf. Cic. *Caecin.* 4 § 11 *Maritus, cum uteretur uxoris dote numerata, quo mulieri res esset cautior, curavit ut in eo fundo dos collocaretur.*

herself die married without children, the mother cannot sue on the bargain, but if the daughter's heir pay her the dowry, can retain it against the husband's suit. If however the mother stipulated for it, she could sue (D. xxiii 4 fr 26, § 4, fr 29, § 2).

After a dowry has once been given and marriage has taken place, the dowry is acquired by the wife, and both giver and wife must join to modify its terms. If a father having given a dowry make a bargain by himself, it avails for and against himself, but does not affect her interest, though he sue with his daughter joined (*mihi filiaeve*). If a wife under her father's power bargains by herself, her father may benefit but not be hurt by it, in accordance with the regular principle of the father gaining through those in his power: if, however, he sue with his daughter joined, the bargain made by her may then damage the father's suit (D. xxiii 4 fr 1, 7; cf. xxiv 3 fr 29). If a father is mad or captured by the enemy, his son or daughter under power can make bargains by themselves (fr 8).

Any bargain made in connexion with the grant of dowry by the giver required no stipulation: others did. If a second bargain be made, rescinding a former one and reviving the normal terms of dowry, it is good, even though the bargain rescinded was more favourable to the wife (D. ii 14 fr 7 § 5, 27 § 2; Cod. v 14 fr 1).

An arrangement is spoken of in two places of the Digest (xxiii 3 fr 73 § 1; xxiv 3 fr 20) by which, for certain purposes, the dowry can be given back to the wife during marriage and such return can obtain a valid discharge for the husband. These purposes are to discharge a debt, to purchase a suitable landed estate, to support herself and hers (*i.e.* her slaves, cf. D. xxiv 1 fr 21 § 1), to give alimony to a parent in exile or captivity, or to assist children by a former marriage, or brothers or sisters in need. The first two purposes are such as may be dictated by prudent business considerations; the third (*ut se suosque alat*) is one for which agreements were sometimes made without entirely doing away with the dowry (*e.g.* D. xxiii 4 fr 4); the others are works of natural charity and affection. It is not difficult to imagine cases in which such action may have been

10—2

perfectly justified (cf. D. xxiii 3 fr 85), but we are given no further explanation, except that the wife, to whom this concession is made, is described as one *non perditura, i.e.* likely to act prudently in the matter. From D. xi 7 fr 27 § 1; Cod. v 19 it is inferred that the permission rested on statutable authority, perhaps the *lex Julia et Papia Poppaea* (cf. Glück's *Pand.* xxvii p. 247; Czyhlarz *Dotalrecht* § 142). If the husband was evidently without means, the wife could, according to the Digest (probably interpolated), by the *actio rei uxoriae* enforce the return of the dowry (D. xxiv 3 fr 24 pr).

Quite distinct from dowry were *parapherna*, 'outside dowry' as the Greeks called them, for which the Gauls used *peculium*, *i.e.* things for the wife's own use, which were either made the property of the husband and on the conclusion of the marriage, recovered by condiction by the wife or her heirs; or were simply brought into the house with a list, which the husband subscribed in recognition of their being the wife's property. The latter mode was usual at Rome (D. xxiii 3 fr 9 § 3; cf. Cod. v 14 fr 8, 11).

V. Fate of dowry on dissolution of marriage.

A dowry, being a contribution from the woman's side for the expenses of the marriage, came to an end as such with the marriage. The marriage ends by death of wife or death of husband or divorce.

i. On the death of the wife during the marriage, the dowry remained with the husband, free from any claim for restoration, unless either it had been given by the wife's father or other ascendant and he survived the husband, or had been given by an outsider and he had stipulated for its return to himself. But where it reverted to the wife's father, *etc.*, the husband could claim to retain one-fifth for each child of the marriage (Ulp. vi 4, 5; Vat. 108); and of course an agreement might have been made for leaving a profecticious dowry with the husband (Cod. v 14 fr 6). If the dowry was partly declared (*dicta*) by the wife's mother but not paid, the husband could not claim that part after the wife's death (Vat. 100).

ii. On the death of the husband during the marriage[1], the wife could claim from his heirs restitution of the dowry, by a suit 'for the wife's estate' (*rei uxoriae judicium*[2], Gai. iv 62). In the absence of any stipulations it mattered not from whom the dowry had come; but if she was under her father's power, he would, as in the case of divorce (see below), bring the action, with her concurrence (which indeed was assumed, unless distinctly refused), against the heirs of the husband, if he was *sui juris*, or against his father if he was under power. The suit was personal to the wife, and if she died before there was any delay in restoring the dowry, her heirs could not bring it, and the husband's heirs retained the dowry. Delay did not count till the wife had brought suit: mere declaration of intention to do so did not suffice (Vat. 95, 97). The time for repayment and the right of deduction for expenses were as in the case of divorce.

It was not unusual for the husband to mention the dowry in his will. But no disposition on his part took away the wife's right, unless she accepted it. If he left the dowry to her in so many words, she obtained by such bequest only the advantage of immediate payment instead of, where a dowry was in money or other fungibles, by three annual instalments. It might be also that he named the original amount of the dowry: if so, he precluded any claim by his heirs for expenses incurred thereon. If he expressly left her something else in lieu of her dowry (*pro dote*), she could make her choice. If, however, he gave her a legacy, or (as we may probably add)

[1] It is noticeable that in the title of the Digest xxiv 3 there is little, and in Ulpian's *Rules* no, reference to the fate of the dowry on the death of the husband. See Bechmann *Dotalrecht* p. 59. Whatever be the explanation, the claim of the wife seems clear.

[2] Servius Sulpicius (according to Gell. iv 3 § 2) said that securities for the wife's dowry (*rei uxoriae cautiones*) were first thought necessary in consequence of the divorce of Sp. Carvilius Ruga (see above, chap. xii B): and in accordance with, or resting on, this Gellius says that for about five hundred years from the foundation of Rome there were neither *cautiones* nor *actiones rei uxoriae* in Rome or Latium. (A *lex Maenia de dote* A.U.C. 568 mentioned by some modern writers is a baseless conjecture of M. Voigt's.)

made her his heir, or had previously given her something *mortis causa*, the praetor's edict *de alterutro* put her to her election, unless testator expressly declared that such legacy or other gift was to be in addition to her dowry (Cod. v 13 § 34; Cod. Theod. iv 4 fr 7 pr; cf. D. xxxi fr 53 pr § 1; Czyhlarz *Dotalrecht* § 138).

iii. Divorce gave occasion to more complicated arrangements. The wife was entitled to demand restoration of her dowry in any case, even against the Crown if her husband's estate was partly confiscated (D. xxiv 3 fr 31 pr). Her heirs could not bring the suit, if she died before her husband had made any delay in the restoration (Ulp. vi 6, 7).

1. The husband had however a right to retain part on various accounts:

(*a*) *Propter liberos*[1]. If the divorce was due to her fault or, if she was under power, to that of her father, one-sixth of the dowry could be retained for each child of the marriage up to the number of three. It could however only be retained; if the dowry was once paid back, it ceased to be dowry and no claim would hold[2]. If the divorce was not the fault of the woman, she could recover the whole dowry[3] (Ulp. vi 10; Paul ap. Boeth. ad Cic. *Top.* iv 19 = Bruns[6] ii p. 76; cf. D. xlviii 5 fr 12 § 3).

(*b*) *Propter mores*. On account of adultery (*mores graviores*) of the wife a sixth is retained; for other faults of conduct an eighth (Ulp. vi 12).

(*c*) *Propter impensas*. Expenditure by the husband on

[1] Cf. Cic. *Top.* 4 § 20 *Si mulier, cum fuisset nupta cum eo quicum conubium non esset, nuntium remisit, quoniam qui nati sunt patrem non secuntur, pro liberis manere nihil oportet.* If there was no right of intermarriage, the children were not recognised as such by the civil law, and the dowry was no dowry.

[2] I take this to be the meaning of the words which Krüger in his note thinks not explicable: *sextae in retentione sunt non in petitione. Dos quae semel functa est amplius fungi non potest, nisi aliud matrimonium sit* (Ulp. vi 10).

[3] Cf. Cic. *Top.* 4 § 19 *Si viri culpa factum est divortium, etsi mulier nuntium remisit, tamen pro liberis manere nihil oportet.*

the property forming the dowry was either necessary or useful or for pleasure.

Necessary expenditure was such as, if not made, the dowry would be depreciated and the husband liable for neglect: *e.g.* repair of buildings, restoration of olive plantations, propagation of vines, institution of seed-plots, throwing out moles into the sea or river, diversion of streams, medical treatment of slaves, in some cases even erection of buildings such as a bakery or granary. Ordinary expenditure on such matters of a moderate amount ought to be defrayed out of the produce of the estate, but considerable and extraordinary expenditure *ipso facto* diminished, as a whole, the amount for which the husband was responsible. If the dowry contained money, such expenditure was charged against the money, but if there was insufficient money and the dowry was land, the husband might claim to retain some or all of the land, if he was not reimbursed by the wife. If such expenditure was made, the husband was entitled to claim even though the particular object perished or was lost; if he neglected to make it, he would be liable only if his neglect was the cause of the loss or destruction.

Useful expenditure was such as improved the value of the dowry, *e.g.* making a vineyard or oliveyard, adding a bakery or shop to a house, teaching slaves various crafts. Such expenditure could be charged against the dowry, but, according to some lawyers, only if done with the wife's consent, as it might be too great for her means.

Expenditure for pleasure (*impensae voluptariae*), *e.g.* making baths, cannot be charged. If the wife desire to keep what has been done, she must pay the cost: otherwise she must allow their removal, so far as is possible without impairing the wife's property (Ulp. vi 14—17; D. xxiii 3 fr 56 § 3; xxv 1).

(*d*) *Propter res donatas.* The husband can set off such gifts to his wife, as are not within the exceptions, against part of the dowry (D. xxiv 3 fr 7 § 5; fr 25). This was in addition to his power of recovery by vindication or condiction (Cod. v 13 § 5 *a*).

(*e*) *Propter res amotas, i.e.* for things carried off by the wife. There was a special action on this account (see D. xxv 2 and below, p. 158).

(*f*) The husband was entitled also to deduct for any expenditure for release from brigands of near relatives of the wife (*necessariae personae*, D. xxiv 3 fr 21).

2. Besides the dowry itself, the wife could (where the dowry was not a 'valued' one, Cod. v 13 § 9 *c*) recover a proportion of the produce for the year in which the dissolution took place. The year was reckoned from the delivery of the dowry or celebration of the marriage, whichever was latest. This apportionment was somewhat difficult in the case of farms, where (usually) the fruits were gathered only once a year and the expenses occurred throughout the year. If the apportionment took notice only of the commencement of possession of the dowry and end of the marriage, the husband might have all the profit and only part of the expense, and the wife have the rest of the expense and no profit, or *vice versa*. Suppose for instance the farm became dowry at the time of the vintage (say 1 October), and after gathering the vintage, the husband let it from the 1st November, and divorce took place on the 31st January: it was not fair that the husband should retain the whole vintage and have in addition one-fourth of the rent (*i.e.* for three months). Papinian gives as the right solution[1], that the vintage and one-fourth of the rent should be added together and that the husband should have one-third of this aggregate, *i.e.* that he should receive, of the total produce credited to the dowry since his possession of it, a sum proportioned to the part of one year which the dowry has been in his hands (four months, 1 Oct.—31 Jan.). On the other hand if the wife handed over the farm in dowry immediately after gathering the vintage (say on 1st Nov.), and the husband let it on 1st March, and divorce ensued on 1st April next following, there would apparently be nothing for the husband except one

[1] The passage seems to me clear as regards Papinian's meaning for the cases put. For various views on this much discussed passage see references in Arndts' *Pand.* § 407 *Anm.*; Windscheid *Pand.* § 501 n. 8; Brinz *Pand.* § 484, and a review of Petrazycki's book by Leonhard *ZRG.* xxvii 275.

month's share of the rent. He ought to have a share of the year's rent proportioned to the duration of the dowry, *i.e.* five-twelfths. Harvest or vintage, taken by the wife before marriage and before giving of dowry, is not reckoned, but the future harvest or vintage should come into account whether included in the rent or not, and the wife may have to give security for it. Similar principles are applied when the harvest takes place twice a year, as in watered meadows (a half-year being then treated as a year), or once in a long period of years, as in coppices, or when besides an annual rent, something extra is paid every five years; or when the produce of a flock of sheep or the hire-money paid for a slave's services for the year has to be apportioned. Expenses of sowing, planting, repairs, *etc.* are chargeable against the year's produce and apportioned accordingly (D. xxiv 3 fr 5, 7, 8; Paul ii 22 § 1).

3. *Judicium rei uxoriae.* The restoration of the dowry, or of so much as was found to be due, would be made, according to its nature, by mancipation, surrender in court, re-establishment of rights, payment of money, *etc.* As a rule the restoration must be made at once, but for money or other fungibles, if there was no special agreement for an earlier date, payment was made in three annual instalments (*annuā, bimā, trimā, die*, 'on that day year, two years, three years')[1]. Any misconduct on the part of the husband was punished by accelerating the time of payment, viz. by substituting periods of six months for a year, if he was guilty of lighter offences, but if guilty of graver misconduct (*i.e.* adultery), he had to pay at once. In the case of land, *etc.* he had to give up fruits to the value of the difference between an immediate payment and a payment by three years' instalments (Ulp. vi 8, 13; D. xxiii 4 fr 17; Cod. v 13 § 7).

[1] This rule of repayment by three annual instalments is by some writers laid down also for the payment of a promised dowry to the husband. Nothing is said of this in the Jurists, and the only basis is (1) the instance of such a payment in Polyb. xxxii 13 which is a case of legacy where payment by instalments was often directed (see Book II), and (2) the case in Cic. *Att.* xi 2 § 2; 4 § 2; 23 §§ 2, 3; 25 § 3 supposed to refer to Tullia's dowry. Probably the mode of payment was a matter of arrangement in each case.

If the husband does not pay at once, he ought to give security. If he cannot do this, he must be condemned in the present value of the amount due (or partly due) in the future. If he can, but will not, give security, he is condemned in the whole amount at once (D. xxiv 3 fr 24 § 2). As regards any dowry-slaves set free by the husband with the wife's consent, he has to give security for restoring to the wife anything he may gain either from the freedman's estate at death or from his services (*ib.* § 4). For anything which through his fraud he cannot restore, he is liable in damages to be fixed by the wife's oath: and he must give security against any fraud or fault in connexion with the restoration of dowry (*ib.* fr 25 § 1). In some cases it appears the wife was sent into possession of her husband's estate to preserve it for dowry account (D. vi 1 fr 9; xlvi 3 fr 48; xliv 3 fr 15 § 4; cf. Cod. v 22; Karlowa *RG.* ii 1183).

Where dowry-property is on lease at the time of divorce, say for five years as usual, reciprocal security is required for loss or profit falling to the husband exceeding his share of the rent (D. xxiv 3 fr 25 § 4).

Restoration where the dowry consisted of a usufruct has been dealt with above.

A husband who was unable to pay in full was granted the usual relaxation. He was condemned only *in id quod facere potest,* no debts being deducted in estimating his means (D. xxiv 3 fr 12, 13, 54; Schol. Sinait. § 12). The time for estimating his means is the time of judgment. If the husband was under power, his father had the like concession (fr 15 pr, § 2). The husband's heirs had no such concession, but they could set off any pecuniary claims such as for expenditure on the dotal property, for gifts and for things carried off, but the conduct of either party did not come into their account (D. fr 12, 15 § 1).

The suit is brought against the husband whether the dowry was actually made over to himself or to another by his order. But if he was under power, the suit lies against the father for the whole amount, if the dowry was actually given to him, or to the son by his order or consent, or was in fact converted into his property; otherwise he was liable only *de peculio* (D. fr 22 § 12; Vat. 102). The son's *peculium* is increased by the amount of any counter-claims he may have, and this must not be deducted from the dowry, if the amount of the *peculium* is insufficient to meet the wife's suit (fr 25 pr).

As in the case of the husband's death, so on divorce the suit is brought by the wife herself, if independent; by her father, *etc.* with her concurrence if she is under power, her concurrence being assumed according to a constitution of Antoninus if she does not oppose. And for repayment the order of both is required. If it be repaid to the wife without adequate reason and she consume it, the father can still sue for it. If she is absent, the father on suing or receiving payment must give a bond for her ratification. If the father is mad, the dowry is paid either to the wife or her agnate caretaker with consent of the other. When the dowry has come from the father and the wife is under his power, it is said to belong to him and her, or to be common to the two (D. fr 2, 3, 22 § 1; xlvi 3 fr 65; Cod. v 13 § 14). This appears to be a rough way of expressing that while the legal control is his, it is intended as her portion. If her father emancipate her, she alone can claim it. If he die, his heirs have no claim to it, even though he disinherit her. If he die intestate, she must bring it into hotchpot; if he has made a will, it bars her right of bringing the plaint of an unduteous will, and especially if it amount to a fourth of the inheritance. And when the dowry is repaid to her father, though no longer dowry, it retains its destination for her benefit in (a future) marriage (Cod. v 13 § 12; D. xvii 2 fr 81). If the husband is bankrupt, the wife's claim by this action has precedence of all but Crown claims and funeral expenses (see Book VI). Her heirs have not this privilege (Cod. vii 74).

The above appear to be the usual incidents and characteristics of dowry as recoverable and protected by the action *rei uxoriae.* It was a suit relating not to the wife's property generally, but to her dowry; it was a *bonae fidei* suit, and came before an *arbiter*; the relations of the two parties were submitted to his consideration, not so much for the application of a strict rule as for an equitable decision as to what was best and fairest for the parties (*quod melius aequius esset*[1]). At least such must have been the character of the old action; allowance for expenses would naturally vary with the circumstances of the case; though practice and precedent would gradually stiffen into general rules much which was indefinite at first. Our chief knowledge of it comes from Justinian's Constitution (Cod. v 13), which amalgamated it with another action arising from verbal covenants.

4. This second action (*ex stipulatu*) was concurrent with the first in some cases; but was not confined to the wife or to her father or other ascendant, and in fact belonged to any one who provided a dowry or added to it and made an agreement with the husband, backed by a stipulation, for the disposal of the dowry when the marriage came to an end. It was (like other actions on stipulation) of a strict nature; it required (in the absence of any special terms), repayment at once of the whole dowry and apportioned profits; it left no opportunity for counter-claims, the dowry however being deemed to be *ipso facto* reduced by the amount of any necessary expenditure for its maintenance. It was a charge on the husband's estate, so that if the wife was made heir by him, it, like other debts, was deducted before the Falcidian fourth could be calculated. If he left her a legacy, she was not put to her election but was entitled to both. Action on the stipulation could be brought by the wife's father without her concurrence, and was transmissible to his heirs; and what was recovered by it passed by

[1] Cicero is fond of referring to these words as occurring in this action and characterising its equitable character (*Top.* 17 § 66 *in arbitrio rei uxoriae in quo est 'quod ejus melius aequius,' Off.* iii 15 § 61). Boethius in commenting on the first passage refers to conditions, sometimes made when a dowry was given, that the husband should retain in case of a divorce so much of the dowry as it should on the whole be 'better and fairer' for him to retain (Bruns[6] p. 77). A reference to these words occurs in an extract from Proculus (D. xlvi 3 fr 82), and in a quotation from Labeo (D. xxiv 3 fr 66 § 7). I hesitate to lay such stress on Boethius' explanation, as some do (cf. Bechmann *Dotalrecht* i p. 72). In *Rosc. Com.* 4 § 12 Cicero speaks of *quantum aequius et melius sit dari repromittique* as if it were a usual part of the *formula* in an *arbitrium*.

his will or to the statutable heirs, the wife taking her chance along with others (Cod. v 13 §§ 4—8, 11, 14).

VI. Two penal proceedings are mentioned affecting dowry.

1. *Judicium de moribus mulieris.*

Gaius mentions a proceeding by this name among those in which defendant is required to give security (iv 102). And a constitution of Constantius speaks of it as personal only, and not good either for or against heirs (Cod. Theod. iii 13 fr 1). It may probably be referred to in D. xxiii 4 fr 5 pr; xxiv 3 fr 15 § 1, though it is there put on a parallel with the husband's claims for gifts, expenses, *etc.* Justinian abolished this proceeding as well as any claim to retention on this account (Cod. v 13 § 5; 17 fr 11 § 2 *b*). We know nothing more of it. In early times mention is made of a family jurisdiction, exercised sometimes by the husband sometimes by the relatives generally. Thus Tacitus speaks of a trial of a lady of high position accused of foreign superstition being conducted *prisco instituto* (*Ann.* xiii 32); and Suetonius tells of Tiberius advising that certain matrons of immodest conduct be punished by their relatives *more majorum* (*Tib.* 35; cf. Dionys. ii 24). These cases and others come rather under the head of criminal law (cf. Mommsen *Strafrecht* pp. 16 sqq.). Marius is said to have been taken as judge between a husband and wife and to have found the woman guilty, but fined the husband of her dower, because though knowing her character he had married her in order to get the dowry (Val. Max. viii 2 § 3). Cato the censor in his speech *de dote* probably referred to this action when he says that 'when a man has made a divorce, the judge plays the part 'of a censor with executive power, fines her for any wrong or 'foul deed, and condemns her if she has drunk wine or disgraced 'herself with another's husband' (Gell. x 23 § 4)[1]. In the time

[1] *Vir cum divortium fecit, mulieri judex pro censore est, imperium quod videtur habet, si quid perverse taetreque factum est a muliere, multitatur; si vinum bibit, si cum alieno viro probri quid fecit, condempnatur.* Some take *vir* as subject to *jud. pro cens. est*, wrongly in my opinion, and Gellius himself seems to take it as I do (cf. § 3). The position of *vir* at the head of the sentence before *cum* is due to a contrast made by Cato between the

with which we are concerned the wife's conduct would come under review in the *rei uxoriae judicium*, perhaps in lieu of any separate proceeding.

2. *Judicium rerum amotarum.*

If in view of divorce (*divortii causa*) a wife carried off things belonging to her husband with the intention of keeping them, and divorce took place, she committed a theft. But the husband was not granted an action *furti* against her; as some lawyers thought, because she was a partner in his life and might be regarded as a part owner; as others thought, because it was not consistent with the respect due to matrimony to allow a disgraceful action against her. Accordingly an action *rerum amotarum* was granted instead. The act however had the characteristic of theft, that anything taken was incapable of usucapion (D. xxv 2 fr 1, 2, 25, 29). If the husband was under power, his father or other ascendant had the same action (*ib.* fr 6 pr). If she stole from a person to whom her husband was heir, or from her husband himself before marriage or during marriage, this action was not available, but a condiction on the ground of theft was: the action *furti* was still not available (fr 3 § 2, 25). If she was under power, her father was liable only *de peculio*, unless he sued for the dowry with her name joined, in which case he was compelled to accept trial *rerum amotarum* to the full amount (fr 3 § 4). If the husband is emancipated from his father's power, there is nothing to prevent the father's bringing the regular action for theft against his daughter-in-law (fr 15 § 1). If the marriage is not lawful, *e.g.* that of a woman with her guardian, the regular action for theft will lie, as it will in the case of a concubine (fr 17 pr). The husband can bring a vindication or condiction instead of this action, whether the thing carried off be his own or dowry property (fr 24). An oath can be tendered to the

positions of man and of woman in the Roman view. Dernburg *Pand.* iii § 142 takes the same view.

Pliny *H. N.* xiv § 90 after mentioning early instances of condemnation to death of wives for drinking wine says *C. Domitius judex pronuntiavit mulierem plus vini bibisse quam valitudinis causa viro insciente, et dote multavit.*

wife, and she is obliged to accept it: she can neither refuse nor retort the challenge. If the woman is under power and the father is defendant, he is not open to the oath; for that would be to make him swear as to another's act. Heirs can sue and be sued, but the heir is not open to a tender of the oath (fr 6 §§ 2, 3; fr 11—13). The suit being based on a tort, defendant is liable without regard to financial means; but as it also aims at recovering property, it is not confined to one year (fr 21 §§ 5, 6).

Ordering a slave to steal, or assisting a thief, makes the wife liable to this action: and she is liable, if the thing is not her husband's, but only pledged to him or honestly bought by him (fr 17 § 3, 19, 21 § 1, 22).

The action was extended, so as to make the husband liable for thefts committed on his wife at the time of divorce (fr 6 § 1, fr 11 pr, *etc.*; Ulp. vii 2).

If the property is not restored, the value is estimated by plaintiff's oath (fr 8 § 1). The damages appear to have been four times the value (fr 16 Hermogenian), and in estimating them, regard is had to any special advantage lost by their removal (fr 21 § 4).

D. Gifts between husband and wife.

It was due to custom, not statute, that gifts by husband to wife or by wife to husband were invalid. The lawyers accounted for it on the ground, that affection might lead to the impoverishment of one for the aggrandisement of the other; and Sex. Caecilius added that if gifts were permitted, they would be made the object of marriage, and the disappointment of expectations would lead to dissension and divorce (D. xxiv 1 fr 1—3 pr).

The rule was logically developed so as to apply (1) to everything in the nature of a gift, whatever form it assumed, but (2) only where the marriage was lawful, and (3) only where the gift operated during marriage, and (4) only where the donor was thereby poorer and the donee thereby richer. Eventually, A.D. 206, the rule was relaxed, so that a gift was not void but voidable by the donor.

1. According to the law before A.D. 206 a gift made by either to the other was absolutely null (*ipso jure nihil valet*). Even as a basis for usucapion, conveyance was of no effect, nor formal promise, nor formal release. Money paid over remained the property of the donor; a direction by a husband to his debtor to pay the wife was not allowed to make her richer; the money paid discharged the debt but became the husband's property (D. fr 3 §§ 10—13; xli 6 fr 1 § 2). If a husband make a sale to the wife for less than the proper price, intending a gift, the sale is void; if, however, the sale is not a mere blind but intended as business, and the reduction of price is only an incidental gift, the sale will stand, but the wife will be liable to repay the amount by which she has been enriched. Non-use of a servitude, or consent to being defeated by a plea put forward by the other against his suit, may also form a gift. In both cases the actual fact cannot be altered, the servitude and suit are lost, but a condiction can be brought to reestablish the servitude or recover the damages in the suit (D. xxiv 1 fr 5 §§ 5—7; cf. fr 31 § 4). If a wife is gaining by usucapion a thing of her husband's, and he learning of it does not interfere, and the woman learns this fact, the usucapion is frustrated by what amounts to a forbidden gift. But her coming to know that the thing was her husband's would not by itself make her acquisition unlawful, because it would not be acquired by his gift (fr 44). If the wife and a third person are liable to the husband for the same debt, and he formally release the wife, the act is null, and neither wife nor third person are freed: if he release the third person, the act is good so far as he is concerned, but the wife (contrary to the general rule in case of a release) remains obliged (fr 5 § 1).

2. Gifts between persons betrothed did not come within the rule, provided they were actually made before marriage. Whether marriage followed or not, such gifts were not reclaimable, unless given on condition that they should be (Vat. 262; Cod. Theod. iii 5 § 2 pr; D. xxxix 5 fr 1 § 1). If given through a third person and not received from him till after marriage, the gift was valid, if he was the agent of the donee (the donor having parted with the gift before the marriage), but if he was agent of the donor, the gift was

invalid (D. xxiv 1 fr 5 pr). A marriage between a freedman and a senator's daughter, or between the governor of a province or military officer of the province and a woman of the province was unlawful, and therefore gifts between the parties did not come within the prohibition. Ulpian however held that gifts in such marriages or even in betrothals between such persons ought to be forfeited to the Crown (fr 3 § 1, 32 § 28).

3. Gifts which were not to take effect during marriage were not within the mischief, and were therefore not invalidated. Such were gifts made in view of divorce or of death. In view of divorce, gifts would usually be made when it took place *bona gratia, i.e.* by mutual agreement, *e.g.* on account of barrenness or old age or health or military service or priestly office. They are valid only if made at the time of divorce, and only if the divorce is *bona fide,* which would be shewn by the party making another marriage or remaining a long time in widowhood (fr 11 §§ 11, 12; 60 §§ 61, 64). Gifts made in view of exile are also allowed, exile being practically equivalent to divorce (fr 43; cf. fr 13 § 1).

Gifts in view of death are valid, provided the donee survive the donor, and the donor has not revoked the gift before he die. Such gifts might, between ordinary persons, be of two kinds. The donor might intend the property to pass either on a resolutive or a suspensory condition, *i.e.* it might pass at once to the donee subject to rescission if the donor revoked it or survived the donee: or it might not pass at all until the death of the donor. In the case of gifts between husband and wife the latter class were alone possible on account of the prohibition, but where by the intention of the donor it would have passed at once, the ownership, though passing only on the donor's death, was thereafter treated as passing at the time of gift (fr 9 § 2—fr 11 § 1, *ib.* § 9, fr 20; xxxix 6 fr 40; Paul ii 23 § 5; Savigny *Syst.* iv p. 247 sqq.). Where the gift was by the intention of the donor on a simple suspensory condition with no retro-action, the position of the parties at the time of the donor's death determines the validity and effect of the gift, *e.g.* if the donee is under power at that time, the gift passes to his or her father: if he (or she) is independent, any attempt to deal with it before is of no effect, for it does not belong to the donee (D. xxiv 1 fr 11 §§ 3, 4).

A Senate's decree introduced by Caracalla (A.D. 206) before his father's death relaxed in some degree the strictness of the law, and put all gifts between married persons, hitherto invalid, on a similar footing to gifts in view of death. It declared that the donor should be free to revoke them, but that if he predeceased the donee and died without having repented of the gifts, they should from thenceforward belong to the donee, *ipso jure* (so far as the *lex Papia Poppaea* allowed, cf. Vat. 294 § 2; Ulp. xv), and stipulations[1] or other obligations should be valid just as if he had confirmed them in his will. And they were so far assimilated to legacies as to be subject to the Falcidian deduction if the heir was overburdened. If a divorce ensued without consent, or the donor pledged or bequeathed the things already given, the donor would be presumed to have revoked the gift. But only where there was clear evidence of the donor's repentance, would the heirs be entitled to revoke it (D. xxiv 1 fr 32 pr—§ 5, § 10). Where husband and wife died together, and it was not known which was the survivor, gifts were held to be good, because neither could be said, in the words of the Senate's decree, to have predeceased the other. If they were both taken captive together by the enemy and did not return, they were deemed to have died together at the time of being taken captive (whether as a matter of fact one survived the other or not), and their gifts were held good. If one returned, he (or she) was deemed the survivor (*ib.* § 14).

If a man committed suicide under the consciousness of crime, or if his memory was damned, any previous gift to his wife as well as any gift to others, *mortis causa*, was revoked (*ib.* § 7).

4. Further, in order to bring a gift within the prohibition, the giver must be thereby the poorer as well as the donee thereby the richer. Non-acquisition does not make the party less rich than he was before. Hence if a husband (I take him only for shortness' sake) repudiate an inheritance or a legacy to which

[1] This was denied by Papinian as reported in D. xxiv 1 fr 23: but cf. Savigny *Syst.* iv p. 184 sqq.; Windscheid *Pand.* § 509 n. 35.

his wife has a claim as substitute or heir on intestacy, the wife may be the richer but the husband's action does not make her gain invalid. So if he be left heir or legatee and be asked to take from the estate or legacy some definite amount, and hand over the rest of a deceased's estate to his wife, he can validly hand it over without deduction as he can validly forego the Falcidian fourth: he will be regarded in each case as simply acting with greater loyalty in the discharge of his trust. Again, he can give his wife ground for burial: it remains his, until she has interred a body there: and it ceases to be his and becomes hers only by this act which makes it religious. She is not thereby the richer, though she is saved from expenditure for the purchase of a burial ground. Similar remarks apply to anything given her by her husband for offering to the gods, even land for the erection of a temple (fr 5 §§ 8—16). If he give her a thing not belonging to him, he is none the poorer, and she can gain the property by usucapion, if he does not recall the gift (D. xxxix 6 fr 13 pr; xli 6 fr 3). On the like ground the gift of a slave by the husband to the wife with the direction to manumit him is not within the prohibition, even though the manumission is expressly deferred for a time. For according to the opinion of Sabinus (which was generally adopted) the property remained with the husband till the manumission; it passes only at the moment when manumission begins, and the wife is not held to be on that account the richer because she gains a freedman, even though she impose services on him (D. xxiv 1 fr 7 § 8—fr 9 pr; Paul ii 23 § 2; cf. xxiv 3 fr 24 § 4). A gift by the wife to her husband on condition that he pay it as dowry to his son in law does not enrich the husband, and is allowable: such a dowry is adventicious (D. xxiii 3 fr 5 § 9). Whether a party has become richer or poorer is a question to be decided in reference to the time of joinder of issue in a suit for recovery or annulling of the gift (D. xxiv 1 fr 7 pr).

5. Partly on this ground and partly to avoid a petty and mean scrutiny, it was held that the use by either of clothes or houses belonging to the other was not invalid. Nor if the wife, using her own wool, employed her husband's female slaves in

making a dress for herself, need she reckon and pay for their services; though if she made men's dress on her husband's account, they are his, but he must pay for the wool. A husband cannot recover money given to his wife for her toilet requisites (*unguenta*), or food for herself and slaves and yoke-beasts, if used in the service of the common household, and for travelling when she is coming to him, or with his consent attending to her own business (fr 18, 21 pr, 28 § 2, 31 §§ 1, 9). Nor is it reckoned as a recoverable gift to pay her a debt before the due day, or to allow her to keep the interest or profit from any money or other thing given to her which itself as illicit is recoverable. But acquisitions by a slave, who has been given to her, pass at once to the husband, and he has to bear the loss if anything given has been consumed (unless fraudulently) or has perished; for the slave and the thing remain his property, and the donee is not the richer for what has been consumed (fr 15 § 1, 17, 28 pr, 32 § 9, 37). If the slave has not been given, but purchased with money given, the acquisitions are recoverable (fr 28 § 5) If he incur expenses for the children of her slaves, he cannot recover them, for he has their services, but the cost of the midwife was recoverable as being expended for the life (*pro capite*) of the infant; like ransom money for slaves taken by robbers (fr 28 § 1). If he spent money for the reconstruction of a house of his wife's which had been burnt down, it was a permitted gift—probably in conformity with the general policy of restoring ruinous buildings (fr 14). Nor were customary gifts (*munera*), if not immoderate, to a wife on the 1st of March[1] or on her birthday invalid, nor (by Antonine constitution) gifts by her to enable him to obtain the broad stripe (mark of senator) or a public horse (mark of equestrian order) or for his other advancement, or to assist him in giving games (Ulp. vii 1; D. fr 31 § 8, 41, 42).

To recover a gift when invalid, vindication or condiction (*sine causa*) are applicable according as the things are still in existence or have been consumed. When money was given and spent on the purchase of things still in existence, an action analogous to a

[1] Cf. Suet. *Vesp.* 19; Juv. ix 53 *Munera femineis tractat secreta kalendis.*

vindication (*actio in rem utilis*) was allowed. If on vindication being brought the possessor does not restore, the damages are estimated at a fair value, and the possessor is entitled to a guaranty against eviction but for the single value only. If the gift to a wife, *etc.* is mixed up with gifts to other persons or gifts of other things, the gift to the wife only is invalid and recoverable, the rest is valid: if however it be not separable the whole is allowed (fr 5 § 2, 6 § 18, 36 pr, 55). If a husband has entered into an obligation for his wife or spent money on her separate property, and there comes a divorce, it was usual for him to get a bond from her on that account. The bond is called *stipulatio tribunicia* (Ulp. vii 3).

It was a principle laid down by Q. Mucius (*praesumptio Muciana*), that if there was any controversy whence a married woman had got anything, and there was no proof, it was both truer and more honourable to hold that it came to her from her husband or someone in his power (D. fr 51; Cod. v 16 fr 6).

The prohibition is not confined to gifts between husband and wife, but extends also to gifts to either from any who are in the same power as the husband or wife respectively, and to gifts by those in whose power they respectively are. Thus the husband's brother cannot give to the wife nor the wife to him; the husband's father cannot give to his daughter in law nor she to him; and the like applies to the wife's relations, provided they are under the same power. The relaxation granted by Caracalla's senate's-decree to gifts between husbands and wives was deemed by the lawyers to apply to gifts between their relatives, and such gifts to be validated by the donor's dying before the donee without having revoked his gift, and without divorce having intervened to destroy the presumed basis of the gift. Thus a gift by father in law to daughter in law (or son in law) is good, if he do not revoke the gift, but die after his son and before the donee, who thus gets the safe enjoyment of the gift only after the marriage has ceased. A gift from husband's father (having power over him) to wife's father (with like power over her) is good, provided the donor die whilst the marriage yet endures and without having revoked it. If the marriage were dissolved, the basis of a gift between such persons being gone would presumably have nullified the gift. A gift by daughter in law to husband's father would fail like others by his death before her, unless the husband was sole heir to his father, and thus might keep the gift not so much by inheritance as by a fresh donation from his wife. A gift by mother in law to daughter in law is not subject to the prohibition, as she is outside the fatherly power. A gift from a mother to her son is within the prohibition, because it would pass to his father who is her husband: but if he is going to military service, this would not be so, and the gift is allowed. Where a father in law has made a gift, and then sent a letter of divorce to the daughter in law against the will of his son, the marriage still continues by a rescript of Severus and Antonine, but the father in law's action is taken as revoking the gift (D. xxiv 1 fr 3 §§ 2—9; fr 32 §§ 16—21; Glück's *Pand.* xxvi § 1254 *b*).

CHAPTER XIII.

ACKNOWLEDGMENT OF CHILDREN.

1. Where a divorced woman thought herself with child, a decree of the senate (*SC. Plancianum*) in or before Hadrian's time provided that she, or the parent in whose power she was or someone by their instruction, should within thirty days from the divorce give formal notice of the fact to the husband or his parent, or, if neither were accessible, leave notice at his house. If the husband did not acknowledge the child as his, he could either send guards to the woman without prejudice to his future action, or he could give formal notice denying the paternity. The effect of the woman's notice is to impose on the husband the necessity of supporting the child unless he take counter steps. The right of the child to be own heir to the father is not thereby decided, and awaits, in case of denial, a judicial decision. If the woman neglect to give notice, the child's claim, both to inheritance and, according to

a rescript of Ant. Pius, to support, is not prejudiced. Another decree of the senate in Hadrian's time provided for proceedings to ensure acknowledgment of a child born while the marriage still subsisted (D. xxv 3 fr 1—3 § 1; Paul ii 24 §§ 5, 6).

If the (supposed) father is dead, the proceedings will be taken against the grandfather; if neither is alive, these decrees are inapplicable, and recourse must be had to the Carbonian edict (D. *ib.* fr 3 §§ 2—6).

2. If a divorced woman disclaimed being with child, and her husband maintained that she was, a rescript of M. Aurelius and his brother directed that the praetor should put the question to her; and if she denied pregnancy, she should be taken to the house of a respectable woman and be examined by three (five, according to Paul) midwives appointed by him, the verdict of the majority to be accepted as decisive, and, if it be in favour of pregnancy, guards to be set. If the woman refuse to appear or answer to the praetor, she is liable to distress or fines. If the verdict is against pregnancy or the woman prove eventually not to have been pregnant, the husband is liable to an action for insult (*injuriarum*), provided his action was not *bona fide* (D. xxv 4 fr 1 pr—§ 9; Paul ii 24 §§ 7, 8).

3. The praetor's edict provided for the case of a woman declaring herself with child after her husband's death, and gave minute rules for inspection and custody. The woman is to give notice twice within a month to the persons (or their agents) who have the next title to succeed to the husband's inheritance whether under a will or intestacy. Such persons are entitled to send five midwives to inspect together, but not to touch the woman without her consent. She is to give notice of the approaching birth thirty days before she expects it; and the birth is to take place in the house of a respectable woman appointed by the praetor. The room is to have only one door; guard is to be kept before it by three freemen and three freewomen with two companions each (*cum binis comitibus*[1]). Whenever the woman goes into that room or to another or to the bath, the guards may previously examine the place and those who have entered, and they may likewise examine any

[1] The Basilica (xxxi 7) has for this δύο στρατιῶται.

who enter the house. When parturition begins, the woman must send notice so that witnesses may be sent. The witnesses are to be five freewomen, and in the room itself there are to be besides two midwives not more than ten freewomen and six slavewomen, all to be examined in the room lest any of them be with child. There are to be at least three windows. The child is to be shewn to the parties concerned or their agents. It is to be brought up where the parent appoints, or, in default of appointment or of willingness on the part of the person designated, then by someone appointed by the praetor after due hearing. The person appointed is to shew the child twice each month till three months old, once a month till six months old, every other month until a year old, once in six months till the child can speak. Any refusal of inspection or of guard or of presence at the birth will lead to the praetor's refusal (after due hearing) of possession to the child; and refusal of shewing the child will lead to his refusal of the actions, which the praetor grants to possessors of the estate.

If these directions are observed there is no need for a further summary inquiry, such as is ordered when a pregnant woman applies for possession of the estate: the child is granted possession at once. And sometimes this course is taken when the directions have not been fully observed, owing to ignorance or inexperience on the part of the woman (D. xxv 4 fr 1, 2).

CHAPTER XIV.

CONCUBINAGE and COHABITATION.

1. Marital intercourse, not merely fugitive, with a freewoman of inferior position or character sometimes took place without marriage being intended. It was recognised by the *lex Julia de adulteriis* under the name of *concubinatus*, and exempted from the penalties for *stuprum* (D. xxv 7 fr 3 § 1; xlviii 5 fr 35), and the parties were liable, just as married persons, for adultery with others (D. xlviii 5 fr 14 pr). Blood-kinship was a bar to concubinage as to marriage, and it was held to be wicked

(*nefarium*) for a father's concubine to be afterwards concubine to son or grandson (D. xxiii 2 fr 56; xxv 7 fr 1 § 3). Paul says a man could not have a wife and a concubine at the same time: penalties for adultery would then be applicable (Paul ii 20). Between a patron and his freedwoman concubinage was regarded as more seemly than marriage. But if the woman was of good character, marriage was usually presumed, at least after the *lex Papia* had allowed marriage with freedwomen for all except senators and their children (D. xxv 7 fr 1 pr, 3 pr; xxiii 2 fr 23, 24). If the woman was freeborn a distinct declaration before witnesses that marriage was not intended was required to bar the presumption (D. xxv 7 fr 3 pr). The difference between marriage and allowed concubinage was thus partly one of social position and relations, but also of legal rights. There could be no legal dowry, gifts between the parties were not revocable, the children would be only natural and belong to the mother. *Semper certa est mater etiamsi volgo conceperit: pater est quem nuptiae demonstrant.* But even such natural children would not be allowed to bring an action against their mother (D. i 5 fr 19, 24; ii 4 fr 4 § 3 fr 5; xxxii fr 49 § 4; xxxix 5 fr 31 pr. Mommsen *Strafrecht* p. 693 sq.).

2. *Contubernium.*

Marital intercourse with slaves was never regarded as marriage[1]: it was only cohabitation (*contubernium* Paul ii 19 § 6). The woman was described as his *contubernalis*: the children as his natural children (D. xxxii fr 41 §§ 2, 5). Marriage was sometimes imitated, *e.g.* a father is spoken of as placing his daughter in marriage to another's slave and giving her a dowry, which in the bond for its repayment is described as a deposit (D. xvi 3 fr 27). And a *quasi dos* is spoken of between slaves (D. xxiii 3 fr 39 pr).

[1] Plautus speaks of slave-marriages in Greece, Carthage and Apulia (*Casin.* 71 sq.).

BOOK III.

INHERITANCE, or
SUCCESSION TO PROPERTY VACANT BY DEATH.

Hereditas nihil aliud est quam successio in universum jus quod defunctus habuerit (Julian in D. L 17 fr 62).

Bonorum possessionem recte definiemus jus persequendi retinendique patrimoni sive rei·quae cujusque cum moritur fuit (Ulpian in D. xxxvii 1 fr 3 § 2).

Praetor bonorum possessorem heredis loco in omni causa habet (Paul in D. L 17 fr 117).

Legatum est delibatio hereditatis, qua testator, ex eo quod universum heredis foret, alicui quid collatum velit (Florentin in D. xxx fr 116 pr).

Fideicommissum est quod non civilibus verbis sed precative relinquitur, nec ex rigore juris civilis proficiscitur sed ex voluntate datur relinquentis (Ulpian *Reg.* 25).

CHAPTER I.

HEREDITAS VACANS.

When a person dies, his property and rights have no visible owner, and appear to lie exposed to the first occupier (*Bona hereditaria vacua sine domino jacent* D. xxxviii 9 fr 1 pr; cf. xliii 24 fr 13 § 5). There is no one chargeable with the payment of his debts. But though the subject of this complex of rights and liabilities is deceased, the inheritance is not derelict: it remains for a time an independent whole, awaiting its disposal or dispersion in accordance with the law. When the heir or heirs appointed under or by the law eventually succeed to the control of the deceased's estate, they are deemed to have succeeded from the moment of the decease (D. xlv 3 fr 28 § 4, 36; xxix 2 fr 54): so that now what was the property or liability of the deceased regains a living owner or owners. Till the heir appears, the deceased remains in some sort the legal subject of the rights and liabilities attached to his person, and the estate is spoken of, sometimes according to the actual fact as the property of no one (D. i 8 fr 1 pr; cf. Gai. ii 9), sometimes, according to the legal aspect, as bearing the person of the deceased (D. xli 1 fr 34), or occupying the place of owner (*Hereditas dominae vicem optinet* D. xliii 24 fr 3 § 5).

The time intervening between the death and the heir's acquisition allows of the estate increasing and diminishing. Besides the natural produce of land, of animals, and of slaves, and their destruction, wasting and death, slaves belonging to the estate might have legacies or inheritances left them, might stipulate and thus acquire rights of action either for the inheritance proper or for their own *peculium*; damage might be done to the slaves or things, or encroachments made by which a right of Aquilian action or *arborum furtim caesarum* or the interdict *quod vi aut clam* or even a suit for *injuria* might be acquired. Again the inheritance might be put under an obligation by some outsider's attending to its business (*negot. gestorum*), and acts done by slaves of the inheritance to other persons or their property might form a basis for suits against the heir when he appeared. The mass of property and obligations, which were a deceased's estate, was thus not inert, and indeed, if slaves were included in it, was in some sort alive and productive (D. iii 5 fr 3 pr; v 3 fr 20 § 3, 28; ix 2 fr 13 § 2, 43; xxv 3 fr 35; xxx fr 116 § 3; xliii 24 fr 13 § 5; xliv 7 fr 16).

It was however incapable of possessing. True possession requires both physical control and intention to hold: there could be no intention (*animus*) without a living and personal subject. As there was no legal possession, there could be no gain by usucapion (D. xlvii 3 fr 1 § 15; xlii 3 fr 25); but, if usucapion had been begun by the deceased, the heir on entry and taking possession could count the period which intervened (D. xli 2 fr 13 § 2; tit. 3 fr. 31 § 5). The absence of a possessor in early times led to *usucapio pro herede* (see chap. iv A), and to the denial that theft was technically possible. This practical want was however remedied by introduction of a special criminal suit for pillaging an inheritance (D. xlvii 19).

There was however an exception to the incapacity of possessing in the case of a *peculium*. As a slave was held to possess and acquire by usucapion for his *peculium* without the knowledge of his master (though of course legally for him), so the slave of a vacant inheritance was held capable of the like (D. xli 2 fr 1 § 5).

Again an inheritance was incapable of holding a usufruct, there being no person to whom it could attach. But a usufruct bequeathed to a slave of the inheritance took effect in his person on the entry of the heir, if the slave thereby became free: if he did not become free at once, and died or was alienated before he became so, the usufruct perished. A usufruct could not be acquired by a stipulation of a slave of the inheritance (Vat. 55, 57. See my note on D. vii 1 fr 6 § 2).

The capacity of a slave to acquire an inheritance depending on the capacity (*testamenti factio*) of his master, an hereditary slave was deemed capable, if the deceased was so, though the eventual heir might not be. The heir, however, took through the slave, only so far as he was himself capable (under the *lex Julia Poppaea, etc.*): the residue passed to those entitled in default. There had been much difference of opinion on the question (D. xxviii 5 fr 53; xxxi fr 55 § 1).

Whether a stipulation by a hereditary slave 'for the future heir' was valid is uncertain. It was maintained by Proculus that, the future heir being at the time an outsider, the stipulation was, in accordance with ordinary rules, invalid and remained so (cf. Gai. iii 103; D. xlv 1 fr 83 § 4). Cassius held that the future heir being deemed to succeed from the death of testator was not an outsider at the time, and the stipulation was therefore valid. Papinian and Paul (in the Digest) follow Proculus; Gaius and Modestin follow Cassius[1]. (D. xlv 3 fr 16, 18 § 2, 28 § 4, 35; and of a *pactum* ii 14 fr 27 § 10.)

CHAPTER II.

INHERITANCE BY WILL.

A. WILL-MAKING.

1. A will (*testamentum*) is the lawful declaration by a person of his will for the disposition of his belongings after his death[2] (cf. D. xxviii 1 fr 1).

[1] Scheurl (*Beitr.* i p. 66), following the gloss, explains the discrepancy in the Digest by understanding the invalidating passages to refer to a stipulation naming the heir, and those validating it to refer to stipulations not naming the heir. But *nominatim* in fr 16 does not necessarily mean that the slave said '*Titio*' but that he spoke *futuro heredi* (which words appear in all the passages) instead of leaving the person to be understood from the stipulant, cf. fr 51 § 1, 15. (For *nominatim* cf. D. xxxii fr 90, xxviii 3 fr 3 § 5 and Brisson's Lex.)

[2] The law of the XII tables gave full sanction to such disposition as a testator made of his property. Cicero gives the words: *Paterfamilias uti super familia pecuniaque sua legassit, ita jus esto* (*Inv.* ii 50). So also *ad Herenn.* i 13 § 23. *Legare* is 'to declare the *lex*' (*legem testamento dicere*, D. xxx fr 114 § 14). Compare the use of *lex* in cases of mancipation,

To be lawful it must be made in conformity with the rules of the civil law by a person of sound mind, who had *testamenti factio*, and it must contain a due appointment of heir (Gai. ii 114—116).

Besides an heir or heirs to continue, as it were, the person of the deceased and bear the complex of his rights and liabilities, so far as they do not expire with him, a will may also distribute specific things or portions of his assets to persons other than the heirs, as well as to the heirs or some of them, may enfranchise some or all of his slaves, may assign his freedmen and freedwomen to one or more of his children, and may appoint guardians to his children so far as they were still under his power and under the age of puberty.

2. Who can make a will?

All Roman citizens, with certain exceptions, above the age of puberty can make a will, but women being under guardianship (unless freed by the *lex Papia Poppaea* or Vestal Virgins[1]) required their guardians' authority. Since a decree of the senate in Hadrian's time, it was not necessary for a woman to go through the form of copurchase for this purpose (Gai. i 40, 115 *a*; ii 112, 113; Ulp. xx 15).

Book IV. *Pecunia* had often a large meaning in early law; thus *Hereditas est pecunia quae morte alicujus ad quempiam pervenit jure, nec ea aut legata testamento nec possessione retenta* (Cic. *Top.* 6 § 29) where *poss. retenta* refers to gifts *mortis causa*. This use of *pecunia* is found elsewhere: *L. Sullae C. Caesaris pecuniarum translatio a justis dominis ad alienos non debet liberalis videri* (Cic. *Off.* i 13 § 43). Cf. *Legg.* ii 20 § 49; 21 § 52; D. L 16 fr 178 pr; Gai. iii 124. (*Familia pecuniaque* originally were 'slaves and cattle.') Pomponius quotes the same passage of the XII tables and comments thus: *Verbis legis duodecim tabularum his 'uti legassit suae rei, ita jus esto' latissima potestas tributa videtur et heredis instituendi et legata et libertates dandi, tutelas quoque constituendi: sed id interpretatione coangustatum est vel legum vel auctoritate jura constituentium* (D. L 16 fr 120).

[1] A vestal virgin, on being taken by the *Pontifex*, at once passed from her father's power and from his family, so that she could not be heir *ab intestato* to anyone and no one could be heir to her if she died intestate. Her property passed to the public (Gell. i 12 §§ 9, 18).

The following were not able to make a will:

(*a*) Sons[1] or daughters under their father or other ascendant's power, because they own nothing. Since Augustus' time, however, sons were capable of disposing by will of anything acquired in military service or given to them for that purpose before entering it (*castrense peculium*)[2]:

(*b*) Persons who are uncertain whether their father is dead so as to make them *sui juris*, or whether they are really free persons, or had been duly emancipated:

(*c*) Persons in captivity to the enemy or uncertain whether they were not so, captives being regarded as slaves for the time. Hostages are in the same position.

(*d*) Persons condemned *ob carmen famosum* are by senate's decree *intestabiles*: they can neither make nor witness a will.

(*e*) Persons interdicted from water and fire, and those deported into an island. But the will of the latter is good, if made before the deportation is approved by the emperor or praefect or deputy praefect of the praetorium, or, according to a letter of Severus and Caracalla, by the praefect of the city.

(*f*) Slaves[3]; but a public slave of the Roman people might dispose by will of half his property.

Criminals condemned *ad ferrum* (to fight as gladiators) or to fight with beasts or to work in the mines are slaves to their punishment (*servi poenae*).

(*g*) Latins, *i.e.* Junian Latins[4] (see p. 38).

(*h*) *Dediticii* (see pp. 19, 32).

[1] A trust (not by will) made by a son or slave, if emancipated or manumitted before death, is valid though made before he became *sui juris* (D. xxxii fr 1 § 1).

[2] Cf. Juv. *Sat.* xvi 51 sqq. *Solis testandi militibus jus vivo patre datur; nam quae sunt parta labore militiae placuit non esse in corpore census, omne tenet cujus regimen pater.*

[3] Pliny (*Ep.* viii 16), speaking of his own practice, says *Permitto servos quasi testamenta facere eaque ut legitima custodire.* See also note 1 (above).

[4] But the inhabitants of certain Latin colonies were able to take under a Roman will and to give to Romans by their will (Cic. *Caecin.* 35 § 102). See above, pp. 19, 32.

(*i*) Sick persons, whose minds are affected (*mente capti*): Madmen (*furiosi*)[1], except during lucid intervals.

(*j*) Spendthrifts (*prodigi*) formally interdicted by the praetor from management of their affairs and not reformed (but a will made before interdiction is good).

(*k*) Deaf[2], because they cannot hear the words of the purchaser of the household: Dumb, because they cannot utter the declaration of will (Ulp. xx 10—16; Paul iii 4 *a*; D. xxviii 1 fr 8, 11, 14, 15, 18; xxxii fr 1 §§ 1—4).

3. How a will is made.

Two modes of making a will were in use in early times.

(*a*) *Calatis comitiis*, *i.e.* at a duly called assembly of the burghers (*populus*), held under the authority of the college of pontiffs (*pro collegio pontificum*). Such assemblies were held twice a year for this purpose, probably 24th March and 24th May (Mommsen *Staatsr.* ii 37).

(*b*) *In procinctu*[3], *i.e.* when the army was drawn up in array for battle (Gai. ii 101; Gell. xv 27).

Both these proceedings evidently belong to a time when

[1] Cicero quotes from the law of the XII tables *Si furiosus escit, adgnatum gentiliumque in eo pecuniaque ejus potestas esto. Inv.* ii 50 § 148. So also *ad Heren.* i 13 § 23. Julian (D. xxix 7 fr 2 § 3) gives as a general rule, *Furiosus per omnia et in omnibus absentis vel quiescentis loco habetur.*

[2] Some lawyers held that complete deafness did not exist: *nullum esse qui penitus non exaudit si quis supra cerebrum illius loquatur* (Cod. vi 22 fr 10, a discriminating constitution of Justinian's).

[3] Cf. Cic. *Orat.* i 53 § 228 *Reprehendebat Galbam Rutilius quod duos filios suos parvos tutelae populi commendasset, ac se, tamquam in procinctu testamentum faceret, sine libra atque tabulis populum Romanum tutorem instituere dixisset illorum orbitati; Nat. D.* ii 3 § 9 *Nulla auspicia, cum viri vocantur, ex quo in procinctu testamenta perierunt.* The last recorded occurrence of this form of will is B.C. 143 (Vell. Pat. ii 5). An old account is given by a scholiast on Vergil printed in Bruns ed. 6 ad Serv. *Aen.* x 241.

An old derivation (apparently first in Festus, see Bruns p. 28; Marquardt *Priv. Alt.* p. 544) connects the expression with the particular mode of wearing the toga called *cinctus Gabinus*; 'when the army was forward-girt.' The Gabine girding however seems unsuitable; cf. A. Müller in Baumeister's *Denkmäler* p. 1834.

the Roman community was relatively small, and the succession to a citizen's place and estate was a matter of public concern. They were out of use in Gaius', perhaps before Cicero's time.

(*c*) A third mode came into use, due, according to Gaius, originally to the emergency of illness which admitted of no delay. This was *per aes et libram*, *i.e.* an adaptation to this purpose of the much used form of mancipation. Testator conveyed his household, that is, his private property (*familiam suam, id est patrimonium suum*), to a friend, and charged him with the execution of his wishes. This mode remained as the regular form in Gaius' time, but was arranged somewhat differently.

At first the purchaser of the household, *i.e.* the friend who took the household by mancipation from the testator, occupied the place of heir, and received his commands for the distribution of his property. But this would often not be convenient, and mancipation once adopted was treated as a mere form, the person intended to be heir often took no part in the ceremony, and another person was got to act as *familiae emptor*. All these forms were oral, and the contents of the will were probably orally declared. But, when Gaius describes the form used in his days, oral wills had become rare, and the ceremony was on this wise:

The testator wrote his will or got it written[1]. In the presence (as in other mancipations) of not less than five

[1] Wills were of course often written or drafted by lawyers; cf. Cic. *Orat.* ii 6 § 24 *Si, Scaevola, nullum erit testamentum recte factum nisi quod tu scripseris, omnes ad te cives cum tabulis veniemus, omnium testamenta tu scribes unus.*

A *SC. Libonianum*, according to a suggestion of Mommsen (*Strafrecht* p. 69) passed in A.D. 16 and afterwards further regulated in Claudius' time (Cod. ix 23 § 3) or Nero's (cf. Suet. *Ner.* 17), forbade any writer of a will to insert, even at the testator's dictation, any benefit to himself; and the penalty of banishment, *etc.* under the *lex Cornelia* was incurred by breach of this decree. A legacy so written was cancelled (*pro non scripto habitum est* D. xxxiv 8 fr 1, cf. xxvi 2 fr 29). But a rescript of Antoninus decided that this should not apply, where the writer was a son who would have been entitled to possession of the estate if there had been no will (Cod. viii 23 fr 1).

witnesses[1] and a balance-holder, all Roman citizens (or Junian Latins) of the age of puberty, and all having notice of the purpose, another similarly qualified, acting as purchaser of the household and holding a piece of bronze, says to the testator, 'Thy household and chattels shall be bought by me with this 'bronze[2], and (as some add) this bronze-balance, into my 'guardianship and caretaking, so that thou mayest rightly make 'a will according to the public statute[3].' He then strikes the balance with the bronze and gives the bronze to the testator as a symbol of price. This was the *familiae mancipatio.* Then the testator, holding the tablets of the will, says, 'These things 'as they are written in these tablets and wax so I give, so 'I bequeath, so I declare, and so do ye, Quirites, bear me 'witness.' This statement by the testator was called *nuncupatio,* that is, an open naming and confirmation in general of what he had written in detail in the tablets; Ulpian calls it *nuncupatio et testatio.* In short (to employ terms of English law), the mancipation is a formal conveyance of the whole estate of the testator to the uses of his will, and the nuncupation is the declaration of uses (Gai. ii 102—104; Ulpian xx 2, 8, 9; D. xxviii 1 fr 21 § 2). A will duly prepared is not a good will, if the intended testator die before declaring it, nor can it be upheld as codicils though it may contain trusts. So Ant. Pius decreed (D. xxxii fr 11 § 1).

[1] More witnesses might be used. Paul (iii 4A § 10), apparently counting the usual company (witnesses, balance-holder, and purchaser) as seven, says *Plures quam septem ad testamentum adhibiti non nocent.* (N.B. *adhibere* is the technical word: Paul uses it eight times in this chapter.)

[2] So in the will of C. Longinus Castor of which a Greek translation is given in *Aegypt. Urkund. aus Berlin* fasc. 10 No. 326 (*apud* Girard *Textes* p. 725, also *ZRG.* xxix p. 198), we have *οἰχετίαν χρήματα ταύτης διαθήκης γενομένης ἐπρίατο Ἰούλιος Πετρωνιανὸς σηστερτίου νόμμου ἑνὸς, etc. i.e. familiam pecuniam hujus testamenti facti emit Julius Petronianus sestertio nummo uno.*

[3] Gaius' MS. requires some correction. I have followed Krüger and Studemund's text in the first part, and Salkowski (*ZRG.* xvi 199) in substituting *tutelam* for *mandatelam tuam* (Salk. has *tutela*). Other modes of correcting are seen in the editions. All come to much the same.

To make any change in the will the whole ceremony must be gone through again; but an explanation to identify a person or the kind of money intended was probably allowable. A will need not be written, but in that case the heirs must be named openly, so that the witnesses can hear them (D. xxviii 1 fr 21 pr § 1).

In theory the whole business lay between testator and purchaser, and, as *domestici testes adhibendi non sunt*[1], no person in the power of either or under the same power, or the father of either at the time, could be witness or balance-holder, for the balance-holder ranked also as a witness. But persons standing in these relations to the real heir or to a legatee, as also the heirs and legatees themselves, were eligible, though Gaius says the heir himself[2], his family-superior, and those in his power ought not to be witnesses. And if a son under power, while still a soldier, made a will respecting his camp-*peculium*, his father or brother could be a witness, but after his discharge neither his father nor anyone in his father's power was a good witness.

Neither deaf nor dumb nor mad nor ward nor woman nor slave[3] could be either purchaser of the household or witness or balance-holder (Gai. ii 103—108; Ulp. xx 7; Dig. xxviii 1 fr 20 §§ 2—7; fr 21 pr § 1).

A will in these times was usually written with a *stylus* on boards (*tabulae*) coated with thin wax and surrounded with a rim of wood. One board (or more if necessary) was coated on both

[1] Cicero appears to have thought differently: see *Att.* xii 18 *Quod scribis Terentiam de obsignatoribus mei testamenti loqui,...equidem domesticos jusseram.* But he does not appear to have had any witnesses who were within Gaius' prohibition.

[2] The rule was not always observed in Cicero's time: cf. *Mil.* 18 § 48 *Cyrum Clodius Roma proficiscens reliquerat morientem. Una fui, testamentum simul signavi cum Clodio: testamentum autem palam fecerat, et illum heredem et me scripserat.* But there may have been sufficient witnesses besides. Ulpian (D. xxviii 1 fr 20 pr) says decisively *Qui testamento heres instituitur in eodem testamento testis esse non potest.*

[3] Where the witnesses were by general consent, at and since the time of the will's being made, held to be freemen, Hadrian held that no question as to their being slaves should be raised (Cod. vi 23 fr 1).

sides, two others on one side only. The three (or more) were so fastened together as to have two bare outsides and four (or more) waxen pages inside. The will was written on the inside pages, the testator's name being written first, and, according to a *SC.* in Nero's time, nothing else on the first two pages (*cerae*)[1]. Strings passed through holes in the rim, tied all the tablets together so as not to shew the contents of the will, which was sealed up (*obsignatum*) by the five witnesses and apparently by the balance-holder and purchaser, making seven in all[2]. Each used a seal, either his own or another's, and his name (in genitive case) was written against it (*adscriptum*). A seal without a name and a name without a seal went for nothing, at least according to the Digest (xxviii 1 fr 22 § 4). It was thought desirable (*convenit*) that each witness should write his own name himself, and even whose will he was witnessing (*ib.* fr 30); but this could not have been insisted on. The expression *tabulae testamenti* could be used whatever the material, *e.g.* paper, parchment, or other skin (D. xxxvii 11 fr 1 pr). One or more duplicates were often executed (D. xxviii 1 fr 24; xxxi fr 47). The date (*dies et consules*) was usually added at the end of the will, but was not

[1] Suet. *Ner.* 17 *Adversus falsarios tunc primum repertum, ne tabulae nisi pertusae ac ter lino per foramina trajecto obsignarentur: cautum ut testamentis primae duae, testatorum modo nomine inscripto, vacuae signaturis ostenderentur.* The earlier use is seen in Horace (*Sat.* ii 5 51) *Qui testamentum tradet tibi cumque legendum abnuere et tabulas a te removere memento, sic tamen ut limis rapias quid prima secundo cera velit versu, solus multisne coheres, veloci percurre oculo.*

The *Lex Cornelia testamentaria* (Cic. *Verr.* II 1 42 § 108) made criminal, if done wittingly and fraudulently, any tampering with a will, or writing or reading aloud a false one (Paul v 25 § 1; D. xlviii 10 fr 1, 2, *etc.*). Cicero says of *Oppianicus*: *Eadem hac Dinaea testamentum faciente cum tabulas prehendisset Oppianicus, digito legata delevit, et, cum id multis locis fecisset, post mortem ejus, ne lituris coargui posset, testamentum in alias tabulas transcriptum signis adulterinis obsignavit* (*Clu.* 14 § 41).

[2] Karlowa (*RG.* ii p. 856) and Erman (*ZRG.* xxxiii p. 189) make the seventh seal that of *antestatus*, not of purchaser. But see my note (Book IV ch. iii D) on *antestatus.* The purchaser is not technically a witness, he seals as a party, in like way as the vendor and surety seal in mancipation-sales (Bruns No. 105 with note). [Theodosius (A.D. 439) directed a will to be sealed at the same time by seven Roman citizens of full age, Cod. Just. vi 23 fr 21.]

necessary to its validity (Fragm. Modest. *Jus Antejust.* ii p. 161; cf. D. xxix 3 fr 2 § 6).

There was no subscription in the modern sense, either by testator or witnesses. The transaction was conceived as oral: the written will was a record originally of the testator's declaration, whether made at the *comitia*, or to his comrades on the eve of battle or to those present at the mancipation, afterwards a record of intention, on tablets shewn to the witnesses and confirmed by nuncupation: closing and sealing was to ensure the document from being tampered with: the name of the witness was added against his seal to shew who should be summoned to the opening of the will. (See Bruns' Essay, *Die Unterschriften, etc.* reprinted in *Kleine Schriften* ii.)[1]

4. CODICILS.

Justinian's Institutes (ii 25) contain an account of the origin of codicils which gives some interesting details. Nothing was known of codicils before the time of Augustus. L. Lentulus on setting out to Africa[2] wrote some small books of tablets (*codicillos*) addressed to Augustus, requesting him to do something by way of trust. The tablets were confirmed by his will, which appears to have appointed Augustus and others heirs. Augustus called together a number of lawyers, among them Trebatius, who was a great authority at that time, and consulted them whether such a practice was not so contrary to the principles of the law as to make codicils inadmissible.

[1] Bruns has shewn that *subscribere, subscriptio* does not as with us denote the writing of the name, but either the date (*e.g. actum Romae Titio Maevio coss.*), or (in letters, *etc.*) the greeting (*Vale, etc.*), or an expression of approval (*e.g. legi*), or is a sign of the copy being true to the original (*recognovi*), sometimes with the writer's name as subject in the nominative (*e.g. L. Titius testis signavi*): it denotes in fact anything added at the end of a completed document. The name alone, as in the modern fashion, appears to be first found (in Roman documents) appended with a seal to a law by the Emperor Romanus in 924 A.D. The Merovingian kings however used it in the 6th or 7th century. See also Mommsen *ZRG.* xxv 252 sqq.

[2] See Krüger's edition. I distrust Theophilus here as elsewhere on historical matters. The account in general is no doubt taken from Marcian or some other good authority. I have given what I think is the meaning.

Trebatius recommended its acceptance on the ground that journeys were often so long that Romans might find it urgent to make a will, but have difficulty in making a formal one, although they might be able to write codicils. Augustus accordingly performed the trusts as he was requested, and so also did the other heirs, and Lentulus' daughter paid some legacies which she was not legally bound to pay. Codicils thus received recognition, and, when Labeo made codicils himself, no doubt was entertained of their legality.

No special form was required for codicils: they might be made more than once: and need not be either written or sealed by the testator, even though in his will previously made he had declared that no others should be valid. But they must be made by one who had the power of making a will and must be intended as codicils, not as a will[1] (D. xxix 7 fr 1, 6 §§ 1—3; xxxi fr 89 pr; xxxii fr 11 § 1).

In the ordinary course codicils presume a will either made or to be made, and an heir or heirs thereby duly appointed: and, if the will is broken or not entered on, the legacies and trusts given by codicils fail[2]. A will may confirm codicils either afterwards by express reference or by clear indication of approval of the contents, or, if made before the codicils, by some such declaration in the will as *quicquid in codicillis scripsero, ratum esto.* A rescript of Severus and Caracalla (Just. ii. 25 § 1) appears to have reversed the burden of proof in case of a trust left by codicils before a will, and allowed the trust to stand if not clearly revoked. Codicils could not disinherit anyone or appoint an heir[3], except where, an heir having been already

[1] A practice grew up (after our period) of adding to wills a clause declaring that, if not valid as a will, it should be taken as codicils (cf. Cod. vi 36 fr 8 = Cod. Theod. iv 4 fr 7). Traces of recognition of such a principle are found in D. xxxi fr 88 § 17; xxviii 3 fr 12 § 1; tit. 6 fr 41 § 3; Cod. vi 36 fr 1; and in a soldier's will D. xxix 1 fr 3 and cf. fr 19 § 1; see also Bruns[6] No. 103; Girard *Textes* p. 727.

[2] Cf. Plin. *Ep.* ii 16 § 1 *Admones me codicillos Aciliani, qui me ex parte instituit heredem, pro non scriptis habendos, quia non sint confirmati testamento. Quod jus ne mihi quidem ignotum est, cum sit iis etiam notum qui nihil aliud sciunt...A me tamen ut confirmati observabuntur.*

[3] Where heirs in substitution were appointed by codicils, and the heir

appointed, the will reserved power to appoint others. If the heir appointed by the will was dead when codicils were made imposing legacies on him, the Sabinians held that they were good against the substituted heir, but the Proculians and Scaevola held that such codicils, whether giving or recalling legacies, being addressed to a non-existent person, were invalid. If two heirs had been appointed and one was dead when the codicils were made, the other would be *prima facie* liable for the whole, but by a plea of fraud could resist a suit for more than in proportion to his share of the inheritance (Gai. ii 270 *a*, 273; D. xxix 7 fr 3 § 2, fr 5, 10, 14; xxviii 5 fr 78; tit. 7 fr 10; Cod. vi 36 fr 1 pr, fr 3). In questions of fact, *e.g. vestis quae mea est,* or the existence or age of the legatee, or the solvency of the testator when enfranchising slaves, the time of making the codicils is decisive. Otherwise the codicils speak as if part of the will (D. xxix 7 fr 2 § 2, cf. tit. 3 fr 11). Freedoms given by codicils are, for the calculation of the *lex Fufia Caninia,* counted with, but rank after, those given by will (Paul iv 14 § 2).

By way of trust codicils might be addressed to the successor *ab intestato,* as if the maker were content, instead of naming an heir by will himself, to take whomever the law eventually assigned. The language would run *e.g. quisquis mihi heres erit bonorumve possessor ejus fidei committo,* and such codicils were not broken by the subsequent birth of an own heir or next agnate, for such persons would come, as statutable heirs, within the succession contemplated by the codicil-maker. So the heir appointed by a will might by codicils be charged to transfer the inheritance wholly or partly to someone else, whether the will confirmed the codicils or not. When a son was born after the date of the codicils, he would not be liable for legacies given by them, but the previously existent heir or heirs *ab intestato* would be liable, though only in proportion to their shares in the inheritance (Gai. ii 270, 270 *a*, 273; D. xxix 7 fr 3 pr, 16, 19).

appointed by will died *impubes,* the mother succeeding *ab intestato* was by a kindly interpretation held to be trustee for the substitutes (D. xxxvi 1 fr 78).

5. Opening a will.

The law was that the will should be opened immediately after the death of the testator. Rescripts of the emperors modified this; so that the rule came to be that, where the persons concerned were on the spot, the tablets should be opened within three or five days from the death; where the persons were absent, then within the same period from their return. Delay was regarded as prejudicial to the interests of heirs, legatees, and slaves freed by the will, as well as to the interests of the revenue; which was interested on account of the 5 per cent. tax (*vicesima hereditatum*) imposed on inheritances by Augustus, to whose law the rules for opening wills are to be attributed.

The ceremony of opening was this. All or the majority of the witnesses who had sealed the will are got together by the praetor's order; the seals are recognised, the thread is broken, the will is opened and read aloud, and opportunity is given for taking a copy. A will made by the father for a child under age is deemed part of the father's will, but, if separately sealed, is not opened unless the praetor order it, as for instance to ascertain who is appointed caretaker to a *venter* in possession. The will is then sealed up with the public seal and deposited in the archives, where on application to the praetor it can be got at and again copied, if the copy taken be lost, or can be inspected by interested parties.

In other places than Rome, whether *municipia, coloniae, oppida, praefecturae, vici, castella, conciliabula,* the rule was for the will to be opened in the *forum* or *basilica* in the presence of the witnesses: or, if they are absent and there is urgent reason for opening the will, then in the presence of some respectable men, between the second and tenth hours of the day (7 A.M. to 4 P.M.?): and read aloud, a copy taken and the will sealed up again by those present[1]. When witnesses could not attend, the will was sent to them to recognise their seals (Paul iv 6; D. xxix 3 fr 4—9).

[1] In Bruns' *Fontes* No. 103 is a protocol of proceedings at the opening of a will at Ravenna A.D. 474, such as in the text.

Anyone who opened a will elsewhere or otherwise than the law prescribed was liable to a penalty of 5000 sesterces (Paul iv 6 § 2 A).

The ownership of the will itself was in the heir, who could vindicate it. But anyone interested could obtain its production before the praetor and inspect or copy it. The praetor however required evidence of the death of the testator; and for fear of forgeries did not permit the date to be inspected or copied (D. xxix 3 fr 2 §§ 4—6). An interdict was issued to heirs and successors to enforce production with damages to the extent of applicant's interest (*e.g.* the amount of inheritance or of legacy), and was not limited to a year. If a legatee thus got damages for the whole amount from the heir, the heir need not pay the legacy. The interdict was not issued when there was a controversy about the inheritance depending on the will, which was then to be deposited in a temple or with a responsible person (D. xliii 5).

6. *SC. Silanianum.*

If a person was said to have been killed by his slaves (*a familia occisus*), a decree of the Senate (*SC. Silanianum*[1]) prohibited any entry on the inheritance or application for possession of the estate until the slaves had been put to the question. An heir, who merely on this account refrained from entry and died, still transmitted his rights to his heir, who could bring *utiles actiones*. The praetor in his edict provided that no one, knowing of the death and the prohibition (*sciens dolo malo*), should have the will or any document thereto belonging opened, read out, or copied before this had been done and the guilty slaves punished

[1] This decree is generally referred to A.D. 10, when Cornelius Dolabella and Junius Silanus were consuls. A further decree was made in the following year. In A.D. 57 another decree subjected to penalty slaves under the same roof set free by the deceased's will (Tac. *An.* xiii 32). This is apparently what is called *SC. Neronianum* in Paul iii 5 § 5; *Pisonianum* (D. xxix 5 fr 8), and *Claudianum* in rubric of D. xxix 5. The consuls of the year were Nero Claudius Caesar and Calpurnius Piso. A severe application of the decree is recorded in A.D. 61, when 400 slaves were put to death, C. Cassius the lawyer being the advocate of severity in the senate (Tac. *An.* xiv 42).

(Paul iii 5 § 1; D. xxix 5 fr 1 § 18). An heir not observing this rule forfeits the inheritance to the Crown (legacies and freedoms however being preserved), and pays a fine of 100000 sesterces, of which half goes to the informer. By a decree of the senate passed A.D. 11 proceedings had to be taken within five years (Paul *ib.* §§ 12 *a*, 13).

Even if it was known who was the killer, the decree still applied in order to ascertain who contrived the act. Moreover it was the duty of the slaves to protect their master, by force if possible, at any rate by shouts for assistance, even at the risk of their own life, as was positively declared by a rescript of Hadrian. All who were under the same roof or attending their master on a journey, perhaps all who were within hearing of a cry, and had not done their best to defend him, were deemed guilty and were punished. Others were punished only if they knew of the attack. Exempt even from the question, as a rule, were slaves on distant parts of the estate or confined so as to be unable to help, or under the age of puberty, or disabled by illness, or deaf, or mute, or blind, or mad, or who were cleared by their master. It was only violent death to which the decree applied: secret poisoning was not within the decree, for slaves could not help against that; and though the heir was bound to avenge the death on those who were guilty or cognisant, the opening of the will need not be deferred. Only a man's own slaves (wholly or partly) were liable: a slave of whom he had the usufruct was not. A father's slaves were liable where his son (even, according to Ulpian, if not in his power) was killed, and a son's slaves, according to the better opinion, were liable, if the father was killed. So also (by a decree in Nero's time), the slaves of the husband and those of the wife living together were liable in the case of either's death; but the mother's were not liable in the case of the death of her son or daughter. A father-in-law's slaves were by some held to be liable, though not within the senate's decree. If a son who was disinherited was killed, the father's slaves were not under the decree, unless the will proved ineffectual, so that if he had lived he would have been owner.

The decree did not apply to cases of suicide, though if slaves were present and could have prevented it, they were punished, unless the suicide was due merely to weariness of life or intolerance of pain. Nor did it apply when a husband killed his wife detected in adultery; but it did apply if husband or wife killed the other in the night, and the slaves heard. A master attacked, but not killed, can deal with his slaves himself, and his case is not within the decree.

Slaves bequeathed or set free by the will, either absolutely or on condition, were still liable to be put to question; but if there was an absolute trust for a slave's freedom Ant. Pius directed that he should not be at once put to question, and perhaps only if proved to be an accomplice. If a slave punished under this decree had been sold, the purchaser was entitled to the value. By a constitution of Trajan freedmen, who had been set free by testator in his lifetime, were liable to the question (Paul l. c., D. xxix 5 fr 1—3, 6, 8—11, 13—15, 25 § 2).

B. Contents of will.

1. Appointment of heir.

Besides a competent testator and due observance of formalities in making a will, it is requisite that there should be a due appointment (*institutio*) of heir. The regular mode is to use these words, 'Titius shall be my heir' (*Titius heres esto*)[1]. And this is a complete will, if testator does not disinherit anyone or leave legacies. 'I bid Titius to be my heir,' had come by Gaius' time to be perfectly accepted.

Most lawyers disapproved altogether of such forms as 'I make' or 'appoint (*facio, instituo*) Titius heir'; and the expression 'I will (*volo*) Titius to be heir' was clearly not accepted (Gai. ii 116, 117; Ulp. xxi; D. xxviii 5 fr 1), no doubt because such expressions indicated rather a present intention or action than the command of a master for the future of his estate. *Legem suae rei dicit* (cf. D. xxiii 4 fr 20 § 1). If the will was

[1] In accordance with a rescript by Ant. Pius the lawyers came to hold even '*Lucius heres*' or '*Lucius esto*' or '*Lucius*' alone to be sufficient, at least in some circumstances (D. xxviii 5 fr 1 § 5).

oral, and the heir was present, the word *hic* was enough (D. fr 59 pr).

2. Own heirs.

According to the XII tables a *paterfamilias* had power to appoint anyone he chose as heir and to make such disposition of his property as he chose (*uti legassit suae rei, ita jus esto* Gai. ii 224; D. L 16 fr 120). But children forming part of his family were recognised both by the civil law and by the praetor as having claims to succeed, which a testator of sound mind must deal with in some way, if his will is to have full effect. They are *sui heredes*, 'own heirs,' because, says Gaius (ii 157), they are of the home (*domestici*), and are in some sort regarded as owners (*domini*) even in the lifetime of their parent[1]. On his death, says Paul (D. xxviii 2 fr 11; cf. *Sent.* iv 8 § 6), they do not so much acquire the inheritance for the first time as come to the free administration of the estate. They are heirs without entry, as a matter of course (*ipso jure*, D. xxxviii 16 fr 14). They are sometimes called *sui et necessarii heredes* (*e.g.* Gai. ii 152, 156), but the expression ceased to be suitable when the praetor allowed them to decline the inheritance, provided they had not meddled with the estate (Gai. ii 157, 163). There is some difference however in the incidents of the several components of this class (Ulp. xxii 14, 15; Gai. iii 2—6; Paul v 8 §§ 4—7). The components are:

(*a*) Sons and daughters in testator's power, whether alive at the date of the will or born afterwards (*postumi*), even, according to the Sabinians (Cod. vi 29 fr 3), though they died

[1] Pliny uses similar language in speaking of the 5 % tax (*vicesima*) on inheritances (see p. 24). He calls it *Tributum tolerabile et facile heredibus dumtaxat extraneis, domesticis grave. Itaque illis inrogatum est, his remissum, videlicet quod manifestum erat quanto cum dolore laturi, seu potius non laturi, homines essent destringi aliquid et abradi bonis quae sanguine, gentilitate, sacrorum denique societate meruissent, quaeque numquam ut aliena et speranda sed ut sua semperque possessa ac deinceps proximo cuique transmittenda cepissent* (*Panegyr.* 37). So Cicero speaks of Verres' treatment of a daughter who was left heir to her father: *Quibuscum bona nostra partimur, iis praetor adimere, nobis mortuis, bona fortunasque poterit?* (*Verr.* ii 1 44 § 113).

without uttering a cry. But a child by one who is not a lawful wife (*justa uxor*) is not 'own heir' (cf. Gai. ii 241).

(*b*) Grandsons and granddaughters by a son of testator, who at the time of testator's death is dead or emancipated (leaving them in their grandfather's power) or in some other way no longer in testator's power[1]. (In the case of captivity rights are in suspense.) Great-grandchildren are in the like position, if their father and grandfather are likewise no longer in testator's power. But a grandchild, *etc.* conceived after his father has left the testator's family or after the death of his grandfather is not an 'own' heir to the grandfather (Gai. ii 241; D. xxviii 3 fr 6 pr; xxxviii 16 fr 1 §§ 4—8; fr 8).

(*c*) Adopted children are in the same position as if they were natural children (*naturalium loco sunt*), but if they are afterwards emancipated by their adoptive father, they cease to be 'own heirs' to him, neither are they counted among his children[2] either by civil law or by the praetor. Thus, while in the adoptive family, they are strangers to their natural father, and, when emancipated, they are as if they had been emancipated by their natural father, without passing through adoption (Gai. ii 136, 137).

(*d*) A wife in hand and a daughter in law in a son's hand are respectively counted as a daughter and granddaughter to the testator (*filiae* or *neptis loco et quasi sua heres*); but the daughter in law is an own heir only if her husband has ceased

[1] Such a grandson is not an 'own' heir so as to require to be noticed in the will, if his father is alive at testator's death, but he is an own heir so as to be entitled to succeed to his grandfather's intestate inheritance, although his father is alive at testator's death, provided he was himself conceived before that date and his father died before the succession was ascertained to be *ab intestato*. Cf. D. xxviii 3 fr 6 pr *Agnascendo is rumpit quem nemo praecedebat mortis tempore; ab intestato vero is succedit cui ante eum alii non est delata hereditas: non fuisse autem filio delatam hereditatem apparet, cum deliberante instituto decesserit. Sed haec ita, si mortis avi tempore in utero nepos fuit. Ceterum si postea conceptus est, Marcellus scribit neque ut suum neque ut nepotem aut cognatum ad hereditatem vel ad bonorum possessionem posse admitti.*

[2] *inter liberos*, for which *ex liberis* is also used (D. xxxvii 4 fr 1 § 6, fr 8 § 12).

to be in testator's power before his death (Gai. ii 139, 156, 159; iii 3).

(*e*) Sons in process of emancipation, after the first or second mancipation revert under their father's power, and become again own heirs. Not so after a third mancipation (Gai. ii 141).

(*f*) Children, whose father has proved his claim to citizenship under the *lex Aelia Sentia* or subsequent senate's decree, or has been granted citizenship by the emperor, are own heirs, if they have thereby become in their father's power. In some cases under the *lex Aelia Sentia* they would not be in his power; and under a grant from the Emperor they would be so only if their father had applied to have them in his power and obtained it (Gai. ii 135 *a*, cf. i 93, 94).

No woman has own heirs (D. xxxviii 16 fr 13).

Own heirs must be noticed in their father's will, either by being appointed heirs (alone or with others) or by being formally disinherited; else the will is, in the case of a son, wholly, in the case of other own heirs partially, invalid (see chap. V B). Disherison may be either express (*nominatim*) or in general terms. For sons whether alive[1] or postumous[2] disherison must

[1] A case is given by Cicero (*Orat.* i 38 § 175) where a father, crediting false news of his son's death while serving in the army, changed his will and appointed someone else heir. The son returning home after his father's death brought a suit for his father's inheritance before the centumviri (*lege egit in hereditatem*) as a son disinherited by the will. Cicero states that the question thereby raised was whether by the civil law a son could be disinherited from his father's estate who had been neither made heir by his father's will nor disinherited in express terms (*possetne paternorum bonorum exheres esse filius quam pater testamento neque heredem neque exheredem scripsisset nominatim*). This seems to me to accord best with the supposition that testator after appointing an heir added *ceteri exheredes sunto* as usual. Karlowa (*RG.* ii p. 889) supposes him to have added nothing to the appointment of heir. That is possible, but *nominatim* at the end of the sentence leads me to differ. Cicero does not mention the court's decision, but speaks of the case as most important.

Augustus by edict prohibited the disherison of a son who was a soldier, but this was repealed subsequently (D. xxviii 2 fr 26).

[2] That the disherison of a postumous son should be express is due apparently to a decree of M. Aurelius; *idem in postumo quod in filio servandum* (D. xxviii 3 fr 3 § 2).

be express, in such words as *Filius meus exheres esto,* the name being either added or not. The disherison must be absolute. Thus *Titius heres esto: cum heres erit Titius, filius exheres esto* is not a valid disherison, any more than *quisquis heres mihi erit, filius exheres esto,* the disherison being in words made dependent on and posterior to the appointment of an heir. For the case of a postumous son the right words are *quicunque mihi filius genitus fuerit, exheres esto,* or simply *postumus exheres esto*[1]. Daughters and grandchildren, if own heirs, may be disinherited either expressly or in general terms, viz. by adding, after the appointment of heirs, *Ceteri omnes exheredes sunto.* It was necessary however, if a postumous daughter was disinherited in such terms, to shew that she was not overlooked by bequeathing something to her. This was by the *lex Junia Vellaea* (Gai. ii 127—132, 134 partly mutilated; Ulp. xxii 16—22; D. xxviii 2 fr 3 § 2; tit. 3 fr 3; tit. 5 fr 69). The disherison of a son might precede the appointment of any heirs, as if to clear the way. If there are two or more grades of heirs (the second succeeding in default of the first, *etc.*), every grade in which a son is neither appointed heir nor validly disinherited (unless appointed heir in a previous grade) counts for nothing, no other heir being validly appointed, if on a right interpretation of the will a son in testator's power has been passed over. And the death of the son before the testator does not cure the invalidity according to the Sabinian school (which was herein followed by the Digest): the Proculians thought, if the son was out of the way, the written heirs could enter without hindrance (Gai. ii 123; D. xxviii 2 fr 3, 7, 14 § 1; tit. 6 fr 43, § 2). Emancipated children could be passed over with impunity according to the civil law, but the praetor required them to be made heirs or disinherited, all males expressly, females either expressly or *inter ceteros*; otherwise he granted *bonorum possionem contra tabulas* (Gai. ii 135 cf. 129; Ulp. xxii 23). See chap. V A.

Postumous children primarily are those born after their father the testator's death[2], but children born in his lifetime

[1] Ulpian (xxii 22) puts postumous grandsons in the same position as daughters, but says express disherison was safer and more usual.

[2] Called by modern writers *postumi legitimi.*

after the date of the will are also reckoned such. Grandchildren, if their father is still in the testator's family, are not own heirs to testator, but if their father die before testator, or is captured by the enemy and does not return, or is emancipated, or otherwise ceases to belong to testator's family before testator's death, his children (even if conceived in captivity) thereby become own heirs to the testator and have a right to recognition. Great-grandchildren may become in the same position, if all the persons intervening between them and testator drop away from his family. All such grandchildren and great-grandchildren will possibly be *postumorum loco*, and, owing to technical difficulties, such as the rule against appointing as heirs uncertain persons, might at one time have invalidated their ancestor's will, without his being able to prevent it. These risks of invalidity were gradually removed. Aquilius Gallus introduced a form of clause[1] for appointing contingently as heirs postumous children of a son alive at the will, if he should die before testator and they be born after testator's death[2]: and a *lex Junia Vellaea* (passed probably about 27 A.D.) provided, if due recognition were made by testator, against his will being invalidated[3] either by the subsequent birth of own heirs in his lifetime[4], or by descendants

[1] The clause is thus given: *Si filius meus vivo me morietur, tunc siquis mihi ex eo nepos sive quae neptis post mortem meam in decem mensibus proximis quibus filius meus moreretur (morietur?) natus nata erit, heredes sunto.* The form would be modified to refer to great grandsons, *etc. Si me vivo nepos decedat, tunc qui ex eo pronepos, etc.* (D. xxviii 2 fr 29 pr—§ 4).

[2] *postumi Aquiliani.*

[3] The invalidation by subsequent birth of a son is treated as certain by Cicero (*Orat.* i 57 § 241) *Num quis eo testamento quod paterfamilias ante fecit, quam ei filius natus esset, hereditatem petit? Nemo; quia constat agnascendo rumpi testamentum; Caecin.* 25 § 72 *Hoc dici non potest: statue, cui filius agnatus sit, ejus testamentum non esse ruptum.* For *agnascendo, agnatio* ('additional birth') see below, p. 207.

Where a will instituted as heirs any son or daughter born *intra decem menses proximos mortis meae* or *intra decem mensuum spatium post mortem meam*, and a child was born after his will but before his death, it was an old dispute whether the will was broken because this child was passed over. Justinian decided that it was not (Cod. vi 29 § 4).

[4] *postumi Vellaeani primi capitis.* These are either testator's own children, born after his will, or his grandchildren, *etc.* born after his will

already born at the date of the will becoming own heirs[1] by the death in testator's lifetime of intervening persons. The lawyers extended the application of this clause to cases of departure from the family otherwise than by death. And Julian applied it to descendants born after the date of the will[2] and becoming own heirs by the death, *etc.* of their father before testator (Gai. ii 133, 134; Ulp. xxii 18—22; D. xxvii 2 fr 9 § 2, 29; tit. 3 fr 3 § 1, 6 § 2; cf. tit. 2 fr 28 § 1. See Vangerow *Pand.* § 468).

3. Who else can be heirs.

Besides children and other members of the testator's family, other persons whether free or slave were capable of being appointed heirs. Of free persons only those could be appointed who, as the Romans expressed it, had will-making with the testator (*testamenti factionem cum testatore habent*), *i.e.* who were fellow-citizens at least in this respect[3]. Such *testamenti factio* must exist at the time of making the will, and at the time of testator's death, and also at the time of cretion or entry on the inheritance; but intermediate disqualification does not affect the validity of the appointment, the maxim being *media tempora non nocent* (D. xxviii 5 fr 6 § 2, 50, 51 pr). Thus a *dediticius*, and, by rescript of Ant. Pius, a deported person were disqualified as being foreigners. A Latin was disqualified by the Junian statute, but if at the testator's death or within the period of cretion he is a Roman citizen, the appointment was valid. And the like held under the Julian statute for unmarried persons (*caelibes*). Under the Voconian statute[4] no woman could be appointed heir to a testator who was enrolled

and after the removal of their father, *etc.* from being an own heir, so that they are own heirs at their birth.

[1] *postumi Vellaeani secundi capitis.*

[2] *postumi Juliani.*

[3] Ant. Pius is said by Pausanias (viii 43) to have enabled Greeks who had become Roman citizens to leave their property to their children, even if not Romans: perhaps by *fidei commissum*, cf. Gai. ii 285; Arndt Glück's *Pand.* xlvi p. 381.

[4] The *lex Voconia*, recommended by M. Porcius Cato and passed probably B.C. 169 (Cic. *Sen.* 5 § 14), besides its restrictions on legacies (chap. viii M), enacted: *Qui post eos censores census esset, nequis heredem virginem neve mulierem faceret* (Cic. *Verr.* ii 1 42 § 107). So (*ib.* § 111):

in the burgess-lists as having 100,000 *asses* (Gai. ii 274, 275, 286; Ulp. xxii 1—3; Cod. vi 24 fr 1).

Deaf and dumb persons were not disqualified for being heirs by will. Madmen can be heirs, as necessary heirs to their father or master, or through a slave. As regards other cases there was much dispute (D. xxviii 1 fr 16; tit. 4 fr 1 § 2; xxix 2 fr 63; Cod. v 70 fr 7 § 3).

Gods can be appointed heirs, but only those expressly allowed by senate's decree or imperial constitutions; viz. Tarpeian Jove, Apollo of Didyme at Miletus, Mars in Gaul, Minerva of Ilium, Hercules of Gades, Diana of Ephesus, the mother of the Gods at Sipyle, (Nemesis) who is worshipped at Smyrna, and the heavenly moon[1] at Carthage (Ulp. xxii 6).

An uncertain person could not be appointed heir, as for instance 'whoever shall first come to my funeral.' On account of this uncertainty, says Ulpian, neither a town[2] nor townsmen (*municipes*) can be made heirs, for they cannot all decide on acceptance or act as heirs. But a senate's decree permitted them to be made heirs by their freedmen. A postumous child not in the class of own heirs (*alienus postumus*), *i.e.* one who is conceived but not born at the time of the will, and when born would not be in testator's power, is counted as an uncertain

Annaea pecuniosa mulier quod censa non erat testamento fecit heredem filiam; (§ 104) *P. Annius Asellus mortuus est C. Sacerdote praetore. Is, cum haberet unicam filiam neque census esset, filiam bonis suis heredem instituit.* In this last case Verres when city praetor extended by his edict the prohibition of the Voconian statute to persons who were not *censi*, and took away the inheritance from the daughter, apparently by refusing her both suit for the inheritance and possession of the estate (§ 113). Gaius (ii 274) restricts the Voconian prohibition to cases where the testator was enrolled as having *centum milia aeris* for which Dio Cassius (lvi 10) gives 2500, meaning probably *drachmae* = 100,000 (silver) *sestertii*. Vangerow (*Lex Vocon.* p. 13) points out that 100,000 *asses* was the minimum qualification for the first class of the Servian organization. *Fidei commissa* enabled the law to be evaded (chap. ix). Vestal virgins were excepted from the law and allowed to receive inheritances (Cic. *RP.* iii 10).

[1] *Selenen* is Böcking's emendation for the MS. *Selinensem.* But *Caelestis* may be a proper name, cf. *Hist. Aug. Pertin.* 4 *Vaticinationes carminum de templo Caelestis emergunt* and others quoted by Muirhead *ad loc.*

[2] Cf. Plin. *Ep.* v 7 *Nec heredem institui nec praecipere posse rempublicam constat.* See also under *praeceptio* (chap. viii A 4).

person. Such a one *e.g.* is a grandson begotten by testator's son after emancipation; a son (of testator's) by a woman who is not deemed a wife by the civil law, *etc.* Nor was it a good appointment to say 'My heir shall be whomever Titius shall have willed' (*heres esto quem Titius voluerit*), the rule being well established by the early lawyers that rights under a testament should be given by the testator to persons of his own and not of others' selection (Gai. ii 241, 242; Ulp. xxii 4, 5, xxiv 18; D. xxviii 5 fr 32 pr). But it is not a bad appointment to leave to some event, *e.g.* marriage with a certain woman, to decide which of certain persons, all known to testator, shall be heir (D. *ib.* fr 9 §§ 10, 11).

Where by a mistake one person has been named heir instead of another, neither is duly appointed, the former not being willed, and the latter not being named. The name is not necessary, if there be an unmistakable and not contumelious designation of the person intended. A wrong description, *e.g.* a wrong *nomen*, *praenomen*, or *cognomen*, or wrong father or country *etc.*, if added, does not vitiate the appointment if the person is ascertained[1]. If there are several persons of the same name, and it is not clear which was intended, the appointment is void (D. xxviii 5 fr 9 pr, § 8, 49 § 3; Cod. vi 23 fr 4).

It was a rule of the civil law that inheritance could not be taken away. Hence no effect was given to words in the same will cancelling an appointment of heir (D. xxviii 2 fr 13 § 1), or to codicils imposing a condition which by its failure might nullify the appointment (*ib.* 7 fr 27 § 1). Where an heir's name was intentionally crossed out, it was deemed never to have been inserted (D. xxviii 4 fr 1 § 4). If a person is appointed as a son, and he really is not, and the testator would not have appointed him had he known the truth, Severus and Antoninus decided the succession should be taken away from him (Cod. vi 24 fr 4; cf. 23 fr 5).

4. Appointment of slaves as heirs.

A slave can be appointed heir, but cannot actually become heir in his own person unless he be free. If he be the testator's

[1] See a curious discussion in Cod. vi 24 fr 14.

own slave, the appointment must be coupled with a grant of freedom: otherwise it is bad. If he be set free before testator's death, he is like any other outsider, free to accept the inheritance or not. If he be the slave of another at the time of the will or become so by testator's alienation, he can accept only by order of his master for the time being (whether the same or not as at the making of the will), who by the slave's entry becomes heir at once, just as if he had been himself appointed by the testator. Testator's slave, appointed heir without a grant of freedom and alienated by the testator in his lifetime, cannot be heir, even if his new master bid him accept, the appointment being bad *ab initio.* But if appointed free conditionally and alienated, he can on the condition being fulfilled enter at the bidding of his master. A grant of freedom to another's slave counts for nothing, even if he be acquired by testator after making his will. Only those slaves belonging to others could be appointed heirs, whose masters had, as above defined, will-making with the testator (Gai. ii 187—189; Ulp. xxii 9, 12, 13; Paul iii 4 § 7; D. xxviii 5 fr 50, 51 pr, 38 § 2).

A testator's own slave is properly appointed heir in such words as 'my slave Stichus shall be free and heir,' or 'shall be heir and free.' If testator in a later part of his will take away the freedom, the slave becomes heir and free all the same, because of the rule that inheritance once given cannot be taken away. If the freedom is deferred to a future time or made dependent on a condition, the heirship, although absolute in the will, is consequently deferred or dependent in the same way, and becomes effective only on the freedom's becoming effective by occurrence of the condition or by manumission in testator's lifetime. But an appointment of a slave to be heir *cum liber erit,* though good for another's slave, is bad for testator's own slave, because one who has the power of giving freedom ought not to make it a matter of chance (Gai. ii 186, 188; Ulp. xxii 11, 12; D. xxviii 2 fr 13 § 1; tit. 5 fr 3 § 1; tit. 7 fr 21, 22). If the usufruct in the slave is alienated by testator in his lifetime, the slave becomes free and heir on the expiry of the usufruct. If the slave is in pledge, by a rescript of Severus he becomes free and heir on satisfying the creditor. A slave who is not testator's in full Quiritary right but only *in bonis*, becomes only a Latin, and as such cannot take as heir. One who is the common property of testator and another becomes free only so far as testator's share is concerned, and theory would make such partial grant of freedom enure only to extinguish testator's ownership of the slave, leaving him by accretion the sole property of the other partner (cf. Paul iv 12 § 1). Much discussion took place on this point, and first a constitution of Severus as regards soldiers' wills, and then a constitution of Severus and Antoninus as regards all wills, directed (in accordance with the opinion of Sex. Caecilius) that, where a partner gave liberty to a common slave, the other owner should be compelled by the praetor to sell his share (D. xxviii 5 fr 9 § 20, fr 30; Ulp. xxii 8, 10; Cod. vii 7 pr § 1; tit. 8).

A slave of testator's, appointed free and heir, becomes heir of necessity, *nolens volens*, and hence is called a 'necessary heir': and this holds good even if he has been alienated by testator and repurchased. A senate's decree[1] required that he should not be less than 30 years old, except when the estate was insolvent and there was no other possible heir by the will. For the appointment of a slave to be heir was often made when testator was doubtful of his solvency, in order that, if his estate had to be sold in order to satisfy his creditors, the disgrace (*ignominia*) of such a sale in bankruptcy might fall on him rather than on testator. In compensation for this unfortunate position he was allowed to retain for himself all property acquired since testator's death, and not to be subjected to further sales by the creditors except for such acquisitions as might accrue to testator's estate, as for instance the property of a Latin freedman of the testator[2]. A slave manumitted in compliance with a trust, or with a condition of purchase, or who had bought his own manumission, is not a necessary heir: he can decline the inheritance if he choose (Gai. ii 153—155, 276; cf. iii 56; Ulp. i 14, xxii 11; D. xxviii 5 fr 9 § 16; fr 85).

1 The relation of this decree (Gai. ii 276) to the *lex Aelia Sentia* (Book I chap. ii B) is not clear. Perhaps it was only to confirm the general rule against doubts arising from the exception. See Muirhead on Gai. *l.c.*

2 This appears to be the meaning of Gai. ii 155.

A person does not cease to be 'necessary' heir because in the interval before the will is opened his *status* has been changed (D. *ib.* fr 3 § 4).

Persons in handtake are strictly speaking 'necessary' heirs, freedom being left them with heirship just as to slaves, but the praetor allowed them to decline. 'Own' heirs were also by the civil law 'necessary' heirs (*sui et necessarii*), but the praetor allowed them to keep aloof (*abstinere se*) from (*i.e.* to decline) the inheritance. All outsiders were free to accept or not as they chose. Children not in testator's power (which is the case with all children of a testatrix) rank as outsiders in this respect (Gai. ii 156—162; Ulp. xxii 24).

5. Conditional appointment of heirs.

Heirs cannot be properly appointed, as from a certain time (*ex die*, or *in diem*), or up to a certain time (*ad diem*). Such additions go for nothing (D. xxviii 5 fr 34). But they may be appointed on a condition. If the condition is a possible one, the appointment is in suspense until the condition is fulfilled; if it be impossible at the date of the will, the condition goes for nothing and the appointment is absolute. The possibility of a condition is a question of fact in the particular case; *e.g.* the condition of getting to Alexandria is possible for one within a mile of it, and may be impossible for one in a distant country in the winter. A condition requiring action contrary to the laws or to the emperor's decrees or to good conduct is bad and goes for nothing. Paul gives as instances of such: 'if you do 'not redeem your father from the enemy, if you refuse support '(*alimenta*) to your father or patron, if you refrain from taking 'a wife, if you shall get (*susceperis*) no children, if you commit 'homicide, if you walk in a procession got up as a ghost[1].' So a condition that the heir should throw testator's remains into the sea was not enforceable. Papinian finely said that all acts which do violence to dutiful affection, to fair repute, to respectful modesty, and generally which are opposed to good conduct,

[1] *Si larvali habitu processeris.* Cf. Sen. *Ep.* 24 § 18 *Nemo tam puer est ut Cerberum timeat et tenebras et larvalem habitum nudis ossibus cohaerentibus.*

should be held to be impossible (Paul iii 4 *b* §§ 1, 2; D. xxviii 5 fr 4 § 1; tit. 7 fr 9, 14, 15, 27).

If a son is appointed heir under a condition which it is not in his power to fulfil, or which ought so to be regarded, the condition is not struck out and the appointment of heir left good, but the appointment is treated as bad, because the son is in effect passed over, and the will is therefore null. If however the condition is within his power, and there is no explicit disherison if he does not fulfil the condition, the validity of the will is in suspense, and coheirs cannot enter. If the condition is one which he or someone on his account could fulfil even when the son is dying (*e.g.* paying money to Titius), his death must be awaited before it can be known whether the will is good or the father was intestate. But if the condition is such, that it clearly cannot now be performed by him (*e.g.* going to Alexandria, when the son is dying at Rome) there is no need to wait: the will is seen to be invalid, and the son himself is heir *ab intestato*, and transmits the inheritance: or if a substitute was appointed in case he should not fulfil the condition, the substitute can enter at once as heir to the testator (D. xxviii 2 fr 16; tit. 5 fr 4, 5, 15; tit. 7 fr 28; xxxviii 2 fr 20 § 4; Cod. vi 25 fr 4). Grandsons, *etc.* could be appointed heirs on any and all conditions, the condition if impossible being disregarded (D. xxviii 5 fr 6 § 1; cf. xxxviii 16 fr 1 § 8).

An appointment on condition of the appointee's doing or giving something usually takes effect if he is willing and is prevented by what is beyond his control. Thus if *A* is appointed heir to two-thirds if he marry a certain woman, and *B* to one-third and *vice versa*, then, if she refuse to marry either, they divide the inheritance equally (D. xxviii 7 fr 23, 24; cf. fr 3, 11, 8, § 7; see chap. viii H; and Windscheid *Pand.* § 92).

The appointment of a coheir, when made by way of penalty on the heir's doing or not doing something, was by some lawyers ('not without reason' says Gaius ii 243) held to be invalid.

The requirement of an oath as a condition of being heir was disapproved by the praetor as likely to deter scrupulous persons from taking up the appointment, and allowing unscrupulous to take the oath and then neglect the performance of what was thus intended to be secured. He therefore by a standing rule remitted the oath[1] in all cases, but refused the heir his rights of action unless he performed what the testator thereby enjoined. In fact he converted the substance of the oath into a condition. (The same rule was applied to legacies, trusts and gifts in view of death; and if a legatee died after the legacy was vested, his heir could sue as if no oath had been imposed: D. xxviii 7 fr 8.)

Captatory appointments, *i.e.* where the condition of appointment of *A* as heir to my estate is *A*'s appointment of someone else as heir to his estate, were disapproved if intended to secure a future appointment, and they were invalidated by a senate's decree. But the appointment of *A* as heir to the same share of my estate to which in his will he has already appointed me is not within the decree. Nor is the open reciprocal appointment by two friends of each other as heir (D. xxviii 5 fr 71, 72).

If a testator has added a condition without intending to do so, the will is read as if it had not been inserted. But if he has unintentionally omitted a condition, or a clerk has omitted or changed a condition without testator's intention, the appointment is bad altogether (fr 9 §§ 5, 6).

6. Distribution among heirs.

A testator can appoint as many heirs as he pleases and give them what shares he pleases. If no shares are mentioned, all take equally. The Romans denoted the shares usually by fractions of the *as*, which was divided into twelve *unciae*[2]. A

[1] Cicero mentions the remission by Verres as praetor of an oath which a testator required his heirs to take to give half their shares to testator's brother who had been proscribed by Sulla. Verres treated testator's intention as illegal and allowed the heirs to have possession without taking the oath; and refused possession to a freedman who took the oath (*Verr.* ii 1 47 § 123).

[2] $\frac{11}{12}$ *deunx*, $\frac{10}{12}$ *dextans*, $\frac{3}{4}$ *dodrans*, $\frac{2}{3}$ *bes*, $\frac{7}{12}$ *septunx*, $\frac{1}{2}$ *semis*, $\frac{5}{12}$ *quincunx*, $\frac{1}{3}$ *triens*, $\frac{1}{4}$ *quadrans*, $\frac{1}{6}$ *sextans*, $\frac{1}{12}$ *uncia* (D. xxviii 5 fr 51 § 2). $\frac{1}{8}$ is *sescuncia*, $\frac{1}{24}$ is *semuncia*.

sole heir was *heres ex asse*; heir to three-fourths was *heres ex dodrante*, to two-thirds *ex besse*, to a half *ex semisse*, to a third *ex triente*, and so on. If the shares named add up to more than twelve, the *uncia* will not be in this case a twelfth, but a sixteenth or twentieth or some other proportion, as the case may be. If they add up to less than twelve, the remainder of the *as* is divided between the heirs in the ratio of their shares. If the shares named make up a complete *as*, and still others are appointed heirs either before or after, without their share being named, they will be held to have half the estate, the former shares being reduced from twelfths to twenty-fourths. If the *as*, or it may be two *asses*, are not complete, the heirs with unnamed shares will divide the remainder equally. But any expressions by the testator implying a different distribution must be regarded; and therefore if the *as* is complete and further heirs are added with the words, 'shall be heirs to the remainder,' testator has miscalculated, and, there being no remainder, their appointment is in fact nugatory. If an heir is appointed and the share left to be named in codicils but not there named, he is still treated as heir (D. xxviii 5 fr 13—20, 36, 80; Paul iii 4 *b* § 6). Heir to a part is heir to the whole, if the other appointments fail through non-acceptance, or non-fulfilment of a condition. If some of the heirs are joined in a common share, even though the share is not named, any failure on the part of one or more increases the portion, not of all the heirs in the will, but of those so joined (D. xxviii 5 fr 17 § 1, 64; xxix 2 fr 53 § 2).

If a clerk wrote in the will a smaller share for someone than the testator dictated, the larger share might be upheld, and this view was supported by some rescripts. But if he wrote a larger share, or even if it could be proved that testator had made this mistake himself, the smaller share was thought to be maintainable (D. xxviii 5 fr 9 §§ 3, 4).

An heir being the successor, in whole or in part, to the whole financial position of testator, it is a mistake, instead of giving a legacy, to appoint an heir to, or exclude him from, a particular piece of property, *e.g. Attius fundi Corneliani heres esto: duo Titii illius insulae heredes sunto;* or *Excepto fundo* (or *excepto usufructu*) *Titius heres esto.* The will is read as if the particular property were not attached to, or excluded from[1], the appointment. Thus, in the above case *Attius* will be heir to one half, and the two *Titii* to the other half of testator's whole estate, whatever be the relative value of the farm and the block; and they will be in the same way liable for deceased's debts, *i.e.* Attius to one half, and each Titius to a quarter. The judge in a suit for dividing the inheritance will however assign to the heirs the properties so given, just as if they were legacies (*praelegata*), and arrange for reciprocal bonds. And the same plan is followed if testator make one heir to all his Italian estate and another heir to his provincial estate, what particular slaves or other chattels go with the one or the other respectively being decided by the permanent uses of the several estates, just as in the case of the legacy of a *fundus instructus*. Thus any money sent from Italy into the provinces for the purchase of goods, and the goods so purchased, belong to the heir of the Italian estate (fr 10, 11, 35, 75, 79 pr). An heir appointed to one thing but without any other heir being named becomes heir to testator's whole estate (D. xxviii 6 fr 41 § 8).

7. Substitution.

1. A testator may direct a person to be heir, and if he do not formally decide to accept, substitute another, and, on his failing, another and so on. Or he may substitute one for several persons so failing or several persons for one. When he appoints two or more heirs, it was not unusual to make them reciprocally heirs to any portion which was not accepted, by such words as *quos invicem substituo.* If two or more persons are substituted for a failing portion, they share it equally in the absence of any specific direction: but by a rescript of Ant. Pius, if they are heirs already with unequal shares, they divide according to those shares; *e.g.* if *A*, *B* and *C* are all appointed heirs and reciprocally substituted, and *C* dies or does not accept, then if *A* was heir to half and *B* to a quarter, *A* will now be heir to eight shares and *B* to four. Substitutes to the instituted heirs

[1] This interpretation is credited to Aquilius Gallus (D. xxviii 5 fr 73).

are spoken of as heirs in the second degree[1]; substitutes to substitutes, in the third. The terms in which substitution was made were of some importance. An ordinary form would be *L. Titius heres esto cernitoque in diebus centum proximis quibus scies poterisque. Quodni ita creveris, exheres esto. Tum Maevius heres esto cernitoque in diebus centum, etc.* (see chap. iv C). Under this form it is of no avail to act as heir (*pro herede gerere*): if a formal decision is not pronounced in due time, the first-named heir is absolutely excluded and the substitute comes in. But if the words of disherison (*exheres esto*) are omitted (*imperfecta cretio*) and the first-named heir does not formally decide, but acts in the capacity of heir, he lets in the substitute to share with him equally. According to Sabinus this is so only if the time for formal decision is past, according to others, even before this period (Gai. ii 174—178; D. xxviii. 6 fr 23, 24, 36; Cod. vi 26 fr 1). Marcus Aurelius however ordained that acting as heir should be as effectual as a formal decision to accept, and should not let in the substitute (Ulp. xxii 34). A substitute's heirs in the absence of express words are not entitled to succeed to testator's estate (D. xxxviii 16 fr 9 *sub fin.*).

2. Substitution is allowed by custom (*moribus*) not only in case of non-acceptance of the inheritance (including death before the testator), but also in the case where children, grandchildren, *etc.*, in testator's power, or postumous children, become heirs but die before they attain the age of puberty[2]. This is

[1] The term *secundus heres* is applied to the substitute in Cic. *Clu.* 11 § 33 *Oppianico testamento legat grandem pecuniam a filio, si qui natus esset; ab secundo herede nihil legat; Verr.* ii 1 43 § 110, 115; *Inv.* ii 21 § 62; *Top.* 4 § 21; Hor. *Sat.* ii 5 49.

[2] Cicero gives instances of pupillar wills. A *paterfamilias* married but without children makes his will and says *Si mihi filius genitur unus pluresve, is mihi heres esto.* Then, after other customary arrangements, proceeds *Si filius ante moritur quam in tutelam suam venerit, tum mihi ille* ('so and so') *heres esto.* No son is born. The agnates claimed the inheritance because the condition of the appointment of the substitute had failed (*Inv.* ii 42 § 122). A similar case *Curius* v. *Coponium* which came before the *Centumviri* is frequently mentioned by Cicero (*Orat.* i 39; ii 6; *Brut.* 39 § 144; *Caecin.* 18 § 53; *Top.* 10 § 44). M'. Curius was appointed by will heir *mortuo postumo filio*, or as it is put in *Brut.* 52 § 195 *Si pupillus ante mortuus esset quam ad suam tutelam venisset.* No postumous son was

pupillaris[1] *substitutio* as distinguished from ordinary substitution (*vulgaris substitutio*). The words used would be these: 'Titius 'my son shall be my heir. If my son shall not be heir, or if he 'shall be heir and die before he becomes his own guardian (*in 'suam tutelam venerit*), then Seius shall be heir.' In such a will the substitute Seius becomes heir to the father, if the son does not become heir; and he becomes heir to the son, if the son have become heir and die before puberty. One will therefore deals with two inheritances, or, it may be said, contains two wills, that of the father and that made for the son by his father (Gai. ii 179—180, 183; D. xxviii 6 fr 2 pr)[2]. If the will made mention of only one case (*e.g.* not becoming heir), the substitute was held in accordance with a constitution of M. Aurelius and Verus to be entitled to succeed in the other also (fr 4 pr). Such pupillar substitution could not be made for any outsiders, but could be made for any or all of testator's children in his power, and for such grandchildren or other descendants as are in his power and will not on his death fall into their father's power. It will take effect at any age named by the testator (*e.g.* 'within his tenth year,' *etc.*), but not later than the age of

born. Q. Mucius was advocate for the heir *ab intestato* on the ground that the condition had failed. M. Crassus won the case for Curius, arguing that the intention was to make Curius heir, if there should be no son who came to years of discretion. In Cod. vi 25 fr 10 we have the reverse case: substitute to child's share appointed, if no child born: child born but dies *impubes*. The mother being appointed as part heir, the lawyers differed whether the substitution took effect or the mother was entitled to all. Papinian held the latter view as more likely to be conformable to testator's intention.

[1] *Pupillus est qui, cum impubes est, desiit in patris potestate esse aut morte aut emancipatione* (D. L 16 fr 239 pr).

[2] In Cic. *Inv.* ii 21 §§ 62—64 a case of this kind is put: a father made by will his son heir, and if he should not come to puberty appointed other heirs (*mihi heredes sunto*). The son had other property besides what came from his father. The agnates claimed this separate property, because the father had not dealt with it in his will, having appointed heirs only to himself. The second heirs claimed it on the ground that the heirs to the father were heirs to the son also, if he died before puberty. The agnates said the estate (*pecunia*) is not one, but two; the second heirs said it was only one, and an estate could not have heirs both by will and intestacy.

puberty, even if testator has named a later date. The provisions for succession to testator himself must precede those for succession to his child; and unless testator's own will has dealt duly with those in his power, and contains a good appointment of heir and be duly entered on by the heir, the pupillar will fails (Gai. ii 184; D. fr 2 pr, §§ 1, 4, fr 7, 10 § 4, 14). But it is not necessary that the son should be appointed heir; he may be disinherited; and in that case the substitute, or rather heir, to the son will have in that capacity only the son's property, *i.e.* what has come to him by inheritances, legacies, or gifts from relatives, *etc.* (Gai. ii 182). The same result will follow if the son, though appointed heir, has not accepted his father's inheritance (D. xxix 2 fr 12 pr). Where an *impubes* has been arrogated and by a pupillar will a substitute was appointed by the arrogator, the substitute will have only what comes to the child in consequence of the arrogation, including the *quarta divi Pii* and gifts from the arrogator's friends (xxviii 6 fr 10 § 6). If a father make his son heir and request him if he die before puberty, to transfer the inheritance to Titius, and the son die before puberty, the statutable heir will be compelled to transfer to Titius all that the son inherited from his father, *minus* the Falcidian fourth; but if the son was disinherited by his father, such a trust has no effect (fr 41 § 3), any more than a legacy imposed on the substitute would have, if neither son nor substitute were appointed by the father heir to himself (D. xxx fr 126 pr, xxxv 2 fr 11 § 8, 87 § 7).

3. Where the son has become heir to the father and dies before puberty, the substitute cannot separate the two inheritances so as to repudiate the father's and accept the son's, unless indeed being a brother he would be entitled to succeed as statutable heir, if the will failed (D. xxviii 6 fr 10 § 2, § 3; fr 12, but cf. Cod. vi 30 fr 20 § 1). If the father appoint in general language his own heirs as heirs also to his son dying before puberty, as *quisquis mihi heres erit, idem impuberi filio heres esto*, only those persons will be heirs to the son who have become directly by the will heirs to the father, even though displaced in the lifetime of the son by a plaint of unduteous will. And therefore a person who has become heir through his son in power, or slave,

is not entitled under the pupillar clause, nor is the heir of the testator's heir: such persons have not been selected by the testator (D. *ib.* fr 8 § 1, 31 pr). If testator has named as heirs his two sons, one of full age and the other under age, with reciprocal substitution (*eosque invicem substituo*), only what is common to both *i.e.* ordinary substitution takes effect: if pupillar substitution is intended for the son under age, this must be expressly stated (fr 4 § 2, cf. Cod. vi 26 fr 2 referring to a rescript of M. Aurelius). If testator named as heirs a legitimate son and a natural son with reciprocal substitution, the like rule applies: for pupillar substitution is not possible for a natural son, who is not in his father's power, and only ordinary substitution can therefore be the effect: and even if the legitimate son die before puberty, his estate will not pass to his natural brother (fr 45 pr). In an analogous case where a testator desired to make a son in his power and another not in his power equal heirs with reciprocal substitution if either died before puberty, Labeo and three other contemporary jurists advised that he should appoint the son in his power sole heir and bequeath a moiety of the inheritance to the other when he came to be his own guardian: and further, should appoint this other to be heir if the son in his power died before puberty (fr 39 pr).

4. A mother is not able to make a pupillar substitution, but can of course appoint a son heir on reaching the age of puberty and appoint another heir in case the son does not become her heir (fr 33 pr).

5. It is not necessary that testator make the pupillar will in the same form as that for himself: one may be written and the other nuncupatory (fr 20 § 1, cf. xxxvii 11 fr 8 § 4). The risk to the child's life, if it was known who was his heir, made certain precautions usual. The ordinary substitution for the case of the son's not being heir at all would be made openly, that is to say in the same part of the will in which the son was appointed heir: the pupillar substitution would be made on lower tablets, sealed up with their own string and wax; and a direction given in the principal part of the will that these tablets should not be opened while the son was alive and under age. During the father's lifetime the contents of the whole will would be

unknown and he could change his will if he chose, and only by the death of the son during this period could the substitute become entitled to the inheritance. Thus the life of the son would be practically secure from the substitute's intrigues. But as it might easily be conjectured that the substitute to the father would be also made heir to the son, Gaius goes on to say that a far safer plan was to name no substitute in the body of the will, but name the substitute in the one case as well as in the other only in the pupillar tablets separately sealed (Gai. ii 181).

C. How wills are broken or invalidated.

Wills are broken or invalidated in several ways (some of which have been referred to before).

1. A will otherwise rightly made is broken (*rumpitur*) by the birth (*agnatione*) of a son, and is modified by the birth of any other own heir, whether male or female, if he or she, whether born in testator's lifetime or not, has been passed over, *i.e.* neither appointed heir nor disinherited in the will. If he or she was appointed heir conditionally, the will is broken if the birth precede the occurrence of the condition.

The same result comes about (*quasi agnatione*) when a person already born at the date of the will, but passed over, becomes own heir to testator by the departure from testator's power, by death or otherwise, of his father or other ascendant in testator's lifetime (Gai. ii 126, 133, 134; D. xxviii 2 fr 22, 24; tit. 3 fr 3 § 1).

It is not sufficient that such own heir should be disinherited in the first part of the will, if it is a second part which, wholly or partially, takes effect. Thus if I and Titius are appointed heirs, and substitutes are also appointed, and Titius dies, the second grade comes in partially; and if a postumous child is born to testator, and has not been disinherited in case of substitutes as well as in case of first-appointed heirs, the will is broken. The chance of such an occurrence makes it impossible for either myself or Titius to enter on the inheritance without the other. But if before the substitution of others Titius and I were reciprocally substituted for each other, the difficulty would not arise (D. xxviii 3 fr 19).

If an own heir passed over in the will keeps aloof from the inheritance, the will though technically broken was allowed to stand. *Voluntas testatoris ex bono et aequo tuebitur* (fr 17).

2. A will otherwise rightly made is also broken by anyone's coming to be an own heir (*quasi agnatione*) in any other way, viz. by adoption or arrogation; by marriage to testator of a woman who thereby comes into his hand[1], or, if she is in his hand already *fiduciae causa*, comes in the place of a daughter; or by a son's return under power after one or two mancipations; or by son or daughter, children of a mother wrongly supposed to be a Roman woman, proving his or her claim under the senate's decree during testator's life. In all these cases the breaking of the will is not prevented by the notice of such persons in the will, presumably because this introduction into the family or the change of their position could not well have been foreseen when the will was made, so that it was not as own heirs that they were either appointed or disinherited (Gai. ii 138—141; Ulp. xxiii 2, 3; D. xxviii 3 fr 8). If a son's claim to citizenship under the *SC.* was established only after his father's death, a senate's decree under Hadrian provided that the will was not broken unless he had been passed over (Gai. ii 142, 143). One adopted by testator in place of a grandson after being appointed heir in the will, and coming to be 'own heir' by the death of his supposed father, does not break the will, for the adoption itself does not make him own heir (D. xxviii 2 fr 23 § 1).

3. A will is also broken by a later will, if rightly made, whether the second will is in its turn broken by a postumous own heir or not. If the heir in the later will is appointed on a condition referring to past or present events (*e.g.* 'if Titius was' or 'is consul'), the later will breaks the former or not according as the condition is or is not the fact. If the condition refer to a future event, the later will breaks the former in any case, for it is enough that inheritance under it should be possible, and, if the condition is impossible, it is treated as not imposed, and the will is therefore unconditional. It is of no consequence whether

[1] Cf. *Laud. Turiae ap.* Bruns p. 283 v 13 *Temptatae deinde estis ut testamen[tum patris] quo nos eramus heredes rup[tum diceretur] coemptione facta cum uxore.*

the heir appointed in the second will decline to enter, or die before or after the testator without entering, or fail in the condition of appointment, or be deprived of the inheritance for childlessness by the *lex Julia*; in all these cases there is an intestacy, the former will being broken by the later, and the later will being invalidated by there being no entry of an heir under it. A rescript of Severus and Caracalla enacted that, even if the later will appointed only an heir to certain things, it should have full force, as if no such limitation were inserted[1] (Gai. ii 144; D. xxviii 2 fr 7; tit. 3 fr 1, 16; xxxvi 1 fr 30; Just. ii 17 § 3). A soldier's will, however made, breaks a previous will (D. xxviii 3 fr 2).

4. A will rightly made is invalidated (*irritum fit*) if no heir enter and there is no own or necessary heir under it (Ulp. xxiii 4; D. xxviii 3 fr 1).

5. A will rightly made is not in strict law invalidated by mere intention on the part of testator to revoke it, or even by his cutting the string, or effacing or crossing out the writing or burning the tablets, though the proof of its contents may become difficult. But anyone claiming under such a will will be met by a plea of fraud or be refused actions to recover. If however there is sufficient evidence of such destruction being unintentional, or of the erasure of certain parts only being intended, effect will be given to testator's intention; and even when the heirs' names have been crossed out, the benefit of the doubt will be given to other heirs and to legacies and freedoms. In one case (A.D. 166) M. Aurelius, following a constitution of his father, refused validity to the appointment of heirs, all their names having been crossed out, but allowed the legacies and freedoms to be valid, and even the freedom of one slave whose name had been crossed out. If, as was usual, a testator ended his will with the words 'the erasures and crossings out I have made myself,' still any accidentally made are not held good. Anything written or crossed out otherwise than by testator's

[1] In the particular case the second will requested that the former will should be valid. Hence the heir by the second was required to retain only the certain things and as much more as might be necessary to make up the Falcidian fourth and to restore the rest to the heirs by the first will.

order is taken as not written or not crossed out (Gai. ii 151[1]; D. xxviii 4; cf. Cod. vi 23 fr 30). If testator was not in sound mind when he cut his will, the will made when he was in sound mind was not invalidated (D. xxviii 3 fr 20).

6. A will rightly made may be called broken, but is usually described as invalidated (*irritum*), when something causing incapacity happen to the testator afterwards, *e.g.* if he lose citizenship, or be condemned to death (unless he appeal successfully: a will made pending appeals is valid), or commit suicide, not from weariness of life or impatience of disease or philosophic self-glorification, but from consciousness of crime. And this applies to a soldier's will also (Gai. ii 145, 146; Ulp. xxiii 4; D. xxviii 3 fr 6 §§ 5—11).

A captive's will was, according to the general law, of no validity: it was the will of a slave, and a slave had no property, no inheritance, no heir, and still less an 'own heir' (D. L 16 fr 3 § 1; xxxv 2 fr 18 § 2). And this remained true of any will (or codicils) made *apud hostes*, *i.e.* during his captivity, whether he returned home or not (D. xxviii 1 fr 1 pr). But a will made before captivity was confirmed by a *lex Cornelia* (of uncertain date[2]), which enacted that the succession to anyone dying in captivity, whether capable of making a will or not, should be in all respects the same as if he had never come into the power of the enemy. That is to say, his will is good, as if his death had occurred when he was taken captive; he leaves an inheritance, which contains what he had at that time and also subsequent accretions, which he would have had if instead of dying he had returned to his country; his will is broken by the birth (in or not in captivity) of an own heir not noticed in the will; and a slave made free and heir by the will becomes so, whether he desire it or not. If he has left no will, or the will is broken, intestate succession or *bonorum possessio* and guardianships take

[1] The text is not certain. See Schirmer against Krüger *ZRG.* xx, xxi.

[2] At one time this *lex Cornelia* was identified with that *de falsis* (D. xlviii 10 fr 1 pr), which dealt specially with forged wills and hence is called by Cicero (*Verr.* ii 1 42 § 108; cf. Just. iv 18 § 7) *testamentaria* (Zimmern, *Geschichte* i § 196, *etc.*); but this view is now not accepted; cf. Schilling *Bemerk.* p. 285; Hase *Jus postliminii* p. 195.

effect as if he had died a freeman (D. xlix 15 fr 22 pr §§ 1, 4; fr 10 § 1; xxviii 1 fr 12; tit. 3 fr 15; Paul iii 4*a* § 8; Ulp. xxiii 5). This is called the 'fiction of the Cornelian law' (D. xxxv 2 fr 18 pr).

If the captive's will contained a pupillar will, the lawyers differed as to its being effective. If the son was not captive, though he died after his father, he had become *sui juris* before his father's death, and a pupillar will was therefore beyond his father's power: if the son died captive, the Cornelian law did not apply, for he had made no will, and the law said nothing of pupillar wills. To which it was replied that the Cornelian law dated back the father's death to the time of his captivity, and that, as it recognized intestacy as well as testacy, the praetor was justified in confirming the pupillar will and granting to the substitute analogous actions. The result of the extracts from Julian and Papinian given in the Digest appears to be that the substitute is entitled, only if the son has survived the father and for a time had the estate vested in him, which would be the case if the son died at home though the father died a captive, or if the son though dying a captive had not been captured till after the father's death (D. xxviii 6 fr 28, 29; xlix 15 fr 10, 11).

D. Plaint of an unduteous will (*Querella inofficiosi testamenti*).

1. There was still further protection given to children by the Roman law, which required not only that testator should distinctly notice his children or descendants in his will, but that he should not disinherit them without cause. The plaint of an unduteous will was a proceeding before the *centumviri*[1], open to those who would be next heirs on an intestacy, *i.e.* to natural children even if postumous, who had been disinherited or at

[1] This plaint is referred to by Quintilian (vii 4 §§ 11, 20); and two cases are discussed by Pliny (*Ep.* v 1; vi 33), all referring to the *centumviri*. Of five earlier cases mentioned by Valerius Max. vii 7 two are before the *centumviri*, one of them being in the time of Pompey (§§ 1, 2); two others are dealt with by Augustus (§§ 3, 4); the fifth by the praetor C. Calpurnius Piso. Cicero uses the expression *fecit testamentum non improbum, non inofficiosum, etc.* (*Verr.* ii 1 42 § 107), but this is scarcely evidence of a recognised plaint in his time.

least had not obtained their due portion in their father's or mother's will. Illegitimate children can bring the plaint against their mother's will. The will is impeached on the ground of its failing in the due regard which a perfectly sane person would have to his children. Parents had the same right to complain of their children's wills. Collaterals, with the exception of brothers and sisters, had no such right. It was applicable also, where one has been not disinherited but overlooked, and was the natural remedy where a mother's will was concerned; but in the case of a father's will, the praetorian remedy of possession against the will was the easier course; and alone applicable, if complainant's son had been retained under power and made heir (D. v 2 fr 1—5, 23 pr; Paul iv 5 § 2). A child given in adoption and passed over in his natural father's will could not bring this plaint effectually according to Papinian and Paul, though others admitted it in some cases (Cod. viii 47 fr 10 pr). Such a child's own will was open to complaint by his natural father (D. *ib.* fr 30). The plaint of a child took precedence of the plaint of a father (fr 14).

2. The suit cannot be brought until the will is entered on, and is then brought against the heir or such of the heirs as complainant chooses, or an heir by trust if possessor. If complainant is possessor, he will use this plaint in reply to the heir's suit for the inheritance (fr 8 §§ 10, 13; fr 25 § 1, *etc.*; Cod. iii 28 fr 1). If the judge pronounces against the will and the written heir does not appeal, the will is thereby at once rescinded[1], possessions granted against the will drop, and deceased

[1] Pliny was made heir with others to the estate of Pomponia Galla who disinherited her own son. The son approached Pliny, and after a full (private) hearing Pliny decided that the mother was justified. On the son's commencing a centumviral suit against the other heirs, Pliny at the request of the other heirs proposed to him that he should accept from them a fourth of the inheritance and added that he would himself give him as much. He put the case to him thus, *Si mater te ex parte quarta scripsisset heredem, num queri posses? quid si heredem quidem instituisset ex asse sed legatis ita exhausisset ut non amplius apud te quam quarta remaneret?...Scis te non subscripsisse mecum et jam biennium transisse omniaque me usu cepisse* (*Ep.* v 1 § 9).

As regards the latter words it may be remarked that this was not

is intestate; complainant (if he would be entitled on intestacy) is recognized as own heir, and can have possession of the estate if he demands it; freedoms given by the will are not valid; legacies direct or by way of trust (even if imposed on the heir *ab intestato*) are not due, and if already paid are recoverable either by the payer or, if they were paid before this suit was begun, then (by an *actio utilis*) by the successful complainant. If the plaint is not brought till more than five years (after entry, cf. Cod. iii 28 fr 36 § 2), as is allowed only for strong reason, freedoms are not revoked, but have to be paid for (at 20 *aurei* each, says Justinian). Trust freedoms on a plaint brought within five years have apparently to be granted at a like price by complainant (fr 6 § 1, 8 §§ 16, 17, fr 9, 13 *ad fin.* 16 § 1). If complainant was successful only against one heir, the intestacy is only partial, and complainant is responsible and entitled only as part statutable heir, but freedoms remain valid (D. v 3 fr 15 § 2; Cod. iii 28 fr 13; cf. fr 19; D. xxxi fr 76 pr). If complainant's son was retained under power and made heir, he will be protected and share with his father (fr 23 pr; cf. p. 246). If collusion is suspected between complainant and heirs, the legatees are admitted to defend the will (fr 29 pr).

3. Complainant has to shew three things:

(*a*) That his conduct has not been such as to justify disherison and that testator has either acted under malign influences, or under a wrong belief; *e.g.* that complainant was not his son, or was dead. If testator were really insane, the will would be invalid from the first: this plaint treats the will as well made, but not *ex officio pietatis* (fr 2, 3, 27 §§ 1, 4, fr 28).

(*b*) That he does not get under the will (*judicio testatoris*) at least one-fourth of his due share of the inheritance. The value of the inheritance is taken as at testator's death, after

a case of a stranger possessing the objects of an inheritance before the heir entered, but that of an heir appointed by will duly entering and being in possession of a certain portion of the inheritance. If however the son was successful in his plaint, the will indeed would be upset, but the judgment to that effect would not bind Pliny as he was not made a defendant, and besides had gained a possessory title, for which in any case two years was enough, whether or not in this case one year only was required.

debts, funeral expenses, and slaves set free by the will, are deducted. His share is reckoned as if on intestacy (*i.e.* the primary division being by stocks). Thus, if there be left one grandson by one son and three by another, the single grandson's fourth is one-eighth of the whole estate: each of the other three grandsons can claim only a twenty-fourth. If the share left to complainant was subject to a trust, still if the trust was not to be executed at once and the share was large, complainant's emolument might be sufficient to give him by the time of restoration the value of his claimable share and its profits. If he were instituted heir to the whole, he could not bring his plaint, because in any case he is secure of his fourth by *Falcidia* or *SC. Pegasianum* (Paul iv 5 §§ 5, 6; D. fr 8 §§ 8, 9). The will is safe if testator has given during his lifetime to complainant as much as will satisfy his share, either in view of death or with the purpose of meeting such a complaint (fr 8 § 6, 25 pr). A person arrogated under the age of puberty, being sure of his fourth under Ant. Pius' constitution, is not generally admitted to this plaint (fr 8 § 15).

(*c*) That he has not accepted testator's judgment; *e.g.* by knowingly taking or claiming a legacy whether bequeathed to himself or to a slave of his (unless in trust for another), or a payment directed to be made to him by heir or legatee or slave as condition of their heirship, legacy or freedom; or by treating the heir as such by buying or leasing from him things belonging to the estate, or paying him a debt due to the estate or suing him for a debt due from it, or even by being advocate or procurator to one suing for a legacy under the will (D. fr 8 § 10; 12 pr § 1, 31, 32 pr; Cod. iii 28 fr 8). A daughter passed over and claiming her share by accretion cannot bring this suit (cf. Cod. vi 28 fr 4 § 4). But a father bringing the suit on behalf of his son under power against the mother's will can take a legacy or enter on the inheritance without thereby barring the success of the son's plaint (fr 22 pr). The father requires the son's consent for suing on his behalf, as the wrong is to the son (fr 8 pr). One who inherits or gets by arrogation a plaint of this kind already begun does not lose benefits received on his own account from the same estate (fr 22 §§ 2, 3).

4. Anyone not successful in his plaint, on the ground of his own conduct, forfeits to the Crown (*fiscus*) anything given him by the will, or if on trust, he forfeits his fourth, the trust not being hurt: but if he was appointed heir with a substitute, the inheritance passes to the substitute. This is so, only if he has carried his plaint to judgment: if he has desisted, or judgment has been passed in his absence and only for his non-appearance, forfeiture does not take place (fr 8 § 14; Paul iv 5 § 9). A rescript of Severus and Antoninus decided that guardians could bring this suit on their ward's behalf without any risk of his losing what was given him by the will (fr 30 § 1).

5. If a complainant has consented to a compromise, the will is not upset, and the legacies, except for the *Falcidia*, and the freedoms are valid. If the heir has not appeared but has allowed judgment to go by default, the like result occurs (by a rescript of Marcus and Verus); there has been no judgment on the merits of the claim (fr 17 § 1, 18, 29 § 2). Sometimes an arrangement is made by complainant with the coheirs to make up to a fourth what has been left him by testator. Such a bargain does not preclude the plaint being brought, if the bargain is not kept (fr 27 pr; Paul iv 5 §§ 7, 8).

Anyone entitled to bring this plaint and declining to do so does not share in the success of complainant. Where a mother left an outsider heir to three-fourths, a daughter to one-fourth, and overlooked another daughter, this last bringing the plaint obtains her full share, *i.e.* one half the estate from the outsider; the other daughter retains her fourth. If she had been disinherited and had refrained from bringing the plaint, the complainant would have obtained the whole inheritance, as if she were the only daughter (fr 17 pr, 19).

6. Anyone bringing the plaint and pressing it to delivery of the petition (*libellus*), or taking up possession of the estate as a step in the prosecution of the plaint, and dying without change of intention, transmits the right to his heir (fr 6 § 2—fr 7; 15 § 1; Cod. iii 28 fr 5).

A pupillar will cannot be attacked unless the father's will be also attacked, with which, if wholly upset, the pupillar will falls also. And being made by the father, it cannot be assailed by the mother, and being the son's will it cannot be assailed by the father's brother; for he is uncle and not within the circle of persons entitled to complain (D. fr 18 § 5).

A soldier's will cannot be assailed on this ground, even by a soldier, within a year from his discharge: but a veteran's will can, though the estate be originally wholly camp-*peculium* (fr 8 §§ 3, 4; 27 § 2). The will of a mother cannot be complained of by one who has been adopted by her as a son without the emperor's order; he is not a son (fr 29 § 3).

This plaint often gave rise to differences of opinion among the judges, not only when plaintiffs and defendants were different (fr 15 § 2; xxxi fr 76 pr; xliv 2 fr 29 pr), but also in the same case. If the judges were equally divided, the will was allowed to stand (D. v 2 fr 10; cf. xlii 1 fr 38).

E. Soldiers' wills.

Soldiers were specially privileged in the making of wills, temporarily by Julius Caesar, afterwards by Titus, Domitian and Nerva. Trajan and his successors made such privilege a standing rule by inserting it in the instructions (*mandata*) given to provincial Governors. 'Let my fellow-soldiers make wills in 'whatever way they will, in whatever way they can, and let the 'bare will of the testator suffice for the distribution of his 'estate' (*bona* D. xxix 1 fr 1 pr; Ulp. xxiii 10). In this case a defect of form, such as insufficient number of witnesses or absence of the ceremonies of sale and nuncupation, was of no importance. But a rescript of Trajan decided in the interest of soldiers themselves that a mere casual statement, 'I make you heir,' or 'I leave you my goods,' was not to be held to be a will: if however a soldier called some men to him for the purpose of witnessing his declaration, and then said whom he willed to be his heir and to whom he gave freedom, it was a good will, and writing was not required (Gai. ii 109; D. *ib.* fr 24). Such a will, destitute of regular forms, could be made only in camp or on expedition (Cod. vi 21 fr 1, 15; Justinian claims to have made this restriction, *Inst.* ii 11 pr; Cod. *ib.* 17), while testator is still a soldier, but its efficacy remains, if he die within a year of his discharge, though the heir may have been appointed on a condition which comes into force afterwards. Superior officers, as praefects and tribunes and others, cease to be soldiers by the entry into office of their successors, and their military will ceases then at once to be valid (fr 21, 38 pr). The will of a soldier dismissed in disgrace ceases to be valid after dismissal. One capitally condemned for a military offence can make a valid military will disposing of his camp-*peculium* only; one captured by the enemy is incapacitated even from a military will (fr 10, 11 pr, 26). Seamen in the fleet and firemen (*vigiles*) had the same privileges in this respect as soldiers. Governors of provinces, legates and other civilians in authority, making wills in an enemy's country, are allowed to neglect forms (D. xxxvii 13).

Besides the simplicity of form a soldier's will had other privileges. It could be made by one who was deaf or dumb, or one doubtful of his being *sui juris*. It is not revoked by *capitis deminutio* or emancipation or adoption or arrogation during service; and though broken by the birth of a postumous child in his power unnoticed in the will, or by the adoption of a son, *etc.*, it becomes valid again if he maintain it (D. xxix 1 fr 4, 8, 11 § 1, 22, 33 pr; cf. fr 36 § 2). It does not require to be complete, for a soldier may die partially intestate (fr 35); and if he has cut or cancelled it, it is revived if the intention to revive is shewn (fr 15 § 1). He can make more wills than one, and one does not repeal another, unless that be intended (fr 19 pr). He can even appoint an heir for a limited time and then substitute another, or on or till the occurrence of a particular event: he can appoint separate heirs for specific things or masses of his property, *e.g.* for town-estate and country-estate, for camp-*peculium* and other property; but if the debts falling on one mass exceed the assets so that the heir declines, the other heir if he enter is responsible for the whole (fr 15 § 4, 17 pr, § 1). He can take away an inheritance by the same will by which he has given it (fr 15 § 1). He can appoint foreigners or Latins as heirs or legatees: and unmarried or childless persons can take in full under a soldier's will (Gai. ii 110, 111, text doubtful). He can make a pupillar will with the age of twenty-five instead of puberty, and apparently without making a will for himself: it will however be effective only for what comes to the child from his father, if the child die after the age of puberty (D. xxviii 6 fr 2 § 1, 15). But a soldier cannot leave bequests either direct or by way of trust to uncertain persons (Just. ii 20 § 25). The *lex Falcidia* did not apply to a soldier's will (D. xxix 1 fr 7 § 4).

When he has left the service his will (respecting the camp-*peculium*) becomes subject to ordinary laws, and if his son now falls under his power by the death of his own father and has not been noticed in the will, the will is broken (D. xxviii 2 fr 28 § 1). If a military will contains in the first grade an appointment of heirs good only by military law, and in the second grade an appointment good by ordinary law, and testator die after a year from discharge, the second only takes effect (D. xxviii 3 fr 7).

In contrast to soldiers' wills, non-soldiers' wills are often called *testamenta paganorum* (*e.g.* D. xl 4 fr 52).

CHAPTER III.

INTESTATE SUCCESSION (TO FREEBORN CITIZENS).

A. The statute of the XII tables gave the estate of a freeborn person, who died without leaving a valid will, on which entry duly took place, to his 'own heirs.'; failing any such to his nearest agnate; failing these to his clansmen. (*Si intestatus moritur, cui suus heres nec escit, agnatus proximus familiam habeto; si agnatus nec escit, gentiles familiam habento*[1], Ulp. xxvi 1; and *ap. Collat.* xvi 4.) Loss of civic position (*cap. dem.*) incapacitated both own heirs and agnates (D. xxxviii 16 fr 11).

1. 'Own heirs' have been described above (chap. ii B 2). Who are such in the particular case, is ascertained at the time when it is ascertained that there is no valid will, or that, there

[1] Cicero gives it thus: *Si paterfamilias intestato moritur, familia pecuniaque ejus adgnatum gentiliumque esto* (*Inv.* ii 50 § 148; so also *ad Heren.* i 13 § 23).

being such, it has not been made operative by due entry of some heir thereby appointed. Grandchildren, *etc.*, conceived before[1] deceased's death are therefore entitled to succeed if at this time (not at the time of his death) their father or other ascendant is dead or emancipated or deported, *etc.* If a son is alive at this time but in captivity or in the power of a redeemer, his sons cannot yet succeed to their grandfather. Their claim is in suspense. If he die in captivity, they become entitled; but if he die in his redeemer's power, he is deemed to have died a freeman, and the grandsons are therefore excluded by not being independent at the moment of intestate succession.

Own heirs are heirs *ipso jure*; they require no entry to perfect their title. Neither madness nor infancy nor absence abroad nor ignorance of deceased's death is any hindrance to their succession. Nor is their right affected by any previous arrangement, *e.g.* by a declaration of a father in an instrument of dowry that his daughter should expect nothing from her father's inheritance. If there are more own heirs than one, whether natural or adoptive, of the same degree of relationship, they share equally. If they are of different degrees, the inheritance is divided by stocks (*per stirpes*), not by heads (*per capita*); if one son or daughter be alive and another son be dead, leaving children in his grandfather's power, the son or daughter takes one half, and the grandchildren take the other half among them; if there are grandchildren by one son and great-grandchildren by another, all in the power of deceased at his death, the grandchildren, one or more, take one half, and the great-grandchildren take the other. Postumous children are equally entitled and share equally with any brothers or sisters born before (Gai. iii 1—8; Ulp. xxvi 1, 2; Paul *ap. Collat.* xvi 3 §§ 1—11; D. xxviii 3 fr 6 pr; xxxviii 16 fr 1 §§ 4, 8, 2 § 6, 14, 16).

2. Agnates are also statutable (*legitimi*) heirs, and so-called by preeminence: they are described above (Book II chap. vii). They are not called to the inheritance as long as there is any

[1] Cf. D. xxviii 3 fr 6 *Si post mortem avi nepos conceptus est, Marcellus scribit neque ut suum neque ut nepotem aut cognatum ad hereditatem vel ad bonorum possessionem posse admitti.*

hope of an 'own heir,' which there would be, *e.g.*, if the intestate had left a wife pregnant, or a son in captivity. Who is nearest agnate is ascertained, if there be no will, at the time of death, but if a will has been made, then at the time when there is found to be no effective will and no own heir who accepts. Agnates in any degree however remote are entitled, if there is none nearer.

The nearest degree among agnates (after the children, D. xxxviii 16 fr 12) are brothers and sisters by the same father as deceased, whether by birth from the same or different mothers, or by adoption or arrogation or coming into hand, or proof of their claim under the *lex Aelia Sentia, etc.* Their relation to one another is not affected by their never having been in their father's power or by his deportation, *etc.* They are called *consanguinei*, and as such are sometimes treated as a separate grade preceding other agnates. Only in this degree have women any claims to inherit *ab intestato* as agnates, for fathers' sisters and brothers' daughters, *etc.* are not admissible. Paul says that the recognition of *consanguinei* as the first grade among agnates was due to lawyers' interpretation, and that the restriction of women as agnate heirs to this class was not in the XII tables and appeared to be due to the policy of the Voconian law.

The rules for agnates' claims are different from those applying to 'own heirs.' For, first, the nearer degree alone is entitled, and thus, if there be left a son and children of another son, the son only succeeds. If there are more than one in the same degree, all are entitled; and if any do not enter, their shares accrue to those who have entered or their heirs. Secondly, those in a remoter degree have no contingent right to succeed, and thus if those in the next degree decline the inheritance or die before entry, more remote agnates do not succeed at all. *In legitimis hereditatibus successio non est* (Ulp.)[1]. Thirdly, among agnates of equal degree the division is by heads, not by stocks. Thus, if there be no brother or sister of deceased, but one or two children of one brother

[1] Hence there was nothing to hinder the 'next agnate' from selling the inheritance; see chap. iv B (p. 228).

and three or four of another, the one or two children take no more each than the three or four do: all take equally. This was well settled (*jam dudum placuit*) by Gaius' time (Gai. iii 9—16, 18—24; Ulp. xxvi 3—6; *ap. Collat.* xvi 6, 7: Paul *ap. Collat.* xvi 3 § 3, 13—20; D. xxxviii 16 fr 1 §§ 9—11, fr 2, 4, 9, 11; Cod. vi 58 fr 6).

Postumous children, though not such as would be 'own heirs,' or capable of appointment as heirs in a will, for instance brothers' sons, are capable of being statutable heirs, as they are capable of possession *sec. tabulas* (D. xxx fr 127 which refers this to Aquilius Gallus; cf. xxxvii 11 fr 3).

Men have the same claim to the inheritance of their female relatives, being agnates, as they have to that of their male agnates. A father's wife if she was in the hand of her husband counted as a sister to his children (Gai. iii 14, 24).

3. In default of own heirs and of nearest agnates accepting the inheritance, deceased's clansmen (*gentiles*)[1] are entitled. Clansmen are said by Gaius to have been described in the first book of his Institutes, perhaps in § 164 now lost; but the whole of clan law had gone into desuetude by his time, and on that account he passes it over in treating of intestate inheritance.

[1] Cic. *Verr.* ii 1 45 § 115 *Minucius quidam mortuus est ante istum praetorem: ejus testamentum erat nullum; lege hereditas ad gentem Minuciam veniebat; si habuisset iste edictum quod ante istum et postea omnes habuerunt, possessio Minuciae genti esset data.* (For *possessio* see chap. v.) Another case of difficulty is mentioned in Cic. *Orat.* i 39 § 176 where there was a dispute about the inheritance of a freedman's son between patrician and plebeian branches of the Claudian clan, the former claiming by the right of the clan, the latter by that of the stock (*stirps*). The difficulty is increased, at least to us, by Cicero's definition of *gentiles* as having no slave among their ancestors; *Gentiles sunt inter se qui eodem nomine sunt, qui ab ingenuis oriundi sunt, quorum majorum nemo servitutem servivit, qui capite non sunt deminuti,* adding that he thinks the definition is complete (*Hoc fortasse satis est, Top.* 6 § 29). Therefore the son of a freedman could hardly be a *gentilis*, and being freeborn himself would seem to be outside of any patronal claims (cf. Cod. vi 4 fr 4 §§ 3, 11): but he was considered within some sort of cognation (*ib.* §§ 14 *a*, 22; cf. Leist in Glück's *Pand.* Pt iv §§ 67, 68). Of course a freedman's son born before his father's manumission would either be a slave or himself also a freedman: he could not be *ingenuus*,

STEMMA AGNATIONIS

(found in MSS of *lex Romana Visigothorum*.

See Huschke, *Jus Antiq.* p. 628 sqq. ed. 5; Krüger, *Jus Antejust.* ii. 168).

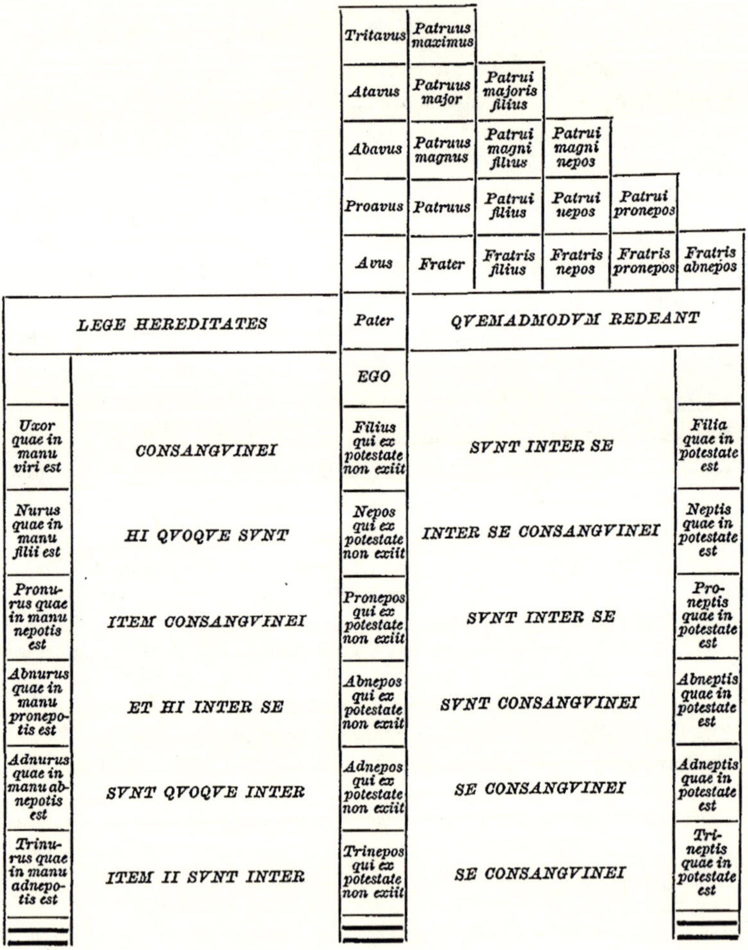

The *lex Julia caducaria* gave to the people an intestate's estate, which had no claimant, either by the civil law or praetorian grant (Ulp. xxviii 7). In imperial times the fisc succeeded, but had to pay the debts of deceased, and the legacies and trusts imposed by the will, from which however it could deduct the Falcidian fourth. If the estate was insolvent, the fisc would apparently not take, but have the estate sold for the creditors (D. xlix 14 fr 1 § 1, 14; xxx fr 96 § 1; xxxvi 1 fr 3 § 5: cf. Vangerow *Pand.* § 564).

The *peculium castrense* of an intestate soldier fell to his father as ordinary peculium, and even if he was punished capitally for a military offence, or if he committed suicide without apprehension of conviction for ordinary crime, was not taken by the fisc if an agnate heir or cognate *bon. possessor* up to the fifth degree claimed it. If there were no cognates it (by a rescript of Hadrian's) passed to his legion (D. xxviii 3 fr 6 § 7; xxxviii 12, cf. xxix 1 fr 11; cf. Leist in Glück's *Pand.* ii 146).

When freedoms were given by a will and the estate was so laden with debt as to be in danger of being sold, M. Aurelius directed any slave thereby freed, who would give security, to have the estate assigned to him. See Book II chap. ii, *ad fin.*

B. *SC. Tertullianum.*

A mother (who had not been in her husband's hand, and thereby made a sister to her children) was not admitted to inherit from her own child, dying intestate, so far as the older civil law was concerned[1]. By the praetor she would be called to the possession of the estate only in the third class (*unde cognati*). The *SC. Tertullianum* passed in the time of Hadrian, and following the lines on which Claudius[2] appears to have proceeded,

[1] So Just. iii 3 § 2. Zonaras xii 1 refers it somewhat doubtfully to Ant. Pius. In D. xxxiv 5 fr 9 § 1 Hadrian is said to have decided a case in favour of a mother who claimed against the agnates to succeed on an intestacy.

[2] *Primus divus Claudius matri legitimam liberorum detulit hereditatem* (Just. iii 3 § 1). Nothing more is known of this.

partially remedied this by providing that a freeborn Roman woman, who had had three children, born alive (not all at one birth), and a freedwoman who had similarly had four children, should be a statutable heir, and succeed to her child's intestate estate after own heirs, emancipated children by birth, brothers by birth or adoption, and the natural father (if such father was either entitled to the inheritance *ab intestato* by statute or to effective possession of the estate *contra tabulas*). If there was only a sister or sisters left, they took half, and the mother the other half. If mother and brother, or mother, brother and sisters, were left, the mother was excluded (Ulp. xxvi 8; Paul iv 9; D. xxxviii 17 fr 2; Just. iii 3 §§ 1—3).

The illegitimacy of the child did not affect the mother's right. Nor if the child was born when the mother was free, did its conception while she was a slave affect her right. But if a child, born in slavery, was manumitted before the mother, the relation of mother no longer existed in the civil law, and she could not claim under this decree. If deceased's son did not enter on the inheritance, or if own heirs did not accept possession of the estate, they did not stand in the way of the mother's succession. A natural lawful father, who had emancipated his son or daughter, could claim possession of the estate as patron (if there were no own heirs) or as nearest agnate. But a grandfather or great-grandfather, even though he had been the emancipator, was postponed under the Tertullian decree to the mother. An adoptive father ceases to be father if he emancipate his son, and is no obstruction to the mother's claim. If the natural father had passed by adoption into another's family, and an agnate of the deceased existed beside the mother, the agnate excluded the father, and thus the mother's claim was admitted. If a sister existed, she and the mother shared the inheritance, and the natural father, whether still adopted or emancipated, was excluded by the claim of the sister (D. xxxviii 17 fr 2 §§ 1—3, 3, 6, 8, 14—18; but cf. fr 5).

A rescript of Severus (confirmed by Severus and Caracalla) provided that a mother, who did not without delay take all proper measures to obtain suitable guardians for her children, should lose the right of claiming their intestate inheritance.

Her exclusion let in the agnates if any; if there was no one with a claim, the estate passed by lapse (D. *ib.* fr 2 §§ 23, 41—47; xxvi 6 fr 2 § 2).

The mother's claim being under statute (*legitima*) was enforced by vindication (D. xxxviii 17 fr 2 §§ 2, 23). If she was under power, she requires of course the order of her father or other ascendant for claiming the inheritance (Just. iii 3 § 2).

C. *SC. ORFITIANUM.*

A reciprocal right to their mother's inheritance was given to her children (not grandchildren) by a *SC. Orfitianum* passed in the time of M. Aurelius and Commodus A.D. 178, which provided that children[1], being Roman citizens (*sui juris* or not), should have a statutable right to their mother's inheritance, if she was not in her husband's hand, in priority to brothers or other agnates or to patron. It did not matter whether they were by the same or different husbands or illegitimate (*volgo quaesiti*), but a child made slave, though set free afterwards, was not entitled, seeing that neither slaves nor freedmen have a mother under the civil law. The child must be Roman, both at the time of devolution of the inheritance and at entry: and entry (at any time within the period of a year) is necessary for acquisition of this statutable inheritance. *Capitis deminutio* (*minima*) does not affect this claim, not being under the law of the XII tables: but condemnation to fight wild beasts or for a capital offence at one time destroyed the claim. Kinder interpretation afterwards admitted both such a one and a son under his power. In default of all qualified accepting the inheritance, the old law prevailed, and the agnate nearest at the time of such default succeeded. The mother had no claim to a son's camp-*peculium* (Ulp. xxvi 7; Paul iv 10; D. xxxviii 17 fr 1, 4, 6 § 1, 10; Just. iii 4).

A constitution of Hadrian granted to the Aegyptians a like right to the estate of a grandmother (see Bruns[6] no. 160 *b*).

[1] *filios* is the word used by Ulpian and Paul; but it appears to be used as equivalent to *liberi* and includes females: cf. *e.g.* Cod. vi 57 fr 1 (besides Dig. and Just.).

D. UNCERTAIN SURVIVORSHIP.

When two or more persons died together, the succession might depend on which was held in the absence of evidence to have survived the other. When father and son died in war, the agnates claiming from the father, the mother from the son, Hadrian held that the father died first. But when a freedman died intestate along with his son, respect for the patron's position makes the statutable inheritance to come to the patron, unless the son is proved to have survived. If husband and wife die together, the dowry will be dealt with on the supposition of the wife's having died in matrimony, unless there be proof to the contrary. If father (or mother) and son under the age of puberty die together, the parent will be held the survivor. If the son is above the age of puberty the reverse is held (D. xxxiv 5 fr 9, 22, 23). When mother and daughter died together, and the question arose whether the mother's heir could claim restitution of the dowry from the daughter's husband, which was repayable by stipulation if she died in matrimony, Ant. Pius held that the heir could not claim, for the mother had not survived the daughter (*ib.* fr 16). If a ward died along with his brother who was the substitute in his father's will, or if two own heirs were reciprocally substituted and died together, in the absence of any evidence as to which survived it was held that neither did (fr 18, cf. xxviii 6 fr 34 pr; xxxvii 11 fr 11 pr). If master and slaves die together, the slaves are not reckoned as part of the estate (fr 18 § 1). If a trust was on a condition that a father died *sine liberis*, and his son died with him, the trust was held to take effect (D. xxxvi 1 fr 18 § 7).

CHAPTER IV.

ACQUISITION OF INHERITANCE.

A. *USUCAPIO PRO HEREDE* is when, there being no necessary heir, a man takes the possession of something belonging to an inheritance before the heir enters[1]. There being no ascertained owner, theft was held to be impossible (cf. Book V chap. vi C); and whether it was a moveable or immoveable, the possessor became owner within one year. Gaius explains this as a relic from the old doctrine, that an inheritance could be acquired by continued possession of the things which composed the deceased's estate[2]; and an inheritance, not being a *res soli*, was included in *ceterae res*, for which the XII tables required only one year's possession. The shortened period was the more readily allowed in order to put pressure upon the heirs to enter, so that neither creditors nor the sacred rites, attached to the inheritance, should suffer delay. Later lawyers abandoned the theory which sanctioned usucapion of an inheritance (*postea creditum est ipsas hereditates usucapi non posse*)[3], but the practice

[1] Cf. Cic. *Orat.* ii 70 § 283 *Scaurus non nullam habuit invidiam ex eo quod Phrygionis Pompei locupletis hominis bona sine testamento possederat.*

[2] By possession of the things the property in them only as single objects was obtained. Consequently all incorporeal rights and credits remained out. Possession and usucapion of the inheritance put the party in the position of an heir: he had the inheritance as a whole, and thus took all the rights and credits and became liable to the debts and the sacral obligations. Discussion has been very busy in modern times with *usucapio pro herede*, but our knowledge is very small. See Leist, Glück's *Pand.* Pt i p. 208 sqq.

[3] The abandonment by the lawyers was apparently later than Cicero's time. He writes to Atticus (i 5 § 6) *De Tadiana re mecum Tadius locutus est, te ita scripsisse, nihil esse jam quod laboraretur, quoniam hereditas usu capta esset. Id mirabamur te ignorare de tutela legitima, in qua dicitur esse puella, nihil usu capi posse* (on the latter part see Book IV chap. iv C 5 c). So he speaks of losing an inheritance by neglect to use: *Tu, T. Vetti, si quae tibi in Africa venerit hereditas, usu amittes an tuum...retinebis?* (*Flac.* 34 § 85. It was a question of a praetor's exercising jurisdiction in his own case

continued of allowing things belonging to an inheritance to be gained by one year's possession. A senate's decree under Hadrian (perhaps the *SC. Juventianum*, chap. vii) directed that this dishonest (*improba*) usucapion, even of single things, should not be allowed as a good plea against the heir's suit for the inheritance. Against third parties the usucapion remained effective. If there was a necessary heir, whether own heir or slave, usucapion was absolutely invalid[1] even under the old law (Gai. ii 52—58, iii 201; cf. D. xli 3 fr 29; xlvii 2 fr 14 § 14, fr 69—71; Cod. vii 29).

B. Transfer of Inheritance.

An inheritance, being incorporal, could be transferred only by surrender in court, only by a statutable heir[2], and only before he had formally accepted the succession by entry or otherwise. An heir by will, before entry going through the form of surrender, transfers nothing and remains as he was. But an heir of either kind, who has once entered, is fixed with the liability; and surrender in court then has the effect of transferring the corporal things to the surrenderee, just as if they had been surrendered severally, but not the obligations whether active or passive. The original heir remains liable to the creditors for the debts due from the estate to them, while the debts due to the estate are lost altogether and the debtors are freed. Whether a necessary heir could surrender was a matter of doubt. The Proculians held that as he was heir

in his province). Karlowa treats these as referring only to usucapion of the contents of an inheritance, colloquially identified with the whole (cf. Sen. *Ben.* vi 5 § 3), the old doctrine having been dropt before Cicero's time (*RG.* ii 900). Not so Pernice *Labeo* i p. 328.

Usucapion of things belonging to an inheritance is mentioned by Cicero in describing the order, under the rules, as taught by Q. Scaevola the pontifex, for liability to perform the *sacra*. See chap. xi, p. 388.

[1] This is one of the instances in which Studemund's reading has essentially altered the meaning: *Necessario tamen herede extante nihil ipso jure pro herede usucapi potest. Nihil* was missed by Goeschen and hence Savigny, *Besitz* § 7 p. 83 ed. 7, was misled.

[2] In statutable heirship there was no succession (Gai. iii 12) and consequently no one to treat the cession as a renouncement of the right and to claim in his turn. See Danz *Gesch. R. R.* ii p. 139; Karlowa *RG.* ii p. 884.

without entry, he was in the position of other heirs after entry, and surrender by him would have the same effect as in their case. The Sabinians held that his action had no effect at all: as necessary heir he had no option to accept or not, and consequently no power of surrender (Gai. ii 34—37; Ulp. xix 12—15).

For the practical transfer of an inheritance by sale see Book V chap. iv F 5 *a*.

C. ENTRY ON INHERITANCE.

1. Entry (*aditio*) on an inheritance is the technical term for acceptance of the position of heir, whether heir to the whole or only to a share of the estate of deceased. Any heir entering is thereby irrevocably fixed with responsibility to the creditors of deceased, not merely within the limit of the assets, but to the full amount of the liabilities (if he be sole heir), or of his share thereof, just as if they were his own. All the property and obligations of deceased pass to him, without conveyance or assignment of any kind, as from the date of deceased's death, either wholly or as yet in undivided shares (D. L 17 fr 59, 138; Ulp. xxiii 4).

In the case of necessary heirs (testator's slaves, if made free and heirs by will) no entry or consent is required; they are heirs and responsible at once. Own heirs are also necessary heirs by the civil law, but if they hold themselves, or are held by their guardian, aloof from the inheritance (*si ab hereditate se abstinuerint*), they are safe without any special application to the praetor: he refuses to grant creditors actions against them, and they are thus practically in the same position as outsiders, who can accept or decline as they please. If, however, they once meddle with the inheritance (*si bonis hereditariis*, or *hereditati, se immiscuerint*), the praetor no longer interposes, their civil liability becomes effective, and withdrawal is henceforth as impossible for them as for outsiders after entry. Exception is made in both cases only for minors under the age of twenty-five. Gaius however mentions one case in which Hadrian allowed an older man to withdraw from an inheritance, which had turned out to be subject to a large debt unknown at the time of entry (Gai. ii 162, 163; 98; D. xxix 2 fr 8 pr, 11, 12, 37, 54, 57; xxvi 7 fr 2; cf. xxviii 5 fr 87 § 1; Just. ii 19 § 6).

2. No one can accept or decline an inheritance before the testator is dead or before the option has duly come to him (*priusquam ei deferatur*). A substitute has to wait till the appointed heir and previous substitutes, if any, are no longer entitled; and the heir *ab intestato* has to wait, if there is a will, until the heirs named therein are out of the way, or the will itself is found to be invalid (D. xxix 2 fr 69, 70). If a man is appointed heir under a condition, his decision cannot be made effectually till the condition have occurred (fr 13 pr). Nor must it be made recklessly or under serious misconception of his position: he must know why he is heir, and must know or believe that the testator is dead, that he was *paterfamilias* and had the power of making a will, that the will was good, and whether he himself is heir absolutely or conditionally; and if heir conditionally on an occurrence of fact, he must know of its actual occurrence, but he need not know the amount of his share, provided he do not assert in entry a wrong amount (fr 13 § 1; 15; 17; 21 § 3; 32—34; 51 pr, 75; xxxvi fr 21). If a woman is or is supposed to be pregnant with an own heir, and the will has not noticed postumous children, the next heir by appointment (and this applies to intestacy also) cannot legally enter, unless he believes she is not pregnant and the event confirms him. An own heir however can enter even if he thinks the woman pregnant, for in any case he will be heir—to the whole, if there be no other own heir, or to a due share, if there be others (fr 30, 84). A deaf or dumb person if intelligent is capable of entry (fr 5; 93 § 1), and a child old enough to be able to speak can enter with the authority of his guardian, even though only an honorary guardian (fr 8, 9, 49). Whether a madman could enter or not was much disputed (Cod. v 70, fr 7 § 3).

A man cannot accept conditionally or for or from a certain time only (fr. 51 § 2; L 17 fr 77); nor can he, at least according to some opinions (cf. Cod. vi 30 fr 20 pr), accept one part and repudiate another (D. xxix 2 fr 1, 2); nor if *B* is heir to *A* can he accept *B*'s inheritance and decline *A*'s (fr 7 § 2). If he is appointed heir to one part of the estate and substituted heir to another, whichever he first accepts after the occurrence of the event which gives him title, brings with it the other: one entry is enough (fr 35 pr, 76). If he has become heir to one part and his coheirs make default, their shares accrue to him necessarily (fr 53 § 1). Where however a minor had become heir and then obtained reinstatement, Severus decided that his coheir should not be further burdened, but the share of the minor should be put into the possession of the creditors (fr 61).

3. A time for decision is usually in the case of outsiders fixed by the will, the ordinary time being 100 days. After the institutory words *Titius heres esto* the testator would add *cernitoque in centum diebus proximis quibus scies poterisque; quodni ita creveris, exheres esto.* This form was called *cretio vulgaris* *i.e.* 'the ordinary limit of deliberation,' the hundred days being counted from the testator's death, or, if the appointment was conditional, from the date (if later) of occurrence of the condition, but excluding days on which the heir was ignorant of the death, or of the appointment, or incapable of making the formal decision. (Time so reckoned, excluding unavailable days, was often called *utile tempus*[1].) If the words *quibus scies poterisque* were omitted, it was a *cretio certorum dierum,* 'a limit of a number of days certain,' and time ran continuously from the death or (in case of substitution) other initial date, whether the heir knew of it or not, whether he was prevented or not, and even whether the condition of appointment had occurred or not. If another's slave (or son) is appointed heir with the ordinary cretion, time runs from the slave's (or son's) becoming aware of his appointment and of the death of testator, and not being prevented from informing his master (or father) so as to accept or not at his bidding (Gai. ii 164, 165; 170—173; 190; Ulp. xxii 25, 27, 31, 32; D. xxix 2 fr 25 § 4). Where the praetor prescribes a time for entering, it is to the slave's master, not to the slave himself, *qui pro nullo habetur apud praetorem* (D. xxviii 8 fr 1 pr).

Where the will contains a *cretio,* a formal declaration is necessary for acceptance and must be made within the period,

[1] Cf. D. xxxviii 15 fr 2 pr and below.

which if unduly long is sometimes shortened by the praetor. Even if the appointed heir has made up his mind to refuse, still, if he repent, he can, so long as the period is yet unexpired, become heir by a formal declaration. This is made by utterance (according to the ordinary practice, in the presence of witnesses, Varro *L. L.* vi 81) of the words: 'Whereas P. Mevius has 'appointed me heir by his will, that inheritance I enter and 'decide on (*eam hereditatem adeo cernoque*)[1].' If he does not make this formal decision, he is irrevocably excluded at the expiration of the period fixed. Action as heir will not supply its place (Gai. ii 166, 168, 170; Ulp. xxii 28, 30).

4. Where there is no *cretio* in the will, it is open to the appointed heir, as it is to the statutable heir, to enter on the inheritance at any time he chooses. In this case entry is made either by a formal declaration as above, or by acting in the character of heir (*pro herede gerendo*), or even by a mere exercise of will. And by a mere exercise of will he can decline the inheritance. An own heir who has declined his father's inheritance can yet, if the estate remains untouched, alter his mind and accept. But in other cases decision either way is irrevocable. If the appointed heir delays in coming to a decision, or in performing a condition within his power, on which condition his appointment rests, the praetor is wont, on the application of creditors of the estate and full hearing, to fix a limit of time for the heir's decision, and in default of decision to allow the creditors to sell the estate. If the condition is beyond his power, the praetor will allow a sale after a certain time. For sufficient cause the time may be extended. Where the estate is large, and some parts are deteriorating or are too expensive to keep up, the praetor allows the heir during deliberation, or an agent appointed by himself, to sell such things without prejudice; and where there are debts under penalty if not repaid, or for which valuables have been pledged, he allows them to be discharged, the amount being raised from cash in

[1] Cf. Cic. *Att.* xi 2 § 1 *Litteras tuas accepi pr. Non. Febr. eoque ipso die ex testamento crevi hereditatem.* Plin. *Ep. Traj.* 75 (=79) *Rogavit testamento ut hereditatem suam adirem cernеremque ac deinde...redderem* (*i.e.* it was to be a trust).

hand or by sale of fungibles or by collection of debts due to the estate, or if necessary by sale of superfluous articles. The like course is followed in the case of a ward, who is not generally required to decide until puberty, but is on cause shewn put under a prohibition not to impair the estate[1], except for his own subsistence or for funeral expenses or necessary maintenance of the property (Gai. ii 167, 169; Ulp. xxii 29; D. xxviii 8 fr 1—9; 5 fr 23 § 1 sqq.; Cod. vi 31 fr 6 pr). A son in his father's power, if he die while still deliberating whether to enter or not, transmits his right to his posterity (Cod. vi 30 fr 19 pr). A son appointed both an heir and legatee does not, by keeping aloof from the inheritance, lose claim to the legacy, unless testator so intended (D. xxx fr 87—90).

'Acting in the character of heir' is dealing with things belonging to the inheritance as your own. Such acts are selling things, giving rations to slaves, making use of slaves or beasts, arranging the cultivation or accounts of the farms, *etc.* Whether this or that act implies acceptance of the inheritance depends not so much on the act itself as on the intention to act in the character of heir. *Pro herede gerere non est facti quam animi.* Even dealing with what does not belong to the inheritance may from the intention shewn fix a man with the position of heir, *e.g.* retaining property which was pledged to the estate, or taking possession as heir of what is not part of the estate. But mere acts of pious affection or desire to safeguard other's goods will not make him answerable to the creditors of the inheritance (Paul iv 8 § 23 (25); D. xxix 2 fr 20 pr, 21 § 1, 88).

5. 'Meddling with the estate' is in the case of an own heir of much the same meaning, only that as a member of the

[1] *Ne bona* or *hereditatem deminuat* is the technical phrase in all such cases. *E.g.* it is used by Cicero in a letter to his brother Quintus, who was reported to have, in his provincial administration, acting in the interest of C. Fundanius, ordered the people of Apollonis in Mysia not to allow the agents of L. Flavius 'to impair the estate' of L. Octavius Nero to whom L. Naevius was heir, until Fundanius' claim on Nero's estate had been paid. Cicero points out to his brother that the debt had not been proved, and that it was an unheard of thing to tie an heir to the payment of a debt, especially one which might not be really due (*ad Q. Fr.* i 2 § 10).

household he may naturally be called to the performance of duties, which in the case of outsiders would more readily imply acceptance of heirship. A son perhaps buries his father or celebrates due rites at his tomb; he repairs buildings, lets houses or farms, feeds the slaves, feeds or even sells the beasts of burden; if he does it, not as heir and owner, but only for due security of the estate, he is not fixed with liability as heir. It was the practice in such cases for him to declare before witnesses that he is not acting as heir. But this was not necessary (*Const.* of Severus *ap.* Krüger iii p. 254). A son is entitled to maintenance (*ali*) during deliberation; but if he carries off (*amoverit*) in bad faith any effects of the estate, he can no longer avoid the position of heir; if he does so after declining, he is liable to the creditors for theft. He may sue for a freedman's services or may ask support from a freedman of his father's without assuming the inheritance; for these acts are open to all sons, but not to all heirs. But if in any way he does that which only as heir he would do, *e.g.* pay a debt of testator's, he becomes responsible as heir to the creditors (D. xxix 2 fr 20 §§ 1, 2, 4 *ad fin.*, 71 §§ 3—9; 87; Cod. vi 30 fr 2). If he holds aloof, but arranges for someone to buy testator's estate on his account, he makes himself liable to the creditors (D. fr 91).

If an own heir decides to hold aloof from the inheritance, and there is a coheir, either own heir also or outsider, who has already become responsible, such coheir has the option to keep or give up all, unless the creditors are willing to pursue his share of the estate only. If he remains on that understanding, they must cede to him their rights of suit against the other share. Any bargain by which creditors agree to take less than the full amount of their debts must have the consent of a majority of the creditors in value (D. fr 55; ii 14 fr 7 §§ 17—19). If the coheir dies before the other decides to stand aloof, the option is given to his heir (D. xxix 2 fr 56). If one own heir meddled with the business, after the other had held aloof, the former has acted with his eyes open and cannot avoid full responsibility (fr 38).

6. Where another's son under his power or another's slave is appointed heir he must await an order from the father or

master, who before giving the order to enter must have the like intelligent knowledge of the situation as if he were appointed heir himself. The order must be for entry on a specified inheritance, and the giver must know whether it is for the whole or for a share, and whether he is instituted or substituted heir. But it still seems that an order to accept part is good for the whole, and an order to accept under a will is good for acceptance *ab intestato*; but not *vice versa* in either case. The order (whether by message or letter or sign) must precede the entry, except in the case of succession under the *SC. Orfitianum*, where ratification will do. It may be conditional on the son or slave's finding himself entitled or on the inheritance's appearing to him worth acceptance; and if the son or slave is aware of a fact necessary to the validity of the entry, the father or master's ignorance does not affect it. The death or insanity or arrogation of the father or master invalidates the order, if entry has not taken place (D. xxix 2 fr 25 § 4 sqq., 30 § 7, 47, 93 pr).

A father or master cannot enter in place of his son or slave, who has been appointed heir; but if a father acts as heir with the son's consent, a series of rescripts decided that he became heir. Neither can validly repudiate such an inheritance without the consent of the other (D. *ib.* fr 6 § 3, 13 § 3; Cod. vi 30 fr 4). A slave's consent is required, though there are cases in which he can be compelled to enter (D. xxxvi 1 fr 67 pr; xxix 4 fr 1 § 3). If a father be appointed heir as well as his son or slave, the son or slave entering by his order makes him heir to his own share as well as theirs; but if the father enters, he does not get their shares, until he has given the order and they have entered (fr 26, 36). If a son is emancipated or slave manumitted after an order but before entry, he becomes heir himself. If the slave be appointed heir to one part absolutely, and to another conditionally, he must enter twice, and, if manumitted before the condition occurs, keeps that share himself (fr 80 § 2). A common slave entering by order of one master makes him heir in proportion to his share in the slave; if the co-owners do not all give an order, their shares accrue to anyone who has ordered; but if the slave has been set free, he can enter and take their shares himself (fr 64, 67). If there is a substitute appointed for the case of the slave's not being heir, and the slave enters on the order of one master only, the substitute is entitled to the other share (D. xxviii 6 fr 48 pr).

7. Entry on an inheritance is an act of the person and not a mere piece of work included in a slave's services. Hence the usufructuary of a slave does not acquire an inheritance left to the slave, nor does a husband acquire an inheritance left to a slave belonging to his wife's dowry, so as to entitle him to retain it against his wife's action for dowry. Nor does a freeman in *bona fide* servitude, entering on an inheritance by order of his putative master, acquire it for him: he acquires for himself, if he wills it as Labeo thought, whether he wills it or not as Trebatius thought. If he was appointed heir on the master's account Julian appears to have thought he might be regarded as acquiring *ex re domini*, and therefore for his master: others held that the inheritance, though acquired by the supposed slave, must be restored to his master (fr 45; xli 1 fr 19; xxviii 5 fr 60 pr).

CHAPTER V.

BONORUM POSSESSIO[1].

A. CHARACTER AND PROTECTION.

1. The praetor exercised a large and salutary jurisdiction over the succession to a deceased person's estate. This was in the interest of the natural heirs, who might otherwise have been excluded by testator's oversight or by failure in the performance or proof of some technicality, or by the superannuated rigidity of the early law. As marriage no longer usually involved the wife's coming into the hand of her husband, as emancipation of sons

[1] This term (*bonorum possessio*) is rare in Cicero. Leist (Glück's *Pand.* Bk 37 1 p. 49) quotes *Cluent.* 60 § 165; Orat. 1 *pro Corn.* Fragm. 37 ed. Müller; *Ep. Fam.* viii 21 (*Verr.* i 4 § 12 *bonorum possessionumque* is not clearly an instance). Cicero's usual phrase is *hereditatis possessio*; *e.g. Verr.* ii 1 45 § 117; 46 § 118; 47 § 124; ii 3 7 § 16; *Ep. Att.* vi 1 § 15; *Part. Orat.* 28 § 98, *etc.*; Valer. Max. vii 7 §§ 5—7.

became more frequent, as the clan ceased to be a living and active institution, and the forms of making wills became out of date, the praetor gave more effect to the claims of relationship by blood and to the presumed intentions of a testator. And this he did, not by directly annulling the rules of the strict law, or by mere arbitrary action, but by granting possession of deceased's estate according to rules previously announced in his standing edict; and protecting the possessors. Such possessors were not heirs, but only in the place of heirs. They were not in strict law owners of the property, or creditors to deceased's debtors, or debtors to deceased's creditors: they had the property only *in bonis*, and required usucapion to perfect their title; they sued and were sued on a fictitious assumption that they were heirs (Gai. iii 80, 81; iv 34; Ulp. xxviii 12). The origin and precise steps of the praetor's action are not known[1], but it appears probable that it sprang from a merely temporary arrangement for the due conduct of a suit or suits for the inheritance among the natural and apparently legal claimants. Other considerations may have assisted.

However that may be, the edict classified this interference under three heads in the following order: (i) *Bonorum possessio contra tabulas*, (ii) *B. P. secundum tabulas*, (iii) *B. P. ab intestato*; the first admitting children who had been overlooked in their father's will, or patrons who had not been given their due share; the second confirming the provision of a will which was

[1] Different theories have been put forward on the origin of the praetorian interference. The principal lines are five. 1. Correction of civil law by adoption of rules of *praetor peregrinus* resting on *jus gentium* (Hugo); 2. Imitation of rules for occupation of public land (Niebuhr); 3. Regulation of *usucapio pro herede* (Huschke); 4. Regulation of the position of parties in the suit for an inheritance (Dernburg, Vangerow); 5. Pressure on the civil heirs to take up the inheritance by warning that otherwise claimants less entitled would be admitted (Leist). See Vangerow *Pand.* § 398; Danz *Rechtsgeschichte* ii p. 143 sqq.; Leist, Glück's *Pand.* Bk 37 i p. 39 sqq.; Girard *Manuel* p. 357 n.

Cicero refers generally to the praetor's action in this matter: *Part. Or.* 28 § 98 *cum hereditatis sine lege aut sine testamento petitur possessio, quid aequius atque aequissimum quaeritur?* Here *sine lege* refers to *B. P. contra tabulas*; *sine test.* to *B. P. ab intestato*.

technically invalid, but (until a rescript of Antoninus) confirming it only if there was no heir *ab intestato* to contest it; and the third enlarging and amending the narrow list and order sanctioned by the XII tables for succession to an intestate inheritance.

The term *bona* 'goods' when used in this connexion denoted the whole estate of the deceased, both corporal and incorporal, its rights and liabilities, its gain and its loss. 'Possession of the goods' was the right of pursuing and retaining the patrimony or any single thing which was deceased's when he died (*jus persequendi retinendique patrimoni sive rei quae cujusque cum moritur fuit* D. xxxvii 1 fr 3 § 2).

2. Acquisition of this right was voluntary. It is generally called 'acknowledgment' (*agnoscere, agnitio*) and corresponded to entry on an inheritance. It could be acquired by oneself or through another, either on previous mandate or on ratification within the prescribed time, and was open to municipalities and other communities, and to companies and clubs. In case of dispute, possession was granted only after due and solemn hearing (*pro tribunali, ib.* fr 3 §§ 3, 4, 7; xlvi 8 fr 24 pr). A slave, or woman, or an absent or even non-applicant person can be granted possession, if the praetor is aware of the fact or *status*. A person under the age of puberty requires his guardian's authority to apply or to repudiate, but the guardian has no power to repudiate a grant for him (D. xxxvii 1 fr 7, 8; xxxviii 9 fr 1 § 4). No grant can be made to one who is by statute, senate's decree, or imperial constitution disqualified from taking an inheritance, or is under capital sentence (D. xxxvii 1 fr 12, § 1, 13). Mute, deaf, blind, persons are capable of accepting possession if they know what they are doing (D. xxxvii 3 fr 2). If there are more than one person with equal claims, all are admissible; if one only accepts, the shares of the others (if under the same title) accrue to him, whether they have died before acceptance or have repudiated, or have not accepted in time (D. xxxvii 1 fr 3 § 9; 4, 5). The time for application is a year for children and parents, 100 days for outsiders. It begins to run from knowledge of deceased's death and ascertainment of applicant's being the nearest relative, whether the will has

been opened or not (Ulp. xxviii 10; D. xxxvii 1 fr 10; xlvi 8 fr 24). In the case of a child or ward, time runs from the knowledge of his father or guardian (xxxvii 1 fr 7 § 2). It does not run so long as the person entitled is mad (xxxvii 3 fr 1).

3. To enable the person to whom the grant was made to obtain what belonged to the estate from anyone in actual occupation, an interdict, called from the initial words *quorum bonorum*, was issued. It ran as follows: 'You are to restore to so and so 'anything belonging to the estate of which possession has been 'granted to him under my edict, which you possess in the charac- 'ter of heir or mere possessor, or would have been possessing, if 'usucapion had not taken place, or which you have fraudulently 'ceased to possess.' The injunction to restore is addressed to anyone who is possessor, either as being heir, or thinking himself to be heir, or who, without any real ground, holds a thing belonging to the estate or the estate itself, though knowing that it does not belong to him. When the grantee of the possession has once obtained possession, this interdict is no longer applicable: he must resort to the ordinary interdicts (*uti possidetis, de vi, etc.*). Nor is it applicable for the recovery of any but corporal things: for debts the grantee must, as stated above, sue with a fiction (Gai. iv 144; D. xliii 2).

The utility of this interdict, probably on account of a shorter and more peremptory procedure than that of the ordinary action, made a grant of possession of the estate desirable even for a rightful heir, whether by will or intestacy. If he did not apply for it, it stood open to anyone who had a remoter possible claim to the inheritance; for instance, to those who would have been entitled if there were no will, or are entitled even against the will. Or supposing the statutable heir to content himself with his statutable right and not to apply for the praetor's grant, then it was open to another agnate, or, if an agnate had entered on the inheritance but not taken the grant of possession, it was still open for a cognate to apply. In all such cases, however, the possessor can be evicted by the rightful heir, and his possession is therefore unreal (*possessio sine re*). Effective possession in contrast to this was described as real (*possessio cum re* Gai. iii 33—37; Ulp. xxviii 13).

4. Another interdict *quod legatorum*[1] was granted to the possessor of a deceased's estate to enable him to get restoration of anything occupied by a legatee without the consent of the *bonorum possessor*. The praetor required that legatees should not take the law into their own hands (*jus sibi ipsos dicere*), but make their demand on the *bonorum possessor* (whether they sued by real or personal action). If it is uncertain in what character the defendant holds possession, whether claiming to be heir or legatee or mere possessor, the course recommended was that the *bonorum possessor* should bring the interdict *quorum bonorum* as well as this interdict, so as to fix defendant with liability in any character, the *bonorum possessor* making a formal declaration that he intended to enforce only one interdict. The interdict ran against even an heir so far as he took a thing specially (*per praeceptionem*), and (in an analogous form) against one to whom a usufruct or use or easement had been left, and against anyone in possession under the praetor's order for due safeguarding of legacies. Moreover it ran not only against the first possessor but his heirs and successors, whether universal or singular. Consent on the part of the *bonorum possessor*, whether previous or subsequent to the occupation, removed the liability so far as the consent extended. But such consent was valid only if given after the *bonorum possessor* had obtained the praetor's grant (D. xliii 3 fr 1; Vat. 90).

The *bonorum possessor* was required to give proper security, either his own or sureties also, if demanded by defendant. He need not offer it, but must be ready to give it when the interdict is issued (D. *ib.* fr 1 § 16—fr 2 § 1).

If the interdict was not obeyed by restoration of the thing occupied, the damages were calculated by the plaintiff's interest in the restoration (fr 2 § 2).

The interdict did not run against one who held under a *mortis causa* gift, the *bonorum possessor*, like an heir, being entitled *ipso jure* to his Falcidian share, though the thing itself be with the donee (fr 1 § 5).

[1] See Leist, Glück's *Pand.* Bk 37 Bd i p. 412 sq.; Lenel *E. P.* § 228; *Palingenes.* ii p. 801. The Digest has made it applicable to the *heir*.

B. POSSESSION OF DECEASED'S ESTATE CONTRARY TO THE WILL.

i. BY CHILDREN.

1. The claims of children, grandchildren, *etc.*, living and postumous, who are, or may by the removal of their fathers become, own heirs, were protected by the praetor no less than by the civil law, but with more regard to kinship by blood than to the strict rules of agnation. If testator had dealt plainly with children under his power by appointing them heirs (either absolutely or on a condition which in fact occurred), or by duly disinheriting them (in the grade to which the inheritance actually came), both civil law and praetor respected his judgment. But if the testator simply passed them by without notice, the civil law invalidated the will, where sons were passed by, and admitted overlooked daughters to share equally with the heirs appointed (*scriptis haeredibus in partem adcrescunt*). If one son was overlooked, all the children became heirs as on intestacy; if children were appointed heirs and a daughter overlooked, the result was the same; but if strangers were appointed heirs, an overlooked daughter or daughters did not oust the strangers from the inheritance as an overlooked son would, but became heir or heirs to a moiety, the strangers having the other moiety. The praetor however treated male and female own heirs alike, and if outsiders were appointed heirs, he granted possession of all the testator's estate to the own heirs in equal shares, and though not displacing the outsiders from being heirs, left them nothing but the name (*heredes sine re*)[1]. M. Aurelius, however, practically restored the old rule as regards overlooked women, limiting their share of the possession of the estate to what they

[1] If an heir entered under a will which overlooked an emancipated son, he had no effectual hold: the son if he applied could draw away the substance of his position from him: a debtor suing him could be met by the plea of the possibility of an emancipated son obtaining a grant of possession *Si non in ea causa tabulae testamenti sint ut contra eas emancipato bonorum possessio dari posset.* Julian uses a strong expression *quamdiu bonorum possessio contra tabulas filio dari potest, heres quodammodo debitor non est* (D. xliv 7 fr 15); cf. Leist in Glück's *Pand.* Bk 37 ii § 5.

would have had by the civil law. Grandsons and granddaughters were treated by the civil law and by the praetor in the same way as daughters (Gai. ii 123—126; D. xxxvii 4 fr 3 §§ 12, 13, fr 8 § 1; Cod. vi 28 fr 4 § 1).

Children by adoption were treated as natural children so long as they continued in the adoptive family: but, if emancipated, they thereby lost all rights in that family (Gai. ii 136, 137).

2. Emancipated children by the civil law were no longer own heirs and were outside their natural family altogether: they could of course be appointed heirs in the will just as any other outsiders, but there was no necessity to appoint or disinherit them, they might be passed by without affecting the validity of the will. The praetor however, by his edict, recognized their full claims as children, and if any were dead leaving children, recognized the claims of the children as representing their father. If any such were overlooked by the will, the praetor gave him or her possession along with own heirs and with others in the same position as themselves. One being overlooked opened the door to all, and the rules of civil law intestacy were followed (Gai. ii 135; Ulp. xxii 23, xxviii 2, 3; D. fr 1 § 1, fr 3). Thus (to take some examples), if a son (or daughter) and two or more grandsons by a dead son are living at the death of testator, and only one has been overlooked in the will, all are admitted to the possession, the son (or daughter) taking one half, the grandsons dividing the other half between them (fr 11 § 1). If said testator having also a grandson by the living son emancipates him and then adopts him in the place of a son, the possession will be granted in thirds to the son, to the grandson as adopted son, and to the two grandsons together (one-sixth each). If he adopt him not only as son to himself but as father to the two grandsons, the division will be in halves, each son taking one half, and the grandsons being excluded by their new father. If after this adoption he emancipates him again, retaining the two grandsons in his power, the original position of all three grandsons is resumed. If one grandson by the dead son does not apply, his share accrues to his brother. If there are two sons (or daughters) and some grandchildren by a dead son, and one

son (or daughter) does not apply, the share accrues both to the other son (or daughter) and to the grandchildren, the possession of the estate being divided into halves (cf. fr 3 §§ 1—3, 12 § 1).

The same view of the continuing connexion of an emancipated son to his original family is shewn by the praetor's allowing his children, if left behind when he was emancipated, to claim (if overlooked in their father's will) possession of his estate provided their grandfather is still alive (fr 7).

3. Sons given in adoption (or arrogated after emancipation) and emancipated by their adoptive father during the life of their natural father are as if they had been simply emancipated by the latter; they are so far connected again with him and have no connexion with their adoptive father (fr 6 § 4; Just. iii 2 §§ 10—12); but sons given in adoption, or arrogated, and remaining in the adoptive family at the time of their natural father's death, and passed over in his will, have no claim to his estate, even if their adoptive father be dead. But the praetor made an exception in some cases where the adoption was into a family not strange in blood. Thus, if a son when emancipated leaves his own son with his grandfather and afterwards receives him back again by adoption, the grandson is, after his own father's death, admissible to the possession of his grandfather's estate. Similarly if an emancipated son beget a son and give him in adoption to his own father and die, the grandson is admissible to the possession of the estate of his own natural father, just as if he were not by the adoption in a different family (fr 3 §§ 7, 8). But an adoptive son given again in adoption by his adoptive father has no claim in any case to share in the possession of such a father's estate. It was only in the case of original blood relationship that the grant could be claimed: he must be *ex liberis* (fr 8 § 12).

4. In another case some difference of opinion prevailed. If a father emancipated his son and then gave himself in adoption and died after his adoptive father, could the emancipated son, if passed over in his father's will claim possession of his estate, seeing that they were in entirely different families? Julian said No. Marcellus thought this hard upon the son, who though separated from his father by an adoption had not got a new

16—2

father, as he would if he himself had been given in adoption. Ulpian (in Dig.) approves the dissent from Julian. Africanus, apparently agreeing with Julian, thought it was a case not for the ordinary edict but for a special decree, and that thus he might be qualified for possession of both his father's and (natural) grandfather's estate (fr 14 § 1, 17).

5. Natural or adoptive children still under power, and natural children emancipated or given in adoption, all, if appointed heirs by their father, share in his estate with those who have been passed over. If they require the possession in addition to their title under the will, the praetor grants it them. If they have accepted testator's judgment by entering on the inheritance, or meddling with it or accepting a legacy or *fidei commissum* under the will, they cannot claim equal shares (*pars virilis*) with those overlooked, but may indeed, so far as they are heirs, have their emolument abridged if it is more than a *pars virilis*. If they have not accepted testator's judgment, they cannot of themselves claim any revision of their lot, but if the matter is thrown open by other natural children (*commisso per alios edicto*) who have been overlooked and (not being in a stranger's family by adoption) have a right of moving against the will, they can claim an equal share. A son given in adoption is not precluded from doing so by his adopted father's having accepted testator's judgment and bidden him enter or take the emolument under the will; and, if emancipated, can claim an equal share of the possession and oust his adoptive father (fr 10 §§ 2, 3; 14 pr).

Where an emancipated son, who had been overlooked, was sued by his father's heir for some debt to the father's estate, and, instead of pleading his right as a son to possession of the estate ('*si non contra tabulas bonorum possessio filio dari potest*'), pleaded fraud in the ordinary way, he was held to have thereby renounced his claim to the possession (fr 15).

6. For the grant of possession against the will, *contra tabulas* (or, as sometimes called, *contra lignum*, an invalid will being no will), it is not necessary that the will should be thoroughly effective. Such grants can be made even when all appointed heirs and substitutes have died before the testator, or were

persons not duly qualified to be heirs. What is necessary as a foundation for this grant is that at the death of a *paterfamilias* a will should have existed, in accordance with which it was possible for entry on the inheritance or possession of the estate to be made or granted (fr 4 pr, 19). Thus if a son has been disinherited by a will duly executed, and passed over by a subsequent will not duly executed, the son can claim possession of the estate only if the later will be established by the praetor, as would be done if the heir therein appointed were superior in claim to the heir named in the former (fr 12 § 1).

7. Sons duly disinherited[1] cannot in any case claim possession against the will: their only chance is a plaint of unduteous will (fr 8 pr; 10 § 5). If a son under power be disinherited, and another be emancipated and passed over, outsiders being appointed heirs, the emancipated son will be entitled to possession of the whole of the estate, whether the outsiders enter or not. If they do enter, the disherison takes effect, but they themselves get no benefit. If they do not enter, there would be an anomalous result; for the disinherited son, though capable of getting possession against the wills of his father's freedmen, would be excluded from his father's estate, and that too by a will which is otherwise ineffective. To avoid this, the case is regarded as an intestacy, and the two sons will practically share the inheritance equally, the disinherited son being sole heir by the civil law, and the emancipated son being sole grantee of the possession[2]. Obviously the outsider heirs are in a position to make a bargain with one or other son: for if they do not enter, the disinherited son will get half: if they do enter, the emancipated son gets all, unless indeed the will be found unduteous (fr 20 pr).

Possession *c. tab.* has nothing to do with women's wills (fr 4 § 2; Gai. iii 71).

[1] Not even if the son be emancipated, then disinherited, and afterwards arrogated by his own natural father (fr 8 § 7; xxviii 2 fr 23 pr).

[2] He would not be called on to make his own property contribute, but he would be liable to pay legacies. The disinherited son would do neither (fr 20, fr 1—3). See another case dealt with by Justinian, where a daughter overlooked would be worse off than if disinherited: she brought the plaint of unduteous will (Cod. vi 28 4 §§ 3—5).

8. In recognising the claims of emancipated children, and by such recognition impairing the share of their father's inheritance which would have otherwise fallen to those remaining in his power till his death, the praetor took account of the whole position and made equitable adjustments:—

(*a*) Joining of children to emancipated father.

On the emancipation of a son some of his children might be left in the grandfather's family and by the departure of their own father become own heirs. But their father's obtaining a grant of possession against the will displaces their claim by his precedence. If the testator did not disinherit them and their father obtain possession either of the whole estate or of an equal share with his brothers and sisters, a special clause of the edict introduced by Julian provided for his sharing whatever he obtained with his children who were in their grandfather's power at his death. If the father gets possession of the whole estate, the grandsons would have one half; if he has to share the estate with a brother who also has not been disinherited, then he has one half and has to divide this half with the grandsons. It is immaterial whether the grandsons have been passed over in the will or appointed heirs to a small part; because when once the door is opened, either by their own father or another, for granting possession notwithstanding the will, the will is set aside and equality of shares between own heirs in the same degree becomes the rule. If the grandsons were passed over by testator, but their father made heir to one-third and their father's brother to two-thirds, the grandsons can apply for a grant of possession, and the result will be that their uncle will be left with one-half the estate, their father with one-fourth and they with one-fourth. If their father is disinherited and the grandsons passed over, they can get possession of a due share for themselves, their father being out of account altogether as if he were dead. A son who has been given in adoption is joined to his children in a grant of possession just the same as one emancipated, but only if he has been appointed heir, and some other own heir has been passed over, so as to bring this part of the edict into play (D. xxxvii 8 fr 1 §§ pr—11; fr 3).

(*b*) *Collatio bonorum.*

Further the praetor required from emancipated sons who were admitted to their share of possession of their father's estate contrary to his will, that if they took thereby from own heirs remaining under their father's power they should in some degree make it up from their own means. Thus, if testator appoints a son heir to three-fourths and an outsider to one-fourth and overlooks another son emancipated, this latter claiming possession obtains one-half the estate and must contribute to his brother in proportion to what he deprives him of; *i.e.* as he deprives him of one-fourth of his father's estate, he must contribute to him one-fourth of his own estate. If the brother under power and the outsider had each a half, the emancipated son simply displaces the outsider, and there is no call upon him to contribute anything to his brother. If this brother was appointed heir only to one-fourth or other share less than half, he benefits by his brother's obtaining a grant of possession and has still less claim to a contribution from him. Nor is the emancipated son any more liable to contribute if he has received a legacy from his father, provided it does not exceed what he can claim as grantee of possession. If a son given in adoption is admitted to possession, his adoptive father must contribute: but not if he emancipate his adopted son before the grant of possession: and in that case neither will the son have to contribute, supposing the emancipation was not fraudulent (D. xxxvii 6 fr 1 to § 8, § 14; Ulp. xxviii 4; *ap. Collat.* xvi 7 § 2). Similarly if a grandson remaining under power claim possession of his emancipated father's estate, the grandfather must either contribute or set the grandson free, so that he himself may take none of the emolument from the grant of possession to the grandson (fr 5 pr). If a son under power is appointed heir and enters and does not apply for the grant, his emancipated brother is not by the terms of the edict bound to contribute to him; but as the son under power could take the like grant if necessary and loses by the grant to his brother, it is fair that contribution should be made (fr 10).

There is no obligation to contribute to other emancipated brothers; they are free to apply for possession or not as they think most advisable; but those who were still under power (including postumous children) at testator's death have to submit to lose by their brothers' admission to possession. So *e.g.* if three sons are emancipated and apply for possession and two sons are remaining in their father's family, each emancipated son obtains only one-fifth of their father's estate and has to share his own estate with the two under power, *i.e.* to contribute one-third of his own estate to each of them, and retain only one-third for himself. Grandsons by a deceased son when other sons are alive contribute and receive contribution collectively to the extent to which their father would (D. *ib.* fr 2 § 5; fr 3 §§ 2, 3; fr 7). An emancipated son coming in and taking a share together with sons of his own left in their grandfather's power has to contribute to them one-half of his own property, *e.g.* a testator leaves one son under power, a grandson by an emancipated son, and an adopted son being a grandson begotten by his emancipated son after emancipation. The emancipated son being passed over obtains possession. The possession of the estate is divided into thirds: one for testator's natural son under power, one for his adopted son, and one divided between his emancipated son and the grandson under power to whom his own father has to contribute (D. *ib.* fr 3 § 6; tit. 8 fr 1 § 13 sqq.).

The contribution, if not paid at once, or if something in lieu thereof is not handed over in satisfaction of the claim, is secured by a stipulation supported either by sureties or pledges. If this cannot be done, a caretaker is appointed for the share of testator's estate due to the person who has to contribute, and the caretaker transfers to him the money raised from the share only on the due contribution being made to his brothers. Giving security is not made a condition of the grant of possession, because of the risks attending delay; for then the death of the contributee would prevent the other's obtaining a grant of the possession (there being no one to take the security), and the death of the contributor would leave no claim to his heir. Contumacious refusal to give security is met by the praetor's refusing actions until it is done. After a year from the time of right to possession accruing, voluntary delay in giving security can rarely be repaired. Sometimes, in lieu of security, the contributor may remit an equivalent portion of his share of the testator's estate (fr 1 §§ 9—13; fr 3 pr, 8).

The amount of the contributor's property is taken, as in other cases, after deduction of debts. Neither camp-*peculium* nor anything given or owed him by his father to support some dignity is subject to contribution. Nor has he to reckon his wife's dowry, for that he takes as a first claim (*praecipuum*), just as a son under power does; nor does he reckon anything which has been lost since his father's death without fault of his own; nor damages for insult (*injuriarum*), that being a matter rather of personal feeling than of property; but damages recoverable for theft come in. Anything due to him on stipulation under a condition is reckoned, for if he were still under power the right of action would belong to his father or his father's heir, and consequently be included in the distributable assets: but a conditional legacy, if the condition did not take effect till after his father's death, would belong to himself, and is therefore not to be reckoned in the contributable property. A legacy to be paid him on his father's death (*cum morietur*) is reckoned. The whole matter is subject to arbitration by a *vir bonus* (fr 1 §§ 15, 16, 18, fr 2 §§ 1—4, fr 3 § 4).

(c) *Collatio dotis.*

An emancipated daughter or one given in adoption has to contribute not only her property but her dowry, whether profectitious or adventitious, to her brothers or sisters still remaining under power, if she obtain a grant of possession of her father's estate, or, according to a rescript of Ant. Pius, if she be appointed heir and meddle with the estate. If she has been given in adoption, her adoptive father has to make the like contribution. A daughter still in her father's power and made heir, if possession is obtained by someone else, can either take a grant of possession also, and, if her share is increased thereby, must contribute her dowry, or can keep the share given her by her father (not being more than a single equal share), and thus accepting her father's judgment is not obliged to contribute her dowry. Nor does she contribute, if she is contented with her dowry and keeps aloof from her father's estate. But an agreement to that effect in the instrument of dowry was not binding on her. The contribution is made only to own heirs of her father (or other ascendant) whose share is lessened by her concurrence, *e.g.* to her brother, if there be only he and her uncle as own heirs, but to her first cousin and uncle if there be no other child of her own father.

The contribution from dowry is calculated after necessary expenses have been deducted. If the dowry has been promised but not paid, the woman (if she has to contribute) must release the concurrents from a proportional share of the amount. If someone other than the woman has stipulated for the return of the dowry to himself, it is not contributable. Interest is payable if there is delay in making the contribution. The contribution is payable only when the marriage is dissolved: if it is still continuing, the woman cannot demand the dowry from her husband for the purpose, but must instead accept a smaller share of the inheritance (D. xxxvii 7 fr 1—5, 9; x 2 fr 20 pr; Cod. vi 20 fr 3, 5).

Some difference of opinion in respect to contribution of dowry to persons who had not remained under deceased's power, is mentioned by Gordian in a rescript of 239 A.D. (Cod. vi 20 fr 4), but the matter is not clear (cf. Arndts in Weiske's *Rechtslex.* iii p. 826; Leist in Glück's *Pand.* Pt iii p. 231).

(*d*) Saving of legacies, *etc.* to children and parents.

When possession of the estate of a deceased person was granted contrary to the will, the will though not technically upset was liable to be nullified by the grantees being protected against the heirs and withdrawing the inheritance from them. If the heirs charged with legacies or trusts did not enter (a result which might easily occur, as they had little to look for) the legacies charged on them failed. Hence the praetor required that the persons obtaining the possession should pay and perform all good legacies and trusts, if charged in the grade against which possession was granted and actually took effect, so far as they were given in favour of children or parents of testator or, on account of dowry, to his wife or daughter-in-law. The class of *liberi*[1] *et parentes* within the saving included all descendants and ascendants at the date of the legacy's vesting, whether men or women, provided they were cognates, including adoptive children remaining in the family as well as children given in adoption. Brothers and sisters were not within the excepted class, and legacies to them were not protected any more than legacies to outsiders. Gifts in view of death were treated as legacies.

Legacies to slaves or others under power of children or parents were not saved: the child or parent might no doubt benefit by such, but he was not the legatee (*Nec enim quaerimus cui adquiratur, sed cui honos habitus sit*). Nor were legacies to children or parents in trust for outsiders saved, but legacies to outsiders in trust or otherwise, intended for children or parents, were saved. If a legacy was to one of the protected class in common with an outsider, the outsider's portion was dropped (D. xxxvii 5 fr 1—3; 24).

The saving extended also by a rescript of Ant. Pius to any shares of the inheritance given to children or parents. If however anyone's share was in excess of the equal share (*pars virilis*) of persons entitled under the praetor's edict, either taken by itself or together with any legacy in his favour, it was cut down to that: if less, it was taken as appointed in the will. The same rule of reduction was applied to legacies. If any heir appointed in the will had legacies charged on him in favour of outsiders as well as of children or parents of testator, the legacies to outsiders were not paid to them, but helped to increase the amounts recoverable by members of the protected class (fr 5 §§ 6—8, fr 6, 7). Any legatee or other beneficiary under the will, if he obtained possession against the will, could not have the legacy or other benefit also, but was put to his election. So if the will made him heir, as substitute to his

[1] On the wide meaning of *liberi* see D. L 16 fr 220; xxvi 2 fr 6.

brother under age, he could not claim his brother's inheritance, if he accepted the possession (fr 5 §§ 3, 4).

Where a will appoints heirs and charges legacies to the protected class on them, and appoints others in substitution and charges legacies against the substitutes, if the appointed heirs or any of them are alive when possession is granted against the will, the legacies charged in the first stage are payable by the grantees whether the heirs have entered or not; if they are not alive or if the condition on which they are appointed heirs fails, the legacies charged on the substitutes are what come to be payable. If neither appointed heirs nor substitutes are alive at the date of testator's death, the possession is granted as *ab intestato*, and no legacies are payable (fr 10 § 1—fr 13).

The protection of legatees is not always limited to the class of children and parents. A son in the power of deceased and therefore an own heir, if appointed heir by the will is liable (in the ratio of his share and deducting the Falcidian fourth) to all legatees in the grade in which he is heir: but if he is overlooked, he succeeds *ab intestato* and is liable to none, whether he rest on his statutable claim or accept a grant of possession: if he abstains, the appointed heirs will on grounds of equity be held liable. An emancipated son, if overlooked and taking the grant of possession, is liable only to the protected class of legatees, but if there is an own heir also overlooked, it is the own heir who invalidates the will and the emancipated son is then not liable to legatees at all. If the emancipated son is appointed heir by the will, but the edict is brought into play by other sons being overlooked, he can either take a grant of possession or stand on the will. In the former case, if others take possession also, he is liable only to the protected class of legatees, but if by others not taking the grant he is left sole possessor he is then liable to all legatees. Again if he stands on the will, he is according to most opinions liable (in the ratio of his share) to all legatees, if there is an own heir who being overlooked is liable to none; but to the protected class only, if there is another emancipated son who being overlooked is also liable to them (fr 14 pr, 15 pr § 1, 16; xxviii 3 fr 17, cf. Gai.

ii 123). Where an emancipated son has been overlooked and another son *impubes* is appointed heir with a substitute, and both sons have the possession granted them, then if the substitute succeeds, he is liable for legacies charged on the *impubes* only within the protected class, but if they are charged on himself he is liable for all. As however he succeeds only to possession of one half of the estate and from that can deduct the Falcidian fourth he will pay three-eighths ($\frac{3}{4}$ of $\frac{1}{2}$) of the whole legacies: and for this matter it is of no consequence what share of the inheritance was left to the *impubes* in the will (xxxvii 5 fr 5 pr § 1; xxviii 6 fr 35).

A daughter overlooked, whether she obtained possession against the will or took by accrual one half of the estate, was liable to all the legatees and kept for herself only the Falcidian fourth, *i.e.* one-eighth of the whole inheritance; whereas if she had been disinherited without adequate cause, she might by the plaint of unduteous will have got a fourth. (Justinian corrected this anomaly; Cod. vi 28 fr 4 § 4, 5.)

A legacy of a dowry (or of a share of the inheritance or anything else expressed to be in lieu of dowry) was regarded as payment of a debt, and not cut down to a *pars virilis* or to the amount of the dowry: but any additional legacy was not payable. It was only to one who was still testator's wife that this applied. In the case of a daughter-in-law (or granddaughter-in-law) repayment of dowry would not be due on testator's death, and a bequest of dowry would therefore strictly be null, but as she could bring an action against her father-in-law's heirs, while the marriage continued, she was allowed a suit for such a bequest (D. xxxvii 5 fr 8 § 3—fr 10 § 1).

Freedoms given by the will fail with it, but, if anyone appointed heir enters, they become effective at once. Hence if a child, who has been overlooked and obtains a grant of possession, gives notice to an appointed heir that he will get his due by a share of the possession, and the appointed heir nevertheless enters, this latter is liable to an action of fraud for diminishing the emolument of the estate by the freedoms taking effect (fr 8 § 2).

ii. POSSESSION BY PARENT (of freeborn person emancipated by him).

A freeborn child in the process of emancipation passes through the state of handtake (*mancipium*) which was a quasi-servile condition, and the manumitter therefore stands to him (or her) in the position of patron. Ordinarily the manumitter would be his father or grandfather, *etc.* (*parens manumissor*). He will now no longer profit by his child's gains; and the technical right of patron to share in the succession to his estate is supported by material grounds as in the case of a slave manumitted. He could therefore claim possession of one half of his emancipated son's estate, if the son's (or daughter's) will had passed him over or left him heir to less than his due share, and he would not be liable for trusts. But if the son left natural children (born before or after emancipation) and had not disinherited them, the parent would be excluded. He was excluded also (by a plea of fraud), if he received money to induce the emancipation of his child or had since received compensation from him or (in a case in Trajan's time) had been compelled to emancipate him because of ill usage. Nor if the son became a soldier, had the parent, according to a rescript of Ant. Pius, this right. The edict gave this right to the father, paternal grandfather and the latter's father. But it did not pass to their children as in the case of a freedman's patron. Nor were the Fabian and Calvisian actions applicable to an emancipated son's inheritance, *quia*, says Gaius, *iniquum est ingenuis hominibus non esse liberam rerum suarum alienationem*. But the parallel with a freedman was carried out where a grandson having been emancipated by his grandfather was arrogated by his own father: the grandfather alone was admitted to the succession, whether the grandson was emancipated by his father or not; for adrogation of a freedman was not allowed, or at any rate would not have impaired the patron's claim. A father only by adoption could not claim possession *contra tabulas* of his emancipated son, the relationship being now at an end.

If the emancipated son had appointed as heirs a disgraced

person, *e.g.* a prostitute, the parent could claim the whole inheritance. The parent's right as manumitter was in addition to his ancient right as father, *i.e.* his right as cognate (D. xxxvii 12; xxxviii 17 fr 2 § 15; cf. Leist in Glück's *Pand.* v §§ 208, 209).

C. Possession of the estate in pursuance of the will.

If children had no claim to possession against the will, the praetor next regarded the heirs named in the will. The will must be the last will of deceased made by one who had the capacity to do so at the time[1] and (as a rule) also at the time of death. But madness or interdiction from fire and water, occurring after making of a valid will, did not bar the grant of possession. If the testator had cut the string, the will was not deemed to be sealed, and possession was not granted. Decay of the string, or destruction by mice, or cutting by another against testator's intention, was not a bar. Nor was the non-production or non-existence of the will a bar, if it was certain that it existed or had existed. If the heir's name had been crossed out, he could not claim possession (D. xxxvii 11 fr 1; 2 pr; xxviii 1 fr 19). A will written in shorthand (*tabulae notis scriptae*) was not a will within the edict (xxxvii 1 fr 6 pr).

A will informally made was however practically recognised by the praetor. Thus, if testator was a Roman citizen whether man or woman, not under another's power, but had not made a due sale (mancipation) of the household or uttered the words of formal declaration (*nuncupatio*), still if the will was produced to the praetor or proved to exist, bearing seven seals of witnesses, he allowed the heirs therein to have possession[2]. If there was a

[1] Cf. Cic. *Fam.* vii 21 *Negare aiebat Servium tabulas testamenti esse eas quas instituisset is qui factionem testamenti non habuerit (? haberet); hoc idem Ofilium dicere.* This was said on occasion of a will made by a woman, *Turpilia.*

[2] Cicero gives an extract from Verres' edict as city praetor: *Ex edicto urbano...Si de hereditate ambigitur et tabulae testamenti, obsignatae non minus multis signis quam e lege oportet, ad me proferentur, secundum tabulas testamenti potissimum possessionem dabo.* He adds *Hoc translaticium est* 'This is the routine-rule' (*Verr.* ii 1 45 § 117). No doubt this refers to the mancipation will for which five witnesses were the minimum

pupillary will, it was sufficient if the father's will had the seven seals. But until a rescript of Antoninus (Caracalla) enabled them to defend their possession by a plea of fraud, any statutable heirs *ab intestato* (*e.g.* a brother by the same father or a father's brother or a brother's son; not mere cognates) could carry off the inheritance from them. Whether the will of a woman made without her guardian's authority comes within the rescript of Antonine and could be maintained against such statutable heirs was doubtful: the statutable guardianship of her father (*manumissor*) or patron of course could not be thus set aside; but a guardian whom she could compel to give his authority stood on a different footing and, as some held, could be disregarded with impunity. Such a possession was also good against the Crown who could not then claim a lapse by the *lex Julia* (Gai. ii 118—122, 149, 150; Ulp. xxviii 6; D. xxviii 6 fr 20; xxxvii 11 fr 7; cf. Paul iv 8 § 2).

The praetor also granted possession *secundum tabulas*, in pursuance of rescripts of Hadrian and Caracalla, to the heir appointed by a will which had been broken in strict law by birth of a child after the will although he died before testator; and to the statutable heir, if appointed heir by a will formally made but broken or invalidated, provided that testator was a Roman citizen *sui juris* and the will had seven seals of witnesses. Legacies and trusts were thus preserved (D. xxviii 3 fr 3 pr; Gai. ii 147, 148; cf. Cod. vi 33 fr 3 pr).

The share of the possession is according to the share of inheritance given by the will, with the right of accretion when some other heir has decided not to take up the possession (D. xxxvii 11 fr 2 § 2, 8). A son appointed heir under a condition can claim the interim possession, which, if the condition fails, may become a possession against the will or on an intestacy,

number required as for all mancipations, but two other persons present, the *familiae emptor* and the balance-holder, usually affixed their seals, thus making seven seals.

From this recognition by the praetor of a will with seven seals arose what was taken to be a new form of will without mancipation (Just. ii 10 § 2); and imperial constitutions came to speak of a civil will with five witnesses and a praetorian will with seven witnesses. See Savigny *Verm. Schriften* i p. 127 sqq.

and in the former case be liable to pay legacies to the excepted persons (fr 2 § 1; 5). If a slave is appointed heir, the possession is granted to his master for the time being, so that a change of masters, before he has been ordered to enter, carries with it the right of possession. *Ambulat cum dominio bonorum possessio.* When the slave has once entered, the possession is fixed and does not shift with subsequent changes of ownership of the slave (fr 2 § 9). Whether a madman or his caretaker could claim possession or not was much disputed (Cod. v. 70 fr 7 § 3).

If testator has lost citizenship or freedom or has given himself in adoption to another and has remained in the adoptive family, the heir named in his will previously made cannot even claim possession of the estate. But if the cause of the will's being broken is the making of a subsequent will, it is of no use for the heirs named in the first will to be put in possession, for they will be ousted by the heirs named in the second will; and if this second will is invalid and yet the heirs get possession, they will be ousted either by the heirs of the first will, if that was valid, or by the civil heirs *ab intestato*, if neither was valid (Gai. ii 147—149).

When any question arises as to a will's being broken or invalid, or, if the heir be appointed on a condition, as to the condition being fulfilled and consequently whether the appointed heir or the substitute be entitled, the heir named or first named in the will, if he applies within a year, is entitled to have the possession till the question is decided. But the will must be duly produced and publicly read, and possession is granted only of what the testator had in actual possession. The substitute can stipulate for security to be given against any impairing of the estate (*ne res hereditarias deminuat*), and can demand as damages double the value of the profits so lost since the date of the stipulation (Paul iii 5 §§ 14—18; v 9 § 1; D. xlvi 5 fr 8; cf. ii 8 fr 12).

D. POSSESSION OF DECEASED'S ESTATE ON INTESTACY (*Bon. poss. ab intestato*).

Application might be made under this head when it was certain that there was no will in existence sealed with the seals of seven witnesses (D. xxxviii 6 fr 3)[1].

The narrowness of the intestate succession as determined by the XII tables (see p. 218 sqq.) is thus particularised by Gaius (iii 18—24):

(*a*) Emancipated children have no right to the inheritance of their parent, since they have ceased to be 'own heirs';

(*b*) Nor have children any right, who have had Roman citizenship granted them along with him, if they have not been reduced into his power by the emperor (Book I chap. iii 3);

(*c*) Nor are agnates who have suffered *capitis deminutio* admitted to the inheritance under this statute, for they have thereby lost the very name of agnates;

(*d*) Nor, if the nearest agnate does not enter, has the agnate following him any more right on that account;

(*e*) Nor have any agnate women, beyond the degree of sisters (*consanguineae*) any claim by statute;

(*f*) Nor are persons akin (*cognati*) through women admitted, so that even a mother had no reciprocal rights of inheritance with her son or daughter, unless she had been in her husband's hand and thus counted as sister to her husband's children under his power.

The praetor remedied, says Gaius, all these unfair restrictions. He called to the inheritance all children who had no statutable claim, just as if they had been in their parent's power at the time of his death, whether there were other children still in his power or not: he allowed succession of remoter agnates in default of acceptance by the nearer agnates: he regarded minor losses of civic position (*cap. dem.*) not as absolute disqualifications but

[1] Cf. Cicero *Verr.* ii 1 44 § 114 *Posteaquam jus praetorium constitutum est semper hoc jure usi sumus: si tabulae testamenti non proferrentur, tum uti quemque potissimum heredem esse oporteret si is intestatus mortuus esset, ita secundum eum possessio daretur. Quare hoc sit aequissimum facile est dicere, sed in re tam usitata satis est ostendere omnes antea jus ita dixisse et hoc vetus edictum translaticiumque esse.*

as grounds for postponing the claims of such persons to those qualified by the civil law: he admitted all agnatic women, and admitted relatives through women, and he allowed the reciprocal claims of husband and wife.

He determined the order of precedence in succession to an intestate estate by arranging qualified claimants in seven grades[1], two however being applicable only to freedmen's estates. The order for admission to inheritance of freeborn persons' estates in general was (1) Children; (2) Statutable heirs; (3) Next of kin; (4) Husband and wife. A last class 'kin of the manumitter' applied only to the estate of an emancipated person. (See Gai. *l.c.*, Ulp. xxviii 7; *Id. apud Collat.* xvi 5—9; D. xxxviii 6 fr 1 § 1.)

1. *Liberi.* All natural lawful children, grandchildren, *etc.*, if born or at least conceived before the death of a *paterfamilias* have first claim to his inheritance, whether they are under deceased's power or emancipated or given in adoption and afterwards emancipated therefrom, or made citizens under the provisions of the *lex Aelia Sentia*; and also persons adopted by deceased and remaining in his power at his death. The rules of the civil law were followed in dividing the possession *per stirpes*; and descendants had no claim, if their father or other ascendant was alive when an effective intestacy was ascertained, unless they had remained in deceased's power while the father, *etc.* was emancipated, in which case if he obtained possession they were joined with him, as in *poss. contra tabulas*, he and they taking each one half of his share and he bringing his own estate into hotchpot with them. A grandson, left in his grandfather's power on the father being emancipated, can claim possession of a share of his father's estate *ab intestato* along with his brothers and sisters, but by rescript of M. Aurelius and Verus the grandfather must contribute from his own estate to

[1] The lawyers (*e.g.* Just. iii 9 § 4) often speak of these grades by reference to the particular clause of the edict whence the title is derived. Thus *possessio unde liberi*, *unde legitimi*. The full expression is *e.g. dare (accipere) bonorum possessionem ex illa parte edicti unde liberi, etc. vocantur*; cf. D. xxxviii 6 fr 2; tit. 17 fr 1 § 5; Lenel *E. P.* § 156; Schirmer *Erbrecht* p. 141.

the son's estate unless he is prepared to emancipate the grandson. A child overlooked could not claim possession *ab intestato*, if he neglected to apply for possession against the will and the appointed heirs had entered, although they had not applied for the possession *secundum tabulas*: he had lost his chance (Ulp. xxviii 8; D. xxxviii 6 fr 1 § 6, fr 2, 4—7 pr; tit. 16 fr 1 § 8). This class did not apply to women's estates. (Cf. Schirmer *Erbrecht* p. 141).

2. *Legitimi* (*heredes*). Under this head come all who have statutable claim to the inheritance, that is, those entitled under the XII tables, namely the agnate nearest in blood to deceased at the time when application in this class is open, who has not undergone *capitis deminutio*, or in the case of emancipated children their manumitter, being a parent by birth; and also the mother who is entitled under the Tertullian senate's decree; and the children, whether lawful or not, who are entitled to their mother's estate under the Orfitian senate's decree. Postumous children are entitled as others. Own heirs, if they have renounced possession as children, have still a claim under this head, and till they are out of the way in both capacities, other agnates have no claim; *i.e.* not so long as the widow of deceased is pregnant, or a son remain in captivity, and the time for an own heir's acceptance has not run out.

The order among agnates is preserved by the praetor, and hence (after children) the first place belongs to brothers and sisters of deceased (*consanguinei*, cf. p. 220); but in the case of a mother's estate her children take precedence as if they were in the class of *liberi*. And a mother who has the *jus liberorum*, in case of her child's estate takes precedence of all in this class except brothers of deceased, and father of deceased.

For agnates entitled after renouncement by the nearest agnate see next class. (Gai. iii 28; D. xxxvii 7 fr 1, 2 pr § 4; v 2 fr 6 pr.)

If the manumitter of an emancipated child was a stranger (Gai. i 134) he had no claim in this grade. The praetor recognizing the practical absurdity of setting aside, in deference to theory, in the case of a freeborn person his own nearest relatives (after his own children), postponed this outsider to the nearest kin, and preferred for possession of the estate those whom he called *decem personae*; viz. father, mother, son, daughter, grandfather, grandmother, grandson, granddaughter, brother, sister (the children having still the first place and coming among cognates only if they have not claimed before, cf. D. xxxviii 9 fr 1 § 11; tit. 15 fr 4 § 1). After these would follow the patron and his family, as in the case of a freedman deceased. (Ulp. *ap. Collat.* xvi 9; Just. iii 3.)

3. *Cognati* or *proximi cognati.* In this grade succeed all kinsfolk who are not entitled to come in the first or second grades. Kinsfolk are created by adoption as well as by blood, but they are kin only to the agnates and only so long as the agnatic relation continues. An adopted son is a member of the adoptive family as created by the civil law, but remains of kin by blood to his birth-family whether the adoption continues or not. Children *volgo quaesiti, i.e.* of illegitimate, but not forbidden unions, are akin to their mother and to her other children and parents. Agnates who have lost their civic position; agnates excluded (according to some lawyers) from claiming in the second grade by one nearer to deceased[1]; women agnates beyond the position of sisters; and all men or women related to deceased through women[2], claim in this grade. Children begotten by soldiers during their time of service were not statutable heirs, because marriage was not allowed, but by a letter of Trajan's were permitted to claim possession of their father's intestate estate in the grade of *cognati* (Bruns[6] p. 381).

There is no representation among cognates. The cognates nearest in blood at the time when the succession comes to this class, although not nearest at the time of deceased's death, are equally entitled. Only cognates conceived in the life of deceased, whether born before or after his death, are entitled (Gai. iii

[1] Gaius speaks of a division of opinion on this head, some leaving them in class 2, some putting them here (iii 28).

[2] Cf. Cic. *Cluent.* 60 § 165 *Intestatum dico esse mortuum possessionemque ejus bonorum ex edicto praetoris huic illius sororis filio datam.* Another reference to the class *unde cognati* appears to be found in *ib.* 15 § 45 *Habitus nullum testamentum umquam fecerat. Id cum Oppianicus sciret, intellegebat Habito mortuo bona ejus omnia ad matrem esse ventura.*

27—31; Ulp. xxviii 9; Just. iii 5; D. xxxviii 8; tit. 16 fr 6—8).

The degrees of kinship are reckoned by the number of births or descents from the common ancestor, *i.e.* one is reckoned for the person whose kinship is sought and one for each intervening person[1]. Thus in the

1st degree are son and daughter, father and mother:

2nd, grandson and granddaughter, grandfather and grandmother, brother and sister:

3rd, great grandson and great granddaughter, great grandfather and great grandmother; nephew, niece by brother and sister, uncle and aunt on father's and on mother's side:

4th, great-great grandson and great-great granddaughter, great-great grandfather and -mother, brother's and sister's grandson and grandniece, great uncle and great aunt on father's and mother's side and first cousins:

5th, father and mother of great-great grandfather and -mother and the sons and daughters of all in the fourth grade:

6th, grandfather and grandmother of great-great grandfather and -mother, and grandchildren of all in the fifth grade (Fragm. ap. *Libr. Antejust.* ii p. 166; D. xxxviii 10 fr 1—3, 10; Paul iv 11).

Only cognates as far as the sixth degree and of the seventh only children of a second cousin (*sobrino sobrinave nati*) were admitted[2]. An agnate in the eighth degree (or further)

[1] Or, reckon one for each step (*gradus*, degree) from the deceased: thus one step from deceased upwards to his father, one step upwards from him to the grandfather, and one step downwards from him to deceased's uncle: the uncle is in third degree.

[2] Paul (D. xxxviii 10 fr 10) gives an enumeration of all the names in the seven grades, and the number in each grade on the supposition of only one person in each position. This is of course right in some cases; a man having only one father and one mother, one father's father, *etc.*, but in most cases it is far below possibility or even probability, as one man or woman may have more than one boy, and more than one girl, and thus more than one father's brother or father's sister or mother's brother, *etc.* Paul's list of persons abridged is as follows:

i. Father, mother, son, daughter. Total 4.

ii. Father's father, mother's father, father's mother, mother's mother;

STEMMA COGNATIONIS.

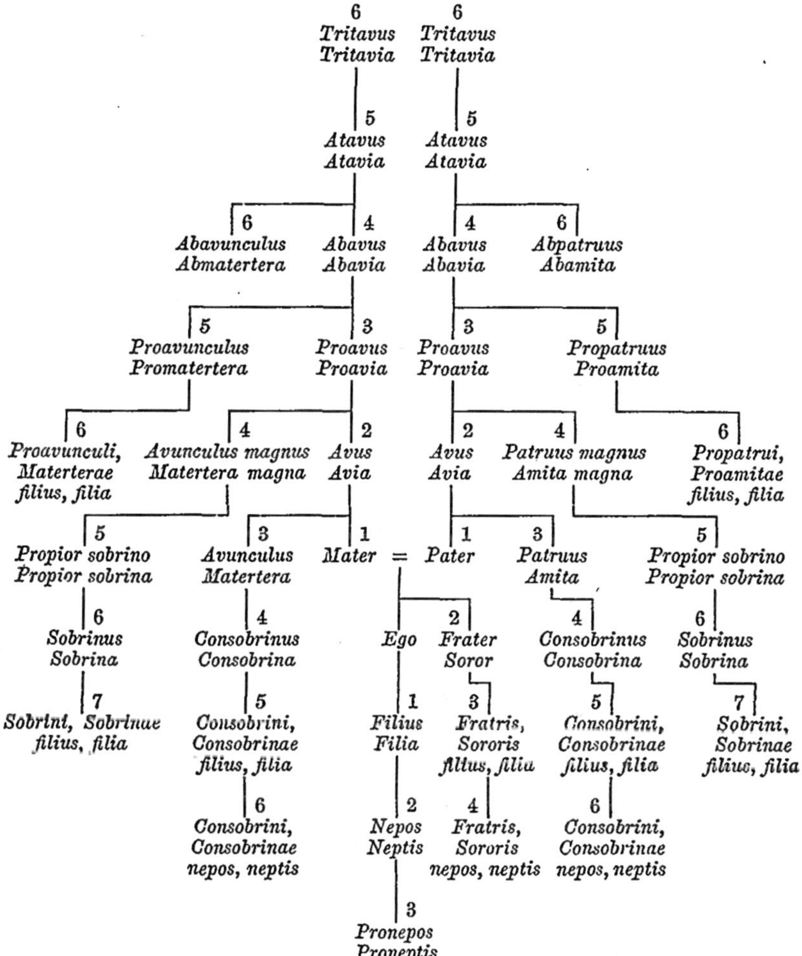

The name given is usually that of the relation to *me*. Where there exists no specific name for this, the relationship to his or her ancestor is given.

Consobrini, consobrinae, first-cousins, denote properly the children of two sisters, but are used also to denote children of two brothers, properly *fratres patrueles*, and of a brother and sister, properly *fratres amitini*. (D. xxxviii 1 fr 10 § 6).

No person beyond the sixth degree is given here, except *sobrini, sobrinae filius, filia*, second cousins' children, who are the only relatives of the seventh degree whom the praetor recognised.

For *propatruus, patruus major*, and for *abpatruus, patruus maximus* are also used. For *proamita, proavunculus, etc.* similar terms occur.

though admissible in the second class is not admissible in this class.

These names of blood-relationship were freely applied to slaves, but there was no legal recognition of them (D. xxxviii 10 fr 10 § 5).

4. *Vir et uxor.* In the order of inheritance by the civil law this class had no place: the only marriage recognised was that whereby the wife and her property passed into the hand of her husband, who retained the latter at her death, while at his death the wife shared his estate as one of his daughters. The praetor, however, recognised free marriage and gave the parties reciprocal rights, but after all blood relations. The marriage must be lawful (*justum*) and still existing at the time of the intestate's death. A divorce though not in the form prescribed by the *lex Julia de adulteriis* is still sufficient to destroy any claim under this head. And so is a divorce by a freedwoman married to her patron, though the divorce is by the *lex Julia de maritandis ordinibus* held invalid, so that she cannot marry again without his consent (D. xxxviii 11).

5. In the case of an emancipated person, who had a stranger for patron (cf. p. 74), a last class is composed of the kin of the manumitter.

Time for deliberation.

Just as there was a *cretio* fixed for heirs named in a will, so the praetor limited the time within which each person, as he became entitled to possession of the estate, had to make up his mind whether to accept or decline it. In the case of children

son's son, daughter's son, son's daughter, daughter's daughter; brother and sister by father, brother and sister by mother (only). Total 12.

iii. 4 *proavi*, 4 *proaviae*, 2 *patrui* (viz. father's brother, father's half-brother by mother's side), 2 *amitae*, 2 *avunculi*, 2 *materterae*, 4 nephews (viz. brother's son, halfbrother's son, sister's son, halfsister's son), 4 nieces, 4 *pronepotes*, 4 *proneptes*. Total 32.

iv. 8 *abavi*, 8 *abaviae*, 4 *propatrui*, 4 *proamitae*, 4 *proavunculi*, 4 *promaterterae*, 8 *abnepotes*, 8 *abneptes*, 16 first cousins (viz. 4 *patrueles*, 8 *amitini* or 8 *amitinae*, 4 *consobrini* or *consobrinae*), 8 great nephews, 8 great nieces. Total 80.

The Totals of the other three classes are: v 184; vi 448; vii 1024.

and parents (whether entitled in their own name or in that of a slave appointed heir) the time was one year, in other cases one hundred days. In both cases it was *utile tempus*, *i.e.* available time. Only those days were reckoned on which the person concerned knew and was able to apply, so that, even if he knew for a time but subsequently had reason to doubt the death of deceased, this period of doubt would not count. If it is a case requiring a formal hearing and a decree by the praetor (*e.g.* under the Carbonian edict) only those days are reckoned on which the praetor sat for applications of this kind. For ordinary grants of possession, taken as matter of course, all days are reckoned. Where it is a son under power who is entitled to the grant, time does not begin to run until he has had opportunity of informing his father, in order that he may order or ratify his acceptance of it. Any decision once come to within the time is final, though the time be not exhausted; and if the possession be declined, or the time has expired, or the deliberant has died, the right passes at once to the next entitled. If another's slave appointed heir by a will is sold while time is running, the new master has only the residue of the time.

A child can not only take the possession under his proper title (*unde liberi*) but if he do not take it, he can claim as agnate, and if he do not take it then, he can claim as cognate, and on each delation is entitled to a year. Acceptance by a nearer cognate precludes later cognates from claiming, even if the nearer one obtain the praetor's allowance to withdraw on ground of youth. The Crown then becomes entitled (D. xxxviii 9; *ib.* 15; Ulp. xxviii 10, 11).

Caracalla confined all inheritance *ab intestato* to persons who had under his law immunity from the tax of 10 per cent. which he had substituted for the old *vicesima hereditatum* (Ulpian *ap. Collat.* xvi 9 § 2; Dion Cass. lxxvii 9). This together with Caracalla's other tax-innovations was repealed by his successor Macrinus (Dion Cass. lxxviii 12).

E. *MISSIO VENTRIS IN POSSESSIONEM.*

The chance of a postumous child being born who would be an own heir was provided for by the praetor. Such a child would have a right to the possession, if not disinherited, as much as any other own heir. *Is qui in utero est pro superstite habetur.* The *venter, i.e.* the pregnant woman, was therefore sent into possession along with the other grantees until the child is born or a miscarriage ensues or it is ascertained that she is not pregnant. Pregnancy both at the time of testator's death and at that of the *missio in possessionem* is requisite; and disherison must be clear and absolute to bar the order. A son's wife has a claim to this protection for her child, if she is pregnant when the son is emancipated. If he has been given in adoption and dies when his wife is pregnant, she is entitled to be sent into possession of the estate of the child's natural grandfather, provided he has been appointed postumous heir and other own heirs have been overlooked (D. xxxvii 9 fr 1 §§ 1, 2, 12, 13, 27; fr 7 pr; xxx fr 1, 21). A claim on behalf of an *alienus postumus,* appointed heir by the will, is admitted only if the woman is unable otherwise to maintain herself (D. xxxvii 9 fr 6).

The edict does not use the term *uxor* because the woman might be no longer a wife at the time, and *venter* properly denotes the unborn child on whose account only (*ventris nomine*) the woman claims the praetor's order. She generally applies for a caretaker for herself and the property. She is entitled whether she has a dowry or not to be suitably maintained out of the estate while in possession, so that not only an own heir may be preserved but the increase of the state by a new citizen be promoted. If the appointment of a caretaker is not made at once, the heir has no right to seal up the things belonging to the inheritance but only to count them and assign them to the woman. She is liable for all expenditure from the estate if she knows she is not pregnant (D. *ib.* fr 1 §§ 10, 17, 19, 28).

If the claim of the woman was disputed on the ground either that her child was not the testator's or was not free, the case fell under the Carbonian edict and required a hearing by the praetor: she could not get the grant of possession in the ordinary way as a matter of course (fr 7 § 1).

Not only an unborn child (of testator) but anyone else who would if born have a claim (*e.g.* as agnate) to the possession *ab intestato* can obtain possession under this part of the edict, but only till birth, *etc.* not, as under the Carbonian edict, till questions of his title are determined at puberty (fr 7 pr, § 1; cf. xxxviii 17 fr 1 § 5; Leist in Glück's *Pand.* iv § 10). The next heir cannot enter until her pregnancy is determined. *Is qui in utero est, quantum ad moram faciendam inferioribus et sibi locum faciendum si fuerit editus, pro jam nato habetur* (D. xxviii 2 fr 30 § 1).

A woman thus sent into possession is protected by an interdict just as is one in possession to guard legacies (D. xliii 4, see chap. viii N). And while she is in possession no one to guard legacies can be there (D. xxxvi 4 fr 7).

On the other hand a woman, who claimed possession while knowing that she was not pregnant, was liable to an action *calumniae causa* to any person who would have a claim to the possession if there were no child. Her parent is also liable, if he caused her to come into possession. The damages, if fraud were shewn, were put at the loss to the plaintiff from the reduction of the value of the inheritance by the expenditure for her support and consumption of the fruits. If a substitute or some other claimant died, while kept out of possession by the woman, his heir could bring this action. So also could legatees, who had an interest in the inheritance being duly entered on. Anyone who gained the suit and recovered full damages was compelled by the praetor to give the freedoms left, whether directly or by way of trust. The action being penal had to be brought within a year (*annus utilis*; D. xxv 6).

If a woman having been put into possession wrongfully transferred it to another, she and her parent, if he abetted her, were liable to a like action, which could be brought against either as the plaintiff chose. This could be brought after a year, because it aimed at recoupment. To remove the person wrongfully brought into possession an ordinary interdict (*quorum bonorum*) would suffice (D. xxv 5).

F. *CARBONIANUM EDICTUM.*

Under a special part of the Edict, called the *Carbonianum Edictum,* provision was made for the case of an infant's (*impubes*) having his claim, as a child, to possession against the will or on an intestacy, disputed. In such a case the praetor gave a summary hearing, and if the child was clearly shewn not to be the testator's or to be a slave, possession would not be granted. But if the case against the claim was not clear, the child was sent into possession just as if his claim were not disputed, but, when he came to the age of puberty, the matter was fully inquired into and decided. Till then the child appeared to the Roman lawyers not to have full power of defending his claim. But if his case was likely to be injured through delay, either by failure of proof or by waste of the estate, and especially if his right appeared to be clear (so a rescript of Hadrian), the praetor would hear and decide at once (D. xxxvii 10 fr 1 pr; 3 §§ 3, 4, 5; fr 7 § 4).

An infant so sent into possession had to give security to his opponent: if he did not, the opponent was sent into possession with him and then had to give security to the infant, or else to be debarred from managing the estate. A caretaker was appointed to manage and sue and be sued. If the opponent was also a child of deceased, he was sent into possession along with the infant, even if the latter gave security. Anyone who asserted himself to be a son ought to take the ordinary possession, and then, if his claim as child of deceased was contested, apply for the Carbonian possession also. Both had to be applied for within a year; but the year ran for the ordinary possession from the time when the applicant knew of the death and was able to act, while for the Carbonian possession it ran from his knowledge of his claim being contested. The infant would thus be possessor till puberty in any case, and if then proved to be child and free, or if opposition dropped, would continue without further order; if proved to be a slave or not testator's child, he would lose all right to the praetor's protection. He was defendant in these proceedings after puberty, if he had given or then offered security; if not, his opponent is put in possession and the infant has to prove his case (fr 1 §§ 2, 13—16; fr 4, 5, 6 §§ 5, 6).

The possession while it lasted was not a mere detention in order to safeguard claims, as in the case of legatees, creditors and others (see chap. viii N), but a practical ownership. And accordingly the infant had a right to be supported out of the estate and to be supplied with education and other necessaries suitable to the means of the estate. Nor was he required to repay this expense, if his claim was eventually disproved. The estate was thus impaired, from fear lest an own heir should suffer or die (fr 4 § 3; fr 15). The opponent when sent into possession had no right to be supported; he was there merely by way of security (fr 6 § 4).

Where testator has appointed a postumous child heir, the claim may be for possession in pursuance of the will, and may be contested on the ground that the child is not free, or not testator's, or even supposititious. In the last case, if the putative mother is subjected to a criminal charge of supposition, and her defence is better conducted at once, a trial would be directed, and the child granted possession or not according to the result. But, except in this case of a postumous child, the Carbonian edict does not apply to anyone appointed heir in the will. Nor does it apply when the claimant is duly disinherited, unless the will itself is disputed. Disherison however is looked at narrowly. If the disherison was coupled with the reason that the child was adulterous, the claimant would not be excluded till this was proved. Or if testator used such words as *quisquis est qui filium meum se esse dicit, exheres esto* it is not enough, for he is not disinherited as a son (fr 1 §§ 8, 9; fr 7 § 6).

It matters little who contests the claim. The Carbonian edict applies even if the child's own father, being emancipated, contests his claim to joint possession of the grandfather's estate, *e.g.* on the ground that he was not retained in the deceased's family, but passed with him on emancipation. Nor does a declaration of testator's, that claimant was not his son, bar the Carbonian edict (fr 1 § 4). But the claim must be to the property as well as to the position. If *status* only be in question, the Carbonian edict does not apply, and if the trial is put off to puberty, that is due to Imperial constitutions (fr 3 § 2; fr 6 § 3).

A rescript of Ant. Pius allowed a similar postponement till puberty of a child's claim to legacy or trust (fr 3 § 1).

CHAPTER VI.

SUCCESSION TO THE ESTATE OF ROMAN FREEDMEN AND FREEDWOMEN DECEASED[1].

A. GENERAL VIEW (from Gaius and Ulpian):

1. Right of the Patron (*a*) in the estate of his freedman.

Under the XII tables a patron had no claim against his freedman's will. Nor if the freedman died intestate, had the patron any claim against 'own heirs,' whether they were such by birth or adoption or by marriage *cum conventione in manum.* If he died intestate and left no 'own heirs,' then the patron succeeded to the estate.

The praetor's edict did not alter this when the freedman left natural children born since his manumission, whether in his power or emancipated or given in adoption, provided he had not disinherited them. Any such children becoming heirs or trust-heirs by his will, to however small an extent, or obtaining possession of the estate sufficed to exclude the patron altogether. But an adopted son or a wife in hand or a daughter-in-law who had been in his son's hand were not allowed to exclude him altogether. For when the freedman had no natural children, the patron was entitled to one moiety of the estate, whether the freedman had made a will and left him nothing or less than half, or had died intestate. If he left no own heirs or natural children at all, the patron's right to the whole estate remained. A patron (or his children), made heir by will to half the estate, had to bear a fair share of the debts.

The *lex Papia* did not interfere with this in the case of small estates, under 100,000 sesterces. Nor did it do so in larger estates, if the freedman left three or more natural children heirs;

[1] Discussion and literature will be found in Leist, Glück's *Pand.* Pt v, §§ 172—174.

but if he left fewer, the patron was to have one equal share (*pars virilis*), *i.e.* if he left two only the patron was granted one-third of the estate; if he left one only the praetor had a moiety. Any alienation by the freedman, for the purpose and with the effect of reducing the estate below 100,000 sesterces, was *ipso facto* invalid as a fraud against the law (see Book v chap. viii 8).

(*b*) Over the estate of his freedwoman the patron had full control. She could not make a valid will, except by his authority; and, if she disposed of any of her property to others, the patron had only himself to blame. She could not have own heirs, and therefore if she died intestate the patron took all. The praetor made no alteration. But the *lex Papia* freed from her patron's guardianship any freedwoman who had the privilege of four children. Hence she could make what will she chose, and the patron might get nothing. The law therefore gave the patron one equal share, according to the number of children she left, *i.e.* if she left all four, one-fifth. If she died intestate without children the patron no doubt took all.

2. The patron's son, son's son, and this latter's son had the same rights as their ancestor both in freedmen's and freedwomen's estates.

3. (*a*) The patron's daughter, son's daughter and son's son's daughter had by the XII tables the same rights as he in the estate of a freedman. But the praetor did not grant them the additional rights against own heirs who were not such by birth, which he gave to the patron and his male descendants. The *lex Papia* however gave them those rights, provided they had the privilege of three children.

(*b*) As regards the estate of a deceased freedwoman dying intestate, whether she left children or not, a patron's female descendant (through males) had by the XII tables the same claim as the patron or his male descendant. The praetor did not alter this; but the *lex Papia* gave one who had three children a claim to possession, if the freedwoman left no natural children. If however the latter had had four children, the patron's female descendant (with three children) could only claim one equal share, and some lawyers thought she could claim nothing. If the freedwoman made a will the case was altered, for a female descendant had no right of guardianship, and consequently no control over the freedwoman's will, and therefore no claim against it. But three children gave her a better position, and she then obtained under the *lex Papia* the same rights against the will of a freedwoman, that male descendants or the patron himself had against the will of a freedman, *i.e.* both the rights granted them by the praetor and also the additional rights conferred by the *lex Papia.* Gaius complains that this part of the *lex Papia* was badly drafted.

The heirs of a patron who were outsiders had no such rights as the patron in freedmen's estates, either on an intestacy or against the freedman's will.

4. Right of a Patroness (*a*) in the estate of her deceased freedman.

A patroness by the law of the XII tables had the same rights as a patron. The praetor gave her no such right as he gave to patrons to the possession of a moiety of the estate, either of an ungrateful freedman notwithstanding his will or of an intestate freedman who left no natural children. But the *lex Papia* gave a freeborn patroness who was privileged by two children (*duobus liberis honorata*) much the same rights as a patron had under the praetor's edict, and if she was privileged by three children, put her in the same position as a patron under the *lex Papia.* A freedwoman patroness with three children was given the same rights as a freeborn patroness with two children.

(*b*) As regards the estate of a deceased freedwoman, who died intestate, a patroness had her right under the XII tables to the inheritance whether the deceased left children or not; but neither the praetor nor the *lex Papia* altered her position; and therefore her right was liable like other privileges under the XII tables to be destroyed by herself or her freedwoman's suffering *capitis deminutio.* If this took place, the freedwoman's children by the right of blood-relationship succeeded their mother to the exclusion of the patroness. If the freedwoman made a will, a patroness who was privileged by children was granted by the *lex Papia* the same rights against it, as the praetor gave a patron against the will of a freedman, *i.e.* possession of a moiety of the estate, where deceased left no natural children.

5. A patroness' son, if he had a child or children, was given by the *lex Papia* the rights of a patron.

6. As the *SC. Orfitianum* gave a statutable inheritance, not liable to be affected by *capitis deminutio*, to the children of an intestate mother, the old rights of patron or patron's children or of patroness to the inheritance of an intestate freedwoman who left children, were either excluded altogether or perhaps cut down to a share with them (*pars virilis*) as in the case of a freedwoman with four children under the *lex Papia*. Gaius wrote his Institutes before this *S. Consultum* (Gai. iii 39—54, and shorter in Ulp. xxvii and xxix; Paul iii 2; D. xxxvii 14 fr 16; Unterholzner *ZGR.* v 33 sqq.).

B. PATRON'S CLAIM TO POSSESSION OF HIS (ROMAN) FREEDMAN'S ESTATE AGAINST THE WILL.

Further details on the rules of the praetor's protection of the patron's claim are found in the Digest.

(1) A patron has, as above stated, a right, subject however to the *lex Papia*, to one half of his freedman's estate, if the freedman left no lawful natural children by birth or if he disinherited them by a valid and effective will. If a moiety was left him by the will, his claim was satisfied: if not he could obtain against the will possession of his moiety (D. xxxviii 2 fr 3 § 10). The will was upset only to that extent. As long as the patron's claim was not satisfied, debtors to the estate could plead that fact in reply to a suit by the heir (fr 25). The patron's claim is satisfied, if he is appointed heir absolutely or on a condition which is fulfilled by the time at which the inheritance is entered on, or if he becomes heir through his slave, or has the estate restored to him under a trust by the heir at law, or being left heir to less than his due share has the amount made up by legacy, or gift in view of death, or other gift, or by payment imposed as a condition on another heir or legatee, or by release from debt

(fr 3 §§ 15—19, fr 19, 50 pr § 6). His sons should be appointed to the same share as substitutes in case of his predeceasing the freedman (fr 5 pr). His share must not be burdened with a trust, except so far as he may have been left more than his due (fr 41, 45). The value of the patron's moiety is taken as at the time of the freedman's death (without deduction for fraudulent alienation); subsequent accessions to the estate do not disturb it (fr 3 § 20, 44 § 2). If a patron has not his due share, he can claim it *pro rata* against the heirs, including any other patron who has more than his due share (fr 10 pr, 34, 43). If a patron has obtained possession to one half against the will, and the appointed heir obtains possession to the other half according to the will, there is no accrual between them if the appointed heir does not apply; the patron requires a second application to get the second moiety (D. xxxvii 1 fr 6 pr).

(2) A patron who has obtained possession against the will is thereby barred from any benefit under the will, directly or through others, and from any gift in view of death, but he may receive anything in trust for others. On the other hand if he has entered on the inheritance (even by compulsion, suspecting its insolvency), or has accepted anything under the will, directly or through his son or slave (which has not been evicted), or has since the freedman's death accepted any gift in view of death, he is debarred from obtaining possession against the will (D. xxxviii 2 fr 6 § 4—fr 8; fr 16 §§ 5—8; 50). An unsuccessful attempt to prove the will to be forged barred patron's claim (fr 19).

The insolvency of a freedman's estate is no bar to a patron's claim, as he may have other than economic reasons for desiring to preserve it (fr 36). For his right to revoke a freedman's acts in fraudulent impairment of his due share of the estate see Book v chap. viii, 8.

Patron is barred, if he has claimed the freedman as his slave (unless he has done so only in order to establish his claim against the person who sold him as a slave), or if he has claimed a usufruct in him. In either case he is not barred, if he has not persisted in the claim up to judgment. He is barred, if he has accused the slave of a capital crime, unless by the direction of his father, or to avenge his father's death, or if he has given evidence against him on a like charge. But retorting a charge made by the freedman against the patron, or acting as advocate on such a charge, does not debar him, nor any proceeding short of final judgment, even if that be prevented only by the freedman's death (fr 14, 16 pr—§ 3, 30; xxxvii 14 fr 9, 10). Nor can he obtain possession if he has taken money for the manumission, or has sold back to his freedman all claim to gifts or services (*donum, munus, operas*), or has failed to support his freedman in need (this is due to the *lex Aelia Sentia*). The loss of claim extends to the patron's children also (D. xxxviii 2 fr 3 § 4, 33, 37 pr; cf. xxxvii 14 fr 20). It was decided by a rescript of M. Aurelius and his brother, following the opinion of Julian, that a grandson is not disqualified from claiming possession of the estate of his grandfather's freedman, because his father had brought a capital charge against him (D. xxxvii 14 fr 17).

(3) If a patron dies before his freedman, his lawful children[1], and in the case of a female patron even illegitimate children, have the like claim to possession of the freedman's estate against the will. And a grandson begotten after his grandfather's death, but during the life of his freedman, can, if his father do not precede him, claim the possession of the freedman's estate, though he has no right to that of his grandfather himself (D. xxxviii 2 fr 2 pr, 18, 47 § 3). Disherison by his father excludes a son from the possession of the estates of his father's freedmen but not from those of his grandfather, provided that his grandfather has not also disinherited him, and that either his father has predeceased his grandfather, or he himself is emancipated. Disherison of his father by his grandfather does not affect the grandson's claim to the estate of his grandfather's freedmen, nor does disherison by a grandfather affect the grandson's claim to the estate of his father's

[1] Verres under a new edict of his own granted the claim of a patron's daughter to possession of one-sixth of a freedman's inheritance, which had been a year before entered on under the freedman's will by one who was apparently no relation (Cic. *Verr.* ii 1 48 § 125). The claim of one-sixth is probably explicable by her having two brothers or sisters.

freedmen. Disherison bars claim through son or slave as well as direct claim. But it does not bar if it is only from one particular grade; nor if the freedman is expressly assigned to the disinherited claimant, or his right to the freedman is expressly preserved; nor if it is due not to any disapprobation but to some other cause (*e.g.* to the son's lunacy); nor if the will proves ineffective; nor if he be pronounced not disinherited, however erroneous the judgment may be (fr 10 § 1—fr 13, 40).

C. PATRON'S RIGHT TO HIS (ROMAN) FREEDMAN'S OR FREEDWOMAN'S INHERITANCE, DYING INTESTATE.

i. By civil law.

The succession to the inheritance of a Roman freedman dying intestate was, by the XII tables, first to his own heirs. Failing these, in the case of a freedman and in all cases (except under the *lex Papia*) in the case of a freedwoman, the estate passed to the patron (or patroness), and if he was dead to the patron's children, or, if they also were dead, to his grand-children (or great-grandchildren) through sons. If there were two patrons they took in equal shares, notwithstanding that they might before manumission have been owners in unequal shares. If the son of one and only grandsons of the other survived, the agnatic rule prevailed; only the nearer degree succeeded: and if one son left three children and another left only one, they took by heads, every grandson having an equal share. If two or more were entitled and some declined to accept their shares, they accrued to the others in equal shares (Gai. iii 58—62; Ulp. xxvii 1—4; xxix 2).

Assignment of a freedman under the Claudian decree (Book II chap. ix B) made some difference. If one of two patrons has two sons (*A* and *B*) and another has one son (*C*), and a freedman is assigned by the former to *A*, he will have two-thirds of the freedman's inheritance, and *C* one-third; but if *B* died or lost civic position before the freedman's death, there would then be only two in the same degree, and *A* and *C* would therefore share equally. The same result would occur if *A* died leaving a son and *B* survived: *A*'s son would have one half, his uncle

B's share having been absorbed by *A*, and *C* would have the other half. So if a patron had a son (*B*) and grandson (*A*) and another patron had a son *C*, and the former patron assigned his share in the freedman to his grandson, this grandson (*A*) would have an equal share in the inheritance with *C*, provided that *B* (whose rights are absorbed and represented by *A*) survived and had not lost status; but if *B* were dead or had suffered *cap. dem.* the agnatic rule gave *C* the right to the whole, and an assignment to one of a more distant degree (*A*) would have no effect (D. xxxviii 4 fr 1 § 8—fr 3 pr).

One who has manumitted a slave in accordance with a trust, though he has no title to services, can claim statutable succession. So also can one who has bought a slave with the condition of manumitting him, even if he have not done so, and the slave become free by the constitution of M. Aurelius. A husband manumitting a dowry slave, burghers manumitting a slave of theirs, a soldier manumitting a slave belonging to his camp-*peculium*, the emperor manumitting a slave of his own, all can claim statutable succession (D. xxxviii 16 fr 3 §§ 1—3, 6—8). But a patron suffering *capitis deminutio*, or (contrary to the *lex Aelia Sentia*) compelling his freedman or freedwoman to swear not to marry or to marry only under certain restrictions, or failing to support his freedman, or bringing a capital accusation against him, has no claim to the statutable inheritance (D. xxxvii 14 fr 11, 15; xxxviii 16 fr 3 § 5 fr 11).

ii. By praetorian grant of possession.

For succession to an intestate estate the praetor made seven grades, all of which might be applicable to a freedman. The order was (1) children; (2) statutable heirs; (3) next of kin; (4) patron's household; (5) patron's or patroness's patron or patroness, or their children and parents; (6) husband and wife; (7) manumitter's kin. (Ulpian *ap. Collat.* xvi 8 § 2, 9 § 1; Just. iii 9 § 3.)

(1) *Liberi.* Their claim has been already stated. Children born before the freedman's manumission were not counted (cf. Just. iii 6 § 10).

(2) *Legitimi.* A freedman has no agnates of the ordinary

kind, but this class is in his case represented by the patron or patroness, the sons and daughters of a patron, and his grandsons and granddaughters through sons, provided they have not suffered *capitis deminutio*.

(3) *Proximi cognati* presume a common free ancestor, whereas a freedman is the commencement of a lawful family[1], and therefore is without cognates, except such as are descended from him after his manumission.

(4) *Familia patroni* (*tum quam ex familia*, Just. iii 9 §§ 3, 6) included probably all agnates[2] of the patron male or female, those coming under the class of *legitimi* having in this a second opportunity. So Theophil. iii 9 § 3 (p. 304 Ferrini); Cod. vi 4 fr 4 § 23.

(5) *Patronus patrona, item liberi et parentes patroni patronaeve* appears to mean the patron or patroness (with their children and parents) of the patron or patroness, and applies only when the patron was himself a freedman[3].

(6) *Vir et uxor* applies only where the freedman has contracted a lawful marriage since his manumission, all matrimonial relations formed in slavery being merely cohabitation, and not recognised by the law as a source of rights.

(7) *Cognati manumissoris* are the patron's kin, but they were limited to persons who by the *lex Furia* were allowed to take by will more than 1000 asses, *i.e.* kin within the first six grades and second cousins (Vat. 301). The term *manumissoris* instead of *patroni* is used to include the case of an emancipated son's inheritance as well as a freedman's proper.

[1] Cf. Ulpian xii 3 *Libertinus nullo modo patri heres fieri potest qui nec patrem habuisse videtur, cum servilis cognatio nulla sit* (Just. iii 6 § 10; D. xxxviii 8 fr 1 § 2; Theophil. *Inst.* iii 7 pr).

[2] Leist in Glück's *Pand.* v p. 360 sq. differs. Agnates of the patron who have suffered *cap. dem.* would I conceive come in class 7, not here. Cf. Huschke *Studien* p. 115, *etc.*

[3] *Liberi* and *parentes* of the freedman's own patron would come in class 2 or 4. Hence these words appear to mean the children and parents of the patron's patron. So Cod. vi 4 4 § 23 ὁ τοῦ πάτρωνος πάτρων καὶ ἡ συγγένεια αὐτοῦ.

D. SUCCESSION TO THE ESTATE OF LATIN FREEDMEN AND WOMEN.

By Latin freedmen are here meant slaves informally manumitted, whose freedom was protected by the praetor but who under the civil law remained slaves, and consequently were subject as regards their property both during their life and on death to the will of their master[1] (see above, pp. 37, 38). The *lex Junia* gave statutable protection instead of praetorian, and declared that they should be as free as Roman citizens who had become members of a Latin colony, but that their goods should belong to their manumitters just as much as before the law was passed, *i.e.* in other words that they should still be regarded as a slave's *peculium*. Hence there were several points of difference between the succession to the inheritance of a freedman who was a Roman citizen, and the succession to the goods of a freedman who was a Junian Latin.

The inheritance of a Roman freedman passed after the patron only to the patron's descendants through males, even if disinherited by their parent; if there were two or more patrons, they had equal shares, though their shares in the slave before manumission had been unequal; a surviving patron excluded the children of a deceased patron; and, if both were dead, the nearer degree among their descendants excluded the remoter, and in the same degree all had equal shares: if one patron declined the inheritance or died before entry, the other or others took the whole.

The goods of a Latin freedman passed to the patron's heirs whether by will or intestacy, whoever they might be, and not to disinherited children of the patron: if there were more patrons than one, they had the same shares in the inheritance that they had had in the slave: and their descendants took these shares *per stirpes*, one patron not excluding the son of another, and the son of one not excluding the grandson of another, no respect being paid to comparative nearness: and if one patron declined or died before entry, his share passed as lapsed to the people (Gai. iii 54—62).

[1] Cf. Plin. *Ep. Traj.* 104 *Valerius Paulinus, excepto Paulino, jus Latinorum suorum mihi reliquit.*

A senate's decree in the consulship of Lupus and Largus (A.D. 42) made some provisions on this matter which were differently interpreted by the lawyers. It gave the goods of Latin freedmen first to the manumitters; failing them to their children, not expressly disinherited, in the order of their nearness: then according to the former law (*antiquo jure*) to the heirs of their manumitters notwithstanding the manumitter had left children. Pegasus interpreted this enactment as putting the goods of Latins on the same footing as the inheritance of Roman freedmen. This is clearly wrong, says Gaius, for in the case of a Roman freedman outsiders have no claim at all, and disherison has no effect on the children of the manumitter. The real effect of the senate's decree is only to give children not expressly disinherited a preference over outsiders. It thus assists an emancipated son who has been passed over, but has not applied for possession against the will; and daughters and other own heirs who have been disinherited in a general clause; and also children who have kept aloof from the inheritance of their fathers (Gai. iii 63—67; § 68 is illegible).

A nice question arose where a patron leaves an outsider heir along with his own children. The outsider no doubt was excluded in favour of the children; but did the children take equal shares in the whole inheritance or only in that part which had been left to the outsider, while retaining in the rest of the inheritance the shares their father had assigned them? Caelius Sabinus maintained the former: Javolen the latter view. Again does the senate's decree give a preference over outsiders to the children of a daughter or granddaughter of the patron? and again in the case of a mother's Latin freedman, have her children a preference over outsiders? Cassius said yes to both questions; but most lawyers disagreed from him, on the ground that the decree speaks of disherison and therefore should be understood to refer only to cases where express disherison was required. It was not required in the case of married daughters as they had left the patron's family: nor in the case of a mother's or grandmother's will, for she is not required either by civil law or by the conditions of the praetor's grant of possession against the will to disinherit a child or grandchild, if she does not appoint him heir. She may simply pass him by (Gai. ii 69—71).

Where a Latin freedman has obtained from the emperor full Roman citizenship saving the patron's rights, as for instance if the grant were made against the wish or without the knowledge of the patron, the effect was that during life he is a Roman citizen as much as any other freedman, but he dies as a Latin, *i.e.* his children are not his heirs and his right of making a will is good only for making his patron heir, and, if his patron did not accept, for substituting another. Hadrian provided by a senate's decree that in such cases the freedman should not be debarred by the saving from obtaining full rights, if he proved his case under the *lex Aelia Sentia* or the supplementary senate's decree. On the case of *dediticii* see Book I chap. ii C ii 4 *c*.

CHAPTER VII.

A. *Hereditatis petitio.*

1. Any heir, who found another person in possession of deceased's estate or of any part or thing corporal or incorporal belonging to it, sued for the inheritance (*hereditatem petit* or *vindicat*[1]). If heir to the whole (*ex asse*) he sues for the whole (*suam esse hereditatem*); if heir to a part (*ex uncia, ex quadrante, etc.*) he limits his claim accordingly, in order to avoid an excessive claim. But his statement of claim does not vary according as defendant is in possession of all or part or only some single thing. If plaintiff succeeds, it is for the judge to apply the claim of the plaintiff to the facts of defendant's position, and order him to restore the whole or part of whatever he has under his control, or would have if he had not fraudulently parted with it (D. v 3 fr 9, 10; tit. 4 fr 1 § 1; Paul i 13 b § 5).

[1] So Pliny (*Ep. Traj.* 84=88) in mentioning a grant by Augustus to the people of Nicaea in Bithynia of the intestate estates of their own citizens calls it *intestatorum civium suorum concessam vindicationem bonorum.*

This action is the same whatever be plaintiff's title, whether he sues in his own right or in that acquired through his son or slave or in that of one to whom he is heir[1], and whether his right is by will or on intestacy, as child, agnate or patron (D. v 3 fr 2, 3). All minor actions, such as actions for a legacy or freedom given by a will, were postponed to this, so as to leave the main question of representation to the deceased unprejudiced (fr 5 § 2—fr 7).

The action was usually[2] brought before the *centumviri* (Cod. iii 31 fr 12). There was an alternative procedure as in the ordinary *rei vindicatio*[3] (see Book IV chap. iii F 1).

2. The heir is entitled to recover by this action:

(*a*) All things and rights forming the estate of the deceased at his death.

(*b*) Things at his risk, as pledged or lent to him or deposited with him.

(*c*) Things which, though not his own, he had the right to retain, *e.g.* such as had been the object of suit against deceased, but which he had sworn were not the suitor's.

(*d*) Additions to the estate since deceased's death, such as produce (*fructus*), offspring of women slaves, rents, slaves' earnings and all others which arise from the inheritance (not from outside *e.g.* inheritances and legacies left to slaves, since defendant's entrance on the inheritance, for they are accessions personal to the holder). All such produce could be claimed as might have been collected by a diligent business man, whether actually collected by defendant or not; and double value is due in case of neglect. The costs of collection are deducted.

[1] Provided he had begun the suit, says Paul (i 13 § 4), but Arndts doubts this (Glück's *Pand. Th.* 48 p. 208).

[2] It has been suggested that they had exclusive competence in estates over the value of 100,000 sesterces and that in case of dispute a *praejudicium* determined this point (cf. Paul v 9 § 1; Lenel *E. P.* p. 415).

[3] Cicero refers to the two methods of proceeding (*Verr.* ii 1 45 § 115) *Si quis testamento se heredem esse arbitraretur quod tum non exstaret, lege ageret in hereditatem, aut pro praede litis vindiciarum cum satis accepisset sponsionem faceret et ita de hereditate certaret.* The first method is the *legis actio per sacramentum*, which was afterwards, at least in the case of vindications of single objects, superseded by the *formula petitoria*: the second process continued (see Book VI chap. vi J).

(*e*) Rights of suit, *e.g.* under the *lex Aquilia,* but only for the simple value (so Julian, as reported in Digest); and claims to an inheritance, provided deceased had joined issue.

(*f*) Things procured by defendant out of his own money for the service of the estate and of great importance to it, defendant receiving of course their cost (D. fr 18—19 § 2, 20—§ 4, 25 § 20—fr 29, 36 § 5, Paul i 13 *b* §§ 1, 8, 9).

Additions subsequent to the judgment have also to be surrendered to the successful plaintiff (fr 41).

Servitudes are not sued for by this action, but by their own proper suit (fr 19 § 3).

3. Besides the claim for the delivery or transfer of the inheritance, both its contents and adjuncts, account had to be taken of the possessor's dealings with the inheritance. In some cases, as where an heir was instituted only on condition, and a substitute was appointed in case of the condition's failing, if the instituted heir claimed possession of the estate, the substitute could demand his entering into a stipulation, binding heirs, procurators, cognitors, and sureties, against any diminution of the inheritance (Paul v 9 § 2). And a decree of the senate under Hadrian A.D. 129 called the *SC. Juventianum* (from P. Juventius Celsus, the lawyer, one of the consuls) laid down principles in the case of estates lapsed to the Crown, which were interpreted and extended by the lawyers to other cases also. A distinction was drawn between honest and dishonest possessors. An honest possessor was one who believed himself to be heir, and held the estate in that character (*pro herede possidet*). A dishonest possessor was one who had occupied the estate or something belonging to it with full knowledge that he had no right to it, and without professing to have any—a mere grabber (*praedo*), who had no tittle of claim beyond the fact of possession (*pro possessore possidet*). Even if he appeared to have taken it as dowry, but knew the wife to be under the age of puberty, or as gift, but from his or her consort during marriage, he held as mere possessor, conscious of having no lawful title. The law regarded the honest possessor with much indulgence, as having innocently occupied a false position. But if after a time he became aware of his absence of right, and in all cases

after joinder of issue, the law regarded him thenceforward as a dishonest possessor or at least as entitled to no more indulgence (D. v 3 fr 11—13 § 1, 20 § 6, 25 §§ 5, 7; Cod. iii 31 fr 1 pr).

Thus where the possessor has sold things belonging to the inheritance, he is *prima facie* liable for the price obtained, even if the things sold would never have come to plaintiff, having perished or been gained by usucapion (*deperissent deminutaeque fuissent*, cf. fr 21), before defendant had any notice of the suit. For interest on the price he is liable only from the date of joinder of issue. But a dishonest possessor is liable, not for the price but for the things themselves and their fruits; he must recover them from the purchaser or others if they still exist, and if he cannot get them, he is liable for damages as fixed by plaintiff's oath; if they do not exist or had been gained by usucapion, he must pay their true value. If the auctioneer who sold them has not paid over the sale-money and has become insolvent, such a possessor is none the less liable. A sale after notice of suit makes any possessor liable as dishonest (D. fr 18 pr, 20 §§ 11, 21, fr 21; Cod. iii 31 fr 1).

An honest possessor is however liable, only so far as he has been (at the time of judgment) enriched by the sale; and for this estimate any penalty or forfeiture which he may have got for delay in payment of the purchase-money must be taken into account. He may have spent or given away the sale-money, or other money belonging to the estate, but still he will not be liable to plaintiff, unless, as M. Aurelius decided in an analogous case, he has thereby saved what he would have otherwise taken from other sources and so far may be held to have been enriched (fr 23 § 1, 25 pr §§ 11, 16, fr 36 § 4). If he have lent money of the estate on interest, he is liable to refund both money and interest if collected, or if they be not collected, to surrender his actions (fr 30). If he has got a judgment and received double damages under the *lex Aquilia*, he must pay over the whole (fr 55).

Again an honest possessor has a right of property in the fruits gathered, and is therefore not liable for any which he has consumed or for the produce from them up to the date of joinder of issue, except so far as he became and remains the richer thereby. A dishonest possessor does not make the fruits his own at any time: they are all additions to the estate for which he is liable (D. fr 40 § 1; Cod. iii 31 fr 2).

4. Further an honest possessor can deduct anything that was due to him from the estate, and all payments made to creditors of the estate (guarantying at the same time the plaintiff against any demand from them in that behalf). The dishonest possessor has no right to deduct for any debt due to himself; but as he has no right of action against debtors to the estate, he is not responsible for the non-collection of any debts due to the estate, even if they become superannuated or the debtors become insolvent. Both possessors alike are liable to pay over any payment actually made to them on account of the estate (fr 31). Recoupment for necessary or useful expenditure can be in practice claimed by both, though the dishonest possessor, as a mere intruder, has no strict right to it; still it is the duty of the judge to allow it, without being aided by a plea of fraud; but there is this difference, that the dishonest possessor can get recoupment only if the object of expenditure is still there and improved by it; the honest possessor can get it even without these conditions. By a plea of fraud he can also get repayment for ornamental expenditure, whereas the most obtainable by the dishonest possessor is the right of removal, if it can be effected without injury (fr 38, 39, 53). For deterioration from neglect both are liable (fr 54 § 2). For anything which he has wrongfully (*dolo*) ceased to possess either possessor is liable and judgment against him does not free the actual possessor, but the liability drops if this latter makes restoration (fr 13 § 14; xlvi 3 fr 95 § 9).

5. Not only the possessor of a corporal object was liable to this action but all debtors to the deceased or to the estate, whether debtors on contract or from delict, by promise to a slave, by *negotium gestio, etc.* or by theft or injury to the persons or things of the inheritance before entry or after. They are as it were possessors of (another's) right (*quasi juris possessores*). If the day or condition on which fulfilment of a promise is due has not arrived at the time of judgment, the defendant must give security for payment when due. If the possessor had been

forcibly ejected from land, he is a *juris possessor*, because entitled to an interdict. If he had restored the inheritance or some thing belonging to it under a trust, he is again a *juris possessor,* for he has a condiction to recover them. In such cases where the things still exist, it is enough if he cede his actions; the forcible ejector or recipient by the trust is liable also as actual possessor (fr 13 § 13—fr 16).

A purchaser of an inheritance is liable under an analogous action as well as the vendor (fr 13 § 4).

If a son under power or a slave is in possession of corporal objects belonging to the inheritance, or of the purchase-money of any such as have been sold, the father or master is liable in full, and continues so even if the son or slave be dead or emancipated or manumitted more than a year before. But if the purchase-money has been consumed, or if the son or slave were a debtor to the estate and not an actual possessor, the action will be limited to the *peculium* and subject to the father's or master's right of deduction and to the ordinary period of a year (see Book v chap. vii). A son under power may be sued directly, when he has the power of restoration, just as he is directly liable to a suit *ad exhibendum* (fr 34 § 1—fr 36 § 1).

6. Where plaintiff is heir not to the whole but only to a part of an inheritance, he sues for that part however much or little defendant may possess, even if it be a single object (see above, p. 281). If there are two heirs and two possessors, each heir has to sue both possessors, his right and their occupation being alike undivided. If a partial heir and an outsider possess the inheritance, and the partial heir has no more than his own share, say an undivided half or third, logic (*ratio*) requires that the other partial heir should sue both, but it was thought more convenient, that he should sue for his share the outsider only, and the judge should make the outsider restore not in proportion to the plaintiff's share, but all that he possesses (D. v 4 fr 1 § 1—§ 3). A defendant, if heir also, can give up the share demanded and retain his own, but such a division is ideal: for real division, so that plaintiff and defendant may no longer hold in common, resort must be had to the *judicium familiae erciscundae* (*ib.* fr 7, 8).

Where a plaintiff is, or may turn out to be, only one of two or more with equal rights (*e.g.* one of several children), and there is a pregnant woman whose child would be equally entitled, it is impossible to say what is plaintiff's lawful share, for the woman may give birth to more than one, four being said to have been born at one birth in Greece and five in many cases in Egypt. The lawyers decided to assume a birth of three, so that plaintiff sues as heir to a fourth, if there be no other equal claimant alive. According to the actual result his fourth would be increased or reduced, or, if the woman is not really pregnant, he will have been heir to the whole. Sometimes the praetor allowed a plaintiff in such cases to claim for an uncertain share (fr 1 § 5, 3—5).

A patron is liable to a proportionate share of the burdens of the whole inheritance (fr 6 § 1).

7. Like actions were granted to one who had *possessio bonorum* as to the civil heir (D. v 5): and to the heir by trust who has had the inheritance transferred to him under the Trebellian senate's decree (D. v 6); and to one who had purchased the whole or part of an inheritance from the Crown (D. v 3 fr 54 pr).

If the person sued made no defence, an interdict '*quam hereditatem*' was issuable to enforce transfer of possession to the plaintiff (Ulp. *Fr. Vind.* Krüger vol. ii p. 159; cf. Lenel *E. P.* § 227).

B. *Familiae*[1] *erciscundae judicium.*

1. This was an old judicial proceeding sanctioned by the XII tables 'for partitioning the household,' *i.e.*, for the due division of deceased's estate among the coheirs whether by will or intestacy. It was also available for *bonorum possessores*, and for

[1] The *familia* was originally the body of *famuli*, and is so used of slaves in Cic. *Caecin.* 19 § 35: the *familia publicanorum* included all servants whether slaves or free (D. xxxix 4 fr 1 § 5). In old language it meant the whole household, children, slaves and other belongings. Hence *paterfamilias*, *filius familias*, *etc.* See also the aediles' Edict D. xxi 1 fr 1 § 1; 25 § 2. Cf. Cic. *Mur.* 7 § 15 *Sunt amplae et honestae familiae*

transferees under the Trebellian senate's decree; and could be applied to a soldier's camp-*peculium*, which by the grant to the soldier of power to make a will had been changed from a *peculium* to a heritable estate. An analogous action was granted where deceased left a son by arrogation entitled to a fourth by Ant. Pius' Constitution (D. x 2 fr 1 pr, 2 pr—§ 2, 24 § 1, 40). Any coheir could claim to initiate the proceeding, and may perhaps specially be spoken of as plaintiff, but practically all concerned are alike plaintiffs and defendants. It is not necessary that all should take part, if they have no claim on anything which requires division or allotment (fr 2 § 3; tit. 3 fr 2 § 1). This suit aimed at a complete division, once for all, between all those concerned, assigning corporal things in several ownership, and settling reciprocal claims (*condemnando, i.e.*) by directing payments or other performance, and, where necessary, security to be given. All the participant coheirs were acquitted or condemned as might be required in each several matter, so that the respective obligations might be completely cleared; but there was no objection to condemn one of two coheirs to pay to the other the balance, rather than each to pay the other (D. x 2 fr 27, 52 § 2). This action could only be brought once, except on special cause approved (fr 20 § 4). It was a *bonae fidei* action; the judge is often called *arbiter*. Each party had to swear to his good faith (*de calumnia*) both in his claims and his non-admissions (fr 20 pr, 25 § 20, fr 30, 44 § 4; Just. iv 6 § 28; Cod. iii 36 fr 9). Until the award is made,

plebeiae; Tac. *H.* i 16 *Sub Tiberio et Gaio et Claudio unius familiae quasi hereditas fuimus*, where it is our 'family.' Slaves and goods together are meant, at least in the later conception of such old phrases, as *vendere familiam, familiae emptor*, Gai. ii 104 (supra, p. 177); *adgnatus proximus familiam habeto* (supra, p. 218). See D. L 16 fr 195 and my *De usufructu* p. 48 sq.

Erciscundae is no doubt rightly explained by Gaius ii 219 as *dividundae.* In the *Lex Rubr.* 55 we have the modern word added to the ancient: *de familia erciscunda dividunda judicium.* In Cic. *Or.* i 56 § 237 *quibus verbis herctum cieri oporteat*, *herctum* or *erctum* is supine: 'in what words a summons to divide the inheritance should be couched.' *Ercto non cito* in Gell. i 9 is probably a mistake for *erctum non cito* 'when there has been no summons for division.'

the several coheirs can act in protection of the property by notice *operis novi*, or vindication of land, or suit for theft, *etc.*, and the results will be appropriately dealt with by the arbiter in his award (fr 47).

2. The suit embraced all things belonging to the inheritance, except debts due to or from deceased. These were by the XII tables divided automatically (*ipso jure*) in the ratio of the several shares: but the judge may for the convenience of the coheirs assign a debt or credit wholly to one, due compensation to or by the others and reciprocal delegations being made in the award. He does not thereby take away from the creditors of the estate their right to sue each coheir, but arranges among the coheirs which shall sue or accept suit or at any rate be responsible on behalf of all, in form partly on his own account, partly as procurator of the others; in substance for himself only (fr 2 § 5, 3; Cod. iii 36 § 6; cf. D. xxxi fr 77 § 18).

Any stipulation by deceased for a right of way gives each coheir a several claim for the whole, and, if the way be denied, a claim for damages in the ratio of his share of the inheritance. It does not therefore enter into this suit for division. And neither does a promise or legacy of a right of way by deceased admit of division, but the judge directs mutual securities to be given, so that, if one coheir is sued and has to pay the whole damages, he may be reimbursed by his fellows. So if deceased has promised money under stipulation for a penalty in default of due payment, though the burden of the sum promised is by the XII tables divided among the coheirs automatically, yet as failure on the part of a single heir to pay his share makes the whole penalty due, the judge in this suit will cause covenants to be entered into between the coheirs not to make default, and if one should have to pay the whole to avoid the penalty, then to pay him their due shares. If the payment of the debt has already been made, the judge condemns the parties at once; and similar treatment is applied where goods have been pledged or legatees have gone into possession and one coheir has redeemed the pledge or paid the legacy; or again when he has paid damages in order to prevent the noxal surrender of a slave (D. x 2 fr 18 § 6, 25 §§ 9—15). Where by the terms of a stipulation (*e.g.*, *neque per me neque per heredem meum fore quo minus quis eat agat*, or *a me heredeque meo dolum malum afuturum* or *Titium heredemque ejus ratum habiturum*) the act of one heir in preventing the use of a road, or in wrongful action, or in bringing suit for what deceased's procurator has already sued for, causes a breach, such heir cannot recover from his fellows for the consequences of his breach either by *fam. ercisc. judicio* or any other action (fr 44 §§ 5, 6), and they on the contrary may have an action against him if damaged thereby (fr 44 §§ 5, 6).

3. All adjudications made by the judge are protected by the praetor who grants to the adjudicatee relative pleas and actions (fr 44 § 1). Immoveable property and some other things can be physically divided, proportionate parts being assigned in severalty to the coheirs: or the judge can give the ownership to one and a usufruct to another; or he can establish temporary usufructs and let the enjoyment shift in alternate years; or he can put it up to auction among the heirs and adjudge it to the highest bidder. And he can impose servitudes in order to meet the convenience of particular lots and can require mutual guaranties against eviction (fr 16 §§ 1, 2, 22 §§ 2, 3, 25 § 21). If a coheir has assigned to him by the judge something given in pledge to deceased, and has accordingly to submit to payments to his fellows on account of it, he needs no guaranty from them, for he has a lien on the property for what he has had to pay them, in addition to his own claim, so as to protect himself against the owner (fr 29)[1]. The destruction of a thing, death of a slave, *etc.* is no obstacle to the due arrangement by the judge of any liabilities of any of the coheirs in respect to it (fr 24 pr; 31).

The arbiter's jurisdiction includes everything belonging to the estate, owned or *bona fide* possessed by the deceased, usufructs reserved by testator or bequeathed to slaves of the estate, gifts to them by outsiders, produce of the slaves or animals or lands before or after entry or joinder of issue, things delivered to deceased and acquired by usucapion by the heirs since, things

[1] On this fragment see Vangerow *Pand.* § 365; Dernburg *Pfandrecht* ii 43.

bequeathed away by him on a condition not yet arrived (fr 9—16 pr, 56). The conduct of the heirs themselves and of their slaves comes under the jurisdiction, but only so far as they have acted or omitted to act in the affairs of the estate, since they were aware of their heirship. They are liable for fraud and fault, but as they are connected with their coheirs by act of the testator, not of themselves, they are bound only for so much care as they shew in their own affairs (fr 16 §§ 4—6, 25 § 16, 49). A coheir, unreasonably withholding his consent to the selection of a slave bequeathed away, is liable for any additional loss thereby caused to his fellows (fr 25 § 17). As between themselves any coheir liable for loss is liable for single value only (fr 17). For any delay in repayment of expenses he is (by a rescript of Severus and Antoninus) entitled to interest (fr 18 § 3).

4. Sons under power had to bring their *peculia* into hotchpot, and by a rescript of Ant. Pius a daughter had to bring her dowry (Cod. iii 36 fr 13; D. x 2 fr 20 pr; xxxvii 7 fr 1 pr). On the other hand anything directed by the testator to be taken before division (*praeceptio*) is assigned accordingly. If a thing in pledge is so left, the charge of redemption is on the heirs generally (D. x 2 fr 25 § 22, fr 26, 28). A son has a claim to take before division (*praecipere*) the amount of any debt incurred by his father's order, or arrears of a public office which was undertaken with his father's approval and discharged during his father's life. He can similarly take the dowry of his own wife, and of his daughter in law (fr 20 §§ 1, 2, 6, 7; fr 46). If testator specially laid on one heir the burden of a debt, he must discharge it without contribution from his coheirs, so however as to retain at least a quarter of his share of the inheritance, just as if the debt had been a trust imposed (fr 20 §§ 5, 8). An emancipated son who for the purpose of study abroad has received gifts from his father does not bring this into hotchpot (fr 50).

If deceased has either during life or by will allotted to his children or heirs specific farms or other things and the burden of specific debts, so as to make an exhaustive division of his estate, the division will be carried into effect. If there turn out to be something left undivided and not appertaining to the allotments, the coheirs will share it in the ratio of their shares of the inheritance. Due regard is paid to the latest intentions of deceased, even if modifying his will and not expressed in writing (fr 20 § 3, 32, 39 §§ 1, 5; xxxi fr 77 § 8; Cod. iii 36 fr 5, 10). Agreements between the coheirs for division made before the arbiter's award will also be given effect to, subject to the right of minors to apply for a cancel (fr 57; Cod. iii 36 fr 1, 12).

Any directions by the testator for the sale of a slave into foreign parts, or the erection of a monument, *etc.* will be given effect to and secured by the judge (fr 18 § 2). Any goods which have been obtained by peculation or sacrilege or violence or robbery will not be divided, nor ought the judge to deal with poisonous drugs or books of magic and other forbidden reading; such things should be destroyed at once (fr 4 §§ 1, 2). The will itself and any documents of importance should, after facilities for copying have been afforded to the others, be left with the principal heir (who has to promise to produce when required) or deposited in a temple. If all are equal heirs, agreement or lot, not bidding, should decide on the depositary (fr 4 § 3, fr 6).

5. Possession of the inheritance or of a part of it is not necessary for accepting suit, but if one in possession denies that a claimant is coheir, he can exclude him from this suit by pleading that it might prejudice the trial of his claim to be heir (*si in ea re qua de agitur praejudicium hereditati non fiat*; cf. p. 282). If, however, the claimant is in possession of his share, then it is the duty of the judge to hear and decide the question of heirship: otherwise he can adjudge nothing to him nor condemn his opponent to pay him anything, this suit lying only between coheirs. If *A* and *B* have proceeded under this suit on the supposition that one or both were coheirs when that was not the case, and adjudications and payments have been duly made, neither can recover things or money from the other; as between them at least the decision stands good. If a division had been made by private arrangement under a similar misconception, there is nothing to hinder recovery (fr 1 § 1, 25 § 2, 36; cf. fr 37, where text is disputed).

If there are several inheritances in which the same parties

are interested, even with the addition of another party, the division of all can be conducted in one proceeding (fr 25 §§ 3—5). If during the proceeding of a suit of this kind one coheir die leaving several heirs, they must be treated as one, a procurator, if necessary, being appointed to act for them (fr 48).

6. The question whether a particular thing is parcel of the deceased's estate or the private property of one of the coheirs or of an outsider is not within the scope of this suit (fr 45 pr).

The assignment of freedmen is outside this suit; and so are the rights to tombs (fr 30, 41).

If any corporal thing and matters therewith connected is undivided, resort can be had to the *judicium communi dividundo*, which is open to coheirs as to all tenants in common, and can be brought as often as required. But its scope is much narrower than the *jud. fam. ercisc.* (fr 44 pr; tit. 3 fr 3, 4 pr § 2, *etc.*).

CHAPTER VIII.

LEGACY.

In making a person heir I make him my representative, and in that capacity he takes all my property and is responsible for all my surviving obligations. If, instead of selecting one person, I select several for this position, they represent me collectively, and are entitled and responsible according to the shares which I have assigned them. A legacy (or bequest) is a gift by will of some particular thing or of some quantity to a person, who (in the absence of a trust) is not thereby fixed with any further privilege or responsibility. If the testator bequeathed him a certain share of his estate, he had to arrange with the heir for the collection of his share of the assets and defrayal of his share of the debts, not being, as a partial heir would be, in direct relation to third parties.

A. How legacies are made.

There were two principal modes of making a legacy, either a direct assignment of the property or a charge upon the heir to execute the gift. The former mode is a legacy *per vindicationem*, the latter *per damnationem*. Two other forms are modifications of these.

1. *Per vindicationem*. This mode is when the testator uses the words, 'I give and bequeath' (*do lego*)[1]. But either word will do alone; and the better opinion was that 'he shall take' (*sumito, capito*), or 'he shall have for himself' (*sibi habeto*) had the same effect. When such words were used, the full ownership (*ex jure Quiritium*) passed to the legatee immediately (not through the heir) on the will's coming into force by the heir's entry, and the legatee could claim (*vindicare*) the thing bequeathed either from the heir or from anyone else who had it. He sued for the thing as his own. There was however a minor dispute between the schools of lawyers[2]: Sabinus and Cassius thought that the legatee acquired, whether he knew of it or not, but that if he declined to accept, the bequest was null: Nerva and Proculus thought there was no acquisition until the legatee (mentally) accepted, and this latter view was held to be confirmed by a constitution of Ant. Pius in reference to the bequest of a Latin[3] to a colony. 'It is,' he said, 'for the 'decurions of the colony to consider whether they choose the man 'to belong to them' (*an ad se velint pertinere* Gai. ii 193—195; cf. D. xlvii 2 fr 65). The emperor's words seem to have been interpreted too narrowly, as *pertinere* may mean 'continue to belong,' quite as well as 'begin to belong.' In any case, if a man has not repudiated the legacy and it is unconditional, the legatee succeeds immediately to the testator without the heir's ever

[1] These words are often used to describe this form of legacy, *e.g.* Vat. 47 (Paul) *per do lego legatum et per in jure cessionem ususfructus et deduci et dari potest; ib.* 57, 75, 83, *etc.*

[2] The Sabinian view was generally supposed to have been accepted by Justinian, but of late this has been contested. See the discussion by Arndts, Glück's *Pand.* Pt 48 1 p. 266; Windscheid § 643. *Contra*, Ihering *Jahrb.* x p. 476 points out the practical difficulties of the Sabinian view.

[3] A similar bequest (or trust bequest, cf. *apud fidem tuam*, in Trajan's answer) was made to Pliny (*Ep. Traj.* 104, 105).

having been owner (D. xxxi fr 80; cf. xxx fr 44 § 1; xxxviii 5 fr 1 § 6). And if the legatee die after the opening of the will, although before the heir's entry on the inheritance, and without having made up his mind to accept, he transmits the claim to his heir (Paul iii 6 § 7). If the legacy is conditional, the Sabinians held that until the condition took effect the ownership of the thing is in the heir, as in the case of a slave conditionally freed (*statuliber*): the Proculians held that in the interim it is no one's, just as an unconditional legacy is no one's until the legatee accepts (Gai. ii 200). Any alienation by the heir, pending the legatee's deciding to accept, or a condition's taking effect, does not impair the legatee's rights (D. xxx fr 69 § 1; xxxiv 5 fr 15; cf vi 1 fr 66).

As this form of legacy acted as an immediate conveyance of ownership, it applied only to things which were the testator's *ex jure Quiritium* both at the time of making his will and at the time of his death[1], excepting however that a bequest of things lying in weight, count or measure, as wine, oil, corn, coins, was valid, if they were his at the date of his death, whatever may have been the case at the date of the will. A decree of the senate proposed by Nero came in aid of such bequests, as would have failed by the strict civil law, because the things had never been the testator's or had been his only at one of these times[2]. It enacted that a bequest not made in apt words should be treated as if it had the fullest right, in fact as if the form *per damnationem* had been adopted, in which case the testator's ownership is immaterial. Where however a testator had bequeathed a thing and afterwards parted with it, the bequest was, according to most lawyers in Gaius' time, bad by the civil law, and was not practically helped

[1] This was also required for manumission directly by will (Gai. ii 267, D. xl 4 fr 35).

[2] This is the only undisputed application of the very general words of the *SC.* which are reported by Ulpian thus: *ut quod minus aptis verbis legatum est perinde sit ac si optimo jure legatum esset* (cf. Gai. ii 197, 212, 218). The application to legacies *per praeceptionem* and *sinendi modo* was also disputed. That a valid legacy *per vind.* could not also be treated at the will of the legatee as a damnatory legacy is strongly argued by Salkowski, Glück's *Pand.* Pt 49 p. 27 sqq.

by the Neronian decree; for even a claim under a damnatory legacy would according to them (see however below, p. 297) be defeated by a plea of fraud (Gai. ii 196—198; Ulp. xxiv 7, 11 *a*). Slaves, previously mortgaged away in trust (*fiduciae dati*), did not pass by a bequest in the *do lego* form (Paul iii 6 § 69).

Where the same thing is left by a *do lego* bequest to two or more persons and all accept, each has a claim to the whole, and it is only by the concurrence of claims that each is reduced to a share (*partes concursu fiunt*). If therefore anyone fail, his share accrues to, or rather is no longer subtracted from, the others. And it makes no difference whether the form of the bequest is joint (*conjunctim*), *e.g. Titio et Seio hominem Stichum do lego* or several (*disjunctim*), *e.g. Titio hominem Stichum do lego; Seio eundem hominem do lego* (Gai. ii 199; Ulp. xxiv 12; D. xxxii fr 80).

2. The most flexible and far-reaching mode of bequest was *per damnationem*, which imposed a personal obligation on the heirs or one of the heirs to carry out the will of the testator in favour of the particular legatee. The words used were such as 'my heir shall be bound to give Stichus to so and so' (*heres meus Stichum dare damnas esto*, or *heredem dare jubeo*) or simply 'my heir shall give' or 'do' (*heres meus dato* or *facito*). It did not matter at one time whether the thing bequeathed was the testator's own, or the heir's, or an outsider's, whether it was mortgaged by testator or not, whether it existed now or only would exist at some future time (*e.g.* 'the fruits which shall be produced on that farm'): the legatee had a personal action of a peremptory character (*certi* or *incerti ex testamento*) against the heir. If the thing be mancipable, the heir must mancipate it or surrender it in court, and also deliver the possession; if the thing is not mancipable, it is enough if he deliver it. And if he cannot or will not do this, he is liable for the value. If the legacy be for something certain and the heir dispute the claim, he is liable for twice the value, as upon a judgment debt (see Book v chap. v). Meantime the thing, if part of the testator's estate, is the heir's (Gai. ii 201—204, 282; Ulp. xxiv 4, 8).

If the thing bequeathed was neither the testator's nor the

heir's, a rescript of Ant. Pius allowed the legacy to stand, only if the testator was aware of this; and this was for the legatee to prove. If he was not aware of it, the legacy was bad, except (by a rescript of Alex. Severus) where it was in favour of a wife or near relative to whom testator would have given it in any case (Just. ii 20 § 4; Cod. vi 37 fr 10; D. xxxi fr 67 § 8). If the thing was testator's, but already pledged to a creditor, the legacy was good, and the heir had to redeem the pledge and hand it over to the legatee, provided in accordance with a rescript of Severus and Caracalla the testator was aware of the pledge (Paul iii 6 § 8; Just. ii 20 § 5). If, since the will was made, testator pledged (*pignori vel fiduciae dedit*) or alienated the thing, rescripts of the same emperors decided that, unless the intention of the testator was shewn to be different, this legacy was still good and the heir had to redeem or repurchase. The matter was disputed in Gaius' time (Gai. ii 198; Paul iii 6 § 16; Just. ii 20 § 12; Cod. vi 37 § 3). As regards trusts the matter seems doubtful (Paul iv 1 § 9, D. xxxii fr 11 §§ 12, 13). A damnatory legacy of another's slave could not be enforced, if the slave had been freed by his master: if the slave was the heir's, the heir is liable for the value (D. xxx fr 35, 112 § 1).

By this form of legacy the heir might be bound to do other things for the legatee, *e.g.* to build him a house, or free him from debt; or sell something to him or buy from him at a reasonable price or at a price fixed by testator (Paul iii 6 § 10; D. xxx fr 66).

Where the same thing was left to two or more persons jointly, each was entitled to a share only (*partes damnatio facit*), there was no accrual, and therefore any share which lapsed remained with the heir (before the *lex Papia*; see chap. x C). But if the legacy is several, each legatee was entitled to the whole, so that the heir had to give the thing to one, and, unless the slave or thing perished before demand, had to give the value to each of the others (Gai. ii 205; Ulp. xxiv 13; Vat. 85; D. xxx fr 36 § 3; xxxi fr 7, 13 § 1; cf. xxx fr 16 pr).

3. A modification of this form occurred when the testator instead of binding his heir to give, bound him to allow the legatee to take: *Heres meus damnas esto sinere L. Titium hominem*

Stichum sumere sibique habere. This form was called *legatum sinendi modo* ('Permissive legacies') and was good for bequests of corporal things and also incorporal; *e.g.* a release to a debtor. It was certainly applicable to bequests of things belonging to the heir, as well as to things belonging to testator, at the time of death, whether they were so or not when the will was made: it was doubtful whether it applied to things acquired by the heir since testator's death: most lawyers held such a legacy invalid, but Gaius appears to differ, and points out that the Neronian senate's decree made it applicable as widely as the damnatory form. The legatee *sinendi modo* has no immediate claim to the thing bequeathed, but only a personal action for *quidquid heredem ex testamento dare facere oportet.* And accordingly the heir had to mancipate it or surrender it in court or deliver it in order to make it the legatee's. There was however another view held that the heir was not bound to do more than was expressed in the words of the form, viz. to allow the legatee to take and keep. Another disputed point was the heir's duty where the same thing was bequeathed to two or more persons severally. Some lawyers thought each had a claim to the whole, others that the heir was only bound to let the first comer have the thing and had no further obligation: if one took it, the heir could meet later applicants with the answer that he no longer had the thing for another to take, and he had not acted fraudulently in parting with it (Gai. ii 209—215; Ulp. xxiv 5, 10; Paul iii 6 § 11).

4. A fourth form of legacy was that *per praeceptionem*[1], *i.e.* where the testator used *praecipito* instead of *capito, e.g.* L. Titius *hominem Stichum praecipito.* The Proculians held that the *prae* was a superfluous syllable, and that this form did not differ from a *do lego* legacy. If the thing bequeathed was the testator's *ex jure Quiritium,* the legatee could claim it at once: if

[1] Pliny mentions a case in which he was left heir, and the borough of Comum also left heir to a fourth, and afterwards in lieu of that to a *praeceptio* of 400,000 sesterces. The borough was not capable of taking, but Pliny waived technicalities and carried out the deceased's will (*Ep.* v 7). Again he is made heir and is directed *praeceptis quinquaginta milibus nummum* to hand over the rest to the communities of Heraclea and Tianum (*Ep. Traj.* 75 (79)).

it was the testator's only *in bonis*, and was left to an heir, the judge would assign it to him in a suit for the division of the estate; if it was left to an outsider, the Neronian decree would come in aid, as it would if the thing in no way belonged to the testator. The Sabinians held that *praecipere* was only applicable to an heir who was to have a bequest before and above his share of the inheritance. It could therefore be sued for only by the suit for division of the inheritance, and was applicable only to things belonging to testator's estate, including however things mortgaged to testator's creditor in trust (*fiduciae datum*). Anything left by this form to an outsider was an invalid legacy, incurable even by the Neronian decree, which remedied faults of wording but not personal disqualifications. Julian however pointed out that there was here after all only a fault of wording, for an outsider could have taken the bequest, if the wording had been that of any of the other three forms; whereas personal disqualification, such as that of a foreigner for instance, would be fatal to the legacy, the Neronian decree notwithstanding. A rescript of Hadrian was said to have favoured the Proculian view. On either view a bequest to two or more persons, whether joint or several, gave them only equal shares, just as in a vindicatory legacy. And this was so, even if they had unequal shares in the inheritance (Gai. ii 216—223; Ulp. xxiv 6, 11; Paul iii 6 § 1; D. xxx fr 67 § 1).

B. Who is liable to pay or discharge legacies?

1. A legacy of anything which is the property of testator could, if the legacy was direct (*do lego*), be enforced by vindication against the possessor, who would usually be the heir or heirs. Actions (*ex testamento*) to enforce damnatory and permissive legacies were of course against the heir or heirs. If there be no express direction, or if the direction be in general terms, *e.g. quisquis mihi heres erit, damnas esto Titio dare centum* (D. xxx fr 104 pr); *Stichum aut decem heredes danto* (D. xxxi fr 15); or simply *heres meus dato*, though several persons are appointed heirs (*ib.* fr 44 pr), all the heirs will be liable in proportion to their shares in the inheritance. But if the testator, as was

frequently done, charged legacies on particular heirs by name, no liability attached to the others, and the heirs so named were liable for the whole legacy in equal shares, not in proportion to their shares in the inheritance (D. xxx fr 54 § 3, 124; cf. xxx fr 67 § 1; xl 7 fr 8 § 1, 12; xlv 3 fr 37). Paul however with others appears to have held that naming makes no difference, and that liability of heirs was always according to their shares in the inheritance (D. xlv 2 fr 17; cf. xl 7 fr 22; xxviii 6 fr 32). Testator's intention was really decisive (cf. D. xxxvi 1 fr 25; Vangerow *Pand.* § 521). If some heirs are unable to pay their share of the legacy, the others are not liable to make it up (D. xxxi fr 33 pr). If the estate is not sufficient, legatees have to abate proportionally (D. xxx fr 80). A legacy imposed on two heirs is according to Sabinus due wholly from one, if the other does not become heir (fr 122 § 1); but if it is imposed on one heir expressly and his share of the inheritance accrue to another who is a son of testator, it comes without the burden, the son being heir taking the legacy as a lapse *jure antiquo* (D. xxxi fr 29 § 2; cf. Ulp. xviii; Brisson's *Lex s.v. antiquum*). Where a statutable heir was charged with trusts (*quisquis mihi heres erit, etc.*) and renounced, his coheir was, since the rescript of Severus and Caracalla, held, as if he were a substitute, to take the burden along with the accrual (D. xxxi fr 61 § 1).

2. When a substituted heir came to the inheritance, he had, according to a rescript of Severus and Caracalla, to pay the legacies imposed on the appointed heir. This was interpreted to apply only where a different intention of the testator did not appear, as, for instance, might be inferred, if he had charged the substitute with a different legacy to the same person, or there was some special reason for charging the appointed heir with the legacy. If legacies were repeated, the substitute was only bound to pay once, and if the legatee had taken or declined the legacy from the appointed heir, the substitute was not bound to pay at all (D. xxx fr 74 pr, 81 § 7). A pupillar substitute was not bound to pay legacies imposed on him, if the pupil was disinherited and he himself was not among the instituted heirs; for legacies could be imposed only

on heirs[1]. And therefore if a legacy had been left to the disinherited pupil, the substitute was not bound any the more (D. xxx fr 126 pr; xxxv 2 fr 87 § 7; xxix 1 fr 41 § 3; cf. Cod. vi 37 fr 24).

3. This principle was strictly observed, where the heir appointed was a son under power or a slave. Although the inheritance passes to the father or master on the son or slave entering by his order, no legacies can be imposed by the will on the father or master (Ulp. xxiv 21).

4. On the other hand where a legacy is given to an heir, it may be charged specially on his coheirs, in which case he gets the whole benefit, or on the whole inheritance, in which case he gets no benefit as legatee so far as it falls on his share of the inheritance, and in claiming from his coheirs must deduct his own proportion. If he keep aloof from the inheritance, he then can claim the whole legacy (Ulp. xxiv 22; D. xxx fr 17 § 2, 18, 104 § 3; Cod. vi 37 fr 12). A legacy to two persons, one of whom is heir, passes wholly to the other: if both are heirs, say one to a twelfth, the other to eleven-twelfths, they will be entitled to the legacy in inverse proportion. If a farm be left to one of two heirs and to two outsiders, the heir-legatee can claim only so far as his coheir is charged: he will get therefore one-sixth (*i.e.* one-third of the half imposed on his coheir); the outsiders will get two-thirds of that half, as well as the half imposed on the heir-legatee, *i.e.* five-sixths of the farm between them (D. xxx fr 34 §§ 11, 12; 116 § 1). Where a legacy to an heir is not specially charged on the other heirs, the testator is often said *praelegare*[2] 'to make a precedent bequest,' and if, as is usual, testator gives it directly (*per vindicationem*) it is a *praeceptio*, and the heir takes it before the division of the inheritance (see above, p. 298). Damnatory forms are naturally rare for this purpose (fr 104 § 3; xxxii fr 34 § 1). Such precedent legacies were, if disputed, matter for settlement by the judge in a suit *fam. ercisc.*

[1] A trust differs from a legacy in these respects (Gai. ii 271; D. xxx fr 11).

[2] Cf. Val. Max. vii 8 § 4 *magna ex parte heres frater erat scriptus, praelegebaturque ei centies et quinquagies sestertium.*

5. Sale of the inheritance left the heir or heirs still liable for legacies and trusts: he or they must protect themselves by covenants with the purchaser (Cod. vi 37 fr 2). If however the estate was insolvent, and the heir still succeeded in finding a purchaser or in getting debtors to take a percentage only, he was not liable to legacies or trusts for anything he thereby saved: he got it from the folly of the purchaser, not from the estate of deceased (D. xxxv 2 fr 3). Where possession of the estate was granted against the will, legacies to children and parents had to be paid (see p. 250 sqq.). Where the will was upset as unduteous or otherwise invalid, legacies and freedoms failed with it (cf. D. xl 5 fr 47 pr). If the inheritance lapsed under the *lex Julia* to the Crown or others, or was forfeited to the Crown, because the heir entered before putting slaves to the question, or did not duly avenge testator's death, the Crown (or others, as the case might be) were bound to pay legacies and grant the freedoms charged thereon (Ulp. xvii 3; D. xxx fr 50 § 2, 96 § 1; xxxiv 1 fr 24).

6. If a person, appointed heir in a will, with legacies charged on him, repudiates or disregards the title given by the will (*omissa causa testamenti*) in order to avoid the legacies, and obtains the possession of the whole or part of the estate or of any single thing belonging to it, as statutable heir or praetorian possessor or perhaps on some fictitious claim, or through a slave or child in his power who has been substituted for him in the will, he will after a due hearing of the matter be compelled by the praetor to pay the legacies: and if there be a pupillar will which would otherwise fail with the principal will, the substitute will also be protected. Such disregard is found not only if a person does not himself enter, but also if he refrain from ordering his slave or son or daughter to accept an inheritance which has come to them. Or if he take possession of the estate as on intestacy, instead of against the will, in order not to pay the legacies to children and parents, which are incumbent in the latter case, he is (according to the better opinion) liable to pay these legacies all the same. If he has taken a bribe from the substitute or statutable successor, or acted from favour to them, and has passed by the inheritance

in order to kill the legacies, he was, by a rescript of Hadrian's, to be treated as if he possessed the inheritance *ab intestato* after neglecting the will, and thus is liable to the legatees. But if he took no money to induce his neglect, and has not any share in the inheritance, the legatees must proceed (*utili actione*) against the possessor. Whether, when money had been taken, he or the successor was primarily liable, seems doubtful (D. xxix 4 fr 1 pr §§ 1, 9; fr 2, 4, 6 §§ 3, 9; fr 13—16, 25, 26). If both the instituted and the substituted heirs disregard the testamentary title and are both possessors, they are liable respectively for the legacies charged on their shares: if only one is possessor, he is liable for all, unless the other has taken a bribe (fr 10 § 2).

The heir of the person so passing the will and getting the inheritance otherwise is liable to the legatees in full; but, if his predecessor was liable only for fraud and did not get the inheritance, the heir is liable only so far as he has benefited. The Falcidian fourth can be deducted in all cases under this edict. If a person refuses an inheritance in good faith, without any such intention to kill legacies, and gets no possession, he is not within this edict. A patron who has been left heir to less than his due share after deduction of legacies, and who acts *bona fide* in upsetting the will is not within the edict (fr 6 § 8, 17, 18 § 1).

Freedoms and trusts are preserved as well as legacies (fr 12 pr, 28 § 1, xl 4 fr 23). But one, to or for whom the heir was to pay or do something as a condition of taking the inheritance, is not a legatee, and cannot claim protection if the heir disregard the title by will (fr 8, 9).

C. What legacies are invalid.

1. The appointment of an heir being essential to a will, no legacy or gift of freedom which precedes such appointment is valid. If legacies are inserted after the appointment of some heirs and before others, whether one or both sets entered, the legacies, says Paul, were held to be good for half the amount if left by vindication, for the whole if left by damnation

(iii 6 § 2; Gai. ii 229; Ulp. xxiv 15). (Presumably in the latter case they would be charged upon the heirs whose appointment preceded, whereas vindicatory legacies were subtracted from the inheritance as a whole and their amounts were reduced, because the inheritance had been only half dealt with when they were inserted.) If freedom was left to a slave in the midst of the appointment of heirs and both sets of heirs entered, the freedom was null; but if only the preceding heirs entered, the freedom was good: after the Papian law it was good only if the preceding heirs were duly qualified to take as heirs (Ulp. i 21).

2. A legacy to take effect after the death of the heir (*e.g. cum heres meus mortuus erit, do lego* or *dato*) was invalid, for that would be leaving it from the heir's heir, which, says Ulpian, is contrary to the principle of the civil law. But a legacy is good if it is to take effect at the time of the heir's death (*cum morietur do lego*, or *heres dare damnas esto*), but bad if to take effect on the day before (*pridie quam heres meus morietur*), for which last rule Gaius saw no good reason. No doubt the reason was, what he gives in the case of stipulations (iii 100), that the day is not known until after the death. The same rules apply also to the grant of freedom to slaves (Gai. ii 232, 233; Ulp. xxiv 16; Paul iii 6 § 6).

3. A legacy by way of penalty (*poenae causa*) is invalid. Such a legacy is when the testator, in order to induce his heir to do or not do something, *e.g.* to give or not give his daughter in marriage to a particular person, or to erect a monument to the testator within a certain time, imposes the duty, in case of non-compliance, of paying a legacy. Nor could a grant of freedom be made by way of penalty on the heir, though this point was the subject of some dispute (Gai. ii 235, 236; Ulp. xxiv 17). Whether a particular provision is a penalty or an ordinary condition or gift over, is a question of testator's intention (D. xxxiv 6 fr 2).

4. A legacy of anything attached to a house or other building, *e.g.* a column, marbles, statues, doors, bookcases, beams, tiles, *etc.* is invalid by a senate's decree, A.D. 122. This was part of the same policy which forbad the sale of buildings to pull down. But it was not unlawful (so rescripts of Severus

decided) to transfer things attached to the freehold from one house to another of the same owner's; and hence any legacy which would only have that effect (*e.g.* bequeathing a house but reserving the marbles for a house of the heir) was not wholly invalid; the legatee was entitled to the value, but the transference was not allowed (D. xxx fr 41 §§ 1—4; cf. xviii 1 fr 52). A legacy of such things for a public building of the same town was allowed (D. xxx fr 41 § 5). A legacy of what is attached to a building, if the legacy is dependent on a condition, was valid or not according as the statue, *etc.* was separate or part of a building at the time of occurrence of the condition (fr 41 § 2). A trust for the removal of the columns or beams of a house was good only for what could be removed without injury to the house (D. xxxii fr 21 § 2).

5. The invalidity of a legacy was sometimes consequent on the person of the legatee. For a valid legacy he must be one who, or in the case of a slave-legatee whose master, had (at the dates of the will, of vesting, and of making entry) will-making with the testator, *i.e.* he must not be a foreigner, nor a Junian Latin, nor a captive in the power of the enemy, nor interdicted from fire and water, nor deported into an island, nor condemned to chains, mines or wild beasts (Gai. ii 218, 275; D. xxviii 1 fr 18; tit. 5 fr 60 § 4). For the incapacity of childless persons under the Papian law see p. 379 sqq. A legacy to another's slave of something belonging to the slave's master (*per damnationem*) is not invalid if such as he could take if free, but it will be effectual only if the slave be free when the legacy vests[1] (D. xxxi fr 82 § 2; cf. xxxiii 3 fr 5).

6. A legacy to one who was in the power, hand, or hand-take of the heir was a subject of much discussion. Servius held that the legacy was good in itself, but became worthless if at the time of vesting the legatee was still under power.

[1] Pliny (*Ep.* iv 10) relates that a lady had made him and another heirs, and although she had not directed her slave Modestus to be free had left him a legacy in these words *Modesto quem liberum esse jussi.* He consulted the lawyers: '*Convenit inter omnes nec libertatem deberi quia non sit data nec legatum quia servo suo dederit.*' Pliny proposed to his coheir that they should allow the slave *morari in libertate* and *frui legato*, as if the will had contained the requisite provisions.

The Sabinians (and Ulpian) held that this was so in a conditional legacy, but that an unconditional legacy was bad; it was absurd to think that a legacy, which would have been invalid if the testator died immediately after making his will, became valid just because he lived longer[1]. The Proculians held that all such legacies were bad, whether conditional or not (Gai. ii 244; Ulp. xxiv 23; cf. D. xxxiii 5 fr 13; xxxvi 2 fr 17).

7. If a son under power or a slave is appointed heir, a legacy to his father or master is good, but if he become heir while still in the legatee's power, the inheritance passes to the father or master and the legacy is therefore merged. The like holds of a legacy to such an heir's brother or son or slave. If however the son be emancipated or the slave set free or alienated to another, the inheritance does not pass to the legatee and the legacy is due (Gai. ii 245; cf. D. xxx fr 25, 91 pr. Ulpian xxiv 24 differs, if our text is right).

8. A legacy to an uncertain person, *i.e.* a legacy to a person not distinctly before the mind of the testator, is invalid. Such a legacy is 'my heir shall give 10000 sesterces to whoever shall be first at my funeral,' or generally 'to anyone who shall come to my funeral,' or 'to whoever shall give his daughter in marriage to my son,' or 'to whoever shall be first appointed consuls after my will is made' and so on[2]. But a legacy to one of a known class, although the particular individual is uncertain, is good (*legatum sub certa demonstratione incertae*

[1] This is an application of what was called the *regula Catoniana*, given by Celsus in these words: *Quod, si testamenti facti tempore decessisset testator, inutile foret, id legatum, quandocumque decesserit, non valere.* All that the title in the Digest (xxxiv 7) under that name tells us, is that the rule did not apply to inheritances, nor to such legacies as did not vest at the time of death but after entry (see p. 314), nor to conditional legacies (cf. xxx fr 41 § 2), nor to any new statutes (*e.g. lex Papia Poppaea*), nor to some other cases. The rule appears to be simply an application to legacies of the general principle *Quod ab initio vitiosum est, tractu temporis convalescere nequit* (D. L 17 fr 29). Whether the rule drew its name from Cato the Censor, or from his son who had more renown as a jurist, we know not. See Vangerow *Pand.* § 540; Windscheid *Pand.* § 638.

[2] Cf. Suet. *Dom.* 9 *Legatum ex testamento Rusci Caepionis qui caverat, ut quot annis ingredientibus curiam senatoribus certam summam viritim praestaret heres suus, irritum fecit* (*Domitianus*).

personae), *e.g.* 'a legacy to that one of my relations now living who shall be first at my funeral' (Gai. ii 238; Ulp. xxiv 18). So the heir may be given the choice of legatee, *e.g. Titio aut Seio utri heres velit*, or *libertis meis quibus voles*. If the heir chooses, others have no claim: if he does not, all may claim (D. xxxi fr 16, 24). That freedom could not be given to an uncertain person is clear; for the *lex Fufia Caninia* required mention *nominatim* of any slave to be freed (Gai. ii 239). But a description by business (*e.g. obsonatorem meum*), or by the name of his mother, was by the *SC. Orfitianum* sufficient, if there was only one to whom it applied (Paul iv 14 § 1). Where freedom is given to Stichus and there are two of the name and no indication which testator meant, neither is freed (Vat. 227).

9. Nor can a legacy be given to an alien postumous child any more than such a one can be made heir (Gai. ii 241, 242; see p. 194).

10. Legacies to towns (*civitates*) within the empire of the Roman people are valid, whether for distribution among the citizens, or for a feast to them, or for the support of old people or children, or for education or for public buildings or shows. This was first allowed by Nerva, and afterwards carefully settled by a senate's decree under Hadrian. A rescript in Gaius' time extended this allowance to smaller places (*vici* Ulpian xxiv 28; D. xxx fr 73 § 1, 117, 122 pr; cf. xxxi fr 30). A legacy (or trust) given to the citizens of *A* is a legacy, *etc.* to the town (D. xxxiv 5 fr 2). *Collegia* were allowed by M. Aurelius to receive legacies (D. xxxiv 5 fr 20; see Book V chap. iv E 2).

11. A mistake in description did not vitiate a legacy if the real meaning was ascertainable. 'I leave the slave Stichus, which I bought from Titius,' or 'the Tusculan farm which was given me by Seius' may be good legacies, though the first was not bought and the second was not given. And it was held that, if a testator said, 'I bequeath to *A* a hundred thousand sesterces which I owe him,' the legacy might be claimed though he did not owe it[1]. A legacy of 'Stichus cook,' or

[1] The like in the case of a trust; D. xxxi fr 88 § 10.

'Stichus shoemaker' may be well given, though the descriptions were wrong. Nor if the legatee is falsely called brother or sister or grandson, *etc.* (if he be the person intended, cf. D. xxviii 5 fr 9 pr) is the misnomer any hurt, as was decided by a constitution of Severus and Caracalla (D. xxxv 1 fr 17 pr § 1; 33 pr, 34; xxxiv 2 fr 10; tit. 3 fr 25; cf. xxviii 5 fr 49 § 3; Cod. vi 37 fr 7 § 1). A legacy of 'what is due to testator under the will of Sempronius' is not vitiated by testator's having novated his claim so that it is no longer due under the will (xxxi fr 76 § 3). But a direction to pay Seius fifty sesterces out of what testator had left to Titius does not entitle Titius to a legacy which as a fact had not been left (fr 72 § 8).

12. Nor does a mistaken reason vitiate a legacy, *e.g.* 'I leave that farm to Titius because he has attended to my business,' or 'Titius shall have that farm over and above, because his brother has taken so much money out of my money-chest' may be good legacies, though the facts were not as stated. (If they had been stated as conditions, of course the legacies would have failed.) But if it is shewn that the testator would not have made the legacies if he had known the facts, the heir would be entitled to meet the claim with a plea of fraud (D. xxxv 1 fr 17 §§ 2, 3; 72 § 6).

13. A legacy (or trust) left by an insolvent testator is not due (D. xxxvi 1 fr 70): and legacies to persons who were not capable, especially under the *lex Papia Poppaea*, often failed altogether; see below, chap. x.

D. Renouncement (*repudiatio*) of legacy.

A legacy *per vindicationem* may be renounced by the legatee, and, if left to a slave, by the legatee's master. But it can be renounced only as a whole: the legatee (or legatee's master) cannot accept one part and refuse another. If he die after the legacy is vested and leave more than one heir, each heir acts for himself in accepting or renouncing his share. So with the masters of a common slave, to whom a legacy has been left. But there is no accrual to the other, if one does not accept. A legatee of two things is not obliged to accept both: if however he repudiate one which carries no emolument (*e.g.*, a slave to be freed) he may have to bear the Falcidian deduction on both (D. xxx fr 7, 38 pr § 1, 81 § 1; xxxi fr 4, 5, 20, 58). If a legacy is left on condition or from a future time, it cannot be renounced till the condition occur or the time arrives: till then, it does not belong to the legatee (D. xxxi fr 45 § 1). Renouncement puts the legatee in the same position as if there had been no such legacy; and anything bequeathed is as if from the first it was the property of the heir (Gai. ii 195, D. xxx fr 38, 44 § 1, 86 § 2).

A legacy *per damnationem* can also be practically renounced by the legatee by his simply not claiming from the heir; but for an extinction of the claim he must give a formal release; or if the claim be for a quantity certain he can resort to the old *solutio per aes et libram* (see below, chap. xi, and Book v chap. v).

E. Repetition of legacy.

Where the same thing is left to the same person more than once in the will, an imperial rescript (of Ant. Pius) declared that the heir was bound only to give it once, as once given it could not be given again. But if the bequest repeated the same amount of money or other fungible, there was no reason why it should not be due twice over. If the legacy repeated not the same sum but the same collection of money, *e.g.* 'the money in my chest,' the difficulty of giving again specifically what has already been given recurs (D. xxx fr 34 §§ 1—6; xxxi fr 66 pr). A legacy imposed on each of the heirs in favour of the same legatee is due from each either *in specie* or in value, just as if it had been bequeathed in two persons' wills. Further, the same legacy, bequeathed in the same will to a man and again to his son under power or his slave, makes two legacies, both of which are due (xxx fr 53 § 2). But a legacy imposed by the will is not made void by a legacy of the same thing to the legatee's slave (fr 108 § 1). All such cases are subject to the general principle that the intention of the testator is to prevail.

It is on that account that such repeated legacies do not

always fall under the rule that a person could not avail himself of two titles for the same thing, unless he had given valuable consideration for one (*Traditum est duas lucrativas causas in eundem hominem et in eandem rem concurrere non posse,* Just. ii 20 § 6). If he got the thing once, whether from the testator or other, he could not enforce the other claim, whether due on stipulation or by will. But if he had bought the thing, he could sue on the will for the amount of the price given. So if he had it by dowry or on trust to restore to someone else, he could claim under the will; for in neither case were there two *lucrativae causae* (D. xxx fr 34 §§ 7, 8, 82 §§ 4, 5, 84 § 5, 108 §§ 4, 5; xxxi fr 22; xliv 7 fr 17, 19). If he had obtained only part of the thing by other means, he could claim under the will for the rest (D. xxx fr 82 § 2, 3; fr 83); or if under one will a Falcidian deduction had been made, he could obtain so much under the second will (fr 108 § 5). Or if he had the thing by an insecure title, the legacy would act as a confirmation of the title (fr 82 pr § 1). So if an heir bound to give over a thing to a legatee in two years, die within the period, leaving it to the legatee immediately, the legatee can only claim the thing or its value once (fr 84 § 2). And the same is the case when a legacy is imposed by the will on one heir and by codicils on all the heirs (fr 86 § 1; xxxi fr 66 § 5).

F. Ademption and transference of legacy.

A legacy may be revoked in the same will in which it is given or in subsequent codicils. Ulpian (xxiv 29) requires that the revocation be made in the same manner in which the legacy was given, a rule which probably referred primarily to the differences between the vindicatory and damnatory and other forms of legacy, but in other respects might be necessary in order to put the testator's intention beyond doubt. The same rule is given for the revocation of grants of freedom to slaves (Ulp. ii 12; D. xl 5 fr 50). Thus a vindicatory legacy would be withdrawn by the words *Quem fundum Titio legavi neque do neque lego;* a damnatory by *quod Titio heredem meum dare damnavi heres meus ne dato* (cf. D. xxxiv 4 fr 2, 3 § 8, 6 § 1).

The same result may be effected by crossing out in the document the words giving the legacy (*ib.* fr 16).

So any change may be made by subsequent correction of the words written or by appropriate words referring to them. A legacy may be transferred to another person, or may be changed in amount or character (*e.g.* usufruct instead of ownership, money instead of land, *etc.*), or may be subjected to a condition, or may be made absolute instead of conditional (though this last was doubted by Papinian), or may be imposed on a different heir from the one first charged (*ib.* fr 2, 3 § 9; fr 6, 17). In all such cases the question may arise whether the subsequent gift is additional, or in lieu of the former one, and the intention of the testator has to be ascertained: usually the later words prevailed (D. xxxv 1 fr 89). A change of intention may also be inferred from the testator's parting while alive with the thing bequeathed (see above, p. 297), or by his making a different disposition of it in a later part of the will, or even by using expressions respecting the legatee which were inconsistent with his being the object of favour (D. xxxiv 4 fr 9, 18, 29, 30 § 1, 31; fr 13 contains a rescript of Severus and Caracalla on the last point; see also Cod. vi 37, fr 23). A legacy to a wife whom the testator afterwards divorces is not thereby necessarily taken away: it is a question of fact what the testator intended (D. xxxiv 2 fr 3).

If a slave is bequeathed and subsequently in the will set free directly or by trust, the freedom takes effect: if the bequest of him is subsequent to the freedom, the freedom is withdrawn only if that appear clearly to be the intention (D. xl 4 fr 10 § 1, 11; tit. 5 fr 50).

Where a testator having directed a slave to be free, or bequeathed him to another and given him a legacy, sets him free in his lifetime and formally revokes the direction of freedom or the bequest to another, the revocation is superfluous and the slave takes the legacy according to the better opinion. But where with a similar will the testator afterwards alienates the slave the freedom drops and purchaser does not get the legacy intended for the slave when free; where the slave was bequeathed, this bequest drops by the slave's no longer being the testator's; the legacy to him apparently requires express revocation if it is not intended to follow the slave (D. xxxiv 4 fr 26, 27). Freedom cannot be taken away by codicils from one who becomes necessary heir (D. xxviii 5 fr 6 § 4).

G. Vesting of legacy (*dies cedit*).

1. A legacy or freedom may be given absolutely (*pure*) or conditionally (*sub conditione*). An absolute legacy vested in the legatee, *i.e.* he was provisionally entitled on the death of the testator, but the Papian law postponed vesting till the opening of the will (Ulp. xxiv 31). If the legatee is not alive at this time, the legacy drops altogether[1]. But if he survive[2], though he die before it is paid, the legatee's heir is entitled. As soon as the will is rendered effective by the entry of an heir, the legacy is payable without any unreasonable delay. If it be left by vindication, the legatee at once becomes owner. In the language of the Romans vesting is expressed by *dies cedit*, 'time goes' or 'begins to run,' the person entitled being ascertained: *dies venit*, usually *vēnit*, 'time has come,' *i.e.* payment is due[3] (D. xxxvi 2 fr 5 pr; 7 pr; Paul *ap. Consult.* vi 9).

2. A legacy, given on a condition which has in fact been fulfilled, as intended, before the opening of the will, becomes absolute: but if the event which is made a condition is one which may recur, and testator knew of its occurrence, he will be held to have referred to a later occurrence (D. xxxv 1 fr 11).

[1] An exception to this rule was made by Caracalla in the case of legacies left to the emperor. If he died before the legacy vested, his successor was entitled. Legacies to the empress (Augusta) were not so excepted (D. xxxi fr 56, 57).

[2] Paul *ap. Consult.* vi 5 adds the condition that he should have claimed it (*cujus litem contestatus*). This seems unsupported, at least as a general rule. Cf. Arndts, Glück's *Pand.* xlviii p. 208.

[3] Cf. Ulp. in D. L 16 fr 213 *'Cedere diem' significat incipere deberi pecuniam; 'venire diem' significat eum diem venisse quo pecunia peti possit. Ubi pure quis stipulatus fuerit et cessit et vēnit dies; ubi in diem, cessit dies sed nondum vēnit; ubi sub condicione, neque cessit neque vēnit dies pendente adhuc condicione.*

An absolute legacy may be postponed by testator till some certain day later than the opening of the will. Such postponement affects not the vesting but the due date of the legacy, for there is nothing contingent so long as the will is not upset: and previous payment of the legacy is good (fr 1 § 1).

3. A conditional legacy is one dependent on an event of which either the occurrence itself or its occurrence within the life of the legatee is uncertain. 'If a son shall be born to me' is an example of the former: 'on the death of my heir' is an example of the latter. A conditional legacy vests only on the occurrence of the condition during the life of the legatee and is then payable: if the legatee die first, his heir has no claim. If the legacy be by vindication, the legatee is owner on the occurrence of the condition, notwithstanding any alienation by testator's heir. A legacy '*cum legatarius morietur*' is held to be given within the legatee's life and passes to his heir. It is considered as *purum* (D. xxxi fr 12; xxviii 7 fr 28; xxxvi 2 fr 4; 5 § 2; xxxv 1 fr 41, 75, 79 pr; cf. Gai. ii 232). A legacy imposed on a substituted heir vests on the opening of the will and does not wait for the death or repudiation of the instituted heir (xxxvi 2 fr 1, 7 §§ 3, 4).

4. A legacy is none the less conditional, because the condition is only implied, *e.g. cum Titius consul factus fuerit; Fructus qui ex illo fundo percepti fuerint, heres dato; Vestem quae mea erit*; are all conditional (fr 22 pr; xxxii fr 85; xxxv 1 fr 1 § 3). A damnatory legacy of Stichus *qui meus erit cum moriar* is treated as conditional, and if testator owned only a share, Trebatius and Cassius held (against Labeo) that the share only was due. If the slave was wholly testator's at time of will but had been subsequently alienated wholly or partly, the legacy failed, or was due only for the part (D. xxx fr 5 §§ 1, 2, fr 6). But it is not conditional where there is neither expression nor implication of the condition, although it is in fact dependent on something, *e.g.* on the capacity of testator or of legatee, or the entry of an heir, *etc.* (D. xxxv 1 fr 99). An absolute legacy becomes conditional, if there is a clause in the will withdrawing it on a certain event: it is then given only on the contrary event (fr 107).

5. Freedom given to a slave absolutely, whether in vindicatory

or damnatory form, dates from the entry of the heir or, if there are more than one named, then from the entry of anyone who is heir in the grade on which the freedom is charged. If there is a necessary heir, the freedoms are good notwithstanding his keeping aloof from the inheritance, provided they are not in fraud of the Aelian Sentian statute. If freedom is given only from a certain day or on a condition, then it dates from the arrival of the time or occurrence of the condition, if subsequent to the heir's entry (D. xl 4 fr 23 § 1, 25, 32).

When a legacy was given to a slave the intention presumably was to benefit him rather than his master. The chance of his becoming free, and thus able to retain the legacy was in view; and accordingly such a legacy did not vest until the entry of the heir: where an own heir or necessary heir succeeds by the will, the will takes effect on the opening, and the legacy (if unconditional) vests at once. Where the slave-legatee is set free unconditionally by the will or has been freed by testator previously, he takes the legacy[1]; where he is not thus freed by the testator, the legacy drops, for it would be due from the heir to the slave's master, *i.e.* to himself. Nor can it revive if the slave obtain freedom in some other way after testator's death (so a rescript of Caracalla). If the slave is bequeathed away, the legacy of the slave would vest on the opening of the will (or, if conditional, on the occurrence of the condition), and the legacy to the slave would pass to the owner of the slave at the date of the heir's entry, unless, the legacy being conditional, the slave had been freed before the occurrence of the condition. Where a legacy is given to another's slave, it also vested only on the heir's entry, and then passed to his master or was retained by himself, according as he was then slave or free: a direction that he should be free was a mere nullity and had no effect. If such a legacy were postponed till the death of the slave's master (*post mortem domini*), it would pass to the master's heir, even if the slave were freed by the master's will; for the freedom would not take place till the heir's entry, whereas the legacy

[1] Where there was a trust for freedom and a direct legacy, the vesting of the latter was postponed till the heir had manumitted the slave (D. xxxi fr 84).

would by the terms of the will have already become part of the inheritance. If however the slave's master was succeeded by an own or necessary heir, the slave, becoming free at the same time that an heir to his master existed, was given the preference and took the legacy (D. xxx fr 68 § 1, 69 pr, 108 § 9; xxviii 5 fr 38 § 4; xxxvi 2 fr 5 § 7, 7 § 6, 8, 17; Cod. vi 37 fr 4; tit. 51 § 6). On the legacy of a *peculium* see below, L 9.

6. A legacy to a son under power would pass to his father or other superior at the time of vesting, and would remain with him even if the son were subsequently emancipated. But if it was directed in express words to be paid to the son, the father could not claim it. A person *sui juris*, arrogated after the vesting of a legacy but before it was paid, carries this with other credits to his new father (D. xxxvi 2 fr 5 § 7; tit. 14 §§ 2, 3).

7. An usufruct or other life interest (*usus, habitatio, etc.*) being attached to the legatee's person could not in any case pass to the heir, and did not vest till it could take practical effect by the heir's entry. This was law, whether the usufructuary was free or slave, *sui juris* or not (D. xxxvi 2 fr 2, 3, 9; Vat. 55, 59, 60).

The legacy of a slave's services (*servi operae*) vested only on demand (D. xxxiii 2 fr 7).

H. Fulfilment of condition of legacy or freedom.

1. If several conditions are attached to the same legacy or freedom and are united (*conjunctim datae*), they must all be fulfilled; if they are put disjunctively, it is enough if any one be fulfilled (D. xxviii 7 fr 5; xxxi fr 27; xl 4 fr 45).

2. The intention of testator here as elsewhere is the fundamental rule of interpretation (D. xxxv 1 fr 19 pr). Hence when the same legacy is given with diverse conditions in different parts of the will, or at least not in connexion with each other, or is given absolutely in one place and conditionally in the other, the last mentioned was taken as conveying the real intention in cases of legacies, as it was in appointment of guardians; but in the case of freedoms the slave was allowed to choose whichever he thought the easiest. If a legacy be

given absolutely and is immediately followed by a damnatory injunction or request to the heir to give it on a condition, the legatee can either vindicate it at once, or await the condition occurring and then sue the heir, unless the testator add words to imply that the second mention was intended to correct the first (D. xxx fr 12 § 3; xxxv 1 fr 51, 87—89; xl 4 fr 5).

3. Conditions consist either in the requirement of acts of the legatee, or of acts of third persons, or of other events in the world. Mere exercise of will is not a good requirement: it is surplusage to make the consent of the legatee into a condition. Mere consent of a third person (*si Titius voluerit*) is too indeterminate and irrelevant to be regarded. *In alienam voluntatem conferri legatum non potest.* To make the consent of the heir a condition is inconsistent with the imposition of a legacy as an obligation. But the approval of the heir (*si comprobaverit heres*, or *si justum putaverit*) is a good condition: for the matter is taken to be submitted to his judgment as a reasonable man. Nor can a legacy be made dependent on an act of the heir's, for that would be to impose it as a penalty (D. xxx fr 75 pr; xxxv 1 fr 52; Ulp. xxiv 17). The same rules apply to legacies by trust; and to grants of freedom by will, unless by way of trust, when the consent of a third person or of the heir is a valid condition (D. xxxii fr 11 § 7; xl 5 fr 46).

Where the consent of the legatee (*si voluerit*) is expressly required for a legacy, it must be given by the legatee himself, else his heir cannot claim the legacy (xxxv 1 fr 69).

4. If the heir, or anyone who has an interest in a condition's not being fulfilled, acts so as to prevent its fulfilment, the condition is treated as if fulfilled. And where freedom depended on some act of the slave, the practice was to allow the freedom, whether the heir hindered or not, if the failure of the condition was in no way due to the slave. If a slave was ordered to perform five services to an outsider, the heir was recommended by the lawyers to hinder him from performing them: the slave would become free, and the outsider would not get his services (D. xxxv 1 fr 57, 78, 81 § 1, xl 4 fr 55 pr). Where placing statues in the forum was a condition of inheritance or legacy, and the burghers granted no place for the statues, Sabinus and

Proculus agreed that, if the person was ready to place them, he fulfilled the condition (xxxv 1 fr 14).

5. An impossible condition was by the Sabinians (whom the Digest follows) counted as null, and the legacy or freedom thus becomes absolute. By the Proculians it was held to nullify the legacy, as it nullifies a stipulation, and Gaius seems inclined to agree (Gai. iii 98; D. xxxv 1 fr 3, fr 6 § 1; xxx fr 104 § 1). Where a slave is made free by will, if he pay 1000 sesterces to Attia, Labeo and Ofilius held that by her dying before the testator the condition had become impossible and the slave could not be free: Trebatius agreed, if Attia died before the will was made, but if she died afterwards the slave would be free. Javolen (in Digest) approves Labeo's logic, but says the practice was in favour of the freedom (D. xl 7 fr 39 § 4). Where the condition became partially inexecutable, as the manumission of certain slaves some of whom are dead, partial fulfilment was deemed by Servius sufficient (xxxv 1 fr 6 § 1). A legacy (or trust) to a woman, on condition of her marrying testator's son, failed, if the son died before marriage (Cod. vi 46 fr 4; cf. D. xxxv 1 fr 31; 101 pr). If testator desired the heir to erect a monument to him and his instructions were impracticable, the heir is bound to erect a suitable monument (fr 27).

6. A disgraceful condition is disregarded; and this often applies to the case of an oath's being made a condition; but the legatee will be compelled to do what was the subject of the oath (fr 20, 26; xxxii fr 14 § 1). Conditions contrary to the laws or edicts or of a merely derisory character are regarded as non-existent (*pro non scriptis*, D. xxviii 7 fr 14; xxx fr 112 §§ 3, 4).

7. A legacy was sometimes coupled with a condition in restraint of marriage. Such a condition is good, if it be limited to a certain time or against marriage with a particular person or persons (*si neque Titio neque Seio neque Maevio nubserit*), but it is bad, as being in fraud of the law, if it be general (*si non nubserit*). In such a case the woman may marry and take the legacy (D. xxxv 1 fr 63 pr, 64 pr, 72 § 5, 79 § 4, *etc.*; cf. xxxvi 1 fr 67 § 1; Cod. vi 40 fr 2, 3); and if there be a gift over in trust, she has not to pay it (D. xxxv 1 fr 22): otherwise, if the legacy be to one who is a wife already (xxxii fr 14 pr). If the condition

be not to marry at Aricia, it is bad, if in the circumstances it appear equivalent to a general restraint and thus be a fraud upon the *lex Papia* (xxxv 1 fr 64 § 1). So a condition that legatee's father or daughter does not marry is bad, and the legacy becomes absolute (fr 79 § 4). A condition to marry a particular person is not bad unless the person is an unsuitable match (fr 63 § 1). A legacy to a woman if she marry with Titius' consent (*arbitratu Titii*) is good even if she marry without his consent or he die in testator's lifetime: and if 200,000 sesterces be left to a woman if she do not marry, and 100,000 if she do, she can marry and claim the larger amount (fr 72 § 4; 100; xxx fr 54 § 1).

8. When the non-performance of something by the legatee is made the condition of a legacy (*e.g.* 'if the legatee shall not ascend the Capitol,' 'if he shall not manumit Stichus'), as until his death the condition is not certainly fulfilled, there seems to be no benefit to the legatee but only to his heir. The legatee was therefore allowed, if there was no other condition for postponement, to claim the legacy on the heir's entry, provided he gave the heir or other party entitled in default a bond to restore legacy and profits if he made default. This bond was called *Muciana cautio*, probably suggested by Q. Mucius, but generally adopted and sanctioned by Antoninus Pius (D. xxxv 1 fr 7, 18, 73, 77 §§ 1, 2; xxxi fr 76 § 7; and cf. xxxvi 1 fr 67 § 1). Where however the condition though negative may yet obtain fulfilment in the lifetime of the legatee, *e.g.* legacy to a woman 'if she shall not marry Titius,' the bond is not appropriate; if Titius die or she marry someone else the condition is deemed fulfilled, and she can claim the legacy. Similarly a condition 'if she shall have remained my son's wife,' though tantamount to a negative ('shall not have left my son'), may be fulfilled by the husband's death (D. xxxv 1 fr 106, 101 § 3; cf. 72 § 2). A legacy to a woman *si a liberis non discesserit* could be fulfilled by the children dying, but this was so ill-omened an interpretation of the rule about the Mucian bond, that she was allowed to give the bond and take the legacy. The same was held if a patron left a legacy to his freedman on condition of his not leaving the patron's children (fr 72 pr, § 1).

9. Conditions imposed on a slave in order to obtain freedom were treated generally as were conditions for taking a legacy, but there was a leaning in favour of freedom which sometimes made a difference. Thus, if the person (other than the heir) to whom a payment is to be made as a condition of a slave's becoming free and receiving a legacy, dies before payment, the legacy fails; but (if the money be ready or even afterwards provided) the freedom takes effect. Similarly if the condition is testator's son completing his fourteenth year, and he die before doing so, the legacy is lost, but the slave becomes free at the time named (D. xl 7 fr 19, 20 § 3; tit. 4 fr 16).

For a slave's freedom three conditions frequently occur: to give services, to give money, to give accounts.

(*a*) Services (*operae*) cannot be performed by deputy. If a slave is required, as the condition of freedom, to serve for a certain time, he must serve the whole time, though absence from illness or other lawful causes will be allowed. But if he run away, he cannot obtain his freedom until he has made up the whole number of days required (*ib.* fr 4 § 4, 14 § 1, 39 § 5).

(*b*) Where a condition consisted in some performance by legatee (or slave who was to be freed), it ought to be fulfilled at the first opportunity, and according to the terms. If he had to give something to the heir, and the heir is another's slave, he must give it to the slave, not to his master; and generally if ordered to give to a slave, he must give to the slave; if to the master, he must give to the master. If ordered to give to the heir, who is under a trust to transfer the inheritance, he must give to the heir, not to the transferee, and the heir will retain it (D. xxxv 1 fr 44 pr—§ 5). But if ordered to give to a ward or a madman, he must give it, not to them but, to the guardian or caretaker (D. xlvi 3 fr 68). If ordered to give to a person who is incapable of taking, he is still bound to give, just as he would be bound to throw the money into the sea, if so ordered as a condition of acquiring a legacy (xxxv 1 fr 55). If ordered to give money without the recipient being mentioned, the condition is fulfilled by giving to the heir; and if there be more heirs than one he must give in proportion to their shares, unless they are mentioned merely by name, when some lawyers held that they must receive equal amounts (D. xl 7 fr 8 § 1, 12, 22, and see p. 300). If he is heir himself, he can deduct his own share (D. xxx fr 104 § 4). Partial performance does not entitle one, to whom the whole is left, to claim a share of the legacy, though it was not necessary for all to be done at once (D. xxxv 1 fr 23, 44 § 8). But if the same thing is left to several, each can perform and claim his share (fr 56). Payment to the heir is satisfied by payment to the heir's heir, if that appear to be testator's intention. In the case of a slave's freedom this intention was assumed (D. xl 7 fr 20 § 4).

For giving money it was an established rule that a slave might use his *peculium*, whether left him by testator's will or not, but it must be strictly his *peculium*; he could not take money due to his master, or any part of the *peculium* which on his master's purchase of him had been reserved by the vendor. If he were ordered to pay to someone other than the heir, he did not require the heir's knowledge or consent to make the payee owner of the money paid. If he has to pay to the heir, he can hand over the money, or set off any debt of the heir's to him against the sum to be paid. If the heir prohibit his use of the *peculium*, or delay his freedom, by not paying him any debt due by the testator to him, or refusing to collect for him debts due from outsiders, he can claim his liberty on account of the refusal or delay of the heir. His services are due to the heir naturally, and the heir is not bound to allow him to raise money by services to others, but cannot prevent his using for such a purpose money so obtained, or indeed obtained in any other way. Prohibition by an outsider to whom services or payment is due under the condition, or by a guardian or caretaker or procurator, on his ward or principal's behalf, has the same effect as prohibition by the heir (D. xl 7 fr 3 pr—§ 2, §§ 8—10; fr 13 § 1, 17, 20 § 1, 35 pr).

If payment was to be made by instalments (*e.g. annua, bima, trima die*) and the slave offer the whole at once, a kindly interpretation allowed him to become free at once (fr 3 § 14). But as a rule where the condition either for payment of money or performance of services involved a lapse of time, and the slave was hindered by the heir or other from due performance, he had to wait the expiry of the time before he became free. So if the condition was the slave's going to Capua, and the heir hindered him, he became free only after the time necessary for going to Capua had expired (fr 3 § 13, fr 20 § 5).

If the heir sold or otherwise alienated the slave before the condition was fulfilled, the slave carried with him his title to freedom, and was allowed to make a good fulfilment of the condition by paying or performing to the purchaser or other alienee. So the XII tables prescribed. But if the heir made it a condition of the sale that the payment or performance should be to himself, or if the performance was of a strictly personal character, *e.g.* teaching the heir's son, the original terms of the condition must be observed notwithstanding the alienation (*ib.* fr 6 §§ 3, 7; fr 15 § 1, 29 § 1; Ulp. ii 4).

(*c*) When the condition of freedom was the slave's 'giving accounts' (*si rationes reddiderit*), it included payment of any balance due on them: and if it was 'paying the balance' (*si reliqua reddiderit*) it included giving satisfactory accounts. Both terms were reasonably interpreted; complete exaction of all moneys due from farmers or other debtors to testator or precise payment was not necessarily required, but full information, absence of fraud, restoration of anything belonging to testator, handing over of all deeds and documents were included (D. xxxv 1 fr 32, 82; xl 5 fr 41 §§ 7—17; tit. 7 fr 13 § 3, 31, 40). If the slave made investments for his master, he need not shew that the debtors were good up to the testator's death but that they were such as a careful man would trust (xxxv 1 fr 41). If the freedom was left without such a condition, but the slave had had the management of such accounts, he would be freed at once, but required to give accounts as above. So M. Aurelius in a rescript on a trust case (D. xl 5 fr 37). If two slaves are given freedom on this condition and their accounts are separate, each can comply with the condition by himself and become free; but if their accounts are really one, or inextricably connected, they stand or fall together (xl 4 fr 13 § 2; tit. 7 fr 13 § 2). This is in fact in accordance with the general principle, that if two slaves are given freedom on condition of executing some indivisible piece of work, *e.g.* building a house, erecting a statue, painting a limb, *etc.*, it depends on testator's intention whether the execution of the work done by one only is a sufficient fulfilment of the condition for him or for both or for neither (xl 4 fr 13 pr § 1). If testator forbad giving accounts, the slave was not thereby given the balance but was excused any non-fraudulent negligence (D. xxx fr 119).

(*d*) Where testator gave freedom on a condition which could not be fulfilled till death, *e.g. Stichus cum morietur liber esto*, testator was held to have intended the slave never to be free. And thus if he was freed '*si non ascenderit in Capitolium*,' the Mucian bond was deemed inapplicable, and the freedom dropped (D. xl 4 fr 61 pr § 1). So also if the condition was giving an impossible amount (100,000,000 sesterces = £850,000, D. xl 7 fr 4 § 1).

10. Where what might be made a condition is only expressed as a purpose (*sub modo legatum*), the legacy can be withheld till security is given, the freedom takes effect without waiting, but the legatee or freedman is compelled to execute the purpose, *e.g.* erect a monument, give a banquet to the burghers, perform rites to the dead, *etc.* (D. xxxii fr 19; xxxv 1 fr 17 § 4; xl 4 fr 44). If there is a gift over in default of due performance, it can be enforced (xxxiii 1 fr 21 § 3). A legacy to Titius in order that he may marry the widow Maevia is good, and security will be required, but a promise of paying money if he do not marry her will not be enforced (D. xxxv 1 fr 71 § 1). Such legacies usually however took the shape of a *fideicommissum* (cf. xxxiii 1 fr 6; tit. 2 fr 17).

J. Place and time of payment of legacy.

A legacy of any specific thing or specific collection of money or other fungibles ('money in my chest,' 'corn in my barn,' *etc.*) must be paid or otherwise discharged at the place where the thing or collection was left by testator, in the absence of any indication of a different intention. If the heir has fraudulently removed it, it is due at the place of suit; if he has removed it innocently, it is due at the place where it is. A legacy of fungibles is due at the place of suit (D. xxx fr 47 pr § 1; fr 108 pr).

As regards time for payment, in the absence of any express direction by testator all absolute legacies are due on the entry of the heir charged. It was not unusual for testator to add a clause to his will making bequests of money payable in three instalments, *e.g.* at the expiration of one, two and three years, (*annuā bimā trimā die*), which would date from the heir's entry. But such a clause however general in terms was taken not to apply to bequests to which a time or condition was attached, nor to such legacies as 'the money which is in my chest,' or 'the wine in my store-room' which are not quantities but wholes (D. xxx fr 30; xxxi fr 32 pr). If nothing was said in the will, and the heir did not contest the legacy, he ought to have a reasonable time for payment (D. xxx fr 71 § 2).

Whether interest was due from the date of the heir's entry is not clear (see p. 328).

When the will fixed a certain period (*e.g.* ten years) for the performance of something or the payment of a legacy, the time ran from the heir's entry. The performance or payment was due on the last day of the period (D. xxxv 1 fr 46, 49). 'Coming to the 16th year of age' was decided by M. Aurelius to mean 'completing the 16th year'; but 'coming to the 20th year' was decided by Caracalla, in what he thought a hard case, to be satisfied by 'commencing the 20th year.' This latter decision was apparently against the advice of Paul (D. xxxv 1 fr 48; xxxvi 1 fr 76 § 1). If to a legacy at such a period of age payment by three yearly instalments was added, and the age was attained at or before testator's death, one or more instalments might be due at once. If testator knew that the age was already attained, the three years would be reckoned from the date of the will (D. xxx fr 49 pr § 3).

The words *cum is in tutelam suam pervenerit* appear strictly applicable only to one under guardianship, and the time denoted to be that of puberty. If applied to an *impubes filius familias*, puberty appears to be understood. But in the will of a mother who was divorced from the father it is more likely that they are intended to denote the date of freedom from the father's power and not merely puberty. If the legatee is already *sui juris* and *pubes*, they will no doubt refer to his coming to the age of twenty-five and being freed from *curator* as well as *tutor*. The time of freedom from such control, whenever it may occur, will be meant when the words are used of one out of his mind or a spendthrift. If a legatee be *sui juris* but *impubes*, the intention of the intestor must decide whether puberty or 25 years is the time meant (D. xxxii fr 50).

Cum suae aetatis factus fuerit may refer either to puberty or to the age of twenty-five years (*ib.* § 6); *cum sui juris fuerit factus* may refer to either of these ages, or to the time of becoming free from *potestas* (*ib.* § 4).

K. Contents of legacy.

All things which are the subject of private property and commerce can be subjects of a legacy, whether they are corporal, single or aggregate, or incorporal rights or servitudes. Debts of others to testator (*nomina*) and release from debts or other obligations can be bequeathed, and these and any other dispositions of testator's property, creations of usufructs, annuities and charges, *etc.* will be executed according to the circumstances. Slaves can be set free or bequeathed, with or without their *peculium* (D. xxx fr 39 §§ 8—10; 41 § 1; xxxiii 1, *etc.*; xliv 3 fr 1, *etc.*).

The general rule of interpretation of all parts of a will was to ascertain and give effect to the intentions of the testator so far as he has expressed them. It is only when questions arise outside the will that the consideration of what is fair and reasonable comes in. If the words are not ambiguous, the question of intention does not as a rule arise (D. xxxii fr 25 § 1; xxxv 1 fr 16, 19 pr).

A will spoke as a rule from the date of making, not from the date of death. Hence *vestem meam, servos meos do lego* refer only to what was testator's at the time of making his will. *Quae dedi, donavi, comparavi, etc.* do not include what testator has given or got since; *quae parata sunt* includes only what has been got at the date of the will; *quae parata erunt* takes in all to the time of death (D. xxxii fr 33 § 1, 34 § 1, 41 § 4; xxxiv 2 fr 2, 7). But a whole like *peculium* is taken as at the time of vesting, whether increased or diminished. So also *familia,* whether general or *familia rustica* or *urbana,* any change among the components or their duties being disregarded. So *lecticarii* or *pedissequi* or *quadriga,* though a bearer or horse might have died and another taken his place (D. xxxi fr 65 pr, § 1).

A legacy might consist (1) in a share of the estate, or (2) in some specific thing or things, or (3) in something only generically described, or (4) an option. Some particular legacies will be treated separately afterwards.

1. As has been mentioned (p. 293) a legacy might consist in a share of the inheritance, both assets and liabilities (D. xxxvi 1 fr 23 § 5)[1]. The usual words are 'my heir shall share and divide (*partitor, dividito*) my inheritance with Titus'; in which case each would have a moiety (D. L 16 fr 164 § 1). But a smaller or larger part might be thus bequeathed. Such a legatee is called *legatarius partiarius.* As he is not heir and therefore not in direct connexion with deceased's creditors and debtors, covenants had to be entered into between the heir and legatee, the legatee stipulating for his due share of the emoluments and the heir stipulating for a proportionate contribution to the liabilities. Such covenants were called *partis et pro parte stipulationes* (Ulp. xxiv 25; xxv 15; Gai. ii 257). The jurists differed whether a division of the assets themselves or of their value was required, the Proculians contending for the former, the Sabinians for the latter. The choice appears to have been left to the heir, who was at any rate justified in paying a share of the value, where division was impossible without injury. By agreement he might satisfy the legatee without dividing everything. By a rescript of Hadrian's no deduction was allowed for the value of slaves manumitted or for funeral expenses, unless the testator had limited the legacy to a share of his estate 'as at the time of his death,' which expression would allow deduction also of dowry (D. xxx fr 26 § 2; xxxi fr 8 § 5, 9; cf. D. L 16 fr 39 § 1).

[1] Cf. Cic. *Clu.* 7 § 21 *Cn. Magius heredem fecit Oppianicum, sororis suae filium, eumque partiri cum Dinaea matre jussit; Caecin.* 4 § 12 *Heredem P. Caesennium fecit; uxori grande pondus argenti matrique partem majorem bonorum legavit. Legg.* ii 20 § 49 may or may not belong here.

2. When a specific thing or things is bequeathed, the heir must if possible give the thing itself, and cannot at his choice substitute the value. If it is not part of testator's estate nor his own, and the owner will not sell it except at an extravagant price, or if it be a slave belonging to the estate but nearly akin to the heir, payment of the value may be allowed, but a sentimental affection for a particular cup or other thing is no ground for such a concession to the heir to retain the thing (D. xxx fr 71 §§ 3, 4; cf. xxxv 2 fr 61). If a slave bequeathed has run away before testator's death, the expense of recovering him falls on the legatee; if since the death, then on the heir (xxxi fr 8 pr, xxx fr 108 pr). If the slave cannot be recovered at the time, or has been taken by the enemy, or anything bequeathed cannot be found, and there has been no carelessness or delay or other fault on the part of the heir, he is liable only to guaranty delivery of the thing or value if it be recovered; if the slave or animal has died naturally, or the land has been lost by earthquake, he is liable for nothing. *Mortuo bove qui legatus est neque corium neque caro debetur.* But if he has killed the slave (except for a crime), or incited him to a capital offence, or surrendered him for a noxal fault, or allowed a house to be duly seized from neglect to give security *damni infecti*, or slaughtered a beast, or made bequeathed land religious by burying therein someone other than the testator, or even testator, if testator did not intend it, he is liable to pay the value (D. xxx fr 47 §§ 2—6; fr 53 §§ 3—8; xxxi fr 49 pr). And if he has made delay in discharging the legacy, he is liable in any case, notwithstanding the death of the slave or destruction of the object (*ib.* fr 39 § 1; xxxiii 2 fr 6). If some change has taken place (without the heir being concerned) in the object of the bequest, *e.g.* melting a cup, making metal bequeathed into a cup, building on a vacant plot, addition or subtraction of land to or from a farm (*fundus*), the heir must give up the thing as it is (D. xxx fr 24 § 2, 44 §§ 2—4, xxxii fr 88 § 3). If a house (or ship) bequeathed has been gradually renewed so that all the original material is gone, the legacy is still good: if it has been entirely pulled down and another built, the legacy drops, unless there is evidence of the testator's having intended the legacy to

stand. If a house has been burnt to the ground, the site is still due. A legacy of a herd (*grex*) is good, though there may have been changes in the components, or even one ox only left (xxx fr 21, 22, 65 § 2; xxxii fr 88 § 2). If wool has been made into a garment[1], or timber into a ship, neither wool nor timber being reproducible in their former state, Paul held that the object bequeathed was gone and the legacy failed (D. xxxii fr 88 pr § 1, cf. 78 § 4; xli 2 fr 30 § 4; Paul iii 6 § 85). If a farm or a slave is bequeathed and the usufruct is out in the heir or another, the legatee can still demand it from the heir (D. xxxi fr 26, 66 § 6, 76 § 2).

If anything bought by testator but not delivered has been bequeathed, the heir must cede his action *ex empto* (xxx fr 39 § 3). If the bequeathed object is evicted, the heir must pay the legatee what he may have recovered from the guarantor of title, or cede his actions to the legatee (cf. D. xxi 2 fr 59)[2]. When a *statu-liber* is bequeathed, the heir need only hand him over, whereas if he had to pay the value it would be estimated as if the slave had no freedom in prospect (xxx fr 44 § 8; xlvii 2 fr 81 § 1). If the contents of a chest are bequeathed, and there is nothing in it at the time of death, nothing is due; if less than the testator described, the description does not increase the heir's obligation (D. xxx fr 108 § 10; xxxiii 4 fr 1 § 7). When a corn-ticket (*tessera frumentaria*) entitling to a free or cheap distribution of corn is left (cf. Suet. *Jul.* 41; *Oct.* 41) the heir has to give it, if still testator's, or pay the value. And the same is true of a bequest of a post in the Imperial service, the heir having also to pay the entrance fees (*militia*[3] D. xxxi fr 22; 49 § 1; xxxii fr 102 §§ 2, 3).

[1] Julian said that the legacy still held and the garment must be handed over (D. xxx fr 44 § 2). A specific lot of wool or timber bequeathed a testator may intend to give, whatever form it takes: a bequest of a certain amount of wool would hardly give rise to such presumption of intention. But the diversity of opinion is probably only the old difference between Sabinians (Julian) and Proculians (Gai. ii 79). Cf. Czyhlarz, Glück's *Pand.* D. xli p. 302, *etc.*

[2] See Salkowski, Glück's *Pand.* 49 p. 356.

[3] See Cujac. vii p. 1301 (ad D. xix 1 fr 52 § 2); Bethmann-Hollweg *Civil Pr.* iii pp. 135, 138, *etc.*; Mommsen *Staatsr.* iii Th. 1 p. 450 ed. 2.

A legatee has a right to accretions by alluvion, or voluntary act of testator, and to the appurtenances of a thing, but not to the plant of a farm or the furniture of a house, unless expressly left (D. xxxiii 10 fr 14; but cf. Paul iii 6 § 34). If the bequest was by vindication, he is entitled to all profits accrued since the inheritance was entered on, or, in a conditional or deferred legacy, since it vested, whether fruits of lands or animals, offspring of female slaves, hire of slaves or beasts, rents, legacies or inheritances which have come to slaves bequeathed, right to the Aquilian action for death or injury to a slave or beast. The only exception seems to be profits taken by the heir in good faith ignorant of the legacy[1]. In a damnatory legacy profits, *etc.* would be due only from the date of the heir's delay. Interest on pecuniary legacies was not due[2], except (as Julian laid down and was followed in practice) when the legacy was left *sinendi modo* (Gai. ii 280; D. ix 2 fr 13 § 3; xxx fr 23, 24 § 2, 39 § 1, 86 § 2, 91 § 7, xli 1 fr 40; Paul iii 8 § 4; Vat. 44). The rate of interest was according to the custom of the particular district (fr 39 § 1 *cit.*). All acquisitions to the inheritance since testator's death and before the heir's entry belong to it, though obtained from bequeathed objects (D. xxxi fr 38; ix 2 fr 15 pr); and all taxes or rates already due from land at the heir's entry have to be paid by him (xxx fr 39 § 15 pr).

On the other hand the heir can claim compensation or guaranty from the legatee for any loss or risk caused before or after entry by the bequeathed slave or other object to the heir's own property or to the rest of testator's estate, *e.g.* where a slave has stolen something from the heir (D. xxx fr 70 pr § 3). If any servitude between the legacy and the heir's property has been merged by the heir's holding both, it should be reserved or restored on the legacy being delivered, the heir

[1] Cod. vi 47 fr 4 is probably interpolated. There is a full discussion by Salkowski, Glück's *Pand.* Pt. 49 pp. 479—496, 510 sq.

[2] The Digest allows interest generally and dates interest and profits from joinder of issue. Paul dates from delay, which would usually come to much the same. A rescript of Severus and Caracalla (Cod. vi 47 fr 1) agrees with Digest, but the identification of all forms of legacy and trust by Justinian makes the matter very uncertain for the classical times.

being able to enforce his rights by a plea of fraud, the legatee his by action on the will (*ib.* fr 70 § 1, 84 § 4, 116 § 4).

3. If 'a house' or 'a slave' is bequeathed *per vindicationem* in general terms, the legatee has the choice which of testator's houses or slaves to claim: it ought not to be either the best or the worst. This rule is supported by a rescript of Severus and Caracalla. But if the legacy is *per damnationem* and the heir is directed to give 'a house' or 'a slave,' the heir has the choice with the like restriction, but is responsible for the title, and must also in the case of a slave guaranty his freedom from thefts and noxal acts, which might make the legatee's tenure uncertain. He need not guaranty the slave's soundness, for that has nothing to do with title. The heir has a right to notice from the legatee, if any suit for eviction is brought against him (D. xxx fr 37, 45 § 1, 56, 71 pr, 110; xxxii fr 29 § 3; xxxiii 5 fr 2 § 1). The legatee's action in case of eviction is the ordinary action on the will, if the heir had handed the legacy to him without waiting to be sued. But if the legatee had to bring that action to obtain the legacy, the judge would require the heir to give security against eviction, and the legatee would sue on the stipulation (xxx fr 71 § 1). Till the choice is made, the heir or legatee, as the case may be, can change his mind, and a rejection of this or that slave or thing has no effect: he can still choose what he has thus rejected (D. xxxiii 5 fr 18). When testator intended to give a specific legacy but has not made the particular gift clear, the legacy becomes in effect general, and the heir has the choice (xxx fr 37 § 1).

When a quantity of some fungible is bequeathed, if the quality is not named, the heir has the selection (D. xxxiii 6 fr 4).

4. An option may be given in so many words to the legatee, *per vindicationem Titius hominem optato, eligito.* The choice cannot be made till after the heir has entered, and once made is final, unless by some mistake he has chosen one who was a freeman or another's slave. The legatee can call for the production of all the slaves or other things included in the option, and the heir can obtain from the praetor a limit of time in which the option must be made, and, if not made, is lost. Option by a son

under power requires his father's order (Ulp. xxiv 14; D. xxx fr 10, xxxiii 5 fr 2 § 2, 6, 8 § 3, 16, 20). The heir cannot frustrate the legatee's option by manumitting some or all of the slaves, whether the option be given in so many words or a generic legacy be made. If the heir did so, the slave's liberty would be contingent on his not being opted (xxxiii 5 fr 14; xl 9 fr 3). Where an option of slaves is left without the number being fixed, a rescript of Ant. Pius limited it to three (xxxiii 5 fr 1).

Sometimes a choice is given limited to two or more alternatives, the legatee having the choice in a vindicatory legacy, the heir in a damnatory one. Or the chooser may be expressly stated, *e.g. Titius Stichum aut Pamphilum utrum volet, do lego* or *utrum heres meus volet, dato.* If without knowing of the alternative Stichus is sued for by the legatee or given by the heir, the choice cannot be reopened (D. xxx fr 84 § 9, xxxi fr 19, xxxii fr 29 § 1). If the heir does not make his choice within a time limited, the legatee can choose (xxxi fr 11 § 1). If more than one heir is charged, they must agree on the choice (fr 15). If the legatee die without choosing after the legacy is vested, his heir can choose (D. xxxiii 5 fr 19).

L. Special legacies.

1. The testator's will often contained arrangements for the continued support or convenience of members of his family or household or dependents. Usufruct is fully discussed elsewhere, (Book IV chap. V A), its character being the same, whether established by will or by a living person. The usufruct might apply to the whole of his property or to his houses and their contents, or to a particular farm, or to such farms as would produce a named income, or to a part of a farm; and might be limited to a certain number of years, or coupled (often by way of trust) with a condition of maintenance of children or others (D. xxxiii 2 fr 24, 25, 32 §§ 2, 6, fr 35, *etc.*). If he left a farm to one and the usufruct to another, they would share the usufruct: if the farm were left to two persons and the usufruct to another, the two owners would enjoy half the usufruct between them (fr 10, 19). A bequest of a usufruct held by testator is ineffective, unless he subsequently acquire the propriety (D. xxx fr 24 § 1).

2. If the 'revenue every year' (*reditus omnibus annis*) of his estate were left, the effect would be the same as a usufruct *i.e.* a continuous enjoyment, or as an annuity, *i.e.* a series of annual enjoyments (D. xxxiii 2 fr 22). A right of residence, or of support as in the testator's lifetime (*quae vivus praestabam*) (which would usually include residence), was another form of legacy to dependents: and in all such cases the practice of the testator was often a key to his intention (fr 33). The services (*operae*) of a slave or freedman were also found as legacies (fr 2, 3, 7).

3. An annuity (*in singulos annos legatum* or *annuum*) might consist in a series of usufructs of land, *etc.*, or in annual payments of money or articles of consumption. It would vest on the testator's death and thereafter at the commencement of each year, being absolute for the first year and conditional on the life of the annuitant[1] for subsequent years. The heir (of the annuitant) would be entitled to the residue of the last year, whereas a usufruct leaves nothing to the heir unless the fruits have been actually gathered. Moreover an annuity is not affected by *capitis deminutio* (D. xxxiii 1 fr 2, 4, 8). It was regarded not as one legacy but as several, and the capacity of the annuitant or of the annuitant's master to take would be determined at the beginning of each (*ib.* fr 11). Any conditions attached (*e.g.* for the annuitant to remain with testator's wife) would be enforced strictly, or modified according to circumstances, in the reasonable discretion of the judge (fr 3, fr 13 § 1). If the heir did not enter till some years after testator's death, payments for the back years must be made (D. xxxvi 2 fr 12 § 3).

Whether *annui* (*e.g. decem denarii*) or *in singulos annos* or *quotannis* was used made no matter. If there was a limit of years (*e.g. dena usque ad annos decem*), the bequest might be meant as a gift of the whole sum, to be paid by instalments: the whole would then vest at the testator's death and unpaid parts be transmissible to heir (D. xxxvi 2 fr 12 §§ 4, 6; fr 20).

4. Instead of a money annuity, a testator frequently directed aliment to be given to his freedmen or others. *Alimenta*

[1] A stipulation for an annuity (*in singulos annos*) was perpetual (D. xlv 1 fr 16 § 1).

included food (*cibaria*), dress and lodging and where water was scarce, as in Egypt, that also. *Diaria* or *cibaria* did not carry with them either dress or shoes or lodging (D. xxxiv 1 fr 6, 14 § 3, 21). All the heirs were liable, but the burden was generally charged on certain persons, and rescripts of Antoninus Pius and others directed that, where this was not done, the court should arrange for someone to receive the money necessary for the purpose and distribute it to the freedmen, the receiver giving a bond for restoring any part which ceased to be necessary owing to the death or other failure of a freedman. If the amount of aliment was not fixed by testator, the court would fix it, having regard to the practice of the testator and other circumstances (fr 3, 22). If no duration of aliment was fixed by testator, it would be for life, and, where for a time application had not been made, arrears would be payable (fr 14 pr, 11, 18 § 1, 19). If the testator directed aliment to the age of puberty, Ulpian thought that the principle of rescripts of Hadrian and others should be followed in making 18 the limit of age for boys and 14 for girls (fr 14 § 1). Conditions were favourably interpreted for the legatee (fr 13 § 1, fr 20 § 3). If the *alimenta* were charged by trust on a gift *mortis causa* or bequest, any deduction for the *Falcidia* was to be taken from the gift or legacy and not deducted from the *alimenta* (D. xxxi fr 77 § 1). Most cases mentioned are cases of *fideicommissum*.

5. *Legatum nominis*.

Debts due to deceased (*nomina*) passed to the heir with the rest of the estate. If they were bequeathed, it was the duty of the heir to hand over the relative documents and to cede his rights of action (D. xxx fr 44 § 6, 75 § 2, 105). If a document of debt (*e.g. chirographum*) is bequeathed, this is equivalent to bequeathing the debt itself (*ib.* fr 44 § 5; xxxii fr 59). Documents of this kind did not pass under general words leaving the contents of a house, *etc.*, it being unlikely that the testator would have so intended (see p. 340). If the debt bequeathed was not really due on any ground, the legacy drops altogether; and even if the sum of the supposed debt is named (*decem quae mihi Seius debet*), the matter is not mended, if nothing is due at all: the words *quae...debet* are not a mere false description but contain a condition (D. xxx fr 75 §§ 1, 2). If a debt is left separately to two persons and *in solidum*, whether one or more persons are liable for it, both legatees are entitled, and the heir must surrender his actions to one and pay the amount of the debt to the other (D. xxxi fr 13).

One who had redeemed a Roman from captivity and held him in pledge for the redemption money could bequeath him to himself, *i.e.* acquit him of the debt (D. xxx fr 43 § 3).

6. *Liberatio legata.*

Another form which a legacy may take is the release of an obligation. This is done by a damnatory or permissive legacy (*damnandi aut sinendi modo*). The words may be such as *damnas esto heres meus quod Titius mihi debet non petere,* or *Titium debitorem meum liberare,* or *quicquid Titium mihi dare facereve oportet oportebitve, damnas esto heres meus sinere Titium sibi habere* (cf. D. xxxiv 3 fr 7 §§ 1, 2, 16, cf. fr 25, *etc.*). A direction to restore to the debtor the acknowledgment of debt comes to the same thing (D. xxx fr 84 § 7). If the debt has been already discharged before testator dies, the bequest comes to nothing; if partially discharged, it is good only for the residue (fr 7 § 4 21 pr). Or a part of the debt only may be directed by testator to be remitted (fr 7 pr). The heir is liable under the will, not only if he sues for the debt, but also if he sets it off or deducts it (D. xlvi 8 fr 15). Subject to any special words or the intention of the testator otherwise shewn, such a release refers only to what the testator knew at the time to be due. If a testator frees an agent or a guardian from giving accounts or from liability to the action of guardianship, the agent *etc.* will not be entitled to retain money already collected for his principal and will be liable for fraud. If release from such claims was intended, distinct reference to them must be made (D. xxxiv 3 fr 8 § 6, 9, 12, 20 § 1, 28 §§ 1—4, cf. §§ 7, 9; 31 §§ 1, 2, 5). So with distinct words a testator may release by bequest his claim to recover rent or a deposit or loan or pledge or damages on the ground of theft (fr 1, 8 § 7, 16). If the testator uses general language (*in rem*), the release is good for the debtor's heir as well as himself; and the testator's heir's heir cannot sue either. It is different if the testator limits it, *e.g. heres meus a solo Titio ne petito* (fr 2 § 1, 8 § 3, 15). A release of a debt due on condition may be sued for by the debtor at once. If the debt be paid before the condition occurs, the debtor can sue on the will for recoupment (D. xxxvi 2 fr 19 § 3; xxxiv 3 fr 7 § 7, 21 § 2).

A release by legacy may be intended for one only of several persons under the same obligation. If testator's heir is forbidden to sue a surety, he can still sue the principal debtor, but if forbidden to sue the latter, he cannot sue the surety; for the surety would then have recourse upon the principal (fr 2 pr). The duty of the heir varies. A single debtor can plead the will against the heir's suit, or can sue him for a formal release. But if he is one of several debtors equally liable (*e.g. rei promittendi*), all would be freed by a formal release given to one, and, if this was not intended, the heir must simply agree not to sue him. In the case of partners, there is no effectual freeing of one without also freeing the others, and a formal release can be therefore claimed. If a surety only is intended to be freed, the heir must simply agree not to sue him (fr 2, 3 § 3, 5 pr § 1). If the heir is directed to release two co-promissors and one of them is incapable of testamentary benefit (by *lex Papia*), the heir should delegate him to the person entitled to the lapse: by this person's suing on the promise and getting payment the other co-promissor is released (fr 29: cf. Keller *Lit. Cont.* § 54).

A testator may direct the release of another's debtor whether the heir's or anyone's else. If he bequeath to Titius what I owe to Titius, both Titius and I will have an action on the will against the heir, who will be required to satisfy the creditor Titius, and protect me against his suit (fr 3 § 5, 4).

7. *Legatum debiti.*

A legacy to his creditor of what testator owes him is superfluous and therefore practically ineffective, unless it puts the creditor in some way in a better position, as by giving him a civil action instead of a praetorian, or by removing a valid plea which the debtor had, or removing a condition, or giving some advantage in place or time or mode of payment (D. xxx fr 28, 29; xxxiv 3 fr 13). A legacy to Titius coupled with a request to pay testator's creditor is of no interest to the creditor, but the heir being debtor has an interest and right to enforce the trust: and if the debt was secured by a surety, the surety would have a like interest and right, for it saves him from being sued and having to sue the debtor. Similar considerations apply when a surety bequeaths to the creditor (or leaves in trust for him) the amount of the debt for which he is responsible (D. xxx fr 49 §§ 4—7). If testator directs his heir to set his surety free, the surety gains by being freed from the chance of having to pay, and then to recover the payment from the debtor (D. xxxiv 3 fr 11).

If testator directs a debt due by him to be paid by some of his heirs, the creditors have no interest in enforcing this direction and have no action against such heirs specially, but against all. The coheirs have an action for relief or reimbursement against the heirs so charged (D. xxx fr 69 § 2).

A bequest to a slave (made free by the will) of *quinque aureos quos in tabulis debeo* was held bad by Servius, because a master could not owe his slave anything, but was held good by Javolen as being intended by testator to refer to a natural, though not a civil, debt (D. xxxv 1 fr 40 § 3).

A legacy of a debt is not liable to diminution to raise the Falcidian fourth, except so far as it may make the payment immediate instead of deferred (D. xxx fr 28 § 1; xxxv 2 fr 1 § 10). Action can be brought on the will not merely for the difference between an immediate and a deferred payment but for the whole debt (xxxv 2 fr 5).

8. *Legatum dotis.*

A legacy of dowry (*dos relegata*, 'bequeathed back,' or sometimes *praelegata*, 'bequeathed before other charges') might be made by a husband to his wife. The object was not specific things but the *universitas dotis*, and was identical with whatever could be recovered by the dowry action (*rei uxoriae*). But the action on the bequest could be brought by a wife's heir, whereas the dowry action was confined to the wife. Being thus the bequest of a debt, the only benefit to the wife was the advantage of immediate payment instead of in three annual instalments (if the dowry was in money or other fungibles). Such expenses of the husband's as *ipso facto* reduce the dowry, and losses, *etc.* of slaves (in a non-valued dowry) were deducible from the amount of the dowry, whether bequeathed, or recovered by the wife's ordinary action. The heir cannot hold back the legacy in order to enforce other claims, *e.g.* for the repayment of invalid gifts or of non-necessary expenditure. But if the husband named in the bequest the original amount of the dowry, he was held to have intended that the dowry should be paid in full without any deduction at all. Only to the extent to which the wife gained any benefit by the bequest above what was recoverable by the dowry action could she be burdened by a trust. If the legacy of the dowry was made to a third person in trust for the wife, and the Falcidian fourth was retained by the heir, the wife could claim the deficit from the heir by her ordinary dowry action (D. xxxiii 4 fr 1 pr §§ 2—6, 12, 13 fr 2 pr 5, 8; xxxi fr 41 § 1; xxxvi 1 fr 80 § 14). If any part of the dowry was pledged, the heir is not bound (as in an ordinary legacy) to redeem the pledge, unless the pledge was since the constitution of the dowry (D. xxxiii 4 fr 15). If the dowry was already duly paid, a bequest of it to the recipient was null (fr 1 § 11).

Where the husband or the wife was under power, the father of either, if holder of the dowry, might bequeath it to either. If bequeathed to the husband without making him heir, the heir could require from him a guaranty against the wife's dowry action. If bequeathed to the wife and the marriage was still subsisting at the testator's death, the wife, if she received the amount of the dowry, could be required to guaranty the heir against the husband's action for the dowry (fr 1 §§ 9, 10).

If instead of a legacy of the dowry something was left the wife 'as for dowry' (*pro dote*) this might be more or less than the dowry. The wife would be able to elect: she could not, without clear intention being shewn, claim both. If the legacy was imposed on one out of several heirs, the woman's action, even if she chose dowry and not legacy, would be against him (D. xxxi fr 53 pr § 1; cf. xxxiii 4 fr 2 pr, 6 § 1, *etc.*).

9. *Legatum peculi.*

It was usual when a testator directed a slave to be free to bequeath to him his *peculium*, and whether the freedom or the bequest was actually named first in the will was of no importance if they were united, *e.g. Pamphilus servus meus peculium suum cum moriar sibi habeto liberque esto* (D. xxxiii 8 fr 14). The *peculium* was taken like other legacies as at the time of vesting, *i.e.* death of testator, if bequeathed to another: but if bequeathed to the slave himself, as at heir's entry. If a slave was bequeathed along with his *peculium*, and before the testator's death was alienated or set free or died, the bequest of *peculium* was extinguished. If a slave was bequeathed along with his vicars, there were two bequests and the perishing of one did not destroy the other (fr 1, 4, 8 § 8). The *peculium* did not pass without express mention or manifest inference, as Severus and Caracalla decided when a slave was freed and ordered to pay something to the heir (fr 8 § 7, 24).

The legacy of a slave's *peculium* included his vicars and their *peculia*, corporal objects, and investments. If left to a slave *per vindicationem* he could not sue for it as a whole under that name, but must sue for the several corporal objects less their proportion of any debt due to the master: the investments (*nomina*) would be recovered for the legatee by the heir or by action in the heir's name. And the heir would pay any debt due from himself. The *peculium* is *ipso facto* diminished by anything due from the slave to testator or his fellow-slaves (not being his own vicars); and the heir could deduct also anything due to himself; and, if the slave was made free, could require security against the slave's peculiar creditors[1]. It is also liable to deduction for any injury done by the slave to his fellow-slaves. If the master had paid damages for a noxal injury caused by the slave's vicars, this also would be deducible from the *peculium* of the slave himself, so far as it was not covered by the *peculium* of the vicar; for the defence of the

[1] There was difference of opinion whether heir or manumitted slave with *peculium* was liable to the slave's creditors for debts previously contracted. For liability of heir, D. xv 2 fr 1 § 7; xxxiii 8 fr 18; against, D. xxxiii 4 fr 1 § 10. Cf. xiv 4 fr 9 § 2.

vicar was chargeable to the slave his master. Other debts of the vicars would be deducible only from their own *peculia*, a master slave, like any other master, being liable for his vicar's debts only to the extent of their *peculium* (D. vi 1 fr 56; xxxiii 8 fr 5, 6 pr § 5, 16, 18, 25). If the testator desired to bequeath the *peculium*, and to remit any debts due by the slave to him, he cannot do it by the simple words *peculium lego, non deducto aere alieno* (for the *peculium* as a whole is only the balance due to the slave), and the words added to the bequest go for nothing; but he can signify his remission of all debts; or he can bequeath specially all the components of the *peculium* (fr 6 § 1, 10).

As regards any debt due to the *peculium* by the slave's master a rescript of Severus and Caracalla denied a slave any claim on account of the bequest of his *peculium* to repayment of money expended by the slave on his master's account. Ulpian apparently thinks this denial wrong, and that, at any rate where such was the intention of the testator, such a credit could be set off against a debt of the slave to his master. The mere entry by a master in his accounts of something as due to his slave, would not, according to the rescript, justify a claim to it as part of the *peculium* (fr 6 § 4).

Accessions by natural growth (*e.g.* young of women or cattle) since vesting of the legacy pass with it, whether the slave be left to another or be set free, but accessions from the slave's own services or other matters pass with the *peculium* only when that is bequeathed to the slave himself. This was supposed to be testator's probable intention (fr 8 § 8; xv 1 fr 57).

10—20. There were some comprehensive terms under which many parts of the corporal property of a deceased person were bequeathed, and the content of which gave rise to much discussion among the republican, as well as later, lawyers. The most important of these are *instrumentum, fundus, etc. instructus, suppellex, aurum et argentum, penus, vinum*. The testator is supposed to use these and all other words in their ordinary meaning, and, if he used one ordinary term, not to have intended what was the proper content of another ordinary term. Testator's own special practice or the practice of the district might be called in aid of interpretation in some cases. But it was recognized that testators do not always speak precisely, and often enumerate some of the components in addition to the comprehensive expression which includes them (D. xxx fr 69; xxxiii 7 fr 12 § 46, fr 18 § 3; tit. 10 fr 7 § 2, 9 pr).

10. *Instrumentum* is the 'plant,' *i.e.* the things, not affixed, but necessary or usual for the working or enjoyment of a farm, or house or shop, *etc.* Thus the *instrumentum* of a *fundus* included what was used for cultivating the land, gathering the fruit, and preserving it, *i.e.* slaves, cattle for manure and draught, ploughs, sickles, pruning knives and other tools, baskets, casks, vats and various receptacles, oil-presses, mills, carts, boats, *etc.* With the labourers go their wives and children, if resident on the estate, and slaves employed in baking, spinning and weaving garments, and otherwise providing for the establishment (D. xxxiii 7 fr 8, 12 pr—§ 12). Fruits already gathered belong as a rule to the heir, but if intended for seed or generally consumed on the farm pass to the legatee (Paul iii 6 §§ 42, 46). So the *instrumentum* of a house included what was necessary for cleaning, or protection against storm or fire, *e.g.* ladders, poles, hooks, vinegar for extinguishing fire, tiles kept to replace those lost, matting, *etc.* But what is for ornament is not included, nor are fixtures, nor pipes and basins for fountains, nor locks and keys, for they are rather to be considered part of the house (D. fr 12 §§ 16—26). The plant of a tavern (*tabernae cauponiae*) would be simply the butts, jars, jugs and drinking-vessels, whereas the plant of a *caupona*, *i.e.* the business of a tavern-keeper, would include the slaves who managed (*institores*, *ib.* fr 13; cf. however Paul iii 6 § 61). The plant of baths, of baking, of butcherings, *etc.* would be analogous (fr 17 § 2, fr 18 pr § 1)

11. *Fundus instructus* had a larger meaning than *fundus cum instrumento*: it meant the farm as equipped for its owner's use and enjoyment, and included furniture (*suppellex*), robes (*vestis*), ornaments, plate, glass, utensils, books and book-cases, wines and other things intended not for stores but for use on the place. Slaves for house service, usually resident there,

were also included; in fact anything kept there not merely for working the estate, but for the owner's own use and convenience, *ut instructior paterfamilias esset* (fr 12 §§ 27—36). Such expressions as *fundus cum omni instrumento rustico et urbano et mancipiis quae ibi sunt*, or *fundus ita ut optimus maximusque est*, or *fundus ita ut possedi*, or *sicut est*, have much the same content (D. xxxiii 7 fr 27; Paul iii 6 §§ 44, 45, 53). Arrears of rents due from farmers did not pass under such terms any more than money or securities (D. xxxii fr 78 § 3; fr 91 pr § 1). A farm left *uti optimus maximusque est* must be freed from servitudes[1] by the heir (D. xxx fr 69 § 3; cf. L 16 fr 90, 169).

Domus instructa is similarly wider than *domus cum instrumento* (Paul iii 6 § 56; D. xxxiii 7 fr 12 § 43, fr 18 § 14).

In the absence of special words these expressions were taken to refer to the (normal) state of plant or equipment of the farm or house at the time when the legacy vested (D. *ib.* fr 28).

12. A legacy of a house or farm and its contents (*domus quaeque mea ibi erunt cum moriar*) gave rise frequently to two questions; (1) whether the contents were to be taken strictly as at the moment of death; and (2) whether it included money or the ledger of investments (*kalendarium*) or documents of debt. On the first point Labeo's view was followed, that what was accidentally there was not part of the legacy, and what was accidentally not there was yet included (D. xxxii fr 78 § 7, 86; cf. xxviii 5 fr 35 § 3). On the second point, however general the words (*e.g. quicquid in patria Gadibus possideo; domus meas in quibus habito nullo omnino excepto cum omni instrumento et repositis omnibus*), it was held that money intended for investment and instruments of debt touching other parts of the estate (*kalendarium, nomina, cautiones, instrumenta, chirographa*) were not included (D. xxxi fr 86 pr (Paul); xxxii fr 41 § 6, 44, 78 § 1, 86, 92, 101; xxxiii 7 fr 12 § 45); Paul however in the *Sententiae* (iii 6 § 59) differs here as in the case of *peculium, etc. ib.* § 34.

13. A legacy to a wife of *quae ejus causa parata sunt* includes not only what has been expressly got for her, but things assigned for her use, whether from stock or from provision for a former wife or even from a valued dowry. It may

[1] Cf. Cic. *Agr.* iii 2.

include all kinds of things, beasts of burden, sedan chairs, sedan bearers, toilette-slaves, *etc.* But the legacy fails, if she is not testator's wife when he dies (D. xxxii fr 45—49, 78 § 6).

14. *Suppellex* is defined as *domesticum patrisfamilias instrumentum* consisting of inanimate moveables intended for ordinary use, excluding wrought gold and silver (which formed another general head) and robes (*vestis*). In fact it was furniture, including eating- and drinking-vessels, whether of wood or clay or glass, and couch bolsters. It did not matter of what material a thing was, provided it was properly an article of furniture; ornaments of gold or silver attached, however valuable, did not take it out of *suppellex*. And couches, tables, candlesticks, and basins, even if wholly of silver, were still reckoned as *suppellex* (D. xxxiii 10 fr 1—7 pr, 9 § 1).

15. A legacy of *gold* or *silver* did not include money. Not even *argentum factum* or *argentum signatum* or *argentum omne*[1] included it unless that could be shewn to be testator's intention (D. xxxiv 2 fr 19 pr, 27 § 1). *Argentum* included all silver wrought or unwrought left by deceased (*ib.* fr 19 pr, 78 § 4, but cf. Paul iii 6 § 85). *Argentum factum*, 'wrought silver,' was negatively defined as being silver neither in bulk nor in sheet nor stamped nor part of furniture nor toilet-ware nor personal ornaments. It in fact comprised what we should call 'the silver plate' with the exclusion (as a rule) of what belonged properly to furniture, such as lamps and of polished mirrors, which were either furniture or toilet ware (*ib.* fr 27 § 6, 19 § 9). The fact that the work was not completely finished did not prevent a cup or dish *etc.* being included under *argentum factum*; and gold insertions (*emblemata*) or jewels in a silver

[1] This was scarcely settled law in Cicero's time. At least he gives as a rhetorical argument: *Quoniam argentum omne mulieri legatum est, non potest ea pecunia, quae numerata domi relicta est, non esse legata; forma enim a genere, quoad suum nomen retinet, numquam sejungitur; numerata autem pecunia nomen argenti retinet; legata igitur videtur* (*Top.* 3 § 13). See also *ib.* 13 § 53 where he makes *argentum* include *pecunia signata*.

That *argentum* did not include investments is clear from Cic. *Top.* 3 § 16 *Non, si uxori vir legavit argentum omne quod suum esset, idcirco quae in nominibus fuerunt legata sunt. Multum enim differt in arcane positum sit argentum an in tabulis debeatur.*

cup, *etc.* passed with it. Wrought silver broken up, so that it could not conveniently be used, was included with the raw metal under *argentum infectum*, 'unwrought silver' (fr 19 §§ 5, 11, 13, fr 27 § 3). *Argentum signatum* referred to such things as foreign coins or medals (fr 27 § 4).

If the legacy was of a certain weight of silver without specific designation, it was satisfied by payment of the value at the price of the time. But if it was of a certain weight of wrought silver, wrought silver could be claimed, and any lead used in the construction must not be reckoned. Vessels that go together must not be separated (fr 9, 19 §§ 1—4).

A legacy of *gold* was similar, but the question more often arising in the case of gold related to its use in ornaments, *e.g.* whether the gold setting went with jewels or the jewels followed the gold: and the answer depended on which was regarded as the principal. If the gold was merely to hold the jewel, the jewel was principal, and a legacy of jewels carried the gold setting: if the gold formed the work of art, and the jewels were only for decorating it, a legacy of wrought gold carried the jewels. Gilt things were not included in a legacy of gold, unless the testator counted them as such (*auri numero habuisset, ib.* fr 19 §§ 13—20, fr 21, 32 § 1).

16. A woman's jewels along with hairpins, buckles, and headgear, passed under the title of *ornamenta*.

17. *Mundus muliebris* were the articles of her toilet, and included, what was sometimes left as a separate bequest, *unguenta* (fr 25 § 10, 21 § 1). A stool for the bath (*sella balnearis*) was also included (Paul iii 6 § 83).

18. *Vestis* or *vestimenta* included all dress, rugs, skins, cushions, excepting such bolsters (*toralia*) as practically formed part of a couch and belonged to *suppellex* (fr 22—24 § 8; cf. xxiii 10 fr 5).

19. Another comprehensive term was that of *penus*[1], *i.e.* household supplies, originally perhaps only eatables and drinkables, but extended after discussion to include spices, firewood, charcoal, candles, and even paper for accounts, grease, scents,

[1] Cf. Cic. *Part. Or.* 31 § 107 *cum ex testamentis quid sit penus...quaeritur, verbi interpretatio controversiam facit.*

incense, with the vessels or boxes necessary to hold them. If the testator was in the habit of storing such things to sell as well as to use, the legacy would cover not the whole store, but as much as would make a year's supply for testator, his family, household and guests, and for his beasts of burden (*jumenta*) (D. xxxii fr 60 § 2; xxxiii 9 fr 3, 4 § 2, 5; Gell. iv 1 §§ 7, 8, 17—23).

20. *Wine* covered all kinds and states which were counted as such by testator. It would not include vinegar, or must, or mead or beer or cider unless testator reckoned them as wine. Old wine includes wine of the year before, unless the testator's use of the term was known. The legacy carried with it the jars or barrels (*amphorae* and *cadi*) in which it was kept for use, but not large butts (*dolia*), especially if sunk in the ground. If a hundred jars at legatee's choice are left, he has a right to taste in order to judge. If a hundred jars of wine from a particular farm are left, and so much was not produced, he cannot claim others, but if the bequest was for 'so much yearly,' the previous year's supply might be called on to make up the deficiency in the present year. If the *penus* was left to one and *vinum* to another, the legacy of *penus* will carry all the other supplies but not any wine (D. xxxiii 6 fr 2, 3, 5, 9—14). If a certain weight of oil is bequeathed without the quality being named, the heir can give what he chooses, without inquiry into the practice of the testator or the district (*ib.* fr 4).

21. Of other expressions it may be noted that *jumenta* did not include *boves* (D. xxxii fr 65 § 5); nor did *oves* certainly include rams or lambs, but *grex ovium* did (fr 81 §§ 4, 5). What should be considered lambs was determined by the custom of the district; usually at one year old or shearing they ceased to be lambs (fr 60 pr, 65 § 7); *pecora* were fourfooted gregarious beasts (fr 65 § 4); *pecudes* included oxen and *jumenta* (fr 81 § 2; Paul iii 6 §§ 73, 74). The male term usually included the female[1], *e.g. equi, muli, pueri*, and, according to most, *servi*, but not *vice versa* (fr 62, 65 § 6, 81 pr); *mulieres* included virgins; *ancillae* sometimes included their male children (fr 81 § 1; Paul iii 6 § 69). *Ligna* included anything intended for fuel, though not yet cut up, but scarcely charcoal or torches or matches

[1] So *fratres* included *sorores* (D. xxxii fr 93 § 3).

(*sulpurata*), nor yet stakes or rods (fr 55, 56). *Lana* includes wool, fleeces, hair of goats and hares, goosedown, and cotton, whether spun or not, but unwoven and undyed. Paul allowed dyed wool to pass: properly it would come under the head of *versicoloria* (fr 70 pr—§§ 9, 12; Paul iii 6 § 82). *Linum* included flax, spun or not, dyed or not, and even what was on the loom (fr 69 § 11). *Libri* included all books of whatever material (paper, parchment, lime-bark, ivory, wax, *etc.*), but not unwritten books, nor did it carry the bookcases (fr 52 pr—§§ 3, 5). *Chartae* did not as a rule include books, but in the will of a student bequeathing to a student 'all his papers,' and having only books, these would pass (fr 52 § 4).

22. When a testator left 'his own slaves' (or other things), positive ownership is not required if testator counted them as his (*suorum numero habuit*); and thus he would be held to include what he had in common with others, those of which another had the usufruct, and probably slaves *bona fide* in his service, certainly those which he had pledged, but not those which were pledged to him or of which he had the usufruct, nor the vicars of his own slaves. Slaves of his own but usually hired out would be included, but, if testator was a slave dealer, he would scarcely include such as were bought merely like merchandise to sell again (fr 71—74, 85).

M. Restrictions on amount of legacies.

1. The power of leaving legacies and freedoms by will was originally unlimited. It rested on the XII tables, which gave validity to whatever disposition a testator might make of his property. 'As he shall have enacted for his estate, so shall the law be' (*uti legassit suae rei ita jus esto*). The result was that a testator could exhaust his estate in legacies, and the heir seeing no profit in the inheritance declined to enter; the will took no effect, and thus many died intestate. Three laws in succession aimed at finding a remedy for this. The *lex Furia* (older than Cicero[1]) provided that no one except relatives within

[1] Mentioned by him *Verr.* ii 1, 42 § 109; *Balb.* 8 § 21.

the sixth[1] degree (second cousins), or persons in their power or in whose power such relatives were, should take by will or gift in view of death more than 1000 asses. It did not rescind the disposition, but enacted a penalty of four times the amount, recoverable by a stringent procedure from anyone who took such legacy or gift, contrary to the law (Gai. ii 224, 225, iv 23; Ulp. § 2[2]; Vat. 301). But this law left it open to a testator to leave nothing to the heir, supposing he made a sufficient number of legatees up to the statutable limit. The *lex Voconia* (169 B.C.) put the maximum receivable by anyone as legacy or gift in view of death not at a certain sum, but at not more than the heirs took[3]. The heirs therefore would be sure to have something, but if the legacies were numerous it might be insignificant, and yet the heirs would remain liable for all the debts and burdens of the inheritance. The third law, *lex Falcidia*, was far more effective and remained in force as a permanent part of Roman law, and was the subject of much comment by the lawyers (Gai. ii 227; Ulp. xxiv 32). On the emancipation of slaves by will a limit was put by the *lex Fufia Caninia*; see above Book II.

This *lex Falcidia* was passed in the year 40 B.C. and while confirming the right of every Roman citizen in making his will to leave either money or things to whomever he chose, either directly or by imposing a duty on the heir, required that the amount should be restricted so as to allow the heirs under the will to retain not less than a fourth part of the inheritance. This is all that we have of the law itself, but we are told that

[1] See above, p. 80 note.

[2] Ulpian gives it as an instance of a *lex minus quam perfecta*.

[3] *Quid si plus legarit quam ad heredem heredesve perveniat? Quod per legem Voconiam ei qui census non sit, licet* (Cic. *Verr.* ii 1, 43 § 110). Taken without regard to the particular case, this differs from Gaius' account, as the former limits the total amount of legacies, the latter limits only the amount taken by each legatee. Quintil. *Decl.* 264 gives as law '*ne liceat mulieri plusquam dimidiam partem bonorum suorum relinquere*,' and this seems to be the point of Cic. *RP.* iii 10 § 17. That the maximum legacy of which an only daughter was capable was one half is the result of Gaius' account also, but he does not confine the rule to women (see above, p. 193), and presumes more legatees than one. In Cic. *Balb.* 8 § 21 Cicero says *Tulit legem Q. Voconius de mulierum hereditatibus*. On this *lex* see above.

a legacy of things bought and procured for a woman (see p. 340) was expressly excepted from reduction by this law (D. xxxv 2 fr 1 pr, 81 § 2).

2. The effect of this law, as interpreted by the lawyers, was that the heir, if only one, each heir if there were more than one, was entitled to reduce the amount of legacies charged on the inheritance or on his share, if payment of them in full would leave him less than one-fourth of the inheritance or of his share of the inheritance, as the case might be. The value of the inheritance is taken as at the time of testator's death. Debts, funeral expenses (so far as they fall on the heir), costs of realization are deducted. So also is the value of slaves either of his own manumitted by the testator, or directed by him to be manumitted, whether belonging to the heir or to be purchased by him from others, or slaves either freed by the praetor as a reward for detection of crime, or punished for crime. All diminutions or accretions of the estate between testator's death and the heir's entry are to the loss or gain of the heir in this account. That is to say, deaths of slaves or animals, losses by theft, robbery, fire, housefall, shipwreck, violence of public enemies or brigands or pirates, failure of debtors, do not entitle the heir to demand a reduction of legacies, if his fourth was there at the time of testator's death. Whether the particular loss or gain falls actually upon the heir or the legatee, depends on its affecting what remains to the heir or what was part of a valid legacy. On the other hand, produce of land or animals or slavewomen, gains by the contracts of slaves or delivery to them, or by legacy or inheritance to slaves, gifts, release or abandonment of servitudes to which the land of the inheritance is subject, rights of action for theft or Aquilian damage, *etc.*, may so increase the value of the estate, that though there was not a fourth remaining for the heir over the legacies at first, yet now, if these were taken into account, the estate would be large enough to leave him his fourth without reducing the legacies. But these things are not taken into this account: the reduction of legacies, if required at the time of death, must proceed all the same. Slaves returned from captivity are taken into account, as by the law of reverter (*postliminio*) they

are deemed to have been part of the estate all the time. To illustrate the above, suppose a testator with an estate worth £4000 leaves legacies to the amount of £5000; first one-fifth must be struck off the legacies as excessive anyhow, then one-fourth must be struck off for the heir. If the legacies amounted only to £3500, they must be reduced by one-seventh[1] in order to increase the £500 surplus of the estate over the legacies to the £1000 required for the heir. Possibly in the interval between the deceased's death and the heir's entry the estate may have been depreciated by £1000, so as to be worth only £3000; the legacies can be reduced only by the fourth or seventh shewn to be necessary at the time of death; the heir gets nothing or only £500. He can, however, decline to enter or meddle with the inheritance, if he thinks in the circumstances it is not worth his while to do so; and the legatees may find it advisable to reduce their claims in order to prevent their legacies dropping altogether by the will's not taking effect. On the other hand, if the estate has appreciated, the heir is so much better off, and reduces the legacies all the same in the proportion determined by the value at death (D. xxxv 2 fr 30 pr, 36 § 2, 37, 39, 43, 72, 73 pr, § 5, 77). Legacies imposed on the heir or his slave in favour of himself are not reckoned among the legacies, any more than legacies which are null (fr 20, 30 § 8).

In making the calculation the heir has to debit himself as part of his fourth with every emolument which being parcel of the inheritance comes to him as heir (*jure hereditario*). Consequently (unless testator has intended thereby to free the legatees from deductions), the heir does not include in his fourth any legacy he may receive from the testator or anything which may come to him in fulfilment of a condition imposed on a legatee or slave manumitted: except that, if a slave makes such payment from his *peculium*, the heir must reckon it, so far as it falls on his share, the *peculium* being part of the inheritance. So also if legacies fail and drop into the residue, the heir gets these as heir and must debit himself in the Falcidian account

[1] *detrahitur octava* (fr 73 § 5), meaning an eighth of the whole inheritance (*i.e.* £500), must be taken from the legacies.

(fr 50, 51, 74, 76, 91). So also with all profits accruing after entry and before the due time for transfer of the legacy (cf. fr 24 § 1).

3. Where the heir-at-law has to restore the inheritance under a trust, the case is reversed. What he takes as heir-at-law in any way from the inheritance is to be handed over to the trust-heir, subject to his retaining a fourth; and this fourth may be made up out of any legacy (direct or by way of trust) from testator or anything he is authorised by testator to take first (*praecipere*), or deduct or retain, so far as it falls on or is taken from his own share (by law) of the inheritance: so much of it as falls on or is taken from his coheirs he takes as additional to his fourth. Where testator said, without specifying the source, that the heir-at-law on receiving a certain sum of money should transfer the inheritance, a rescript of Hadrian or Ant. Pius decided that the whole sum should go to satisfy his Falcidian claim, as if he were retaining it out of the estate. And this held good of a partial heir *A*, requested to receive money and transfer his share of the inheritance to a coheir *B*. But if it were land that the coheir *A* was to receive, this could not be regarded as wholly retained; for the other coheir *B* being part owner has to contribute a portion: and if the value of the land was in excess of the share of the inheritance which *A* has to transfer to *B*, *B* can claim a Falcidian fourth of the excess, just as if to that extent *B* were paying *A* a legacy. If anything which an heir-at-law is to receive as a condition of transferring the inheritance is itself made subject eventually to a trust for transfer, it will not (so the above rescript) count towards satisfaction of the heir's Falcidian claim. Nor does anything paid to the heir-at-law in fulfilment of a condition count, for it was not part of the inheritance; and if it be paid by a legatee, the whole amount of the legacy (without deducting such payment) is to be reckoned with other legacies in calculating the burden on the inheritance, which may entitle the heir to apply the Falcidian law (fr 91, 93; xxxvi 1 fr 60 § 3; cf. xxxi fr 77 pr)[1].

[1] There is much dispute about the matters in this paragraph; cf. Cujac. iv p. 2456 sq.; Vangerow *Pand.* § 536; Windscheid *Pand.* § 652 n. 17; Brinz *Pand.* § 417.

If, however, the heir-at-law is directed to sell the estate to the intended heir by trust at an amount less than the real value, though the transaction is like in result to restoration on the receipt of the same sum, yet the character appears different; the price now represents the inheritance and will tend to satisfy the Falcidian claim (D. xxxv 2 fr 19, 30 § 7; cf. fr 87 pr). For the treatment of profits see below (chap. IX.).

4. In taking the value of the estate, or of anything bequeathed from it, each item is to be reckoned at its true value as an article of commerce, without regard to any special circumstances, such as a slave's being natural son of the heir or of some likely purchaser, or his being guilty of a noxal offence; but of course having regard to the place where a thing is and to the state of the markets. A debt due to the estate is worth only as much as the debtor can be forced to pay (fr 42, 63). If the debtor is insolvent and a release is left him by testator, the release will be reckoned at the full amount of the debt: if the debt is bequeathed away, the legacy is not reckoned at all (fr 22 §§ 3, 4).

In the case of legacies, their value has to be estimated not only for determining whether the Falcidian law is to be applied, but also in order to make the due deduction. Everything which is the object of a legacy has *prima facie* to be subjected to this reduction, both corporal things, certain or uncertain, fungibles, debts and rights. For the division of corporal things the proceeding *com. div.* might be resorted to; and if the application of the *Falcidia* was uncertain, the judge would incidentally decide that question, or the legatee might bring a vindication for an unascertained share (D. x 3 fr 8 § 1). A usufruct may be valued and divided. A servitude cannot be divided, and therefore the right can be withheld by the heir, until the legatee pay him the due part of its estimated value (D. xxxv 2 fr 1 §§ 7, 9, 80 § 1). If a slave is bequeathed with a trust for manumission, the trust must be executed even if there be nothing else bequeathed, either to legatee or to bequeathed slave, out of which the legatee can take his claim: if there is, the claim for his fourth of slave and of additional bequest can be satisfied wholly from the latter. If a slave is bequeathed (without such trust for manumission) and a farm is bequeathed to the slave, some lawyers held that the same plan could be followed, and the Falcidian claim for both be satisfied wholly out of the farm. But Paul says that the practice (assisted by a rescript of Ant. Pius) followed Cassius, who pointed out that the right to a fourth of the slave made heir and legatee tenants in common, and that any legacy to a common slave belonged wholly to the one who could take: the heir could not take such a legacy to himself, and therefore could not claim any share of the farm, which passed to the legatee, subject only to a deduction for the Falcidian share of the value of the slave (fr 33, 35, 36 § 3, 49 pr). If payment of a debt is left to the creditor and, owing to the payment being anticipated, there is pecuniary value in the legacy, this also is subject to Falcidian deduction (fr 1 § 10). If the legacy consist in an annuity, and there is at first no cause for the *lex Falcidia*, the payments will be in full: if a year comes in which, owing perhaps to a conditional legacy becoming due, the law has to be applied, the heir is entitled to a reduction on the payments already made (fr 47 pr, cf. fr 16). The value of an annuity or usufruct according to Ulpian was taken at 30 years purchase for all annuitants under the age of 20 and on a reduced scale at intervals above that age[1]; at 60 and upwards, the value was taken at five years purchase. But Macer says the usual mode was to take the value at 30 years purchase for all ages up to 30, and above that age at the difference between the age and 60. This method would give a somewhat higher value than the first mentioned (fr 68, cf. fr 55). If the heir was required to sell or buy a thing at a certain price, the value of the legacy was the difference between that and the real price (fr 30 § 1, 87 pr). Where a legacy was under a condition still pendent at testator's death, or testator had made a stipulation on such a condition, the value for the Falcidian account might be taken at what it

[1] Viz. from 20 to 25 at 28 years; from 25 to 30 at 25 years; from 30 to 35 at 22 years; from 35 to 40 at 20 years; from 40 to 50 at one year less than the difference between the age and 60; from 50 to 55 at 9 years; from 55 to 60 at 7 years. See a comparison of these scales with modern scales in my edition of *De usufructu* p. 190 sq.

would sell for; but the more usual course was for heir and legatees to enter into reciprocal guarantees for rectifying the account according as the condition occurred or failed, the heir meantime according to agreement treating the legacy or stipulation as due unconditionally or not at all (fr 31, 45 § 1, 73 § 1).

5. Where a person becomes entitled to more than one share of the inheritance, and such shares are unequally burdened with legacies, the question arises whether they are to be treated in respect of the Falcidian deduction together or separately. Where two heirs are appointed by the will to equal shares and one has at least a fourth of the whole estate free from legacies and the other has his half exhausted by legacies, the former must pay legacies charged on him in full, the latter can claim a deduction of 25 per cent. If now the former fail to take, and the latter become by accrual sole heir he has no longer any claim for the Falcidian concession, and will pay all the legacies in full, retaining for himself at least a fourth of the estate. But if the latter fail to take, and his rights thus accrue to the former, it would be contrary to the policy of the Falcidian law for the accrual to bring burden only; the former takes with it the right to deduct the 25 per cent. (fr 77, 78). Where the will after appointing the two heirs substituted them, each to the other, in case of either's failure, then whichever failed, the two shares must for the purposes of this account be treated as a whole, and the whole of the legacies paid in full (if a fourth of the whole estate was clear), that being in the absence of anything to the contrary taken as testator's intention. So where testator's *impubes* son and Titius are made equal heirs, and Titius is substituted for the son, if he die before the age of puberty, whether he become heir or not, Titius, succeeding to the son's share as well as to his own, has to bear the legacies (with or without deduction) just as if he were originally appointed sole heir, provided the son never became heir (*i.e.* died before testator). If however the son became heir, his share of the father's estate becomes now a separate estate, and Titius takes the burdens upon it with the same right of deduction as the son would have had (fr 1 § 13, 87 §§ 4—8). Where an *impubes* son is

appointed heir, and by a pupillary will a substitute is appointed for him, and legacies are charged both on son and substitute, the substitute has to pay both sets of legacies, subject, if necessary, to the Falcidian deduction. The estate is still taken as at the time of the father's death, subsequent gain or loss by the son being disregarded in this account (§ 79; tit. 3 fr 1 § 1).

Another case is when there are two substitutes for an *impubes*, *e.g.* suppose a father with £4000 leaves his son heir, subject to legacies amounting to £2000, and in case he die under age, appoints Titius and Seius equal heirs, but charges Titius with legacies to the amount of £1000. The son dies, and Titius and Seius succeed. Each is entitled to £2000, but charged in each case with £1000 legacies, and Titius charged in addition on his own account with another £1000. Seius will have £1000 left after paying legacies, and has no right to the Falcidia. Titius on the other hand would have nothing left, and can therefore deduct £250 from the £1000 legacies, part of those charged on the son and £250 from those charged on himself (80 pr, cf. fr 11 § 6; xxxv 3 fr 1 § 1)[1].

If testator's whole estate consists in one debt of £4000, and he bequeaths a release to his debtor and £4000 in legacies, the Falcidian law comes in. The heir is entitled to his fourth, and the debtor and legatee (or legatees) divide the rest. That is to say the debtor will pay £1000 to the heir, £1500 to the legatee and will retain £1500 himself, the heir giving him a formal release. If the debtor is insolvent and can pay only £1000, this will be divided, £250 to the heir and £750 to the legatee. Of the remaining £3000 half is cancelled, being due from and to himself: the other half due will be sold as a debt, and anything obtained for it will be divided between heir and legatee as above (fr 82).

6. Gifts in view of death were subject to the Falcidian deduction (D. xxxix 6 fr 42; xxiv 1 fr 32 § 1; Cod. viii 56 fr 2). And so were trusts even when charged on the heir *ab intestato*. This was due to Ant. Pius (D. xxxv 2 fr 18 pr).

[1] A full discussion of the various cases of this and the preceding paragraphs will be found in Vangerow *Pand.* § 535. There is much dispute. Cf. Windscheid § 653.

Where a son and heir had received gifts from the testator largely exceeding his due share and was ordered to pay from the profits a legacy to other children, he was not allowed to invoke the Falcidia (D. xxxi fr 87 § 4).

It is not strictly applicable to persons who do not claim under the will, but get possession of the inheritance otherwise: the praetor's edict however required them to pay legacies and authorised the reduction as by the Falcidian law (D. xxxv 2 fr 1 § 2).

The testator can discourage the application of the Falcidian law by making the heir a gift or giving him a legacy on that condition (fr 56 § 5, 75). The heir can then elect. But a stipulation or appointment of heir with a penal clause, conditioned on not making use of the Falcidia, will not be enforced (fr 15 § 1; cf. fr 27).

The law does not apply to soldiers' wills if made outside the forms of ordinary law (D. xxxv 2 fr 92; Cod. vi 50 fr 7).

It is not applicable to a bequest of a woman's dowry, because that is practically a mere restitution of what is her right (D. *ib.* fr 81 § 1).

Legacies to municipalities or to gods are not exempt (fr 1 § 5).

7. Whenever a doubt was felt whether, owing to the number of slaves freed, or the amount of debts likely to fall on the estate, or other contigencies affecting it, the value of the estate was sufficient to pay the legacies and trusts in full without deduction under the *lex Falcidia* or otherwise, the heir was authorised by the praetor to require from the several legatees, before or even (by a rescript of Ant. Pius) after payment, a bond with sureties for the repayment of any excess which they may have received above what they were entitled to have. The Crown and petty annuitants were not required to give this bond. If the estate was diminished, not all at one finding, but in several, the bond could be put in force *toties quoties*. A usual course was, on the announcement of a Falcidian reduction being required, for an arbiter to be appointed to ascertain the value of and charges on the estate (D. xxxv 3 fr 1 §§ 4—12; 3 §§ 4, 5).

N. Protection of legatees.

1. Legatees had a right to be protected against the heir. The praetor accordingly directed a stipulation to be entered into with the heir for his conveyance or performance within the time willed by the testator, and for the absence of all fraud. Every heir, whatever his rank or means, was required to give this promise and support it with sureties. The stipulation should embrace successors of the heir as well as of the legatees, and it might be given by or to a procurator. It is applicable to trusts, to partial heirs as well as universal heirs, to substituted as well as instituted heirs, to conditional as well as absolute legacies and trusts. If the legatee is dead when the condition occurs, the stipulation drops along with the legacy. If the legacy is given to one under power, the stipulation will be made both with him and with his father (D. xxxvi 3 fr 1 §§ pr—7, 12, 14, 20, fr 3, 11, 14; xl 5 fr 47 § 3, 48). A son under power or slave cannot require security from the heir, if he be father or master; but if the son or slave be emancipated, or set free before the condition of the legacy occur, he can demand security by a hypothek of the father's or master's property without sureties (fr 7). By a rescript of M. Aurelius any indication of testator's desire to remit giving security would be given effect to (Cod. vi 54 fr 2; xxxv 1 fr 77 § 3).

Security can be demanded if it is doubtful whether the inheritance has been entered on. If it is clear that no entry has been made, security cannot be asked. If the inheritance is repudiated or omitted or the necessary heirs have abstained, security cannot be asked, for the legacy or trust fails. If testator has forbidden security to be taken, and the heir in ignorance of the fact or in the belief that security cannot be dispensed with has given the security, he can bring a condiction for release; and sureties, if sued on the stipulation, can plead 'not owing' (D. xxxvi 4 fr 1 pr, § 4, fr 2).

2. If security was not forthcoming (whether from fault or absence of the person burdened with the legacy) the legatee (or trust-legatee) obtained an order for taking possession of the goods of the estate (*missio in possessionem*). The only condition

was that the legatee (or trust-legatee) was not to blame for the security's not being obtained (*per legatarium, etc. non stare quominus ei caveatur*). Other legatees could obtain a like order, and would be in possession concurrently. The possession was only for the preservation of the estate, and the heir was not turned out. By the goods of the inheritance were meant all things in the ownership of the heir, lands held on long lease (*vectigales*), pledges, fruits, offspring of cattle and female slaves. Things deposited or lent to the deceased did not count in the inheritance, but things honestly bought with bad title did. The private property of the heir could also be taken possession of and the fruits used to satisfy the legacy, provided application had been made to the court on approved grounds, and six months elapsed without security being given. The fruits would be applied, first, to pay interest and then to reduce capital. The legatee would have the right to sell fruits of a perishable nature, and store the other property in the testator's house, or, if there were none, in some suitable warehouse. If the heir refused admittance to the legatee, the magistrates or an official would put him in. If there was a trust imposed on a legatee, and he did not give security, the most convenient course is for the trust-legatee to get payment from the heir, and himself to give security to the legatee, to refund, if the condition turned out against him. If there is no property belonging to the inheritance, the legatee can obtain from the praetor a surrender of the heir's actions. However small the legacy may be, the legatee is entitled in default of payment or security to be sent into possession of all the goods of the inheritance (D. xxxvi 4 fr 1 § 1, 5, 10, 13; Paul iv 1 §§ 15, 17).

Towns (*municipia*) are open, like any other heir or legatee, to have their property taken possession of in this way. If they require to enforce a legacy or trust, the praetor gives an order to their manager (*actor* fr 12).

3. Anyone thus sent into possession was protected by the praetor, who issued an interdict against anyone who unlawfully (*dolo malo*) hindered him from taking or keeping possession. One who interfered, because he believed the estate to be his own or mortgaged to him or at any rate not the person's against

whom possession had been ordered, was not liable to this interdict. An action on the case was granted against anyone, if of age to be *doli capax*, disobeying the interdict, with damages covering the interest of the legatee or other creditor, and thus yielding him nothing, if he was not really entitled. The heir or other successor could bring it but not against an heir, except so far as the latter had got something on this account from his predecessor. The action must be brought within a year (D. xliii 4 fr 1).

If the person sent into possession claimed under a trust, and was refused admission, this interdict was applicable; but the more appropriate course was for the magistrate who took cognisance of the trust to execute his own decree *extra ordinem*, and if necessary put the claimant into possession by main force (fr 3 pr).

CHAPTER IX.

TRUSTS (*FIDEICOMMISSA*).

A. 1. Trusts were at first merely solemn requests and were without any legal sanction. They appear to have been originally used in order to put an inheritance or legacy into the hands of persons legally disqualified to take by will[1], and were afterwards

1 Several instances are mentioned by Cicero. A. Trebonius had a brother proscribed by Sulla, and a *lex Cornelia* forbad aid to be given to the proscribed. Trebonius in writing directed his heirs to take an oath to secure to his brother at least one half of their several shares. Of the heirs only a freedman took the oath; the others went to Verres, who (in accordance with praetorian practice, see above, pp. 199, 200) excused them from the oath, and granted them the possession of the estate (*Verr.* ii 1 47 § 123). Q. Fadius Gallus made P. Sextilius Rufus heir, and wrote in his will that he had requested him to pass the whole inheritance to testator's daughter. Rufus consulted his friends, Cicero among others, telling them that Gallus had really never made this request, and that he himself had sworn to the Voconian law and could not act contrary to it. Of the older friends none advised him to do so; Cicero says he ought to have handed over the whole estate. Madvig is probably right in supposing

used, partly in connexion with codicils, in order to avoid some restrictions which attached to dispositions by will. Augustus first gave them legal force, and gradually they obtained so firm a footing, that a special praetor was appointed (by Claudius or earlier[1]) to deal with them (*qui de fideicommissis jus diceret,* Just. ii 23 § 1; D. i 2 fr 2 § 32 ff.; xlix 14 fr 3 § 3; Gai. ii 285). Where the intention was clear, the courts were not disposed to stickle at words, but contrived to give effect to testator's will.

The effect of a trust was that a person duly appointed heir or legatee is thereby made by testator a channel for passing the inheritance or a legacy, wholly or partly, as the case might be, to another. This latter is regarded so completely as the real owner, that the inheritance or legacy is said to be restored (*restitui*) to him. But (unless the trust be imposed on the statutable heir, or made by codicils) there must be an heir duly appointed by valid will, and the heir must enter on the inheritance: else the trust with the will itself fails altogether (D. xxix 7 fr 3 pr; xxxi fr 81; Gai. ii 270, 283)[2].

2. The language used in creating a trust differs greatly from that in which a testator in the exercise of his old statutable right lays down the law for his own property. It is precative, not imperative. Instead of *jubeo* and *esto, do lego* and *damnas esto,* a trust is couched in words of entreaty. The form is such as this: 'L. Titius shall be my heir. I ask you, L. Titius, and beg 'of you (*rogo te petoque a te*) that as soon as you can enter on 'my inheritance, you give it up and restore it (*reddas*[3], *restituas*)

that Gallus had bequeathed to his daughter as much as the Voconian law allowed (see p. 345), and in understanding the oath mentioned by Rufus to have been a general oath to observe the laws, taken by him when entering on some office (Cic. *Fin.* ii 17 § 55). Sex. Peducaeus having received a secret request from C. Plotius told Plotius' wife of the request and gave up to her the whole estate (*ib.* 18 § 58). See also Val. M. iv 2 § 7. Justinian in his Institutes (ii 25 pr) says L. Lentulus was the first person who made a *fidei-commissum,* as he was the first to make codicils.

[1] Cf. Suet. *Claud.* 23 *Jurisdictionem de fideicommissis, in urbe delegari magistratibus solitam, in perpetuum atque etiam per provincias potestatibus demandavit* (*Claudius*).

[2] See exceptions D. xxxi fr 77 § 23, 88 § 9.

[3] *Reddendi verbum quamquam significationem habet retro dandi recipit tamen et per se dandi significationem* (D. xxx fr 21).

'to C. Seius.' But though a request, it was a request which was intended to be followed, whether the heir wished and approved it or not. *Si volueris* was as much out of place here, as in an appointment of heir or gift of a legacy (D. xl 5 fr 46). And the request was equally valid if communicated through a third person as if in form addressed to the person charged with the trust (D. xxxi fr 77 § 26). Apt words to create a trust are *peto* (*ut illi des, ut illi fideicommissum relinquas, ut illi libertatem adscribas, etc.*, D. xxxi fr 18 § 3), *rogo, volo, fidei committo.* Others add *mando, deprecor, cupio, injungo, exigo, desidero, impero*, but *relinquo* and *commendo* are not effectual. *Contentus esto illa re* indicated that all else given was to be treated as in trust for others (Gai. ii 246—250; Paul iv 1 §§ 5, 6; D. xxxii fr 11 §§ 2, 4; xxxi fr 69 pr). So also a trust is expressed by *credo te daturum, scio te restiturum* (D. xxx fr 115, 118); and a trust for release, *Quod Sempronius mihi debet, peti nolo* (xxxiv 3 fr 22). Even a nod in the case of one unable to speak was in practice sufficient to create a trust, if its application was clear (Ulpian xxv 3; D. xxxii fr 21 pr). Papinian highly praises a rescript of M. Aurelius directing that a statement of testator 'that he did 'not doubt that his wife would hand over to his children what- 'ever she took by his will' should be taken as creating a trust (D. xxxi fr 67 § 10). Severus too had authorised the inference of a trust from the contents of a will generally (*ib.* § 9; cf. xxxii fr 39 pr). A trust once created can be enforced by the persons entitled, notwithstanding any disposition of the property affected contrary to the testator's intention, the value being payable if restoration is impossible (*e.g.* D. xxxi fr 88 § 16, 89 § 6; xxxvi 1 fr 26 §§ 2, 3). The heir charged with a trust was called *heres fiduciarius*, the person in whose favour the trust was created was called *heres fideicommissarius*. I call the former 'the legal heir,' or 'heir-at-law' or 'trustee'; the latter, 'the heir by trust' or 'trust-heir.'

3. Anyone may be charged with a trust, who will get some benefit from the testator at his death, whether it be something made over to him or which testator allows him to retain. Such are an heir, alive or postumous, or legatee under the will, whether direct or substitute, or the heir of an heir or of

a legatee, a statutable heir *ab intestato*, a *bonorum possessor*, the statutable heir or *bonorum possessor* of testator's son dying before puberty, a donee *mortis causa*, the master of a slave or father of a son under power, if such slave or son are made heir or legatee[1], the appointed recipient of money to be given by a *statuliber*, a debtor of testator's, and even under circumstances the emperor or fisc (D. xxx fr 11, 77, 92 § 2, 96 § 4, 114 § 2; xxxi fr 162; xxxii fr 1 § 6 sq., fr 5 § 1). Any inability to take for themselves is no hindrance to their taking a trust for persons with the requisite capacity (D. xxxi fr 42, 49 § 3; xxxii fr 28). A trust is sometimes imposed generally on all successors by the use of the words *quisquis mihi heres bonorumve possessor, ejus fidei committo* (*e.g.* D. xxix 7 fr 3 pr; xxxi fr 87 §§ 3, 10, 11), or *ad quemcumque ex testamento vel ab intestato bona mea perveniant, rogo, etc.* (D. xxxii fr 9).

The trustee is not supposed to bear himself the expense of the trust, *i.e.* to give more than he has received (Gai. ii 261). The legacy of a slave with a request to set him free is good (the *lex Falcidia* notwithstanding, D. xxxv 2 fr 33), but no further trust can be imposed in virtue of this legacy, unless the freedom is so postponed, that the legatee has the benefit for a time of the slave's services. So a legacy by a husband to his wife of her dowry justifies a trust only to the extent to which she benefits thereby, *i.e.* by the difference between immediate payment and payment by three annual instalments, or, if the legacy be so expressed or intended, by the waiver of claim for recoupment of expenses. A woman, who having stipulated for the return of her dowry, gives her husband a formal release by way of gift *mortis causa*, can impose a trust on her husband, for he thereby gains. A surrender *mortis causa* of a usufruct to the proprietor is a sufficient basis for the imposition of some trust. But the legacy to a creditor of what testator owes him will not bear a trust, unless the debt is due only after a time, or on a condition, or is exposed to some plea, and thus the creditor gains by not having to wait or by being sure of his

[1] If the beneficiary under the trust is the slave or son, the Falcidian fourth will not be retained by the superior; if he be an outsider, it will (D. xxx fr 11).

money. A legacy on condition of giving the heir a certain sum which is the value of the legacy is no basis for a trust. Nor is the release of a pledge such a basis (D. xxxii fr 3, 7 § 2; xxx fr 122 § 2; xxxiii 4 fr 2).

Manumission by itself without further advantage will not support a trust on the freedman (D. xxx fr 94 § 3). A freedman who leaves his patron no more than his due share of the inheritance can impose no trust thereby on the patron: if the patron refuse to take his share, others who claim it can be held to the performance of the trust. If a freedman die intestate, he can impose on his patron a trust covering one-half of his estate (D. xxxi fr 28; xxx fr 114 § 1).

4. A legatee burdened with a trust who has not received the legacy can, by a rescript of Caracalla, only be called on to surrender his actions to the trust-legatee (xxxi fr 70 pr). If he is asked to restore just what he receives, he will not be liable for negligence but only for bad faith in the performance of his trust: if asked to restore a larger sum, he is liable only for the amount received, and if restoration was postponed by testator, the profits: the excess is invalid (Gai. ii 26; D. xxx fr 78, 108 § 12; xxxi fr 70 § 1). But one who is asked by will to take a certain sum and restore to another a thing belonging to the legatee, cannot, if he accept the legacy, refuse to perform the trust, though the thing be of greater value than the legacy (fr 70 § 1). If a legacy on which a trust is based drop into the residue, or the legatee die before fulfilment, the heir or legatee's heir is bound to fulfil (xxxi fr 29 pr, 32 § 4).

A trust like a legacy should be executed specifically, if possible, and only when that is impossible should the value be substituted (D. xxxii fr 11 § 17; but cf. xxx fr 114 §§ 3—5). If the impossibility arise from the death or destruction of the slave or other thing left by trust, the trust fails: if from the death of the trust-legatee, the legatee keeps the thing (D. xxxi fr 17, 60). If the trustee make delay, he is responsible for all loss which the beneficiary incurs (xxxii fr 26). A legatee asked to set free another's slave keeps his legacy, if the slave's master refuses to sell (xxx fr 92 § 1; xl 5 fr 51 § 2); and some lawyers held that a trust for the conveyance of another person's property dropped, if the owner refused to sell (Gai. ii 262). A trust should not be executed before the day of vesting; for the effect may thereby be altered, *e.g.* a trust to restore to testator's brother's sons may if prematurely performed give the inheritance to the brother, or to more sons than will be found at the due time (Rescript of Severus and Antoninus, D. xxx fr 114 § 11): but where the trust is for the benefit of children and expressed to be performable on the death of their father, it was held that, if the children were emancipated, the trust might be performed at once (xxxvi 1 fr 23 pr).

5. A trust to appoint Titius heir was invalid; by senate's decree it was interpreted as a trust to transfer the inheritance of testator to Titius (xxx fr 114 § 6). A trust for the emancipation of trustee's sons according to Papinian and others could not be enforced: no money value can be put on fatherly power. Ulpian however thought, in accordance with a rescript of Severus, that the praetor on an application *extra ordinem* ought to compel emancipation, if the father had accepted a legacy which testator had left with that view (D. xxx fr 114 § 8, xxxv 1 fr 92).

6. A general direction by a testator not to alienate the property has no effect, unless some reason be given or some person is found whose benefit was contemplated, such as children, descendants, freedmen, heirs, *etc.* If the heir's estate is sold on account of testator's debts, or claimed by the Crown (*fiscus*), trust-heirs as well as legatees lose their claims, notwithstanding any such direction. A rescript of Severus and Caracalla was to that effect (D. xxx fr 114 § 14; xxxii fr 38 § 4; = 93 pr). A direction to the heir 'not to pledge, sell, or give a farm as long as he lived: otherwise the farm to go to the Crown,' is no bar to his leaving it to outsiders by will, though testator desired it to remain in his name (xxxii fr 38 § 3). A frequent direction by way of trust was, that the heir or heirs should not alienate a particular farm, but when he died leave it in the family, or that it should not pass from the testator's name (which would include freedmen[1]). In the absence of any further special

[1] Papinian even includes freedmen who had been manumitted under a trust by testator's outside heirs (D. xxxi fr 77 § 11), and the son and heir of a freedwoman who had a share (*ib.* § 28).

direction, the heir could select at his death such members of the family as he chose, with such shares as he chose, and the person selected would take as by the original testator's will, though it may have been expressly left by the heir also. In fact the heir had the property only for his life with the power of selecting one or more reversioners out of the family who would take exclusively of others. If the heir alienated it from the family, either while alive or by will, persons duly entitled, either those named in the will or, in default of such, those in the next degree of relationship can petition for the trust farm at his death: and all with the same claim will take, and take in equal shares. Even if the alienation has been by a sale in bankruptcy for the holder's debts, the purchaser can hold it only until the bankrupt's right of enjoyment was extinguished by death or otherwise; after that those entitled under the trust can claim. In a trust 'for testator's family' the claimants, after those named in the will, are persons of testator's name at the time of his death, and their children in the first degree, unless testator expressly provided for further degrees. 'Family' included emancipated members[1]. Anyone thus taking precedence by nearness of kin can be called on, by way of additional security for the family, to give a bond to restore on death. Emancipation does not disqualify from benefiting by a family trust, nor does disherison bar a suit, if the trust to keep in the family is not duly observed. If an heir leave the farm to a member of the family in trust for a stranger, the stranger may have a claim for the value (if the legatee had consideration) but this will not oust the family from their title to the farm. A gift *inter vivos* to one of the family gives him an interest only during the donor's life, and does not count as a selection, if the trust require the selection to be made at his death. If the farm were left to several, and some sold their shares, those who did not sell can claim the others' shares. In another case[2]

[1] Cf. D. L 16 fr 195 § 2 *Omnes qui sub unius potestate fuerunt recte ejusdem familiae appellabuntur.*

[2] D. xxxii fr 38 § 2; see Cujac. *Obs.* xv 4. On D. xxxi fr 77 § 27 see Cujac. vol. iv p. 2341 (ed. Prati), who comparing xxxii fr 38 § 5 thinks a coheir who has bought from another could alienate that from the

where the beneficiaries were expressly named, it was held that there was no accrual. If the trust be for children and their descendants, and all die out, the last holder can leave the farm to a stranger (D. xxx fr 114 §§ 14—18; xxxi fr 32 § 6, 67 pr—§ 7, 69 §§ 1, 3, 4, 77 §§ 10, 27, 78 § 3; xxxii fr 94; xxxiii 2 fr 34 pr).

7. In expressions of dying *sine liberis* other descendants were included and not merely the first grade (D. L 16 fr 220). One child was sufficient (xxxv 1 fr 101 § 1). Whether legitimate children only were meant was a question answered in the negative by Papinian in the case of a freedman. According to Ulpian it depended on the testator's understanding of the term, and that was to be gathered from his rank, intentions, and circumstances (D. xxxvi 1 fr 18 § 4; cf. fr 79 § 1). Children begotten after the father had been deported or become *servus poenae* did not count as such (*ib.* fr 18 §§ 5, 6). Nor did adopted children or children who predeceased their father without leaving offspring (*ib.* § 7, xxxv 1 fr 76). It was not necessary that the children should be heirs (D. xxx fr 114 § 13).

Posteri did not include *liberti* (*i.e.* the freedmen's freedmen), even in a trust for *liberti* and their *posteri* (xxxii fr 83 § 1).

8. Trusts to give freedom to slaves were very common, and if the intention of the testator was clear, difficulties were not allowed to prevail. Thus the scruples about making a legacy dependent on the heir's or other's will largely disappeared. A request to the heir to set Stichus free was not vitiated by the condition *si volueris*: nor by *si Stichus voluerit*, nor by *si Seius* (another person) *voluerit.* But to make the heir's consent necessary to another's setting free a slave invalidated the request, as in the case of a legacy, unless what was meant was a reasonable, not a capricious consent, an appeal to his judgment as a *vir bonus* on the conduct of the slave. That the heir should fix the particular time or select the particular slave out of several was quite allowable (D. xl 5 fr 46).

The intention to give freedom was often indirectly expressed, *e.g.* by such expressions as *nolo alii quam tibi Stichus serviat, ne Stichum alienes, Stichum vēnire nolo.* In such cases the slave

family. I doubt this: certainly the language of the trusts is different, and in fr 38 the freedmen are named.

could claim his freedom at once, if alienated voluntarily by the heir. But it was otherwise where the object of such expressions was rather to retain the slave's services for the heir, or to punish him by preventing his getting a better master (*ib.* fr 9, 10, 24 § 8).

9. A trust for freedom like other trusts and legacies (not charged on the statutable heir) drops, if the will giving them is broken or invalid. But it does not drop because the slave had been bequeathed to someone not in existence, or to one in the power of the enemy, or criminally condemned, and the bequest therefore treated as not written. He who by such lapse has got the slave will be bound to give the freedom (fr 24 § 11, 26 § 6, 47 pr, 51 pr; xxxiv 8 fr 3). Where a legatee is asked to give freedom to one of his own or another's slaves, and the legacy is not equivalent to the slave, he is still bound, if he accept the legacy, to free his own slave: but not bound to purchase and free another's, if he cannot do so with the amount which has come to him from the testator (*ex judicio testatoris*). If the legacy has received increase from the heir's delay, or the value of the slave has decreased, the balance may be restored. If he is asked to free several, the legacy may be adequate to the freedom of part, and the selection can be made by following the order in the will, or by lot, or by serious estimation of the respective merits of the slaves in question. If the legatee has accepted the legacy and trust under a notion of its value, which owing to some unexpected occurrence has been disappointed, and the value is no longer adequate, the legatee may be excused from the trust on refunding the legacy. If he has been asked not only to free one of his own slaves but to hand over to him the legacy, he cannot (at least in the opinion of some lawyers) be compelled to free the slave; for then he must also pay over the legacy and himself have nothing. If however he is allowed by the terms of the trust to defer the payment, the freedom will be in abeyance till the profits or interest make the legacy adequate (D. xl 5 fr 24 §§ 12—20; xxxv 2 fr 36 pr § 2).

A good trust for freedom will be enforced notwithstanding any alienation or usucaption of the slave. If it be conditional, alienation is not barred, but the slave carries with him his title to freedom, and if the condition takes effect, he must be freed. Constitutions of Hadrian and Ant. Pius gave the slave a right to be heard why he should not, instead of being freed by his present master, or, if already freed, continuing as his freedman, be remitted to the original trustee (xl 5 fr 24 § 21). Incapacity to alienate is no bar to executing a trust for freedom (fr 12, 51 § 1).

10. A series of senate's decrees from and after Trajan's time were passed to remove difficulties in executing trusts for freedoms. The *SC. Rubrianum* A.D. 103 provided for the case when persons (heir, legatee, purchaser, *etc.*) charged with the trust kept out of the way. They were to be summoned by notice, edict, and letter: the praetor heard the case on the application of the slave himself, and, if he found the trust effectual, declared the slave free, just as if he had been freed directly by the will: he will be *orcinus libertus*. The *SC. Dasumianum* applied the same remedy where the person charged with the trust was not hiding or unwilling to appear, but absent for good cause; *e.g.* where the trust was charged on an infant or madman, or captive, or wards who had no guardians, or where the absence of either the person himself or his guardians was due to danger to life, reputation, or property, or indeed for any cause not fraudulent. The *SC. Vitrasianum* and a rescript of Ant. Pius provided for the case of the trust's being charged on some only of the heirs, and empowered them to free the slave, fixing them with liability as for a judgment debt to the other heirs for the value of these others' shares in the slave. The *SC. Articuleianum* A.D. 123 empowered Governors of provinces to act in such matters, though the heirs charged were not of their province. And the *SC. Juncianum* applied the *Rubrianum* to cases where the slave to be freed was not at the time of death the property of testator. Where there was no heir or successor, or an own heir had kept aloof from the inheritance, a senate's decree in Hadrian's time (*Dasumianum*?) ordered that application be made to the praetor to grant the freedom: and in that case, as under the *Rubrianum*, the slave would be freedman of testator (*orcinus*), and testator's family would be patrons and guardians. Where the *Rubrianum*

did not meet the case because the trust was imposed on a legatee who, though present, could not free the slave, because the heir had not conveyed him and was absent, special application to the emperor was necessary (D. xl 5 fr 5, 26 § 12—fr 30 § 14, fr 36, 51 §§ 4—11; xxvi 4 fr 3 § 3).

11. Extraordinary favour was shewn to claims for freedom. Freedom given directly by will to a slave who was pledged was in strict law invalid; but it was upheld, as if given by a trust (D. xl 5 fr 24 § 10). Freedom given by a trust, imposed on the appointed heir and substitute, was upheld, though both died without entry on the inheritance: and where a soldier had in the same way left a trust for the slave to be free and heir, his freedom and heirship were both upheld (fr 42). Where a pregnant woman was left free by trust, and in consequence of delay her child was born before she was freed, the child was ordered to be made over to the mother to be manumitted by her, and to have *status* as freeborn from the day of application. Marcian (in the Digest) says that the rule became established that such a child should be held freeborn from the due date of the trust: if the trust was conditional and the child was born before the condition took effect, he should be freed by the mother (fr 13, 26 § 1, 53). And generally Marcus Aurelius directed that trust-freedoms should not be destroyed or impaired, nor the position of the freedman worsened by the age or condition or delay of those charged with the trust (fr 30 § 16; fr 51 § 3).

On the other hand a trust to free a slave who had carried off some of testator's goods was (by a rescript of Hadrian) not to be enforced until an arbiter had reported what was due to the heir, but this was to be done at once in order that freedom might not be delayed (D. xl 12 fr 43).

B. Differences between direct disposition and trusts.

Trusts, as was natural from their nature, being originally mere requests destitute of necessary form or legal force, were free from the various restrictions to which legal dispositions of property at death were subject; and though some of this freedom was after a time removed, they always had much wider application than legacies, until Justinian assimilated them. Gaius (ii 263—289) and Ulpian (xxv 1—13) set out the differences:

1. Thus as regards form a trust may be expressed in Greek (or Punic or Celtic or other language, D. xxxii fr 11 pr), whereas Latin was requisite for a legacy. It does not require the previous institution of an heir but may be expressed generally, and, even where there is no will, it may be imposed on the successor *ab intestato* (*ad quem bona ejus pertinent*). A legacy must be imposed on an heir, whereas a trust could be imposed either on a heir or on a legatee, whether legatee by law or by trust. A legacy may not, but a trust may, be imposed on the father or master of a son (under power) or a slave, if son or slave are heirs or legatees. By codicils no heir can be appointed and no one can be disinherited, and unless they are confirmed by a will either in anticipation or subsequently, no legacy can be given: but a trust by codicils, confirmed or not, is good for securing the transference of the inheritance or of any single object to another (Paul iv 1 § 10). An oral declaration by a dying woman of her will that certain slaves be free was held binding as a trust on all statutable successors (D. xl 5 fr 47 § 4).

2. As regards the *personal* recipients of the benefit, foreigners were at first allowed to take under a trust (as indeed, says Gaius, this was the chief origin of trusts), but afterwards it was forbidden; and by a senate's decree in Hadrian's time things left to foreigners by trust lapsed to the Crown (*fisco*). The *lex Junia* prohibited Latins from taking inheritances or legacies, but they could take them by trust. The *lex Voconia* forbad women being appointed heirs to anyone registered in the census as possessing 100000 *asses*, but, if he left a trust for a woman to be heir, the incapacity dropped. Unmarried persons (*caelibes*) were forbidden by the *lex Julia* to take inheritances or legacies, but for a time they were thought capable of taking them by a trust. Married but childless persons (*orbi*) were mulcted by the *lex Papia* of half an inheritance or

legacy: trusts they were thought capable of taking whole; but this was afterwards forbidden by the *SC. Pegasianum* which treated them as lapses. An uncertain person, which term included an alien postumous child (cf. p. 194), could not be made heir or have a legacy left him: a trust in his favour was good, until a senate's decree under Hadrian put trusts in this matter under the same rule as direct legacies and inheritances. Townsmen (*municipes*) could not be made heirs directly, but could take under a trust. This applies (by a *SC. Apronianum*) to all communities in the empire: for the purposes of suits they had to appoint an *actor* (Ulp. xxii 5; D. xxxvi 1 fr 27).

3. A will can directly appoint not only an immediate heir, but provide for another to be heir, if he fail to become so. Only in the case of a child under puberty can a testator provide a successor to one who has actually become heir. But by way of trust he can go further. He can request his heir, after due entry on the inheritance, either then or at some later time or when he dies, to transfer the inheritance in whole or in part to someone else. Or he may effect the same purpose more directly by using such words as these: 'On the death of my heir Titius I will my inheritance to belong to P. Maevius.' In both cases the heir is under an obligation to restore the inheritance to the person named. In this way, by any words indicating his intention, he can impose on a father made heir the obligation to pass the inheritance to his son on death (D. xxxii fr 11 § 10). A trust-legacy *pridie quam morietur* was good: a direct legacy was not (Paul iv 1 § 11), cf. p. 304.

4. Again, in the case of freedoms. A senate's decree forbids a slave under thirty years old being made free and heir by will, but the general opinion was that he might by will be declared free on attaining that age, and a trust be imposed for the restoration of the inheritance to him. If freedom were given to the same slave on different conditions in the same will, the slave could choose the easiest; if it were given by trust, the last mentioned was, by a rescript of Caracalla, authoritative (D. xxxv 1 fr 90).

As has been said above (pp. 28, 82) any slaves who are set free by direct words are the freedmen of the testator; whose children, or such one or more as the testator chose to assign them to, had a statutable right of guardianship over them and inheritance to them. But only such slaves could be directly set free as the testator owned in full right both at the time of making the will and at the time of death. In trusts it was different. Any slave whatever whether testator's or another's (subject to his master's consent to sell him) could be the object of a trust as of a damnatory legacy for his purchase and manumission; and when freed becomes the freedman of the trustee, who however has only rights to inheritance, not to services. If the owner declines to sell, the trust drops altogether, without any allowance or deduction, freedom being inestimable in money.

5. Other differences between direct disposition and trusts by will were that legacies were sued for by the regular issue tried by a judge; trusts were dealt with at Rome by the consul or a praetor specially appointed for this jurisdiction in the provinces by the Governor; suits for legacies were not heard in vacations; trusts were heard (at Rome) all through the year. Interest and fruits were due on trusts if the trustee made delay in discharging them: but on legacies, as a rescript of Hadrian declared, interest was not due, except probably in the case of legacies *sinendi modo* (see p. 297). There was no doubling the amount claimed under a trust, as there was under a damnatory legacy if the claim was disputed; and money which was not due, if paid under a trust, could be recovered, which was not the case in damnatory or, as Ulpian and Paul say, in any legacies.

The imposition of a trust by way of penalty was by Gaius' time (there were doubts before) held invalid as in the case of legacies. So a trust for adoption of a particular person, to be enforced by disinheritance or revocation of legacy in case of disobedience, was held invalid (D. xxxii fr 41 § 8).

A guardian could not be appointed by trust (Gai. ii 289).

Protection by requiring security, sending into possession, interdict, or other proceeding *extra ordinem*, was given to legatees by trust as to direct legatees; see p. 354.

C. Transference by heir-at-law to heir by trust.

1. A trust may relate to all or only a part of the inheritance: it may be absolute or conditional, to take place at once or on a future day. It has however no strictly legal effect of itself. The heir who has entered is not by the trust or by any action under the trust divested of his rights and obligations as heir; but by the aid of the praetor (who could give or refuse actions and pleas), practical effect was given to the trust. The method adopted was for the heir-at-law to sell the inheritance for a nominal consideration (*nummo uno*) to the heir by trust, and the two parties entered into the covenants usual on the sale of an inheritance. The heir-at-law stipulated that the heir by trust should indemnify him for anything he might be adjudged to pay or might have otherwise given in good faith on account of the inheritance, and generally that he should be duly defended in any action brought against him as heir. And the heir by trust stipulated that the heir-at-law should hand over (*restitui*) to him anything which might have come to the heir-at-law from the inheritance, and allow him to use as his *procurator* or *cognitor* the usual actions of an heir (Gai. ii 250—252). If the trust affected only a part of the inheritance, the position of the two parties was like that of the heir and the legatee of a share, and corresponding covenants (*partis et pro parte, i.e.* claiming a part and liable in proportion) were entered into between them for sharing in due proportion the gains and losses of the common inheritance (*ib.* 254).

2. The cumbrous method of a sale and covenants was rendered superfluous by a decree of the senate in the reign of Nero and consulate of Trebellius Maximus and Annaeus Seneca (25 Aug. A.D. 57 probably: so Mommsen). By this decree it was enacted that 'in cases of trust-inheritance all suits dependent by the 'civil law on deceased's estate, should follow the transfer of right 'and profit rather than imperil the person who had fulfilled 'the testator's trust, and consequently that all actions which 'were usually allowed for and against the heirs should not be 'allowed for and against those persons who had restored as 'required by the will, but should be allowed for and against

'those persons to whom the inheritance had been duly restored, 'in order the better to establish the last will of the deceased.' The praetor accordingly granted analogous (*utiles*) actions to and against the trust-heirs just as if they were heirs by the civil law, and they were set forth in the edict (Gai. ii 253; D. xxxvi 1 fr 1 pr and § 1 which is fuller than Gaius). For any other actions resting on praetorian authority, which the heir-at-law would usually have, the praetor required no authority from a decree of the senate: he would naturally adjust those to the wants of the trust-heirs (D. *ib.* fr 41 pr).

3. But while both heir-at-law and heir by trust were thus protected and the creditors and legatees of deceased also protected if the trust took effect, there was no protection for the trust itself. The same difficulty arose here which had arisen in the case of heir and legatees and had finally led to the enactment of the *lex Falcidia*. If an heir was called upon to restore the whole or greater part of the estate, he had little or no inducement to enter, and, if he suspected the estate to be insolvent, he might decline to enter whether he had to restore less or more. In any case, if he did not enter, the will failed and the trust with it. To remove these causes for the heir's reluctance and make the heir by trust secure of the option, a senate's decree was passed in the reign of Vespasian and the consulship of Pegasus (the well-known lawyer) and Pusio (cir. 70 A.D.) by which the heir-at-law was authorised to deduct, as he might do under the *lex Falcidia* in the case of legacies, a fourth part of the inheritance. And in practice this principle was applied also to cases where the heir-at-law was only heir to a part, and was requested to hand over the whole or part of his share: he could retain one-fourth of it. A further provision of the decree was that if the heir-at-law thought the inheritance was insolvent and on that or other grounds declined to enter, the heir by trust might apply to the praetor, who could then order the heir-at-law to enter and restore the inheritance, analogous actions being granted to and against the heir by trust, as if the transfer had been made under the Trebellian decree. The heir-at-law in this case retained nothing and ran no risk (*ib.* 254, 258, 259; Ulp. xxv 16; D. xxxvi 1 fr 4).

4. There were thus two procedures[1]. If the heir-at-law was willing to enter and restore in conformity with testator's request whether the whole or part of the inheritance or of his share, there was no need of any stipulations between him and the heir by trust; the Trebellian decree met the case. In civil law he remained capable of suing and liable to suit for the whole, but the praetor controlled and protected him, so that in fact he sued and was sued only so far as he retained any share of the estate, while the heir by trust sued and was sued by analogous actions for what he received. If he declined to enter at all, the heir by trust could compel him and the principle of the Trebellian decree applied: the heir-at-law under the control of the praetor parted with everything, both emolument and liability, and the heir by trust took all. But if the heir-at-law, being left by testator heir to less than one-fourth, claimed his full fourth under the Pegasian decree, he must secure himself by covenants with the trust-heir, and the trust-heir, like the legatee of a share, must get reciprocal covenants from him (Gai. ii 255—257; Ulp. xxv 14, 15; Paul iv 3 §§ 1—3).

5. If the heir was asked to restore, after reserving or taking (not a proportionate part but) some specific thing (*deducta aut praecepta aliqua re*) or things, or a certain amount of money, and he restored accordingly, he was not liable for any actions against the inheritance: they all passed (*in solidum*) to the trust-heir, even if the thing retained was more than the Falcidian fourth or even contained the bulk of the deceased's estate. The inheritance might thus become worthless to the heir by trust or dangerous to accept (D. xxxvi 1 fr 31 § 3; fr 1 § 16; cf. Just. ii 23 § 9).

6. The Trebellian decree and the Pegasian decree were applicable whenever the trust was imposed on an heir, whether heir by will or a statutable heir, or an heir by trust; and their heirs or the possessors of their estate, or a father or master who has acquired the inheritance through his son or slave, could all act

1 Justinian speaks of the *captiosas et ipsis veteribus odiosas Pegasiani senatus consulti ambages.* He amalgamated the two decrees and treated all as referable to *SC. Trebellianum* (Const. *Tanta* § 6 *a*). So in the Institutes ii 23 § 7.

under the decree. It applied also to the will of a son under power in respect of his camp-*peculium* (D. xxxvi 1 fr 1 § 5—§ 8; fr 41 § 1; fr 57 § 2). The restoration of the inheritance is effected by allowing the heir by trust to take possession of the things of the estate on that account, or by approval of his action in doing so, or by transfer to another at the request of the heir by trust. And the heir's allowance may be signified either by word or letter or message. Restoration may be made by the heir's heir if the heir be dead; or by a father or master who has acquired the inheritance by his son or slave; or with the authority of his guardian by or to a ward or to a ward's slave on his account, or according to a rescript of Ant. Pius by the caretaker of a madman (fr 36, 38, 41 § 1, 66 § 2, 67 §§ 3, 4). These decrees do not apply to a legatee of a share of the inheritance who is asked to restore it to another (fr 23 § 5).

Even if the heir by trust has not actually taken possession, the assets of the inheritance become by the act of the heir-at-law part of the trust-heir's goods (*in bonis fiunt ejus*), and the actions will be transferred either wholly, if the whole inheritance was the subject of the trust, or partially, if the trust affected only a portion, even though the heir actually transferred more. And the like partial transfer occurred when the heir-at-law or the heir by trust died before it could be effected, leaving several heirs who did not act all at once (fr 65 pr § 3, 66 § 2). If the trust was to transfer the inheritance, partly to one, absolutely or at a fixed time, and partly to another under a condition, the heir-at-law will transfer the whole to the former, and on the occurrence of the condition, if the latter accept, the rights of action for his share shift to him as of course (fr 1 § 9). The restoration may be made in the absence of the heir by trust to his procurator, who if there be doubt as to his authority must give security for his principal's ratification. The actions will pass to the heir by trust only when he accepts (fr 68 § 1). If there be a temporary action in the inheritance, time will run against the heir by trust from the time at which it was first in the power of the heir-at-law to sue (fr 72 § 2). The actual presence of the heir-at-law is not necessary for the transfer (fr 13 § 1).

If the heir by trust is another's slave or son, restoration to him requires his master's consent, but not necessarily before, as in the case of accepting an inheritance: ratification is sufficient, as in the case of *bonorum possessio,* and the actions then pass by the Trebellian decree. The consent or service of the slave is not necessary here, as it is in both the other cases (fr 31 § 2, 67 pr). If the heir-at-law is requested to manumit some of his own slaves and restore the inheritance to them, he will be entitled to deduct their value besides a fourth of the inheritance after such deduction (fr 28 § 17).

7. Whether the heir-at-law was bound to hand over fruits, rents, and interest on investments taken since testator's death, was much discussed. All fruits, offspring of slaves, *etc.* gathered before the heir's entry, must be restored along with it. And acquisitions made by stipulation or mancipation by slaves belonging to the inheritance are in the same position. After the heir's entry, until application is made to him to restore to the heir by trust, all such gains made by himself, or slaves belonging to the inheritance, including inheritances and legacies left to them and accepted by him, but not including offspring of slaves, become his property by the act of perception, and (unless testator has otherwise directed) he is not bound to hand them over, and if entering voluntarily can claim his fourth besides (Paul iii 8 § 4; D. xxii 1 fr 3 pr; xxxvi 1 fr 19 pr, 23 §§ 2, 3, 28 § 1, 46 § 1). If the trust was not to take effect until some future time, or on the death of the heir-at-law, or on the occurrence of some condition, so that the heir-at-law would by the authority of the testator (not by neglect of the trust-heir) have for some time the enjoyment of the estate, he must set them off against his claim to a fourth of the inheritance, and the profits thereof; if they exceed that, he is entitled to keep the excess over what may be necessary to make up the inheritance (so far as transferable under trust) to the value as left by testator (D. fr 19 §§ 1, 2; 23 § 2; 28 § 16; 34; 60 § 5; cf. xxxii fr 83 pr). As soon as demand to restore in accordance with the trust is made, delay begins, and from that date all profits and gains accruing due from the estate, less proper expenditure on it, must be handed over to the heir by trust, who is entitled to sue debtors to the inheritance

for all unpaid arrears, and is liable to creditors for the like (Gai. ii 280; Paul iii 8 § 4; D. xxii 1 fr 3 pr; xxxvi 1 fr 60). Losses, unless caused by his gross negligence (*culpa quae dolo proxima est*), the heir-at-law is not bound to make up (except as above), but for alienations, manumissions, or damage, committed by him, he is responsible by petition on the trust (fr 23 § 3, 72 § 1). A right of action acquired by him under the Aquilian statute for injury to a slave of the inheritance does not pass to the trust-heir; for the Trebellian decree passes only actions belonging to deceased's estate, *i.e.* acquired before the heir's entry (fr 68 § 2)[1]. Nor has the trust-heir actions (*e.g. Serviana*) for pledges taken by the heir-at-law to secure estate-money lent either by him or by testator; but by suit on the trust he can get surrender of these actions (fr 75 pr). Rights concerned with tombs remain with the heir-at-law (fr 43 § 1). Servitudes which were due between land or houses of the heir-at-law and testator are held to be still good, notwithstanding the temporary merger (fr 75 § 1). Accretions to land by alluvion or the rise of islands pass to the legatee by trust as part of the corpus of the trust (D. xxxii fr 16).

When the trust is to restore 'what shall be left of the inheritance,' *e.g.* at the heir-at-law's death, the heir by trust has a right to demand not only the replacement of anything spent or alienated with a view to reduce the trust fund, but also to have the heir-at-law's expenditure apportioned reasonably between the trust-fund and his own estate. This was by a decree of M. Aurelius (fr 56).

8. The heir-at-law is not bound to give any guaranty against eviction: the goods and land pass as they are, but on the contrary he is entitled to be secured against eviction of any he may have sold (fr 71). And if he has retained a farm by testator's wish, he can claim security against eviction: or else, as Julian suggested, the farm could be valued at what it would

[1] See Doneau's *Comment.* vii 25 (vol. i p. 661, ed. Florent. 1821). F. Mommsen (*Erörter.* i 103) holds that the heir-at-law would be bound to surrender this to the trust-heir. So also A. Pernice (*Sachbeschädigungen* p. 189). If the right was acquired before delay, why should it be transferred any more than other acquisitions?

fetch if purchaser took the risk of eviction, and if the value be less than a fourth of the estate the heir by trust should make it up (fr 1 § 16).

So far as any legacies or freedoms are charged on the inheritance or part of the inheritance transferred, the trust-heir is liable wholly or proportionately (fr 1 §§ 17, 20, 21).

Dowry is subject to its own rules and though found in the property passing to the heir-at-law, whether as a *praelegatum* or not, is not part of the estate so as to come under the obligation to restore (fr 53, 61 § 1, 64 pr).

An heir-at-law who has restored an inheritance without deducting his fourth, has *prima facie* no right to recover by *condictio indebiti*, but he can recover if he prove that his action really was due to mistake; or, if he come into possession of any of the inheritance, he can retain it till satisfied (fr 22, 70 § 1; Paul iv 3 § 4).

A legatee by law or trust to whom the inheritance has also been transferred cannot claim the Falcidian deduction from legacies he may have to pay (D. xxxv 2 fr 47 § 1).

9. The second provision of the *SC. Pegasianum* gave further protection to the trust. The heir-at-law might well prefer, if he could only expect a fourth of the inheritance, which perhaps might be loaded with debt, to decline altogether. On the application of the trust-heir he could be compelled to enter and restore the inheritance. He was not bound to shew that the inheritance was insolvent or in fact to give any reason for his refusal. If he were doubtful, he might obtain time for deliberation even after entry, and then, if he accepted the inheritance and duly restored, he would be deemed to have entered voluntarily and be entitled to claim a fourth. Otherwise he would be ordered to restore and would practically be relieved from all responsibility, but would take neither his fourth nor anything from the inheritance, unless expressly left him in view of this case. Anything directed by testator to be given to the heir by a slave as a condition of his freedom is taken and retained by the heir. If the heir-at-law was ordered by testator to enter in some special place and declined to

accept, he could be compelled to go there and enter, his travelling expenses being paid. But for restoration his presence was not necessary: and the application to the praetor might be made by a procurator for the trust-heir (D. xxxvi 1 fr 4, 6 pr, 9 §§ 1, 2, 6, fr 7, 9 § 1, 11 § 2, 28 § 15, 73; xxxv 1 fr 44 § 5). The effect of the entry and restoration would be to uphold the will including a pupillar will, legacies and freedoms, the trust-heir taking the place of the heir-at-law as regards rights and liabilities (xxxvi 1 fr 15 § 2, 57 § 2; xxviii 6 fr 38 § 3).

This power of compulsion on the heir to enter only applied to one who was asked to restore the inheritance or part of it, not merely to restore some definite thing: in the latter case the heir-at-law would be transferring emolument but not thereby gaining any relief from liability to action. The precise term used to denote the inheritance was unimportant, but it must be one which meant the *universitas* or complex of rights and liabilities and not a separate thing. Thus besides *hereditas, bona* or *familia* or *pecunia* or *universa res mea* or *omnia mea* or *patrimonium* or *facultates* or *quicquid habeo* or *census meus* or *substantia mea* or *peculium meum* (testator speaking depreciatively of his property) would all imply the succession as a whole (including actions), unless a different intention was manifest. Such an expression as *quidquid ad te ex hereditate bonisve meis pervenerit rogo restituas*, strictly taken, denotes only the balance after burdens have been discharged, but it was held that *pervenire* was used loosely, and that the whole succession was meant. So *hereditas deducto aere alieno* or *deductis legatis* was thought by some lawyers to involve the absurdity of subtracting definite quantities from an ideal whole: but Julian held that the heir-at-law should transfer the estate under the Trebellian decree, and if he paid the legacies and debts and claimed his fourth, he should guaranty the heir by trust against the legatees and creditors. A soldier's will was privileged in this respect as in others, and, if it contained a trust for the transfer of some particular thing or collection of things (*e.g. res Italicas*), the heir-at-law was compellable to enter and transfer, and actions relating thereto would pass as if under the Trebellian decree (D. xxxvi 1 fr 15 § 5—17 §§ 3, 6, 31 § 1).

10. A patron appointed heir to his due share and asked to restore it to testator's disinherited children can, if necessary, be compelled to enter and restore. A son under power or other necessary heirs can be compelled to intermeddle with the inheritance and restore, and in all these cases the actions will pass to the trust-heir. So also the Crown and townsmen and in practice heirs on intestacy and praetorian successors were held compellable (fr 6 §§ 1—4; 66 §§ 1, 3). An heir can be compelled to enter and restore to his own son or to another's slave, whether the slave was freed directly or by trust: but he could not be compelled to restore to his own slave, even if someone was ready to guaranty him against loss. If however he choose to enter, he must give the freedom and the inheritance according to the trust. A mere trust for freedom (without inheritance) is not sufficient basis for compulsion (fr 17 §§ 11, 13, 14, fr 23 § 1, 54 § 1). Where the heir by trust is an infant or mute, the praetor will on the application of the guardian or caretaker compel the heir-at-law to enter and restore to them; and they will be held capable under the authority of the guardian or caretaker of accepting the inheritance at their own risk, as they are held capable of taking a grant of possession of the estate or of *pro herede gerere* (fr 67 § 3).

If the appointment of heir-at-law is conditional, and the condition is within the power of the heir and neither difficult nor expensive to perform, the trust-heir can force its performance, by tendering money for the cost. If the condition is disgraceful, the praetor will discharge it, and order the heir-at-law to use analogous actions or apply for possession of the estate in accordance with the will and then transfer estate and actions to the trust-heir. If the heir was directed to bear the testator's name, the condition is not disgraceful, but if desired the praetor will discharge it. No application for compulsion can be made by a trust-heir, until the occurrence of the condition on which his own title is based (fr 65 §§ 7—10, cf. 28 § 4).

11. Where there are several trust-heirs entitled, the rule was that the whole inheritance passed to anyone who applied to the praetor for a compulsory order, the others being left to claim from him. In this case even if they did not join in

the application, the heir-at-law could not claim his fourth. But if the applicant did not ask for the whole inheritance, but only for his own share, he obtained only that, and the heir-at-law was not debarred from claiming a fourth from the rest, if he voluntarily transferred to them (fr 17 §§ 4, 8, 9).

If an emancipated son has already got possession of the estate *contra tabulas*, the heir-at-law is no longer compellable to enter or to perform the trusts (fr 28 § 6).

If the heir-at-law enter on a compulsory order, the trust-heir cannot escape liability by declining to take up the inheritance. And where testator has given a slave freedom and made him heir by trust, and the heir-at-law is compelled to enter, the freedman's heir cannot avoid taking up the trust. The heir by trust is liable to be sued either where he lives, or, if he desire it, where the larger part of the restored inheritance is (fr 46 pr, 68 § 4, 69 pr; v. 1 fr 50 pr, § 2).

CHAPTER X.

A. Restrictions on the capacity of unmarried or childless persons.

The provisions of the *lex Julia* (18 B.C.) and *lex Papia Poppaea* (9 A.D.) have come down to us imperfectly (they were abrogated by Constantine), and affect many parts of the law[1]. Some of the provisions may best be given here (see also, p. 90).

1. Unmarried persons (*caelibes*) were incapable by the *lex Julia* of taking either inheritances or legacies, and the *SC. Pegasianum* extended this prohibition to trusts (Gai. ii 111, 286).

[1] The precise relation of the two laws is not known, and the date of the *lex Julia de maritandis ordinibus* (as sometimes called) is disputed. Horace's words in the *Carmen seculare* 17 *Diva producas subolem, patrumque prosperes decreta super jugandis feminis prolisque novae feraci lege marita* (B.C. 17) make B.C. 18 the date at which the law was either carried or at least approved by the senate, though rejected by the people (cf. Suet. *Oct.* 34; Tac. *An.* iii 25; Dio Cass. liv 16; lv 2). The *lex Papia Poppaea* was passed in the consulship of *M. Papius Mutilus* and *Q. Poppaeus Secundus* (Dio Cass. lvi 10; Tac. *An.* iii 28). It was modified under Tiberius (Tac. l.c.). See also Girard *Dr. Rom.* p. 852 note.

Married but childless persons (*orbi*) were incapable of taking more than one half of either inheritances or legacies or (since the *SC. Pegasianum*) trusts (Gai. ii 286 *a*).

A man who has before completing his sixtieth year obeyed neither law, though now freed from the obligation to marry, remains by the *SC. Pernicianum* under perpetual incapacity, unless (by the *SC. Claudianum*) he marries a woman under fifty years of age.

A woman who before completing her fiftieth year has obeyed neither law is in a similar position, and is not benefited by afterwards marrying a man under sixty. She remains by the *SC. Calvisianum* incapable of taking even her dowry, which therefore becomes a lapse (*caduca* Ulp. xvi 3).

2. The following were excepted from the incapacity of taking by will or intestacy, the ground for exception being relationship by blood or marriage to the deceased.

By the *lex Julia* were excepted

Relatives (*cognati*) within the sixth degree; and of the seventh degree, a second cousin's child: (the term *natus* is in the law, but the lawyers interpreted it to include *nata*);

All persons in the power of such relatives and all such relatives of those in power of the deceased;

Husbands and wives of such relatives, and such relatives of the deceased's husband or wife.

By the *lex Papia* were also excepted

Husband, wife, son- and daughter-in-law, father- and mother-in-law, step-father, -mother, -son, -daughter at any time of the deceased, or of those who have been at any time in deceased's power or married to deceased (Vat. 216—219).

By the *lex Julia* a woman was allowed to abstain from a second marriage for a year from the death of her husband, or six months from divorce. The *lex Papia* extended each of these periods by an additional year (Ulp. xiv).

3. The capacity of husband and wife of taking from each other on death was as a rule restricted, viz.:

On the ground of marriage husband or wife could take

one-tenth, and the usufruct in one-third of the estate. If they have had children[1], they could take the ownership, instead of the usufruct, and the woman could take her dowry, if left to her.

If they have had a child but lost it after the ninth[2] day, they can take an additional tenth; if they have lost two, they can take two-tenths. (The ninth day was the day on which boys were named: girls were named on the eighth according to Fest. p. 120 ed. Müller).

If either has children by a former marriage still alive, he or she can take an additional tenth for each (Ulp. xv).

4. There are cases however in which they have unlimited capacity of taking on each other's death (*inter se solidum capere possunt*), viz.

(*a*) if both or either are under the age from which the law requires children: that is to say, the husband under 25 years, the wife under 20;

(*b*) if both have exceeded in marriage (*i.e.* lived and are married) the years defined by the *lex Papia*, viz sixty for the husband, fifty for the wife;

(*c*) if they are within the sixth degree of relationship to one another;

(*d*) if the husband be absent, then during his absence or within a year after his return;

(*e*) [3]if they have obtained from the emperor the *jus liberorum*[4];

[1] Cf. *lex munic. Malac.* 56, 57 (*temp. Domit.*), which enacts that in any elections to office made within the borough, if the votes be equal for two or more candidates, preference shall be given to a married over an unmarried man without children; to one having children over one who has not; to one who has more children over one who has fewer. Two children dead after name-giving, or one dead after reaching puberty or being marriageable, are to count as one alive.

[2] So the MS., and Mommsen *Staatsr.* iii p. 202. Krüger with others reads both in chaps. xv and xvi *nominum i.e.* the name-day.

[3] The subsequent conditions follow after an insertion *Libera inter eos testamenti factio est.* I think no difference is meant in capacity from that under the former conditions.

[4] The grant of the privileges attached by the Papian law to the parentage of three or more children was sometimes made to individuals on petition. Cf. Suet. *Galb.* 14 *Civitatem Romanam raro dedit, jura trium*

(*f*) if they have a common child alive;

(*g*) if they have lost a common child aged 14 years if a boy, or 12 years if a girl; or two children three years old; or three children who survived the ninth day; or even one child under the age of puberty within the last year and six months;

(*h*) if the wife gives birth to a child by her husband within ten months from his death she has unlimited capacity (Ulp. xvi 1).

5. On the other hand if they have contracted a marriage forbidden by the law (see p. 130), *e.g.* if a senator has married a freedwoman or others have married one disgraced (*famosam uxorem*), they are wholly incapable of taking from each other (Ulp. xvi 2).

Incapacity did not affect a person who took only to restore under a trust (D. xxxi fr 42); or who was appointed heir by an insolvent (D. xxviii 5 fr 73). No inquiry into incapacity was needed till the inheritance or legacy became vested (*pertinet*) (D. xxxi fr 52).

B. LAPSES (*CADUCA*[1]).

Anything left by will which a person could take under the civil law, but owing to some special statute or the failure of

liberorum vix uni atque alteri ac ne is quidem nisi ad certum praefinitumque tempus. Martial obtained it from Domitian (ii 91, 92; in iii 95 *Caesar uterque* is obscure). Statius (*Silv.* iv 8 20) mentions a grant of the same period. Pliny refers to grants by Trajan (*Ep.* ii 13 § 8 *Quanquam parce et cum dilectu daret,* cf. x 96); and obtained them for himself (*Ep. Traj.* 2) and for Suetonius (*ib.* 94, 95). The privileges were (1) exemption from disabilities of this law; (2) contingent claim to lapses (p. 384); (3) diminution of patron's claim to inheritance (p. 271); (4) freedom (of a woman) from guardianship (p. 102). Two or more natural children exempted freedmen from promised services (p. 90). A preference in election to office and choice of provinces was given to persons having children (Tac. *An.* ii 51; xv 19; Plin. *Ep.* vii 16); and priority between consuls in taking the *fasces* was decided by number of children (Gell. ii 15 §§ 3—8). Confiscation of the property of one condemned was sometimes waived in favour of the children (D. xlviii 20 fr 7 § 3).

[1] Cicero's phrase *Antonium in via caducae hereditates retardarunt* (*Phil.* x 5 § 11) means 'Inheritances which had fallen to him delayed him on the road,' as if he had stopped to pick up fallen fruit (*Glans*

some condition or other cause does not take, is called in a general way 'lapsed' (*cadūcum*). A distinction was however made. If a disposition was written by anyone in favour[1] of himself or anyone in his power, or was made in favour of a person who turned out not to be in existence or to be in captivity at the time of writing, whether a will or codicils (as the case might be), the legacy was counted *pro non scripto*; it had been written by mistake, and was void from the first (D. xxxiv 8; xlviii 10 fr 6, 10, 14, 15, 22). If the legatee died, or a condition of the legacy failed, between the date of the will and the death of testator, it was counted *in causa caduci*, *i.e.* in the same position as a lapse. If the failure of the condition was subsequent to the death of testator, it was a proper lapse, *caducum* (Cod. vi 51 fr 2 *a*).

In all such cases according to the old law the inheritance, part-inheritance, or legacy passed to the substitute if there was one appointed, or if it was given jointly to two persons and failed in one case, the other, if it was a legacy by vindication, took the whole by accretion. If there was no substitute and no one jointly entitled, it remained with the heir. The Papian law however altered this. It deferred the vesting until the opening of the will, and thus increased the chance of a lapse (*in causa caduci*). Further it made lapses of bequests to a childless person who did not within one hundred days from the opening of the will comply with the Papian law, or to a Junian Latin who did not within the same period obtain Quiritary rights. And it gave the lapses (1) to such children or parents of the testator (as far as three degrees[2]) as were appointed

caduca est quae ex arbore cecidit, D. L 16 fr 30 § 4). The general use of *caducum* in law is due to the *lex Julia* and *Pap. Popp.* Ulpian (xix 17) speaks of *caducum vel ereptorium ex lege Papia Poppaea.* Cf. Juv. ix 86 sqq. (an adulterer is speaking to the husband) *Jam pater es, dedimus quod famae opponere possis: Jura parentis habes, propter me scriberis heres, legatum omne capis, nec non et dulce caducum.*

[1] This was by a decree of the senate called *SC. Libonianum* which made persons so acting punishable under the *lex Cornelia de falsis.*

[2] A grandfather had not such rights in the inheritance of a daughter's child unless his son was a veteran: the exception being due to M. Aurelius (Vat. 195).

heirs in the will; (2) failing these, then to such heirs or legatees (as the case might be) as had children, (3) failing these, to the people. If however a legacy was given jointly, and one legatee failed, the co-legatee if he had children took before the heirs: and, as most lawyers thought, this applied to damnatory as well as to vindicatory legacies. A constitution of Caracalla however deprived the second class of legatees of their contingent claim; and, subject to the claims of heirs who were children or parents of testator, gave all lapses to the Crown (*fiscus*). In either case the lapses passed with their burden, *i.e.* freedoms, legacies and trusts; and any other payments or services, imposed on the inheritances or legacies which had lapsed, were to be paid or performed by the receiver of the lapse, so far as performance was not peculiar to the legatee, *etc.* (Ulp. xvii, xviii; Gai. ii 206, 207, 286; D. xxx fr 96 § 1; xxxi fr 49 § 4; 61 § 1; xxxv 1 fr 60 § 1; Cod. vi 51, esp. §§ 1—3, 9). Where the same thing is bequeathed to a man absolutely and to his slave on condition, and he renounces the legacy to himself, but, on the condition occurring in the life of the slave, chooses to take his slave's legacy, some held that one half of the legacy lapsed, others (including the Digest) that he took the whole (D. xxxi fr 59). An insolvent estate not accepted by the Crown would be sold in bankruptcy (D. xlix 14 fr 1 § 1), unless taken by a slave under M. Aurelius' constitution (D. xl 5 fr 2).

C. Forfeiture of legacies and inheritance.

From the time (apparently) of Ant. Pius and especially in that of Severus and Caracalla rescripts were issued, which declared in certain cases the forfeiture of legacies and inheritances on account of acts which made the legatee or heir unworthy to take them (D. xxxiv 9). The following are the principal cases.

1. A freedman who has accused his patron after his death of contraband trade is deprived of anything left him by the patron (fr 1).

2. One who charges a will with being false or unduteous cannot take anything which comes to him therefrom directly

or through his son or slave. The like forfeiture is incurred by one who assists the accuser or is surety or has given evidence for him. Not only legacy or inheritance or trust but also gift to be made by a legatee or *statuliber* as a condition of legacy or freedom, and the benefit of the Falcidian law are thus forfeitable. A person appointed guardian by the will and excusing himself of his own motion forfeits a legacy, but if he has already got the legacy, his excuse is not admitted. If he accuse the will as false, he loses the legacy, but his charge is no sufficient excuse for declining the guardianship.

A guardian who brings the charge only on behalf of his ward at the instance of the mother or freedman does not forfeit his own legacies. Nor does anyone who has brought the charge, but claims as heir to a legatee or to the heir named in the will.

A contention that the will is not duly made (*non jure factum*) does not involve forfeiture (fr 5, 7, 22, 24; Cod. vi 35 fr 2).

3. An heir who has made away with part of the estate cannot claim his fourth from that part (D. *ib.* fr 6).

4. Capital enmity arising between testator and legatee justifies the view that the testator would not wish the legacy to be maintained; and the better opinion was that the legatee could not sue for it. The same, if he has openly abused the testator, or disputed his *status* (fr 9).

5. Any fraud on the law by a promise to transfer the estate of a deceased or anything else to one legally incapable of taking, or by accepting a silent trust for the purpose forfeits the benefit of the Falcidian law, so far as the amount of the fraudulent transfer is concerned. And the transgressor is disqualified for taking any lapse under that will as one who has children. These provisions are due to a *SC. Plancianum.* The whole of the property under a silent trust and its profits are forfeited to the Crown (fr 10, 11, 18; cf. xxx fr 123 § 1; xxxv 2 fr 59; Ulp. xxv 17). An heir however remains heir though deprived of emolument (D. xxviii 6 fr 43 § 3), but is treated as a *praedo* in possession of the inheritance (D. v 3 fr 46).

6. An heir more than 25 years old who neglects knowingly

to avenge the testator forfeits to the Crown the inheritance and any legacy he may have, and, as a *mala fide* possessor, has to restore all the fruits with 6 per cent. interest on all moneys which have come to his hands (xxix 5 fr 15 §§ 1, 2; xxxiv 9 fr 17; Cod. vi 35 fr 1, 6). The Crown has to satisfy the legatees and to confirm freedoms of all slaves excepted from the Silanian senate's decree (D. xxix 5 fr 9).

7. An heir clearly shewn to have compassed by negligence the death of his testatrix forfeits the inheritance (D. xxxiv 9 fr 3).

8. If an adulterer marry the adulteress and make her his heir, the inheritance is forfeited to the Crown. The like if she make him heir. The marriage is not lawful (fr 13).

9. An official disregarding the imperial instructions (*mandata*) and marrying a woman from the province, where his official duties are, forfeits to the Crown any inheritance she leaves him. But the woman can inherit from him (fr 2 §§ 1, 2).

10. A guardian contrary to the senate's decree marrying his ward incurs the like forfeit, but she can inherit from him (fr 2 § 1).

11. In this connexion may be mentioned that by the praetor's edict, following a constitution of Hadrian, anyone who *dolo malo* prevented a will being made or changed, was refused all actions for obtaining inheritance or bequest under such will, whether for himself or his child or slave. This rule applied whether it was a draftsman (*testamentarius*) or witnesses that he prevented from getting access to testator. If a legacy was left him only in trust, he was allowed to take it and restore. In the other cases the Crown took, subject, if the inheritance was in trust, to the right of the heir by trust, the Crown retaining the Falcidian fourth. The lawyers extended the refusal of actions to the children, if they ceased to be under power and to the slave if emancipated (D. xxix 6; xxxvi 1, fr 3 § 5; xxxviii 13).

CHAPTER XI.

CONNEXION OF *SACRA* WITH A DECEASED'S ESTATE.

The death of a *paterfamilias* left not only a mass of property, rights, and obligations without an owner, but sacred rights awaiting regular performance on behalf of the family now deprived of its head. If a son was sole heir, he represented his father in the control of the estate and in liability to human and divine obligations. But if there were several heirs, the matter was not so simple. As regards the estate, resort to the *arbitrium familiae erciscundae* would settle any disputes which the deceased had not obviated by the terms of his will. The sacred rites would presumably be discharged by the heirs in proportion to their share in the inheritance, and subject to rules sanctioned by the College of Priests. But when a testator gave legacies, whether a legacy of a share of the estate, or of considerable sums of money, or portions of his landed property, the heir or heirs might find themselves with all the sacral obligations and but little of the means which had hitherto borne them. For a legatee did not, like an heir, represent the person of the deceased; he was a mere recipient of a specified gift, and, unless the testator had imposed on him any duty as a condition of the gift, his legacy was wholly and purely gain: he was responsible for nothing thereby. If no heir was found to take up the inheritance, the sacred rites were in danger of perishing altogether. The priests being the original guardians and formulators of the civil law dealt with both matters—the succession to the estate and the preservation of the *sacra*. Gaius tells us that their anxiety for the latter made the old Romans tolerate usucapion of an inheritance, even by one who had no claim to it (ii 55). Cicero attacks the lawyers, and especially the lawyer priests P. and Q. Mucius Scaevola, for a perverted ingenuity in applying principles of the civil law to the rules for the maintenance of the *sacra*. The principal passage, which indeed contains almost all we know of the subject, is *Legg.* ii 19 § 47—21 § 53[1].

The older priests laid down that persons were bound to the maintenance of the *sacra* of a family in three ways: (1) by inheritance; (2) by taking more than a moiety of the money; (3) if more than a moiety was given in legacies, then by taking any of it[2]. The persons liable are therefore (1) heirs, and with them either (2) donees *mortis causa* or usucapients, if any one such has got more than a half of the estate, or (3) any legatee, if the legacies altogether amount to more than one-half of the estate. The principle of taking heirs as the proper representatives of the testator was thus infringed, only when they had less than a moiety of the estate, and therefore could not be deemed by themselves to stand in the deceased's place. Donees, usucapients or legatees, as the case might be, were called in aid.

The *lex Voconia* (B.C. 169) by forbidding legacies to exceed the amount left to the heirs (so Cic. *Verr.* II I 43 § 110, but see above, p. 345) made some amendment, at least of the third class, necessary. The Scaevolae made new rules, but retained the attachment of the *sacra* to the *pecunia*,—an attachment which Cicero says rested on no statute but solely on the authority of the priests (*Legg.* ii § 52). The new classification was fivefold. Liable to the *sacra* are

(1) Heirs:

(2) Anyone who takes on the ground of death or under the will as much as all the heirs together (this includes *mortis causa* gifts and legacies[3]):

(3) If there is no heir, then anyone who has taken most by possession (*i.e.* usucapion) of the goods belonging to deceased at his death (*qui de bonis quae ejus fuerint quom moritur usu ceperit plurimum possidendo*):

[1] For full discussion and references to others see Leist, Glück's *Pand.* Bk 37 Th. I pp. 164—208; Burckhard *ZRG.* xxii p. 286 sqq.

[2] *Antiqui his verbis docebant, tribus modis sacris astringi; aut hereditate aut si majorem partem pecuniae capiat, aut si major pars pecuniae legata est, si inde quippiam ceperit* (§ 49).

[3] This suits excellently a legacy of a share (above, p. 325): see Cicero's use of *partitio* in § 50.

(4) If there is no heir and no one who has thus taken any thing, the creditor who recovers most of his debt (*qui...plurimum servet*):

(5) Lastly, any debtor to deceased, who has paid no one on that account, should be treated as if he had taken that money from the estate.

A testator aware of these rules and desirous of leaving some-one a legacy, not large enough to make him liable to the sacral obligation, would sometimes provide in the will for the deduction of 100 sesterces so as to make the legacy just less than what the heirs took[1]. But if the testator did not give this direction himself, the legatee was advised by the lawyers (not formally to repudiate part of the legacy—that he could not do, but simply) to take only so much as would not bring him within the rule of liability. The Scaevolae admitted that in this case the liability to the *sacra* did not attach. Cicero (§ 50) taunts them with the inconsistency of this decision with the principles on which they proceeded as jurisconsults in matters of civil law. If a son under power makes a gift with the approval of his father, the gift is valid: if the gift is made without the father's knowledge, it is not valid, unless the father approves it. But in the case of the legatee the action of omitting part of the legacy is not approved by the testator beforehand, and is done without his knowledge and of course without his subsequent approval[2]. Yet the lawyers allowed it to be effectual to defeat the attachment of the *sacra*.

A legatee thus quietly omitting to claim the whole legacy did not extinguish the right. If his heir or one of his heirs

[1] Burckhard (l.c. p. 303) suggests these words: *deductis centum nummis heres meus hereditatem meam cum Titio partito.*

[2] This seems to me clearly Cicero's meaning. Apparently Manutius so took it. For other very different explanations, not treating the reference to a gift as a mere analogy, see Burckhard l.c. p. 289. B. Kübler (*ZRG.* xxiv p. 41 sqq.), referring to the power of a son with his father's permission to make a gift *mortis causa*, but not a will (D. xxviii 1 fr 6 pr; xxxix 6 fr 25 § 1), takes the gift here to be a *mortis c. don.*; and the priests not to allow the evasion. But he seems to me to overlook the abstract character of Cicero's language and to give little significance to the words *quod eo insciente factumst*, which form the point of Cicero's remark.

claimed the neglected portion, the claim was good, but the priests held that he made himself thereby solely liable to the *sacra*, if the amount obtained by the heir added to the amount received by his predecessor was equal to the sum left by the will.

Another plan to avoid the sacral obligation was this. The legatee by an arrangement with the heirs liable to pay the legacy, gave them a formal release by bronze and balance, and at the same time stipulated the like amount from them. The legacy and its obligations were thus entirely extinguished, and he who was previously legatee was now entitled by verbal contract to the same amount of money, without incurring any liability to the *sacra*. According to Gaius iii 175 the release by bronze and balance is confined to what can be weighed and counted, *i.e.* money. Its use therefore seems hardly applicable to a legacy of a share, unless we suppose a valuation of the inheritance (Burckhard, p. 314), but to a legacy of a definite sum of money.

A further mode of avoiding the *sacra* is named by Cicero in *pro Mur.* 12 § 27 so briefly as to be very obscure. See p. 71.

The burden of the sacred rites made *sine sacris hereditas* a synonym for 'a piece of good luck' (Plaut. *Trin.* 484).

CHAPTER XII.

BURIALS AND GRAVES.

1. The duty of disposing of the body of a deceased person fell in the first instance on any person named by him. If he did not perform it, he lost any emolument left him by the deceased on that account but was not otherwise liable unless he got and kept the emolument. The duty next devolved on the heirs named in the will; if there were none such, on the statutable heirs or kinsmen in the order of succession to an intestate estate (D. xi 7 fr 12 § 4, fr 14 § 2).

2. The expense of the burial was properly defrayed from deceased's property. It was a first charge upon it in precedence of legacies and debts, and should be defrayed out of any money left, or by the sale of perishable objects, or by sale or pledge of gold or silver, or by collection of debts due to deceased. Things specifically bequeathed could be taken for this purpose, the legatee having a claim on the heir for compensation, if he entered and there was means. The expense included what was required for the body itself, its dress, conveyance from a distance and its formal conveyance to the grave (*elatio*), for its protection, temporary deposit if any, sometimes a sarcophagus, and the grave itself and monument. The expense was fixed if necessary by the praetor or municipal magistrate on a scale suited to the rank and means of the deceased. Any foolish directions given by deceased could be disregarded. Ornaments should not be buried with the body. The erection of a monument was not a strict legal duty of the heirs, unless directed by the testator, and then, if the cost was immoderate, would not be recognised as a legal claim. If the burial was performed by one who had not control of deceased's property, and was not done out of mere generosity, the expense could be recovered by a suit (*actio funeraria*) against those *ad quos funus pertinet, i.e.* heirs or other successors, including a patron. When a child or other possible heirs did it before the inheritance was entered on, they sometimes made a formal declaration of their motives in so doing, lest it should be treated as *pro herede gestio* or as voluntary liberality (*ib.* fr 12 § 2—fr 14 §§ 10, 17, fr 15, 37; v 3 fr 50; Paul i 21 § 15). In the case of a woman, burial was a charge on the dowry, whether it was in the hands of the husband or father or an outsider. If she had property beside, the expense was to be defrayed from this and the dowry proportionately, neither legacies nor manumitted slaves nor debts being deducted for this estimate. If the husband was sued, there was the usual limitation *in id quod facere potest.* If the dowry was small, the father could be called on to pay the excess (D. xi 7 fr 16—30; Paul i 21 § 10, 11).

3. The effect of burying a dead body or bones, whether of

freeman or slave, was to make the actual grave[1] religious; provided the ground belonged to the deceased, or its owner or owners, and others, having rights therein as fructuary or wayholder, consented. If the way could conveniently be diverted, or the usufruct was created by bequest of the deceased and there was no other so convenient a place, the dissent of the wayholder or usufructuary would not prevent the place becoming religious. An owner was not prevented from burial in his own ground by its being mortgaged: a co-owner did not require his fellows' consent to his being buried himself in the ground belonging to them. Gaius makes a further proviso that the burial should be by the person entitled to perform it. Presumably his subsequent consent would have the same effect: if he did not consent, the body would be removed, as it would be if put into another's ground without the due consents: and the ground would then be deemed pure. Anyone burying in others' ground was liable to an action *in factum* to compel removal or pay the value of the ground, the action running without limit for and against the heir. Even the owner of the ground could not however disturb or remove the body so wrongfully buried, without a decree of the chief priests: otherwise he would be liable to an action for insult. Anyone, prohibited from burying in a place where he had a right, could at once bring an interdict, or bury elsewhere, and bring an action on the case for compensation; but this action, though directed to

[1] *Sepulchrum est ubi corpus ossave hominis condita sunt: Celsus autem ait: non totus, qui sepulturae destinatus est, locus religiosus fit, sed quatenus corpus humatum est* (D. xi 2 fr 2 § 5). The limits of ground made religious were probably subject to rational interpretation. Cf. D. xviii 1 fr 22 *Hanc legem venditionis 'si quid sacri vel religiosi est, ejus venit nihil' supervacuam non esse, sed ad modica loca pertinere.* Where dimensions are given on a tombstone, probably the whole enclosure (often containing gardens, *etc.*) would usually be deemed 'religious,' though legally capable of restriction if circumstances required it. Cf. Mommsen *ZRG.* xxix p. 204. See also the judgment, relative to a sale of ground containing tombs, in Bruns p. 361 no. 158; D. xviii 1 fr 73 § 1. In Hor. *Sat.* i 8, 12 *Mille pedes in fronte, trecentos cippus in agrum* (1000 feet frontage by 300 deep) *hic dabat, heredes monumentum ne sequeretur* the dimensions relate to a burial ground founded by endowment for a number of persons. For the last words see below.

reimbursement, not to punishment, did not run for or against heirs (at which Gaius expresses his surprise). Anyone burying in a public place wrongfully was liable to moderate punishment as well as to an action. A cenotaph had, according to the better opinion, the effect of making the ground religious, until Marcus Aurelius decreed otherwise (Gai. ii 6; D. xi 7 fr 2—4, 6 § 1, 7—9, 41; x 3 fr 6 § 6). No right of burial could be acquired by usucapion (D. xi 8 fr 4).

If a body was divided and the parts buried in different places, only that spot where the head was buried was religious (fr 44). No body could be buried or burnt within a town[1], lest the sacred rites of the town be defiled (*funestentur*, Paul i 21 §§ 2, 3). Nor must a tomb be built near another person's house: he can proceed against the builder by *operis novi nunciatio* or *quod vi aut clam* (D. xi 8 fr 3 pr). No one is allowed to live close to or above a monument, that being an offence to the religion: severe punishment is inflicted on an offender (Paul i 21 § 12; D. xlvii 12 fr 3 pr, § 6).

An early law (*lex regia*) forbade any woman in child to be buried: the child must first be removed (D. xi 8 fr 2).

4. A family tomb (*sepulcrum familiare*) is one constructed for self and family; an hereditary tomb, for self and heirs[2], or one which has come by inheritance. In both family and hereditary tombs, unless the deceased has otherwise ordered, heirs and successors of all kinds[3] and degrees have a right to

[1] Cicero (*Legg.* ii 24 § 61) says that it was from fear of fire that the XII tables forbad *rogum bustumve novum propius sexaginta pedes adigi aedes alienas invito domino.* He quotes also from the same *Hominem mortuum in urbe ne sepelito neve urito.*

[2] Specimens of various inscriptions on tombs are given in Bruns' *Fontes.* They describe the persons for whom the tomb is intended, prohibit alienation or violation under a fine to be paid to the pontifices or the state treasury or the borough, and provide for due access for sacrificial and other purposes.

[3] By the pontifical law those outside the Agnates or the clan would not be allowed to be buried there. Cic. *Legg.* ii 22 § 55 *Tanta religio est sepulchrorum ut extra sacra et gentem inferri fas negent esse.* The word *familia* had often a wide sense, cf. D. L 16 fr 195 § 2 *Communi jure familiam dicimus omnium agnatorum...Omnes qui sub unius potestate fuerunt recte*

bury and be buried, and so have all children, whether emancipated or not, and whether acting heirs or not; but freedmen have a right only if heirs, notwithstanding that the monument may be inscribed 'for self and freedmen.' Disinherited children may be buried there themselves (unless justly forbidden by testator) and so can their posterity; but they cannot put others there. On a sale of the land containing religious places, they do not pass to the purchaser; and if the vendor declared that he reserved the tomb for himself and descendants, this carries with it a right of access. If an owner gave up the right of burial for all persons entitled, there must be a stipulation to that effect or a direction by will; a mere pact was not enough. If a man had a tomb but no right of way, he might by a rescript of Severus and Caracalla obtain one through the adjoining land by application to the Governor of the province and payment of a just price (D. xi 7 fr 5, 6 pr, 10—12 pr; xlvii 12 fr 3 § 3; Cod. iii 44 fr 4, 8, 13; Paul i 21 § 7). It was the practice to allow owners of tombs, in land which had been sold, to visit them for the performance of funeral rites (D. xlvii 12 fr 5).

5. Violation of a tomb (*sepulcri*), under which term is included every place of burial, if done wrongfully (*dolo malo*) was by the edict ground for an action for damages, which were to be estimated fairly, having regard to the insult, the actual damage, and the gain and temerity of the violator. Condemnation involved infamy. Violation included any interference with the structure or inscription, or removal of anything therefrom, or exposure of the body to the sun's rays, or introduction of a corpse not entitled to burial there. One who dwelt or built on a grave was also liable to this action; which could be brought by any one, the person or persons rightly entitled having the preference, if desirous of bringing the action. An outsider could not recover more than 100 guineas (*aurei*) on a charge of violation, 200 guineas on a charge of dwelling or building: for those entitled by right this was the minimum. The amount recovered was regarded as mere penalty for a

ejusdem familiae appellabuntur, qui ex eadem domo et gente proditi sunt. Tombstones often bore the words *hoc monumentum heredem exterum non sequetur.* Cf. Mommsen *ZRG.* xxix pp. 215, 216.

public offence, and creditors of the deceased had no claim to it, nor could one absent on public business complain of another's having brought the action (D. xlvii 12 fr 1, 3, 6, 10; Paul i 21 §§ 4—9). Under the *lex Julia* violation was punished criminally, such offences coming under the head of acts in prevention of funeral rites and burial (D. fr 8; Paul *l.c.*). Spoliation of corpses or ejection of them or of bones was punished still more heavily (D. fr 3 § 7, fr 11).

Rescripts of M. Aurelius and Severus provided for the removal of bodies which had been only temporarily deposited (fr 3 § 4). And even bodies permanently buried might, in consequence of the overflow of a river or apprehended collapse of the tomb, be removed elsewhere by night and after the usual sacrifices (Paul i 25 § 1). For removal on other grounds the chief priests would have to be consulted: but Trajan sanctioned provincials applying to the Governor instead (Plin. *Ep. Traj.* 69 (74)).

APPENDIX TO BOOK III.

Cretio in Ciceron. *Att.* xi. 12; xiii. 46.

1. A short passage from Gaius explains the term (see above, p. 231).

Extraneis heredibus solet cretio dari, id est, finis deliberandi, ut intra certum tempus vel adeant hereditatem, vel si non adeant temporis fine summoveantur. Ideo autem cretio appellata est, quia cernere est quasi decernere et constituere. Cum ergo ita scriptum sit, 'Heres Titius esto,' adicere debemus, 'cernitoque in 'centum diebus proximis quibus scies poterisque: Quodni ita 'creveris exheres esto.' Et qui ita heres institutus est, si velit heres esse, debebit intra diem cretionis cernere, id est, haec verba dicere, 'Quod me P. Mevius testamento suo heredem instituit, eam hereditatem adeo cernoque.' Quodsi ita non creverit, finito tempore cretionis excluditur; nec quicquam proficit, si pro herede gerat, id est, si rebus hereditariis tamquam heres utatur. At is qui sine cretione heres institutus sit, aut qui ab intestato legitimo iure ad hereditatem uocatur, potest aut cernendo aut pro herede gerendo vel etiam nuda voluntate suscipiendae hereditatis heres fieri. (Gai. *Inst.* ii 164—167). Very similar language is found in Ulpian xxii 25 sqq.

Cernere is thus to 'decide' on accepting an inheritance. *Heres cum constituit se heredem esse, dicitur cernere et cum id fecit, crevisse* (Varr. *L. L.* vii 98). *Cretio* is the 'decision,' and hence is used for the time allowed for coming to a decision. This limitation of time is the real object of prescribing *cretio*, and the main difference between an inheritance with and without *cretio*. *Adeo cernoque* is 'I enter on the inheritance and I express my decision as required by the testator.'

2. Cicero in *Epist. Att.* xi 12 *sub fin.* writes:

Galeonis hereditatem crevi: puto enim cretionem simplicem fuisse, quoniam ad me nulla missa est.

Ibid. xiii 46 § 3:

Ex Balbo cognovi cretionem Cluvii—o Vestorium negligentem—liberam cretionem, testibus praesentibus, sexaginta diebus. Metuebam ne ille arcessendus esset: nunc mittendum est ut meo iussu cernat; idem igitur Pollex. Etiam de hortis Cluvianis egi cum Balbo: nihil liberalius, se enim statim ad Caesarem scripturum, Cluvium autem a T. Hordeonio legare et Terentiae HSIↃↃↃ *et sepulcro multisque rebus, nihil a nobis. Subaccusa, quaeso, Vestorium: quid minus probandum quam Plotium unguentarium per suos pueros omnia tanto ante Balbo, illum mihi ne per meos quidem?...Vestorium nihil est quod accuses; iam enim obsignata hac epistola noctu tabellarius noster venit, et ab eo litteras diligenter scriptas attulit et exemplum testamenti.*

In the next letter 47:

Tu velim e Pollice cognoscas rationes nostras sumptuarias.... Idem Pollex remittendus est ut ille cernat. Plane Puteolos non fuit eundum, quum ob ea quae ad te scripsi, tum quod Caesar adest.

The letter about Gallio's inheritance was written from Brundisium; those relating to Cluvius from Tusculum.

Pollex was a slave of Cicero's (*Att.* viii 5 § 1); Vestorius was a man of business at Puteoli, perhaps a banker. Cicero says in the 45th letter of this book that he could not have chosen anyone more careful, more attentive or more devoted to him. Balbus was acting on behalf of Caesar, who was coheir with Cicero in Cluvius' estate.

3. Schilling in his *Bemerkungen* p. 200 (followed by Rein (*Privatrecht* p. 829 note) and several editors of Cicero), dealing with the passage from the 11th book takes *cretio simplex* to mean 'an acceptance and nothing more.' *Nulla* is supposed to mean *nulla hereditas.* 'Cicero got nothing by the inheritance.' Others following Manutius, who rightly understands *cretio* with *nulla,* take the passage to mean, 'I think I am sole heir, for I have received no notice from other claimants.'

Both these interpretations are wild: *Cretio simplex* could not have either meaning: *hereditas nulla ad me missa est* is nonsense. Besides, why should Cicero accept an inheritance from which he got nothing? And when was it usual for heirs or claimants to send round notices to one another?

I take *simplex* to mean 'simple,' 'without any special requirements.' If there had been any such, the form in which the *cretio* was conceived by the testator would have been sent to Cicero. Accordingly he accepted the inheritance without more ado. (So also Karlowa *R. G.* ii p. 897; Tyrrell *Letter* 427.)

4. The other passage has more difficulty. But *liberam* I take in the same sense as *simplicem*, 'unrestricted by any special directions[1].' The only varieties of *cretio* that we know of are in the addition or omission of the words after *diebus*, '*quibus scies poterisque*' (which does not seem likely to be referred to under *liberam*); and the addition of a gift over in case the decision was not duly made (see p. 203, Gai. ii 174—178). It is not impossible that by *liberam* Cicero meant that there was no gift over, *i.e.* no substitute appointed in the will; but it is more likely that he referred to the absence of any special directions as to place, number of witnesses, and other circumstances, which testators may have been found to make in other cases. Schilling has suggested that *liberam* might include a release from the necessity of a personal declaration by the heir: but that seems to me an unnatural meaning.

The words in letter 46 *Cluvii—o Vestorium negligentem—liberam cretionem* are not in the Medicean MS. but are found among the readings given in the margin of Cratander's edition, and in one MS. Otto E. Schmidt (*Briefwechsel des M. T. Cicero* p. 341 sqq.) omits them as being an insertion of Bos resting on no good authority[2]. For my part I can see no adequate reason for anyone inventing and inserting them: the repetition of *cretionem* gives an easy explanation of their omission; they suit the passage very well, and are Ciceronian in style. Moreover it

1 Comp. *libera legatio*, *libera administratio peculi*, *etc.* and of this very matter: *ei qui sine cretione heres institutus sit, liberum est, quocumque tempore voluerit, adire hereditatem* (Gai. ii 167).

2 Schmidt is disposed now to believe the words genuine. See *Philologus* for 1896, pp. 709 and 717, and C. F. Müller's edition 1898, Pref. p. cxxvi.

is difficult to justify *ille*, if Vestorius had not been mentioned. It is true a like *ille* occurs in the next letter without Vestorius having been there named, but, as it is in the same connexion as in this epistle, where he is named more than once, the omission is comparatively unimportant. Schmidt's notion that *cretio testibus praesentibus* was a 'technical' expression for 'acceptance through an agent' seems to me baseless, and the expression quite unsuitable. I am sorry to see that Tyrrell and Purser in their excellent edition have (evidently rather against their own judgment) allowed themselves to be partly persuaded by Schmidt. Müller retains the words which Schmidt omits.

5. I translate the principal portions of the quoted passages thus: 'I learnt from Balbus the acceptance directed by 'Cluvius—how careless of Vestorius (not to have sent me 'word)—a free acceptance in the presence of witnesses, within '60 days. I was afraid I should have to send for him (Vestorius) 'to come here: now I must send to him to accept on my order: 'this same Pollex then must go.'

In the next letter: 'That same Pollex must be sent back 'to Puteoli to get him to accept. Clearly *I* could not go 'there.'

Except for the uncertainty as to the precise meaning of *liberam*, the passages seem straight and clear enough. Vestorius was to accept the inheritance by Cicero's order, and Pollex was to take him the order. Cicero was appointed heir along with some others, Caesar apparently being one; the testator left some legacies but none were charged on Cicero's share. Whether *nobis* refers to Cicero only or to Cicero and Caesar is not clear.

Karlowa (*RG.* ii 899) and Tyrrell take the subject of *cernat* to be Pollex. In that case we must remove the punctuation after *cernat* in the first letter, and then the position of *igitur* near the end of the sentence becomes strange. In the second letter, as Pollex is mentioned in the principal sentence, it seems impossible to refer *ille* in the final clause to him. And Cicero would hardly have written *mittendum* in the first letter instead of *mittendus* as in the second. Boot in his note on this letter takes, as I do, Vestorius to be the subject of *cernat*.

Karlowa apparently takes Pollex to have been made heir by Cluvius and Cicero therefore to become heir through him. I see no hint of such an institution. If Pollex acted in the *cretio*, it must have been as messenger only: and it is in a capacity analogous to that of a messenger that I conceive Vestorius to have been meant to act. For this purpose a freeman was as suitable as a slave, possibly more so in the case of an inheritance. But there are objections, which have been brought or might be brought against a freeman like Vestorius being supposed to act in this matter on Cicero's behalf.

6. The first objection is that Cicero would then acquire the inheritance in some sort 'through a free person,' whereas it is a well-known rule *per extraneam personam nobis acquiri non posse*[1], all persons being 'outsiders' who are not our slaves or our children. The only exception according to Gaius (ii 95) is possibly that of possession. By Paul's time the doubt was removed. He says (v 2 § 2) *per liberas personas quae in potestate non sunt adquiri nobis nihil potest; sed per procuratorem adquiri nobis possessionem posse utilitatis causa receptum est.* See also D. xli 1 fr 54 pr; xiii 7 fr 11 § 6; Cod. iv 27 § 1. There is no doubt that the primary reference of this maxim is not to the use of free persons in the process of acquisition, but to the transference *ipso facto* of their acquisitions to us. A son or slave was as it were a hand of his father or master: what he took was no sooner acquired by him than it passed to his superior. If he were instituted heir and accepted the inheritance, he thereby became heir, but the inheritance did not rest with him for a moment but passed at once to his father or master (D. xxix 2 fr 79). So if he stipulated, it made no matter whether he stipulated for himself or his superior; the latter in either case at once acquired the right to the promise (D. xlv 3 fr 1 pr). In the case of mancipation, as the usual form required the mancipatee to assert that the thing was his own by the law of the Quirites, and no slave could be such an owner, the slave used a modified form, asserting the ownership on the part of his master. *Hanc*

[1] It is amusing to see the ever-present dread lest one should be thought guilty of violation of this principle: cf. D. ii 14 fr 27 § 1; xxii 1 fr 24 § 2; xlii 5 fr 12 pr; xliii 24 fr 3 pr.

rem ex jure Quiritium L. Titi domini mei esse aio eaque ei empta esto hoc aere aeneaque libra (Gai. i 119; iii 167)[1].

In none of these cases could a procurator or other free person acquire in this direct way for his principal. An inheritance given to the procurator remained with him; a stipulation for another was invalid; *alteri stipulari nemo potest* (D. xlv 1 fr 38 § 17; Gai. iii 103); nor by mancipation or any other form could he acquire an obligation for his principal. But where his action was not of a legal or abstract but of a physical character, as by taking delivery of an object, by occupying land, by putting a borrower in possession of his principal's money, in such cases, if the action was intended for his principal, the principal acquired the right, whatever it was (D. xli 1 fr 53; xlv 1 fr 126 § 2). And further an agent lending his own money to another by his principal's wish and in the name of his principal acquired for his principal the right of requiring repayment of the loan from the borrower (D. xii 1 fr 9 § 8). Compare the acquisition of a *precarium* (D. xliii 26 fr 6 § 1; cf. fr 4 § 2). Nor are cases wanting which relate to the acquisition of a deceased's estate. For *bonorum possessio* could be acquired through an outsider (D. xxxvii 1 fr 3 § 7 and xxix 2 fr 48): and the acceptance of *bon. poss.* involved acting as heir (*pro herede gestio* Cod. vi 30 fr 12)[2]. And the transference of an inheritance from the heir by law to the heir by trust could be effected not only by passive acquiescence on the part of the former and apprehension on the part of the latter, but by a letter or a message (D. xxxvi 1 fr 38 pr). These cases are however of a different character from a formal entry on an inheritance by cretion.

7. Without going into the whole question of representation, it may be well to observe that three things require to be kept distinct: (1) representation by my son (under power) or my slave; (2) representation by my mandatee or procurator, *etc.* who acquires for himself but is answerable to me his principal, and

[1] As regards *in jure cessio* a slave could not act at all, because it was a form of suit, and slaves could not appear as suitors in court.

[2] See Köppen *System d. Erbrechts* p. 387. *Contra* Brinz *Pand.* iii 188 n. 25.

must by separate subsequent proceeding give me the benefit of his acquisition: and (3) representation by someone acting by my order and on my behalf and acquiring nothing for himself, *i.e.* in the main as a mere messenger (*e.g.* in making a *constitutum*, D. xiii 5 fr 15), but in some cases having a certain choice as to the particular action to be taken[1]. It is in such a capacity that a procurator took possession. *Procurator alienae possessioni praestat ministerium* (D. xli 2 fr 18 pr). And in a similar capacity he acts when giving a formal prohibition (D. xliii 24 fr 3 pr). Is there anything in *cretio* which would be incompatible with representation in this last sense?

Our information respecting *cretio* is scanty, because *cretio*, having been partly abolished by a constitution of A.D. 407, was wholly abolished by Justinian, and hence does not further appear in his law books (Cod. Theod. viii 18 fr 8 § 1; Cod. Just. vi 30 fr 17). The argument against Vestorius being employed by Cicero to do the act of *cernere* for him, so far as derived from the nature of cretion, may perhaps be put thus. (*a*) *Cretio* has a solemn unalterable form of words given by Gaius and Ulpian; (*b*) it requires, to use the words of these constitutions, 'a scrupulous ceremony'; and (*c*) the declaration is suited only to the heir himself speaking in the first person (*me heredem instituit, hereditatem adeo cernoque*). Moreover (*d*) *cernere* includes *adire*; *aditio hereditatis* was an *actus legitimus* (D. L 17 fr 77); and *nemo alieno nomine lege agere potest* (*ib.* fr 123). I deal with these points in order.

8. (*a*) I see no reason to suppose that the words of *cretio* given us are intended to be taken as the only apt words without admitting any modification or addition[2]. They are actually given somewhat differently by Ulpian, who omits *testamento suo* from Gaius' formula, and does not direct the heir *cernere, id est, haec verba dicere* (as Gaius expresses it) but *verba cretionis ad hunc modum dicere* 'to speak words of acceptance in this fashion.' They are simple natural words, but, if used by a procurator declaring his principal's acceptance, would require modification,

[1] See similar language in Savigny *Obl.* ii p. 56 sqq.

[2] See a similar case in Vat. 318.

just as the ordinary form of mancipation was modified when used by a slave (see above, p. 400).

(*b*) Allowing for the grandiloquent style of the imperial constitutions, *scrupulosa solemnitas* is abundantly satisfied by an heir being compelled to gather witnesses and utter a formula. Had there been any further ceremony required, Gaius and Ulpian would not have described *cernere* in such simple terms. It would be natural for an important declaration to be made before witnesses (else how could it be proved?), and Varro tells us that testators or 'people' generally directed this, as in our case (*L. L.* vi 81 *itaque in cretione adhibere jubent testes*), but our legal authorities say nothing about it. Again it would be natural to make the acceptance at the abode of the testator[1], but again our authorities are silent. In truth whatever may have been customary or natural or prudent, we have no right to assume (unless special directions were given by the testator) that anything more was required by law for the validity of the act than the utterance of such a declaration as above within the time prescribed[2]. The Autun interpretation of Gaius (Krüger, 4th ed. pp. l—liii) makes no mention of anything else.

(*c*) Kuntze (*Cursus* § 856) makes a point of the personal character of the declaration. No doubt the acceptance of an inheritance was an act of will, and the will had to be expressed. There are three ways at least in which this could easily be done: First, A letter declaring his acceptance might be written and sent by Cicero. Roman declarations were however usually oral, though a written record might be made of them. Thus, secondly, Cicero might collect some witnesses where he was, and in their hearing utter the words of acceptance. A protocol (*testatio*) might be drawn up, communicated to Vestorius, and

[1] Voigt asserts that this was essential, but he has no authority beyond this passage of Cicero (*Die XII Tafeln* ii 372).

[2] Cujas (*Obs.* vii 19; also in *Op.* iv 1700) has a curious notion that both *aditio* and *cretio* were accompanied by a snap of the fingers. The notion arose from a misunderstanding of Cic. *Off.* iii 19 § 75 found in St Ambrose (*Off.* iii 11 § 70) *Non ego in hereditatibus adeundis digitorum percussiones et nudi successoris saltationes notabo*, to whom Gibbon also refers (*Decline, etc.* ch. xliv).

read out at Puteoli for the information of those concerned. But if this were intended, Cicero would have given some hint of it, and neither this nor the preceding suggestion could properly be described as sending off Pollex to Vestorius *ut ille cernat.* Even if Cicero had mainly in mind certain practical arrangements with his coheirs, such as the division of the cash in the house and other like matters (see preceding letter, No. 45) requiring prompt attention, *cernere* could scarcely be used of those exclusively and not imply that the agent was to do the formal act itself.

A third way therefore seems to be most likely, viz. that Vestorius should at a suitable time and place declare Cicero's acceptance in some such words as these: *Quod Cluvius testamento suo M. Tullium Ciceronem heredem instituit, eam hereditatem jussu ejusdem M. Tulli, nomine ejus, adeo cernoque.* As Cicero was only part heir, possibly the share would be mentioned after *heredem, e.g. ex triente, ex quadrante, etc.*

(*d*) The fourth argument seems to be made much of generally, but, I think, breaks down on examination. Entry on an inheritance was no doubt a statutable proceeding (D. L 17 fr 77), *i.e.* it was part of the old civil law which was supposed to rest on the authority of the XII tables (see p. 95 n.). Papinian says in accordance with the ordinary doctrine that it did not admit of a conditional or anticipatory performance; but he does not say that it could not be done by a procurator[1]. And as a matter of fact we are practically told that one of these so-called statutable proceedings, viz. *acceptilatio* (though it could not be done by a slave, D. xlvi 4 fr 22), could be done by a procurator (*ib.* fr 3, where the suggested omission of *sine* seems to me to leave an intolerable sentence, and is against the Basilica). Nor is the argument improved by bringing in D. L 17 fr 123;

[1] Cujas (*Op.* iv 1697) does say so, and gives an artificial explanation of D. xlvi 4 fr 3. But his view was no doubt largely influenced by supposing that in D. xxix 2 fr 90 entry by a procurator was expressly denied. (In commenting on the passage however (*Op.* v 1946) he reads *per curatorem* but argues *a fortiori* against a procurator having the power.) The Florentine reading *per curatorem* is now accepted. That a madman's or youth's *curator* could not accept for his charge is a widely different case from acceptance on a sound fully-grown man's order.

for the meaning of that passage when Ulpian wrote it doubtless had reference to the old *legis actio* as a judicial proceeding. (Accordingly Lenel *Paling.* ii p. 494 puts it among matter relating to the centumviral jurisdiction.) What was meant by Justinian is difficult to say, but does not concern the interpretation of Cicero. I cannot think that Justinian could have declared entry by a procurator invalid when in his legislation, no less than before, absolutely no form was required, and mere will (*nuda voluntas*) was sufficient (D. xxix 2 fr 88, fr 95, *etc.*; Gai. ii 167, 169). As Doneau (*Com.* vii 9) says, an order to a procurator to accept is an *indicium voluntatis* (cf. D. xxix 2 fr 88). Moreover acceptance by a messenger is incidentally mentioned in the Digest (xxxvi 1 fr 67 § 3 *hereditatem adire, quomodo absentis per nuntium*). See Vering *Erbrecht* p. 497 and notes.

9. The result is that so far as *aditio* was concerned, no form was necessary, which a procurator acting on the heir's order could not fulfil. And as regards *cretio* I see nothing to make a personal oral declaration by the heir necessary; else how could a dumb person ever have become heir *cum cretione*? And even if it was, Cicero could have supplied the deficiency by an utterance of the supposed magical words in his villa or anywhere before despatching Pollex. But all doubt may reasonably give way under the plain words of Cicero, who speaks of deputing Vestorius to *cernere* as the natural course of procedure, when he did not find it convenient to go to Puteoli himself. It is impossible to suppose that he did not perfectly well know what he was about.

10. The ordinary conception or misconception of the matter is due, I suspect, to the false reading of *procuratorem* instead of *curatorem* in D. xxix 2 fr 90[1]; and to forgetting that the sense in which the Roman lawyers speak of *acquirere per servum* and deny *acquirere per liberum hominem* is quite different from an acceptance by a procurator in the name and by the previous order of the heir named in the will.

[1] The Florentine MS., supported by the Basilica, has *curatorem*, and this is retained by Mommsen. See also Windscheid *Pand.* § 596 n. 11. (Vangerow even in his last edit. (§ 498) quotes the passage with *procuratorem.*)

Neither of two recent writers on Representation refer to this passage of Cicero. Hellmann (*Stellvertretung* p. 106) is favorable to the possibility of representation in acceptance of an inheritance and interprets Cod. vi 30 fr 4 as referring to *cretio.* Mitteis (*Stellvertretung* p. 19; cf. p. 76) is unfavorable[1], but his argument appears to ignore the fact that a slave can take by mancipation distinctly in the name and on the account of his master.

[1] So also in *ZRG.* xxxiv p. 200.

BOOK IV.

PROPERTY

AND

(PRINCIPAL) SUITS *IN REM*.

In rem actio est, cum aut corporalem rem intendimus nostram esse aut jus aliquod nobis competere, veluti utendi aut utendi fruendi eundi agendi aquamve ducendi vel altius tollendi prospiciendive: actio ex diverso adversario est negativa (Gai. *Inst.* iv § 3).

In rem actio est per quam rem nostram, quae ab alio possidetur, petimus: et semper adversus eum est qui rem possidet (Ulpian *Inst.* ap. D. xliv 7 fr 25 pr).

CHAPTER I.

WHAT THINGS ARE NOT PRIVATE PROPERTY?

1. Some things are beyond human control (*extra nostrum patrimonium*), such as the sea and air and flowing water. Others again are put beyond human control by being devoted to the gods.

Subject to the rights of the gods (*divini juris*) are *res sacrae, res religiosae* and in some degree *res sanctae.* Such things are not part of the estate of any individual (*nullius in bonis sunt*), or a possible subject of private acquisition.

(*a*) *Res sacrae*[1] are such as are consecrated to the gods above; *res religiosae* are such as are abandoned to the Gods *Manes, i.e.* to the Beings of after-life.

Nothing is considered to be *sacred* except what has been made so by the authority of the Roman people either by a law or by a senate's decree passed therefor[2]. In the provinces there may be things which have not been consecrated by

[1] Gallus Aelius (ap. Fest. pp. 289, 318, Bruns[6] pp. 32, 34) agrees generally with Gaius (who may have taken it from him or other republican jurists) but points out that the words *sacer, religiosus, sanctus* can also be used in more general meanings. He defines *sacer* thus: *sacrum esse quodcunque more atque instituto civitatis consecratum sit, sive aedis sive ora sive signum sive locus sive pecunia sive quid aliud quod dis dedicatum atque consecratum sit: quod autem privati suae religionis causa aliquid earum rerum dedicent, id pontifices Romanos non existimare sacrum. At si qua sacra privata suscepta sunt...ille locus ubi ea sacra privata facienda sunt vix videtur sacer esse.*

[2] Cicero refers to a *lex Papiria* forbidding any temple, land, or altar being consecrated without the order of the Commons (*injussu plebis*), and to the practice in this respect (*Dom.* 49—53). In accordance with this practice his own house was declared by the *Pontifices* to be unaffected by Clodius' consecration (*Ep. Att.* iv 2).

authority of the Roman people; but by their former lords, and these are not properly sacred but are counted as such (*pro sacro habetur*)[1]. A *sacrarium*, made in a private place to contain sacred things, is not sacred.

(*b*) A place is made *religious*[2] by private will, *i.e.* by placing therein a corpse, provided that the soil is our own (or conceded for the purpose by the owner) and that his burial duly belongs to the person so acting. As regards the provinces, the ownership of the soil being in the Roman people or the emperor, and private persons seeming to have only the possession or usufruct thereof, the soil is held by most lawyers not to become strictly religious, but anyhow it is counted as religious. The burying-places of public enemies are not recognised as religious, nor are Roman burying-places, when and so long as they are captured by the enemy. See above, p. 392 sq.

(*c*) Inviolable things (*res sanctae*) are such as the walls and gates of a town; the violation of these, as by crossing the wall instead of passing through the gates, was prohibited under capital penalties (Gai. ii 1—8; D. i 8 fr 2, 6 §§ 3, 4; fr 11; xi 7, fr 36; xlvii 12 fr 4).

Purus locus is that which is neither *sacer*, nor *sanctus*, nor *religiosus* (D. xi 7 fr 2 § 4).

2. Of things subject to human rights some seem not to belong to the estate of anyone, for they are believed to be the property of the community as a whole; others are private, *i.e.* are the property of individuals (Gai. ii 11).

The sea and its shores, a river and its banks, are common to all to use; and hence ports and banks are open to all for the usual purposes of navigation, putting in to land, depositing loads, drying nets, fastening boats, even to the trees on the banks, fishing, *etc.* But the ownership of a river's banks and

[1] A question having been raised by Pliny whether a temple at Nicomedia could be moved, Trajan replied *Nec te moveat quod lex dedicationis nulla reperitur, cum solum peregrinae civitatis capax non sit dedicationis quae fit nostro jure* (*Ep. ad Traj.* 50).

[2] Cf. Cic. *Legg.* ii 23 § 58 *Ut in urbe sepeliri lex vetat, sic decretum a pontificum collegio non esse jus in loco publico fieri sepulchrum....Statuit collegium locum publicum non potuisse privata religione obligari.* The connexion of *religio* with burials is spoken of throughout *capp.* 22, 23.

of the trees on it is private, and is in the proprietors of the adjoining land (D. i 8 fr 4 § 5). The seashore extends to the line reached by the highest flow (*maximus fluctus*, D. L 16 fr 96, 112)[1]. A river's banks are from the line of fullest stream, *i.e.* from the commencement of slope from the level, down to the water (D. xliii 12 fr 3).

3. Protection of public and sacred places.

(*a*) The rights of the public were protected and regulated partly by public officers, partly by interdicts (which could be brought by any member of the public) or by other suits of law. Permission to build on a public place, to lead water from a navigable river, to take the profits of some public place, is granted by the emperor or public officers (D. xliii 8 fr 2 §§ 10, 16; tit. 9 fr 1; tit. 12 fr 2). Special city officers are charged with the oversight of the streets and their protection from being dug up, occupied or obstructed, the inhabitants being required to keep their buildings from falling, and their watercourses and the parts of the streets opposite to their houses clean. The levelling of the streets, the cleansing of the streams, and provision of bridges where necessary, are for the public officers (D. xliii 10; cf. xviii 6 fr 13). If highways in the country are blocked wholly or seriously, the magistrates interfere (D. xliii 8 fr 2 § 25; Paul v 6 § 2). A senate's decree (B.C. 7) provided for the water-commissioners to take earth, stones, sand, wood, *etc.* for the repair of the aqueducts from private lands in the neighbourhood against compensation, and for rights of way for the purpose (Frontin. *Aq.* 125).

(*b*) Anyone could build in the sea or on the seashore, unless it was to the injury of others. Eventually a decree of the praetor's was required to authorise it. Fishermen can build on the seashore houses of refuge, and are owners so long as the houses stand; but if they fall or are removed, the ground reverts to the public (D. i 5 fr 1, 2 pr; xli i fr 14, 50; xliii

[1] Celsus in the Digest (L 16 fr 96, cf. fr 112) refers the first establishment of this definition according to common report (*aiunt*) to Cicero himself, acting as arbitrator. But this is, as Mommsen notes, probably a mistaken reference to Cic. *Top.* 7 § 32 *Solebat Aquilius...cum de litoribus ageretur, quae omnia publica esse voltis...ita definire litus, 'qua fluctus eluderet.'*

8 fr 2 § 8, fr 3, 4). The free use of the sea is protected by the action *injuriarum*; anyone likely to be damaged by a mole, *etc.* can bring an interdict (D. xliii 8 fr 2 § 8).

(*c*) All rivers which have a perennial flow are public: and lakes with perpetual water are also public. The free navigation in them is protected by an interdict; and so is the right of driving cattle to them. If the fishing of a lake or port is let out to a *publicanus*, he is similarly protected (D. xliii 14). Repairs to their banks are open to anyone to effect, if he give security to the neighbours against possible injury to the navigation within ten years. After the work has been done, no interdict will lie, but anyone injured must resort to the *lex Aquilia* (D. xliii 15; cf. xxxix 2 fr 24).

Interdicts run against anyone who does anything on or puts anything into a public river or its banks so as to impair the navigation or mooring (*statio*) or change the measure or character of the stream from what it was in the summer of a year back (cf. chap. vii 2). Subject to such limits, building is open (D. xxxix 2 fr 24 pr). An owner of both banks has no right to build a private bridge over the stream. Other interdicts run to compel anyone, who keeps such construction whether done by himself or others (*factum vel immissum habet*), to restore the former condition. Nor according to the better opinion had defendant a right to a plea that it was done only 'for repairing the banks,' though such a plea might be allowed after due hearing of the case: he had a right according to Labeo to the plea of the work being done 'as was allowed by statute' (D. xliii 12, 13; Gai. iv 159).

(*d*) Public (country) roads and their free use are similarly protected by interdicts couched in the same language. Discharge of drains into a public road, building so as to prevent the water on it from passing off, allowing cattle to feed there so as to injure it, altering its character, building on it whether a monument or anything else, come within the interdicts. If a tree fall on to the road, the owner, unless he choose to abandon it, must as in other cases remove it and restore the road. Not only main highways (*viae praetoriae* or *consulares*) but also public footpaths (*iter*) and many country roads (*vicinales*), which are for the general uses of villages (*vici*) and have not been made at private expense or have been made in immemorial times, are public roads within these interdicts. Repair of a road by private contributions does not make them private. In private roads the soil is the property of private persons: in public roads the soil is public. Anyone can bring the interdict, the damages being limited to his interest. If a person has not done the work, or ordered it or approved it, he is not bound to restore but only to allow restoration (D. xliii 7; 8 fr 2 §§ 20—45). Anyone is allowed to repair a road, if he does not make it worse; but he must not alter its character by putting gravel on, or paving an earth road, or substituting earth for pavement (D. xliii 11).

(*e*) Public places generally are protected by a similar interdict against anything being done or put in them which damages a person, unless the doer has a right granted by statute, senate's decree, edict or decree of the emperor. 'Public place' includes occupied or unoccupied ground in the city or country intended for the public use, but not what is the property of the Crown (*fiscus*). Injury consists in the deprivation of the convenience or advantage afforded by the public place; *e.g.* obstruction or lessening of access or prospect or light. The interdict goes only to forbid, and to require security against doing; not to require restoration. If a building has been erected on public ground without anyone's objecting, the owner is not required to pull it down: that might make the city unsightly; but if it is found to obstruct the public convenience, the state officer will either remove it or impose a rent (*vectigal, solarium*, D. xliii 8 fr 2 pr—§ 18 fr 7). If such buildings, *e.g.* bankers' shops, are sold, the purchaser acquires only the use (xviii 1 fr 32). Statues or pictures (*imagines*) for the ornament of a town are usually allowed to be placed in public (xliii 8, 9 fr 2).

(*f*) Sacred places are protected both by a prohibition of similar character and (on religious grounds) by a requirement of restoration (D. xliii 6 fr 1; 8 fr 2 § 19; Gai. iv 159).

CHAPTER II.

DISTINCTIONS OF THINGS, AND OF RIGHTS OVER THEM.

1. An important distinction among things (*res*), which are the subject of private rights, is between tangible or corporal things and certain aggregates or claims which relate to concrete things but are themselves abstractions[1]. Corporal or tangible things are such as land, houses, slaves, dress, gold, silver, *etc.* Incorporal things are such as *jure consistunt*, *i.e.* whose substance is not physical matter, but matter of legal conception, for instance, an inheritance, an usufruct, an obligation. An inheritance (or succession to the estate of a deceased person) no doubt includes the land or slaves or cattle or other corporal things which belonged to the deceased: an usufruct contains a taking of the fruits of the earth; an obligation often includes demanding and getting land or slaves or money; but the right of succeeding to a deceased's estate, the right of using and taking the fruits, the right of control over the acts and services of one who is under an obligation are in themselves incorporal. So also is the right of control over others' land or houses, which right is called *servitus*, 'easement' (Gai. ii 12—14). This distinction comes especially into prominence in reference to acquisition and transfer.

2. The principal rights recognised by Roman law in and over things are ownership (*dominium*) and *servitutes*. Pledge gave rise to a limited right over things and will be treated in connexion with contracts. *Emphyteusis* and *superficies* were long tenancies of land and houses arising from lease (see Book v). Possession is a fact, which is usually a consequence and cause of rights: it will be treated below (chap. iv).

[1] Cf. Cic. *Top.* v § 27 *Duo genera prima; unum earum rerum quae sunt, alterum earum quae intelleguntur. Esse ea dico quae cerni tangique possunt, ut fundum, aedes, parietem, stillicidium, mancipium, pecudem, supellectilem, penus et cetera. Non esse rursus ea dico quae tangi demonstrarive non possunt, cerni tamen animo atque intellegi possunt, ut si usucapionem si tutelam si gentem si agnationem definias, quarum rerum nullum subest quasi corpus.*

CHAPTER III.

OWNERSHIP (*DOMINIUM*).

A. Ownership is the full right of doing whatever one likes with a thing, using, alienating, destroying. In Rome it was limited[1] in the case of land and houses (1) by such control as the public authority imposed in the interest of the people at large, (2) by the rights of neighbours, (3) by the previous voluntary action of the owner himself or his predecessors in title. Otherwise the owner of land has the full and free use of all above and below his land.

As examples of the first may be taken the prohibition of (buying or) selling houses in order to pull them down, which was made by a senate's decree under Claudius A.D. 44 (Bruns[6] No. 51; D. xviii 1 fr 52; cf. xxxix 2 fr 48; *lex Urson.* 75); and again by Vespasian (Cod. viii 10 fr 2. See also D. xxx fr 41 §§ 1—6). Or again the prohibition of an occupier's allowing anything to remain on the eaves or a projection from his house which might fall and injure passers by (see Book V chap. v ii 3). Or the town-rules for a certain space to be left round each *insula* (2½ feet?; cf. Fest. *s.v. ambitus*; D. viii 2 fr 14 *legitimo spatio*); and for limiting the height of houses, *e.g.* 70 feet for houses on public roads: so Augustus ordered (Strab. v 3, 7); similarly Nero (Tac. *A.* xv 43), *etc.* See also divers rules respecting interments (Book III chap. xii).

Examples of the second are seen in certain old proceedings of the civil law (chap. viii); in numerous interdicts (chap. vii); and in *finium regundorum actio* (chap. iii F 4), *etc.* Examples of the third are servitudes.

Interference with ownership of slaves is seen in the prohibition by senate's decree of the sale or gift of a slave while he was still in flight (D. xlviii 15 fr 2; Cod. ix 20 fr 7).

The ownership of a thing may belong to two or more persons in common. So long as the common farm or slave or thing is undivided or unallotted, none is full owner of the

[1] See a careful list of limitations in Böcking *Pand.* § 140.

whole (*in solidum*); but the rights of each extend in due proportion over every part of it: *totius corporis pro indiviso pro parte dominium habet* (Celsus, *ap.* D. xiii 6 fr 5 § 15). The common ownership may arise by descent, or legacy, or gift, or contract, *etc.* It is sometimes joint, so that the survivor becomes exclusive owner; sometimes tenancy in common, so that the share does not accrue to the survivor but passes to successors.

Ownership is acquired in different ways, which may be classed under two heads, as original and derivative. Under the former come cases in which appropriation takes place of what has not previously been private property of any Roman, or, if it has, has apparently ceased to be so. Under the second head come cases in which, either by one-sided action or judicial decision or voluntary transference, we acquire what was wholly or partly others' property. Voluntary transference by, or in pursual of, agreement between the parties may well be treated as a separate head. Acquirement by usucapion or adverse possession is best treated after voluntary transference, to which it often formed a sequel and complement.

B. ORIGINAL ACQUISITION is made in several ways.

1. Occupation[1]. We become owners by seizure of what we catch on earth, or in sea or sky, whether we are on our own ground or not, provided the thing does not belong already to someone else.

[1] For original occupation of land there was in Gaius' time little opportunity; but Cicero refers to it (*Off.* i 7 § 21) *Sunt autem privata nulla natura sed aut vetere occupatione, ut qui quondam in vacua venerunt, aut victoria, ut qui bello potiti sunt, aut lege, pactione, condicione, sorte; ex quo fit, ut ager Arpinas Arpinatium dicatur, Tusculanus Tusculanorum, similisque est privatarum possessionum descriptio.* Here *lege* may refer to the XII tables with its sanction of wills, intestate inheritance, mancipation, *etc.* or to laws distributing land among colonists (cf. Sic. Flac. p. 163 Lachmann); *pactione, condicione* to public arrangements with allied or subject states (cf. Cic. *Balb.* 6 § 15), or to land held on terms from the State (*e.g.* Liv. xxxi 13 §§ 7—9; Cic. *Verr.* ii 36 § 12), or in private matters to purchase of land; *sorte* to distribution of public land by lot (cf. Hygin. Grom. p. 200 Lachm.).

(*a*) Such are wild beasts, birds, fish; they are ours as soon as we have caught them, and continue ours so long as we have them under our control. If they escape they recover their natural liberty, and anyone else may seize and own them unless they have been tamed. Escape is when they have got beyond our sight, or at least beyond our power of following and securing them. In the case of animals like pigeons, bees, deer, *etc.*, which are accustomed to go away and return, the traditional rule is that they continue ours, so long as they have the disposition (*animum*), that is to say the habit, of returning. Domestic fowls and geese remain ours, although they may have flown whither we know not. A swarm of bees ceases to be the owner's if it has passed out of his sight and ready capture: if it settles in our land, it is not thereby ours but becomes the property of whoever hives it: and any honeycomb which the bees have made belongs to him who seizes it. Of course one who goes on another's land and catches any wild animal is liable to be stopt and may be liable for trespass[1], but that does not affect the question of ownership of what he has caught (Gai. ii 66—68; D. xli 1 fr 3—5; xlvii 2 fr 26 pr).

(*b*) Precious stones and other things found on the seashore become the property of the finder by taking (D. i 8 fr 3). The same is the case with anything which has been intentionally abandoned (*derelictum*) by its owner. According to Proculus, it did not cease to be his property till taken by another, according to Julian (following Sabinus and Cassius), it ceased as soon as abandoned. But goods thrown overboard for lightening a ship in a storm, or accidentally fallen from a carriage, *etc.* are not to be regarded as derelicts, and seizure with a view to appropriation may be an act of theft (D. xli 1

[1] All that our authorities say is *potest a domino si is providerit jure prohiberi ne ingrederetur* (D. xli 1 fr 3). It is not clear that there is any legal redress for mere trespass for such a purpose. If injury is done, the Aquilian action is available: if a prohibition is defied with insolent purpose, the *actio injuriarum* applies; if the trespass is repeated, as if to claim an easement, the *negatoria* could be brought; if the owner's use of his own land is obstructed by the hunter, the interdict *uti possidetis* can be used (D. xliii 17 fr 3 § 2; cf. tit. 16 fr 11). See Czyhlarz, Glück's *Pand.* Book xli § 1727 *c*.

fr 9 § 8, 58; tit. 7 fr 1, 7; xlvii 2 fr 43 § 5). Things thrown among a crowd become the property of the seizer, either because they have been plainly abandoned, or because they are intentionally transferred as a gift to a previously unascertained person (D. xli 1 fr 9 § 7; tit. 7 fr 5 § 1).

(c) Treasure trove belongs to the finder, if it is in his own ground. (This rule is referred to a constitution of Hadrian.) If it is accidentally found in another's ground, then, by a constitution of M. Aurelius, one half goes to the finder and one half to the owner of the ground, whether a private person or the Crown or the public. If a husband find it in dowry land, one half is treated as part of the dowry. If it was found in sacred or religious ground, Hadrian appears to have given it all to the finder, but M. Aurelius to have given half to the Crown (Just. ii 1 § 39; D. xxiv 3 fr 7 § 12; xlix 14 fr 3 § 10. On the distribution when treasure is found by a common or fructuary's slave, see D. xli 1 fr 63). By treasure trove is meant an old deposit of money not recorded and therefore ownerless.

If money has been buried for safe-keeping and the depositor or owner is known, to take it is theft (D. xli 1 fr 31 § 1). If it be buried in another's ground, the owner of the treasure can bring an interdict to compel the owner of the ground to permit him to dig it up and take it away, giving guaranty against any damage caused thereby: an action *ad exhibendum* does not lie if the ground owner has not taken possession of it (D. x 4 fr 15). So money left in a house by a former owner through mistake or ignorance belongs to him, not to the purchaser of the house (D. vi 1 fr 67).

(d) Where land has been surveyed and distributed by the State, and thus has boundaries definitely set out (*ager limitatus*)[1], an island formed in a public river, or the old bed left by its changing its course belongs to no one and becomes the property of the first occupier (D. xliii 12 fr 1 §§ 6, 7).

2. Alluvion relates only to *ager non limitatus*. Anything washed on to our land, *i.e.* added by a river to our land so gradually that we cannot estimate how much is added in each moment of time, becomes ours. It is a kind of restoration

[1] See my article *Agrimetatio* in Smith's *Dict. Antiq.* ed. 3.

of what the stream has at other times carried away. But the case is different when a definite portion of land is cut off by a river from another's land and attached to mine: your property in the severed portion continues, unless and until in the course of time its trees put their roots into my land (Gai. ii 70, 71; D. xli 1 fr 7 §§ 1, 2). So also in the case of land slipping on to another's land (D. xxxix 2 fr 9 § 2).

If in the middle of a river a new island is formed, it is an accession to the land opposite, and is thus the property of the several owners of the banks on each side of the river, the middle line of the river and the length of the opposite bank owned by each determining the portions accruing to them respectively.

If the island is not in the middle of a river, it belongs to those who own land on the nearest bank. But if an island is formed by the river's taking a new course, the ownership of this land is not changed, and the old bed of the river becomes the property of those who own the adjoining land (Gai. ii 27; D. xli 1 fr 7 §§ 3—5; fr 29, 30, 38). Temporary inundation does not affect the property (fr 7 § 6).

3. Fruits and other produce, such as the young of animals and children of female slaves, belong to him who at the time of production owned the land, or mother. When separated from the parent stock they belong to him, or to anyone to whom (*e.g.* a farmer) he has granted the right to take and use as his own. But this is not always so.

The fruits of anything purchased or otherwise acquired in good faith, even though it turns out to have been acquired from one who was not the owner, become the property of an honest possessor as soon as they are separated from the parent stock[1]. Whether the seed or plants were his own or not, and whether he sowed them or not, does not affect the question. One who is a *bona fide* possessor does not, according to Julian, cease to be so, and to have this right, until he is evicted. But

[1] The matter is much debated, Savigny (*Besitz* § 22 *a* p. 279) holding that the *b. f. possessor* acquired only possession until usucapion; others that he acquired a true ownership (Vangerow *Pand.* vol. 1 p. 621); others again that he had a limited ownership (Windscheid *Pand.* § 186). But the position in the time of the classical jurists is still more doubtful.

others inclined to think the right ceased as soon as he became aware of his want of title. If evicted, he was perhaps liable to restore all fruits still unconsumed, and certainly all fruits whatever from the date of joinder of issue (see below G I). A fructuary is in the same position except that mere separation is not enough: he must gather or appropriate them in some way (*percipiat*) to make them his own. Of animals the milk, hair, and wool, and the young (lambs, kids, goats, foals) are all reckoned as fruits and follow the same law. The offspring of female slaves is not reckoned among fruits[1], and does not belong to a *bona fide* possessor or to a fructuary until he has acquired it by usucapion.

These rules apply (with some limitations, see chap. iv C i 5) even if that which produces the fruits has been stolen or taken by force; or has been acquired from a ward without his guardian's authority (before it was sold or otherwise passed to the *bona fide* possessor); or has been acquired from a woman knowingly without her guardian's authority, a woman having power to part with the possession, which is not a *res mancipi* (D. xli 1 fr 48, 66; tit. 3 fr 33 pr; xxii 1 fr 25, 28; Vat. 1; cf. Just. ii 1 § 37).

4. Capture from the public enemy is a good title to property (Gai. ii 69); and this applies to land, persons and moveables. All these when taken in war became the property of the State, but were often sold by auction to the highest bidder, or distributed to the soldiers or to colonists in full property. Besides, things belonging to the enemy might be in a Roman's possession, and, on war breaking out, became the property of the first occupant (D. xli 1 fr 51).

C. Derivative acquisition.

1. Combination. When two things belonging to different persons are joined together, the question of ownership of the combined product depends on the nature of the junction, on the relative importance of the things, and on the knowledge or consent of the parties. If the junction is readily dissoluble, so

[1] On the reason of this see my note on D. *de usufructu* fr 68 pr, p. 242.

27—2

as to restore the things to their original form, *e.g.* a silver cup with another's handle merely fastened to it by solder (*adplumbatum*), or something made by melting together my bronze and your silver, the ownership is not affected, and an action *ad exhibendum* will secure the production and separation of the things. But if the junction is indissoluble, as where the cup and its handle are joined by welding or fusion, especially of the same material (*ferruminatum*)[1], or my wool has been dyed with your purple, or you have written on my paper, even with letters of gold, the owner of the principal thing (in these cases the cup, the wool, the paper) becomes owner of the whole. The same is the case when plants belonging to one man have been put and become rooted in another's land, or corn has been sown in it; the owner of the land owns all. When however neither of the two things can be regarded as a mere accessory to the other, it is a question, probably in each particular case, whether they are still several properties, as Proculus and Pegasus thought, or common to both, or whether the whole is the property of the person on whose account the combination has been made. If the owner of the principal thing has wittingly taken another's accessory, he would be liable to an action for theft, and for production (as having fraudulently put it out of his power to restore), and vindication (or condiction). If he did it unwittingly, he is, according to the Digest, liable to an action on the case (*in factum*). If the union was made unwittingly by the party who has, under the rules stated, lost the ownership, he can, if in possession and sued for the whole, plead fraud, and thus recover the value of his thing, at least if a necessary or useful addition: if he acted wittingly, he will be taken to have waived his right: in neither case has he, if not in possession, any remedy.

Two cases require special notice, viz. building and painting.

(*a*) If a building be erected on one man's ground with another's materials, the building as a whole, unless otherwise agreed, is the property of the ground owner. *Superficies solo*

[1] Cf. Marquardt *Priv. Alt.* p. 663 note; Windscheid *Pand.* § 189; Dernburg *Pand.* § 209.

cedit. No vindication or action for production and separation is open to the owner of the materials. For the XII tables forbad the removal of a stolen beam fixed in a building or vineyard, and interpretation extended the prohibition to all materials in a building, not originally the owner's, whether actually stolen or not[1]. But under the statute the ground owner by a special action *de tigno juncto* (see Book V chap. VI B) was liable, if he took the materials, to pay twice the value, and if he had done so knowingly, he was liable also (as above) for production and vindication or condiction. On the other hand, if the house is pulled down, the other's right to the materials can then be reasserted, and all question of usucapion is excluded. If the owner of the materials built, knowing the ground to be another's, he thereby passed the property in them at once; if he built in the *bona fide* belief that the land was his own, he can, if in possession, plead fraud and recover his expenses.

(*b*) Painting on another's panel occasioned much dispute. According to Gaius (ii 78; cf. D. xli 1 fr 9 § 2) the better opinion was *tabulam picturae cedere,* that the painter became owner of the panel (though Gaius himself could hardly justify the anomaly), others keeping to the general rule that as the picture could not exist without the panel, the panel when painted remained the property of the original owner. Either party when suing, the painter, if owner, by a regular *vindicatio,* the other as not being the owner, by a *utilis vindicatio,* could be forced to repay the other the value of the panel or cost of the painting (Gai. ii 73—78; D. vi 1 fr 23 §§ 2—7, fr 39 pr, 59; x 4 fr 6, 7 pr—§ 2; xii 6 fr 33; xix 1 fr 45 § 1; xli 1 fr 7 § 10—fr 9 § 2, 12 § 1, 26—27; xlvii 3; Fest. *s.v. tignum*)[2].

2. Specification. Similar considerations arise when a person gives a new form to something belonging to another, *e.g.* if he makes wine or oil or corn out of another's grapes or olives or

[1] See D. xlvii 3 fr 1 § 1 for meaning of *tignum,* and comp. *tignum furtivum* of that fragment with *tignum alienum* of Gai. *ap.* D. xli 1 fr 7 § 10; Just. ii 1 § 29. Where consent was given, the double value was not obtainable (D. xxiv 1 fr 63).

[2] On some further questions see Pernice's *Labeo* ii 1 p. 319 ed. 2, and a full dogmatic statement in Schmid's *Handbuch* i pp. 137—167.

heads of grain; or makes a cup out of another's gold or silver; or a ship or cabinet or bench out of another's boards; or a woven dress out of another's wool, or mead out of another's wine and honey, or a plaster or ointment out of another's drugs. Whose is the new product? The Sabinians held that it belonged to the owner of the materials. The Proculians held that it belonged to the maker, the owner of the materials having an action for theft against one who had taken the materials secretly, and a condiction besides; a vindication was impossible, as the things had ceased to exist in their old forms. Some others held that the Sabinians were right, if the new thing could be reduced to the old form, as a silver cup by melting down; but that in other cases, as wine, the Proculian view must be taken (Gai. ii 79; D. xli 1 pr 7 § 7). Where the owner of the material consented to the operation, the thing belongs to the person on whose account it was made (D. *ib.* fr 25).

To this head may be referred buildings erected for fishing purposes on the seashore. They are the property of the builder so long as they last, but if they fall down the ground reverts to the public use. Eventually the praetor's consent appears to have been required for any erection, but the absence of this did not prevent the acquisition of ownership (D. i 8 fr 6 pr; xli 1 fr 14, 50). An erection in the sea, on piles or not, belongs to the builder (D. xli 1 fr 30 § 4).

3. Adjudication. In the three judicial proceedings for dividing what was in common between two or more persons, viz. for settling boundaries (*finibus regundis*), for partitioning a deceased's estate (*familiae erciscundae*), and for dividing anything held in common (*communi dividundo*), the judge had the power of assigning things in severalty to one or other of the parties, who thereupon became at once by adjudication owner of it, without any further formality (Ulp. xix 16).

4. By will we may acquire both an aggregate of rights and liabilities (Inheritance) and the property or rights in separate objects (Legacy). Acquisition of *caduca, etc.* under the *lex Papia Poppaea* has been treated in connexion with this (p. 382). On intestacy, the law or the praetor's action supplied the place of a will. (See Book III chapp. iii and v D.)

D. VOLUNTARY TRANSFERENCE among the living.

The natural modes for transfer of property are, as regards corporal things, delivery from hand to hand, or visible acquiescence in another's taking possession: as regards rights, which from their own nature are incapable of delivery or of visible possession, a transference may naturally be effected by assertion of the right by the one who is to be the gainer, and a declared acquiescence on the part of the other. Roman law, when first we find it, contains these two modes, but stiffened by tradition and practice into special forms. The former was *mancipium*[1], 'handtake,' or, as called later, *mancipatio* (*mancipium* then denoting usually not the act, but the right acquired by the act): the latter was *in jure cessio*, 'surrender in court'; both are older than the XII tables. The former was a fictitious sale; the latter a fictitious lawsuit. Things transferable by mancipation were called *res mancipi*; other things *res nec mancipi*[2].

(*a*) Mancipation was thus. The parties meet in the presence of not less than five witnesses[3], all Roman citizens of the

[1] Cf. Cic. *Top.* 5 § 28 *Abalienatio est ejus rei quae mancipi est aut traditio alteri nexu aut in jure cessio, inter quos ea jure civili fieri possunt.* (For *nexu*=*mancipio* see Essay on *nexum*, Book v.) Horace speaks of mancipation *Ep.* ii 2 158 *Si proprium est quod quis libra mercatus et aere est.* (On the different uses of *mancipium* see my *Lat. Gr.* Pt ii Pref. p. L *a*.)

[2] *Mancipi* is genitive of *mancipium*, 'things capable of handtake.' *Nec* is the older form of the negative particle. So in *nec manifestum furtum*.

[3] The epitome of Gaius i 6 § 3 speaks of five witnesses, a *libripens*, and *qui antestatus appellatur*. This last person is simply the person first called to witness (*ante-testatus*) and is included in the five witnesses. *Antestari* is found in the XII tables (*ap.* Porphyr. *ad* Hor. *Sat.* i 9 76), Plaut. *Curc.* 623, *Pers.* 747, *Poen.* 1230, Horat. *l.c.*, Plin. *H. N.* xiv 251; cf. Cic. *Mil.* 25 § 68, of asking a person, by touching his ear, to bear witness to a notice to appear in court. Aelius (or some other writer) is quoted by Priscian viii 16 as using the verb passively *impubes libripens esse non potest neque antestari* προδιαμαρτυρηθῆναι (cf. Ulpian xx 3 *testis aut libripens adhiberi non potest*), and it is used in a marble inscription (3rd cent. p. Chr.) of conveyance of a gift by mancipation (Bruns[6] no. 112). In two other earlier

age of puberty or upwards. An additional witness, called *libripens*, 'balance-weigher,' holds a bronze balance[1], as if for the purpose of weighing the metal. The acquirer by handtake (*qui mancipio accipit*) or purchaser (as still called in English conveyancing) holds a piece of bronze as a symbol of the price; and seizing the thing to be acquired, for instance a slave, says, 'This man I assert to be mine by the law of the Quirites, and it shall be bought for me with this bronze and bronze balance' (*Hunc ego hominem ex jure Quiritium meum esse aio isque mihi emptus esto hoc aere aeneaque libra*); then he strikes the balance with the bronze[2] and hands it to the other party (or vendor). This was the regular form between Roman citizens for the conveyance of those things which constituted in primitive times the principal subjects of ownership, viz. land and houses on Italian soil[3]: slaves; beasts of burden and draught, or, as the Romans expressed it, beasts tamed by neck or back, *i.e.* oxen, horses, mules, asses. The Sabinians considered such beasts to be always *res mancipi*, but the Proculians held that they were not so until they were either tamed, or, if too wild to be tamed, came to the age at which such beasts were usually tamed. The former view appears to have been generally

inscriptions of the same character (Bruns[6] nos. 111, 114) it is used actively *antestatus est Ti. Erotem, etc.* So in the Greek translation of a will made by C. Longinus Castor A.D. 189 we have ἀντεμαρτύρατο Μάρκον Σεμπρώνιον Ἡρακλίανον (*ZRG.* xxix 198; Girard *Textes* p. 728). The classical lawyers have no such word. In a will *per aes et libram* the testator with them bids all witnesses *testimonium perhibere* (a technical phrase), and this (with other mancipations) is what is referred to in the XII tables *Qui se scierit testarier libripensve fuerit, ni testimonium fariatur* (*fatiatur* some conjecture), *improbus intestabilisque esto* (Gell. xv 13 § 11).

1 The scales and witnesses were remnants of a time when there was no coined money, and they were in fact necessary to make the tender of metal into a tender of price properly ascertained. The witnesses represented the people. Cf. Bekker *Act.* i 23.

2 An old phrase is reported by Festus p. 265 *In mancipando cum dicitur 'rudusculo libram ferito,' asse tangitur libra.*

3 Italian soil had these legal qualities: it was mancipable, admitted of usucapion, was entered in the census and thus liable to the burghers' taxation; and was taken as security for public contracts (see Cic. *Flac.* 32 § 80 quoted below, p. 479, note 1). On the *jus Italicum* see Mommsen *Staatsr.* iii. 1. p. 806 foll. ed. 2.

adopted. Elephants and camels became known to the Romans too late to be included in this class. One class of incorporal things were also so conveyed, viz. servitudes attached to land, obviously because they were usually for convenience conveyed along with the land itself and regarded as accessory to it. Slaves and animals had to be present, when the mancipation was performed, and each had to be seized, alone or together: land and the servitudes thereto attached could be mancipated at a distance and several at the same time, some clod or other symbol no doubt being used (Gai. i 119, 120; ii 14—17, 104; Ulp. xix 1, 3—6).

(*b*) Surrender in court (*in jure cessio*) was thus. The parties appeared before a magistrate of the Roman people, usually the praetor; in the provinces before the governor. The acquirer holding the thing says: 'This thing I assert to be mine by the law of the Quirites' (*Hunc ego hominem ex jure Quiritium meum esse aio*). After he has thus formally claimed it (*vindicavit*), the praetor asks the other party whether he makes any counter-claim, and if he says no, or is silent, the praetor assigns (*addicit*) the thing to the claimant. This form was applicable both to corporal and to incorporal things, but mancipation being done anywhere, and surrender in court requiring the attendance before the magistrate, the former was usually adopted (*plerumque et fere semper*), when it was possible. Moreover slaves could be used for mancipation (the slave saying not *meum esse*, but *e.g. L. Titi domini mei esse aio*, Gai. iii 167). For surrender in court, which professed to be a judicial proceeding, slaves were not competent. Nor could any persons under power take a surrender in court, for nothing could be 'their own' in strict law. For incorporal rights (except rural servitudes) mancipation was not applicable, and it is for the creation and transference of these, especially urban and personal servitudes, that surrender in court was chiefly used. But it was not applicable either to provincial lands or to servitudes of any kind in them (Gai. ii 24, 25, 31, 32, 96; Ulp. xix 9—11)[1].

[1] Varro (*R. R.* ii 10 § 4) gives an enumeration of the principal modes in which a vendor of slaves may have got and therefore could give a good title: *In emptionibus dominum legitimum sex fere res perficiunt; si heredi-*

As the form of mancipation was gone through for many purposes, and it was often necessary or desirable to state the particulars and terms of the contract, a declaration usually preceded or accompanied it, at first oral (*nuncupatio*), afterwards reduced to writing. This formed the *lex mancipi* and was taken to be made authoritative as between the parties by the XII tables. *Cum nexum faciet mancipiumque, uti lingua nuncupassit ita jus esto* (Cinc. *apud* Fest. *s.v. nuncupatio*). Something of the same kind must have taken place when *in jure cessio* was the form used, a form also confirmed by the XII tables (Vat. 50). In practice no doubt the formal conveyance was preceded by negotiations and agreements between the parties, which would be a *pactum* (or *pactio*) and might perhaps be simply referred to in the *nuncupatio* and thus incorporated into the conveyance. See the case of wills (above, pp. 177, 178).

(*c*) All things which did not come within the restricted class of *res mancipi* were *res nec mancipi*. This negative class therefore included all chattels except slaves and farm cattle; all land except Italian land; and all servitudes except rural servitudes in Italian lands. For all corporal things in this class the regular form of conveyance was delivery (*traditio*), *i.e.* the formal transfer of possession[1].

For mancipable things delivery, if not effected in the process of mancipation itself, would be its natural consequent, as a transfer of possession in pursuance of transfer of title: for non-mancipable things it stood alone, but was to be effected formally as a conveyance of title. In both cases it was the external mark of the change of ownership. If the transferor

tatem justam adiit; si ut debuit mancipio ab eo accepit a quo jure civili potuit; aut si in jure cessit qui potuit cedere et id ubi oportuit; aut si usu cepit; aut si e praeda sub corona emit; tumve cum in bonis sectioneve cujus publice veniit (*bona* when the estate was sold to the broker, *sectio* when the broker sold the items of the estate), cf. Cic. *Inv.* i 45 § 85.

[1] If a non-mancipable thing was made the subject of mancipation, according to Cicero, it had no effect: the ownership was not transferred, and the transferor was not liable on any guaranty of title: *Finge mancipio aliquem dedisse id quod mancipio dari non potest. Num idcirco id ejus factum est qui accepit? aut num is qui mancipio dedit ob eam rem se ulla re obligavit?* (*Top.* 10 § 45).

was owner, and intended to transfer his property, and the ground of delivery was good and the transferee willing to acquire (which would usually be presumed), this act vested full ownership in the transferee (Gai. ii 18—21; Ulp. xix 7; D. xli 1 fr 35). But in sales, at least when mancipation did not take place, ownership did not pass till the vendor had received the price or had consented to wait for it (D. xviii 1 fr 19). When anything, for instance land (after mancipation, if in Italy), is delivered it passes with all its rights of servitude and obligations of servitude: the owner transfers what he has in it and only what he has. If he has professed to transfer something else than it is, he may thereby render himself liable for the mistake or fraud, but does not alter or augment the actual transfer (D. xli 1 fr 20 pr § 1). What constitutes delivery is treated below, chap. iv 3.

These methods of transfer by agreement and delivery were applicable and sufficient in the case of non-mancipable things, and something of the kind was no doubt used in the provinces between foreigners. We know also that they were sufficient for the transfer of provincial lands to or by Roman citizens (Gai. ii 21). As regards slaves and other mancipable animals in the provinces, it seems strange that mere delivery was enough between foreigners or between foreigner and Roman, but that mancipation or usucapion was required between Roman citizens. Presumably the burden was, in the eyes of a Roman, compensated by the greater security. At any rate the distinction between *res mancipi* and *res nec mancipi* was important for Roman citizens, with whom must be classed also Latin colonists, Junian Latins and such foreigners as had the *jus commercii* granted them (Ulp. xix 4). Caracalla's grant of citizenship to 'all persons in the Roman world' (see above, p. 24) did not remove the importance of the distinction of Italic and provincial soil, and *mancipi* and *nec mancipi*. They remained apparently until abolished by Justinian (Cod. vii 31).

(*d*) If then a Roman citizen bought a slave or an Italian farm, and the form of mancipation (or surrender in court) was not gone through, delivery did not make him owner by the law of the Quirites. Yet the vendor might have been owner and everything else might have been in order. The vendor however was held to remain owner, and the purchaser had the thing only among his goods (*in bonis*[1]). To meet this case, which appears to have often occurred, the XII tables allowed a certain length of possession to supply the defect in conveyance. Two years was the period fixed for land, one year for other things. At the end of this period the purchaser became full owner *ex jure Quiritium: usuceperat, i.e.* he had got it by use, *i.e.* by possession (see chap. iv and Gai. ii 40—42). And he was protected in the interim against third parties by a special Praetorian action (*Publiciana*), and against the legal owner by a plea *rei venditae et traditae* (cf. D. xxi 3), or an action on the purchase.

This division of the ownership into a bare technical right, which the informality of the transfer left in the transferor, and the practical ownership which the transferee was recognised to have got, is often in modern writers denoted by the words Quiritarian and Bonitarian[2] ownership. It is to some extent analogous to the distinction in English law between the legal and equitable estate, and I may have occasionally used those terms. It did not, as Gaius says, exist in early Roman times, or ever among foreigners. It must not be confounded with the distinction of ownership and possession. A man may be owner in the fullest sense and not possess: he may possess (in some

[1] The Digest uses *in bonis* to include things practically the property of a person, even though by insufficient title, and also *choses in action* (D. xx 1 fr 9, 15; xlvii 2 fr 12 § 2, *etc.*, L 16 fr 49, *etc.* *In bonis nostris computari sciendum est non solum quae dominii nostri sunt, sed et si bona fide a nobis possideantur vel superficiaria sint. Aeque bonis adnumerabitur etiam si quid est in actionibus petitionibus persecutionibus: nam haec omnia in bonis esse videntur* (Ulp.); xli 1 fr 52 *Rem in bonis nostris habere intellegimur, quotiens possidentes exceptionem aut amittentes ad reciperandam eam actionem habemus* (Modest.)). In order to include things lent or pledged to a person the term *ex bonis* 'of the goods' is used in D. xlvii 8 fr 2 § 22; Just. iv 2 § 2: cf. also D. xxxiii 2 fr 1. So *ex rebus* D. xliii 33 fr 1 pr. Cf. *ex liberis* D. xxxvii 5 fr 5 §§ 3, 6.

[2] This barbarous word is due to the Byzantine Theophilus, *Inst.* i 5 (p. 25 ed. Ferrini). The distinction was abolished by Justinian, Cod. vii 25.

senses) and not be either owner *ex jure Quiritium* or have the thing *in bonis* in the old Roman sense. But one who has had a slave or farm delivered by the owner to him, whether as a gift or in fulfilment of a contract for value, but without mancipation, has all the other conditions of ownership, except that; he has a good title in fact, but not in strict law: he has the physical control or concrete possession, just as if he were technically owner; and the law so far recognised this as to treat him as inchoate owner, and facilitate the completion of his title. Usucapion was held to be peculiar to Romans and not applicable to provincial lands. (Gai. ii 40, 65.)

Those whom the praetor recognised as practical heirs by giving them possession of a deceased's estate (*bonorum possessio*) and protecting them therein, are at first not owners of the things belonging to the inheritance, but have them only *in bonis*, and usucapion is required to give them full ownership. The same is the position of the purchaser of a bankrupt estate (Gai. iii 80, 81); and that of the holder of a noxious slave led away into his place of control by the praetor's order for want of due defence, instead of being duly conveyed by his owner (D. ix 4 fr 26 *fin.*); and that of the (real) owner of a slave whom he has been compelled by force to mancipate (Paul i 7 § 6 compared with D. iv 2 fr 9 § 6; cf. Gradenwitz *ZRG.* xix 66).

(*e*) Land in the provinces did not admit of the same ownership *ex jure Quiritium* as Italic land. The owner was the Roman people as a whole, or (in certain provinces) the emperor. Private persons were held to have a kind of possession or usufruct. The provincial lands paid a tax or tribute (*vectigal, stipendium, tributum*; whence the lands in the ownership of the Roman people were called *stipendiaria*, those in the ownership of the emperor *tributaria*, though without any substantial distinction so far as we know, Gai. ii 21; Mommsen *Staatsrecht* ii p. 964); and this tax seems to have been compared in theory with the rent paid by the lessee of a farm, and to have required lawyers to refuse the title of owner in the strict sense to all holders of land in the provinces. But the theory had no practical effect; distinctions of owner, possessor, usufructuary, lessee, *etc.* with analogous (*utiles*) actions of vindication, *etc.* were in as full use in provincial as in Italic land: the forms of conveyance were different (cf. Frontin. ii p. 36[1] *Agrimensores* ed. Lachmann = Bruns ii p. 89; D. xxxix 2 fr 15 § 26).

(*f*) Of incorporal things, an inheritance (*i.e.* the aggregate assets and liabilities of a deceased person) could be transferred only by surrender in court, see above, p. 228. For the practical transfer of an inheritance by sale see Book V chap. iv F 5.

For transfer of usufructs see below, chap. v, and for the transfer of obligations, Book V chap. iii A 7.

E. Restrictions on alienation by women and wards *etc.*

1. A woman cannot alienate mancipable things without the authority of her guardian. And any land which has been settled as dowry, although legally made the property of the husband (by mancipation, surrender in court or usucapion), cannot be alienated by him without her consent. This is by the *lex Julia*. Whether the rule about dowry was confined to land in Italy or applied to provincial land also was a matter of doubt (Gai. ii 63, 80). Provincial land was non-mancipable (Gai. ii 27; Vat. 259). Non-mancipable things, *e.g.* money, she can alienate without her guardian's authority, and therefore in making a loan she can make the money the property of the borrower and thus oblige him to repay the amount. Possession of land can be alienated by her without her guardian's authority,

[1] Frontinus describes *stipendiarii agri* as *qui nexum non habent neque possidendo ab alio quaeri possunt, possidentur tamen a privatis sed alia condicione, et veneunt sed nec mancipatio eorum legitima potest esse; possidere enim illis quasi fructus tollendi causa et praestandi tributi condicione concessum est. Vindicant tamen inter se non minus fines ex aequo ac si privatorum agrorum; nam et controversias inter se tales movent quales in agris immunibus et privatis solent evenire. Videbimus tamen an interdicere quis possit de ejusmodi possessione.* Here *ex aequo ac si* is 'just as if,' not as some take *ex aequo* 'equitably,' a meaning never denoted by *ex aequo* (see my note on D. *de usufructu* p. 31). Gaius in an almost illegible passage (ii 27) says to the same effect: *provincialis soli nexum non esse:... solum Italicum mancipi est, provinciale nec mancipi.*

and the purchaser is entitled to appropriate the fruits he gathers, and can gain the ownership of the land by usucapion unless she offer him the price before completion of usucapion (Vat. 1). She requires no authority from her guardian to better her condition, *e.g.* to receive anything whether mancipable or not; and if she receive payment from a debtor she can give a valid release; for the release of an obligation is alienation of a non-mancipable thing. But she cannot of herself give a formal release (*acceptilatio*) without receiving money; because a formal release was one of the statutable civil acts (Gai. ii 81, 83, 85; Ulp. xi 27; D. L 17, fr 77).

2. A ward without his (or her) guardian's authority can alienate nothing mancipable or non-mancipable. If he hand over money on loan, it still remains his and he can vindicate it: if however it has been consumed, there was doubt how it could be recovered, though probably a *condictio indebiti* would apply, if the receiver was in good faith; if not, an action *ad exhibendum* (Gai. ii 82 mutilated; Just. ii 8 § 2). If he paid a debt the money still remained his: if however the creditor spent it, he was freed from his debt (D. xlvi 3 fr 14 § 8). But a ward can receive anything without his guardian's consent; for that is to better his condition. Thus if a debtor pay the money to the ward, it becomes the ward's property, but the debtor is not discharged[1], for that would be for the ward to release an obligation, which he cannot do by himself. If however he is enriched by the money and should sue for his debt, the debtor could defeat him by a plea of fraud (Gai. ii 84). The time for estimating the enrichment is usually the time of suit: and even if the thing paid him has perished before suit the plea will still hold, provided that the thing was necessary for him (D. xlvi 3 fr 47).

[1] The difference of a ward's position from a woman's in this respect is noted by Cicero (*Top.* xi § 46); *Non quemadmodum quod mulieri debeas recte ipsi mulieri sine tutore auctore solvas, item quod pupillo aut pupillae debeas recte possis eodem modo solvere*; where *recte* means 'duly' 'with full legal effect.'

F. Alienation by non-owners.

Gaius mentions three cases in which a non-owner can convey with good title. (1) The caretaker of a madman can by the XII tables alienate the madman's things. (2) A procurator can do so under some circumstances, *e.g.* if he has a free power of management during his principal's absence, and even without such power, if the things are likely to spoil. (3) A creditor can sell with good title things pledged to him, if the debtor has given him a power of sale, to be used in case of the debt not being paid (Gai. ii 64 mutilated; D. xli 1 fr 9 § 4, iii 3 § 63).

G. Acquisition through others:

i. Through persons *in potestate*.

A man can acquire ownership or other rights, not only by his own direct action, but through the action of those who are members of his family. These may be divided into four classes, being severally subject to certain limitations:

1. Children and slaves under his power (*in potestate*).

2. Women in hand and persons in handtake (*in manu mancipiove*).

3. Slaves of whom he has the usufruct.

4. Persons in good faith possessed by him as slaves, although really freemen or slaves of someone else.

1. Children under power and slaves can hold nothing as their own, and whatever is acquired by them, whether thing or right or obligation, passes to their father or master, whether they receive it by mancipation[1] or get it in virtue of delivery or

[1] Cf. Cic. *Att.* xiii 50 § 2 *Vestorius ad me scripsit ut juberem mancipio dari servo suo pro mea parte Hetereio cuidam fundum Brinnianum ut ipse ei Puteolis recte mancipio dare posset. Eum servum si tibi videbitur ad me mittes.* Cicero appears to have been one of several heirs of Brinnius, and a farm belonging to the inheritance had to be conveyed to Hetereius. Vestorius (Cicero's man of business at Puteoli) proposed to send his slave round to the coheirs to receive by mancipation each coheir's share; these would pass at once to Vestorius, who could then make a proper mancipation of the whole farm to Hetereius. The dative *Hetereio cuidam* is apparently 'for the benefit of Hetereius,' but I think it should be transferred

stipulate for it or acquire it on any other ground. It passes at once, without staying for a moment with them. If an inheritance is left to my child or slave, he enters on the inheritance only by my order, and the effect then is the same as if it had been left to me and I had entered. Any other acquisition, *e.g.* by legacy, gift, *etc.* is made without my consent being required; and his stipulation binds a promiser to me, even if I have forbidden him to stipulate. He can take and hold possession for me, and the possession is good for usucapion (Gai. ii 87; D. xxix 2 fr 79; xli 1 fr 32, xlv 1 fr 62). A slave or child stipulating under a condition acquires for his then father or master, though he be afterwards emancipated or manumitted or pass under another's power, the time regarded in stipulations being the time of contract, whereas in legacies the time of vesting decides (D. L 17 fr 8, xlv 1 fr 78 pr). A slave informally manumitted holds neither for himself nor for others, but if he take possession in the name of someone, he acquires for him (D. xli 3 fr 31 § 2). If a slave be legally (*ex jure Quir.*) the property of one but equitably (*in bonis*) the property of another, the latter only acquires through him: the former can acquire nothing, not even, according to some opinions, if the slave take by mancipation or stipulate expressly for him (Gai. ii 88, iii 166; Ulp. xix 20). If a slave is bequeathed or set free by a will, the heir who knows of it can acquire nothing by him (D. xli 1 fr 40).

If a slave expressly declare for whom he is acquiring, the expression is decisive where there are several persons for whom he is capable of acquiring. If he is owned by one person only, it does not matter whether he expressly declare for his master or for someone in his master's power or for himself; in all these cases he acquires for his master. If he be owned in common by two or more masters, he acquires for them in the ratio of their respective shares in him, notwithstanding that he

to just before *Puteolis* and *ei* struck out. It seems clear that Cicero by *juberem* meant that he was to order one of his own slaves to mancipate to Vestorius' slave, cf. D. xxi 2 fr 39 § 1. I cannot agree with Mitteis's handling of these passages in order to prevent their supporting mancipation by a representative (*ZRG.* xxxiv p. 210).

may have used the goods of one only for the business. But express statement of his acting for one or some of his masters ousts the others altogether. Whether a previous order to the slave from one or some of his masters had the like effect was disputed: the Sabinians held that it had, the Proculians held that the order went for nothing, and that the acquisition was for all, if the slave made no declaration to the contrary. There was a like dispute if one master gave the order and the slave declared for another (Gai. iii 167; D. xli 1 fr 37 § 2; xlv 3 fr 5, 6, 27, 28 § 3; Cod. iv 27 fr 2); or if a donor delivered to a common slave for one of his masters and he accepted it as for the other (D. xxxix 3 fr 13; xli 1 fr 37 § 6). If a slave stipulated for his masters by their names, the acquisition is shared by them, not in the ratio of their shares but equally (D. xlv 3 fr 37)[1]. (Where the acquisition has been made at the expense of one or some, an action *pro socio* or *com. div.* will make the necessary adjustment: D. xli 1 fr 45; xlv 3 fr 28 § 1.) If a common slave stipulated for something which could be taken by one and not by another, *e.g.* if he stipulated for a dowry when only one of the partners was about to marry, or for a slave who already belonged to one of the partners, or for a right of road when one of the partners had no neighbouring farm to which it could be appurtenant, the stipulation was not nullified by the partial impracticability, but was good for the partner (or partners) who was about to marry, or to whom the slave did not belong, or who had the requisite farm (D. xlv 3 fr 1 § 4, 7 § 1—fr 9 pr). So a legacy or *fidei commissum* given to a common slave by one of his owners enures wholly to the other (D. xxxv 2 fr 49 pr).

If a slave stipulated expressly for an outsider, the stipulation is null; if he name also another, who is not an outsider, *e.g. aut mihi aut Titio,* the stipulation is null so far as the outsider is concerned, except that payment to the outsider frees the debtor; the outsider having then to account to the slave's master (D. xlv 1 fr 38 § 17; xlvi 3 fr 10; Gai. iii 103).

2. Through persons in hand or handtake ownership is acquired in the same way, but there is a question, says Gaius,

1 For a similar principle in legacies, but disputed see D. xxx fr 124 and pp. 300, 319.

whether their superior can gain possession by them, seeing that he does not possess them. They cannot take by surrender in court (*in jure cessio*) any more than slaves or children under power (Gai. ii 90, 96).

3. Through slaves in whom we have the usufruct we can acquire only so far as the acquisition rests on their services or our property (*ex operis suis vel ex re nostra*), *e.g.* by our hiring them out, or their buying something with our money. This may take place by mancipation or delivery or stipulation: and the fructuary may through them obtain a formal release or a plea of bargain. Any other acquisition made by them, as for instance an inheritance or legacy or gift, passes to the owner, not to the fructuary, for entry on an inheritance cannot be counted as a slave's service, and legacies and gift are still further from coming within the grounds of a fructuary's claim. Some lawyers however appear to have held that if the testator or donor had the fructuary in view, the legacy or gift to the slave passed to him (Gai. ii 91; Vat. 71 b; D. vii 1 fr 22; xxix 2 fr 45 pr § 3). An express declaration by the slave that he is stipulating or in some other way acting for the owner, ousts the fructuary, even though the business rests on the use of his property. And an order from the owner has the same effect. (The fructuary can recover from the owner by condiction.) But if the fructuary's property or the slave's services are not the basis of acquisition, the fructuary gains nothing, unless (as said above) a gift to the fructuary is intended by the promiser. The express declaration of the slave, that he is acting for the fructuary, has no effect (D. vii 1 fr 24, 25 § 3, xli 1 fr 37 § 5, xlv 3 fr 39). As the fructuary does not properly possess the slave, of whom he has the usufruct, it is, says Gaius, a question whether he can possess through him and thus acquire by usucapion (Gai. ii 94), but Paul and Papinian say he can, Paul producing the analogy of a son, and Papinian resting on the fructuary's holding being after all a practical possession (D. xli 2 fr 1 § 8, fr 49). But the fructuary cannot like a *bonae fidei* possessor acquire the ownership of the slave himself, for he knows that another is the owner (Gai. ii 93).

By a slave of whom we have only the use, we cannot acquire

on the ground of his services, for we cannot let them out; but we can acquire if our property is used (D. vii 8 fr 14 pr).

4. The same rules in general as those for slaves in usufruct applied to persons possessed by us in good faith as our slaves, whether they are really freemen or some other's slaves, only that there is no doubt that through them we can both possess and gain by usucapion. Anything acquired by them otherwise than from their services or our property does not belong to us, but to themselves if they are freemen, to their owner if they are slaves. Except that, if they are slaves, acquisitions of or by possession cannot fall to their owner, for he is out of possession, nor to their possessor if they are not due to his property: if they are freemen, being themselves possessed by others, they cannot possess. As regards an inheritance left them, one who is a freeman, entering either of his own accord or on our order, acquires for himself, if he is conscious of his freedom and acts with that intention; if not, he acquires neither for himself nor for us (Gai. ii 92—94; D. xli 1 fr 19, 21, 54; Ulp. xix 21). The slave or freeman purchased *bona fide* is deemed to be possessed *bona fide* until he is evicted (so Julian, D. xxii 1 fr 25 § 2; cf. fr 40; but Pomponius and Ulpian require actual *bona fides* to be continuous, D. xli 1 fr 23 § 1, 48 § 1).

If another's slave *bona fide* served two masters, he acquired for the one whom he expressly named: if he acted only on order from one he probably acquired for him. If there was neither express declaration nor order, but the acquisition was based on the property of one, he acquired for him either wholly, as some thought, or partly for him (as he was only part possessor) and partly for his owner, who however would apparently be liable to a condiction from the possessor whose property had been used.

If one master is capable and others not, he acquires wholly for the capable (D. xli 1 fr 23 § 3; xlv 3 fr 33; vii 1 fr 25 § 6, on which see my note).

5. Through another's slave simply pledged to us we acquire nothing: he is possessed by us only as a security (D. xli 1 fr 37 pr).

6. Another's slave, when possessed *bona fide* for the time

required by usucapion, became the property of the possessor and thenceforth acquired for him only (Gai. ii 93).

A freeman in *bona fide* slavery is bound as of course to his possessor by promises, or by buying, selling, or other business: and is liable also for Aquilian damage if of a serious nature (D. xli 1 fr 54 §§ 1—3).

ii. ACQUISITION THROUGH PERSONS NOT *IN POTESTATE*.

From the above it appears (says Gaius) that in strict law we acquire through free persons, only if they are either legally subject to us (*i.e.* belong to one of the first two classes) or are *bona fide* possessed by us as slaves: through slaves belonging to another we acquire only if we have either the usufruct or the lawful possession. This is expressed by the ordinary maxim that nothing is acquired for us by an outsider (Gai. ii 95).

An exception was however made in practice, and eventually confirmed by a rescript of Severus and Antoninus, by which a procurator could acquire on his principal's account the possession of anything, which if ratified by his principal enured for usucapion from the date of the principal's knowledge. A similar immediate acquisition of possession for their ward, *etc.* by guardians or caretakers, *etc.* was allowed (Paul v 2 § 2; D. xli 1 fr 20 § 2; tit. 2 fr 1 § 20; Cod. vii 32 fr 1). For taking delivery, *i.e.* acquiring possession, in completion of a contract any free person could be used, the action being regarded not as one of technical law but of physical handling, just as a deposit might be made or a purchase concluded or a loan contracted through the hands or voice of a third person acting as a messenger and so putting the parties legally in direct connexion with each other (D. xvi 3 fr 1 § 11; xviii 1 fr 1 § 2; xii 1 fr 9 § 8, 15; xli 1 fr 13; cf. Vang. *Pand.* iii p. 289 sq.; Savigny *Obl.* ii § 57). The acquisition would however date only from the time when the thing reached the hands of the principal, unless its acceptance by the agent was previously authorised or subsequently ratified by him (D. iii 5 fr 23; xli 1 fr 59; tit. 2 fr 42 § 1; cf. Savigny *Besitz* p. 397 ed. 7). A thing could be received in pledge through a procurator, but the obligation could not as a rule be acquired through him (D. xiii 7 fr 11 § 6).

If a procurator sold a thing on the mandate of his principal, and entered into the usual covenants, Papinian held that the principal could sue and be sued by actions analogous to those in the case of an *institor* (xix 1 fr 13 § 25). And the praetor after a hearing would allow a principal to proceed on his procurator's stipulation *damni infecti* (xxxix 2 fr 18 § 16).

H. Actions to recover or ascertain property.

1. *Rei vindicatio.*

The regular action for recovering property was called "vindication." The plaintiff asserts *rem qua de agitur suam esse*, 'that the thing in question is his own.' Its ordinary application is to single physical objects, *e.g.* a farm, a slave, an ox, a ship, a cup, *etc.*, but it also could be used where a number of such things came under one name, *e.g.* a herd. Other applications of the term, viz. to claims for an inheritance as a whole, and for servitudes both personal and real, will be found elsewhere. A *peculium* could not be sued for as a whole: the components must be claimed separately. A father's power over his children was in old days so like ownership, that this action was held applicable to a claim for a child, the formula being modified accordingly, *e.g. hunc puerum*, not *suum esse* but, *filium suum esse* or *in potestate sua esse ex jure Quiritium.* But for this class of cases a *praejudicium* or an interdict was more usual (D. vi 1 fr 1, fr 56. See above, p. 64).

The object of the action must be described sufficiently for identification, *e.g.* a slave by his name, or, if his name is not known, by that of his mother or the inheritance to which he belongs, *etc.*, a farm by its name and district, dress by its colour, silver plate by its character and shape, coined money by count, raw metal or other substance by its weight. If a whole is not claimed, the portion must be stated, lest the penalty of a *pluris petitio* (Book VI chap. vi B 1) be incurred. If however there was good cause (*e.g.* ignorance of the deduction which the *lex Falcidia* would make in a legacy), an undefined share might be claimed. Where plaintiff's property has been combined or mixed with that of others, separation should first be procured by the action *ad exhibendum*; or, if the whole is common property, the action *communi dividundo* must be resorted to instead of a vindication (fr 3 § 2—fr 5 pr, 6, 76). A herd may be claimed as such, although not all, but the majority of the animals, are plaintiff's: restitution however will be confined to those which are his own (fr 1 § 3, 2, 7).

Plaintiff is anyone who has acquired the ownership but is not in possession, either by himself or through another holding for him. A purchaser who has not yet had delivery is not competent to bring this action: he is not yet owner (fr 23 pr, 50 pr). But ownership until a certain time or until the occurrence of a condition is enough (fr 41 pr, 66). The proof of ownership is on the plaintiff (Paul i 13 B §§ 6, 7).

Defendant is anyone who is possessor, be the ground what it may. Some lawyers maintained that only those could be defendants, who were qualified for the interdicts *uti possidetis* and *utrubi*, and that consequently depositaries, borrowers, hirers who held the possession for others, and those who were merely in possession to secure legacies or dowry or on behalf of an unborn child or on account of apprehended damage, were not liable to this action. The prevalent opinion however was that anyone was liable who had such a control of the thing sought as to be able to restore it to the plaintiff. The judge had to satisfy himself of this (fr 9). If defendant makes no defence, an interdict *quem fundum* was issuable to enforce transference (Ulp. *Fr. Vind.*; *ap.* Krüger *Jus Antejust.* ii p. 159).

Besides contesting plaintiff's ownership, defendant can defeat his suit by pleading a valid right to retention of the thing, such as that he is usufructuary or pledgee. Even if the right is not valid against every claimant, it may be good against this plaintiff, *e.g.* if he has himself sold and delivered the thing to defendant, or if he is heir of one who has done so (D. xxi 3 fr 1 pr § 1). A hirer or borrower or depositary cannot assert such a claim against the owner's vindication, but a hirer, by pleading fraud, can obtain equitable compensation.

When defendant has lost the possession, after joinder of issue, by negligence or other fault but not by fraud, he is still liable to the action, but if condemned can claim from plaintiff surrender of his right of action. If he has lost it fraudulently (after joinder of issue), he is liable for such damages as plaintiff may fix on oath without any limit from the judge. This is regarded as a settlement of the suit, and defendant becomes owner as soon as he can get possession, plaintiff guarantying to do nothing to prevent it; but as a punishment for the fraud, plaintiff is not bound to cede him his actions, nor is defendant entitled to bring an action analogous to the *Publiciana* (fr 46, 68—70). If defendant had parted with possession fraudulently before joinder of issue, he was (as Paul says, on the analogy of the *SC. Juventianum*, see above, p. 283)[1] still liable to this action: and the heirs of such a person were liable to be sued by an action *in factum*, so far as they had been enriched by their predecessor's fraud (D. vi 1 fr 27 § 3, 36 pr, 52).

Anyone who without cause accepted suit (*liti se obtulit*), plaintiff being ignorant of his position, is liable to condemnation under this action (fr 25—27 pr).

If plaintiff won his case, he was entitled to restitution of the thing and of profits, and to compensation. Of these, in order:

(*a*) Restitution of the thing itself, or, if it has been sold, of its true value. It should be restored to plaintiff, in ordinary cases, where it happens to be at the time of joinder of issue; but if it is a moveable, plaintiff can, on paying the cost of the carriage, have it restored at the place of action (fr 10—12). If since joinder of issue the thing (*e.g.* a slave) has perished without fault on the part of defendant, this head of the claim drops, if defendant was an honest possessor. But if fraud or even negligence is proved, defendant is still liable. Acts of negligence are such as sending a slave into dangerous places, letting him fight in the arena, sending a ship to sea with incompetent persons or at a dangerous time, insecure keeping of a runaway slave (fr 16, 96). If since joinder of issue defendant has completed usucapion of the thing sued for, he

[1] Probably the liability of one who *dolo desiit possidere* is much earlier than the *SC. Juventianum*. Labeo appears to have applied the principle to several actions; cf. D. x 4 fr 15; xliii 8 fr 2 § 42; tit. 13 § 13 (Demelius *Exhibit.* p. 188).

is none the less liable to restore, and must formally convey the thing, and guaranty plaintiff against his having pledged it, or (if a slave) having manumitted him. If it be a runaway slave, he must cede his actions to plaintiff (fr 18, 21). If, instead of giving up the thing, defendant prefer to pay damages, he cannot call on plaintiff to guaranty him against eviction, for he chooses to take the risk (fr 18, 21, 35 § 2).

(*b*) Further, defendant has to restore all profits of whatever kind, which the plaintiff could have had, if restitution had been made at the time of joinder of issue. *Causa omnis praestanda est.* This includes vegetable produce, whether actually gathered or which reasonably might have been gathered (what remains ungathered is still part of the farm, fr 44); the young of animals and slaves, rents of houses, freight of ships, earnings of slaves, legacies and inheritances which have come through a slave, rights of suit under the *lex Aquilia, etc.* If only a part of the thing was claimed, the claim for profits would be proportional. If claimant was bare owner, he could claim only such profits as did not belong to the fructuary (fr 17 §§ 1, 20, 33, 76 pr, 78; xxii 1 fr 19 pr). An honest possessor was liable for no fruits before joinder of issue, unless[1] he had them still unconsumed. A dishonest possessor was liable for all fruits from the time when he took possession (Cod. iii 32 fr 22). It would appear also that fruits had to be paid twofold, but the matter is not certain[2]. An honest possessor is from the time of joinder of issue, if unsuccessful, treated as a dishonest possessor (cf. D. v 3 fr 20 § 11, 25 § 7).

(*c*) Further, defendant has to make compensation for loss (*e.g.* death of a slave) or deterioration (*e.g.* by wounding or beating a slave) due to his fault. If it is such as to make

[1] Whether this exception was true so early as Antonine times appears doubtful. See Pernice *Lab.* ii 1 p. 356 sq.; Czyhlarz, Glück's *Pand.* i p. 561 sq.; Dernburg *Pand.* i § 205.

[2] So the XII tables ordered, cf. Fest. *s.v. vindiciae*; Paul i 13 B § 8 says this of fruits neglected; v 9 § 2 (cf. D. ii 8 fr 12) of the heir's bond to a conditional substitute. Cod. Theod. iv 18 fr 1, tit. 19 is express for the double fruits, and very likely in this respect did not make new law. The constitution iv 18 = Cod. Just. vii 51 fr 2 is of the year A.D. 369. Compare Lenel *EP.* pp. 411, 412.

defendant liable under the *lex Aquilia* (which gives double damages), plaintiff can elect, and it will be the judge's duty to secure defendant against further liability on this score (fr 13, 14). An infant or madman is not responsible for acts of this kind (fr 60).

On the other hand an honest possessor can call upon the plaintiff to repay or set off any reasonable expense defrayed by him in connexion with the object of the suit, *e.g.* payment of the principal or interest of a mortgage on it, payment of damages to avert noxal surrender of a slave, cost of training or educating a slave (provided the slave is for sale and has thereby acquired greater money value), planting the land, erection of buildings on it, gathering and storing the fruits, *etc.* And if defendant has had to give a guaranty against apprehended damage (*damni infecti*), the plaintiff will give him a counter guaranty (*his rebus recte praestari* Gai. ii 76; D. vi 1 fr 19, 27 § 5—30, 65 pr; cf. L 16 fr 71). Even a dishonest possessor can get some relief in such cases, *e.g.* he can be allowed to remove in a reasonable way any additions he may have made to a building (unless plaintiff will give him what they would be worth on removal), but he cannot remove what he has planted (fr 53). In all these matters it will be for the judge to decide equitably according to the particular circumstances; *e.g.* a poor man recovering his ancestral farm cannot be required to pay for expensive buildings erected by the defendant (fr 37, 38). On the other hand if defendant has got profits before joinder of issue, their amount may be set off against his improvements on a farm (fr 48).

There were in Cicero's and Gaius' times three modes of bringing this suit.

(*a*) The old *legis actio* could be used before the *centumviri*. It was distinguished from the other modes *inter alia* by a challenge from both parties to a *sacramentum* or stake of 125 sesterces (so fixed by a *lex Crepereia*), which was exacted from the loser as a penalty, and by the condemnation being for the thing itself and not as in the formulary system for damages (Gai. iv 95, 48). See Book VI chap. iv A.

(*b, c*) The other modes were *per formulam petitoriam*[1] and *per sponsionem* (Cic. *Verr.* II I 45 § 115; Gai. iv 91—95). The former was no doubt a continuance of the direct claim (*petere*) with a formula adapted to it, directing the judge, if the plaintiff proved his ownership and defendant did not make due restitution, to condemn defendant in the value of the thing and of the profits. The latter was an indirect proceeding by wager (see Book VI chap. vi J). Security was required in each case from the possessor, *judicatum solvi* in the former procedure, *pro praede litis et vindiciarum* in the latter (Gai. iv 89—94. See Book VI chap. vii B). We do not know the reasons for there being two forms (they seem to be different modifications of the old sacramental procedure), nor the circumstances which directed the choice of one rather than the other.

Practically it was considered to be the most advisable course for one claiming the ownership not to bring a vindication at first, but to get the possession, if possible, by means of an interdict. Claimant can then wait quietly in possession and leave to his adversary the task of evicting him by proving ownership (D. vi I fr 24; Cod. iii 32 fr 13). Even after commencing a vindication a person can obtain the interdict *uti possidetis*, a claim of ownership being quite distinct from a claim of possession (D. xli 2 fr 12 § 1).

2. PUBLICIANA IN REM ACTIO.

Analogous to vindication was an action (presumably first granted by a praetor named Publicius; so Just. iv 6 § 4) to protect honest acquisition in one who was not yet legal owner but was in the way to become so by usucapion. The action is granted, says Gaius (iv 36), to one *qui ex justa causa traditam*

[1] Cicero evidently gives us part of the *formula petitoria* in shewing Verres' method of so framing the issue as to leave the judge no power of deciding otherwise than as Verres wished: *Si paret fundum Capenatem quo de agitur ex jure Quiritium P. Servili esse neque is fundus* (not *P. Servilio*, but as Verres directed) *Q. Catulo restituetur*, *i.e.* if *A* is proved to be owner and the estate is not restored to *B*, then condemn defendant in the value, *etc.* Such an issue is just, only if *B* be agent of *A* (cf. Book VI chap. vi G 4).

sibi rem nondum usucepit eamque omissa possessione petit[1]. The defect which usucapion was expected to cure might be either in the form of conveyance or in the title. The purchaser of a mancipable thing (*a*) may have had delivery from the owner but not either mancipation or surrender in court. The thing is his, but only *in bonis*, not by the law of the Quirites (Gai. ii 41). Or (*b*) he may have had the thing duly mancipated to him and delivered, but if the vendor was not the owner of the thing, neither is the purchaser owner, notwithstanding his ignorance of any flaw in the vendor's title (*ib.* 43). In both cases he can in the course of time become full owner by usucapion, but meantime he has no proper protection if he loses possession. Against the owner *ex jure Quiritium* in the first case he can bring an action *ex empto*, or sue on the covenant against eviction: in the second he must, if evicted by the owner, bring these actions against the vendor; the owner is not liable to him at all. Against third parties he uses this Publician action. The issue for trial is framed on the fictitious assumption that usucapion had been completed (Gai. iv 36. See Book VI chap. V G).

Purchase is the most common ground for the delivery but other good grounds are exchange, bequest, gift (whether absolute or *mortis causa*), dowry, judgment, payment (in discharge of an obligation), noxal surrender or apprehension by the praetor's order, judicial assignment (*adjudicatio*), retention on payment of damages (D. vi 2 fr 1—7 § 1, § 5, fr 13 pr). Nothing more than lawful ground of acquisition and delivery on that account are required, where the defect was in the form of conveyance, but if the acquisition was made from one who was not owner, there must have been good faith in the acquirer, *i.e.* he must have honestly believed that he was dealing with the owner both at the time of contract and at the time of delivery. The honest acquirer can bring the action, even if his vendor (or other *auctor*) was dishonest; and the heir of an honest acquirer can bring it, even if he himself is aware

[1] The words given as from the edict in D. vi 2 fr 1 are generally considered due partly to Tribonian. See Lenel in *ZRG.* xxxiii p. 11 sqq.; Huschke *Recht der Public. Klage*, etc.

of the vendor's defect of title (fr 7 §§ 11—17). The action is applicable also where the acquisition was made from a madman[1] or minor, if the acquirer was unaware of the madness or minority; or from a ward, if the acquirer supposed the person giving authority to be the ward's true guardian (fr 7 § 2, fr 13 § 2).

The Publician action applies (besides ordinary objects of vindication) to usufructs, servitudes, long leases of lands (*vectigalia*), building leases (*superficies*), provincial lands and other things the alienation of which is not prohibited by statute. A child of a stolen or runaway slavewoman, conceived and born while with the possessor, may be the object of suit if the possessor sue in ignorance of the mother's being stolen, *etc.*; but the thief's heir cannot sue, nor can the mother herself be the object of suit (fr 11 §§ 2—4).

Whether it be the purchaser himself or his heir that has had delivery, the heir can sue, and so can anyone to whom delivery has been made by the purchaser's order (fr 9 pr, 11 pr). An heir can sue for what a slave of the inheritance has bought and got delivered and lost before the heir entered; and the burghers can sue on a thing bought on peculiar or other account by their slave and lost after delivery (fr 9 § 6, fr 10). Delivery *brevi manu* (p. 458) is good for this suit; and accessions follow their principal in this as in other cases. Generally this action is similar to a vindication, and rests on the same conditions as usucapion; but a moment's possession is all that is required to qualify (fr 7 §§ 6, 8, fr 11 §§ 4, 7, 12 § 7). Where two persons have bought the same thing from a non-owner, the one to whom the thing was first delivered has the best right to bring this action: if they bought from different non-owners and one is in possession, he can defeat this action if brought by the other: if neither is in possession, (apparently) the praetor will give the preference to the one who had first delivery (fr 9 § 4; xix 1 fr 31 § 2; much disputed).

If the real owner is in possession and this suit is brought against him, he must plead his ownership (the plea being framed *e.g.* thus '*si ea res possessoris non sit*'). If however he

[1] Paul (D. xli 4 fr 4 § 16) denies this.

had consented to the sale, or had since become heir to vendor, a replication would be allowed (*si non auctor meus ex voluntate tua vendidit, etc.*), and an order to his procurator not to deliver would not avail against the fact of the previous consent (fr 14, 15; 72). Nor is the owner's claim good against an injured party's right to a slave, whom his *bona fide* possessor had surrendered noxally (D. ix 4 fr 28). Where a mandate to sell another's slaves had not been executed before it was revoked by the mandatee's death, and his heirs ignorantly sold them and the purchasers had gained the full ownership by usucapion, the former owner on returning from abroad was held entitled to dispute the grant of a plea of ownership to the purchasers[1], on the ground of his having given no mandate to the heirs but only to the dead man whom he trusted (D. xvii 1 fr 57).

3. *ACTIO AD EXHIBENDUM*[2], 'For production.'

This action is to compel the production in public of some chattel which is the object of a claim by the plaintiff, or at least to obtain free access to it. It is as a rule preparatory to some other action, usually a vindication, but is open not merely to persons claiming the ownership but to fructuaries and pledgees. So also to a legatee who has an option left him and requires the production of the slaves, *etc.* in order to make his selection; and to one who has a noxal action and requires production of slaves in order to identify the particular culprit. The only other obligatory claim which can be assisted by this action is that of theft, but it appears to be probable that in this case production is preparatory only to a vindication of the stolen object or to a noxal action against the thief (D. x 4 fr 1,

[1] In this case the action is often called *Publiciana rescissoria* and is thought to be referred to in D. xliv 7 fr 35. I see no ground for making such an application of the suit into a special action. Where there has been a reinstatement (as in D. iv 6 : see Book v chap. viii B) any suitable action may be brought, *Publiciana* or other. Just. iv 6 § 5 does not authorize our extending the term *Publiciana* from § 4 into § 5.

[2] Pliny (*Ep.* v 10) in a letter to Suetonius makes a playful allusion to the *formula ad exhibendum*.

2, 3 §§ 1—7, fr 12 § 2; xiii 1 fr 7 § 1; xlvii 1 fr 1 pr; xliii 29 fr 3 § 8; Demelius *Exhibitionspflicht* § 29). It is also preparatory to interdicts—at least to the interdict *utrubi* (fr 3 § 5; Demelius § 27). It is not available where a freeman is said to be detained in custody, for there is no pecuniary interest in the plaintiff; nor where someone other than an heir desires to see a will, for there is a special interdict for that purpose; nor can the production of an adversary's accounts be demanded, for that is not reasonable as a rule; nor can one who has fraudulently parted with the possession of a thing bring this action, for that would be to assist a wrong-doer (D. x 4 fr 2 § 8; 3 § 11; fr 13, 19). The general statement that all can sue for production must, says Paul, receive an intelligent meaning; else a student might sue for the production of books on the ground that he would be wiser by reading them (fr 19). It is the duty of the judge to make a summary inquiry whether the plaintiff has such a lawful and reasonable ground of action as requires for its establishment the production demanded. Plaintiff has to set forth his grounds, and defendant can state his objections. The judge has to decide all pleas such as bargain, fraud, oath, matter judged, and any others raising a simple issue, but to defer more difficult questions to the trial of the main action (fr 13, 3 § 1). Production is allowed where a slave is claimed into freedom, though the claimant can have no pecuniary interest: the reason being perhaps that this was a vindication, and that the courts were ready to favour the cause of freedom (fr 12 pr). In criminal cases it was allowed in order to subject the slave produced to the question and ascertain his confederates (fr 20).

The action lies against anyone who has possession or is in possession at the time of judgment, even if not so at joinder of issue. And anyone who had the power of production at the time of joinder of issue but has since fraudulently lost the power, *e.g.* if he have killed a slave, poured away oil or wine, broken an article up, or parted with the possession to another, is liable to condemnation (fr 3 § 15—fr 5 pr, § 6, fr 7 §§ 4—6, fr 9 pr). Indeed if a slave since joinder of issue has died from no fault of the possessor, the latter was sometimes held liable, especially if the death would not have occurred had the slave been duly produced at the time (fr 12 § 4, cf. fr 7 § 5). A thing is not deemed to be duly produced if it is in a worse condition than it was at the time of joinder of issue. Hence if defendant has since then become owner by usucapion, he must consent to accept a trial of ownership as before the completion of usucapion (*repetita die intentionem suscipere* fr 9 §§ 5, 6). If a slave, whose production is demanded, has run away or is residing in a distant place, defendant must guaranty his production when he get the power to do so, and may be required by the praetor to fix a time for it (fr 5 § 6, 12 § 5).

Production must be made at the place where the thing was at joinder of issue, unless the plaintiff defray the cost of production elsewhere, or defendant have intentionally sent him away to throw difficulties in plaintiff's way (fr 11 § 1) or even without such intention have created difficulties (D. xix 2 fr 19 § 5).

The action for production, though contemplating a further action, might sometimes be sufficient in itself, as for instance where there is no real contest as to the ownership. Thus a purchaser of land may decline to give up the building materials (*ruta caesa*) which he finds there; or a riparian proprietor may decline to allow the owner to fetch away a raft which has been carried by the stream on to his land; or a neighbour may be refused permission to carry off the ruins of his house from the adjoining plot, or the manure which he has piled on to an adjoining field; in such cases the decision of the judge allowing production, *i.e.* the desired access, may settle the dispute, defendant having no real ground for contesting the ownership (D. x 4 fr 5 § 2—5; xix 1 fr 25; tit. 5 fr 16 pr). If acorns from my trees have fallen into your land and you refuse me permission to take them or you send cattle in to eat them, I can sue you by this action (D. x 2 fr 9 § 1).

Where specification has taken place, *i.e.* where defendant has made plaintiff's jewel into a ring, or put his wheel into a carriage, or used his timber for a cupboard, or his purple for a dress, *etc.*, plaintiff cannot claim his property, because it is part of another article, but he can apply for its production, and defendant will have to separate it. If condemned on this issue, he will probably not contest the ownership of the extracted article (fr 6—7 § 2). This action is not applicable in the case of a *tignum junctum* (above, p. 421).

When plaintiff has a treasure in another man's land, and the other has not touched it and perhaps is quite ignorant of it, no action for theft will lie against him, and he is not possessor so as to be liable to a suit for production: but on taking an oath of good faith and giving security against possible damage plaintiff may obtain an action or interdict to enable him to dig it up and remove it (fr 15). Production of documents cannot be demanded unless they are written on plaintiff's paper; but in a fit case an action *in factum* would be granted (fr 3 § 14).

Defendant by producing obtains an acquittal. The action gives him the choice (*arbitrium*), by the insertion in the formula of *nisi exhibeat*. If he refuse production, the damages will be estimated at the value of plaintiff's interest in the production, *i.e.* whatever he would have had if production had duly been made. This will include the offspring of a female slave whether conceived before or after joinder of issue; the loss of an inheritance or option which could have been accepted or exercised, *etc.* (fr 9 §§ 7, 8, fr 10, 11).

The action although directed against the possessor was personal: it called for a performance, and did not claim a thing (fr 3 § 3). Heirs can sue and be sued, not as heirs but as possessors like anyone else. As heirs however they are responsible for their ancestor's fraud, if the inheritance was thereby enriched (fr 12 § 6).

Whether the action was civil or praetorian is not clear (Demelius *Exhib.* § 5).

4. *Finium regundorum judicium*[1].

This was a proceeding between adjoining proprietors of country lands to settle their boundaries. It was resorted to

[1] Cf. Cic. *Top.* 10 § 43 *Quemadmodum si in urbe de finibus controversia est, quia fines magis agrorum videntur esse quam urbis, finibus regendis adigere arbitrum non possis, sic si aqua pluvia in urbe nocet, quoniam res tota magis agrorum est, aquae pluviae arcendae arbitrum adigere non possis.* He mentions the suit again in *Muren.* 9 § 22. For *arbitrum adigere* see note to Book v chap. iv E 1 *a*.

only on occasion of a dispute about the precise line of the boundary, when the old marks were obliterated, or differently read by the neighbours. It is sometimes spoken of as a dispute *intra pedes quinque*[1], because the XII tables directed that usucapion should not be allowed for neighbours within 2½ feet from the boundary line of each. This space of five feet was in fact treated as neutral, for either to turn his plough, *etc.*, or as a road. Such disputes were to be decided by three experts as arbiters, for which the *lex Mamilia* (apparently identical with the *lex Julia Agraria,* see Bruns) substituted one. Any dispute about a larger piece of land was called a dispute *de loco*: it raised questions of title, not of boundary-marks, and was consequently left to ordinary vindication or to interdicts, and conducted before the regular tribunals (Frontin. *ap. Gromat.* pp. 37, 44, *etc.*, ed. Lachmann; D. x 1 fr 2, fr 4 § 10). In later times the regulation of boundaries came like other disputes before a judge, who if necessary sent surveyors to the place to decide the matter on the spot (Ulpian D. *ib.* fr 8 § 1).

This proceeding did not apply to houses with a common wall or to lands separated by a river or a public road. It might be used even for boundaries in a town, if there was a considerable extent of adjoining gardens; and in the country it was not used where buildings were continuous. The judge had the power, if no other convenient boundary could be made, of drawing a new line and consequently assigning land to one party to which he had no previous claim, and making him compensate the other in money. And he took notice of any claims of either party for profits derived since joinder of issue from land found to belong to the other; and he could condemn to damages either party, who refused to cut down a tree or pull down a building which obstructed the proper line of boundary. The proceeding could take place between more persons than two, if they had adjoining lands, and usufructuaries and pledgees as well as owners

[1] Cicero plays on this in reference to disputes of the philosophers: *ex hac verborum discordia controversia est nata de finibus, in qua quoniam usus capionem duodecim tabulae intra quinque pedes esse noluerunt, depasci veterem possessionem Academiae ab hoc acuto homine non sinemus, nec Mamilia lege singuli sed e XII tres arbitri finis regemus* (*Legg.* i 21 § 55).

were competent to proceed. The action was *in personam*: each party was at once plaintiff and defendant (D. *ib.* fr 2 § 1, fr 3; 4 §§ 1—3, § 11).

Some old rules, said to be based on a law of Solon's at Athens, were confirmed by Gaius as to be regarded by the judge in this proceeding. It was prescribed that anyone erecting a rough stone wall[1] at the boundary should keep it in his own land; if he made a mortared wall (*τειχίον*), he should leave an interval of a foot in breadth; if he erected a house (*οἴκημα*), two feet; if he made a ditch, he should leave a space equal in breadth to the depth; if a well, he should leave the breadth of a fathom; olives and figs to be planted seven feet from the boundary, other trees five feet (D. *ib.* fr 13).

CHAPTER IV.

POSSESSION AND USUCAPION.

A. Possession. 1. Different Kinds.

Possession is a term used in a variety of senses, determined by the context and especially by what is in thought opposed to it. It is sometimes used as if equivalent to ownership, and owners of land are spoken of as possessors (*e.g.* D. ii 8 fr 15 pr; xli 1 fr 7 § 3; L 9 fr 1; tit. 16 fr 78). It is sometimes used of mere physical control irrespective of title. But its special technical use in Roman law is confined to such cases of control of things mediate or immediate, as are of lawful origin and recognised to be worthy of legal protection. It is a possession, which, if not that of an owner, is good against all the world except the owner, and may, as in the case of a first occupant, or when continued under certain conditions, give valid title as owner.

A creditor may be put in possession of a bankrupt's estate for the purpose of sale: he has only the custody, and no claim to acquire the ownership merely by continued possession. A slave may hold a thing, but he is himself in law a chattel,

[1] *αἱμασία*. Cf. Sandys on Dem. *c. Kall.* § 11.

owned and possessed by others, and has no rights of property at all, but is a mere instrument for his master. A thief may hold a thing, and intend to keep it for himself, but his possession is altogether wrongful, and cannot obtain any legal recognition. A farm tenant has possession of a farm, but this is only by agreement with the owner and in his place for the time, tilling the land and taking the fruits. A depositary has possession, but only for the convenience and at the will of the owner. A creditor may have a pledge in his possession, but that is only for the security of his claim on the debtor, and the pledge cannot thereby become his property except by further act or default of the debtor. A usufructuary has practical possession, but only because in no other way can he exercise his right to the use and enjoyment: the owner bides his time, and the usufruct becomes again merged in the ownership.

True technical possession, *i.e.* civil possession, requires both physical control (or detention, *poss. naturalis*) and lawful intention to hold for oneself. It is opposed to ownership (whether *ex jure Quiritium* or only *in bonis*) as occupation *de facto* is opposed to the right of exclusive independent occupation and disposal: it is opposed to mere detention as occupation in one's own right, though exercised either by oneself or through representatives, is opposed to physical control under some other's authority for a limited and temporary purpose: it coexists with a usufructuary's use and enjoyment, but is as it were in a state of suspended animation. Further it is distinguished from *bonorum possessio* as being a general term applied to all corporal objects, whereas the latter is a fictitious or *de facto* heirship, a succession granted by the praetor into the complex of rights and liabilities which make up the estate of one deceased.

Civil possession is important in two relations: it gives under certain conditions ownership of the thing possessed; and it makes the possessor secure in his holding without proof of title, till others shew a superior title. For acquiring, retaining and restoring the position of possessor the praetor granted interdicts[1], which in some cases were available for possessors who

[1] Cicero playfully reproaches Volumnius for not having prevented other people's jokes being fathered on him: *Parum diligenter possessio salinarum*

had not full civil possession (D. vi 1 fr 9). The trial of an interdict did not ascertain a right of ownership or of usufruct or of easement; but at most enjoined restitution of the holding or enjoyment or forbad interference with it (cf. D. xliii 1 fr 1 § 3; xix 1 fr 35). See also the Publician action p. 443.

It may be convenient to enumerate the various classes of persons who have possession of some sort but not full civil possession.

i. The following have wrongful[1] possession:

1. A thief as regards moveables, who however is included under the more general designation of

2. A dishonest, *i.e.* forcible or clandestine, possessor of land or moveables: commonly called *praedo* (cf. D. v 3 fr 11 § 1—fr 13 pr; x 3 fr 7 § 4; xli 2 fr 5, *etc.*).

ii. The following are sent into possession by the praetor merely for safekeeping: *Non possident sed sunt in possessione custodiae causa* (D. xli 2 fr 10 § 1; 3 § 23).

3. Creditors in possession of an insolvent's or absent person's estate (D. xlii 4).

4. A person put in charge of a deceased's estate, when there is no apparent heir willing to give security, for the protection of legatees' and creditors' claims (D. xxxvi 4).

5. A pregnant woman whose child will or may have a claim to an inheritance (D. xxxvii 9).

mearum a te procuratore defenditur. Ais enim, ut ego discesserim, omnia omnium dicta in me conferri....Urbanitatis possessionem, amabo, quibusvis interdictis defendamus (*Fam.* vii 32 written from Cilicia).

[1] *Justa* and *injusta possessio* are not technical terms, but mean generally a possession to which one has, or has not, a title, as *e.g.* a mortgagee has *justa possessio*, a thief has *injusta*. But in relation to certain interdicts *uti possidetis, etc. justa possessio* is a possession which has not been obtained *clam, vi* or *precario* from the other party (D. xliii 17 fr 2, 3 pr). Neither are *bonae fidei* or *malae fidei possessio* generally technical terms; they mean that the holder believes himself to be entitled or does not believe himself entitled to hold (cf. Savigny *Besitz* § 8). The legal character of possession in itself is independent of moral characteristics: *in summa possessionis non multum interest juste quis an injuste possideat* (D. xli 2 fr 3 § 5): but the rights which it brings and the protection which it gets from the law depend in various ways and degrees on the mode of its acquisition.

6. The holder under praetor's order of a house to which damage is apprehended from the ruinous state of a neighbouring house, the owner or other occupant of which refuses to give security (D. xxxix 2). The edict sharply distinguishes *in possessione esse* from *possidere* (*ib.* fr 7 pr). See below, pp. 510, 513.

iii. The following are *de facto* in possession as the only means of using and enjoying: *non possidet sed potius fruitur* (Vat. 70, cf. Gai. ii 94). *Naturaliter videtur possidere qui usum fructum habet* (D. xli 2 fr 12 pr). They are holders, not possessors (D. xliii 3 fr 1 § 8); *quasi in possessione* (cf. D. *ib.* 16 fr 3 § 17). The owner has civil possession all the while (D. xli 2 fr 52).

7. Usufructuary.

8. Usuary (cf. D. xliii 16 fr 3 § 16).

9. Superficiary (D. xliii 18).

iv. The following have a limited possession for certain purposes but not for usucapion.

10. Pledgee has possession, for that is of the essence of his contract with the owner, and he can claim protection against the world. But his holding does not prevent the owner from confirming his own title by usucapion (D. xli 3 fr 16, 33 § 4).

11. Holder on sufferance (*precario*) is in a similar position towards the world, but has no right against his grantor, who alone is counted to have possession for the purpose of usucapion (D. xliii 26 fr 4 § 1; 16 § 2, 17).

12. A stakeholder (*sequester*) has possession so as to exclude any of the depositors from gaining by usucapion, if such exclusion be intended by the depositors: otherwise he holds for the future victor, who counts the stakeholder's possession with his own for usucapion (D. xli 2 fr 39; xvi 3 fr 17 § 1).

v. The following are put in possession by agreement with the real possessor, who holds the civil possession through them. He possesses; they are in possession by his consent and as it were on his account. *Possidere videmur non solum si ipsi possideamus sed etiam si nostro nomine aliquis in possessione sit, licet is nostro juri subjectus non sit* (Gai. iv 135). *Sunt in praedio et tamen non possident* (D. xliii 26 fr 6 § 2; xli 2 fr 3 § 20; fr 25 § 1). *Possidet cujus nomine possidetur, procurator alienae possessioni praestat ministerium* (fr 18 pr).

13. The holder of a thing lent (*commodatum*).

14. A depositary.

15. A lessee or hirer, especially a lodger in town (*inquilinus*), a farmer in the country (*colonus*). And the position is not altered if he have occupation free of rent (Gai. iv 153).

16. Procurator, guest, friend (D. xli 2 fr 9).

vi. The subordinates of a *paterfamilias* are regarded as mere hands and instruments: they have neither property nor possession of their own, but acquire and hold both in his name (Gai. ii 89); *Qui in aliena potestate sunt rem peculiarem tenere possunt, habere possidere non possunt, quia possessio non tantum corporis sed et juris est* (D. xli 2 fr 49 § 1). Such are

17. Children under power.

18. Slaves owned by him either wholly or at least *in bonis*.

19. Slaves of which he has the usufruct,

and

20. Slaves of others but in good faith possessed by him.

2. Conditions of possession through others.

All acquisition, *etc.* by the last two classes (19, 20) is subject to the regular limitation that it must arise from the use of the superior's property or their own services. Gaius (ii 94) records a doubt, whether possession could be acquired through a slave in usufruct, 'because we do not possess the slave himself.' So also Ulpian (D. L 17 fr 118). But Paul (D. xli 1 fr 1 § 8) rejects the doubt, adducing the fact that we acquire possession through children although we do not possess them. A like doubt is mentioned by Gaius (ii 90) respecting persons in hand or handtake, and the same counter-argument applies. Possession cannot be acquired for his owner through a slave handed over to a creditor in pledge, nor, according to some, through a slave in flight, but general convenience put aside the latter objection (D. xli 1 fr 2 §§ 14, 15). In all these cases however it is necessary that the slave or child should have intelligence[1]. A slave owned by more than one person acquires possession for his masters or some of them on the same principles as he acquires ownership (*ib.* §§ 7, 9, 19). See above, chap. iii G i. 1.

Through free persons (except children in power) we acquire possession, (*a*) if they are in our possession *bona fide* as slaves, and act on our account, or (*b*) if they are our agents, guardians or caretakers and act with the intention of acquiring for us. Acquiry through the latter class was doubted in Gaius' time, and eventually accepted, not as logically justifiable, but only on the ground of practical convenience (Gai. ii 94, 95; Paul v 2 § 2; D. xli 2 fr 1 § 20, fr 18 pr; and in very general language D. xli 1 fr 53; Cod. vii 32 pr). An agent requires a mandate: otherwise the possession is acquired by the master only on ratification (D. xli 2 fr 42 § 1). A slave belonging to another, but not possessed by anyone, could acquire for one who is not his master, if he took possession in his name (D. xli 2 fr 34 § 2). See above, chap. iii G ii.

We can hold possession through anyone: farmer, lodger, agent, guest, friend, if he be actually in possession in our name (fr 9). A captive could not hold possession, either himself or through a slave (fr 23 § 1; tit. 3 fr 11). The burghers of a town, not having a single will, cannot properly possess; they enjoy and use in common: practical convenience, however, allowed of their acquiring and holding possession through a slave or free agent (fr 1 § 22; fr 2).

A ward, at least if of intelligent age, could both acquire and hold possession without his guardian's authority, physical possession being a matter rather of fact than of law (fr 1 § 3; 32 § 2).

3. Acquisition of possession.

Possession is acquired *corpore et animo*, *i.e.* by corporal apprehension, either by ourselves or others for us, combined with knowledge and intention of the act. In the case of lawful

[1] According to D. xli 2 fr 2 § 19 the assent of the slave is necessary. But this probably refers to cases where the slave could acquire for more than one person. Gradenwitz suspects an interpolation (*Interp.* p. 220).

acquisition by children in our power or slaves for their *peculium*, it was eventually held that no knowledge on the part of the *paterfamilias* was required: but his knowledge either at the time or subsequently was required whenever child, slave or free agent acquired possession for him directly (D. xli 2 fr 1 § 5, 24, 44 § 1). An heir does not acquire possession of the inheritance merely by entry, he requires actual apprehension of the components. If there are slaves belonging to it and he get possession of one, he can through him acquire possession of the rest. (The republican lawyers doubted this.) And the same method is applicable to a donation of land and slaves (fr 1 § 16, 23 pr, 30 § 5, 48). Possession of part of a thing can only be possession of a known definite share (*e.g.* one third, *etc.*), except in land, where possession of a certain bounded area is possible; but there can be no possession of what is uncertain, *e.g.* 'whatever part of the land is yours.' Nor is possession of a house or ship or cupboard, *etc.*, possession also of the contents (fr 3 § 2, 26, 30 pr; vi 1 fr 8). Nor does possession of land count as possession of treasure buried in it, as Brutus and Manilius thought, unless there be also knowledge, and probably actual handling, of the treasure (D. xli 2 fr 3 § 3). Two or more persons cannot be possessors at the same time of the same thing *in solidum* (fr 3 § 5).

Apart from first occupation, the usual mode of acquiring possession is, as regards moveables, taking delivery[1], as regards immoveables, being put into possession when vacant, *i.e.* when there is no one there to oppose his entrance or assert an adverse claim. For good delivery it is not always necessary for the parties themselves to hand over and receive the object. Putting it in sight so that the other can take it without

[1] *Tradere rem* (*e.g.* Gai. ii 20, 43) and *tradere possessionem* (*e.g.* Vat. 2; D. vi 1 fr 77) are both used. Of land *tradere vacuam possessionem* (D. xxii 1 fr 4), *inducere* or *mittere in vacuam possessionem* (D. xli 2 fr 33, 34), *etc.* are also used. Cf. *ad Heren.* iv 29 § 40 *Necesse est, cum constet istum fundum nostrum fuisse, ostendas te aut vacuum possedisse, aut usu tuum fecisse, aut emisse aut hereditate tibi venisse. Vacuum, cum ego adessem, possidere non potuisti; usu tuum etiam nunc fecisse non potes; emptio nulla profertur; hereditate tibi me vivo mea pecunia venire non potuit; relinquitur ergo ut me vi de meo fundo dejeceris.*

hindrance is good delivery *quasi longa manu* (D. xlvi 3 fr 79). If I bid a seller deliver something which I have bought and which is in my presence, to my agent, or put it into my house, or if he, or someone by his order, deliver me the keys of the repository when I am at the place, the delivery is good, and I acquire possession. If the thing is already in my possession as hirer or borrower or depositary, and I buy it, mere consent to my retention on my own account supplies the place of any formal delivery. (This is called by modern writers *brevi manu traditio*[1].) Similarly if I possess a thing and consent to hold it for the future as for you (in consequence of sale, gift, *etc.*) you become possessor. (This is called by modern writers *constitutum possessorium.*) To take delivery of land it is not necessary to walk over or round the whole, it is enough to enter a part as for the whole; or for the seller, if the land is so near as to be clearly identifiable, to point out the land to me from some place in my land commanding it, and declare that he gives me vacant possession of it (D. xli 2 fr 1 § 21, 3 § 1, 18 pr § 2; 51; xviii 1 fr 74; xix 1 fr 2 § 1; xli 1 fr 9 §§ 5, 6). In all cases of delivery the parties must agree on the thing though not necessarily on the name: if it be made to my agent, agreement either on my part or on my agent's is enough (D. xli 2 fr 34 § 1). Delivery on condition is good, if the condition occur; possession dates from the occurrence (fr 38 § 1).

4. Loss of possession.

Possession is lost *animo* if I consciously give up the intention to hold for myself: it is lost *corpore* if I am ejected, or it is stolen, or I abandon it, or if a change occur in the thing's character, *e.g.* by specification, as when wool is made into a dress, or land becomes religious by the interment of a dead body, or when a river or the sea covers it (fr 3 § 6, 9, 17, fr 30 § 1, 3, 4). Actual violence is not necessary to cause ejectment from land: one who flees on finding it occupied against him in force loses his possession. The adverse entry of another

[1] In contrast with *longa manu traditio* D. xlvi 3 fr 79. *Brevi manu* is found in D. xxiii 3 fr 43 § 1 in a different sense.

on our land does not affect our possession until we know of it and neglect to remove him. This specially applies to mountain pastures and the like, which are wholly deserted at times: our intention is sufficient to retain our possession, so long as we are not aware of any intrusion, just as it is if we leave our farm or house with the intention of returning. If our tenant die or become mad or leave[1], we still retain possession, unless and until someone else has gained it (fr 3 § 8, 44 § 2—46). If our tenant sublets, we hold through the sublessee; but if he formally deliver or abandon to another, so that the other holds on his own account and not on ours, our possession is lost; at least, according to some opinions (D. xli 3 fr 33 § 4; Cod. vii 32 fr 12 pr). The same distinction applies where, instead of letting, we have deposited or lent a thing (*ib.*).

A slave who runs away is considered to be still in our possession, and to hold for us anything he carries off, until he is either taken possession of by another person or asserts himself to be free (D. xli 2 fr 13 pr, 15, 50 § 1). But a slave, not actually free, though claiming his freedom openly, remains in our possession until his claim is proved (fr 3 § 10).

Moveables (other than slaves) are possessed by us only so long as they are under our control or can be put so at our will. Cattle that have strayed or articles that cannot be found or got at, or which having been lent or deposited with others are held by them against our consent, are no longer possessed by us. Wild animals kept in cages or fish in stews, tame birds or pigeons that have the habit of returning, are possessed by us, but animals kept in large enclosures or parks or pools, so as to be in fact in a state of natural liberty, are not possessed by us (fr 3 § 13—16, 47).

[1] On this point D. xli 2 fr 40 § 1 gives apparently a different decision.

B. Protection of Possession.

1. *Interdictum uti possidetis.*

For securing a person in possession two interdicts are of special importance, called from the first words *uti possidetis*[1] and *utrubi*. The former was concerned with immoveables (land and houses), the latter with moveables. They were chiefly used as preparatory to a suit for ownership, when in default of agreement it was necessary to settle which of the parties was to be plaintiff and which defendant. These interdicts were addressed to both parties, who were considered equally plaintiffs and defendants (Gai. iv 148, 149; D. xliii 17 fr 1 § 3, 3 § 1; cf. xli 2 fr 35).

The form of the interdict for land or houses is given by Ulpian, *Uti eas aedes, quibus de agitur, nec vi nec clam nec precario alter ab altero possidetis, quominus ita possideatis vim fieri veto.* The question thus turned on the character of the possession each asserted; and the decision recognised that one of the parties as possessor, who shewed that at the time of the issue of the interdict he possessed, without having used either force or concealment or request to obtain it from the other. It did not matter whether the possession had been obtained by one of these means from a third party; or whether in the abstract it was lawful or unlawful possession; the reciprocal relations of the two parties were for this matter alone in question (Gai. iv 150; D. fr 1 § 9—fr 3 pr). Nor was a successor's possession affected by his predecessor's having obtained it by force, even though he knew the fact (D. fr 3 § 10). The interdict is applicable to the whole of a farm or to a plot or to an undivided fraction (fr 1 § 7).

It is also usable to prevent encroachments on the owner's free use and cultivation of his land or dealing with his house, *e.g.* if he be hindered in building. Or if a lodger hinder him from repairing the house, the owner can bring this interdict, making at the same time a declaration that he does not thereby seek to

[1] Cicero (*RP.* i 13 § 20) makes Laelius allude playfully to this interdict on the occasion of two suns being seen in the sky, *ut ita caelum possideant, ut uterque possederit.*

interfere with the tenant's right of occupation but only with his claim to possession. If my neighbour's predecessor[1] in title has trained my vines on to his trees, I can give my neighbour notice, cut the vines and use this interdict to prevent his interference, which would be a forcible interference with my possession of the land in which the vines are planted (D. fr 3 §§ 2—4). A projection from my house is liable to this interdict from anyone who possesses the ground under it; so my putting plaster on my side of your wall is cause for the interdict (D. fr 3 §§ 6, 9). On such use of this interdict see also D. viii 5 fr 8 § 5, xxxix 1 fr 5 § 10; xlvii 10 fr 14, and below, p. 524.

Though as a rule the owner of the ground has legal possession of any building above it, yet if the building has an entrance from the street (*ex publico*), the owner of vaults below is not deemed to possess the building for the purpose of this interdict. And superficiaries have special actions and analogous interdicts allowed them by the praetor according to the terms of their holding (D. xliii 17 fr 3 § 7). Usufructuaries can use it against the owner or against a usuary and *vice versa* (fr 4). Creditors sent into possession by the praetor do not possess, and cannot therefore use this interdict (fr 3 § 8).

The damages are laid at the value of the thing (*quanti res est*). Servius took this literally, but later lawyers interpreted it to mean the interest of the possessor in retaining the possession (fr 3 § 11).

The general principles of possession *per alios* and of retaining possession not necessarily *corpore* but *animo*, apply to this interdict (Gai. iv 153; see pp. 455—459).

The interdict had to be brought within a year from the suit's being possible (*intra annum quo primum experiundi potestas fuerit*, D. fr 1 pr).

2. *Interdictum utrubi.*

The interdict for moveables ran thus, *Utrubi hic homo quo de agitur majore parte hujusce anni fuit, quominus is eum ducat, vim fieri veto.* The principle of decision between the

[1] If my neighbour did it himself, the interdict *quod vi aut clam* would apply (see p. 521).

rival claimants did not, as in *uti possidetis*, turn on who possessed at the time, but who had possessed for a greater part than his opponent of the year ending with the issue of the interdict; so that if I possessed for the last seven months and you for the eight months preceding that, I am entitled to the possession, for you cannot count more than five months of your possession. In this reckoning each party can count not only the time of his own possession but also that of his predecessor in title, *e.g.* the deceased to whom he is heir (even though not possessing at his death): so a purchaser can count his vendor's possession, a donee can count his donor's, a legatee that of testator and his heir, a husband that of the person from whom he received it in dowry, *etc.* But such additional possession (*accessio possessionis*) can be counted only by one who has possession of his own; and eventually (*obtinuit*) it was required that, as with *uti possidetis*, both his and his predecessor's possession must be faultless as against his opponent, but need not have been continuous. Possession *per alios* and retention of possession *animo* apply here also (Gai. iv 151—153; D. xliii 21; cf. xli 2 fr 13 §§ 1—13; L 16 fr 156).

3. *Interdictum de vi*[1].

This interdict was the principal means for recovering lost possession of immoveables, and appears to have run as follows in Julian's edict[2]: *Unde in hoc anno tu illum vi dejecisti aut*

[1] On *vis* see Essay on *pro Caecina* (Vol. II).

[2] In Cicero's time it appears to have run: *Unde tu aut familia aut procurator tuus illum aut familiam aut procuratorem illius in hoc anno vi dejecisti, cum ille possideret quod nec vi nec clam nec precario possideret, eo restituas* (Cic. *Tull.* 19 § 44; *Caecin.* 31 § 91). Another form is also given in Cic. *Tull.* 12 § 29 *Unde dolo malo tuo ille aut familia aut procurator ejus vi detrusus est, etc.*

This interdict is also referred to in Cic. *Agrar.* iii 3 § 11 *Promulgare ausus est, ut quod quisque possidet...jure teneret. Etiamne si vi dejecit? Etiamne si clam, si precario venit in possessionem? Ergo hac lege jus civile, causae possessionum, praetorum interdicta tollentur.* And in the *lex Agrar.* of 111 B.C. (Bruns[6] p. 77) § 18 we have (*sei quis eorum quorum ager*) *supra scriptus est ex possessione vi ejectus est, quod ejus is quei ejectus est possederit, quod neque vi neque clam neque precario possederit ab eo quei eum ea possessione vi ejecerit, etc.* Cf. *ad Heren.* iv 29 § 40.

familia tua dejecit, cum ille possideret quod nec vi nec clam nec precario a te possideret, eo illum quaeque ille tunc ibi habuit restituas (cf. Lenel *EP*. pp. 370—374).

This interdict relates only to forcible dispossession from land or buildings, whether farm, uncultivated land, house or flat (*superficies*), or even a wooden building (*qualequale sit quod solo cohaereat*). What was on the land at the time is included in the restoration required (D. xliii 16 fr 1 §§ 3—8).

Actual possession at the time of ejection is requisite to qualify for using the interdict. The possession may be exercised through a slave, an agent, a tenant, a lodger or any other person in our name; it may be held *corpore* or *animo, i.e.* by physical possession or, in temporary absence, by the intention and power to return. Forcible dispossession takes place whenever a man, or the occupant for him, is forcibly turned out of the place, or prevented from re-entering it, either by actual force or, provided[1] the threatener actually occupy the place at the time or directly afterwards, by adequate threat of force. But a person, who has not yet had possession, and is about to take it for the first time and is forcibly prevented, cannot be said to be ejected (*deici*) and cannot bring this interdict. The force may have been used either by defendant himself or his slaves or servants or agents, whether one or more. If it was done by his slaves without his consent, he is liable only for any profit accrued and for the surrender of the slaves: a volunteer agent (*falsus procurator*) is liable himself: in the case of a true agent, acting with or without consent, both agent and principal are liable to the interdict, but damages can be recovered from one only. Neither ownership nor civil possession is necessary to qualify; *e.g.* a wife possessing by gift from her husband has sufficient possession (fr 1 §§ 9—26, 29; Gai. iv 154; Paul v 6, §§ 3, 4, 6). If slaves or other occupants are turned out or subjected to bodily or mental restraint (*si vinxit aut imperavit*) the master is deemed to be ejected and has the right of interdict; but if his slaves are allowed to remain without constraint and in his service, he is not entitled to the interdict, even if personally ejected: he retains possession through them (fr 1 §§ 45—47,

[1] This proviso is omitted in a passage from Julian D. xli 3 fr 33 § 2.

fr 8, 20). A usufructuary or usuary has an analogous interdict (Vat. 90, 91; D. *ib.* fr 3 §§ 14—17). A pledge creditor, and tenant by permission (*precario*) have special interdicts. For ejection from a ship or waggon or moveables generally an action analogous to *vi bon. rapt.* or *injuriarum* or theft, according to circumstances, is applicable (Paul v 6 § 5; D. xliii 16 fr 1 §§ 6, 7).

One who has gained possession by force or stealth or permission is not protected against eviction (*impune deicitur*) by the former possessor: but is entitled to use the interdict against others than the person from whom he has obtained it: and as force may lawfully be repelled by force, a possessor is not held to possess by force who has so acted, nor is one disqualified from using this interdict who, after recovering by force the land from which he was forcibly ejected, is again ejected by the same person (Paul v 6 § 7; D. *ib.* fr 1 §§ 27, 30, fr 17). A farm tenant has no right to the interdict as a rule, but, if he has refused to admit a purchaser sent by his landlord to take possession, he is deemed to have ejected his landlord, and then if ejected by the purchaser can bring the interdict as an independent person against this latter. He is himself liable to the interdict from his landlord (fr 12, 18).

The scope of this interdict[1] is to restore to the ejected possessor all he has lost by the ejection, not merely the land or buildings itself, but everything which he had there at the time; not merely his own property, but anything on loan or hire or pledge or deposit with him; not merely in the particular spot from which he was actually ejected, but in the whole of the farm or building. It includes probably slaves and cattle which have died and buildings burnt since the ejection (although

[1] On the scope of this and the interdict *de vi armata* cf. Cic. *Caecin.* 13 § 36. Cicero is there arguing for the applicability of the latter to a case there put, and speaks of the insufficiency of an action *injuriarum* (which is however applied in some cases, see chap. vii); 'that does not touch the possession but only gives personal compensation.' *Praetor quemadmodum te restituat in aedes tuas non habebit? Qui dies totos aut vim fieri vetat aut restitui factam jubet, qui de fossis, de cloacis, de minimis aquarum itinerumque controversiis interdicit, is repente obmutescet, in atrocissima re quid faciat non habebit?*

without any fault on the part of the ejector), the fruits since the day of ejection (not, as in other interdicts, since the issue of the interdict), and any other advantages which have been lost (D. fr §§ 33—41). The valuation of damages is calculated on the interest of the plaintiff in retaining the possession (*ib.* fr 6).

The interdict must be brought within a year from the time it was first available (*annus utilis*, fr 1 § 39). After that time, and at all times against the ejector's heir, there is an action on the case limited to the restoration of any profit accrued (*de eo quod ad eum pervenit*, fr 1 pr, § 48, fr 2). It could not be brought by children against their father or by a freedman against his patron: an action on the case was substituted (fr 1 § 43).

4. *INTERDICTUM DE VI ARMATA.*

If the ejection is done by armed men a similar interdict (*de vi armata*)[1] is granted, but without the words requiring plaintiff's possession to have been free from fault. The arms may be only sticks and stones[2], they may not have been prepared beforehand, but picked up at the time; they may not have been actually used: but, if men so armed by force or terror effected the ejection or prevented the entrance of the possessor, and occupied the place, it is armed force within the meaning of this interdict. The defendant is liable, whether he has taken part himself, or ordered or approved the ejection, or contrived it *dolo malo*. Armed force may be used to repel armed force[3], or to reinstate the possessor, provided it be done at once, so as to make it part of the same proceeding. The interdict runs, after a year[4] and against heirs, only for what has reached the defendant's hands (Gai. iv 155; D. xliii 3 pr—fr 12). It could be brought against parents or patron (fr 1 § 43).

[1] In the time of Cicero this interdict ran as follows: *Unde tu aut familia aut procurator tuus illum vi hominibus coactis armatisve dejecisti eo restituas* (*Caecin.* 8 § 23; 19 § 55; 21 §§ 59, 60; 30 § 88). In an older form *detrudere* was used for *deicere* (*ib.* 17 § 49; *Tull.* 12 § 29). On this interdict the case of Caecina turned. See Essay on Cicero's speech (Vol. II).

[2] The same is stated by Cicero in argument, *Caecin.* 21 §§ 60, 61.

[3] See Cic. *Fam.* vii 13 quoted at end of Essay on Cic. *pro Tullio* (Vol. II).

[4] Cf. Cic. *Fam.* xv 16 § 3, where writing to Cassius, who had lately become an Epicurean, Cicero says *Postulabimus ex qua* αἱρέσει '*vi armatis*

Neither of these interdicts, any more than any other interdict, involves civic disgrace (D. *ib.* fr 13).

5. *Precarium.*

Tenure by permission or on sufferance, or, as the Romans called it, by request[1], exists whenever a person obtains by request (oral or written) the use of anything for so long as the grantor allows it. It is very similar to a loan, but, being regarded as due to favour and rather of the nature of a gift than of a contract, it is not the subject of any specific (*eo nomine*) civil action (D. xliii 26 fr 1, 14)[2].

Tenure by permission may exist in moveables or immoveables, in things or in servitudes. Whatever may have been the arrangement when the request was acceded to, the grantor can recall it at any time, and the praetor gave him an interdict to compel restitution. An action on the case *praescriptis verbis* is also said to have been allowed (D. fr 2, 4 § 1, 12 pr).

The interdict goes against the person who holds on this tenure or has fraudulently parted with it, whether he made the request himself or through his slave or son or (if confirmed by him) his procurator. The owner himself may hold a thing on this tenure, if ('as often happens') he has pledged it and retains the physical possession only by permission of the creditor. The grantee by permission had possession, so as to be able to use the interdict *uti possidetis* against every one except the grantor. The grantor was held to have possession for the purpose of usucapion, at least so far as to be able to count this period when he had put an end to the grantee's tenure. If the grantee had asked only to be in possession, not to possess, he would not have more possession than a farmer or lodger (D. fr 4 § 1, 6 § 2, 15 § 4, 17; xli 2 fr 10 § 1).

hominibus' dejectus sit, in eam restituare. In hoc interdicto non solet addi 'in hoc anno': quare, si jam biennium aut triennium est cum virtuti nuntium remisisti delenitus illecebris voluptatis, in integro res nobis erit.

1 Cf. Cic. *Orat.* iii 41 § 165 *Verecunda esse debet tralatio ut deducta esse in alienum locum, non inrupisse, atque ut precario, non vi venisse videatur.*

2 In another place (*Sent.* v 6 § 11) Paul says expressly *Et civilis actio hujus rei (i.e. precarii) sicut commodati competit.* Probably he referred to a *condictio.*

The precarious holder was responsible to the grantor or his heir or assignee for fraud, but not for ordinary fault. The interdict went to restore to the grantor his former position, and carried with it the fruits from the day of the interdict being issued. Damages were estimated for the interest of the grantor as on that day, and delay in restitution made the holder liable for the whole risk, for fault as well as fraud (D. fr 8 §§ 2—6).

The heir of the grantee or holder did not inherit the position, but was regarded as a clandestine possessor: he was liable to the interdict just the same: for his predecessor's fraud he was liable only so far as he was thereby benefited (fr 8 § 8, 12 § 1; Paul v 6 § 12). The interdict could be brought after more than a year (D. fr 8 § 7).

Such a holding may be granted by one who owns but does not possess, and by one whose possession is maintainable by the interdict *uti possidetis,* though he may not prove to be the owner (fr 7, 18; cf. xli 2 fr 21 pr).

C. Usucapion.

i. General.

Possession, if continued without interruption, for two years in the case of land or house in Italic soil, for one year in the case of a moveable, makes the possessor owner *ex jure Quiritium*[1], provided the possession has been honestly acquired, and the

[1] Cic. *Caecin.* 19 § 54 *Lex* (*i.e.* XII tables) *usum et auctoritatem fundi jubet esse biennium: at utimur eodem jure in aedibus, quae in lege non appellantur.* In *Top.* 4 § 23 after making a similar statement, he adds, that a house is, according to the actual language of the XII tables, included in the general class for which a two years' possession is required, *et sunt* (*aedes*) *ceterarum rerum omnium, quarum annuus est usus.* Gaius gives the obvious meaning of the term: *usucapio mobilium rerum anno completur; fundi vero et aedium biennio; et ita lege XII tabularum cautum est* (ii 42); *lex XII tabularum soli quidem res biennio usucapi jussit, ceteras vero anno* (*ib.* 54). Cf. D. L 16 fr 211 *'Fundi' appellatione omne aedificium et omnis ager appellatur, sed in usu urbana aedificia 'aedes'; rustica 'villae' dicuntur.*

The XII tables appear to have meant by *usum et auctoritatem* that the actual possession (by the purchaser) and the guaranty of the vendor

thing is not under special disability. The possessor was said to take the thing by use (*usu capere*). So short a period was, says Gaius, allowed to have this effect in order to prevent the frequency of uncertain titles.

Usucapion was required to complete a man's title to property in two cases; (1) where the forms of conveyance had not been duly observed, as where a mancipable thing had been only delivered and not either mancipated or surrendered in court (see above, p. 427 *d*); and (2) where it had been acquired from one who was neither the owner nor had an owner's right of conveyance. Usucapion in the first case cured a defect in form though the title was substantial; in the second case it cured a defect in substance, however correct may have been the form of acquisition[1] (Gai. ii 41—44; Ulp. xix 8).

1. The possession required must be civil possession; that is to say, physical control combined with conscious intention to hold for oneself. It must be possession of something certain: the usucapient must know, not merely that he claims some part of a thing or some animals of a herd, but how much, or which. If he knows that part is another's, but not which

were to last for two years: after that, if the possession was uninterrupted, the possessor became owner, and the vendor's guaranty became unnecessary. So also Pernice, *Labeo* ii² p. 328. In the Digest xxi 2 fr 76 *auctoritas* is explained by *actio pro evictione*, which would suit here exactly. In the XII tables *adversus hostem aeterna auctoritas* (Cic. *Off.* i 12 § 37; cf. D. xli 3 fr 4 § 6) and in the *lex Atinia*, *quod subruptum erit, ejus rei aeterna auctoritas esto* (Gell. xvii 7 § 21), the meaning is, that the guaranty by the vendor of a thing afterwards captured or stolen continues, because usucapion is impossible, and a fresh title cannot therefore be acquired (not merely because an enemy and a thief are incapable, but because the thing itself has been stolen or taken by force). If *hostis* means *peregrinus*, as Cicero takes it, then the foreigner having no right of usucapion has to rely only on the vendor: or (cf. Karlowa *RG.* ii 406) if a *peregrinus* was the real owner, the purchaser cannot gain from him by usucapion.

[1] Cicero dwells with force on the advantages of usucapion. *Fundus a patre relinqui potest, at usucapio fundi, hoc est, finis sollicitudinis ac periculi litium, non a patre relinquitur sed a legibus; aquae ductus, haustus, iter, actus a patre, sed rata auctoritas* ('confirmed title') *harum rerum omnium ab civili jure sumitur* (*Caecin.* 26 § 74). Horace in inexact language speaks of use being as good a title as mancipation: *Quaedam, si credis consultis, mancipat usus* (*Epist.* ii 2, 159).

part, he acquires none. A herd cannot be acquired as a whole; each individual stands by itself (D. xli 3 fr 30 § 2, 32 § 2; tit. 4 fr 4).

Only in the case of things belonging to a *peculium* can usucapion take place in ignorance on the part of the master or father. Where possession is acquired by a procurator, the period for usucapion runs only from the time of the principal's knowledge (D. xli 3 fr 47; Cod. vii 32 fr 1). A madman or infant can acquire by usucapion, only through a slave to whom delivery has been made, but madness supervening does not prevent usucapion ripening into ownership. A ward in possession can acquire, though he have not guardian's authority. In case of acquisition by a slave, if belonging to a vacant inheritance, time does not run for usucapion until the heir's entry (D. fr 4 §§ 1—4; fr 28, 44 §§ 3, 6; cf. Cod. vii 32 fr 3).

2. The possession must continue for the full period of 365 (or twice 365) days; in reckoning which however any part of the last day is counted as if it were the whole (D. xli 3 fr 6, 7; xliv 3 fr 15 pr; cf. L 16 fr 134). But an heir was allowed to count the period during which the deceased possessed, and also the time elapsed after his death until the heir entered, and after the entry on the inheritance until he took possession himself. If usucapion is begun by deceased, it may be completed before the heir's entry (D. xli 3 fr 31 § 5, 40, 44 § 3; tit. 4 fr 6 § 2). A remoter heir was allowed to reckon the deceased's possession although an intervening heir had not taken possession (D. xli 4 fr 2 § 18). A constitution of Severus and Caracalla gave the like privilege to a purchaser; he could count his vendor's possession and that of his vendor's vendor (Just. ii 6 § 13). Whether any further extension of this principle, *e.g.* to donees, or to a husband in case of dowry, *etc.* was made in Antonine times, is not clear[1].

A freeman cannot count the time he was in possession, nor the real owner of a slave count the time his slave possessed, while such freeman or slave was *bona fide* in slavery to another

[1] The extracts in the Digest, D. xli 2 fr 13, 14; xliv 3 fr 14, related to the interdict *utrubi.* Justinian (cf. Cod. vii 31) applied them to usucapion, probably following a practice which may have begun in classical times.

(D. xli 2 fr 13 § 3). If a house has been pulled down, you cannot count for usucapion of the materials the time during which you possessed the house. If however you have begun usucapion of the materials while separate, you can complete it if you have put them into a house and possess that (*ib.* 3 fr 23, 30 § 1).

3. The possession must be uninterrupted by adverse seizure or loss. It is interrupted if the possessor is ejected by anyone, owner or not, from land, or prohibited from returning to it, or if he retires in dread of armed men approaching it; in the case of a moveable, if it is stolen from him or lost; also in the case of a slave, if he runs away and is prepared to assert his freedom legally against his master (D. xli 3 fr 5, 15 § 1, 33 § 2). Capture of the possessor by the enemy interrupted usucapion, whether the captive returned home afterwards or not; but this did not apply to usucapion by his sons or slaves for him, nor, if their *peculium* was concerned, to a usucapion begun while he was in captivity (*ib.* fr 15 pr; xlix 15 fr 12 § 2; 29). Possession is interrupted by the owner's regaining it in any way, *e.g.* if one holding a thing as heir lets or sells it to the real owner, notwithstanding that the letting or selling are really nullities: or if he pledge it to him by actual transfer, for though the pledge is a nullity, the possession is interrupted (*ib.* fr 21, 33 § 5). If a usucapient has lent or deposited a thing, his possession is uninterrupted, so long as it is held for him by the borrower or depositary, but if they formally deliver it to another, the usucapient's possession is broken (fr 33 § 4).

Mere notice from the owner, or even joinder of issue, does not break usucapion honestly begun[1] (*ib.* fr 2 § 21; fr 13), but a usucapion completed after joinder of issue is no bar to restoration, if the owner wins his suit (D. vi 1 fr 18). Nor is

[1] A passage in Cicero (*Orat.* iii 28 § 110) appears to refer to some symbolical mode of asserting a claim against one who was in possession and might otherwise deprive him of the ownership (cf. § 108): *Hac divisione utuntur, sed ita, non ut jure aut judicio, vi denique recuperare amissam possessionem, sed ut jure civili surculo defringendo usurpare videantur.* For such a meaning of *usurpare* 'break the use,' see D. xli 3 fr 2. But the passage is not clear, and probably not quite sound.

pledge incompatible with the continuance of usucapion by the pledgor, nor, if it be formed by agreement without corporal possession, is the pledge creditor deprived of his rights by the debtor losing the ownership by subsequent usucapion on the part of a purchaser or heir (D. xli 3 fr 44 § 5). If a pledge is in the corporal possession of the creditor, its abstraction by a slave, whether creditor's or debtor's slave, does not interrupt usucapion begun by the pledgor (fr 33 § 6).

If possession be interrupted and resumed, usucapion has to commence afresh without relation to the former possession (*ib.* 3 fr 15 § 2; tit. 4 fr 7 § 4).

4. The possession must have been honestly acquired. The usucapient must be *ignorant* that the thing was really another's[1], and the acquisition must be based on what appears to the acquirer to be a lawful proceeding. A person may stipulate for something which is not the property of the promiser; or he may contract for the purchase of something which is not yet the property of the vendor; but, if at the time of delivery he believes the thing to be vendor's, the possession has an honest beginning and time runs in favour of the acquirer. *Optinuit Sabini et Cassii sententia traditionis initium spectandum* (D. xli 3 fr 10 pr; tit. 4 fr 2 pr § 1). The commencement of possession in the case of a slave-child born after the acquisition of his mother is its birth, but Papinian held that, if the possessor had acquired the mother in good faith, usucapion of the child was not prevented by knowledge of the title being bad before the birth of the child (tit. 3 fr 44 § 2). Where the mother had been stolen a different view prevailed (see below, p. 476).

The innocent acquisition of another's property might occur in several ways. Moveables might be found among a deceased person's things, which had been lent him or hired out to him or deposited with him, and the heir might give or sell them under the belief that they were the deceased's. Or one who had the usufruct of a female slave, being ignorant that her children were not in law part of the fruits but belonged to her owner, might give or sell them. In both these cases and others the transferor commits no theft, for there was no thievish

[1] For some exceptions see below, pp. 473, 474.

intention, and the transferee, if ignorant of the circumstances, can acquire by usucapion. Or suppose land lying neglected and unoccupied, perhaps because its owner is dead without successor or absent from the country: a man might occupy it without any force, and though himself unable to acquire a good title by usucapion owing to his being aware that it was not his own, he might convey it to another who, possessing no such guilty knowledge, consequently could by usucapion acquire a perfect title (Gai. ii 50, 51; D. xli 3 fr 36—38). A slave, *bona fide* serving another than his master, may commit a noxal offence and be duly surrendered. The surrenderee has him only *in bonis*, but usucapion perfects his title, though the owner may claim him; for the claim can be met by a plea of fraud (D. ix 4 fr 28).

Civil possession is in itself the same in all cases whatever was the mode of acquisition. But one who gained possession by force or stealth, *i.e.* against the will or presumed will of the possessor (even though he had a claim to delivery), or who possessed without any good ground and knew it, was said to hold as a mere possessor, *pro possessore possidet* (Gai. iv 144; Vat. 1; D. v 2 fr 12 § 1—fr 13 § 1; xli 2 fr 5), in contrast to one who held as purchaser (*pro emptore*) or heir (*pro herede*) or legatee (*pro legato*) or donee (*pro donato*) or husband (*pro dote*), or first occupant (*pro suo*), or had seized a thing as derelict (D. xli 2 fr 3 § 21). But, whatever the mode of acquisition, it must, if usucapion is to proceed, be good in the eyes of the acquirer. If he thinks he has no right to take, or that there is no good ground for delivery, it matters not what the deliverer thinks, time will not run in his favour. If the ground be purchase, there must have been good faith at the time of contract as well: and further there must be a good basis for his faith and his acquisition. He must either have purchased absolutely, or the condition on which he purchased must have been fulfilled; he must have intended to purchase what was actually, or would be before delivery, the property of the vendor; he must take delivery of what he believed to be his property: the thing delivered must be the thing agreed on. A possessor as of a gift must be receiving what was a gift and not merely what he supposed to be a gift. One who possesses as heir (*pro herede*) cannot gain by usucapion, if testator is still alive, or he himself is incapable of inheriting, or if there be a necessary heir, or an heir in possession already. One who possesses *pro legato* cannot gain by usucapion, when no such legacy was left him, or he himself was disqualified from taking. A gift by a father to a son under his power is no true gift; and is no basis for usucapion even after his father's death. A gift by husband to wife or *vice versâ* is not a valid gift (*pro possessore possidet* D. xli 2 fr 16), and time does not run even after divorce unless the gift be then confirmed. Possession of a supposed dowry is of no avail for this purpose, if there was no valid marriage. Possession by a non-owner of goods thrown into the sea is not available for usucapion, if the goods had been jettisoned but not abandoned. Where however the transaction took place under some error of fact, and the error was honest and reasonable, usucapion may proceed. Such a case is where a slave or agent has been instructed to buy something and delivers it to his master or principal accordingly, though he has not really bought it; or where a thing not the testator's, was taken by the heir under the belief that it was testator's; or where a thing really was testator's and had been bequeathed, but the bequest had been revoked by a codicil unknown to the legatee (D. xli 3 fr 27, 29, 48; tit. 4 fr 2 pr—§ 2; 7 § 5, 11; tit. 5 fr 2 § 2—4; tit. 6 fr 1; tit. 7 fr 7; tit. 8 fr 2, 4, 7; tit. 9 fr 1 § 3; tit. 10 fr 3, 5; xviii 1 fr 74). But an error in law vitiates the possession; and thus a purchase from a ward without his guardian's authority is bad, if purchaser thinks the authority not requisite, but good if he thinks the youth to be of full age (xli 3 fr 31 pr; 4 fr 2 § 5).

Where a slave acquires possession for his *peculium*, his honest intention is requisite for usucapion, and any subsequent knowledge on his master's part of the acquisition being bad does not hinder it; but if he is acquiring not for his *peculium* but directly for his master, and the master know at the time that the thing is another's, or if he take away the slave's *peculium* and know that the acquisition was bad, usucapion will not proceed (D. xli 4 fr 2 §§ 11—13; cf. xviii 1 fr 12). An heir or other successor may know that something purchased by the deceased was not the vendor's, but if deceased was in good faith and had had delivery, usucapion will run from the date of his possession; if it was not delivered to him but to the heir, the heir's knowledge prevents usucapion (*ib.* § 19; tit. 3 fr 43).

A title to possession, bad at the time of acquiry, cannot be made good for usucapion by the mere intention of the possessor: *nemo causam possessionis sibi ipse mutare potest* (D. xli 2 fr 3 § 19); the original fact cannot be altered. But this does not prevent a new ground of possession being acquired. Thus, if a possessor without good ground proceed to buy the ownership, he now holds by a good title, even if he be in error and the vendor was not owner. So if he become heir, legal or praetorian, to the owner, or even with good reason believe that he is, or obtain in any way the owner's consent, he now holds by a good title, and time for usucapion begins to run (D. xli 3 fr 33 § 1). But a depositary or borrower cannot convert his mere detention on other's account into a lawful possession for himself, by assuming himself to be heir or asserting a purchase which has never taken place (D. xli 5 fr 2 § 1; xliii 26 fr 6 § 3).

5. Certain classes of things were incapable of usucapion. These were:

(*a*) All things incapable of private ownership, *e.g.* free persons, things sacred or religious, or belonging to the Roman people or to other communities; or to the fisc (Gai. ii 48; D. xli 3 fr 9; Cod. vii 30 fr 2).

(*b*) Lands in provincial soil (Gai. ii 46; cf. Cod. vii 31). On these see above, pp. 427, 429.

(*c*) Before the *lex Claudia* (which abolished agnatic guardianship of women) mancipable things belonging to a woman in the guardianship of her agnates, unless they had been formally delivered by her with her guardians' authority. This prohibition was referred to the XII tables (Gai. ii 47).

(*d*) By the Julian law *repetundarum*, all presents to the governor or praetor contrary to the law (D. xlviii 11 fr 8 pr).

(*e*) Things stolen. This restriction was also due to the XII tables. It applied only to moveables: *fundi furtum non fit* (Gai. ii 45, 51).

(*f*) Things taken by force (*res vi possessae*). This restriction applied both to moveables and immoveables, and was due to the *lex Julia et Plautia* (Gai. ii 45; D. xli 3 fr 33 § 2).

Of these cases of disability most discussion is concerned with the last two. The thief or forcible occupier of course could not gain by usucapion, because he was acting dishonestly, but neither could any innocent acquirer from him or his successors. The thing or land was as it were tainted, until it once more got into the hands of its lawful owner and was thereby purged of its taint (Gai. ii 49). According to the words of the *lex Atinia*, the disability was removed if the stolen thing came back to him from whom it was stolen; but this was interpreted to mean that it must come back to its owner; and further it must have come back lawfully, and with the knowledge that it was his and had been stolen. A thing in pledge or borrowed must return to the pledgor or lender. If however the pledgor himself had stolen it, some held that it must return to the pledgee. Things in a slave's *peculium*, if stolen without the master's knowledge and returned to the slave, are capable of usucapion; if the slave stole something from his master and replaced it as before, the taint from theft is purged: but if the master knew of the theft, he must also know of the return, and in the former case must be willing that it should still remain in the slave's *peculium* (D. xli 3 fr 4 §§ 6—9, 21, fr 49). Return to a procurator without the principal's knowledge of something stolen from the principal does not cure the theft (*ib.* fr 41), but return, within the knowledge of guardians or caretakers or to them, of things stolen from a ward or madman is sufficient (fr 4 § 11; D. xlvii 2 fr 57 § 4). So also is delivery to another with the owner's approval (D. xli 3 fr 4 § 14). And where the thief purchases it from the owner, or becomes heir to him, or the owner has brought an action for it and received the damages, the taint is purged and the possession honest (fr 32 pr, 42 § 1; xlvii 2 fr 85, 87). One who purchased from the enemy a stolen slave cannot gain it by usucapion (D. xlviii 15 fr 27).

Wool shorn from a stolen sheep while in the thief's possession is incapable of usucapion, and so, according to the better opinion, is a dress made of such wool. But if the sheep was in the hands of a *bona fide* holder for value, unaware of the theft, the wool when shorn and the young at birth, both being fruits, became at once the property of the holder, at least so as to admit of consumption without eventual liability to compensate the owner of the sheep. The like held with regard to other animals (D. xli 3 fr 4 §§ 19, 20; tit. 1 fr 48 § 2; xlvii 2 fr 48 §§ 5, 6; xxii 1 fr 28 pr[1]). If a slave woman was pregnant when stolen or if she conceived while in the thief's possession, the child was tainted with the theft and therefore incapable of usucapion[2]. An heir, though ignorant of his predecessor's theft, was affected by his fault, and was disqualified from gaining by usucapion a child of a stolen woman, though conceived and born in his possession (D. xli 3 fr 4 § 15; i 5 fr 26). Whether a master receiving, as the price of his slave's freedom, or otherwise for value, a slavewoman stolen by his slave, was affected in the same way, was a point variously decided (D. xli 3 fr 4 §§ 16, 17; tit. 4 fr 2 § 14, 9, 10). An honest purchaser or other holder for value is in a more independent position than an heir; and if a stolen slavewoman in his possession conceive and bear a child, it is free from taint both for himself and others, and if unaware of the theft at the time of birth[3] he can gain it by usucapion. Subsequent knowledge of the mother's being stolen did not in the opinion of most affect the matter. But Pomponius held that if he became aware of the theft before usucapion was completed and did not do his best to inform the real owner, his possession became stealthy (*clam possidere*) and did not avail for usucapion. A donee, legatee or other *bona fide* holder, though not for value, is in the same position as a purchaser (D. xli 3 fr 4 § 18, 33 pr; tit. 10 fr 4; xli 1 fr 48 § 1; xlvii 2 fr 48 § 5).

Land occupied by force was incapable of usucapion though the ejected was a dishonest possessor and though the ejector was the lawful owner, for even he would have to give it up

1 It is difficult to reconcile the texts. See *e.g.* Karlowa *RG.* ii p. 420.

2 Scaevola (on the ground that *partus* is not *pars*) held a different view (D. xli 3 fr 10 § 2).

3 In the passage of Papinian (fr 44 § 2) referred to above, p. 471, it is not said that the woman was stolen.

under the interdict (*unde vi*), and therefore it could not be said to have returned into his power (D. xli 3 fr 4 §§ 23—25). If the occupant of a vacant possession forbids the owner to enter, this is not counted as forcible occupation. If one has expelled a possessor by force but not occupied, and another has occupied it when vacant, the land is capable of usucapion, for though the interdict *unde vi* would apply, because the former possessor was *vi dejectus*, yet the land was not *vi possessus*. If the owner fled on sight of the approach of armed men, though none of them actually entered, he is *vi dejectus* but the land is not tainted (fr 4 §§ 22, 27; fr 33 § 2).

(*g*) A right of road is not capable of physical possession and ejection (fr 4 § 26). Servitudes cannot be gained by usucapion separately from the buildings or lands which they serve, nor can a building (*superficies*) be gained separately from the ground (fr 10 § 1, 23 pr, 26, 39). Nor can a usufruct be gained by this means; but both personal and real servitudes can be lost by non-use (fr 4 § 28, fr 44 § 5).

ii. SPECIAL CASES OF USUCAPION.

Gaius mentions three cases in which usucapion was, at least at one time, allowed to proceed, notwithstanding knowledge on the part of the possessor that the thing was another's.

1. The first is *usucapio pro herede* on which see p. 227.

2. The second (as well as the third) case is called *usureceptio* (or *usus receptio* as sometimes *usus capio*, probably two nominatives) because the former owner recovers his property, which he has mancipated or surrendered to another in trust (*fiduciae causa*). If the former owner regained possession and kept it for one year (even if it was land) he regained the ownership without any reconveyance. This applied both to a deposit and a pledge, provided the debt had been discharged. If however it was not discharged, usucapion ensued only if his reacquisition of the possession was independent of his creditor, for if he got it by request or hire he would be holding the thing for his creditor and not as of right for himself (Gai. ii 59, 60). Abstraction of a thing by the debtor from a fiduciary creditor did not therefore render him liable for theft (iii 201): but such

abstraction of an ordinary pledge or even sale of a hypothek was treated as theft of the possession (Gai. iii 200; D. xlvii 2 fr 12 § 2, 67 pr; *Scaevola ait possessionis furtum fieri*, xlvii 4 fr 1 § 15), but it did not, according to the better opinion, render the thing furtive and incapable of usucapion by others, for the theft had put it into the hands of the owner (D. xli 3 fr 4 § 21, tit. 4 fr 5, but cf. Cod. vii 26 fr 6; D. xliv 3 fr 5 § 1).

3. The third case is *ex praediatura usureceptio.* Gaius says (ii 61) that if the people sell a thing which is bound (*obligatam*) to them and the owner get possession of it, he is allowed to regain it by a two years' use. This requires some explanation. It was the practice of the Romans to put out to contract their chief matters of public business. The collection of the revenues (*vectigalia*) was thus farmed out: and the erection or repairs of state buildings was done through contractors[1]. The farmers of the revenue had to give security for the due payment of the sum agreed on: the contractors had to do the same for the due performance of their contract. The *duoviri* or *quaestores* who had control of public money in a town had to give the like security *pecuniam municipio salvam fore.* The security consisted of persons as sureties, and lands besides. The former were called *praedes*, the latter *praedia*[2]. The contractor was

[1] In the case spoken of by Cicero *Verr.* ii 1 50 § 130 sq. the repair of the temple of Castor at Rome had been undertaken by Junius, who died. Verres found the execution unsatisfactory, and put it out to contract again with more onerous conditions, the cost to be defrayed by Junius' heirs. The cost was fixed by auction, as Cicero says, at an amount fourteen times more than the proper cost on regular conditions. Cicero maintains that it ought according to the regular practice to have been assigned to the old contractors, who had already given security: *Ubi illa consuetudo in bonis* (i.e. *mancipis*) *praedibus praediisque vendundis omnium consulum, etc., ut optima condicione sit is cuja res, cujum periculum sit?...Locatur opus id quod ex mea pecunia reficiatur, ego me refecturum dico, probatio futura est tua qui locas; praedibus et praediis populo cautum est* (§ 142). Verres by an express edict had excluded Junius' son from taking the job and also forbad the contractor to have any partner. It is difficult to say how much of this was usual, how much due to Cicero's rhetoric, how much to Verres' peculiar methods of proceeding.

[2] In the same way Cicero, on relinquishing his provincial government, speaks of leaving public money at Laodicea and taking *praedes, ut et mihi*

manceps (Fest. *s.v. Lex agrar.* 46), who was said *praedibus praediisque cavere* (Cic. *Verr.* ii 1 54 § 142). The fullest account that we have of this proceeding is in the charter given by Domitian to the borough of Malaga in Spain, of which some chapters have been preserved on bronze. The terms (*lex*) of each contract, the sureties accepted, the lands submitted, undersealed and bound (*subdita, subsignata, obligata*)[1], the examiners (*cognitores*) of the lands were all to be entered in the books of the community and also to be kept exposed to public view during the whole time of office of the duumvir, who presided over the law court. All these and all their then lands and later acquisitions, except so far as they might be honestly freed (by payment or arrangement), were to be bound

et populo cautum sit sine vecturae periculo (*Fam.* ii 17 § 4). In the charter of Malaga cap. 60 provision is made for all candidates for the duumvirate or quaestorship to give *praedes* for the security of any public money with which they may have to deal if elected (Bruns[6] pp. 150, 151). Similar provisions are found in the fragment of a charter for Tarentum lately discovered and published with notes by Scialoja and Petra in the *Monum. Antichi dei Lincei*, vol. VI (1896), (also issued separately at Rome). The term was regularly applied at one time to the surety given to the Court for forfeits in private suits (Gai. iv 16, 94). There is no evidence of *praes* being ever used of a surety in contracts between private persons. Cf. Plaut. *Men.* 593; Cic. *Att.* xii 52; xiii 3; *Fam.* v 20 *Docuit me Camillus... praedes Valerianos teneri. Erat enim curata nobis pecunia Valerii mancipis nomine.*

[1] Cicero alludes to this in criticising Rullus' agrarian bill. *Soluta praedia meliore in casu sunt quam obligata; eodem capite* (by this clause of the bill) *subsignata omnia, si modo Sullana sunt, liberantur* (*Rull.* iii 2 § 9). In *pro Flacc.* 32 § 80 he speaks as if only mancipable lands could be made security to the public: *Quaero, sintne ista praedia censui censendo, habeant jus civile, sint necne sint mancipi, subsignari apud aerarium aut apud censorem possint. Subsignare* is used of securities in *lex Agrar.* 73, 84 (Bruns[6] no. 11); *lex Puteolana* 7, 15 (Bruns[6] no. 142). The undersealing would be by the person pledging the land in question, and would take the place of our signing. Compare the undersealing of *chirographa* found at Pompeii noted by Zangemeister (*Corp. I. Lat.* IV supplem., pp. 420, 433). (In Plin. *NH.* xviii 34; *ib.* 61 it means simply 'subjoin.' In Plin. *Ep. Traj.* 4 § 4 it is used metaphorically: *subsigno apud te fidem pro moribus Romani*, 'I pledge my honour for the conduct of Romanus'; so *Ep.* iii 1 § 12.)

Things pledged to the fisc could yet be vindicated, alienated, and have servitudes imposed on them by their owners (Pompon. *ap.* D. L 17 fr 205).

to the borough fund of Malaga in the same way as were like sureties, examiners and lands at Rome. The examiners were to be liable only in case of anything false being found in their report. The *duoviri*, on a decree of the borough council, made when not less than two-thirds were present, were empowered to sell the sureties, examiners and lands according to the terms observed at Rome, and if no buyer should be found on those terms, then they were to be sold *in vacuom*[1] and the money to be brought into the borough chest. The borough courts were enjoined to give the purchaser every proper facility for suing the sureties and examiners and obtaining the lands pledged (*Lex munic. Malag.* 63—65). Other references and allusions appear both in laws (*lex agrar.* A.U.C. 643 §§ 46—48, 53; *lex Puteol.* Bruns[5] no. 142); and in classical writers[2] but do not add substantially to our information. The *cognitores* were no doubt persons who certified to the existence and value of the lands taken as security, and to the charges, if any, upon them. The persons who bought the securities were called *praediatores* (Gai. *l.c.*), their act or business was *praediatura*, the rules regularly observed were called *lex praediatoria*, and the law and practice in this matter formed a special branch of law (*jus praediatorium*, Cic. *Balb.* 20 § 45).

The exact relation of the *praedes* and *praedia* to the *manceps*, the terms of the first offer for sale, and the meaning of a sale *in vacuom* and other questions have been much discussed[3]. Mommsen holds that the *manceps* though liable *ex*

1 Suetonius says of Claudius (cap. 9) *Sestertium octagies* (*cir.* £6800) *pro introitu novi sacerdotii coactus impendere ad eas rei familiaris angustias decidit, ut cum obligatam aerario fidem liberare non posset, in vacuum lege praediatoria venalis pependerit sub edicto praefectorum*, *i.e.* 'his name was put up as a Treasury debtor, whose estate was to be sold without limitation.'

2 For the redemption of the prisoners taken at Cannae some people suggested that money should be advanced on loan from the public treasury; *dandam ex aerario pecuniam mutuam praedibusque ac praediis cavendum populo* (Liv. xxii 60 § 3). So later under Augustus *facta mutuandi copia sine usuris per triennium, si debitor populo in duplum praediis cavisset* (Tac. *Ann.* vi 17).

3 See Mommsen *Stadtrechte der Salpensa, etc.* pp. 471, 472; Ihering *Geist* III 1, Pref. pp. xi—xxvii, and note 240 *a* (ed. 4); Kuntze's *Excurs.* ii

locato conducto, was not liable in the first line, nor so stringently as the *praedes*: the liability was first on the *praedes*, including their *praedia* (cf. *lex Acil. repet.* 56; *lex agr.* 47, 84; Cic. *Rab. P.* 4 § 8, 13 § 37; Gell. vi (vii) 19; Liv. xxxviii 58). Ihering holds that in old Roman law there was no direct *obligatio faciendi* (only *dandi*), and that, in order to obtain a man's promised performance, the practice was to have other persons bound in penalties to secure it. So with *praedes, vades, obsides*: the *manceps* himself promised neither performance nor penalty: the *praedes* had every motive to see that he duly performed. Karlowa holds the *manceps* liable in the first line, referring especially to Cic. *Verr.* ii 150 § 130 cited *supra*. And this seems to me probable for Cicero's time at least.

The *praedia* probably belonged to the *manceps* or to the *praedes*, and were specified, not to make them liable for the debt—all their property was liable—but to shew that the guarantors were substantial, and to facilitate execution. The lands were not necessarily, I imagine, free from previous charges. The first offer for sale was probably at a minimum upset price equal to the debt to the State, and the purchaser would have to meet previous charges on the property, and possibly (though nothing is said of this) be bound to retransfer to the previous owners within a certain time at the same or some reasonable price. Actual possession may have been deferred. If no purchaser was found on these terms, the lands were offered probably at anything they would fetch, and (as Karlowa suggests) clear of any right of redemption by the former owner[1]. Previous charges on the lands would not be swept away, any more than in sales by the fisc (cf. D. xlix 14 fr 3 § 5, 11, 22 § 1, 41, *etc.*)[2]. The State sold only what was

pp. 506—512 (where many extracts from Rivier's tract are given); Karlowa *RG.* ii pp. 47—59.

[1] *In vacuom vendere* is 'to sell on clear terms,' cf. *in incertum decernere* 'in reference to what is uncertain' (Liv. xliii 12); *in universum quaerere* 'to inquire generally' (*ib.* ix 26).

[2] On the sale of confiscated property, to which *sectio* is usually applied, see Book VI chap. xiii B. Both of this and of the sale of estates pledged to the State are used the phrases *publice bona mercari* Gai. iv 146, compare (same section) *publice bona emere* (MS. *publica*); iii 154 *si bona publice*

pledged to them, and the contractor could pledge only the surplus value over previous charges. If the sale fetched more than the debt due to the State, the overplus would presumably be paid to the debtor (cf. D. xlix 14 fr 45 § 12). In early days perhaps the *manceps* and *praedes* themselves, like judgment debtors, were given up to the purchaser (see Book VI chap. xiii A). Afterwards the sale of a *praes* would mean the sale of his estate (cf. *sector Pompei, etc.* Cic. *Phil.* ii 26 § 64, quoted Book VI chap. xiii B 3). The purchaser (*sector*), at any rate when the sale was *in vacuom*, would get full ownership and possession of the lands and property (cf. Varr. *RR.* ii 10 § 4) and had an interdict (*sectorium*) to get hold of them (Gai. iv 146). If the lands did not belong to the persons reported by the examiners, the real owner, if his property was sold, would probably be in some way reimbursed from the examiners' pocket.

The usucapion spoken of by Gaius was perhaps allowed in the case of the *praedia*, only when they were sold *lege praediatoria* and not *in vacuom*: but as regards his other effects, a *praes* may have often been left in possession of things overlooked by the estate-broker: he was not bound to disclose all his estate; and public opinion would allow his reacquiring the ownership by possession for the ordinary period, notwithstanding his knowledge of the public sale. Or this practice might have prevailed simply as saving the trouble of a reconveyance, the *praediator* being a friend[1] or not caring to interfere. It was not every estate-broker who would care to push his rights to an extreme, and it was better for general business that titles should be clear. Hence this 'reacquisition by use after a sale of State pledges' is mentioned by Gaius without any blame.

aut privatim venierint; Cic. *Flac.* 18 § 43 *fratris bona, quod populo non solvebat, praetore Flacco publice venierunt. Publice* does not mean 'publicly,' but 'by authority,' or 'on behalf,' of the people.

[1] There appears to have been a friendly arrangement made for the purchase of Milo's estate (which was sold, owing to the great mass of debts, *semuncia, i.e.* at $4\frac{1}{6}$ per cent. Ascon. p. 159). See Cic. *Att.* v 8; 10 § 4. Perhaps too this was the cause of Quinctius being *socius* of Naevius in the purchase of Alfenus' estate (a case of *sectio*). See the Essay on Cic. *pro Quinctio* (Vol. II).

D. PRESCRIPTION.

Usucapion made a man owner *ex jure Quiritium* and gave him all the rights and protection due to an owner. But, as has been mentioned, there were many things to which usucapion was not applicable, and of these land in the provinces was very important. There grew up (we do not know the commencement or the steps) protection for possessors in some of these cases also[1]. But it was protection only, not a positive acquisition of ownership. It was a plea under the name of *praescriptio* (see Book VI chap. vi F), and may have been prefixed to the *formula* in some words restricting the contention to what had not been possessed for a long time by the defendant. There must have been a rightful origin of the holding, and uninterrupted possession by the holder or his predecessors in title for a period of ten years if the parties lived in the same province, or twenty years if they lived in different provinces. If suit was commenced, that at once broke the possession, but if the property was transferred to a new purchaser after the commencement of the suit and he continued in possession for twenty years, he had a right to the *praescriptio*. This protection by twenty years possession was good against the State (*res publica*), which was granted a remedy by action for the value of its interest against those who had allowed the adverse possession to grow (Paul v 2 §§ 3—5; cf. Vat. 7; D. xliv 3 fr 14). The prescription appears to have been good against any claim of a creditor to recover his pledge from a third party (D. *ib.* fr 5 § 1; Cod. vii 36 fr 1).

An edict of Marcus Aurelius provided for the protection of anyone who had bought from the Crown what did not belong to it. The lapse of five years since the purchase was sufficient as a plea to defeat the owner's claim (Just. ii 6 § 14).

[1] The matter was the subject of so many imperial constitutions between the Antonines and Justinian, that the Digest is little to be relied on for details of the previous law.

CHAPTER V.

SERVITUDES are rights exercisable over another's property. As regards him they are diminutions of the full control which belongs to an owner in favour of another who exercises some control in place of or beside him. Servitudes are of two kinds, according as they are attached to persons or are attached to land or houses. *Servitutes personarum* are rights attached to particular persons over the property of others, as, for instance, a usufruct; *servitutes praediorum* ('easements') are rights attached to certain *praedia* (*i.e.* farms or houses) over neighbouring farms or houses, as for instance a right of road, or a right to prevent another obstructing the lights of your tenement.

PERSONARUM SERVITUTES.

1. *Usufructus.*

(*a*) The principal personal servitude is usufruct, which is the right of making use and taking the fruits of anything without destroying its substance or altering its character (D. vii 1 fr 1). It corresponds largely to a life-interest[1] in a thing, being usually tenable for the life, natural and civil, of the grantee. The owner remains owner as before the creation of the usufruct, but his practical enjoyment is suspended until the usufruct is ended: and the ownership may be changed without the usufruct being affected.

(*b*) Rights of usufructuary.

A usufruct may exist in any material thing which can be used without being destroyed (for the case of consumables see p. 488), but the usufructs generally spoken of are in land, houses, and slaves. The usufructuary, or, as he is often called, the fructuary, was entitled to have the physical possession, to use the thing in the ordinary way according to its character, and

[1] Cf. Lucr. iii 971 *Vita mancipio nulli datur, omnibus usu.*

to take and dispose of its natural or usual produce. If he did not use it himself, he could let it or allow another to use it. If it is let already and the tenancy is not excepted, the fructuary can turn out the tenant. He must maintain it in proper condition, keep up its rights and discharge all dues regularly falling on the occupant (*e.g.* rates for water, drainage, roads, produce for a passing army, or (at a low price) for the burghers if that be customary, and taxes (*fusiones*) due to the Crown), but is not responsible for its loss or destruction except from his own fraud or fault. The fructuary of a farm, besides his right to its ordinary produce for all purposes, can take stone or lime or sand or timber for the repair of the homestead, poles and withies for fences and vineyards, even from land (of the grantor's) not actually part of the farm but which was generally resorted to for the purpose. If there are bees he can take their produce. If there is a coppice or reed-bed on the farm, he can cut for sale; if there are regular quarries or mines he can sell the produce also, and even establish in suitable places new mines or works if more profitable than agriculture, provided they do not foul the air or require an expensive staff. But he must not cut down fruit trees or timber trees, unless necessary for firewood, or turn pleasure grounds into kitchen gardens. If there be a nursery garden, he can sell the plants, but must keep it restocked. Trees that have fallen belong to him, and any game and fish that he can catch. He has a right to use the plant (*instrumentum*) which was required for working it, whether slaves, oxen, or farming implements, presses and vats. He must not deteriorate but may improve the farm, acting as a sensible business man (*bonus paterfamilias*) would do in dealing with a farm of that character (D. vii 1 fr 9—fr 12 pr, 13 § 4—§ 6, 27 § 3; 59).

The usufructuary of a house may embellish it with painting and statuary, *etc.*, and may put in windows, but may not alter the rooms, or reverse the entrances, or raise the building, or divide it into apartments for letting, or generally alter the style and arrangements. He must keep it in repair (*sarta tecta habeat*, the former referring to the walls, the latter to the roof), and renew ornamental plaster and pavements; but is not liable to rebuild what has fallen from age. If he add to the building, he cannot remove the additions (D. fr 7, 12 § 7—15 pr; cf. xxxix 2 fr 20). The usufructuary of vacant ground (*area*) cannot build generally upon it (Paul iii 6 fr 21), but may put up a cottage for a caretaker (D. vii 1 fr 73).

The fructuary of a slave[1] is similarly entitled to the services of the slave, and restricted by regard to his worth and qualifications. He must not send a scribe (*librarius*) to do farm work, or make a bandsman into a butler, or set a trained gymnast to clean sewers. He has full power of discipline, but must be moderate in correcting a slave, not torture or whip (*flagellis caedere*) or injure him. He must feed and clothe him in a way suited to his value, and give him medical attendance (D. vii 1 fr 15 §§ 1—13; fr 17 § 1, 45; Paul iii 6 § 23). Acquisitions through a slave by one who has the usufruct in him are limited to what is procured either by his services or by use of the fructuary's property, or is due to others' desire to benefit the fructuary through him (D. fr 21, 22, see p. 435). The child of a slave-woman is the property of the owner, not of the fructuary, who has not even the usufruct in the child (D. fr 68 pr; v 3 fr 27; xxii 1 fr 28; cf. Gai. ii 50)[2].

The fructuary of a herd of animals is entitled to the young as his own, subject to the duty of maintaining the herd in

[1] Curius writes playfully to Cicero (*Fam.* vii 29) *Sum* χρήσει μὲν *tuus,* κτήσει δὲ *Attici nostri; ergo fructus est tuus, mancipium illius, quod quidem si inter senes comptionales venale proscripserit, ègerit non multum.* Cicero replies (*ib.* 30) *Attici quoniam proprium te esse scribis mancipio et nexo, meum autem usu et fructu, contentus isto sum; id enim est cujusque proprium quo quisque fruitur atque utitur,* the last sentence being philosophically, not legally true. Curius puns on *mancipium,* 'property' in the first clause, 'slave' in the second. For *mancipio et nexo* see Essay on *nexum* (Vol. II).

[2] Whether the offspring of a slave, the object of usufruct, belonged to the fructuary was a matter in early times much disputed; cf. Cic. *Fin.* i 4 § 12 *Partus ancillae sitne in fructu habendus, disseritur inter principes civitatis P. Scaevolam M. Manlium ab iisque Brutus dissentit.* By the time of the Digest lawyers it was decided in favour of Brutus' opinion, that a fructuary had no right either of ownership or use in a child, but he had the ownership of the offspring of animals. See my note on Tit. *de usufructu* fr 68.

full strength. When an animal is definitely placed in the herd (which is a question of fact in the particular case), it belongs to the owner; meanwhile the property is in suspense, till the event decides: if the herd is full, the young are the property of the fructuary. The fructuary of a single animal takes the young, and is not liable to supply the place of the animal, if it dies (D. vii 1 fr 68 § 1—fr 70). Both of a herd and of single animals the milk, hair, and wool, when taken, belong to the fructuary (D. xxii 1 fr 28).

If the usufruct of robes (*vestis, vestimentorum*), *e.g.* such as are used for theatrical representations or funerals, is left to a person, the fructuary may let them out, and is not responsible for ordinary wear and tear, but ordinary dresses he would not be expected to let but only to use (D. vii 1 fr 15 §§ 4, 5; tit. 9 fr 9 § 3).

(*c*) Usufructuary's bond.

The fructuary had to bind himself by stipulation to use in a proper manner (*boni viri arbitratu usurum*, or *ac si optimus paterfamilias uteretur*), and on the expiration of his usufruct (he or his heir) to restore whatever then remained. And the usual clause against fraud (*dolum malum abesse afuturumque esse*) was added. If this guaranty is not given, although the fructuary has had the thing delivered to him, the owner can bring a vindication, and thereby either recover the thing or damages, or get a proper guaranty (D. vii 9 fr 1—3; Paul iii 6 § 27).

(*d*) Special usufructs.

A usufruct in the whole or part of testator's estate is often spoken of. It was a natural means of making a provision for a wife, and might be coupled with care of the children. If 'a part' was left, a moiety was understood. A third part is sometimes mentioned: and the usufruct of a third part of the estate was permitted by the *lex Papia* to be taken as legacy by wife from husband or *vice versa* (D. vii 1 fr 43; xxxiii 2 fr 24, 32 § 8, 37; Ulp. xv 3). It made no difference whether the word *bonorum* or *rerum* was used: in either case debts would be deducted before dividing into thirds (D. xxxiii 2 fr 43). Such bequests would naturally lead to the senate's decree about to be named. In Cicero's time money and consumables appear not to have been included[1].

By a senate's decree bequests were allowed of the usufruct of everything which was the property of the testator (*ut omnium rerum, quas in cujusque patrimonio esse constaret, ususfructus legari possit*), and hence a bequest of the usufruct, or rather quasi-usufruct, of consumables (*e.g.* wine, oil, corn) was admitted. The legatee thereupon became owner, but had to guaranty the restoration, of the like quality and quantity or their agreed value, on the lapse of the usufruct by his death natural or civil (*cap. dem.*). The same principle was applied to a bequest of the usufruct of money, the benefit consisting in the use of the money without paying interest. Such a bequest came to be allowed also when the consumables or money were not the property of the testator, the heir being then bound to obtain them for the legatee (D. vii 5 fr 1, 2, 5, 7, 9, 10; tit. 9 fr 7 § 1; cf. xxxiii 2 fr 1; Ulp. xxiv 27). There was also allowed (after some discussion) a usufruct of investments (*nomina*), by which the fructuary would obtain the interest and presumably have the power of reinvestment. If such a usufruct were left to the debtor himself, it would save him from paying interest. The fructuary would have to give the usual guaranty (D. vii 5 fr 3, 4; xxxiii 2 fr 24; Vat. 46).

There was no usufruct in a right of way, for *servitus servitutis esse non potest*: nor was it rendered possible by the senate's decree; for a right of way is neither included in a person's goods, nor wholly outside them (*neque ex bonis neque extra bona*). But the legatee was granted an action against the heir to allow him his full rights of *uti frui*, including

[1] Cicero (*Top.* 3 § 17) gives an argument: *Non debet ea mulier, cui vir bonorum suorum usum fructum legavit, cellis vinariis et oleariis plenis relictis, putare id ad se pertinere: usus enim, non abusus* ('using up,' *i.e.* consumption, cf. D. vii 5 fr 5 § 2) *legatus est: ea sunt inter se contraria.* Cf. D. xxxiii 2 fr 32 § 2. An instance of such a general bequest occurs in Cic. *Caecin.* 4 § 11 *Testamento facit heredem quem habebat e Caesennia filium; usum et fructum omnium bonorum suorum Caesenniae legat, ut frueretur una cum filio.* This son soon dies and leaves a large quantity of money, which therefore was probably not deemed to be included in the usufruct (*ib.* § 12).

a road, during the legatee's life, or else formally to constitute such a right, subject to a guaranty of restitution on his death natural or civil (D. xxxiii 2 fr 1). If a right of access, through other parts of the testator's or grantor's land or otherwise, was necessary for the fructuary of a farm, although not named in the will or grant, he could claim it from the heir, and even in spite of the testator's having declared that the heir need not give it (Vat. 54; D. vii 6 fr 1 §§ 1—3).

A usufruct extends over imperceptible accretions, but not over an island in a river which has arisen by itself, though its proximity may make it an accretion to the ownership of the land (D. vii 1 fr 9 § 4).

(*e*) Creation of usufruct.

The most usual way in which a usufruct was created was by legacy; which vested only on the entry of the heir (D. vii 3 § 2). A direct creation by will might take place in two ways. The testator either granted and bequeathed (*do lego*) the usufruct, or in granting and bequeathing the ownership, reserved (*recipit, deducit, excipit*) for the heir the usufruct (D. vii 1 fr 36 § 1). *Inter vivos*, it was either created directly by surrender in court, or could be reserved (for the grantor) either by that conveyance or by mancipation. The reservation must be made in express words; for otherwise, if a usufruct is bequeathed or granted to one and the ownership to another, the owner and fructuary would have a joint right of using and enjoying. A usufruct might also be established by the judge in a suit for dividing an inheritance or for dividing common property. All these methods —legacy, surrender, deduction on mancipation, adjudication— being proceedings by the civil law, were applicable for establishing usufructs in Italic land, or in mancipable things anywhere, between Roman citizens. Land in the provinces was incapable of mancipation or surrender; and therefore for provincial land, for non-mancipable things, and for establishing a right of usufruct for foreigners other means were required. A stipulation confirming a bargain was resorted to, and created a practical holding (*tuitione praetoris*) though not a legal tenancy of the usufruct.

By will the same end might be effected by imposing on the heir (*per damnationem*) the duty of establishing, or of permitting, a usufruct or its equivalent. The form *fidei commissum* might also be used. When the usufruct was once established by the heir, the usufructuary was in the same position as if it had been left him by *do lego*[1]. An usufruct could not be gained by usucapion.

Whether a usufruct could be made dependent on a condition, or restricted in length, or made to commence at a future date, depended on the mode of establishment. Bequest admitted of all these modifications, whether the usufruct was established directly or by reservation. Surrender in court and adjudication being dependent on a proceeding by statute (*legis actio*) probably (but cf. D. x 2 fr 16 § 2) could not be applied to create directly a usufruct in the future (*ex certo tempore et condicione*). Whether it could by these means be created by way of reservation was not certain. But there was no objection to the usufruct being limited *ad certum tempus*. So by mancipation such a limited usufruct (*e.g. hic fundus mihi emptus esto deducto usufructu usque ad Kal. martias*) could be made, according to Paul, who speaks of it however as a matter of theory rather than of practice. Pomponius denied its establishment whether by mancipation or by surrender: a practical transference of the thing was alone possible (Vat. 47—50, 82; Gai. ii 31, 32; D. xxxiii 2 fr 19; xli 3 fr 44 § 5).

(*f*) Extinction of usufruct.

A usufruct is attached to a person (*cohaeret personae* D. xxxiv 3 fr 8 § 3) and is therefore wholly lost by his death, or by forfeiture of his civil position (*capitis deminutio*), which in some cases amounted to civil death (cf. Gai. iii 153): Paul

[1] A usufruct once established stood on its own basis: cf. Cic. *Top.* iv 21 *Si paterfamilias uxori ancillarum usum fructum legavit a filio neque a secundo herede legavit, mortuo filio mulier usum fructum non amittet. Quod enim semel testamento alicui datum est, id ab eo invito cui datum est auferri non potest. Repugnat enim recte accipere et invitum reddere.* I understand the son to have become heir and to have died before puberty but after the usufruct was established by his entry: the pupillar substitute then became heir, without affecting the wife's usufruct.

mentions deportation, penal servitude, arrogation, and adoption (iii 6 § 29). But any *cap. dem.*, even when purely technical, was regarded as changing the person (see my note on *De usufr.* fr 25 § 2). Such a loss occurred whether the usufruct was established by one of the civil law forms or under praetorian protection, *e.g.* in provincial land. It is obvious that this might lead to much practical inconvenience; for instance when a woman having a usufruct passed into hand, or either man or woman passed into handtake. In order to meet the difficulty conveyancers adopted the plan of adding, at least in wills, to the grant of a usufruct such words as *quotiensque capite minutus erit, ei lego*, or *quotiens amissus erit, etc.*: thus reconstituting the usufruct afresh as often as it was lost. This was confirmed by a rescript of Caracalla (D. xxxiii 2 fr 23). Or much the same end was obtained by bequeathing the usufruct *in singulos annos*, for loss of usufruct being loss only of what was already established, at the end of the year a new usufruct arose under the terms of the will, unaffected by the cause of the previous loss. A usufruct vested (*dies cedit*) only when the time for actual exercise came, and, if bequeathed by will, vested, not on the death of the testator (as Labeo held), like other legacies, but (if unconditional) on the heir's entry, and was thus not affected by a previous *cap. dem.* (Vat. 60—64; D. vii 1 fr 25 § 2; tit. 4 fr 1, fr 3 pr).

A usufruct was lost by the destruction, or complete change, total and permanent, of the object; *e.g.* by the burning down or fall of a house, even though it were rebuilt afterwards. If the usufruct of a vacant plot (*area*) is left, and a house is built on it, the usufruct is lost (the builder being liable to a suit by the usufructuary). But the usufruct of a farm is not lost by the fall of the homestead, nor that of land by the establishment or removal of vineyards, or by temporary inundation. The usufruct of a wood is lost by its being cut down and the ground sown: that of a mass of metal by its being made into a cup, or *vice versa*; that of a bath-house by its being made into a dwelling-house or shop; that of a slave, who was an actor, by testator's having turned him to other services; that of a four-in-hand by the death of one of the horses, unless the horses themselves, and not the *quadriga*, were the subject of the usufruct (D. vii 4 fr 5 §§ 2—12, 23, 24; Paul iii 6 § 31).

A usufruct is also lost by neglect to exercise the right for the period of two years in the case of land, of one year in the case of a moveable. This applied to a practical holding in fulfilment of a trust as well as to a fully established usufruct. The exercise need not be by the fructuary himself: it was enough if someone enjoyed it on his account. If he has sold or leased the usufruct, the use of the money-value was regarded as a constructive use of the thing, and therefore it mattered not whether the purchaser or lessee actually used the thing or not (Paul iii 6 § 30; D. vii 1 fr 38; tit. 6 fr 3). If a slave ran away, the usufruct in him was not lost, any more than the civil possession of the owner (Vat. 89).

If the owner acquire the usufruct, or the fructuary acquire the ownership, the usufruct is merged. No one can have a usufruct in his own property (*nulli res sua servit*). It is often said that the usufruct when lost returns to the ownership, but this only means that the owner is now no longer hindered by the temporary right of another from using, enjoying and disposing of the thing as he pleases (Paul iii 6 § 28; D. vii 1 fr 3 § 2; tit. 6 fr 5 pr; xxiii 3 fr 78 pr).

(*g*) Transfer of usufruct.

No personal servitude is capable of being transferred by the holder to anyone else so as to attach it to that person and make it dependent on the transferee's life instead of on the transferor's. If a fructuary goes through the form of surrender to anyone except the owner, the surrender goes for nothing, the usufruct continues in the surrenderor, and on loss by him passes to the owner. If he surrenders to the owner, the usufruct is at once merged (Gai. ii 30; Paul iii 6 § 32). The bequest of a usufruct is only good if the testator have the full ownership or acquire it before he die (D. xxx fr 24 § 1). If a usufruct was bequeathed to one person in trust for another who was accordingly put into possession by the legatee, in strict law the usufruct was dependent on the legatee's life, but the praetor protected the trust by treating the legatee by trust as if he were himself fructuary. He could not give him the right under the civil law (*dominium ususfructus*) but he gave him the possession of the usufruct, *i.e.* the practical usufruct (D. xxxiii 2 fr 29; vii 6 fr 3).

When a fructuary sold or leased his right, the purchaser or lessee obtained, not the right itself, but the practical exercise of it, so long as the fructuary retained it. He had at most, as in English law it might be called, an estate *pur autre vie.* This was the means adopted to effect a practical transference, the consideration being real or nominal (*nummo uno*) according to circumstances (D. xxiii 3 fr 66; Vat. 50).

(*h*) Acquisition of usufruct through others.

A town could acquire a usufruct by bequest to its burghers (*municipes*), not *ipso jure* but by the praetor's protection. As no man could be supposed to live longer than 100 years, this period was taken for the duration of a town's usufruct (D. vii 1 fr 56; xxxiii 2 fr 8).

When a slave (or son under power) acquired a usufruct by stipulation, it was at once established in the person of his master or father: the slave could even stipulate for it to commence after his own death. But if it was bequeathed to him, it appears to have been established in his person. So also if he was made heir, and the propriety was unconditionally bequeathed away and the usufruct reserved: if the propriety was bequeathed away on condition, then the full ownership having been acquired through the slave by his master, the usufruct would remain with the master when the condition occurred and the bare propriety passed away (Vat. 57, 82; cf. Cod. iii 33 fr 17; and my note on D. vii 1 fr 6 § 2). A slave was incapable of acquiring a usufruct by surrender in court or adjudication. By mancipation a usufruct could be acquired through a slave, only if the ownership was mancipated to him, and his master then remancipated it, reserving the usufruct of course for himself (Vat. 51). There was much debate whether, when a usufruct was acquired through a slave, its continuance was affected by the total or partial alienation of the slave. Julian held that it was not (Cod. iii 33 fr 15).

(*j*) Division and accrual of usufruct.

A usufruct is divisible: it may be created in shares to several persons and each share may be lost separately from the others; it may be created in a thing which is owned in common by several persons, and the usufructuary and each co-owner or co-heir will be mutually responsible according to their shares; if the promiser of a usufruct dies, each of his heirs will be liable to the stipulator for his share of the obligation: and, by the *lex Falcidia,* the heir can claim a fourth part of any usufruct bequeathed (D. vii 1 fr 5). It may be actually (or practically) divided, either (in the case of land) by dividing the land into portions and restricting the usufruct of the co-fructuaries to one of such portions; or by selling or letting the usufruct and dividing the proceeds; or by arrangements for occupation in turns (cf. D. x 3 fr 7 § 10).

When a usufruct is left by *do lego* bequest jointly (*conjunctim*) to two persons, on one losing it his share accrues to the others. The same is the case when it is left to a slave, the common property of two persons; and also if it be left by a *do lego* bequest separately to two persons, for then each has a right to the whole, and it is only by the existence of an equal right in someone else, that he is for the time limited to enjoy only a share of it (*concursu divisus est ususfructus*). Nor is accrual prevented by the fact that one of the fructuaries may have acquired the ownership: the praetor granted an analogous action, *i.e.* treated the case as if (partial) merger had not taken place. If a testator appointed two heirs and bequeathed the ownership of something away, reserving the usufruct, the heirs were held to have from the commencement only a share in the usufruct; and there would consequently be no accrual to the other, if the one lost it (Vat. 75—79; Paul. iii 6 § 26). When a usufruct is given by a damnatory legacy or *sinendi modo* or *fideicommisso* to more than one person jointly, the heir was bound only to establish partial usufructs and there is no accrual (Vat. 85). But if it were given to several persons separately, the heir is bound alike to all, and will have to establish the whole usufruct for one and pay the value to each of the others (Gai. ii 205; D. xxxiii 2 fr 14).

(*k*) Usufructuary's action.

When once a usufruct is established in a person the fructuary had an action (*civilis* or *utilis*) *in rem* to enforce his right to use and take the fruits. It was a vindication (*petit* or *vindicat usumfructum*), and was sometimes called *confessoria* as calling on the defendant to admit (*confiteri*) plaintiff's right. It is not available when time or other circumstances have determined the usufruct. It lay not only against the owner but against anyone in possession. If there was a right of road or water or any other servitude belonging to the land or house of which one had the usufruct, and his neighbour obstructed him, he brought this action, claiming not the servitude itself in so many words, as he would if he were owner, but the right to use and enjoy the thing and all belonging to it. (*Si vicinus non patiatur eum ire agere, tenetur quasi non patiatur uti frui.*) The action carried with it a claim for all past fruits which he had been prevented from taking; and, if his usufruct expired during the process of the action, he was entitled not only to its reestablishment, but to a guaranty against any difficulties from the conduct of the possessor, who might for instance have pledged it. As in other real actions *omnis causa restituenda est* (D. vii 6 fr 1 pr, fr 5 §§ 1—5, viii 5 fr 2 pr; Vat. 46). It was disputed whether this action could be brought after one or (in case of land) two years (Cod. iii 33 fr 16 pr). A usufructuary could also bring the *Publiciana* (p. 442 sqq.).

On the other hand the owner had an action, called *negatoria*, against anyone who asserted a right to the usufruct. The owner did not claim the usufruct; he could not claim as a separate right what was already included in his rights as owner: his claim was that defendant had no right *uti frui* without his consent; or that he had himself the right of prohibiting defendant. The action carried with it a right to compensation for any fruits taken (D. vii 6 fr 5 pr, 6).

Interdicts could not be brought in the ordinary terms by or against a usufructuary. If forcibly prohibited from enjoyment, he could not bring the interdict *de vi*, because he was not properly *dejectus*. Nor could an interdict be brought against him simply as possessor, for he did not possess. Analogous (*utilia*) interdicts were allowed, *i.e.* the language of the interdicts was altered either by adding or substituting *uti frui* to or for *possidere* (Vat. 90—93).

2. '*Fructus*' always included *usus*, so that a bequest of *fructus deducto usu* was an impossible bequest; and if a usufruct be left and the *fructus* is taken away, the whole is taken away. If *usus* be left to one and *fructus* or *ususfructus* to another, the two will be sharers in the use (Paul iii 6 § 24; D. vii 1 fr 42 pr; tit. 8 fr 14 § 1). '*Annui fructus*' is the same as *ususfructus* (D. xxxiii 2 fr 41).

3. *Operae* (*servi*) had the same content as *ususfructus*, but did not perish by death, or by *cap. dem.* of the person entitled, or by nonuse. If however the slave became by usucapion the property of another, the *operae* were lost (D. vii 7 fr 2—5, xxxiii 2 fr 2).

4. *Usus* (or *nudus usus*, *i.e.* without *fructus*) was a personal servitude made and ended in the same way as usufruct (D. vii 1 fr 3 § 3). But it could not be divided: nor could it be sold or let or granted gratuitously to another (D. vii 8 fr 11, 19). There was a good deal of discussion as to the rights of the usuary; but on the whole it was held that the use of a house was the right of dwelling there with a person's family and dependents, though there was some difficulty at first in conceding this to a woman usuary. But lodgers could be allowed only if the usuary dwelt there himself. The owner could be excluded, even though the house was too large for the usuary's requirements (fr 2—6, 22 § 1). The use of a country estate (*fundus*) carried, besides this, the right of taking, for daily use of the family and guests, ordinary products, such as vegetables, fruit, flowers, wood, straw, and perhaps also wine and oil, and even of carrying such if plentiful to town. The usuary could prevent the owner's using the estate except to see to the cultivation, but could not forbid the farm servants being there (fr 10 § 4—fr 12 § 1). The use of cattle (*pecus*)

included only the manure and a little milk: the use of slaves or oxen or horses included all their usual work (fr 12 § 3—§ 6, 15 § 1).

The usuary (by bequest) of a house will share with the heir the duty of repairs, but if the heir *fructum accipiat* (*i.e.* have the rent ?) the whole duty falls on him, while if the heir can from the nature of the thing get no produce, the legatee must repair (fr 18).

Hadrian decided that the usuary of a wood had the right of felling and selling, for otherwise he would get nothing from the bequest (fr 22 pr).

5. *Habitatio* did not differ practically from the use of a house. It was disputed among the republican lawyers whether the right was for one year or for life; the latter opinion prevailed (D. vii 8, fr 10 pr § 3; see an instance in xxxix 5 fr 27, and cf. fr 32). The right was not lost by non-use or by *capitis deminutio* (D. vii 8 fr 10 pr).

CHAPTER VI.

SERVITUDES (*continued*).

PRAEDIORUM SERVITUTES, 'Easements'.

1. Servitudes, like usufruct, are *jura in re aliena.* They entitle the owners of the land or buildings to which they are appurtenant to make certain use of others' land or buildings, or to restrict these others in their own use and dealings with them. Servitudes appurtenant to lands are called *servitutes praediorum rusticorum,* those appurtenant to buildings are *servitutes praediorum urbanorum.* The name[1] is derived from their being chiefly in use in the country or in town respectively, but wherever situate the character of the easements is the

[1] Similarly in legacies *urbani (servi), urbana penus* refer not to the place where they are, but to the character of the service or of the supply (D. xxxii fr 99; xxxiii 9 fr 4 § 5; L 16 fr 166, 210).

same (D. viii[1] 4 fr 1; L 16 fr 198). What is a right (*jus*) as regards the dominant tenement is a servitude as regards the other, which is therefore said *servire*, while the dominant tenement is said *acquirere, retinere, amittere, etc., servitutem.* Servitudes cannot exist in gross, *i.e.* otherwise than appurtenant to particular lands or houses (D. 1 fr 15; cf. xxxiii 3 fr 5).

Ownership includes control over the land or building, and freedom from interference with the air above and the ground below. Apart from any restrictions made by the State, or anything threatening danger or injury to neighbours, an owner can keep others from his place and deal as he chooses with it himself (2 fr 9). So far as he is bound to admit others or is restricted in his own action, his land or buildings are under some servitude, which has been duly established by him or his predecessors in title and continues until duly extinguished by waiver or neglect to use.

2. Principal easements. The principal rural servitudes are rights of way and of leading and drawing water (*aquae ductus, aq. haustus*[2]). *Iter* or *jus eundi* is a right of passage on foot or horseback over others' land, including carriage in a sedan; *actus* or *jus agendi* is a right of driving *jumenta, i.e.* horses, mules, asses, whether yoked to a waggon or carriage or not, and includes *iter*; *via* is a general right of road for all purposes, walking, riding, driving, and (as most lawyers thought) of drawing, so however as not to injure the crops or interfere with fruit trees overhead[3] (3 fr 1, 7, 12). If a right of road is granted without other indication, the grantee can go

[1] References unless otherwise stated are all to the various titles of this viiith book of the Digest.

[2] The two expressions are found together in Cic. *Q. Fr.* iii 1 § 3 where it was proposed to lead water from one farm to another: *Aiebat aqua dempta et ejus aquae jure constituto et servitute fundo illi imposita tamen nos pretium servare posse* 'If water be taken (from farm *A*) and a right of leading the water established (for farm *B*) and a servitude (for the supply of the water) imposed (on farm *A*), still we should get our price (for farm *A*).'

[3] *Qui viam habent eundi agendique jus habent: plerique (putant) et trahendi quoque lapidem aut tignum, et rectam hastam ferendi jus, modo fructus non laedat* (3 fr 7; cf. 6 fr 11). Böcking (*Pand.* § 170 n. 29) compares the phrase of German country-folk 'to pass with a laden hay-cart.'

on any vacant part that he chooses in a reasonable manner (*civiliter*[1]), and the owner of the servient tenement must not hinder him; but if a way be once laid out, thenceforth the servitude is limited to that. The breadth sufficient is determined in case of disagreement by an arbiter. For a *via* the XII tables prescribed a minimum breadth of eight feet, and at an angle sixteen feet (1 fr 9; 3 fr 8, 13). But a smaller breadth was allowed (3 fr 23 pr). If it be required, the road may be made solid (1 fr 10), but must not (without special direction) be paved (5 fr 4 § 5): and the right of passage or driving (*iter*, *actus*) does not authorise the erection of a bridge over a stream (D. xxxix 3 fr 11 pr). A right of passage over a lake was sometimes created (3 fr 23 § 1). For leading water, pipes may be laid without special agreement, and may be carried under rivers, but paved conduits, being unusual, require agreement, and cannot be taken under a river for fear of percolation; nor should water be led in an arch over others' road (D. *ib.* fr 11 pr; fr 17 § 1); nor along a public road without the permission of the emperor (*ib.* fr 18 § 1).

Other rural servitudes are such as pasturing cattle (*pascendi*), driving them, or a certain number of them, to water (*pecoris ad aquam appulsus*), burning lime (*calcis coquendae*), digging sand, taking sticks from a coppice, depositing materials (D. viii 3 fr 1 § 1, fr 4—6; cf. xliii 20 fr 1 § 18). A right of pasturing cattle might perhaps be accompanied by a right of having a refuge-hut on the pasture ground (3 fr 6 § 1). Quarries were sometimes subject to a custom, by which, on a certain payment being made, anyone could cut and remove stone in a reasonable way (4 fr 13 § 1).

The principal urban servitudes are rights of light and prospect (*ne luminibus*[2], *prospectui*, *officiatur*), of passing streams of water or raindrip into or over your neighbour's house or area (*fluminum* or *stillicidii avertendi servitus*[3]), of resting your

[1] Cf. Cic. *Caecin.* 19 § 54 *Si via sit immunita, (lex) jubet qua velit agere jumentum.*

[2] A *servitus luminum 'ut vicinus lumina nostra excipiat'* is difficult clearly to distinguish from *ne lum. officiatur* (tit. 2 fr 4).

[3] Cf. Cic. *Legg.* i 4 § 14 *Quid hortaris? ut libellos conficiam de stillicidiorum ac de parietum jure?*

beams on another's wall (*tignum immittendi* or *oneris ferendi*), of projecting a balcony over others' ground, or sending your sewer through others' land, or your smoke through his house. The first two are often expressed by *altius tollendi*[1] or *nequid altius tollatur*; and such a prohibition may also prevent a neighbour from throwing back the raindrip, *etc.* into your place (2 fr 1, fr 2; 5 fr 8 § 5).

3. Nature of easements. A servitude consists not in the performance of some act by the owner or occupier of the servient tenement, but in his refraining from taking action and his acquiescence in action taken on the part of the dominant tenement. Hence the owner of the servient tenement has no duty of repairing the road or water-course, but must give facilities for this being done. If however the wall or building, which is under a servitude bound to support a neighbour's beams, is ruinous, the owner of the servient tenement is in this case (by Servius' opinion prevailing over Aquilius') bound to repair by the character of the particular servitude, or else to abandon the servient tenement (2 fr 33; 4 fr 11; 5 fr 6 § 2).

A servitude must be for the permanent service of the dominant tenement, so far as it really requires such service, not for the accidental convenience or casual caprice of its owner. Hence a servient tenement must be neighbouring, though not necessarily contiguous (1 fr 15; 2 fr 38; 5 fr 5): water must be led or drawn from a permanent natural spring or stream, not a mere local pool with stagnant water (2 fr 28; cf. tit. 4 fr 2 pr; xliii 22 § 4). A right of taking brick-earth or potters' clay is a servitude, if the bricks are for the farm or homestead, and the pots are for holding or exporting the produce of the farm: if the bricks and pots are for sale, the right is rather usufruct than rural servitude (3 fr 6 pr).

[1] A *jus altius tollendi* is sometimes spoken of by Gaius (D. viii 2 fr 2; *Inst.* ii 31) but it is not easy to explain why the exercise of an owner's ordinary rights should be regarded as a special privilege, and as the result of a neighbour's being under a servitude. Such cases probably arise when freedom is acquired (so as to appear a new right) by the waiver or other extinction of a servitude (cf. D. viii 2 fr 21; and my note in *De usufructu*, p. 192).

Urban servitudes could not be pledged. Rural servitudes could; at least an agreement could be made that so long as the debt was not paid the creditor having a neighbouring farm might use the servitudes and have an eventual power of sale to a neighbour (D. xx 1 fr 11 § 3, 12).

4. Creation of easements. Subject to such conditions various other servitudes may be created, and a special *modus* may be attached to ordinary servitudes, limiting the time of their exercise, or the kind of animals used or of load carried on a road (1 fr 4 § 1). They cannot in strict law be created from or only till a future date, or under a condition: but a plea of bargain agreed or of fraud would be allowed against anyone suing in defiance of an agreement to that effect (1 fr 4 pr). And an agreement may provide against obstruction of future lights, or for a servitude for a future building (2 fr 22, 23), or for finding and then leading water (3 fr 10). But in a conditional legacy of a farm and an absolute legacy of a right of road for it, there may be, when the legacy is due, nothing to support the appurtenance, and the road would therefore be lost (D. xxxiii 3 fr 3).

On Italian soil servitudes are created by surrender in court (*in jure cessio*), and rural servitudes can also be created by mancipation (Gai. ii 17, 29). Both rural and urban servitudes can be reserved (*recipi, excipi*) on mancipation[1]; *i.e.* an owner in disposing of a house or land can impose on it a servitude in favour of another house or other land which he retains; or he may impose a servitude on what he retains in favour of the other. But he cannot impose a servitude on what is not his own, nor can he reserve a servitude for any but his own tenements (4 fr 3, 6, 8). Servitudes are also created (and this is the regular mode in provincial land) by bargain confirmed by stipulation (Gai. ii 31); and the creation of them can be imposed on an heir by will (4 fr 16). Servitudes can also be created by adjudication in the proceedings for dividing an

[1] A case of reservation of a servitude on mancipation is given in Cic. *Orat.* i 39 § 109 where the vendor of a house *in mancipio lumina uti tunc essent ita recepit.* The purchaser took *recepit* in the sense of 'guaranteed,' and based an extravagant claim on it. See Essay appended to this Book.

inheritance or common property (D. x 2 fr 22; 3 fr 7 § 1). The usual form in creating a positive servitude is *jus illi esse, ire, agere,* or *stillicidium in tectum illius avertere,* or *aquam per illius fundum ducere, etc.* In negative servitudes the form is *jus illi non esse invito me (vicino) tectum altius tollere,* or *luminibus officere*: and a person is *invitus* who does not consent (2 fr 5, *etc.*). Servitudes duly created, whether by stipulation or otherwise, run with the tenements (3 fr 25; fr 36; 4 fr 12; 5 fr 20 § 1). The legacy of a house, which rests on another of testator's, in such words as *tabernam meam uti nunc est do lego,* carries with it the right to support by the other, whether such right existed before or not (D. xxxiii 3 fr 1).

A right of road or of water or an urban servitude being granted to one does not preclude a like right being granted to others, if compatible with the first (3 fr 2 § 2; 4 fr 15; xliii 20 fr 4). In granting a right of leading water, the consent, not only of all the owners of the land, but of all entitled to water therefrom, is required, but subsequent assent is sufficient. If a public road or river intervene, it may be crossed, but a sacred, religious or inviolable (*sanctus*) place may not (D. xxxix 3 fr 8, 9, 17 §§ 2, 3). One of several co-owners cannot acquire or impose a servitude for or on the common property (1 fr 2; 3 fr 19; fr 27; 4 fr 5); all must join, and if they do not join at once, then the acquisition dates from the act of the last co-owner (3 fr 11; 4 fr 6 § 2; fr 18).

A servitude is a whole and not divisible. Each co-owner of the dominant tenement can claim the right; each co-owner of the servient tenement has to allow the right (1 fr 17; 3 fr 19). It cannot be partly lost or partly gained (1 fr 3; fr 8 § 1; 3 fr 18, fr 34; 4 fr 6 § 1; cf. D. xliii 20 fr 1 §§ 17, 18); one co-owner cannot gain *e.g.* a right of road for the common farm unless the other co-owner has a title also (D. xxxiii 3 fr 3). But this does not prevent a dominant owner from giving up the right so far as concerns a part of the servient land (1 fr 6), or prevent the whole road necessary for access to some place being gradually acquired by a series of grants or stipulations over different pieces of land (3 fr 38, cf. fr 7 § 1).

There can be no relation of servitude between two tenements of the same owner. If the owner of a dominant tenement become owner also of the servient tenement or *vice versa*, the servitude is merged, *i.e.* extinguished by confusion. But not if the confusion affect part only; the part not confused retains the servitude as a whole (2 fr 30; 3 fr 27; 4 fr 10).

Servitudes cannot be acquired (separately from the buildings or lands) by use, not only because of the impossibility, as the lawyers came to consider, of continued possession of an incorporal right, but because the *lex Scribonia* abolished such an acquisition (1 fr 4; D. xli 3 fr 4 § 28; fr 10 § 1). A right of leading water and of protecting lower lands from the rush of water, by the maintenance of banks and drains in the lands above, were however exceptions so far that the claimant need not prove the origin, but only the long continued use without force, concealment or request (5 fr 10): and such a presumption of legal origin was allowed for other servitudes also (*ib.* xxxix 3 fr 1 § 23; xliii 19 fr 5 § 3; Cod. iii 34 fr 1, 2).

5. Loss of easements. Urban servitudes are lost by a two-years' maintenance of defiant freedom[1] from the servitude claimed (D. viii 2 fr 6, 18 § 2), provided the house maintaining the freedom be possessed by the same person for the two years (2 fr 32 § 1). Rural servitudes are lost by non-use for two years (Paul i 17). To prevent the loss, the servitude must be exercised according to the terms of its constitution; if it is for a road by day, it must be used by day; if for a particular beast or vehicle, no other kind of beast or vehicle will do (1 fr 4 § 1; 6 fr 7, 11). The use may be exercised either by the owner or his slave or guest or tenant or by a fructuary or any other person, (rightfully or not) using it as a servitude of right belonging to this particular farm or building (6 fr 5, 12, 20—25). *Satis est fundi nomine itum esse* (6 fr 6 pr). A road to a tomb is not lost by non-use (6 fr 4).

6. Actions. Actions may be brought to claim or enforce the observance of servitudes, or to deny a right to servitudes. The former is called (as in the case of usufruct)

[1] *e.g.* by blocking up the hole in which the dominant party claimed to insert beams; by building higher in contradiction of a servitude not to do so; *etc.*

confessoria, the latter *negatoria* or *contraria*. But they can be brought, the first only by the owner of the land or house to which the servitude is attached, the second only by the owner of that which is alleged to be servient, and against the obstructor, who will usually from the nature of the case be the owner of a neighbouring house or land. Owners in common have each a right to bring these actions. The aim of the action was to have the servitude, or freedom from servitude, recognised and respected, and obstructions removed, and sometimes security given for future conduct, and compensation for any damage sustained. Refusal was punishable by the plaintiff's being allowed to fix the amount of damages on oath (D. viii 5 fr 2 pr, § 1; fr 4 §§ 2—4; fr 7, 10 § 1, 12). Where the claimant of a servitude brings his action declaring that his neighbour has no right to build higher, and no defence is made and the building is not begun, the judge will simply have to direct the defendant to give his bond (*cavere*) not to build higher until he has brought an action and proved his right to do so. So if an intended builder brought an action to establish his right to build higher, without his neighbour's consent, and no defence is made, the judge will simply direct the defendant to give a bond not to give him 'notice of new work' or forcibly to obstruct his building (D. xxxix 1 fr 15). The pledgee of a farm has an analogous action to enforce servitudes due to it (D. viii 1 fr 16).

The '*possessor*,' *i.e.* the party who has the right to stand on his defence, is the one who is in the practical enjoyment of the servitude claimed, or of the freedom from the servitude alleged: *e.g.* in the case of a servitude by which I must be allowed to raise my house if I wish, the possessor is the owner of the alleged servient tenement before the house is raised, but after it is raised, the possessor is the owner of the dominant house (5 fr 6 § 1; 8 § 3).

To protect the enjoyment of servitudes (which is analogous to possession of land by its owner) until, if necessary, a suit for determining the right can be tried, interdicts were issued on proof of recent actual enjoyment for a time. (See the following sections.) Judgment on trial of an interdict does not rank as a decision on the right, but only as an allowance or bar of the use (D. xix 1 fr 35).

CHAPTER VII.

PROTECTION OF EASEMENTS AND THE LIKE.

1. *Interdictum de itinere actuque privato*[1].

This interdict is open to anyone who has used a foot or bridle path (*iter*) or cart road (*actus*) for at least thirty days[2] within a year preceding its issue, provided he has used the way, as against his adversary, without force, concealment or permission. His right is not inquired into, but he must have used it as of right, either himself or through another (his farmer, guest or friend) using it as his road. A use free from fault for and within the period is not the less available because subsequent use has been contrary to prohibition or stealthy or permissive: nor, if my own use is faulty throughout, is the use of another in my name as of right any good to me. A fructuary (of a neighbouring farm) can have the interdict as well as the owner, if each has made the required use. And a purchaser, legatee in possession, donee, husband with dowry, can avail himself of his predecessor's use. If the purchase was by mandate, the purchaser can allege the mandatee's use (D. xliii 19 fr 1 §§ 2—4, 11, 12; fr 3 pr—§ 10, fr 7).

If the land through which the way passes has been inundated one year, the claimant can obtain a reinstatement so as to avail himself of his use in the previous year. If in consequence of inundation or other inconvenience he has used a different road, he does not thereby acquire any right to the new road, and his non-use of the old road both in this and the previous year prevents his claiming this interdict (*ib.* fr 1 §§ 6, 9). The damages are reckoned on the basis of the plaintiff's interest in not being obstructed in the use (*ib.* fr 3 § 3).

[1] These and other interdicts are referred to in Cic. *Caecin.* 13, quoted in note, p. 464.

[2] *i.e.* as most take it 'on thirty separate days': or, as some take it, 'for a period of thirty days,' cf. fr 1 §§ 2, 12.

Another interdict was open to anyone who desired power to repair the road, but in this case he must shew not merely use but a right to repair in the way or to the extent which he is exercising it. And such a right includes as of course a right to bring the materials over a suitable part of the land, and if necessary to erect a bridge. Plaintiff can be called on to give security against damage (*ib.* fr 3 § 11—fr 5 § 1). This interdict is not merely possessory: it protects the right of a quasi-owner (D. xliii 1 fr 2 § 2).

2. *INTERDICTUM DE AQUA COTTIDIANA ET AESTIVA.*

Similar interdicts were available to protect a right of leading water. Such a right might be either for leading it on any day in the year, or only in summer, *i.e.* the six months from the vernal to the autumnal equinox. The former was called *aqua cottidiana,* whether used or not on some days or during some part of the year; the latter was *aqua aestiva,* though the water might as a fact be obtainable at all seasons of the year. Both interdicts were available, if a single day's or night's use as of right, not *vi aut clam aut precario,* could be shewn; even though plaintiff had also used it not as of right. The use for the former interdict must be within the preceding year (*ŭti hoc anno*) from the date of the interdict; for the latter, within the preceding summer (*ŭti priore aestate*), so that if the interdict were brought in autumn or winter, not the last summer but the one before that would be referred to, *priore* being the former of two (D. xliii 20 fr 1 §§ 1—4, 20, 31—34). An analogous interdict was allowed if the right was claimed for a winter use only; or if the uses were shewn to be in the present or last summer, not the preceding (*ib.* fr 1 §§ 35, 36). Successors and purchasers are entitled to the use of the interdict as in the case of a right of road (*ib.* § 37).

A right to the water properly established is not necessary for this interdict, if the applicant shews a use under what he believed to be a right, though he were mistaken in fact (not in law, fr 1 § 10). The use must be according to the character and within the limits of the presumed right; and must be claimed according to its character (fr 1 §§ 15, 22). Any interference with the use, either direct or incidental, by operations on the land interrupting or vitiating the water, justify the interdict (*ib.* § 27). If more than one person has a right of this kind, a double interdict will lie to determine their respective claims; and arrangements between them for use of each other's right will not impair their own right as against the land-owner (fr 1 § 26; fr 5).

The interdict is available though the water be led into buildings (*urbana praedia*; cf. D. L 16 fr 198) and not used only for irrigation: and it may be in or outside the city. Nor does it matter whether the water is cold, or, as at Hierapolis, warm (fr 1 §§ 11—14).

A similar interdict was open to one who had a right, whether attached to his person or to his land, to take water from the public reservoir (*castellum*). Such a right could be obtained only by grant from the emperor. In this case the interdict does not merely, as in former cases, prepare the matter for a regular suit on the right, but ascertains the right finally (*ib.* fr 1 §§ 38—44).

3. *Interdictum de rivis.*

An interdict to permit clearing and repairs of the cuts, channels, and protecting sides of a watercourse was granted to one proving a use without inquiry into his right. But the repair must be limited to the use claimed and the character of the channel, which must as a rule, according to the early lawyers, not be lowered or raised or widened or extended or covered if open, or opened if shut, though Ulpian considered that covering or opening might be allowed, if not shewn by the opponent to be injurious to him. The change of an earth course by putting tiles or cement, or *vice versa*, was apparently allowed, at any rate where there was no substantial objection. A new canal or a course of pipes in the stream might be made under the protection of an analogous interdict. All streams whether on public or private soil admit of this interdict. Ditches and wells are also within its scope. The person using the interdict may be called on to give security against possible damage. He cannot be stopped by notice of objection to a new work (*op. novi nuntiatio*), but is of course liable to an action denying his right to the servitude (D. xliii 21).

Similar interdicts (*de fonte*) apply to prevent interference with the use or repair of any spring, lake, basin, or well containing spring water, which a person claims the right of drawing water from or of watering cattle at. The qualifications for obtaining this interdict are the same as *de aq. duc.* (D. xliii 22).

4. *Interdictum de cloacis.*

An interdict was also obtainable to permit one whose sewers passed into others' houses or buildings to cleanse or repair them, and if necessary to take up the pavement for the purpose. He had to give security against possible damage, and of course to restore the place. The interdict applied also, if the sewer passed into a field. The great importance of the work to the general health and security of the buildings made the praetor omit the requirement *quod non vi, non clam, non precario ab illo usus es*: the sewer should be cleansed or repaired, however little right to the possession the applicant had.

Anyone who desired to make a sewer opening into the public sewer was to be permitted to do so, without injury to the public service. The control lay with the caretaker of the public roads (D. xliii 23).

The following interdicts deal with similar matters to servitudes.

5. There were two interdicts *de arboribus caedendis* to free a person from trees in his neighbour's ground overhanging his own house or land. The former dealt with trees from one man's house overhanging his neighbour's house and gave the latter the right, if the owner would not cut down the tree, himself to cut it down, either so far as it overhung, or, as most lawyers held, from the roots; and to keep the wood. A usufructuary had the same right; if the injured house was the property of two persons, either had the right to take action in full. Vines were included under trees. The other interdict was based on the XII tables and provided that, if a tree in country land hung

over neighbouring land, the owner of the latter, in default (after summons) of the owner's doing it himself, might clear (*sublucare*) up to fifteen feet from the ground, so as to prevent his being overshadowed (D. xliii 27). Any *dominus* (usufructuary, Publician possessor ?) has this right (Paul v 6 § 13).

6. On the other hand the owner of a tree had a right protected by an interdict *de glande legenda* to pick up acorns (extended by interpretation to include all fruits) which fell upon another's land, but not oftener than every other day. The owner of the tree might be called on to give security against possible damage. If the owner of the land where the acorns lay sent in cattle to eat them, he was liable to an action *ad exhibendum* or on the case (D. xliii 28; x 4 fr 9 § 1; xix 5 fr 14 § 3).

CHAPTER VIII.

PROTECTION AGAINST DAMAGE FROM NEIGHBOURING BUILDINGS AND AGAINST INTERFERENCE WITH POSSESSION.

There were four general proceedings (besides any special claims to servitudes) for securing land and buildings against danger or injury from others' action, and especially from erections or works on neighbouring lands. The first three are only precautionary, and are directed chiefly against buildings or works on neighbouring land: the last (*quod vi aut clam*) is of wider scope and is concerned with the past. All these proceedings rest chiefly on the natural claim of an owner or other interested person, that his neighbours or others shall not interfere injuriously with his land, nor so work their own land, or so omit to repair their buildings, as to put the former to unnecessary loss or peril.

1. *Damni infecti.*

(*a*) The damage to a neighbour which might result from the ruinous condition of buildings or faulty work was a subject of the old *legis actio*, and was the only matter for which that procedure was still possible[1] in Gaius' time, except in

[1] See Wlassak's suggestion as to the cause of this retention (below, Book VI chap. v).

suits before the *centumviri* (iv 31). But in practice, as he says, it was superseded by the remedy which the praetor's edict supplied. The provisions of the edict on this head are preserved to us by Ulpian in the Digest (xxxix 2 fr 7 pr). The matter is constantly referred to as *damnum infectum, i.e.* loss or damage not yet suffered[1], but apprehended (*ib.* fr 2). It included all loss which was likely to arise from the faulty condition (*vitio*) of a house, or of a work which was being done on a house or in any place, in city or country, private or public (fr 19 § 1).

(*b*) On application (*postulatio*) to the praetor and oath of the person who stood in fear or of his representative, that the application was made in good faith, the praetor required the owner of the dangerous building to give the applicant a bond or recognizance (*cavere*) to make good to him, so far as his interest extended, any damage which might ensue. A part-owner need not give a bond to cover more than his own share of the damage. If there was dispute as to the ownership, the possessor was called on to give the bond with a proviso dealing with the case of his not being owner. An owner gave only his own promise (*repromisit*); others had to give a surety also (*satis dedit*). The praetor after hearing the case decided for what period the bond should extend: and, if he thought fit, renewed it when expired. In the case of damage from erections on a public river or on its bank, the regular period was ten years. If such bond was not given, the praetor directed the applicant to take possession of the building in question (*in possessionem ire jussit*). If the owner refused admission, the praetor did not coerce him by taking pledges, but granted the complainant an action (*in factum*) against the owner for the full amount to which he would be liable if he had duly given the bond. If, while complainant was in possession, anyone else made a like application, and complainant did not give security (*i.e.* promise with surety), the praetor directed the second complainant to be in possession along with the first (Edict ap. D. fr 7 pr, 4 § 2, 15 pr; x 3 fr 6 § 7).

[1] *damnum facere* is usually, as here, to make a loss, *i.e.* to suffer it: *damnum dare* is to cause loss, cf. D. *ib.* fr 26.

Notice of the application had to be given to the owner or to his agent or to lodgers, or left at his house, and, if it was part of an inheritance the heir of which had not yet entered, it was thought advisable to affix a notice to the building itself (fr 4 §§ 5, 6).

(*c*) The oath of good faith was sufficient to qualify an applicant: he was not questioned as to his interest or the vicinity of his house. The praetor however could refuse, if he thought fit. Neighbours, even though there might be other houses intervening, even lodgers or their wives or persons living with them, could apply. An analogous bond was obtainable, at least in Antonine times, by superficiaries and usufructuaries (fr 13 §§ 3—5 § 8). And a similar right belonged to anyone, whether in possession or not, who was responsible for the endangered house (*e.g.* a vendor before delivery), the damages for breach being always measured by the interest of the applicant (fr 18 pr §§ 7—10). A procurator could apply and take oath of his principal's good faith, but must give security for his principal's ratification: the principal was allowed after explanation (*causa cognita*) to sue on the bond so obtained (fr 18 § 16; 39 § 3). Similarly usufructuaries and superficiaries, unless the owner gives his bond, could be called on to give security: if they do not do so, whether the owner is therefore compelled to do it, or the complainant is sent into possession, they will be excluded from the enjoyment of their rights (fr 9 §§ 4, 5; fr 10). Whether a pledge-creditor, or *bona fide* purchaser with bad title, could claim such a bond, was disputed: they were liable to give a bond, but there were doubts whether they had to give a surety also (fr 11, 13 pr § 9). Mere casual visitors in the endangered house had no right to apply (fr 13 § 4). As between owner and superficiary or usufructuary or lodger no such right existed: they had their own actions against each other (fr 18 §§ 2, 3). And generally the proceedings (*damni infecti*) are justified only when other actions do not avail (fr 32).

(*d*) The bond is made to bind the promiser and his heirs or successors and those whom it concerns (*ad quos ea res pertinet*), *i.e.* all successors, whether universal or singular, as purchasers, *etc.*

It is conditioned on any damage occurring to the stipulator through fault of the house or the place or the work, sometimes of the trees; but this is understood not to extend to any natural fault such as the marshy or sandy nature of the soil or to *vis major* such as earthquake, hurricane, violent flood, fire, *etc.* If however the promiser has allowed the foundations of his building or his trees to become so weak as to be incapable of due resistance, and they fall and damage the stipulator's house or crops, there is liability (fr 24 §§ 2—11). But he is not liable, if he digs a well on his own ground, or carries up his buildings higher, provided he is under no servitude and is acting within his rights, though he may thereby be drawing off his neighbour's water or obstructing his light or prospect. In such a case even a promise *damni infecti* actually given cannot be enforced. The stipulator is properly said not to be making a loss (*damnum facere*) but to be no longer enjoying an unearned advantage (fr 24 § 12—fr 26; fr 30).

(*e*) In suing on the bond for damages each plaintiff (if more than one) sues only for his own share, and each defendant is liable only for his own share. This limitation is presupposed in respect of the stipulators: a man stipulates only for what is his own and the mention of a part would mean a restriction to part of his share; but, if there are several co-owners of the faulty building, each when promising must limit his liability in express words (fr 27, 40 §§ 2—4). A superficiary will claim and be liable only so far as his building or flat is concerned; the (bare) owner only so far as the ground is concerned; but a complainant is entitled to security for the whole, and if he does not get it, will be sent into possession (fr 23, 39 § 2). A reasonable estimate will be made of the damage, without too much regard to expensive decorations (fr 40 pr). But the loss of rent, by lodgers' leaving and by others being deterred from taking rooms owing to the fear of accidents, is fairly included in reckoning the damage (fr 28, 29, 37, 43 § 1). The stipulator may bring the action more than once, if the damage is repeated (D. xlvi 8 fr 18).

(*f*) If the building fell before the bond was given, an interdict was granted to the sufferer to compel the owner to remove the fallen materials and repair the damage, or else to abandon the ownership. But if the complainant had negligently omitted to apply to the praetor, or had without good cause omitted to use the order, or had left the place, unless from fear of imminent peril, he would not be assisted by the praetor (D. xxxix 2 fr 7 § 2—fr 9 pr). An action *ad exhibendum* lies for the owner of the materials against the possessor of the land where they have fallen (D. x 4 fr 5 § 5).

(*g*) When, the bond not being given, the applicant is sent into possession, the owner is not turned out, but anyone (*e.g.* pledgee or pledgor) who might have given security and did not, was not allowed to exercise his rights against those in possession (D. xxxix 2 fr 15 §§ 20, 24, 25). If more than one applicant is in possession, they have equal rights although their risk may be unequal (*ib.* § 15, 18). If the dangerous tenement, whether land or building, is very large, the possession will sometimes be limited to a part only, if the whole is not under suspicion (*ib.* §§ 12—14; fr 38). Until damage actually occurs or the praetor issues a second decree, it is open to the owner to give his bond and free his possession. There is no obligation in practice on those in possession to do the required repairs. If repairs are made or if damage occur, the owner can obtain discharge only by recouping the cost or loss (fr 15 §§ 30, 33, 34, fr 16).

(*h*) If the bond was still refused, and after a sufficient interval the matter seemed to require settlement, the praetor put an end to the state of suspension by a second decree. He bad the applicant or applicants in possession to possess (*possidere jussit*). Just as, when animals have caused injury, their owner has the choice of paying damages or of abandoning his ownership of the animal to the injured person (*noxae dedere*), so the owner's refusal to give a bond in the case of dangerous buildings or to repay any damage caused is treated as abandonment of his rights. The praetor cannot confer civil ownership, but his second decree puts the complainants into the position of owners (*domini constituuntur*): they hold the tenement *in bonis*, and by usucapion become full legal owners. The tenement is discharged from all claims of pledge or even of dowry, unless a creditor, desirous of retaining his pledge, recoups the complainants for all their cost or loss. The owner is ejected altogether (fr 7 § 1, 15 § 16, 44 § 1; xxiii 5 fr 1; xli 2 fr 2 § 23). The applicant, now praetorian owner, is liable like any other owner to give a bond *damni infecti* to other applicants. Any expenses for repairs made by one of the applicants in possession will be apportioned among the applicants (if more than one are made owners) by a suit *communi dividundo* (fr 15 § 19). If a fructuary of the endangered tenement is sent into possession and eventually becomes praetorian owner, he holds for himself irrespective of the duration of his usufruct (D. vii 1 fr 7 § 1). If the dangerous tenement is perpetual leasehold (*praedium vectigale*), it is not susceptible of usucapion, and the praetor therefore varies the phrase; he does not bid the complainant, whom he has sent into possession, to possess, but decrees that he shall hold by the same right as the lessee who had not given security (D. xxxix 2 fr 15 § 26).

(*j*) When an unsafe party wall[1] was common to two houses, it was usual to exchange bonds for apprehended damage, but it was not necessary to do so unless one of the owners undertook the repair alone or had a more valuable house, so that the interests of the two owners were unequal. If either demolished a wall which was adequate for the burden, he was liable not only for the cost of a new wall, but for any loss suffered by the other (fr 36, 37, 39 pr).

Where a private erection in a public river or on its bank was dangerous, the bond is limited to damage arising to neighbours from the erection and takes no account of fault in the ground. The like applies to any paving (*munire*) of the public roads which private persons may have done in a way to endanger

[1] Compare Cic. *Top.* 4 § 22 *Omnibus est jus parietem directum ad parietem communem adjungere vel solidum vel fornicatum. Sed qui in pariete communi demoliendo damni infecti promiserit non debebit praestare quod fornix vitii fecerit: non enim ejus vitio qui demolitus est damnum factum est, sed ejus operis vitio quod ita aedificatum est ut suspendi non posset*, *i.e.* where a person has built an arch at right angles to a common wall and resting on it, the co-owner of the common wall in pulling it down to make a stronger one is not bound to make good damage to the arch; because his neighbour ought to have built his arch so as to stand by itself.

the neighbouring houses. In erections, *etc.* on public roads and rivers the bond must be supported by a surety (fr 15 §§ 2—8; fr 24, 31 pr; cf. xliii 15). Interdicts (see pp. 411, 412) dealt with the protection of public ways, *etc.* on public grounds.

(*k*) Where the occasion for this proceeding arose at some distance from Rome[1], the praetor, if local inquiry was necessary, referred the matter to the local magistrates so far as related to the bond and the order to take possession, but the second decree (conferring ownership) or the discharge of the first decree he reserved to himself. An action was granted against any local magistrate who did not attend to a proper application (fr 1, 4 §§ 2, 3, 7), and this action ran for and against heirs without limit of time (*ib.* § 9).

2. *AQUAE PLUVIAE ARCENDAE ACTIO.*

Special precaution was taken against injury from the flow of rainwater, if it was due to a neighbour's act. In a hilly agricultural country like Italy such occurrences must have been frequent, and a remedy was provided in early times by the XII tables (D. xl 7 fr 21 pr).

The suit 'for keeping off rainwater' applied whenever work done by hand on a man's own land interfered with the natural flow of the rainwater (or of waters swollen by rain), so as to make the stream larger or quicker or more violent, or by damming it up make it overflow, and by such changes make it dangerous to a neighbour's land. But furrows made by the plough and drains, if not merely beneficial to the land but necessary to prepare for sowing and planting, did not justify the action. The precise limits of this exception were the subject of discussion among the early lawyers (D. xxxix 3 fr 1 pr—§ 9). The damage might be caused either by a work on upper land increasing or turning the flow on to lower land, or by work on lower land preventing water from running off higher land. In

[1] In the *lex Rubria* c. 20 the local magistrates in Cisalpine Gaul are directed to exercise this jurisdiction of requiring recognizances (whether by personal promise or additional surety) and of giving an action for damage suffered, when recognizances had been demanded but not given. Conformity to the rules and *formula* set out by the *praetor peregrinus* at Rome is expressly enjoined.

some cases lands were subject to statutable regulations, imposed by the State or leader of a colony, by which the owner of certain lands had a right to the protection of banks or trenches in another's land: but as a rule lower lands were held to be under a natural servitude to higher lands and bound to receive the flow of water, unless caused by works done within the memory of man[1]. It was not necessary to shew when such works were done, nor to produce witnesses to anything but the tradition of the fact (fr 1 §§ 10, 22, 23; fr 2 pr § 8).

The suit lay only between the owners of the land concerned; it related only to the future (*si aqua pluvia nocet* = *nocere poterit* D. xl. 7 fr 21 pr), and aimed at compelling the owner of the land, on which the work was, to restore effectually the previous condition and to compensate for any damage occurring since joinder of issue (D. xxxix 3 fr 3 § 4, fr 4 pr, 6 § 6). If the damage was due to the natural clogging of a drain, the action might be brought to compel the owner of the land at least to allow the party injured to clean it; if a bank, either natural or artificial but ancient, had given way, some held that this or an analogous action could be brought for the same purpose; but if an earthquake or violent tempest so altered the lie of the ground as to cause damage, only the later lawyers allowed the party injured to claim entrance and permission to repair (fr 2 pr—§ 6). But this proceeding did not apply if damage was done to a building or in a town[2] (that was matter for an action denying a servitude): nor for retention of water which would otherwise flow down to a neighbour; nor for intercepting springs which had previously supplied a neighbour (fr 1 §§ 11, 12, 17, 23; fr 2 § 9; cf. xxxix 2 fr 26). If the work was done on public ground, the action did not apply: resort must be had to proceedings *damni infecti*. For damage caused before action the interdict *quod vi aut clam* was available (fr 3 § 3; fr 14 §§ 2, 3).

[1] Cf. Cic. *Top.* 9 § 39 *Genus est aqua pluvia nocens: ejus generis formae loci vitio et manu nocens* (*i.e.* two species, one injurious by fault of the ground, the other by handwork), *quarum altera jubetur ab arbitro coerceri, altera non jubetur.*

[2] Cf. Cic. *Top.* 10 § 43 *Si aqua pluvia in urbe nocet, quoniam res tota magis agrorum est, aquae pluviae arcendae adigere arbitrum non possis.*

Where a farmer or procurator did the work without the knowledge of the owner, the latter was only bound to allow restoration to be made; the farmer or agent himself was liable for the expense and for the damages by the interdict *quod vi aut clam* (fr 4 §§ 2, 3, fr 5). Where either the offending or the injured land belonged to several persons, each could sue or be sued, but be condemned only for his share; if one restored the work and paid the damages, the others were liable only to him by *com. div.* (fr 6 § 1; fr 11 §§ 1—3). If the owner parts with the land injured, he loses his right to sue by this action, which relates to the future only and must therefore be brought by the purchaser or donee or other owner for the time being. If the owner of the injurious work part with the land before action is brought, this action lies against the purchaser, partner, legatee, donee, *etc.*, either to restore if he choose, or to permit the restoration; the vendor or donor is liable only by *quod vi aut clam* to compensate for past injury and the expense of restoration (fr 6 § 4; fr 12, 13). A fructuary cannot strictly sue or be sued, but possibly an analogous action will lie (fr 3 § 4; fr 22). The owner of a farm which has a right of way can bring this action for injury to the road, because his farm is thereby injured (fr 25).

The action is called an *arbitrium*, and the judge *arbiter* (fr 23 § 2; 24 pr; and Cic. l.c.). It was not *in rem sed personalis* (fr 6 § 5), *i.e.* not to assert a general right against the world, but a special duty of the owner of a particular piece of land to repair a wrong he had done.

3. *Operis novi nuntiatio.*

(*a*) This was a proceeding under the praetor's edict, when a person anticipates danger to, or interference with his rights, from new works, whether on public or on private ground, in town or country, in Italy or in the provinces (D. xxxix 1 fr 1 § 14, fr 3 pr). The work must be building or demolition of building or some construction in or on the ground which gives it a new character. Necessary repairs to old buildings, or (from regard to public health) cleansing of foul sewers or streams are not within the edict. Nor are cutting trees, pruning vines, reaping crops (fr 1 §§ 11, 12, fr 5 §§ 11, 13; cf. Burckhard, Glück's *Pand.* 39, p. 16). Works already completed are objects for interdicts such as *quod vi aut clam* or *quod in loco sacro* or *quod in flumine publico*, not for this proceeding, which looks to the future (fr 1 § 1).

This proceeding consists in a notice of objection given on the spot or spots where the work is being done to the occupant, whether owner or not, or to anyone engaged in executing the work, or to any person (slave, woman, boy, girl) there on account of the responsible person, so that it may come to his knowledge. Notice to the owner or master himself not on the spot is not good. The notice may be given on any day by the objector or his deputy (fr 1 §§ 3, 4; 5 §§ 2—4), and must specify whether the objection extends to the whole work or else to what part of it (fr 5 § 15). The effect of the notice is to impose on the person concerned the necessity either of at once discontinuing the work or of giving his recognizance for the removal of it, if shewn to be beyond his rights. No previous application to the praetor is required, but the notice once given, if the matter is not settled by agreement, puts it under the praetor's jurisdiction (fr 1 §§ 2, 9; fr 8 § 4). The recognizance provides as usual for obedience to the judgment, for due defence, and for absence of fraud. If the recognizance is given, the notice is practically discharged (*remittitur*), and the work if on private ground can proceed: the praetor by an interdict prohibits any interference with the doer. If the plaintiff refuses to receive the recognizance, the praetor formally discharges the notice. If the recognizance is not given, and the work is continued, the edict is infringed, and the praetor issues an interdict directing the doer, whether he had a legal right to do the work or not, to remove everything constructed, until the notice should be discharged or deserve discharge, which latter phrase includes the case of the recognizance being given after all. Both interdicts can be brought by heirs: against heirs, some lawyers thought, instead of the interdict for restoration, an action on the case should be brought, to make the heirs allow destruction of the work by the notice-giver, and pay damages to the extent to which they have benefited (*in id quod ad eos pervenit*, fr 20—22).

(*b*) The exact procedure for final determination of the respective rights is not in all respects clear[1], but appears to be as follows. Plaintiff substantiates his application to the praetor by taking an oath of good faith; if he is acting on another's behalf, he must give security for his principal's ratification (fr 5 §§ 14, 18). The praetor after a preliminary hearing, if he found further inquiry into the rights of the parties to be necessary, formally declared that, so far as plaintiff's consent was legally necessary to the work in question, he held the notice binding, otherwise he discharged it (*missam fecit*). He would then probably send the parties before a *judex*, and the notice-giver would have to prove his right of prohibiting defendant's work. If he gets judgment for restoration or damages in default, he could then proceed to enforce it by means of an arbitrator under the recognizance. The damages would be for the value of the plaintiff's interest in the work's not being done. If he is unsuccessful, the notice would be held discharged, and the recognizance would drop. The discharge of the notice would not bar any other actions which plaintiff might have (D. xliii 25 pr—§ 2, xxxix fr 19, 21 §§ 4, 7).

(*c*) The notice to be successful must be based either on a public or a private right of the giver. All citizens have a right to stop encroachments on public ground, or on a river bank, or in a sacred or religious place, or any building contrary to statutory regulations (D. xxxix 1 fr 1 § 17). In such cases the doer of the work need give only his own recognizance (*repromissio*). A private right may justify the notice in two cases: (1) if another builds on the notice-giver's ground or lets something into his house, *etc.*; (2) if on ground in his possession he put works likely to damage the notice-giver, or infringe the rights to which he is entitled either as owner or by way of easement. In both cases the recognizance must be supported by a surety (*satisdatio*). In the former case however it is in practice better to protest by throwing a pebble against the work, and, if the doer persist, then to bring the interdict *quod vi aut clam* or *uti possidetis*, because by these means the complainant does

[1] Cf. Burckhard, Glück's *Pand.* p. 277 sq.; Hesse *Rechtsverhältnisse zwischen Grundsstücknachbarn* § 82; Windscheid *Pand.* ii p. 686 sq. note.

not put his opponent into the position of possessor, as he does by the *op. nov. nuntiatio* (fr 1 § 17; fr 5 §§ 8—10; fr 8 §§ 2, 3; xliii 25 § 3; xlvi 5 fr 1 § 6).

Besides owners, superficiaries were eventually allowed to use this notice. A usufructuary could give it only as agent for the owner: on his own account he could proceed against such works only by bringing the ordinary vindication against the doer of the work. A pledge creditor could give notice for interference with a servitude. A right of road does not justify the notice against one who builds on the road (fr 1 § 20, 3 § 3, fr 9, 14). When there are several owners of the land affected, each must give notice, and each is entitled to security, though it is more convenient for one only to take it for all. But if there are several owners of the site of the work, notice given to one is good for all, and only one need give security (fr 5 §§ 5, 6; fr 21 §§ 5, 6). The effect of the notice is general (*in rem*), and not confined to the possessor at the time: it is objection not to a person but to the work, and follows a purchaser of the ground, and is effective though the owner be an infant or a madman, provided it be given to an intelligent person (fr 10, 11).

The effect of the notice expires after a year (Cod. viii 10 fr 14), or on the death of the giver or his alienation of the land affected (fr 8 § 6).

When the notice is given, if the work has already been substantially commenced, the notice-giver should have a protocol (*testatio*) to declare the fact, and the work should be measured so as to put beyond dispute what is new work (fr 8 §§ 1, 5; cf. fr 21 § 3).

4. *Interdictum quod vi aut clam*[1].

(*a*) This interdict, so called from the initial words, was in full probably as follows: '*Quod vi aut clam factum est, qua de re* '*agitur, id si non plus quam annus est cum experiendi potestas est,*

[1] Cicero mentions this interdict in his speech *pro Tullio* 23 § 53 *Ego ipse, tecto illo disturbato, si hodie postulem quod aut vi aut clam factum sit, tu aut per arbitrum restituas aut sponsione condemneris necesse est.* (On the procedure in interdicts see Book VI chap. xiv.)

'*restituas.*' 'Anything that has been done by force or stealth 'in the matter now in question you are to restore, if it is not 'more than a year since there was the power of suing' (D. xliii 24 fr 1 pr: cf. Lenel *EP.* § 256). Like the *operis novi nuntiatio* it is directed not merely against building, but against works of all kinds done on land; it aims not merely at stopping works begun but at undoing, or securing remedy or compensation for injury done by works whether in progress or completed: it applies whether the work is on the doer's land or on the complainant's or on public or religious land (fr 20 § 5); it does not matter whether the doer had or had not a right to do it (fr 1 § 2); the fact that it is done in defiance of actual objection, or so as to elude the observation of possible objectors, justifies this peremptory interference.

(*b*) Force (*vi facere*) was defined by Q. Mucius as doing a thing after being forbidden to do it, and this definition was approved by later lawyers. A man might be forbidden by simple words, by a formal declaration before witnesses, or by any symbolical act, such as a motion of the hand or the cast of a pebble against the work: and a slave or procurator or tenant or lodger might forbid on behalf of the party objecting. Force used by the doer to prevent the prohibition (*e.g.* threats, shutting the door in his face, *etc.*) counts as force in the doing (D. *ib.* fr 1 §§ 5—8, fr 3 pr, 17, 20 pr, § 1). Stealthy action (*clam facere*) is action kept from the knowledge of the other party, or action without notice given to one from whom the doer has reason to expect prohibition. If notice be given, but does not convey sufficient information, or is given when the other party has no opportunity of forbidding the work, or if the work is not begun till long after the notice, or is done in a different way from that declared, the action is stealthy (fr 3 § 7—fr 5 § 1, fr 22 § 5). Where the party himself is not accessible, notice should be given to his friends or procurator or at his house (fr 5 § 2). Some works might be done partly *vi*, partly *clam* (fr 11 § 5).

(*c*) Any work on or connected with land comes within the interdict: erecting buildings, pulling them down, removing tiles, statues, *etc.* which are on or affixed to the buildings, digging a trench, ploughing, throwing stones on land, cutting trees or reeds or withes or vines, or a coppice before it is ready, removing vine props, polluting a well, breaking open or injuring a tomb or piling earth on it or removing a statue, even spreading dung on rich land if it is thereby injured; turning the rainfall on to a tomb or making a projection over it, even though it be not touched, for all above the tomb up to the sky belongs to it (fr 7 §§ 5, 6, 9, 10, fr 9 pr § 2, fr 11 pr §§ 2, 3, fr 15 §§ 1, 2, fr 22 §§ 1, 4). But meddling with the fruit, or burning or dispersing a loose heap, or walking or carrying dung or pursuing game through a neighbour's land without doing any injury, or carrying off bolts or keys or mirrors or lattice work not fixed to the building, are not within the scope. Nor is cutting down a coppice, when ripe for the purpose, nor doing any agricultural work which benefits the farm (fr 7 § 7; 9 § 1, 18 pr, 22 § 3).

If a work done *vi aut clam* is demolished *vi aut clam*, it is for the judge to decide whether the second action is justified by the circumstances. If a house is pulled down to prevent a fire reaching the doer's house, and a magistrate has not authorised it, the doer will be condemned unless the fire actually reached the house. So Servius against Aquilius (fr 7 §§ 3, 4; cf. fr 22 § 2).

(*d*) The works which form the subject of this proceeding are usually works done by defendant on plaintiff's or on public ground, not on defendant's own ground. But not only the owner of the land affected prejudicially, but anyone interested in the work not being done, is entitled to the interdict. If trees are cut, a fructuary is interested, providing they are fruit-bearing or useful to him for shade or ornament, and, whether they are cut by a stranger or by the owner, he is entitled to this interdict as well as to the Aquilian action. A farm tenant is in the same position. Co-owners can use the interdict against one another. An heir can bring it for works done before his entry, *vacante hereditate*. And use of it by one, *e.g.* fructuary or farmer, does not preclude further use for a further interest, *e.g.* by the owner (fr 11 § 14—fr 13 pr § 5, fr 16 pr § 1). When land on which such work is done is in process of sale, the vendor can bring the interdict on account of any work done before delivery, but if the work be done after the sale, he will have to account for anything gained by his suit to the purchaser. If the sale was on a resolutive condition, the right to the interdict is with the purchaser, if he is in possession even as tenant or by permission, but if and as soon as the occurrence of the condition resolves the sale, the right is with the vendor (fr 11 §§ 8—13).

(*e*) The person liable to the interdict is the doer of the work (*semper adversus possessorem operis hoc interdictum competit*), but if the work is done by order of someone else, this other is the responsible person. If it is done, say by a tenant who throws the stones into a neighbour's field, the tenant is liable to the interdict; his lessor is only bound to allow restoration to take place and to cede any action he may have. If it is done in common by several persons, each is liable in full, but suit against one frees all. If a slave has done the work without his master's knowledge, he can be surrendered noxally: if he is sold, the purchaser is liable but can surrender him: and even a ward or madman is bound to permit restoration and surrender the slave. A slave who acted on the order of a guardian or caretaker may (as is usual when the action is not of an utterly wrong and wicked character) be excused; the guardian or caretaker will be liable to an analogous interdict (fr 7 § 1, 11 §§ 6, 7, 13 § 7, 15 pr, § 1; 16 § 2).

(*f*) The interdict must be brought within a year from the completion or cessation of the work. If, however, the work is in a tomb or underground (*e.g.* in a sewer), so that it is not readily observed, a longer time may be granted on consideration of the case. If a person is absent on State business, the year for use of the interdict begins with his return. It runs against heirs and other successors only so far as they have got anything thereby (*in id quod ad eos pervenit*). The damages are regulated by the plaintiff's interest, and the duty of the judge is to put the plaintiff in the position he would have been in if the work had not been done. This may involve restitution of usufruct or of servitudes lost or impaired in consequence of the work. The amount is fixed by oath of the plaintiff or, in default, by the judge. If plaintiff has recovered the value of his interest by another action (*e.g.* the Aquilian), he takes nothing by this interdict (fr 15 §§ 3—12; fr 21 § 3).

(*g*) The interdict *quod vi aut clam* has several sides, and may be concurrent in concrete cases with other proceedings. If plaintiff is building on his own ground and is interfered with by his neighbour, or by someone who has a show of interest in the building or land, he can apply for the interdict *uti possidetis* on the ground of his neighbour's act being an encroachment on his possession. And the like if the neighbour meddles with the training of his vines, or puts plaster on plaintiff's wall, *etc.* (D. xliii 17 fr 3 § 2, 4, 9; viii 5 fr 8 § 5). If the neighbour alleges that plaintiff's building is an infringement of his servitude, plaintiff can bring the *negatoria*, and shew that the neighbour has no such right (D. viii 5 fr 2 pr, 4 § 7). If the neighbour should give him notice of 'new work,' plaintiff can either suspend his operations for a time and proceed to establish his right, or give security and then continue his work, leaving his opponent to prove his right of interference, presumably on the ground of having a servitude over plaintiff's land or house (fr 3 § 5).

If someone attempts to build on plaintiff's ground or commits a trespass on his ground or buildings, so as to cause him practical annoyance or injury, plaintiff can give him notice of objection, and, if he persist openly or underhand, can bring against him the interdict *quod vi aut clam*, and defendant cannot save himself by alleging a right: if he rely on a right, he must declare his readiness to defend his conduct and give security (D. xliii 24 fr 1 § 2, 5; fr 3 § 5). If any such trespass conveys an insult, defendant is liable to an action *injuriarum*; if it causes sensible injury, he is liable to the Aquilian action.

In short, if I am interfered with on my own ground I have, besides the more personal and semi-penal proceedings of *injuriarum* and *lex Aquilia*, the interdicts *uti possidetis* and *quod vi aut clam* which protect my possession, and the *negatoria* which protects my property from any unfounded claim of servitude (D. xxxix 1 fr 5 § 10). If I have rights of servitude over my neighbour's land or house, I can bring the *confessoria* to vindicate my right, and I have the interdicts *de itinere, de aqua, etc.* for more summary protection. Against any new buildings which menace my rights of servitude or my necessary conveniences I have the proceeding of *operis novi nuntiatio,* and if the building is erected without my knowledge I can bring the interdict *quod vi aut clam.*

Usufructuaries had like modes of protection but with modifications.

CHAPTER IX.

GIFT (*DONATIO*).

A. *DONATIO (INTER VIVOS).*

1. It is not easy to satisfy oneself as to the proper position[1] of Gift in a treatise like this. It is not usually a ground of obligation; nor is it, like mancipation, a mode of acquisition. But it is certainly a ground of acquisition, and has affinity to occupation of what is abandoned by its owner, only that the abandonment (in the case of gift) is made in favour of a particular person, and evidence of such abandonment is required. Hence this Book is not an unsuitable place.

In the most common sense of the term a gift is the voluntary transfer during life to one person by another of something belonging to the latter, so that it becomes the former's property without his giving any consideration for it. In a wider sense it is used of any act whereby one person is made better off at the expense and by the consent of another. *Donari videtur quod nullo jure conceditur* (D. xxxix 5 fr 29 pr). Release of a debt or other obligation[2], grant of free lodging or of a servitude,

[1] Savigny (*System* vol. iv) and others put it in the General Part. Windscheid (*Pand.* § 365 n. 18) puts it among separate agreements under the head of Obligation. See also on the subject generally Schilling *Institutionen* ii p. 741 sqq.

[2] Cf. Plin. *Ep.* ii 4 *Quidquid mihi pater tuus debuit, acceptum tibi fieri jubebo* ('I will formally release'); *nec est quod verearis ne sit mihi onerosa ista donatio.*

refusal of a legacy, non-execution of a judgment, non-use of an easement, consent to an unfavourable division of common property, even the cultivation or improvement of others' land, and other acts, may, if done with the intention not of compromising a suit or paying for services, but of free enrichment of another at our expense, be regarded as gifts from us to him (fr 9 pr, 14, 17; xxiv 1 fr 5 §§ 6, 13, 14, *etc.*).

2. What constitutes a gift was discussed by the Romans chiefly in two connexions, one that of gifts between husband and wife (on which see Book II, p. 159 sqq.), and the other that of the *lex Cincia*[1]. This law recommended by Q. Fabius Maximus was passed in the year B.C. 204 on the proposal of M. Cincius Alimentus. Besides forbidding gifts to advocates, it forbad all gifts above a certain amount and it required full execution of the gift[2]. There was no penalty for breach, but gifts not in conformity to the statute were revocable by the donor during his life (Ulp. *sub init.*; Vat. 294 § 1). The maximum fixed by the law is not known. Gifts between certain classes of relatives were excepted from the provisions of the law.

The relatives excepted are (*a*) cognates up to the fifth degree

[1] Cicero speaks of the law in general terms, calling it *lex Cincia de donis et muneribus* (*Sen.* 4 § 10; *Orat.* ii 71 § 286). Tacitus (*An.* xi 5) refers to its bearing on fees to advocates; *Consurgunt patres legemque Cinciam flagitant qua cavetur antiquitus ne quis ob causam orandam pecuniam donumve accipiat*; xv 20; Livy (xxix 20; xxxiv 4) speaks of it as caused by the fear of the plebs' becoming *vectigalis et stipendiaria senatui* (the nobles being the usual advocates).

By a senate's decree in Pliny's time (105 p. Chr.) *omnes qui quid negotii haberent jurare prius quam agerent jubebantur, nihil se ob advocationem cuiquam dedisse promisisse cavisse: peractis tamen negotiis permittebatur pecuniam dumtaxat decem milium dare* (*Ep.* v 9 § 4, cf. *ib.* 13 (14) §§ 8—10). The *lex Cincia* appears to have been superseded by Constantine (Vat. 249). To disguise payment to an advocate it was sometimes promised under the fiction of repayment of a loan (Cod. ii 6 fr 3).

[2] Pliny applied to Nerva to make Voconius Romanus a senator, whose mother wrote to the Emperor that she would give her son 4,000,000 sesterces (£40,000) to support the rank. Difficulties arose. Pliny applies to Trajan to grant it and says: *mater liberalitatem nondum satis legitime peregerat; quod postea fecit admonita a nobis: nam et fundos emancipavit* (see above, pp. 77, 78 note) *et cetera quae in emancipatione inplenda solent exigi, consummavit* (*Ep. Traj.* 4).

and also (from the sixth) second cousins (*sobrinus sobrinave*); (*b*) all persons who were in the power, hand or handtake of such relatives, or in whose power, hand or handtake such relatives were; (*c*) those who were at the time of gift step-son, step-daughter, step-father, step-mother; father-in-law, mother-in-law, son-in-law, daughter-in-law; husband, wife, betrothed man and betrothed woman. These might both give and take. Further (*d*) guardians might give to their wards without regard to the Cincian limit; a freedman[1] or one who had been a *bona fide* slave might give to his patron or former master, and according to some lawyers to his patron's children. Any relative of any degree might give by way of dowry to woman or girl (Vat. 298—309). One rescued from robbers or the public enemy might give to his deliverer to any amount (Paul v 11 § 6).

3. A distinction has consequently to be made, as regards the validity of gifts, between these classes: (*a*) persons under power of donor; (*b*) relatives within the exceptions as above; (*c*) persons independent and not excepted.

(*a*) Gifts to persons under the donor's power are absolutely invalid. If however the donor confirmed the gift by any clear words in his will, and the gift left for others enough to satisfy the Falcidian law, and to exclude the plaint of an unduteous will, the gift was good, and, if not, was good up to that limit. Mere non-revocation was not sufficient, even for a title to usucapion as against the other children, if the donee remained under power until the donor's death (Vat. 256 *a*, 280, 281, 294—296; cf. Paul iv 1 § 11). But a gift for dowry was good, if properly executed (Vat. 258).

(*b*) Gifts to persons not under the donor's power, but within the exceptions as above, are complete, if mancipated though not delivered, or if gained by usucapion though not mancipated, or, in the case of non-mancipable things, whether provincial lands or other things, if delivered only. A promise in reply to stipulation was also effective, and could be enforced against the donor. A son or daughter, from whom his *peculium* is not taken away on emancipation, can obtain full ownership by usucapion,

[1] Paul interpreting a clause of the law '*Si quis a servis accipit*' says: *Servis liberti continentur* (Vat. 307): cf. Mommsen *Staatsr.* iii[2] 428.

but in order to enforce debts, requires either delegation or surrender of actions. Payment to him without dissent from his father, whether the debtor knows his change of *status* or not, discharges the debtor (Vat. 254, 260, 294, 310, 314). A declaration of gift entered on the court records (*apud acta professio*) was not in itself sufficient to pass the property (Vat. 266*a*, 268). But a statement in a deed of gift to a son that delivery had been duly made was held to be sufficient evidence (Vat. 314). A mother could not give to her children while under their father's power except for dowry or on the ground of marriage (*in honorem nuptiarum*); for such a gift was in effect a gift to her husband (Vat. 254, 269; Paul v 11 § 1).

(*c*) Gifts to persons not within the excepted list require more complete execution. Land in Italy requires mancipation and delivery, or usucapion; provincial land still requires delivery only: moveables, whether mancipable or not, require, besides mancipation and delivery, or delivery only as the case may be, possession for the greater part of one year before or afterwards, so as to be superior in the interdict *utrubi*. Investments (*nomina*) require to be duly transferred (Vat. 259, 293, 311—313).

Whether there has been due delivery is a question of fact rather than of law. Presence of the object, when mancipation or announcement of the gift takes place, or corporal possession of the object, if the donee knows of the gift, are sufficient evidence (Vat. 264, 265; Paul v 11 § 2; D. xxxix 5 fr 10). Delivery, as a gift, of deeds of purchase of slaves was by a rescript of Severus taken to be delivery of the slaves themselves (Cod. viii 53 fr 1). If the same thing be professedly given to two persons, the corporal possession and not the prior acceptance of the gift decides who is effective donee, whether the persons are in the excepted list or not (Paul v 11 § 4; Vat. 291). Payment to a common slave, as a gift to one of his masters, is good as a gift to that one, though the slave may receive it as for another or for both. If a procurator receive for himself what is intended for his principal, the principal acquires notwithstanding (D. xxxix 5 fr 13[1]).

[1] On D. xli 1 fr 37 § 6 see Waechter *Pand.* ii p. 69.

Mere entry in his accounts by an intended donor of his owing the donee something does not make a gift (*ib.* fr 26).

4. A donor is not liable to give a guaranty of title, nor, if he has promised it, can he be compelled to do so (Paul v 11 § 5). Even in mancipation a substantial guaranty was avoided by mancipating *nummo uno* (see Book v chap. iv c 1). Nor is a donor liable for delay in executing his promise: and by a constitution of Ant. Pius, if sued he can be condemned only *in id quod facere potest*, debts for value being deducted in estimating his means (Vat. 267; D. xxxix 5 fr 12, 22).

5. Where a gift has not been duly made in accordance with the Cincian law, the donor can revoke it during his life or by will. If a suit is brought to enforce delivery or execution in accordance with promise, he can plead that there was no consideration for the mancipation or promise (*si non donationis causa mancipavi vel promisi me daturum*); if the amount was in excess of the legal maximum, he could plead the Cincian law. If he has actually executed his gift, he could bring a vindication or condiction to recover it and meet any pleas by a like replication. If he has not revoked his gift, his heir has no such pleas or right to recover, for *morte Cincia removetur*. And the donee could plead fraud by way of answer or replication (Vat. 259, 310, 312). The plea 'contrary to the Cincian statute' could, as the Proculians held, be used during the donor's life by anyone resisting the donee's claim (Vat. 266; cf. Schilling *Inst.* iii p. 883 *kk*). A surety for a promise of an excessive gift could plead the Cincian law, without any consent from the donor (D. xxxix 5 fr 24).

6. A gift may be made by a creditor's delegating his debtor to the intended donee. If the gift is above the legal limit but not above the debt, the debtor has no plea against the donee's suit, for he is in fact only paying by his creditor's order what he owes; but the donor can sue his debtor for rescission of the excess if he has not yet paid, or the donee if he has already received payment in full (D. xxxix 5 fr 21). If the person delegated for the purpose of a gift is not really in debt to the donor and acted by mistake, he can resist the donee's suit by a plea of fraud, and can sue for release (fr 2 § 3).

7. A gift may be made for a particular purpose. If such

purpose is made a condition, the gift may be recovered if the condition on whatever ground is not carried out: but if it be merely a motive of the donor's, the gift is still good, notwithstanding that effect has not been given to the purpose. Whether a purpose be condition or merely cause is a question rather of fact than law (fr 2 § 7). A gift to one person for a time and thereafter to another is best secured by the latter making a stipulation with the former. If this was not done and the transfer over is not duly made, the donor or his heir could bring a condiction for the recovery of the gift. Eventually the second donee was allowed a *utilis actio* against the first (Vat. 286 = Cod. VIII 54, 3).

8. A son under power even if he have free administration of his *peculium* has no right to make gifts, unless he has express permission to do so, or his position in the world (*e.g.* a senator) may justify such a presumption (D. xxxix 5 fr 7). There is no such restriction on a *castrense peculium* (D. xxxix 5 fr 7).

In calculating the amount of a gift accrued profits (slave-children, fruits, rents, hire) are not reckoned unless expressly named (fr 9 § 1; fr 11).

Anything paid in remuneration of services (*e.g.* to a surety, or for help or influence, *etc.*) is not mere gift. Nor is repayment by a freedman of money lent to him as a slave; nor gift of a slave to be at once set free; nor promise to a man on condition of his swearing to bear promiser's name. What is given or promised *ob rem*, *i.e.* for a consideration, is not gift (D. i fr 19 §§ 1, 4—6; fr 18 § 1). Nor does anyone acquire by gift what he declines to accept (fr 19 § 2; cf. Cic. *Top.* 8 § 37).

B. *Donatio mortis causa.*

1. A gift made in view of death is a special form of conditional gift, made to take full effect only on the death of the donor before the donee. Such a gift is naturally made when the donor is seriously ill, or about to undertake a perilous journey[1], or going to war, or in fear of attack of brigands or of

[1] The lawyers quoted an instance in Homer (*Odyss.* xvii 78 sqq.) of a gift *mortis causa* by Telemachus to Piraeus.

some powerful enemy, or in fact when, from some cause or other, he is apprehensive of death and desirous, if that occur, to secure to the donee the thing given (D. xxxix 6 fr 2—6). In the epigrammatic language of the lawyers *magis habere se vult quam eum cui donat magisque eum cui donat quam heredem suum* (fr 1; fr 35 § 2). Special terms may provide for the donor's having no power of revocation, if he survive the special emergency or if he survive the donee: if there be no reversion at all to the donor, it is not properly a *mortis causa donatio* but only an ordinary gift, though occasioned by an apprehension of death (fr 13, 27). Usually a gift *mortis causa* is revocable by the donor at any time during his life (Paul iv 7; fr 16, 30). A son under power could make a gift *mortis causa* by permission of his father (fr 25 § 1).

2. A gift of this kind may be as various in its nature as any other conditional gift, and requires due execution. It may be made either on a suspensive or resolutive condition, *i.e.* the property may pass only on the death of the donor, or may pass at once, subject to reversion if the donor alters his mind or survives the emergency or survives the donee. In the former case the donor can always bring a vindication for the thing: in the latter case the donee had a vindication for the time, and then on the condition occurring either (as was doubtingly held) the property shifted back to the donor, or he had a condiction or action *in factum*, to secure its return from the donee (D. fr 18 § 1, 29, 35 § 3; xii 1 fr 19 pr). If the donee parted with the property to another, the donor could still bring a condiction against the donee for the value; and the same if the gift was a slave and the donee freed him. If the donee was a son under power, the action would be against the father *de peculio* (D. xxxix 6 fr 19, 37 § 1, 39). A condiction would apply also if the gift consisted in the delegation of a debtor, or in the release of a debt (fr 18 § 1; 24). All fruits, offspring of slaves, and accretions acquired by the donee in the interim are recoverable by the donor along with the thing itself (D. xii 4 fr 12; xxii 1 fr 38 § 3), the donee being entitled (by a plea of fraud) to get allowance for any necessary and useful expenditure (D. xxxix 6 fr 14). If the condition took effect by the donor's

death, the rights of the donee (if capable of taking) would be deemed to accrue from the time of the gift (fr 40). A gift in view of death might at any time have a trust attached to it by the donor (D. xxxi fr 77 § 1); and it might be made to one person with a proviso for it to pass to another if, when the time came, the first were incapable of taking. This would be secured by stipulation between the two donees (D. xxxi fr 50 pr).

3. A gift in view of death was regarded as in many ways the same as a legacy. By the pontifical law the two were classed together as creating an obligation to maintain the sacred rites of the family (Cic. *Legg.* ii 19 § 48). The restriction by the *lex Furia* and *lex Voconia* on the amount which could be withdrawn from the heir applied to both (Gai. ii 225, 226); and the provisions of the *lex Falcidia* were extended to such gifts by a constitution of Severus (Cod. viii 56 fr 2 § 2; D. xxxix 6 fr 42). In case of the donor's insolvency such gifts were rescinded as well as legacies, even though the donor had no fraudulent intention (fr 17); and the same rule was adopted (unless the gift was to children) when *bonorum possessio contra tabulas* was granted (D. xxxvii 5 fr 3 pr, *etc.*).

4. *Mortis causa capere* is properly correlative to *m. c. donare* and is often so used, but the term itself is much wider and includes not only inheritance, legacy and *fidei commissum* but also any sums taken as a condition of accepting or refusing an inheritance or of refusing a legacy or of obtaining freedom, *etc.* (D. xxxix 6 fr 8, 21, 31 § 2, *etc.*); and other cases of a different character where a death is the occasion of money, *etc.* passing (*e.g. dos recepticia*, fr 31 § 2: cf. fr 12). The incapacity of taking inheritance or legacies imposed by the statutes in promotion of marriage (Gai. ii 286, 287) was applied to gifts in view of death by a decree of the senate (D. fr 35 pr). For this purpose, and in case of gifts between husband and wife, the time regarded is the time of death, not the time of gift (D. xxxix 6 fr 22; xxiv 1 fr 11 § 2).

5. If an annuity was granted a man by stipulation (*in annos singulos quoad viveret*) to commence on donor's death, it was one gift, and the capacity of donee was ascertained at donor's death, once for all; whereas in a legacy to the same

effect, the capacity was subject to question every year (D. xxxix 6 fr 34, 35 §7; xxxiii 1 fr 11).

C. *POLLICITATIO.*

A mere offer or promise by itself was not enforceable (Paul v 12 § 9; Vat. 264 *a*, 267). But offers (*pollicitationes*) of a service to the public were in some cases enforceable. By a constitution of Trajan anyone who, on account of the grant of a public office (*honor*) to himself or another, whether before or after the grant, offered to give some money or other thing to a town or to erect a building[1] for the public, was bound to fulfil his offer. So also if, without regard to such a grant, he had actually commenced the performance of his promise, *e.g.* by part payment of the money, clearance of the ground, depositing materials or apparatus on the spot; or if the community had taken some action in consequence of his promise. And if the promise was made on account of a fire or earthquake or collapse of a public building, it could be enforced even if not part performed. In one case an offer was enforced, notwithstanding the promiser's being banished by the city praefect for three years.

By a rescript of Severus and Antoninus a promise made on account of a public office, if the work was commenced and the promiser became poor, was enforceable only to the amount of one-fifth. If a promiser died before entering on office, and the work had been commenced by himself or the community, his heirs were bound, but if the estate was insufficient, children were bound only for a tenth, outsider heirs for a fifth. Interest was due only after delay. Conditions attached to the offer were enforced only if useful to the State (D. L 12).

A vow binds the person making it, if independent and of the age of puberty, and binds his heir; but does not bind the thing vowed, it does not become sacred. If a man vows the tenth of his property, the tenth remains part of the estate, until actually separated by himself or his heir.

A son or slave was not bound by a vow made without his father's or master's authority (*ib.* fr 2).

[1] Pliny mentions such offers in connexion with the building of a theatre at Nicaea: *Huic theatro ex privatorum pollicitationibus multa debentur, ut basilicae circa, ut porticus supra caveam* (*Ep. Traj.* 39 § 3).

APPENDIX TO BOOK IV, CHAP. VI.

RECIPERE applied to servitudes.

[Reprinted with slight alterations from *Journal of Philology*, vol. XV (1886).]

Cic. *Orat.* i 39 § 179. *Quo quidem in genere familiaris noster M. Buculeius, homo neque meo judicio stultus et suo valde sapiens et ab juris studio non abhorrens, simili in re quodam modo nuper erravit. Nam cum aedes L. Fufio venderet, in mancipio lumina uti tum essent, ita recepit. Fufius autem, simul atque aedificari coeptum est in quadam parte urbis, quae modo ex illis aedibus conspici posset, egit statim cum Buculeio, quod, cuicumque particulae caeli officeretur quamvis esset procul, mutari lumina putabat.*

The case of *Fufius* v. *Buculeium* respecting the lights in a house bought by the plaintiff from the defendant, has received a good many comments, but I think there is still room for another. For though Prof. Wilkins, in his note on the passage, has taken the right view, the matter requires a fuller explanation than he has given.

Crassus is represented by Cicero as desirous of shewing the necessity of a knowledge of law to public orators, and for this purpose he instances one case after another in which the arguments turned not on matters of ordinary life and interest, but on strictly legal questions. In the case mentioned just before ours, Marius Gratidianus the vendor of a house, had not declared in the statement accompanying the conveyance that a part of the house was subject to an easement in favour of another. Crassus had argued on behalf of the purchaser Orata that the vendor ought to have disclosed any fault or defect in the house which was in his knowledge. The mention of this case suggested to Crassus another, which had occurred, as he said, lately. It was of the same class (*quo in genere*), and occurred to a friend, viz. M. Buculeius, a man, whom Crassus thought no fool, who thought himself very clever, and who moreover was a bit of a lawyer. Here we come to a difference in the reading. Some of the best MSS. have *simili quodam modo erravit*; others have *simili in re quodam modo erravit.* The former of these two readings makes the blunder of Buculeius to have been somewhat like that of the vendor in the other case, the latter makes him to have blundered but only in a like matter. If this last reading be adopted, we have to find a meaning for *simili in re* as well as for *quo in genere,* unless the one be taken as a careless repetition of the other. But there is no necessity to suppose carelessness. *Quo in genere* may refer to the incompleteness of a declaration, and *simili in re* to the question of sale of a house, or, more specifically, to questions respecting an easement arising on the sale of a house. If the latter reading be adopted, we have to find a similarity in the blunder as well as in the subject-matter. But then we can take *quo in genere* of sales of houses and *simili modo erravit* of incomplete declarations by the vendor. And therefore whichever of these readings be adopted, there is no decisive help gained for the precise interpretation of our passage. The case relates on either supposition to the sale of a house, to the existence or nature of an easement, and to the imperfect or erroneous declaration of the vendor.

It is always venturesome to explain a law-case unless one has a full report by a competent hand. In a speech of Cicero's we have no doubt a number of facts, or matters intended to be taken as facts, but we know not whether other facts may not have been suppressed altogether, and whether the statement of those which are given is so full, so accurate, and so fair, as to justify the inferences which we should be inclined to draw. In the brief mention of a case, such as we have here, we can only expect to have one point or aspect presented, and it is therefore of some importance to ascertain from what point of view the narrator regards it. In our passage it is not stated that Crassus was himself engaged in the case on either side, nor is it said that it led to an elaborate legal discussion. The mention of it at all appears to be due to the similarity of the matter, and possibly of the blunder, to that of Marius; but it is reasonable to suppose that the case was instanced, like the rest, to prove Crassus' thesis, that in such a matter there was ample call for thorough knowledge of law. Yet we cannot assume that we have in the statement here given all the important points of the case. For the case of Marius as given in § 178 is certainly deficient. Cicero has referred to it again in the *de Officiis* iii 16 § 67, and there he mentions, what is not told here, that the house now sold to Orata by Marius had a few years before been purchased by Marius from Orata, and that this fact formed the pivot on which Antonius' defence turned. It was absurd, he argued, for Orata to complain that Marius had not told him of this easement on the house, when Orata had owned the house and knew of the easement as well as Marius could tell him. With this example before us of the incompleteness of Cicero's statements in incidental references to law-cases, we must hesitate before we assume that *Fufius* v. *Buculeium* has been adequately reported.

In a city like Rome, where the buildings were close to one another and the streets were narrow, the comfort and indeed habitability of a residence largely depend on its neighbours. One house may actually require the support of another, or it may have no other way of carrying off its rainwater, except over the roof or into the area of its neighbour. Its prospect or its light may be open, only so long as the neighbours do not build in a particular direction or to a particular height. Yet each owner is *prima facie* entitled to do what he likes with his own building or area, to pull down or to build higher, to stop his neighbour from sending his drains through or over his (the first owner's) premises, or in any way interfering with the first owner's arrangements. But sometimes an owner can be induced to secure to his neighbour such conveniences, and to impose on his own house a servitude to some specific effect in favour of his neighbour's house. And nothing can be more natural than for the owner of two neighbouring houses in selling one or both to impose upon one or both a servitude in favour of the other. While the houses were in the same ownership, these rights may have been mutually enjoyed, and may have become necessary for their convenient use as residences. A purchaser would require them, and a vendor would guaranty or reserve them.

The explanation of our passage taken generally by lawyers is set forth by Rein *Civil-Recht* p. 322, and more fully by Griesinger *de servitute luminum* 1819, pp. 128—154. On one point there is a slight divergence (see Rein p. 323 and Voigt, *Ius naturale* iii p. 306).

Griesinger's view is as follows. The house of Buculeius enjoyed a servitude *ne luminibus officiatur* granted by a neighbour either to Buculeius himself or to a former owner of Buculeius' house. This grant would be in the usual words (cf. D. viii 2 fr 23; xviii 1 fr 33) *lumina, uti nunc sunt, ut ita sint.* The effect of this servitude was that the particular neighbour was prevented from so building as to interfere with the lights of Buculeius' house. Buculeius now in selling to Fufius used exactly the same formula, *i.e.* he undertook that the lights should always be as they then were. Buculeius (according to Griesinger) meant to guaranty only the servitude previously granted by his neighbour. But his words, taken strictly, had a wider meaning; and Fufius took advantage of it, maintaining that he was thereby guarantied against any obstruction of any portion of the sky visible from his house. On a building being erected a long way off, but just visible from his house, Fufius at once brought an action against Buculeius for this interference with his lights. Buculeius' error was this. In the mouth of a neighbour constituting a servitude the words could only relate to his own house, and impose this restriction of rights on himself and subsequent owners of the servient house only. But Buculeius as seller of the dominant house might, wisely or unwisely, undertake a personal liability to the purchaser for any privileges or advantages he chose to connect with the house. If he promised Fufius security against interference with his lights, not from one or more persons, who owned servient houses, but from all the world, he might not, it is true, be able to keep his bargain, but he would be liable on his covenant[1], and must compensate Fufius. And it was a principle of the law that ambiguous words should be construed against the vendor (cf. D. ii 14 fr 39). Some such case is apparently referred to by Pomponius in D. xviii 1 fr 33. *Cum in lege venditionis ita sit scriptum 'flumina stillicidia uti nunc sunt, ut ita sint,' nec additur quae flumina vel stillicidia, primum spectari oportet quid acti sit: si non id appareat, tunc id accipitur quod venditori nocet: ambigua enim oratio est.*

Voigt (with others) supposes that Buculeius was not covenanting for the continuance of an already existing servitude (he doubts this being the practice), but that by the use of the words *lumina uti nunc sunt ut ita sint* he imposed a servitude on another of his own houses in favour of that he was selling.

Griesinger thinks that Fufius would win on account of the strict construction of words in early times. Voigt apparently thinks he would lose his case, because there could be no doubt of Buculeius' real meaning.

Had Cicero's words been different, I should have thought such an explanation, whether Griesinger's or Voigt's, probable and reasonable. But Cicero does not say *lumina uti tum essent ut ita essent,* and he does not use the word *promisit* or *spopondit,* but *recepit.*

Ita recepit is rather too short an expression for *recepit ita futura esse*; and it is at least as probable that *ita* does not relate to the favourable position of the lights but to the accurate representation of the formula. That is to say *ita* may mean 'in these words,' quite as well as 'in this arrangement.' Instances may be found to justify either interpretation, *e.g.* both occur in the passage of Pomponius just quoted.

Recipere in Law Latin is used in several senses. It means 'to recover,' 'to receive' physically (*e.g.* receiving produce of robbery D. xlvii 9 fr 3 § 3; receiving on deposit D. xvi 3 fr 1 § 10 sqq.) and metaphorically (*e.g. receptum est* 'it is accepted as law'). It also means 'to undertake,' *e.g. obligationem alienam, in*

[1] Is this so? If it were a formal stipulation, Griesinger may be right. But if it was in the *lex mancipi* or an attached *pactum,* it would I think be cut down to what properly concerned the convenience and commercial interest of the house sold (cf. D. viii 3 fr 5 fin. fr 6 pr).

se recipere periculum, etc. In this last sense it is used not unfrequently by Cicero, chiefly in his letters, *e.g. omnia se facturum recepit* (Cic. *Att.* v 13 § 2), *in me recipio fore eum tibi voluptati* (*Fam.* xiii 10 § 3). Several times it is combined with *spondeo, etc., e.g. et ipse spondeo et omnes hoc tibi tui pro me recipiunt maximum te fructum facturum* (*ib.* 50 § 2); *Promitto, recipio, spondeo C. Caesarem talem semper fore civem, qualis, etc.* (*Phil.* v 18 fin.); *de aestate polliceris vel potius recipis* (*Att.* xiii 1 § 2). So the substantive *receptum, e.g. satis est factum officio ac necessitudini, satis promisso nostro ac recepto* (*Verr.* v 53 § 139), *ille promissum et receptum intervertit ad seque transtulit* (*Phil.* 2 32 § 79). Both verb and noun are found in this sense in the Digest though not very often, *e.g.* D. xxviii 5 fr 47; and in the rubric of iv 8 *de receptis: qui arbitrium receperint ut sententiam dicant, i.e.* 'Of undertakings: herein specially that those who have undertaken an arbitration, should declare their award'; and several times in iv 9 fr 1 pr *quod cujusque salvum fore receperint*; *ib.* § 8; fr 5 § 1; xlvii 5 § 4. Bekker has discussed this use of the word in *ZRG.* xvi 1 sqq.

The construction of *recipio* in this sense is either absolute, or with an infinitive object sentence, or with *de,* or with abstract words like *causam, periculum, mandatum, etc.* None of these usages resembles that in our text; *lumina uti tum essent ita recepit.* Nor have I noticed this sense of *recipere* to occur of an agreement between vendor and purchaser.

But there is yet another meaning of *recipere* which suits the passage, and is free from these objections. It is best illustrated by such passages as the following, which I take from just those parts of the Digest which naturally deal with our present subject-matter. The first is from the title on general rules affecting servitudes: the second from that on the action to enforce the mutual obligations of vendor and purchaser, the third from that on the purchaser's claim for double damages when he has not got quiet enjoyment of the object purchased. The regular meaning of *recipere* in such matters is 'to reserve' from the conveyance. The word was synonymous with *excipere, detrahere, deducere* (cf. D. vii 1 fr 36 § 1).

D. viii 4 fr 10 (Ulp.) *Quidquid venditor servitutis nomine sibi recipere vult, nominatim recipi oportet: nam illa generalis receptio 'quibus est servitus utique est' ad extraneos pertinet, ipsi nihil prospicit venditori ad jura ejus conservanda: nulla enim habuit, quia nemo ipse sibi servitutem debet, i.e.* a vendor wishing to reserve to himself a servitude over the property sold must do so in express terms. A mere general clause of reservation—'for those who have servitudes and as they have them[1]'—is good to preserve the rights of third parties, but not good for the vendor, who cannot have a servitude over his own property and cannot therefore be included in the words *quibus est.*

D. xix 1 fr 53 (Labeo) *Si habitatoribus habitatio lege venditionis recepta est, omnibus in ea habitantibus praeter dominum recte recepta habitatio est.* (Paul) *Immo si cui in ea insula quam vendideris gratis habitationem dederis et sic receperis 'habitatoribus ad (aut* MS.) *quam quisque diem conductum habet,' parum caveris, nominatim enim de his recipi oportuit, itaque eos habitatores emptor insulae habitatione impune prohibebit, i.e.* a right of free lodging cannot, according to Paul, be reserved on a sale, unless it be by express words for particular individuals.

D. xxi 2 fr 69 § 5 (Scaev.) *Qui fundum tradit (mancipat*

[1] I take *utique* here as adverb of manner (*uti*) with the copulative *que* (cf. *e.g.* Lex Jul. Mun. 5; Edict ap. D. xxi 1 fr 38; SC. ap. D. xxxviii 4 fr 1 pr, *etc.*), and the sentence to require for completeness the expression of an apodosis in some such words as *recte recipitur.* (See the passage of Scaevola, below.) Such imperfect quotations are common *e.g.* D. xviii 1 fr 7 pr; fr 59; fr 66 § 2; xxi 2 fr 48; *etc.* The Greek commentators apparently, unless merely paraphrasing, took *utique* as meaning 'of course,' for they translate οἷς ὁ ἀγρὸς δουλεύει, δουλευέτω Tipucitus ap. Heimb. Bas. v p. 197 (and similarly in Bas. xix 2 fr 68 ed. Zachar. = D. xxi 2 fr 69 § 5). Hence Mommsen in his larger edition of the Digest suggested *utique esto.* In the later stereotype edition he has not repeated this suggestion. *Utique* 'anyhow,' 'of course,' is a conversational expression and is common enough in the Digest in jurist's arguments, *e.g.* D. xxi 1 fr 1 § 8; fr 31 § 12, but I doubt altogether its occurrence in a formal conveyance. The Greek translation corresponds better to such a phrase (very different from ours) as we find in D. xix 1 fr 39 *Qui sic exceperat: si quae servitutes debentur debebuntur*, which is referred to a case from an ante-Augustan jurist (*apud veteres*).

Scaev.) *et, cum sciat certam servitutem deberi, perfusorie dixerit 'itinera actus quibus sunt utique sunt recte recipitur,' evictionis quidem nomine se liberat, sed quia decepit emptorem empti judicio tenetur, i.e.* a vendor with knowledge of a definite servitude to which the house, *etc.* is subject must inform the purchaser of it. Mere general words by which due reservation is made for all who have rights of road and driving according to the character of such rights, are not enough to free the vendor from responsibility. The purchaser cannot indeed claim double damages as having been so far evicted, but he can claim full compensation on the ground of being deceived by the vendor.

Other instances of *recipere* in this sense in the Digest are vii 1 fr 36 § 1; viii 3 fr 30; 4 fr 5, 6 fin.; xviii 1 fr 40 § 3, § 4; xxxix 6 fr 35 § 2, 42 pr. It is also found in Plaut. *Trin.* 157 of reserving part of a house; in Cic. *Or.* ii 55 § 226 and also *Top.* § 100 of reserving *ruta caesa,* and in Cato ap. Gell. xvii 6 § 1 of reserving money in making a dowry; and in *de Re Rust.* 149, where, among the clauses of an agreement for the sale of the winter pasture, comes *bubus domitis binis, cantherio uni, cum emptor pascet, domino pascere recipitur. Holeris asparagis lignis aqua itinere actu domini usioni recipitur, i.e.* 'Right is reserved for the owner to pasture along with the purchaser's cattle, two yoke of oxen and one gelding. Right is also reserved for the owner to take vegetables, firewood, water, and to have a road.' The phrase *recte recipitur* was so common that it was denoted by initials *R. R.* See Probi *Notae* iv p. 276 ed. Keil, cf. p. 327.

It seems strange that this use of *recipere* should not have been mentioned by earlier interpreters of Cicero[1]. There is no doubt of its meaning; it occurs not infrequently, and occurs just in relation to conditions made in conveyance. The form of our sentence is very similar to D. xviii 1 fr 77 *In lege fundi vendundi lapidicinae in eo fundo ubique essent exceptae erant* where *exceptae* is much the same as *receptae,* as

[1] *E.g.* Voigt (*Die* XII *Tafeln* ii p. 154) adheres to his old view, though treating of cases of reservation on sale in the next pages. But Voigt's judgment is very inferior to his learning and industry.

is well shewn by D. viii 3 fr 30. *Qui duo praedia habebat, in unius venditione aquam quae in fundo nascebatur et circa eam aquam late decem pedes exceperat; quaesitum est, utrum dominium loci ad eum pertineat an ut per eum locum accedere possit. Respondit si ita recepisset 'circa eam aquam late pedes decem' iter dumtaxat videri venditoris esse*, *i.e.* 'The owner of two estates sold one, but excepted in the contract of sale some water which rose in it and ten feet wide adjoining[1]. Alfenus was consulted whether the effect of this was that the vendor retained the property in the ground for a distance of ten feet adjoining the water, or had only a right of access over the purchaser's ground to that extent. Alfenus answered that, if the reservation was made just in those words, the vendor had only the right of access[2].

I think then, following the suggestion of D. xxi 2 fr 69 § 5 quoted above (p. 540), that Buculeius inserted in his conveyance a general *reservation* in some such words as *lumina uti nunc sunt recte recipitur* or possibly *lumina quibus sunt, utique nunc sunt, recte recipitur*, *i.e.* 'Due reservation is made of the lights as they now are' or 'due reservation is made for all who have lights according to their present condition.' Buculeius probably used them from excess of caution without any definite reference or even any distinctly conceived purpose. Perhaps he liked to show off his acquaintance with legal *formulae*. Or he may have thought that they would protect his own lights or the lights of some neighbouring house against Fufius. Cicero says that he *erravit*, which may very well apply to an erroneous use of a common general form. Fufius however, ignoring the technical sense of *recipitur*, chose to take it as a *guaranty* of his own lights against the world. This was doubly wrong, as the law is in the Digest and probably was in Cicero's time also. For (1) *recipitur* did not mean in such

[1] Cf. D. xliii 15 § 1 *opus facere ripae agrive qui circa ripam est tuendi causa licet.*

[2] The decision went presumably on the ground that the words pointed to what was necessary for a water course and facilities for cleaning it, and that more would have been said if a long strip of land were intended to be reserved in ownership.

formulae 'a promise is given,' but 'a right is reserved,' and (2) he would have to shew not merely that some portion of the sky which was previously visible from his house was now obscured by the new building, but that his light was thereby lessened (cf. D. viii 2 fr 15, 16, 38, 39). There would still remain the important question *quid actum esset* (D. xviii 1 fr 33, 40 § 3, 77; L 17 fr 34, *etc.*), *i.e.* 'what was the real contract between the parties,' and this was a matter which would require in the rival advocates a good knowledge of forms of conveyance, of the practice in sales, and of the respective provinces of verbal expression and other evidence in determining the real meaning of the parties.

CAMBRIDGE: PRINTED BY J. AND C. F. CLAY, AT THE UNIVERSITY PRESS.

ROMAN PRIVATE LAW

IN THE TIMES OF CICERO AND OF THE ANTONINES

by

HENRY JOHN ROBY

M.A., Hon. LL.D. Cantab., Hon. LL.D. Edinb.,
Honorary Fellow of St John's College, Cambridge

Volume II

THE LAWBOOK EXCHANGE, LTD.

UNION, NEW JERSEY

2000

ISBN 1-58477-074-0

Printed in the United States of America
on Acid-Free Paper

The Lawbook Exchange, Ltd.
965 Jefferson Avenue
Union, New Jersey 07083-8605

Please see catalogue at rear of this volume
or our website http://www.lawbookexchange.com
for a selection of our other reprints.

Library of Congress Cataloging-in-Publication Data

Roby, Henry John, 1830-1915.
Roman private law in the times of Cicero and of the Antonines / by Henry John Roby.
v. ; cm.
Originally published: Cambridge: Cambridge University Press, 1902.
Includes bibliographical references and index.
ISBN 1-58477-074-0 (cloth : alk. paper)
1. Roman law—History. I. Title.

KJA147 .R63 2000
340.5'4'09—dc21 99-059270

ROMAN PRIVATE LAW

IN THE TIMES OF CICERO AND OF THE ANTONINES

In two Volumes,
Vol. II

Book V. Obligations.

Essays on
Litterarum obligatio.
Nexum.

Book VI. Procedure.

Appendix.
Essays on Cicero's speeches
Pro Quinctio.
,, *Roscio Comoedo.*
,, *Tullio.*
,, *Caecina.*

London: C. J. CLAY AND SONS,
CAMBRIDGE UNIVERSITY PRESS WAREHOUSE,
AVE MARIA LANE,
AND
STEVENS AND SONS, LTD,
119 AND 120, CHANCERY LANE.

Glasgow: 50, WELLINGTON STREET.
Leipzig: F. A. BROCKHAUS.
New York: THE MACMILLAN COMPANY.
Bombay and Calcutta: MACMILLAN AND CO., LTD.

ROMAN PRIVATE LAW

IN THE TIMES OF CICERO AND OF THE ANTONINES

by

HENRY JOHN ROBY

M.A., Hon. LL.D. Cantab., Hon. LL.D. Edinb.,
Honorary Fellow of St John's College, Cambridge

Volume II

Cambridge:
at the University Press
1902

Cambridge:
PRINTED BY J. & C. F. CLAY,
AT THE UNIVERSITY PRESS.

CONTENTS OF VOLUME II.

Book V.

Chap. I. Classification.

Criticism of Gaius' division, p. 2.
Classification in this book, p. 3.

Chap. II. Agreements.

A. *Pacta*, p. 6.
B. Compromise (*transactio*), p. 8.

Chap. III. Strict obligations (*Stricta judicia*):

General character, p. 10.

A. Verbal obligation (*Stipulatio*), p. 11:

1. (*a*) form, p. 11; (*b*) conditions of validity, p. 13;
(*c*) impossibility of performance, p. 17;
(*d*) options, p. 19; (*e*) heirs how far bound, p. 20;
(*f*) drafting and interpretation, p. 22; (*g*) action, p. 24;
(*h*) who can enter into stipulation, p. 25;
2. Correal obligation, p. 26;
3. Adstipulation, p. 28;
4. Sureties: three kinds, p. 29:
sponsor, *fidepromissor*, p. 29;
lex Appuleia, *lex Furia*, *lex Cicereia*, pp. 30, 31;
fidejussor, p. 31; Hadrian's letter, p. 31; *lex Cornelia*, p. 31;
details of suretyship, pp. 32—37;
5. Novation (by stipulation), p. 38;
6. Delegation, p. 42;
7. Transfer of obligations, p. 45:
(*a*) by stipulation, p. 45; (*b*) by representation, p. 47;
8. Payment or discharge of obligation, p. 49;
what is payment? p. 50;
to whom should payment be made? p. 52;
marshalling of debts, p. 54;
other modes of discharge, p. 55;
9. Verbal Release (*acceptilatio*), p. 55;
10. Quittance or receipt, p. 59;
Pompeian tablet, p. 59;
11. *Pactum de non petendo*, p. 61.

B. *Litterarum obligatio* (Book-entry), p. 64.

C. 1. Cash-loan (*mutuum*), p. 66;
2. interest on loans, p. 72;
3. loans on bottomry (*trajectitia pecunia*), p. 75.

D. *Condictiones*, p. 76:
1. *ob rem dati, re non secuta*, p. 77; 2. *indebiti*, p. 79;
3. *sine causa*, p. 82; 4. *ob turpem causam*, p. 82;
5. *furtiva, i.e. ex causa furtiva*, p. 82;
6. *incerti* (?), p. 84.

E. 1. *Actio de eo quod certo loco dari oportet*, p. 86;
2. *pecuniae constitutae*, p. 86; 3. *recepticia*, p. 88.

Chap. IV. *Obligationes bonae fidei:*
1. general character, p. 89; 2. enumeration, p. 90;
3. classification, p. 90.

Loan, Deposit, Pledge, p. 91:

A. Loan (*Commodatum*), p. 92.

B. Deposit: 1. ordinary, p. 94; 2. with banker, p. 96;
3. with stakeholder (*sequester*), p. 97;
4. under *fiducia*, p. 97.

C. 1. *Fiducia*, p. 97; as pledge, p. 98;
Baetic tablet, p. 101;
2. *Pignus* and *Hypotheca*, p. 102;
definition, p. 102; what can be pledged, p. 103;
pledge of others' property, p. 104; tacit pledge, p. 105;
creditor's duty, p. 106; ἀντίχρησις, p. 107;
power of sale, p. 108; forfeiture, p. 110;
successive pledges, p. 111; end of pledge, p. 112;
pledge of pledge, p. 113; creditor's actions, p. 113;
3. *Pignoris capio*, p. 115.

D. 1. *Mandatum*, p. 116;
mandator as guarantor, p. 121;
Jussus, p. 122;
2. *Negotiorum gestio*, p. 123;
direct action, p. 124; counter-action, p. 126.

E. *Societas:* 1. ordinary Partnership, p. 127;
2. companies: tax-farmers, p. 133;
clubs, towns, *etc.*, p. 134;
3. *judicium communi dividundo*, p. 135.

F. Purchase and sale (*Emptio, venditio*):
1. contract of sale, p. 138;
2. obligation under contract of sale, p. 142;
vendor's duty, p. 143; what sale carries, p. 145;
vendor's liability for faults, p. 147; purchaser's duty, p. 148;

3. AEDILES' EDICT, p. 149;
judicium redhibitorium, p. 151; *quanti minoris*, p. 151;
4. liability for want of title, p. 157;
stipulatio duplae, p. 158;
5. action *ex empto*, p. 160;
6. special subjects of sale:
(*a*) *venditio hereditatis*, p. 162; (*b*) *venditio nominis*, p. 163;
7. sales on condition, p. 164;
(*a*) *in diem addictio*, p. 165; (*b*) *lex commissoria*, p. 165;
(*c*) *si displicuerit*, p. 166; (*d*) *sub modo*, p. 166;
(*e*) *ita ut*, p. 167;
8. specimen record of sale, p. 167.

G. LETTING AND HIRING (*LOCATIO, CONDUCTIO*), p. 169;
1. *loc. cond. rei*, p. 171; 2. *operarum*, p. 174;
3. *operis faciendi*, p. 174; 4. carriage, *etc.* of fungibles, p. 176;
5. *SUPERFICIES*, p. 176; 6. JETTISON (*lex Rhodia*), p. 177;
7. *Receptum nautarum, etc.*, p. 178.

H. ACTIONS ON THE CASE (*in factum, praescriptis verbis*), p. 179:
1. *Aestimatoria*, p. 180; 2. barter, p. 181;
3. *do ut des, etc.*, p. 181; 4. various, p. 182;
5. delictal, p. 182.

CHAP. V. SEMIDELICTAL OBLIGATIONS, p. 183:
i. 1. *actio judicati*, p. 184; 2. *depensi*, p. 184;
3. *de sponsu*, p. 185; 4. *legati certi per damn.*, p. 185.
Liberatio per aes et libram, p. 185.
5. *DAMNI INJURIA*: *lex Aquilia*, p. 186;
cases under law, p. 187; analogous, p. 188;
good defence, p. 189; who is plaintiff, p. 190;
measure of damages, p. 191; injury to freeman, p. 192;
concurrent actions, p. 193; second clause of law, p. 193.
Dare damnas esto, p. 194.

ii. 1. *Arborum furtim caesarum*, p. 194;
2. *de dejecto effusove*, p. 195;
3. *de suspenso, exposito, etc.*, p. 196;
4. *qui naves, cauponas exercent*, p. 197;
5. *PAUPERIES*, p. 198; keeping dogs, *etc.*, p. 199.

CHAP. VI. *OBLIGATIONES EX DELICTO*, p. 199:

A. *FURTI.* What is theft? p. 201;
ope consilio, p. 203; who can sue, 205;
damages, p. 209; *f. manifesti*, p. 209;
noxal surrender, p. 211.

B. Other actions for theft:
1. *de tigno juncto*, p. 212; 2. *de pastu pecoris*, p. 212;
3. *abigeatus*, p. 212; 4. *oneris aversi*, p. 213;
5. *rerum amotarum*, p. 213.

C. Abstraction from vacant inheritance, p. 213;
(*a*) *expilatae hereditatis*, p. 214;
(*b*) fraud by slave freed, p. 214.

D. 1. *Furti concepti*; 2. *f. oblati*, p. 215;
3. *f. prohibiti*, p. 215; *non exhibiti*, p. 216.

E. 1. *Vi bonorum raptorum*, p. 216;
2. *ex incendio, etc. rapti recepti, etc.*, p. 217;
3. *damni in turba facti*, p. 218.

F. *Servi corrupti*, p. 218.

G. 1. *Injuriarum*, p. 220; Criminal insults, p. 224;
2. *interdictum de hom. libero exhibendo*, p. 225;
3. *patronum in jus vocandi*, p. 225.

H. Intimidation, p. 226.

J. Fraud. *Doli mali actio*, p. 228;
doli mali exceptio, p. 231.

K. *Pecuniae acceptae calumniae causa*, p. 234;
calumniae judicium, p. 234.

L. Fraudulent allowance of sale of self, p. 235.

M. Publicans' exactions, p. 235.

N. Action against land surveyors, p. 236.

Chap. VII. A. Liability on contracts of persons under power:
1. *actio quod jussu*, p. 237; 2. *de peculio*, p. 238;
where *peculium* passes, p. 241; vicars, p. 243;
3. *de in rem verso*, p. 245; 4. *tributoria*, p. 247.

B. Liability on others' contracts:
actio exercitoria et institoria, p. 248.

C. Liability on torts of persons under power:
noxal surrender of slaves, p. 252; of children, p. 258.

Chap. VIII. Reinstatement of persons and cancelment of transactions, p. 258:

A. Reinstatement of minors, p. 259.

B. Reinstatement of *majores*, p. 262.

C. *Postliminium*, p. 264.

D. *Capitis deminutio*, p. 266.

E. *SC. Macedonianum*, p. 267.

F. *SC. Velleianum (Vellaeanum)*, p. 268.

G. *Actio Pauliana*, p. 273.

H. *Actio Fabiana vel Calvisiana*, p. 276.

I. *De alienatione judicii mutandi causa*, p. 277.

APPENDIX TO BOOK V.:

A. *LITTERARUM OBLIGATIO*, p. 279;
terms used, p. 288;
pararii, p. 293; Cicero *Att.* IV 17, p. 295;
Valer. Max. viii 2 § 2, p. 295.

B. *NEXUM*, p. 297:
1. use in Livy, p. 297; 2. in XII tables, p. 303;
3. in Cicero, p. 304; 4. in Varro and Aelius Gallus, p. 305;
5. *nexum aes*, p. 306; 6. use in Gaius, p. 306;
7. use in Digest and Codes, p. 306; 8—9. result, p. 307;
10. *lex Poetelia*, p. 310.

BOOK VI.

CHAP. I. COURTS:

A. Praetor, p. 312. B. Consuls, p. 313.
C. *Centumviri*, p. 314. D. *Decemviri*, p. 315.
E. *Recuperatores*, p. 315. F. *Arbiter*, p. 318.
G. *Arbiter ex compromisso*, p. 320. H. *Judex*, p. 322.

CHAP. II. TIME AND PLACE OF LEGAL BUSINESS:

A. Time: 1. of year, p. 323; 2. of day, p. 324.

B. Place, p. 325.

CHAP. III. DISQUALIFICATIONS FOR SUING:

A. General, p. 326; *Infames*, p. 327.

B. for appointing representatives, p. 329.

C. Special disqualification of gaming-house keepers, p. 330.

CHAP. IV. PLACE AND TIME OF SUING:

A. Where suit should be brought, p. 331.

B. When suit should be brought, p. 332.

CHAP. V. PROCEEDINGS *IN JURE*:

A. Summons, p. 333.

B. *Vadimonium*, p. 336.

CHAP. VI. PROCEDURE *PER LEGIS ACTIONES*, p. 339:

A. *Sacramento agere*, p. 340.

B. *Per judicis postulationem*, p. 345.

C. *Per condictionem*, p. 345.

CHAP. VII. PROCEDURE *PER FORMULAS*:

1. history, p. 346;
2. framing the issue, p. 349;
3. appointment of judge, p. 351;
4. praetor's general functions, p. 352;
5. *si quid novi juris (magistratus) statuerit*, p. 353.

CHAP. VIII. PLEADINGS:

A. General form of statement of issue:

1. *demonstratio, intentio, condemnatio*, p. 354;
2. modifications of form, p. 354;
3. damages, p. 355;
4. *formula in jus* or *in factum concepta*, p. 356;
5. *praejudicium*, p. 359.

B. Error in plaintiff's statement:

1. in the claim, p. 359; 2. in the condemnation, p. 361;
3. in the demonstration, p. 362.

C. Set-off (*compensatio*), p. 363: 1. by banker, p. 363;
2. *deductio* by *bonorum emptor*, p. 363.

D. Pleas (*exceptiones*):

1. general character, p. 364; 2. mode of statement, p. 365;
3. peremptory or dilatory, p. 365.

E. Replications, *etc.*, p. 367.

F. Praescriptions:

1. in periodical payments, p. 368; 2. other cases, p. 368;
3. in suretyship, p. 369; 4. on behalf of plaintiff, p. 370.

G. Fictions:

1. general, p. 371; 2. *damni infecti, etc.*, p. 372;
3. *bonorum emptor*, p. 372; 4. *cognitor, tutor, etc.*, p. 373;
5. *actio exercitoria*, p. 373.

H. *Sponsiones*, p. 374.

CHAP. IX. A. REPRESENTATION OF PARTIES:
1. under *legis actio*, p. 376; 2. *cognitor*, p. 377;
3. *procurator*, p. 378; 4. distinction between them, p. 380;
5. disqualifications, p. 381.

B. SECURITY to be given by suitors:
1. by parties, p. 381; 2. by agent, p. 382;
3. what is security, p. 382;
4. *ratam rem dominum habiturum*, p. 383;
5. *judicatum solvi*, p. 384; 6. *pro praede lit. vindic.*, p. 385.

CHAP. X. CHECKS ON LITIGATION:

A. General, p. 386.

B. *Exceptio rei judicatae*, p. 388:
1. *eadem quaestio*, p. 388; 2. *inter eosdem*, p. 390;
3. *etiam non eadem actione*, p. 391; 4. special cases, 392;
5. by authoritative judge, p. 392.

C. Small question not to prejudice larger, p. 393.

CHAP. XI.

A. OATHS: 1. voluntary, p. 394;
2. necessary, p. 395; 3. judicial, p. 396.

B. ADMISSION (*confessio in jure*), p. 397.
Failure in due defence, p. 398.

C. *INTERROGATIONES in jure*, p. 399.

CHAP. XII. JOINDER OF ISSUE (*lis contestata*), p. 401:
1. importance and form, p. 402; 2. *legitima judicia*, p. 403;
3. *judicia imperio continentia*, p. 405;
4. effect of joinder of issue, p. 405.

CHAP. XIII. PROCEEDINGS *IN JUDICIO*:

A. Parties' action, p. 407. B. Evidence, p. 408.

C. Judge's action, p. 410.

D. Interlocutory findings (*pronuntiationes*), p. 410:
1. in actions *in rem*, p. 411; 2. in *bonae fid.* actions, p. 411;
3. in actions on torts, p. 411; 4. on plea of fraud, p. 412;
5. surrender of actions, p. 412;
6. in concurrent actions, p. 412;
7. action *de peculio*, p. 413; 8. *compensatio*, p. 413.

E. Satisfaction after joinder of issue, p. 414.

F. Taxation: *litem suam facere*, p. 415.

G. *In litem jurare*, p. 415.

H. Condemnation *in id quod facere potest*, p. 416.

J. *Ire in consilium*, p. 417.

Chap. XIV. Appeals:

A. 1. procedure, p. 419; 2. judge, p. 420;
3. who allowed to appeal, p. 420; 4. conduct of appeal, p. 421;
5. effect of success, p. 421.

B. Correction without appeal, p. 421.

C. *In duplum revocare*, p. 421.

Chap. XV. Execution: *actio judicati*, p. 423.

A. Attachment of person:
1. under *legis actio*, p. 423; 2. *manus injectio*, p. 425;
3. result and position, p. 426; 4. local jurisdiction, p. 429;
5. *manus injectio pro judicato*, p. 429;
6. arrest and imprisonment in later times, p. 430;
7. English analogy, p. 431.

B. Attachment of property:
1. *missio in possessionem*, p. 432;
2. bankruptcy proceedings, p. 433;
3. sale of estate, p. 435; 4. privileged claims, p. 436;
5. *separatio bonorum*, p. 437;
6. persons liable to sale of estate, p. 438;
7. jurisdiction, p. 439; 8. composition, p. 439.

C. 1. Distress by authority of Ant. Pius, p. 440;
2. specific performance, p. 441.

Chap. XVI. Interdicts and their procedure:

A. Classification of interdicts, p. 441.

B. Procedure, in single interdicts, p. 443;

C. in double interdicts, p. 444.

D. Did Gaius write *non faciat* in iv 170? p. 446.

Chap. XVII. Procedure *extra ordinem*, p. 449:

Interdiction of spendthrifts, p. 449.

Appendix to Vol. II. Essays on Cicero's private orations.

Cicero speaks as advocate, p. 452.

A. *pro P. Quinctio*, p. 453.
Statement of the facts, p. 453.
Argument: 1. no ground for application, p. 463;
2. praetor's order not justified, p. 465;
3. execution ineffectual, p. 469.

Text of § 60, p. 471.
Special points:
1. had Quinctius failed to appear? p. 475;
2. must procurator give security? p. 477;
3. appeal to tribunes, p. 479;
4. execution of order, p. 480;
5. must possession be complete? p. 481;
6. was seizure of Gallic land illegal? p. 483;
7. was eviction of Quinctius illegal? p. 484.

B. *pro Q. Roscio comoedo*, p. 486:
Statement of facts, p. 487;
argument from absence of legal ground, p. 490;
from position of partners, p. 491;
charge of theft, p. 494;
nature of suit, p. 496;
not founded on book-entry, p. 497;
object of second part of speech, p. 498;
Conclusion, p. 500;
v. Mayr's view, p. 501; Bethmann-Hollweg's objections, p. 502.
Date of speech, p. 502.

C. *pro M. Tullio*:
Statement of facts, p. 503;
Argument: 1. armed violence cannot be justified, p. 505;
2. why *dolo malo* is in *formula*, p. 506;
3. *dolus malus* applicable to a *familia*, p. 506;
4. further reply to objections, p. 507.
Conclusion, p. 509.

D. *pro A. Caecina*, p. 510:
Statement of facts, p. 510;
character of suit, p. 513;
argument of opponent, p. 518;
reply: 1. rejection is dejection, p. 518;
2. intimidation is force, p. 518;
3. possession not necessary, p. 520;
examination of Cicero's argument, p. 521;
4. Caecina was owner, p. 530;
5. Volaterrans are not disqualified, p. 532.
Conclusion, p. 535.

CORRIGENDA IN VOL. II.

p. 116, line 19 from top, *for* chap. xiii *read* chap. xv.
p. 289, line 19 from top, *for* (*Font.* 2 § 3 (17)) *read* cf. *Font.* 2 § 3.
p. 306, line 24 from top, after *mancipi est* add (ii 27).

BOOK V.

OBLIGATIONS.

Obligationum substantia non in eo consistit ut aliquod corpus nostrum aut servitutem nostram faciat, sed ut alium nobis obstringat ad dandum aliquid vel faciendum vel praestandum (Paul *ap.* D. xliv 7 fr 3 pr).

In personam actio est, qua agimus cum aliquo qui nobis vel ex contractu vel ex delicto obligatus est, id est, cum intendimus dare facere praestare oportere (Gai. *Inst.* iv 2).

In personam actio semper adversus eundem locum habet (Ulpian *ap.* D. xliv 7 fr 25 pr).

Naturales obligationes non eo solo aestimantur, si actio aliqua eorum nomine competit, verum etiam eo si soluta pecunia repeti non possit (Ulpian *ap.* D. xliv 7 fr 10).

Servi ex delictis quidem obligantur, et, si manumittantur, obligati remanent: ex contractibus autem civiliter quidem non obligantur, sed naturaliter et obligantur et obligant (Ulpian *ap.* D. xliv 7 fr 14).

Creditorum appellatione non hi tantum accipiuntur, qui pecuniam crediderunt, sed omnes quibus ex qualibet causa debetur (Gai. *ap.* D. L 16 fr 11).

CHAPTER I.

CLASSIFICATION.

Gaius, who is followed by Justinian in his Institutes, divides obligations into two classes, according as they arise *ex contractu* or *ex delicto*. Obligations from contract arise in four ways; *re, verbis, litteris, consensu*[1]. Contracts arising *re* are divided by Gaius, in his book of 'Golden things,' from which extracts appear in the Digest (xliv 7), which are followed in Justinian's Institutes, into four; *mutuum, commodatum, depositum, pignus*. Consensual contracts are also divided into four; *emptio venditio, locatio conductio, societas, mandatum*. Finally obligations *ex delicto* are also four; *furti, bonorum raptorum, damni injuriae, injuriarum*. The symmetry of these four groups of four excites suspicion of their artificial character, and we are not surprised to find that Justinian (following Gaius' *Aurea*) has to add another division consisting of obligations *quasi ex contractu*; viz. *negotiorum gestorum, tutelae, communi dividundo, familiae erciscundae, legati, indebiti* (a motley collection); and another of obligations *quasi ex delicto*; viz. *litem suam faciendi, dejecti effusive* and *recepti* (against innkeepers, *etc.*). Even thus some important actions find no place in the classification and are inserted, if at all, in strange places; *e.g. actiones praescriptis verbis, pecuniae constitutae* (Just. iv 6 § 8), *de pauperie* (*ib.* iv 9), *doli* (D. iv 3), *servi corrupti* (Just. iv. 6 § 23), *rei uxoriae* (by Justinian combined with an action *ex stipulatu*, Cod. v 13

[1] This division is referred to by Ulpian in D. ii 14 fr 1 § 3; xlvi 1 fr 8 § 1; tit. 2 fr 1 § 1 (literal contract having been of course struck out by Tribonian). Cf. A. Pernice *ZRG* xxii 220 foll.

fr 1), *etc.* But a worse fault of this classification is, that it puts together obligations widely different in character and history, such as *mutuum*[1] and *commodatum*, and neglects a far-reaching distinction such as that between *stricta judicia* and *bonae fidei judicia*[2]. Who was the author of this classification in fours we do not know, but it is noteworthy that no such classification is followed in the Digest (which mainly follows the order of the praetor's edict), or is mentioned in any other ancient authority extant, and that no adequate justification is alleged. The groups *quasi ex contractu* and *quasi ex delicto* are not suitably composed or labelled, there being in at least several of the former little or nothing analogous to contract, and of the latter, two being cases of liability for the delicts of others, and the first being as much *ex delicto* as the Aquilian action itself. Hence I have abandoned a classification which seems arbitrary and unfruitful, and an arrangement which interposes verbal and litteral contracts between real and consensual. Nor am I satisfied with the position of Aquilian damage along with theft and other obligations of a semi-criminal or malicious character. In the Edict and the Digest its place was far removed from theirs: and while theft, robbery, and insult rendered infamous those condemned and those who have bargained to avoid condemnation, Aquilian damage had no such effect (Gai. iv 182).

A better classification is suggested by Gaius in dividing actions according to their aim. *Agimus interdum ut rem tantum consequamur, interdum ut poenam tantum, alias ut rem et poenam.* The first class are contracts, the second torts, the third

[1] It is noticeable that Gaius in his Institutes gives *mutuum* alone as an instance of real contract, and omits altogether the other three which are classed with it in the *Aurea*. But the praetor's edict put *commodatum* and *pignus* along with *mutuum* under the title of *de rebus creditis*.

[2] Gradenwitz (*Interpolationen* p. 110) shews that *bonae fidei judicium* is a usual expression, but *actio stricti judicii* occurs only once (D. xii 3 fr 5 § 4). The use of *stricti juris* is a mistake due to Justinian. The opposite to *b. f. judicium* is naturally *strictum judicium*, which however is only found in Just. iv 6 § 30 and perhaps in D. xiii 6 fr 3 § 2. (*Stricto jure*, in another sense, as we say 'in strict law,' occurs D. xiii 5 fr 30; xxix 2 fr 86.)

an intermediate class where prompt admission and discharge of the obligation were demanded by its nature (Gai. iv 6—9). Following this suggestion, but dividing contracts again into those enforced strictly, and those treated by the rules of fair dealing, we get this arrangement:

1. Obligations leading to *stricta judicia*, viz. *stipulatio*, *litterarum obligatio*, *mutuum*; and I add (with Gaius iii 91) other *condictiones*, where there is at most a constructive contract, or claim analogous to that on a money-loan. Suretyship comes under stipulation. Two obligations, *operarum jusjurandum* and *dotis dictio* (cf. Gai. iii 95, 96), might claim a place by the side of stipulation as being verbal obligations, though made by a simple declaration (or oath), instead of by a promise in reply to a question, but they are applicable only to special classes of persons, and I treat them therefore in Book II (vol. I pp. 86, 140). To stipulation, partly as the abstract type of contract, I append the change, transfer, discharge, and release of obligations.

2. Obligations leading to *bonae fidei judicia*. This important class contains all the obligations *ex consensu*, and the remaining three of the *obligationes re factae*, as classed by Gaius in his *Aurea*, and by Justinian in his Institutes. The actions *tutelae* and *rei uxoriae* are also *bonae fidei*, but, like dowry and services due on oath, are more conveniently dealt with in Book II (vol. I pp. 109, 153). The suits for division, *familiae erciscundae* and *communi dividundo*, are also called *bonae fidei*, but are not really cases of contract. The former naturally belongs to Inheritance (vol. I p. 287): the latter I append, partly by way of contrast, to Partnership. Similarly I append *negotiorum gestio* to *mandatum*.

3. Having thus disposed of obligations from contract which give actions *quibus rem tantum persequimur* and the modes of fulfilling, transferring and extinguishing such rights, we come to cases of semi-delictal obligation, in which by the act of defendant or others, but without necessarily any conscious malfeasance on his part, plaintiff is so notably out of his property or rights, as to give rise to a peremptory obligation calling for discharge without dispute or delay. They are often spoken of

as a class where non-admission doubles the damages (*quae infitiando crescunt, adversus infitiantem in duplum agimus*), one value being for reimbursement, and the other as penalty for disputing the claim. In these cases *rem et poenam persequimur*. The type is the obligation arising from a judgment: other cases were expressly referred to this type, the statute either saying that the person obliged was to be treated as if he were judged (*pro judicato*), or directing the obligation to be created in the old words *dare damnas esto*, as in actions under the *lex Aquilia*.

Other actions of similar import to those under the *lex Aquilia* but without the same consequences are appended.

4. Having thus disposed of all obligations or actions *quae rei persecutionem habent*, we come to the last class, comprising obligations *ex delicto*, *i.e.* arising from wrongful and criminal acts, considered not as offences against the State, but as injuries to individuals. Such are theft, robbery, intentional insult, intimidation and fraud (all which involve disgrace), besides others of less importance.

5. A further section takes cases of liability on the contracts and delicts of persons other than the defendant himself, and especially of children under power and of slaves. They are not distinguished from other obligations by difference in the subject-matter, but are in fact enlargements of the capacity of persons to sue and be sued. The qualifications and conditions of their enforcement require however common treatment.

6. Last come proceedings for cancelling rights and liabilities which have been acquired in consequence or under the influence of the other party's insufficient age or experience, or absence, or captivity, or through a bankrupt's or freedman's fraud.

CHAPTER II.

AGREEMENTS[1].

A. It is not every agreement that forms a contract good in law. There is no limit to the agreements which one person may make with another. They may be legal or illegal, moral or immoral, fair or unfair, practicable or impracticable, serious or trifling; but it is clear that they do not all deserve to be enforced by law. The Romans acknowledged three classes as justifying in some degree the protection of the law.

1. The first class is composed of such as are sanctioned by statute or other quasi-legislative authority or long-recognised custom. Practically this includes all such agreements as are clothed with a special form, viz. mancipation (and others accompanied by the formality of the bronze and balance), stipulation, book-entry, declaration of dowry (*dotis dictio*). In these the serious intention of the parties is vouched for by the adoption of a special form of words or ceremony. A freedman's

[1] *Conventio* is the most general word for agreement; but is not technical (cf. D. ii 14 fr 1 § 3). *Pactum* is very general, especially of agreements to settle a question without carrying it, or continuing to carry it, before the Courts. It is often found side by side with *conventum* (adj.?). So *ex pacto jus est: si quidquid inter se pepigerunt, si quid inter quos convenit. Pacta sunt quae legibus observanda sunt hoc modo: 'Rem ubi pagunt, orato: ni pagunt, in comitio aut in foro ante meridiem causam coicito.' Sunt item pacta quae sine legibus observantur ex convento* (*ad Heren.* ii 13 § 20, quoting XII tables). *In foro tabulae, testimonia, pacta conventa, stipulationes, cognationes, etc.* (Cic. *Orat.* ii 24 § 100). *Quod foedus aut pactio, quod, ut ad privatas res redeam, testamentum, quae judicia aut stipulationes aut pacti et conventi formula, etc.* (Cic. *Caecin.* 18 § 51.) *Ait praetor; pacta conventa...servabo* (D. ii 14 fr. 7 § 7), *etc.* *Contractus* is not in Cicero, but is the technical phrase in the Jurists for contracts on which suit can be brought; cf. Gai. iii 88, 89; D. xii 1 fr 1 § 1, *etc.* Cf. Serv. Sulpic. ap. Gell. iv 4 *is contractus stipulationum sponsionumque dicebatur sponsalia.* In Cicero *rem contrahere* of business transactions is common; *Off.* i 5 § 15 *rerum contractarum fide*; 17 § 53; ii 18 § 54 *in omni re contrahenda, vendundo emundo, conducendo locando, etc.* See Pernice *ZRG.* xxii 196 sq., 218 sqq.

oath, pledging himself to the performance of certain services, may be classed with them.

2. The second class is composed of such as belong to the *jus gentium, i.e.* as are recognised by the law of the world as regular parts of the business of life. They have often their own special names, *e.g.* sale and purchase, letting and hiring, loan, deposit, pledge, partnership, mandate, *etc.* No special form is required to entitle the parties to the help of the law. But where there is no such regular name, still, if there is precise agreement or definite ground (*causa*) for the agreement, the praetor granted an action on the facts of the particular case (*in factum* or *praescriptis verbis*, cf. D. ii 14 fr. 7 §§ 1, 2; xix 5 fr 8; see chap. iv H). Some such cases were sufficiently important and frequent to make the praetor mention them specially in the edict, *e.g. constitutum debiti.*

3. The above two classes comprise all to which the law granted full effect. They gave rise to actions. They had either a special form, or they were of certain definite character, or they were accompanied with good consideration. To other agreements, not being illegal or immoral or fraudulent, the praetor gave a limited protection. They did not entitle either party to sue on them, but they could be pleaded in bar of a suit by the other. The praetor practically said: 'If you go outside of the regular forms and business agreements of the law, the law will not in all cases lend either of you its active assistance against the other to enforce the agreement. But still less will it enable you to act contrary to your own agreement, and therefore if you agree to give up any claim you may have against the other, I will bar any action to enforce the claim.' *Nuda pactio obligationem non parit, sed parit exceptionem* (D. ii 14 fr 7 § 4; cf. Gai. iv 116 *b*); *i.e.* a bare agreement, standing by itself without either formal words of the parties present, or regular book-entry, or real consideration in fact, produces no right of action, but may be pleaded as a surrender of rights of action. It is in this sense that the praetor declared in his edict that he would support agreements made without fraud, and not conflicting with or evading the standing law (D. *ib.* fr 7 § 7; Paul i 4). Hence an agreement not to sue on a

particular matter became practically tantamount to a formal release of an obligation. (See below, p. 61.)

4. Covenants, consistent with the character of the contract, and made in immediate connexion with a sale, or lease, or pledge, or grant of dowry, or other *bonae fidei* obligation, are regarded as part of it. There is good consideration for the covenant, and it does but arrange details or terms to give precision and effect to the contract. *Ea pacta insunt bonae fidei judiciis quae legem contractui dant, id est quae in ingressu contractus facta sunt.* The same rule held in the case of all conveyances of property, whether performed by mancipation, or delivery, or counting out money for a loan: but a bargain, *e.g.* for repayment of more than the sum lent, was invalid. Agreements intended to affect the business, but made afterwards, must be clothed with a stipulation[1], otherwise they will not avail for a plaintiff, for they produce only a plea. A bargain may be made to rescind a former bargain, and then, if the former is pleaded in bar, the latter is a good answer (*replicatio*), and the plaintiff can proceed. (Paul i 1 § 2; D. ii 14 fr 7 §§ 4—6; fr 17 pr, 48; xii 1 fr 7.)

As contrasted with stipulations, bargains do not create a right of themselves, but require the support of actual business (*in stipulationibus jus continetur, in pactis factum versatur*, D. ii 14 fr 27 § 2). But both alike as a rule must be taken to affect only the parties to the agreement, and only in reference to the matter in hand: at any rate other persons and other matters are not in any way directly prejudiced. *Ante omnia animadvertendum est ne conventio in alia re facta aut cum alia persona in alia re aliave persona noceat* (*ib.* fr 27 § 4).

B. Compromise (*transactio*).

An agreement made between parties for the arrangement or compromise of disputes was called *transactio*[2]. It might

[1] The *Constitutum* was an exception (p. 86).

[2] *Transigere* is often used for the settlement of any claim or dispute. Cf. Cic. *Att.* iv 16 § 8 speaking of clearances for the enlargement of the forum: *cum privatis non poterat transigi minore pecunia*; *Rosc. C.* 18 § 55 of the compromise of a suit; for which *decidere* is used *ib.* 11 § 32; *Rosc.*

take shape as an agreement only (*pactum conventum*), or might be, and usually was, confirmed by an Aquilian stipulation, *i.e.* a general renewal of all preceding claims accompanied with a formal release (see p. 58), and by a covenant of penalty for breach. Any suits not in the contemplation of the parties are not included in the settlement, however general the words of the stipulation or bargain may be. It was good only between the parties, and did not affect the rights of others. It presumed doubts to exist: *de re dubia et lite incerta neque finita transigit.* If a suit has been brought to judgment and no appeal is made or possible, there is no basis for a compromise, and (as a rescript of Caracalla decided) the judgment stands; but what has been actually paid under the compromise is allowed to reduce the amount of the judgment (D. ii 15 fr 1, 2, 7 pr, § 1, 9, 11; xii 6 fr 23). If defendant does not abide by the compromise, plaintiff can continue the original action, at least in some cases (D. v 2 fr 27 pr).

Where alimony (*alimenta*) was left by will or given *mortis causa*, a senate's decree, made at the instance of Marcus Aurelius, invalidated any compromise which was not made after full hearing by the praetor, who was to inquire into the cause of the arrangement, the sufficiency of the allowance, the necessities of the recipient, and the solvency of the person charged (D. ii 15 fr 8).

In two cases an agreement for settlement of a cause of suit not merely gains a plea *pacti conventi*, but extinguishes the action altogether (D. ii 14 fr 17 § 1). These are *injuriarum* (D. xlvii 10 fr 11 § 1) and *furti.* In the latter case a settlement is called *pro fure damnum decidere* (D. xlvii 2 fr 46 § 5).

Am. 39 § 114. (The English words *transaction* and *compromise* (from *compromissum* 'a common agreement to abide by an arbitrator's settlement of terms') differ widely in meaning from their Latin originals.)

CHAPTER III.

STRICT OBLIGATIONS (*STRICTA JUDICIA*).

The first class of obligations are characterised by their definite nature, and the suits to enforce them have a clearly defined claim. Plaintiff is entitled to judgment for the whole or none: if the contract was made at all, defendant must pay: there is no adjustment of recognised claims: one or other of the parties is wholly wrong in the particular matter. Cicero's contrast between *judicia* and *arbitria* applies closely to the relative positions of the parties in strict and in *bonae fidei* actions: *ad judicium hoc modo venimus ut totam litem aut obtineamus aut amittamus: ad arbitrium hoc animo adimus ut neque nihil neque tantum quantum postulavimus consequamur* (Cic. *Rosc. Com.* 4 § 10). When issue was once joined, the object sued for was ascertained; if it was money, the amount is thereby given; if it was not money, the value had to be estimated as at that time (D. xiii 6 fr 3 § 2, *etc.*, tit. 3 fr 3: see Lenel *Paling.* ii 575). The claim was, at least before the time of the Antonines, separate and irrespective of any other, so that no set-off was admissible, and in early times (before C. Aquilius, cf. Cic. *Off.* iii 14 § 60) the contract once made bound by its terms, whether fraud had induced the contract, or the precise interpretation was harsh and inequitable, or not[1]. The plea of fraud and the action for fraud once introduced (it is uncertain when) could be used so as to modify this rigorous character, and M. Aurelius authorised the use of the plea of fraud in order to

[1] Cf. Cic. *Caecin.* 3 § 7 *Si quis quid spopondit, qua in re verbo se obligavit uno, si id non facit, maturo judicio sine ulla religione judicis condemnatur; qui per tutelam aut societatem aut rem mandatam aut fiduciae rationem fraudavit quempiam, in eo quo delictum majus est, eo poena est tardior? 'Est enim turpe judicium.' Ex facto quidem turpi.* The *stricta judicia* did not involve *infamia* on condemnation (D. xliv 7 fr 36).

admit set-off[1] (Just. iv 6 § 30). But in substance these actions remained types of the contract of freemen, who had a right to lay down a law for themselves, and a duty to abide the consequences of their own free disposal.

The three principal obligations of this class are contract by oral question and answer (*stipulatio*), contract by book-entry (*litterarum obligatio*), contract by cash loan (*mutuum*), which Cicero enumerates (*Rosc. Com.* 4 § 13) as alone giving a claim for money certain. The first of these naturally served the Roman lawyers with the opportunity for discussing the general principles of contract; for the contents of a stipulation were anything that the parties chose, and the uses to which a stipulation was put were as varied as its contents. Accordingly I put in this part the sections treating of renewal, transfer, fulfilment and release of obligations. With loan of money are closely connected, at least by analogy, actions (*condictiones*) for money, *etc.*, which has become another's property without due cause for retention, and is therefore subject like a loan to a claim for repayment (cf. Gai. iii 91). And I append such natural developments by the praetor as are found in the actions *de eo quod certo loco dari oportet* and *de pecunia constituta*.

A. Verbal obligation (*Stipulatio*[2]).

1. (*a*) Form.

The only general and universally applicable mode of making an agreement which should be legally enforceable was by oral procedure between the parties present at the same place[3]. Writing was however frequently used not to make

[1] Seneca *Ben.* vi 4, 5 contrasts the legal practice of refusing 'set-off,' and trying each matter separately with the principles of benefit and gratitude.

[2] For conjectures on the history of the form and origin of the terms *stipulari*, *spondere*, *etc.* see *e.g.* Girard *Manuel* p. 472 sq.; Muirhead *Hist.* § 29.

[3] How usual it was for a record of a stipulation to be made is seen from Cic. *Top.* 25 § 96 *Ista sunt tria genera quae controversiam in omni scripto facere possint: ambiguum, discrepantia scripti et voluntatis, scripta*

but to prove the contract. It took the shape of a record either of the stipulation or of a declaration of the same before witnesses. A senate's decree in the time of Nero prescribed that all documents (*tabulae*) containing record of contracts whether public or private should be pierced in the middle of the margin, and tied with threefold thread, and the thread be sealed by the witnesses, the object being to have one copy of the agreement secured against alteration, while another on the outside was available for use. If this was not done the tablets were not to be allowed any weight in court[1] (Paul v 25 § 6; Suet. *Ner.* 17).

A stipulation consisted in a question and answer, the question being put by the person who was to acquire a right, the answer being given orally by the person who undertook the obligation. The matter of the agreement being stated, the binding words were usually simple; those used by (and peculiar to) Romans being *Spondesne?* or *spondes? Spondeo.* A stipulation made with a foreigner in these terms was invalid (Gai. iii 93, 94, 179). The questioner was called *stipulator*, sometimes *reus*[2] *stipulandi* ('person concerned with stipulating'), the answerer usually *promissor* (or *reus promittendi*), the natural word *sponsor* being practically confined to a particular class of stipulations (see p. 29). Other words used by Romans and

contraria. Jam hoc perspicuumst non magis in legibus quam in testamentis, in stipulationibus, in reliquis rebus, quae ex scripto aguntur, posse controversias easdem existere. Part. Or. 37 § 130 *Scriptorum privatum aliud est, publicum aliud: publicum: lex, senatusconsultum, foedus; privatum: tabulae, pactum conventum, stipulatio; ib.* 31 § 107 *In gravissimis firmamentis etiam illa ponenda sunt, si quae ex scripto legis aut testamenti aut verborum ipsius judicii aut alicujus stipulationis aut cautionis opponuntur defensioni contraria; Caecin.* 18 § 51; *Rosc. Com.* 13 § 38 *Quis est hujus restipulationis scriptor;* Quintil. vii 5 § 6; Dig. L 17 fr 92; Paul in D. xliv 7 fr 38 says *placuit non minus valere quod scriptura quam quod vocibus lingua figuratis significaretur.* Cf. Sen. *Ben.* iii 15 § 1 *utinam nulla stipulatio emptorem venditori obligaret, nec pacta conventaque inpressis signis custodirentur.*

1 Examples of such tablets exist, and a copy of one is given in Bruns' *Fontes* p. 371 sqq.

2 Cf. Fest. p. 273; Cic. *Orat.* 43 § 183; 79 § 321, and my note on D. *de usufructu* p. 46.

foreigners alike were *promittis* or *fide promittis? promitto*; *dabis? dabo*; *facies? facio*; *etc.* Greek or other languages, with the aid if required of an interpreter, might be used even by Roman citizens. The essential was clear understanding and expressed agreement (Gai. iii 92, 93; D. xlv 1 fr 1 § 6). In records of stipulations the question is described by *f. r.* for *fide rogavit*, the answer by *f. p.* for *fide promisit* (see Bruns nos. 105—108, 127, and cf. Gai. l. c.). See also p. 29 n. 2.

The promise must be in reply to a question, in order that the intention of both parties to make a legal contract might be in evidence. To meet any doubts on this point a rescript of Severus decided that, if a document stated a promise to have been made between persons present[1] it should be taken to have been made in a formal stipulation (Cod. viii 37 fr 1; cf. Paul v 7 § 2; D. xlv 1 fr 134 § 2). And similarly it was held as a general rule that if a man wrote that he had bound himself as surety (*fidejussisse*), it should be presumed that all requisite formalities had been observed (D. xlv 1 fr 30).

(*b*) Conditions of validity.

The answer must follow the question without any considerable interval or any interpolation of other business. A day's interval would prevent any obligation arising (D. xlv 1 fr 1 § 1; tit. 2 fr 12 pr).

The answer must fit the question. There must be agreement as to the object-matter, though a variance in the name given or the addition of superfluous language does not invalidate. If the question is absolute (*dabis?*), the answer must not be conditional (*si illud factum erit, dabo*). A different time or place in the answer from that named in the question spoils the stipulation from lack of agreement. A variance in amount only was held by some not to be fatal, because the larger sum includes the less, so that if the stipulator says, 'Will you give me twenty?' and the answer is 'I will give ten,' or *vice versa*, the agreement is good for ten only. Gaius however held such

[1] Paul does not mention the condition of presence of the parties, but I take the omission to be accidental or due to the Visigothic editors. Justinian gave a further extension to the rule (Cod. viii 37 fr 14).

stipulations to be invalid in accordance with the general rule[1] (Gai. iii 102; D. xlv 1 fr 1 §§ 3, 4, 83 §§ 1—4, 137 § 1).

A contract can be enforced only by one who has an interest (*i.e.* a money interest[2]) in it and is a party to it[3]. Hence every stipulation must be in the interest of the stipulator or of those in whose power he is[4]. Any stipulation framed wholly in the interest of an outsider is invalid. But a guardian giving up the management of his ward's affairs could, it was thought, stipulate from his fellow guardian *rem pupilli salvam fore*, for he is still responsible so far. And a stipulation by a contractor from a subcontractor for the due execution of work on another's house, which the contractor has himself undertaken to build, is valid. So is a stipulation for something to be paid to one's own son under power, or slave, or agent, or creditor; or for the building of a temple or tomb, though neither can be his property (Gai. iii 103; D. xlv 1 fr 38 §§ 20—25 fr 39). Any difficulty that might arise from the principle that stipulations are only for the stipulator could be removed by attaching a penalty to non-performance. Thus *dabisne Titio servum illum* (Titius being an outsider) shews no interest for the stipulator; but if there be added *si non dederis, centum nummos mihi dabis?* there is interest in the penalty, and this becomes the content of the stipulation, which is therefore valid (D. xlv 1 fr 38 § 17; xlvi 5 fr 16).

In view of this principle a stipulation for oneself and another (*mihi et Titio*) was of questionable validity. The

[1] Justinian (iii 19 § 5) follows Gaius: not so in the Digest. It is possible that Gaius meant only that the contract was not good *as framed* by the stipulator.

[2] Cf. D. xl 7 fr 9 § 2 *Ea in obligatione consistere quae pecunia lui praestarique possunt*; cf. D. xvii 1 fr 54. A. Pernice's criticism of these passages (*Labeo* iii p. 189 sqq.) seems to be overstrained.

[3] *Quaecumque gerimus, cum ex nostro contractu originem trahunt, nisi ex nostra persona obligationis initium sumant, inanem actum nostrum efficiunt: et ideo neque stipulari neque emere vendere contrahere ut alter suo nomine recte agat possumus* (Paul D. xliv 7 fr 11). *Nec paciscendo nec legem dicendo nec stipulando quisquam alteri cavere potest* (Q. Mucius, D. L 17 fr 73 § 4).

[4] For stipulations by slaves and others under power see vol. I p. 432 sqq.

Sabinians held that it was good for oneself only, the addition of another name being disregarded. The Proculians agreed that it was good for oneself, but held that it was good only for half the amount (Gai. iii 103; cf. D. xlv 1 fr 110). A stipulation for oneself or another (*mihi aut Titio*) was quite valid, but the stipulator alone had the right to sue on it and take the benefit, or to novate or release it: the other name was deemed to be put in merely to facilitate payment, Titius being treated as having no interest, but being merely an agent of the stipulator duly authorised to discharge the debtor by accepting payment or delivery. Unless allowed to retain it as a gift, Titius was compellable by an action of mandate to pay it over to the stipulator (D. xlv 1 fr 131 § 1; xlvi 3 fr 10). A different time or place could be inserted for payment to stipulator from that for Titius; nor did a different condition invalidate the stipulation, provided that the condition for the stipulator took effect. Again, payment to the stipulator might be stipulated unconditionally and payment to Titius conditionally, but if the reverse was done, and the condition did not take effect, the stipulation was invalid. Some lawyers held that the content must not be different, *e.g. mihi decem aut Titio hominem*; but if such a stipulation were made, payment to Titius would either discharge the obligation, or at any rate would support a plea (D. xlv 1 fr 141 §§ 5—9; tit. 3 fr 34 § 2, fr 98 §§ 4—6).

On an analogous principle the stipulation must be aimed at an action of the promiser's, not of some outsider. *Alius pro alio promittens daturum facturumve eum non obligatur; nam de se quemque promittere oportet* (D. xlv 1 fr 83 pr). General words were thus restricted by interpretation. If a stipulation for quiet enjoyment of property conveyed is in the simple terms *habere licere spondes?*, it was held to give only a guaranty against any interference with the stipulator's (and his heirs') enjoyment by the promiser (or his heirs). If a guaranty against others' interference was desired, a clause with penalty for interference must be added. So the ordinary covenant against fraud *dolum malum abesse afuturumque spondes?* without the addition of a penalty clause, such as *si hujus rei dolus malus non aberit, quanti ea res est* (or *xx milia sestert.*) *dari spondes*, includes only fraud on the part of the promiser or his heirs (fr 38 pr—§§ 2, 5, 13; xlvi 7 fr 19). A promise, *e.g.* by an agent for the appearance of another (his principal) in court, is taken to mean that the promiser will procure his appearance (*qui alium sisti promittit, hoc promittit id se acturum ut stet*). And a negative form such as *per te non fieri quominus illud fiat* is not always satisfied by mere passive abstinence, but may require exertion of the promiser to secure fulfilment (D. xlv 1 fr 50 pr, 81).

A stipulation for something to be paid or done for me after my death or the promiser's death is bad: no obligation should begin with the heir (for at the time of stipulation he would be an outsider to the contracting parties). A stipulation for payment on the day before death meets with the same difficulty, for 'the day before' cannot be ascertained until death has taken place. But it is valid to stipulate for payment or performance at the time of death (*cum moriar* or *cum morieris*), the obligation being then put on the last of life. What has been said of natural death applies also to civil death (*capitis deminutio* Gai. iii 100, 101; cf. Cod. iv 11). A slave can stipulate for something 'after his death,' because the person really concerned with the acquisition is his master, and thus a usufruct stipulated for by a slave enures for his master's, not for his own, life (Vat. 57).

A stipulation which leaves performance (not merely the time of performance) entirely to the will of the promiser is nugatory (D. xlv 1 fr 17, 46 §§ 2, 3, 108 § 1). If a stipulation require the mode of performance to be at the discretion of a third party and he do not exercise the discretion, suit cannot be brought on it (fr 43, 44).

A stipulation to procure or reward an act permanently forbidden by statute or contrary to good customs, *e.g.* for the commission of a crime, or to procure a particular marriage (under a penalty for breach), or to get the promiser to make one his heir, or for the sale of a freeman 'when he shall become a slave,' is invalid (fr 27 pr, 61, 97 § 2, 123, 134 pr).

(c) Impossibility of performance.

A stipulation for what is impossible (not merely for promiser but for anyone) is bad; *e.g.* to stipulate for the conveyance to us of one whom we believe to be a slave but who is really a freeman; or of a slave whom we believe to be alive but who is actually dead; or of what is already our own property, under the belief that it belongs to others; or of a fabulous monster *e.g.* a hippocentaur; or of what is sacred or religious or public land, though supposed at the time to be ordinary land. And a stipulation on an impossible condition, *e.g.* 'if the sky be touched with the finger,' is on the same footing. So a stipulation for a usufruct by a slave belonging to a vacant inheritance is invalid even though conditional, for there is no person to whom it can attach; and the validity is judged at the time of stipulating, though suit may be postponed to some future time. And no stipulation (even expressly for the heir) by such a slave is valid or due, unless and until the inheritance is entered on (Gai. iii 97—99; Vat. 55; D. xlv 1 fr 73 § 1, 137 § 6; tit. 3 fr 16, 25). A stipulation for a right of road by one who has no neighbouring farm at the time, or has parted with it before the constitution of the servitude, is null (fr 98 pr, 130).

Whether a slave could covenant in the ordinary terms *habere licere* against eviction was disputed. Julian maintained that *habere* was a term technical to ownership, and inasmuch as a slave could neither hold nor alienate anything as civil owner, the covenant was null. Ulpian (in Digest) allowed the stipulation to be good both for slaves and sons under power, but interpreted *habere* as referring only to possession. A stipulation for a right of way (*non per promissorem fieri quominus sibi ire agere liceret*) was not open to the same doubt, because *ire, agere* denoted acts, not legal position (D. xlv 1 fr 31 § 6).

Performance of a stipulation may become impossible, although not so when made, *e.g.* by the stipulated object perishing or a slave becoming free before the due time for delivery. If the promiser was not in fault, the obligation drops. But if he has himself killed or destroyed the object (unless it be a criminal slave caught in the act) or has manumitted a slave promised, or has made promised land religious or sacred, or has alienated it to one who has done so, he remains liable on his stipulation. It was an old rule that *quotiens culpa intervenit, perpetuari obligationem,* and it applied to sureties as well as to the principal. If the promiser of another's slave or building-plot (*area*) could not buy in consequence of the refusal of the owner to sell, the stipulation was still good for the value; but if the owner had manumitted the slave or he had died so that he no longer existed as an article of commerce, the promiser was free. If the owner had built on the plot its delivery is now impossible, at least for a time, but as it still exists it can be the object of a suit and the promiser is still liable (D. xlv 1 fr 33, 37, 83 § 5, 96, 137 § 4; xlvi 3 fr 92; Paul v 7 § 4). The promiser was freed, if the stipulated object had already become the property of the stipulator without cost (*ex lucrativa causa* D. xlv 1 fr 83 § 6; 98 pr).

Where the perishing of the promised object was attributable to the promiser's neglect (*non-feasance*) the promiser was not liable under the stipulation; he had not promised to *do* anything, and therefore was not in fault by the want of active exertions; and as the slave or other object no longer existed, it was impossible to give him or it; *ad dandum non ad faciendum tenetur* (fr 91 pr). The circumstances might however be such as to give the stipulator an action for fraud: and if a penalty clause had been added to the stipulation, the promiser would be liable for that.

The impossibility of performance, however it arose, did not free the promiser, if he had failed to perform at the due time. Delay was fault, and thenceforth the promiser bore all the risk. If no time is prescribed by the stipulation, the performance is due as soon as it can reasonably be executed. One who promises money is not bound to have it with him at the moment; if the performance is to be at a distant place, he is not bound to travel there night and day in all weathers; if he contracts to build a house, he is only bound to the ordinary speed and exertions of an active builder (D. fr 41 § 1, 72 § 2, 82 § 1, 137 §§ 2, 3; cf. xlvi 3 fr 105). If the stipulation included a positive promise to perform (*e.g. Rhodum te iturum; si non ieris, tantum dari spondes?*) it was held by Sabinus and others that suit could be brought as soon as promiser was able to perform and did not. If however the negative condition and consequent penalty stood by itself (*Rhodum si non ieris, etc.*), and no limit of time was specified, suit could not be brought until the performance of the action had become impossible (D. xlv 1 fr 10, 115; cf. xvii 2 fr 71 pr). And if a time is named for execution of a promise, suit must await the time, though performance has become impossible, *e.g.* by death of the slave who was to be delivered on a named future day (D. xlv 1 fr 8, 99 § 1). Before issue has been joined, delay could, as good lawyers held, be purged by performance or tender of the thing promised (fr 84, 91 § 3).

(*d*) Options.

When a promise is in the alternative ('this or that') the impossibility of one makes the promise of the other absolute, the performance of one makes the other no longer obligatory. If the condition of a promise is in the alternative, *e.g.* 'if this happen or that,' the stipulation is due whichever first happens; and the result is the same if the alternative be the not happening of this or that; as soon as it is clear that one cannot happen, the stipulation is due. A combination of two events ('if both this and that') requires, if positive, both to happen; if negative ('if neither this nor that,' or 'if this does not and that does not') neither to happen (fr 63, 129).

The option, when nothing is expressed to the contrary, is with the promiser, whether specific alternatives are named, *e.g.* 'to give Stichus or Pamphilus,' or the promise is general, *e.g.* 'to give a slave' (fr 106, 109, 138 § 1, cf. xxiii 3 fr 10 § 6). Where a son under power or a slave stipulates and reserves the option (*illud aut illud quod ego voluero*) the election must be made by himself, not by his father or master (D. xlv 1 fr 76 pr, 141 pr).

A promise to make over (*dare*) a specific object is satisfied by giving it as it is, without any guaranty: but a promise to give a slave or other object of which promiser has the choice is not satisfied without a guaranty of title, and in case of a slave, of his freedom from thefts and noxal acts. It is not necessary to guaranty *servum sanum esse*, for soundness has nothing to do with title (D. xxx fr 45 §§ 1, 46).

(*e*) Heirs, how far bound by a stipulation.

Whether heirs and *bonorum possessores* are entitled to claim the performance of their predecessor's stipulation or are bound by their predecessor's promise, without being named in the stipulation, was a disputed question (at least as regards stipulations *ad faciendum*), until Justinian settled it in the affirmative (Cod. viii 37 fr 13). But they could always be expressly included even in a stipulation for usufruct (D. xlv 1 fr 35 §§ 12, 14), and no doubt often, perhaps usually, were so added. When the stipulator or promiser left more heirs than one, the execution of the stipulation was sometimes difficult, and the character of the stipulation became important.

Stipulations lie *in dando* or *in faciendo*, in giving (*i.e.* making over, conveying), or in doing. The payment of money, the conveyance of a farm or slave, the constitution of a usufruct or other servitude, lie in gift (or conveyance): the erection of a house, the excavation of a trench, the delivery of possession, the grant of a release, lie in act (or performance). A third class might be made, so far as form goes, of stipulations requiring abstention from act, such as the common clause against fraud *dolum malum abesse afuturumque esse*, or even the constitution of a servitude in such words as *neque per te neque per heredem tuum fieri quominus mihi ire agere liceat*, but these may be held to be brought under the class of stipulations lying in act by the jurists' doctrine that the promiser was bound to secure the result promised (D. fr 2 pr, 50 pr, 72 pr, 83 pr; L 16 fr 189; cf. xvii 1 fr 45 § 5).

As regards the mass of stipulations lying in gift, a plurality of heirs is quite compatible with due execution. Money and other things stipulated for *in genere* admit of easy division by count, weight, *etc.*, and each heir of the stipulator can demand his share, and each heir of the promiser is liable for his share, proportionate to their respective shares in the inheritance. If however the promise has been made by testator under a penalty, or a pledge has been given, the penalty becomes due unless the whole sum promised has been paid, and the pledge can be retained until this is done. In the case of a stipulation for a specific slave or horse or dish, ideal not material parts are alone possible; and the stipulator is not duly paid, if he has from the promiser's heirs halves or portions of different slaves or different horses: nor is one of the promiser's heirs discharged by conveying his share unless or until the other shares in the same horse or slave are also conveyed. If one convey the whole, or one of the stipulator's heirs receive the whole, the obligation is duly discharged; and the *judicium familiae erciscundae* in this as in other cases will secure due distribution among the coheirs of the burden or benefit, and the interchange of mutual guaranties of indemnity among the coheirs of the debtor. Whichever heir of stipulator sues first, will sue for the whole of the slave or horse: if he obtain a part, any subsequent suit by the others must be for the remainder only. In the case of land, as material division is possible, there was this difference: all promiser's heirs are liable in the first instance, but each is freed on conveying his share, unless the whole was due under a penalty (D. xlv 1 fr 2 § 1; 54 pr, 85 §§ 1—6; xlvi 3 fr 41 § 1; x 2 fr 25 §§ 13, 14).

Stipulations for what lies in act and also those for easements occasion more difficulty, though the Romans held that difficulty of performance was no reason for nullifying the obligation. In these cases each heir of the stipulator can *prima facie* demand the right of way or the erection of the house stipulated for, as they are indivisible; and each heir of the promiser is liable for the whole, the damages payable to each heir of the stipulator being however proportionate to his share of the inheritance. If only one heir of stipulator is prevented from enjoying the right of way, the others will have no effectual suit, for they have no grievance, and consequently no interest: they would be met by a plea of fraud. If however a penalty be attached to the infringement of the right of way, then the question of interest in the right of way itself drops: any breach of the right of way makes the penalty due from all the heirs of promiser, and gives a claim to all the heirs of stipulator, the *jud. fam. ercisc.* rectifying, after payment to one or by one, the claims or liabilities of his coheirs. Even if there be no penalty, obstruction by any one of the heirs of promiser was held sufficient to make them all liable to the obstructed heir (D. xlv 1 fr 2 §§ 2, 4—6, 85 §§ 2, 3; x 2 fr 25 §§ 9, 10).

In the case of the judicial stipulations, for ratification (*Titium heredemque ejus ratum habiturum*) and for freedom from further suit (*amplius non agi*), division is automatic: only he who is sued or who suffers from the want of ratification has any interest in suing on the stipulation; and only he who has sued or refused to ratify, can be called on to fulfil it. As regards the common stipulation for double value in case of eviction, each heir of the stipulator who is evicted from his share has a proportionate claim to redress, but whether the whole or part be evicted, the vendor's heirs are liable each for his share of the damages. In such cases the words of the formula run *quanti ea res est*, and thus fix the claim by the value of the particular claimant's interest (D. xlv 1 fr 4, 85 § 5; x 2 fr 44 § 6; xlvi 5 fr 2 § 2; cf. xxxix 2 fr 18 § 10).

Where the stipulation lay in act and was indivisible (*insulam fabricari, etc.*) some lawyers[1] suggested that a value should be put upon it so as to enable a division of claim and liability to be effected, but how far this plan was followed, we do not know (D. xlv 1 fr 72 pr). A stipulation for a freedman's services admits of division by the number of days' service; if one service has to be divided, the readiest way is for the freedman to offer money value (fr 54 § 1). As regards grants of release see p. 57.

A stipulation for payment by promiser and his heir Titius did not operate so as to exempt promiser's other heirs from their share of payment (fr 56 § 1). And a guaranty against any interference with stipulator's enjoyment of a road by promiser or his heir Titius was good against interference by Titius's coheirs also (fr 131 pr).

(*f*) Drafting and interpretation.

In framing a stipulation it is desirable to state all special

[1] Celsus following Tubero. He makes a like suggestion in the case of *operae serviles* D. xii 6 fr 26 § 12.

points: if not stated either in the recital of agreement or in the operative words, they would not be taken to be part of the agreement. As the stipulator has the framing, the presumption in case of doubt is generally against him (fr 99 pr; 110 § 1, 134 § 1; xxxiv 5 fr 26; cf. xix 1 fr 21, 33). The interpretation was strict; *e.g. quicquid te dare facere oportet* includes only what is due at the time of stipulation[1]: if subsequent obligations are to be included, the words *oportebitve*, or *praesens in diemve* must be added. Again by a stipulation for *illud aut illud quod ego voluero* the choice is given to the stipulator (or his heir), but once made cannot be altered; if *volam* were used instead of *voluero*, the choice could be changed at any time before joinder of issue (fr 76, 89, *etc.*). If words are ambiguous and the parties took them in different senses, there was no agreement and the stipulation does not hold (fr 83 § 1). If the intention was not fully apparent, the usual habit of the district was followed (D. L 17 fr 34). It is rarely allowable to introduce by interpretation time or condition into a stipulation when it was not expressed (D. xlv 1 fr 126 § 2 *ad fin.*).

Stipulations for separate things or separate amounts are separate stipulations, though some words may comprehend a number of objects (*e.g. familia servorum, pecunia*) without thereby making separate stipulations for them to be necessary. Nor does the fact that a number of covenants may be embraced under one stipulatory question and answer (*Ea omnia quae dixi*, or *quae supra scripta sunt, dari fieri praestari spondes?*) prevent their being separate stipulations and capable of separate suit (fr 29 pr; 134 § 3, 140; xxi 2 fr 32). A stipulation containing alternatives (*Stichum aut decem dabis?*) is one only, being satisfied by performance of one of the alternatives (D. ii 14 fr 27 § 6). A stipulation for repayment of loan and interest is two stipulations. And one for payment by instalments, *e.g. annua bima trima die*, is three stipulations (fr 75 § 9, 140 § 1).

In stipulating for something to be done under a penalty,

[1] The same is true of a legacy (D. xxxi fr 46). Paul notes that the case is different in issues for trial (D. xlv 1 fr 76 § 1).

the usual words were *si ita factum non erit*, or *si non feceris*; for something not to be done, *si adversus ea factum erit* or *feceris* (D. xlv 1 fr 137 § 7).

In the praetorian stipulations (see Book VI chap. ix B) a clause against fraud was regularly inserted (*clausula doli*), and was held to refer not to what was expressed but to what was unforeseen (fr 53, 119). Consequently it had not the effect of putting stipulations on the same footing as *bonae fidei* obligations. But where a stipulation was contrary to the real agreement, even without actual fraud on the other's part, a plea of fraud could be used, bringing suit on such a stipulation being of itself a fraud (fr 36).

(*g*) Action to enforce a stipulation.

The form of action which was to enforce a stipulation depended on whether the stipulation was certain or uncertain. A *certain* stipulation (*certa* or *certi stipulatio*) is one which contains as its object what is certain in substance, quality and quantity (*quid quale quantumque sit*), *e.g.* two sovereigns (*aurei*), my, your, *etc.* Tusculan farm, my slave Stichus, a hundred bushels of the best African wheat, a hundred gallons of the best Campanian wine, the wine in my cellar, the wheat in my granary, *etc.* An *uncertain* stipulation is one covenanting for a slave or farm without any distinctive name being given, or for a hundred bushels of good African wheat, or for a hundred gallons of good Campanian wine, or for the produce or (probably) for the usufruct of a farm (though the farm itself be certain), or the future child of a female slave, or for what Seius owes to Titius, or for what is due to Titius under Seius' will[1]; or for one of several alternatives, unless the stipulator have the option, or for anything which lies not in conveyance (*in dando*), but in performance or non-performance (D. xlv 1 fr 74, 75). In the case of a certain stipulation the claim is made for the thing itself as described in the stipulation (or in default for its value

[1] Even, says Ulpian, though the promise or legacy was for a sum certain; but he appears to retract this immediately afterwards. I suppose Ulpian's first view was caused by the certainty not appearing on the face of the stipulation.

at the time of suit); in the case of an uncertain stipulation the thing requires further ascertainment, and the claim therefore can only be *quicquid eum dare facere oportet* or *quanti ea res est, i.e.* the amount of his interest in there being default (D. xlvi 5 fr 2 § 2, 11; xlv 1 fr 113 § 1, 114 *lex Rubr.* 20). The former was enforced by a *condictio certae creditae pecuniae* or *certae rei* with its advantages of summary procedure (see p. 71); the latter by an action *ex stipulatu* (D. xii 1 fr 24). On the *formula* see Gai. iv 53, 136, and below (Book VI chap. viii A 3).

Action on the stipulation can be brought until full satisfaction is obtained, *e.g.* an action for a thing promised is not concluded by delivery, if some right attached to the thing remain out. The form of action will still be for the thing (*ipsa res petenda est quamdiu aliquid juri rei deest* D. xlvi 3 fr 27).

(*h*) Who can enter into stipulations.

A mute or a completely deaf person cannot make a stipulation or promise, for they cannot utter or hear the words. A madman cannot for want of intelligence. A ward is competent for all business; but, if it is to bind him, he needs the authority of his guardian, though he can bind another without such authority. This of course only applies to such wards as can speak and are old enough to have intelligence. Infants and those of an age next to infancy have really not much more capacity than madmen, but practical convenience has prevented this being pressed in the case of those who are above the age of infancy. Women having guardians are in the same position as other wards (Gai. iii 105—109; cf. Just. iii 19 § 10; D. xlvi 6 fr 6). Minors above the age of puberty are capable of being bound without the consent of their caretakers (D. xlv 1 fr 101).

Slaves, persons in handtake, women under power or in hand, can stipulate for themselves or for those in whose power they are, the superior in both cases obtaining the right of action. But they cannot be legally bound by a promise either to him under whose power they are or to anyone else. Nor can a son under power enter into a stipulation with his father, but with other persons he can (Gai. iii 104; D. xliv 7 fr 39; xlv 3 fr 1 pr). If a son makes a stipulation under a condition, and when the time comes he is emancipated, the right of action remains with the father, the date of stipulation ruling such matters (D. xlv 1 fr 78).

2. Correal obligation.

If two or more persons stipulate together for the same thing or two or more persons promise together the same thing, it would generally be taken that they are jointly, not separately, entitled and liable. But all depends on the intention, and it may be that each stipulator is to have a several as well as a joint claim to the thing, and each promiser to take a several as well as joint liability for it. Still, the obligation being one only, payment to or by one discharges all. Payment of two halves of the same due object to two stipulators or by two promisers is also effectual. Such legal relation usually arises from stipulation, whether the questions and answers are several or joint, *e.g. spondesne* and *spondesne?* or *spondetis? spondeo* and *spondeo*, or *spondemus*. It might be created by a common slave, if couched in appropriate words. It is not necessary that the double obligation should be made at the same time, but there must be no such interval and no such other business interposed as to make either two separate transactions instead of a single joint one, or the later to be regarded as a novation of the earlier (D. xlv 2 fr 2—4, fr 6 § 3; tit. 3 fr 29; xlvi 3 fr 34 § 1). The parties are spoken of as *duo* (or *plures*) *rei stipulandi* or *rei promittendi* (D. xlv 2 fr 1); and once the term *correus* is used (D. xxxiv 3 fr 3 § 3), whence the modern terms of *correal* and *correality* are derived.

This joint and several obligation is not vitiated by some difference in the terms. One may promise absolutely, and another conditionally; one promise payment immediately, another at some future day; one may have a surety, another not; but they must promise the same thing or the same amount, and it must be clear that the obligation is for one performance or one payment only, according to their respective terms (if there be a difference). The obligation was probably expressed by such words as *eandem rem dari fieri* or *eosdem centum aureos dari* or *eandem summam, etc., ita ut duo rei stipulandi* (or *promittendi*) *essent* (D. xlv 2 fr 6 § 1, 7, 9 § 2, 11 §§ 1, 2; 12). In such an obligation each stipulator may at his choice demand the whole from any one promiser, or part from one and part from another. Discharge of one, and thereby of all, results not only from complete performance but from formal release, from novation, or joinder of issue on the part of any one stipulator. A bargain not to sue, though in general terms made by one joint stipulator did not affect the other's right to sue, but made by one joint promiser with a common stipulator freed the other promisers, if the bargaining promiser would otherwise be affected. Delay or obstructive action of one promiser does not hurt the others. Nor does the freedom of one promiser by *capitis deminutio* affect the liability of the others (fr 16, 18, 19; xlvi 2 fr 31 § 1; cf. ii 14 fr 25 pr). If one joint stipulator becomes heir to the other, there is no merger: each obligation continues to exist and can be exercised at choice (D. xlvi 3 fr 93 pr).

The like obligation is said to be also possible by other means than stipulation, *e.g.* by deposit, by loan, sale and purchase, letting and hiring, or by will (D. xlv 2 fr 9 pr).

The advantage of such arrangements was almost entirely on the side of the stipulator, who thus gained greater security by having more than one person fully liable as promiser. If he had another as co-stipulator, he had a fully competent representative in case perhaps of his own absence, but he was also liable to suffer by his acts. Whether one co-stipulator was always compellable to share with the others any payment obtained, and one copromiser who paid could obtain contribution from his fellows, is a question only incidentally touched in our authorities and the subject of much debate in modern times. Probably the circumstances which caused the joint stipulation, *etc.* to be made would determine this. If the relation of partnership or mandate existed between them, as would often be the case, contribution or sharing would clearly be obtainable (see Savigny *Oblig.* 1 §§ 23—26; Vangerow *Pand.* § 573 *anm.* 3, *etc.*).

3. ADSTIPULATION.

In co-stipulation the stipulators are on an equal footing; but if one stipulator employs another merely as accessory, the latter is called *adstipulator*. He is not *reus stipulandi*, for he has no direct interest in the matter (Fest. p. 273). The form was for the adstipulator (after the principal's stipulation, *e.g. dari spondes?*) to say to the promiser *ĭdem spondes?* or *ĭdem fide tua promittis?* or some other appropriate words. The adstipulator can sue, and the debt can be paid him just as effectually as to the principal, but he is accountable for it to the principal or his heir by an action *mandati*. The accessory must not stipulate for more in quantity or for earlier payment than his principal: if the principal stipulates for ten, he may stipulate for five, or if the principal stipulate unconditionally, the accessory may stipulate conditionally, but not *vice versa*. The adstipulator's heir cannot sue. A slave adstipulating and, according to the better opinion, a person in handtake adstipulating, go for nothing. A son in the power of his father does not thereby, as in other cases, acquire for his father, but cannot sue on his adstipulation, unless and until he has passed from his father's power without changing his civic status (*sine capitis dem.*), *i.e.* not by emancipation, but by his parent's death or by being inaugurated as *flamen Dialis*. The like is true of a daughter under power or in hand.

The use of adstipulation[1] was, in Gaius' time, pretty well confined to cases where a stipulation was entered into for something to be given (*dari*) after the principal's death, so that there might be someone to enforce it (Gai. iii 110—114, 117, iv 113; cf. D. xvii 1 fr 59 pr). If an adstipulator played false, and gave the promiser a formal release, he was liable under the second clause of the *lex Aquilia* to an action for corresponding damages (Gai. iii 215). See below, p. 193.

[1] An *adstipulator* is mentioned in Cicero *Quint.* 18 § 58 in connexion with a *vadimonium*. In Pseudo-Cic. *ad Octav.* § 9 *Octavian* is referred to as one *cujus avus fuerit argentarius, adstipulator pater, uterque precarium quaestum fecerit.* Some such contemptuous reference to mean services is seen in Cic. *Pis.* 9 § 18. In *Acad.* ii 21 § 67 the technical meaning has receded.

4. SURETYSHIP.

(*a*) Accessory promisers, *i.e.* sureties, were much more common than accessory stipulators, and were indeed the usual form of security for engagements, when a creditor was not content with the debtor's own promise (*repromissio* or *promissio*). Sureties differed from copromisers. Copromisers were liable on one and the same obligation, but were independent and one as fully liable as another. Sureties depended on their principal, *i.e.* the person whose obligation they were to secure; they were affected by his conduct and could use his privileges, though they were equally liable with him to the creditor. On the other hand they could call upon their principal to repay them.

In Gaius' time there were three kinds of sureties, *sponsor*[1], *fidepromissor*, *fidejussor*, corresponding to the words used in the stipulation, which, following on the engagement of the debtor, was such as *ĭdem dari spondes?* or *ĭdem fide promittes*[2]*?* or *ĭdem fide tua esse jubes?* But the stipulation might take the simple forms *ĭdem dabis? ĭdem promittis? ĭdem facies*, and in such a case there is no special name for the surety (Gai. iii 115, 116), but the term *adpromissores* (cf. D. xlvi 3 fr 43) would include all. *Fidejussores* (and no doubt *fidepromissores*) could give their guaranty in Greek (D. xlvi 1 fr 8 pr).

(*b*) None but Romans could be *sponsores*, *spondere* being a word peculiar to them, and a stipulation by or with foreigners,

1 Cf. Hor. *Ep.* i 16. 43 *Vir bonus est quis?...quo res sponsore et quo causae teste tenentur*; ii 2. 67 *Hic sponsum* ('to guaranty') *vocat*; *Sat.* ii 6. 23 *Romae sponsorem me rapis.*

2 In Plaut. *Men.* 894 (of an ordinary promise) we have *mea ego id promitto fide* (cf. Sall. *Cat.* 47 *fide publica dicere jussus est*). Of the principal debtor's answer to a stipulation *fide* (without *sua*, *etc.*) *promittere* is often in the Transylvanian documents; cf. Bruns[6] nos. 105, 106, 107, 108, probably all of provincials. Of sureties *fide tua jussit* is found in nos. 105, 107, 110. Cicero does not (apparently) use either *fide promittere* or *f. jubere*, but speaking of a loan with a surety says *pecuniam credidit P. Fulvi Nerati fide* (*Flac.* 20 § 46); *Hermippi fide pecuniam sumpsit a Fufiis* (*ib.* § 46); *Hermippus Fufiis satisfacit et fidem suam liberat, hunc judicio persequitur* (*ib.* § 47). In rhetorical language we have *Audebo obligare fidem meam vobis populoque Romano...Promitto, recipio, spondeo, etc.* See Pernice *Labeo* i p. 408 sqq.

using *spondes spondeo*, was null (Gai. iii 93, 179). Foreigners were however capable of taking and being sureties, and the term *fidepromissor* was no doubt first and chiefly applied to them (cf. *ib.* 120), *fide* 'on my credit,' 'faithfully' being prefixed to distinguish a solemn promise in reply to a stipulation from other promises. The *sponsor* and *fidepromissor* were in the same legal position (Gai. iv 118).

These two kinds of sureties were accessory only to verbal obligations, that is, only when the principal debtor had himself promised in reply to a stipulation. Their heirs were not liable, at least by Roman law, though Gaius hints that the heirs of a *fidepromissor* being a foreigner might be liable under the laws of his own community (Gai. iii 119, 120, iv 113). The risk of the sureties themselves was mitigated by several statutes, all of uncertain date, but probably earlier than Cicero[1].

At first, if there were more sureties than one, each was liable in full. The *lex Appuleia* however made them to some extent partners in the obligation, and gave any who had paid more than his share an action against the others for contribution. This law extended beyond Italy to the provinces, *i.e.* to the Romans in the provinces (Wlassak *PG.* ii 157). The *lex Furia* (*de sponsu*, Gai. iv 22) divided the obligation among the sureties, whatever their number, at the time of the debts becoming due, so that each was liable for one equal share only; and to insure this, it gave a summary remedy against any creditor who exacted from a surety anything more than his share (see p. 185). Another clause freed all sureties from their obligation at the end of two years[2]. But this law applied only to (the Romans

[1] Cf. Girard *Dr. Rom.* p. 739 n. 4, p. 740 n. 2.

[2] Cicero speaks of having been called on to pay as a *sponsor*, although the engagement was made twenty-five years before. *Quod pro Cornificio me abhinc amplius annis xxv spopondisse dicit Flavius, etsi reus locuples est et Apuleius praediator liberalis, tamen velim des operam ut investiges ex consponsorum tabulis sitne ita* (*Att.* xii 17 § 2; cf. 14 § 2, 19 § 2). Huschke (*Beitr. zur Gaius*, p. 86) suggests that Cicero though really freed by the *lex Furia* thought it better not to plead the statute, as the principal was a man of means. See also Karlowa *RG.* ii p. 735. Others hold the *lex Furia* to be subsequent to Cicero's time.

in) Italy, practically superseding there the provisions of the *lex Appuleia.* The *lex Cicereia* aimed at securing the benefit of these restrictions on a surety's liability, by making it obligatory on everyone who took sureties to announce openly beforehand the matter of the obligation and the number of sureties intended to be taken. If this was not done, the sureties were allowed within thirty days to demand a preliminary trial (*praejudicium*) whether the law had been obeyed, and, if due announcement had not been made, the sureties were freed. None of these laws mentioned *fidejussores.*

(*c*) A *fidejussor* was a surety different in some important respects from a *sponsor* or *fidepromissor.* The words appear to be of a stronger type. 'I bid it be done on my credit' (*fides*), *i.e.* 'on my guaranty,' as if the attitude were that of a *mandator* ordering the business and taking the responsibility (cf. D. xvii 1 fr 60 § 1), but differing from a *mandator* in being necessarily present on the spot and making a legal contract in strict form. Accordingly a *fidejussor* was used to guaranty any kind of obligation, verbal, litteral, real, consensual, and not only civil but also merely natural obligations, as for instance a sale or promise by a slave or son to an outsider or to his own master or father. His liability is transmitted to his heir (Gai. iii 118, 119; D. xix 1 fr 24 § 2; xlvi 1 fr 8 §§ 1—6; 16 § 3, 4; 56 § 1).

A *fidejussor* whether alone or with others was liable in full. He obtained no relief under the *lex Appuleia* or *Furia*, but a letter of Hadrian's (followed by the edict, Paul i 20) directed creditors who had several *fidejussores* to claim from each only an equal share; but, as in reckoning the shares insolvent sureties were to be disregarded, those solvent might still have more than their own share to bear. (This letter of Hadrian's might also relieve in some degree *sponsores* and *fidepromissores* in the provinces where the *lex Furia* was not in force.) It was perhaps in consequence of this letter that the practice prevailed of announcing the number of *fidejussores*, as required for other sureties by the *lex Cicereia* (Gai. iii 121, 123; D. xlvi 1 fr 26—28).

(*d*) A restriction of a different kind was enacted by the *lex*

Cornelia for all kinds of sureties. It limited the total amount of money on credit, for which any one surety could be bound in the same year for the same principal debtor to the same stipulator (*idem pro eodem apud eundem eodem anno*). The limit was 20,000 sesterces. Any excess was invalid. The law used the term *summa creditae pecuniae*; and under this term the lawyers included not only money actually lent but all money which at the time of obligation was certain to be due (though the time for suing might be deferred), *i.e.* all that is stipulated for unconditionally, whether to be paid now or at a certain future time. And 'money' (*pecunia*) in this law was taken to include wine, or corn, or land, or slaves[1]. The only cases in which the law allowed security to be unrestricted in amount were when the security was given for a dowry, or for something left by will, or when it was given by a judge's order. And the *lex Julia* exempted also any security required by that statute for the 5 per cent. tax on inheritances[2] (Gai. iii 124, 125).

(*e*) A surety is not bound, if there is no principal bound, *i.e.* if the principal is not under a lawful obligation recognised by the civil law as actionable or as so natural as to make payment of it irrecoverable (D. xlvi 1 fr 16 pr §§ 3, 4). It was questionable whether there was any obligation which could support suretyship in a promise by a slave or a foreigner using the word *spondeo*

1 Cf. Savigny *Syst.* v. p. 536.

2 Augustus A.D. 6 imposed a tax of 5 per cent. (*pars vicesima*) on all inheritances and legacies taken by Roman citizens, except the children of the deceased. Newly made citizens whether by Latin right (vol. I p. 23) or grant of the emperor were exempt only if they obtained specially the right of kinship (*cognatio*). Nero and Trajan extended the exemptions, without special grant, to inheritances of children from either parent and *vice versa*, in the case of Roman citizens, and also to cognates in the second degree (*i.e.* between brothers and sisters), and freed small inheritances and legacies altogether. Caracalla doubled the tax, abolished exemption of near relatives, restricted succession *ab intestato*, and to swell the proceeds of the tax gave Roman citizenship to all (see vol. I p. 24). Macrinus restored the tax arrangements to the State before Caracalla. Plin. *Paneg.* 37—40 (partly quoted vol. I p. 188); Dio Cass. lv 25; lxxvii 9; lxxviii 12. Some points are doubtful. See Huschke *Beitr. zur Gaius* p. 16 sqq.

(Gai. iii 119); and there was none in a promise by a father or master to his son or slave, for that is in fact a promise to himself, and no one can be surety for and to the same person (D. xlvi 1 fr 56 § 1), or in an oath to perform services by one who is not a freedman (fr 56 pr), or in an obligation which has by efflux of time ceased to bind (fr 37), or which has been nullified by the debtor being condemned to deportation (fr 47 pr), or in a professed loan where the money was not the lender's, was not spent and was not accompanied by any stipulation (fr 56 § 2). Nor does a stipulation between thieves for sharing the booty or paying the penalty allow of a surety (fr 70 § 5). A madman or spendthrift could hand over nothing and could not be bound by a promise: their action went for nothing and consequently there could be no surety in such a proceeding (fr 70 § 4; xlv 1 fr 6). A woman or ward promising without the authority of their guardian contracts a natural but not a legal obligation: it is however sufficient to allow of a surety. And the same, says Gaius, applies to a promise for something to be done after the promiser's death, which in itself is an invalid stipulation (Gai. iii 119).

(*f*) No surety can be bound for a different thing or for a larger amount than the principal debtor is; what is accessory should not be greater than the principal. But a surety may be bound for less than the principal debtor (Gai. iii 126). Nor can the principal be engaged only from a certain time or on condition, and the surety be engaged absolutely or at once. If the principal is engaged on one condition and the surety on another, the surety is bound only if the principal's condition occur first. If the surety is engaged on a condition additional to that on which the principal is engaged, he is bound only if both conditions occur; otherwise there would be more chance of his being bound than of the principal's being bound. If the principal promise 'Stichus or ten pounds,' surety can be liable only if the option be his. If principal promise only to give Stichus, surety cannot be bound for 'Stichus or ten pounds,' for if Stichus die the principal debtor may not be liable at all, and the surety would be responsible for ten pounds. But if the principal promised a farm, the surety may promise only the usufruct, that being regarded for this purpose as a share of the same thing. And generally the engagement of the surety may be lighter, but must not be harder, than that of his principal (D. xlvi 1 fr 8 § 7 sqq., 34, 42, 70 pr—§ 2). A surety for a slave is bound in full whatever be the amount of the *peculium*. A surety for the master in a suit against him *de peculio* is bound only for the amount of the *peculium* at the time of judgment (fr 35: cf. D. xix 1 fr 24 § 2).

(*g*) If the principal's obligation determines by course of law, that of the surety or sureties determines likewise (D. xlvi 1 fr 16 pr). Payment in full by either debtor or surety or co-surety frees all. If the debtor is freed by judgment or creditor's will, or by compromise, or novation, or formal release, or oath (affecting the liability of both), or any cause not special to the person of the debtor but extinguishing the debt morally as well as legally, the sureties are freed also (fr 37, 49 pr, 60, 68 § 2; tit. 3 fr 43; tit. 4 fr 16; ii 14 fr 22; xii 2 fr 42; Cod. viii 40 fr 4). If debtor become heir to creditor or creditor to debtor, the debt is extinguished by merger (*confusio*), and sureties taken for the debt now merged are freed: they cannot be liable for and to the same person (*pro eodem apud eundem*), and there is no existing debt to support their suretyship (fr 21 § 3, 38 § 1; cf. xxi 2 fr 40, 41 § 2). If surety become heir to creditor or creditor to surety, the debtor remains bound (xlvi 3 fr 43). If surety become heir to debtor or *vice versa*, and the debtor was under a civil obligation, surety's obligation no longer exists independently, and if the debtor was a minor and deserved reinstatement, the surety now could obtain reinstatement as his heir. If however a debtor was bankrupt, and became heir to his surety, the latter's creditors might demand separation of the estates, as if surety's obligation still existed (D. xlvi 1 fr 21 § 2; tit. 3 fr 93 §§ 2, 3, fr 95 § 3; xlii 6 fr 3 pr). Where the debtor was a minor and surety was not his heir, the reinstatement of the minor or his heir did not necessarily involve the reinstatement and consequent liberation of the surety: it was a question for the praetor to decide on the circumstances, who if he retained the surety's obligation would refuse him the right of recouping himself by action of mandate against the minor (D. iv 4 fr 13 pr). Formal release to a surety, or judgment in his favour, or oath, on a point affecting the liability of both, frees the debtor to the same extent (D. xlvi 4 fr 13 § 7; xii 2 fr 42 §§ 1—3). But where the intention is to benefit surety only, the creditor may release him or receive payment from a third party on his behalf without relieving debtor from surety's action on the mandate (D. xvii 1 fr 10 §§ 13—fr 12 pr, 26 § 3).

(*h*) In the absence of any special agreement with surety, the creditor can, when the debt is due, sue either debtor or surety at his own choice. If he has also a pledge, he is not bound to realize that first, but if he sue surety, he must transfer to him the right over the pledge (Cod. viii 40 fr 2; D. xlvi 1 fr 51 § 3, 57). If he elect to sue debtor, he thereby frees all sureties[1], unless the surety was bound expressly for so much as should not be recovered from the debtor (Paul ii 17 § 16; D. xlv 1 fr 116; xii 1 fr 42). If he sue a *fidejussor*, the other *fidejussores* and the principal debtor appear (from Cod. viii 40 fr 28 § 1) to have

[1] The fact that joinder of issue with the principal or his procurators frees the sureties is mentioned in Cicero *Att.* xvi 15 § 2: *Etsi sponsores appellare videtur habere quandam* δυσωπίαν ('looks rather shamefaced on my part'), *tamen hoc quale sit consideres velim: possumus enim, ut sponsores appellemus, procuratores introducere, neque enim illi litem contestabuntur, quo facto non sum nescius sponsores liberari. Sed et illi turpe arbitror eo nomine, quod satisdato debeat, procuratores ejus non dissolvere, et nostrae gravitatis jus nostrum sine summa illius ignominia persequi.* Cicero is trying to recover from Dolabella the dowry which he had given with his daughter Tullia, and wishes to combine strong action against him with consideration for the sureties (which Dolabella had given for the restoration of the dowry, see vol. I p. 154), and also not to involve Dolabella in the disgrace of bankruptcy. Cicero therefore proposes to summon Dolabella's agents into Court, and thus shew the sureties that he does not proceed against them as he might do, in the first instance, but only on finding it hopeless to recover from Dolabella. The agents would be sure not to join issue, because then they would have to give security *judicatum solvi* (Book VI chap. vii B), and would never be repaid by the moneyless Dolabella. Then Cicero could proceed against the sureties, and Dolabella would have the practical disgrace of having exposed his sureties to loss without the legal ignominy which would follow if the suit were continued against himself, judgment obtained and execution issued. This is Huschke's explanation *ZRG.* xiv 42 sqq. See also Keller *Lit. Contest.* § 54.

been thereby freed[1], but this consequence was in practice often averted by previous bargain (Cod. *l.c.*; cf. Just. iii 26 § 2). A bargain in general terms against suit, if made with the principal debtor, supplies a plea to sureties also; for the debtor, being contingently liable to them, has an interest in their freedom; but such a bargain made with a surety does not as a rule benefit any other surety or the principal debtor; for the bargaining surety has no interest in their being freed (D. ii 14 fr 21 § 5—fr 26; cf. xxxiv 3 fr 5 pr, § 1). See below under section 11.

(*j*) A surety can meet the creditor's suit with any plea connected with the matter (*rei cohaerens*) which the debtor could use, such as 'matter brought to issue or decided,' 'fraud,' 'oath,' 'intimidation,' 'bargain in general terms not to sue,' 'burdensome services on a freedman,' 'loan contrary to the senate's decree in Macedo's case,' *etc.*: but a purely personal plea like that of (debtor's) 'inadequate means,' or 'a bargain limited to debtor' is not open to a surety. Nor is debtor's consent necessary to surety's use of a plea (D. xliv 1 fr 7; xlvi 1 fr 32). On the other hand the conduct of the debtor, *e.g.* in not paying when due, perpetuates the claim not only against himself but also against his sureties (D. xlvi 1 fr 58 § 1). Delay of the surety perpetuates the claim against himself (D xxxviii 1 fr 44).

(*k*) Sponsors had a specially stringent action (*depensi* p. 184) to enforce recoupment (Gai. iii 127; iv 22). Sureties in general have an action *mandati* (or in some cases *negot. gestor.*) against

[1] That suit against sureties freed the debtor is generally stated absolutely, *e.g.* by Baron *Inst.* § 118, 8; Keller *Lit. Contest.* p. 436, who however limits the freeing of cosureties to the case of *fidejussores*, as others were *ipso jure* liable only for a share. But a *fidejussor* might be expressly bound only for a part (D. xlvi 1 fr 8 § 7). Should this case be excluded? It is difficult in our ignorance of the details of formular procedure (see Book VI chap. viii F 3) to draw a precise doctrine from Cod. viii 40 fr 2. Justinian's alteration of the rule on this point, and omission of *sponsor* and *fidepromissor*, and consequent alterations in the Digest make the ground very slippery. Other passages quoted (*e.g.* D. xlv 2 fr 2; xlvi 2 fr 31 § 1) do not really apply: and Paul's omission of this point in *Sent.* ii 17 § 16 is very noticeable.

the principal debtor for relief or reimbursement, but cannot sue before they have either been condemned or have satisfied the creditor, unless the debtor long delay payment, or be running through his property (Gai. *l.c.*; D. xvii 1 fr 10 § 11, fr 38 § 1; cf. Cod. iv 35 fr 10). If they have paid before the due date, they must await this before suing their principal (D. xlvi 1 fr 31). After condemnation they can sue for due defence against the action on the judgment: after payment, for the amount paid, even if they have waived, or through some ignorance of fact have omitted, an effective plea (D. xlvi 1 fr 45, xvii 1 fr 29; cf. xii 6 fr 47). A surety who has become such *donandi animo* has no action for recoupment, nor right to use the plea of 'bargain not to sue,' which his principal may have obtained (D. ii 14 fr 32).

Against his cosureties a surety had no right of action except under the *lex Appuleia*, which applied only to sponsors and fidepromissors. A fidejussor, if sued for the whole debt and not disputing his liability[1], could by the edict under Hadrian's authority plead the solvency of his cosureties (*si non et illi solvendo sint*) and demand that he should be sued only for his share (D. xlvi 1 fr 10 § 1, 28). Or he could bargain with the creditor (by threatening the *doli exceptio*[2]) that if he pay the whole, the creditor should cede to him his actions against the cosureties and debtor: he is then regarded not as having paid the debt (for that would at once extinguish the actions against the others) but as having purchased the actions (fr 17, 26, 36, 39; Gai. iii 121—123).

(*l*) A woman cannot be a surety (D. xlvi 1 fr 48): nor can a slave without his master's authority; and anything paid by him as such unauthorised surety can be recovered by his master unless paid from his *peculium* on a matter concerning his *peculium* (fr 19, 20).

As written documents became usual, it came to be held that no proof was required of the oral ceremony, if a person stated

[1] The like rule is found in partnership, D. xvii 2 fr 67 § 3; xlii 1 fr 22 § 1.

[2] Cf. D. xxi 2 fr 65; xxx fr 57; x 2 fr 18 § 5; Savigny *Oblig.* i 242, 275; Vangerow *Pand.* § 573, *Anm.* 3 (vol. iii p. 74); Girard *Dr. Rom.* p. 742 sqq.

in writing that he had made himself surety (D. xlv 1 fr 30). See above, p. 13.

(*m*) A guaranty of another's debt might be given in two other ways:

(1) By a *constitutum debiti alieni* (see p. 87), which does not put the constituent in the position of a surety: his obligation is independent and limited only by its own terms.

(2) A guaranty may also be effected by mandate to a person to lend money or give credit to another at the mandator's risk (p. 121). [Justinian treats of *mandatores* in this sense along with *fidejussores*: *sponsores* and *fidepromissores* he ignores entirely.]

5. Novation (by stipulation).

(*a*) Novation is a renewal of an obligation, in this sense, that the old obligation is extinguished, and a new one relating to the same matter takes its place (*Novatio est prioris debiti in aliam obligationem transfusio atque translatio*, D. xlvi 2 fr 1 pr). Such a change was effected by three different legal acts; by stipulation, by book-entry, and by joinder of issue: but the term *novatio* is in the Digest regularly applied to the first only, book-entry being struck out of the Digest altogether. So also Gaius distinctly applies it to transfer by stipulation (ii 38), does not use it of book-entry (iii 128 sqq.), and clearly separates it from *litis contestatio* (iii 176—180; cf. D. xxvi 7 fr 22).

(*b*) For such renewal to take place it is unimportant of what nature the former obligation was, whether civil, or natural, or honorary (*i.e.* of Praetorian creation), whether it was verbal, litteral, real or consensual; but it is essential that the new obligation should be good, though, as happens in a few cases, it may not be valid for all purposes. Three cases are given by Gaius, a stipulation from Titius for something to be done or paid after his death, and stipulations from a woman or a ward without guardians' authority. Such stipulations though not enforceable are sufficient to kill the former obligation.

But a stipulation from a slave is a mere nullity in the eye of the law and leaves (though Serv. Sulpicius thought otherwise) the old obligation undisturbed (Gai. iii 176, 179; D. xlvi 2 fr 1). If however the slave owed as much to the former debtor as he was promising now, and was thus only transferring a (natural) obligation from one creditor of his to another, the stipulation was upheld as a pact not to sue the former debtor (D. ii 14 fr 30 § 1). A stipulation from a foreigner, made by the word *spondeo*, is null and cannot novate (Gai. iii 179).

(*c*) A stipulation does not novate, unless it relate to the same object, and this relation or identity will usually appear in the form of the stipulation. Nor does it novate if it is a mere repetition of a former stipulation; there must be either a new creditor (*e.g. quod Titius mihi debet, id dare spondes?*), or a new debtor, or a new condition, or a new time, *etc.* Whether a new surety was sufficient to allow of novation, was a matter of dispute between the schools: the Sabinians said, 'Yes'; the Proculians held that neither the withdrawal nor the addition of a surety affected the continuance of the former obligation. Again, where a new condition was made, the former obligation was not extinguished, unless and until the condition occurred, which gave life to the new obligation. Serv. Sulpicius however held that the old obligation was extinguished at once by the creation of the new obligation, whether the latter ever came into operation or not. Gaius suggests that even on the other view (which prevailed) any attempt to put the old obligation into force before the occurrence of the condition could be defeated by a plea of 'fraud' or 'bargain agreed,' on the ground of its being the intention of the parties that no suit should be brought unless the condition took effect (Gai. iii 177—179; D. xlvi 2 fr 8 § 1, 14 pr; cf. xii 6 fr 60 § 1). If the old obligation contained a condition, and the new one was absolute, novation took place only if and when the condition existed (fr 14 § 1).

(*d*) It is essential to novation that the second obligation should be intended to be established not beside, but in place of, the old obligation. It must be made *novandi animo*[1]. A

[1] Salpius argues that the jurists older than Papinian regarded novation

stipulation from *C* to guaranty (*fidejubere*) to *A* whatever amount of *B*'s debt he shall not have got from *B* does not affect *B*'s obligation, because that is not the intention; but a stipulation from *C* for defrayal of *B*'s debt to *A* would (if so intended) set *B* free. If a plaintiff takes the ordinary security *judicatum solvi*, he does not thereby novate and thus extinguish his action on the judgment; because his intention is only to get sureties for the judgment, not to waive defendant's obligation to perform the judgment. Where money is paid down for a loan, and a stipulation, whether immediately before or after, is made for due repayment, the intention in both cases is to create one obligation only, that of stipulation, and the payment down of the money is merely the fulfilment of what was contemplated in making the stipulation (D. xlvi 2 fr 6, 7, 8 § 3). If I have stipulated from you to convey to me the Cornelian farm, and afterwards stipulate for its value, and novation is not intended, there are two stipulations in force, one for land and the other for money. If the farm is conveyed to me, or if I sue for it and join issue, in either case the second stipulation remains unaffected, but the damages in the suit for the farm will be estimated according to the present value, in the suit for the value of the farm they will depend on the value of the farm at the time when the stipulation was made, which might be more or less than the present value. By avoiding novation the stipulator would be able to take his choice; he could not exact both, unless indeed he could shew that that was the intention of both parties (fr 28). If someone else promise to my creditor what I owe him, there is novation if that be intended, and I am freed whether I wish it or know it or not: if novation is not intended, both stipulations are good, and my creditor can sue which he pleases, but if either I or the other promiser pay, both are freed. On the other hand if another stipulates from my debtor what he owes me, be their intention what it may, it cannot affect my claim on the debtor without my consent (fr 8 § 5, 91; iii 5 fr 38). If I bid you stipulate for a usufruct which another

as taking place from the form of the stipulation, without reference to any intention on the part of the stipulator. See his book, esp. pp. 187, 192, 356. Justinian altered the law largely (Cod. viii 41 fr 8).

owes me, the nature of a usufruct, as adherent to a person, prevents actual novation (in which case you would have the usufruct for your life in place of my having it for mine), but you will by virtue of the stipulation have a usufruct for your life, and I shall be prevented, by a plea of fraud or a special plea on the case, from exercising my right of usufruct, even if I survive you (D. xlvi 2 fr 4). A stipulation may destroy a *condictio furtiva,* but the condiction does not revive if the stipulation loses its effect by after events (D. xlv 1 fr 29 § 1).

(*e*) As novation destroys the former obligation, all accessories such as pledges and sureties in connexion with it are discharged (unless severally renewed), and interest on anything due on it, if not secured by a separate stipulation, ceases to run (D. xlvi 2 fr 18; *tit.* 1 fr 60). The privilege which dowry and wardship have over other creditors is lost, if the woman after divorce stipulate for her dowry, or the ward after puberty similarly novate his action against his guardian. For in these cases the novation is deliberate. But where a somewhat like change takes place, made by joinder of issue in prosecuting their claims, there is no intention of giving up any pledges or privileges, and the procedure has no such effect (D. xlvi 2 fr 29). Sureties are however discharged by creditors joining issue with the debtor, as by novation (Paul ii 17 § 16).

(*f*) Stipulations by sons under power or by slaves, if made at the bidding of their fathers or masters or afterwards ratified by them, are valid, and consequently can novate a former obligation of their superior. Practice also allows (*receptum est*) of a procurator's novating an obligation at his principal's bidding, or in virtue of his general authority (Paul v 8; D. xlvi 2 fr 20 § 1). A son under power or a slave, if they have the control of their *peculium,* can themselves novate debts in connexion therewith, especially if they thereby improve their position; but they cannot do so in order to give things away (D. *ib.* fr 34 pr). A guardian or agnate caretaker of a madman or of a spendthrift has power to novate, if it be expedient for his charge (*ib.* fr 34 § 1).

6. DELEGATION[1].

Delegation[2] (*i.e.* assignment, deputation) is technically used of one person deputing another to pay, or enter into an obligation to pay, a third person on behalf of the delegant. *A* desires to pay *C* a sum of money and deputes *B* to pay it for him, not as a messenger with money supplied by *A*, but with money of his own. Or perhaps *C* is willing to receive, instead of actual money, *B*'s formal promise to pay, and to treat it as equivalent to money. In either case *A* is said to delegate *B* to *C*. In our times *A* might give *C* a cheque on his banker *B*, and *B* might pay *C* in cash or give him a promissory note. *A* is said *delegare,* or *jubere promittere,* or *reum dare. B delegatur, solvit* or *promittit jussu alterius: C* is *cui delegatur*, delegatee; he stipulates from *B* at the bidding of *A*. (*Mandare* is rarely used in this

[1] See v. Salpius *Novation und delegation* (1864). I have thought it desirable to give separate sections to Novation, Delegation, and Transfer of Obligations, notwithstanding that this plan involves some repetition. They are all distinct, though often intermixed. Novation may or may not be produced by delegation: it may occur between the same persons. Delegation may not involve any novation or transfer of obligations but may relate to a simple payment or the creation of a new obligation altogether. Transfer of obligation is always between different persons, but may be effected either by stipulation, or by representation in joinder of issue.

[2] Cf. Cato *RR.* 149 *Donicum pecuniam* [add: *solverit aut*] *satisfecerit aut delegarit, pecus et familia quae illic erit pigneri sunto*, *i.e.* until he has paid the money or contented the owner or deputed another to pay; Sen. *Ben.* vi 5 § 2 *Nam et pecuniam dicimur reddidisse, quamvis numeraverimus pro argenteis aureos, quamvis non intervenerint nummi, sed delegatione et verbis perfecta solutio sit.* Cicero uses the word metaphorically in *Font.* 8 § 18 *Quid si hoc crimen optimis nominibus delegare possumus, et ita non ut culpam in alios transferamus?* 'What if we can transfer this charge to 'excellent names (very good accounts) without imputing any blame to 'others,' *etc.*; cf. *Dom.* 7 § 16. But it is used in a literal sense in *Att.* xii 3 § 2 *Nomen illud, quod a Caesare, tres habet condiciones aut emptionem ab hasta...aut delegationem a mancipe annua die...aut Vettieni condicione semissem; i.e.* I have the choice of three ways to deal with the claim on Caesar (as confiscator of some Pompeian, who owed Cicero money); either buy the whole estate at the auction, or take an assignment from the purchaser of the estate and wait a year for my money, or sell the debt to Vettienus for 50 per cent.

sense for *jubere*[1], *e.g.* D. xlvi 3 fr 56 *Qui mandat solvi, ipse videtur solvere.*)

The payment thus made to *C* by *A*'s order counts in law as if payment were made to *A* himself. *Quod jussu alterius solvitur, pro eo est quasi ipsi solutum esset* (D. L 17 fr 180; xxiv 1 fr 3 § 12). And if *C* accepts as payment a promise to pay from the person deputed, even though such person prove insolvent, it is as if he received payment: *solvit et qui reum delegat* (D. xvi 1 fr 8 § 3); *bonum nomen facit creditor, qui admittit debitorem delegatum* (D. xvii 1 fr 26 § 2)[2]. The most frequent case of delegacy is where *B* is a debtor to *A*, and *A* is a debtor to *C*. Then *B*'s payment on *A*'s order discharges at once both debts to that amount. *Qui debitorem suum delegat, pecuniam dare intelligitur, quanta ei debetur* (D. xlvi 1 fr 18).

The relations of *A* to *B* and to *C* may be of various kinds. *B* may be owing money to *A*, or may be making him a gift, or a loan: and a like variety may be the cause of *A*'s deputing him to *C*. Or the money may be paid on *A*'s account, and may form the dowry of *A*'s wife (D. xxiii 3 fr 19) or the dowry of *C*'s wife (fr 5 § 8). And the variety of purpose which is found in actual payments is found also in promises to pay (*ib.* fr 59; xlvi 1 fr 18, *etc.*).

There may be a further delegation added to the first. *C* may not desire to receive the money or the promise himself but to pass it on to *D*, so that *B* on *A*'s order may pay or promise *D* on *C*'s order. In modern times *C* would endorse to *D* *A*'s cheque in *C*'s favour on *B* (*Delegare est vice sua alium reum dare creditori vel cui jusserit*) 'to his creditor or order,' *i.e.* creditor's order (D. xlvi 2 fr 11 pr; cf. Goldschmidt *ZRG.* xxiii 387). In this case of double delegation the one payment (or promise) by *B* to *D* is in law equivalent to payments by *B* to *A*, by *A* to *C* and by *C* to *D*. Whether such payment discharges a debt or constitutes a loan or a gift or anything else, depends on the arrangements between the several parties leading to the payment (fr 19).

The delegation consists simply of the order by the delegant

1 For the difference between these terms see below, p. 122.

2 Cf. Windscheid *Pand.* § 412 n. 17.

and the performance by the person delegated. The order may be in any form, oral, or written or even a nod where the delegant is unable to speak (fr 17). If payment is made, no consent on the part of the delegatee is required in law[1]: if a promise is made, the delegatee stipulates and the delegated person promises. If he was under an obligation to the delegant, the stipulation (if so intended) novates this obligation, *i.e.* extinguishes the obligation of *B* to *A* and establishes in place thereof a new obligation of *B* to *C*, which is judged by its own terms. A similar delegation is given effect to by book entry (Gai. iii 130; see p. 65).

The content of the new obligation is usually the same as the previous obligation and subject therefore to the same restrictions. It would then refer to the previous obligation in some such terms as *quod Titio debes, mihi dabis?* or *quicquid ex vendito Titium dare facere oportet, mihi dare facere spondes?* (cf. D. xlvi 2 fr 27, 34 § 2, *etc.*). But the creditor is new to the debtor, and many pleas available against the former creditor are not good against the present one. If a debtor in name, who has however a complete answer (*e.g.* a plea of fraud) against his creditor's demand, chooses to submit to delegation by him in payment of a debt to another, he has thereby waived the plea, and made as it were a gift to his creditor: his new creditor stands on his own stipulation, and the debtor's promise to him is absolute within its own terms. If the debtor consented to delegation in ignorance of his not being indebted or of not being effectively indebted, he can sue—not the new creditor (*ille enim suum accepit*), but the delegant—either for relief from the new obligation, if he has not paid, or fulfilled the obligation (*condictio incerti*), or, if he has paid, he can sue him by a *condictio certi* for the amount paid (*ib.* fr 12, 13). The case is different if the old creditor was not in debt to the new creditor, but was either making him a gift or acting under a mistake; for then the promiser can defeat the new creditor's claim by a plea of fraud and can sue him for a release (D. xliv 4 fr 7).

[1] Cf. Sen. *Ben.* vii 18 § 2 *Obligare non possum nisi accipientem, liberari tamen si reddidi possum.*

If the delegatee decline, unless the delegant guaranty the fulfilment of the new promise, to credit the person delegated (*nomen* or *fidem ejus sequi*) and to stipulate from him, the delegant's guaranty is a mandate accompanying the obligation. He delegates *suo periculo* and is liable to the delegatee for whatever the latter cannot recover from the person delegated (D. xvii 1 fr 28 § 2, 45 § 7; cf. xxi 2 fr 68 § 2)[1].

7. TRANSFER OF OBLIGATIONS.

An obligation is not susceptible, as a thing is, of bodily transference from the possession of one to the possession of another[2]. An active obligation is a right to have some performance made by another: a passive obligation is a liability to make some performance at the will of another. To take the simplest case of obligation, a right of *A* to receive money from *B*, and a corresponding duty of *B* to pay money to *A*: how is *A* to put *C* into his shoes so that *C* shall be entitled instead of *A* to receive the money, or *D* to be put into *B*'s shoes so as to be bound instead of *B* to pay the money to *A* (or to *C*)?

The Romans managed this in two different ways (Gai. ii 38, 39; D. xlvi 2 fr 11).

(*a*) By stipulation. *A*, *B* and *C* all meet. At *A*'s bidding *C* stipulates from *B* for the debt that *B* owes to *A*. *B* promises it and is thereby freed from his debt to *A*, and becomes bound for the same amount to *C*. This is the transfer of a credit or active obligation (the creditor being changed, the debtor remaining the same), and is a case of *delegatio*. It may be

1 When the verb *delegare* is used, not with a person as object, but with *nomen* or *actionem*, it means (but compare Vat. §§ 260, 263) to transfer the debt or action to another by appointing him representative in the action (see *e.g.* D. xv 1 fr 51; xix 5 fr 9; xxi 2 fr 68 § 1). *Mandare actiones* or *praestare actiones* are used in the same sense.

2 It is, in the English law-phrase, 'chose in action': cf. D. xxxiv 2 fr 34 pr *Si aurum suum omne paterfamilias uxori suae legasset, id aurum quod ei deberetur ex stipulatu non pertinet ad uxorem: id enim quod suum esset, non quod in actione haberet, legavit.*

expected to take place most frequently when *A*, the old creditor, is a debtor of *C*, the new creditor of *B*.

For the transfer of a debt or passive obligation *A*, *B* and *D* meet. *A*, say at *B*'s request, stipulates from *D* for the debt which *B* owes to *A*, *D* promises it, and thus accepts *B*'s position of debtor to *A* while *B* is freed. This is a case of *expromissio* (the debtor being changed, the creditor remaining the same). It may be expected to take place most frequently when *D*, the new debtor to *A*, is a debtor to *B*, *A*'s old debtor[1].

But the presence of all three persons is not requisite. In the first case *A* may signify by letter or message his order to *B* to give the promise to *C* (D. xlvi 2 fr 17): and in the second case *B* may take no part at all. If *D* promise to *A* in so many words to pay the debt which *B* owes *A*, *B* is freed even though ignorant of the proceeding and against his consent (D. xlvi 2 fr 8 § 5 *sub fin.*; iii 5 fr 38; Cod. viii 41 fr 1).

The transference of a debt is thus easier than the transference of a credit, because *B* in the second case gains his freedom, while in the first case *A* loses a credit. But in both cases the parties who are to enter into the new obligation *i.e.* *C* (or his slave) and *B* in the first case, *A* (or his slave) and *D* in the second, have to meet in order to go through the oral stipulation.

As any obligation can be dealt with by stipulation, all obligations are transferable in this way, but the old obligation should be referred to in the new stipulation so that it may be clear that the intention is to create a new obligation in place of, and not in addition to, the old one. And the new obligation will then be subject to the same conditions and limitations that the old one was. Pleas available against suit on the old obligation will be good against suit on the new, only if they relate to the matter of the obligation and not to the person of the debtor or creditor (D. xliv 1 fr 7; xlvi 2 fr 19).

[1] To use modern illustrations, if *A* have money at *B*'s bank, he can pay *C* with a cheque on *B* (transfer of credit): if *B* desire to pay off *A*, he can do so by sending *A* a cheque on *D* (transfer of debit). Or if *A* has got a mortgage on *B*'s property he can assign the mortgage to *C* (transfer of credit): if *B* desire to free his property he may get *A* to accept a mortgage on *D*'s property instead (transfer of debt).

The disadvantages of this mode of transference are (1) that the parties have to meet in person; (2) that the transfer of an active obligation requires the debtor's consent (D. xlvi 2 fr 8 § 5); and (3) that by the novation sureties and pledges cease to be bound (D. xlvi 2 fr 18; tit. 3 fr 43).

(*b*) By representation. *A*, wishing to transfer to *C* his right to be paid a sum of money by *B*, appoints *C* his agent to collect the debt, and, if necessary for that purpose, to sue *B*, and agrees that *C* shall have what *B* is bound to pay. *C* is said to be appointed *A*'s *cognitor* (or *procurator*) *in rem suam*, 'agent on his own behalf.' (See Book VI chap. viii G 2.) So, if instead of *A* transferring his credit to *C*, *B* wishes to transfer his liability to *D*, *B* appoints *D* his agent on his own behalf to conduct the defence against *A*'s suit. The claim itself is not affected and is subject to the same pleas as before.

The appointment of *C* is by *A*'s order (*jussus*), and is enforced on either side if necessary in accordance with the arrangements between them which led to the representation, *e.g.* by action *ex vendito* or *empto* if the representative has bought a *nomen*, by petition if he is trust-heir, *etc.* There is no suit *mandati* when a person is bidden to act *in rem suam* (D. iii 3 fr 42 § 2). *D*'s acceptance of liability in place of *B* may have, but does not require, *B*'s consent (D. xlvi 3 fr 23). In some cases the cession of an action or the acceptance of another's liability is imposed by the praetor or judge.

The position of agent is assured by the issue for trial being made to contain in the condemnation-clause the name of *C*, instead of *A*, as the person to whom the damages should be paid (Gai. ii 39). In the same way, if *B* gets *D* to accept his liability, *D*'s name is inserted in the formula instead of *B*'s, as the person who will be condemned to pay the damages. This is just as it would be, if *C* and *D* were intended to be really only agents on behalf of *A* and *B* respectively: the agents have the conduct of their respective cases, and are entitled (at least when on their own behalf) to receive, and liable to pay, the result of the trial as expressed in the condemnation-clause. Of course, if in the trial it be found that *A* was not entitled to the payment supposed from *B*, *C* will lose his suit and have to come again upon *A*, according as the agreement between them may be.

The consent of the other party is not, at least as a rule, required to the change of opponent. But he has a right to protection against the principal's again bringing the suit which he has fought out against his representative: and against an insolvent defendant taking the place of a solvent one. An agent appearing as plaintiff in the absence of the person entitled to the action is required to give security for the latter's consent (*de rato*), and all agents appearing as defendants, whether their principal is present or not, are required to give security *judicatum solvi*, Gai. iv 84, 88—101; Vat. 317, 331—333; D. iii 3 fr 25.

It is not necessary that the matter should actually come to trial. In ordinary cases notice being given to *B* by *A* or *C* of the assignment of the credit, *B* will pay to *C*, and, if notice is given to *A* by *B* or *D* of the assignment of the debt, *D* will pay to *A*. But only by joinder of issue in a trial, *i.e.* by establishment of the formula containing the new names, does the position of transferee become assured[1].

The advantage of this method is that it does not require the presence of the parties, nor the consent of the debtor (*B*) for the transfer of a credit, nor, if due security be given, the consent of the creditor (*A*) for the transfer of a debit (cf. D. x 2 fr 3; cf. iii 3 fr 29). The disadvantage is that until joinder of issue the suit and consequently the assignment may be revoked by the will of the principal and may be extinguished by either's death. Moreover the position of the transferee is dependent generally on the conditions which attached to it in the person of the principal: it is another's claim that he is enforcing (though for his own interest): it is another's liability that he has accepted: the transferee is not in his own shoes but in his principal's. Pledges are not affected either by joinder of issue or judgment (D. xiii 7 fr 11 pr; xx 1 fr 13 § 4).

[1] When acknowledgments of debt (*chirographa*) were bequeathed, the debt was understood to pass to the legatee, but he would require the heir to cede his actions (D. xxx fr 44 § 5, 75 § 2, 105).

The Romans spoke in the first process (as said above, p. 42) of *qui delegat* (*A*), *delegatus* or *qui delegatur* (*B*), and *cui delegat* or *delegatur* (*C*). And in the second process of *qui cedit*, *qui ceditur*, *cui cedit* or *ceditur*; and the process is commonly spoken of as *cedere actione*, or *actionibus*, *alicui*, or *mandare* or *praestare actiones* (*e.g.* D. x 2 fr 2 § 5).

In passive obligations the new debtor is *expromissor*[1] in the first process, *defensor* in the second, but the general terms *procurator* or *cognitor in rem suam* are used both of the new creditor and of the new debtor indifferently; and the general terms *creditor*, *debitor*, *stipulator*, *promissor* are of course also found applied to the transferers and transferees of obligations.

Eventually a *utilis actio* was granted to the transferee of an obligation so that he could thereafter bring the appropriate suit in his own name. This appears to have been first allowed by Antoninus Pius in the case of the purchaser of an inheritance and gradually extended (D. ii 14 fr 16 pr; xviii 4 fr 2 § 8; cf. Cod. iv 10 fr 1, 39 fr 5; Savigny *Obl.* i 243 foll.).

A transfer was often the object of *litt. obligatio* (see p. 65).

Concerning the effect on obligations by the transfer of the whole (*universitas*) containing them, see the case of adoption (vol. I p. 62); of wife coming into hand (vol. I p. 70); of transfer of an inheritance (vol. I p. 228); of sale in bankruptcy of a person's whole estate (Book VI chap. XV B).

8. Payment or discharge of obligation.

(*a*) *Solutio*[2] 'loosening,' opposed to *obligatio* 'tying up,' or *contractus* 'drawing together,' is a general term applicable to

1 *Expromissor*, *expromittere* are not confined to the case where one becomes debtor in place of another. They mean simply to take by promise (*stipulatio*) the position of debtor: cf. D. xv 1 fr 11 § 1; xxiii 3 fr 55; xxxviii 1 fr 37 § 4, *etc.*; Varr. *R.R.* ii 2 § 5; cf. Salkowski *Novation* p. 124. Some modern writers confine the term to cases where the promise is made without delegation (Arndts' *Pand.* § 268).

2 *Solvere* is used like our 'pay' (properly 'pacify') both of the debt discharged and of the money or other thing given to discharge it: *solvere debitum* or *obligationem*: *solvere pecuniam* or *equum*.

every kind of discharge of an obligation, and not merely to the payment of money. The mode of discharge will usually follow the mode of contract: if a particular thing has been lent or deposited or pledged, the proper discharge is the return of the thing to the lender, depositor or pledger; if money has been lent, the same amount of money should be returned; if the contract was in words, the discharge should be made either by the performance of the content of the words or by a formal verbal release; if sale or letting was the subject of agreement, agreement to the contrary will reverse it (D. xlvi 3 fr 54, 80). And any form of satisfaction counts as discharge. An order to another to pay (if fulfilled), counts as payment by the person who gives the order (fr 52, 56).

(*b*) What is payment?

Payment in full requires both the right amount and the due date to be observed; but payment before the time is good. The debtor is discharged by payment when, and only when, his creditor has received what is due, without any cost to himself and without any liability to repay it (fr 61, 70, 85). It does not matter who pays a debt: neither the knowledge nor consent of the debtor is necessary for his discharge, provided it is paid on the debtor's account. The maxim applied *licet etiam ignorantis invitique meliorem condicionem facere* (fr 17, 23, 53; iii 5 fr 38). But if a husband bid his debtor pay something to his wife as a gift, the debtor is not discharged, because the money does not become the wife's property: the husband can still demand the debt, but the debtor can obtain a plea *doli*, if he surrender to the husband his action (*condictio indebiti*) against the wife for repayment. If the *bona fide* holder of a deceased person's estate pays the creditors, the real heir is not discharged, for the creditors are liable to repay the money which was paid them not on account of the heir but on account of another, who thought himself to be heir (D. xlvi 3 fr 38 §§ 1, 2 *fin.*; v 3 fr 31 pr).

Property pledged to another, a farm afterwards evicted, a slave entitled to freedom on condition (unless the condition fails, while the slave is alive), a slave of whom another person has the usufruct, or who is liable to be surrendered noxally, or is seriously wounded, are not good payments, unless of course the express terms of the obligation provided for such temporary or restricted benefit, or the restriction in the event disappears (fr 20, 33, 38 § 3, 98 pr). If however a freedman has fully paid his creditor, the debt is not revived because his patron under the Fabian statute carries off the payment from the creditor (fr 98 § 1).

The debtor is not discharged if the thing delivered in payment is not accompanied by its accessories and securities. The creditor can still bring his action for the thing, whether bequeathed or promised on stipulation (fr 27).

Payment in another form than that promised or due (*datio in solutum* 'conveyance to effect discharge') is good payment, only if accepted by the creditor. Whether in such a case the debtor was discharged in strict law (*ipso jure*) or only entitled to a plea of fraud, was disputed, the Sabinians declaring for the former, the other school for the latter (Gai. iii 168; D. xii 1 fr 2 § 1; xiii 5 fr 1 § 5).

Part payment if accepted effects a partial discharge. If the debt was ten, payment of five leaves five only due. So if the slave Stichus was promised, the promiser by conveying one half is relieved of half, and only the other half of Stichus can be sued for. But if the promise was for a slave generally, and half, say of Stichus, is conveyed, the creditor will sue not for the other half of Stichus but for a slave generally, which may be met by conveyance either of the other half of Stichus or of the whole of some other slave (fr 9 § 1). If a man promises either ten or a slave and gives two sureties, neither surety is discharged if one only pay five, or if one pay five and the other convey half of a slave (fr 34 § 10). If a man had promised two slaves and handed over one, discharge may be effected, supposing the promiser to have again become owner of this slave, by handing him over again (fr 67). It was disputed whether a creditor was bound to accept part-payment but it was held the kinder course for the praetor to compel the acceptance (D. xii 1 fr 21).

If payment is made with the money or other property of

another than the payer, without the knowledge or consent of the owner, the payer commits a theft. The money, *etc.*, if neither spent nor inseparably mixed, remains the owner's; if inseparably mixed, it becomes the property of the payee; and the payer on his own account is discharged. If it is separable, he cannot demand payment of his debt without offering the money back. If the money paid was partly payer's, partly others' (whether the community extended to each coin or only to the amount), the payer gets partial discharge (fr 17, 78, 94 pr § 1). If a thing thus handed over to *A* in payment of *B*'s debt is evicted by the real owner, the original obligation remains in full, whether the eviction be whole or only partial; but if *A* gains it by usucapion, *B*'s debt is discharged (fr 46, 60). If I bid your slave discharge my debt to you and he borrow money for the purpose and pay you or put it to your credit in your accounts, my debt is not discharged, unless it was lent to the slave expressly on my account for that purpose (D. xvii 1 fr 22 § 8).

(*c*) To whom payment should be made.

Payment to the creditor himself, or to anyone by his order, or without his order but with his ratification, is good. And even if he has withdrawn his order or is dead or has forbidden payment to the person, it is good, if the payer was not aware of such fact. Payment to a guardian (not interdicted or under suspicion), or caretaker, or procurator appointed (not merely for conduct of suit, but) for general purposes or for receipt of money, is good (D. xlvi 3 fr 12 § 9; 34 §§ 3, 4, 86; L 17 fr 180). Payment to an acting pro-guardian is good if the money passes into the ward's estate (D. xlvi 3 fr 28). Payment to a mother, although managing her son's business according to the father's desire, does not discharge the son's debtor (D. iii 5 fr 30 § 6). Payment to a ward without his guardian's authority is not good[1], unless the ward be expressly named in the stipulation; but payment by a ward's debtor to the ward's creditor,

[1] Cf. Cic. *Top.* 11 § 46 *Non, quemadmodum quod mulieri debeas recte ipsi mulieri sine tutore auctore solvas, item quod pupillo aut pupillae debeas recte possis eodem modo solvere.*

by the ward's order, though without the guardian's authority, is good to discharge the ward, but only gets a plea of fraud for the paying debtor (fr 66). Where payment has been made to the possessor of an inheritance the debtors are discharged as of course, if the possessor hands over the money to the rightful heir (D. v 3 fr 25 § 17).

A slave, as he cannot alienate property, so he cannot give a good discharge, unless he is acting by the order of his master, or his act is ratified by his master, or he is dealing with his *peculium* and has the free management of it; but even then he cannot make a gift. If he has lent money on account of his *peculium* and is repaid, the debtor is discharged, but only if the money comes into his own (and therefore into his master's) hands, not if it is paid by his directions to someone else. If he is acting in his master's affairs and is manumitted or alienated, payment to him on his master's account is good, if the debtor did not know of his changed position; if he is acting on peculiar account, and his *peculium* has been withdrawn, it is enough if the debtor was ignorant of his *peculium* having been withdrawn (fr 18, 19, 32; xlvi 2 fr 34; xvi 6 fr 11; Gai. iii 160).

If the stipulation required payment *mihi aut Titio*, payment according to the terms of the stipulation to Titius (if he has not been adopted or has not otherwise gravely lost civic position) is a good discharge to the debtor, but payment to Titius' heir is not good (D. xlvi 3 fr 38 pr, 81 pr). And if payment was to be to me or Titius' slave Stichus, payment to Titius is not good unless the slave consented (fr 9 pr, 95 § 7). Titius' position in this class of stipulation is simply that of my agent, the terms of the stipulation being equivalent to an order to pay: and if payment was after all not due, the payer would bring his action to recover, not against Titius but against me (fr 59: see also p. 15).

If a debtor tenders payment and the creditor without good cause refuses to accept it, the praetor will refuse the creditor leave to sue for it afterwards, and if the money be lost or the slave or other thing duly tendered perish without fault of the debtor, the debtor is discharged (fr 30, 72 pr). On a creditor's refusal to take payment, it was customary to seal up the money and deposit it in a temple, and, on this being done, interest would cease to run (D. iii 3 fr 73; iv 4 fr 7 § 2; xxii 1 fr 7; xxvi 7 fr 28; Cod. viii 42 fr 9)[1]. If the money was deposited at a money-changer's for examination, it would lie at the risk of the party who required this step and selected the money-changer (D. xlvi 3 fr 39).

(*d*) Marshalling of debts.

If the debtor owes the creditor on more accounts than one, it is for the debtor to specify to which debt the payment should be appropriated: if nothing is said by debtor, the creditor must appropriate it as he would if he were debtor. The appropriation must be made at the time, not afterwards: either party can object to the appropriation, taking of course the consequences of refusing or withdrawing the payment tendered. If nothing is said as to the appropriation by either party, it will be deemed to be appropriated in the order of importance or pressure of the several debts (D. xlvi 3 fr 1—3). Where interest is legally due, that should first be covered, and the principal be reduced by the surplus; but this does not apply when interest is due only by simple agreement (*pacto*, fr 5 § 2; Cod. viii 42 fr 1). The Antonines decided that when interest was due some on stipulation and some on simple agreement, any money paid without appropriation should be applied to both, not *pro rata* but equally (fr 5 § 2). The order of importance given by Papinian was (1) debt involving disgrace (*infamia*); (2) debt involving penalty for non-performance; (3) debt for which a mortgage (*hypotheca*) or pledge has been given; (4) debt due on one's own account rather than as surety; (5) and in other cases an earlier rather than a later debt (D. xlvi 3 fr 97). So also preference should be given to what is secured by sureties rather than on simple promise; for what is due on a judgment

[1] The Salaminians (of Cyprus) claimed to be allowed to deposit, but Cicero as proconsul, declined at the time to order it (*Att.* v 21 § 12; vi 1 § 7). In *Fam.* xiii 56 § 3 Cicero addressing a propraetor says (of another debt) *Caunii aiunt se depositam pecuniam habuisse. Id velim cognoscas, et si intellexeris eos neque ex edicto neque ex decreto* (*i.e.* neither under the general edict nor by special order) *depositam habuisse, des operam ut usurae Cluvio, instituto tuo, conserventur.*

rather than on a contract; for what is not disputed rather than for what is disputed; for what is actually due rather than what is not yet due (fr 3—7). If all debts are equal in time and character, the payment is deemed to be appropriated proportionally (fr 8). The like marshalling of debts applies when the money is raised by sale of a pledge not specifically appropriated (fr 96 § 3).

(*e*) Other modes of discharge.

Obligations could also be discharged by formal release (below) by the bronze and scales in some cases (p. 185); by delegation (p. 142); by novation (p. 38); by set off, *compensatio* (Book VI chap. xiii D 8).

They were also discharged by merger (*confusio*) *i.e.* by the credit and debt meeting in the same person, as when creditor becomes heir to debtor or *vice versa* (D. xxxiv 3 fr 21 § 1; xlvi 3 fr 95 § 2, 107). If only one of several creditors or of several debtors becomes heir, the merger is only partial. The sureties are also freed when by the merger they become bound to and for the same person (D. xlvi 1 fr 71 pr). See above, p. 34.

Joinder of issue technically discharged the obligation concerned (Book VI chap. xii), and 'Bargain not to sue' supplied a plea which reduced the obligation to impotence (p. 61).

A natural (though not legal) obligation is discharged as of course by payment of money, or a lawful bargain (*justo pacto*) or an oath (D. xlvi 3 fr 95 § 4).

9. VERBAL RELEASE (*ACCEPTILATIO*).

A verbal obligation could be entirely dissolved by a verbal release composed of oral question and answer. The party who is to be released says to the other, 'What I have promised you, have you received?' and the other replies, 'I have' (*Quod ego tibi promisi, habesne acceptum? Habeo*). Or the form might be of this kind, 'Do you treat ten pounds as received? I do' (*Accepta facis decem? Facio*)[1]. Such a release was called by a

[1] *Acceptum fers? fero* is not found. In descriptive language the regular terms for a verbal release in the Digest are *acceptum facere* and *acc. ferre*:

name taken from book-keeping, *acceptilatio* 'entering a receipt: *i.e.* carrying to credit.' The releasing words had strictly to correspond to, or clearly cover, the expressed obligation, and if the obligation did not exist, the release was of no effect. If the release was general, *e.g.* 'what you have promised me,' then every stipulation which you have made me is released, unless it was shewn that the parties intended to refer to one or two only (Gai. iii 169; D. xlvi 4 fr 6, 7, 14). It must itself be absolute in terms; but if it related to an obligation due on the occurrence of a condition or at a future time, the release took effect only when the condition occurred or the time arrived (fr 4, 5, 12; L 17 fr 77). It counts as payment (*est velut imaginaria solutio*) at least for some purposes, and hence frees all who are under the same obligation, *i.e.* sureties and copromisers as well as the principal debtor (D. xlvi 4 fr 16; xxxiv 3 fr 5 § 2, 3). So a debtor for a loan, who had not entered into a stipulation, but had given sureties, was still held to be freed, if his sureties were released; but if a surety were bound in anticipation for a loan not yet made, a release to him would not affect the debtor's obligation on the subsequent loan. Again, if an heir charged with a conditional legacy gave promise and sureties for its due payment, a release to the sureties did not free the heir, when the condition arose, for though freed from the obligation created by his own promise, he still remained liable by testator's direction (D. xlvi 4 fr 13 § 7—9). One who had the same object promised to him by stipulation absolutely by one promiser and

the latter appears not to be used in this sense before Gaius (except Celsus, D. xlvi 3 fr 71 § 2, which see).

In lay writers the former is found in Cic. *Verr.* iii 60 § 139 *Scandilium cogis sponsionem acceptam facere*; Catull. 36, 16 *Acceptum face redditumque votum*; Plin. *Ep.* ii 4 *Acceptum fieri* (or *ferri?*); vi 34 *acc. fieri. Acceptum ferre* in lay writers is used only of book-keeping 'to credit'; cf. Plin. *NH.* xxxiv 138 *culpa ejus non naturae fiat accepta.* See Append. on *Litt. obligatio*; and Erman *Röm. Quittungen* p. 25 sq.

Accepto (probably a predicative dative) *facere, fieri, ferre, rogare* are found in the law writers in the same sense as *acceptum facere, etc.* of a verbal release. In two places only of the Digest (xxxv 2 fr 15 § 6; xlvi 3 fr 96 § 3 both from Papinian) *accepto facere* is used of simple crediting (*Vocab. Jur. Rom.* s.v. *accipio*).

conditionally by another, could release the former without losing the right of claiming it from the other if the condition arose (D. xlv 1 fr 56 § 8).

A son under power, as he can put himself under an obligation by promising in reply to a stipulation, so is capable of putting the question to obtain a formal release: his father is not put under a direct civil obligation by his son's promise and therefore is not required to effect the release, but is freed as well as his son. Similarly a slave can obtain a formal release from an obligation touching his *peculium*, and it is good to bar any suit *de peculio, etc.* against his master. A slave common to two masters can by express words obtain a release for one of his masters even on a debt due from him to the other. A slave of a fructuary or of a vacant inheritance can also obtain a release for the fructuary or for the inheritance (fr 8 §§ 1, 2, 4, fr 11 § 1). But a slave cannot give a release even by his master's order (fr 22), nor a woman without her guardian's authority (Gai. iii 171). A procurator can neither give nor obtain a release for his principal without a mandate (fr 3).

Whether a release of part of an obligation was good was a subject of doubt in Gaius' time (iii 170); later it appears to have been decided in the affirmative, provided the object was materially or ideally divisible. Thus if ten were due, five (or half) could be released: if a slave was due, a share could be released as is done when one heir of a promiser receives a release (fr 9, 10). A predial easement was not divisible: a usufruct of a farm was divisible in the sense that after release of a part, the usufruct continued in the remainder of the farm. But neither a usufruct nor a right of road was itself deemed to be part of the ownership, and therefore if a farm was due, the release of either of them was wholly ineffective. When a stipulation was for the usufruct, a release of the use was good[1], as that can exist without the usufruct. If one who had stipulated

[1] The result would be that the *fructus* could not be exercised; for *fructus sine usu esse non potest.* Accordingly a legacy of *fructus sine usu* was invalid, and an ademption of the use after a legacy of the usufruct was, according to Aristo, of no efficacy—a decision accepted by Ulpian as *benignior* (D. vii 8 fr 14 § 1).

for the transfer (*dari*) of a slave, without particularising, releases the promiser from transferring Stichus, the release extinguishes the obligation, for the transfer of Stichus would have been a good discharge of the stipulation. If the stipulation was for Stichus or ten pounds on a certain condition, the release of the promiser from giving Stichus would not discharge the obligation, if Stichus died before the condition occurred; for then the only obligation would be the payment of ten pounds, and that was not released (fr 13 §§ 1—4, 6; xlv 1 fr 2 § 3).

This formal release applied strictly only to verbal obligations. If the obligation was otherwise created, such a release had no effect in strict law, but founded a plea of fraud or bargain agreed (fr 8 § 3, fr 19 pr). But by novation any obligation can be made a verbal one, and then a formal release can be given. Again, if a guardian or caretaker of a madman or a procurator desires to release a debt due to his principal, he cannot do so directly because it is not in his own but in his principal's name; he can however novate the obligation, and then release it: and the same plan can be adopted to release an obligation due from the madman or other principal (Gai. iii 170; D. *ib.* fr 13 § 10).

In this way a general release might be made of all claims by first collecting them in a stipulation and then releasing them. A form for this purpose is stated to have been composed by Gallus Aquilius. We have it in the shape of a written record. 'Whatever you are or shall be bound to give 'me or do for me, whether due now or not until a future day, 'and for whatever things I have or shall have an action against 'you or claim to get or exact from you, and what of mine you 'have, hold, or possess; so much money as each thing of these 'things shall be worth Aulus Agerius stipulated, Numerius 'Negidius engaged should be given him. What Num. Negidius 'promised or engaged to give to Aulus Agerius, Num. Negidius 'asked A. Agerius whether he had received it from him. Aulus 'Agerius treated it as received to the credit of Num. Negidius' (fr 18; cf. Just. iii. 29 § 2). Such a proceeding was in practice in cases of compromise (*transactio*). However general the words, claims not intended to be released are not released (D. ii 15 fr 4; cf. fr 9 § 1).

A promise of services by a freedman on oath was held capable (without novation) of release by this form (fr 13 pr). Such a promise was part of the old civil law, as was *acceptilatio.*

10. Quittance or Receipt.

Quite different from *acceptilatio,* which required oral question and answer, was a quittance (*apocha*), *i.e.* a document given on receipt of money in such words as *accepi,* or *persolutum, numeratum habeo,* the latter being probably confined to freemen who alone could be said *habere* in a full legal sense (cf. D. xlv 1 fr 38 § 6). Such a quittance was merely evidence of payment: a formal release was a complete discharge in itself without payment or performance (D. xlvi 4 fr 19 § 1), just as in book-keeping *acceptum ferre* or *referre,* from which use comes (oral) *acceptilatio,* discharged the book obligation created by *expensum ferre* (see p. 65).

An instance of a quittance on receipt of money (probably a loan) is given in D. xlvi 3 fr 89 pr. *Titius Maevius dico me accepisse et habere et accepto tulisse a Gaio Titio reliquum omne ratione posita ejus pecuniae quam mihi Stichus Gaii Titii servus caverat.* 'I T. M. declare that I have received and have and 'have carried to credit from G. T. all the balance on the account 'of the money which Stichus his slave had acknowledged to 'be due.'

As examples of a quittance or receipt may be taken those found in 1875 in a box at Pompeii (and now fully and carefully edited by Zangemeister in a supplement to *Corp. I. L.* vol. iv[1] (1898). A selection is given in Bruns' *Fontes*). Most are quittances given by various persons to the auctioneer L. Caecilius Jucundus, who had sold for them certain property, had entered into a stipulation for the proceeds, and had paid over to the former owners the full amount either at once or by degrees, less his commission. They are written on wax tablets folded in the regular way and contain (usually) in the inside a statement of

[1] They are discussed by Mommsen *Hermes* xii p. 88 foll.; Bruns *ZRG.* xiii p. 360 foll.; Karlowa *RG.* i 798 foll.; Zangemeister *l.c.* p. 417 foll.; Erman *Römische Quittungen* (1883) p. 5 sqq. and a later discussion in *ZRG.* xxxiii p. 172 sqq.

the vendor's declaration of due receipt and on the outside an autograph acknowledgment of receipt by the vendor (or someone by his order). I give one numbered by Zangemeister xl (= No. 34 ed. Petra; Bruns[6] p. 316).

Internal. HS n IↃↃ ∞ ∞ ∞DLXII *quae pecunia in stipulatum L. Caecili Jucundi venit ob auctionem Tulliae Lampuridis mercede minus persoluta habere se dixsit Tullia Lampyris ab L. Caecili(o) Iucundo. Act. Pomp. x. k. Januar. Nerone Caesare* II *L. Caesio Marti(ale) cos.*

External. *Nerone Caesare* II[1] *L. Caesio Martiale cos x. k Januarias Sex. Pompeius Axiochus scripsi rogatu Tulliae Lampyridis eam accepisse ab L. Caecilio Iucundo sestia nummum octo [milia] quingenti sexages dupundius*[2] *ob auctionem ejus ex interrogatione facta tabellarum signatarum.*

Affixed are eight seals, one being that of Sex. Pomp. Axiochus.

Int. 'Tullia Lampuris said that she had 8562 sesterces 'fully paid, less the commission, by L. Caecilius Jucundus which 'money came into stipulation with L. Caecilius Jucundus on 'account of the auction sale of Tullia Lampyris. Done at 'Pompeii 23 Dec. A.D. 57[3].'

[1] *Act(um) Pompeis* is here (at the end of a line) inserted subsequently.

[2] A blunder of the slave for *quingentos sexaginta duos* (Mommsen).

[3] In the external writing I should translate *ex interrogatione, etc.* 'in 'accordance with the stipulation made (by her and recorded) in the sealed 'tablets,' the stipulation being one made by the vendor with the auctioneer (cf. D. xlvi 3 fr 88), and loosely called in the inner writing 'Jucundus' stipulation,' as being one in which he took part (as promiser). Cf. *e.g.* D. xxvii 9 fr 5 § 6. Mommsen, Zangemeister and Bruns understand *stipulatum* of Jucundus' stipulation with the purchasers. This seems to me (and to Karlowa) to have nothing properly to do with this receipt. It could thus be only a roundabout way of describing the amount realised by the sale. But further, did an auctioneer really make a stipulation for every separate item in the sale, or at least with every purchaser for the total amount of his purchases? I doubt it. Delivery only against payment, or to well-known purchasers on credit, as nowadays, seems to me the safer and more likely course of business.

Mommsen, Zangemeister and Karlowa take the interior writing to be the record of an *acceptilatio*. I agree with Bruns and Erman (so also Benno Trese in *ZRG.* xxxi p. 255) in rejecting this view and taking it to be

11. *PACTUM DE NON PETENDO*[1].

(*a*) A bargain not to sue had practically, at least in many respects, the same effect as a formal release and required no formality. The plea of 'bargain agreed' was fatal to the suit. The bargain might be *in rem* or *in personam*, *i.e.* might be couched in general words 'not to sue for a particular debt' or might be special to a particular person, 'not to sue Titius for the debt': but the fact that a person was named in the bargain was not conclusive as to the promise being confined to him. All depended on the intention: the words were not interpreted as strictly as if it were a stipulation. As a rule a promise not to sue Titius is no hindrance to a suit against Titius' heir, nor a promise that '*I* will not sue Titius' any hindrance to my heir's suing him (D. ii 14 fr 7 § 8, 57 § 1).

(*b*) The benefit of these agreements, as of stipulations, is as a rule confined to the parties making them. If I bargain that you do not sue Titius, or that you do not sue me or Titius, Titius has no right to plead the bargain, even if he become my heir. And as I am not named in the former bargain, I have no plea either, even if you sue me on his account (fr 17 § 4, 21 § 2). But a son under power or a slave (or a *bona fide serviens*) can bargain that his father or master be not sued,

a simple acknowledgment of receipt. My reasons are: (1) an *acceptilatio* (*i.e. veluti imaginaria solutio* Gai. iii 169) was not required and was probably very unusual, when actual payment of the full sum was made in a simple case of loan, sale, lease, *etc.*, and not in a complicated matter involving a variety of claims (cf. D. xlvi 3 fr 80 *vel re vel verbis*—not both); (2) *habere acceptum* or *facere acceptum* appear to be the technical words in an *acceptilatio*, not, as in these tablets, *numerata* or *persoluta habere*, which indeed are the natural words for a receipt of actual money to close a transaction as opposed to receipt of money as a loan, *habere* being opposed to *debere* (cf. Bruns[6] no. 127); (3) The external writing is more naturally taken to refer to the same acts of payment and receipt as the internal, and not as a distinct acknowledgment of receipt superadded to the formal release. *Ex interrogatione* may well refer, as I have taken it, to *stipulatum* mentioned in the internal writing (cf. D. xlv 1 fr 1 §§ 1—3; iii 5 fr 6), but could hardly stand for *acceptilatio*, when the internal writing has no allusion to any 'question' for that purpose.

[1] Some such bargain appears to be alluded to in Cic. *Rosc. Com.* 9 § 26 *Dic pactionem fecisse* (*Roscium*) *ut absolveretur: non pepigit.*

and the bargain is good, whether it relate to contracts made with them or with himself. If a son under power bargain for himself not to be sued, it avails to bar an action against his father *de peculio* or *de in rem verso* or as defender of his son, or a suit against his father's heir, so long as the son is alive, but after the son's death the plea is no longer available. The bargain of a slave for no suit to be brought against himself is of no force, but his master will have a right to a plea of fraud. If he bargain in general terms, *i.e.* that no suit be brought in the matter, then the plea of bargain agreed is available for his master and his master's heir. If a father or master bargain against any suit being brought against his son or slave, it is good not for his son or slave, but only if he himself be sued on their account: if a father bargain against any suit against himself or his son, his son will be only able to use the plea of fraud. *His qui in nostra potestate sunt paciscendo prodesse non possumus* (fr 17 § 7—fr 21 § 2).

(*c*) A debtor's bargain in general terms for no suit to be brought in the matter bars a suit against his surety, for, as he is liable to his surety on the mandate, he has an interest to that extent. Similarly bargains against suit, made in general terms by one of a number of joint promisers or bank-partners, bar actions against the others. But a bargain by surety or cosurety for no suit to be brought bars suit against himself only, there being no interest in him to support a bar to suit against the principal debtor or his cosureties. If however the intention was to bar suits against them also, a plea of fraud can be used (fr 21 § 5—fr 26, 32). On the other hand the indirect interest of the principal debtor was after some dispute held to bar a suit against surety, where debtor had bargained directly for this and not even named himself (fr 27 § 1). A ward's bargain against suit, made even without his guardian's authority, is good; and so also a caretaker's bargain is good on behalf of a madman or spendthrift (fr 28 pr § 1), and a guardian's on behalf of his ward (fr 15). A procurator's bargain against a suit creates for his principal a plea of fraud (fr 10 § 2).

(*d*) The burden of such bargains is still more strictly confined to the person making them. Neither a joint stipulator nor a bank partner agreeing not to sue, whether *ne ipse petat* or (in general terms) *ne petatur*, bars a suit by the other stipulators or partners. An agreement by a son or slave *ne ipse petat* is worthless, for he cannot sue in his own person; an agreement *ne petatur* bars a suit by the father or master, only if it relate to the *peculium* of which the son or slave has full power of management, and if it be made in consideration of adequate advantage, and not by way of mere gift (fr 27 pr, 28 § 2). In the case of an insult to the son, who as well as his father, has an action *injuriarum*, he can bar his own suit, but not that of his father (fr 30 pr). A procurator's agreement not to sue bars his principal, if the procurator have full general powers, or have a special mandate for this purpose, and be not a mere representative in an action (fr 10 § 2—fr 13). A ward's bargain not to sue is of course invalid without his guardian's authority (fr 28 pr). And so is a like bargain made by a care-taker on behalf of his ward (fr 28 § 1).

(*e*) A bargain against a suit for future fraud or theft or injurious insult is not good, but a bargain against suit for past offences is good (fr 27 §§ 3, 4).

A bargain against suit can be revoked by a subsequent bargain, except in the case of a suit *injuriarum* or theft, which are killed altogether by a bargain not to sue (fr 17 § 1, 27 § 2).

(*f*) An agreement not to sue may be inferred, as for instance if a bond be returned to the debtor; but the like inference cannot be drawn from the mere return of a pledge (fr 2 § 1, fr 3). If I stipulate from a slave for a debt due from Titius, I am understood to agree not to sue Titius, but this is so only if the slave was not a mere surety but had an adequate ground for undertaking the obligation (*e.g.* because he owed Titius as much) so as to make his master responsible *de peculio* (fr 30 § 1). One who receives future interest on a loan is taken to agree not to sue for the principal within that time (fr 57 pr). A formal release (*acceptilatio*), if invalid as such, may yet be taken as an agreement against suit (fr 27 § 9).

A bargain not to sue for ten pounds, when I have stipulated for either ten pounds or the slave Stichus, is properly a bar to my suing on the stipulation at all, just as much as if I had received payment or brought suit or given a release for one of the alternatives. But if the bargain was understood between us to negative only suit for ten pounds, I can sue for Stichus without being barred by the plea. A bargain not to sue for an inheritance is good against any suit for its components (fr 27 §§ 6, 8).

(*g*) Such words as *rogavit Titius spopondit Maevius* are often found subjoined to a record of a bargain; and generally mean that a stipulation was made; and consequently an action on the stipulation arises, special proof being required to shew that a formless agreement only was intended (fr 7 § 12). Where a bargain not to sue is followed by a stipulation for a penalty on breach, and the promiser sues, the stipulator can either sue for the penalty or (at his choice) meet promiser with a plea of 'bargain agreed,' but must then release the stipulation (fr 10 § 1).

(*h*) As in some cases already mentioned, a plea of fraud is often available where parties are not entitled to plead a bargain. Thus where a bargain with creditors is made by an own heir before meddling with an inheritance, or by an outsider, or slave made unconditionally free, before entrance on an inheritance, the bargain can be well pleaded against suit by the creditors. But if the slave is made heir conditionally, his bargain is null; for what is done while in slavery is not as a rule good for him as a freeman. He can however use a plea of fraud. So also (as was held after some doubt) can a son under power who made such a bargain and entered on an (outsider's) inheritance after emancipation, or who bargained with his father's creditors while his father was yet alive (fr 7 §§ 17, 18).

B. *Litterarum obligatio*[1].

Besides verbal contracts made by stipulation and promise, the Romans had another form of strict obligation which arose from book-keeping. Gaius is our only trustworthy source of

[1] See full explanation in Appendix (p. 279): also the Essay on Cic. *pro Q. Rosc. Comoedo*.

direct information, and he treats it very shortly. The obligation was made by book entries of transfer (*nominibus transcripticiis*). The transfer might be *a re in personam*, when a debt on account of purchase or hire or partnership was entered as if it had been money paid out; or it might be *a persona in personam*, when Titius gets you to undertake his debt to me, and I in the same way enter it in my books, as if I had paid out the money to you instead of to Titius. That is to say, taking the first case, I have you in my books entered as owing me money for a farm, which I have sold you or leased to you, or for my share of the profits of some joint transaction. I close this account and enter the amount against you as debtor for a liquidated sum of money, of course with your agreement (else how could there be a contract?). In the second case I close the account against Titius and enter the amount against you as a debtor, instead of against him, he having, as the Romans said, delegated you to me, in other words got you to promise to pay me and got me to accept you as a debtor instead of him. There is in each case a transfer from the existing account to another, and this transfer creates a new obligation[1] wholly independent of the previous obligation and resting simply on the book entry against you. Actual cash loans (*arcaria nomina*) though entered in the creditor's books derive their obligation from the payment of the money: the book entry is then only evidence. In the case of *litterarum obligatio*, it is unimportant whether any money has been actually paid. The entry in the ledger, declaring the fact of debt and disclosing no special cause, is in itself the cause and only cause of obligation. It supplies a formal element distinguishing it from a pact, and binds the debtor as much as he would have been bound by the words of promise in reply to a spoken stipulation. The parties were not required to meet to make the entry. Suit would be brought as for *certa credita pecunia* (cf. Cic. *Rosc. Com.* 5 § 14).

[1] In both cases there appears clearly to be a change analogous to that of novation, but Gaius uses that term only of stipulations: nor does he mention the extinction of the former debt *acceptilatione*, no doubt because this expression in his time applied to a *verbal* release. See p. 55.

There was a doubt among the lawyers whether this was so specifically a Roman form of obligation as not to be open to foreigners. Nerva (the lawyer) held that it was not open to them: Sabinus and Cassius held that foreigners could be bound by the former class of transfers (*a re in personam*)[1], but not by the latter. *Arcaria nomina* were of course applicable to foreigners as much as to Romans.

Gaius notes that *litterarum obligatio* is a phrase which might be used of a written acknowledgment of debt, or promise to pay, such as the *chirographa* ('notes of hand,' *i.e.* autographs), and *syngraphae*[2] ('bonds,' 'agreements') of the Greeks. In his time probably these were frequent, and the custom of relying on a book entry only had dropped out of regular use.

C. 1. *Mutuum.*

(*a*) *Mutuum* is cash-loan, *i.e.* a loan of money (*pecunia numerata*) or of other things lying in weight, count or measure[3], such as wine, oil, corn, bronze, silver, gold. The principle of the contract is that they are counted, measured or weighed over to the borrower and become his property, with the obligation of

[1] This might be considered as a mere restatement of the debt and hence common to all nations; but the latter involved a change of debtor and required some mutual understanding and custom of a particular community.

[2] Such *syngraphae* are often mentioned by Cicero, *e.g. Fam.* viii 2 § 2; *Att.* v 21 § 11. Their precise character is a matter of doubt. Mitteis (*Reichsrecht* pp. 459—485) holds that the term was specially, though not exclusively, applied to debt-agreements which of themselves proved the debt, whether the money had passed or not. But he rests much on Pseudo-Ascon. *ad Verr.* ii 1 § 91, a writer whom I believe to have had no independent knowledge either of law or business; and I doubt the word in itself having such special meaning.

[3] Such things are often called by a mediaeval term 'fungibles,' derived from such expressions as D. xii 1 fr 2 § 1 *in genere suo functionem recipiunt per solutionem quam specie* 'they admit of discharge by payment in kind rather than specifically.' Savigny (*Syst.* vi p. 123) calls them 'quantities,' quoting D. xxx fr 34 § 3 where *corpus* and *quantitas* are contrasted; vii 1 fr 15 § 4; xlvi 3 fr 94 § 1. So too in a constitution of Gordian. ap. *Jur. Antejust.* iii p. 233 *debitores quantitatum debitarum.*

returning at some time the same count of money, measure of corn, weight of silver, *etc.*, but not the identical coins or corn or silver (Gai. iii 90). The contract is of a different character from *commodatum*, the loan of an article which is to be carefully used and itself restored[1]. In that case the owner, besides having an action on the loan, can vindicate the thing itself. But in *mutuum* it matters not whether the coins or wheat, *etc.* lent exist or not, whether they are still with the borrower or not, their free use or consumption is intended or expected, or is at any rate indifferent to the lender: his right is not thereby affected: they have become the property of the borrower, and the risk of loss or robbery is his: the lender's claim is to have these or other coins or other wheat, of the like fineness and count or weight, made over to him in due time in full ownership (D. xii 1 fr 3).

(*b*) This kind of loan involves and requires a transfer of property, and consequently, besides the intention to contract and convey, there must be delivery actual or constructive of the money or other thing lent. Physical transfer for this purpose by the lender as owner of the money was not always necessary (see vol. I p. 458): if a man has money of mine deposited with him, I can authorise him to use it and sue him as on a loan (D. xii 1 fr 9 § 9). Further it was held in practice that, if my debtor by my order paid money to another, I could sue this other for the loan thereby made, although the actual money had never been mine. Where however my agent has collected money on my account and proposes to treat it as a loan to himself, the lawyers differed, Africanus holding that there was no loan but only an obligation on mandate, Ulpian declaring for a loan (D. xii 1 fr 15; xvii 1 fr 34 pr). And the like difference is found where a man intending a loan, but not having the cash, hands over some article to sell[2] and use the proceeds as a loan (D. xii 1

[1] The two kinds of loan are both named in Cato *RR.* 5 § 3 *satui semen, cibaria, far, vinum, oleum mutuum dederit (vilicus) nemini. Duas aut tres familias habeat unde utenda roget et quibus det.*

[2] The plan of a sale was adopted sometimes by usurers in order to avoid the usury laws. The usurer sold something to the borrower at a high value and at once repurchased it from him at a low value and gave

fr 11 pr; xvii 1 fr 34 pr; cf. xxiv 1 fr 3 § 12; Savigny *Syst.* iv p. 594).

(*c*) But further it came to be recognised as a general rule that if a man pay his own money to some one as being my money and as a loan on my account, whether I have actually requested him to advance it in the particular instance, or am absent and ignorant of the matter, I can sue the recipient on the loan (D. xii 1 fr 9 § 8; cf. tit. 6 fr 53). This is stated broadly by Paul: *plane si liber homo nostro nomine pecuniam daret vel suam vel nostram ut nobis solveretur* (*i.e.* with the instruction to repay me) *obligatio nobis pecuniae creditae acquireretur* (D. xlv 1 fr 126 § 2; cf. Cod. iv 27 fr 3). It is in fact the ordinary case of a banker making investments for his customer whether he happen to have at the time and to use money which has passed through his customer's hands or not: *cottidie credituri pecuniam mutuam ab alio poscimus ut nostro nomine creditor numeret futuro debitori nostro* (xii 1 fr 9 § 8) 'it is an every day occurrence 'that when we are going to make a cash-loan we ask another to 'pay the money as creditor on our account to the person who is 'to be our debtor.'

(*d*) On the other hand, if I profess to make you a loan on my own account and hand over another's money, it does not become your's; there is no cash-loan; the owner can claim the coins. And the same is the result, if a runaway slave or any other slave of mine contrary to my intention hands over my money to you as a loan. I can claim the coins, but I have no action as on a loan. But if you without any fraudulent intent spend (*consumpseris*) the money, it has passed beyond my power of claiming it, and I can sue you for the amount as if I had lent it you and made you owner of the coins. So a ward cannot without his guardian's authority alienate his money for a loan or any other purpose, but if he has done so (or rather professed to do so) and the borrower has spent it, he can sue (by a condiction) just as if the loan were valid (D. xii 1 fr 11 § 2, 13 § 1, 19; tit. 6 fr 29).

him cash, the borrower remaining debtor for the difference in value. This kind of contract was in the middle ages called by an Arabic term *Mohatra*. Pascal refers to it in the eighth of his 'Letters to a Provincial.'

(*e*) The paying or, as the Romans described it, the weighing out[1] (*expendere, dependere*) or counting out (*numerare*) of the money is the ground of the obligation, but the intention of the parties to give and receive as a cash-loan is also necessary to make the contract. (*Non satis est dantis esse nummos et fieri accipientis ut obligatio nascatur, sed etiam hoc animo dari ut obligatio constituatur* D. xliv 7 fr 3 § 1.) If I hand money over to you as a gift or as a deposit, and you receive it as a loan, there is no proper gift or deposit or loan[2]. Again, if you ask for a loan from me and from Titius, and I tell my debtor to promise it you, and you think it is Titius' debtor who promises it, there is no contract between us. But in all these cases, if you spend the money, I can sue for the amount (D. xii 1 fr 18, 32). And the result is similar where the want of agreement between the parties is due to one being insane (though supposed not to be so) or becoming insane before the completion of the contract (fr 12). The completion of the contract dates from the handling of the money by the borrower or from the agreement, whichever is latest. If the agreement was conditional, the occurrence of the condition must be waited for (fr 9 § 9, fr 10, 19 pr).

(*f*) The intention of the parties in thus giving and receiving money would be in some way stated, usually at the time, probably in an oral declaration, then or afterwards reduced to writing, and containing the conditions of the loan. *Omnia, quae inseri stipulationibus possunt, eadem possunt etiam numerationi pecuniae* (D. xii 1 fr 7). Such agreement might fix the condition, if any, on which the money paid should become a loan, the date and place for repayment, the person to whom

[1] In early times the metal was weighed, *asses, semisses, dupondius, etc.* being primarily weights. The *lex Rubria* (B.C. 49—42) describes *mutuum* as *pecunia certa credita signata forma p(ublica) p(opuli) R(omani)*, *i.e.* bearing the public stamp of the Roman people = lawful Roman coin. Cf. D. xviii 1 fr 1 pr.

[2] It was not clear to the lawyers in the Digest, when both parties intended a transfer of ownership but differed as to the ground (*e.g.* one intending to make a gift, the other taking as a loan), whether the ownership of the money passed. Julian said it did (D. xli 1 fr 36): Ulpian inclined to think it did not (D. xii 1 fr 18 pr *magisque, etc.*).

it should be repaid; but it could not fix a larger sum to be repaid than the amount actually paid; for the contract would be *nudum pactum* as regards the sum; but it might fix a smaller (fr 11 § 1, 22, 40; ii 14 fr 17 pr).

A stipulation was often made to confirm such agreements, and, though good, was held not to novate the obligation arising from the payment, or to constitute a separate contract: the payment whether before or after was regarded as merely supplying content to the verbal obligation (*non duae obligationes nascuntur sed una verborum* Paul). And if the payment was not accepted, a stipulation made in anticipation had no effect. If payment had been made and for some cause or other the stipulation proved to be invalid, it was possible to fall back on the payment, and enforce the natural obligation thence arising (D. xii 1 fr 9 §§ 4, 5, fr 40; xlv 1 fr 126 § 2; xlvi 2 fr 6 § 1, fr 7; Cod. viii 37 fr 3; cf. xliv 7 fr 44 § 6). Where a ward received a loan without his guardian's authority, the lender could not recover, until Ant. Pius by a rescript granted him an action to recover so far as the ward was at the time of the action thereby enriched (D. xxvi 8 fr 5 pr; xlvi 3 fr 47 pr).

(*g*) A cash-loan did not carry interest unless special stipulation was made (D. xix 5 fr 24). Just as other real actions contemplated originally only the return of the thing lent, deposited, or pledged, so a cash-loan by itself contemplated only the return of the same quantity, and therefore interest could not become due on a mere bargain, as if it were part and detail of the loan (D. xxii 1 fr 41 § 2 probably relates to some provincial loan.)

(*h*) In early Roman times a loan of money, or rather of metal not properly coined, was made with the bronze and balance as in mancipation, they being necessary to ascertain the amount, and the accompanying declaration shewing the nature of the transaction. This was called *nexum*[1]. If the debtor made default in due repayment, his person was liable to be seized, and he was compelled, legally or practically, to work for his creditor. Admission of the debt was equivalent to judgment.

In later times the technical term in describing a suit for

[1] See Appendix (p. 296).

a loan of money appears to have been *pecunia certa credita*[1] (Lex Rubr. 21; Gai. iv 171). By a *lex Silia* a summary mode was introduced for recovery of a sum of money certain (*certa pecunia*), 30 days' notice (*condictio*) of trial being substituted for the old sacramental procedure (Gai. iv 18, 19), and this summary procedure was probably applied[2] to loans of money (*certa credita pecunia*). From the position of the title *de jurejurando* in the Digest (xii 2) and from the rubrics of Paul *Sent.* ii 1 *de rebus creditis et de jurejurando* and of Cod. iv 1, it is generally inferred that plaintiff could put defendant on his oath as to the fact of the loan or of its repayment; and probably this was the leading use of compulsory oaths[3]. Further the defendant, if defeated, might be mulcted in a penalty of one-third of the money lent (in addition to the sum itself), by being forced at the commencement of the suit to wager on the justice of his cause. The plaintiff would have to submit to a restipulation to the same effect (Gai. iv 13, 171). The *lex Calpurnia* extended the summary procedure to suits for any definite thing (*de omni certa re*). The oath was probably admissible in this case also (so said in D. xii 2 fr 34 pr), but the wager was not (cf. Gai. iv 19).

This action by summary notice was called *condictio* and was the regular action in the case of cash-loans or other claims for money certain, whether based on payment, or on book credit, or on stipulation (Cic. *Rosc. Com.* 4, 5 §§ 10—15; D. xii 1 fr 24).

(*j*) Defendant if sued on his bond (*cautio*, *i.e.* record of stipulation) when he had not received the money, could plead the non-payment (*exceptio non numeratae pecuniae*) and then

[1] The expression (without *pecunia*) occurs in Quintil. *Inst.* iv 2 § 61; viii 3 § 14 (speaking of the difference of style required from an advocate in different causes) *an non pudeat certam creditam periodis postulare aut circa stillicidia affici aut in mancipii redhibitione sudare;* xii 10 § 70. *Certa credita pecunia* is in Quintil. iv 2 § 6. Cf. Lenel *EP.* p. 186. In *lex Julia munic.* 44 the procedure for recovering a loan (*uti de pecunia credita judicium dari oporteret*) is applied to the recovery of expenses to which a town was put in discharging duties neglected by individual citizens, *e.g.* cleaning the streets.

[2] Karlowa argues against it (*RG.* ii 594).

[3] Cf. D. xii 2 fr 14 and note on *abjurare* Book VI chap. iii; Demelius *Schiedseid* p. 73.

the plaintiff had to prove payment. This plea is mentioned as early as the Antonines (Cod. iv 30 fr 1, 3); and a like plea was allowed when the amount named in the bond was larger than the sum actually lent: the creditor could recover only the latter sum (Cod. *ib.* fr 2). Where a liquidated sum of money was acknowledged in writing (*chirographum*) to be due, though not actually paid down, and there was a just cause of debt, this plea was not good (fr 5). A plea of fraud (*doli*) was also available, but that threw the burden of proof on the defendant (*ib.* 13, Gai. iv 116 *a*; D. xliv 4 fr 2 § 1).

The bond on payment was usually destroyed or given up to the debtor, but its retention whole gave the creditor no rights, if the debt had been fully paid, nor did its loss defeat his right, if the debt was not paid (Const. of Severus and Antoninus in Cod. Greg. iv = *Jur. Antejust.* iii 232).

2. INTEREST ON LOANS.

Interest may be defined as the amount to be paid to the lender for the use of his money, and for the risk which he runs of not being repaid. It was called *faenus*[1] or *usurae* (sometimes *usura* sing.): *faenebris pecunia* is money on loan at interest. The capital is usually called *sors*.

The strict action on a money loan was for repayment of the capital sum lent, and, as has been said above, did not carry with it any claim for interest. A stipulation was required in order to create an obligation for this, and if the capital was stipulated for at the same time, still the two obligations were distinct: the claim for the capital was for an ascertained amount (*certum*); that for the interest was dependent on the length of time it remained unpaid, and consequently was, at the time of stipulation, for an unascertained amount (*incertum*, Paul ii 14 § 1; D. xix 5 fr 24; xlv 1 fr 75 § 9).

It appears to have been sometimes the practice to fix a near day (next Kalends ?) for the repayment of the capital, and, as a penalty for the non-repayment of the capital on that day, to

[1] Cf. Plaut. *Asin.* 243 *Interii si non invenio ego illas viginti minas...Si mutuas non potero, certumst sumam fenore; Pseud.* 286 *Si amabas, invenires mutuom; ad danistam devenires, adderes fenusculum.*

stipulate for interest at so much per month (30 days), which might be made to run either from that day or from the day of the stipulation. At other times we find stipulation to be made for repayment on demand (*qua die petierit*). Sometimes the capital was to be repaid by instalments, and then interest would only run for the unpaid instalments, as they became due. Action for the loan or an instalment would not stop the interest continuing to run, that being conditioned on due payment or on satisfaction not having been made (D. xii 1 fr 40; xlv 1 fr 90, 126 § 2; Bruns no. 127). Tender of payment when due prevents interest running (see pp. 53, 54). For some purposes interest on money was put in the same class as *fructus* (D. xxii 1 fr 34): but *in fructu non est, quia non ex ipso corpore sed alia causa est, id est nova obligatione* (D. L 16 fr 121).

The rate of interest was fixed by the stipulation. It was not unusual to fix a lower rate of interest for punctual payment and an increased rate if payment were delayed. If payments on the lower rate continued for a time to be made and accepted when the higher rate might have been demanded, a bargain was presumed for the lower rate to continue. And when punctual payments for some years had been made, a bond providing for retrospective increase of the rate in case of unpunctuality was (by a rescript of M. Antoninus) not allowed to be enforced (D. xxii 1 fr 9 § 1, 12, 13 pr, 17 pr; Cod. iv 32 fr 5, 8). Delay exists as soon as claim has been made on the debtor in a suitable place for payment and payment has not been made (D. xxii 1 fr 32 pr).

The fact of stipulation for interest having been duly made admits of proof, even if it should not have been mentioned in the bond (Cod. iv 32 fr 1, 7). If no stipulation has been made, but interest has been paid as agreed, the money cannot be reclaimed or set against capital, unless in excess of the legal rate. And a pledge can be retained, until interest has been paid, though the agreement has not been confirmed by a stipulation (Cod. fr 3, 4). Loans by municipalities did not require a stipulation (D. xxii 1 fr 30); nor was it required for the demand of an accession in the nature of interest, in case of a loan of corn or barley (Cod. fr 11).

A maximum rate of interest was laid down by law. By the XII tables the maximum was one-twelfth of the principal (*unciarium fenus*), *i.e.* 8⅓ per cent. (Tac. *Ann.* vi 16). The history of the subject is obscure[1], but in the times of Cicero and of the Antonines the maximum was one per cent. per month of 30 days (*usurae centesimae*), *i.e.* 12 per cent. per annum. This was 'statutable interest' (*legitima usura*). Any agreement for interest above this rate was void as regards the excess (by a rescript of Severus), and the excess if paid went in diminution of the principal: if the principal was repaid, the surplus interest (or the principal itself, if repaid after being already covered by surplus interest) could be recovered as *indebitum* (Paul ii 14 § 2; D. xii 6 fr 26 pr; xxii 1 fr 29). Five per cent. and four per cent. or even less are also mentioned as usual in some cases and districts; and 'statutable interest' regarded as heavy (D. xxvi 7 fr 7 § 10).

Compound interest was forbidden altogether by Justinian, who tells us it was forbidden by ancient laws but ineffectually (Cod. iv 32 fr 28; vii 54 fr 3 pr)[2]. In the time of the Antonines interest left to accumulate and compound interest, together exceeding the amount of the capital, could neither be stipulated for nor exacted. The excess if paid could be recovered (D. xii 6 fr 26 § 1; Cod. iv 32 fr 10).

[1] Livy mentions (B.C. 347) *Semunciarium tantum ex unciario fenus factum;* a temporary measure? (vii 27 § 3); in B.C. 342 *Invenio apud quosdam L. Genucium trib. pl. tulisse ad plebem ne fenerare liceret* (vii 42 § 1). The restrictions on lending at interest which applied to loans made by Romans were extended in B.C. 193 to loans made by any of the allies or Latins to Romans (Liv. xxxv 7 § 5). Tacitus (*Ann.* vi 16) apparently refers to these statements. Cato (*RR.* 1) says *majores nostri sic habuerunt et ita in legibus posiverunt furem dupli condemnari, feneratorem quadrupli.* We know no more of this. Probably it was penalty for exceeding *unciarium fenus.*

[2] Cicero in his provincial edict for Cilicia said he should allow *centesimas cum anatocismo anniversario, i.e.* 12 per cent. per annum with annual rests (Att. v 21 § 11). In the case there related of a loan by Brutus and others to the Salaminians in Cyprus, the bond was drawn for 48 per cent. A decree of the senate about this time forbad compound interest (*ib.* § 13), but whether it was a general prohibition or limited to certain places or transactions we do not know.

3. *Trajecticia pecunia.*

The maximum rate of interest might be exceeded lawfully in loans on bottomry (*trajecticia pecunia*), *i.e.* when money is lent for a mercantile adventure beyond sea, on the condition of repayment only if the ship got safe to its destination. The creditor's risk in this case justifies a higher than the usual rate of interest, and no limit was put to *nauticum fenus* or *usurae maritimae* (Paul ii 14 § 3): but the higher rate was allowable only for the period over which the creditor's risk in the voyage extended. It was usual for the creditor to send a slave in the vessel to watch the shipper's proceedings and demand, if necessary by process of law, repayment of the loan as agreed. If the money and interest were not forthcoming on the agreed day, it was usual for further interest to be paid at a rate not exceeding 12 per cent. for the time after the goods had got safe, and also, by way of penalty, a sum per day for the slave's services (who might have to wait some time in a distant port), both amounts to be reckoned from the due date, the amount for services not to exceed the amount of legitimate interest[1]. The goods first embarked and any goods purchased with the proceeds of sale were pledged for the loan. A stipulation was usually made, but the principal sum could be recovered as a loan, and the additional sum by an action *praescriptis verbis* (see Chap. IV H) on the agreement. The claim for penalty was good on any delay in payment, unless the borrower was free from fault: subsequent offer did not purge the delay (D. xxii 2 fr 4, 7; xliv 7 fr 23; cf. xlv 1 fr 122 § 1; xix 5 fr 24).

[1] *Quod in singulos dies in stipulatum deductum est ad finem centesimae non ultra duplum debetur. In stipulatione faenoris post diem periculi separatim interposita, quod in ea legitimae usurae deerit, per alteram stipulationem operarum supplebitur* (Papin. in D. xxii 2 fr 4 § 1): *i.e.* 'the amount 'stipulated for the slave's services must not do more than double the 'interest at the maximum rate, unless a lower rate is agreed for interest, in 'which case the amount for services may be increased up to the limit afore-'said.' It is not clear whether each payment (for interest and for services) is limited by the amount of the maximum rate or both payments together. Ihering *Jahrb.* xix p. 16 takes the former view. Sieveking (*Das Seedarlehen* 1893, p. 44) with others takes *duplum* to mean double of the capital sum lent; as *supra duplum* in D. xii 6 fr 26 § 1.

Some other conditions of a similar character are mentioned as occurring in loans: *e.g.* loan to a fisherman for apparatus, payment to be dependent on a catch of fish: loan to an athlete for training expenses, to be repaid if he won in the contest. In these cases also a bargain (*pactum*) would suffice to support an addition to the amount of the loan as compensation for risk (D. xxii 2 fr 5).

Loan on bottomry differed in several ways from an ordinary loan of money (*mutua pecunia*): for in the latter the creditor's claim was absolute or at least not dependent on the result of the debtor's employment of the money; the rate of interest was limited by law; the action a *condictio certi*; and interest was not recoverable except on a separate stipulation.

D. *Condictiones.*

Condiction was a form of legal procedure, as mentioned above, first applied to the recovery of a loan of a definite sum of money, and afterwards applied to a loan of other things ('fungibles') where the return of the loan was required in quantity and quality, but not the identical things; in fact, where the borrower undertook to repay not *this*, but *so much* of the article and quality received. When condiction was applied to such things, it was said to be called *triticaria* ('relating to wheat') from one of the most important subjects, but this action (*condictio triticaria*) was afterwards extended so as to include all cases where things certain, other than coined money, were redemanded (D. xiii 3 fr 1). In practice the term *triticaria* was not used, or Justinian has cut it out.

The characteristic of the situation was that the property in the thing had been the lender's and had passed to the borrower. Whether the borrower retained the thing or consumed it or spent it was immaterial: vindication was not applicable, for whether the thing existed or not, it was no longer the lender's, but he had a right to an equivalent. An analogous situation occurred when money had been paid for a purpose not afterwards realized; or had been paid under the belief that it was due when it really was not; or when it had got into the hands and ownership of someone without any real or sufficient ground at all; or when the purpose for which it was given was so unlawful or disgraceful that the law could not regard the recipient as entitled to retain it. The conditions under which a condiction is allowed are much the same as those which justify a plea of fraud (*exceptio doli*). In other words, where unfair enrichment, if it took place, would give rise to a condiction, a plea of fraud is allowed to prevent its taking place (cf. D. xliv 4 fr 2 § 3, fr 7, *etc.*).

Nor was either the inequitable situation or the remedy by condiction confined to cases where money or other fungibles had passed. If any defined thing had under such circumstances passed from the ownership of *A* to the ownership of *B*, *A* had a condiction to recover it (*repetere*), whether the ground was bad or insufficient originally, or turned out to be bad or to fail. *Constat id demum posse condici alicui quod vel non ex justa causa ad eum pervenit vel redit ad non justam causam* (D. xii 7 fr 1 § 3). If ownership had not passed, condiction was not applicable (D. xii 1 fr 14).

The action was strict in procedure, although resting on an equitable principle (D. xii 1 fr 32; tit. 6 fr 66); and the claim included any profits which had accrued to the receiver from the thing since acceptance of the issue for trial, so that plaintiff should have what he would have had, if defendant had discharged the obligation at that time (D. xii 1 fr 31; tit. 4 fr 7 § 1; tit. 6 fr 15 pr, 65 § 5).

The cases of condiction were referred by the lawyers to four[1] principal heads, not always clearly distinguished from one another.

1. *Condictio ob rem dati, re non secuta*[2], *i.e.* a condiction

[1] A fifth head is found in the rubric of D. xiii 2 *condictio ex lege*, but appears to be due to Tribonian.

[2] The name which I have given is taken from Celsus (in D. xii 4 fr 16) and Paul (*ib.* fr 9 pr, 14; xix 5 fr 5 § 1). In the rubric of D. xii 4 this is called *condictio causa data causa non secuta*, a phrase not elsewhere found and difficult to explain. In Cod. iv 6 the rubric is *de condictione ob causam datorum* which points to the meaning, that the action is for the recovery of what has been given for a purpose which has failed. The

for something handed over for a purpose which has failed, *e.g.* for the emancipation of a son, or manumission of a slave, or for securing a dowry, or settlement of a law suit, or as a condition of acceptance of a legacy or inheritance. If the son or slave is not freed, or the marriage does not take place, or the suit is pressed on, or the inheritance is not accepted, or the will is upset, the money or other property passed can be recovered, as a rule, subject to exception in cases where there is no fault on the recipient's part, and he has not in fact been enriched by the transfer. But if the owner of the slave would have sold him, had it not been for this bargain for his manumission, and he fled or died without there having been any fault or delay on the owner's part, there is no ground for refunding the amount paid. Condiction is also allowed where the event did not fail to follow, but the supposed ground for payment was a mistake, as where the slave who was to be manumitted is found to be a freeman, or the condition of acceptance of a legacy is found to be revoked by a codicil, *etc.* (D. xii 4 fr 1—fr 3 § 7, fr 5 §§ 3, 4). If a formal release was given and the consideration fails, a condiction will lie for the old debt (fr 10). A gift in view of death can be recovered in the same way by the donor on his becoming well again (fr 12).

language in the Digest makes *pecunia* or the like, not *causa*, subject to *data*; see this title fr 1, 14, 16, tit. 5 fr 1, tit. 6 fr 23 § 3, 65 §§ 2, 3; Cod. iv 6 fr 5, 10, *etc.* Yet it is hardly possible to suppose the expression in the rubric to be contracted for *causā (pecuniā) datā causa non secuta.* I have no doubt that it is a corruption for *causā dati, causa n. s.*, so that *condictio dati* is parallel to *condictio indebiti. Causā* is probably to be taken as dependent on *dati* and used absolutely, 'for reason,' 'on a consideration'='*ob causam*': compare *exemplo* in Cic. *Verr.* ii 2, 42 § 102 *dixerat se exemplo fecisse quod fecisset*, 'had done on precedent.' [To take *causā datā* as 'cause declared' would be a very unusual sense of *dare* and not well suited to the conditions of the action. Karlowa (*RG.* ii p. 769) takes *causā* as 'consideration,' but with *datā* it would refer to a different thing in the two clauses: Schilling's suggestion (*Institutionen* iii p. 592 followed by Voigt and Dernburg) that *data* is acc. plural (*dătă*) dependent on *secuta*, is right in meaning, but hardly possible in such a combination of words. Baron (*Condict.* p. 70 sq.) gives an enumeration and criticism of different views. I see there that others have also held the view that *data* is a corruption for *dati.*]

Mere general expectation of kindness or reward in consequence of the transfer is not sufficient to justify a disappointed donor in trying to recover his gift (fr 3 § 7). Nor probably was repentance of an offer or promise or gift sufficient basis for a condiction in Antonine times. (The cases in fr 3 and fr 5 are probably due to Tribonian: see Gradenwitz *Interpol.* § 18; and Lenel *Paling.* ii pp. 390, 391.)

2. *Condictio indebiti.* What has been paid in error as to matter of fact without being due[1] can be recovered from the person to whom it has been paid (Gai. iii 91). Thus if I pay in virtue of a supposed compromise, and the compromise has not been made or has been abandoned or is null, because made after judgment in the suit had been already given (D. xii 6 fr 23 pr, § 1); or if believing myself erroneously to be heir or *bonorum possessor*, I pay a creditor of the estate (fr 19 § 1); or, being freeborn, pay sums as condition of freedom given by will (fr 67 pr); or, being heir, have sold and delivered the inheritance without deducting a debt due to me from the testator (fr 45); or have paid a trust which turns out not to be due (fr 58); or pay a debt due only on an uncertain condition before the condition occur (fr 18, 48); or pay interest on what was supposed to be a debt but was not (fr 26 § 2); or pay (unless fraudulently, D. xlvi 3 fr 50) the wrong thing (fr 19 § 3), or an excessive amount (fr 19 § 4, 31), or pay one who is neither creditor (fr 65 § 9) nor creditor's agent (D. iii 5 fr 5 § 11; xlvi 3 fr 58 pr), and in other cases, I can recover what I have thus unduly paid. And it makes no difference whether I did not owe it at all, or owed it in strict law but had a perpetual plea to protect me (D. xii 6 fr 26 §§ 3, 7); nor whether the money or other thing paid was mine or not: in any case the possession had been transferred and is recoverable by me; unless indeed the owner vindicates the money (fr 15 § 1, 46).

If the excess over the real amount is not separable (*e.g.* in case of a farm) the whole can be recovered, the original obligation reviving in consequence (D. L 17 fr 84; xii 6 fr 26 § 4).

[1] The rules as to the burden of proof given in D. xxii 3 § 5 are generally held to be largely due to Justinian. See Lenel's *Paling.* i 1188 and others.

But mere repentance of a payment, made with eyes open, gives no claim to recovery, though the payment was not due (fr 24, 50, 62; cf. xxii 6 fr 9 § 5). Nor, if a person has received what he is entitled to (*qui suum recepit*), can he be called on to repay it because it was not paid by the true debtor; *e.g.* a legatee receiving his legacy from the inheritance by the hands of one who falsely supposed himself to be the heir (D. xii 6 fr 44; xliv 5 fr 1 § 10). Nor is recovery allowed, if there be a natural justification for the payment, though it may not have been legally enforceable. Such a case is that of a real debtor paying after joinder of issue but before judgment; for even if acquitted he is morally debtor (fr 60 pr); or of payment by a freedman to his master for manumission in accordance with an agreement made by him whilst a slave (fr 13 pr); or of a son under power taking a loan contrary to the *SC. Macedonianum*, and repaying it after he has become independent (fr 40 pr); or of a ward taking a loan without his guardian's authority and repaying it after puberty (fr 13 § 1; xxxvi 1 fr 66 pr); or of a father or master in debt to his son or slave, and paying the debt after the relationship of power has ceased (D. xii 6 fr 38 § 2); or a person paying interest on a loan, though interest had not been stipulated (fr 26 pr); or a debtor paying before the due date, or before the occurrence of a condition which is certain to occur (fr 10, 18, 56); or a father or master paying a debt of his son's or slave's in excess of his *peculium* (fr 11); *etc.*

If a freedman, erroneously thinking he owed services to his patron, paid them, he can bring a condiction for the amount at which the patron would have hired such services, provided they were industrial services; but if they were dutiful, he cannot; for they are natural to the relationship (D. xii 6 fr 26 § 12).

Payments made contrary to the *lex Cincia* were irrecoverable (Vat. 266). So also payments made in execution of a judgment, or of a damnatory legacy, or under the *lex Aquilia*, being for peremptory obligations (Just. iii 27 § 7; D. v 1 fr 74 § 2). The like is true of penalties for crime (D. xii 6 fr 41). Error in law does not form a basis for recovery, except in minors (under 25 years), D. xxii 6 fr 9 § 6.

According to some lawyers' opinions, money paid by mistake

to a woman or ward without guardian's authority, and consequently without raising any obligation, was not recoverable (Gai. iii 91): but a rescript of Ant. Pius gave an action against the ward who had received a loan without authority, to the extent of his enrichment (D. xxvi 8 fr 5 pr).

Payments by a ward without his guardian's authority, or by a madman or spendthrift interdicted from managing his estate, are as a rule recoverable by condiction if spent, by vindication if the moneys remain unspent (D. xii 6 fr 29).

A woman, who has made herself surety and has paid, can recover the money, because the protection given by *SC. Velleianum* is continuous through her life, whilst the *SC. Macedonianum* was intended only to protect persons while under age (fr 40 pr).

If payment was made expressly on behalf of another, this other (if anyone), not the payer, will have the right of recovery (fr 46, 53, 57 pr). Similarly if payments be made to legatees under a will which is afterwards upset, or if the payments be found to be excessive on account of the liabilities of the inheritance proving heavier than was thought at first, or hidden codicils being found which reduced the legacies; or the heir being under 25 years old obtain a cancelling of his acceptance (*in integrum restitutio*), the whole or the excess of the legacies can be recovered from the legatees by the person eventually taking the place of heir. Rescripts of Hadrian and Ant. Pius established this in some cases (fr 2—5; v 2 fr 8 § 16). So if guardians in good faith have paid some creditors of their ward's father, but finding the assets insufficient, have declined the inheritance on their ward's behalf, the other creditors will have the right of recovering the excess paid (xii 6 fr 61).

The person against whom the condiction is brought is as a rule the person who received the money (fr 49), but if the payer acted as a delegate under the wrong belief that he was debtor to the delegator and thereby discharged a debt due from the delegator, he must sue not the payee but the delegator (D. xlvi 2 fr 12). One who, though not his debtor, pays the ward's creditor at the ward's bidding, without the guardian's authority, cannot bring a condiction against the creditor with whom he dealt only on the ward's account, nor against the ward except so far as he was enriched (D. xlvi 3 fr 66). If the payee was entitled on a stipulation to receive but not to keep (*e.g.* Titius in a stipulation *mihi aut Titio*), the condiction must be brought against the stipulator (fr 59). If a man in wrongful possession of another's houses lets them and takes the rents, he is liable on a condiction to the owner; but if he takes rents on lettings made by the owner, the tenant is not discharged and can recover his payments by condiction (fr 55).

3. *Condictio sine causa* is said to occur when payment is made or promised with no good ground either real or supposed, *e.g.* a gift from husband to wife or *vice versa* (D. xxiv 1 fr 6). The expression however seems to be used rather as a general one to include any cases which may seem not properly to come under the first two heads (D. xii 7; cf. tit. 6 fr 66 *Quod alterius apud alterum sine causa deprehenditur condictio (indebiti) revocare consuevit*).

4. *Condictio ob turpem vel injustam causam.* When money is paid or promised for a disgraceful or wrongful object, suit cannot be brought either for payment or for recovery of payment. But if money has been paid to induce a person to abstain from sacrilege or theft or murder, or to return a deposit, a condiction lies to recover it. So also to recover a payment which has been made on a stipulation extorted by force. The case is different when the payer is himself guilty. And thus payment made by a thief to prevent information being given, or by an adulterer to escape the consequences of detection, or payment on the ground of past adultery or other immoral connexion, is not recoverable. A suitor with a good case, who gave money to the judge to decide in his favour, was by some thought to have a right to recover, but Severus decided he should be treated as a wrong-doer (D. xii 5 fr 2—7).

5. A further case of condiction differs from the above-named classes by the absence of legal change of property. This is called *condictio ex causa furtiva*, sometimes shortened to *condictio furtiva*. Theft does not make the thief owner, but only deprives the owner of possession; who therefore, besides bringing an action (*furti* or *vi bonorum raptorum*) against the

thief or robber for double or quadruple damages, can claim his property by a vindication against the thief or anyone else who may happen to be in possession of it. Gaius recognises the anomaly of allowing condiction in this case, and accounts for it by the natural desire of accumulating penalties on thieves (*plane odio furum receptum est* iv 4). But something more than this may be urged for the *condictio furtiva.* What is stolen is often mingled with other moneys or goods so that identification is impossible; or it is spent and thus in fact appropriated by the thief. Hence the practical position being so far the same as if ownership had passed, there was no good reason for withholding from the owner any advantages which this special form of action might confer. And if the thing stolen was money or other fungible there was no anomaly in a claim *si paret furem dare oportere.* The anomaly lay rather in giving the action generally, whether the object was fungible or not, and whether it existed or not; instead of confining it to cases of consumption. Obviously convenience required that consumption should not need to be proved. Nor was it any answer to the suit that the slave or thing had perished from natural causes, a thief being always 'in delay.' The only defence was immediate delivery on demand.

Condiction went against the thief himself and his heir, but not, like the *actio furti,* against aiders and counsellors: they had not had the stolen thing and consumed or lost it. But theft had the same import in both actions. The measure of damages was the owner's interest in the thing stolen, the value of the thing being taken at the highest amount it had since joinder of issue, and incidental advantages (*e.g.* an inheritance falling to a stolen slave) being added. If a son under power was the thief, the action lay against him in full: against the father (*de peculio*) for what had come to him. A slave (in early times, a son also) could be surrendered noxally for the remainder which was not covered by the *peculium.* Condiction and vindication could not both be brought with effect. Condiction could not be brought against one who, when slave, had committed theft; unless he had handled the thing since he became free.

Plaintiff must be owner and have had possession before the theft. A legatee cannot sue, if he has not yet actually acquired the property. Nor can a usufructuary, if the thief gathered the fruit before the usufructuary severed it. Parting with the ownership or reacquiring the possession disqualify one from suing (D. xiii 1 esp. fr 1—11, 15; xlvii 1 fr 2 § 3; tit. 2 fr 81 §§ 5, 7; vii 1 fr 12 § 5). Celsus thought that a condiction for the possession would lie against one who had forcibly evicted plaintiff from land (D. xlvii 2 fr 25).

Condemnation on a condiction, though arising from theft, did not attach infamy to the defendant. It aimed at recoupment for loss (*rei persecutionem habet*), not punishment of the offender (D. xliv 7 fr 36; xiii 1 fr 7 § 2).

6. *Condictio incerti*[1].

In all the above-named cases the object of the suit is some definite thing: the action is either a *condictio certae pecuniae* or *condictio certae rei*. It is, in general words, an *actio qua certum petitur* and the claim[2] in the formula runs *si paret dari oportere*. But a *condictio* may also have a claim *si paret dari fierive oportere*, and it is enough to prove *fieri* only (Gai. iv 5; D. L 16 fr 53 pr)[2], and *fieri* ('performance') has not the definite character of *dari*. A stipulation too may be certain or uncertain (see p. 24); on a certain stipulation (*certa* or *certi stipulatio*) a condiction is the proper suit; on an uncertain stipulation the action appears to have been called simply *ex stipulatu* (D. xii 1 fr 24), or *actio incerti ex stip.* (D. xxii 1 fr 4 pr). So we find in the Digest beside the *condictio certi*[3] a *condictio*

[1] It is the claim (*intentio*) which makes an action into certain or uncertain. A claim for a thing certain may have an uncertain condemnation clause, the judge having to assess the amount of damages; cf. Gai. iv 51.

[2] Savigny v p. 589.

[3] The term *condictio certi* is found in D. xii 1 fr 9 pr and § 3 (a passage which appears to have been largely interpolated and altered by Tribonian); xlvi 2 fr 12 (also not free from suspicion): in both cases it appears to refer to money; cf. D. xiii 2 fr 1 where the *actio si certum petetur* is contrasted with *condictio triticaria* (see above, p. 76). *Condicere certum* is found

incerti. Its object was sometimes to recover an amount of money not yet ascertained (D. xxiii 3 fr 59 § 1; xxx fr 60); but generally to secure the performance (*facere, fieri*) of something unintentionally omitted at the proper time, *e.g.* the imposition of a servitude in selling and delivering a house or farm (D. viii 2 fr 35; xii 6 fr 22 § 1; xix 1 fr 8 pr); a usufructuary's usual bond (D. vii 9 fr 7 pr); a bond for due restoration under a special trust (D. iv 4 fr 16 § 2); release from an obligation (D. xii 7 fr 3; xxxix 5 fr 2 § 3; xlvi 2 fr 12); restoration of a pledge (D. xiii 1 fr 12 § 2); or of possession (D. xii 6 fr 15 § 1; xiii 3 fr 2); giving a surety (D. xvi 1 fr 8 § 8); *etc.* (In the three last passages *incerti* is omitted.) The action is also referred to simply as *incerti agere* (*e.g.* D. iv 8 fr 27 § 7; xxxix 5 fr 2 § 4). And in the case of legacies the suit is, according to the character of the legacy, sometimes a *condictio* if the claim be certain (D. xii 1 fr 9 § 1) and sometimes an *actio incerti* (D. vii 5 fr 8).

Gaius gives us information of the formula in suits on uncertain stipulations (iv 136, 137). Whether in uncertain condictions generally the same lines were pursued, we do not know. Some recent jurists throw doubts on the name and even on the existence of an *incerti condictio* (apart from stipulations) in Antonine times, and are inclined to treat them, not without reason, as due to Justinian only[1].

in D. xii 2 fr 28 § 4; *certi condicere* D. xxv 2 fr 17 § 2, and nowhere else (Lenel *EP.* p. 185; Pernice *ZRG.* xxvi p. 252).

[1] See Pernice *Labeo* iii p. 203; Trampedach *ZRG.* xxx p. 113 sqq.; Pflüger *ZRG.* xxxi p. 75 sqq. The last ingeniously suggests that what Justinian accomplished by granting a *condictio incerti* was often accomplished in a less direct way by the Antonine jurists by a *condictio certi*, *e.g.* by suing for the whole legacy, or the whole house or farm (cf. D. L 17 fr 84 pr; xii 6 fr 24 § 4); defendant, consenting to repay the overplus or to give the bond or allow the servitude, and thus having satisfied the plaintiff, claims an acquittal (*ib.* pp. 79, 80). It must be admitted that many of the passages naming *condictio incerti* seem to betray Tribonian's handling, but to get rid of *incerti condictio* altogether requires very slashing treatment of the text.

Earlier writers on the subject are Savigny *Syst.* v p. 687; Huschke *Darlehen* p. 212 sq.; Lenel *EP.* p. 121.

E. Three other actions, the first two at least of praetorian origin, are closely connected with stipulation and cash-loan.

1. *De eo quod certo loco dari oportet.* Where a sum of money is due to be paid at a particular place and is not paid, the creditor is allowed by the praetor to sue for payment elsewhere; and an arbiter will be appointed to fix how much more or less should be paid at the place now proposed, according as the change is for the interest of the debtor or of the creditor. If the debtor shews that he has already offered the money at the agreed place, or has it there on deposit, or can easily pay it there, the judge will probably acquit him, first taking security for the payment at the place agreed. If he finds for plaintiff, he will weigh the circumstances of the two parties, and allow in some cases a higher than the statutable rate of money interest, *e.g.* if the loan was on bottomry, or the delay in payment has led to forfeiture or to forced sale or loss of usual profit in business. The action can be brought against a surety, but not for any addition due to debtor's delay. Debtor cannot claim to discharge his obligation by payment elsewhere than originally agreed, if creditor objects.

This action applies when money is due on a strict obligation, as a stipulation, or money loan, or legacy, not on a sale or deposit or other *bonae fidei* contract, since, if a change is required in such matters, it can be effected under their proper actions. This action is specially called *arbitraria*[1] (D. xiii 4).

2. *Pecuniae constitutae*[2] 'money appointed to be paid.' An action was granted to enforce a definite engagement, though

[1] The Digest gives this term to one other action *quod metus causa*, and that only once (iv 2 fr 14 § 11; Lenel *EP.* p. 195 n. 1; Gradenwitz *Interpol.* p. 99).

[2] An instance of *pec. const.* occurs in Cic. *Quinct.* 5 § 18 *Quasi domi nummos haberet, ita constituit Scapulis se daturum.* It is not clear whether we should refer here Cic. *Att.* i. 7 § 1 *L. Cincio* HS $\overline{\text{XX}}$CD *constitui me curaturum Idibus Februariis*, the word *curaturum* looking rather like practical arrangements for payment (as *e.g.* Cic. *Quinct.* 4 § 15). So in *Att.* xvi 15 § 5 *scis me pridem jam constituisse Montani nomine* HS xxv *dissolvere* we may understand *constituisse* either of a resolution of Cicero's or of a promise to his son or to Montanus (cf. *ib.* xii 52 § 1) or a formal appointment to Montanus' creditors. See Bruns *Kl. Schr.* i p. 226.

without stipulation, to pay or perform a debt previously contracted and yet unpaid, though, as was held after some doubt, the original debt might not yet be due. The debt must consist of money or other things lying in count, weight or measure; it might be one's own debt or another's, legal or only natural (unless barred by perpetual plea), civil or praetorian, arising from any contract or other cause (dowry, guardianship, *etc.*), even from a liability for theft, robbery or insult (D. xiii 5 fr 1 §6—fr 3, fr 5 § 2; 29; Cod. iv 18 fr 2 § 1). The appointment (*constitutum*) might vary the time or place or form of payment, or add a pledge or surety, but could not increase the amount, or add interest on a loan (fr 1 § 5, 4, § 5 pr, 11 § 1—14 § 2). If no time for payment was named in the appointment, there were doubts apparently whether the agreement was void or whether suit could be brought at once; but by the Digest a moderate delay, at least ten days, was allowed (fr 21 § 1). The appointment must be for payment by the appointor and to the appointee, whether the original debt was or was not due by the one or to the other. The original debtor need not consent (fr 5 §§ 2—6, 27). The appointment created a distinct obligation, and bound by its own terms, even if the old obligation ceased by time or other cause; and it left the old obligation standing, at least until joinder of issue in this, and as some thought, until the debt was paid (fr 28; xv 3 fr 15; cf. xlvi 3 fr 59). But in the case of two joint stipulators an appointment by debtor to pay one disabled the other from receiving for his own account payment of the debt (D. xiii 5 fr 8—10). An appointor was not in strict law excused from payment at the time appointed by anything whatever (even *per rerum naturam*) except fault of the appointee, nor by subsequent offer before joinder of issue, but equitable considerations were allowed to prevail (fr 16 § 2—18).

The appointment might be made at an interview or at a distance, by words or letter[1] or messenger, slave or free, by any form of words or by oath duly tendered or retorted, affirming an

[1] Thus a letter to this effect: *Decem quae Lucius Titius ex arca tua mutua acceperat salva ratione usurarum habes penes me* (D. xiii 5 fr 26) was held to be a *constitutum*.

existing debt. But an oath denying an appointment does not of course affect the existing debt. Neither parent nor patron were exempt from the obligation to take an oath, if tendered by plaintiff (fr 14 § 3, 15; xii 2 fr 14, 36). Guardians, caretakers (of madmen) and borough managers (*actor*) could be appointees, and their principals were in practice allowed to sue, if the appointment was to pay the principals: if such agents were appointors, they were liable themselves. An appointment to a slave vested at once in his master. An appointment for payment *de peculio* was not affected by subsequent increase or decrease of the *peculium* (fr 5 §§ 7—10, fr 1 § 8, 20). What is bad as a stipulation, cannot be treated as a *constitutum*: it was not so intended (fr 1 § 4).

Like the *condictio certae creditae pecuniae* the suit on an appointment (probably an *actio in factum*) might be accompanied by a wager, so that defendant if condemned had to pay half as much again as the sum appointed (Gai. iv 171).

3. *Actio recepticia.* There was another action of somewhat similar character to the last, called *recepticia,* because it was 'based on an undertaking' (*receptum*), which action was free from some of the limitations of the *actio constitutae pecuniae.* It was not restricted to fungibles, but could relate to land or any moveable: it did not require as its ground a previously existing debt: it was not limited in duration, and ran for and against heirs; but could be brought only against a banker, and in a regular form (*sollemnibus verbis*). So much may be gathered from Cod. iv 18 fr 2 § 1; and Theophil. *Inst.* iv 6 § 8. See Lenel *ZRG.* xv 62.

CHAPTER IV.

Obligations *bonae fidei.*

1. Obligations of this class are as various as are the services required by one man from another in society. They were regarded by the Romans as in no way peculiar to themselves, but common to the world. Hence no special formalities were

used; consent of the parties was alone requisite; the judge had a larger discretion, and the standard set before him was what was fairly to be expected from business-like men dealing with one another in good faith[1]. Subsidiary agreements (*pacta adjecta*) are to be regarded as part of the contract, if made at the first in close connexion with the original contract (D. ii 14 fr 7 § 5; L 17 fr 27; xviii 5 fr 3, *etc.*); and the whole was to be interpreted not so much by the words used as by the real intention of the parties (D. L 16 fr 219): any action brought was to be tried with consideration of the equities[2] involved. In execution of this principle defendant was accountable for the fruits and other accessions of anything in his charge, not merely as in strict actions from the time of joinder of issue (D. xxii 1 fr 38 § 7), and if it was a female slave, he had to deliver up her offspring with her (D. xvi 3 fr 1 § 24). The value of any object of suit was taken as at the date of the judgment; not as in strict actions at the date of joinder of issue (D. xiii 6 fr 3 § 2). Interest was payable, as of course, when there was delay in fulfilling the obligation, and from the date of delay, not merely from joinder of issue (D. xxii 1 fr 32 § 2). Counter-claims could, if

[1] Cicero often dwells on the legal embodiment of the principles of good faith in business transactions: *Off.* iii 17 § 70 *Q. quidem Scaevola, pontifex maximus, summam vim esse dicebat in omnibus iis arbitriis in quibus adderetur 'ex fide bona,' fideique bonae nomen existimabat manare latissime, idque versari in tutelis, societatibus, fiduciis, mandatis, rebus emptis venditis, conductis locatis, quibus vitae societas contineretur; in iis magni esse judicis statuere, praesertim cum in plerisque essent judicia contraria, quid quemque cuique praestare oporteret: Nat. D.* iii 30 § 74 *Inde tot judicia de fide mala, tutelae, mandati, pro socio, fiduciae, reliqua quae ex empto aut vendito aut conducto aut locato contra fidem fiunt*; cf. *Top.* 10 § 42; 17 § 66.

[2] The regular phrase for 'equity' was *aequum et bonum* (not *aequum* by itself). See *e.g.* Pl. *Curc.* 65; *Men.* 578; Cic. *Caecin.* 23 § 65; *Top.* 17 § 66; *Brut.* 39 § 145, 53 § 198; *ad Heren.* ii 10 § 14, 11 § 16, *etc.*; Sen. *Clem.* i 18 § 1; ii 7 § 3. In Pl. *Most.* 682 we have the order inverted *bonum aequomque oras*; Gai. iii 137 *Ex bono et aequo* and regularly in Digest; *e.g.* i 1 fr 1 pr *jus est ars boni et aequi*; *ib.* § 1; ix 4 fr 30 *ex bono et aequo*; xii 6 fr 66; xxi 1 fr 18 pr; xliv 7 fr 34 pr, *etc.* (In xvii 1 fr 12 § 9; xl 4 fr 22 *ex aequo et bono*; i 1 fr 11 *quod aequum ac bonum est.*) *Aequitas* is also found in the same sense, Cic. *Caecin.* 23 § 66; 27 § 77; 29 § 83, *etc.*

the judge thought fit, be set off to diminish the amount of the damages adjudged[1] (Gai. iv 63). Fraud justified the damages being fixed by oath of the plaintiff, which was not usual in strict actions (D. xii 3 fr 5; xiii 6 fr 3 § 2). The formula in these actions contained *ex fide bona* (or some such words) in the claim (*intentio*, cf. Gai. iv 47), and it was not necessary for defendant to have an express plea of fraud inserted. *Doli exceptio inest in bonae fidei judiciis* (Vat. 94; D. xxiv 3 fr 21). No one could contract out of responsibility for fraud (D. L 17 fr 23). If anything was left to a person's discretion, a reasonable, not arbitrary, discretion is meant (D. L 17 fr 22 § 1).

2. The actions (*judicia*) enumerated as *bonae fidei* by Gaius (iv 62) are *ex empto vendito, locato conducto, negotiorum gestorum, mandati, depositi, fiduciae, pro socio, tutelae, rei uxoriae*: to which may probably be added, as part of Gaius' original text, *commodati, pigneraticium, familiae erciscundae, communi dividundo*, which are given with the others in Justinian's *Institutes*, and may well have been omitted here by error of the copyist[2] (Just. iv 6 § 30).

3. Obligations of a *bonae fidei* character have several points of connexion or contrast with one another.

The first group is composed of such as are concerned with the transfer of possession without any payment being made therefor. The transfer may be for the transferee's convenience (*commodatum*), or the transferor's convenience (*depositum*), or as a security to the transferee for some loan or other obligation of the transferor (*pignus*).

The second group is where services of one are employed by or given to another, either by this latter's request (*mandatum*), or without any commission from him but in his interest (*negotiorum gestio*).

No payment is made for the services in this group any more than in the first. But expenses are chargeable in both groups.

[1] A constitution of M. Aurelius authorised 'set-off' in all strict actions by a plea of fraud (Just. iv 6 § 30).

[2] So Krüger and others. The line *mandati—uxoriae* is twice written in our MS. of Gaius, probably by confusion of the terminations of *mandati* and *commodati*.

The third group is where there is a community of interest; property, possession, and services being in common. This is partnership (*societas*). But only when this relation arises by voluntary agreement is there any contract: where it arises by operation of law (*commune sine societate*) each person may have duties to the other enforceable by law, but they are not mutually intended and obligatory in consequence of the consent.

The fourth group contains transfers for money, either transfer of property from one to another (*emptio venditio*), or transfer of the use of property, or of services (*locatio conductio*).

LOAN, DEPOSIT, PLEDGE.

The first group of *bonae fidei* obligations is composed of such as arise out of the transfer without payment of the physical possession of a thing. A man may lend for instance his silver plate to another for him to use; or he may deposit it with him for safekeeping; or he may put it in his power as security for a debt. In all these cases, loan, deposit, pledge (*commodatum, depositum, pignus*), the contract was held to be formed *re*, *i.e.* by the transfer into the other's possession. They are primarily one-sided contracts; the lender, depositor or pledgor having an action (*rectum judicium, actio directa*) to recover possession of the thing in good state, at the time or in the circumstances agreed on, the other party having no counterclaim, except for any incidental expenses he may have been put to in safekeeping (*contrarium judicium, contraria actio*). Loan is for the benefit of the borrower; deposit for the benefit of the depositor; pledge is primarily for the benefit of the creditor who thus gets security, but secondarily for the benefit of the debtor who thereby gets credit (Modest. in *Collat.* x 2 §§ 1, 2; Just. iii 14 § 4). In all any use of the thing, except as agreed on or approved by the lender, depositor, or pledgor, makes the user liable *furti* (D. xlvii 2 fr 55 pr § 1; xiii 1 fr 16). Any payment (rent, interest, *etc.*) for the loan or deposit converts the contract into one of letting and hiring or of *mutuum*; or in some circumstances an action *praescriptis verbis* may be the right remedy (cf. D. xvi 3 fr 1 § 9).

A. LOAN (*COMMODATUM*).

1. This contract is also denoted by the words *utendum dare*[1], *accipere*, which are equally applicable to moveables and immoveables. Labeo wished to confine *commodare* to moveables, but this theory was not accepted, though the gratuitous use of other's land is more often the subject of *precarium* (cf. D. xliii 26 fr 1). What is consumed by the use (*e.g.* corn) is not subject of *commodatum* but of *mutuum*; nor is money, unless the coins themselves are intended to be returned, as when it is lent for mere show or for use as a symbol of price (D. xiii 6 fr 1 § 1; 3 § 6, 4).

2. Loan being entirely for the benefit of the borrower, he is responsible not only for fraud (*dolus*) but also for fault (*culpa*). That is to say he is bound to exercise the greatest care, to make only such use as was understood and intended by the lender, and to return the thing lent in safety according to the arrangement made, with all its belongings. Any profit which has been made from it, is usually returnable to the lender, but in the case of the article's being stolen and the borrower's recovering penalty in addition to the thing or its value, there was much doubt whether the borrower must give up the penalty to the lender: Papinian's final opinion was that, as the risk was the borrower's, he ought to have the benefit of the penalty (fr 5 §§ 2, 3, 9, fr 13 § 1; Cod. vi 2 fr 22 § 3*a*). If the thing be stolen by the borrower's own slave, the borrower remains responsible, but no action of theft is possible (D. xlvii 2 fr 54 § 2; see p. 205). The conditions of use should be laid down at the time of lending, not afterwards, so as to change a contract already formed. The borrower is not responsible for mere fault, if the loan is really for the benefit of the lender, as for instance in the case of a praetor's giving a dramatic

[1] Cf. Plaut. *Asin.* 444 *Scyphos quos utendos dedi Philodamo rettulitne?... Non? si velis dare, commoda homini amico.*

show and lending dresses to the actors. Nor is he responsible for the sickness or death of a slave lent him, or for loss or damage by some irresistible occurrence, as fire, shipwreck, the falling of a house, a landslip, or pirates or brigands, where there has been no use of the thing beyond or other than was authorised, and no fault on his part (D. xiii 6 fr 5 § 10, 17 § 3, 18 pr). If a slave lent runs away, the borrower is responsible, provided the slave is of an age or character or in circumstances evidently requiring safekeeping (fr 5 §§ 6, 13, fr 18 pr). Where a loan, *e.g.* of a carriage, is made to several persons, each is responsible for the whole, but payment by one clears all (fr 5 § 15). If a borrower is sued for theft, he is not liable also to suit on the loan; and *vice versa* (D. xlvii 2 fr 72 pr).

3. The borrower has a counter action against the lender to recover any proper expenses, if at all considerable, to which he has been put in keeping or recovering the thing lent. The food of a slave is not chargeable to the lender: it is regarded as a set-off against his services. But if the slave has stolen from the borrower, or damage has been done to him by the thing lent (*e.g.* a cracked or tainted vessel), the lender is liable (by the counter action) if he knew of the vicious quality. If he did not know, he is still liable on a noxal action for theft (D. xiii 6 fr 18 §§ 2, 3, fr 22). Unreasonable withdrawal of the thing lent may render the lender liable (fr 17 § 3). A counter claim can be enforced either independently or as a set-off against a direct claim (fr 17 § 1, 18 § 4).

4. The lender retains not only the property but the civil possession of the thing lent; the borrower has only the physical possession. But his liability duly to return the object gives him a sufficient interest to entitle him to sue for theft anyone who abstracted the thing: for any injury to the thing by an outsider the lender alone can sue under the *lex Aquilia* (fr 5 § 15, fr 8, 19; ix 2 fr 11 § 9).

Borrower's heir is liable only so far as his share in the inheritance extends, unless he happens to have the physical power of restoring the whole and does not do so (D. xiii 6 fr 3 § 3).

The issue of an action *commodati* might be either *in jus* or *in factum concepta* (Gai. iv 47. See Book VI chap. V iii 4).

B. Deposit (*depositum*).

1. Deposit is the transfer of a thing to the possession of another for him to keep for the depositor and return on demand, or as agreed. Instead of *deponere, commendare*, or *servandum* or *custodiendum dare* are common expressions (Paul ii 12 §§ 2—4; Scaev. ap. Gell. vi 15). If any use is intended to be made of the thing deposited, the contract may be *commodatum* or *mutuum*: if any payment is to be made by either party, it would be a contract of letting and hiring.

(*a*) There was an action for deposit granted by the XII tables for double damages (Paul ii 12 § 11)[1]. The action in use was from the praetor's edict and was for single damages in ordinary cases, but for double if the deposit was made in consequence of an emergency such as fire, shipwreck, housefall, public tumult, or robbers (D. xvi 3 fr 1 § 1).

(*b*) The depositary was liable only for fraud or such gross negligence as was akin to fraud. No agreement could affect the liability for fraud; and fraud once committed makes the depositary liable whatever may happen to the thing. Otherwise (except by special agreement) he bears no risk, if the thing is lost or perishes. The depositor has only himself to blame if he has chosen a careless depositary (Paul ii 12 §§ 6, 10; D. xvi 3 fr 1 §§ 6, 7, 35, fr 14 § 1, 32; xliv 7 fr 1 § 5). Any use or handling of the thing contrary to what the depositary believes to be the depositor's intention makes the depositary liable for theft, as well as on the deposit (D. *ib.* fr 29 pr; xlvii 2 fr 77 pr). He is bound to restore all the produce of the thing, whether fruits, offspring of slaves or other accessions; and if there is any delay in restoring on due demand, he is liable for interest of money deposited (D. xvi 1 fr 1 § 24, fr 24).

[1] Ihering suggests that the action really meant was that for *furtum nec manifestum*, the XII tables having no action for dealings with deposit short of this (*Schuldmoment* p. 32).

Justinian (*Inst.* iv 6 §§ 23, 26) speaks of the damages being doubled in certain cases of deposit, if the action was disputed. I do not find this elsewhere.

(*c*) Restoration must be made of the thing itself, a set-off for it not being allowed. If it is in a damaged condition, the restoration may be treated as fraudulent non-restoration (Paul ii 12 § 12; D. xvi 3 fr 1 § 16). It should be made at the place where the thing is, or would be but for fraud on the part of the depositary (fr 12 § 1); and should be made as a rule to the depositor. If a slave deposited it, it should be returned to the slave, unless there be reason to think the slave's master would object, or the slave have been manumitted or alienated since the deposit. If the thing turns out to be the depositary's own, or to have been stolen and the owner claims it, the depositor has no right to the return. Otherwise the depositor is not disqualified from suing by want of rightful claim to hold: his responsibility to others gives him a lawful interest (fr 1 § 39, 11, 31).

(*d*) Where there are two, or more, depositors, they can claim their shares, or, if so agreed, either can claim the whole. If there are two or more depositaries, they are not discharged from their obligation, until the depositor has received back in full what he deposited, whether one or both have returned it. Where the depositor is dead, leaving several heirs, each can claim his share. Where some have received their shares and the depositary is (without fraud) unable to pay the rest, it was a disputed point whether these latter could claim from the former. But if the deposit is not divisible it should be returned to the heirs present, as soon as the majority in value have entered, security being given to the depositary against claims by the others; or in default of security the thing or things should be deposited in a temple (fr 1 §§ 37, 43, 44, fr 14; Cod. iv 34 fr 12).

(*e*) A depositary's heir is responsible to the full for depositary's fraud, not merely to the extent of what has come to him. If there be more heirs than one, each is responsible in the ratio of his share in the inheritance. In case of deposit on emergency, where the depositary was liable for double damages, his heir is liable only for single, unless the heir act fraudulently, when it becomes double, *i.e.* either double his share, if the deposit was divisible, or double the whole, if indivisible (D. fr 1 § 1, fr 22).

If a depositary has further deposited the thing with someone else, both he and the original depositor can (the latter by an analogous action) sue the second depositary (Paul ii 12 § 8).

A son under power can sue or be sued for a deposit made by or with himself. If a father or master is sued (*de peculio*) on a deposit made with his son or slave, he is liable not only for their fraud, but also for his own (fr 1 § 42, 19). Some lawyers held that if a slave when manumitted retained a thing deposited with him, he could be sued directly. Certainly in the case of an emancipated son suit should be brought against him and not against his father, even within a year from emancipation (fr 21).

(*f*) A counter action (*contrarium judicium*) can be brought by the depositary, similar in other respects to that brought by a borrower (*commodator*), but he can charge the depositor with a slave's or animal's maintenance (*Collat.* x 2 § 5).

Both the direct and the counter action are *bonae fidei*: but in the direct action only were the damages assessable on oath, and condemnation caused infamy (Gai. iv 62, 182; D. fr 1 §§ 23, 26; fr 5 pr, iii 2 § 1).

(*g*) The praetor set forth in his edict two forms of issue in cases of deposit, on which see Book VI chap. viii 4. In the *formula in factum concepta* it appears to have been necessary to specify the article deposited in precise terms, *e.g.* of gold and silver, the form and weight; of wool, the weight and dye; of a box containing several articles, then the description of each, unless the box was sealed and contents not disclosed; but even then the depositor might sue not only for the box but for any individual article contained in it (D. xvi 3 fr 1 §§ 40, 41).

2. Where money was deposited with a banker or other person, with the understanding that the amount, not the identical coins, was to be returned on demand, the transaction was not strictly a deposit. (Modern writers call it *depositum irregulare.*) But the suit *depositi* still applied; interest was not due, unless, as in other *bonae fidei* contracts, delay occurred in returning the amount. If however payment of interest was part of the understanding (*lex contractûs*) it could be enforced.

Such a deposit might by agreement easily be converted into a regular cash loan (D. xvi 3 fr 24, 25 § 1; xix 2 fr 31; xii 1 fr 9 § 9, fr 10).

Where a banker fails, ordinary depositors can claim before those who have put their money at interest with him or through him, and before privileged creditors. As between themselves all such depositors rank equally (D. xvi 3 fr 9, §§ 2, 3).

3. A special use of deposit was when an object of dispute was handed over to a stakeholder (*sequester*) to keep, produce and deliver according to instructions. There was an action called *sequestraria actio* to compel the *sequester* to fulfil the agreement (D. xvi 2 fr 5 § 1, 6, 7, 12 § 2, 33). The stakeholder was considered to have civil possession of the thing so as to prevent either party from gaining the property by usucapion. The successful party on obtaining possession would however be able to count the time during which the thing was held by the stakeholder (fr 17 § 1; xli 2 fr 39).

4. In early times deposit was sometimes accompanied with conveyance of the ownership in trust for restoration (*fiduciae causa mancipio dare, quo tutius nostrae res apud amicum sint* Gai. ii 59, 60). Similarly Boeth. *ad* Cic. *Top.* 10, in Bruns[6] *Fontes* p. 77. Of this we know no more: see below, C.

C. *Fiducia*: especially of pledge.

'Trust' (*fiducia*) occurred in several parts of the law, when a permanent relation was created which was intended to have only a special or temporary effect. A woman made a copurchase, and thus passed into the hands of a stranger, merely to change her guardian or enable her to make a will. A son or daughter passed into the power of an outsider, as a step towards emancipation. To evade the restrictions of the law, a man was made heir or legatee with instructions to pass on the property to another or to manumit a slave. So anything might be conveyed to another by mancipation or surrender in court in trust for reconveyance on a certain event or on request. This was done, we are told, for two purposes, either as a mere deposit for safekeeping or as security for a loan. The friend in the first case, the creditor in the second case, was thus made owner, and had in law all the rights of an owner to hold and protect the property during his friend's absence or until the loan was repaid. And in order to facilitate the re-entry of the old owner into his rights, if he regained possession (subject in the case of a creditor to certain restrictions) a year's possession was held to be sufficient for usucapion, even if the thing was land (*res soli* Gai. ii 59, 60; cf. vol. I p. 477). Probably the words *fiduciae causa* or something to that effect[1] appeared, at any rate after the first fearless innocency had passed, in the formula of mancipation or surrender (cf. Gai. *l.c.* and i 114); or a distinct declaration was made at the time, as one of the terms of mancipation (*lex mancipii* i 140), to shew the limited purpose. Eventually the praetor granted an action (*judicium fiduciae*), at any rate in cases of pledge, to compel restitution of the object. It was *bonae fidei judicium*, and condemnation involved infamy (Gai. iv 62, 182).

1. (*a*) *Fiducia*[2] was one of three forms of pledge in use among the Romans, *fiducia, pignus, hypotheca.* The essential of pledge is that a creditor is put into control of a thing in order to insure, either by the desire of the debtor to re-possess his property, or by sale of the thing, if necessary, the total or partial satisfaction of his claim. If the claim is otherwise satisfied, the control of the creditor is removed. In the case of *fiducia* the

[1] The formal words used in *fiducia* are not known, but references to such are found in Cic. *Off.* iii 15 § 61 *Reliquorum autem judiciorum haec verba maxime excellunt; in arbitrio rei uxoriae 'melius aequius'; in fiducia 'ut inter bonos bene agier': ib.* 17 § 70 *Quanti* (how precious!) *verba illa 'uti ne propter te fidemve tuam captus fraudatusve sim'* (perhaps from the *lex mancipii*, cf. D. xvi 3 fr 1 § 42); *quam illa aurea 'ut inter bonos bene agier oportet et sine fraudatione.'* Cf. *Fam.* vii 12 § 2; see Lenel *EP.* § 107.

[2] *Fiducia* originally 'trust,' 'confidence,' reposed in the depositary or creditor and so used in the phrases *pactum fiduciae, fiduciae causa,* came to be applied to the thing conveyed in trust. See Cic. *Flac.* 21 § 51 (below, p. 100 n.). Gaius (ii 59; iii 201) has *fiduciae causa dare*, or *mancipare, etc.*; Paul (ii 13 § 6; iii 6 § 69) has *res fiduciae data* (like *pignori data, etc.*) where *fiduciae* may be either the thing (pred. dative) or the contract 'given to trust' (cf. *pignus contrahitur* D. xiii 7 fr 1 pr, *fiducia contrahitur* Gai. ii 60).

creditor is made owner[1]; in that of *pignus* he is made possessor; in *hypotheca* he has only a power of sale. The differences between them appear to have been only such as arose naturally from the difference in their character, but our information is very imperfect, because *fiducia*[2] went out of use with mancipation and surrender in court, and the Digest expressly treats *pignus* and *hypotheca* as differing only in name (D. xx 1 fr 5 § 1). Some passages relating to *fiducia* appear to have been incorporated in the Digest with little change beyond the substitution of *pignus* for *fiducia*[3].

(*b*) In *fiducia* the creditor has no occasion for a power of sale to be expressly given him: that is one of his rights as owner; and even an agreement not to sell is not binding, only that before proceeding to exercise his right he must give the debtor notice, probably at three different times, and allow opportunity for repayment. For the debtor's right to redeem and have a

[1] The English mortgage forms a striking analogy to the Roman and was probably derived from it. In early times there were two kinds of pledges of estates, *vivum vadium* and *mortuum vadium*. A living gage was where an estate was granted to the creditor to hold till the debt was repaid by the profits (cf. ἀντίχρησις p. 107). This is an estate conditioned to be void as soon as such sum was raised. A dead gage, or mortgage, is where the estate is granted to the creditor on condition that, if payment be made on a certain day, the debtor may reenter or may demand reconveyance, but, if payment be not made, the debtor forfeits all claim, and the estate is dead to him: the creditor is absolutely entitled. So the law continued till the end of the fourteenth century, when the Courts of Equity interfered, and the debtor's equity of redemption, even after the day was passed, became recognized, and either party could apply to the Court for an account of the debt and interest, or of the profits, and then either payment was made and the estate reconveyed or else foreclosure took place. But the usual course was for a power of sale to be given by deed to the mortgagee in case of default. The mortgagor continued to have an estate in the land, which could be devised, granted and entailed, but he had not the possession, except perhaps as tenant at will (*precario*) (Butler's notes to Co. Litt. p. 205 a; Blackstone ed. *Kerr*, Bk ii ch. 10).

[2] It is said to be last named in Cod. Theod. xv 14 § 9, A.D. 395, and Sidon. Apoll. *Ep.* iv 24 § 1 A.D. cir. 470.

[3] See Lenel *ZRG* xvi 104; but I am not convinced as to all his instances, *e.g.* compare Gai. iii 201 and Paul ii 31 § 19 with his view of D. xiii 7 fr 22 pr. Karlowa (*RG.* ii 563) also disagrees from Lenel as to fr 22 and fr 24 (D. xiii 7).

reconveyance of the thing on payment of his debt was fully recognized by law. In some sort he was regarded still as owner, potential if not actual; he could bequeath his 'equity of redemption' as we should call it, by the form called *praeceptio:* and he could sell the thing itself, tender the creditor payment of his debt out of the purchase money, obtain reconveyance, and transfer the thing to his purchaser. Any profits which the creditor might have made as owner of the thing (*e.g.* through a fiduciary slave) had to be deducted from the debt. And the debtor's rights of latent ownership were further recognized by his not being liable for theft, if, having obtained possession of the thing without any agreement or permission of the creditor, he retained it without having paid his debt. Continued use, notwithstanding his knowledge of the formal ownership being in another, enabled him to reacquire the ownership (Gai. ii 59, 60, 220; iii. 21; Paul ii 13 §§ 2, 5).

(*c*) The creditor if he sold for more than the amount of the debt had to pay the excess promptly to the debtor. He could not be purchaser himself, being already owner, and if the sale was made to another for him without the debtor's consent, it was not a good sale and the debtor's right of redemption was not barred. It appears however to have been usual for a clause of forfeiture (*lex commissoria*)[1] to accompany the conveyance to the creditor, giving him the right of foreclosing the equity of redemption, if the debt were not fully extinguished by a certain day[2]. Such a clause was forbidden altogether by Constantine (Cod. viii 34 fr 3; Paul ii 13 §§ 1, 3, 4).

(*d*) The possession of the thing often remained with the debtor by the consent of the creditor, either gratuitously or for hire. Whether the *fiducia* was security for interest as well as for principal would depend on the agreement. The practice too

[1] Cf. Cic. *Flac.* 21 § 51 *Pecuniam adulescentulo grandi fenore, fiducia tamen accepta occupavisti. Hanc fiduciam commissam tibi dicis: tenes hodie ac possides* (where *fiducia* is probably the translation of a Greek provincial term for pledge, perhaps ὑποθήκη; Voigt *Jus Nat.* ii 418; Karlowa *RG.* ii 575): *Fam.* xiii 56 *Philocles* ὑποθήκας *Cluvio dedit. Eae commissae sunt. Velim cures ut aut de hypothecis decedat easque procuratoribus Cluvii tradat aut pecuniam solvat.*

[2] See below, p. 110, and Mitteis *Reichsrecht* p. 441.

of warranting the title when the thing was sold might vary with the circumstances of the case, but would presumably be necessary in order to get a good price. The *actio fiduciae*, mentioned above, would settle equitably the rights of creditor and debtor and would run for and against the heirs of both. If the creditor had improved the property, he could claim recoupment of the cost (Paul ii 13 § 7; cf. D. xlvii 4 fr 13). The debtor's heirs had no action against a creditor who had sold a thing pledged or mortgaged (*pignora vel fiducias*) unless the action was begun by the debtor himself (Paul *ap. Consult.* vi 8[1]). If the creditor bequeathed the property, the debtor's action would lie not against the legatee but against all the heirs (Paul ii 13 § 6).

(*e*) A tablet found at San Lucar in the Roman province of Baetica (Bruns ed. 5 no. 110), probably of the first century after Christ, may be quoted as illustrative of fiduciary contracts. It contains a form or precedent used by a banker for securing advances past and future. The first part is a record of a mancipation of a farm and slave, made in trust to a slave who *fidi fiduciae causa mancipio accepit*[2] on payment of one sesterce each. Subjoined is a *pactum conventum*[3] explaining the purpose and conditions of the mancipation. All advances made or to be made in actual cash or in credit (*credidit*)[4] or by book entry (*expensum tulit*), and all liabilities incurred by the

[1] Arndts (Glück's *Pand.* xlviii p. 210) questions this. See also Dernburg *Pfandrecht* i p. 15.

[2] The like combination occurs in Plaut. *Trin.* 117 *tuae mandatus est fide et fiduciae.* In the tablet *fidi* is an old form of the genitive of *fides*.

[3] The *pactum conventum*, explaining the absolute *fiducia*, resembles in an English mortgage the defeasance which is sometimes separate from the conveyance, though referred to its date and recorded together with it. But usually the condition of the conveyance is inserted in the conveyance deed itself (Kent *Comm.* iv 141—158 ed. 9).

[4] *Credidit* is taken by the expositors generally to refer to stipulations, on the ground of the parallelism in Cic. *Rosc. Com.* 4 § 13, 5 § 14; and Gai. iii 124. But there stipulation had a due place: in our case I do not see that the banker would necessarily or always make a stipulation with the debtor whenever he gave him credit on a purchase or other business. I take *credidit* to refer to any credit in general, other than book-entry which is mentioned separately.

banker in becoming surety for the mortgagor are covered by the mortgage. On any default of the debtor at the due day in repaying advances or discharging the banker's liability, the banker or his heir has the right of selling such of the mortgaged property as he chooses, where and when he chooses, for cash. He is not obliged to mancipate them for more than one sesterce, nor to give a surety for the guaranty of title (*satis secundum mancipium dare*), nor personally to warrant the title in the usual words, nor to promise either the single or double value in case of eviction. Here the tablet breaks off: probably another tablet contained a covenant for remancipation to the mortgagor on payment of advances in full. The mancipation for one sesterce is to shew that the transaction is not sale, but in this case pledge. The mortgagee is not required to sell for more than one sesterce: this is in order to reduce his obligation to a minimum, in case eviction took place. (See the essays referred to by Bruns; also Karlowa *RG.* ii 378.)

2. *Pignus* and *hypotheca* will be treated together as they are often put together in our authorities. If a corporal object was passed into the possession of the creditor as security for the discharge of an obligation, it was properly *pignus;* if it was not put into his possession but treated by agreement as such security, it was *hypotheca*. *Pignus* was of immemorial antiquity; *hypotheca* was, as the name shews, of Greek origin, and, though once mentioned by Cicero in connexion with the province of Asia, was, as a Roman institute, probably later than his time. Not being confined to corporal objects, it admitted of much wider application, and in practice would be the more readily resorted to, because the use and possession of the thing hypothecated was not withdrawn from the debtor until sale. When a pledge was in the creditor's possession, the debtor could enforce his rights by an *actio pigneraticia,* the creditor could enforce his against the debtor by a counter action (*contraria pign. actio*). When the pledge was not in the creditor's possession, he could obtain it by an interdict or *actio hypothecaria.*

(*a*) Pledge was a contract made by agreement (*pactum conventum*), either verbal or in writing, with or without delivery real or constructive, of the object pledged. But the object must be agreed on (D. xiii 7 fr 1 pr; xx 1 fr 4). Pledge may be made as security for the fulfilment of any obligation, whether one's own or another's, whether a money-loan (which is the most common case) and the interest on the same, if that be agreed to be covered also, or dowry or purchase or hiring or mandate or suretyship, *etc.*, whether the obligation be present or future, absolute or conditional, civil, praetorian, or natural; and it may cover the whole or part of an obligation. If the pledge is for a conditional obligation, it exists only if the condition occur (D. xiii 7 fr 9 § 1; xx 1 fr 4, 5). A testator could also establish a pledge by way of legacy: this was decided by rescripts of the Antonines. A magistrate could do so by sending a person into possession of some object (xiii 7 fr 26; xxxiv 1 fr 12); or by seizure in execution of a judgment (D. xlii 1 fr 15). On tacit pledges see below (*d*, *e*).

(*b*) Anything saleable can be pledged, not merely corporal things, but a usufruct, or (if the creditor has a neighbouring farm) rural servitudes, but not urban servitudes. An undivided share of a common thing may be pledged, and division will still leave both parts subject *pro rata* to the pledge. A flock or herd may be pledged and will remain so, although all the individual components may be changed. Similarly a shop and its contents (D. xx 1 fr 9 § 1, 11 § 2—fr 13 pr, 34 pr, tit. 6 fr 7 § 4). Fruits not yet gathered, children or animals not yet born, may still be pledged either by full owner or by usufructuary (xx 1 fr 15 pr). A general charge might be created on all the goods (*bona*) of the debtor, what he had and what he should afterwards have; and a clause of this kind was often added in contracts after certain things had been specifically pledged. Such a general charge was held not to include things which a debtor would not be likely to pledge specifically, *e.g.* his dress, furniture, necessary slaves, concubine, natural children, *etc.* (*ib.* fr 6—8; cf. fr 34 § 2). Nor did it preclude manumission of slaves (Cod. vii 8 fr 3).

An investment (*nomen*) might be pledged; and in such case the praetor granted the creditor an action (*utilis*) to get in the money, which would then be set off against the debt, or if the investment yielded something else than money, this would be held by the creditor in pledge. The praetor would also protect the person whose debt was thus pledged against his original creditor. The document shewing the debt would naturally be put into the creditor's hand, just as the purchase deed sometimes was on a pledge of the property (D. xiii 7 fr 18 pr, 43; Cod. viii 16 fr 2, 4).

(c) A pledge of what is the property of someone else is not a good pledge unless the owner consents. Anyone knowingly pledging such, or pledging what is already pledged to someone else, unless there be an ample margin in value over the first debt, is liable to criminal proceedings for 'geckotry' (*stellionatus*[1]), if he have not informed the pledgee or second pledgee of the fact (D. xiii 7 fr 1 § 2, 20 pr, 36 § 1). The creditor pursuing a pledge in the hands of others is not bound to prove that it was the debtor's own, but only that at the time of pledge it was *in bonis ejus*, *i.e.* acquired *bona fide* by the debtor, though his title may prove to have been bad (cf. D. L 16 fr 49). Such proof of the thing's being *in bonis* at the time of agreement is of course not required when the pledge was general and related to subsequent acquisition. If the slave or thing was not then in existence, the proof relates to the mother of the child or young, or to the land on which the fruit was produced (D. xx 1 fr 3 pr, 15 § 1; tit. 4 fr 11 § 3; L 16 § 49). If the debtor sue the creditor for return of his pledge, the creditor cannot object that it is not the debtor's: that point has nothing to do with the contract between them, provided the debtor pays his debt. As between them the contract is good to support their respective actions against one another (D. xiii 7 fr 9 pr, § 4, 32). As regards third parties the pledge is good, only if and when the pledgor afterwards acquire and retain the ownership, or if he was at the time entitled to the Publician action. Unless the pledge was intended

[1] From *stellio* (*stelio*) a kind of lizard (cf. Plin. *HN.* xxx 89; Verg. *G.* iv 243). Any criminal fraud, not coming under a regular name, was so called and was punished severely *extra ordinem* (D. xlvii 20). Specially mentioned are fraudulent alienation of things pledged, spoiling them, making away with them, substituting other goods, and imposture or collusion to ruin another (*in necem alterius*).

to operate only in the contingency of the debtor's acquiring ownership and the creditor knew of the debtor's having no right to pledge, subsequent acquisition of ownership does not remove the original invalidity of the pledge, but a *utilis* action is granted to the creditor (D. xx 1 fr 1 pr, 9 § 3, 18; xiii 7 fr 41; cf. xliv 4 fr 4 § 30; Vangerow *Pand.* § 372 *Anm.* 2, and others). Whether the owner of a thing, becoming heir to one who has professed to pledge it, thereby becomes subject to the creditor's action in respect thereof, was disputed (D. xiii 7 fr 41; xx 1 fr 22). A pledge of what is already the creditor's is no pledge at all (D. L 17 fr 45).

A temporary or conditional ownership is good basis for a pledge; *e.g.* a *statuliber*, or land subject to a rent (*vectigale*), may be pledged, but on the condition being fulfilled or the land being forfeited, the pledge ceases (D. xx 1 fr 13 § 1, 31).

(*d*) Fruits of farms (*praedia rustica*) were held to be pledged to the lessor without express agreement (D. xx 2 fr 7 pr; Cod. viii 14 fr 3). So also the offspring of slaves and, at least when owned by the pledgor, the young of animals (D. xx 1 fr 26 § 2, 29 § 1) according to the Digest, but Paul (ii 5 § 2) denies this of *fetus aut partus*. If a wood was pledged and a ship or other things were made out of the timber, they were not subject to the pledge, unless express words had been used to include them (D. xiii 7 fr 18 § 3). All legal accessions to the thing pledged, such as alluvion to land, or buildings erected on it, or the usufruct falling in after the bare ownership has been pledged, are included in the pledge (D. xiii 7 fr 18 § 1, 21). The *peculium* does not follow the pledge of a slave (D. xx 1 fr 1 § 1).

In tenancies of buildings in towns (*praedia urbana*) the practice was that whatever was brought in with the intention of its staying there (*e.g.* furniture, *etc.*) was without any express agreement deemed to be pledged for the rent, and for any damage caused by the tenant: but this rule did not apply to things brought in only temporarily. The most general terms are used: *illata, inducta, invecta, importata, ibi nata*. A lodger's things were held to be pledged only for his own rent, and if he was granted his lodging for nothing, they were still not pledged for the general rent of the building. Such tacit pledge was no hindrance to the emancipation of a slave, unless rent was actually due and the house was shut up by the landlord to enforce payment (D. xx 2 fr 2—6, 8, 9; xiii 7 fr 11 § 5). A lodger, who has paid the full rent for the period of his lease and desires to move, has a special interdict (*de migrando*) to prevent the landlord detaining any of his things, and this protection extends to things lent or hired out to him or deposited with him (D. xliii 32). In tenancies of farms (*praedia rustica*[1]) only those things which were brought in by agreement with the lessor (*voluntate domini*) were deemed to be so pledged (Cod. iv 65 fr 5; see Dernburg *Pfandr.* 1 p. 312).

(*e*) By a senate's decree under Marcus Aurelius anyone who, at the owner's request, supplied money either to him or to his contractor for reconstructing a building in Rome and its territory, had thereby the house pledged to him (D. xx 2 fr 1, xii 1 fr 25; cf. Cod. viii 14 fr 7). For taxes or contracts with the fisc the whole property of those liable was held to be pledged (Cod. viii 14 fr 1, 2).

(*f*) When the pledge has been handed over to the creditor, he is responsible both for fraud and fault, as in the case of *commodatum*; he is bound to keep safely and without injury to the thing pledged, but he is not responsible for *vis major* (D. xiii 7 fr 13 § 1, 24 § 3; Cod. iv 24 fr 5, 6). His possession is protected, and he retains it even if he leases the thing to the owner, but he cannot gain ownership by usucapion, because he does not possess as his own, but as another's (D. xli 2 fr 37; tit. 3 fr 13 pr, 33 § 6). The debtor has no right to demand restoration of the thing pledged or of any part of it until he (or someone for him) has paid (or at least offers in court) the whole of the debt, including interest, if interest was intended to be covered by the

[1] In Cato's treatise on farming we find forms of contract containing somewhat similar covenants for pledges, *e.g.* in that for selling the olive crop ungathered (*olea pendens*) the purchaser is to gather, and his implements to be pledged till the crop is paid for; *Donicum solutum erit aut ita satis datum erit, quae in fundo illata erunt pigneri sunto: nequid eorum de fundo deportato: siquid deportaverit domini esto* (*RR.* 146 § 2). So for the sale of winter pasturage: *Donicum pecuniam (solverit aut) satisfecerit aut delegarit, pecus et familia quae illic erit pigneri sunto* (*ib.* 149).

pledge. It is at the creditor's choice whether he will accept anything in lieu of payment, *e.g.* another pledge, or sureties, or a new debtor, or surrender his claim on the thing altogether (D. xiii 7 fr 9 §§ 3, 5; xx 6 fr 6 § 1; xlvi 3 fr 40). If however, though the pledge was handed over, the pledgee had never actually paid the loan, or had given a formal release, or had bargained not to sue for it, or the condition of the intended obligation had never occurred, the debtor could bring his action at once for return of the pledge (*ib.* fr 11 § 2). If without payment the debtor carries off the pledge, he is liable to the creditor for theft of the possession (Gai. iii 204). On the other hand if the creditor make use of the thing pledged, he is liable for theft (D. xlvii 2 fr 56 pr).

(*g*) Sometimes a special agreement was made for the creditor to take the fruits and set them off against the interest and principal. This was called ἀντίχρησις. Or, instead of actually working the estate or occupying the house, *etc.* himself, he might let it and set off the rent. The debtor can, after payment has thus or otherwise been taken in full, obtain redelivery of the thing by the ordinary *actio pigneraticia*, but the creditor, if he have lost possession, must obtain an action *in factum* for its recovery, there being in fact no proper pledge, so as to enable him to use the *Serviana* (D. xiii 7 fr 33; xx 1 fr 11 § 1; Cod. iv 24 fr 1; viii 27 fr 1). If a pledge is given for a loan on which debtor pays no interest, the creditor was allowed to retain fruits up to the amount of lawful interest (D. xx 2 fr 8). And generally whenever a creditor, except under some special agreement, retained produce from the pledge whether fruits or timber, or offspring, or rents of land and houses, or wages of slaves, *etc.*, or indirect gains, *e.g.* such as would come from an action or condiction for theft, he has to account for them to the debtor, as he has also for any damage done to the pledge (Cod. iv 24 fr 1—3, 7). On redelivery of the pledge a debtor can call on the creditor for a guaranty against any fraud, or, in the case of land and houses, against any easements having been lost by nonuse (D. xiii 7 fr 15).

(*h*) On the other hand the creditor by the counter action can claim, even if the pledged object has perished, reimbursement for any proper expenses to which he has been put for the maintenance of the thing: *e.g.* medical attendance for a slave, repairs to a house or highway, *etc.*, and for any improvements, not being excessive, made by him (*ib.* fr 8 pr; fr 25: Cod. viii 13 fr 6), and for any impairment of the value made by the debtor (D. xx 1 fr 27).

A creditor of a slave in pledge, who steals from him, can sue the debtor (*furti*) and get noxal conveyance, and the debtor, if aware of the slave's thievish propensity, can be forced (by the counter action) to make full compensation for the creditor's loss (D. xiii 7 fr 31). The creditor can sue by this counter action if the debtor has pledged what does not belong to him, or what has been pledged to someone already, or in any other way has acted fraudulently (*malitiose* fr 9 pr 16).

(*j*) By pledging a thing the debtor did not lose his power of selling or otherwise dealing with it, but any disposition that he makes is subject to the pledge[1]. He has limited his own rights as owner, and subsequent transactions affect only what remains of them, until he has redeemed the pledge and thus regained his full power. Meanwhile he cannot emancipate a slave who is specifically pledged, and, if he disposes secretly of a pledged slave or other moveable, he is liable to the creditor for theft (D. xiii 7 fr 18 § 2; xl 1 fr 13; xlvii 2 fr 19 § 6). Whether an agreement with his creditor not to sell rendered a sale made by the debtor null is much disputed: it appears to be affirmed in the Digest (xx 5 fr 7 § 2).

(*k*) The creditor on the other hand has usually, as part of the agreement of pledge, a right to sell and convey unrestricted ownership in the thing pledged, so far at least as the debtor was owner (Gai. ii 64). Even if the right of sale was given, not generally (*in rem*), but to the creditor, it availed for his heir unless expressly excluded. And unless express agreement was made to the contrary, the right of sale was presumed to

[1] There is a question, whether the child of a pledged slavewoman, born after the debtor had sold her, was subject to the pledge (so D. xiii 7 fr 18 § 2; xliii 33 fr 1 pr) or the free property of the purchaser (so D. xx 1 fr 29 § 1; cf. fr 1 § 2). See Czyhlarz, Glück's *Pand.* on D. xli 1 p. 418, who takes fr 29 to be interpolated.

accompany a pledge, at least in later times (see however D. xlvii 2 fr 74). But the creditor can sell[1] only if the debt and interest remain unpaid on the due date; and only after notice (three notices ?) to the debtor, and after waiting some time (one year? *annus luitionis* Cod. viii 33 fr 3 pr) to give debtor a chance to redeem. If more things than one are the subject of the pledge, he can sell all or which he likes. He is not compelled to sell. If he sells in any way contrary to his agreement, he is liable for theft (of a moveable), and the sale is invalid (Paul ii 5 § 1; D. xiii 7 fr 4—6[2]; 8 § 4; xx 5 fr 8; xlvii 2 fr 74; Cod. viii 27 fr 5). Apart from special agreement with the purchaser the creditor is not responsible for the debtor's title or for faults in the thing, and the purchaser cannot if evicted[3] reclaim the price; nor, if the price is not yet paid and vendor has expressly guarded against being held responsible, can he resist a demand for it. But the creditor is responsible for concealment of defect in the title and for any fraud of his own, and cannot resist redhibition in a proper case (D. xix 1 fr 11 § 16; xx 6 fr 10; xxi 2 fr 68). The purchaser takes the thing free from all obligation to the selling creditor or subsequent creditors, or, unless a right of repurchase was specially reserved, to the debtor. The proceeds of the sale must be applied, first to the payment of interest (if the pledge covered it) and of expenses incurred on the thing; next to discharge of the principal debt: the surplus (if there be no other pledgees) belongs to the debtor, who has a right to be paid without delay in cash and not by delegation of the purchaser. If the debt is repaid completely and there is no chance of redhibition, the debtor is freed from the creditor: if it is not repaid, the creditor retains a claim for the residue. If on the creditor's offering the thing for sale, the debtor purchase at

[1] A notice of intended sale appears to have been affixed to the property. Such a notice put up maliciously was held by Servius Sulpicius to justify an action for insult (D. xlvii 10 fr 15 § 32).

[2] On the interpolations in these see Gradenwitz *Interpol.* p. 22; Eisele *ZRG.* xxiii 304.

[3] The better opinion was that the creditor could be made to cede to the evicted purchaser the creditor's actions against the debtor (D. xxi 2 fr 38).

a price less than the debt, he gains nothing thereby (D. xiii 7 fr 7, 8 § 5, 35, 40 pr, 42; xx 5 fr 7 pr § 1, 9 pr; xlvi 3 fr 26; Cod. viii 27 fr 3).

(*l*) Sometimes, instead of a power of sale being given to the creditor, it was agreed that if by a certain day the debt (and interest) were not paid, the creditor should become owner—in fact be the purchaser at the price of the debt and interest. There was no legal objection to a sale of the pledge to the creditor at any time and whether conditionally or not, but the price must be fixed. In the case supposed the price is in fact fixed by the rate of interest and duration of the loan. In another case the price was left to be determined when the time for payment of the loan arrived; it was to be a fair price (*justum*); and this was confirmed by a rescript of Severus and Antoninus (Vat. 9; D. xx 5 fr 12 pr; tit. 1 fr 16 § 9; cf. xviii 1 fr 81 pr). The practical difference of such arrangements from the clause of forfeiture (*lex commissoria*) in mortgages was apparently that on a sale the debtor could secure by the *actio venditi* a fair account between him and his creditor, whereas on forfeiture the creditor was not accountable for any part payments made by the debtor, or any produce he might himself, if in possession, have got. (See Dernburg *Pfandrecht* ii p. 283.)

Sometimes when no purchaser for the pledge could be found, the creditor obtained from the emperor or praetor the right of retention as owner (D. xiii 7 fr 24 pr; xxxvi 1 fr 61 pr; Cod. viii 33 fr 1, 2, *etc.*).

(*m*) An unsecured creditor (*chirographarius, i.e.* having a written acknowledgment only) has no right forcibly to seize pledges from his debtor without an order from the governor (*praeses*). He is liable under the Julian law for private violence. If however he was authorised by a clause in the agreement, and proceeds to take possession, he is not liable for violence, but he ought first to obtain a magistrate's order. Where he has had a pledge or *fiducia* put into his possession by the debtor, he requires no order to justify him in recovering it if lost (Paul v 26 § 4; Cod. viii 13 fr 3[1]).

[1] This constitution (of Severus and Antoninus, A.D. 205) may refer merely to possession or to (eventual) ownership: *creditores qui non*

(*n*) The same thing may be pledged to two or more persons for different debts: if the later creditor is informed of the previous pledge, or if the value be ample to cover both, the proceeding is lawful; if otherwise, the debtor is liable to a criminal charge. As against third parties each pledgee can claim the whole: as against the debtor they can claim only for the amount of their debt (and interest), and only after earlier pledgees have been satisfied. Whether general or special they rank in order of date of valid constitution of pledge, and, if the money has been actually paid, it does not matter whether the pledge is absolute, or depends on a condition independent of pledgor's will but not yet realised, or on a time not arrived before the constitution of a later pledge; but the mere payment of the money without any constitution of pledge does not entitle the creditor to priority (D. xiii 7 fr 36 § 1; xx 1 fr 16 § 8; tit. 3 fr 1, 2; tit. 4 fr 9 § 1, 11 pr, § 1, 12 § 2; Cod. viii 17 fr 1—8). The first creditor has priority only for advances made before the pledge to others; and for interest (if the pledge covered it), whether accruing before or after subsequent loans. He cannot claim priority if he has consented to such subsequent pledging: but he does not lose his priority by novating his debt and getting additional pledges; and he alone has the right of selling the pledge (D. xx 4 fr 12 §§ 3—6, fr 16, 18). Subsequent creditors with a pledge on some object are entitled to pay off the first or earlier creditors, and stand in their place for the whole amount of the payment so made as well as of their own prior claims, but if they pay sums due for interest, they cannot charge the debtor with interest upon those. This right of a subsequent creditor to obtain his pledge by settling earlier claims cannot be enforced against a purchaser from the creditor, but can against a purchaser from the debtor who has paid the first creditor with the purchase money, or against

reddita sibi pecunia conventionis legem, ingressi possessionem, exercent, vim quidem facere non videntur, attamen auctoritate praesidis possessionem adipisci debent (Cod. viii 13 fr 3). Mitteis (*Reichsrecht* p. 431) shews that agreements giving the creditor rights over the debtor's property without further application to the courts (καθάπερ ἐκ δίκης, sometimes ὡς ὠφληκὼς δίκην) were common in the eastern half of the Mediterranean from cir. 200 B.C. to 200 A.D. and later; cf. Arndts' *Pand.* § 379 n. 2.

a surety who on discharging his own obligation gets the pledge as if by purchase (Paul ii 13 § 8; D. xx 5 fr 2, 3; Cod. viii 19 fr 1; cf. D. xvii 1 fr 59 § 1). A later creditor obtains priority over those preceding for any expenditure required for the preservation of the thing pledged; *e.g.* if a ship be pledged, then for money spent on its repairs or on food of the sailors; if goods be pledged, then for freight or carriage or warehousing, *etc.* And a minor had priority if the pledged thing had been bought with his money (D. xx 4 fr 4—6 pr). The Crown, in all matters except taxes, has no right to priority on property acquired by debtor before the Crown pledge was established (fr 21; Cod. iv 46 fr 1).

In case of death of either creditor or debtor the debt (or credit) is divided among heirs automatically, but pledges belong to each coheir, and the consequent arrangements are matter for a suit *fam. ercisc.* (D. x 2 fr 18 § 7, 29; xx 5 fr 11, 14; Cod. viii 31 fr 1, 2).

(*o*) A pledge is extinguished by destruction of the thing pledged, or by payment of the debt, or by acceptance of a surety for the whole debt in lieu of the pledge, or by a bargain not to sue for the debt, or by an oath duly tendered and taken denying the debt, or by novation, or by consent of the creditor to waive it, whether he waive the debt itself or not. If creditor consent to debtor's sale or disposal of the object pledged, it is a question of fact whether he does so knowing that the pledge remains, though the ownership is changed, or intending to give up his claim. The latter appears to be assumed in the absence of special circumstances or expression. If the sale is for the purpose of paying off the creditor, the safer course is for him to require a written undertaking (*cautio*) from the intending purchaser to pay him out of the purchase money (D. xiii 7 fr 11 § 1; xx 6 fr 4, 5, 6 pr, 8 §§ 10, 15; L 17 fr 158). If a sale is rescinded, the parties re-enter into their previous rights (D. xx 6 fr 10). A creditor may sell his rights without in any way impairing them (fr 5 § 2). Nor is the pledge affected by creditor's obtaining judgment against the principal debtor or surety (D. xx 1 fr 13 § 4); nor by anyone obtaining the ownership by usucapion (D. xx 1 fr 1 § 2; xli 3 fr 44 § 5).

(*p*) A ward could not take or waive a pledge without his guardian's consent, nor could a procurator or slave appointed manager (*actor*), waive one, unless this was specially allowed them; nor could a son under power or slave waive a pledge for a peculiar debt, unless they got value for the waiver (D. xiii 7 fr 38; xx 6 fr 7 pr § 1; fr 8 § 5). A procurator can receive possession of a pledge for which his principal has contracted, but cannot make his principal liable on a contract of pledge: nor can he give anything of his principal's in pledge, unless he have previous mandate or his act be ratified, or he have the general management of the estate of one who was in the habit of taking loans on pledge: even then it is the procurator himself who will have the right to bring the pledge-action (D. xiii 7 fr 11 § 6 fr 12; Cod. iv 27 fr 3; but cf. D. xx 1 fr 21 pr). A debtor can resist the pledgee's suit by pleading a bargain of waiver made for him by his slave, or by a plea of fraud, if the bargain was made by his procurator (D. xx 6 fr 7 § 2).

(*q*) Where a creditor who has a pledge is himself in debt to another, it is possible for him to make this pledge a security to his own creditor; but it is good only so long as both debts are unpaid: if the first debtor pay off his debt, he can recover the pledge, and the second creditor must look to the money or other thing so paid to satisfy or secure his own claim (D. xx 1 fr 13 § 2; xiii 7 fr 40 § 2).

(*r*) Creditor's actions.

Where a thing was pledged, but was neither in the ownership (*fiducia*) nor the possession (*pignus*) of the creditor, he had his action on the loan or against the debtor, but originally no actual hold over the thing, and no power of recovering it from third parties or from the debtor himself. To meet this want, the praetor provided gradually several remedies:

Where a farmer had pledged his goods for the rent, the landlord had an interdict (*Salvianum interdictum*, first granted by a praetor Salvius?) to recover the goods from the farmer

(Gai. iv 147). Whether this interdict could be brought against third parties is not clear[1].

An action called *actio Serviana* (author and date unknown) was also granted to the lessor in the case of farm tenancies, and apparently not only where there had been an express agreement of pledge, but in all tenancies. And it ran against third parties as well as against the farmer himself (Just. iv 6 § 7; D. xx 1 fr 10). On the analogy of this an action was granted to all creditors who had not received payment to get or re-get possession of hypothecated goods. It was called *quasi-Serviana* and also *hypothecaria* (Just. *l.c.*; D. xvi 1 fr 13 § 1). Both the *Serviana* and *quasi-Serviana*, practically treated as one, were actions *in rem* available against any possessor, and the creditor was said *vindicare pignus*. Defendant is condemned, if he possessed the pledge and did not either restore or pay the damages: he is also condemned, if he has fraudulently parted with the possession: and in this case the damages are fixed by plaintiff's oath. If defendant pay damages and debtor sue for the pledge, he cannot recover without offering the value of the debt for which it was pledged. If the debtor possesses the pledge, and the Servian action is brought against him, the damages will be, not as in the case of other possessors for the full value of the thing, but only for the amount of the debt (D. xx 1 fr 16 § 3, 21 § 3; tit. 4 fr 12 pr; tit. 5 fr 1; tit. 6 fr 2; xiii 7 fr 43 pr). If this action be brought by a second creditor against the first, being in possession, he would be met by the plea *Si non mihi ante pignori, hypothecaeve nomine, sit res obligata*: if brought by the first against the second, being in possession, and the second plead *Si non convenit ut mihi res sit obligata*, the first can retort in the words of the previous plea (*si non mihi, etc.* fr 12 pr). A purchaser from the creditor could not bring the Servian action, at least in his own name (D. xxi 2 fr 66 pr).

Where a debt had been pledged, the praetor (as stated above *b*) eventually granted an *actio utilis* to the creditor to enable him to recover from the debtor's debtor (D. xiii 7 fr 18 pr;

[1] Cod. viii 9 fr 1 says expressly, no: but D. xliii 33 fr 1 says, yes. Lenel (comparing this latter with xx 1 fr 10) supposes the passage corrupted by Tribonian. See *ZRG*. xvi 180 sqq.

Cod. viii 16 fr 4; iv 39 fr 7). So one who lent money for the repair of a house, and by agreement was to recoup himself out of the rents, had an analogous action against the lodgers (D. xx 1 fr 20).

3. *PIGNORIS CAPIO.* 'Levying a distress.'

An old right of 'taking a pledge' is mentioned by Gaius. *Pignoris capio* was authorised by custom in the case of soldiers against the persons charged with giving them either their pay (*aes militare, stipendii nomine*), or the money for the purchase of a horse (*aes equestre*) or of barley for the horse (*aes hordiarium*). The soldier might seize something by way of pledge[1], if the distributor made default. What would happen, if the distributor did not ransom it, we are not informed.

By the XII tables a like right was given in two cases: against one who had bought a victim for sacrifice and did not pay the price; and against one who had not paid the hire-money for a draught horse (*jumentum*) which had been let out in order to raise thereby money for a sacrificial feast (*in dapem, id est, in sacrificium*).

By the censors a like right was granted to the farmers of the public taxes of the Roman people against those who made default in payment[2]. But later the tax-farmer had a regular action to recover the same amount, as defendant would have had to pay in order to redeem such a pledge, if it had been taken.

In all these cases the levying of a distress[3] was accompanied

[1] There is an allusion to this in Plaut. *Poen.* 1285 *Pro majore parte prandi pignus cepi, abii foras: sic dedero: aere militari tetigero lenunculum;* cf. *Aul.* 526 sqq.

[2] Comp. Cic. *Verr.* iii 11 § 27 *Omnibus in aliis vectigalibus...publicanus petitor aut* (most MSS. have *ac*) *pignerator, non ereptor neque possessor solet esse.*

A similar right is given in certain cases to a company which farmed a mine at Vipascum in Spain (Bruns[6] no. 97 lines 16 and 35. The date is about end of first cent. p. Chr.).

[3] On English and other analogies see Maine's *Early Hist. of Institutions,* Lect. ix.

by a declaration in a set form of words, so that most lawyers, says Gaius, considered it was a *legis actio*, which in the sense of a proceeding authorised by statute it was; but, as other lawyers pointed out, it lacked the characteristics of a judicial procedure: it was done out of court; it was mostly done in the absence of the other party; and it could be done on a non-religious day (*die nefasto*), *i.e.* when judicial *lege agere* was not permitted. It was obsolete in Gaius' time (Gai. iv 26—30, 32; cf. Wlassak *PG* i 251).

A magistrate in some cases levied a distress in order to compel obedience to his orders (*pignora capere, pignoribus cogere, coercere*)[1]. Thus in the *lex Quintia* (B.C. 10) providing for the protection of the Roman aqueducts, breaches of the law may be punished either by a fine or by taking pledge (*multa pignoribus cogito coerceto* Bruns[6] p. 116); so in cases of alimony (D. xxv 3 fr. 5 § 10 *pignoribus captis et distractis cogetur*). And a procedure by such a levy of distress was made part of ordinary execution for debt by Ant. Pius (D. xlii 1 fr 15, 31). See below, Book VI chap. xiii C.

If municipal magistrates took pledges and allowed them to spoil, or if they thus took cattle and did not allow the owner to feed them, they were liable to an action under the Aquilian statute (D. ix 2 fr 29 § 7).

D. 1. (*a*) *MANDATUM* is a commission or order given by one person to another to do something on the mandator's account without payment for his services. If payment for the service is a condition and is fixed in amount, the business is one of

[1] This exercise of executive power is recorded of consuls, praetors, censors, tribunes, and aediles (Mommsen *Staatsr.* i² 152). So of the *decemviri* Liv. iii 38 § 12. In Cic. *Orat.* iii 1 § 4 the consul Philippus is recorded to have taken this step as a retort to Crassus' speech against him in the senate: *graviter exarsit pignoribusque ablatis Crassum instituit coercere.* The pledges so taken were often destroyed by the magistrate; hence Crassus retorted: *An tu cum omnium auctoritatem universi ordinis pro pignore putaris eamque in conspectu populi Romani concideris, me his existimas pignoribus terreri;* cf. Liv. xxxvii 51 § 4; xliii 16 § 5; Suet. *Jul.* 17.

letting and hiring; if the payment is not fixed, an action on the case might be the mode of enforcement (D. xvii 1 fr 1 § 4; xix 5 fr 22). But occasionally remuneration was made for such services (*honorarium* or, if continuous, *salarium*), and could be demanded only by an extraordinary application to the praetor or governor. It is spoken of chiefly in connexion with the conduct of a suit at law. A bargain for a share of the proceeds of a lawsuit before it was decided was illegal (D. xvii 1 fr 6 § 7, fr 7; L 13 fr 1 § 12; Cod. iv 35 fr 1, 20).

(*b*) A mandate may be given orally or by letter or message: no special form of words is required. It may be conditional or to take effect only from some future time (*in diem*). Present knowledge and acquiescence, or even subsequent ratification may be tantamount to a mandate and make a person liable. Consent on the part of the recipient is of course necessary (D. xvii 1 fr 1; L 17 fr 60).

A mandator has an action (*directa mandati actio*)[1] against the mandatee (*cui mandatum est*) to secure the due fulfilment of the commission: the mandatee has a counter-action (*contraria mand. actio*) to recover his expenses and in some cases to enforce release from his charge. Condemnation made either party infamous (Gai. iv 182; D. iii 2 fr 6 § 5). For fraud of either party his heir was liable in full[2] (D. xliv 7 fr 12).

[1] Cicero shews the principle of the Roman law of mandate: *In privatis rebus si qui rem mandatam non modo malitiosius gessisset sui quaestus aut commodi causa, verum etiam negligentius, eum majores summum admisisse dedecus existimabant. Itaque mandati constitutum est judicium non minus turpe quam furti, credo propterea, quod quibus in rebus ipsi interesse non possumus, in iis operae nostrae vicaria fides amicorum supponitur: quam qui laedit, oppugnat omnium commune praesidium, et quantum in ipso est, disturbat vitae societatem. Non enim possumus omnia per nos agere: alius in alia est re magis utilis. Idcirco amicitiae comparantur, ut commune commodum mutuis officiis gubernetur. Quid recipis mandatum si aut neglecturus aut ad tuum commodum conversurus es? cur mihi te offers ac meis commodis officio simulato officis et obstas? Recede de medio: per alium transigam etc.* (*Rosc. Am.* 38 § 111 sqq.; *Top.* 17 § 66).

The judge was *arbiter* (Cic. *Rosc. Am.* 39 § 114).

[2] Cf. *ad Heren.* ii 13 § 19 *Fit ut de eadem re saepe alius aliud decreverit aut judicarit, quod genus; M. Drusus praetor urbanus, quod cum herede mandati ageretur, judicium reddidit, Sex. Julius non reddidit.* We know

(*c*) The death of either party while the mandate is still unexecuted puts an end to it, and if mandatee's heir executed it, he could not sue the mandator. If the mandator died and mandatee in ignorance proceeded with the mandate, practical convenience was held (*utilitatis causa receptum est*) to require that he should be able to sue the mandator's heirs (Gai. iii 160; D. xvii 1 fr 26 pr, 27 § 3).

A mandate for something to be done after the mandatee's death[1] is invalid; for no obligation should commence with the heir. And a mandate for the performance of what is immoral, *e.g.* to despoil a temple or to wound or kill a man, is also invalid. So execution of a young man's mandate to lend money to a prostitute, or be surety for her, gives the mandatee, knowing the facts, no right of action against the mandator: it is simply helping him to throw away his money (Gai. iii 157, 158; D. xvii 1 fr 12 §§ 11, 17, fr 22 § 6).

(*d*) A mandate may relate to the business of the mandator himself or to that of others or to that of the mandatee. The last case gives rise to doubt. If I tell you to invest your idle money, or to make some purchase for yourself, the question arises whether this is mere counsel or proper mandate. If it is counsel and you choose to follow it, you take the consequences, and I am not responsible, however it turn out. Servius appears to have held that instruction however specific

nothing of the circumstances of these decisions nor whether, as commonly supposed, it was in a suit against the heir of a mandatee.

[1] The reading in Gaius iii 158 is somewhat awkward but it appears to relate to the mandatee's death. (The MS. has *si quis post mortem meam faciundum mandet.*) A mandate for something to be done after mandator's death is taken by many (*e.g.* Huschke *Gaius ad loc.*; Arndt's *Pand.* § 294, *etc.*) to be valid, and not revoked by his death, on the strength of D. xvii 1 fr 12 § 17, 13, 27 § 1. I am inclined to think that such a mandate is no exception to the general rule of revocation by death, but it is not invalid *ab initio*, and consequently supports an action whenever execution has proceeded in mandator's life (cf. Cod. iv 35 fr 15). This would explain the first and third passages and perhaps fr 13 if we had the detail. D. xlvi 3 fr 108 is clear for revocation where the mandate has not been already carried into a stipulation by a third party. Justinian altered the old rule (Cod. iv 11); and the Digest is therefore open to suspicion on this matter (cf. Windscheid *Pand.* § 411).

to anyone to act on his own behalf never made the giver responsible to the doer. Sabinus held that it amounted to mandate if the doer acted only on account of the instructions. The mandatee then relied on the mandator's guaranty (Gai. iii 155, 156; cf. D. xvii 1 fr 2). See below, p. 121.

(*e*) The terms of the mandate must be closely followed: otherwise the mandatee cannot claim reimbursement (at least in full), and the mandator, if damnified, can claim the amount of his interest in having the mandate executed as undertaken. A mandate to lend money, taking proper security (*cautio idonea*), is not followed if neither pledge nor surety is taken. A mandate to buy a farm for 100,000 sesterces may be well fulfilled by purchasing for less, but not for more, not even, according to the Sabinians, if the mandatee is willing to let the mandator have it for the sum he named; for that would be to make a contract exist or not at the will of one party. The Proculians however held that he could compel acceptance at that price. If one is commissioned to sell a thing at a certain price and sells at less, the sale will be upheld only if mandatee make up the amount (Gai. iii 161; D. xvii 1 fr 3 § 2—5 § 3, 33, 59 § 6; Paul ii 15 § 3). The principle was that the mandatee might improve the position of his mandator but might not make it worse: and it is only if the mandator can shew that he is damnified by mandatee's improper action or neglect that mandator can sue (D. *ib.* fr 8 § 6; cf. fr 49 pr). The mandatee is liable for any breach of good faith or for gross negligence in the matter: he is bound to deliver up all profits from the business, is chargeable with interest if he has delayed the payment of what he has obtained, and is bound to hold, transfer, or deal with, any property or obligation he may have acquired in the matter as mandator may direct, or, if no direction be given, then for his best interest (fr 8 § 9—fr 10 § 3, § 6).

(*f*) On the other hand a mandatee can recover from mandator all expenses *bona fide* incurred, though more than the mandator himself might have spent; and suit need not be postponed till the conclusion of the business. Sometimes he will have an equitable claim to interest on any money which he has found it necessary to advance for the discharge of his commission. But if he has in pursuing the business been robbed or shipwrecked and lost his goods, or if he himself or his servants have fallen ill and caused medical expenses, he cannot charge the mandator with what is his own bad luck and not properly incidental to the business (D. fr 12 § 9; 26 § 6; 27 § 4; 56 § 4). If however mandator has commissioned him to buy a particular slave and the slave steals from him, mandator is bound to make up the loss in full (D. xlvii 2 fr 62 § 5; xxx fr 70 § 2).

(*g*) A mandatee may in some cases claim release from his engagement, or that his mandator should take upon himself the obligation he has incurred, as for instance if he has bought a thing by instructions and has no ready cash to pay the price; or has become bail for mandator's appearance to a suit and mandator has failed to appear; or has undertaken another's obligation either by his direction or as *negotiorum gestor*, and has been condemned to pay (D. xvii 1 fr 38 § 1, 45 pr—§ 5). Of his own motion mandatee can renounce the charge, only if it be untouched, and he give timely notice to mandator so that he can conveniently commission someone else: the mandator then would not be damnified. Any renunciation without these guards would require good reason, such as mandatee's sudden illness, a necessary journey, a quarrel between the parties, the hopelessness of success (*inanes rei actiones*), or unfair loss (*captio*) resulting to the mandatee. The mandator can revoke his mandate so long as the matter is untouched. The equities of such cases, as of all occurring in a *bona fide* contract, would be for the judge to settle on action being brought (Gai. iii 159; Paul ii 15 § 1; D. fr 22 § 11—fr 5, 27 § 2).

(*h*) If two persons give the mandate, either may be sued for the whole amount, but if judgment be given expressly against both, each is then liable only for his own share. Of two mandatees each is liable for the whole, but only one whole can be exacted (D. fr 59 § 3, 60 § 2).

A mandatee can employ others to do the business, and is responsible to them on the mandate he has given, and to his own principal for its proper execution. His obligation to his own mandatee is the measure of his claim on his mandator. The principal can demand surrender of the middle man's actions against the actual executant (D. iii 5 fr 20 § 3, 27).

(*j*) In two cases of mandate the mandatee is generally called *procurator* and the mandator *dominus*: (1) when the subject-matter is not one piece of work only but a regular part of a man's business (D. iii 3 fr 1): and (2) when it is the conduct of a lawsuit (Gai. iv 84). For the latter see Book VI chap. ix.

(*k*) In two other cases the relation created by the mandate is that of surety or guarantor. A *fide promissor* or *fidejussor*[1], if he duly discharges the debt, and sometimes before discharging it, had a right of action as mandatee against the principal debtor: provided that he became surety at the debtor's request or at least with his knowledge or acquiescence (D. xvii 1 fr 40, 50, 53). But a like relation in some respects may be created by a mandate to the creditor to lend money or otherwise trust the debtor[2]. The mandator in effect guarantees the account. The difference however between a *fidejussor* and a *mandator* is, that the surety is bound to the creditor by a stipulation, and recoups himself for anything paid by a counter action (*mandati*) against the debtor, the guarantor is bound to the creditor by a formless agreement, and recoups himself only by getting a surrender of the creditor's actions against the debtor. The obligation of a surety is accessory to that of the debtor, and is destroyed, if the creditor joins issue with the principal: the obligation of a guarantor is independent and therefore unaffected by the fact of suit against the debtor: he remains liable for any balance of the debt which the principal is unable to meet. Or the creditor can, if he choose, sue the mandator without first suing the debtor or selling pledges, and the debtor is not thereby released. Suit against one co-surety in certain cases frees all, but suit against one co-guarantor leaves the others still liable, until payment is made in full (Paul ii 17 § 16; D. xvii 1

[1] A sponsor had a special action (*depensi*). See p. 184.

[2] The mandator used such expressions as *negotium mihi gere, periculum est meum, periculo meo crede, etc.* The mandatee was said *fidem mandantis sequi* D. xvii 1 fr 12 § 13, 48 § 1; 60 § 1, iii 2 fr 6 § 5.

fr 27 § 5, 28, 56 pr, 60 pr.; xlvi 1 fr 13, 41 § 1, 52 § 3, 71; Cod. viii 40 fr 28 pr)[1].

Jussus[2]. 'Order.'

Mandate must be distinguished from order (*jussus*), though the words are often used loosely of the same business. *Mandatum* is a contract: *jussus* a one-sided declaration of will. In the execution of the business a mandatee may have dealings and make contracts with third parties, but they are not thereby in relation with the mandator: whereas a person receiving and acting on an order puts third parties into direct relation with the person giving the order, but has himself no contract with him (cf. D. xlvi 3 fr 66). *Jussus* is used (not to speak of orders by public authority such as the senate or praetor) of an order which directly affects the giver's financial position, as of a testator making his slave free and heir, *liberum et heredem esse jubet* (Gai. ii 186); or of a father or master directing his son or slave to enter on an inheritance; or authorising anyone to contract with his son or slave, whence the outsider gets an action *quod jussu* against the father or master (Gai. ii 188—190; iii 167 *a*; iv 70); or of an order to a procurator to novate an obligation (Paul v 8); or of a creditor's directing his debtor to promise someone on a stipulation (Gai. ii 38); or to pay the debt to a third party: *Cum jussu meo id, quod mihi debes, solvis creditori meo, et tu a me et ego a te liberor* (D. xlvi 3 fr 64; cf. L 17 fr 180).

[1] Where a slave is said to give a third person a mandate to buy him from his master with the slave's money and then manumit him, there is no real mandate. A slave cannot buy, or give a real mandate; nor can he be conceived as acting for his master, for that would be for the master to give a mandate to buy his own slave. The purchaser is liable for the price, and if the price is taken from the slave's *peculium* it is in law the vendor's own money, and only by his knowledge and consent can it be treated as effective payment. If the purchaser does not manumit the slave, an action on the mandate can be brought by the vendor, based, according to Papinian, on his affection for the slave, who may be supposed to be the vendor's natural relative.

[2] Cf. Salpius *Novation* p. 50 sqq.; Pernice *Labeo* i 504 sq.; Brinz *Pand.* ii § 282, p. 375 n. ed 2.

An order should precede, not like a guardian's authority await, the performance of the action ordered (D. xxix 2 fr 25 § 4). It may be oral or by letter or messenger or formal declaration before witnesses (*testato*): and may be revoked before being acted on (D. xv 4 fr 1 § 1) and is revoked by the death of the giver (D. xlvi 3 fr 32). If the order is given by the medium of another, the person responsible is he on whose account it was given (*cujus nomine jusserit* D. xliii 24 fr 5 § 12).

2. *NEGOTIORUM GESTIO.* 'Unauthorised agency.'

(*a*) Management of another's business was recognised by the praetor as a good basis for suits between the parties. The edict on this matter was couched in quite general terms; *Si quis negotia alterius gesserit*[1], *judicium eo nomine dabo.* But as mandate, guardianship, *etc.* had special actions, the action for 'business done' was used where the agent had no authority, either special or general, but was justified by the risk of serious loss to the absentee if no one volunteered to act for him. The swift process of the law courts in the case of absent and undefended debtors gave frequent occasion for a friend's interference. Or again a pledge might be sold by a creditor, a penalty on a stipulation might be incurred, a right of returning a faulty slave might be lost, or some injury might be done to a person's rights or property, if no one interfered in time, when the principal had been suddenly called away or been unexpectedly detained. Nor was it only conscious action for a particular person's benefit that justified the suit against him. Misapprehension whose business it really was, or wrong belief that he had a commission to do it, did not prevent an obligation arising. But there must be an intention to put someone under an obligation, and this action would then serve to adjust the matter between him and the real principal (D. iii 5 fr 1—3 pr § 10, fr 5 § 1; x 3 fr 14 § 1; xliv 7 fr 5 pr).

The person, whose affairs had thus been handled without his authority, has a direct action to call the agent to account

[1] These words were originally not technical, cf. Cic. *Inv.* i 26 §§ 37, 38.

for any failure in the duty which he has undertaken, and for any retention of what belongs to the principal. The agent has a set off and, if necessary, a counter action to recover any useful expenditure he has made, and to be held harmless for any obligation he has properly incurred on the other's account (fr 2, 7 § 2).

(*b*) Direct action. As special instances of liability to this action may be mentioned a mother's interfering in the affairs of her son who is under guardianship; a father's managing his son's property after emancipation, the property being given him without reserve; a guardian continuing in the administration of his ward, after the guardianship is really ended (Paul i 4 §§ 2, 4, 7); a caretaker managing the affairs of a madman or spendthrift or of a minor above the age of puberty (D. xxvii 3 fr 4 § 3, fr 13). If a father by will appoint a guardian for his postumous son, and the person appointed acts in the affairs but no postumous son is born, he is not liable to a suit for guardianship, for he was no guardian, but is liable for business done (D. iii 5 fr 28). If I order a freeman in *bona fide* slavery to me to do something, there will be no relation of mandate between us, for he acts, not as in a voluntary contract but under supposed compulsion; he will be liable however to this action (fr 18 § 2). If under a mistaken belief that Titius owes you money, I collect it for you, and you ratify my conduct, you thereby make the business yours, and can sue me for business done: Titius can recover the money from you by *cond. indebiti* (fr 5 §§ 11, 12). If you have sold what you erroneously believed to be in the *peculium* of a slave whom you have bought, or in a bequest to yourself, the real owner or legatee can claim it, and, if it has perished, can sue for the price by this action, or by a condiction (fr 48, xii 1 fr 23). I can sue by this action anyone who has received money or anything else and undertaken to bring it to me (D. iii 5 fr 5 § 4).

If a son or slave manages another's business at his father's or master's command, the latter is responsible by this action in full: if without such command, the action is good only to the extent of the *peculium*. Similarly in the reverse case, if another manages business for a son or slave, looking to the father or master, this latter is responsible in the action; if however the *negot. gestor* does so, looking only to the son or slave himself or from friendship to them, the limitation to the *peculium* comes in (Paul i 4 §§ 5, 6; D. iii 5 fr 5 § 8). A slave who becomes free is not himself responsible for management of another's affairs any more than for other acts done whilst a slave, unless it was so continuous with his management afterwards that it could not be separated. The Proculians however held that if he retained in his *peculium* what was due to the person whose business he had managed, he should be liable just as a freeman would on the principles of good faith. Sabinus appears to have agreed that he should be liable for anything actually due in his accounts, but not for any fault or fraud committed while in slavery (fr 16—18 § 1).

(*c*) As a volunteer, whose action moreover might prevent others more competent from interfering, such an agent is as a rule responsible not only for fraud but for fault also, though if the emergency be great, some fault may be excused (fr 3 § 9; L 17 fr 23). He cannot without good cause drop business which he has taken up, nor can he confine himself to certain matters only, if a careful man would be expected to do other things as well. He must act for the other's interest against himself, whenever the other was entitled so to act, especially if speedy action is important: must collect any debt due from himself, and, if the debt was without interest originally, it will carry interest from its due date, at such rate as the creditor was getting on other loans (D. iii 5 fr 5 § 14, fr 34, 37). Having no mandate, he cannot usually collect debts from others by legal process, but in some cases, *e.g.* if the business is his son's or father's or kinsman's or patron's, he does not require mandate, provided he offer security for ratification; and then it may be his duty to do this and sue on their behalf (fr 7 pr; cf. tit. 3 fr 35 pr). He must pay interest on any of his principal's money remaining after deduction of expenses; and must as a rule bear the risk of any investments he may make for him, if, when issue is joined in this action, they are found to be bad. And if he has made purchases or entered into business of any kind not usual with his principal, he may have to bear any loss which may accrue (fr 10, 30 § 3, 36 § 1; Paul i 4 § 3). The fact that he is managing the other's affairs does not disable him from gaining by usucapion the property in a thing belonging to the other, which he has bought in ignorance of the real owner; but if he has discovered, before usucapion is completed, whose it was, he ought to get someone to sue for it in the absentee's name so that the usucapion may be broken, and he may be entitled to reimbursement from his vendor under the stipulation for eviction (fr 18 § 3).

(*d*) Counter action. A *negotiorum gestor* can claim reimbursement for expenses of management only so far as it has really been for his principal's interest (*utiliter gestum*), or (whether useful or not) has been approved by him. But he cannot charge more expenses than were really necessary, although he may have spent more, nor can he, at least in Julian's opinion, recover any expenses, however useful, incurred after the principal has forbidden him to interfere. But it is not necessary that his action should have been successful; *e.g.* if he has repaired (*fulsit*) a house or tended a sick slave and his action was right, the fall of the house or death of the slave does not impede his claim (fr 8, 9, 21, 26; Cod. ii 18 fr 24 § 1). He is not entitled to any payment for his own services, and if he has meddled with a view to his own profit, he can charge only so much as he has enriched his principal (fr 5 § 5). Nor can he recover at all, if he has acted from affection or duty to children or parents or patron's children, and not as a matter of business. Thus a mother cannot recover from her son's estate for the cost of his nurture or his household, unless she has declared, or the facts shew, that she intended not a gift, but an advance to be repaid afterwards (fr 33; Cod. ii 18 fr 1, 5, 11).

(*e*) Some instances of the cases where the doer of the business can sue the principal may be given. If I defend your slave in a noxal action without your knowledge, I can sue you for the full amount, not merely *de peculio* (fr 40). If in the belief that I am heir, I hand over to legatees things of my own, the real heir is thereby cleared of an obligation, and I can recover the value from him (fr 48). Where a person has acted in business common to him and others, he can recover expenses by the partnership action or that *communi dividundo,* provided he could not separate his interest; if he could, as for instance in giving security *damni infecti,* limit it to his own share of the suspected house, but has not so limited, he can get contribution only by the action *negot. gest.* (D. x 3 fr 6 §§ 2, 7). Where one of several owners of water-rights defends the right in a suit, the action *com. div.* not being applicable to incorporal things, he must use the action *negot. gest.* to recover from his co-owners (D. iii 5 fr 30 § 7). Where of three captives one was released by the Lusitanians on condition of bringing ransom for all three but did not return, and the two others had to pay for him as well as for themselves, Servius held that the praetor ought to grant them an action against him (fr 20 pr). Where a loan of money has been made to *A* on the faith of a letter from *B* or on other evidence of its being intended to pay *B*'s debts, the creditor can pass over *A*, and sue *B* instead, by an action *negot. gest.*, on the analogy of an action by the creditor of an *institor* (fr 31 pr; D. xvii 1 fr 10 § 5; cf. xxvi 9 fr 5 § 1). Where *A* is a recognised procurator of *B*, the creditor can sue *B*, but not *A* (D. iii 5 fr 5 § 3). A surety without mandate can sue the principal by this action (D. xvii 1 fr 20 § 1).

(*f*) Both actions are *bonae fidei*: just as in mandate, the parties *aeque invicem experiri possunt de eo quod ex bona fide alterum alteri praestare oportet* (D. xliv 7 fr 5 pr; cf. iii 5 fr 2, 17).

Both women and heirs could sue and be sued, either by direct or by counter action (D. iii 5 fr 3 §§ 1, 7). The edict expressly recognised action on behalf of one who was dead, *i.e.* a vacant inheritance, and it did not matter whether the heir turned out to be of full age or not: he takes over this obligation along with others (fr 3 § 6, 20 § 1). The *actio funeraria* is an action of this nature (cf. D. xi 7 fr 14 §§ 7, 11, 13).

E. *Societas.* 1. Ordinary partnership.

(*a*) Partnership is a contract whereby two or more persons agree to work together for common profit, or to acquire and hold property in common, sharing the gains and the losses.

They may combine only for one particular piece of business, or to carry on a continuous trade or enterprise, or they may even agree to put all they have into a common stock and share each other's fortunes of whatever kind[1]. In the absence of any wider intentions clearly shewn, the partnership will be taken to relate only to business matters and to the gain and loss thence arising, in which case inheritances, legacies, gifts will be outside the contract. The technical expression for forming a partnership was *coire societatem*[2]. For any failure in the performance of the contract the proper remedy was an action, usually called *judicium pro socio, i.e.* 'a suit in the character of partner,' brought against the offending partner or partners. It was an action *bonae fidei*; and condemnation brought infamy[3] (D. xvii 2 fr 1, 5, 7—9; Gai. iii 148; iv 62, 182). The judge was often called *arbiter*[4] (D. fr 38 pr).

[1] It is probable that this thorough-going partnership sprang from the position of brothers and sisters living together as joint heirs to their father. *Consortes* appears to have this special application. Gellius (i 9) speaking of the Pythagoreans says, *quod quisque familiae, pecuniae, habebat, in medium dabat, et coibatur societas inseparabilis, tamquam illud fuit anticum consortium, quod jure atque verbo Romano appellabatur 'Ercto non cito'* (?*erctum non cito*, 'where there was no summons to divide the inheritance'). Cf. Ovid *Her.* iii 47 *Vidi ego consortes pariter generisque necisque tres cecidisse.* Dig. xvii 2 fr 52 § 8 *Si inter fratres voluntarium consortium initum fuerat*; cf. *ib.* § 6 (Leist *röm. societas* p. 20). An instance appears to be found in Plin. *Ep.* viii 18 § 4 *Consors frater in fratris potestatem emancupatam filiam adoptionis fraude revocaverat.*

[2] Cf. Cic. *Quinct.* 24 § 76; *Rosc. Am.* 8 § 21; *Rosc. Com.* 18 § 55; Suet. *Aug.* 32; Gai. iii 148; D. xvii 2 fr 1; *etc.*

[3] Cf. Cic. *Rosc. Am.* 40 § 116 *In rebus minoribus socium fallere turpissimum est, aequeque turpe, atque illud de quo ante dixi* (*i.e. mandatum negligere*); *Rosc. Com.* 6 § 16 *Si qua enim sunt privata judicia summae existimationis, et paene dicam, capitis, tria haec sunt fiduciae, tutelae, societatis. Aeque enim perfidiosum et nefarium est fidem frangere, quae continet vitam, et pupillum fraudare qui in tutelam pervenit, et socium fallere qui se in negotio conjunxit*; *Top.* 10 § 42; 17 § 66.

[4] Cf. Cic. *Rosc. Com.* 9 § 25 *Cur non arbitrum pro socio adegeris Q. Roscium, quaero*, 'why you did not drive him before an arbiter on a partnership action.' *Quinct.* 3 § 13 *Quasi qui magna fide societatem gererent, arbitrium pro socio condemnari solerent* (Cicero is speaking ironically). The expression *arbitrium...condemnari* is strange (see note in Orelli

(*b*) Partnership is formed by simple consent without any formality, either by words, writing or message, either for a definite period or not, and may commence from a future time. Whether its existence could be made conditional on the occurrence of some event was a disputed point (D. fr 1, 4; Cod. iv 37 fr 6). It can always be dissolved by consent, or by one of the parties renouncing; but, if the renunciation is made unseasonably or with the view of securing unfair advantage, the renouncing partner is liable (*a se liberat socios, se autem ab illis non liberat*): and accordingly if the other be absent at the time, the one renouncing must share all gain he receives and all loss occurring to either, and has no claim on any gain coming to the absentee, up to the time when knowledge reaches him. Even if the partnership arrangement provided against dissolution within a certain period, circumstances may justify earlier renunciation. Partnership is dissolved by the death of a partner, by his bankruptcy, by confiscation and sale of his estate, by the conclusion of the business, or destruction of the thing which was the object of the partnership, or by the action *pro socio* being brought (D. fr 14—17, 63 § 10—65 § 6, §§ 9, 10; Gai. iii 151—154).

A partner's heir did not become a partner, even if it were so provided at the commencement of the partnership, but he should assist in winding up the business, and can claim and is responsible under the action *pro socio* for fraud and negligence, and for anything accruing from the common property or business until his predecessor's death, though not received till afterwards (D. fr 35, 36, 40, 53 § 8, 65 § 9). *Capitis deminutio* was also said to dissolve partnership, but the dissolution in this case might be got over at once by consent of all to continue. According to the Digest indeed, a partner continued notwithstanding arrogation or emancipation, but the arrogator did not become a partner (Gai. iii 153; D. fr 14 § 1, 63 § 10, 65 § 11). A partner could himself take a partner so far as he was himself concerned, but he does not thereby make him a partner with the

ed.). *Arbitrum adigere* to compel a person to go to an arbiter, *i.e.* accept an arbitration, is frequent and technical; cf. Cic. *Top.* 10 § 43; *Off.* iii 16 § 66.

others, and is alone responsible to him and for him to them; *socii mei socius, meus socius non est* (fr 19—22).

(*c*) Each partner is bound to be as careful in conducting matters of partnership, as he is in his own business, and is responsible to his partners for any loss arising either from fraud or from fault. His diligence and success in some matters cannot (as was clearly decided by M. Aurelius) be set off against the loss from negligence in others (fr 23—26, 72). Any costs or loss rightly incurred by a partner on the partnership business, the interest of any money advanced out of his own pocket, and even, as was eventually held, his medical expenses for hurts received in the defence of the partnership property, are chargeable against the partnership. A partner is not responsible for loss of what is under his charge by brigands, fire or shipwreck, *etc.*, where there was no fault of his own; but he might be responsible for loss by thieves, as being due to his negligence. And if he does not contribute what he has received on the common behalf, and especially if he has used it for his own affairs, he is liable to make them compensation in the nature of interest (fr 52 §§ 3, 4, 15, 60 pr; Paul ii 16).

Where there is a universal partnership, gains even from actions for Aquilian injury to himself or son, or from insult to himself, must be paid to the partnership, which is however not bound to take upon itself any payment he has been condemned to make for his own insulting conduct or crime, unless his condemnation was unjust. Gains from theft or other crime should not be paid to the partnership: if they are paid, then they become common property, but if paid with the knowledge of the partners, they can be drawn upon by the contributor for any damages and penalty payable by him in the like cases; if paid in without his partners' knowledge, they can be drawn upon for damages only. A partnership for the purpose of crime (*maleficium*) is no partnership at all (D. fr 52 § 16—fr 57).

A partner is liable to his fellows for theft or Aquilian injury of the common property, both by those actions and by the partnership action. The whole damages in the action *furti* are additional; in *damni injuria* and *condictio furtiva* they are good only for the excess over what is obtained by the action *pro socio.*

The case however must be very clear to justify a charge of theft, the presumption being that a part-owner is exercising only his right (fr 45—51).

(*d*) The shares of partners, in the absence of any special agreement, are taken to be equal: but they can agree on unequal shares, or on one contributing money and the other services, or on one having a larger share of profits and a smaller share of loss, or even no share of loss, if for instance his services were so valuable, or he be so exposed to personal trouble and danger as to justify the arrangement. Some old lawyers disputed this last as being contrary to the nature of partnership, and as being unintelligible, unless the accounts were kept separate for each transaction, profit being only the balance after deducting loss. A leonine[1] partnership, *i.e.* where one took all the profit and the other all the loss, was held to be no partnership. If only the share of profit or of loss is expressed, the other is taken to be the same (Gai. iii 149, 150; D. fr 29, 30; Just. iii 25 § 2). If the shares were left to be fixed by some arbitrator, he must make a reasonable decision; *ad viri boni arbitrium res redigenda est* (D. fr 6, 76—80).

(*e*) The relation between partners was regarded as approaching that of brothers, and consequently claims could not be pressed without regard to their pecuniary position. The judge was to condemn only *in id quod facere possunt*, provided they did not deny their partnership and had not fraudulently reduced their means. This privilege was certainly granted to universal partners, but its application to partnerships in a single matter appears to have been disputed. It was confined to the partner himself, and not extended to surety or heir, or to the father who may have ordered him to form the contract. His means are estimated, without deduction of his debts to others, as they stand at the date of judgment, and he has to promise to pay in full, if his means afterwards admit it (fr 63 pr—§ 7; xlii 1 fr 16, 22).

[1] Alluding to the fable: cf. Phaedr. i 5.

(*f*) The action *pro socio* could only be brought once. The judge took account not merely of property in hand but of debts due to the partnership, liquidated the partnership concerns, settled the mutual claims of the partners, took the accounts as between them, condemned them to pay one another according to the result, and directed reciprocal guarantees to be given where future claims were expected. He had no power to adjudge any property in ownership to any of the partners. If that were necessary, it could be done by the action *communi dividundo* (D. xvii 2 fr 27, 43).

(*g*) In a universal partnership the things belonging to the several members become common property without any actual delivery by one to the others. Debts remain as they were, and if my partner is to sue for a debt due to me, he requires a cession of my action just as if he were not a partner. Where the partnership is only for a particular business, the contributions of the partners become common property only by actual or personal delivery. As regards all dealings with third parties, the partners act as individuals; they cannot alienate more than their own share of a thing, and if they profess to be alienating the whole, and the alienee is evicted, they are liable of course themselves, not their partners. If they buy anything, it becomes the buyer's only; he is bound, if it be bought on partnership account, to make it common to his partners, but that is not the vendor's concern. The contract of partnership like other contracts affects only the parties to it: to the world in general the partners are only single persons and cannot act for each other, unless duly authorised (fr 1 § 1—3 pr, 68 pr, 74, 82; xlvii 2 fr 52 § 18)[1].

(*h*) Bankers (*argentarii socii*) were however an exception

[1] In *Rosc. Com.* 17, 18 §§ 51—56 Cicero argues that a partner sues only for himself, and only if appointed *cognitor* (see Book vi) can he sue for his partner. He compares the position of a partner with that of an heir: *Ut heres sibi soli, non coheredibus petit, sic socius sibi soli, non sociis, petit; et quemadmodum uterque pro sua parte petit, sic pro sua parte dissolvit, heres ex ea parte qua hereditatem adiit, socius ex ea qua societatem coiit* (§ 55). Cicero is here ignoring the ultimate liability of a partner to account, but his language is hardly stronger than D. xvii 2 fr 62.

to this. They could severally both sue and be sued *in solidum*[1]. A bargain for their creditor not to sue if made with one partner in general terms could also be pleaded by the other, but a bargain by one partner not to sue the debtor did not prevent the other from suing him (D. ii 14 fr 9 pr, 21 § 5—27 pr).

(*i*) The term *socius* is frequently applied to tenants in common[2], who have become so by external causes (inheritance, legacy, gift, *etc.*) without any contract between them. The action *pro socio* is not open to any except such as are partners by voluntary agreement. *Ut sit pro socio actio societatem intercedere oportet, nec enim sufficit rem esse communem...Communiter autem res agi potest etiam citra societatem, ut puta, cum non affectione societatis incidimus in communionem* (D. xvii 2 fr 31).

2. Companies.

The large companies of tax-farmers differed in many respects from private partnerships. They were not dissolved by a partner's death, and, if the company registered (*adscripsit*) the share of the deceased as belonging to his heir, the latter became thereby partner (*adscitus*). Without this the heir would be in the ordinary position of a partner's heir. In these companies it was possible on particular matters to sue *pro socio* without winding up the company (D. xvii 2 fr 59, 63 § 8, 65 § 15). Such companies were said *corpus habere, i.e.* to form a corporation; they had a common chest and a manager (*magister* usually in the case of tax-farmers, *actor* or *syndicus* in other cases) to sue and be sued or make bargains on behalf of the body. Other cases of such corporations, authorised by senate's decrees or imperial constitutions, were those for working gold and silver mines, or saltbeds. At Rome there

[1] The writer *ad Heren.* ii 13 § 19 says *Consuetudine jus est id quod sine lege, aeque ac si legitimum sit, usitatum est, quod genus* (as for instance) *id quod argentario tuleris expensam ab socio ejus recte petere possis:* 'What you have debited a banker with you can lawfully sue his partner for.' I see no reason for confining this statement to cases of contract by book-entry.

[2] Cf. Cic. *Quinct.* 16 § 52 *Quis ad vadimonium non venit? Socius. Etiam gravius aliquid ei deberes concedere quicum te aut voluntas congregasset, aut fortuna conjunxisset.*

was an association of bakers (*collegium pistorum*), and others (D. iii 4 fr 1; ii 14 fr 14).

No *collegium*[1] was lawful without permission of the public authority, except for religious purposes, not contrary to the senate's decree. Burial and dining clubs existed, and statutes for some of these or others are preserved wholly or partly in inscriptions (Bruns[6] no. 146 foll.). Slaves are named as members of a burial club (no. 147), a thing which was illegal without the consent of their masters (D. xlvii 22 fr 3 § 2). All lawful *collegia* could own slaves, and were enabled by M. Aurelius to manumit them (D. xl 3 fr 1).

Towns and other civil communities had common property and a common chest and could manumit slaves (D. *l.c.*) and be trust heirs of an inheritance (D. xxxvi 1 fr 27). They had a council (*decuriones*), two-thirds of which formed a quorum, and a majority of the quorum was required for important acts. A manager (*actor*) was appointed to conduct their suits, and, as a consequence, also to defend them. He had much the same powers as a private agent, but could not sue upon the judgment: he was not however as a rule required to give security *ratum haberi*. A *constitutum debiti* made with him was valid, and if he made a stipulation on behalf of the community, the administrator of the community had a *utilis actio*, but usually for any security to be given to the community a public slave was preferred as the medium. A community might be liable for interest on delay in executing a trust, and for costs of litigation (D. xxxi fr 78 § 2). Execution was made on the common property, and, if necessary, on the debts due to the community. *Si quid universitati* ('to the corporation') *debetur, singulis non debetur, nec quod debet universitas, singuli debent* (D. iii 4 fr 7; comp. fr 2, 10; *lex Malac.* (*ap.* Bruns) 29, 61, 67, *etc.*). A community could not commit fraud, but if they benefited by their agent's fraud, an action would lie: for councillors' fraud the individuals could be sued (D. iv 3 fr 15 § 1). If a legacy was

[1] Cf. Suet. *Jul.* 42 *Cuncta collegia praeter antiquitus constituta* (*Caesar*) *distraxit; Aug.* 32 *Plurimae factiones titulo collegii novi ad nullius non facinoris societatem coibant: igitur...collegia praeter antiqua et legitima dissolvit.*

left them (*'municipibus'*) conditioned on taking an oath, the oath might be taken by those who managed their business (D. xxxv 1 fr 97). If a usufruct was left to a town, it expired in 100 years, that being taken as the period of longest life (D. vii 1 fr 56).

Towns, clubs and other like bodies could possess and gain by usucapion and were subject to suits *ad exhibendum* (D. x 4 fr 7 § 3). Since Hadrian's time towns, since M. Aurelius' clubs, could receive legacies (see vol. 1 p. 307). A town was bound by a cash-loan, if the money was applied to its benefit: otherwise those who made the contract were alone liable (D. xii 1 fr 27).

3. *JUDICIUM COMMUNI DIVIDUNDO*[1].

This was a proceeding open to all who in any way, by legacy, by gift, by purchase, *etc.*, find themselves owners, or possessors with good title, in common of corporal things. While tenants in common they share in every part of the thing, and only by agreement or judicial proceeding can they become exclusive owners of a portion. As in the proceeding for division of an inheritance, possession is not required in either party: all the partners are in an equal position, and not properly either plaintiffs or defendants. The judge is often called *arbiter* (*e.g.* D. x 3 fr 7 § 1, 18, 26); the proceeding is *bonae fidei*, and the judge has large powers of making an equitable settlement (*e.g.* fr 14, 24 pr). The suit is confined primarily to the division of the things held in common, or of such of them as the partners or some partners desire to be divided, and secondly to making the partners mutually contribute for any loss or damage caused by them to the common property, or by their slave, *etc.*, to the private property of a partner, or for any expenses incurred or gain obtained in respect of it (D. x 3 fr 1—4 § 3, 8 § 1, 30; xvii 2

[1] Cicero rallying the lawyer Trebatius on his becoming an Epicurean says: *Quod jus statues communi dividundo, cum commune nihil possit esse apud eos qui omnia voluptate sua metiuntur?* (*Fam.* vii. 12 § 2). Trebatius might have replied that a jurisconsult or judge is not a litigant, and that *com. div.* regards not the philosophy of tenants in common or their motives of action, but only whether their actions were authorised or necessary so far as they affected the common property.

fr 34; xlvii 2 fr 62). Only such expenditure can be charged as has been incurred by common agreement, or as a partner has necessarily made on the common property in the protection of his own share. Nor is the suit excluded by the fact of the thing itself having perished. But if a partner went beyond what was necessary for the proper dealing with his own share, he can get contribution from the others only by suing them for business done (*negot. gest.* D. x 3 fr 6 § 2, 14, 25). Although suit for Aquilian damage cannot be brought against an heir, yet, if his predecessor has committed such damage on a thing held in common, the heir is liable to account by this proceeding to his predecessor's partner (fr 10 pr). Any partner condemned on account of a common slave can sue for contribution before he performs the judgment (fr 15).

This proceeding applies when expenses are incurred on property in common, though the person spending is ignorant or mistaken who his partners are. But if he believes the whole to be his own, he has no *animus obligandi*, and has therefore no right either to this action or to that for business done. If however a vindication or a suit *comm. div.* is brought against him by his partner, he can under a plea of fraud (*exceptio doli*), retain the property until reimbursed for a due share of the expenditure, and, if he part with his share of the common thing, the purchaser can exercise the like right of retention (fr 14 § 1, 29 pr).

This suit can be brought as often as may be required, and is open to coheirs when their proper procedure for division (*fam. ercisc.*) has taken place, and something is found undivided (D. x 2 fr 44 pr); and to voluntary partners within its own limits; but it is not concerned, like the action *pro socio*, with the duties of the partners, except incidentally (D. xvii 2 fr 43, 65 § 13). Where a corporal object has to be divided between heir and legatee, either by the terms of the will or in consequence of the *lex Falcidia*'s applying, the judge may have incidentally the duty of examining whether and to what extent the *lex Falcidia* applied (fr 8 § 1).

It is the duty of the judge to make as fair a division as possible, and to give effect to any agreement of the partners in connexion therewith. He has the power to assign in severalty parts to each, or to give, for instance, the ownership to one and a usufruct to another, or to give the whole to one at a price determined by competition among the partners, or even to extend the competition to outsiders. He has to determine the payments to be made to the others by way of compensation, or the guaranties to be mutually given (Ulp. xix 16; D. x 3 fr 6 §§ 9, 10, fr 19 § 3, 21; Cod. iii 37 fr 2, 3). Acquisitions made by a common slave from the property of one of the owners are in common, but by this action will be appropriated to him (D. fr 24 pr). Things whether mancipable or not, so legally adjudicated, become at once the assignee's (Ulp. xix 16).

Persons entitled in common to a usufruct or a pledge, or to possession *ventris* or *legatorum causa*, or to an aqueduct, have an analogous (*utile*) procedure for severing their connexion, or adjusting their relations, or apportioning common loss or gain. The judge may *e.g.* allot usufructs in different portions of the land, or may let the usufruct to one and divide the proceeds, or may arrange for alternate enjoyments, and may require reciprocal securities (D. x 3 fr 7 §§ 3—10; xliii 20 fr 4). A common right of water may be divided by allotting to each certain quantities and prescribing certain times of enjoyment (D. x 3 fr 19 § 4). Breaches of such arrangements may be dealt with by this suit (fr 23). If a thing held in common is pledged by one of the owners, a division can still take place, the creditor's right will be unaffected, and its value will be charged against the pledgor. If a thing is pledged to two persons in common, it may be adjudged at the value of the debt only, power being reserved to the debtor to redeem (fr 6 § 8, 7 § 12).

The division made affected only the parties, and did not alter the rights of others (cf. D. xxxiii 2 fr 31). If property not belonging to the litigants but to someone else was adjudicated to one of them, he did not thereby acquire it as his own, but his ground of possession was such that he could gain it by usucapion (D. xli 3 fr 17). A person claiming a share of something could bring this action to get his right to the share affirmed and the thing apportioned (D. xxi 2 fr 34 § 1). Where there was no real title to the holding, as between farmers (*coloni*) or depositaries or *praedones* or holders on sufferance, or when one or both were alleged to be holding by force or stealth, this proceeding was not available (D. x 3 fr 7 §§ 4, 5, 11).

F. Purchase and sale (*Emptio, venditio*).

1. Contract of sale.

(*a*) Purchase and sale (one thing under two names[1], D. xix 1 fr 19) is an exchange of commodities by mutual consent, one of such commodities being money[2]. The purchaser is he who makes over the money, the vendor is he who makes over the thing. At one time it was a subject of dispute whether anything but money could be the price, the Sabinians maintaining the affirmative, and quoting Homer[3] in proof of the antiquity of barter as a mode of purchase; the Proculians maintaining the necessity of money to make it clear which of the commodities exchanged was the thing sold, and which was the price given. Where a thing was for sale, and by consent of the parties a slave or something else was made over as and for the price, some lawyers at least held the contract to be purchase and sale (Gai. iii 141; D. xviii 1 fr 1 § 1; cf. Cod. iv 44 fr 9). Where the consideration in such a contract was not, at least partly, in money, the action *ex vendito* did not apply, and resort must be had to an action on the case: where there was no transfer of property, the contract was loan, not sale (D. xix 1 fr 6 §§ 1, 2).

[1] The double description of this contract, as also of lease, is found in Cicero (*Off.* ii 18 § 64) *Conveniet in omni re contrahenda vendundo emendo, conducendo locando, vicinitatibus et confiniis aequum facilem esse.*

[2] Paul's account of money is worth quoting: *Olim unusquisque secundum necessitatem temporum ac rerum utilibus inutilia permutabat...Sed quia non semper nec facile concurrebat, ut cum tu haberes quod ego desiderarem, invicem haberem quod tu accipere velles, electa materia est, cujus publica ac perpetua aestimatio difficultatibus permutationum aequalitate quantitatis subveniret. Eaque materia formā publicā percussa usum dominiumque non tam ex substantia praebet, quam ex quantitate; nec ultra merx utrumque sed alterum pretium vocatur* (D. xviii 1 fr 1 pr).

[3] *Il.* vii 472 sqq. Paul (D. xviii 1 fr 1 § 1) rightly says this only mentions barter as in vi 235, and that *Odyss.* i 430, where πρίατο is the word used, would have been a better quotation for the Sabinians.

(*b*) The contract rests on agreement only, and requires neither special words nor writing nor earnest money[1] nor formalities of any kind. It may be formed between parties at a distance, by message or by letter. It is complete without actual payment of the price or delivery of the thing sold, provided that both the price and the thing are ascertained, and that, if the sale be made on a condition, the condition has occurred (D. xviii 1 fr 1 § 2, 2 § 1, 7 pr, 9 pr; Gai. iii 139). Gaius implies that at one time doubts were entertained whether a thing could be sold (or let) under a condition (Gai. iii 146 *fin.*).

Special agreements may be made at the time, and will be regarded as part of the contract and enforced by vendor's or purchaser's ordinary action: *Solemus dicere pacta conventa inesse bonae fidei judiciis...Ea pacta insunt quae legem contractui dant, id est, quae in ingressu contractûs facta sunt* (D. ii 14 fr 7 § 5). Such agreements[2] may provide for this or that being included in, or excluded from, the purchase, or for a guaranty of or against this or that servitude, or for or against some special use of the thing sold. Or they may provide for the rescission of the contract, if by a certain day the price is not paid or the thing delivered, or if better terms are offered by someone else, or if the thing sold prove unacceptable, or on other grounds. Any such agreement may be revoked or varied by new agreement, and the whole contract may be rescinded by

[1] A ring was sometimes handed over as an earnest (*arra, arrabo*) or pledge (*pignus*) for the payment of the price, and on the contract being fully executed its return could be enforced by *actio empti* or *condictio* (D. xix 1 fr 11 § 6). Sometimes the earnest was a substantial part of the price itself; *e.g. Arraboni has dedit quadraginta minas* (Pl. *Most.* 647), which is spoken of afterwards as a *pignus* (*ib.* 978). *Arra, arrabo* are also used of pledges for loans; Ter. *Haut.* 603; Apul. *Met.* i 21; and (esp. of a ring) in betrothals; Pl. *Mil.* 957; D. xxiii 2 fr 38; Cod. v 1. In Plin. *HN.* xxxiii § 28 a *consuetudo volgi ad sponsiones etiamnum anulo exiliente* is spoken of by which a ring was used as *arra* in connexion with loans of money, so that *sponsiones* is probably 'stipulations.'

[2] A special agreement on the sale of half a farm was that the purchaser should have a lease of the other half for ten years at a fixed annual rent. The question arose whether the vendor could enforce this by action *ex vendito*. Labeo and Trebatius said no. Javolen said yes, provided that the price taken for the half sold was a reduced one in consideration of the lease. The practice followed Javolen (D. xviii 1 fr 79).

agreement, provided that matters remain as they were, or, though part performance has taken place, have by agreement been replaced in their old position. In the interpretation of the contract the first question always is, *quid inter contrahentes actum est?* 'What was the real intention of the parties?' The action to enforce the sale, *i.e.* the vendor's action, is *actio venditi* or *ex vendito*; the purchaser's action to enforce the purchase is *actio empti* or *ex empto* (D. xviii 1 fr 3, 6 §§ 1, 2; tit. 5 fr 2, 3, 5 § 1; xix 1 fr 11 § 1; ii 14 fr 58).

(*c*) Anything can be a subject of sale which can be a subject of private property. Not only moveables and immoveables, but incorporal rights (as a usufruct or right of way) and collective unities (such as an inheritance) and even rights of action are saleable. But a sale was invalid, when, for instance, it was a sale of sacred or religious land, or of a moveable which had been stolen, or of a supposed slave who was a freeman, or of what was the purchaser's own already. If the purchaser knew that a thing was stolen and the vendor did not, the former would be liable to the other on the contract, supposing the other were prepared to perform his agreement. Whether the vendor knew or not of the unsaleable character, the purchaser, if ignorant, could sue on the contract for the amount of his interest in not having been deceived: if both knew, the contract was invalid (D. xviii 1 fr 4, 6 pr, 34 §§ 1—4, 62 § 1). If a man ignorantly bought that of which he had already the usufruct, the sale was not invalid, but the judge would cut down the price. If he owned part of the thing, the sale would be good for the other part only (fr 16 § 1—18 pr). A thing which is at the time the object of a suit (*res litigiosa*) could not be alienated by either of the parties (D. xliv 6). Some decrees of the senate (A.D. 44, 56) made null any sale of buildings for the purpose of making a profit by pulling them down or as a speculation (*negotiandi causa*), the purchaser being liable to a fine of double the price (D. xviii 1 fr 52; cf. Bruns no. 51)[1]. Poisonous drugs were unsaleable, if incapable of being made useful or harmless (fr 35 § 2).

[1] See also Book III chap. viii c 4 (invalid legacies). It was part of the same policy to make it the duty of a provincial governor to inspect

(*d*) A guardian was disqualified from buying anything belonging to his ward; and the like rule applied to caretakers, procurators or other managers of others' business. A public officer could not buy anything from what was under his charge, under a penalty (by a constitution of Severus and Caracalla) of fourfold, besides the loss of the thing (fr 34 § 7, 46). Sale by one who is interdicted from dealing with his property or is otherwise incapable of alienation, will not enable a purchaser, knowing the fact, to acquire the property (fr 26).

(*e*) There must be agreement on what is sold (*in corpore consensus*). If the vendor is thinking of one farm or slave and the purchaser of another, the sale is null; but a difference in the name is of no consequence. If a farm is sold and Stichus is to go with it, and there are several slaves of the name, the sale of the farm is good, and Labeo held that the Stichus sold is the one intended by the vendor. A mistake as to the material, *e.g.* brass for gold, lead for silver, vinegar (not merely sour wine) for wine, a woman slave for a man slave, is fatal: but if a thing is covered with gold and is not stated to be solid gold, the contract may still be good, subject to compensation if there be fraud (fr 9—11, 14, 34 pr, 41 § 1, 45; xix 1 fr 21 § 2). A difference in the quality or quantity does not vitiate the sale, where the parties are agreed on the *corpus*. Thus if a particular farm or plot of land is sold at so much per acre according to measurement, the purchaser must take and pay for the acreage actually found, though slightly more than what was stated by the vendor (D. xviii 1 fr 40 § 2). In reckoning the acreage of a farm, only what is saleable is included as a rule; and if public roads, shores, balks, or sacred or religious ground are to be reckoned in, express words are required (fr 51).

If the thing is adequately defined, it is unnecessary that the precise contents should be known. Thus the contents of a box, the fish caught by the next throw of a net, the game within a certain drive, are all good subjects of sale, though nothing be found there. The purchase of a 'catch' is sometimes called *emptio spei* (D. xviii 1 fr 8 § 1; xix 1 fr 11 § 18). If an alternative

buildings and compel the owners (after due hearing) to repair them (D. i 18 fr 7).

is sold (*illa aut illa res*) the choice is the vendor's (D. xviii 1 fr 25 pr).

(*f*) The price must be ascertained, or ascertainable by the rule agreed between the parties. If it was left to be fixed by some other person, Labeo and Cassius held that there was no contract: Ofilius and Proculus held that there was a contract (Gai. iii 140; cf. Cod. iv 38 fr 15). Probably these latter required that the person named should actually fix the price: whether they held also that there was any remedy against a wholly unreasonable price so fixed, as was apparently Proculus' opinion in an analogous matter (cf. D. xvii 2 fr 76—80), we do not know. Sale at a reduced price by way of gift is a good sale none the less (D. xviii 1 fr 38). But see vol. 1 p. 160.

(*g*) In the case of goods sold by weight, measure or count, the contract is not complete (at least according to Sabinus and Cassius) until the weighing, measuring or counting is done, as that ascertains both the thing and the price. If however they were sold in block (*per aversionem*), *i.e.* at a price for the whole, the contract is complete at once (D. xviii 1 fr 35 § 5). What measure should be used was in the choice of the parties. So a rescript of Antoninus and Verus in a sale of wine (fr 71).

2. Obligation under contract of sale.

(*a*) When the contract is complete, the parties may proceed to put it into force; that is to say, they may enforce whatever has been actually agreed on, and, in default of any special details, they may enforce what is naturally involved in a *bona fide* sale and purchase (D. xix 1 fr 11 pr). Here as in other consensual contracts, *alter alteri obligatur de eo quod alterum alteri ex bono et aequo praestare oportet* (Gai. iii 137). The duty of the vendor is to secure to the purchaser the full possession and enjoyment of the thing sold: the duty of the purchaser is promptly to pay the price; and if it is not wholly paid, when he sues on the purchase, he must tender it (D. xix 1 fr 13 § 8).

(*b*) The vendor is bound to deliver the thing purchased to the purchaser or to his order at the place agreed on, or, if there be no such agreement, at the place where it is (D. xvi 1 fr 12 § 1). If the price is not paid, vendor has a lien until he is satisfied (D. xix 1 fr 13 § 8). Besides delivery, if the thing is mancipable, vendor can be called on to mancipate it[1] or surrender it in court, and in the case of incorporal rights to surrender them, or make the necessary promise on stipulation. If the vendor is himself the owner, he thereby transfers the property to the purchaser: if he is not owner, he by delivery puts the purchaser into the position of acquiring the ownership by usucapion, and meanwhile of using the Publician action to protect himself against third parties. If the vendor become owner subsequently or the owner become heir to vendor and attempt to claim the thing sold, the purchaser can defeat his claim by pleading the sale and delivery (*exceptio rei venditae et traditae*, D. xxi 3 fr 1 pr § 1). And further he is bound to guaranty the purchaser quiet and lawful possession (*habere licere*); but he is not bound to make him owner[2]. The purchaser lies under a different obligation: the price is to be paid in money, and the use and enjoyment of money lies in its free disposal and alienation. Hence the purchaser must make the vendor owner of the money, and either pays it down, or gives a pledge for the payment or surety or *expromissor*, or in some way satisfies him. In the case of both parties, the transference, whether of the thing or of the money, is with intent to fulfil the mutual contract of sale; and if the vendor has neither received the price nor agreed to give credit for it, the purchaser does not become owner of the thing: if the purchaser has neither got the thing nor acquiesced in the vendor's retention or disposal of it, the vendor does not become owner of the money[3] (D. xix 1 fr 11 § 2; tit. 4 fr 1 pr; xviii 1 fr 19,

[1] Cf. Plaut. *Trin.* 420 sqq. *Minas quadraginta accepisti a Callicle et ille aedis mancipio aps te accepit?* Le. *Ad modum.* Ph. *Pol opinor adfinis noster aedis vendidit.*

[2] It is otherwise where one has promised a farm or other thing in reply to a stipulation (D. xlv 1 fr 75 § 10; xviii 1 fr 25 § 1).

[3] Varro *RR.* ii 2 § 6 (speaking of sheep) *Cum id factum est* (*i.e.* agreement), *tamen grex dominum non mutavit, nisi si est adnumeratum* (money paid down): *nec non emptor pote ex empto vendito illum damnare, si non tradet quamvis non solverit nummos, ut ille emptorem simili judicio, si non reddit pretium.*

25 § 1, 53, 74; Ulp. xix 7; cf. Gai. iv 131 *a*). The person on whose account the purchase is made, not the person who merely pays over the price, is deemed to be the owner, provided he has got delivery (Paul ii 17 § 14; cf. Cod. iv 50 *passim*). In case of non-delivery by vendor's fault the purchaser can sue for the value of his interest in having the thing at the time agreed on; and thus if meanwhile the thing has risen in value, the purchaser can claim the increased value, but cannot claim for remote consequences of the delay, *e.g.* for the loss of a favourable sale, or the death of slaves starved to death from want of the purchased corn[1] (D. xix 1 fr 1 pr, 21 § 3).

(*c*) No delivery frees the vendor from responsibility unless the purchaser is thereby given possession of the thing sold, free from all interference, not only by persons claiming a legal possession as owners, pledgees, or others, but also by persons claiming to occupy on behalf of legatees or creditors[2]. If anyone can lawfully withdraw the possession, there has been no proper delivery (D. xix 1 fr 2 § 1, 3 pr). And if eviction is threatened, the purchaser cannot be compelled to pay, even though sureties are offered (Vat. 12, reversed in D. xviii 6 fr 19 § 1). If an agent sells a thing for less than he was authorised, the property does not pass to the purchaser (D. xxi 3 fr 1 § 3). If a slave, either by mistake or malice, in shewing the bounds or delivering vacant possession, shews a larger plot of land than the vendor intended to sell, the excess does not pass to the purchaser (D. xviii 1 fr 18 § 1): but if the vendor himself shewed

[1] Paul says the vendor is liable for *omnis utilitas emptoris*, but limits it by adding *quae modo circa ipsam rem consistit, neque enim si potuit ex vino puta negotiari et lucrum facere id aestimandum est etc.* The matter has given rise to much discussion. See Vangerow *Pand.* iii pp. 44, 45 who holds that the indirect consequences which are excluded are such as were only possible and could not be foreseen. Cf. D. xiii 4 fr 2 § 8; xviii 6 fr 20.

[2] The usual course as regards land was for the bounds to be shewn (*fines demonstrari*) to the purchaser and vacant possession (*vacua possessio*) to be given, *i.e.* the purchaser entered on the estate when there was no one claiming title on the place. (See vol. 1 pp. 457, 458.) Cf. Cic. *Tull.* 7 § 17 *Fines Acerronio demonstravit neque tamen hanc centuriam Populianam vacuam tradidit* (the *cent. Pop.* being land adjacent to that sold). Cf. D. xix 1 fr 48; xxi 2 fr 45.

the bounds, he was liable if part were evicted, although what was left was more than he had stated (D. xxi 2 fr 45).

(*d*) From the date of completion of the contract, though delivery has not taken place[1], the risk (as well as the fruits or other gain) belongs to the purchaser: and therefore the vendor is bound, so long as the thing is not delivered, to such care for safekeeping as, or even more than, a good housefather (*bonus paterfamilias*) uses to his own things (D. xviii 6 fr 3, 8 pr; Vat. 15). If the thing sold should be stolen from him, the vendor must cede to the purchaser his actions of vindication and condiction (D. xviii 1 fr 35 § 4). If a slave dies or is injured, or if land has been seized by the State, or if a house has been burnt down, *etc.* after contract for sale completed and without fault of the vendor, the purchaser must still pay the vendor the agreed price (D. xviii 5 fr 5 § 2; tit. 6 fr 12; xxi 2 fr 11). If wine has been sold for price certain but has not been definitely marked or set out, the purchaser does not bear the risk of its turning sour or mouldy; but if a specific lot of wine has been sold, the purchaser bears the risk, even though the condition of the purchase does not actually occur until later (Vat. 164; D. xviii 1 fr 35 § 7; tit. 6 fr 4 §§ 1, 2). Where vendor has made delivery impossible, *e.g.* by manumitting a slave whom he has sold with his *peculium*, he is liable to the purchaser for all the slave had in his *peculium* and his future acquisitions, which would otherwise have come to the purchaser; and he must give him a bond for whatever should come to him from the inheritance of this freedman (D. xix 1 fr 23).

(*e*) The thing sold (and the same is true if it is bequeathed) carries with it all natural appurtenances. Thus the sale of a house includes many things which are not physically attached to it, but are of permanent use with it, such as well-covers, wheels for raising water, troughs, pipes, leaden cisterns (*castella*), keys, tiles or other things waiting to be replaced where they were in use before. So also pipes leading water to the house, even if the right to the water is lost by non-use.

[1] The apparently discrepant passages D. xviii 6 fr 13—14; xix 2 fr 33 *med.* are perhaps best explained by assuming that there was fault on the part of the vendor. Cf. Fr. Mommsen *Beitr.* i pp. 332—336.

Warehouses carry with them jars (*dolia*) sunk in the ground. Land carries as a rule only what is fixed to the soil, and does not include the plant (*instrumentum*), *e.g.* oil-presses, sunk jars, *etc.*, nor trees fallen before completion of the contract; but vine poles temporarily pulled up, and beds of straw or dung intended for use on the farm and lying there, pass to the purchaser. *Ruta et caesa*[1], *i.e.* sand, chalk, timber, charcoal, or other things won or cut, and still remaining unused above the ground, do not pass with the land, though it is usual for greater certainty to reserve or except them (*recipere, excipere*). Fruits, ungathered though ripe, pass with the land, unless expressly excepted (D. xviii 1 fr 47—49, 76 pr; tit. 6 fr 9; xix 1 fr 13 § 10, fr 15, 17; L 16 fr 205, 241). A reservation of all the fruits includes reeds and underwood (xviii 1 fr 40 § 4). The rents of lands and houses, already due, do not pass to the purchaser unless promised; nor in strict law do the future rents under a lease made before the sale, for the purchaser is no party to the personal contract between his vendor and the lessee. If nothing is said about the lease in the contract of sale, the purchaser can ignore it, and turn out the lessee, leaving him to his remedy against the vendor for breach of contract. Or, if he cannot do that, he can sue the vendor for failure to deliver vacant possession, or for breach of his covenant of quiet enjoyment (D. xviii 1 fr 68; xix 1 fr 13 § 11; tit. 2 fr 25 § 1; Cod. iv 65 fr 9). In the case of lands belonging to towns or other communities and let by them for a perpetual rent, any sale of the lands must be subject to the rights of the lessee (D. vi 3 fr 1). The benefit and burden of servitudes duly constituted pass (though not mentioned) with the estate to which they are

[1] Cf. Cic. *Top.* 26 § 100 *Feci quod saepe liberales venditores solent, ut cum aedes fundumve vendiderint, rutis caesis receptis concedant tamen aliquid emptori quod ornandi causa apte et loco positum esse videatur.* In the last words Cicero probably referred to rocks or pebbles, or trunks of trees, not permanently affixed, but disposed by way of rustic ornament, or perhaps to wooden buildings not affixed to the soil, for such were counted among *ruta et caesa* (D. xix 1 fr 18; Cic. *Orat.* ii 55 § 256). Cf. Cic. *Part. Or.* 31 § 107 *Cum ex testamentis quid sit penus, aut cum ex lege praedi quaeritur, quae sint ruta caesa,...verbi interpretatio controversiam facit.*

attached; but the vendor, if cognisant of a burden of the kind, is liable to the purchaser for fraud if he does not name it expressly—not merely in general terms[1] (D. xli 1 fr 20 § 1; xix 1 fr 39). So also acquisitions of any kind since the contract, whether fruits gathered, moneys for hire of slaves or of beasts or of ships accruing due, the offspring of animals and children of female slaves born since, inheritances and legacies acquired through slaves, actions acquired such as *damni infecti, aq. pluv. arcendae, quod vi aut clam,* or *legis Aquiliae,* come to the purchaser (D. xix 1 fr 13 §§ 12, 13, 18; xxii 1 fr 4 § 1; Vat. 15). A slave's *peculium* did not pass with him, unless that be agreed (D. xviii 1 fr 29). In general the rule holds that *abalienatio cum fit, cum sua causa dominium ad alium transferimus, quae esset futura, si apud nos ea res mansisset; idque toto jure civili ita se habet, praeterquam si aliquid nominatim sit constitutum* (fr 67; xli 1 fr 20 pr), *i.e.* apart from any special agreement, the purchaser steps into the vendor's shoes from the date of the contract's being duly completed, and is entitled and subject to all natural or duly constituted accessories and restrictions, benefits and burdens of the ownership: but personal obligations whether active or passive remain with the vendor.

(*f*) The vendor is liable to the purchaser for any serious defects which he has not declared and of which the purchaser was reasonably ignorant, either in the thing sold or in any accessory. And he is especially liable if he has declared what was not true. The liability is much more onerous, if he has known of the fault and has concealed it. If he has been ignorant, for instance, that the cattle were diseased, or the timber faulty, or the slave a runaway, or the

[1] In selling a farm or house, if the vendor declared that he sold it *ita ut optimus maximusque* (cf. Bruns[6] no. 108), *i.e.* 'in the largest extent and best condition,' it was held by Q. Mucius that the vendor guaranteed its freedom from servitudes to others, but if nothing of the kind was said, it was sold for what it actually was, the vendor taking no liability on this score either for beneficial or burdensome servitudes (D. xviii 1 fr 59; xxi 2 fr 75). A dispute on this point is mentioned in Cic. *Orat.* i 39 § 178; *Off.* iii 16 § 67; in which latter place the important fact of the purchaser's having been at one time previously owner of the premises is named, though omitted in *Orat.* See vol. 1 p. 536.

wine bad or not likely to remain good till the time of delivery, or the land, or house subject to easements or water rate, *etc.*, he is liable to the purchaser for so much as the purchaser would have given less if the facts had been known to him. But a fraudulent vendor is liable for all the loss which the purchaser has suffered from the purchase, *e.g.* for the value of the house, if it fell in consequence of the timber being rotten, for the value of cattle which had caught a disease by contact with those sold, for the value of things stolen by the runaway slave or of other slaves whom he may have induced to run away also. And one who without knowledge of a slave's fault makes bold assertion to the contrary is nearly as bad (D. xix 1 fr 1, 6 § 4, 11 § 17, 13 pr—§ 3, 27, 41; xviii 1 fr 45; tit. 6 fr 16; xxi 1 fr 4 § 4, 33).

If purchaser brings action more than once on account of several defects or breaches, vendor is not liable in account for more than the purchaser's interest (*quanti emptori intersit*), and therefore damages in later actions will if necessary be reduced by what has been paid on former ones (D. xix 1 fr 11 § 10).

(*g*) Purchaser is bound to take delivery at the time agreed on. Thus wine bought from the cask (*doliare*, 'jar-wine') must be taken without unreasonable delay and at any rate before the vintage, if vendor is a grower and requires the jars. If purchaser delays, vendor can, after notice given, pour out the wine, or charge the purchaser with the cost of hiring other jars (D. xviii 6 fr 1 § 3—fr 2; xix 1 fr 9). So if purchaser of a slave does not take delivery, he can be charged with the cost of keeping him (xix 1 fr 38 § 1). Purchaser is liable for interest on unpaid purchase money from the time of delivery—such delivery as enables him to take the fruits (Paul ii 17 § 9; Vat. 2; D. xix 1 fr 13 §§ 20, 21). Any bargain for interest exceeding the lawful rate was invalid for the excess (Vat. 11). Purchaser is liable for any expenses reasonably incurred by vendor on the thing sold (fr 13 § 22).

(*h*) [A rescript of Diocletian allowed the vendor, if he or his father had sold for less than half the value, to claim rescission of the sale or payment of the deficiency, the purchaser having the option (Cod. iv 44 fr 2, 8). This rescript was followed in practice, and in modern times became the subject of much discussion, the loss to the vendor being spoken of as *laesio enormis.*]

(*i*) As sales rest on informal agreement and are similarly dissoluble, a formal release (*acceptilatio*) has no proper application, but is evidence of agreement to dissolve (D. xviii 5 fr 2, 3, 5).

Two matters require further treatment in some detail: viz. the vendor's liability (i) for defect in the thing sold; (ii) for want of title. Both were part of the ordinary law, but the obligation was further secured and accentuated, for the former by the Aediles' Edict, for the latter by a stipulation.

3. AEDILES' EDICT.

Liability for faults was recognised by the XII tables, so far as the vendor had made any declarations at the time of mancipation. The lawyers extended this liability to the case of any suppression of facts important for the purchaser to know, and applied it to sales in general, whether made by mancipation or otherwise[1]. The (curule) aediles in their edict made special regulations for the sale of slaves, and certain animals; and these, so far as applicable, were extended to

[1] Cic. *Off.* iii 16 § 65 *De jure quidem praediorum sanctum apud nos est jure civili ut in iis vendendis vitia dicerentur, quae nota essent venditori. Nam cum ex duodecim tabulis satis esset ea praestari quae essent lingua nuncupata, quae qui infitiatus esset dupli poenam subiret, a jurisconsultis etiam reticentiae poena est constituta; quicquid enim esset in praedio vitii, id statuerunt si venditor sciret, nisi nominatim dictum esset, praestari oportere. ib.* 17 § 71 *Nec vero in praediis solum jus civile ductum a natura malitiam fraudemque vindicat, sed etiam in mancipiorum venditione venditoris fraus omnis excluditur. Qui enim scire debuit de sanitate, de fuga, de furtis, praestat edicto aedilium. Heredum alia causa est* (heirs' position being different because responsible not for their own knowledge but for that of their predecessor). The extension by lawyers is put by Cicero as relating to land; and he gives a further instance in the case of one who sold his house after he had notice from the Augurs that it obstructed their view and that he must pull it down (§ 46). Labeo (see text, p. 151) made the principle general, doubtless on the analogy of the curule aediles' edict.

other sales; but the special actions given by this edict did not oust the general action *ex empto,* except so far as satisfaction may have been got.

(*a*) Under this edict the vendor was to declare plainly at the time of sale any disease or vice a slave had, and whether he was a runaway or truant or liable to be surrendered for thefts or injuries committed[1]; whether he had committed any capital offence or had attempted suicide or had been sent into the arena to fight with beasts. An old hand was not to be sold as a novice (*veterator*[2] *pro novicio*). If such declaration was not made, or if the slave was found to have faults not declared (perhaps unknown to the vendor), the purchaser or other person concerned (*e.g.* heir, *etc.*) could, within six months from the sale, require the slave and all accessories and profits to be taken back (*redhiberi*), and could demand restitution of the price and of any accessory to the price[3]; or, within twelve months, could demand compensation for the inferior value of the slave on these accounts. A like rule was laid down for the sale of *jumenta* (*i.e.* horses, mules and asses), and was further extended to other cattle (*pecus*). If the trappings (*ornamenta*)[4] of the animals worn at the time of sale were not delivered, the purchaser could within two months sue for them, or return the animals on that account; and if a pair were sold,

1 Varr. *RR.* ii 10 § 5 *In servorum emptione solet...intercedere stipulatio sanum esse furtis noxisque solutum.*

2 The distinction between 'new' and 'old hands' is in some cases made by length of service in the city, one year's service being that which makes an old hand (D. xxxix 4 fr 16 § 3). But in interpreting the aediles' edict more weight was attached to the kind of employment and the state of education. The new hands were thought preferable because more easily governed and more readily adaptable to a master's wishes (D. xxi 1 fr 37, 65 § 2).

3 Cf. Pl. *Pers.* 669 where, after the sale of a (supposed) slave has been agreed upon, an accession both to the slave and the price is proposed: *Heus tu, etiam pro vestimentis huc decem accedent minae.* Cf. Cat. *RR.* 144—146; Cic. *Verr.* iii 32, 36, 49, 50; *Rab. P.* 11 §§ 30, 31.

4 Plautus alludes to this *Stich.* 171 *Nunc si ridiculum hominem quaerat quispiam, venalis ego sum cum ornamentis omnibus.* *Pseud.* 342 *Jam pridem vendidi* (*tuam amicam*). Ca. *Quo modo?* Ba. *Sine ornamentis, cum intestinis omnibus.*

both could be returned on account of the faults of one (D. xxi 1 fr 1 §§ 1, 2, 18 § 6, 37, 38 pr § 5). The times named are all *utiles* and run from the day of sale or declaration or promise.

The lawyers are said by Labeo (in Digest) to have extended the edict so as to comprehend all other things whether moveable or immoveable (*ib.* fr 1 § 1; cf. fr 49, 63).

(*b*) The action to have the purchase rescinded and the price returned was *judicium redhibitorium.* If the price was not repaid or the surety for the price not released, the damages were double the amount of the price and of any accession to the price. The action for compensation was called *jud. aestimatorium* or *quanti minoris.* Both actions ran for and against heirs (*ib.* fr 18 pr, 23, § 5, 45, 48 § 5). Within six months purchaser could bring either action at his choice, and, if he sued by the latter and the defect were shewn to be such as would have prevented the purchase altogether, he can demand that the slave, *etc.* be taken back (D. xliv 2 fr 25 § 1).

(*c*) What particular defects or infirmities came under the names of *morbus vitiumve* were discussed in detail. Both terms related to the body; and the criterion was whether the use and service of the slave was thereby hindered[1]. When the defect was palpable or betrayed by ordinary indications, so that an intelligent purchaser was in no risk of deception, the edict hardly applied. For faults of character (*animi vitia*), redhibition was not granted, unless the vendor had denied them, and on this account the edict required[2] a distinct statement

[1] Thus, where the defect was no practical hindrance to the use or service of the slave, the following were held not to be cases for redhibition: *gutturosus, gibberosus, curvus, varus, vatius, balbus, blaesus, lippus, pruriginosus, scabiosus, impetiginosus, spado,* having too many fingers or toes, unequal eyes or jaws or arms, squinting, *etc.* On the other hand the following were generally considered subjects for redhibition: lame, having tongue cut out, or fingers or toes cut off, or fingers joined together, *varicosus,* near-sighted, having a *clavus,* or diseased tonsils, by malformation incapable of bearing children, having tertian or quartan fever, or gout, or epilepsy (D. xxi 1 fr 4 § 6—fr 15, 50, 53).

[2] Cicero, putting a case of conscience, says *In mancipio vendundo, dicendane vitia, non ea, quae nisi dixeris, redhibeatur mancipium jure civili, sed haec mendacem esse, aleatorem, furacem, ebriosum* (*Off.* iii 23 § 91).

Cf. Hor. *Sat.* ii 3 284 *Sanus utrisque auribus atque oculis; mentem,*

whether the slave was a runaway or truant (*fugitivus errove*); a truant being one who often loiters and stays out, a runaway one who leaves his master's house or service with the intention of not returning (*animus fugitivum facit* and cf. D. L 16 fr 225). Flight to an asylum or Caesar's statue does not make a runaway. Nor is a slave returnable who for the first time runs away at the buyer's. When there is no other evidence attainable, credit will be given to the slave's own answer on the point of this being his first running away (D. xxi 1 fr 17 § 12, 54, 58 § 2; Paul ii 17 § 12). The vendor had also to state the slave's nation. Mere puffing of a slave's good qualities is no ground for these actions, and even distinct declarations must be interpreted reasonably; but any serious difference of character from what was asserted or promised by the vendor is ground for suit; and if such assertion was made in order to deceive the purchaser, an action for fraud could be brought. Suicide, if attempted not from guilt but merely from physical pain, is not ground for suit. Condemnation or having incurred penalty for criminal offence ought to be declared (D. *ib.* fr 1 §§ 6—8, 4 §§ 3, 4, 14 § 10, 17 pr—§§ 16, 19, 18 pr, 19 pr—§ 4 fr 31 § 21; iv 3 fr 37; cf. xviii 1 fr 43). If a farm is malarious (*pestilens*), redhibition applies: if it was subject to an undeclared servitude *quanti minoris* applies (fr 49, 61).

(*d*) The scope of the redhibitory suit is to restore the parties to their old position. The purchaser has to restore the slave and anything which accompanied him and all that he has gained by the slave, including *partus ancillae*; and damages recovered on account of robbery of, or injury to, the slave, but excluding damages for insult through him (*injuriarum*) and any gains made by use of the purchaser's own property (*ex re mea*). Further he must give security against any fraud of his own, and must compensate the vendor for any

nisi litigiosus, exciperet dominus cum venderet. (In the particular case however it is a freedman who is spoken of: Horace is supposing him a slave.) *Ep.* ii 2 14 sqq. where a vendor of a slave says *Semel hic cessavit et ut fit in scalis latuit metuens pendentis habenae. Des nummos, excepta nihil te si fuga laedat. Ille ferat pretium poenae securus, opinor: prudens emisti vitiosum: dicta tibi est lex.*

deterioration either in the slave's body or character, which has been occasioned by his or his people's[1] or manager's treatment of him (*operae familiae procuratorisve*). If the manager was in fault, it is enough if the purchaser surrender his action. If the purchaser has pledged the slave, he must redeem him. On this restitution being made, in accordance with the judge's decision, or if vendor be regarded as impecunious, on a bond being given by the purchaser to this effect, the vendor has (under a penalty of double the value if he refuse) to repay the price and anything given with it as part of the bargain, and also accrued interest and expenditure (*e.g.* tax or rent charge, *vectigal*) made by purchaser, and to free him from all obligations in that behalf. Further the purchaser is entitled to retain the slave until he is reimbursed by vendor for the expenses of the slave's illness (not his keep), the value of things stolen from him by the slave, and any payment he may have made as damages for the slave's delicts. If the vendor declines to pay these expenses as allowed by the judge, he must give up his claim to the slave (who will remain with the purchaser), and condemnation will then be for the amount of the price and accessories only (D. xxi 1 fr 21 § 1, 23 pr §§ 1, 7—fr 31 pr, 45, 58; xxx fr 70 § 2). If the slave is dead before trial without any fault on the purchaser's part, the purchaser's claim is still good (D. xxi 1 fr 31 § 13).

(*e*) The vendor is responsible for the good condition of the accessories to the thing sold, provided that they are ascertained either by name or description (*e.g.* 'all the slaves on the estate'); but not if they are merely part of a general term, *e.g.* an inheritance, the working stock (*instrumentum*) of a farm, the *peculium* of a slave (none of which necessarily includes slaves). On the other hand a slave, though not diseased or vicious, may be returned, if appendant to the principal thing sold and found deficient, or if he be one of a band; or a near blood-relation of a slave returned. A similar rule obtained in the case of yoke beasts (fr 33—35, 38 §§ 13, 14, 39).

1 For the corruption of the slave by the purchaser's own slave, the purchaser could not make a noxal surrender of his own slave, for the harm was done to one who was at the time his own slave also (D. xxi 1 fr 25 § 7).

(*f*) Knowledge by the purchaser of the fact of flight, *etc.* is fatal to any claim against the vendor based on non-declaration (fr 48 § 4). Where the purchaser of a slave, *etc.* was himself a slave, whether buying for his *peculium*, or by his master's order, the master's suit cannot be met by a plea alleging the master's knowledge of an undeclared fault; the slave's knowledge is alone of importance, unless the master knowing of the actual fault directed this very slave to be purchased. In the case of a procurator, his knowledge defeats his suit, his principal's knowledge does not (fr 51).

(*g*) If a master sue by the *redhibitoria* in respect of a slave, *etc.* purchased by his slave, the whole that he has gained with or by him must be returned, irrespective of the amount of his *peculium*. But if a slave (or son under power) be vendor, and the master (or father) is sued on his behalf, he is liable only to the amount of the *peculium* (in which however the value of the slave sold is reckoned): so that if the slave is much in debt to his master, the result may be that the purchaser will have returned the slave and get nothing back (fr 57).

If the purchaser gives back the slave and accessories, and the vendor receives him, the redhibitory suit is no longer necessary, and the purchaser has an action on the case (*in factum*) for repayment of the price, *etc.*, in which the only issue for trial is, whether the slave, *etc.* has been actually returned (fr 31 § 17; cf. Vat. 14).

(*h*) The suit '*quanti minoris*' can be brought more than once, if a new cause occur, *e.g.* first for a slave's running away, then for discovered disease, *etc.*; but the total damages should be controlled, so as not to let the purchaser make a gain (fr 31 § 16; xxi 2 fr 32 § 1). This suit can be proceeded with notwithstanding that the redhibitory has been defeated by a plea of more than six months having elapsed (D. xxi 1 fr 48 § 2).

(*i*) Where the purchaser leaves several heirs, the consent of all is required for redhibition, and they should act by the same procurator: each can claim separately his share of the price and the accessories, and each is separately liable for damage; but if the damage has been caused by one only, he is liable in full. Where the vendor leaves several heirs, each can be sued in proportion to his share of the inheritance; the purchaser would not redeliver the slave until he had been wholly repaid or secured. The same is the case where a slave common to several owners has been bought by separate shares, but if each or one professed to sell the whole, he will be liable to redhibition for the whole (fr 31 §§ 5—10). Where a number of slave-dealers are the vendors and act as a company, the redhibitory suit can be brought against that one of them who has the largest share or at least as large a share as any of the others. Action on the purchase lies against each for his own share only (fr 44 § 1).

(*k*) Redhibition was not in practice allowed in cases of such small value that the single value only was demanded for their eviction (*simplaria venditio*); and it was also inapplicable to sales by the fisc; which indeed never paid more than the single value (D. xxi 1 fr 48 § 8, fr 1 § 3; xlix 14 fr 5 pr).

(*l*) In order to secure further the obligation of the vendor under this edict it was usual to add to or include in the stipulation against eviction (*stipulatio duplae*) a guaranty of the truth of the vendor's declarations[1]: and action on the stipulation was not limited to the six (or twelve) months of the edict; and once acquired was not lost by eviction or the death or manumission or flight of the slave. Such an engagement came to be regarded completely as a part of the *bonae fidei* contract, so that the purchaser could sue *ex empto* to compel the vendor to make it, or could within two months make redhibition, or within six months sue *quanti minoris*, to have

[1] Varro gives such covenants in the case of many animals, *e.g. Cum emptor dixit 'tanti sunt mi emptae?' et ille respondit 'sunt' et expromisit nummos, emptor stipulatur prisca formula sic: 'Illasce oves, qua de re agitur, 'sanas recte esse uti pecus ovillum quod recte sanum est, extra luscam surdam 'minam (id est ventre glabro) neque de pecore morboso esse habereque recte 'licere: haec sic recte fieri spondesne'* (*RR.* ii 2 § 6). *Boves cum emimus domitos, stipulamur sic: 'Illosce boves sanos esse, noxisque (solutos) praestari?' cum emimus indomitos, sic 'Illosce juvencos sanos recte deque pecore sano esse, noxisque (solutos) praestari spondesne.' Paulo verbosius haec qui Manili actiones* (*i.e.* the forms drawn by the jurist Manilius) *secuntur lanii qui ad cultrum bovem emunt; qui ad altaria, hostiae sanitatem non solent stipulari* (*ib.* ii 5 §§ 10, 11).

the price reduced on account of the absence of this stipulation (D. xxi 1 fr 28, 31 § 20; tit. 2 fr 16 § 2).

(*m*) Where the vendor had wrongly magnified the quantity of land sold, he was liable for the difference as if the purchaser had been evicted to that extent. The value was estimated in proportion to the number of acres if the price had been fixed per acre or for the whole without distinction: but if the acreage had been given separately for vineyard or oliveyard, *etc.* the estimate had regard to the particular quality of the land. And the like regard was paid when a specific portion of the farm was evicted. If the vendor had lied respecting the quantity, he had to pay double value[1] (Paul ii 17 § 4; D. xix 1 fr 4 § 1; xxi 2 fr 1, 53 pr, 69 § 6).

(*n*) It was allowable for the parties to contract themselves out of this edict by a bargain (*pactum*) made at the time or subsequently (D. ii 14 fr 31).

4. Liability for want of title.

(*a*) Liability for eviction was of the very essence of a *bonae fidei* contract. Sales by mancipation carried with them a guaranty of title to double the value[2], and, when there was no mancipation, a stipulation of the like amount was usual. It is doubtful whether surrender in court had the same effect as mancipation[3], but for the conveyance of mancipable things mancipation was the almost invariable practice (Gai. ii 25). The vendor in his character of guarantor of title was called *auctor*, and the action against him to enforce the

[1] Paul in i 19 speaks of an *actio de modo agri* which is classed with those which *infitiatione duplantur*. This classification is by Krüger and others taken to be a mistake. So also Mitteis (*ZRG.* xxxv 111). On such a separate *actio* see Lenel *ZRG.* xvi 190 (who holds that it was originally of a delictal character); Pernice *Labeo* iii 115; Karlowa *RG.* ii 576 who makes two actions.

[2] Cf. Pl. *Pers.* 524 *Suo periculo is emat qui eam mercabitur: mancipio neque promittes neque quisquam dabit,* the girl being sold without any guaranty of title. The usual practice is given by Varro *RR.* ii 10 § 5 *In servorum emptione, si mancipio non datur, solet dupla promitti, aut, si ita pacti, simpla.*

[3] It had not according to Bekker *Act.* i 33; and Karlowa *RG.* ii 383.

guaranty was *auctoritatis actio*[1]. At one time it was the practice for the vendor to give bail (*vades*) for his due appearance to defend the purchaser when the title (to land) was attached[2]. Afterwards sureties for title were usual, at least in sales for value by mancipation (*satisdatio secundum mancipium*); but the ordinary practice, in imperial times, even in sales by mancipation, was for the purchaser to stipulate, without requiring sureties, for twice the value in case of eviction of the whole or part, or for the single value only when the value was small. More than twice the value was occasionally promised. Where no mancipation or stipulation or special bargain was made, the vendor would not be liable *ex empto* for more than the purchaser's interest in not being evicted (Paul ii 17 §§ 1—3; Vat. 8; D. xxi fr 4 pr, 37 pr, 56 pr, 60, 70; Varr. *L. L.* vi 74; *Tab. Baet.* vv 16, 17 *ap.* Bruns[6] no. 110).

[1] Cicero refers to this in *Mur.* 2 § 3 *Quod si in iis rebus repetendis quae mancipi sunt is periculum judicii praestare debet qui se nexu obligavit, profecto etiam rectius in judicio consulis designati is potissimum, consul qui consulem declaravit, auctor beneficii populi Romani defensorque periculi esse debebit.* In *Caecin.* 19 § 54 *Actio est in auctorem praesentem his verbis 'quandoque te in jure conspicio.'* See Val. Prob. 4 who refers the words to the *legis actio* and completes them with *postulo anne far (fuas?) auctor.* Plaut. *Curc.* 498. In D. xiii 7 fr 43 pr we have *instrumentum auctoritatis* 'title deed of sale.' To 'name' or 'call on' the authority for the title was *laudare auctorem* D. xix 1 fr 6, 25; xxi 2 fr 63 § 1; Cod. viii 44 fr 7, 14; cf. Gell. ii 6 § 16 *Laudare significat prisca lingua nominare appellareque. Sic in actionibus civilibus auctor laudari dicitur, quod est nominatus.* Cf. Cic. *Orat.* iii 18 § 68; *Brut.* 11 § 44.

[2] Cf. Varr. *L. L.* vi 74 *Consuetudo erat, cum reus parum esset idoneus inceptis rebus, ut pro se alium daret. A quo caveri postea lege coeptum est ab his qui praedia venderent 'vadem ne darent'; ab eo adscribi coeptum in lege mancipiorum 'vadem ne poscerent nec dabitur.'* Cic. *Att.* v 1 § 1 *De satisdando te rogo, quoad eris Romae, tu ut satisdes: et sunt aliquot satisdationes secundum mancipium, veluti Memmianorum praediorum vel Attilianorum.* Cicero no doubt had sold some lands and had to give security for title to the purchaser in accordance with the terms of mancipation.

A surety for title was commonly called *auctor secundus* (D. xxi 2 fr 4 pr). The stipulations on sales given in Bruns[6] nos. 105—108 are all supported by a *fidejussor*, who in no. 107 calls himself σεκοδο αυκτωρ. For this habitual practice in Greek sales see Mitteis *Reichsrecht* p. 503 sqq.

By the contract of purchase the purchaser could demand the acceptance of such a stipulation: and a refusal to make the promise gave the purchaser a right to double damages (D. xxi 2 fr 2). An agreement for no guaranty or for the addition of sureties could be made, but would only serve as a plea, unless made at the time of the original contract (D. xviii 1 fr 72 pr).

(*b*) The ordinary stipulation against eviction (*stipulatio duplae*) imported (in accordance with the ordinary law) not that the vendor was owner, or conveyed the ownership of the thing sold, but that he guarantied to the purchaser lawful holding (*recte habere licere*), and in case of disturbance, double the value. The terms of the stipulation varied, the vendor sometimes guarantying (by a penalty attached) the purchaser against any interference from any quarter with his hold of the thing (which would be the effect of a simple promise *habere licere*), sometimes giving a guaranty only against interference by himself and his successors (*per se venientesque a se personas nihil fieri quominus emptori habere liceat*). Even in the latter case vendor would still be liable on any eviction of the purchaser, if he knew that he was selling what was not his own. If he did not know it, and was acting in good faith, it was held, or at least suggested, by Julian, that the purchaser if evicted by outsiders, could at any rate claim the return of his purchase money, not under the stipulation, but on the general equity of the contract. Julian puts on the same footing a definite bargain by vendor that no claim at all against him should be brought in case of eviction. It is much disputed[1] whether Ulpian approved or dissented[2] from Julian, and Julian's suggestion is not adopted by modern lawyers. That it was possible for the parties to agree that the purchase money should or should not be returnable, cannot be doubted (D. xix 1 fr § 18; xlv 1 fr 38 pr—§ 5). When a slave is sold, the eviction-clause should contain the addition *partemve*; otherwise if someone established a claim to a share in the slave, the purchaser would not be protected, as the slave (being physically indivisible) would not have been evicted (D. xix 1 fr 56 § 2).

[1] Cf. Vangerow *Pand.* § 610 Anm. 4.

[2] The words *ex empto non tenebitur* favour the view of Ulpian's dissent.

(*c*) The stipulation comes into play (*committitur*) only if by rightful judicial decision the purchaser is deprived of all or part of his rights, whether it be that he has to give the thing (or part) up to a claimant, or is condemned to pay damages for its value, or that the possessor is acquitted, when the purchaser sues for it (D. xxi 2 fr 16 § 1, 51 pr); or if by judicial proceeding the thing is shewn to be under pledge, or only partly the property of vendor, or subject to a usufruct in favour of another, or to an easement when he asserted it to be free (fr 10, 34 §§ 1, 2, 46 pr, § 1, 48); or if the purchaser has resold the thing and the second purchaser is evicted for want of title in his vendor (fr 33, 39 § 1). Or further, if a slave is sold and purchaser is not informed that he is *statu-liber*, or if the purchaser is deceived as to the condition of the slave's contingent freedom, or if a purchased slave has to be surrendered noxally for fault committed before the sale; in all these cases the vendor is liable on the stipulation (fr 46 §§ 2, 3, 54 § 1). But the purchaser cannot recover from the vendor, if the loss of the thing or its possession is really due to himself; *e.g.* if he has let judgment go by default; or has consented to an arbitration and been defeated; or has neglected to secure himself by usucapion; or has broken the conditions of the sale of a slave (*e.g. ne prostituatur*) so that he or she becomes free; or has allowed vendor to be buried in the land purchased and thereby lost its ownership (fr 29 § 1, 34 pr, 51 § 2, 55 pr, 56 §§ 1, 3). It is only an eviction by rightful decision after fair defence by the purchaser, that makes the vendor liable on his guaranty (Vat. 8, 10).

(*d*) The purchaser if sued on the point of title should give notice (*denuntiare*) to the vendor time enough before the judge's decision to enable him to defend. If the vendor is absent, or shirks notice, or declines to defend the title (*defugiat auctoritatem*), and judgment goes against the purchaser, the vendor is liable. Vendor's heirs are each entitled to notice and each is liable to be sued for the whole amount, and anyone avoiding (*defugiens*) defence of the title makes all liable to payment in the ratio of their shares in vendor's inheritance. If one appears and defends and the rest purposely keep aloof, the success or defeat of the one is good for all. Notice to the vendor or his heirs was as a rule a necessary condition of purchaser's right to recover from them (fr 29 § 2, 53 § 1, 62 § 1; xlv 1 fr 85 § 5, 139; Cod. viii 44 fr 8). If vendor was a slave, notice must be given to him, not to his master; and if eviction takes place the master can be sued only *de peculio* (D. xxi 2 fr 39 § 1). Notice is not essential, if vendor purposely avoids it or is absent or purchaser cannot ascertain where he is (fr 55 § 1, 56 §§ 4—6).

(*e*) When vendor is a creditor selling things pledged to him, he is responsible for his title to sell as creditor, but is not liable for eviction on account of the debtor's want of title, not even to restore the price, unless he knew that the pledgor was not owner (D. xix 1 fr 11 § 16; xx 5 fr 10, 12). If creditor has without fraud expressly guarded himself against any liability for eviction, purchaser has no plea to resist demand for the price (D. xxi 2 fr 68).

5. Action *ex empto*.

The general action *ex empto* is wider than the action *ex stipulatu*, and applies to all cases where, owing to vendor's fault, purchaser has not obtained by the purchase the benefits which he had a right to expect from the vendor's conduct and declarations. The stipulation was not as a rule intended to novate all obligations arising from the contract, and therefore the action on the purchase remained often available, where the stricter action on the stipulation was not available or effective. The action *ex empto* can be brought as soon as a defect is ascertained, without waiting for actual damage as an action on the stipulation requires (D. xix 1 fr 4). It can be brought on the ground of fraud before eviction, if vendor knew and purchaser was ignorant that vendor had no title; and this power would be especially useful, if the purchaser required not merely the possession but the ownership, *e.g.* in order to manumit a slave or to pledge the thing (fr 30 § 1). Declarations made by vendor may afford sufficient protection to him against the stipulation, but if the purchaser was reasonably deceived by them, would not be good against a suit on the purchase (D. xxi 1 fr 69 § 5). Easements the vendor is not held to guaranty, unless he has declared them, but if he knows of their purtenance to the land or house sold, and his silence leads the purchaser to neglect their use, the better opinion was that the vendor was liable to an action on the purchase (D. xviii 1 fr 66 pr § 1). If a purchaser of a farm, with the understanding that there was no right of way for others through it, is defeated on an interdict by a stranger asserting a user of such a way, he cannot sue on the stipulation (which would be broken only by the success of an adverse claim of right), but his quiet *de facto* possession being disturbed, he can sue *ex empto* (xix 1 fr 35). On the other hand if purchaser has become heir to the real owner or has otherwise obtained the ownership without cost, his possession will not be disturbed, but he has got nothing for his money, and action on the purchase is his remedy (D. xxi 2 fr 9, 41 § 1; cf. fr 57; Paul ii 17 § 8). If a farm has improved or deteriorated since the purchase and is evicted, suit on the stipulation will lie for the value as at the time of purchase[1], whereas suit on the contract is for the amount of loss to the purchaser by his vendor's want of title; and this amount may be less, but may also be much more than the original value (fr 16 pr, 64 pr). Fruits of a thing plucked by vendor, young of an animal or slave born since the sale, and other accessories since obtained (*e.g.* an inheritance through a slave), do not come strictly within the terms of the regular stipulation (*rem dari, vacuam possessionem tradi, habere licere*), but if they are not delivered by vendor, or if they are delivered and subsequently evicted, their value could be recovered by action on the purchase (D. xix 1 fr 3 § 1; xxi 2 fr 8, 42, 43; xxii 1 fr 4).

A *bonae fidei emptor* like any other *bonae fidei possessor* holding as owner takes and keeps as his own all fruits separated from the tree or ground, the produce and young of animals, and, if usucapion of the mother has proceeded, the young of female slaves, but his right to take or keep becomes doubtful as soon as issue is joined in suit for eviction (D. xli 1 fr 48 pr; vi 1 fr 20; xxii 1 fr 25 § 1, 28). On this doctrine, much disputed, see Windscheid *Pand.* § 186; Czyhlarz, Glück's *Pand.* § 1732 e. For the consequences in this respect if purchaser is evicted see vol. I p. 441.

[1] Including however any alluvial accession though subsequent (D. xxi 2 fr 15 pr).

6. Some special subjects of sale require notice.

(*a*) *Venditio hereditatis.* Transfer of the position of heir altogether could only be effected in the case mentioned in vol. I p. 228. But any heir after full acceptance of heirship could sell to another the inheritance, *i.e.* the complex of assets and debts, rights and liabilities. As between themselves the transfer was complete, but as regards third parties it had no effect. The heir was liable to them as before: and the purchaser could until the time of Antoninus Pius (who granted a *utilis* action D. ii 14 fr 16) sue them only in the heir's name: since that time a bargain made with the purchaser could be used as a plea against suit by the heir. The corporal assets of the inheritance were transferred by delivery.

As with other sales the contract varied with the intention of the parties. Sale of the inheritance of one who is alive or does not exist is null. There may however be a sale of the prospect of an inheritance, and in that case, if vendor is not heir he is liable for nothing. But usually it was understood to be the sale of a known inheritance, which belonged to vendor, who guarantied its existence but not any particular contents. Vendor sells his right and that only. Apart from special agreement or particular exception purchaser took over all incomings[1] and outgoings from the death of testator including the funeral expenses. If the inheritance contained a house which was the subject of security for possible damage (*damni infecti*), and the vendor excepted the house from the sale, the liability for damage caused up to the date of the contract would presumably be the purchaser's; subsequent liability would be the heir's. If vendor reserved a slave but not his *peculium*, he would be entitled to reimbursement by the purchaser for what he has had to pay to the slave's creditors suing him *de peculio* or *in rem verso*, so far as their claims were for what had been expended on the master's own property or were chargeable on such part of the *peculium* as ordinarily accompanied a slave when sold. If the

[1] *Non solum quod jam pervenerit sed et quod quandoque pervenerit restituendum* (D. fr 2 § 4). This appears to include any share of the inheritance which may accrue to the share sold. The matter is much disputed. Cf. Vangerow *Pand.* § 494 n. 6.

slave with his *peculium* was excepted and nothing further was expressed, the vendor would be understood to take all the responsibility for the slave's debts, so far as the *peculium* extended. If vendor excepted a farm, the exception is interpreted very strictly, and thus if vendor afterwards acquired something in virtue of the farm he must cede the accession to the purchaser, unless the intention be shewn to be otherwise. If vendor, besides being heir to testator, was also substituted heir to a child of testator's under age, this inheritance does not necessarily go with testator's own, though for some purposes the will is regarded as one only. But if the pupillar inheritance has already fallen in at the date of the sale, in the absence of proof of contrary intention, the sale would be taken to carry both. All actions acquired by vendor in connexion with the inheritance sold have to be surrendered to the purchaser, who on the other hand has to reconstitute servitudes between testator's and heir's properties which have been lost by temporary merger. Any claims which the heir may have had against testator and could have enforced against anyone else as heir, though merged temporarily, will in equity be enforceable against the purchaser; and reciprocally the purchaser will be able to enforce testator's claims against the vendor, and so far as their *peculium* extends, against vendor's son or slave (D. xviii 4 fr 1, 2, 7—13, 14 § 1, 25; ii 14 fr 16 pr; Cod. iv 39 fr 2).

The relation of vendor and purchaser of an inheritance came especially into notice in its use as the mode of transferring, before the *SC. Trebellianum*, an inheritance from heir by law to heir by trust (Gai. ii 252; see vol. I p. 370).

Where an inheritance was sold by the Crown (*fiscus*) on account of debts or confiscation, the purchaser became directly answerable to creditors, and could directly sue debtors by analogous actions (Cod. iv 39 fr 1; D. xlix 14 fr 41; v 3 fr 13 § 9, 54 pr).

(*b*) *Venditio nominis*. Upon the sale of a debt, the vendor was held to guaranty the existence of the debt but not the solvency of the debtor. The purchaser had a right to all pledges given for the debt, and to a surrender by the vendor of his actions against the principal debtor and sureties if any. Should the vendor obtain any payment in satisfaction of the debt or a set-off, he must surrender it to the purchaser (D. xviii 4 fr 4—6, 23). The consent or knowledge of the debtor is not required for the sale of the debt (Cod. iv 39 fr 3).

(c) The sale of a usufruct is an ambiguous expression. It may mean the establishment for the purchaser in return for his payment, of a usufruct in something belonging to the vendor, in which case the usufruct would last for the purchaser's life, natural or civil. Or it may mean the exercise in return for payment by the purchaser of the right of usufruct in a thing of which vendor is not owner but has only a duly established usufruct, which therefore expires with the vendor's life (D. xviii 6 fr 8 § 2).

7. Sales on condition.

Sales are sometimes made subject to a condition. Much depends on the character of the condition, *i.e.* whether it is suspensive or resolutive. If the condition be suspensive, the contract awaits the condition and is not formed until that occurs. If the condition be resolutive, the contract is complete, and the occurrence of the condition rescinds it. In the former case although the terms of the contract may have been agreed, no rights have passed from the vendor, whether he has made delivery or not, and nothing has yet been gained by the purchaser. In the latter case the vendor has parted with his rights in the thing, and the purchaser has got them instead: he is entitled to the fruits and accessions, can pledge it, bears the risk, and is in a position, if the vendor was not owner, to gain the ownership by usucapion. If the condition occur, both vendor and purchaser re-enter their original position: any pledge of the thing made by the purchaser drops, and he has to give back to the vendor all that he has got by the sale, and the vendor has to refund the purchase money if received. But the purchase and sale, though rescinded, were so far recognised as to entitle the parties to the actions *empti* and *venditi* to enforce the terms of the rescission (D. xviii 1 fr 6 § 1; tit. 2 fr 2 § 1; tit. 3 fr 4 pr; tit. 6 fr 18 § 5).

Certain special conditions of sale may be noticed:

(*a*) *In diem addictio*[1], 'assignment for a future day,' is a contract of sale subject to the condition that vendor has no better offer before a day named. Usually, but not necessarily, this is intended and treated as sale completed but subject to rescission, if the vendor gets a better offer. If such an offer is not made, or if vendor die and no heir be ascertained before the agreed day, the sale stands good and the purchaser cannot be ousted, whatever offer be made subsequently. If a better offer be made the vendor may still disregard it, and the purchaser will then be unaffected (unless indeed by the terms of the sale he was in that case to have the right to throw up the purchase). But if vendor deem the proposal worth accepting, he must give notice of it to purchaser, so that if he choose he may improve his own offer. Whether the vendor accepts the offer of the second purchaser or the new offer of the first, the old contract is rescinded, and the first purchaser must surrender to the vendor all fruits and other gains and rights of action acquired in the meantime, but can by a rescript of Severus claim reimbursement for any necessary expenses incurred upon the thing purchased and any part of the price which he may have paid (D. xviii 2 fr 2, 4 §§ 3—5, fr 6—9, 15 pr, 16; cf. xlix 14 fr 50). Better terms (*melior conditio*) may consist in higher price, easier or quicker payment, a more convenient place for payment, a more substantial purchaser, or one offering lighter terms or requiring no sureties. If higher price be offered by one who is insolvent or otherwise unsuitable, still the vendor was entitled to accept him and rescind the sale. But the right to claim from the first purchaser the mesne profits does not make an offer of the same price as the first purchaser a better offer within the meaning of this agreement (fr 4 § 6, 14 §§ 2, 5).

(*b*) *Lex commissoria*, 'terms of forfeiture,' occurs where the vendor bargains for the rescission of the sale if the purchase money is not paid by a certain date (*si ad diem pecunia soluta non sit, ut fundus inemptus sit*). This also was usually

[1] Cf. Plaut. *Capt.* 179 where a parasite proposing himself to dinner, says *Age sis roga emptum, nisi qui meliorem adferet quae mi atque amicis placeat condicio magis, quasi fundum vendam, meis me addicam legibus*, *i.e.* 'on my own terms.'

understood as a sale on resolutive condition. It was usual also to bargain that if the vendor in consequence have to sell elsewhere at a less price, the defaulting purchaser should be liable for the difference. If any part of the price or earnest money had been paid, it was usually agreed that this should be forfeited to the vendor, and any fruits gathered should be surrendered, or (at least according to some lawyers) so much of the fruits as were not covered by the forfeiture of part price. To prevent forfeiture purchaser must tender the price. The rescission is at the vendor's discretion, but he must elect, once for all, as soon as the due date arrives: and acceptance of the price or demand for it after that date is a waiver of the forfeiture (Vat. 3, 4; D. xviii 3; cf. iv 4 fr 38 pr).

(*c*) *Ut si displicuerit, res inempta sit*[1], 'purchase on approval,' *i.e.* that the buyer should have the right of returning the thing and its fruits if he did not like it. This also was held to be sale on a resolutive condition, and resolution could be enforced and return of price and earnest obtained by action on the purchase (D. xviii 1 fr 3; xix 1 fr 11 § 6; cf. Vat. 14). If no time was fixed, the purchaser under the aediles' edict was allowed to bring, within sixty available days (or longer if good cause be shewn), suit (*in factum*) to compel the vendor to take the thing back (D. xxi 1 fr 31 § 22).

In the case of wine the sale is often made dependent on approval after tasting: if no delivery takes place the condition is suspensive; and the risk remains with vendor until tasting (D. xviii 6 fr 1 pr, 4 pr § 1).

(*d*) A condition is sometimes attached to a sale by way of limitation of the purchaser's use, and may be intended either to compel or to forbid certain dealings with the thing sold. In modern writers this is called *modus* (cf. D. xxviii 5 fr 93; *hoc modo vendidi* D. xix 5 fr 6; *sub modo legatum* xxxv 1 fr 17 § 4). Its due observance would be enforced either by an action *ex vendito*, if it were made a *lex mancipationis*, or a *pactum* in connexion with the sale; or, if a stipulation were entered into, by an action on that. Sometimes the vendor reserved

1 Cf. Plaut. *Merc.* 420 *Dixit se redhibere* (*ancillam*) *si non placeat* 'that he takes her back if she does not give satisfaction.'

the right, in case of breach, of seizing the slave as forfeited (Vat. 6). Instances frequently occur on the sale of slaves, the *modus* or bargain being (*ea lege ut manumitteretur, etc.*) that the slave should be manumitted immediately, or after a certain time or event, or should not be alienated so as to have any other master than the purchaser; or, in case of a female slave, that she should not be prostituted. The first seller under such an agreement could enforce it, even if the woman has been sold repeatedly. A condition against manumission altogether was held not lawful (D. xviii 1 fr 56; tit. 7). But a condition that the slave should not reside in a particular place (*e.g.* Rome, Italy, *etc.*) was good. If the purchaser manumitted the slave, and he returned to the forbidden place, he might be reduced to perpetual slavery; the vendor however for whose protection such a condition was deemed to be made could waive it, and manumit the slave (Vat. 6). The sale even of criminal slaves for fighting with beasts was declared unlawful by M. Aurelius (D. xviii 1 fr 42).

(*e*) The particles *ita ut* are ambiguous, *Erit mihi emptus fundus ille, ita ut eum intra Kal. Jun. a Titio liberes* may either mean 'I buy the farm, you undertaking to redeem Titius' mortgage before June 1st,' or 'I buy, provided you redeem, *etc.*' On the former meaning the purchaser can sue on his contract for the redemption of the mortgage as well as for the delivery of the farm: on the latter meaning the purchase is conditional on the mortgage being already redeemed by the time named (D. xviii 1 fr 41).

8. It is well here to give one of the documents found in Dalmatia which shew the form of a record of sale dated 162 A.D. (edited by Mommsen and Zangemeister *C.I.R.* iii p. 941, see Bruns *Fontes*[6] p. 288).

Dasius Breucus emit mancipioque accepit puerum Apalaustum sive is quo alio nomine est n(atione) Graecum apocatum pro uncis duabus[1] ✱ DC *de Bellico Alexandri, f(ide) r(ogato) M. Vibio Longo. Eum puerum sanum traditum esse furtis noxaque*

[1] The meaning of these words *apocatum pro uncis duabus* 'receipted for two ounces,' is not clear.

solutum, erronem fugitivum caducum non esse, prestari; et si quis eum puerum q(uo) d(e) a(gitur) partenve quam quis ex eo evicerit q(uo) m(inus) emptorem s(upra) s(criptum) eunve ad q(uem) ea res pertinebit uti frui habere possidere(que) recte liceat, tunc, quantum id erit, quod ita ex eo evictum fuerit, t(antam) p(ecuniam) duplam p(robam) r(ecte) d(ari) f(ide) r(ogavit) Dasius Breucus, d(ari) f(ide) p(romisit) Bellicus Alexandri, id(em) fide sua esse iussit Vibius Longus; proque eo puero q(ui) s(upra) s(criptus) est pretium eius ✳ DC *accepisse et habere se dixit Bellicus Alexandri ab Dasio Breuco.*

Actum kanab(is) leg(ionis) XIII *g(eminae)* XVII *kal. Junias Rufino et Quadrato cos.*

(*Signatores septem.*)

We have here

(1) Purchaser (Dasius Breucus);
(2) Fact of purchase and conveyance by mancipation;
(3) Description of thing sold, *i.e.* name and nation of slave;
(4) Price (600 *denarii*);
(5) Vendor (Bellicus Alexandri);
(6) Surety (M. Vibius Longus);
(7) Delivery in sound condition;
(8) Guaranty of absence of (mental) faults; also that he is not epileptic (*caducus*);
(9) Promise of double value if purchaser or person concerned is disturbed in his quiet enjoyment by total or partial eviction;
(10) Promise by surety;
(11) Acknowledgment of receipt of price;
(12) Date and place of contract (*kanabae* are huts or barracks for soldiers and sometimes grew into towns);
(13) Seals of five witnesses and of surety and vendor (so described).

G. *Locatio conductio*, 'letting and hiring,' is an agreement for the use of a thing belonging to another or for the use of another's services in consideration of an agreed payment. It is in many respects under similar rules to those which regulate purchase and sale, being indeed a purchase and sale not of a thing itself but of its use. The price is called *merces* 'hire-money,' which we should translate 'rent' in the case of land or houses, and 'wages,' *etc.* in the case of personal services. The contract is formed by consent, without any special form of words or writing or other formality being required. It may be made subject to condition, though this was at one time doubted, and is complete when the subject-matter and the amount of hire or rent is agreed on (Gai. iii 142, 146; D. xix 2 fr 1, 2 pr, 20 pr). The *locator* has an action called *locati* or *ex locato*; the *conductor* an action *conducti* or *ex conducto*.

If the *merces* was left to be fixed by someone else, it was an open question in Gaius' time whether the contract was good. So also if it was left to be fixed by agreement of the parties after the job was done; or if, instead of money, the use of one thing was to be the consideration for the use of another. In the case of land we hear of the rent being sometimes partly in corn: and of a letting on the metayer system (still common in Italy) where the rent consists in a certain share of the produce (Gai. iii 143, 144; D. xix 2 fr 19 § 3, 25 § 6; cf. Cod. iv 65 fr 8, 21)[1]. The question was not whether such agreements were enforceable by action but whether the action would be the ordinary one of lease and hire. Eventually there was a special action *praescriptis verbis*. In the case of payment by share of produce the action *pro socio* might sometimes apply (D. xvii 2 fr 52 §§ 2, 3 and below, p. 176).

Three cases are mentioned by Gaius in which doubt was entertained whether they belonged to sale or letting. The first is land let for ever (*in perpetuum*). Thus lands belonging to towns were let on the terms that so long as the ground-rent

[1] The farmer is called *colonus partiarius*. Cf. Cato *RR.* 136, 137; Liv. xxvii 3 § 1 *Agrum qui publicatus erat locavit omnem frumento;* Plin. *Ep.* ix 37 *Medendi una ratio si non nummo, sed partibus locem.* Hence when the rent is in money we have *qui nummis colit*, D. xlvii 2 fr 26 § 1.

(*vectigal*)[1] was paid (cf. D. xx 1 fr 31) the lands should not be taken away from the tenant (*conductori*) or his heir. (They passed also to legatee, D. L 16 fr 219; cf. xxx fr 71 §§ 5, 6.) The better opinion was that this was lease. (Zeno and Justinian made it a special contract *emphyteusis* Just. iii 24 § 3.) The second case was where one man supplies gladiators to another on the terms that for each one who survives unhurt (*integer*) 20 *denarii* should be paid for his toil, but for each one killed or crippled (*debilitatus*) 1000 *denarii*. The better opinion was that this was lease so far as the men were unhurt, sale so far as they were killed or crippled; the contract being conditional till

[1] Cicero writes on behalf of the borough of Atella which owned land in Gaul and derived such a rent from it: *Locutus sum tecum de agro vectigali municipii Atellani. Velim existimes, quod res est, municipii fortunas omnes in isto vectigali consistere* (*Fam.* xiii 7 § 2).

Pliny the younger (*Ep.* vii 18) wishing to settle an endowment for poor freemen at Como of the value of 500,000 sesterces, mancipated one of his farms to the town agent, who then restored it to Pliny, reserving a perpetual annual rent of 30,000 sesterces, *i.e.* 6 per cent. on the capital (*Agrum actori publico mancipavi, eundem vectigali imposito recepi, tricena milia annua daturus*). The land would thereafter be subject to this rent-charge, and being itself of much greater value would, as Pliny thought, always find a holder (*dominus*), and the town would be sure of a fixed payment; whereas if he paid over the capital sum it might gradually be lost or spent; if he made over land absolutely for the amount it might be badly managed and not produce the amount required. Pernice thinks the bare ownership of the land actually conveyed would remain in the town, like any other land which a town lets for a perpetual fixed rent (*Labeo* iii p. 162). So also Karlowa *RG.* ii 1273 n. 4, who says *recepi* does not imply 'received back by mancipation.' This may be so, but the word *dominus* (cf. D. vi 3 fr 1 § 1) rather suggests that the ownership was in Pliny, subject to what in Manchester would be called an annual chief-rent. (So Huschke also, quoted in Karlowa.) In an inscription at Ferentinum (Bruns[6] no. 125) an endowment for doles is made by the founder's purchasing (*redemit*) land belonging to the town and giving it back charged with a payment of 4000 sesterces a year for doles, *in avitum rei publicae reddidit* (so in some Greek inscriptions εἰς πατρικά, see Karlowa); cf. Bruns[6] no. 131 where *ob avitum et patritum* is apparently 'on account of land subject to a permanent (as it were, "hereditary") rent'; or as Karlowa takes it *ob avitum, etc. vectigal*. Another plan for endowments was to lend the endowment money to owners of lands who then paid interest and 'undersealed' the lands to the communal treasury; cf. Bruns p. 305.

the fact was ascertained. The third case was of a contract with a goldsmith to make some rings of a certain weight and shape, he to supply the gold, for the sum of 200 *denarii*. Cassius held that this was purchase of the gold, hiring of the service. Most lawyers held that the contract was purchase. But all were agreed that if the customer supplied the gold, the contract was hire of his services (Gai. iii 145—147; D. xviii 1 fr 20). Analogous to the second case is that of farm-plant or slaves of agreed value (*aestimatum*) being let with the farm (D. xix 2 fr 3, 54 § 2).

This contract of lease and hire was treated by the Roman lawyers as one, but there are clearly three principal varieties in its application, and these differ in some of their incidents. The subject-matter (1) may be a thing, slave, land, *etc.* (*locatio rei*); or (2) it may be personal services (*loc. operarum*); or (3) it may be a work to be effected (*loc. operis faciendi*). The *locator* is the person who provides the thing, or services, or the subject of the work (*e.g.* land to be built on, house to be repaired, *etc.*). We should call him in the first case the lessor; in the second the hireling or employee; in the third the employer or putter out of a contract. The *conductor* is the person who gets the use of the thing or of the services, or effects the work. We should call him in the first case the lessee or hirer; in the second the employer; in the third the contractor. The third class is distinguished from the first two by the fact that in them the *locator* receives the rent or wages, and his action is *ex locato*: in the third he pays it and his action is *ex conducto*. In the second case the *locator* does the service, in the third the *conductor* does it.

1. *Locatio conductio rei.* The lessor was bound to grant and maintain to the lessee quiet use and enjoyment of the land (with its fruits), house, *etc.* for the term of the lease. The lessee of land is frequently called *colonus*, of a house *inquilinus* ('lodger'). The lessee, if turned out from want of title in the lessor or from the lessor's own action, can claim the value of his interest; and the same rule holds if the thing let was plainly unsuited for its known purpose, *e.g.* leaky casks for wine. If land containing poisonous herbs is let for pasture, the lessor with knowledge is

liable for loss of the cattle, if ignorant, he cannot claim rent. If the lessor was ignorant of his want of title, *e.g.* to a house, and was ready to provide the lessee with another equally convenient, he could demand acquittal. If the house let was confiscated by public authority or burnt down or destroyed by earthquake or other irresistible force, the tenant could only claim remission of rent for the time of non-use. If it was not fit for habitation at the time for commencing the tenacy and for months after, or if it had its lights obscured by a neighbour's building, the lessee could throw up the contract, and rent would cease (D. xix 2 fr 9 pr, 15 § 8, 19 § 1, 25 §§ 1, 2, fr 33, 60 pr). But the lessor may effect necessary repairs during the term, only he must remit the rent or provide other accommodation, if the inconvenience to the tenant is so great as to justify him in removing (*ib.* fr 27, 28).

In letting a farm the lessor was required to provide a farm house and stabling fit for tenant's use, and necessary plant (*instrumentum*) in good repair, such as an olive press and tackling, cauldron, oil jars, wine casks, *etc.*, but not moveables such as baskets (fr 15 § 1, 19 § 2). If irresistible damage was done, *e.g.* by rivers, or jackdaws, or starlings, or locusts, or earthquake, or landslip, or blight, or unusual heat, or sudden fire, or by an invasion of the enemy, the lessor (in the absence of special agreement) has to remit the current rent. But if the wine produced on the farm turn sour, or the standing crops are spoilt by worms or weeds, or if any other misfortune occur of an ordinary character arising from the nature of the farm, the loss is the tenant's and he must pay rent all the same. Against the barrenness of one year the landlord has a right to set off the fertility of subsequent years, and the rent may then be demanded which had been previously remitted (Ulp. in D. fr 15, quoting for the main principle Servius; cf. Cod. iv 65 fr 8).

The lessee was bound to pay the rent as agreed, to maintain the property unimpaired both physically and in rights (*e.g.* to keep in use a right of road, *etc.*), duly to cultivate (if it be an agricultural tenancy), and to deliver up at the expiration of the term. In the absence of any special agreement, good faith and the custom of the district rule the contract (fr 11 § 2, 25 § 3;

Cod. iv 65 fr 11). The lessee cannot cut down trees (being liable to other actions as well as this), and is even responsible for his neighbour's doing so, if such cutting down was occasioned by quarrelling with his neighbour (fr 15 § 4). Generally a tenant is responsible for damage caused by his slaves or guests, and if there was any want of care on his part in introducing them or otherwise, he is responsible in full and cannot free himself by surrendering slaves noxally (fr 11 pr). If a lessee having taken a house or farm for a term (five years was usual) at periodical payments abandons it before the time without good cause, or is not allowed to enjoy, he can be sued or sue at once for the whole (fr 24 §§ 2, 4, 55 § 2).

Necessary or useful additions or improvements, though made without agreement, are ground for a suit *ex conducto*. The tenant can as a rule recover his expenditure. Other additions he can remove, making good any damage caused thereby (fr 19 § 4, 55 § 1; cf. fr 61 pr). All things or animals brought on to a farm by the tenant with the lessor's consent are deemed to be pledged for the rent: things, *etc.*, brought into a house and intended to remain there are pledged whether the lessor was aware of them or not (*ib.* fr 5). In the absence of agreement a tenant can sublet. A sublessee's things are not so pledged, but the fruits are pledged just as if the original lessee had gathered them (fr 24 § 1; Cod. iv 65 fr 6).

The contract of lease and hire is personal to the contracting parties and their heirs, and does not run with the land or house, *etc.* A purchaser or legatee (*per vindicationem*) of anything in lease cannot (without special covenant) claim the rents, but can gather the fruits and turn the lessee out, leaving him to his remedy against the lessor or lessor's heir (D. fr 25 § 1, 32; tit. 1 fr 13 § 11; Vat. 44; Cod. iv 65 fr 9, 10; cf. D. xxxiii 4 fr 1 § 15; xxiv 3 fr 25 § 4). If a fructuary has let for a term of years and dies before the term expires, his heir is not liable for the continuance of the tenancy unless he has represented himself as owner: nor is the reversioner bound by the lease (D. xix 2 fr 9 § 1).

If a tenant remains after the term of the lease without express agreement, in the case of a farm a new contract for a whole year is deemed to be made, in the case of a house (*praedium urbanum*) the new contract is only for so long as he actually occupies. This presumes that the parties are capable of consent (not lunatic, *etc.*). Pledges remain bound (fr 13 § 11, 14; cf. Vang. *Pand.* § 644).

2. *Locatio conductio operarum.* This applies to the hire of a freeman's services, *i.e.* of his daily labour (cf. Paul ii 18 § 1)[1]; and practically to the hire of a slave's services if he is acting for his own *peculium*: otherwise a slave's services come under *locatio conductio rei.* The hirer of the services or his heir is bound to pay for the full term agreed on, whether he use the services or not, if the person hired (*locator*) is ready to render them (D. xix 2 fr 14 § 9, fr 38). Negligence or fault on the part of the person hiring himself out makes him liable for the consequences (fr 60 § 7).

A special contract of this kind was that of a freeman hiring himself out for fighting in the arena (*auctorari*)[2] when he engaged himself '*uri vinciri ferroque necari.*' He was no longer capable of conducting another's suit (D. iii 1 fr 1 § 6), or being witness in criminal cases (*Collat.* ix 2 § 2; Gai. iv 3), and, like a slave, could be object of theft (Gai. iii 199).

3. *Locatio conductio operis faciendi*[3]. In this case the engagement is for the performance of a particular piece of

[1] Some hire-notes are given in Bruns[6] p. 328. They provide for fines for each day's absence from work or delay in payment of wages.

[2] An oath of a *quasi*-military character was taken by the gladiator: cf. Sen. *Ep.* 37 int. *Promisisti virum bonum; sacramento rogatus es. Deridebit te si quis tibi dixerit mollem esse militiam et facilem; nolo te decipi: eadem honestissimi hujus et illius turpissimi auctoramenti verba 'uri vinciri ferroque necari.' Ab his, qui manus arenae locant et edunt ac bibunt quae per sanguinem reddant, cavetur ut ista vel inviti patiantur: a te, etc.* Petron. 117 *In verba Eumolpi sacramentum juravimus 'uri vinciri verberari ferroque necari' ...tanquam legitimi gladiatores, etc.* Hor. *Sat.* ii 7 58 *Quid refert uri virgis ferroque necari auctoratus eas an, etc.*

[3] Pernice suggests that in contracts *opera* (sing.) was the technical expression for the work of the contractor; cf. D. xix 2 fr 2 § 1 *Si aurum dedero mercede pro opera constituta, etc., ib.* fr 22 § 2 *Locat enim artifex operam suam* (in building a house) *id est faciendi necessitatem,* Plaut. *Trin.*

work, as for the erection of a house, the teaching and training of a slave, tending and feeding of cattle, carriage of merchandise, making of a gold ring, setting of jewels, making cloth into clothes, cleaning of clothes. Usually the *locator* supplies the material or the principal material; if the *conductor* supplies it, the contract is rather purchase and sale. In a contract for building a house, though the *conductor* may supply the materials, the *locator* supplies the site, and the house being only an accession to the site, the business as a whole comes under *locatio conductio* (D. xix 2 fr 2, 22 § 2; xviii 1 fr 20).

The contractor (*conductor*, *redemptor*) is liable by action *ex locato* for non-execution of the work, for want of due skill, and for negligence of himself or his employees (D. fr 9 § 5, 13 § 5, 25 § 7, *etc.*). If a fuller loses clothes given him to clean, or allows the mice to gnaw them; if a driver races with other vehicles and upsets the gig and kills or hurts the slave whom he has contracted to carry; if a shipmaster transships the goods which he has to carry in order to get them up a river and does so against the will of the *locator*, or at a wrong time, or in a bad boat, and the boat is lost; or if one undertaking to train a slave takes him abroad without consent, and he is captured by the enemy or killed; or if a shoemaker corrects his apprentice so violently as to injure him; in all these cases the contractor is liable *ex locato* as well as in some of them under the *lex Aquilia* (D. fr 13 pr—§ 6; cf. xiv 2 fr 10 § 1). But the contractor is not liable for *vis major* or otherwise, when there is no fault on his part (D. xiv 2 fr 10 § 1; xix 2 fr 13 § 8, 24 § 7, *etc.*).

When a work is to be done subject to the *locator's* approval as a whole (*aversione*[1] *locatum*) it is at the risk of the contractor until approval: if the contract is at so much per certain measure, it is at his risk until measured. 'Subject to the *locator's* approval' is interpreted to mean subject to a reasonable, not arbitrary, approval (D. fr 24 pr, 36; xvii 2 fr 77).

843 *Ego operam meam* (as sycophant) *tribus nummis hodie locavi ad artis nugatorias, etc.* (*ZRG.* xxii 246). *Opera* is really an abstract term for service: *operae* is either different kinds of service or, usually, 'days' labour' (see vol. 1 pp. 86, 87), and therefore appropriate for employment of handwork by time.

1 'At a sweep' (from *averrere*).

Where cattle are put out to pasture on the terms of the owner and farmer sharing the young (and other produce?) the contract was usually deemed to be partnership (D. xvii 2 fr 52 §§ 2, 3; cf. Cod. ii 3 fr 9).

4. When corn was shipped by several parties and was not kept in separate partitions, it was held to become the property of the carrier, who was liable only for the like quantity. So with money deposited at a bank and not made up or sealed separately. The same rule applied with silver or gold given to be made into vases or rings: the goldsmith was liable only for giving due weight, not for using the metal actually supplied. An old action brought against carriers *oneris aversi* 'for making away with the load' (from *avertere*) was held by some lawyers to be superfluous, the carrier's act being theft if he was bound to deliver the precise thing and did not do so, but if he was liable only for the due amount, not for the specific article, the action *locati* was sufficient for any failure of delivery (D. xix 2 fr 31).

5. *Superficies.*

A special case somewhat like that of *emphyteusis* (above, p. 170) was when a man had erected a building on another's ground, under an agreement to pay him a ground-rent (*solarium*). The relation is similar to what we should call a building-lease[1]. If, instead of lease for periodical payment, the builder bought the surface for one sum, the relation was not essentially altered. In either case the builder and groundowner can maintain their rights against each other by action on the lease or the sale, or by a plea on the facts. And a purchaser of the ground, if evicted by the superficiary, can of course proceed on the warranty of title or on the purchase, like any other acquirer. But against third parties the superficiary (or builder) could at first protect himself only by getting a surrender of the groundowner's actions. Later however the praetor allowed all superficiaries an interdict, by

[1] Cf. D. xxxix 1 fr 3 § 3 Ulp. *Si ego superficiarius sim et opus novum fiat a vicino an possim nuntiare? movet* (there is a doubt) *quod quasi inquilinus sum sed praetor mihi utilem in rem actionem dat, etc.*

which they could recover possession without any necessity of shewing their title, provided that (as in the case of the interdict *uti possidetis*) they had not obtained it from their adversaries by force, stealth or entreaty. And further, on cause being shewn, the praetor granted to all superficiaries who were not merely temporary lessees (*non ad modicum tempus*) an action *in rem*, such as a usufructuary would have. In this way a building-lease became a limited ownership subject to the payment of the ground-rent; the right could be sold or given or bequeathed or pledged, and servitudes could be established in relation to it and other rights against neighbours, with analogous (*utiles*) actions for their protection. If two persons had the right in common, an analogous action *com. div.* would be granted them (D. xliii 18; 17 fr 3 § 7; xx 4 fr 15; xxxix 1 fr 3 § 3). The right of *superficies* could not be gained by usucapion apart from the ownership of the ground (D. xli 3 fr 26).

6. Jettison (*lex Rhodia de jactu*), 'general average.'

The actions *locati conducti* were applied in the special case of sea carriage. The law of Rhodes on this point was adopted by the Romans, and provided that, if goods carried on a ship labouring at sea are thrown over in order to lighten it and are lost, the owner has a right to a *pro rata* contribution from the property saved by this sacrifice. The goods jettisoned were valued at their cost price. The goods saved whether cargo or personal effects of a passenger (*vector*) are valued at their selling price; the ship itself is also valued: provisions intended for consumption on the voyage are alone exempted. If a mast or other tackling of the ship is sacrificed for the same purpose the ship-owner is entitled to contribution. But contribution is due only if the ship is saved and the goods are thereby saved also. If goods are put into a boat to lighten the ship and come safe, while the ship is lost, no contribution is due from the saved goods. But if the boat be lost and the ship come safe, the owner of the goods in the boat is entitled to contribution just as if they had been jettisoned. If in making the jettison other goods are damaged by exposure, they must still make a contribution but only at their damaged value. Goods saved, not by the preservation of the ship, but by their owners' exertions or by paid divers, are not called to contribute, unless the ship now lost had in a previous part of the voyage been saved by a jettison. Passengers being freemen are not liable to contribution, as a freeman's person is deemed incapable of pecuniary valuation. Damage to the ship itself or its equipment or repairs to the same give no claim to contribution, any more than injury to a workman's tools in the performance of his contract. Goods jettisoned are not deemed to be abandoned: they remain the property of their owners; but if they are recovered, any contribution already made can be reclaimed.

If a ship is ransomed from pirates, the cargo, *etc.* must contribute to the ransom, but ransom of particular goods or robbery gives no claim to contribution.

The contribution is enforced by the owner of the jettisoned goods suing the skipper (*magister*), either *ex locato* if his contract was for the carriage of the goods, or *ex conducto* if it was for a place on the ship. The skipper will either retain the goods saved, until contribution is made, or will sue their owners *ex conducto* or *locato* as the case may be. If some do not pay, the skipper is not liable for the deficit (D. xiv 2 fr 1—9; Paul ii 7; see also D. xix 6 fr 1 § 1).

7. *Receptum nautarum, etc.* 'Shipmasters', innkeepers' *etc.* undertaking.'

Special liability was attached to shipmasters, innkeepers, and stablekeepers, or, if those actually in charge were only deputies, then to the principals. By the praetor's edict they were made responsible for the safe delivery of everything which in the ordinary way of their business they had undertaken to carry or keep safely (*quod salvum fore receperint*[1]). It was not necessary that the master should receive the goods himself; any officer with general management or appointed for this purpose could bind. Whether any disclaimer of responsibility was allowed is not said; the rule was, that no special consignment was necessary, but the placing in the vessel or inn or even on

[1] Lenel (*ZRG.* xxvi 403) suggests that the undertaking was by an announcement on the house, *e.g. sarcinae salvae erunt.*

the shore, if defendant has accepted them, was enough[1] to make him responsible not only for his own act, but for his servants or passengers or travellers, although not himself to blame; and he could not free himself by surrendering a slave noxally. But he was not liable for loss due to shipwreck, pirates or *vis major*. Clothes, *etc.* of travellers had also the benefit of the guaranty. The action was *in factum*, and ran for and against heirs. It was wider than an action *locati conducti*, because no fault was necessary to found the action, and than *depositi*, where it is necessary to prove fraud. When concurrent with other actions it was subject to the usual treatment. It could be brought by anyone who had an interest in a thing's being safely kept, *e.g.* a lender on bottomry (D. iv 9 fr 1—5 pr). An action on the case was also granted for delicts; see p. 182.

H. Actions on the case.

Agreements are sometimes made which do not come strictly under well-known descriptions and yet are not confirmed by stipulation. If, however, they are of a definite character, containing mutual engagements and intended to raise obligations, the party who performs his engagement was recognised by the Roman law as entitled to the performance by the other or to compensation for his failure. Many such cases bordered on sale or hiring or mandate or partnership, or other contracts. The want of a short title was supplied in framing the issue for trial by a statement of the facts of the case. This appears to have been denoted by two expressions: the plaintiff *agit praescriptis verbis*[2] or *agit in factum*: and sometimes both were combined (*in factum praescriptis verbis*). *Praescriptis verbis* refers to the mode of prefixing to the ordinary formula a brief explanation of the case or incorporating it with the demonstration

[1] Ude (*ZRG.* xxv 66) gives a somewhat different view, but he is dealing with the Justinian law which has half amalgamated two actions in this title (D. iv 9).

[2] *Agere praescriptis verbis* is a correct expression: but there was probably no such phrase in Antonine times as *actio praescr. verb.*, certainly no such action as a common type. Gradenwitz *Interpol.* p. 123.

as a limiting clause (*e.g.* Gai. iv 130—137); the claim was put as one of right (*formula in jus concepta*) but of uncertain character (*quicquid paret N. Negidium A. Agerio dare facere oportere*) and hence came under the general class of *civiles*[1] *incerti actiones*; cf. Gai. iv 45—52, 54, 60.

The other expression *agere in factum* is more general, and is frequently applied to a somewhat different class of untitled actions, where there was little or no appearance of a contract or agreement, but the facts of the case shewed a wrong deserving of a remedy. In these cases the praetor did not profess that it was a matter of civil law, but stated the facts themselves and directed the judge to condemn the defendant in damages to the plaintiff if he found the facts to be so. These were praetorian, not civil actions; they were pre-eminently *actiones in factum*; the claim (*intentio*) was contained in the facts stated, and only the condemnation clause was uncertain (*quanti ea res erit*). This kind of action was sometimes adopted in the case of relatives in order to avoid the infamy which attached to condemnation in a civil action (cf. Cod. v 12 fr 1 § 2).

The limits of these expressions are not clearly ascertainable, as Justinian endeavoured to make only one such class of actions and to fuse the expressions (D. xix 3—5; cf. Pernice *ZRG.* xxii 253). Earlier lawyers seem to have differed in opinion on the matter, Julian proposing an *actio in factum* where Ulpian and others gave an action *praescriptis verbis* (D. ii 14 fr 7 § 2; cf. xix 5 fr 5 § 2).

1. *De aestimato,* or *aestimatoria praescriptis verbis actio*[2]. When a person was given a thing to sell with a price affixed, the usual agreement was that he could keep for himself any excess which he might obtain, but he bore the risk of whatever happened, and was liable either for the return of the thing in

[1] *Civilis* added to *in factum* in fr 1 pr § 1 and fr 5 § 2 is held to be an interpolation by Polkrowsky *ZRG.* xxix 88 foll., and so is *praescriptis verbis* in fr 15, 27, *etc.* by Gradenwitz *Interpol.* pp. 125, 135, whom see on the title generally, esp. on fr 17 and 20.

[2] Cf. Plaut. *Merc.* 93 *Quas merces vexeram omnis vendidi: lucrum ingens facio praeterquam meus pater dedit aestimatas merces: ita peculium conficio grande.*

good condition or for the affixed value. The case was not one of sale, for there was no obligation on the receiver to take the thing at the price; nor was it *conductio venditoris* or *locatio rei vendendae* for there was no fixed *merces*, and even if a *merces* was agreed on, the distributor's chance of gain by asking a higher price than the value affixed was too important to be disregarded; nor was it mandate, for the receiver was not presumed to act gratuitously; nor was it partnership, for there was no arrangement of definite shares in the gain, and the thing never became the common property of giver and receiver. Doubts were settled by making it a special action and giving it a separate place in the edict (Lenel *EP.* p. 238). It was deemed to be *bonae fidei* (D. xix 3; cf. 5 fr 13). Where no agreement as above was expressed or implied, the seller would be liable only for fraud or fault; if the transaction was solely at the request of the seller, for fraud only (D. xix 5 fr 17 § 1; Paul ii 4 § 4).

2. Another class of cases which occasioned much doubt as to its character was barter (*permutatio rerum*). The Sabinians, fortified by Homer[1], thought it a form of sale; the Proculians held that it differed essentially, by there being nothing to decide which of the parties was purchaser and which of the commodities was price (Gai. iii 141). A purchaser has to make the vendor owner of the money-price; a vendor has only to covenant for quiet enjoyment by the purchaser. But in barter each party has to make the other owner; and mere consent is not sufficient to ground an action, but part performance is required. The action goes to the due performance by the other party, or for damages to the amount of our interest in it (*in id quod interest nostra, illam rem accepisse de qua convenit*). The liability for faults appears to be the same as in sale (D. xix 4). A condiction would also lie (as an alternative action) for restoration of the thing (D. xix 5 fr 5 § 1).

3. Analogous cases are where the exchange is not of thing for thing (*do ut des*) but of thing or services for services (*do ut facias* or *facio ut facias*)[2]. Thus, I give you a house on condition

[1] See above, p. 138 n. 3.

[2] The famous division of such cases into four: *do ut des*, *do ut facias*,

that you repair another for me (D. xix 5 fr 6); or I give you a vacant plot of land to build on in consideration of your erecting a house on it, and giving me a part (fr 13 § 1); or I lend you my ox for ten days at a time in consideration of your lending me yours for like periods (the *actio commodati* is not applicable, because the loans are not gratuitous, and there is no fixed *merces* to make it *locatio conductio*, fr 17 § 3; cf. D. x. 3 fr 23 and Gai. iii 144). Or I put a slave for safekeeping in your bakery and agree that you shall be compensated by his services (D. xvi 3 fr 1 § 9). The due performance of the agreement, or responsibility for ill-treatment of the ox or slave will be secured by a civil action *praescriptis verbis*. So also if I bargain with you to manumit a certain slave, and in consideration give you another slave, or agree to manumit one of my own, and I perform my part, I can sue for compensation if you do not manumit as agreed (D. xix 5 fr 5 pr and § 1), as you can sue me if *e.g.* the slave I have given you is evicted (*ib.* § 2 and cf. ii 14 fr 7 § 2). If I give you money to manumit your slave, it is not hire, for manumission is not a hireable service; and I must sue in the same way (*ib.* fr 7).

4. Other cases are various. I release a debt of yours on your agreeing to delegate a debtor of yours to me (fr 9); or you happen to know where my runaway slave is, and I agree to pay you a certain sum, if you give me information which will enable me to seize him (fr 15); or instead of money for a loan I give you a thing to sell, and you either do not sell it, or sell it and decline to accept the price as a loan (fr 19 pr); or I give you a slave, with value affixed, to be put to the question on an accusation of theft; he is not convicted, and you return neither the slave nor his value (fr 8). Where I have given money or a thing, I can recover it by a condiction, but to enforce the agreement I require to sue *praescriptis verbis*.

5. One-sided obligations of a delictal character were enforced by an *actio in factum, e.g.* without good cause to throw others' goods overboard in order to save one's own; to strip

facio ut des, facio ut facias, attributed to Paul in D. xix 5 fr 5, is, with much else of this fragment, the creation of Tribonian, according to Gradenwitz *Interpol.* p. 131. See however Lenel *ZRG.* xxii 181.

another's slave so that he dies of cold; to throw another's silver cup into the sea for mischief's sake: and if such acts were done in order to make a gain, the doer would be liable for theft. If acorns fall from your trees into my land, and I admit cattle which eat them, I am not liable under the XII tables (*de pastu pecoris*), for they are not trespassing on your land; nor is the act *pauperies*, for the animals are acting quietly and naturally; nor is it under the *lex Aquilia*, for I have done no direct act of violence. An action *ad exhibendum* might apply; or, if there was any fraudulent intent, an action *de dolo*; otherwise an action *in factum* is the remedy (fr 14; x 4 fr 9 § 1; cf. Cod. v 12 fr 1 § 2). Other cases are mentioned under Aquilian damage. See also *de recepto nautarum* (p. 178), *calumniae causa* (p. 234), *si quis mensor* (p. 236).

(Some cases named in this title (xix 5) for *actio in factum* are however not of the character of delicts: *e.g.* of an agreement (fr 12); of a one-sided matter where a condiction would appear suitable (fr 10); of hiring, with price to be fixed by subsequent agreement (fr 22; cf. Gai. iii 143).)

CHAPTER V.

SEMIDELICTAL[1] OBLIGATIONS.

i. These obligations are characterised by the rule that if restitution was disputed and judgment obtained, the defendant had to pay double damages, *i.e.* once for reimbursing the plaintiff, and the like amount again as penalty for non-admission of the claim. They consisted in Gaius' time (so far as we know) of obligations (or actions) *judicati, depensi, de sponsu, damni injuriae* (under the *lex Aquilia*) and *legati per damnationem certi*, including no doubt *legatum sinendi modo*. The history of these actions, at least as regards the first three, is given by Gaius in treating of execution *per manus injectionem*, and will be found below (Book VI ch. XV A). They all had these characteristics: non-admission (*infitiatio*) doubled the damages; a mere bargain (*pactum*) was not sufficient to

[1] This term seems convenient, but I have no authority for it.

settle the case; any money paid in excess of what was due was not recoverable (Gai. iv 9, 171; Paul i 19; Just. iii 27 § 7). The first two (*judicati* and *depensi*) had the further marks of stringency, that the *vadimonium* was put at the full amount of the judgment debt, or of the money paid down, and that defendant was required to give security *judicatum solvi*. The *actio de sponsu* was probably in the same position, but we know little of it (Gai. iv 22, 25, 102, 186; iii 127; *lex Urson.* 61). The first three would be strict actions; *damni injuriae* probably at first relatively strict (the measure being given by statute); an action on a legacy would be strict or not, according as the object was certain or uncertain. Only *certa legata* belong to this class (Gai. iv 9).

The damages were not doubled if defendant admitted the claim before suit or tendered an oath to plaintiff who thereupon swore to the debt (D. xii 2 fr 30 pr). An heir could bring these actions, but was not liable under the *lex Aquilia*, unless his predecessor had joined issue (Gai. iv 112; Just. iv 12 § 1), or the heir had any profit from the act causing the loss to plaintiff (D. ix 2 fr 23 § 8). To the other actions the heir was liable.

1. The *actio judicati* was not limited to any time; it was *perpetua* (D. xlii 1 fr 6 § 3). For the procedure see under Execution, Book VI ch. XV.

2. *Actio depensi*[1], 'on money paid down by weight,' was granted by the *lex Publilia* against a debtor who had not within six months repaid his surety (*sponsor*). The law expressly gave the right of *manus injectio pro judicato*, and thus made the debtor liable to arrest, and disabled him from conducting his own case in court (Gai. iv 22, 25).

[1] For the use of *dependĕre* cf. Plaut. *Trin.* 425 *Trapezitae mille drachumarum redditae. Nempe quas spopondi. Immo 'quas dependi' inquito*: and metaphorically Cic. *Fam.* i 9 § 9 where Pompey says to Q. Cicero, *Nisi cum Marco fratre diligenter egeris, dependendum tibi est quod mihi pro illo spopondisti*; also *Ep. ad Brut.* i 18 § 3; Sen. *Ben.* iii 8 § 2 *Hic pecuniam pro addicto dependit.*

Eisele (*Beitr.* p. 30) suggests that the money paid by a sponsor was paid with the formalities of the bronze and balance. Karlowa (*RG.* ii 773) argues that the expression belongs to a time when *aes grave* and not coined money was used, *i.e.* before 486 B.C.

3. *Actio de sponsu* was granted to sponsors by the *lex Furia* (see p. 30): it was against any creditor who had made a sponsor pay more than his share of the debt: and made him liable to *manus injectio pro judicato* (Gai. ii 121; iv 22).

4. *Legati certi per damnationem relicti, i.e.* for a legacy left in such words as *Heres meus Stichum servum meum dare damnas esto,* though Gaius says the word *dato* was sufficient of itself (ii 201). Probably this was a relaxation of the old formula, when the full significance of *damnas esto* was no longer realised. The claim of the legatee in the formula was *heredem sibi dare oportere* (Gai. ii 204; iv 55).

Liberatio per aes et libram.

There was an old form of release[1] by a fiction of payment (*imaginariae solutionis*) which was applicable to a judgment debt, to legacies bequeathed in the damnatory form, and also to contracts made by the bronze and balance, *i.e.* by mancipation and *nexum* (see p. 308). It consisted in the application of a form like that used in mancipation (cf. D. L 17 fr 35 *nihil tam naturale est quam eo genere quidque dissolvere quo colligatum est*), and was thus. Five witnesses and a balance holder are present. The person whose obligation is to be released says, 'Whereas I am condemned to thee in so many thousands 'I now loose (*solvo*) and free myself from thee in that matter 'with this bronze and bronze balance[2]. This pound[2] I weigh 'out to thee as first and last[3] in accordance with the public 'law.' He then strikes the scale with an *as* and hands it over to the creditor by way of payment (*solvendi causa*). When the release is given by a legatee to the heir, the words *testamento*

[1] For the application of this old form of release to free a legatee from the obligation under the priestly code of keeping up the sacred rites attached to an inheritance see vol. I p. 390.

[2] *libra* is used for both 'balance' and 'pound.'

[3] The bit of bronze is to represent the whole sum supposed to be paid. Cf. the old formula in Livy i 24 § 7 *Ut illa prima postrema ex illis tabulis cerave recitata sunt etc.*; D. xxxviii 16 fr 2 § 4 *Idem primus postremusque qui solus occurrit.*

dare damnatus are substituted for the simple *condemnatus* of the judgment debtor. It is however only a legacy consisting in a certain weight or certain count of things that is released by this form; but some lawyers thought that it could be applied also to the legacy of a certain measure (Gai. iii 173—175). Evidently measure was at first deemed inconsistent with the original conception of scales and money.

---

5. *DAMNI INJURIA* (*i.e. damni injuria dati*[1]), or *DAMNI INJURIAE*.

(*a*) The *lex Aquilia* of early but uncertain date[2] (stated by Ulpian to have been a plebiscite proposed by a tribune of the Commons) granted an action for any loss wrongfully (*injuriā*) caused to another by injury to his slave or animal or other thing. It superseded previous enactments on the subject, even that of the XII tables. The first and third clauses (the second being comparatively unimportant) were apparently in the following terms (though in more archaic language):

I. *Qui servum servamve alienum alienamve quadrupedemve pecudem injuria occiderit, quanti in eo anno plurimi ea res fuit, tantum aes dare domino damnas esto.*

III. *Ceterarum rerum (praeter hominem et pecudem occisos) si quis alteri damnum faxit, quod usserit, fregerit, ruperit injuria, quanti ea res fuerit in diebus* XXX *proximis, tantum aes dare domino damnas esto.* And it was added

Adversus infitiantem in duplum actio erit (Gai. iii 210—218; D. ix 2 fr 2 § 1, 27 § 5).

The first clause therefore provided for the case of anyone killing wrongfully another's slave or fourfooted farm-animal, *i.e.* horse, mule, ass, ox, sheep, goat, pig. Elephants and camels

[1] For *dare* used with *damnum* in this sense see Gai. iii 211, 218, 219; D. ix 2 fr 5 § 2, *etc.* The short phrase without *dati* is also used by Cicero; *judicium damni injuria constitutum, Rosc. Com.* 11 § 32 and again in 18 § 54. Gaius has *damni injuriae actio* (iii 210; iv 76) where *injuriae* may be an attraction into the genitive, or a simple combination of the elements of loss and wrong as *uti frui; ruta caesa, etc.*

[2] Theophilus (iv 3 § 15) refers it to the time of a secession of the *plebs*. This seems to be merely an inference from what Ulpian says here (D. ix 2 fr 1) and what Pomponius says in D. i 2 fr 2 § 8.

were also held by the lawyers to be within the terms, but dogs, bears, *etc.* were not.

The third clause provided for the case of any wrongful wounding of any slave or animal of the above class, and for the case of killing or wounding any other animal, or damaging any thing belonging to another person. The old (*i.e.* republican) lawyers took *ruperit* to mean *corruperit,* and gave a wide interpretation to the terms used in the statute so as to include cutting, burning, breaking, bruising, tearing, smashing, letting out (of liquids), in fact spoiling of any sort (Gai. iii 217; D. fr 27 §§ 13—17). 'Wrongfully' included negligence, even though slight (*et levissima culpa* fr 44; cf. xl 12 fr 13 pr), and was not restricted to cases of malice or evil purpose; for it included *damnum culpa datum etiam ab eo qui nocere noluit* D. ix 2 fr 5 § 1: nor had it here, as in the *actio injuriarum,* any special connexion with 'insult' (*contumelia* fr 5 § 1). But killing or hurting in self-defence, *e.g.* killing a robber by night, whom one could not seize, is not within the statute. Nor does action lie against a madman, or infant, or an *impubes,* who is not intelligent of wrong (Ulp. in *Collat.* vii 3; D. fr 5 pr § 2; xlvii 2 fr 23; tit. 4 fr 1 § 2).

(*b*) Thus liability attaches to one who uses excessive violence in training or correcting pupils, or strikes a slave when ill, so that he dies in consequence, or to a surgeon who performs on a slave unskilfully or administers a wrong drug; or to a muledriver who from incompetence to control his mules crushes some slave; or to sailors who by their bad management collide with others' ships or nets, or cut others' ropes; or to a porter who has taken too great a load or walks so carelessly that he slips, and his load kills or hurts someone; or to one who strikes a pregnant woman or mare so as to cause miscarriage; or who corrupts another's slave girl, being an immature virgin. So also the act covers one who is practising with missiles in a place not intended for the purpose and kills or hurts a passing slave or animal; or who is lopping a tree near some road or path and does not cry out to warn people, with the result that a branch falls and injures them; or who digs pits or puts nets in the roads without notice or precautions so that cattle, *etc.* fall into them and are injured (D. ix 2 fr 5 § 3, 7 §§ 2, 5, 8, fr 8 pr §§ 1, 8, fr 9 § 4, 11 pr, 27 § 22, fr 28, 29 pr—§ 2, 31; Paul i 13A § 6). Again, one who tears or soils another's dress, or throws another's corn into the river, or mixes it with sand, or casts tares or oats into cornfields[1], or fouls or turns sour another's wine, or lets it run to waste, or cuts down standing corn or vines, or gathers another's olives before the grain or fruit is ripe (if it be ripe, there is no cause for suit as he only saves the owner trouble), or cuts another's fowling nets, or cuts off the beams of another's house which without right project over his own house, or so repairs the banks of a public river as to injure the riparian proprietors, are all liable under this statute. So is even a wife who without her husband's consent pierces (so as to string them) pearls lent her by him; or anyone who rubs out or obliterates another's will, or documents containing proof of debt (D. ix 2 fr 27 §§ 15, 18—20, 25, 30, 31, fr 29 §§ 1, 3, 41, 42; xliii 15 § 5). But consumption of another's wine or corn was not matter for a suit under the statute itself[2], but for an analogous (*utilis*) action (D. ix 2 fr 30 § 2).

(*c*) Strictly speaking the law required the injury to be caused *corpore corpori* (cf. Gai. iii 219; D. fr 51; Just. iv 16), *i.e.* by direct physical force causing physical injury; and hence arose much discussion among lawyers and subtle distinction (see *Collat.* xii 7). Thus, if a man threw a slave into the river and the slave was drowned, still, though the death was only indirectly caused by the force used, the Aquilian action was held to lie. But if he had persuaded a slave to go up a tree or down a well, and the slave in doing so had fallen and been killed; or if he had irritated a horse which the slave was riding, so that it threw him off into the river and he was drowned, the *lex Aquilia* did not apply. Nor did it apply if a man only held a slave, or led him into an ambush, and another killed him; nor if a midwife gave drugs, without actually administering them, to a woman, and the woman

[1] Oats were thought to cause barley, *etc.* to degenerate, tares to cumber the ground (Plin. *HN.* xviii 149, 153); cf. Verg. *Buc.* v. 37.

[2] Apparently because consumption of food, being its natural use, hardly comes under the terms of causing damage to a thing.

died thereof; nor if a patient died from his surgeon's or another's neglect after a skilful operation; nor if a person set fire to his own stubble or sticks without due care or watching, and the fire caught and burnt a neighbour's farm; nor if a person confined slaves or cattle so that they were starved to death; or drove another's beast so fast that it was injured; or smoked another's bees so as to put them to flight or kill them (Gai. iii 219; D. fr 7 § 7, 8 pr, 9 pr §§ 2, 3, 30 § 3; *Collat.* xii 3). If a farmer's slave lighted a furnace, and another who had to watch it fell asleep, and the farmhouse was burnt down, it might be said that the farmer was not responsible for either; one slave had done what he ought, the other had done nothing. If a man set a dog at another and held the dog, the Aquilian law applied, but if he did not hold him, Julian considered the case was not within the statute. The praetor however in all cases coming within the spirit of the law granted an action 'on the precedent of the Aquilian law' (*ad exemplum legis Aquiliae* Gai. iii 219; Ulp. in *Collat.* xii 7 §§ 6, 7; D. fr 53). Such an action is usually called *in factum* (D. fr 33 § 1, *etc.*), sometimes *utilis* (fr 27 § 32, *etc.*).

Mere continued neglect of duty, *e.g.* neglect to plough land, to prune vines, to clear water-courses, is not within the statute at all (D. vii 1 fr 13 § 2).

(*d*) It is a good defence that the doer took due precautions, or was acting in self-defence against plaintiff (if plaintiff and not innocent third persons were injured), or was acting only under irresistible force, or was exercising his own right, or did the injury while engaged in an honourable athletic contest[1], or was in such a position that if anyone were to blame, it was the injured rather than, or as much as, the injurer. A slave hurt while crossing a place intended for shooting at the time of practice, or going on private ground, where there was no right of road, and falling into a pit made for catching stags or bears, gives his owner no right of action (D. ix 2 fr 9 § 4, 28 pr, 52 § 1)[2]. A sudden gust of wind on a calm day causing fire to spread, a storm driving vessels against one

[1] Cf. D. xi 5 fr 2 § 1, 3.

[2] For other interesting cases see fr 11 pr, 52.

another or making it necessary for sailors to cut others' cables, a push by a third party causing defendant involuntarily to do the injury, are recognised as grounds for excuse (fr 7 § 3, 29 § 3, 30 §§ 3, 4, 52 § 2; cf. fr 11 pr). A man cutting waterpipes laid by another without right through defendant's house is not liable under this law (fr 29 § 1). Nor is one liable under this statute (according to Servius and others against Labeo) who, to stop a fire from reaching his house, breaks down a neighbour's house, whether the fire actually reach his house or not; but if it does not, he is liable to his neighbour under the interdict *quod vi aut clam* (fr 49; xliii 24 fr 7 § 4; xlvii 9 fr 3 § 7). A man finding another's cattle on his land is not justified in shutting them up or driving them off otherwise than he would treat his own cattle (D. ix 2 fr 39).

(*e*) Plaintiff is primarily the owner of the slave or thing hurt, or heir to the owner. One who has the use or usufruct is entitled to an analogous action, even against the owner himself, if he has caused the death or injury (fr 11 §§ 6, 10, fr 12, 43), as is the owner also against him in the like case (D. vii 1 fr 15 § 3). If the slave be in pledge and the debtor is insolvent, or the time for creditor's action on the debt has passed, the creditor can sue under the Aquilian law, being of course liable to the debtor for any excess recovered above the amount of the debt (D. ix 2 fr 30 § 1). If a slave belonging to an inheritance is killed before the heir enters, the heir can sue, and, even if the slave have been bequeathed away, retains the right of action (the legacy having failed with the death of the slave). If the slave be only wounded, the heir must cede his action to the legatee. If he be slain after the heir has entered, and the legatee has not yet accepted the legacy[1], the legatee has no claim (fr 13 § 2—fr 15 pr). If the killer is a slave, his owner is liable to the action, even though the slave be in flight: it does not lie against the master of one serving *bona fide*. But it does lie against one who, having the right to command, orders another freeman to commit an injury (fr 27 § 3, 37 pr). An owner is liable, if he has killed his slave or animal, to a *bona fide* possessor or to a pledgee (by an action *in factum*): a pledgee is

[1] See vol. I p. 294, where the dispute about acceptance is mentioned.

liable by the Aquilian law as well as by the pledge action (fr 17—19). Any co-owner can sue for his share of the damages (fr 20, 27 § 2). The action can be brought against heirs of the injurer, only so far as they have been enriched (fr 23 § 8).

(*f*) The measure of damages for killing under the first clause was the highest value of the slave or animal at any time within the year (*i.e.* 365 days) preceding the death, or if the death was not till long afterwards, within the year preceding the fatal wound. Under the third clause the measure was the depreciation caused in what was the value to the plaintiff within the last thirty days. The word *plurimi* being here omitted, some thought that the judge had the power of taking the lower estimate, but the practice followed Sabinus in treating the omission of *plurimi* as accidental (Gai. iii 218; D. fr 21, 29 § 8, 51). Two wounds inflicted at one time by the same person counted as one offence; not so, if inflicted at different times. But if suit be brought and damages obtained for a wound to a slave and he afterwards die of the wound, suit can be brought again, but only for the residue (after deduction of these damages) of what the owner would have obtained if suit had been originally brought for the killing (fr 32 § 1, 46, 47). If a slave, being mortally wounded by one, is after a time killed by another, both are liable, though the estimate of damages may differ in the two cases on account of the differences in reckoning the period of value (fr 51). Where several persons are directly concerned in the same offence, all are liable, and the penalty on one did not relieve the others, unless they were all of the same family of slaves,—an exception due to unwillingness to excessive cumulation of penalty on the owner (fr 11 §§ 2, 4, fr 32).

(*g*) In estimating the value or loss by a slave's death or injury, all has to be included that would have been gained through him and all cost to which plaintiff has consequently been put. Thus the damages would be increased if the slave had an inheritance left him, and he was killed before he could accept; or if his manumission was the condition of his owner's becoming heir; or if he had committed frauds in his accounts, and his death prevented his being put to the question to reveal his confederates; or if he was one of a band of comedians or musicians, and the rest were depreciated by his loss; or again if a mule was killed which was one of a pair, or a horse which was one of a four-in-hand. If suit be brought against the owner of an animal which has caused damage (*pauperies*) and the animal is killed, the owner can sue under the *lex Aquilia* for so much as was his interest in not paying damages but surrendering the noxious animal (Gai. iii 212; D. fr 22, 23 pr §§ 2, 4, fr 33 § 1, 37 § 1). Mere sentimental considerations, *e.g.* ties of relationship or affection, were not regarded: the loss must be of a substantial character such as would be felt by any owner (fr 33 pr). Again, at the time of injury a slave might be lame or have lost the use of an eye, or of a thumb, and thereby the slave being a painter have lost his value as an artist; but if he was sound within the period prescribed, the higher value was taken. If a slave proved eventually none the worse for the injury, still the action was good for the cost of healing (Gai. iii 114; D. fr 23 § 3, 27 § 17; cf. *Collat.* ii 4). In any case if defendant disputed his liability and was condemned, the damages were doubled. If he admitted the fact and disputed only the estimate of damage, double damages were not due, and the trial was confined to the determination of the value (Gai. iv 9, 71; D. fr 23 § 10, 25 § 2, 26).

(*h*) Injury to the body of a freeman did not come within the *lex Aquilia*, which dealt only with damage done to others' property. Moreover *nemo membrorum suorum dominus videtur* (*i.e.* limbs are not property) and it was a maxim that *liberum corpus aestimationem non recipit.* But an analogous action was granted (D. fr 13 pr; cf. xiv 2 fr 2 § 2). The measure of damages would be in this as in some other cases the costs of healing and the loss of services. Disfigurement would not come into the calculation (D. ix 1 fr 3; tit. 3 fr 7; cf. xxi 1 fr 42). A father could however sue for damage to a son in his power (D. ix 2 fr 7 pr).

(*i*) If a slave appointed free and heir by will be killed before testator's death, neither the substitute (if any) nor statutable heir to testator can sue under the *lex Aquilia.*

If he be mortally wounded, but die after testator, the wounded man's heir cannot sue where he himself had no action; if however he was only part heir, his coheir can sue for the diminution of his share of the inheritance, the right once acquired to the testator by the wounding of the slave not being lost by his manumission (D. fr 23 § 1, 36; xliv 7 fr 56).

(*k*) For offences under this statute committed by a slave or son under power, or by a vicar at his slave master's order, the owner for the time being was liable (*noxa caput sequitur*), and he could, instead of paying damages, surrender the delinquent. See below, chap. vii c.

(*l*) In many cases other actions are available concurrently with this, *e.g.* pledge, hire, loan, theft, spiteful injury, or *ad exhibendum*. If one suit was successful, another could be brought only for the excess thereby recoverable (D. fr 18, 27 §§ 11, 34, fr 42; xliv 7 fr 34). If a slave were killed maliciously (*dolo*) the killer would be liable also to criminal proceedings, but there might be a question whether both should be allowed (Gai. iii 213; D. ix 2 fr 23 § 9; xlvii 10 fr 7 § 1).

(*m*) The second clause of the *lex Aquilia* gave an action against an *adstipulator* who formally released the promiser so as to cheat the stipulator. The damages were to be *tanti quanti ea res est*. The connexion of this clause with the first and third is obscure. Gaius himself is puzzled at this grant of a special action, when, as he says, the action *mandati* was sufficient, though it was true (he adds) that by the *lex Aquilia* he could get double damages if the defendant denied the act (Gai. iii 215, 216). Modern writers are inclined to doubt whether in those early days an action *mandati* would have been good. But I think it possible that the real solution of the difficulty may be that the second clause was due to some particular circumstances which led to Aquilius' proposing this law. An *adstipulator* was chiefly used when the promise was to be performed after the stipulator's death (Gai. iii 117), in order that there might be someone to enforce the contract. Suppose such a stipulation to have been made by a slave, the slave to be killed and the master to die before bringing suit: suppose the *adstipulator* to be persuaded by the promiser (himself perhaps the killer of the slave) to give him a release. Nothing could be more natural than that Aquilius should provide that in such a case (the case on my theory actually before him at the time) the *adstipulator* should be liable to the full amount for the loss caused by the death of the slave and his own fraud. But without knowledge of the actual words of this clause (of which indeed even Gaius may have had only a brief traditionary account) it is useless to speculate further.

The words *dare damnas esto* are often used in exacting fines for breach of public statutes. See *lex Jul. Agrar.* 54, 55; *lex Julia municipalis* vv. 19, 125; *lex Quinct.* 25; *lex Urson. passim etc.* and sometimes in private inscriptions on tombs, Bruns[6] p. 338. In an old inscription on a grave in Luceria the right of *manus injectio pro judicato* is given against offenders. Actions for exacting the fines were *populares, i.e.* could be brought by anyone, like English *qui tam* actions (*lex Jul. Agrar.* 54 *ejus pecuniae qui volet petitio hac lege esto*). The fine under such actions was not doubled by non-admission.

That *damnas esto*, used in a public statute, had originally the same effect as *judicatus*[1] I do not doubt (cf. Gai. iv 21): but how long this continued is a more difficult question. And it is doubtful what was the effect of it when used in a private will or in an inscription by a private person *qui legem suae rei dicit* (cf. D. xxiii 4 fr 20 § 1; Mommsen *ap.* Bruns[6] p. 259).

---

ii. There are other cases of semidelictal obligation similar in general character to those under the *lex Aquilia*, but the amount of damages was not affected by admission or denial of the offence. In several however the damages are put from the first at double the value.

1. *ARBORUM FURTIM CAESARUM.*

This was a special action against one who stealthily cut trees. The XII tables had a like action with a penalty of 25 *asses*. It was an old dispute whether vines were included

[1] This is contested by Monro (see his edition of D. ix 2, App. II.), and very recently by Mitteis (*ZRG.* xxxv 113).

under trees. Most of the old lawyers (cf. Gai. iv 11) said they were. Ivy, reeds, and osiers were held to be included. Not only cutting down, but any cutting (*caedere, subsecare*) or ringbarking (*cingere*) was within the law: pulling up by the roots was not. If my tree puts its roots into a neighbour's land, he must not cut them, but bring an action denying my right to let the trees do it (*immissum habere*). The damages are laid at double the owner's interest in not having the trees hurt: the value of the wood is deducted from the amount of the damage. The action did not lie against an heir; and is not open to a usufructuary. It could be brought at any time (*perpetua est*). The *lex Aquilia* will apply where this action fails, and is concurrent with this where it lies, but if both are brought, that brought second is good only for the excess over what has been recovered. If the wood or branches cut are carried away, an action lies for theft (D. xlvii 7). Paul appears to extend this action to the cutting of standing corn (*Sent.* ii 31 § 24; cf. D. xlvii 2 fr 21 pr).

For the right of an owner to cut a neighbour's overhanging trees see vol. I p. 508.

Other actions for damage similar to that which was the subject of the *lex Aquilia* were granted by the praetor against persons who had not themselves caused damage but were presumed to have had the power to prevent it. Such are (2) *de dejecto effusove*, (3) *de suspenso, exposito, etc.*, (4) *de damno in nave aut caupona facto.* (5) To these may be added some old actions granted by the XII tables for damage caused by animals. Denial did not involve double damages.

2. *De dejecto effusove.* If anything was thrown down or fell or was poured out so as to cause damage to a person in a place where people in general pass or stand, the occupier of the house or apartment, whence the damage came, was liable to an action on the case. It was not necessary to prove fault. The damages were double the estimate of the injury, irrespective of confession or denial. If a freeman was killed, the damages are fixed (by Justinian) at fifty *aurei*; if he was only hurt, then at whatever the judge shall think fair, reckoning the fees

to doctors and other cost of his illness, and the value of his services for the time, and, if he is disabled, for the future also, but not reckoning anything for scars or deformity. The action did not run against heirs, but could be brought by an heir, except where the damage was done to the person of a freeman. In that case he himself could sue at any time, others must sue within a year, whether he was killed or only wounded. It was open to anyone to sue, parties interested or related to him by blood or marriage being however preferred; but heirs as such had no claim, where as in this case the matter was not regarded as compensation for a pecuniary loss, but as a matter of justice only (D. ix 3 fr 1 §§ 1—6, fr 5 § 5, 7).

The occupier is alone chargeable, even though he may have given gratuitous lodging to clients or freedmen, or may use the house as a workshop or school, or may have let off a small part of it in apartments, but if the bulk is let off all the occupants are chargeable; the praetor however will find it reasonable in some cases to allow the action only against the person actually occupying the chamber whence the mischief was caused. Occupiers in common are all liable: payment by one frees the others, who can then be made to contribute. Where an occupier has had to pay for the act of his guest, *etc.*, he can recoup himself by an action on the case against the offender (who is also liable under the *lex Aquilia*). A son under power occupying separately is responsible himself, as there is no contract to make his father liable *de peculio*. If a slave was occupier, his master was not liable either *negot. gest.* or *de peculio*, and hence he was dealt with *extra ordinem*. If he actually committed the offence, without his master's knowledge, he could be surrendered noxally (D. *ib.* fr 1 §§ 4, 7—fr 5 § 4).

3. *De suspenso, exposito, etc.* A like action was granted against anyone whether owner or lodger, dwelling there or not, who allowed anything to be placed on, or hang from, the eaves or a projection, which might fall and hurt passers by in a public place. If harm was actually done, the person who placed the thing there, instead of the occupant, was liable. And a like action was granted against one who exposed in a booth a picture or jar, *etc.*, so that it fell and did hurt. The penalty

was put (by Justinian) at ten *solidi.* Anyone could bring the action, but being penal it did not run against heirs (D. ix 3 fr 5 §§ 6—13). (N.B. *aureus* = *solidus* fixed by Caracalla at $\frac{1}{72}$ lb. gold.)

4. A somewhat similar action (*in factum*) was granted by the praetor against shipmasters, innkeepers and stablekeepers (*qui naves, cauponas, stabularia exercent*, cf. p. 178) for acts of theft or damage committed in the ship or tavern, *etc.*, by their sailors or servants or lodgers, not being merely travellers or passengers. The liability attaches where there is no fault on the part of the principal except for a bad selection of servants or other residents. If the offender is one of his own slaves, the master is entitled to some indulgence, because they are not chosen for this purpose, but are a family plague (*quasi domesticum malum*): he can therefore free himself by noxal surrender. If another's slave be employed in the ship or tavern and do theft or damage to his owner, the owner can sue the *exercitor* by this action (as well as by an *actio furti* or *Aquilia*). But damage done by one sailor or employee to another is not ground for this action. The injured person can proceed directly against the offender (if ascertained) by the *actio furti* or *Aquilia*; but, if he prefer to sue the principal, he must cede to him his actions against them: if the principal be acquitted on this action, the other actions will be barred. Damages by this action are for the double value, and the action is not limited to a year. It lies for the heir but not against him. If a slave be working the ship or tavern without his master's consent, the master is liable *de peculio* for such offence committed by an assistant, but if it have been committed by the slave *exercitor*, the master can surrender him noxally. If the slave die, suit *de peculio* cannot be brought at all. A master or father, whose slave or son is working the ship or tavern with his consent, is liable in full. Notice to the passengers of non-liability and their assent to it free the shipmaster (Paul ii 31 §§ 16, 18; D. xliv 7 fr 5 § 6; xlvii 2 fr 42 pr, tit. 5; iv 9 fr 6, 7).

5. *PAUPERIES.* 'Damage caused by an animal.'

An action was granted by the XII tables against the owner of a fourfooted animal, which had caused any damage (*pauperies*) without provocation. If the beast was irritated by any harsh treatment or by the difficulty of the road or the weight of an excessive burden, this action would not lie, but resort must be had to an action under the *lex Aquilia* or an analogous action *in factum*. It does not matter whether the mischief is caused by the horse, *etc.* himself, or by the cart or anything else to which he is attached. But, only when the beast does harm spontaneously from his own wildness or temper (*commota feritate*), is the owner liable under this action. If another beast excited him, the owner of this other beast is responsible. If two rams or oxen fought and one was killed, the owner of the aggressor if surviving was liable. Paul makes this or like action applicable if a horse or other animal with the mange was allowed to mix with neighbours' herds, so as to communicate the disease. And grazing on another's pasture was ground for this action (*si quid depasta sit* Paul i 15 § 1). It was the owner of the animal for the time being (*noxa caput sequitur*) who was liable to suit, not the owner at the time of the hurt. And not only the owner could sue, but anyone who was interested in keeping the damaged thing safe, *e.g.* one to whom it had been lent. It ran both for and against heirs in their capacity as owners. The claim was in the alternative: defendant had either to make compensation or to give up the animal; *aut noxam sarcire aut in noxam* (or *noxae*) *dedere*. If the animal died before joinder of issue, the action dropped: if after joinder of issue the animal was killed by someone else, the defendant must either pay the damages or make over to plaintiff his action under the *lex Aquilia* against the killer. If a free person was damaged, it was eventually decided that he (or his father) could sue, not for any disfigurement, but for the expense of his cure and the loss of his services present and future (D. ix 1).

6. (*a*) The case of dogs was specially dealt with by a *lex Pesolania*. If a dog was in a square or public road and not tied up in the day-time and did mischief, the owner was liable: and if a dog was led by one incompetent to hold him or in

a place where he ought not to be and did mischief, the leader, not the owner, was liable (Paul i 15 § 1; D. ix 1 fr 1 § 5).

(b) An analogous (*utilis*) action to that *de pauperie* was granted in case of mischief done by animals not fourfooted. Wild animals (*e.g.* a bear) are not properly within the scope of the law, for if they escape from confinement they cease to have an owner (D. ix 1 fr 1 § 10, 4).

(c) The aediles' edict forbad keeping, unless securely tied, in any place where people commonly pass, a dog, boar, wild boar, wolf, bear, panther, lion or any other hurtful animal. In case of injury to a slave the penalty was double the damage; in the case of a freeman, if hurt, what the judge thinks right, if killed, a fine of 200 *solidi* (20,000 sesterces? cf. Just. iii 7 § 3). This action would be concurrent with that *de pauperie*, both being penal (Just. iv 9 § 1; D. xxi 1 fr 40—42).

The praetor forbad keeping such animals in such places even if tied; and for any damage caused by them, or on account of them, gave an action according to the offence (especially if a man was killed) either against the owner or the keeper. This was granted *extra ordinem*. And any damage caused through fright of snakes made those who carried them about liable to suit (Paul i 15 § 2; D. xlvii 11 fr 11).

CHAPTER VI.

OBLIGATIONES EX DELICTO (TORTS).

Obligations, arising from a wrong act of one person which causes loss or injury to another, have certain common characteristics which do not apply to contractual obligations.

1. They do not run against the heirs of the offender, unless issue has been joined with the predecessors. But if the heirs retain any profit arising from the delict, they are liable to restore it. If the obligation arise from taking a thing by fraud or violence, they are liable to an action for production and consequent vindication (D. xliv 7 fr 33, fr 59; xlvii 1 fr 1

pr; L 17 fr 38, fr 164). All delicts, except insult, could be subject of action by heirs (Gai. iv 112).

2. If several torts are combined in one proceeding, the actions arising therefrom are concurrent, but do not destroy one another. Thus if a man has stolen and killed or wounded a slave, he is liable to an action for theft and also under the *lex Aquilia*. So if he took the slave by force, he is liable for robbery, and also under the *lex Aquilia*. If he stole him and whipped him, he is liable for theft and insult; if further he killed him, he is liable under a third action for that (D. xlvii 1 fr 2; xliv 7 fr 60).

3. If the offender is a slave, the master is liable not *de peculio* but in full. On the other hand he can free himself from the penal actions, whether one or more, by surrendering the slave noxally, provided he had neither ordered the wrong deed nor had guilty knowledge of it. It is the owner at the time of action, not at the time of offence who is liable. The action for fraud is not always noxal (D. xlvii 1 fr 1 § 2; ix 4 fr 2 pr, fr 7, fr 20).

4. Condemnation for the principal delicts makes the offender infamous. This is declared of theft, robbery, insult, fraud, violation of a tomb; and, in the case of the first three, infamy follows not only condemnation but bargain to avoid condemnation (Gai. iv 182).

5. In most delicts condemnation was to damages of twofold or fourfold the value, *viz.* in theft, robbery, damage in a crowd, corruption of a slave, calumnious bribe, intimidation; but not in fraud or the action against land-surveyors. Insult had a special estimation of damages. Set-off was admissible in all delictal actions for damages (D. xvi 2 fr 10 § 2).

6. All arise from acts done maliciously, *i.e.* with evil intention and consciousness of wrong-doing; *maleficia voluntas et propositum delinquentis distinguit* (D. xlvii 2 fr 54 pr).

The action for Aquilian damage resembles delicts in the first three points, but it did not involve infamy, nor did it inflict double damage, unless the charge was contested, nor was it at all confined to cases of evil intention: it included mere negligence. A partner who had injured partnership property was liable to the Aquilian action as well as *pro socio*, but to condemnation only under one: whereas if he stole it, he could be condemned for theft in addition to *pro socio* (D. xvii 2 fr 45, 50).

A. *FURTUM.* THEFT.

(*a*) Theft is taking, secretly or forcibly, anything moveable, with the intention of appropriating it without the owner's consent: and not only the fraudulent appropriation of the thing itself, but the like appropriation of its use or possession is also theft. *Furtum fit, non solum cum quis intercipiendi causa rem alienam amovet sed generaliter cum quis rem alienam invito domino contrectat* (Gai. iii 195). Forcible taking is, however, usually subject of another action (p. 216). To make theft there must be not merely an intent or thought but actual dealing with the thing (D. xlvii 2 fr 1 § 1; xli 2 fr 3 § 18); not mere dealing in words or writing but in physical touch (fr 52 § 19); not merely wrongful action but handling with intent to make gain thereby (fr 1 pr, 54 pr); without the owner's consent and without a belief that the owner would consent[1]. If the owner consents, there is no action for the theft; if the owner is believed to consent, or the taker believes the thing to be his own, there is no fraudulent purpose, and no *actio furti* (Gai. iii 197, 198; ii 50; D. fr 46 §§ 7, 8). In some cases the owner himself may be guilty of theft, if he furtively resume possession in spite of others' rights (fr 54 § 4, *etc.* see below).

(*b*) Thus, besides ordinary cases of stealing, theft is chargeable if a man make any use of what is deposited with him merely for safekeeping; or borrows from another's slave, when he knows that the owner is not consenting; or if a borrower lend to another what has been lent to him only, or use it otherwise than the lender intended or is believed to approve, *e.g.* if a man borrow plate for a dinner party and then take

[1] Gellius (xi 18 § 19) quotes from Sabinus *ex libro juris civilis secundo* as follows: *Qui alienam rem adtrectavit, cum id se invito domino facere judicare deberet, furti tenetur*: and from another chapter: *Qui alienum jacens lucri faciendi causa sustulit, furti obstringitur sive scit cujus sit sive nescit.*

it abroad with him, or borrow a horse for an ordinary ride, and take it to battle or to a long way off (Gai. iv 196; D. xiii 6 fr 14; xlvii 2 fr 40, 55 § 1, 77 pr; Scaev. *ap.* Gell. vi 15); or if a fuller or tailor use clothes given them only to clean or mend (fr 83 pr). It is theft, if a creditor use what is only pledged to him, or after the debt is paid, do not return but conceal the pledge, or when he has no power of sale, sell it (fr 52 § 7, 55 pr, 74); or if a debtor, before paying the debt, surreptitiously take the pledge away from his creditor or sell it, even though the creditor were not in possession of it (fr 19 §§ 5, 6, 67 pr; Gai. iii 200). So if a farm tenant who has agreed as usual that the fruits should be pledged to the lessor for the rent, secretly carries them off, or sells them to one who gathers and removes them, both farmer and purchaser are chargeable with theft, for the fruits are the farmer's only if gathered with the lessor's consent (fr 62 § 8). It is theft if, after the expiration of his lease, a farmer gathers the next year's crops; or if an owner secretly takes the fruits or conceals the thing from one who has its usufruct or is in *bona fide* possession, or secretly takes back a thing borrowed by another who has a lien on it for expenses (fr 15 §§ 1, 2, 20 § 1, 60, 68 § 5; Gai. iii 200). It is theft for the owner of a thing to take by force the price from the thief who has sold it (fr 48 § 7; cf. ix 4 fr 38 § 2). One who picks up anything lying in the road is not chargeable with theft, if it has been abandoned or he believes it to have been abandoned by its owner, or if he intends to return it to anyone who may prove to be its owner: and the same applies to the case of goods thrown overboard (fr 43 §§ 4—11). Resuming without fraud what has been conveyed to another in trust (*fiduciae causa*) is not theft (Gai. ii 59, 60; iii 201).

(*c*) Anyone pretending to be creditor, and receiving money as such, is chargeable with theft, and the money does not become his. So there is theft if the owner by mistake deliver a thing to another, who knowing it not to be his appropriates it; or if a man, instead of himself receiving money not due to him, directs it to be paid to another in his presence. If, however, it be paid in his absence, he cannot be charged with theft, when he has never handled or seen the coins. If one, assuming to be agent for another, receives payment on his behalf and keeps it for himself, it is theft, provided the debtor gave him the money for delivery to the creditor, or if the false agent assumed the name of the real agent; but it is not theft if the agent was intended to be owner of the actual money and to account for the sum to his supposed principal (D. fr 43 pr—§ 2, 44 §§ 1, 2, 81 § 6; cf. xlvi 3 fr 18). It is theft if a man receives money from me to pay my creditor, and does pay him, but on account of a debt of his own (fr 52 § 16)[1]. One who gets a loan for himself by false pretences, such as that he is solvent, or is going to invest it in goods, or will give good sureties, or will repay directly, or being a slave professes himself a freeman, or being a son under power professes himself *sui juris*, is deceitful, but does not commit theft: if liable in no other way he can be sued for fraud (fr 43 § 3). Nor is obtaining by fraud a promise to pay, or mere denial of a deposit, theft (fr 76, 88 pr). Carrying off or concealing a female slave, who is a prostitute, is not theft, because the motive is gratification of passion; but if she is not a prostitute, although the motive is the same, it is held to be theft and also plagiary (fr 39, 83 § 2; Paul ii 31 §§ 12, 31 seems to differ on the former point).

(*d*) Aid or counsel to a thief for the purposes of theft makes the giver liable as for theft[2], provided theft be actually committed (*ope consilio alicujus furtum factum*). This liability attaches to one who directs his son or slave to commit a theft (Gell. xi 18 § 24); or who knocks money out of your hand that another may carry it off, or blocks your way that another may rob you, or frightens your sheep or oxen (*e.g.* with a red

[1] So if *A* gives a thing to *B* to present on *A*'s behalf to *C*, and *B* presents it as from himself, he commits a theft, and the property in strict law does not pass; but as *C* was intended to have it, he was allowed (by a kindly construction) to resist by a plea of fraud any action of *A*'s to reclaim it (D. xxxix 5 fr 25). (In the earlier issues of Mommsen's stereotype edit. D. xlvii 2 fr 52 § 16 there is a typographic error *furtum non facere* for *furtum eum facere*, which has probably misled Lenel *Paling.* i 376, ii 676 to give *non* for *eum*).

[2] Cf. Cic. *N. D.* iii 30 § 74 *Inde illa actio 'ope consilioque tuo furtum aio factum esse.'*

cloth) that another may catch them; or lends tools or a ladder knowingly for the purpose of a theft; or lends a purchaser over-heavy weights in order to cheat a vendor; or conceals a runaway slave, or persuades a slave to run away, if the slave carry off things with him or be himself stolen by someone else[1]. But merely shewing the road to a runaway slave, or refusing information of his whereabouts, or frightening cattle in mere sport or from malice to the owner, or from pity setting free a fettered slave, may be in some cases subjects for action (*in factum, lege Aquilia, etc.*) but not *furti*, if there is no thievish intent (Gai. ii 202; D. fr 39, 48 § 1, 50 §§ 1, 4, 52 §§ 13, 19, 22, 55 § 4, 69; iv 3 fr 7 § 7; cf. Paul ii 31 § 33). If when you intend to make a loan to a respectable man Titius, I substitute a needy man of the same name and divide the money with him and he knows it and takes the money, he is guilty of theft, I of aiding and counselling (fr 52 § 21, 67 § 4). The republican lawyers (*veteres*) held that a man who with a fraudulent intent (*dolo modo*) summoned a muledriver into court was chargeable with theft if the mules meanwhile were lost (fr 67 § 2). If Titius persuades my slave to carry off chattels of mine and bring them to him, and the slave tells me of the plan and performs his part by my instructions in order that I may catch Titius in the act, Titius is not liable to me for theft, for I consented to his handling of the goods, nor is he liable for spoiling my slave (p. 219), for my slave is not spoilt (Gai. iii 198; Justinian iv 1 § 8 says some lawyers held him guilty of theft).

(*e*) When a thief has taken part of a larger whole, *e.g.* part of a cask of wine, some of the articles in a cupboard, part of the contents of a bale or box which was too heavy for him to carry off, he is (as was held eventually) chargeable with theft only of the part or things taken, but if he handled all and could carry the whole, he is chargeable with theft of the whole. So several persons combining to steal and carry a heavy beam are each chargeable with stealing the whole (fr 21). A man digging

[1] Gellius tells us that Sabinus mentions the case of a man judged guilty of theft who, when a fugitive slave happened to be passing before his master, prevented his seeing the slave by holding up his *toga* under pretence of putting it on (xi 18 § 14).

sulphur or chalk or cutting timber or taking stones or fruit in another's land is liable for theft if he carry it off (fr 25 § 2, 52 § 8, 58). An immoveable is not capable of being stolen, though at one time some old lawyers thought *fundi furtum fieri posse*[1] (Gai. ii 50, = D. xli 3 fr 38).

(*f*) Free persons might in some cases be stolen, viz. a child under power, a wife in hand, or a person in a quasi-servile condition, such as an adjudged debtor or one hired out as a gladiator (*judicatus vel exauctoratus meus* Gai. iii 199). But though an action *furti* may thence arise, there is no *condictio furtiva*, at least in the case of a child or wife (D. xlvii 2 fr 38 § 1).

(*g*) The right to sue for theft belongs to him who has a lawful interest in the safekeeping of the thing stolen (*cujus interest rem salvam esse*), whether it be the owner for the time being or fructuary or anyone in honest possession of others' things and effectively responsible for them. The suits of such are independent of one another, as one co-owner's action is of another co-owner's. Thus a hirer or fuller or tailor or borrower can sue for theft of the thing given him to use or clean or mend, and the owner in these cases has not the action, for he can recover the value from them by the ordinary actions (*locati, commodati, etc.*). But if they are insolvent (at the time of the theft; cf. Cod. vi 2 fr 22 § 1), or if he has given them a release from liability, the interest has shifted back to him and he can sue the thief. If the borrower have paid him for the loss, and the thief turn out to be a slave of the lender, repayment by the lender is sufficient to destroy the borrower's action for theft. A depositary is responsible for fraud only, not for safekeeping (unless he has expressly promised it), and has therefore no lawful interest upon which to base an action for theft (Gai. iii 203—207; D. fr 10, 12, 14 §§ 3, 4, 16, fr 46 § 5, 47, 54 § 1; cf. xlvii 8 fr 2 § 23). A holder on sufferance is not responsible by the ordinary law; but if an interdict *de precario* is issued

[1] Gellius (xi 18 § 13) mentions that in a book of Sabinus 'on thefts' a generally unexpected proposition was laid down *fundi quoque et aedium fieri furtum*, and that a farmer who rented a farm and sold it was condemned for theft because he had done his landlord out of the possession (*quod possessione ejus dominum intervertisset*).

against him, he becomes responsible and then has an interest to justify his suing the thief (D. xlvii 2 fr 14 § 11). One who farms at a money-rent so as to be entitled to the crops when gathered can sue for theft of them when standing (fr 26 § 1). The bearer of a letter, if hired or otherwise responsible for its safekeeping, or if its contents were intended to benefit him, has sufficient interest (fr 14 § 17). The owner of a bond or receipt can sue for the full value of the amount named therein, even if the document be cancelled, for it may be necessary to prove payment (Paul ii 31 § 32, fr 27—32). If a thing in pledge is stolen, not only the debtor (if the thing is of greater value than the debt) but the creditor also (if his debt is unsatisfied) can sue, whether the debtor be solvent or not, and for the full value of the thing, having of course to account to the debtor for the surplus over the debt (fr 12 § 2, 14 § 6, 15 pr, 46 § 4). One who has only a claim to a thing by will or stipulation cannot sue for theft of what is not yet his either in ownership or possession (fr 13, 86; cf. fr 81 § 7). A purchaser before delivery cannot sue for theft, but can call on the vendor to surrender to him his actions, or if vendor has already got damages, to pay over the amount (fr 14 pr: according to Paul (ii 31 § 17) both vendor and purchaser can sue). One who of his own motion manages others' business or acts as guardian (*pro tutore*) has no right to sue for theft, but if he is himself sued by the owner for the loss, can claim a surrender of the owner's actions (fr 54 § 3, 86). A thief has no action against one who steals the same thing from him: the owner will have an action against both; and if there be no owner to sue, still (though Servius had a different opinion) the thief cannot sue for what is in no way his: but if a stolen slave steal from the thief, it was held that to prevent the mischief of the master being enriched by the fraudulent increase of the slave's *peculium* the thief might sue the master (fr 14 § 4, 68 § 4, 77 § 1). One who without title is possessing a thing in the character of heir has in his hope of gain by usucapion no such interest as would enable him to sue for theft of the thing (fr 72 § 1).

(*h*) A father or master can sue for theft of a thing from his son or slave as he is the legal owner of their *peculium*, and liable to others so far as it extends. If, however, there be nothing in it, his interest ceases; and thus if a slave has undertaken to clean clothes and they are stolen from him, the master has in such case no right of suit, and only the owner of the clothes can sue (Paul ii 31 § 20; D. fr 52 § 9). A son is however in a different position: he can always be sued for the full amount of a debt (as well as his father *de peculio*), and can himself sue on a loan (*commodati* D. xv 1 fr 44; xliv 7 fr 9, 39): if therefore a thing lent him be stolen, as he is liable for its safekeeping, he, not his father or surety, will have the title to sue for its theft (D. xlvii 2 fr 14 § 10; cf. §§ 14, 15). If a slave in usufruct (or use) be stolen, the fructuary (or usuary) can sue for the loss of his services or other fruits accruing to him, the owner can sue for the value of his propriety (fr 46 §§ 1, 3). Guardians and caretakers of lunatics could bring and settle an action for theft from their wards and also bring a condiction on their account (fr 57 § 4). For theft from dowry the husband has the right of suit, though the risk is really the wife's (fr 49 § 1).

No one can sue his children under power or his slaves, not because of any law forbidding it but from the nature of the case: they are part of his family; what is theirs is his; and he has power to deal with their offences himself. Nor if they be alienated or set free does a right of action arise, which did not exist when the act was committed (fr 16, 17 pr § 1). Nor can a part-owner of a slave who has stolen from him sue for the theft, even if he acquired the share of ownership since the theft (fr 43 § 12, see p. 211). If a son has a camp-*peculium*, he is responsible for his slave's thefts from his father, and possibly, as he has property of his own, responsible by an *actio utilis*. for thefts of his own: his father will be responsible to him for thefts from such a *peculium*. A wife is not liable *furti* for theft from her husband, except on account of her slave: for her own theft she is liable in an action *rerum amotarum*. Anyone who aids his son or slave or wife when committing a theft, is liable to this action even though the principals may not be sued (fr 52 §§ 1—6; 36 § 1). A patron cannot sue for theft his freedman or client; nor a hirer sue his hired servant (fr 90).

An *impubes* according to the better opinion was chargeable

with theft, only if he was near the age of puberty, and therefore understood that he was doing wrong (Gai. iv 208). He was not held capable of aiding and counselling theft (fr 23).

(*i*) An heir could sue for theft from his predecessor (D. xlvii 1 fr 1 § 1). If a slave of the inheritance stole from the heir before the inheritance was entered on, the heir could sue the man himself if made free by the will, or the legatee, if he was directly bequeathed, as in neither case was the slave ever the property of the heir (D. xlvii 2 fr 44 § 2, 65). On theft from a vacant inheritance see p. 213.

An heir was not liable to be sued for his predecessor's theft, but if he possessed or had fraudulently parted with the thing, he was liable *ad exhibendum*, and also to vindication and condiction (D. xlvii 1 fr 1 pr). A usufructuary of a slave was not liable for the slave's thefts but could sue the owner (D. xlvii 2 fr 18).

Whether a *bona fide* possessor of another's slave was liable to suit for a theft committed by the slave was disputed, but eventually, as appears, decided in the affirmative; and, this being so, he was held to have no action against the real owner for theft committed by the slave, until this last had returned to his owner's power (Cod. vi 9 fr 21 § 1; D. xlvii 2 fr 17 § 3).

(*k*) Destruction of the thing stolen, or death or manumission of a slave stolen, is no bar to action for theft; nor is its capture by the enemy or abandonment by the owner subsequent to the theft. The action once arisen continues as long as the thief lives, until it is either settled for (*dum quis pro fure damnum deciderit*[1]) or judgment is obtained (fr 46 pr; cf. § 5). If the thief be *sui juris* he is liable himself; if he is not, the action is against whoever is his father or master at the time of suit; if he becomes free since the theft, the liability shifts to him (*noxa caput sequitur* fr 41 § 2; xliv 7 fr 14; Paul ii 31 §§ 8, 9). The settlement (*pro fure decidere*) could be made by a simple agreement, and was operative *ipso jure* (D. ii 14 fr 17 § 1).

[1] The phrase *damnum pro fure decidere* 'to settle the loss in the character of thief' was used of defendant in the *intentio* of the *formula* (cf. Gai. iv 37).

(*l*) The amount of damages varied according to the title of the plaintiff and the character of the theft. If plaintiff was not owner, the measure of damages was his interest in the thing not being stolen (fr 50 pr). If he was owner, the measure was the maximum true value which the slave or thing stolen had at the time of or since the theft. If however he was not permanent owner, but owner only till some condition occurred which made the slave free or transferred the ownership to a legatee, the measure was what a purchaser would give for the slave in the circumstances. A slave, stolen when a child, is estimated at its worth when grown up (if still stolen). The value of any inheritance falling to the slave or of any penalty due for non-delivery of him before a certain day, comes into the estimate, if he be stolen and die before entry or be not delivered as due (fr 50 pr, 52 § 29, 68 §§ 1, 2, 81 § 1). But it is not the single value that forms the damages, but a multiple according to the character of the theft.

(*m*) Ser. Sulpicius and Masurius Sabinus made four kinds of theft; *manifestum, nec manifestum, conceptum, oblatum*. Labeo more rightly rejected the latter two as not theft but only connected with it (see p. 215). Theft manifest was defined (1) by Sabinus and others to be when the thief is caught (*deprehenditur*), not merely seen (cf. D. fr 7 § 1), in the act; (2) by others again to be when the thief is caught while still on the spot, *e.g.* theft of olives or grapes, while the thief is yet in the oliveyard or vineyard; theft of articles in a house, detected while the thief is still there. Another (3) definition made it theft manifest, if the thief was caught before he had brought the thing stolen to the destination he intended. A fourth (4) still further extended it to include whenever the thief was seen anywhere in possession of the thing (*rem tenens*). Gaius tells us that this last definition was not approved, and that the third seemed not to be approved, because of the doubt whether it should be limited to cases where the thief is caught within one day or in several, especially where a thief had carried the thing off to a different town or province. Of the first two definitions the second, he considered, met with most favour (Gai. iii 183, 184). Paul accepts the first three (*Sent.* ii 31 § 2). Julian and Ulpian (in D. fr 3—5) agree with Paul. Aid and counsel to a thief was never considered to be theft manifest: robbery was clearly so (D. fr 34, 81 § 3). A carrier of goods, knowing them to be stolen, is if caught with them guilty of theft manifest (fr 35 pr).

Theft manifest was a capital offence by the law of the XII tables. They permitted a thief to be killed, if he was caught stealing in the night, or if in daytime he defended himself with a weapon, but before killing there was to be a cry as a kind of notice to the public. If the theft was in the daytime and there was no armed defence, a freeman could only be beaten (*verberatus*) and assigned (*addictus*) to the person on whom the theft was committed. It was a question with the old lawyers (*veteres*), whether the thief was thereby made a slave or was in the same position as a judgment debtor assigned to his creditor (*adjudicati loco*). A slave who committed theft was beaten, and, if *pubes*, thrown from a rock; if *impubes*, was liable to be given up noxally. The praetor however substituted an action for fourfold the value in each case; and the action (contrary to the usual rule) was not limited to a year. Theft not manifest was subject to an action for twofold the value (Gai. iii 189, 190; iv 111; *Collat.* 7 § 2; D. ix 2 fr 4; Gell. xi 18 §§ 6—10).

Both the quadruple and the double were regarded as penalty only[1], the owner having the right also to recover the thing or value either by vindication against the possessor whoever it might be, or by condiction (*furtiva*, see p. 82) against the thief or his heir if not in possession (D. xlvii 2 fr 48 pr, 55 § 3). But it would be the judge's duty to restrict the plaintiff to the produce of one of these two actions (fr 9 § 1). If the thief be brought by the plaintiff before a police magistrate (*praefectus vigilibus vel praeses*), and the thing or its single value recovered, the civil action for theft was deemed to be waived, especially if punishment was inflicted as well (fr 57 § 1). Settlement for

[1] Quintil. vii 6 § 2 gives as an instance of obscurity in the law: *Fur quadruplum solvat. Duo subripuerunt pariter decem milia; petuntur ab utroque quadragena: illi postulant ut vicena conferant; nam et actor dicit hoc esse quadruplum quod petat, et rei hoc quod offerant.*

theft (*si pro fure damnum decisum sit*) did not bar vindication or condiction (D. xiii 1 fr 7 pr).

(*n*) Both condemnation and settlement in an action for theft made the defendant infamous; and this consequence followed *ipso facto* without the praetor or governor having power to prevent it (Gai. iv 182; Paul ii 31 § 15; D. xlvii 2 fr 64).

(*o*) As in the case of other torts, when a slave has committed a theft, his owner unless having himself guilty knowledge could escape payment of damages by surrendering the slave (*noxae servum dedendo*, see p. 252). Ordinary actions of contract were often sufficient to compel the slave's master either to settle for the loss or to give up the culprit (*aut damnum decidere aut pro noxae deditione hominem relinquere*). Thus if a slave in pledge stole from the creditor, the counter pledge-action was enough for this purpose. If a slave is bought and is to be given back by the purchaser, the latter can call on the vendor in the proceedings for redhibition (for he has no interest to support an action for theft) either to compensate him for any theft which the slave has committed, or to abandon to him the slave. A like use may be made of the actions on hire and loan in the case of a slave committing theft when hired or lent. But if a man has directed his agent to buy a particular slave for him, and the slave turn out to be a thief and steal from the agent, the *mandator*, whether he knew of the slave's character or not, is compellable by the counter action of mandate to compensate the agent without having the alternative of noxal surrender. And the like applies in the case of deposit, as both agent and depositary are acting for their principal's benefit and not for their own. If a slave steal from one of his co-owners, the sufferer can by the action *com. div.* force the other to repair the loss or surrender the slave (D. xlvii 2 fr 62 pr—§ 7, 68 § 3, 17 § 2).

(*p*) The issue had to describe the thing stolen sufficiently for practical purposes. If a dish or plate or cup was stolen, its weight need not be given, but the metal should. If unwrought metal was stolen, the weight and kind of metal must be stated; the number and metal of medals or coins, the colour (if remembered) of robes. If silver has been stolen and wrought into cups, either the weight or the wrought article may be given: if grapes have been stolen and crushed, the demonstration may name them either as grapes or must or raisins (fr 19 §§ 1—4, 52 § 14).

(*q*) Besides the private action for theft criminal proceedings might be taken, and Ulpian (fr 93) says that in his time this was the more usual case. Thieving by night or stealing in public baths were punished by being put to public labour for a term; burglars or thieves who defended themselves with a weapon were sent to the mines or relegated according to their rank. Killing a thief was not allowed unless it was necessary in self-defence (*Collat.* vii 2—4).

B. OTHER ACTIONS FOR STEALING.

1. Where a beam had been stolen and joined to a house or vineyard the XII tables directed that it should not be capable of vindication, but he who joined (*junxit*)[1] it to the building (*i.e.* practically the ground owner) should be liable to an action for double the value (*actio de tigno juncto*). An action for production (*ad exhibendum*) would also lie against one who joined it knowing it to be another's, on the ground of his fraud in precluding himself from being able to restore. All building materials (stone, tiles, pots, lime, sand) and all things necessary for vines (props, poles) were held to be included (D. xlvii 3 fr 1).

2. There was an action given by the XII tables against anyone who sent in his cattle to feed on another's land, but we know no more about it (*Act. de pastu pecoris* D. xix 5 fr 14 § 3).

3. Cattle-lifting (*abigeatus*) was generally punished criminally, being taken out of the category of private theft by its frequent practice as a business, by the scale on which it was done, and by the use of armed force in defence. Driving off one horse, two mares or oxen, ten goats or sheep, five pigs, came within the law. But driving off a straying ox or horse in desert places, or fewer goats, sheep or pigs than this number

[1] Pernice suggests that the XII tables had not *junxit* but *junctum habuit*; cf. D. xli 1 fr 7 § 10 (*Labeo* ii 1 p. 320).

was merely theft (Paul v 18; *Collat.* xi; cf. D. xlvii 14 fr 3 *de abactoribus* or *abigeis*).

4. An old action (*oneris aversi*) against carriers is mentioned by Alfenus (lawyer of Cicero's time) but regarded as superfluous (see p. 176; D. xix 2 fr 31).

5. Theft by a wife and some other persons was the subject of an action *rerum amotarum*, the relationship making a disgraceful action unsuitable (D. xxv 2).

6. Theft in a tavern, *etc.* (*in caupona, etc.*) was the subject of a special action against the proprietor, see p. 197.

C. Abstraction of things belonging to a vacant inheritance was the subject of two special procedures. Theft (as Q. Mucius Scaevola said) was concerned only with possession; an inheritance before the heir entered was not possessed by anyone, and, though for some purposes regarded as a legal person, had no power to hold, and no *animus* to act, as possessor of the things belonging to it. When the heir enters he acquires all the rights of the deceased, and all the things belonging to the inheritance, but possession of them is not included under either category; and, until he actually takes possession, there is no possessor against whom theft could be committed. It was therefore a recognised principle that *hereditariae rei furtum non fit*[1]. But things lent or hired out or pledged by the deceased had a *de facto* possessor in the borrower or hirer or pledgee; and the like was true where another had the usufruct: in these cases therefore the heir (as well as the borrower, *etc.*) after entry was held capable of suing for theft. But in other cases the heir could only sue for production (*ad exhibendum*) so as to vindicate the thing stolen. (See D. xlvii 2 fr 14 § 14, 69—71; tit. 4 fr 1 § 15; tit. 19 fr 2 § 1, 6.) Special means were therefore

[1] Cicero probably refers to this doctrine when he wrote to Trebatius (*Fam.* vii 22) to prove that there was an old dispute *possetne heres quod furtum antea factum esset furti recte agere*. Trebatius maintained that no one had ever thought he could. Cicero produced opinions of Sex. Aelius, M'. Manilius and M. Brutus to that effect, and mentions Q. Mucius Scaevola's opinion to the contrary. This opinion is apparently given in D. xlvii 4 fr 1 § 15 as above.

taken to prevent thefts before the heir entered or actually got possession.

(*a*) By a decree made under Marcus Aurelius anyone who pillaged an inheritance before the heir's entry or taking possession was liable to criminal proceedings *extra ordinem* (*crimen expilatae hereditatis*), but Severus and Antoninus declared the heir to have the option of either prosecuting the offender or vindicating the things stolen (D. xlvii 19 fr 1, 3). It could not be brought against the wife nor against a coheir (fr 5; Cod. iii 36 fr 3).

(*b*) An action for double the heir's interest (*dupli judicium*) was given by the praetor against anyone, declared free in a will, whose fraud (*dolus malus*) prevented anything which was included in the goods of the testator from coming to the heir. The fraud must have been since testator's death and before any heir's entry. A slave in this position might, it was thought (so Labeo), act with less scruple, because, even if the inheritance be regarded as his mistress, he could not be controlled and punished as a slave, and no action lay for a mistress against her freedman for torts committed in slavery. The language was so general as to include all fraudulent damage as well as abstraction, and was applied whether the freedom was given directly or by way of trust; and also when the doer remained a slave but was unconditionally bequeathed. If there was a condition either of freedom or legacy he remained a slave and was subject to chastisement (D. xlvii 4 fr 1, §§ 2—7, fr 3). Nor was it confined to loss or damage of things actually *in bonis* of the deceased; things lent or pledged or honestly possessed by others and fruits come within the action—wherever in fact an action for theft could have been brought if the slave had been a freeman and the inheritance a living person. The action must be brought within a working year, and was open to heirs, and did not exclude vindication; but if deceased's heir could come to his own in other ways this action did not lie. If several slaves so acted, they were each liable for the double, and payment by one did not free the others (fr 1 §§ 10, 16—19).

D. Further actions not for theft, but connected with theft, are the following:

1. *Furtum conceptum*[1], 'taking to oneself,' 'receiving,' was when a stolen thing was found, witnesses being present, in the possession of a person (*apud aliquem*). The penalty was threefold, both by the XII tables and the praetor's edict (Gai. iii 183, 186, 191).

2. *Furtum oblatum*, 'putting a theft on to another,' was when a stolen thing was given to someone in order that it might be found with him (*concepta*) rather than with the giver and was so found. The person with whom it was found had an action *f. oblati* against the giver. The penalty was the same as for *f. concepti* (Gai. iii 183, 187, 191).

3. *Furtum prohibitum*, 'hindering (search for) theft,' was when a person desirous of searching for a stolen object was hindered from doing so. The hinderer was liable to an action for fourfold by the praetor's edict. The XII tables affixed no penalty, but provided that anyone who wished to search should search naked, having his loins girt with a linen cloth, and holding a dish; and that if he found anything, the theft should be theft manifest. Gaius criticises this regulation severely. If a man meant to hinder the search, he would hinder a naked man as much as if he were clothed, and all the more because of the increased penalty on detection. What use is carrying the dish? to put the stolen thing on? or to occupy the man's hands so that he cannot bring the thing in secretly and declare it to be stolen? The thing may be too big to suit either hypothesis. One thing however, says Gaius, is certain, that the law is satisfied, whatever the material of the dish: and though the discovery of a thing under these circumstances may perhaps not strictly turn the theft into theft manifest, all agree that the law can prescribe the same penalty (Gai. iii 188, 193[2]).

[1] All these expressions belong to the class where gerundives often, and sometimes participles, are used to denote not the thing or person acted on, but the action itself; *e.g. dubitabat nemo quin violati hospites, legati necati, fana vexata efficerent vastitatem* (Cic. *Pis.* 35). Lat. Gr. § 1410.

[2] Gellius (xi 18 § 9) says *Ea quoque furta quae per lancem liciumque concepta essent proinde ac si manifesta forent decemviri vindicaverunt.*

Paul apparently gives the later practice, that one who means to search had first to declare what he sought, giving both its name and description (*Sent.* ii 31 § 22). Certainly in a suit name, colour, weight, number, *etc.* were required to be stated (D. xlvii 2 fr 19, 52 § 25; above, p. 211).

4. Justinian mentions an analogous action *furti non exhibiti, i.e.* for non-production of a stolen object; but the practice of search in this fashion becoming obsolete, these actions went out of use, anyone who knowingly received or concealed a stolen thing being guilty of theft not manifest (D. xlvii 2 fr 48 §§ 1, 3; Just. iv 1 § 4).

E. 1. *VI BONORUM RAPTORUM*, 'ROBBERY BY FORCE.' This action was introduced by the praetor, M. Lucullus[1], probably in 76 B.C., in order to meet the lawless acts committed by large bands of slaves who were kept in farms and pastures at a distance from Rome. The early form of the edict appears to have been directed against anyone who forcibly and maliciously collected or armed men, and inflicted loss or carried off goods. (*Si cui vi dolo malo hominibus coactis armatisve damni quid factum esse dicetur sive cujus bona rapta*[2] *esse dicentur, etc.*, comp. Cic. *Tull.* 3, 4.) In the Digest (xlvii 8 fr 2 pr; cf. § 7) *vi* and *armatisve* are omitted, but the omission does not appear to have affected the statement of the law. Force indeed characterises the action throughout and distinguishes it from mere theft. If there is not actual force, there must be contrivance to use it, by getting people together for the purpose. Acts of mere stealth are not within the edict. The men may be armed or not; they may be free or slave; collected by defendant or another; they need not be numerous, one is sufficient; nor need defendant be with them in person. It did not require participation in the act to make the contriver liable.

[1] See Cic. *Tull.* 4 § 8 and my essay on this speech (vol. II, Appendix).

[2] Keller arguing from the formula given in Cic. *Tull.* 3 § 7 thinks *bona rapta* was originally included in *damnum*, and this clause added in the edict, only when *damnum*, by its use in the Aquilian *lex*, came to be used specially of damage other than robbery (*Semestr.* pp. 578—584).

Carrying off one's own goods or one's own runaway slave is not within the mischief. Nor is a tax-farmer liable if he carry off my cattle under a mistaken idea that I have committed a breach of the revenue-law; for the act is not malicious; but otherwise, if cattle have been carried off forcibly, one who shuts them up so that they die of hunger, is liable also. As regards the goods, it is not requisite that they should be part of plaintiff's estate, if only they are in his *de facto* possession[1], so that he has an interest in them (as a usufructuary, *etc.*), or in their safekeeping, as depositary, pledgee, *etc.*

The action could be brought by an heir, but not against one, condiction sufficing, if the heir has been enriched. It must be brought within a working year (*annus utilis*), and lay for fourfold the value of the things (not of the plaintiff's interest)[2]. Slaves who were concerned in the robbery could be surrendered noxally, and their owner thus relieved. Besides vindication and condiction the actions for theft and Aquilian injury are often applicable, but fourfold damages is the maximum recoverable (D. xlvii 8 fr 1, 2). Restitution before trial was not enough to avoid the penalty (D. fr 5).

Goods taken by force were incapable of usucapion until they had returned to the possession of the owner (D. xlvii 8 fr 6). The incapacity was created by the *lex Julia et Plautia* (Gai. ii 45; D. xli 3 fr 33 § 2); the extinction of the incapacity apparently by a *lex Atinia* (D. xli 3 fr 4 § 6). See vol. I p. 475.

An analogous action was granted against anyone who forcibly ejected another from a ship and carried off any goods, or who seized and carried off a carriage or horse (Paul v 6 § 5).

2. *EX INCENDIO RUINA NAUFRAGIO, ETC. RAPTI RECEPTI DOLO MALO DAMNIVE DATI.* Robbery or other damage, on occasion of a fire or fall of buildings or shipwreck or violent attack on a raft or ship, subjected the offender by the praetor's edict to an action for fourfold damages, if action be brought

[1] For the distinction of *in bonis* and *ex bonis* see vol. I p. 428 note.

[2] Under the interdict *de vi* the whole interest was recoverable but not fourfold. See vol. I p. 464.

within a year from the suit being possible; if after a year, for single damages. The attack on a ship, *etc.* (*navis expugnata*) might consist in sinking, scuttling, cutting ropes or sails or anchors. Any kind of malicious damage or removal, whether by force or not, came within the edict. But it must be on the spot and at the time of the fire, *etc.* though not necessarily from the house or ship itself, but also from adjacent parts. A guilty receiver was also chargeable. Labeo extended the edict to the occasion of an attack on a house or villa. Where a person broke down (*dissipavit*) a neighbour's house to save his own catching fire and had no other way of preventing it, Celsus and Ulpian (against Labeo) held him not to be liable under this edict: there was no malice. A senate's decree made anyone who robbed persons shipwrecked liable, besides the amount recoverable by the individual, for as much more to the fisc (D. xlvii 9 fr 1—3, 6; Paul v 3 § 2).

There were criminal proceedings with severe penalties for such offences, especially against wreckers (D. *ib.* fr 4, 7, 10).

3. *DAMNI IN TURBA FACTI.* Damage suffered in or by occasion of a crowd or insurrection (*seditio*), if due to malice, was the subject of an action under the praetor's edict. The crowd might be collected purposely or might have gathered of itself on hearing cries or seeing some act of violence. Anyone who caused the damage, or wrongfully caused the crowd which afforded occasion for it, came under the action, which lay for twofold the value, if brought within a year, afterwards for the single value. Loss of goods or damage, not robbery, was the subject. Personal injury was the subject of extraordinary proceedings. Three or four persons were held not to make a crowd, ten or fifteen did. The action lay against a slave or body of slaves, who presumably could be surrendered noxally as in case of robbery; which action is the same as this as regards the liability of heirs (D. xlvii 8 fr 4; Paul v 3 § 1).

F. *SERVI CORRUPTI.*

The praetor granted an action against anyone who fraudulently harboured another's slave, or persuaded him to any act which made him worse (*qui recepit persuasitque ei dolo malo quo eum deteriorem faceret*). It lay against anyone, even a partner or fructuary, who harboured a slave, not in order to deliver him to his master or from mere humanity, but with fraudulent intent; or who persuaded him to any wrong act, or to run away or to embarrass his *peculium*, or destroy or falsify his master's accounts, or confuse accounts of which he had the management, or be contumacious to his master, or become seditious, or a lover, or go much to shows, or take to a wild, extravagant or shameful life. Malicious persuasion to an act which led to his injuring his body was also within this action. Whether defendant confessed or denied, the damages were laid at double the amount both of depreciation of the slave and of the value of anything he may have carried off. Account will be taken also of any other loss or risk for which his master is liable, *e.g.* theft or Aquilian injury to another, or compensation to one who has hired the slave from me (before deterioration). If the slave is utterly spoilt, plaintiff can at his option keep him and get the damages, or make defendant take the slave and pay him the price. In this last case if the slave is not in his possession, plaintiff must surrender his actions to defendant. The action remains after alienation, death, or manumission of the slave. It may be brought effectively as well as theft (*ope consilio*) and condiction. If a slave has committed the offence, the master is liable but can surrender him noxally. A fructuary can sue the owner and has an analogous action against a stranger. The action can be brought at any time and lies for but not against heirs. If during marriage it be brought by a husband against his wife, the damages are for single value only (*favore nuptiarum* D. xi 3).

An analogous action was granted for the like conduct to a son or daughter under power, though in their case it is not a mere pecuniary loss but the dignity and reputation of the house that is chiefly concerned. The judge has to decide the proper amount of damages (*ib.* fr 14 § 1).

(The admission and protection of runaway slaves in country estates was punished by a fine; and facilities were given on application to the magistrates for the owners to pursue them on private land. This was by a decree of the senate, apparently A.D. 228, but the *lex Fabia* (before Cicero *Rab. ad pop.* 3 § 8) had provisions for the same purpose. The same statute (and the Antonines still more severely) punished any concealment or sale of freemen whether freeborn or freedmen (D. xi 4; xlviii 15; *Collat.* xiv).)

G. 1. *INJURIARUM*, *i.e.* insulting conduct.

(*a*) The XII tables[1] gave actions for ruptured limbs, broken bones, libellous writings, spoken abuse, and evil incantations (see Bruns p. 28). For ruptured limbs the penalty was retaliation, for broken bones a fine of 300 asses, if the sufferer was a freeman; 150, if he was a slave. For other injuries 25 *asses*[2] (Gai. iii 223; *poena* 25 *sestertium*, *Collat.* ii 5 § 5; Paul v 4 § 6). For libel and abuse other writers say beating with clubs was inflicted (Cornut. *ad* Pers. *Sat.* i 137; Porph. *ad* Hor. *Ep.* ii 1 152). The Antonine lawyers mention the XII tables in connexion with the *actio injuriarum*, but in part refer to the class of offences which were more fully dealt with by the *lex Aquilia*.

(*b*) The praetor's edict gave an action *injuriarum*[3], which

1 Cf. Cicero *R. P.* iv 10 (*ap.* August. *C. D.* ii 9) *Nostrae contra duodecim tabulae, cum perpaucas res capite sanxissent, in his hanc quoque sanciendam putaverunt, si quis occentavisset sive carmen condidisset, quod infamiam faceret flagitiumve alteri*; *T. D.* iv 2 § 4; Hor. *Epist.* ii 1 153 *Lex poenaque lata, malo quae nollet carmine quemquam describi*; *Sat.* ii 1 82 (quoted below). See also the notes in Bruns *Fontes* (on XII tables). A person condemned *ob carmen famosum* was made by a senate's decree *intestabilis* 'incapable *testandi*,' which is explained by Ulpian to be one who could not make or witness a will, and by Gaius to be incapable of being a witness or having others as witness (D. xxviii 1 fr 18 § 1, 26).

2 A. Gellius xx 1 § 13 quotes Labeo *L. Veratius fuit egregie homo improbus atque inmani vecordia: is pro delectamento habebat os hominis liberi manus suae palma verberare. Eum servus sequebatur, ferens crumenam plenam assium; ut quemque depalmaverat, numerari statim secundum duodecim tabulas, quinque et viginti asses jubebat. Propterea, inquit* (*Labeo*), *praetores postea hanc abolescere et relinqui censuerunt injuriisque aestumandis recuperatores se daturos edixerunt.*

3 Cicero mentions the action *Caecin.* 12 § 35 *Actio injuriarum dolorem imminutae libertatis judicio poenaque mitigat*; Quintil. vii 4 § 32 *Alia*

shewed a more reasonable appreciation of the nature of such wrong (*ex bono et aequo est* D. xlvii 10 fr 11 pr). It was distinguished from the Aquilian, so far as bodily injury was concerned, by the slight physical character of the wrong act in comparison with its significance. There were three principal classes of injury: blows, abuse, and anything else of an insulting character (*quae ad infamiam alicujus fiunt*). The insulting act might be done to a person himself, or to his children under his power, or to his wife (whether in hand or not[1]); or to his betrothed (*sponsae*) or daughter in law, or to his slaves; and an insult to a corpse may give a right of action to the heir. Any kind of personal violence (*e.g.* throwing filth, tearing clothes), any public abuse (*convicium*) or shouting against a person, even at his house or shop in his absence, come within the law, if improper (*contra bonos mores*), and calculated to throw disgrace on a person or excite odium against him[2] (Gai. iii 220, 221; D. xlvii 10 fr 1 pr—§ 4, 15 § 2—12; cf. Paul v 4 § 13). The third general head included very various acts: indecent or improper soliciting, following, molesting respectable women or youths, or withdrawing their attendants from them. (fr 15 §§ 15—23, 9 § 4); wearing mourning clothes[3] or letting hair or beard grow so as to excite odium against anyone; writing, issuing, or singing an insulting composition (*carmen* fr 15 § 27); doing any act to reflect on another's financial position, *e.g.* wrongfully seizing

quoque multa controversiarum genera in qualitatem cadunt; injuriarum; quamquam enim reus aliquando fecisse negat, plerumque tamen haec actio facto atque animo continetur, i.e. 'sometimes it is a question of fact but generally both fact and intention are concerned.'

[1] Gaius appears to have *cum in manu nostra sint*; which Mommsen regards as a gloss. Krüger gives in text *quamvis in manu nostra non sint.* Paul v 4 § 3 has simply *aut uxori.*

[2] *Mimus quidam nominatim Accium poetam compellavit in scena. Cum eo Accius injuriarum agit. Hic nihil aliud defendit, nisi licere nominari eum cujus nomine scripta dentur agenda* (*ad Heren.* i 14); *C. Caelius judex absolvit injuriarum eum, qui Lucilium poetam in scena nominatim laeserat; P. Mucius eum, qui L. Accium poetam nominaverat, condemnavit* (*ib.* ii 13 § 19).

[3] One of the elder Seneca's specimens of rhetorical treatment is on the theme of a poor man in mourning following a rich man whom he suspected of having killed his father (*Contr.* x 1 30).

his goods, calling upon his sureties when he himself is ready to pay, affixing a notice of sale to a pledge given by him, demanding payment when he owed nothing, preventing him from selling his own slave (*ib.* §§ 31—33, 19, 24); summoning another wrongfully before a court of law; not allowing him to fish in the sea, or bathe in the public baths, or sit in the amphitheatre, or in any way interfering with the exercise of his private or public rights (fr 13 §§ 3, 7; xix 1 fr 25; xliii 8 fr 2 § 9); beating improperly another's slaves or putting them to the torture or doing any other act to them which the praetor shall consider offensive to the slave's master and unjustifiable in a slave of such character and position. Even a municipal magistrate ordering a man's slave to be flogged without proper reason is liable to this action (xlvii 10 fr 15 §§ 34—45). Some lawyers held that the occupant of a lower floor smoking one above, or a higher neighbour throwing something into a lower house, incurred liability to this suit, if he did it to give offence (fr 44).

(*c*) Intention was necessary to constitute this offence. *Pati quis injuriam, etiamsi non sentiat, potest, facere nemo nisi qui scit se injuriam facere, etiamsi nesciat cui faciat* (fr 3 § 2). A blow in an athletic contest or in fun, or given to a freeman mistaken for one's own slave, is not insult. If insult is intended, but as in some libels the person at whom it is aimed is not named, the offence is best met by a criminal indictment (fr 6). On the other hand, if on receiving the insult a person passes it over, he cannot afterwards take it up again and bring an action: it had caused no such abiding sense of insult as to justify action of a penal character. And thus it was thought equitable that a bargain not to sue, or a settlement or an oath, should bar a suit of this kind. A man is liable to suit, who has promoted or encouraged an insult, or ordered or persuaded or hired one to do it, as much as the doer himself (fr 11 pr—§ 6; Paul v 4 § 20).

(*d*) The praetor required the nature of the insult to be properly described, so that its importance might be estimated, and in some cases the admissibility of the suit be decided. The description should be positive not alternative; if a blow is charged, plaintiff must specify the part of the body struck and the instrument, whether a hand, or a stick or a stone, but it was not necessary to say which cheek was struck or with which hand. If an incorporal insult is charged, it should be stated whether the insult was by word or writing, so that the issue may be precise (Paul ap. *Collat.* ii 6). If several offensive acts were done at the same time, they should be combined in one action (D. fr 7 § 5).

(*e*) An insult may be aggravated (*atrox*) either from its own nature as wounding or beating so as to cause pain (*verberatio*, distinguished from a painless blow, *pulsatio*) or striking with rods, especially if in the face or the eye; or from the place, as if it be done in the forum or theatre or before the praetor; or from the time, as during the public games or in the open day; or from the dignity of the person insulted, as a magistrate or senator or decurion or other person of distinction; or from the disparity of the parties, as when a person of low rank insults any of the above or a Roman knight or aedile or judge. A blow is not necessary in such circumstances to make the insult aggravated; tearing (another's) dress, withdrawing an attendant, abusive cries are sufficient (Gai. iii 225; *Collat.* ii 5; Paul v 4 § 10; D. fr 7 § 8—fr 9). Justification of an insult, as addressed to a guilty person, was allowed (fr 18 pr).

(*f*) No action could be brought by one under power against his father; nor, unless the insult be aggravated, by one no longer under power. Nor could a freedman sue his patron for any slight correction, whether with words or blows, but severe beating or wounding will justify the suit. 'One who was a 'slave yesterday though free to-day cannot be allowed to complain 'of trifles' (fr 7 §§ 2, 3). Nor can he sue his patron on account of slight insults or correction given to his son or wife, though they themselves are not necessarily prevented on that account from suing in their own person (fr 11 §§ 7, 8). A freeman, or one claiming to be free, has an action *injuriarum* against anyone claiming him as his slave, though knowing the contrary (fr 11 § 9, fr 12).

The same act may give rise to more than one action. If a married woman still under her father's power is insulted, her father can sue for her and also for himself, and her husband can sue also: and one action does not bar the other. Except under the *lex Cornelia* a son cannot sue for insult to himself, unless his father is incapable or absent or otherwise unfit, and his father's procurator is negligent or not adequate to the occasion. Whether one under power should sue is for the praetor to decide after hearing the case (fr 17 §§ 10—22; Gai. iii 221).

The owners of a common slave can sue severally for insult sustained through him, and recover damages proportioned to their share. They cannot on his account sue one another for beating their slave, nor can owner and fructuary sue one another on that account. As between the latter, suit for beating or torturing the slave belongs to the owner (fr 15 §§ 36, 37, 47). There can be no insult to a slave, but only to others through him (Gai. iii 222).

(*g*) The damages were assessed by the plaintiff, subject to the judge's decision to take a lower estimate, but if, as was usual in aggravated insults, the praetor himself assesses it for the purpose of fixing the bail (*vadimonium*), the plaintiff takes this estimate, and the judge, though not bound to the full amount, usually defers to the authority of the praetor. Condemnation involved infamy (Gai. iii 223, 224; iv 182, Paul ap. *Collat.* ii 6). Where the offender is a slave he may be surrendered noxally, or, if the owner chooses, he may instead produce him to receive a beating (*verberandum*), such as the discretion of the judge may think right (D. fr 17 § 4). If he was emancipated, he was personally liable, even, as Labeo thought, if he had acted on his master's order (Gai. iv 77; D. fr 17 § 7). A plaintiff could be met by a counter suit in which the damages were laid at one tenth (Gai. iv 177, see p. 234).

(*h*) Some insults were dealt with under one of Sulla's laws (*lex Cornelia*). Blows, beating, forcible entry into another's house; writing, composing, publishing anything to throw disgrace on another, or causing such things to be done, were liable to be punished criminally; and a decree of the senate made the like punishable, although no one was named. An oath could be tendered to the accused, and this was allowed in the praetorian action also under the influence of this law. Under this law a son could prosecute for himself, and his father could not sue for him. Criminal prosecution when brought barred private suit, and *vice versa*. The praetor will however prefer criminal indictment, whenever the offence is of so grave or public a character as to make it rather an offence against public order than an injury or insult to an individual (D. xlvii 10 fr 5, 6, 7 § 1). Paul treats the subject mainly from the criminal side. Deprivation of rank, banishment, and death are penalties named (v 4).

2. *INTERDICTUM DE HOMINE LIBERO EXHIBENDO.*

The wrongful retention of a freeman in confinement would probably justify an action for insult. But the case was specifically met by an interdict to compel production of any one, male, female, old, young, *sui juris* or not, known to be free and concealed or confined against his will. If defendant shewed that he had ransomed the freeman, he was justified in retaining him until the price was tendered. If he shewed that he was his own child though not under his power, or his nursling, and was acting from affection, or that he had been surrendered noxally, the retention is not wrongful. Nor if defendant was unaware of his being a freeman, or if he contested the fact, or had bought him *bona fide* as a slave, did the interdict apply. For a trial of contested *status* see vol. I p. 46.

It was open to anyone to bring the interdict, even to a woman or one under the age of puberty, if the person confined was a parent or near relative. If more than one applied for the action, the praetor would select. If defendant was absent, without being defended, his estate would be taken possession of. The interdict could be brought at any time, but not more than once unless good reason be shewn. If the man was not produced, and defendant paid damages, the interdict could be repeated (D. xliii 29).

For *lex Fabia de plagiariis* see above, p. 220.

3. *PATRONUM IN JUS VOCANDI.* Action against a freedman for summoning his patron into court.

This action was in the praetor's edict and could be brought only by the patron himself: it could not be brought by or against the heir, and was limited to one year. In Gaius' time it was tried before Recoverers. The formula is given in Gaius iv 46. Ulpian in the Digest (ii 4 fr 24) speaks of a penalty of 50 *aurei*. See Book vi ch. ii.

H. Intimidation.

In cases of intimidation or fraud[1] the praetor exercised a salutary jurisdiction by granting according to circumstances an action or a plea, so as to prevent the user of such methods from benefiting by his conduct. Intimidation was dealt with still more severely than fraud, and, besides possible criminal proceedings under the *lex Julia*, involved a heavy penalty on anyone who did not comply with the judge's order for restitution. In other respects there was much similarity in the way in which the law dealt with such acts.

The edict ran: *Quod vi metusve causa gestum erit ratum non habebo.* 'Business done under force or fear I will not allow to stand.' In Ulpian's time *vi* was omitted as superfluous, all fear being accompanied by force (D. iv 2 fr 1). The edict did not apply to lawful force used by magistrates, or to force or threats used by brigands (*latrones*), or by the public enemy or the people (popular tumults are probably referred to); and anything, given or promised under such influence to one who himself took no part in it, was regarded as the price of protection or deliverance, and not a subject for legal interference (Paul i 7; D. fr 9 § 1). But in other cases the edict applied, provided there was serious danger to life, liberty or body of

[1] Cf. Cic. *Off.* i 10 § 32 *Jam illis promissis standum non esse, quis non videt, quae coactus quis metu, quae deceptus dolo promiserit? quae quidem pleraque jure praetorio liberantur, non nulla legibus. Flac.* 36 § 89 *Si vis erat, si fraus, si metus, si circumscriptio, quis pactionem fieri, quis adesse istos coegit?* A formula for such cases had been drawn by a praetor Octavius: cf. Cic. *Verr.* iii 65 § 152 *Postulavit ab L. Metello ut ex edicto suo judicium daret in Apronium, 'Quod per vim aut metum abstulisset,' quam formulam Octavianam Romae Metellus habuerat.* The Octavius was apparently C. Octavius, father of the Emperor Augustus, cf. Cic. *Q. Fr.* i 1 § 21. For rhetorical dealing with this matter see Sen. *Contr.* ix 3 (=26) §§ 8, 9.

oneself or children, and the apprehension was such as would be felt by a reasonable person. Paul gives as instances, shutting a person up in a house or chaining him or putting him in prison in order to force him to mancipate or deliver or promise or sell a slave or other chattel or extort anything, *e.g.* a release from obligation (Paul i 7 §§ 8—10; D. fr 3—6, *etc.*). Even one detected in theft or adultery, if the circumstances are not such as to justify his being killed on the spot (see p. 210), is not excluded from the benefit of the edict. On the other hand the language of the edict is general (*in rem*), and applies not only to the intimidator himself but to anyone who has taken advantage of the violence or threats exercised (fr 9 § 1).

If property has been transferred under intimidation, the praetor regarded it as still part of the intimidated person's estate (*in bonis*), and accordingly was ready to allow a vindication (*utilis*) or other action for its recovery, and for the recovery of all fruits accrued which might have been taken but for the intimidation—such as children of slaves, offspring of cattle, fruits of land, acquisitions of a slave, *etc.* Plaintiff can demand also that defendant should give a guaranty against fraud in his treatment of the thing. If money has been paid, the amount must be given back. If a debt or obligation or pledge or sureties have been released, the former position must be fully restored. If full restoration was not made, as the judge ordered, before he gave final judgment, plaintiff was entitled to damages of the amount of fourfold the value of the thing or of the plaintiff's interest in his former position. If several persons were liable for this offence, payment by one, according to the better opinion, freed the others. The value could be established if the judge thought fit by an oath *in litem,* subject to a limit fixed by him. If the intimidation was by slaves, the owner could escape the penalty by surrendering them noxally, but was still liable to surrender any profit or advantage he had gained by their act (D. fr 9 §§ 4—7, fr 10 pr, 12 pr, 14 §§ 1, 14, 15; tit. 3 fr 18 pr).

Plaintiff had to prove that force or threats of force had been used (not necessarily by defendant), that he had been damnified thereby and that defendant had been enriched. If a thing had been lost without defendant's fraud or fault, or a slave who had been taken was in flight, defendant might be acquitted on giving a guaranty for restoration of the thing or slave if recovered and for exertion to recover. The action could be by heirs, and lay against them, so far as at joinder of issue it was found they were enriched, and, this once established, the action runs against heirs of heirs. After a year, on cause being shewn, action could still be brought, but for the single value only. The quadruple included the value of the thing, the triple only being for penalty (fr 14 §§ 1, 3, 10, 11, fr 16, 17, 20).

This action was granted only if there was none other adequate (fr 14 § 2). Where the payment of a just debt was taken by force, the edict did not apply, for the debtor suffered no loss: but a decree of M. Aurelius declared the creditor's right forfeited, *i.e.* the creditor would be subject to a condiction for the thing or money exacted as if it had not been owed (fr 12 § 2, 13).

If criminal proceedings were taken under the *lex Julia* the penalty was one third of defendant's estate; and infamy followed conviction (D. xlviii 7 fr 18).

A plea (*si in ea re nihil metus causa factum est*) was granted when a person was sued on a stipulation or other engagement extorted by intimidation whether of plaintiff or anyone else, excepting only of a person in whose power defendant was. Cassius considered this plea unnecessary as being included in a plea of fraud, but other lawyers held a special plea preferable, the plea of fraud being limited to fraud by the plaintiff, *si in ea re nihil dolo malo actoris factum est* (D. iv 2 fr 9 § 3; xliv 4 fr 2 § 1, 4 § 33).

J. Fraud (*dolus malus* or *dolus*)[1]. The praetor promised to grant an issue (*judicium*), where any business

[1] C. Aquilius was the first who introduced this action: cf. Cic. *N. D.* iii 30 § 74 *Inde everriculum malitiarum omnium, judicium de dolo malo, quod C. Aquilius familiaris noster protulit, quem dolum idem Aquilius tum teneri putat cum aliud sit simulatum, aliud actum; Off.* iii 14 § 60 *Nondum protulerat C. Aquilius de dolo malo formulas*, where the same definition is repeated (see below, p. 287). The plural *formulas* may probably refer to his

transaction was alleged to be due to fraud, provided just cause were shewn, and there was no other action. Fraud was defined by Servius, who was followed by Paul, to be 'contrivance 'for deceiving another person, when what is done is different 'from what is professed' (*cum aliud agitur, aliud simulatur*). Labeo's definition, approved by Ulpian, was 'all cunning, covin and device used to get round, cheat or deceive another' (*omnis calliditas, fallacia, machinatio ad circumveniendum fallendum decipiendum alterum adhibita,* Paul i 8; D. iv 3 fr 1 §§ 1, 2).

This action is not granted, unless the fraud is clear and important; nor if there is any other mode of redress or protection, whether by action, plea, replication or interdict, either against the fraudulent person or another. Sometimes even if there is such other action, yet if the defendant to such action is insolvent, so as to be unable to give adequate redress, an action for fraud will be allowed. On the other hand if plaintiff has had such other means of redress, and has lost it by his own neglect (not by the fraud of his adversary), this action will not be granted (D. fr 1 § 4—fr 6, 7 § 10). Action would not be allowed according to the Digest for anything not exceeding two *aurei* (fr 9 § 5—11 pr).

Examples of cases where action for fraud will be granted are—persuading a person to refuse an inheritance by deceitful representation of its being insolvent; or persuading one, who has an option, to choose a particular slave by craftily representing him as the best in the household; obtaining an acquittal by noxal surrender of a slave when he was subject to a pledge; refusing when manumitted in accordance with a bargain to take upon himself the liability for the price of his freedom from one whom he has persuaded to guaranty it; persuading another's slaves to give up possession, provided the occupant is thereby damnified; contesting ownership of something which another is selling until he loses a purchaser, and then abandoning the contest; obliterating or spoiling a will deposited with him; giving permission to dig stone or lime,

allowing a plea as well as an action (cf. Wlassak *Edict* p. 122; Pernice *Labeo* ii p. 198 ed. 2), or perhaps to some differences in the frame of the formula according to the circumstances to which Aquilius proposed its application.

and then, after expense has been incurred, refusing to allow its removal; promising a slave or a farm, and then before delivery poisoning the slave, or imposing servitudes on the farm or cutting down timber; consenting to my depositing a disputed thing with a stakeholder till decision of the dispute, and then refusing to accept trial; *etc.* (fr 7 § 8, 9 §§ 1, 3, 4 fr 31, 33—35). In the last case some held that an action for fraud was needless, because an action on the case might be brought against the stakeholder to compel him to give up the thing, although there had been no decision of the dispute. In the case before, if the promise was accompanied by a clause against fraud, or the slave or farm were purchased, action on the stipulation or *ex empto* rendered an action for fraud needless. If a third person killed the slave, the promiser could not bring an Aquilian action, for he is freed from his promise, and has no interest in the matter; but the promisee would have an action for fraud against the killer (fr 18 § 5).

Plaintiff has to specify both the fraud and the doer. The action aims at restitution, and only if restitution according to the arbiter's order is not made, does condemnation ensue. Damages are for the single value of plaintiff's interest (*quanti ea res est*); if defendant is contumacious, plaintiff can fix the value by oath, subject to limitation by the judge (fr 15 § 3, 16, 18 pr; iv 1 fr 7 § 1). If more than one person has committed the fraud, restitution or even payment of the value frees all. Heirs and other successors are liable only for so much as has come to them (D. iv 1 fr 17). Conviction in the suit brings infamy on the doer, and hence it is not granted to a wife against her husband, or to children or freedmen against their parents or patrons, or to one of low condition against one of high dignity such as a consular of authority, nor to a wild liver against one of upright life. An action on the case is granted instead. Against heirs no such distinction is made, as no disgrace attends their condemnation. A ward is liable for his own fraud, if he is near the age of puberty; and, so far as he has been enriched, is liable for his guardian's fraud. So is a principal for his agent's fraud. Burghers if enriched are liable for their manager's fraud: members of the council (*decuriones*) are also liable for their own fraud (fr 11—15; Cod. v 12 fr 1 § 4). If the action is on account of a slave's fraud, it may be noxal or *de peculio* according to the character of the fraud (fr 9 § 4 *a*). Where the fraud consisted in preventing an action being brought within the proper time, Trebatius held that the judge should not allow restitution of the action, as that would be against the policy of the law, but should condemn in damages for the plaintiff's loss (fr 18 § 4).

Action for fraud must be brought within a year against the doer: against heirs and others who are sued for enrichment it is perpetual; and so also against the doer so far as he is enriched (fr 28, 29; xliv 7 fr 35 pr).

DOLI MALI EXCEPTIO.

Fraud was frequently pleaded to defeat an action. Examples of cases in which this plea could be used are—where plaintiff sues on a stipulation for which there was no ground or no still subsisting ground; or for a loan of money which has never actually been paid; or against a plaintiff who sues in breach of an agreement made by defendant with plaintiff's superior; or against a ward's suit for debt of which he has received payment, though without his guardian's authority, and is still enriched; or against a fructuary who has consented to the sale of the estate and now claims the usufruct; or against one who claims both the object itself and the penalty for non-delivery within a certain time; or against suit for a penalty for non-appearance at an arbitration, when the non-appearance was caused by illness; or against a coheir by will who has sold his share and sues for the price, while a trial to prove the will forged is yet undecided; or against a creditor suing for a debt, when he has by his own fault lost the pledge given him for it; or against a suit for execution of a judgment made by bribing the opponent's agent; or against an heir who sues for a debt for which testator has forbidden him to sue; *etc.* (D. xliv 1 fr 4; tit. 4 fr 2 § 3, fr 4 §§ 2, 4, 7, 12, fr 8, 9, 17 § 2; ii 14 fr 16 § 1). If sureties for a debt plead the *SC. Vellaeanum*, alleging that they were directed to become sureties by debtor's mother, creditor can meet it with a replication of fraud, if he was ignorant of the mother's intervention (D. xvi 1 fr 6). If under the belief that I owe you money, I submit to delegation by you to someone to whom you purpose making a gift, and my belief is wrong, I can plead fraud against the delegatee's suit, and I can also bring a condiction to obtain a release. The same holds also if, by the delegation, you meant to pay the delegatee a debt which, as it turns out, you did not owe; but if you owed the debt, I cannot resist the suit, for the delegatee is in his right (*suum petit*). If I delegate to my creditor one who is desirous of making me a gift in excess of the statutable limit, and my creditor sues on the stipulation, the statute cannot be pleaded against him; for he is only seeking his due, and the fraud is not his (D. xliv 4 fr 5 § 5, fr 7).

This plea is often available to compel reparation of a neglected duty such as a deduction for the Falcidian fourth, which has not been offered by plaintiff in suing for a right of way bequeathed him; or the cost of an erection made on other's land in the builder's possession, even (as most held) on an erection by husband or wife on land given by one to the other; or when the heir, without offering security for repayment in case the condition occur, sues for a debt which has been conditionally forgiven (fr 5 pr § 1, 10, 14). A surrender of plaintiff's actions may often be obtained by this plea (*e.g.* D. xlvii 2 fr 81 §§ 5, 7).

It was necessary to specify whose fraud it was that grounded the plea, but it was not necessary that it should have been fraud against the defendant; it sufficed that it should have been fraud in the matter concerned and committed either by plaintiff or someone in his power or his procurator. But a fraud by a subordinate is not always a good plea against the principal. Against a plaintiff himself a plea is good which rightfully alleges his fraud in bringing this very action if it is not just, *i.e.* if he thereby seeks to get what he has no true claim to get or no true claim to keep. *Dolo facit quicunque id quod quaqua exceptione elidi potest petit* (Ulp.). *Dolo facit qui petit quod redditum est* (Paul). So that an action which can be defeated by any other plea is therefore also liable to the plea of fraud. And even if plaintiff's fraud has been committed since joinder of issue, or, though committed some time before, has led to the suit in question, this plea is good. If the suit is *de peculio*, any such pertinent fraud by a son or slave is good basis for the plea, for they are the real principals. The same responsibility for all frauds is true also of a procurator suing on his own account and also of one's universal procurator. But if the suit is not *de peculio* and the fraud pleaded is the fraud of plaintiff's son or slave, it is not allowed when the fraud is past or subsequent, but only if it be fraud in the matter then in suit. And this applies also to a procurator appointed for the particular suit, except that as by joinder of issue he may be considered to have made the suit his own, subsequent fraud on his part may, if proved, justify the plea. Fraud on the part of a guardian or caretaker may be pleaded against the ward or minor's suit, if it was committed in respect of the matter in question and is found at the time of suit to have enriched him (D. xliv 4 fr 2 §§ 1—5, fr 4 §§ 17, 18, 23, 25; xlvi 3 fr 47 pr).

If my debtor by false pretences gets you to accept his liability to me (*te mihi reum dederit*) and I accordingly stipulate from you, it was the better opinion that you could not plead my debtor's fraud against my suit, but must pay me and sue him (fr 4 § 20). Nor can the fraud of his predecessor in title be pleaded against a purchaser for value. Thus if I am heir by will, and you being statutable heir fraudulently induce me to renounce, and you then sell the inheritance and pocket the price, I cannot plead your fraud against the purchaser's suit for the inheritance. But if a man claim as legatee or donee, fraud on the part of his testator or donor can be effectively pleaded to defeat a claim which has no support independent of the fraudulent predecessor (fr 4 §§ 28, 29).

The plea of fraud could not be met by a replication of fraud, for no one should be allowed to enforce the results of his fraud (fr 4 § 13). Nor was it subject, as the action of fraud was, to any limitation of time, the time of bringing suit being in plaintiff's not in defendant's power (fr 5 § 6).

K. *PECUNIAE ACCEPTAE CALUMNIAE CAUSA.*

An action was granted by the praetor's edict against anyone who took a bribe for bringing or not bringing a lawsuit maliciously (*ut calumniae causa negotium faceret vel non faceret*). The right of action on account of a bribe to bring a suit belonged to him against whom the suit was to be brought: action on account of a bribe to suppress a suit could be brought by the person who gave the bribe. Defendant was the person who took the money or ordered or ratified its payment to another, or made any disgraceful bargain (*qui depectus est*) of this nature, whether before or after joinder of issue, and whether he did as was intended or not. The bribe might consist in money or anything else, or in a release from obligation, or in reduction of price for a purchase, or in a gratuitous loan, *etc.* The reasonable compromise of a suit was not interfered with by this action. A condiction could also be brought to recover the money by the heir of the giver or, if given from pity to another without any corrupt intent, by the giver himself. In that case the receiver is liable to both actions, but not to a greater extent than fourfold, which was the amount of damages under this action, if it was brought within a year. After a year single damages only could be demanded, and not those if a condiction lay. The year was reckoned in the case of one who gave money to avoid a lawsuit from the date of payment; in the case of one against whom a suit was to be brought, from the date of his knowing of the payment of money for the purpose. This action did not lie against parents or patrons, or patrons' children or parents: an action on the case (*in factum*) was substituted (D. iii 6; xxxvii 15 fr 5).

CALUMNIAE JUDICIUM.

An action so called is mentioned by Gaius as one which may be challenged by defendant in reply to any action. Plaintiff in the principal action is not condemned in this trial of his good faith, unless shewn to be aware of the injustice of his claim and to be suing only to harass his adversary. The penalty is usually one tenth of the amount claimed in the principal action, but against an *assertor* of a person's freedom, one third. It is quite a different action from *pec. acc. cal. causa* (Gai. iv 174, 175, 178).

L. Fraudulent allowance of sale of oneself.

If a freeman over twenty years old, in order to deceive a purchaser, allowed himself to be sold as a slave and shared the price, he became a slave (vol. I p. 43). But if he did not share the price, although knowing his freedom, he was not prevented from afterwards claiming his freedom and thereby ousting the purchaser (D. xl 12 fr 7 pr—§ 3). The purchaser or each purchaser, if more than one, has an action *in factum* granted by the praetor's edict against the person so supposed to be purchased. The damages were double the price and double anything accessory to the price. The action was additional to the purchaser's ordinary action against the vendor for double in case of eviction, and being penal, payment of damages by one did not lessen the damages recoverable from the other. If however the purchaser knew of the freedom at the time, he has no case. If the purchaser was a son under power, and either he or his father knew of the freedom, the father has no action, unless the purchase was on peculiar account, and the father knew nothing about it. If the purchase was by a procurator on mandate for the purchase of the particular man by an innocent principal, the procurator's knowledge will not prevent his principal's having the action. The action has to be brought within a year. The heir and other successors can bring an action which their predecessor could have brought: their own knowledge or ignorance does not affect the question (fr 14—22).

M. Publicans' exactions[1].

The large companies for farming the public revenues with their numerous retainers were the subject of several clauses in the praetor's edict not clearly distinguishable from one another with the meagre information before us.

[1] Compare Cic. *Verr.* iii 10 sqq.

1. If a publican or his staff (*familia*) took anything by force on account of a public tax (*publici nomine*) and did not restore it, he was liable to an action for the double value, or after a year for the single value. The value of the thing itself was included in the double. A similar suit was available if any wrongful damage was done by them or any theft committed. If restitution was offered after joinder of issue, though the offender was strictly liable, he would be acquitted. Only one penalty was exacted, though several persons were concerned in the offence. Under the term *familia* were included not only the publican's own slaves, but also others, or freemen who were employed in this particular service. If plaintiff required the production of the persons charged, and defendant did not produce them, the company were liable for the whole amount without having the right to surrender slaves noxally. No excuse was admissible for non-production: defence of the absent was not allowed.

If plaintiff preferred, he could bring the ordinary actions for robbery or theft or Aquilian injury instead (D. xxxix 4 fr 1—3, 5; cf. fr 12 § 1; Lenel *EP.* §§ 138, 183).

2. Any unlawful exaction, whether made publicly or privately, was the subject of a suit for double the value; and, if it was extorted by force, for triple the value, besides criminal proceedings (D. xxxix 4 fr 6, 9 § 5).

3. If a publican retained slaves (belonging to private persons) and received money on that account which was not due, he was liable to an action on the case for fourfold the value for having got money on a false charge (*calumniae causa* D. iii 6 fr 7 § 2; see above, p. 234).

N. Action against land surveyors and others.

The praetor granted an action *in factum* against a land surveyor who had *dolo malo* made a false report of the acreage of land, which he was appointed either by the judge or by agreement of the parties to measure. Only fraud or gross negligence (*lata culpa*), or the fraud or gross negligence of one deputed by him to do the measurement, made him liable (D. xi

6 fr 1, 2). The action was open to anyone who was interested in the report being true, that is either to vendor or to purchaser or to litigant provided they were injured. But if the purchaser paid too much on account of the report, he could bring a condiction or sue *ex empto* for the money over-paid, and if the vendor delivered too much land, he could sue *ex vendito* for the excess, and therefore neither has any real interest to enable him to sue the surveyor, unless the other party is insolvent, or plaintiff has not recovered the full excess (fr 3 § 1—4; 5 § 1). The action can be brought by, but not against, an heir, and at any time (fr 3 § 5, 4). If a slave made the false report, he could be surrendered noxally (*ib.* fr 3 § 6).

The praetor extended the action to include measurements not only of land but of anything else; *e.g.* measurement of buildings or of breadth of roads, or projection of beams in connexion with a servitude; or of beams themselves, of stones, corn, wine, *etc.* Severus applied it also to architects and contractors; and Ulpian thought it applicable to accountants (fr 2 § 2, 6, 7).

CHAPTER VII.

A. Liability on contracts of persons under power.

1. *Actio quod jussu.*

Any business conducted with a slave (or other person under power) at the bidding of the master (or father) makes the master liable in full, for it is to him that the creditor looks. There is no special form required for the order: it may be in writing or by messenger or oral before witnesses, or a subscription to a slave's acknowledgment of debt; it may be special for a particular business or quite general. Subsequent ratification counts as an order. The action applies not only to an order given by the owner but to one given by a fructuary or by the master of a *bona fide serviens,* or by the caretaker of a madman or spendthrift, by a ward with his guardian's authority or, if for the benefit of the ward, by the guardian. An order by a true procurator binds his principal in this action; if the procurator is not really appointed, he himself only is bound. But if a contract is made with someone else's slave at my bidding, I am not bound *quod jussu*, even though I afterwards purchase the slave. Nor, if I become surety for my own slave, am I bound *quod jussu*; for I am acting not as his master but as an outsider: as surety I am liable on the same conditions as any other surety (D. xv 4 fr 1, 2).

This action cannot be brought after that *de peculio*, unless the creditor has been deceived (D. xiv 5 fr 4 § 5).

2. *ACTIO DE PECULIO.*

(*a*) The nature of a *peculium* has been described above (vol. I p. 54 foll.)[1]. It was in fact the slave's (or son's) private property, though held on a precarious tenure, but recognised by the praetor, with due regard both to the rights of the master or father, and to the practical necessities of daily life, in which slaves and sons played inevitably a great part. They acted in economic matters sometimes as representatives of their superior, making him liable in full, sometimes for themselves, in which case his liability was limited to the amount of the slave's property *i.e. peculium*. (For convenience I speak of slaves, and defer to the end any difference between them and sons.)

(*b*) If a slave made a contract or incurred an obligation by his master's order or on his account, or in connexion with a business or a ship of which he had appointed the slave manager or skipper, the master was responsible. In other cases the slave

[1] Cf. Cic. *Cael.* 7 § 17 *Nam quod aes alienum objectum est, sumptus reprehensi, tabulae flagitatae, videte quam pauca respondeam. Tabulas qui in patris potestate est nullus conficit. Versuram numquam omnino fecit ullam, etc.* Karlowa (*RG.* ii 757) concludes from this that a *filiusfamilias* who had a *peculium*, had entries of expenses and receipts in his father's books, but kept separate. I conceive the son would keep books like anyone else if he had transactions requiring them, though in law the books would be his father's. I take Cicero to be speaking rhetorically with an eye to the particular case. Caelius was a young man with no business to conduct and no investments: he kept no books.

was taken as acting for himself, and his creditors had a claim against him just as they might have against an independent person to the extent of his property. But slaves were not recognised as persons, and had no footing in a law court. Any action to enforce their contracts or other claims against others had to be brought in the name of their master: any action to enforce others' claims against them had to be brought against their master *de peculio, i.e.* in respect of the slave's *peculium*, he being its owner in law and its very existence and amount being dependent on his actual or presumed will. But while it existed, or if it had existed, he could not decline the suit of the slave's creditors and is liable even if the slave was *impubes*, provided he has been thereby enriched, and even if he has forbidden contracts with the slave (D. xv 1 fr 1 § 4, 21 § 3, 29 § 1, 41, 49 pr). He is liable *de peculio* on a condiction for a slave's theft, so far as the *peculium* has been thereby enriched: for the rest, he can surrender him noxally (fr 1 § 1; xiii 1 fr 4). In the case of *bona fide servientes, i.e.* freemen or others' slaves honestly taken to be slaves of another, actions will lie on their contracts against their apparent master until the real ownership becomes known. And where a person has the usufruct of a slave, action lies primarily against the fructuary according to the usual distinction respecting acquisitions (vol. 1 p. 435). The sex of the owner or fructuary or of the person under power does not affect the question (D. xv 1 fr 1 § 3—3 § 2, 50 § 3).

(*c*) A slave has a *peculium* only if allowed by his master. The establishment of it requires the will of a sane master of full age, but once established it continues though the heir be under age or mad. No special form or declaration is required for its establishment: tacit allowance was thought by some lawyers at least to be sufficient. But a thing does not pass from the master into his slave's *peculium* without delivery, nor is one made debtor to the other without definite ground, such as would be required in the case of a freeman under the civil law (fr 4 § 1, 7 § 1, 8, 49 § 2 *Nuda ratio non facit debitorem*).

(*d*) Included in a slave's *peculium* may be anything moveable or immoveable, slaves (*vicarii*) and their *peculia*, debts due from outsiders or fellow-slaves, inheritances and legacies, obligations to him of others than his master for theft or damage, debts due from his master (*e.g.* for expenses in the master's service or moneys collected by his master by suits on *peculiar* account). The value of the slave himself is not counted as part of the *peculium*; nor is a vicar's debt to the master of both slaves chargeable against the *peculium* of his slave-master (D. xv 1 fr 7 §§ 4—7, fr 9 pr, 38 § 2). From the (apparent) *peculium* must be deducted for the purposes of this action everything due by the slave to the master himself or to anyone in his power (excepting to the slave's own vicars) or to his wards or others under his care or administration, whether on contract or delict or otherwise; *e.g.* moneys collected by him with his master's approval or ratification. For any theft committed by the slave from his master, only the simple value, not penal damages, can be deducted. Anything paid to a creditor, or due on stipulation or judgment obtained on the slave's account, diminishes the amount of the *peculium* for subsequent creditors, the principle being first come, first served (*occupantis melior est condicio*). If two suits are pending, priority is determined not by date of joinder of issue, but by date of obtaining judgment. The master however himself is regarded as always on the spot and claiming before anyone else, privileged or not. Where the master is under an obligation on the slave's account, but has not yet paid anything nor been condemned, some lawyers held that the master should not deduct for his possible liability on this head, but take security from the creditor to refund the amount for which judgment might be got. Where a creditor of the slave has been made heir, and the slave himself is bequeathed or manumitted by the will, the creditor can deduct his debt from the *peculium*, although he has not been even for a moment owner of the slave (Gai. iv 73; D. xv 1 fr 9 § 2—11 § 2, § 9, fr 52). Debts due to a slave by outsiders are not always to be taken into account at their full amount, as there may be costs of collection and delay and uncertainty of result to be considered. Hence a master sued *de peculio* may be allowed in such a case to claim acquittal on surrender of his actions to plaintiff (fr 51).

(*e*) Any fraudulent withdrawal or diminution of the *peculium* on the part of the master, *e.g.* if made in contemplation of a suit, is not good against the slave's creditors; but payment to one creditor is not fraud against the others. Fraud ought to be charged within the time which is allowed for an action of fraud. Sale while a suit *de peculio* is pending makes vendor liable to the extent of the *peculium*, including all acquisitions made since the sale (fr 21 pr, 30 § 6, 43). Heirs, purchasers, *etc.* are not responsible for the fraud of their predecessors except so far as it has brought them some profit (fr 21).

(*f*) An action may be brought even if there is nothing in the *peculium* when issue is joined. That does not affect the right: and condemnation may follow if there is something in the *peculium* at the time of judgment. Whether in such circumstances, if the father kept out of the way, possession could be taken of his estate was answered in the negative by Papinian, in the affirmative by Ulpian (fr 30 pr, 50 pr; xlii 4 fr 7 § 15).

(*g*) When a slave is manumitted or sold or otherwise alienated (*e.g.* by legacy or dowry) his *peculium* may be retained by vendor, *etc.* or allowed to pass with him. In the former case, the vendor is liable (within one working (*utilis*) year from the alienation) on any action *de peculio* for debts incurred by the slave before alienation, and he cannot deduct any debts of the slave to him incurred since. The *peculium* will be reckoned with allowance of natural increase or decrease since the alienation. If the vendor sold the slave with his *peculium* and delivered it, he is not liable to any action *de peculio* even within a year, unless he has received a price for the *peculium*, in which case he and not the purchaser is considered to hold the *peculium*. In transferring the *peculium* vendor is deemed to have deducted or not transferred any portion which is due to himself in repayment of a loan or otherwise, the *peculium* being always lessened *ipso facto* by any amount due to the slave's master. The vendor has therefore no action *de peculio* against the purchaser for any debt before the sale took place. And this is true whether the loan, *etc.* was made to the slave while he was the vendor's, or when he was another's slave before purchase by vendor. If however vendor has in fact not deducted the amount due to him, he can bring a condiction (*indebiti*) against the purchaser as for so much overpaid, or sue him *ex vendito*, if the *peculium* contained at the time of sale sufficient to discharge what was due to vendor. On the other hand the purchaser, if he has made a loan to the slave before purchase can within a year from the purchase sue vendor *de peculio* for the amount, less the amount of *peculium* now with purchaser. The like holds generally between alienor and alienee (D. xvi 1 fr 11 § 8, 28 §§ 4—7, 32 § 2—35, 47 § 4; tit 2 fr 1, 3).

The new master (purchaser or other) is always liable to be sued *de peculio* by the slave's creditors, if the slave has had his old *peculium* confirmed to him, or has acquired a new or additional *peculium*; but creditors cannot sue at the same time the old and new master. If however they have not been fully satisfied by the suit against one, they can sue the other for the residue (fr 27 § 2, 30 § 5, 47 § 3).

If a slave has been set free by will or bequeathed with his *peculium*, neither slave nor legatee are liable in strict law for his previous debts: the heir is liable (within a year), but is entitled before delivery of the *peculium* to require a bond from the legatee to discharge any liability which may arise (D. xv 2 fr 1 § 7; xxxiii 8 fr 17). If a slave received a deposit and after manumission retained it, he only could be sued by the depositor, at least according to Trebatius. There was no doubt about this, where a *filiusfamilias* was the depositary (D. xvi 3 fr 21).

If a slave die, his *peculium* becomes extinct; but his master is liable *de peculio* for one year. A usufructuary is liable for a year from the extinction of the usufruct (D. xv 2 fr 1).

(*h*) The heirs of a person responsible *de peculio* are each severally liable to be sued *de peculio*, but cannot be condemned to more than the amount of the *peculium* with them after deducting what is due to them or theirs. If one heir be sued, all are freed, though the amount of damages does not cover the creditor's claim[1]. And the like is true where

[1] The cause probably was that the frame of the formula put the whole debt in suit. In the Digest we are told that equitable considerations were allowed to prevail over this strict law, and the creditor was allowed to sue

there are several fructuaries or *bonae fidei* possessors of one slave. The case is different when a slave is common to two or more joint owners, so that the whole *peculium* wherever it may be belongs to one as much as to the other. Creditors can sue each for a share or one for the whole: and the one who may thus be condemned to pay for both can get contribution by a suit *pro socio* or *com. div.* Whichever co-owner is sued can deduct what is due to his partner as well as to himself. It may however happen that one of the co-owners is entitled to all the *peculium* (*e.g.* if the other co-owner had (without fraud) simply withdrawn the *peculium* so far as he was concerned, *etc.*), and in that case is of course alone liable to the creditors (D. xv 1 fr 11 § 9, 14, 15, 27 § 8, 30 § 1, 32 pr; cf. x 3 fr 9).

(*j*) Some complications arise in case of vicars (*i.e.* slaves' slaves), or of slaves in usufruct. Vicars' *peculia* are included in their master's, the ordinary slave's, *peculium*. If I am sued in respect of my slave's vicars' *peculia* I can deduct not only all debts due by them to me or to my slave, but also all debts due by him to me (because the vicars' *peculia* are liable for the slave their master's debts). On the other hand any debt due to them by their master goes to increase their *peculia*; and any debts due by them to me are not deducible, if I am sued in respect of their master's *peculium*, their debts not being chargeable against him (otherwise than *de peculio*) any more than my ordinary slave's debts are chargeable against me (fr 17, 18, 38 § 2). A slave in usufruct may have two *peculia*, one arising from his relations to the fructuary, another arising from his relations to the owner. Outside creditors can sue the fructuary or owner whose *peculium* was primarily involved, and if not satisfied can then sue the other. And so the fructuary himself, if the slave's *peculium* with him is not sufficient to satisfy a debt due to the fructuary, can sue the owner for the balance and *vice versa*, persons

the other heirs for what was still unpaid to the extent of the *peculium*. But this is held with good reason to be an interpolation by Tribonian (cf. *ZRG.* xxxii p. 243, xxxiv p. 194; *Vocab. Jur. sub voce* '*Aequitas*'). Whether in classical times any other remedy was granted (*e.g. in integrum restitutio;* cf. Keller *ap.* Bekker's *Jahrb.* iii p. 166) we do not know.

contracting with a slave usually looking to the whole of his *peculium* without distinction. Similar is the position of a husband who has a slave in the dowry, the *peculium* partly relating to him, partly to his wife (fr 19 §§ 1, 2).

(*k*) There is a difference between the position of a son under power and a slave. A slave's creditor has only one person to sue, viz. the master *de peculio*: a son's creditor can sue both him in full and his father *de peculio*. Moreover a slave is not liable for a penalty on an agreement for arbitration, nor as a surety of any kind for any debt or business unconnected with his *peculium* or his master's property. And consequently no action lies against his master *de peculio* on these accounts. But a son is capable in all these as in other cases of incurring an obligation, and his father is therefore liable *de peculio*. Even if no action could originally have been brought against the father, yet, if the action is brought against the son and he is condemned, the father is liable (*de peculio*) on the judgment (fr 3 §§ 5—11). Again, if a slave of testator's is one of several coheirs, and an action is brought for a debt incurred by him before testator's death, he is liable only for his share: but if it be on a son's *peculium* that the action is brought, the son though only one of several heirs is liable for the whole. He is however allowed to purchase the liability of his coheirs, *i.e.* to obtain a cession of the creditor's actions against them so as partially to recoup himself (fr 30 §§ 2, 3).

(*l*) If a son under power is emancipated (or otherwise becomes *sui juris*), he is liable in full for his delicts. For his contracts before emancipation, whether made by order of his father or of his own will, and whether on his father's or his own account, he is liable also, but, said the praetor, only so far as his means permits (*in id quod facere potest*). The same applies to the execution of a judgment, already passed while he was under power. In estimating his means no deduction must be made for debts contracted before emancipation, *etc.*, unless they are privileged, the rule being still as regards all ordinary contracts, first come, first served. Debts contracted after emancipation can be deducted. The same limitation on his liability applies to a son disinherited, or who has declined his father's inheritance, or has been made heir only to a very small amount. But if he is restored to the inheritance under a trust, or if he has when contracting professed to be *sui juris*, he is liable in full like any other heir (D. xiv 5 fr 2 pr).

(*m*) A daughter under power, a person in handtake and a woman in hand were incapable of being bound by a stipulation (Gai. iii 104), and presumably by any other obligation any more than a slave. As regards any debts actually incurred by the two latter, if their superior declined to defend them in full (*in solidum*) the praetor allowed their creditors to sell, and divide the proceeds of all property which would have been theirs if they had not passed into his power (Gai. iv 80; cf. iii 84; iv 38).

Whether an arrogator was liable *de peculio* for the arrogatee's debts incurred previously was disputed. Sabinus and Cassius held that he was not (D. xv 1 fr 42). But the praetor's action in making the arrogatee's property liable just as if he had not suffered *cap. dem.* was more effective (Gai. iv 38; see vol. I p. 62).

3. *De in rem verso.*

Whenever a slave (or son) contracted a debt really for his master's service, the master was liable for the full amount, and not merely to the extent of the *peculium*. Anything spent on the cultivation of the master's land, the support or repair of his buildings, the maintenance or clothing of his servants, the payment of his creditors, the purchase (at a proper price) of a farm or any other thing necessary or really useful to him, was for his service and deemed to be converted into his property (*in rem domini versum*). The test was whether the expenditure was such as would entitle a procurator or *negotiorum gerens* to recover from his principal without order or ratification. Any loss (*e.g.* the death of a slave or loss of money or destruction of corn, *etc.* purchased for the master) or mistake in such application was at the master's risk and charge. Ratification is not required, but it is required that the creditor who furnished the money should have given it for the master's service, and he should look to its application. It is not for the master's service if the slave did not so intend it and the creditor was credulous. If money borrowed for such a purpose was lost and the goods were obtained on credit, both lender of money and vendor of goods would have an action *de in rem domini verso*, but the master having paid on one would not be further liable to the other. If a son under power borrows and gives his daughter or sister or granddaughter a dowry, such as his father would have given, the creditor can claim the whole as laid out on the father's estate. And the same if a slave does it: but in both cases he must be doing it as and for the father or master, *patris* or *domini negotium gerens*. So if a son (under power) accepts suit on his father's behalf and is condemned or is surety for him and pays, the amount is chargeable to the father (Just. iv 7 § 4; Paul ii 9; D. xv 3 fr 3, 4, 5 pr, 7 § 5, 8, 10 pr, § 1, 12, 17 pr; cf. Gai. iv 73).

This action does not cover a loan to a slave to pay debts due by him to his master or any other contract on his own account, nor a payment from a surety on the slave's account, nor payment for the slave's manumission. It is only the new and unearned gain of the master that counts as 'converted into his property.' If the slave is in debt to his master, any expenditure on his master's property up to the amount of his debt will not be *in rem versum*. If he is not in debt at the time but become so after the expenditure, the expenditure ceases to be *in rem versum*, as it does if the master repay the slave for it. Nor, if the master take away the slave's *peculium* entirely, or sell something belonging to it and keep the price, has anything thereby been converted: it was his before. The master would of course remain liable *de peculio* to the slave's creditors. In fact this action was not a separate action from that: under the same formula the judge first inquires whether any part of the money has been *in rem domini versum*, and condemns the master for so much, if any: and then, if the claim is not satisfied, inquires into the amount of the *peculium*, and up to that amount condemns the master further (D. xv 3 fr 2, 5 § 3, 10 §§ 6—8, fr 11; cf. Gai. iv 75; Just. iv 7 § 4).

The liability *de in rem verso* was not limited, like that *de peculio*, in case of alienation or manumission or death of the slave, to one year (D. xv 2 fr 1 § 10).

4. *TRIBUTORIA ACTIO.*

(*a*) Where a business is being carried on by a slave (or other person under power) appointed by his master, the master is liable under the *institoria actio* in full. He is also liable in full if the master has given an order either for the particular piece of business or a general order for all business done with the slave. Or again if the business has been done for the master's account so that he is thereby enriched (or was intended to be enriched), the master is liable in full. Otherwise he is liable only as the legal representative of his slave, and only to the extent of his slave's *peculium*; and before paying anyone else he pays or deducts what is due to himself from the slave whether for a loan of money or anything else. But this deduction is not allowed if the master was aware of the slave's carrying on business with his *peculium* and did not forbid it. In that case he has no privilege as master. Whatever goods there may be in the business, or profits accumulated from it, must (if the slave is insolvent) be divided (*tribui*) rateably among all the creditors, including the slave's master. *In tributum vocatur* 'He is summoned to division.' This proceeding is called *tributoria actio*. Not only our own slaves but any *bona fide* servient whether free or slave, and any in whom we have the usufruct, if trading with our goods, may subject us to this action (D. xiv 4 fr 1, 2). And this applies to the case of a ship where the *exercitor* is acting with the knowledge but not with the consent of his master (D. xiv 1 fr 6).

(*b*) A guardian or caretaker's knowledge makes the ward or madman liable to this action: for their fraud the ward or madman is not responsible, except so far as he has profited by it; and he is held also liable to transfer his action against the guardian. A procurator's knowledge or fraud affects his principal (fr 3 § 1—5 pr).

(*c*) Only so much of the slave's *peculium* comes into division under this action as is employed in his business or has been gained from it (Gai. iv 74 *a*). Creditors only for a particular class of goods or at a particular shop are entitled to a distribution separately from more general creditors or from those at another of his shops, the credit being really given not to the slave's total *peculium* but to the special stocks. Pledge-creditors have a preference even over the slave's master. If anyone has sold the goods to the slave and passed the possession but not the property, he can vindicate them. Otherwise creditors are all in an equal position: the rule is not 'first come, first served'; and those who are paid their share can be called on to give security (*cavere*) to make a rateable refund, if other debts unknown or conditional call for payment (fr 8 § 7—fr 17 pr). The distribution belongs to the master: if he decline the task and surrender his claim, the praetor will appoint an arbiter to divide the property liable (fr 7 § 1).

(*d*) The action may be brought at any time and against the heir or other successors so far as they have received anything. If the slave is manumitted by will and his *peculium* bequeathed to him, the heir must deduct from the *peculium* what is to be distributed or take security from the slave for its refund; else he will be liable to this action on the ground of fraud. No one can sue both by this and *de peculio* in reference to the same goods, and if the slave is trading only with part of his *peculium*, the action *de peculio* may be preferable, notwithstanding the master's being thus able to deduct for his own debts (Gai. iv 74*a*; D. fr 8, 9, 11).

B. Liability on others' contracts.

Actiones exercitoria et institoria.

(*a*) As a rule direct liability on others' contracts is found only in case of contracts made by persons under power, and then only to the extent of their own (so-called) property: but there were two cases where there was no such restriction and for which, in addition to any other actions (*e.g. de peculio, redhibitoria, mandati, etc.*), the *actiones exercitoria* and *institoria* were granted by the praetor (Gai. iv 71; Paul ii 6, 8; D. xiv tit. 1 *de exercitoria* (esp. fr 5 § 1); tit. 3 *de institoria* (esp. fr 17 pr)).

(*b*) When a person provided a ship and appointed a skipper in charge of it, he was held liable in full for the skipper's contracts in connexion with it, if the person contracting chose to sue him instead of the skipper. The person working (*qui exercet*) *i.e.* providing or employing the ship, whether owner or hirer of the ship, was called *exercitor*[1], the skipper was *magister*. So also when a person had a shop (*taberna*) or business and appointed a manager (*institor*) the manager's contracts bound him who appointed the manager (*qui institorem praeposuit*). In both cases this rule held, whether the person appointing was man or woman, slave or free, under or over age, under power or independent, though of course in some cases with restrictions. A ward acting without the authority of his guardian was bound only so far as he was enriched by the contract. In the case of a son under power or a slave having a shop the father or master was not liable (except *de peculio*) on the contracts of the manager appointed by the son or slave. But in the case of a ship, the great importance of the shipping trade made an exception to this, and the father or master was liable in full on contracts made either with any skipper appointed by his son or slave, or with the son or slave himself, provided his son or slave was carrying on the business with his superior's consent. Mere knowledge was not enough to make the superior liable in this action. Prohibition of employment of a particular person did not remove responsibility in the case of ships (D. xiv tit. 1 fr 1 pr—§ 5, § 15, § 19—23; tit. 3 fr 1, 7 § 1, 8, 10).

Similarly it mattered not whether the person put in charge of the ship or shop was free or slave, or of what age or condition he was. That was at the risk of the person who appointed him. In the case of a shop, boys or women or girls were not unusually appointed in charge (D. tit. 1 fr 1 § 4; tit. 3 fr 7 § 1, 8).

(*c*) A ship was taken to include boats and rafts, either on sea, river or lake. A shop was only one of many businesses included. The *institor* might be manager of a block of dwellings (*insula*), a bank, a farm, a laundry (*fullonica*), a stable, a bakery, or carry on the business of a tailor, an undertaker (*libitinarius*), a corn dealer or other merchant, a mule keeper, or he might be a shopkeeper's traveller or hawker. So the skipper might be appointed

[1] *Exercitor* is also used in the praetor's edict of the manager of a bank, D. ii 13 fr 4 pr.

to carry goods or passengers or to trade. But in all cases the skipper or manager bound his principal only within the limits of his charge; if appointed to sell, he could not buy; if to lend money, he could not borrow and *vice versa*; if to lend money on pledges, he could not (as a rule) guaranty others' purchases. A skipper appointed only to take goods could not take passengers; if he was only to let the accommodation, he could not take the fares or the freight and *vice versa*; if he was only to carry hemp and seeds, he could not take marbles; if appointed only to voyage on a river or for the cross passage to Greece, he could not bind his principal for other voyages. If not expressly forbidden, both skipper and manager might be justified in borrowing money for the purpose of the business, especially a skipper, as from the nature of the case he is often forced to buy what is required for the service of the ship. But anyone who lent money to either skipper or manager must, if he is to sue the principal, satisfy himself of there being reasonable cause for the loan. If nothing is said by the borrower of the loan being for the ship's needs, and the borrower applies the loan to his own purposes, it is a question whether the principal will be liable. If a person is put in charge of a shop but without power of sale, notice in clear letters ought to be put up and kept up on the place, and then he will not be considered an *institor*. If restrictions are put on an *institor's* power of making contracts, such as by requiring the approval of another person or the taking of a pledge or by forbidding any dealings with certain persons or classes of persons, it must be so done as to prevent purchasers from being misled (tit. 1 fr 1 §§ 6—14, fr 7; tit. 3 fr 3—5 § 15, fr 11 §§ 2, 6, fr 16, 18; tit. 5 fr 8; xii 1 fr 29). A manager is bound in full by the contracts of his foremen or apprentices appointed in charge of the business or workshop (Paul ii 8 § 3; D. xiv 3 fr 5 § 10). An *exercitor* would usually be liable on the contracts of a deputy appointed by his skipper; or of a manager appointed by his agent, or (so far as the ward is enriched) by his guardian or caretaker (tit. 1 fr 1 § 5; tit. 3 fr 5 § 18). A surety of skipper or manager might sue by these actions (tit. 3 fr 5 § 16).

(*d*) When two or more persons appoint a skipper or manager, whether one of themselves or not, all are liable in full, and the one who has to pay can make his partners contribute by an action *pro socio* or *com. div.* (tit. 1 fr 1 § 25—fr 4 § 2; tit. 3 fr 13 § 2). If they act separately in making appointments, each is liable only for his department: they are not regarded as each appointing the others (tit. 1 fr 4 pr). If a man appoints a slave as *institor* and dies, giving freedom to him, his heirs, having now no right to the action *com. div.*, should be sued only for their several shares (tit. 3 fr 14).

Both actions ran for and against heirs; and when a slave has provided the ship with his master's consent and dies, the master can be sued without limitation to a year (tit. 1 fr 4 § 4; tit. 3 fr 15).

(*e*) If a slave (or other person under power) of one man is put in charge of another's ship or business, there is nothing to prevent the owner of the slave from making contracts with him and suing by these actions the proprietor of the ship or business. This latter will of course have a right of suing the owner of the slave by action on mandate or hire, so far as the slave's *peculium* extends. Other persons who make contracts with such a slave as skipper or manager can sue either the person who appointed him by these actions or the owner *de peculio* (tit. 1 fr 5; tit. 3 fr 11 § 8, 12, 17 § 1).

It is only the original obligation which justifies suing by the *institoria* (or *exercitoria*?): if anyone novates it by stipulating from the manager or anyone else, he can no longer bring the special action (tit. 3 fr 13 § 1).

(*f*) Neither of these two actions had counterparts for the owner of the ship or business. If he worked them through his own slave or a *bona fide serviens*, he acquired rights of suit through them. If he worked through another's slave or a freeman, he could sue, according to circumstances, either the slave's master or the freeman himself *conducti* or *mandati* or *negotiorum gestorum* so as to get their actions ceded to him. Some lawyers however held that, if he could not get what was due to him in any other way, the praetor would grant him an action against the purchaser (tit. 1 fr 1 § 18; tit. 3 fr 1 § 2).

Analogous to these actions is the practice of allowing a creditor who has lent money to my mandatee on the strength of my letter to the latter, to sue me for the loan, as business done on my account (D. iii 5 fr 30 pr; above, p. 127).

C. Liability on others' torts. (*Noxales actiones.*)

(*a*) When a son under power or a slave committed a delict without the knowledge of his father or master, these latter were liable to suit on account of the son or slave, and the damages were not limited to the amount of the *peculium*, but they had the right of freeing themselves by giving up the delinquent, instead of paying the damages. (I speak first for brevity's sake of slaves.) It was, says Gaius, unfair that a master should have to bear any greater loss for the wrong acts of his slave than that of the slave's own person. The condemnation clause was therefore couched in the alternative, *aut noxam sarcire* (*i.e.* as Gaius puts it, *litis aestimationem sufferre*) *aut noxae*[1] *dedere*, and the option of surrendering the slave was open until the owner was

[1] *Noxa* (from *nocere*) meant originally 'hurt,' 'harm.' This regarded from the side of the injurer is 'fault' or 'guilt'; *noxius* is 'harmful' or 'guilty,' *noxia* 'harmfulness' or 'guilt.' The injured requires compensation; hence the old phrases were *noxam nocere* 'to do harm' (*e.g.* Liv. ix 10 § 9); *noxam sarcire* 'to make good the harm' (Gell. xi 18 where the reading varies *noxiam*, *noxam*, D. ix 1 fr 1 § 11). A natural way of making compensation was to hand over the offender to the offended person. This was *noxae dedere* 'to give up to the hurt.' A hurt done leaves the offender liable to make amends, and this side of the *noxa* is expressed in *noxā solutus* 'freed from guilt,' not liable to make amends; *noxa caput sequitur* 'the guilt or liability follows the agent.' Plautus, Terence and Cicero do not use *noxa* but *noxia*, though even this is rare in Cicero; Livy has both, but chiefly *noxia*. In the lawyers *noxa* is most usual. There is no clear distinction in meaning. *Noxam mereri* (Liv. viii 28 § 8) is not 'deserve punishment' but 'get guilt,' *i.e.* 'commit a guilty act.' *Noxae dare* is not a Latin phrase, but a very common blunder arising from a confusion of the perfect of *dare* (*dĕdi*) with the forms of *dēdere*. See fuller details in my commentary on *De usufructu* fr 17 § 2. (I see Gradenwitz *ZRG.* xxi 257 agrees with me that *noxae dare* is a blunder.) Pernice (*Lab.* ii 2 1 p. 16) takes *noxae* as genitive '*der Schuld wegen*,' comparing *quadrupli manum inicere* (Plaut. *Truc.* 762); *damni infecti in possessionem mittere* (D. xxxix 2 fr 15 § 16), *etc.* To take *noxae* as dative (see above) seems to me more natural and easier.

sued on the judgment (Gai. iv 75; D. v 3 fr 20; cf. xlvii 2 fr 62 § 5). The XII tables gave this right in the case of theft; the *lex Aquilia* in the case of wrongful damage; the praetor in the case of insult, robbery, and other acts, *e.g.* where a slave refused admission to one sent into possession *damni infecti*, or had done some work which injured a neighbour's field by the flow of rain water (Gai. iv 76; D. xxxix 2 fr 17 pr; 3 fr 6 § 7; xliii 24 fr 7 § 1). The theory appears to have been that the primary liability for such acts was personal: an independent freeman ransomed his person by a money payment: a slave (or other person under another's power) was at his master's disposal, and the master could either ransom him or not as he chose.

(*b*) Suits of this character were called *noxal*, and lay against the owner for the time being, the liability following the delinquent under any change of ownership or status (*noxa caput sequitur*). If he is alienated after commission of the offence, the new master is liable on his account; if he is emancipated, he becomes directly liable himself, just as if he had been independent at the time of committing the act; unless he had acted on his master's order and his action had not been criminal. If he was independent at the time and afterwards came under the power of another (*e.g.* by arrogation or otherwise; cf. Gai. i 160), the injured person's right of suit shifts from suing the delinquent himself to suing the person in whose power he now is, with the consequent alternative of surrender (Gai. iv 76; D. xliv 7 fr 20). The death of the slave before joinder of issue (if there was no delay on the part of the owner), or his becoming free without fault of the owner, removes liability to a noxal suit (D. ix 4 fr 14 § 1—fr 16, fr 39). It was against rule to surrender a dead slave, but if it was done and the slave had died a natural death the owner was freed (Gai. iv 81: text mutilated and uncertain: see also the Autun interpretation prefixed to Krüger's 4th ed. p. LIX).

(*c*) If several slaves of the same master joined in the offence, he is *prima facie* liable on all, but as this might mean his ruin, the praetor allowed him to admit his slaves' offence and, if he preferred to retain the slaves, to pay only so much damages as a single freeman would have to pay (D. xlvii 6 fr 1 pr; ix 2 fr 32).

If, having been sued on account of one or more slaves and having surrendered them, he is sued again for others for the same offence, he is liable only if the prices got from sale of those surrendered do not amount to as much as the double in the noxal suits and the single in the condiction added together (D. ix 4 fr 31).

(*d*) If the master knew of the offence at the time, that is to say, knew and could have prevented it, still more if he actually ordered the slave so to act, he is liable in full, as for an act of his own, without being allowed the alternative of surrendering the delinquent slave, and remains liable even after alienation or manumission or death of the slave, and notwithstanding that the manumitted slave may have been sued and paid damages. If several slaves of the same master were concerned in the offence and he knew of it, he is liable both on his own account and for all of them, and cannot claim the benefit of the above-named provision of the praetor's edict for reduction of the damages. When a slave is alienated after the offence, the present owner is also liable, but penalties cannot be exacted from both. One who knew of the offence at the time and afterwards purchased the slave is allowed to surrender noxally. If the slave is owned in common by several persons, any of them is liable to suit: if all were ignorant, the surrender of the slave or payment of damages frees all: if all knew, any of them is liable to be sued for the whole damages without the alternative of surrender, and suit against one does not free the others. If one knew and the others were ignorant, suit against him frees the others, but his payment of damages gives him no right to contribution from them in excess of their share of the value of the slave who is thus preserved to them: if these others were sued and paid, they could recover from him his full share of the damages, and sue him besides for having spoiled the slave: if instead of paying damages they surrendered the slave, the partner with guilty knowledge could also be sued for so much of the damages as might exceed the value of the slave, and could not get any relief for this from his partners, besides being liable to them in an action *pro socio* or on the case. If he not only knew but ordered the guilty act, he is not entitled to any contribution from them. If, all being ignorant, one is sued, he can free himself by surrendering his share of the slave before issue is joined: after issue joined, he must surrender the whole slave, or pay the damages and recover from his partners by an action *com. div.* or *fam. ercisc.* There was however a question whether, if defendant surrendered his share before joinder of issue, plaintiff who thus became a part owner of the slave could then sue the others for their share by the action *com. div.*, seeing that one partner has no noxal action against his partners, and *com. div.* does not usually apply to wrong acts committed before community arose: Ulpian (in Digest) was disposed to allow it (D. ix 4 fr 3—5, 8, 9, 17 pr, 39 pr; cf. x 3 fr 15; xlvii 6 fr 1, 5; Sell, *Noxalrechte* p. 203).

(*e*) If your slave is a shipmaster, and one of his vicars, employed on the ship, does damage to someone, the action will lie against you in respect of the *peculium* of your slave, but allowing the surrender of the vicar. If however the vicar acted on his master's (your slave's) order or with his knowledge and allowance, the action is against you with the alternative of surrender of your slave (D. ix 4 fr 19 § 2).

If several persons are entitled to sue for a noxal offence, the rule is first come, first served: surrender of the slave may in some cases be made to all together, but if this is not done, surrender to the one who first gets judgment frees the owner from all (fr 14 pr, 19 pr). Successive actions for several delicts of the same slave can be brought against his master, only if he has chosen to pay damages and retain the slave (fr 20).

(*f*) It is the owner (or father) who is liable to a noxal suit but in order to be condemned he must either have not only the legal power but the present control so as to be able to deliver, or have fraudulently put it out of his power to deliver. A slave in flight or abroad was held not to be in his (physical) power: a slave pledged or lent or deposited was in his power. The practice was to interrogate the defendant in court whether he had the slave in his power[1]. If he admitted this, he had to produce him

[1] See generally Demelius *Conf.* § 23; Lenel *EP.* § 58 and *Nachträge* p. xiii. *Habere in potestate* was certainly ambiguous. Apparently the distinction was left to the defendant to put forward in reply to the interrogatory.

or to give security for his production as soon as he could, and either surrender or defend him or be treated as contumacious. If he denied it, the praetor's edict gave plaintiff the option either of challenging him to swear that the slave was not in his power and that his being out of his power was not his fault, or of taking an issue for damages without the alternative of surrender. If defendant took the oath, or if on the trial of the issue plaintiff did not prove defendant's denial to be false and thus lost his case, he could yet sue again, if he contended that the slave had afterwards come into defendant's power. Defendant's denial of having the slave in his power could be revoked before joinder of issue. A guardian or caretaker was admitted to swear: a procurator was not (D. ix 2 fr 27 § 3; tit. 4 fr 21, 22 § 4, 26 § 5; ii 9 fr 2; xi 1 fr 8; L 16 fr 215).

(*g*) In case of surrender it was the owner's duty to convey the ownership and deliver the slave to plaintiff. If the slave was lent or deposited or pledged, *etc.* so that he had not the actual possession, he was bound to get it; if the slave was pledged, he must redeem him, at least if he have the money, but is not bound to sell other property to raise it. The pledge creditor, if not willing to defend the slave, loses his right of pledge, the praetor refusing him an action. A usufructuary, if not willing to defend, will be compelled by the praetor either to contribute to the damages proportionally to his interest, so as to avert the surrender, or to give up (*cedere*) his usufruct: else the praetor will refuse him an action and the usufruct will die by non-use. If a slave was actually serving another than his owner, the possessor, whether in good faith or not, was liable to suit[1]; and if he surrender the slave, the owner in this as in the case of a pledgee, *etc.* will be barred by a plea of fraud from claiming the slave, unless he offer the full amount of damages *i.e.* the double or quadruple, *etc.* according to the offence (D. ix 4 fr 11, 13, 17 § 1, 22 pr—§ 2, 27, 28; vii 1 fr 17 § 2; xlvi 3 fr 69).

(*h*) If the master has alienated or set free the slave so as no longer to have him in his power, he is liable as well as the new

[1] If the offence was under the first clause of the *lex Aquilia* (killing a slave, *etc.*), the owner, not the person whom the offender was *bona fide* serving, is liable (D. ix 2 fr 27 § 3).

master or the manumitted slave, and the plaintiff can elect which to sue. But if the new master or manumitted slave are willing to accept suit, the old master is protected by a plea (fr 24, 25). If several slaves were concerned in a theft and one of them is manumitted, action against him will not bar subsequent action against the master *familiae nomine* (D. xlvii 6 fr 3). If the slave was a *statuliber* at the time of judgment, Sabinus and Cassius and others held that surrender freed the master: if the slave become free before surrender, the praetor transferred the suit on to him (fr 14 § 1, 15; xl 7 fr 9 § 2).

If the owner is absent and no one else (*e.g.* fructuary, pledgee) undertake the defence, the slave could be led off by plaintiff under the praetor's order, and then becomes his *in bonis*. An owner, or other person entitled, returning after *bona fide* absence, could obtain permission to defend the slave (D. ix 4 fr 26 § 6; 28 *ad fin.*, 30; vi 2 fr 6).

(*j*) Noxal actions are perpetual and can be brought by heirs. As owners they can also have such actions brought against them (fr 42 § 2).

A person who has paid damages for a noxal offence of one supposed to be slave, but afterwards found to be free, can sue him for the amount by an action on the case so far as the defendant had acted wrongfully. For an act done *culpa*, not *dolo*, he must sue by the Aquilian action (D. xl 12 fr 12 § 6, 13 pr).

(*k*) No delict committed by one under power against his father or master gives rise to any action: plaintiff and defendant would be the same person. Nor does it arise for his previous act if such delinquent afterwards pass under the power of another or become independent. Whether if another's slave or child commit a delict against me and then come under my power the right of action is lost altogether or only suspended, was a disputed point, the Sabinians holding that it was lost altogether, because it had now come into a position with which it was incompatible, the Proculians holding that it revived, if the delinquent subsequently passed from my power (Gai. iv 78; D. xlvii 2 fr 62 pr). If I had joined issue on the delict with his master, my subsequent acquisition is no hindrance to the condemnation of his former master (D. ix 4 fr 37).

(*l*) Children were in theory as liable to be surrendered for delicts as slaves were, and the same rule no doubt applied to persons in hand and in handtake. (Gaius' text is mutilated.) Papinian said that, when as much had been acquired through a freeman so surrendered as amounted to the damage he had caused, the praetor should compel his manumission; but the noxal receiver was not liable to an action *fiduciae* (*Collat.* ii 3), the surrender being an absolute conveyance. The lawyers in Gaius' time disputed whether one mancipation was enough for due conveyance of a son surrendered, as it sufficed in the case of a daughter or grandchild or slave. The Proculians held that the words of the XII tables requiring three mancipations applied to sons in all cases; the Sabinians held that they referred only to voluntary emancipations. In Justinian's law noxal delivery of children is indignantly rejected as an ancient but unworthy practice. And the Digest accordingly in the case of sons speaks only of their being liable, if not defended by their fathers, to be sued themselves, and their fathers being liable to pay damages on their account only to the amount of their *peculium.* One can hardly think that in Antonine times the surrender of a child could be anything but exceptional (Gai. i 140; iv 79; Just. iv 8 §7; D. ix 4 fr 34, 35).

CHAPTER VIII.

REINSTATEMENT OF PERSONS AND CANCELMENT OF TRANSACTIONS.

In a number of cases, partly by the praetor's edict[1], partly by senate's decrees, the law sanctioned the annulment of acts

[1] An early instance of such interference on the part of the praetor is found in Cic. *Verr.* II ii 25, 26 §§ 62, 63, Metellus as praetor of Sicily cancelling wholesale judgments of his predecessor Verres and acts done by his order: *Fecerat Metellus ut omnes istius injurias quas modo posset rescinderet et irritas faceret.* Metellus enforced it by summary arrest of any who did not obey. *Quod Heraclium restitui jusserat ac non restituebatur, quisquis erat eductus senator Syracusanus ab Heraclio, duci jubebat; itaque permulti ducti sunt.*

of a legal character and the reinstatement of persons, injuriously affected by such acts or by adverse circumstances, into their former position. The justification of such proceedings was the intimidation or fraud of others, infirmity of sex or age, change of civic *status*, capture by the enemy, absence from home.

Intimidation and fraud were subjects of special delictal suits which have been already dealt with (pp. 226, 228). But fraud is a very important allegation in many other proceedings.

A. Reinstatement of minors.

Any business transaction with one less than twenty-five years of age[1] was subject on due application to review by the praetor, who, if the minor appeared to have been done (*captus*[2], *circumscriptus*), or to have acted in a way in which a vigilant person of full age would not have acted, and if no ordinary remedy was open, cancelled the transaction and restored the minor to his former position. It was no bar to this interference that the minor had honest guardians or caretakers and had acted with their authority. On the other hand the fact that the business had turned out badly was no sufficient ground as a rule for interference if it had been done with reasonable prudence. The praetor did not grant the application lightly or as a matter of course, for then people would decline altogether to do business with minors: he summoned (*evocavit*) the parties affected to the hearing and either granted an issue for trial of the question or gave other directions according to the circumstances (D. iv 4 fr 1, 11 §§ 3, 4, 16 pr, 24 §§ 1, 5, 29 § 2, 44, 47 pr; Cod. ii 41 fr 1). Express or tacit approval of the act after attaining majority barred the minor's application (Paul i 9 § 3; D. fr 3 §§ 1, 2).

1 In reckoning minority a different principle prevailed from that used in reckoning the age under the *lex Aelia Sentia*. The act of a minor must be done earlier than the birth hour of the day on which the twenty-fifth year is completed (D. iv 4 fr 3 § 3).

2 *Captus* 'caught' was almost a technical word in such cases: cf. Cic. *Off*. iii 17 § 70 *Quanti verba illa 'ne propter te fidemque tuam captus fraudatusve sim'* (see p. 98); D. xvi 3 fr 1 § 42 *Si eorum nomine qui sunt in potestate agatur, veniat in judicium et siquid per eum in cujus jure sunt captus fraudatusve est;* iv 6 fr 28 § 1; xix 1 fr 39. Hence the use of the word *captiosus*.

Almost any act might be cancelled, on a sufficient case. Acts mentioned are arrogation, constitution of a dowry, sale, purchase, borrowing money, partnership, becoming surety or giving a pledge, accepting an impecunious debtor for a solvent one, exercise of an option, repudiation of a legacy, acceptance or non-acceptance of an inheritance, or possession of a deceased's estate, agreement to an arbitration, miscarriage of a suit, either as plaintiff or defendant, failure to appeal in due time, sale at an undervalue of his estate or of specific assets to satisfy a judgment, or of property mortgaged by his father, *etc.*[1] (D. fr 3 §§ 5—8, fr 7 §§ 1, 3—8, 11, 12, fr 9 § 1; Cod. ii 33, 38, 39, *etc.*; Paul i 9 § 8). But reinstatement was not granted where the minor had committed a delict or acted fraudulently in a business transaction, except that if he had failed to settle for theft (*pro fure damnum decidere*), or to admit Aquilian injury, he might be restored so as to avoid the multiple penalties. An offence against the revenue laws was not regarded as a delict incapable of reinstatement (fr 9 §§ 2, 5). A minor could not get reinstatement to enable him to prosecute a penal action *e.g. injuriarum* (fr 37 pr). Where an act was invalid, *e.g.* contract with a ward without his guardian's sanction and without his being enriched, there was no need for this extraordinary remedy (fr 16 pr). Where a minor had declined an inheritance and the substitute had entered and the estate been distributed, the minor's prayer for reinstatement was held to be too late (fr 24 § 2).

The reinstatement was effected as thoroughly as circumstances admitted. If a minor had sold land at an undervalue, he recovered the land and its profits and repaid the purchase money so far as he had gained by it. If he had bought land at too high a price, he restored the profits which had accrued to him and received back the purchase money and all interest which had or might have been got from it. If he had given a formal release, he recovered his right of action, not only against the debtor but against his sureties and recovered his pledge. If land sold by him had been resold, the minor could claim it

[1] Paul gives an interesting account of a case in which, contrary to his advice, the emperor (from dislike of a forfeiture clause) granted reinstatement (see D. iv 4 fr 38).

back from the second purchaser, if he knew of its being bought from a minor; if he did not know, then the minor could claim its value from the first purchaser if solvent; but if he was not solvent, then the minor was allowed to claim the land from the second purchaser though ignorant of the circumstances, and leave him to his remedy for eviction (fr 13 § 1—15, 27 §§ 1, 2; Cod. ii 47; cf. Paul i 9 § 7). If the minor had received money either as loan or in payment of a debt, and had spent it, the praetor would refuse an action to the creditor or cancel the discharge of the debtor, who has himself to blame for putting the money into the minor's hands instead of depositing it in a temple (cf. p. 54) or paying it to the minor's caretakers. If the minor had lent the money to someone in need, he must cede his actions to his own creditor (fr 7 §§ 1, 2, 27 § 1). Where a minor after entry on an inheritance obtains reinstatement, he is not called on to repay the legacies which he may have paid or the prices of slaves who by his entry have obtained their freedom (fr 22). If the business lay between two minors and both had been done, reinstatement was not granted (fr 11 § 6).

Reinstatement of a minor does not release one who has been surety for him with his eyes open; nor, if a minor has been surety, does his reinstatement free the principal debtor (Paul i 9 §§ 5, 6). One who has employed a minor in doing his business cannot on that account get reinstatement; but if the minor acted for him without mandate, the case is different, and if the minor refuse to apply for reinstatement, he will have no protection against the principal's suit *negotiorum gestorum* and may be compelled to allow his principal to apply for reinstatement in his name (fr 24 pr).

A son under power, being a minor, can rarely obtain reinstatement, for the father is really responsible. But if the son be sued in his own person or has lost some advantage which he might otherwise have had, reinstatement is possible; and if the son die, his father might obtain it, as if he were his heir (fr 3 §§ 4—9).

A slave once emancipated could not be put back into slavery by a minor's reinstatement. All that could be done was to grant the minor an action (of fraud or an analogous action) for the value of what he has lost by the manumission, the action being against the manumitted slave himself or whoever had done the minor (fr 9 § 6—11 pr, 48 § 1; Cod. ii 30).

Application for reinstatement was made by the minor himself, or with his consent. His father however, if the minor was still under power, could apply even without his consent. Other relations could apply only with the minor's consent, unless he be such as to require interdiction as a spendthrift (fr 27 pr). An exile can make application to the praetor by a procurator, or to the governor of the province (fr 20). Application has to be made within one year after completing the age of twenty-five (fr 19 pr).

No magistrate could grant reinstatement by cancelling a decision of a superior magistrate, but he could do so against a former decision of his own. The praefects of the *praetorium* could cancel decisions of their own, notwithstanding that their judgments admitted of no regular appeal. The jurisdiction in this matter was not in the nature of an appeal from an erroneous decision of a court, but was a petition for relief from the consequences of the minor's own blundering or the fraud of the other party to the transaction (fr 16 § 5—18 pr).

B. Reinstatement of *majores*.

Reinstatement (*in integrum restitutio*) was also granted by the praetor to persons above twenty-five years of age in two classes of cases.

The first class is where persons have either suffered positive loss either of a thing or a right, or have been prevented from bringing a suit within the time limited in consequence of absence due to intimidation or to the public service, or of being in prison or chains or in slavery or in the power of the enemy. Intimidation must be serious, causing fear of death or torture. Absence on the public service must be *bona fide* absence from one's domicile, and obligatory, not optional. It includes service in the army, even at Rome, but magistrates at Rome are not reckoned absent. Confinement may be either in a public prison or in an island or by brigands: and a person is deemed to be in chains, if so bound as to be unable to appear in public without disgrace. 'Slavery' applies to a freeman serving *bona fide* or to one forcibly detained, but not to actual slaves, who have no property; nor to slaves made heirs and free by will, until the will takes effect; nor to persons suing for freedom, for they are treated as freemen while the suit is in progress. 'In the power of the enemy' includes those captured as well as those born in captivity, and relief is given to themselves if they return, or to their successors if they die in captivity. But the applicant must have used due diligence to prevent the loss: and the relief is granted to enable a person not to gain by another's loss, *e.g.* by completing usucapion, but to retain or recover what was his own (D. iv 6 fr 1—7, 9—13, 15, 16, 19—20, 36, 40). If the applicant had an adequate representative, an appeal only was granted (D. iv 1 fr 8; 6 fr 39). Besides those whose cases are specifically mentioned in the edict, others on just grounds might obtain the like relief, *e.g.* persons summoned from home to give evidence, or to prosecute an appeal, or persons who had given sureties not to leave a certain place, or absent students whose procurator has died, *etc.* (D. iv 6 fr 26 § 9, fr 28 pr § 1).

The second class consists of those who have incurred loss owing to the absence of others without leaving a proper representative, to whom notice could be given or against whom suit could be brought. The result might be that the absentee might complete usucapion or gain freedom from a servitude or from an action. And not only absence, but confinement in chains, or keeping out of the way, or appeal to a higher court, or privileged exemption from compulsory summons, or extraordinary holidays preventing the sitting of the courts, might enable one's opponent to make an unfair gain calling for the praetor's interference (fr 1 § 1).

In this second class of cases any absence however caused may justify the relief, provided the absentee is not duly defended. It is the duty of the applicant to call upon the friends of his absent opponent to defend him. Cases for relief are the more numerous because usucapion may proceed through the possession of persons in the power of the absentee as well as through himself, and even when he is in captivity, although he himself is unable to possess. This relief is often a better means of redress than the ordinary remedy of being sent into possession of a defendant's estate who fails to appear, for that would only be granted when a defendant was wrongfully hiding (fr 21—25).

The reinstatement may consist according to circumstances in the grant of an action or of a plea or in the suspending of the opponent's usucapion for the minimum of time which has been lost by his absence or by the non-sitting of the courts, *etc.* Where fruits have been gained, reimbursement may be required to complete the reinstatement (fr 26 §§ 7, 8, fr 28 § 5, fr 23 § 2). Where the condition of a legacy or stipulation is presence in Italy at a particular time, the praetor will reinstate a person absent on public business (fr 17 § 1, fr 41, 43).

Application for reinstatement must be made within a year from the earliest opportunity to apply (fr 1 § 1).

C. *Postliminium.* 'Reverter.'

1. Persons who had been taken captive by the enemy and had returned to their own country with the intention of remaining, re-entered *ipso facto* into their old position as if they had never been captive. This was the law of *postliminium* (on which as regards *status* see vol. 1 p. 42). A captive's children, whether born at home or in captivity, became again in his power, either as children or grandchildren as the case might be. If the captive's father had been arrogated, the captive on his return would fall into the power of the arrogator, even if the father be emancipated. During a captive's absence the position of his children is in suspense; if he return, or die while still in the power of a redeemer, they are held to have been in his power all along, and anything acquired by them is acquired for him; if he die in captivity, they are held to have been *sui juris*, not merely from the date of his death but from the moment of his capture (Gaius had doubts on this point, i 129), and their acquisitions are consequently not part of his estate but their own (D. xlix 15 fr 12 § 1, 13, 22 § 2). Acquisitions by

slaves whether by stipulation or release or otherwise, form part of his estate (D. xlv 1 fr 73 § 2; xlvi 4 fr 11 § 3).

A captive appointed heir or legatee by another's will can accept and enter if he return; and is entitled to possession of his deceased father's estate as if he had not been captured, bringing into hotchpot what his estate amounted to at the time of the death. If he does not return, the appointment or legacy drops. If his slaves are appointed heirs, they can accept at his bidding if he return, at the bidding of his heirs if he die in captivity. (D. xxviii 5 fr 32; xxx fr 108 § 5; xxxvii 6 fr 1 § 17.) As to the validity of his own will see vol. 1 p. 210.

This law of reverter cannot alter facts, and therefore possession by the captive himself is interrupted, and new possession cannot be begun while he is in captivity. But possession through slaves or children in his power is effective for usucapion so far as their *peculia* are concerned, for knowledge on his part is not required. If he does not return, children's usucapion avails for themselves (D. xlix 15 fr 12 § 2, 29; iv 6 fr 19, 23 §§ 1, 3; xli 3 fr 44 § 7).

A caretaker was usually appointed to look after a captive's property (D. iv 6 fr 15 pr). Actions in respect of business done for him are good for and against him or his successors according to the event (D. iii 5 fr 18 § 5, 19). For theft, whether committed before or during his captivity, he can sue on his return (D. xlvii 2 fr 41 pr, § 3). His son and daughter were not precluded from marrying during his absence, if three years had elapsed, and even before, if the marriage was one which he would have consented to if present (D. xlix 15 fr 12 § 3; xxiii 2 fr 9 § 1, fr 11). His own marriage was dissolved by his captivity[1] as by death, except, according to the better opinion, in the case of a freedwoman married to her patron. Of course the marriage could be renewed by a fresh consent (xlix 15 fr 8, 12 § 4, 14 § 1; xxiii 2 fr 45 § 6; xxiv 2 fr 1; fr 6 is interpolated).

2. The law of reverter (*postliminium*) applied to chattels as well as to persons. Land, slaves, horses, warships, if taken by

[1] Cf. Hor. *Od.* iii 5, 41 of Regulus, *Fertur pudicae conjugis osculum parvosque natos ut capitis minor ab se removisse.* In the eye of the law he was a slave, and a slave's marriage was no marriage.

the enemy, revert on being freed to their former owners[1]. Arms and dress do not; for disgrace attends their loss (D. xlix 15 fr 2, 3, 20 § 1). The case of slaves, probably from its frequency, received much attention. A slave who re-entered the Roman territory resumed his old position with his Roman master, subject to any mortgage or usufruct or trust for freedom or disability for freedom or to punishment which attached to him before. Anyone who redeemed him from captivity had a lien for the ransom, and a constitution (unknown) made him the property of the ransomer at once, but on the old owner's tendering the amount the slave reverted to him. A creditor of the old owner who had lent money on the slave could tender the ransom, obtain the slave, and add it to the amount of his mortgage. The slave, if a *statuliber*, could not apply to be freed under the trust, till that was paid. And any punishment to which a captive slave may be liable would be in abeyance, until the fisc paid it. If the redeemer had bought the slave without knowledge of his being a Roman's slave in captivity, he could by usucapion extinguish the owner's right of redemption; and, if he had knowledge himself, still a *bona fide* purchaser from him was not bound by the former owner's claim. How far manumission by the ransomer conferred full freedom or only relinquished the manumitter's right, so that the old owner could yet claim him as a slave if found in Roman territory, was a question of some difficulty, except where usucapion had proceeded. But even a ransomer with knowledge appears to have been held to confer full freedom, where no offer of repayment had been made and there was no opportunity of calling on the former owner to make it (fr 12 §§ 7—17; vii 4 fr 26).

D. *Capitis deminutio.* When a person's *status* is changed *e.g.* by adoption, emancipation, coemption, it was provided in the praetor's edict that his obligations of whatever kind, contracted previously, might be enforced, just as if he had not experienced *capitis deminutio* (D. iv 5 fr 2 § 1). Where citizenship or liberty

[1] Cf. Cic. *Top.* 8 § 36 *Postliminio redeunt haec: homo navis mulus clitellarius equus equa quae frenos recipere solet.*

was lost, actions were granted against the possessors of the goods, including the fisc, and if the case was not defended, plaintiffs were sent into possession (fr 2 pr, 7 § 2; xlix 14 fr 11).

E. The *SENATUS CONSULTUM MACEDONIANUM* made in the time of Claudius (Tac. *A.* xi 14) or Vespasian (Suet. *Vesp.* 11) in consequence of the usurious practices of one Macedo decreed that 'no one who gave money on loan to a son under 'power should be granted any suit (*actio petitioque*) even after 'the death of the parent in whose power he was.' Its avowed object was to prevent any loan of money to such a person being a good debt (*bonum nomen*) at any time (D. xiv 6 fr 1 pr; Paul ii 10). The decree was treated as applicable (*a fortiori* says Ulpian) to a *filiafamilias* (fr 9 § 2) and to grandchildren and further descendants (fr 14; Cod. iv 28 fr 6). It was strictly interpreted to refer only to loans of money actually paid down to such a person, not to sales on credit, or to novations by the son of loans to others, or to other transactions, provided they were not used to evade the law. It protected, if necessary by a peremptory plea, not only the person under power but also his heirs, father, and any surety or guarantor (*mandator*) that may have been given for the loan (D. fr 3 § 3, 7 § 6, 9 §§ 3, 10, 13). It applied however only where the creditor knew, or might have known, that the borrower was not independent (fr 3 pr, § 4, fr 19). It did not apply if the loan was really for the father, or had passed into his property, or where the father (being independent) knew of, or acquiesced in, or had recognised the loan. Whether subsequent ratification by the father took the loan out of the statute was disputed (fr 7 §§ 12, 15; Cod. iv 28 fr 7). Nor did it apply where the loan was for an object within the duty of the father; *e.g.* for a daughter's dowry, or for the usual expenses of a student away from home, or for necessary expenses (fr 7 § 13, 17; xlvi 3 fr 47 § 1; Cod. iv 28 fr 11 pr; cf. D. xiv 6 fr 7 § 2); nor to pay a debt which could certainly be enforced (fr 7 § 14); nor where the loan did not exceed the borrower's camp-*peculium*; nor where he openly acted in every way as if independent; but the mere fact that he was consul or otherwise in high office does not bar the senate's decree (fr 1 § 3—3 pr). If a son under age was put in charge of a shop and took a loan, the decree barred any suit against him, but not against the principal (whether father or not) who appointed him as *institor* (fr 7 § 11). Loans to a *filiusfamilias* who farmed the public taxes (*qui vectigalia conducta habebat*) were not within the decree (fr 3 § 1). Whether the loan was to bear interest or not did not affect the question (fr 7 § 9).

If a *filiusfamilias* repaid the loan, his father could vindicate the moneys, but if the creditor had spent them, the father could not bring a condiction: at least so Marcellus held. If a son after becoming independent repays part of the debt, the rest can be sued for; and any payment made by the borrower or his sureties cannot be recovered, whether paid in error or not: there was a natural, though not a legal, obligation. If however the creditor got judgment for the money, because this decree was not pleaded, the plea could be used against suit on the judgment (fr 7 § 16, 9 § 4—fr 11; xii 1 fr 14).

F. *Senatus consultum Velleianum* (*Vellaeanum*).

1. Edicts of Augustus and Claudius are said by Ulpian (in the Digest) to have been directed against women's intervening (*ne intercederent*) on behalf of their husbands. The praetor appears to have extended this prohibition; and in A.D. 46[1] a decree of the senate was passed, at the instance of the consuls M. Junius Silanus and C. Vellaeus Tutor, which 'directed the 'praetors to refuse as heretofore actions against women who 'contracted cash loans or offered security on behalf of other 'persons who were under legal obligations. Such engagements 'were in the opinion of the senate men's business and unfit 'for women' (D. xvi 1 fr 2 pr § 1).

2. Interpretation of this decree was wide in some respects, and strict in others. The edict was held to nullify a woman's intervention for this purpose in whatever form of contract it was

[1] So Mommsen: but it is usually referred to A.D. 27 which had consuls of these names. That date however would be inconsistent with Ulpian's putting it after Claudius. *Velleianum* is an old corruption for *Vellaeanum*.

attempted (fr 2 § 4; Paul ii 11 § 1); and not only the woman's obligation was cancelled, but all other obligations which were attendant or consequent upon it. On the other hand the edict did not stop a woman from making gifts or from any form of payment on behalf of others; nor from incurring obligations in favour of persons who were not themselves under an obligation in the matter; nor from obligations or expenses on her own affairs; nor from being sued on a prohibited obligation, if her creditor was innocent of any offence against the decree. For an obligation to come under the decree, it must be an obligation contracted by a woman to a person who acted wittingly, such obligation being intended to relieve another from a valid obligation already contracted or about to be contracted, and imposing on the woman financial risk without compensation. The theory of the law was that women might easily be induced to give a promise or guaranty to relieve others from embarrassment, while more consideration would be given, if they were to pay money or make a gift on the spot. But fraud disentitled her at once to the protection of the law: *infirmitas feminarum, non calliditas, auxilium demeruit.* So rescripts of Ant. Pius and Severus (fr 2 § 3, 4 pr).

3. Thus a woman could not defend in a suit even her husband or son or father, for she would thereby be liable to the damages in their place (fr 2 § 5). Nor could she authorize persons to be sureties for the defender of her absent son. If she did, both she herself and the sureties could plead the decree against suit to enforce the mandate or stipulation. But if the plaintiff, who accepted the sureties, was ignorant of the woman's mandate, he could defeat the plea by a replication of fraud. The sureties who had to pay might however fairly claim an action *negotiorum gestorum* against the defender who had been freed by their money. They could not sue the mother on the mandate for they were cognisant of the breach of the decree (fr 6, 7). If a woman intervened on behalf of another's debtor and gave the creditor a surety, both are released by the decree, and the old action will be restored against the debtor (fr 16 § 1). If a woman borrows money as for her own purposes, and lends it to another, this comes within the decree, provided her creditor was

not deceived in her purpose of intervention; if he was, the decree cannot be pleaded, for otherwise no one would enter into business with a woman at all (fr 11, 12). If a person wishing to lend money to Titius' heirs distrusts them, and lends it instead to testator's wife and takes pledges from her, and she gives the money to the heirs, the creditor is debarred by the decree from suing her, and the pledges are not bound: it was however thought reasonable that the heirs and any pledges that they had given to the woman should be held liable to the man who advanced the money (fr 29 pr). A woman who in order to pay *C*'s debt to *A* delegates *B* to *A* is protected by the decree, if she thereby becomes obliged to *B*; but if *B* was her own debtor for that amount, she is then incurring no obligation, but simply paying off *C*'s debt to *A* by this transfer of *B*'s debt, just as she might have done by so much cash of her own. *Solvit enim et qui reum delegat.* If *B* was not her debtor, he can plead the decree against *A*'s suit, who would then have to sue his old debtor *C*, notwithstanding any discharge he may have given him. If the woman had obliged herself to *A* in order to relieve *C*, and now either pays money or delegates a debtor to *A* in fulfilment of the obligation, the obligation being invalid under the decree, the woman (at any rate if previously ignorant of the invalidity) can bring a condiction against *A* for the money he has received from her or from her debtor; or she can bring it against *C*, but in that case must guaranty him against any claim from *A* in respect of the old debt which she assumes to have paid (fr 8 §§ 3—7, 31; Cod. iv 29 fr 9). If a woman being in debt to *A* is delegated by him to his creditor *B* and promises to pay *B*, the senate's decree does not come into play: she has novated her debt to *A*, is freed from him, and is bound only to *B*. But if she is not delegated by *A*, and yet promises to pay *B* what *A* owes him, she thereby undertakes *A*'s obligation to *B* while remaining obliged to *A*: the decree nullifies her obligation to *B* (D. fr 24 pr § 1; Cod. fr 2).

4. A mother urging her son's guardians not to sell his land, and undertaking to indemnify them if they follow her advice, is not within the decree, for she is not adopting another's

obligation but creating one for herself (fr 8 § 1; Paul ii 11 § 2). If *A*'s guardian dies leaving *B* as heir, and *B* from fear of the ward *A*'s claims against his guardian's estate hesitates to enter, but does so on getting a guaranty of indemnity from *A*'s mother, the case does not fall within the decree; there is no proper intercession where the guaranty is given to *B* on behalf of himself. If the ward were guarantied against *B*'s failure by the ward's mother, the decree would apply and the guaranty be cancelled (fr 19 pr). If a woman buy an inheritance and guaranty the seller against claims, or if she has given a surety and takes his obligation on herself, in neither case is her obligation liable to be cancelled by the decree; for she is acting in her own interest. The same is the case if a woman slave undertakes after manumission the obligation which some person has incurred with her master as the price of her freedom (fr 13 pr). If a woman and another, co-owners of an estate, borrow for the necessities of the estate, the decree does not apply if she would have suffered greater loss by not obtaining the joint loan (fr 17 § 2). If a woman obtain a loan for another, who however expends it on the woman's own estate, she cannot plead the decree against her creditor. If I give money to a woman for her either to pay it or to promise it to my creditor and she promise it accordingly, she will not be relieved of her liability to my creditor by the senate's decree, for by the promise she fulfilled the mandate and has payment beforehand (fr 21 pr, 22). If a mistress authorized a loan to her slave, she is liable for the loan under an action *quod jussu*: but if he borrowed on his own account and she became his surety, she can plead the decree to a suit by the creditor (fr 25).

5. Many cases depend for their validity or invalidity on the intention of the woman, whether it is an actual gift that she intends or only relief of another from the immediate pressure of a debt. A woman may borrow money from *B* and pay it over to *A* or pay it to *A*'s creditor *C*, or may hand over to *C* something of her own in satisfaction of *A*'s debt to *C*, or may sell a farm to *D* and give the price to *C*, or instead of receiving the price herself delegate *D* to *C* in discharge of *A*'s debt to *C*, or may sell a farm to *C* the creditor himself and direct him to credit *A*

with the price. In all these cases if the woman from the first means to make *A* a gift, the senate's decree does not apply and the transaction is unimpeachable (so far as any gift from the woman to *A* is unimpeachable). But if in all these cases she undertook *A*'s obligation to *C*, and in order to discharge that incurred another obligation either by borrowing, or by a contract of sale, without deliberately intending a gift to *A* but taking the risk of not being repaid, the transaction is void under the decree. The woman is then freed from obligation to pay; if she has paid, she can bring a condiction to recover the money; and if she has delivered or mancipated in order to fulfil the contract of sale, she can vindicate the thing sold; as she can also, if she gave a pledge and the creditor sold the pledge (fr 4 § 1, 5, 32 § 4; vi 1 fr 39 § 1). It is assumed in such cases that the woman has been guilty of no deception when she borrowed money or made any other contract for this purpose, and that in paying money or making delivery she has acted in ignorance of her full rights; and that the lender or purchaser was not in ignorance of her purpose (cf. D. xvi 1 fr 12, 17 pr, 23, 28 § 1, 30 pr; Cod. iv 29 fr 1, 5, 7, 9).

6. The actions which were given by the praetor to restore the position as before the woman's intercession, were often called *restitutoriae*, but were really the old actions which were capable of enforcement, if she had not interfered. If her interference prevented an obligation being formed, which otherwise would have been formed, the praetor granted an action against the person relieved by the woman similar to that which lay against the woman, *e.g.* if she had promised in reply to stipulation, the other was treated as if he had entered into the stipulation, but if she had promised conditionally and the original debt was unconditional, the restitutory action would be unconditional. And such restitutory actions were granted to and against heirs, *etc.* without limit of time. If the person for whom the woman had made herself liable was a ward, he would be now made liable only so far as he had been enriched: if he was a minor, he could apply for *in integrum restitutio*; if he was another's slave, the action would be against the master (D. fr 8 § 12—fr 10, 13 § 2). If pledges had been given by the original debtor, the

creditor could regain them by the *quasi Serviana* without any fresh action, because his claim (*intentio*) would still be true *i.e.* 'that the pledges had been given by agreement with the debtor 'and the debt had not been paid' (fr 13 § 1; Cod. iv 29 fr 8 § 1). If sureties had been given for the debt, the actions against them would be revived also (fr 14).

7. It appears from Justinian's constitutions (Cod. iv 29 fr 22, 23, 24) that in former times doubts were entertained whether a woman was bound notwithstanding the decree (1) if after intercession she gave a bond or pledge or surety to support it; or (2) if she at first or afterwards received some compensation; or (3) if she promised money on condition of another manumitting one of his slaves.

G. *ACTIO PAULIANA*[1].

1. When a debtor's goods had been taken possession of by his creditors, no dealing with them calculated to defraud the creditors was permitted. Both an interdict (*int. fraudatorium* D. xlvi 3 fr 96 pr) and a suit were granted to effect the restoration of anything wrongfully alienated, and the revocation of any deed or proceeding (*quae fraudationis causa gesta sunt*) which had the effect of impairing the bankrupt's estate. The suit is called in one place *Pauliana* (D. xxii 1 fr 38 § 4). The relation of the interdict and suit is obscure: the Digest treats them together under the style of an action. I have no choice but to follow.

2. The suit is of a practical, not punitive, character. It is brought by the caretaker of the estate or other whom it may concern within a year after its being first possible (D. xlii 8 fr 1 pr, § 1, 10 pr, § 1, 25 § 1). The acts specifically mentioned as

[1] This action is apparently referred to by Cicero, who had been requested by Atticus' uncle Caecilius to assist a suit against Satyrus, who had in fraud of Varius' creditors received a conveyance of some of Varius' property. *Caecilius A. P. Vario cum magna pecunia fraudaretur, agere coepit cum ejus fratre A. Caninio Satyro de iis rebus quas eum dolo malo mancipio accepisse de Vario diceret. Una agebant ceteri creditores, in quibus erat L. Lucullus, P. Scipio, et is quem putabant magistrum fore, si bona venirent, L. Pontius...Rogavit me Caecilius ut adessem contra Satyrum* (*Att.* i 1 § 3).

modes of fraud for this suit are alienation, *e.g.* by way of gift, or of sale at an inadequate price, release of a debtor or surety, either formally or by agreement, paying a debt before it is due, giving up a pledge, giving a pledge for an old unsecured debt, payment of legacies by a necessary heir, constitution of a usufruct or dowry, incurring an obligation, preference of a creditor, deliberate non-appearance in court, or failure to demand payment so that a claim expires, deliberate non-use of a servitude or usufruct, abandonment of a thing as derelict (D. xlii 8 fr 1 § 2—fr 5, fr 6 § 13, 10 §§ 12—14, fr 25 §§ 1, 2). But simple non-acquisition or declining to do what would improve the estate (*e.g.* accepting an inheritance or legacy) or non-fulfilment of a condition to bring a stipulation into force is no ground for this suit (fr 6 pr, § 2; xxxvi 1 fr 69 § 1).

3. The suit can be brought against anyone who dealt in such matters with the insolvent, provided he knew of the fraud or at least knew the estate was insolvent. But the suit lay, irrespectively of knowledge, against a master or father whose slave or son was aware of the fraud, or who was enriched thereby; against a donee or a ward whose guardian or caretaker was aware; or against a legatee, to whom a necessary heir has paid the legacy from an insolvent estate (fr 6 §§ 8, 10—13, fr 10 § 5). None of the above-named acts are frauds within the scope of the law, if done before the estate was seized by the creditors. And a creditor who, with full knowledge of the debtor's insolvency, still enforced a lawful claim before seizure, is not acting fraudulently but is only vigilant for his own interest; *sibi vigilat; jus civile vigilantibus scriptum est* (fr 6 §§ 6, 7, fr 24). Even after the estate has been seized, a *bona fide* purchaser from a fraudulent purchaser is not within the scope: nor one who handed over a trust inheritance without taking the Falcidian fourth; he was regarded only as a faithful executant of the trust. Nor is one within the scope who at the instance of the heir by trust entered on an inheritance and restored it to him, if the inheritance was wholly outside of the estate on which the creditors had a claim (fr 9, 19, 20; xxxvi 1 fr 69 § 1). The praetor will on sufficient cause being shewn grant a special action against one who had no knowledge of the fraud (fr 10 pr).

4. The existence or knowledge of fraudulent intention was not enough to found the action, unless the creditors were actually defrauded. If the insolvent satisfied those who were his creditors at the time of the fraudulent act, subsequent creditors could not claim the revocation, unless, as Severus and Antoninus laid down, the first creditors were paid with the money supplied by the second. It is only the creditors who sell up the insolvent who have a right to this action. If a fraudulent insolvent makes his will giving freedom to slaves[1] and afterwards pays off his then creditors, and has others before he dies, the freedoms are valid; there was no fraudulent intent against the latter, and no fraud against the former: *Libertates ut rescindantur, utrumque in eorundem persona exigimus et consilium et eventum* (fr 10 § 1, 15).

5. The action aims at complete restoration both of property and of rights of action, so that all may be in the same state as it was before the fraudulent act. Whatever was part of the thing before it was alienated and all produce and profits, which could have been taken since joinder of issue, must be restored. Produce whether of land or slaves, wholly grown in the intermediate period, could not be part of the insolvent's estate (*in bonis*), and therefore does not come into the action. Interest on debts improperly collected or remitted[2], and interest naturally due on a *bonae fidei* contract was recoverable, but not other interest which had not been made the subject of stipulation. All necessary expenses must be repaid to defendant (fr 10 §§ 19—23, 25 §§ 4—6). A fraudulent purchaser cannot recover the price he has paid, unless the actual money is found in the estate (fr 7, 8). Where the fraud consisted in the establishment of a dowry, whether by the wife, or her father or an outsider, both husband and wife are liable to this action, if they knew of the fraud, and the wife as a donee, if she did not know: an innocent husband is not liable, as he would not have taken a wife without dower (fr 25 §§ 1, 2).

If the insolvent had squandered property beyond chance of recovery, the action would be granted against him, by way of penalty (fr 25 § 7).

[1] This was forbidden by the *lex Aelia Sentia*. See vol. I p. 32.

[2] *medii temporis commodum* (fr 10 § 22).

H. *Actio Fabiana vel Calvisiana.*

On allegation of any act of a freedman done to defraud his patron of his due share of the inheritance, whether the freedman dies with or without a will, the praetor hears the case and applies a suitable remedy by cancelling the act or otherwise. A gift in view of death can be cancelled without proving fraud, but if made to a son is not revoked, being within the freedman's rights; if made to a copatron, he has to share it. If a sale has been made at less than the real value, the purchaser has his choice either to surrender the thing or pay the additional price. If a purchase has been made at an exorbitant price, the vendor has the choice of receiving his thing back at the price given or of repaying the excess. But the patron cannot insist on rescinding a sale made by the freedman if the price was fair, though it may have been land for which he had a special affection on sentimental or other grounds. Lease or exchange are in the same position as purchase and sale. If the freedman borrowed money and gave it away, the patron can sue the recipient, but if he squandered it, there is no remedy; for the lender has a right to recover from the inheritance. Nor has the patron any action against a creditor to whom the freedman has become surety or given a pledge for another, but he can sue the debtor on the mandate, or, if the freedman was making a gift so as to have no action of mandate, the patron can use the Fabian action. A gift by the freedman to a slave or son under power gives the patron a right to sue the master or father: if the slave be manumitted or alienated or dies the action must be brought as usual within a year: there is no action against the slave himself if manumitted. If the freedman has given a dowry to someone not his daughter, the patron can sue either husband or wife according as the dowry is still with the husband or has been repaid.

In all cases the only fraud to be proved is fraud by the freedman; whether the other party was aware of his being a freedman or not, does not affect the patron's right to sue him. If the freedman both sold at too low a price with intent to defraud his patron and gave the price away to another, the patron can sue both purchaser and donee. Failure to acquire is not fraud: but the freedman's abandonment of a suit or consent to a verdict against him, if fraudulent, entitles the patron to sue.

The action is personal, not general (*in rem*); it is not penal and can be brought at any time; it goes for and against heirs and other successors, but is special to the patron and not for other claimants to the freedman's estate generally. All fruits gathered since joinder of issue are recoverable. If restitution is refused, the damages can be fixed by oath of the plaintiff. If the thing fraudulently alienated no longer exists, the action cannot be brought; nor can the thing be followed in the hands of a *bona fide* purchaser from the donee. Two or more patrons or patronesses can each sue for an equal share: the shares of those who do not sue accrue to the others (D. xxxviii 5; Paul iii 2 § 3; Frgm. *de form. Fab.* in *Jus Antejust.* iii p. 299).

The *lex Fabia* (or *Favia*) and the *lex Calvisia* had the same import, but applied the first to testate, the second to intestate inheritances (fr 3 §§ 2—4). Neither applied to the inheritance of an emancipated child *a parente manumissi* (D. xxxvii 12 fr 2).

Where a freedman alienated property in order to reduce the amount of his estate under 100,000 sesterces (see vol. I p. 271) the alienation, being in fraud of the Papian law, was *ipso facto* invalid, provided it would have had the effect intended. But if the estate was still 100,000 sesterces, the alienation was not void, but only gave ground for suit under the Fabian or Calvisian statutes as being in fraud of the patron. If several things together were alienated, the alienations were all void, though the revocation of one or two only might have sufficed. But if the alienations were at different times, those later, if they left the estate still of the value of 100,000 sesterces, were not *ipso facto* void (D. xxxvii 14 fr 16).

I. *De alienatione judicii mutandi causa.*

Anyone who, anticipating a law suit respecting something which he owns or possesses, alienates it maliciously, in order to put difficulties in the way of his opponent, is liable to an action on the case for the amount of his opponent's interest in the alienation not having taken place. Such a case is found if you alienate it to a man of greater influence or to one in a different province; or manumit a slave whom I am claiming (because the praetor favours freedom); or where, having carried out some work on your land, which makes you liable to me by the interdict *quod vi aut clam*, or by the action for keeping off rainwater, you alienate it; for then I cannot make the new proprietor remove it at his expense as I could you, but can only get the right of removing it myself; or, when I have given you notice not to carry out some work (vol. I p. 518), you alienate it, and the purchaser carries it out, for then I cannot sue him because I have not warned him, nor you because you have done nothing in it (D. iv 7 fr 1—3). Alienation of a rural or urban servitude is within the edict (fr 4 § 4). For the purpose of this edict alienation will include transfer of a thing not really one's own (fr 8 § 2); and transfer of possession where the transfer is made maliciously (*dolo malo*), to give the other a troublesome opponent. But a transfer to another from dislike of continual litigation or from ill health or age or necessary business is not within the edict (fr 4 §§ 1—3). Nor does the edict apply to dealing with a thing by will; or to alienation followed by taking the thing back; or to one who has returned it under the aedile's edict to the vendor from ordinary motives, or has paid it in discharge of an obligation to another, notwithstanding my intention to claim it (fr 8 § 3—fr 10 pr).

The action is not of a penal character, but aims at recovering the position. The judge has it in his discretion to make condemnation dependent on failure to restore (fr 4 § 6, fr 7 pr). Indeed the action will not be granted at all, if the intended defendant offers to accept an analogous (*utilem*) action to that contemplated before alienation (fr 3 § 5).

The action can be brought by an heir, but not against an heir nor after a year (fr 4 § 6—fr 6).

APPENDIX TO BOOK V.

A. *Litterarum obligatio* (Obligation by Book-Entry). (See p. 64.)

Until the discovery of Gaius' Commentaries there was no professed account of this matter except in Pseudo-Asconius and Theophilus, two late unsatisfactory authorities, to whom I think no attention is due on such a question. But Gaius gives a definite and trustworthy account (iii. 128—134, 138), and since the publication of his book many writers have treated of it[1]. Notwithstanding this there still appears to students an air of mystery about it. They think that *obligari litteris* meant that *A* by entering in his ledger *B* as a debtor for a certain sum of money thereby made *B* a debtor for that amount, and could call on the courts to compel *B* to pay. Not unnaturally this has seemed a strange state of the law. Perhaps, too, Gaius' over-neat classification of contracts has contributed to some misapprehension. *Litt. obl.* is distinguished from contracts made *re*, where there was delivery of something as the basis of the contract; and from contracts made *consensu*, where there were reciprocal obligations; and from contracts made *verbis*, where the person bound had made a formal promise. It looks, therefore, as if *litteris obl.* rested on a one-sided act of the

[1] See Danz *Gesch.* § 151 vol. ii p. 43 foll. The most important are Savigny *Verm. Schrif.* i 205 foll., Keller *Inst.* § 125 p. 102 foll., and Karlowa *RG.* ii § 66 p. 746 § 99. Voigt, *Die Bankiers*, is as usual elaborate, but he is quite wrong in his principal new contentions. See the excellent review by T. Niemeyer *ZRG.* xxiv 312 sqq. I am amazed that Czyhlarz (who so well exposed Voigt's construction of a *lex Maenia de dote*) should have adopted (*Instit.* 1889) Voigt's theory of a special *codex*, and his absolutely baseless invention of *expensum referre* for the debtor's entry of his debts. Sohm who adopted it in the 3rd and 4th editions of his *Institutionen* has now (7th ed., 1898) reverted to Keller's view, and Czyhlarz later (see 4th ed. 1899) has also abandoned Voigt, and given a very cautious account of the matter.

creditor, without value having passed, without reciprocal obligations to counterbalance, and without acknowledgment on the part of the debtor.

Cicero, in his speech *pro Roscio comoedo*, speaks of accurate bookkeeping as a criterion of an honest Roman. Many writers have taken his rhetoric (which is on a par with Macaulay's references to the knowledge of school-boys) as a statement of fact, and spoken as if every Roman *paterfamilias* kept books as fully and regularly as a banker. It is probably true that many Romans kept a ledger[1], just as many Englishmen have a copying-press for their letters. But many Englishmen have not the latter, and many Romans, doubtless, did not do the former. Business men with capital to put out, and especially bankers, kept ledgers; and perhaps the circumstances of Roman business made it necessary for private persons to do so, to an extent which is not now required. There were then no public stocks in which a man might invest his capital, and be saved from trouble by receiving his interest regularly, and getting his principal repaid or selling his stock. The usual period for loans was apparently very short, and therefore reinvestment was going on frequently.

A ledger is not a record of transactions but only a statement of the result of such transactions expressed in money. For the purpose of the ledger it is immaterial what the nature

[1] Keller and Savigny speak of a *codex accepti et expensi* as a *cashbook*, and distinguish it from a ledger (*Contocurrentenbuch*). I do not think anything really turns on the distinction, if the cashbook is a regular and orderly book and not a mere collection of hurried temporary entries (*adversaria*). Bankers would have several permanent books; ordinary persons probably only one. These litteral-contract entries would, in such a system of bookkeeping as I am acquainted with, probably not go into the cashbook, which is confined to entries of actual money, but into the ledger, which collects all entries from the journal (of invoices, *etc.*) and from the cashbook, and enters them in separate accounts for each debtor or creditor. Transfers from one account to another would be made directly in the ledger. I see no necessity for assuming a separate part of the *codex* for *res*, nor an invariable system of double entry, but otherwise I agree largely with Karlowa (*RG.* ii § 66), whose book was published long after I first wrote this essay.

of the transaction was. If it claims a place in the ledger at all, it must be because on some day or other, past or future, it produced, or in its nature would or will produce or extinguish, an obligation on the one part or the other to pay a sum of money. An orderly ledger, as now kept, has usually a separate page or portion of the book giving the results of transactions between the owner of the ledger and each person in constant business relations with him. Whether the owner pays him money, or pays money for him to someone else, or gives him goods, or has been promised money by him, and the time has come for payment without payment being made, in each case the owner enters the amount as a debt against him in a separate line, and in fact treats the matter as if he had in each case paid out that sum of money to the debtor. To make such an entry as if of a loan the Romans called *expensum alicui ferre*. On the other hand if the owner of the ledger has received money from a person, or from another on his behalf, or taken goods from him at a certain price, or has promised him money, and the time has come for payment without payment being made, in each case the owner enters the sum to his credit, or as the Romans said 'as received (by himself) for the other,' *acceptum alicui referre* (or sometimes *ferre*). If the ledger is regularly kept and in due order, persons being kept separate, and transactions duly dated and arranged accordingly[1], it is *prima facie* entitled to credence, at least as much as any other document in the owner's possession. Nay, it is entitled to more credence than most such documents, because of the importance of a regular record, and the probability of its being accurately kept for the owner's personal information. But any document may be false, and got up for the purpose of establishing a fictitious claim; and so each entry in the ledger may be fictitious, and the order cunningly devised for fraudulent purposes. Whether it is so or not is a matter for evidence and argument, whatever be the reason for the production of the books in a law-court. If no ledger is kept, the same transactions may be recorded, but

[1] The letters *AFPR* were often added to an entry which was made later, out of its right place. They stood for *ante factum, post relatum*, 'done before, entered afterwards' (Cic. *Orat.* ii 69, § 280).

dealings with one man are not kept separated from dealings with others.

If a person is debited with a loan of money or with the value of goods purchased, and if the borrower or purchaser refuse payment, the lender or vendor must of course prove payment of the money or delivery of the goods: if there is an entry debiting a man with interest, the lender must prove loan, agreement for interest, and accrual due: if there is an entry debiting a man with a sum for services rendered, or expenses incurred on his behalf, the claimant must prove the fact of their being rendered or incurred, and his right as *locator* or mandatee, or *negotiorum gestor* or *tutor* or the like, to charge him with them. The ground of obligation in these cases is the money actually paid down (*pecunia numerata*), or the sale, or the agreement for interest, or the *mandatum, etc.* In the case of a loan the Roman lawyers said the debtor was bound *re, i.e.* by actual transfer of physical object, viz. the coins; in the case of interest, that he was bound on an express verbal agreement (*verbis i.e. stipulatione*); in the other cases, *consensu*, by agreement to reciprocal benefits. The entry in the ledger might be used as evidence, but it was evidence only. The borrower, or purchaser, or hirer, or person otherwise served was not in any way, more or less, bound by such a book entry; he was not *obligatus litteris*. Possibly he might more easily be proved to be a debtor by the production of a ledger shewing the entry in due place, just as the direction of the wind may be more easily shewn by a weathercock; but the weathercock does not cause the wind, and the ledger does not create the obligation. Both exist independently.

But now suppose the moneys thus entered in the ledger to be due. If they are paid, the ledger-keeper enters on the credit side of his debtor's account the fact of payment, the two entries balance each other, and the matter is squared. But perhaps they are not paid, and some arrangement is made for delay. The creditor may of course refrain from enforcing payment, and simply wait and do nothing, or if there are several claims he may submit an account, get it confirmed or amended, and carry the balance to a fresh account. Or he may desire to close this transaction or series of transactions, and arrange for a definite settlement. In modern times he might get his debtor to accept a bill of exchange. In Rome he made an entry to the debtor's credit, just as if he had received the money from him, and then made another entry to the debtor's debit of the same amount, as if lent him (*creditum*). The debtor then was bound not by any actual delivery of the money lent to him, not by the old business transaction which had first led to this matter and was agreed to be closed, not by any formal stipulation, but simply by the entry in the ledger (*ipso nomine* Gai. iii 132). He was *litteris obligatus* 'bound by writing.' That this entry was justified by the agreement of the parties had of course, if necessary, to be proved as any other contract might have to be proved. But the proof need not go further back than the ledger to give a *prima facie* good ground of action. It was not a mere vague understanding, nor an informal *pactum*, but had the requisite legal requirements of being definite and intentional. If disputes arose, what had to be proved or disproved was the defendant's consent to the entry, not plaintiff's having given consideration for the debt.

Suppose again that the creditor, *A*, was unwilling to give his debtor, *B*, any further delay, but was willing to give credit instead to a friend, *C*, of the debtor's. The arrangement then might be that *A* should enter the amount on the credit side of *B*'s account, and thus close the transaction with him, but enter the like amount to the debit of *C* in another account. *B* was now free, and *C* was now *litteris obligatus* to *A*[1]. In modern times a banker would do the same in receiving a cheque on himself from *C* to be put to *B*'s credit. Gaius mentions both cases, the first is a transfer *a re in personam*: the second a transfer

[1] In Livy xxxv 7 *Via fraudis inita erat (a feneratoribus) ut in socios qui non tenerentur fenebribus legibus nomina transcriberent: ita libero fenore obruebant debitores.* The object here was to substitute a non-Roman creditor for the real creditor, so that the rate of interest might be free from restriction. Probably the Roman creditor booked to the credit of the debtor an acceptance of the money lent, and debited the non-Roman ally with the same amount, who in his books debited the Roman debtor with principal and usurious interest and credited the original Roman creditor with it.

a persona in personam. And the second case might equally well occur when *B* had previously been in *A*'s books as *litteris obligatus*, or as *re* or *verbis*, or *consensu obligatus.*

It must be remembered that the use of forms and the legal value attached to them was a matter of growth and not of skilful device. The Romans did not say, 'we want a form of 'valid obligation for oral contracts, and another form of valid 'obligation for parties in commercial relations at a distance.' The first (*stipulatio*) arose from recognition of the clearly expressed intention of the parties; and just as mancipation was simply the dry residuum of a sale in public, with delivery of the object by one party, and delivery of the price in metal of full weight duly ascertained by the other, so *litteris obligari* was the result of the practice of merchants and bankers, and the usages of bookkeeping. The Roman lawyer found entries produced which, on the face of them, disclosed no independent ground of action, no purchase, no actual cash loan, no formal stipulation. But they were entries of a definite character, usual among business men, they were not mere oral agreements (*pacta*), but had a recognised precision and formality from their place in a regular ledger, which was analogous to the precise question and answer of a stipulation. The custom of business men procured them legal validity. The obligation was deemed to be created by the book-entry, because there was nothing else to base it on; and that an enforceable obligation should exist was the intention of the parties.

Of course the debtor, if he kept books, ought to make a corresponding entry in his own ledger[1], and the production of his books would form a natural part of the evidence (cf. Cic. *Rosc. Com.* §§ 1, 2; *Verr.* ii 1, 39 § 102). But creditors often keep much more complete accounts than their debtors, and their books are not on that account less worthy of acceptance, because their debtor has been negligent or dishonest. The entry which created the obligation is that made by the creditor in his own books (Gai. iii 137), just as in other cases, *e.g.* manci-

[1] A mere entry in a man's ledger that he owed *B* money did not avail as a gift: *nuda ratio non facit aliquem debitorem* (D. xxxix 5, l. 26).

pation (Gai. i 119), surrender in court (*ib.* ii 24), stipulation (iii 92, 116), formal release (iii 169), release by the bronze and balance (iii 174), it is the party who thereby gains a right or release, not the party who is to be charged, or from whom the right is gained, that gives as it were voice to the transaction. In these other cases the parties had to meet; in obligation by book-entry the debtor was not required to be present (Gai. iii 138), bookkeeping would not usually be so conducted, and the entries would often be the result of correspondence, and not of personal intercourse at the time.

It is easy to see that this one fact would give a reason in the interests of commerce for the acceptance of book-entries as a ground of obligation. And the convenience to the creditor especially, but really to both, of having only a claim or liability for an ascertained sum of money instead of a balance of claims and counterclaims, of debts and credits, would be a further reason. The law treated suits on book entries as it treated suits on actual cash loans: both came under the description of *certa pecunia credita* (Gai. iii 124; D. xii 1 fr 1 § 1, 2 § 3); and hence the procedure allowed a wager to be made which involved the condemned debtor in a fine of one-third the amount, and (probably) an oath to be peremptorily tendered. (Cf. Cic. *Rosc. Com.* 4 § 10; 5 § 14; Gai. iv 171; above, p. 71.)

Gaius (iii 128) speaks of *litt. obligatio* as created *veluti nominibus transcripticiis* 'for instance by transferred entries of debts.' The use of *veluti* does not imply in this case any more than in others[1], that there are other modes of obligation *litteris* than those given: it is merely a cautious expression in a popular lecture or treatise, where the writer does not choose to consider or discuss whether the enumeration is exhaustive[2]. I believe *litt. obl.* was confined to such cases of transfer. In original entries there was the cause in the actual payment, or actual business, or formal promise, and this cause was probably made part of the entry; it was only when a transfer took place that the entry constituted the ground of the obligation. But

[1] *E.g.* Gai. iv 141. See Schmidt *Interdicten-verfahren*, p. 234. Savigny *Verm. Schr.* i p. 251 note.

[2] Even if anyone presses *veluti*, the mode mentioned in § 134 is sufficient to satisfy such a supposed implication.

though original entries of business were presumed, I imagine they did not always exist. Accommodation bills in modern times afford an easy analogy. They may be drawn up just as if a sale of goods had taken place, and yet may be accepted without real value received. And so it may have suited Romans to make entries of feigned transactions, or otherwise arrange their books so as to make the real debt appear only as a transfer. How far in a suit for payment it was possible to go behind a book-entry, admitted to have been made by agreement for a liquidated amount, and contest the consideration which gave it birth, or the circumstances and intention of the parties, is a matter on which we have little information. It can hardly have been usual, and seems to require a plea of fraud. See the case of Otacilia, p. 295.

Gaius contrasts these 'book-entries' or 'debts' with *arcaria nomina*, 'box' or 'cash debts,' *i.e.* ordinary entries of loans or investments booked as such. The obligation, arising in the eye of the law, not from the entry of debt, but from the actual payment of the money (*numeratione pecuniae obligantur*) was of a character not specifically Roman, but part of the business of the world generally. I see no reason (quite the contrary) for supposing always a separate book for the different kinds of entries. That would depend on the particular person's choice, and on the extent of his transactions. Nor was there any special form of words required for a book-entry, or used by others in describing it. Inspection of the ledger shewing such a transfer professing to debit a person with a definite amount of money, and proof or presumption of such transfer having been made by consent, were enough to find a ground of obligation without any proof of payment, or sale, or other transaction. Such transfer or entry was no mere *pactum*; it stood by the side of stipulation as creating a legal obligation.

An anecdote given by Cicero (*de officiis* iii 14 §§ 58—60) has been rightly cited by Savigny as a case of *litterarum obligatio*. Canius goes to Syracuse for amusement, and is entrapped into purchasing a seaside villa from Pythius, a banker of the place. *Emit homo cupidus et locuples tanti quanti Pythius voluit et emit (hortos) instructos; nomina facit, negotium conficit, i.e.* Canius is wealthy and impatient, he accepts the price named by Pythius, and agrees to buy the villa with its appurtenances and furniture just as it was. He desires to complete the purchase and become owner at once: for this purpose he must either pay the money down or give security or get Pythius to give him credit without security (D. xviii 1 fr 19). He has not the money with him, but Pythius is willing to give him credit. Accordingly Pythius[1] makes in his ledger three entries. 1. He debits Canius with the purchase money. 2. He credits him with the price as if received. 3. He debits him with a loan to the same amount. This is described generally as *nomina facit* 'he makes entries.' The second entry at once closes the sale and entitles Canius to demand delivery of the villa. The third entry binds Canius to the payment of the liquidated sum irrespective of the prior proceedings. With this last entry Pythius closes the business (*negotium conficit*), the result being that Canius owns the villa and gardens, and Pythius has invested their value in a loan to Canius. Canius afterwards finds his expectations disappointed and sees that Pythius has fraudulently made the villa appear more valuable than it really was. But he had no remedy; the sale was complete, and the loan was agreed on and duly entered in the ledger. He has himself to blame for his impatience and credulity. Cicero implies that if it had occurred in his own time Canius would have had a remedy. He might either have brought an action for fraud, or he might have pleaded fraud so as to defeat Pythius's demand for payment of the so-called loan. These remedies were introduced by Aquilius. In a somewhat similar case (but without book-entry) Papinian said the *actio empti* would apply to remedy the fraud (Vat. 13). But law had made progress between Cicero's time and Papinian's.

This special form of obligation went out of use before Justinian's time (Just. iii 21[2]), probably as Savigny (after

[1] I take Pythius to be subject to *facit*. Others (cf. Madvig *Verfassung* ii p. 187) take Canius as the subject. No doubt Canius is the last named subject; but the inference from this is rebutted by the repetition of Canius in the next succeeding sentence, as if Pythius had been just referred to. For the use of *nomina facit* see below, p. 291.

[2] Compare D. xliv 7 fr 1 § 1 (Gaius) with Gai. iii 89.

Schüler) suggests (pp. 244, 248) in consequence of the full development of the *constitutum debiti*[1], and perhaps the more frequent use of Greek bankers and Greek forms of commercial engagements. Gaius himself speaks of what might be considered (*fieri videtur* iii 84) as an obligation by writing (*litt. obl.*), viz. an acknowledgment of debt testified by promissory notes or written agreements (*chirographis et syngraphis*, cf. Cod. Theod. ii 4 fr 6), which are said by Gaius properly to belong to foreigners; *i.e.* they were the ordinary mode of dealing between parties who were not both Roman citizens. Justinian speaks (*Inst.* iii 21) of the applicability of the term to the case of a person who has given an acknowledgment of debt without having actually received the money. In this case he was not allowed to dispute the debt or its amount after five years according to Cod. Hermog. i 1 (p. 234 ed. Krüger) or after two years according to Justinian (Cod. iv 30 fr 5, 10, 13, 14, *etc.*). After this period the writing was unimpeachable, and hence might be considered to constitute for the future the ground of the obligation.

Something may be said on the terms used, and some special passages may be quoted and explained.

The terms *litteris obligari, litterarum obligatio, litteris* (*sc. facta*) *obligatio* are terms used by Gaius: *scriptura obligari, obligatio nominibus fieri dicitur* are expressions found in Justinian's *Institutes* in speaking of the same thing. *Litterarum obligatio* is also found in Cod. Theod. ii 4 fr 6 of written acknowledgments of debt, as in Gai. iii 134, nowhere else is the expression *litt. oblig.* found. In Cicero and other writers we have only bookkeeping expressions, *expensum ferre* and *nomen* or *nomina facere* being used for these entries of credit as well as for entries of actual expenditure.

Thus *expensum,* (*expensam, etc.*) *alicui ferre* is the regular phrase for debiting a person; *acceptum* (*acceptam, etc.*) *referre* for crediting, *e.g. Quod minus Dolabella Verri acceptum rettulit quam Verres illi expensum tulerit* (Cic. *Verr.* II 1, 39 § 100, cf.

[1] An instance of a *const. debiti* for balance of account is given in D. ii 14, fr 47 § 1.

§ 102): 'the balance of the amount debited against Dolabella by Verres over that credited by Dolabella to Verres.' *Quas pecunias ferebat iis expensas quibuscum contrahebat, eas aut scribae istius aut Timarchidi aut etiam isti ipsi referebat acceptas* (*ib.* 2, 70 § 170): 'all sums which Carpinatius debited 'against those with whom he had business, he used to put to the 'credit of Verres' secretary or of Timarchides or of Verres him-'self'; *i.e.* he was carrying on the business for Verres' account. *Deinde in codicis extrema cera nomen infimum in flagitiosa litura fecit; expensa Chrysogono servo* HS *sescenta milia, accepta pupillo Malleolo rettulit* (II 1, 36 § 92): 'in the last tablet of the 'ledger, the place of the last entry shewed over a criminal 'erasure a debit against Chrysogonus his ward's slave' (so I take him to be) 'of 600,000 sesterces which were credited to his 'ward Malleolus,' *i.e.* he had paid Chrysogonus the amount due to Malleolus. *In argentarii tabulis ei expensa pecunia lata est acceptaque relata* (*Caecin.* 6 § 17): 'in the banker's books he was 'debited with the purchase money, and credited with it when 'it was paid' (*Font.* 2 § 3 (17)). So in other writers *scimus non amplius quam terna milia peraeque in singulos menses ex ephemeride eum expensum sumptui ferre solitum* (Nep. *Att.* 13 § 6): 'we know that the regular amount of Atticus' monthly table 'expenses were not more than 3000 sesterces, the expenses being 'entered in a day-book and then every month summed and 'posted in the ledger under the head of *Sumptus.*' *Pecuniae locupletibus imperabantur, quas Longinus sibi expensas ferri cogebat....Accersit omnes qui sibi pecunias expensas tulerant acceptasque eas jubet referri* (*Bell. Alex.* 39, *i.e.* 'Longinus made 'requisitions of money from the rich and insisted on their 'being entered to his debit (as if on loan); afterwards directed 'them to credit him for them (as if repaid).' *Id quod argentario tuleris expensum, ab socio ejus recte petere possis* (*ad Heren.* ii 13 § 19): 'what you have booked against a banker, you are legally entitled to sue his partner for[1].' *Nec legata percepit Tiberius ulla aliter quam ut peculio referret accepta* (Suet. *Tib.* 15): 'Tiberius, after being adopted by Augustus and therefore

[1] Savigny refers this to 'litteral contract.' *Obl.* i p. 151. I think it is general.

'no longer *sui juris*, credited every legacy he received to his '*peculium*' (as a son under power would do).

In the Digest we have *expensum* (*-sam, etc.*) *ferre e.g.* xx 4 fr 12 § 5; xxxvi 1 fr 23 § 4; *expenso* (predicative dat.?) *ferre* xxxiii 10 fr 10 (where perhaps we should read the dative *supellectili* instead of the genitive); *acceptum ferre, e.g.* xlvi 3 fr 1; *accepto ferre, ib.* fr 3; xiii 7 fr 35; xxvi 7 fr 56; xxxii fr 91 §§ 4, 6; Cod. v 37 fr 3; *acceptum* (*-tam, etc.*) *referre* xxiii 3 fr 48 § 1; xxxii fr 29 § 2; xl 1 fr 6; *in acceptum referre* xlvi 3 fr 10 § 1.

These expressions are sometimes used metaphorically, *e.g.* *Nemo fuit qui mihi non vitam suam fortunas liberos rempublicam referret acceptam* (Cic. *Phil.* ii 5 § 12); cf. *ib.* 22 § 55; Liv. x 19 § 7; and in poets; *Acceptum refero versibus esse nocens* (Ov. *Trist.* ii 10), 'I owe my criminal character to my verses'; *incultis versibus et male natis rettulit acceptos regale nomisma philippos* (Hor. *Ep.* ii 1 234). So *acceptum ferre*[1] in Sen. *Ep.* 78 § 3 and in Plin. *HN.* cited below; *expensum ferre* in D. xxxvi 4 fr 3 § 3; xliii 1 fr 24.

Expensum ferre seems sometimes to mean simply 'to lend,' *e.g.* Liv. vi 20 § 6, *homines prope quadringentos produxit quibus sine fenore expensas pecunias tulerat*; Cael. ap. Cic. *Fam.* viii 4 § 4 *Eam legionem expensam tulit C. Caesari Pompeius.*

It is used of obligatory book-entries in Cic. *Rosc. Com.* 1 § 2; 4 § 13; 5 § 14 *Haec pecunia necesse est aut data aut expensa lata aut stipulata sit: expensam latam non esse codices Fanni confirmant.* So in the Baetic fiduciary bronze (Bruns[6] no. 110) *quam pecuniam Baianio dedit dederit, credidit crediderit, expensumve tulit tulerit* (see above, p. 101); and in Val. M. viii 2 § 22 (quoted p. 295): Papinian in *Vat.* 329 *sub cognitione cognitor non recte datur, non magis quam mancipatur aut acceptum vel expensum fertur; nec ad rem pertinet an ea condicio sit inserta quae non expressa tacite inesse videatur.* In Plin. *Ep.* ii 4 *quicquid mihi pater tuus debuit, acceptum tibi fieri* (*al. ferri*) *jubebo*, a book-credit is apparently intended.

Referre is sometimes used with *acceptum* of obligatory entries, but is of general use for entry in a ledger, *e.g.* Cic. *Verr.* II 1, 39 § 102; *Rosc. Com.* 1; D. xxxv 1 fr 82.

[1] For *acceptum* (*accepto*) *ferre* or *facere* of verbal release, see p. 55 n.

An account book is *codex accepti et expensi* (Cic. *Rosc. Com.* 1 § 4; 2 § 5; 3 § 9), often referred to as *tabulae* 'boards' (*ib.* § 2), of which, covered with wax, it was in fact composed. Into this, especially if kept as a ledger with each customer's account separate, the entries would be posted from the rough day-book (*adversaria*, *Rosc. Com.* 2 § 5), perhaps originally a number of loose sheets or tablets. To post the ledger is *conficere tabulas* (*ib.* §§ 6, 8 *Verr.* ii 1 39 § 102; 2, 76 § 186; *Cael.* 7 § 17).

The separate entries or items were *nomina*, properly 'names of debtors' (or creditors). So *nomina referre in codicem* (*Rosc. Com.* 1 §§ 2, 3, *etc.*). Each account is *ratio*; hence Plaut. *Truc.* 750 *ratio accepti scribitur*; Cic. *Verr.* ii 1, 39 § 100 *Hinc ratio cum Q. et Cn. Postumis Curtiis multis nominibus, quorum in tabulis iste habet nullum*; Sen. *Ben.* iv. 32 § 4 *Apud me istae expensorum acceptorumque rationes dispunguntur* 'are examined' (cf. D. L 16 fr 56 *dispungere est conferre accepta et data*).

Rationibus inferre is to enter an item in the accounts (Suet. *Jul.* 47; D. xl 7 fr 40 pr). The credit and debit sides of each account were usually on separate (facing?) pages, cf. Plin. *HN.* ii 22 *Huic* (*sc. fortunae*) *omnia expensa, huic omnia feruntur accepta, et in tota ratione mortalium sola utramque paginam facit.* The dates were added to the entries *e.g.* Cic. *Verr.* II 2, 77 § 188 *in his tabulis magnam rationem C. Verruci permultis nominibus esse, neque hoc perspicere ex consulum mensuumque ratione* 'looking to the consuls (*i.e.* years) and months'; cf. D. ii 13 fr 1 § 2.

Nomen facere is 'to make an entry,' hence 'to make a loan,' *e.g.* Cic. *Fam.* vii 23 § 1 *Accepi Aviani litteras, in quibus hoc inerat liberalissimum, nomina se facturum cum venisset, qua vellem die* 'that he would make me loans any day I liked.' So in Cic. *Off.* iii 14 § 59 of a contract *litteris* (above, p. 287). It is frequent in the Digest, *e.g.* ii 14 fr 9 pr; xv 1 fr 4 § 1; fr 52 pr *si ex re pupilli nomina fecit vel pecuniam in arca deposuit*; xvii 1 fr 12 § 15; xxvi 7 fr 16; fr 39 § 14; xl 5 fr 41 § 17 *Stichus arcarius probante domino nomina fecit, etc.* (In D. xv 1 fr 4 § 1 it means to debit one's self. In D. xxxiii 1 fr 1 *si ex stipulatu aut nomine facto petatur* it may have meant a *litt. obl.*) The book containing such loans or investments was called

Kalendarium, which was also used for a man's investments collectively *e.g.* D. xxxii fr 64 *cum quis kalendarium praestari alicui voluerit...ipsae quoque pecuniae, si adhuc kalendario id est nominibus faciendis destinatae essent, eidem fidei commisso cedere debeant*; xxxiii 2 fr 37 *calendarii usus fructus*, xxvi 7 fr 39 § 14 *actio kalendarii* 'the right of suing for the investments.' Cf. xxxii fr 34 § 1; fr 41 § 6, *etc.*

Cicero says of himself *bonum nomen existimor* (*Fam.* v 6). So in *S.C. Macedonianum*: *ut scirent qui pessimo exemplo faenerarent, nullius posse filii familias bonum nomen expectata patris morte fieri* (D. xiv 6 fr 1 pr).

The genitive with *nomen* denotes the debtor, very rarely the creditor (v. Salpius *Novation, etc.* p. 98). The debt may be not in money but some other thing; cf. D. xiii 7 fr 18 pr; xx 1 fr 13 § 2.

Three other words, all compounds of *scribere*, and more or less connected with bookkeeping, may be mentioned.

Perscribere[1] is to 'write in full,' 'write out,' *e.g.* Cic. *Verr.* ii 1, 21 § 57; *Cat.* iii § 13, *etc.*; so of writing an acknowledgment of debt and pledge (*chirographum*, D. xx 1, fr 6 § 1); and it and the noun *perscriptio* are specially used in money matters in two senses: (1) of the person, credited or debited with sums of money, writing entries in his account books, *e.g.* *Rosc. Com.* 1 § 2 *Aeque tabulae condemnantur ejus qui verum non rettulit et ejus qui falsum perscripsit*, the former phrase being here used of the debtor, the latter of the creditor; *ib.* 2 § 5. In Cic. *Flac.* 19 § 44 the object of the expenditure is named; *in aedem sacram reficiendam se perscripsisse dicunt.* So also *Verr.* v 19 § 48.

(2) Of writing an order (cheque) on a banker; Liv. xxiv 18 § 14 *a quaestore perscribebatur.* So apparently in Cic. *Att.* xiii 51 *Tiro narravit perscriptionem tibi placere*; xvi 2 § 1 *quod perscribi oportet.* In the wax tablets found at Pompeii, con-

[1] Since writing this I have seen a somewhat similar account by L. Mitteis in commenting on the use of διαγράφειν in some Greek records *ZRG.* xxxii 213 sq. He takes διαγράφειν in these documents regularly to mean 'to pay,' and takes *perscribere* and *perscriptor* often in this sense. 'To give a cheque' is in English use the same as 'to pay,' presuming of course that the cheque is honoured.

taining receipts to an auctioneer L. Caecilius Jucundus for the sale money for different persons' goods sold by him for their account, the external docquet is '*perscriptio*,' which perhaps describes the contents as a warrant for payment to the vendor (framed as a receipt—like Treasury warrants). See Bruns[6] no. 131, and Mommsen *Hermes* xii p. 111 (above, p. 59).

In many places the precise meaning is uncertain, *e.g.* Cic. *Orat.* i 58 § 250 *si de tabulis et perscriptionibus controversia est*; *Phil.* v 4 § 11 *sestertium septiens miliens falsis perscriptionibus donationibusque avertit*; *Att.* ix 12 § 3 *Viri boni usuras perscribunt*, 'are entering up their interest'? 'are giving cheques for the interest?' Suet. *Jul.* 42 *deducto siquid usurae nomine numeratum aut perscriptum fuisset.*

Rescribere is 'to book a credit' or 'give an order for repaying' Ter. *Phorm.* 922 *Transi sodes ad forum atque illud mihi argentum rursum jube rescribi.* PH. *Quodne ego discripsi* (*al. perscripsi*) *porro illis quibus debui?* Cic. *Att.* xvi 2 § 1 *De Publilio quod perscribi oportet, moram non puto esse faciendam; de residuis* $\overline{\text{CCCC}}$ HS $\overline{\text{CC}}$ *praesentia solvimus, reliqua rescribimus*; Hor. *Sat.* ii 3 76 *Dictat* (gives an order for a loan) *quod tu nunquam rescribere possis.* So *scribe decem a Nerio*, 'give a cheque on Nerius for ten' (Hor. *ib.* 69)[1].

Transcribere is to make a transfer in the ledger, *e.g.* D. xvi 1 fr 13 *Si hereditatem emerit et aes alienum hereditarium in se transcribat*, 'debit herself with the debts due from the estate.' (It is also used of transfers of landed property D. xix 5 fr 12; xxxii fr 41 § 9.)

A practice seems to have prevailed, in order to get either greater secrecy or better security, of interposing between lender and borrower, some other persons, called by Seneca *pararii* 'balancers.' Thus *Ben.* ii 23 *Quidam nolunt nomina secum fieri nec interponi pararios nec signatores advocari, chirographum tantum dare.* 'Some persons like as little fuss as possible 'made about a loan, simply an acknowledgment in writing, no 'book entries, no interposition of 'balancers,' no summoning of

[1] Besides the proof thus afforded by the bankers' books (cf. D. ii 13 fr 9 § 2), the creditor adds ever so many acknowledgments drawn up by Cicuta (*adde Cicutae nodosi tabulas centum*).

'witnesses to seal a deed.' *ib.* iii 15 § 2 *Adhibentur ab utraque parte testes, ille per tabulas plurium nomina interpositis parariis facit: ille non est interrogatione contentus nisi reum manu sua tenuit* ('by an autograph bond'?). What the *pararii*[1] were (accountants? brokers?) is not known. Some writers on *litteris obligatio* have imagined book-entries made by one person in another's books and used these passages and Cic. *Att.* iv 17 (quoted below) in illustration. I cannot understand book-entry giving rise to an obligation between parties whose books are not used. There is nothing in any of these passages to prove that entries binding *A* to *B* were made in *C*'s ledger. If book-entries are intended, it could only be by binding *A* to *C* (a banker perhaps) in *C*'s books, *C* to *D* in *D*'s books, and *D* to *B* in *B*'s books. Whether in Cic. *Rosc. Com.* i §§ 1, 3 something of this kind was referred to, is a question insoluble in the present state of the MSS. Borrowing a note-book or blank tablets (*codex, pugillares*) from a person in order to get a written acknowledgment from a debtor (D. xiii 6 fr 5 § 8; fr 17 § 3) is a totally different affair: it is merely what would in modern times be borrowing a sheet of paper[2] for the purpose. Only conceive a merchant's borrowing another merchant's ledger to make binding entries of his own transactions!

A passage in Cicero (*Att.* iv 17) is often quoted in this connexion. He is referring to a monstrous agreement made between the consuls of the year B.C. 54, and two of the candidates for the consulship of the following year. One of the candidates C. Memmius read this out in the senate. The consuls were to use their influence on behalf of himself and Domitius. They in turn were to procure for the consuls the provinces they desired. To do this they were to produce three

[1] *Pariator* is used of one who pays up and thus balances his account D. xxxv 1 fr 81; Inscr. *ap.* Bruns no. 140. I derive both words from *par* not *parare*. L. Havet in Wölfflin's *Archiv* x 525 takes *pararii* to be persons to whom the loan is made in the first instance in different amounts and who then lend these sums to the real debtor.

[2] The difference is due to modern improvements. The ancients used wax tablets in which the wax could be smoothed again and used afresh (analogous to our slates). If we borrow paper, it is a case of *mutuum*, not *commodatum*: we should repay the like, not the same.

augurs to declare they were present when a *lex curiata* was passed to give the consuls the proconsular *imperium*, and two men of consular rank to declare that they were present in the senate when the distribution of the provinces was arranged, no such law having been passed, and no meeting of the senate having been even held on the day named in the fictitious resolution. And they bound themselves to do this under a penalty of 40,000 sesterces to be paid to each consul. Cicero proceeds: *haec pactio non verbis sed nominibus et perscriptionibus multorum tabulis cum esse facta diceretur, prolata a Memmio est nominibus inductis auctore Pompeio, i.e.* The agreement was not made by a stipulation (*verbis*) but by book-entries and orders for payment passed through several persons' (bankers?) books. No doubt the three augurs and two consulars were secured beforehand; book-entries or money orders in their favour were made. When at Pompey's instance the agreement was produced, the names of the consulars and augurs were obliterated (*nominibus inductis*). It is useless to conjecture in what precise mode the bargain was made. Probably there was some further *pactum ne peteretur* to prevent the parties claiming the penalties if the bargain was duly performed[1].

A story given by Valerius Maximus (viii 2 § 2) appears to relate to book-entry. C. Visellius Varro, when seriously ill, allowed a woman named Otacilia, who had been his mistress, to debit him with 300,000 sesterces (*expensa ferri sibi passus est*), his intention being that if he died she should sue his heir for that amount. It was in fact a *mortis causa donatio* made by book-entry. Varro recovered, much to Otacilia's regret: and she sued him for the money. The great lawyer C. Aquilius was *judex*, and having some of the leading men as his assessors gave judgment against the claim. If the case was after C. Aquilius had introduced (as praetor, or advising the praetor on other occasions) the use of a plea *doli* (see Cic. *Off.* above, p. 287), the decision would be easy to understand, provided the

1 Other views may be seen in Rein *Priv. R.* p. 691; v. Salpius *Novat.* p. 94; Tyrrell *Cicero's Corresp.* vol. ii, letter cxlix. See my article in *Class. Rev.* i 67.

issue contained such a plea. It would as Savigny says (*Verm. Schr.* i 255) be justified from the disgraceful ground of the gift (D. xii 5 fr 8), from its being contrary to the rules of the *lex Cincia* (*Vat.* 310, 311), and from its being a *mortis causa don.* (D. xliv 4 fr 4 § 1). True, a condition of payment only after death would render a book-entry nugatory (*Vat.* 329). But Valerius' words (*eo consilio*) seem to point to no such condition having been expressed. As *judex* Aquilius would be bound by the issue, and if the issue alleged debt on book-entry one does not see how the judge was to go behind the simple entry and consider the ground or conditions of the gift, unless fraud was pleaded[1]. Valerius says nothing of this and regards the whole case and judgment as exceptional. But as he confuses book-entry and verbal obligation, by calling the entry *inanis stipulatio* one cannot trust to the accuracy of his report.

B. *Nexum*[2]. (See p. 70.)

1. There is no doubt of the original meaning of *nexum*. *Nectere* is *to tie* or *bind* (*nectere ligare significat* Fest. p. 165) and is used with an accusative both of the thing tied and of the band produced by tying. *Necte comam myrto, nectere colla lacertis, pars brachia nectit* (link their arms), are instances of the first; *Veneris, dic, vincula necto, Medo nectis catenas,* of the second. Both are found in Horace's *Apricos necte flores, necte meo Lamiae coronam.* The metaphorical use is seen in Cic. *N. D.* i 4 § 9 *Est enim admirabilis quaedam continuatio seriesque rerum ut alia ex alia nexa et omnes inter se aptae conligataeque videantur*; *T. D.* 8, 17 *Omnes virtutes inter se nexae et jugatae sunt, etc.*; D. xxvii 4 fr 3 § 8 *quod negotiis tutelae tempore gestis nexum probatur.* Hence *nexum* is a tie or band or link, and *nexus* (subst.) is 'tying' and differs from it no more than 'banding' or 'bandage' does from 'band.' Our English 'bond' used both of a legal obligation in writing and a prisoner's

[1] Cf. Pernice *Labeo* II² pp. 198, 239: Kübler *ZRG.* xxvii p. 85.

[2] The literature of the subject is given in Muirhead's *Hist. Rom. Law* p. 151. An essay by Mitteis has since appeared in *ZRG.* xxxv, principally directed against Huschke's publicist views.

chains illustrates the ambiguity which attends the Latin words in some passages.

Roman history and law furnish at least three uses of the term which deserve attention; the use in Livy's account of the early struggles at Rome arising from the harsh treatment of insolvent debtors which was ended by the *lex Poetelia* B.C. 326; the general use in Cicero and the early lawyers; the use in the Digest and Codes.

2. Livy recounts the public disturbances arising from insolvent debtors in four books of the early history; viz. first, ii 23—32, when the plebs seceded to the *Mons Sacer* and were brought back by Menenius Agrippa B.C. 495; next in vi 14—20 Manlius' sedition B.C. 385, and again *ib.* 27 B.C. 381, and *ib.* 34—36 B.C. 377—371; next in vii 19—21 B.C. 353, 352; last in viii 28 B.C. 326. In three of these books (ii, vii, viii) he uses the term *nexum* and *nexus*; in the vith book though describing similar scenes of distress he speaks of *judicati* and *addicti* but not of *nexi*. It is probable that the difference of language is simply an echo of the authority he had before him.

The principal passages from Livy are as follows:

B.C. 495. Livy ii 23 § 1 *Civitas secum ipsa discors...maxime propter nexos ob aes alienum. Fremebant se foris pro libertate et imperio dimicantes, domi a civibus captos et oppressos esse.* A centurion of advanced age in miserable plight burst into the forum and said (§ 5) *Sabino bello se militantem, quia propter populationes agri non fructu modo caruerit sed villa incensa fuerit, direpta omnia, pecora abacta, tributum iniquo suo tempore imperatum, aes alienum fecisse.* (§ 6) *Id cumulatum usuris primo se agro paterno avitoque exuisse, deinde fortunis aliis, postremo velut tabem pervenisse ad corpus; ductum se ab creditore non in servitium sed in ergastulum et carnificinam esse. Inde ostentare tergum foedum recentibus vestigiis verberum*[1]. *Ad haec visa auditaque clamor ingens oritur. Non iam foro se tumultus tenet sed passim totam urbem pervadit. Nexi vincti*

[1] ὅθεν διαλῦσαί μου τὸ χρέος οὐκ ἔχων ἀπήχθην δοῦλος ὑπὸ τοῦ δανειστοῦ σὺν τοῖς υἱοῖς δυσίν· ἐπιτάττοντος δὲ τοῦ δεσπότου τῶν οὐ ῥᾳδίων ἔργων τι ἀντειπὼν αὐτῷ πληγὰς ἔλαβον μάστιξι πάνυ πολλάς κ.τ.λ. Dionys. vi 26 p. 1099.

solutique[1] *se undique in publicum proripiunt, implorant Quiritium fidem.*

The Volscians making an attack on the Roman territory, the plebeians are reluctant to take arms until the consul Servilius (24 § 6) *edixit ne quis civem Romanum vinctum aut clausum teneret, quo minus ei nominis edendi apud consules potestas fieret, neu quis militis donec in castris esset bona possideret aut venderet, liberos nepotesve ejus moraretur*[2]. (§ 7) *Hoc proposito edicto et qui aderant nexi profiteri extemplo nomina, et undique ex tota urbe proripientium se ex privato, cum retinendi jus creditori non esset, concursus in forum ut sacramento dicerent fieri.*

(27 § 1) After defeating the Volsci, Sabini, and Aurunci, the Roman people *victor tot intra paucos dies bellis promissa consulis fidemque senatus expectabat, cum Appius et insita superbia animo et ut collegae vanam faceret fidem, quam asperrime poterat, jus de creditis pecuniis dicere. Deinceps et qui ante nexi fuerant creditoribus tradebantur et nectebantur alii.* (§ 8) *Desperato consulum senatusque auxilio, cum in ius duci debitorem vidissent, undique convolabant.*

Disturbances take place and eventually a dictator is appointed (30 § 4), viz. M. Valerius, who issues an edict similar to that of Servilius. An army is again formed, and the Volsci, Aequi and Sabini are defeated. Valerius then, (31 § 8) *omnium actionum in senatu primam habuit pro victore populo rettulitque quid de nexis fieri placeret.* The motion is rejected through the influence of the *feneratores* (§§ 7, 9), and a secession to the *Mons Sacer* takes place, which is ended by the institution of the tribunate and by the release both of insolvents from their debt, and of those from confinement who were detained either on account of failure to pay at the time agreed on or for judgment debts[3].

[1] *οἱ πρὸς τὰ χρέα δουλωθέντες κομῶντες ἁλύσεις ἔχοντες οἱ πλεῖστοι καὶ πέδας.* *ib.* p. 1100.

[2] *τὰς τούτων οἰκίας μηδένα ἐξεῖναι μήτε κατέχειν μήτε πωλεῖν μήτ' ἐνεχυράζειν μήτε γένος αὐτῶν ἀπάγειν πρὸς μηδὲν συμβόλαιον.* *ib.* 28 p. 1105—6.

[3] These terms were stated by Menenius, *τοὺς ὀφείλοντας χρέα καὶ μὴ δυναμένους διαλύσασθαι πάντας ἀφεῖσθαι τῶν ὀφλημάτων δικαιοῦμεν καὶ εἴ*

Time passes, the XII tables are enacted, and the next we hear in Livy of disturbances on account of debtors is connected with Manlius in B.C. 385.

Livy vi 11 § 8 *Manlius non contentus agrariis legibus quae materia semper tribunis plebi seditionum fuisset, fidem moliri coepit; acriores quippe aeris alieni stimulos esse qui non egestatem modo atque ignominiam minentur, sed nervo ac vinclis corpus liberum territent. Et erat aeris alieni magna vis, re damnosissima etiam divitibus, aedificando contracta.* (This was in consequence of the destruction of Rome by the Gauls.)

(14 § 3) *Centurionem, nobilem militaribus factis, iudicatum pecuniae cum duci vidisset, medio foro cum caterva sua accurrit et manum iniecit...* "*tum vero ego*" *inquit* "*nequicquam hac dextra Capitolium arcemque servaverim, si civem...in servitutem ac vincla duci videam.*" *Inde rem creditori palam populo solvit libraque et aere liberatum emittit.*

The centurion declared (§ 7) *se militantem, se restituentem eversos penates, multiplici iam sorte exsoluta, mergentibus semper sortem usuris*[1], *obrutum fenore esse.*

Manlius (§ 10) *Fundum in Veienti, caput patrimonii, subiecit praeconi,* "*ne quem vestrum*" *inquit* "*Quirites, donec quicquam in re mea supererit, iudicatum addictumve duci patiar.*"

Summoned before the dictator Cornelius Cossus, Manlius (according to Livy) addressed him (15 § 9) "*Offendit*" *inquit* "*te,*

τινων ἤδη τὰ σώματα ὑπερημέρων ὄντων ταῖς νομίμοις προθεσμίαις κατέχεται, καὶ ταῦτα ἐλεύθερα εἶναι κρίνομεν· ὅσοι τε δίκας ἁλόντες ἰδίας παρεδόθησαν τοῖς καταδικασαμένοις καὶ τούτους ἐλευθέρους εἶναι βουλόμεθα, καὶ τὰς καταγνώσεις αὐτῶν ἀκύρους ποιοῦμεν (Dionys. vi 83 p. 1231). See Schwegler *Röm. Gesch.* ii 259. Livy mentions only the appointment of tribunes.

[1] Moneylending is the same in modern times. The following three cases are from the evidence given before a Committee of the House of Commons in 1897; and the facts were admitted by the moneylender:

A. Loan £115; repaid £175; debt sued for £689.

B. Loan £400; promissory note £648 (Feb. 1888); repaid (by Sept. 1888) £175. 10*s.*; balance £472. 10*s.*; add default interest from Sept. 1888 to Jan. 1889, at ½*d.* per shilling per week; amount still due £787. 10*s.*

C. Loan £460; repaid £456; interest £280; default interest £213. 16*s.* 8*d.*

The moneylender said in defence that he was always open to a reasonable reduction (*Times* July 28 and 30, 1897).

A. Corneli, vosque patres conscripti, circumfusa turba lateri meo? Quin eam diducitis a me singuli vestris beneficiis, intercedendo, eximendo de nervo cives vestros, prohibendo iudicatos addictosque duci, ex eo quod affluit opibus vestris sustinendo necessitates aliorum? Sed quid ego vos de vestro impendatis hortor? Sortem reliquam[1] *ferte; de capite deducite quod usuris pernumeratum est; iam nihilo mea turba quam ullius conspectior erit.*

Manlius is imprisoned (*vinctus in carcere*), and eventually released by the senate. He again recommences (B.C. 384) similar proceedings. *Plebs, dum tam potentem habebat ducem, spem cepit fenoris expugnandi* 18 § 2. Two tribunes of the commons indict him. At the trial (20 § 6) *homines prope quadringentos produxisse dicitur, quibus sine fenore expensas pecunias tulisset, quorum bona venire, quos duci addictos prohibuisset.* Manlius is after trial put to death (§ 12).

In the year B.C. 380 there were no censors, two attempts at creating them having failed, the first from the death of one, the second from informality. A third attempt was prevented by scruples. (27 § 6) *Eam vero ludificationem plebis tribuni ferendam negabant: fugere senatum testes, tabulas publicas, census cuiusque, quia nolint conspici summam aeris alieni, quae indicatura sit demersam partem a parte civitatis, cum interim obaeratam plebem obiectari aliis atque aliis hostibus....*(§ 8) *Quod si sit animus plebi memor patrum libertatis, se nec addici quemquam civem Romanum ob creditam pecuniam passuros, neque dilectum haberi, donec inspecto aere alieno initaque ratione minuendi eius, sciat unusquisque quid sui, quid alieni sit, supersit sibi liberum corpus, an id quoque nervo debeatur. Merces seditionis proposita confestim seditionem excitavit. Nam et addicebantur multi et...novas legiones scribendas patres censuerant. Neque duci addictos tribuni sinebant, neque iuniores nomina dabant. Patribus minor in praesens cura creditae pecuniae iuris exsequendi quam dilectus erat.*

(31 § 4) *Condiciones impositae patribus, ne quis, quoad debellatum esset, tributum daret, aut ius de pecunia credita diceretur.*

B.C. 377. The debts of the commons are increased by

[1] So Madvig (*sortem aliquam* MSS.). 'Take the remainder of the principal sum, having first deducted what has been paid as interest.'

having to pay a tax for building a wall (32 § 1). Then (34 § 2) *Cum iam ex re nihil dari posset, fama et corpore iudicati atque addicti creditoribus satisfaciebant, poenaque in vicem fidei cesserat.*

(35 § 4) *Creati tribuni C. Licinius et L. Sextius promulgavere leges omnes adversus opes patriciorum et pro commodis plebis, unam de aere alieno, ut deducto eo de capite quod usuris pernumeratum esset, id quod superesset triennio aequis pensionibus persolveretur; alteram de modo agrorum, etc.*

B.C. 369. (36 § 12) Licinius and Sextius asked *an placeret fenore circumventam plebem, potius quam sorte creditum solvat, corpus in nervum ac supplicia dare, et gregatim quotidie de foro addictos duci et repleri vinctis nobiles domus, et ubicumqae patricius habitet, ibi carcerem privatum esse.*

Both the above-named laws were carried B.C. 368 (Liv. vi 39 § 2).

In the viith book of Livy the word *nexum* recurs.

In B.C. 357 (16 § 1) a law *de unciario fenore* is carried by the tribunes.

B.C. 354. (19 § 5) *Etsi unciario fenore facto levata usura erat, sorte ipsa obruebantur inopes nexumque inibant.*

A commission of five *mensarii* were appointed to relieve the general insolvency of the commons B.C. 352. (21 § 8) *Tarda nomina et impeditiora inertia debitorum quam facultatibus aut aerarium, mensis cum aere in foro positis, dissolvit, ut populo prius caveretur, aut aestimatio aequis rerum pretiis liberavit.*

In the next year (22 § 6) *Quia solutio aeris alieni multarum rerum mutaverat dominos, censum agi placuit.*

In B.C. 347 (27 § 3) *Semunciarium tantum ex unciario fenore factum et in pensiones aequas triennii, ita ut quarta praesens esset, solutio aeris alieni dispensata est; et sic quoque parte plebis affecta, fides tamen publica privatis difficultatibus potior ad curam senatui fuit. Levatae maxime res, quia tributo ac dilectu supersessum.*

In B.C. 342 (vii 42) a bill is stated to have been brought forward and perhaps carried by L. Genucius a tribune of the commons *ne fenerare liceret,* but Livy's authorities were not agreed.

In viii 28 we have the story of the abrogation of *nexum.*

B.C. 326 *Eo anno plebei Romanae velut aliud initium libertatis factum est quod necti desierunt; mutatum autem ius ob unius feneratoris simul libidinem, simul crudelitatem insignem. L. Papirius is fuit, cui se C. Publilius ob aes alienum paternum nexum dederat*[1]. Papirius attempts to seduce Publilius, but fails, and orders him to be stripped and flogged. The youth after being flogged bursts from the house and excites a tumult. *Victum eo die ob impotentem iniuriam unius ingens vinculum fidei, iussique consules ferre ad populum, ne quis, nisi qui noxam meruisset, donec poenam lueret, in compedibus aut in nervo teneretur; pecuniae creditae bona debitoris, non corpus, obnoxium esset. Ita nexi soluti, cautumque in posterum ne necterentur.*

In B.C. 216 (Liv. xxiii 14 § 3) we hear that the dictator M. Junius Pera *edixit, qui capitalem fraudem ausi quique pecuniae iudicati in vinculis essent, qui eorum apud se milites fierent, eos noxa pecuniaque sese exsolvi iussurum*, a step which Livius calls *ultimum prope desperatae rei publicae auxilium.*

3. It is difficult to imagine that the state of things described in Livy's vi^th book was really different from that described in the ii^nd, vii^th and viii^th. In all we find the disturbances arose from distress, and the distress from debt; the debt was caused by loans payable with interest, and the accumulation of unpaid interest exceeded the amount of the original loan. The debtors were led off into confinement; were put in chains or prison; were slaves in fact though not in the eye of the law, and were disgraced and often ill-used. The difference is that in the vith book they are spoken of as *iudicati addictique*, in the other books as *nexi*. The law described in the viii^th book deals distinctly with *nexi*, and says that the *nexi* were freed and that *necti* was abolished for the future.

There is nothing in Livy which suggests any other than a corporal meaning for *necti* and *nexus*. 'To be bound' and 'bondsman' appear to be the proper translation. *Nexi vincti*

[1] Cf. Val. Max. vi 1 § 9 *Cum propter domesticam ruinam et grave aes alienum P. Plotio nexum se dare* (*T. Veturius*) *adulescentulus admodum coactus esset.*

solutique are 'Bondsmen (or 'prisoners for debt') in chains and at large[1],' confinement being in fact carried out sometimes by shackles (*vinclis, compedibus*) or stocks (*nervo*), sometimes by mere imprisonment, or the *parole* or practical consent of the debtor. *Nexum inibant* and *nectebantur* are 'entered into bonds,' 'became bond' or 'bound,' *i.e.* passed from a state of personal liberty into one of bondage or practical slavery. *Nexum se dare alicui* is like *nuptum se dare* 'to give oneself to someone to bind.' If it were not for other writers than Livy, a metaphorical instead of a corporal meaning would not have been thought of with *necti, nexus, nexum.* Nor can we give any other meaning to the word in Columella i 3 § 12 where he speaks of the overpowerful *qui possident fines gentium, quos proculcandos pecudibus et vastandos feris derelinquunt, aut occupatos nexu civium et ergastulis tenent.* So Justin xxi 1 § 5 *Dionysius nexorum tria milia carcere dimittit; ib.* 2 § 2 *nec, uti pater, carcerem nexis sed caedibus civitatem replet.*

The XII tables were enacted between the events described by Livy in his ii^nd and vi^th books. Gellius (xx 1 § 41) describes the procedure ordained by them, applicable especially to debt on loan. It deals with admissions of loans and with judgments. *Duci* is applied both to taking into court and taking from court into confinement: the debtors are *vincti aut nervo aut compedibus*, and unless they come to terms with their creditors are kept by them *in vinculis* for sixty days; but during this time are produced in the *comitium* on three market days and notice of their debt is given. If at last they are not redeemed they become *addicti* and either *capite poenas dant aut trans Tiberim peregre venum eunt.* With the exception of this last clause the whole procedure agrees well with Livy's description; only that he applies *nexus* to the debtor, and does not make any difference between their state before and after final addiction. The law of the XII tables in this matter probably only confirmed existing practice.

4. One mention of *nexum* in the XII tables has come down

[1] Madvig *Verfassung* ii p. 193 n. Cf. Huschke *Nexum* p. 70; D. L 16 fr 216 *Verum est eum qui in carcere clusus est non videri neque vinctum neque in vinculis esse nisi corpori ejus vincula sint adhibita.*

to us. Festus, p. 177 sub v. *nuncupata* quotes: *cum nexum faciet mancipiumque, uti lingua nuncupassit, ita jus esto.* Here we are placed in a different sphere altogether from that of Livy. *Nexum* is evidently a contract of some sort, a bond perhaps, but a bond not of a physical but of an abstract nature. With this the use of the term in Cicero accords. It is (except in *RP.* ii § 9) used with or for *mancipium*, apparently to denote mancipatory conveyance of property or the legal guaranty of title thence arising. These are the passages.

Caecin. § 102 *Sulla ipse ita tulit de civitate* (*Volaterranorum*), *ut non sustulerit horum nexa atque hereditates.*

Mur. § 3 *In iis rebus repetendis quae mancipi sunt, is periculum praestare debet, qui se nexu obligavit.*

Har. Resp. § 14 *Multae sunt domus in hac urbe...jure optimo sed tamen jure privato, jure hereditario, jure auctoritatis, jure mancipi, jure nexi*[1].

Orat. i § 173 *In causis centumviralibus, usucapionum, tutelarum, gentilitatum, agnationum, adluvionum, circumfluvionum, nexorum, mancipiorum, parietum, luminum, stillicidiorum, testamentorum ruptorum aut ratorum, ceterarumque innumerabilium jura versentur.*

Ib. iii § 159 *Omnes translatis et alienis magis delectantur verbis, quam propriis et suis: nam si res suum nomen et vocabulum proprium non habet, ut pes in navi, ut nexum quod per libram agitur, ut in uxore divortium, necessitas cogit quod non habeas aliunde sumere.*

RP. i § 27 *Huic soli licet omnia, non Quiritium sed sapientium jure, pro suis vindicare, nec civili nexo sed communi lege naturae, quae vetat ullam rem esse cujusquam nisi ejus qui tractare et uti sciat.*

Ib. ii § 59 *Sunt propter unius libidinem omnia nexa civium liberata nectierque postea desitum*[2].

Parad. 5 § 35 *Non ita dicunt eos esse servos ut mancipia quae sunt dominorum facta nexo aut aliquo jure civili.*

[1] These three words, *auctoritatis mancipi nexi*, refer to the same thing (cf. Huschke *Nexum* notes 15 and 269), 'sale mancipation and assurance.'

[2] This is no doubt from the old annalist: cf. Liv. viii 28 above.

Top. § 28 where he gives as an instance of a definition which proceeds by enumeration of all the species of the genus: *Abalienatio est ejus rei quae mancipi est aut traditio alteri nexo aut in jure cessio inter quos ea jure civili fieri possunt.*

Ep. Fam. vii 30 writing to Curio (who had said in *ib.* 29 *sum* χρήσει μὲν *tuus,* κτήσει δὲ *Attici nostri; ergo fructus est tuus, mancipium illius*). *Quoniam proprium* (*Attici*) *te esse scribis mancipio et nexo, meum autem usu et fructu, contentus isto sum: id enim est cuiusque proprium quo quisque fruitur atque utitur.*

5. Cicero's contemporaries Varro and Aelius Gallus give us express information in two important passages.

Varro *LL.* vii 105[1] *Nexum Manilius scribit omne quod per libram et aes geritur, in quo sint mancipia. Mucius quae per aes et libram fiant ut obligentur, praeterquam mancipio detur. Hoc verius esse ipsum verbum ostendit, de quo quaeritur; nam id est, quod obligatur per libram neque suum fit, inde nexum dictum. Liber qui suas operas in servitutem pro pecunia quam debet dat dum solveret, nexus vocatur, ut ab aere obaeratus. Hoc C. Poetelio Libone Visolo*[2] *dictatore sublatum ne fieret, et omnes, qui bonam copiam jurarunt, ne essent nexi, dissoluti.*

Festus p. 165 *Nexum est, ut ait Gallus Aelius, quodcumque per aes et libram geritur, id quod necti dicitur, quo in genere sunt haec, testamenti factio, nexi datio, nexi liberatio*[3]. (For these last two I suspect the real expressions were *nexui* or *nexu* (dat.) or *nexum* (supine) *datio, nexu* (abl.) *liberatio.*)

Notwithstanding the bad state of the text it is clear from these passages that in its legal use *nectere* was *per aes et libram gerere,* Manilius and Gallus Aelius holding mancipation to be a species of *nexum,* and with this Cic. *Orat.* iii 159 agrees; Mucius Scaevola putting *nexum* and *mancipium* side by side as species of *per aes et libram gerere.* Varro supports Mucius' view by an etymology of his own. He does not notice the relationship of *nexus* to *nectere,* but supposes it to be a compound of *nec suus* (!) and thence argues that *mancipium* and *nexum* are opposed: by *mancipium* a thing becomes one's own,

[1] I have followed Mommsen's text as given in Bruns' *Fontes.*

[2] MS. has *C popillio vocare sillo.*

[3] MS. *nexi dando nexi liberando.*

by *nexum* a person becomes for a time a slave and not one's own.

6. Besides the other expressions quoted, Festus p. 165 has *nexum aes apud antiquos dicebatur pecunia quae per nexum obligatur*. I hesitate to assign any definite meaning to this in the absence of an example of its use. It appears not applicable to money paid over as a loan, for that does not remain 'bound,' but is intended to be spent. Nor does it better fit the money claimed in replacement, for that cannot be bound before it is produced. True, Varro (*LL.* v 102) says *qui pecuniam alligat stipulari et restipulari dicunt* as if to get a binding promise to pay money were to bind the money itself, but he gives no instance of its use from which we can see whether it is a phrase of law or of business or of light conversation, satire or comedy. Possibly it is a mere general phrase for a loan secured by the *nexum*. Nor do I think *pecunia nuncupata* 'money named in the declaration of the *nexum*' (Fest. p. 173, Varro *LL.* vi 60) throws much light on the matter, though M. Voigt (XII *Tab.* § 122) elevates it into the title of the action for recovery of a loan!

7. In the only passage in which Gaius speaks of *nexum* (and that passage very imperfectly read) he identifies *nexum* with mancipation. *Admonendi sumus...provincialis soli nexum non esse...solum Italicum mancipi est, provinciale nec mancipi est.* Frontinus (or Aggenus Urbicus) *Grom.* p. 36 Lachmann, has the like. *Stipendiarii* (*Afri*) *nexum non habent neque possidendo ab alio quaeri possunt: possidentur tamen a privatis, sed alia condicione: et veneunt, sed nec mancipatio eorum legitima potest esse.*

Of any money-contract by the use of the bronze and scales Gaius has nothing, but *nexi liberatio* is clearly given us in iii 173. *Est etiam alia species imaginariae solutionis per aes et libram. Quod et ipsum genus certis in causis receptum est; veluti si quid eo nomine debeat quod per aes et libram gestum sit sive quid ex judicati causa debeat.* The ceremony is like that of mancipation, but with a declaration appropriate to release.

8. In the Digest and Codes we find *nexus, nexum* used as equivalent to *obligatus, obligatio,* but especially of pledge.

Thus *Pactum, ut si quis summas propter tributiones praedii pignori nexi factas creditor solvisset, a debitore reciperet* (D. ii 14 fr 52 § 2 Ulp.); *partem nexu pignoris liberam consequatur* (x 2 fr 33 Pap.); *si quis ideo creditorem possessione arcuerit quia rem suam putabat vel sibi nexam vel certe non esse debitoris* (xliii 4 fr 1 § 4 Ulp.); *nexum non faciat praediorum nisi persona quae jure potest obligari* (Cod. Theod. ii 30 fr 2 = Cod. Just. viii 15 fr 8); *qui hypothecae seu pignori rem sibi nexam vendiderit* (Cod. Just. viii 27 fr 2); *sciens alienam rem velut propriam suo nexuit creditori* (*ib.* ix 34 fr 2). But the words are also used in other connexions, *e.g. nexu venditi liberare* (D. xii 6 fr 26 § 7 Jul.); *accepti latio est utriusque ab eodem nexu liberatio* (D. xlvi 4 fr 1 Modest.); *nexu sanguinis teneri* (Cod. Theod. xii 1 fr 122); *etc.*

9. From this review of the use of the words we find three special meanings; (1) physical confinement for debt, which meaning Livy appears to have always given to the words, though probably his early authorities were better informed; (2) mancipation, which was its ordinary meaning to Cicero and his contemporaries, Varro excepted; (3) legal tie or bond such as arises from pledge, used somewhat rhetorically in the lawyers. All these meanings may be said to be combined in the *nexum* which we are seeking. It was a contract, with similar ceremony to that of mancipation, and constantly leading to imprisonment for debt. According to Varro it was a pledge or surrender of a man's personal services until he found means to pay his debt.

It has been seen that Livy speaks of two classes of prisoners, *nexi* and *judicati*, and that the language used of their fate is similar to that of Gellius in describing execution following a judgment debt. Manlius is said (in Liv. vi 14 quoted above) to have seen a judgment debtor (*judicatum pecuniae*) being led off by his creditor to his private prison: he at once takes the position of *vindex* and openly pays the debt to the creditor. On doing this he doubtless acquired an analogous right to that of a *sponsor* (Gai. iv 22, above p. 36), but, instead of exacting repayment, he released him with the bronze and balance. This form of release was applicable not only to discharge judgment debts but also any contract made by the bronze and balance; in other words to discharge

20—2

a *nexum*. Dionysius of Halicarnassus (vi 83 quoted above) speaks of two classes of unfortunates, those whose persons were detained from having made default in the legal times of payment, and those who had lost their private suits and had been given up to their opponents. Gaius (iv 22) mentions a practice in many old laws of making the penalty for breach to be 'arrest as for a judgment debt' (*manus injectionem pro judicato*). Whether these laws were as old as the events in Livy we do not know, but the practice was no doubt old. It is hardly therefore an assumption to say that *nexum* was a contract, especially applied to the loan of money, by which the borrower bound himself, in default of payment at the agreed time or times of a sum covering principal and interest, to accept the position of a judgment debtor[1], possibly in some form of words, accompanying the ceremony of bronze and balance, like *pro judicato damnas ero* (cf. Gai. iii 175). The *nexum* was thus analogous to a warrant of attorney (or *cognovit actionem*) in English law given by a debtor confessing a cause of action[2] and authorising judgment to be entered up against him without further proceeding. Such warrants, says Blackstone (iii 397 ed. Kerr), constitute a very usual form of security for money. (Since 1837 they have been subjected to severe regulation.)

10. Business done by means of the bronze and scales (*quod per libram et aes geritur*) contained in old times two chief species, *mancipium* and *nexum*. Both consisted originally in handing over bronze by weight, as price or as loan, accompanied by some declaration of the purpose and conditions of the transaction. The effect varies with the nature of the business. A purchaser parts with his money, but in return the seller hands over the thing with a warranty of title. A lender parts with his money, and in return the borrower binds himself to repay, or in default to submit his services without more ado to his creditor's will. When money came to pass by count (perhaps dating from the introduction of silver coinage B.C. 269), the balance remained in use as a symbol of

[1] Cf. Karlowa *RG.* ii 549, 559.

[2] Muirhead takes *aeris confessi* in the XII tables to refer to nexal debtors (*Hist. Rom. Law* pp. 157, 205).

the binding nature of the contract[1]. For valid sale the price had still to be definitely ascertained—a certain count of coins, *i.e.* of *materia forma publica percussa* (D. xviii 1 fr 1 pr). So a loan of actual money (which was entitled to a summary remedy for repayment) is called, in the *lex Rubria* 22, *pecunia certa credita signata forma p*(*ublica*) *p*(*opuli*) *R*(*omani*). Sale and loan would be the principal business transactions in a young community: in sale both seller and purchaser can secure themselves by not parting from the money or the thing, until they have the other: but want of title is possible; and therefore it was understood that double the value had to be paid in case of eviction of a thing sold. In a cash loan the lender risks the loss of his money, for he gets nothing immediately in return except a promise to pay: it is natural and inevitable that the lender should be empowered to put strong pressure on the borrower to induce him to keep his bargain. An impecunious debtor may first sell his stock or house or land: after that he has only his services or those of his family to offer: the creditor naturally insisted on having a ready means of compelling the sale or transfer of his property or the use of his or his family's labour, by keeping him in chains or prison. This was Livy's *ingens vinculum fidei* (viii 28). Hence Varro's description of a *nexus* as 'one who 'gives his services *in servitutem* (*i.e.* like a slave[2]) in return for 'money which he owes,' was in terms a true description of the result, though perhaps not so expressed in the original contract. Whether any calculation was made of the value of the services to set against the interest or capital of the debt is a question which, I imagine, must be answered in the negative. The debtor once in the control of his creditor was not in a position to make a bargain or to protect himself from harsh or cruel treatment. Only in so late a time as Papinian's do we hear of something analogous in the statement that a free person (*filius familias*), who has been given up for

1 Compare in England the continued use of seals (now commonly represented by wafers bearing no mark of identity) attached to documents which thereby have superior efficacy as deeds over writings bearing only the parties' signatures.

2 Hence Dionysius xvi 5 (fragm.) calls them οἱ δουλωθέντες.

a noxal offence, will be restored to liberty by the praetor, if the injured party has received through him full compensation (*Collat.* ii 2). In theory the *nexus* did not become a slave, for he was capable of serving in the army (Liv. ii 24); and see Bk VI chap. XV A (p. 428).

11. The *lex Poetelia* according to Livy had the following provisions:

(1) All *nexi* were freed, *i.e.* from chains. Varro however qualifies this by saying that all *nexi* were freed, who declared on oath that they had sufficient means.

(2) For the future no one was to be kept in fetters or stocks, except criminals till they had made amends. (Prison is not abolished.)

(3) A debtor's property and not his person was to be liable to be taken for non-payment of a money loan (*i.e.* when there has not been a proper judgment?).

(4) The *nexum* (*i.e.* any agreement with the creditor beforehand to accept treatment as a judgment debtor) was abolished.

Livy's statement is not precise, and it is to me doubtful in what sense he understood the words which he found in the old annalists *cautum ne necterentur*, for which Cicero gives us *nectier postea desitum.* But in the sense which I believe the law really had, we have a parallel in the abolition by Constantine of the forfeiture-clause (*lex commissoria*) in agreements for fiduciary pledge. (See p. 100.)

The restriction mentioned by Varro implies the existence of *nexi* who yet had property. Such may have been unable to realize their property in time to prevent legal process, or may have been determined to sacrifice themselves in order to preserve the family estate. The relief of debtors by a kind of landbank is mentioned in Liv. vii 21 (quoted above); and was resorted to also by Caesar (*Bell. Civ.* iii 1). Perhaps something of this kind may have been meant by the third provision. The bankruptcy law of the later republic was scarcely so early as 326 B.C.: and execution on the person, though doubtless in some degree modified, was certainly not abolished, as we may see from Liv. xxiii 14 § 3 (above), Sall. *Cat.* 33 and other writers. But there is no trace of the *nexum* with its onerous conditions in subsequent times.

BOOK VI.

JUDICIAL ADMINISTRATION AND PROCEDURE.

CHAPTER I.

COURTS.

A. Praetor.

The principal organ of justice at Rome was the Praetor. The first praetor was created in 367 B.C. *qui jus in urbe diceret* (Liv. vi 42). He was distinguished as *praetor urbanus*, on another being created cir. 242 B.C. *qui inter peregrinos jus dicet* (*Lex repet.* 12, Bruns no. 10), or as described later *qui inter civis et peregrinos jus dicet* (*Ed. Venafr.* Bruns no. 73 *ad fin.*), sometimes *praetor peregrinus* (Pompon. D. i 2 fr 2 § 28; Gai. i 6). The number of praetors was afterwards increased to six, and by Sulla to eight, chiefly for criminal jurisdiction; by the Emperors to sixteen or eighteen. Claudius created two praetors for *fidei commissa*; M. Aurelius, one for guardianships (Pompon. D. i 2 fr 2 § 32). But so far as private law was concerned, the two early praetorships continued to have the chief place, and the praetor (in the singular number) is usually spoken of in the law-books without distinction (cf. Mommsen *St.R.* ii 185 sq.).

The praetor had the arrangement of all trials of private suits and the formal appointment of judges for them. To him was committed a large oversight of guardians and the appointment of such in default of legal acting guardians. Of his edict, and the quasi-legislative functions which he thereby exercised, I have spoken above in the Introduction (vol. I p. 10 foll.). Many important private acts required his presence and authority, *e.g.* adoption, manumission, and in some cases the conveyance of property and especially of incorporal rights.

In the provinces the *proconsul* or *praeses* had as full authority as the praetor in Rome (D. i 16 fr 7 § 2; 18 fr 4).

For public audience in republican times the praetor sat in a curule chair (*sella curulis*) on the front of a raised platform (*pro tribunali*) in the forum or comitium; afterwards in one of the pillared halls (*basilica*) in or near the forum. He was often surrounded by a number of advisers (*consilium*) and clerks. This was for full hearing of a matter (*causae cognitio*), which was followed by his decree or by sanction of an issue for trial. Interlocutory questions, ordinary orders and the sanction of private acts could be decided or made without form, even as he was walking in the streets or at the baths. The former acts are done *pro tribunali*, the latter *de plano* (cf. D. xxxvii 1 fr 3 § 8; xxxviii 15 fr 2 § 1; Gai. i 20). Compare the English distinction between 'in court,' and 'in chambers.'

The sanction of private acts was so much a matter of course, that a praetor (or consul or governor) could emancipate his sons or give them in adoption or manumit slaves *apud se*, *i.e.* without requiring the presence or sanction of any other magistrate. If he was himself a *filius familias*, he could be adopted or emancipated *apud se* (D. i 7 fr 3; tit. 14 fr 1, 2; tit. 16 fr 2), and the like is true of such borough magistrates as have *legis actio*, *i.e.* are competent to give authority to others' acts of this kind (Paul ii 25 § 4; D. i 7 fr 4). A praetor could manumit slaves before a consul as a higher authority, but he could not do so before a praetor, who has no higher *imperium* than he has himself (D. xl 1 fr 14; tit. 2 fr 18 § 1).

B. Consuls.

The Consuls were superior to the Praetors in imperial as well as in republican times, but their jurisdiction was chiefly in trusts (Gai. ii 278, cf. D. xxxv 1 fr 50) and in sanctioning manumissions, and dealing with questions of *status* (D. i 10; xl 12 fr 27 pr; 14 fr 4; 15 fr 1 § 4, *etc.*). Claudius gave them the right of appointing guardians, which M. Aurelius transferred to the Guardianship Praetor first appointed by him (Suet. *Claud.* 23: Hist. Aug. *Mar. Aurel.* 10). Cf. Mommsen

St.R. ii pp. 98, 99. Pliny (*Paneg.* 77) speaks of consuls *jus dicentes*, and Gellius (xii 13 § 1) of their appointing *judices*.

C. The *CENTUMVIRI*[1] or 'Court of the Hundred men' is said by Festus (p. 54) to have been composed of three from each of the 35 tribes of Rome, and called 'the Hundred' in round numbers (Varr. *RR.* ii 1 26). This would make its establishment later than 241 B.C. (Mommsen *St.R.* ii p. 220). A suit did not come before them until after the formal procedure of the *legis actio sacramento* had been gone through before the city or foreign praetor (Gai. iv 31). The Court is mentioned by Cicero in connexion with the case of *Curius v. Coponium* (*Or.* i 39 § 180, *etc.*), and also in *Agr.* ii 17 § 44 as a Court for suits in matters of inheritance. He gives a list of the classes of suits within its jurisdiction (*causae centumvirales*) but adds, in rhetorical fashion, that there were innumerable others (*Or.* i 37 § 173)[2]. What he names are all connected with the old civil law: rights of usucapion, of guardianship, clanship, and agnatic relation; the breaking and confirmation of wills, bonds and handtakes (*nexa, mancipia*)[3], urban servitudes, alluvial acquisitions. In Vespasian's time the number of cases before this Court was so great as to require special assistance (Suet. *Vesp.* 10). Tacitus speaks of

[1] There is an elaborate article on the *centumviri* by Wlassak in Pauly's *Realencycl.* vol. iii new edit.

[2] Cicero is speaking of advocates who are ignorant of law and says: *Volitare in foro, haerere in jure ac praetorum tribunalibus, judicia privata magnarum rerum obire, in quibus saepe non de facto sed de aequitate ac jure certetur, jactare se in causis centumviralibus, in quibus usucapionum tutelarum gentilitatum agnationum adluvionum circumluvionum nexorum mancipiorum parietum luminum stillicidiorum testamentorum ruptorum aut ratorum ceterarumque rerum innumerabilium jura versentur, quom omnino quid suum, quid alienum, quare denique civis aut peregrinus, servus aut liber quispiam sit ignoret, insignis est impudentiae.* Bethmann-Hollweg (*ZGR.* v 369 sq.) brings all these centumviral cases under three heads; actions for property, predial servitudes, and inheritance, referring *nexorum* to the first and *tutela* to the last head. Wlassak seems to approve (*PG.* i 87). In fact they were mainly concerned, at least originally, with vindications (cf. Keller *CP.* p. 27).

[3] See essay on *Nexum*, esp. p. 308.

their having the most important cases (*Dial.* 38). Pliny the younger frequently pleaded before them, though he complains of the Court's being sometimes occupied with trifling cases and stripling pleaders (*Ep.* ii 14). So far as he tells the nature of his cases, all related to inheritance, especially to the *querela inofficiosi testamenti*: and such were perhaps in practice at that time its principal occupation. But we do not know what were the limits of their competence in imperial times, or on what principle suits to be sent before them were selected. Their jurisdiction was concurrent with that of a single judge (Quint. v 10 § 115; cf. Wlassak *Pr. G.* i p. 206 foll.).

The 'Hundred men' appear to have been divided into four sections (*consilia, hastae*), as we hear of *duplex judicium* (Quint. *Inst.* xi 1 78), and *quadruplex*, consisting in one case of 180 judges (Plin. *Ep.* iv 24; vi 33. See also D. xxxi fr 76). A spear was put up in the Court (Gai. iv 16; Quint. v 2 § 1; Mart. vii 63, 7, *etc.*; cf. p. 341). They were presided over by ex-quaestors until Augustus transferred this duty to the *decemviri* (Suet. *Aug.* 36). Pliny (*Ep.* v 9 (21) § 5) speaks of the praetor presiding over them, apparently in the sense not of personal presence but of control of their proceedings.

D. The *DECEMVIRI stlitibus judicandis* were perhaps as old as 449 B.C. (Liv. iii 55) or older, but appear in inscriptions from 139 B.C.[1] Cicero speaks of their deciding a case where a woman of Arretium claimed freedom, and Cicero was advocate (*Caecin.* 33 § 97).

Augustus, as above stated, made them presidents of the *Centumviri*. Pomponius mistook this for the cause of their creation (*qui hastae praeessent*, D. i 2 fr 2 § 29).

E. *RECUPERATORES.*

1. 'Recoverers' are said to have been first appointed in accordance with arrangements made between the Roman people and foreign kings and communities for the restoration and recovery of property and for carrying on private suits between

[1] Mommsen *St.R.* ii 590. Wlassak denies any connexion of the older with the later body (*Pr. G.* i 144 foll.).

them (Fest. p. 274). Three recoverers were appointed by Scipio (210 B.C.) to decide a dispute for a prize of valour between two claimants belonging to one of the legions and the naval allies (Liv. xxvi 48 § 9). And recoverers, five in each case, were named to try charges made by Spaniards against some Roman magistrates, B.C. 171 (Liv. xliii 2 § 3). Plautus in two plays (cir. 192—189 B.C.) speaks of recoverers in suits between foreigners (*Rud.* 1282, on a question of freedom; *Bac.* 270, on a debt). In Cicero's third speech against Verres 'recoverers' are frequently mentioned as appointed by the praetor of Sicily to decide suits of the Sicilian farmers against the tax-farmers (*publicani*, 11 § 28; 14 § 35; 22 § 55; 28 § 68, *etc.*). In Cic. *in Caecil.* 17 § 56 they decide a claim of a Lilybaean woman for some slaves who had been carried off for a band of music in the fleet. We hear also of recoverers in a suit between two citizens of Temnus in Asia (*Flac.* 20 § 47); and Cicero's speech for Tullius on a trial for armed wrong, and that for Caecina on the interdict for armed dispossession were both made before recoverers. Caecina was a Volaterran and his citizenship was one of the points in dispute: Tullius was apparently from *Thurii* (*Tull.* 6 § 14) and his opponent from Asia (*ib.* § 19). Recoverers act on a charge of extortion (*repetundarum*) in Tac. *A.* i 74; and in fiscal cases (Suet. *Ner.* 17); and in a trial whether slave or freeborn (*ib. Vesp.* 3; cf. *Dom.* 8; Cic. *Flac.* 17 § 40).

Gaius speaks of *recuperatores* to try a plaint by patron on account of his being summoned into Court by his freedman (iv 46); of either *judex* or *recuperatores* being used in interdict issues (iv 141); of *recuperatores* being sometimes employed to try at once (*protinus*) a breach of *vadimonium* (iv 185). They were according to Labeo (Gell. xx 1 § 13) promised by the praetor for estimating insults (*injuriis aestimandis*). And so in Cic. *Inv.* ii 20 § 60. They appear as alternative with *judices* in *lex Agrar.* 35 (Bruns no. 11); *lex Rubr.* 21; *lex Anton.* ii 1; *Tab. Bant.* 2; *Frag. Atest.* 15.

2. We do not know the number of recoverers usually appointed, probably three (so in a Sicilian case, Cic. *Verr.* iii 12 § 30; 21 § 54; but cf. §§ 28, 69; and apparently in Asia, Cic. *Flac.* 17 § 40; three or five in Livy *l. c.*; in *lex Agrar.* the text is

uncertain), nor the mode of selection: a power of challenge is given to each party in the *Ed. Venafr.* (Bruns no. 73; cf. *lex Agrar.* 37, *ib.* no. 11) and in Verres' edict for suits against publicans in Sicily (*Verr.* iii 11 § 28). The proceedings appear to have been quicker than with an ordinary judge (Cic. *Tull.* 5 § 10; cf. § 41; Gai. iv 185; Plin. *Ep.* iii 20 § 9); and the municipal charter of Ossuna (*lex Urson.* 95) gives special instructions for getting them to sit and come to a decision at latest within 20 days from their appointment. On the qualifying age (24?) see a papyrus fragment *ZRG.* xxxv 170.

3. In directing a trial before recoverers the praetor was acting not on the old civil jurisdiction, but on his executive power (*imperium*, Gai. iv 105). This accords with the predominant character of Recoverers as being employed where a foreigner is a party. It is generally held that they were also eventually appointed to decide cases between Roman citizens[1]. With the meagre information which we have about the institution in general or the cases in which recoverers are said to have been appointed, it is impossible to be confident. But in no single case is it clear that the suit was between two private Roman citizens. Foreigners, tax-farmers, a municipal or other public authority appear in several cases; where, as in statutes, there is an alternative with *judices*, the case of foreigners may have been in view; where we know only of the subject-matter of the suit, the same remark applies[2]; and questions of freedom imply the appearance or possibility of non-citizenship. *Recuperatores* is the name given to Roman citizens forming the Court in proceedings in the provinces on the manumission of slaves under the *lex Aelia Sentia* (Gai. i 20; Ulp. i 13 *a*); and the same term is used in the general sense of 'Judges' by (the African) Apuleius (*de mundo* cap. 35). The facts seem to point

[1] Wlassak (*Röm. Pr. Gesetz* ii 74) relies on Cicero's speeches *pro Tullio* and *pro Caecina* (so also Madvig *Verf.* ii 256; cf. Soll *Recuperatio* pp. 412 sqq.) and on Gai. iv 105, 109 to prove this. The fragmentary nature of *pro Tullio* makes it difficult to assert anything: Caecina's citizenship (as I have said) is a question in his case. Gaius seems to me to prove nothing, but rather to suggest the contrary to what Wlassak supposes. (I take *interveniente, etc.* in Gaius as properly qualifying only *quae sub uno judice acc.*)

[2] *E.g.* in Gai. iv 46 Latin freedmen may be in contemplation.

to *recuperatores* being employed only when foreigners (*i.e.* non-Romans, Gai. i 79) were concerned, or where it was anticipated they might be concerned.

F. *Arbiter.*

The great mass of cases after preparation by the praetor were directed by him to be tried by a single judge, who is usually called *judex*, but sometimes *arbiter*. The XII tables appear to have spoken of *judex arbiterve* more than once (Gell. xx 1 § 7; Fest. *s. v. reus*, p. 273). The same occurs in the notes of Probus referring to *legis actiones*, in the *lex Julia repetundarum* (D. xlviii 11 fr 7 pr); and in the *fragm. Atest.* (Bruns no. 103) we have *judicis arbitri recuperatorum datio addictio.* Cicero mocks at the lawyers for not having made up their minds whether to speak of a *judex* or *arbiter* (*Mur.* 12 § 27); and both he and they speak of an *arbiter* as a *judex* (*Off.* iii 16 § 66; cf. 17 § 70; Gai. iv 163; Paul i 18). It is clear that *judex* was the more general term, and that *arbiter* was a special kind of *judex*. In Plautus *arbiter* is used both in the early sense of a witness (*Capt.* 211; *Poen.* 663, *etc.*; so also Cic. *Off.* iii 31 § 112; Liv. vii 5 § 4, both doubtless from some early historian) and of a judge formal or friendly; *e.g. Rud.* 1004 *In istunc hodie non feres, nisi das sequestrum aut arbitrum, quoius haec res arbitratu fiat; etc.*

Cicero (in *Rosc. Com.* 4 §§ 10—13, quoted below, p. 361) contrasts a legal *arbiter* with a *judex* at some length. With a *judex* you are bound to your exact claim; you get all or nothing: with an *arbiter* you have a larger consideration of the matter and obtain what is fairer (*aequius melius*) on the whole[1]. In

[1] So Seneca *Benef.* iii 7 § 5 *Ideo melior videtur condicio causae bonae si ad judicem quam si ad arbitrum mittitur, quia illum formula includit et certos quos non excedat terminos ponit, hujus libera et nullis adstricta vinculis religio, et detrahere aliquid potest et adicere et sententiam suam, non prout lex aut justitia suadet, sed prout humanitas vel misericordia impulit, regere.* This may refer to arbitration by agreement: the fact is, an *arbiter*, whether sitting in a legal suit, or appointed by the praetor for subordinate work, or acting by agreement of the parties, was always conceived to have a duty of coming to a fair common-sense decision irrespective of particular wording or technical rules.

the same way Gaius (iv 163) describes the difference in a defendant's position in interdict procedure, if he demands an *arbiter* and does not let the matter go before a *judex*. And so in other cases where the object of a suit is not the payment of a definite sum of money or the performance of a defined duty, but the judicial settlement of a complicated matter, the judge was called *arbiter*. Thus suits for the division of an inheritance among coheirs or of property common to two or more owners, or the regulation of the boundaries of country estates, or plaints for protection against the flow of rainwater are submitted to an *arbiter* (D. x 1 fr 7; 2 fr 43; 3 fr 26; xxxix 3 fr 23 § 2; fr 24 pr; Cic. *Top.* 10 § 43). For the regulation of boundaries the XII tables required three *arbitri*, who were reduced to one by the *lex Mamilia* (Cic. *Leg.* i 21 § 55). Three *arbitri* are also mentioned in another matter in Fest. *s.v. vindiciae* (quoted below, p. 344 n. 1).

Cicero gives the name of *arbitria* to the whole class of *bonae fidei* obligations, partnership, mandate, fiduciary relation (*i.e.* deposit, pledge), purchase and sale, letting and hiring as well as to those of guardianship and dowry (*rei uxoriae*); *i.e.* wherever in fact the suit turned on conduct required by good faith and on due allowance being made for defendant's claims (*Off.* iii 17 § 70). In the Digest we occasionally find the term *arbiter* applied in such cases (*e.g.* xvii 2 fr 38 pr, 76; xxiii 4 fr 1 § 1; xlvi 3 fr 48; xlix 1 fr 28 § 2). It is used of the judge in the actions *de eo quod certo loco dari oportet* and *quod metus causa gestum est* which are the only actions to which the term *arbitraria* is applied in the Digest[1] (cf. p. 86). It is also used when special points require settlement or special inquiries have to be made; *e.g.* into the solvency of a surety (D. ii 8 fr 9; xlix 2 fr 2); the proper height for a new building (viii 2 fr 11), or breadth for a road (*ib.* 3 fr 13); the distribution of a slave's stock-in-trade among his creditors (xiv 4 fr 7 § 1); the accounts of a steward (xxxv 1 fr 50); the reckoning of the Falcidian fourth (xxxv 3 fr 1 § 6); or where perishable goods have to be sold, while rights are undetermined (xlii 5 fr 27); or damages have to be assessed

[1] But in D. xxii 1 fr 3 § 1 a general expression is used: *In his quoque judiciis quae non sunt arbitraria nec bonae fidei, etc.*

(cf. Probus who gives among other abbreviations A L A *arbitrium liti aestimandae*), etc.

G. *Arbiter* (*ex compromisso sumptus*)[1] was also the name usually given to a judge appointed merely by agreement of the parties without any authoritative jurisdiction[2]. The award of such an arbiter had of itself no binding force, and was no bar to a subsequent trial and legal decision of the case. To make it effective, the agreement (*compromissum*) to refer the matter or matters to such a voluntary arbitrator was confirmed by a stipulation, and usually provided a penalty (*poena, pecunia compromissa*) in case of disobedience to the decision (*si arbitri sententiae non stetur*). The penalty might be a fixed sum or *quanti ea res erit*. If no penalty was specified, an action could be brought on the stipulation for the amount of the party's interest in the due execution of the award. The agreement often contained a clause requiring the parties to act in good faith (*doli clausula*): in the absence of such clause, an action *de dolo* or a plea would be available to meet chicanery.

The arbitrator had no power beyond what was given by the agreement, which therefore had to be strictly followed, or the decision was null. If a time is named for the decision, the

[1] Cf. Cic. *Rosc. Com.* 4 § 12 *Quaero quid ita de hac pecunia compromissum feceris, arbitrum sumpseris* (see below in Essay on this speech); *Verr.* ii 27 § 66; *Flac.* 21 § 50 *Q. Naso judex sumitur; qui cum sententiam secundum Plotium se dicturum ostenderet, ab eo judice abiit* (*Hermippus*), *et quod judicium lege non erat, causam totam reliquit*, which possibly refers to such a non-judicial *arbiter*, though called *judex*. Mommsen *ZRG.* xxv 281 understands it of a trial *imperio continens* and consequently expiring with the praetor's term of office (Gai. iv 105); Hermippus lets this occur: cf. *litem mori patietur* D. xlii 8 fr 3 § 1.

[2] To arbitrations of this kind reference appears to be made in Cic. *Caecin.* 2 § 6 *Omnia judicia aut distrahendarum controversiarum aut puniendorum maleficiorum causa reperta sunt, quorum alterum levius est propterea quod...disceptatore domestico dijudicatur, alterum non honorariam operam amici sed severitatem judicis ac vim requirit. Honorariam* means 'complimentary' 'not obligatory,' cf. Cic. *Tusc. D.* 41 § 120 where Carneades is spoken of as intervening between Stoics and Peripatetics *tamquam arbiter honorarius*: so *Fat.* 41 § 120. Cf. Wlassak in Pauly *Encycl.* s.v. *arbiter*, new edit. In Cic. *Rosc. Com.* 5 § 15 *honoraria* appears to refer to appointments by the praetor. Cf. Voigt *Jus Nat.* iv p. 454.

arbiter cannot extend it (*diem proferre*). He cannot be bound down beforehand to any particular decision, he must be free to decide as he thinks right. The award must embrace and definitely decide all the questions submitted, and define any security which has to be given. He cannot delegate his power, unless so provided by the agreement. The award once given cannot be changed. If it be duly made, the parties are bound by it whether fair or unfair[1], so far at least as it contains nothing *inhonestum*. There is no appeal, unless the plea of *doli mali* allowed by Antoninus may practically give such protection. Any failure to execute or abide by the award makes the penalty due. The arbitrator cannot forbid its enforcement. Where there are two (or more) persons jointly and severally bound, or two bank partners or even two sureties who are partners, and an award forbids one to sue or be sued, suit by, or against, the other brings the penalty clause into force. So also if a party's heir sue, when the party was forbidden.

If three arbitrators are appointed, a majority can decide. If two are appointed and do not agree, the praetor will compel them to choose a third. All must be present at the award as well as the parties. Even ill-health or public business preventing a party's appearance is no bar to the penalty becoming due, but the praetor in such a case will bar the action to enforce it.

A slave could not be an *arbiter* or party to an arbitration, but any man of the age of 20 or upwards (this was in conformity with the rule in *lex Julia* for judges), was eligible as *arbiter*. If he has once accepted the appointment (*si arbitrium receperit*) duly made, the praetor will compel him to make an award, unless for such good cause as his own ill-health, insolvency of one of the litigants, defamation or contumelious treatment by them, *etc.* Compulsion would be effected by a fine or perhaps *pignoris capio*.

[1] Cf. D. xvii 2 fr 76 *Arbitrorum genera sunt duo, unum ejusmodi ut sive aequum sit sive iniquum, parere debeamus (quod observatur, cum ex compromisso ad arbitrum itum est); alterum ejusmodi ut ad boni viri arbitrium redigi debeat, etsi nominatim persona sit comprehensa cujus arbitratu fiat*: *i.e.* when any matter is referred to someone to decide, without a formal agreement and stipulation for penalty.

An end is put to an arbitration, not only by the award but by the death of a party (unless his heir was named in the agreement) or of the arbitrator; by a formal release; by a bargain or settlement (*transactio*); or by the case being brought into Court. This last would not prevent the penalty being due.

An arbitration on a criminal matter is invalid, nor will an arbitrator be compelled to give an award on a question of freedom, or *status* of freeborn or freedman, or where there is a popular action (D. iv 8 esp. fr 2, 7, 13 § 2, 15, 17 § 6—fr 19, 27—31, 32 §§ 6—8, 14, 16, 21; fr 41; Cod. ii 55 fr 1; Paul v 5 *a* § 1 who applies the term *judex*).

H. *Judex.*

Judices were according to Polybius (vi 17) taken in most of the important cases from the list of Senators, who however were disabled for this function[1] by C. Gracchus. He put *equites* in their place (*lex Sempronia* B.C. 122: Vell. ii 6; Cic. *Verr.* i 13 § 38)[2]. In Cicero's speech *pro Rosc. Com.* 14 § 42 mention is made of a private suit in which an *eques* acted as *judex*, but the date of the suit is uncertain (see p. 502). In 81 B.C. Sulla as dictator restored the senate to their old position (cf. Cic. *Verr.* iii 41 § 96). In 70 B.C. L. Aurelius Cotta established a separate list from which *judices* were to be taken, composed of three *decuriae*, one of senators, one of *equites* and one of *tribuni aerarii* (Ascon. *in Corn.* p. 78 Bait., *in Pison.* p. 16; Cic. *Att.* i 16 § 4; *etc.*), who appear to have been a class of plebeians of position and property, ranking next to, or even sometimes with, the *equites* (Cic. *Cat.* iv 7 § 15; *Flac.* 2 § 4 with schol. Bob. *ad loc. etc.*[3]). It is supposed that equal numbers were taken from all three classes[4]. The list (*album judicum*) was revised by the

[1] See Madvig *Verfassung* ii pp. 218 sqq.; Mommsen *St.R.* iii 527 sqq.

[2] A consular Fimbria is spoken of as a *judex* in a case told to Cicero as a boy (Cic. *Off.* iii 19 § 77). Fimbria was consul in 104 B.C. but he may not have been a senator at the time of the trial, and he may have been privately appointed.

[3] See Madvig *Verfassung* i 182 sqq.; Mommsen *St.R.* iii p. 192.

[4] Cf. Sen. *Ben.* iii 7 § 7 *De quibusdam et imperitus judex demittere tabellam potest:...ubi vero id de quo sola sapientia decernit in controversiam*

praetors, probably every year (Cic. *Clu.* 43 § 121). Julius Caesar removed the *tribuni aerarii* (Suet. *Jul.* 41), but according to the same writer Augustus found four *decuriae* and added another for cases of small importance (*Aug.* 32), of which the elder Pliny (xxxiii § 30) gives a confused account. Caligula added a fifth *decuria* in order to prevent the judges being overworked (*Calig.* 16). The normal number in each *decuria* was 1000 (Plin. l. c.). It is not clear whether the choice of a *judex* in civil matters was limited to the *album*; but for *legitima judicia* the judge must be a Roman citizen. For some suits, even in Rome, foreigners were appointed, presumably only in suits where foreigners were parties (Gai. iv 105)[1].

The qualifying age was reduced by Augustus from 35, which had been the minimum, to 30 (Suet. *Aug.* 32; see Mommsen *St.R.* iii pp. 534, 537), but according to D. iv 8 fr 41 to the age of 20; and in practice the age of 18 appears to have been held sufficient (D. xlii 1 fr 57). Mutes, deaf, madmen and *impuberes* were disqualified. So also were women, and of course slaves. The position of judge being a public office, a *filius familias* is no less capable than a *paterfamilias*, and in a private suit a father may be judge in his son's case, and a son in his father's (D. v 1 fr 12, 77, 78).

CHAPTER II.

TIME AND PLACE OF LEGAL BUSINESS.

A. 1. Not every day in the year was good for law business. On the *dies nefasti* the praetor was not permitted to use the technical words which were necessary for his regular functions, *do, dico, addico*: on other days law matters were transacted either throughout the day or some part of it. According to Mommsen's computation (*Corp. I.L.* 1 Pt. 1 p. 296, ed. 2) 108

incidit, non potest sumi ad haec judex ex turba senatorum quem census in album et equestris hereditas misit.

[1] Cf. Wlassak *Pr. G.* ii pp. 196, 209, *etc.*

days in the ante-Julian calendar were *nefasti*, partly of a solemn, partly of a cheerful character; 45 were marked as *fasti*; 11 were partly *fasti*; and 191 were days on which both law business and also public *comitia* could be held. In the Julian calendar 55 days were *fasti*. The result is that 247 (or 257) days in the year would be open for law business either wholly or partially, provided they were not required for the public assemblies (Varr. *LL.* vi 29—32; Macrob. i 16 § 14) or for holidays (*feriae*) and public games[1]. These latter, so far as they fell on these days, have to be deducted, and the number of legal days comes down to less than 200, including however those which might be occupied by *comitia*. Extraordinary feasts and games sometimes reduced this number. Augustus added more than thirty days to the legal year (Suet. *Aug.* 32). M. Antoninus increased the total number of days to 230 (Hist. Aug. *Ant.* 10), and while forbidding any compulsory summons at the times of harvest and vintage, unless a thing was perishing or a right of suit would otherwise be lost, or in case of serious delicts, provided for a number of matters being dealt with by the praetors on holidays, such as the appointment, admonishment, or excuse of guardians and caretakers; orders for alimony of children, parents, and patrons; grants of possession on behalf of legatees, fideicommissaries, or a *venter*, or on the ground of possible damage from buildings, securing a trust-freedom, *etc.* (D. ii 12 fr 23).

The sittings of the Courts were at one time divided into a summer and winter season; Claudius joined them. The sittings were called *rerum actus* (Suet. *Aug.* 32; *Claud.* 23; *Ner.* 17; Plin. *Ep.* ix 25)[2].

2. The legal Roman day was reckoned from midnight to midnight (D. ii 12 fr 8; Gell. iii 2); but the ordinary usage

[1] Cf. Cic. *Verr.* Act i 10 § 31.

[2] So Gai. ii 279 *cum res aguntur*: an adjournment or vacation was *res prolatae* (Plaut. *Capt.* 78; 80; Cic. *Mur.* § 28), *rerum prolatio* (Cic. *Att.* vii 12 § 2); the return of the session, *res redeuntes* (Plaut. *Capt.* 86; Cic. *Sest.* 62 § 129). Madvig (*Verf.* ii 240) quotes also Sen. *Rhet. Contr.* vii praef. § 7 *centumviri rebus jam ultimis properabant* 'were in a hurry at the end of the session'; Sen. *Ben.* v 17 § 4 *res proximae* 'the last session.'

was to reckon only the period of light, so that an hour (one-twelfth) varied from $1\frac{1}{4}$ modern hours at midsummer to $\frac{3}{4}$ hour at midwinter. The usual time for law business seems to have been from the second to the tenth hour. So at least for opening wills (Paul iv 6 § 2). The second hour is named in Cic. *Quint.* 6 § 25; Hor. *Sat.* ii 6 35; Ascon. *Mil.* p. 42; the third or fourth hour in Hor. *Sat.* i 9 35; and in Martial: *Exercet raucos tertia causidicos* (iv 8 2), and *raucae vadimonia quartae* (viii 67 3). Judgment against an absent party was not usual till the tenth hour (Cic. *Verr.* ii 17 § 41). Augustus is said sometimes to have continued sitting till nightfall (Suet. *Aug.* 33). The charter for the colony of Ossuna (*lex Urson.* cap. 102) directs both the duovir (corresponding to the praetor at Rome) and the judge not to sit before the first (? or second? see the bronze) hour nor after the eleventh, unless the case was one which that law required to be concluded in the day. (See Marquardt *Privatleben* p. 246 sqq.)

In the XII tables the direction was for both parties to appear and plead their case before midday, and not till after midday was the judge to assign the suit to the victor, being present (*post meridiem presenti stlitem addicito*). Sunset was to be the final time (Gell. xvii 2 § 10).

B. Trials before public officers whether *judices* or *arbitri* or *recuperatores* were usually held in the *forum*, *i.e.* in the old *forum* or those built by Julius and Augustus (Suet. *Oct.* 29), or in the *basilicae* adjoining, or in smaller rooms *auditoria* (Tac. *Orat.* 39). The judge sat on a raised platform (*tribunal*), others assisting on benches (*subsellia*) beside him. The parties and their advocates on benches on the level ground (Suet. *Ner.* 17; Madvig *Verfassung* ii p. 241). For the praetor see above, p. 313.

CHAPTER III.

DISQUALIFICATIONS FOR SUING.

A. It was not everybody who was allowed by the praetor to conduct a case before him. Some classes of persons were prohibited absolutely; others were allowed to appear for themselves but not for others: a third class were allowed to appear for themselves and also for near relatives, but only for those. The prohibition was absolute and could not be waived by consent of opponent. The technical term for making or opposing an application to the praetor was *postulare*[1] (D. iii 1 fr 1 §§ 1, 2; fr 7). The three classes (*ordines*) of persons *qui prohibentur postulare* were these:

i. Prohibited absolutely

Children under 17 years of age complete: and persons completely deaf.

If an advocate was required for them, the praetor assigned one (D. fr 1 §§ 3, 4).

ii. Prohibited from acting on behalf of others

Women; but if there was no one else, they were sometimes permitted to act for parents or near relatives (D. iii 3 fr 41; xl 12 fr 3 § 2);

blind persons; and

a few of those who were commonly called *infames* (viz. those numbered below 4, 9, 11 and 14) (D. fr 1 §§ 5, 6).

iii. Prohibited from acting on behalf of others, except of relatives, viz. parents, patrons, patrons' children or parents, their own children, brother, sister, wife, father-in-law, mother-in-law, son-in-law, daughter-in-law, step-father, step-mother, step-son, step-daughter; and if they have been duly appointed by the parent or majority of guardians or the magistrate to be guardian or caretaker, then they may act for a ward, a madman

[1] Cf. Cic. *Verr.* iii 67 § 155 where one of Verres' favourites speaking to another says *Te postulante omnes vincere solent.*

or an idiot, deaf, dumb, spendthrifts, youths under 25 years of age, and wholly infirm persons (D. fr 1 § 11—fr 5).

The persons in this third class were

(*a*) all that were so prohibited by any general statute, plebiscite, senate's decree, or edict or decree of the Emperor.

(*b*) all *infames* or (as Gaius calls them) *ignominiosi*[1]; unless their disgrace was cancelled (*in integrum restituti*). No such name was given in the Edict: it was the usual short description of the classes contained in the praetor's list (Gai. iv 182). The list appears to have been something as follows[2]:

(1) Persons condemned of having committed theft or having bargained to avoid condemnation for theft. To theft, Gaius and the Digest add, robbery by violence, and insult (*injuriarum*): the Digest adds also *dolo malo et fraude* and limits the whole to condemnation *suo nomine*;

(2) or who have been condemned as trustee (*fiduciae*) or partner or guardian or mandator or for insult or *dolo malo*.

(The Digest puts *injuriarum* and *doli mali* in the preceding clause, omits *fiduciae*, adds *depositi*, and limits the whole to 'condemnation in a direct, not in a counter action': Gaius gives both *fiduciae* and *depositi*, but omits *doli mali*;)

(3) or have been condemned under, or for contravention of, the *lex Plaetoria*;

[1] The usual word in the lawyers is *infamia* (cf. D. iii 2 rubr.; Cod. ii 11); Gaius uses *ignominia*, also of insolvents whose estate has been sold (ii 154), for which Cicero uses *infamia* (*Quinct.* 14 § 46) as well as *ignominia* (*ib.* 40 § 64), both in a general (not technical) sense, as he does frequently. In *Quinct.* § 49 *aut ignominia affectus aut judicio turpi convictus* he appears to contrast ignominy with the result of the cases named by Gaius iv 182 (but cf. *Rabir. perd.* 5 § 16), as he does when applying it to the censor's mark in *Clu.* 42 § 119, which he denies to be judicial: *Quodsi illud judicium putaretur, ut ceteri turpi judicio damnati in perpetuum omni honore ac dignitate privantur, sic hominibus ignominia notatis neque ad honorem aditus neque in curiam reditus esset. Nunc, etc.*; *RP.* iv 6. For the history of *infamia* see Greenidge's '*Infamia* in Roman Law.'

[2] I take it from the list given in the *lex Julia municipalis* 110—123 of those disqualified for the municipal council. A very similar but shorter list is in D. iii 2 fr 1. The Digest omits altogether nos. 3, 5, 6, 7, 8 and 13. Cf. also Frag. Atest. *ap.* Bruns[6] p. 103.

(4) or have hired themselves out to fight in the arena[1];

(5) or have taken an oath in court denying a debt[2];

(6) or have sworn their own solvency[3] when they have reported to their sureties or creditors that they cannot pay their debts in full or have bargained not to do so;

(7) or for whom sureties have had to pay;

(8) or whose estate has been seized and advertised under the praetor's edict, unless they were wards or absent *bona fide* on the public service;

(9) or have been condemned in a public trial at Rome, resulting in banishment from Italy, and have not been reinstated;

(10) or have been condemned in a public trial[4] in their own borough or other community;

[1] The Digest says 'fight with beasts,' cf. *Collat.* iv 3.

[2] The text of the *lex Julia* here is *queive in jure abjuraverit, bonamve copiam juravit juraverit quei sponsoribus creditoribusve sueis renuntiavit renuntiaverit se soldum solvere non posse, etc.* *Abjurare* is 'to swear off,' *i.e.* to deny a loan (cf. Plaut. *Curc.* 496; *Pers.* 478 *ne quis mihi in jure abjurassit*; *Rud.* 14; Sall. *Cat.* 25; cf. Serv. on Verg. viii 263; Cic. *Att.* i 8; so *abnegare* is used of denying a deposit Sen. *Ben.* iv 26; and in English 'repudiate' of refusing to pay a debt). Mommsen's supplement of *bonam copiam* before it is quite wrong (as I see Karlowa *RG.* ii 598 also holds).

[3] To make such an oath of solvency a grave offence it must be false, as in the preceding clause (*quei—abjuraverit*), and therefore I connect it with the following sentence (*quei sponsoribus, etc.*). So also Huschke *Nexum* p. 137. Mommsen adds *ve* to the *quei* before *sponsoribus*, which can be right only if *bon. cop. jur.* was in itself a discreditable proceeding.

[4] Public trials are defined by Macer (in D. xlviii 1 fr 1) as those which are under statutes, viz. *lex Cornelia* on assassins and poisoners, and another on forged wills (cf. D. xlviii 10 fr 16); *lex Pompeia* on parricide; *leges Juliae* on treason, adultery, peculation, private or public violence, canvassing, extortion, corn-supply. We may add the *lex Fabia* on kidnapping (D. xlviii 15). The Digest in the corresponding passage (*de postulando* iii 1 fr 1 § 6) has simply *capitali crimine damnatus* which comes to the same thing, capital charges being those where the punishment was death or interdiction from fire and water (*i.e.* not relegation). Charges which involve only a fine or some punishment to the person are not capital (D. xlviii 1 fr 2). If we trust Cicero's rhetoric (*Quinct.* 2 § 8; 31 § 95) *capitis causa* would have a far wider meaning, cf. D. L 16 fr 103. See Savigny *Syst.* § 81; Mommsen *St.R.* i 469 note 2; *Strafrecht* pp. 994, 995.

(11) or have been judged in a public trial to have brought an accusation or done anything calumniously or in prevarication[1];

(12) or when with the army, have had their rank taken away from them for disgraceful conduct, or have been ordered by the general to leave the army for disgraceful conduct;

(13) or have taken money or any other reward for bringing in (*referundum*) the head of a Roman citizen;

(14) or have traded with their own body (*qui corpore quaestum fecit:* Digest has *qui corpore suo muliebria passus est*);

(15) or have been training-masters or stage-players[2] (*qui lanistaturam artemve ludicram fecit*);

(16) or shall be pandars.

To these the Digest (iii 2 fr 1) adds (probably due to the *lex Julia et Papia Poppaea*);

(17) or have knowing that their son-in-law was dead given in marriage a daughter in their power before she has for the due time mourned her husband; or have knowingly married such a woman, unless by order of their family superior; or have permitted a son in their power to marry such a woman;

(18) or have on their own account, unless by order of the family superior, or on account of either son or daughter in their power, had two betrothments or two marriages established at the same time.

B. Some persons who were *infames* were also prohibited from appointing *cognitores* or *procuratores*[3]. There appears to have

[1] *Calumniari est falsa crimina intendere; praevaricari vera crimina abscondere* (D. xlviii 16 fr 1 § 1).

[2] It is noticeable that throughout the speech *pro Q. Rosc. Com.* there is no allusion to any disgrace attaching to defendant as a stage player: quite the contrary, *e.g.* § 17 *Ita dignissimus est scaena propter artificium ut dignissimus sit curia propter abstinentiam.* Livy refers to some disgrace: *Hoc genus ludorum ab Oscis acceptum tenuit juventus nec ab histrionibus pollui passa est: eo institutum manet ut actores Atellanarum nec tribu moveantur et stipendia tanquam expertes artis ludicrae faciant* (vii 2 § 12, cf. Val. M. ii 4 § 4). See Pernice *Labeo* i p. 242 sq.

[3] Savigny points out that a prohibition *ne dent cognitorem (procuratoremve) neve dentur* would prevent (until Ant. Pius allowed a *utilis*

been a separate list, (part of which is preserved in the Vatican Fragments §§ 320—323)[1], which adds the women themselves who have married before the due time of mourning has expired either for their husband, or parents (both male and female), or children. But Ulpian (*ap.* Dig. iii 2 fr 23) expressly denies the penalty of *infamia* to neglect of mourning for parents, children or other relatives.

The period of mourning is stated to be a year (of ten months) for parents, and for children more than ten years old; as many months of mourning as years of life for children from ten to three years old[2]; slight mourning for a child of one or two years, and none for children less than one year old (Vat. i 1). For a husband the period was ten months, for near relations eight months.

Mourning was abstention from dinner parties, ornaments, purple, and white dress (Paul i 21 § 13, 14). An heir's family was put into mourning (*funesta facta*) from the death of testator (D. xlv 3 fr 28 § 4).

C. Special disqualification of gaming-house keepers.

Here may be mentioned a peculiar declaration in the Edict, that no action would be granted against anyone who beat, or injured any keeper of a dicing house, or stole anything from his house when dicing was going on. Pomponius thought that this last provision referred to the action for theft only, but Ulpian held that the language of the Edict was so general as to imply a refusal of a vindication or condiction or action *ad exhibendum* also (D. xi 5 fr 1).

The senate forbade any games for money, except in manly exercises such as throwing spears or pikes, running, leaping,

actio) surrender of actions by or to *infames* (*Syst.* vol. ii § 82). Who were prevented from appointing representatives is not at all clear. Such a disability is referred to in Quintil. iv 4 § 6; vii 1 § 20; Gai. iv 124; Vat. 322; D. iii 3 fr 43 § 1; Just. iv 13 § 11. Keller (*CP.* n. 640) rightly points out that the fact of Q. Roscius appointing his partner a *cognitor* (*Rosc. Com.* 11 § 32) shews that the list could not be identical with the praetor's third class of disqualified persons. See also Karlowa *ZRG.* ix 223.

[1] The text is not clear. See Savigny *Syst.* ii, *Beilage* vii § 8.

[2] Paul i 21 § 13 gives a different account, but it rests only on a MS. now lost. See Savigny l.c. p. 553.

wrestling, boxing. Money gained contrary to the prohibition could be recovered by a *condictio*, *ib.* fr 2 § 1. Slaves were allowed to play for anything put on the table at a feast (fr 2 § 1—§ 4).

CHAPTER IV.

PLACE AND TIME FOR SUING.

A. Where suit should be brought.

The rule of Roman law was that a person must be sued where he had his home[1], and if he does not duly defend himself, his estate is liable to be seized under the praetor's order.

Home (or domicile) is the place which a man has made the seat of his household property and fortunes, where he means to abide if nothing call him away, and any departure from which is foreign travel. *Singulos habere domicilium non ambigitur, ubi quis larem rerumque ac fortunarum suarum summam constituit, unde rursus non sit decessurus si nihil avocet, unde cum profectus est peregrinari videtur, quo si rediit peregrinari jam destitit* (Cod. x 40 fr 7 § 1, cf. D. L 16 fr 203). For business purposes any shop, office, or warehouse is a sufficient establishment to make one liable to the local jurisdiction (D. v 1 fr 19 § 2).

If for business purposes or the administration of a ward's affairs he has established himself elsewhere, he is liable to be sued there also for any obligation there contracted or arising, or if he has contracted for payment or performance elsewhere, he may be sued in the place so named. An action *in rem* usually had to be brought like a personal action at defendant's domicile (Vat. 326 by Diocletian), but for a legacy had to be brought where the thing was. So an heir sued on a trust for an inheritance, may require the action to be brought where the greater part of the inheritance is. Plaint of an unduteous will was

[1] So Cicero said of Sicilians that it was their fixed right *ne quis extra suum forum vadimonium promittere cogatur* (*Verr.* iii 15 § 38).

brought where the heirs named therein had domicile (D. v 1, fr 19, 20, 38, 50; tit. 2 fr 29 § 4).

An heir is liable to be sued on his predecessor's obligation in the place where it arose; or if the suit has been already begun, then in the place accepted by his predecessor, whatever his own domicile may be (D. v 1 fr 19 pr; 34). And one who himself sues (except for a tort) in a place not his domicile, cannot refuse to be sued there (fr 2 § 5; 22).

Persons who are called away from their homes on public business, as legates or to give evidence, or to act as judges, and have suits brought against them for pressing obligations in the place of their temporary abode for obligations contracted at home, may demand to have the suit brought at their home (*jus revocandi domum*). If required they must give their personal security for appearance at the trial on a day fixed by the praetor (fr 2 § 3, 6; fr 24, *etc.*; cf. *Frag. Atest.* 17).

If a person is summoned by the praetor out of another's jurisdiction, he must appear and submit his objections to the jurisdiction. It is for the praetor to decide upon the limits of his jurisdiction: and this rule applies to legates claiming their privilege (D. v 1 fr 5).

Consent of the parties can give jurisdiction to any duly appointed judge (fr 1).

B. When suit should be brought.

As regards the time within which a suit must be brought, a distinction was made between suits resting on a statute or senate's decree, *i.e.* all suits belonging to the civil law proper, and those which were granted by the praetor on his own authority: *i.e.* (to use Gaius' language on another occasion) between those which *ipso jure competunt* and those which *a praetore dantur* (iv 112). Suits of the former class could be brought at any time after the cause arising; the latter as a rule only within one year. But there were exceptions where the action aimed at restitution (*quae rei persecutionem habet*) and not at mere penalty. And specially possessors of a deceased's estate and other persons in an heir's place were put on the footing of statutable heirs, and thus enabled to bring their analogous (*utiles*) actions, and to be liable to suits more than a year after cause of suit arisen. And the same applied to the Publician action. Nor did the praetor put any limit to the time within which he granted an action for theft manifest, that action being really a milder substitute for the action given by the XII tables, which carried capital punishment (Gai. iv 110, 111; D. xliv 7 fr 35 pr).

When it is said that an action must be brought within *annus utilis*, 365 days must be reckoned without counting any day on which plaintiff's ignorance of his right, or physical hindrance, or non-sitting of the court prevents action. *Tempus utile* in this sense is opposed to *tempus continuum* (D. xxxviii 15 fr 2 pr; xliv 3 fr 1).

The time at which an action is held to be actually brought is joinder of issue (chap. xii): for the time within which it must be brought to judgment see same chapter.

CHAPTER V.

PROCEDURE *IN JURE*.

A. Summons.

The first step in legal process was to summon the defendant to appear in court (*in jus vocare*), *i.e.* before the praetor, to hear plaintiff's ground of action[1]. It is plaintiff's business to make the summons. He may summon him in any public place, at the door of his house or in the streets, at the baths or theatre, but cannot go into his house for the purpose, still less can he take him forcibly from his house. If defendant is visible from outside, or allows access, plaintiff may summon him (D. ii 4 fr 18—21). If on being summoned he does not obey, the XII tables directed evidence of the fact to be procured

[1] Cf. Plaut. *Pers.* 745 Sa. *Age ambula in jus, leno.* Do. *Quid me in jus vocas?* Sa. *Illic apud praetorem dicam; sed ego in jus voco.* Do. *Nonne antestaris?* Sa. *Tuan ego causa, carnufex, quoiquam mortali libero auris atteram?* *Poen.* 1233.

by the plaintiff's touching the ear of some bystander and requesting him to bear witness to his having uttered the summons. If defendant tried to shirk or refused to go, plaintiff was authorised to lay hand on him and take him. If he was old or ill, plaintiff had to provide a beast to ride or a carriage[1] (Fest. *s.v. Struere*, p. 310; Porph. ad Hor. *Sat.* i 9 76; Gell. xx 1 § 25). Defendant had when duly summoned only three courses open to avoid extreme measures: he had either to go into court, or to settle with plaintiff, or to furnish someone to answer for him. Such a substitute was called *vindex*. A defendant who adopted none of these courses was liable to a penalty under the praetor's edict, enforced by an action *in factum* (Gai. iv 46, 183; D. ii 4 fr 22 § 1). This penalty appears to be a substitute for the old fashion of compulsory taking into court; but, though we find no instance of the latter in Cicero[2], its continued existence is shewn by Horace's narrative of the bore, by the action named in Gaius (iv 46) and the Digest (ii 7) against anyone who forcibly rescued a defendant after summons, and by other reference (D. ii 8 fr 5 § 1). In practice no doubt private arrangements often obviated any such peremptory proceedings, at least in ordinary civil cases. Where a defendant kept out of the way to avoid summons, and no one appeared to defend him, the plaintiff could obtain an order from the praetor to take possession of his estate (D. ii 4 fr 19).

We have no information of the precise position and functions

1 The words as restored were (see Bruns p. 17): *Si in jus vocat, ni it, antestamino: igitur em capito. Si calvitur pedemve struit, manum endo jacito. Si morbus aevitasve vitium escit, jumentum dato. Si nolet, arceram ne sternito.* I agree with others (*e.g.* Demelius *ZRG.* xv p. 9; Lenel *ib.* p. 49) that *manum endo jacito* does not import the procedure under the *legis actio* (see chap. xv). *Arceram ne sternito* makes it unnecessary for plaintiff to provide floorcloths or cushions.

2 So Bethmann-Hollweg *CP.* ii 199. Obedience to a summons occurs, *e.g.* in Cic. *Quinct.* 19 § 61 *Vadari vis, promittit; in jus vocas, sequitur; judicium postulat, non recusat.* Cf. *Verr.* ii 76 § 187 and iv 66 § 148. In Plautus we have forcible dragging: *Rud.* 860 Pl. *Age ambula in jus.* La. *Quid ego deliqui?* Pl. *In jure causam dicito: hic verbum sat est, sequere.* La. *Obsecro te, subveni, mi Charmides; rapior obtorto collo: Poen.* 1232 *Moramini: in jus vos voco, nisi honestiust prehendi.*

of the *vindex*[1]. It seems probable that he merely undertook to produce defendant at some future time as the praetor might direct. If he failed to do so, he may have been liable to personal arrest and imprisonment; or to an action by plaintiff for the full amount of his claim. On satisfying this he would no doubt have a peremptory action against the original defendant. Against defendant who had given a *vindex* and kept out of the way, plaintiff had still the remedy of an order to take possession (D. ii 8 fr 2 § 5—fr 4; xlii 4 fr 2; Lenel *ZRG.* xv p. 43 sqq.).

Certain persons were not open to summons without the praetor's permission. Such were a lawful parent, grandparent, *etc.*, an adoptive parent during the adoption, a merely natural parent (*e.g.* a freedman whose child was born in slavery, or the mother of an illegitimate child), a patron or patroness, or the children or parents of a patron or patroness. This respect is due to them even if they are only guardians of the person really sued, but not if the patron is a ward and the suit is therefore against his guardians, or if plaintiff is suing on behalf of a ward. *Capitis deminutio* at least of a minor character does not affect for this purpose the relation of patron and freeman. A slave manumitted by a town or other corporation is not prevented from suing the individuals. The praetor will grant permission to sue, where the suit is not one involving disgrace or insult, or where the patron has abused his rights (D. ii 4 fr 4 §§ 1—4, 10 §§ 2, 4, 12, fr 16; Gai. iv 183). A like prohibition was in force against summoning young girls (*impuberes*) in the power of a parent, or madmen, or infants. And the like protection was extended to a consul or other magistrate with the *imperium*; a priest while performing sacred rites, a judge while sitting in court, a suitor before the praetor; one who is already bound to appear in court or in some fixed place for the purpose of a suit; one who is marrying or being married; one who cannot on religious grounds leave a place; one engaged in a funeral of his family

[1] We cannot assume identical functions with those of the *vindex* in execution. The Digest does not retain the name, but substitutes *fidejussor judicio sistendi causa*, a phrase all the more awkward because the first appearance was before the praetor. But the distinction between *in jure* and *in judicio* had passed away in Justinian's time.

or performing rites to the dead, or escorting a corpse; or being under review on a state horse (D. ii 4 fr 2—4 pr, 22 pr). The penalty for violation of the edict in this matter was 5000 sesterces (50 *aurei* in Digest *ib.* fr 12, 24). Gaius gives the formula for an action before *recuperatores* against a freedman for suing his patron (iv 46).

If suit were brought against parents, patrons, or patrons' children, children or others in plaintiff's power, or wife or daughter-in-law, any *vindex* was held to be sufficient. In other suits only a *locuples vindex,* i.e. one of adequate financial means could be accepted. If a clearly sufficient *vindex* was tendered and refused, both defendant and *vindex* had an action *injuriarum* against plaintiff who had thus insulted them (D. ii 8 fr 5 § 1).

B. *VADIMONIUM*[1].

If defendant appeared and the matter was not finished in one day, he had to make a *vadimonium, i.e.* to promise under penalty appearance on a named day. The edict provided for

[1] In Cicero *vadari* is used of requiring an adversary to promise appearance in court on a certain day, *e.g. Quinct.* 6 § 23 *Ait se jam neque vadari amplius neque vadimonium promittere; si quid agere secum velit Quinctius, non recusare. Hic hominem in praesentia non vadatur: ita sine vadimonio disceditur. Cum ceteris quae habebat vadimonia differt*; *ib.* 19 § 61; *Verr.* iii 34 § 78; Plaut. *Pers.* 289; Liv. iii 13 § 8; Ovid *Rem.* 665. To keep such an appointment is *ad vadimonium venire, vadimonium obire* (Cic. *Quinct.* 16 § 52; 17 § 54); not to keep it *vadimonium deserere* (*ib.* 18 § 56). Bail for appearance was *vas*; to give bail, *vadem dare* (cf. Hor. *Sat.* i 1 11 *Ille datis vadibus rure extractus in urbem*); to accept bail, *vadem accipere* Cic. *Ep. Brut.* i 18 § 2. *Vas* is principally used in criminal cases, *e.g.* Cic. *Off.* iii 10 § 45; Sall. *Jug.* 35 § 9; Liv. iii 13 *Appellati tribuni in vincula conici vetant; sisti reum pecuniamque ni sistatur populo promitti placere pronuntiant...Senatui vades dari placuit...Tot vadibus accusator vadatus est reum. Hic primus vades publico dedit. Vadatus* is used passively in Pl. *Bac.* 180: but probably not in Hor. *Sat.* i 9 36 *respondere vadato debebat* 'he ought to reply, *i.e.* to appear in court to one who had made him promise.' Mommsen (in Bekker and Müller's *Jahrbuch* vi 390) inclines to take *vadato* as ablative (cf. *auspicato, etc.*) 'after bail had been given.'

Other expressions for appearance (as in Liv. l.c.) are used in Gaius and the Digest, viz. *sistere reum* (of the bail) 'to produce defendant'; *sistere*

different cases, defendant sometimes giving a promise only (*vadimonium purum*), sometimes a promise supported by sureties, in other cases a promise on oath. Or again the appearance was secured by the appointment of Recoverers, who would at once if he failed to appear (*si non steterit*) condemn him in the amount of the sum named (Gai. iv 184, 185; D. ii 8 rubric). The amount of the *vadimonium* was usually fixed by the plaintiff on oath, who swears also to his own good faith (*non calumniae causa se postulare*). It is however limited by two *maxima*: it must not exceed either half the value or 100000 sesterces. Suits on a judgment or on money paid down by a sponsor (cf. Gai. iii 127) have the *vadimonium* unrestricted at the full value (Gai. iv 186).

The promise was in the form of answer to stipulation[1] and the action for the penalty was *ex stipulatu*. A surety for this, as for other praetorian stipulations, had to be substantial (*locuples*), and his sufficiency might if necessary be determined (subject to appeal) by reference to an arbitrator appointed by the praetor. A woman or soldier or minor under 25 years or slave is not a good surety (D. ii 8, fr 8 §§ 1, 2, fr 9, 10). Where the suit is of a nature to bring double or triple, *etc.* damages, the sureties are liable for the multiple (*ib.* fr 3).

Persons who could not be summoned without the praetor's consent (see above, p. 335) were also freed from the necessity of making a *vadimonium*, unless the praetor allow it (Gai. iv 187).

Persons in the country, where the suit was beyond the

vadimonium (Nep. *Att.* 9 § 4), *sisti* (of the defendant) 'to be produced,' 'to appear'; for which also *se sistere* (cf. Plaut. *Curc.* 163) and *stare* perf. *stetisse* are found. All the editors of Cic. *Quinct.* have been strangely misled by Gell. ii 14 where it is said that in Cato *quid si vadimonium capite obvoluto stitisses* the text should not be altered to *stetisses*. Of course not; *stare, stetisse* is intransitive and stands by itself as in all MSS. of Cic. *Quinct.* 6 § 25 *Testificatur P. Quinctium non stetisse et stetisse se*; but *vadimonium* would require the transitive *sistere, stitisse*. See full discussion in my *Introd.* Justin. p. ccxxvii. This is a remarkable instance of the way in which editors follow one another without thought, where the matter is at all technical.

[1] The stipulation was of course reduced to writing, cf. Cic. *Q. Fr.* ii 13 (quoted below, p. 347 *n.* 2); Ovid *Am.* i 12. 23 *Aptius hae capiant vadimonia garrula cerae.*

competence of the local jurisdiction, had to give a *vadimonium* to appear in Rome (*vadimonium Romam facere* (*lex Rubr.* 21)). For this purpose (and probably for other cases) the time for appearance was so fixed as to allow one day for every twenty miles of distance (D. ii 11 fr 1).

Non-appearance was excused (by grant of a plea) in case of serious illness (*morbus sonticus*) or age, or tempest, or swollen rivers impeding the journey (provided the defendant started in reasonable time); or absence *bona fide* on public business, or detention by a magistrate, or a family funeral, or capture by the enemy. In such cases and where defendant has been capitally condemned the sureties were not liable. In other cases, if appearance was made a few days after the day appointed, and plaintiff was not damnified, a plea might be admitted (D. ii 11 fr 2, 4 pr—§ 3, fr 6, 8).

Promise for another's appearance is not duly kept, if when he appears he is not in the same legal position as he was, *e.g.* if he has got some new privilege. But economic considerations did not affect the question, *e.g.* if he had incurred additional debt or had lost money. When a slave was to be produced in a noxal suit, the *vadimonium* required that he should be *in eadem causa*, *i.e.* not have been sold to someone more powerful or less accessible to suit than the former owner. Noxal surrender made in the interval on the ground of wrongs previously committed does not affect his position. *Noxa caput sequitur*, and therefore he remains liable for any subsequent injuries. If he have been manumitted, he becomes answerable, as a freeman, *i.e.* answerable in body for a criminal offence, and pecuniarily in full for a civil wrong (D. ii 9 fr 1, 2, 5; tit. 11 fr 11).

What was the consequence of plaintiff's not appearing we do not know, but the charter of Ossuna cap. 95 deprives him of all right to pursue the case further, unless he was prevented by ill-health, a *vadimonium*, a *judicium*, a sacrifice, a funeral in his family, or a feast in honour of the dead (*feriae denicales*): which in fact appear to be standing excuses (cf. Gell. xvi 4 § 4). The charter is supposed by Bruns and Mommsen to be dealing with criminal prosecutions.

C. The parties, often attended by their advocates (Cic. *Or.* i 37 § 168), being before the praetor, the real contention began. It consisted of two parts: (1) the arrangement for the trial, *i.e.* the ascertainment of the plaintiff's claim and of the nature of the defendant's reply, and the appointment of a judge to try the contention; (2) the trial before the judge so appointed. The first was the proceeding *in jure, i.e.* before the praetor or proconsul, *etc.*; the second was the proceeding *in judicio* before a *judex* or *recuperatores, etc.*

The proceedings before the praetor were in early times characterised by a series of formal declarations and symbolical actions of the parties, which were supposed to rest on the statute of the XII tables, and the procedure was hence called *legis actio.* The same name was also given to other procedures introduced by subsequent statutes.

CHAPTER VI.

PROCEDURE *PER LEGIS ACTIONES*[1].

Procedure by statute (*lege agebatur*) was, according to Gaius, in five different ways. Three of these were preparations for the trial of the contention: the fourth was the mode of enforcing

[1] It has been suggested that the proper notion of *agere, actio* in these legal proceedings was legal exercise of his right by plaintiff, and that the determination of questions as to his right was not the object of the proceeding, but arose incidentally on the resistance of defendant. This is seen in the *pignoris capio* and *manus injectio.* Cf. Demelius *Confessio* p. 40 sqq.

Lege agere is used by Cicero of vindications of land (*Or.* i 10 § 42, and perhaps *Mur.* 12 § 26); of suits for inheritance (*Or.* i 36 § 167; 38 § 175; *Verr.* ii 1. 45 § 115); of suits in Sicily (*Div. in Caecil.* 5 § 19; *Verr.* ii 2 16 § 39; *Caecin.* 33 § 97) without precise reference. Some may be referred to the technical *legis actio*, but it may be better to take them all in the general sense of 'according to the statute' whether the XII tables or other (see Bekker *ZRG.* v p. 343). So *lege agito* 'bring a suit'; Plaut. *Aul.* 458; *Mil.* 453; Ter. *Phorm.* 984. In Liv. xxvi 15 § 9 *lictorem lege agere jussit* is 'bade him proceed by law,' *i.e.* execute the prisoner.

execution of a judgment given or deemed to have been given, and will be more appropriately explained later on. The fifth was not properly judicial procedure, but a kind of self-help, classed with the others on account of the requirement of particular words (see p. 115). We know little about any of these statutable proceedings, and that little mainly from Gaius.

A. *Sacramento agere.* This was originally the only procedure and was applied, where no other form had been directed by special statute (Gai. iv 13), both to actions *in rem* and actions *in personam.* It was so called from a *sacramentum, i.e.* a stake of money deposited by each party on the justice of his claim or defence, which may have at one time gone to the priest, but in Gaius' time went to the public treasury. The mutilation of Gaius' MS. has deprived us of most of his description of procedure in a personal action[1], but has left us that in a real action.

Where a moveable object, whether slave, animal, or thing, was in dispute, it was brought into court. If this was impossible or inconvenient, as for instance in the case of a ship or column, a bit was broken off; in the case of a house, perhaps a tile was brought; in the case of land a clod[2]; if a flock or herd

[1] Valerius Probus § 4 gives explanations of certain abbreviations by initial letters for common forms in *legis actiones.* Among these appear three sentences, very probably relating to the *act. sacramenti in personam*: '*Aio te mihi dare oportere*'; '*Quando negas, te sacramento quingenario provoco*'; '*Quando neque ais neque negas*' (*Jus Antejust.* ii p. 144).

[2] Cicero in a witty passage in his speech *pro Murena* 12 § 26 ridicules the forms used in a suit for ownership of land. Plaintiff says 'The farm 'which is in the territory (*ager*) which is called Sabine, that I say is mine 'by the law of the Quirites. Thereon I call thee from court to join hand' (*Inde ibi ego te ex jure manum consertum voco*). Defendant: 'Whereon thou hast called me from court to join hand, thereon I in retort call thee.' Praetor: 'Each party having their witnesses (*superstites*) present, I declare (point?) that road: go the road. Return the road.' This shews the retention of old forms which were originally used at a time when the parties, with (or, later, without) the praetor, went to the land in dispute to identify it and there *in re atque in loco praesenti apud praetorem* both at the same time laid their hands on it (so Gell. xx 10 § 7 quoting the XII tables *si qui in jure manum conserunt*), or perhaps engaged in a symbolical struggle. A later stage, in which the parties took a clod from the place, and on it, as

was in dispute, one sheep or goat, or even some hair from an animal, was produced as a symbol of the object. The plaintiff then with a rod (*festuca*) in his hand laid hold of the thing or symbol, put the rod on it, and said, 'This man (or this thing) I 'assert to be mine by the law of the Quirites according to its 'character. As I have said, see you there, I have put my rod '(*vindicta*) upon it[1].' The rod was in lieu of a spear (*hasta*)[2], the sign of legally recognized ownership, as if the man or thing had been taken in war. If the claim was for the ownership of the thing, no qualifying words would be necessary; where the ownership was subject to a qualification, or where the claim was for the usufruct or use only, or for the ownership *minus* the usufruct, or for a servitude, or for a slave who was *statu liber*, or for an inheritance, or for a free person who was under power

upon a symbol of the land, made their claim in court, is given by Gaius in our text, and also by Gellius. He quotes Enn. *Ann.* viii *Non ex jure manum consertum sed mage ferro rem repetunt* (cf. Cic. *Mur.* 14 § 30; *Fam.* vii 13 § 2). In Cic. *Or.* i 10 § 41 both interdict and ownership suit are alluded to. *Id nisi in tuo regno essemus non tulissem multisque praeessem* ('captained' see Wilkins edit. *ad loc.*) *qui aut interdicto tecum contenderent aut te ex jure manum consertum vocarent, quod in alienas possessiones tam temere irruisses. Agerent enim tecum lege Pythagorei...ceterique in jure sua physici vindicarent...quibuscum tibi justo sacramento contendere non liceret.*

Journeys of the parties accompanied by friends to the spot are spoken of in Cic. *Caecin.* 7 § 20 *placuit constituere quo die in rem praesentem veniretur; Off.* i 10 § 32 *Si constitueris cuipiam te advocatum in rem praesentem esse venturum; Orat.* i 58 § 250.

[1] The words are *Hunc ego hominem ex jure Quiritium meum esse aio secundum suam causam. Sicut dixi ecce tibi vindictam imposui.* Some connect *sicut dixi* with what precedes. So Ihering *Geist* iii 1 p. 102 (4th ed.). For *secundum suam causam* cf. D. xli 7 fr 2 pr; x 2 fr 12 § 2; Karlowa *Röm. CP.* pp. 71, 72. Muirhead (*Hist.* § 34 n. 7) suggests that it is not part of the declaration, but a parenthetical instruction to the speaker to describe what he means by *meum esse.* But would *suam* be used in such a case?

[2] Cf. Cic. *Off.* ii 8 § 27 *Sulla ausus est dicere hasta posita, cum bona in foro venderet et bonorum virorum et locupletium et certe civium, 'praedam se suam vendere'; Phil.* ii 26 § 64; 40 § 103; *etc.* The spear was set up in the forum when the censors put out public contracts (Liv. xxviii 18 § 11; xxxix 44 § 8). It was in fact the traditional sign of a State auction (cf. Liv. ii 14 §§ 1—4).

(*adjecta causa* D. vi 1 fr 1 § 2), the character of the claim (*secundum suam causam*) would be briefly stated (or possibly only hinted at by these very words), the symbol itself being very far from telling its own tale. The defendant made a like claim accompanied by a like gesture. The praetor then intervened and directed both parties to let go (*mittite ambo hominem*). They let go. Plaintiff proceeds 'I demand whether thou sayest on what title thou hast claimed by rod.' Defendant answers 'I have done right so, as I have laid rod thereon. Plaintiff, 'Whereas thou hast wrongly claimed by rod, I challenge thee 'with a stake of 500 of bronze (*D aeris sacramento*).' Defendant said in similar way, 'and I thee.' Something further then followed (the MS. fails) as in a personal action, and then the praetor declared the *vindiciae* in favour of one of the parties: that is, as Gaius tells us, he made one of the parties *ad interim* possessor of the thing, and bade him give his opponent sureties for the suit and the rod-claims (*praedes litis et vindiciarum*[1]), *i.e.* for the due delivery, if he lost the case, of the thing itself and profits accruing in the meantime. The praetor further required from both parties other sureties for the amount of the stake, forfeitable by the loser to the public, the stake being 500 asses, if the claim was for a thing worth 1000 asses or more, 50 asses, if of less value. If the suit was whether a person was slave or free, the stake was only 50 asses, however valuable he might be, for freedom was not estimable in money (D. L 17 fr 106),

[1] Festus, p. 376, following Cincius, explains *vindiciae* to be the things taken from the land into court. I doubt this. Serv. Sulpicius (*apud* Fest.) seems to have taken it as I do. Gaius translates *litis et vind.* by *rei et fructuum.*

As regards *lis*=*res* Cicero ridicules the lawyers for not having made up their minds whether the term (in some proceedings—probably this) should be *lis* or *res* (*Mur.* 12 § 27), cf. Varr. *LL.* vii 93 *Quibus res erat in controversia, ea vocabatur lis; ideo in actionibus videmus dici* '*quam rem sive me litem dicere oportet.*' The more usual meaning of *lis* (old form *stlis*) is 'suit,' *e.g.* D. L 16 fr 36. So in *Decemviri stlitibus judicandis, litis contestatio, etc.* In Cicero it is distinguished from *judicium*, *Verr.* iii 10, 26 *Traducere homines ad insolitam litem atque judicium; ib.* 13 § 32 *Persequi lite atque judicio*, and means perhaps the process before the praetor, or the older process of *legis actio.* Cf. *Orat.* ii 24 § 99; *ad Heren.* iv 23 § 33; Wlassak *PG.* ii p. 12.

and it was important that no claim of personal freedom might be hindered by the largeness of the stake. These amounts were all fixed by the XII tables (Gai. iv 13—17).

The second stage of the proceedings ensued. What was the practice before the *lex Pinaria* we do not know[1], but by that law an interval of 30 days was allowed before the appointment of a judge. On the judge being accepted, the parties gave notice (*denuntiabant*, to one another?) to appear before him on the next day. When they appeared, they first gave a summary or heads of their claim or defence (*causae conjectio*[2]), and afterwards pleaded their case in full (Gai. iv 15 of an action *in personam*).

No doubt witnesses were heard, but we know no more than is above given.

Three fragments of information which Gaius gives us elsewhere respecting the statutable procedure may be noticed here.

(*a*) In iv 108, after speaking of the plea of matter decided and brought to issue, Gaius remarks that in the days of the *legis actiones* there was no such use of pleas as there was in his time. Although his remark may refer only to that particular plea, it may be asked generally, how did defendant who had just objections to plaintiff's suit get them duly regarded? The answer which is given by most is that defendant urged them before the praetor himself so as to get him to refuse the *legis actio* altogether. If the facts required to be ascertained, he would direct a preliminary inquiry by means of a wager.

Possibly also the power of bringing a subsequent action for reimbursement would be some safeguard against exorbitant or unjust demands. The *lex Cincia* and *lex Plaetoria*, it has been suggested, might well be enforced by this latter means[3]. Other matters may have been dealt with by the judge himself, who was probably not in those days bound to so precise an issue as he was under the formulary system, where consequently a worthy plea could not be left out of the instructions, if right was to be done.

1 '*Statim*' in Krüger's text of Gai. iv 15 is conjectural.

2 MS. has *collectio quasi causae suae in breve coactio.*

3 Cf. Ihering *Geist* § 52; Karlowa *CP.* § 46.

(*b*) What form judgment took is much disputed. In iv 48 Gaius[1] apparently contrasts the formulary system with that of the *legis actiones*, in that the former had the decision always directed to damages, whereas in the latter the judge condemned defendant in the thing itself. This may however have been sometimes preceded by an interlocutory pronouncement, *ejus qui petit* (plaintiff's) or *a quo petitur* (defendant's) *sacramentum justum esse.* Indeed in actions respecting personal liberty this was very probably the form of the decision itself (Cic. *Caec.* 33 § 97; *Dom.* 22 § 78). Where the thing in dispute was not producible, or pecuniary damages on any ground required to be awarded, the judge would probably proceed at once to settle them.

The fragment of the XII tables *post meridiem praesenti litem addicito* (Gell. xvii 2 § 10) agrees with Gaius' expression.

(*c*) Gaius (iv 108) tells us that in the days of procedure by statute, a matter once made the subject of a process could not again become so[2]; and that this was as of course (*ipso jure*). Compare *exceptio rei judicatae, etc.* below.

[1] Gaius' words are *Et si corpus aliquod petamus veluti fundum hominem vestem argentum judex non ipsam rem condemnat eum cum quo actum est, sicut olim fieri solebat; aestimata re pecuniam eum condemnat.* Most editors insert *sed* before *aestimata.* Some however have connected *sicut—solebat* with what follows, and thus make the same course to be taken under the process by statute as under the process by formulas. Böcking conjectures *sed ut* for *sicut.* It seems improbable that Gaius should have mentioned the old system at all, unless it was different from the modern. Keller supposes that this condemnation *in rem ipsam* was followed by an *arbitrium litis aestimandae*, and refers to this Fest. *s.v. vindiciae: in XII (tabulis) 'si vindiciam falsam tulit si velit is (praetor) arbitros tres dato, eorum arbitrio (reus) fructus duplione damnum decidito'* (*CP.* p. 74). There is no evidence for Keller's view. Cf. Stintzing *Leg. Act.* pp. 32, 34; Cogliolo notes to Padelletti p. 337.

[2] Cf. Ter. *Phorm.* 403 *Tu magistratus adi, judicium de eadem causa iterum ut reddant tibi, quandoquidem solus regnas et soli licet hic de eadem causa bis judicium apiscier; ib.* 419 *'Actum' aiunt 'ne agas';* Donat. ad Ter. *Ad.* 232 *Actum agam: proverbium,* i.e. *nihil agam: quod enim in jure semel judicatum fuerit, rescindi et iterum agi non potest;* Quintil. *Inst.* vii 6 § 4 *Solet et illud quaeri, quo referatur quod scriptum est; 'bis de eadem re ne sit actio'; id est, hoc 'bis' ad actorem an ad actionem: haec ex jure obscuro.*

B. The second *legis actio* mentioned by Gaius was called *per judicis postulationem.* His account is lost and we know nothing of it. It seems probable that it was used for the authoritative settlement of disputes which were too complicated to admit of a simple issue. Such might be the *judicia fam. ercisc.* and *com. div.* or the action *pro socio* or *rei uxoriae* or *tutelae.* Or it is conceivable that it was applied when defendant admitted liability, and the question was only what should be the damages. Some think[1] it was an alternative course open to the parties in any suit (cf. Cic. *Rosc. Com.* 4). Some connect with this procedure the challenge we often read of in Plautus and others 'to take a judge' (see chap. viii H).

The form of application is apparently given by Val. Probus § 4: *Te praetor judicem arbitrumve postulo uti des.*

C. The *legis actio per condictionem* derived its name from the notice (*condictio* = *denuntiatio*) given by plaintiff to defendant to appear on the thirtieth day (from the notice) to take a judge. Its introduction was due to a *lex Silia,* and under that law it applied only to suits for money certain. A *lex Calpurnia*[2] afterwards extended it to suits for anything certain (*de omni certa re*). Gaius says it was much questioned why this mode of procedure was wanted at all, for a claim *quod dari oportet* could be brought either by sacrament or by application for a judge (Gai. iv 17*a*—20), *i.e.* by one or other of those modes, possibly some by one and some by the other; certainly a choice in all cases is not implied (cf. *ib.* 13).

The commencement of Gaius' account has been lost from the MS. The notice in 30 days is the same as that given by the *lex Pinaria* in the sacramental procedure. Considering the class of cases to which this procedure was applicable, it is reasonable to conjecture that the motive for its introduction was to shorten the proceedings in matters (money loans) where

[1] So Schmidt *ZRG.* xiv 153; Wlassak *PG.* i 105. Against Wach-Keller *CP.* p. 78; Ihering *Scherz* 205. Karlowa (*RG.* ii 576) thinks this was the mode of enforcing *pecunia certa credita.*

[2] Mommsen identifies this law with the *lex repetundarum* of B.C. 149 (*Strafrecht* p. 708).

no long investigation was required and stringency was usual. This might be effected by substituting for the solemn ceremonial before the praetor a simple notice, possibly an extra-judicial[1] notice, given along with the summons, to appear in court that day month. Very likely some specification of the claim might have to be given at the time: and possibly the penal wager, which was part of the procedure for loans of money, was then made by the parties (Gai. iv 171; see above, p. 71; cf. Maine, *Early Hist. of Inst.* Lect. IX. p. 257).

CHAPTER VII.

PROCEDURE *PER FORMULAS*, *i.e.* by issues stated by the praetor.

1. All these procedures by statute came into odium, according to Gaius, from their excessive strictness which made any mistake fatal. The ceremonial words followed the precise terms of the statute, and this appears to have been especially the case with any action founded on the XII tables. Gaius mentions one instance: the XII tables gave an action against one who cut down trees (*de arboribus succisis*); a man had his vines cut down and in stating his plaint named vines and not trees. He lost his case. The law spoke of trees: how was a judge to say that vines were trees? If plaintiff complained of something else than the law gave an action for, he must take the consequence and go without the remedy[2] (Gai. iv 11).

[1] Demelius (*Krit. Viert.* viii 508) and Wach-Keller's *CP.* p. 86 ed. 5 state some objections to this view. In reply to the latter see Voigt *Vadimonium* p. 328.

[2] The doubt was not without real foundation. Vines were in some parts of Italy regularly trained to elms or planes or other trees (*arbores*); *arbustum* was the term for such a plantation, which required more years to grow than a plant like a vine. Hence it seems to me likely enough that the XII tables referred to the destruction of the permanent support (and also olives, *etc.*) and not to that of the easily growing but fruitful plant. Cato distinguishes them; *arbores facito uti bene maritae sint vitesque uti*

There appears to be in Gaius' remarks a lack of distinction between *actio* in the sense of legal procedure generally and *actio* as a ground for judicial protection in a particular class of circumstances. But it seems clear that the procedure or procedures by statute lacked flexibility, and were encumbered with antiquated formalities of an unpractical character and only half understood. The growth of Rome and its commerce increased its intercourse with other cities and nations, and promoted the transaction of business on a more simple and intelligible plan. The institution of a praetor for suits among and with foreigners brought new methods in its train, and the bold judicial legislation of the city praetor modified and extended the old law, and no doubt required the accompaniment of a reformed procedure. This reform was eventually effected by a *lex Aebutia* and two *leges Juliae*[1], which established a system of pleading conducted not by gesture and oral ritual, but by words specially adapted to the particular suit (*per concepta*[2] *verba id est per formulas*). The old procedure was abolished except for suits which were to come before the Hundredmen, and in cases of damage apprehended from ruinous buildings (*damni infecti*[3]).

satis multae adserantur (*RR.* 32); so also Varro; *ex arboribus in arbores traductis vitibus vinea fit* (*RR.* i 8 § 4). Pliny includes vines among trees in a general sense; *Vites jure apud priscos magnitudine quoque inter arbores numerabantur* (*HN.* xiv 9). For the action *de arboribus succisis* see p. 194.

1 Wlassak in a very careful and elaborate investigation has made it probable that the *lex Aebutia* introduced the formulary process for all kinds of actions, but concurrently only with the procedure by statute (*Proc. Gesetz.* i p. 104); and that one *lex Julia* (of Augustus) abolished the *legis actiones* except in the two cases mentioned in the text. Both *Aebutia* and *Julia* dealt only with the proceedings before the *Praetor urbanus*. A second *lex Julia*, he suggests, made the same reform for Roman communities outside Rome, and limited the competence of municipal magistrates (*ib.* p. 191 foll.).

2 For this use of *concipere* 'to draft,' see Cic. *Ep. Q. Fr.* ii 13 § 3 *Negat Trebatius quemquam fuisse* (*i.e.* in his camp in Gaul) *qui vadimonium concipere posset* 'who could draw a bail-bond': Liv. vii 5 § 5 *in quae ipse concepisset verba jurare*; Plaut. *Pseud.* 1077; Cic. *Off.* iii 29 § 108; Gai. iv 119, 131; *etc.*

3 Wlassak makes the excellent suggestion that the *legis actio damni infecti* contained an extra-judicial notice (as in *operis novi nuntiatio*) to the

Of these the former was alone important. No use was made of the second, as the praetor's edict provided a remedy by way of stipulated guaranty which proved more convenient than the old proceeding (Gai. iv 11, 30, 31; Gell. xvi 13 § 8). After the *lex Aebutia* therefore the procedure by statute was in fact confined to cases intended for the Centumviral Court.

We do not know the date[1] of these laws, though the *leges Juliae* were probably passed by Augustus. Nor do we know their respective shares in the reform, nor how far the change which was thus stamped with authority had been gradually developed in practice. Our knowledge of the formular procedure is derived mainly from Gaius, but in essentials it existed in Cicero's time, who speaks of it as in use in Sicily. The principle of the procedure was that the praetor should settle beforehand all such questions of law arising in a suit as did not depend on the facts, should define how far equities should be recognised which were beyond the old or ordinary law, and should leave to the judge the decision on the facts and on the application of the law as known, or as now laid down by the praetor, to the result of the facts[2]. The plaintiff's claim and

owner of the dangerous building which imposed on him a liability, and that this part of the *leg. act.* was not of a nature to be superseded by a *formula*, but was superseded by the praetor's directing a stipulation (*Pr. G.* i 269 sqq.).

[1] The latest inquiry into the date of the *lex Aebutia*, that by P. F. Girard (*ZRG.* xxvii 49, see also *Manuel* p. 36), puts the *lex Aebutia* between 605 and 628 U.C. (149—126 B.C.). The *leges Juliae* he puts probably in the year 17 A.D. (*Manuel* p. 49).

[2] The distinction between proceedings *in jure* and *in judicio* is clearly seen in Cic. *Inv.* ii 11 § 57 *Et praetoris exceptionibus multae excluduntur actiones, et ita jus civile habemus constitutum ut causā cadat is qui non quemadmodum oportet egerit. Quare in jure plerumque translationes* (cf. p. 352) *versantur. Ibi enim et exceptiones postulantur et agendi potestas datur et omnis conceptio privatorum judiciorum constituitur. In ipsis autem judiciis rarius incidunt. Part. Or.* 28 § 99 *Etiam ante judicium de constituendo ipso judicio solet esse contentio, cum aut sitne actio illi qui agit aut jamne sit aut num jam esse desierit aut illāne lege hisne verbis sit actio, quaeritur. Quae etiamsi, antequam res in judicium venit, aut concertata aut dijudicata aut confecta non sunt, tamen in ipsis judiciis permagnum saepe habent pondus, cum ita dicitur: 'plus petisti'; 'sero*

the defendant's answer (if not a simple negative), so far as they were admitted by the praetor for trial, were embodied in one formula, framed on lines set forth in the Edict, but adapted to the particular contentions. This question or complex of questions was the issue which the judge had to try. The praetor *judicia dat* 'gives trials,' or 'grants issues for trial[1]'; the *judex judicat* 'tries and decides the issues' (Cic. *Verr.* II 2. 12 § 30).

2. The course followed in framing the issue is nowhere expressly described. Presumably the plaintiff selected among the *formulae* set forth on the praetor's *album* that which best suited him[2], and informed the defendant of it (*edebat*), *i.e.* either

petisti'; '*non fuit tua petitio*'; '*non a me*'; '*non hac lege*'; '*non his verbis*'; '*non hoc judicio*' (*i.e.* you have claimed too much; you are behind time with your suit; it is not for you to sue; nor am I the party to be sued; your case is not under this statute, nor within the words of this formula, nor in a trial like this). Again *ib.* § 100 *De constituendis actionibus, de capiendis subeundisve judiciis, de excipienda iniquitate actionis, de comparanda aequitate, quod ea fere generis ejus sunt ut, quamquam in ipsum judicium saepe delabuntur, tamen ante judicium tractanda videantur, paulum ea separo a judiciis tempore magis agendi quam dissimilitudine generis.*

[1] *Judicium* 'the declaration of law' includes the whole issue tried before the *judex* or *recuperatores* as authorized by the praetor and accepted by the parties. 'Trial' or 'issue' are the more precise, but 'suit' or 'process' are also sometimes convenient translations. When Wlassak (*e.g. Litiscontestation* p. 14) contends for its not only denoting the whole trial (*Gericht*) but also being technical for the *Schriftformel*, distinguishing this from the issue 'das von den Parteien vereinbarte Processprogramm' (*Proc. Gesetze* ii p. 60, cf. i p. 76 sq.), I cannot follow him, though willing to admit that the tablet containing the issue may often have been spoken of by the word properly denoting only the contents. That it means 'issue' and is often used where *formula* might be used, is clear. See also B. Kübler's examination of Ciceronian usage in *ZRG.* xxix 137 sqq.; xxvii 80; and Lenel *ib.* xxviii 374 sqq. *Formula* generally denotes such model or blank forms for issues as were set out in the praetor's *album*, but also the form filled up to give the issue for a particular trial, *e.g.* Gai. iv 57. Gradenwitz says the latter use is not found in laws and republican writers (*ZRG.* xxii 190).

Wlassak notes that where Cicero uses *judicium* the Digest often puts *actio*; this is strikingly shewn by comparing Cic. *Tull.* §§ 7—10, 38—43 with D. xlvii 8 fr 2, esp. §§ 13—25 (*Proc. Ges.* i p. 80).

[2] Cf. Cic. *Rosc. Com.* 8 § 24 *Sunt jura, sunt formulae de omnibus rebus*

read it to him (*dictare judicium* D. xlv 1 fr 112 pr), or shewed it him, or gave him a copy of it (cf. D. ii 13 fr 1 § 1; xxvi 8 fr 1, 15; xliv 4 fr 4 § 19). Sometimes, *e.g.* where there was a doubt as to the ground on which defendant maintained possession, plaintiff proposed two *formulae*, declaring at the same time that he intended only to use one (D. xliii 3 fr 1 § 4). If defendant made no objection and the case was of an ordinary type, the praetor would allow it. But there might often be circumstances which seemed to one party or the other to demand some addition or modification in order to get an issue which both could accept; and upon these proposals the praetor would have to decide (Cod. ii 1 fr 3; Cic. *Tull.* 16 § 38). It was not for the praetor to dictate[1] to the plaintiff what action he should bring, nor to the defendant in what way he should meet it: each party was presumed to know the law and facts of the case and the probable consequences of his proceeding. But the praetor was free to refuse a trial altogether[2] (see lexica *s. v. denegare*), or to refuse the particular issue demanded, if the circumstances made it unfair or inapplicable[3]. On the other hand if plaintiff shewed the praetor that no ordinary form would meet his case, but that he had *prima facie* been wronged in a way calling for legal redress, the praetor could direct an issue in such a special form as would enable right to be done[4]. So if defendant shewed that the issue insisted on by the plaintiff was too absolute and gave no opening for his answer, the praetor would make corresponding exceptions or requirements, and grant a trial to the plaintiff only if he accepted them as part of the issue. Some

constitutae, ne quis aut in genere injuriae aut ratione actionis errare possit. Expressae sunt enim ex uniuscujusque damno, dolore, incommodo, calamitate, injuria, publicae a praetore formulae, ad quas privata lis accommodatur. Quae cum ita sint, cur non arbitrum pro socio adegeris Q. Roscium, quaero. Formulam non noras? Notissima erat. Judicio gravi experiri nolebas? Quid ita?

[1] This is clearly laid down by Cicero *pro Caecina* 3 § 3.

[2] Cf. Cic. *Flac.* 21 § 49 *M. Gratidius legatus ad quem est aditum, actionem se daturum negavit: re judicata stari ostendit placere.*

[3] *E.g.* the actions *quod metus causa*, and *de dolo* were granted only if there was no other adequate legal remedy (D. iv 2 fr 14 § 2; 3 fr 1 §§ 4—7 pr).

[4] *E.g.* by an *actio in factum.*

pleas if granted by the praetor would be clearly fatal to plaintiff's case: others would not. The plaintiff was free to avail himself of this issue or to proceed no further with his suit. If he chose to take the issue as settled by the praetor, defendant had either to accept it and go to trial, or to admit the justice of the claim and either make an arrangement with plaintiff or be condemned without more ado.

3. The issue was directed to a particular person or persons, as judge or recoverers, named in the formula. Apparently the plaintiff proposed the name of someone duly qualified (*ferre judicem*, Cic. *Rosc. Com.* 15 § 45; *Orat.* ii 70 § 285), who if accepted by the defendant (*accipere judicem*) would be nominated. Plaintiff was then said *sumere judicem* (Cic. *Rosc. Com.* 14 § 42; *Quinct.* 9 § 32; D. x 2 fr 52 § 2); or *arbitrum* (D. x 2 fr 47). But defendant might refuse (*recusare, reicere*) the person proposed, and might be compelled to support his refusal by an oath (*ejurare*) that he believed him to be unfair (*iniquus*, Cic. *Verr.* iii 60 § 137; *Or.* ii 70 § 285; *Fin.* ii 35 § 119). Fresh proposals would be made until an agreement was arrived at. Even in a matter of a small sum of money, says Cicero, no one was appointed judge who was not agreed upon by the parties (*Clu.* 43 § 120). Pertinacious refusal to accept all judges proposed would doubtless be treated by the praetor as failure in due defence[1], and defendant might probably be condemned without trial, or possession of his estate be given to plaintiff (cf. *lex Rubr.* 21, 22). A rescript of Hadrian (where the parties disagreed) disapproves of the appointment of a judge whom one party requested by name (D. v 1 fr 47).

As the function of judging was a public duty, the person named in the formula could only obtain excuse for grave reasons (D. v 1 fr 78; cf. fr 39; Suet. *Oct.* 32; *lex Urson.* 95); or as a matter of privilege, either under the *lex Papia Poppaea* (*Vat.* 197, 198), or otherwise, cf. Plin. *Ep. Traj.* 58 (66).

In the appointment of recoverers[2] it was perhaps usual to

[1] Cf. Cic. *Verr.* iii 60 § 140 where Verres similarly condemns a plaintiff who asked for recoverers taken from the regular assize list and declined to accept Verres' nominees from his own suite.

[2] This was the mode followed in Sicily: *Quid praetor* (Verres)? *Jubet recuperatores reicere; decurias scribamus. Quas decurias? De cohorte mea*

take by lot a number of names out of a list of duly qualified persons, and then for each party to have the right of challenging (*rejiciendo*) a certain number (*Ed. Venafr. sub finem*, Bruns no. 73).

In all cases whether of single judges or of recoverers the actual appointment (*datio, addictio*) was made by the praetor, who might however, and would in some cases, either by general rule or perhaps on the application of the parties, send the matter before the *centumviri* or *decemviri*. Any change of party or representative or judge required the approval of the praetor, who would then alter the *judicium* according. This was *transferre judicium* (D. iii 3 fr 17; v 1 fr 46, 57).

4. The general functions of the praetor in these matters, especially when the contest resulted in a trial, are often mentioned in the laws preserved in inscriptions, the phrases being very similar. *Magistratus ita jus deicito, judicia dato, judicareque jubeto, cogito*, 'the magistrate (*i.e.* praetor, governor of province, *etc.*) shall declare the law, shall grant trials, and bid and compel men to judge the case' (*lex Rubr.* 20); *de ea re juris dictio, judici* (=*judicii*) *judicis recuperatorum datio esto* (*lex agrar.* 35); *juris dictio judicis arbitri recuperatorum datio addictio, etc.* (Frag. Atest. 15 *ap.* Bruns no. 17). The expressions remind one of the three words which the praetor could not utter on an unholy day (Varr. *LL.* vi fr 4 § 30)[1]. But those probably related to his functions under the old statutable actions, perhaps thus, *do judicem, dico vindicias, addico judicatum* (*i.e.* to his creditor), or *addico rem* in surrender in court, *etc.*

All orders made by the praetor could be revoked by him (D. xlii 1 fr 14), and a *judicium* is dissolved by a prohibition of the praetor or of one who had greater authority (*e.g.* consul, D. v 1 fr 58). But neither praetor nor judex could rescind a judgment (*sententia*) once given by him (D. xlii 1 fr 42, 45). All magistrates (not however town *duoviri*) had power to enforce

reicies, inquit (Cic. *Verr.* iii 11 § 28), cf. *Flac.* 4 § 11. In Plin. *Pan.* 36 we have (perhaps referring to *recuperatores*) *sors et urna fisco judicem adsignat; licet reicere, licet exclamare, 'hunc nolo,' 'illum volo.'*

[1] Cf. Ovid *Fast.* i 47 *Ille* (*dies*) *nefastus erit, per quem tria verba silentur; fastus erit, per quem lege licebit agi.*

obedience to their orders by directing an issue for damages *quanti ea res est* (D. ii 3).

Special preparatory or alternative proceedings by means of wagers, orders for giving security, and tenders of an oath might form part of the business before the praetor. In some cases interrogatories were allowed. The appointment of representatives to conduct the suit was included in the issue. These matters together with certain checks on litigation will best be treated after the pleadings have been discussed. Gaius' fourth book is almost our only source of direct information on the pleadings.

When the emperor referred a litigant to the praetor or proconsul, *etc.* (*eum qui provinciae praeest adire potes*) it was for the magistrate to decide whether he would deal with (*cognoscere*) the matter himself or appoint a judge (D. i 18 fr 8).

5. A check upon the praetor's or other magistrate's possibly arbitrary decisions was provided by the edict declaring that if he laid down any new law (*si quid novi juris statuerit*) against a litigant, he and the litigant who demanded and obtained it in his favour must submit to its application against themselves in any suit which either might subsequently be engaged in, if his opponent in such future suit, whoever he might be, demanded it. The heir of the litigant favoured by the decision has to submit to its application also; but it cannot be used by a surety of the litigant. If the magistrate was a son under power, the father, sued on his son's behalf, is not liable to this principle (D. ii 2). The magistrate so applying it, if attacked, could plead *praeterquam si contra eum fecerit qui ipse eorum quid fecisset* (fr 4).

CHAPTER VIII.

PLEADINGS, OR PARTS AND KINDS OF *FORMULAE*.

A. General form.

1. The instructions on an issue for trial contained normally three parts. The first part was a brief statement of the matter giving rise to the suit, and was called *demonstratio*: the second set forth the plaintiff's claim (*intentio*): the third (*condemnatio*) instructed the judge to condemn the plaintiff in so much damages or to acquit him, as he might find to be right on the issue raised.

Thus to take the case of suit on a stipulation for a definite sum of money the issue would be framed thus:

M. Titius[1] *judex esto. Quod A. Agerius de N. Negidio x milia stipulatus est.* (*Demonstratio.*)

Si paret N. Negidium A. Agerio x milia dare oportere. (*Intentio.*)

M. Titi[2], *N. Negidium A. Agerio x milia condemna; si non paret absolve.* (*Condemnatio.*)

2. All these parts were subject to alteration according to the nature of the suit. Thus in a suit *ex vendito* against the buyer of a slave for the purchase money, the demonstration would state the fact of the sale, and the claim might be for the agreed amount: *e.g.*

M. Titius judex esto. Quod A. Agerius hominem Stichum N. Negidio vendidit, si paret N. Negidium A. Agerio L milia dare oportere, etc. But as the claim might in this, as in other *bonae fidei* suits, carry with it further rights for interest, *etc.* due to the delay of the purchaser, or might be subject to equities or counterclaims on behalf of the purchaser, a more general form of the *intentio* was adopted, *quidquid paret N. Negidium A. Agerio dare facere oportere.*

[1] Perhaps *M. Titi*, the vocative; but in Cic. *Verr.* ii 2, 12 § 31 we have *L. Octavius judex esto.*

[2] Gaius has *judex* in the formula, for which I presume the name of the particular judge selected would appear in the issue as actually sent for trial.

Where the suit was *in rem* to recover one's own slave or other thing in the possession of another, there was often no need of any demonstration and the claim would be put forward at once, *i.e.*, *M. Titius judex esto. Si paret hominem Stichum quo de agitur ex jure Quiritium A. Agerii esse.* The condemnation clause would contain not a definite sum of money, but leave the valuation to the judge, *e.g. quanti Stichus est, tantam pecuniam, M. Titi, N. Negidium A. Agerio condemna; si non paret absolve* (Gai. iv 40, 41, 43).

Where again the suit is one for division of property held in common, whether between coheirs by the suit *familiae erciscundae,* or between partners or tenants in common by the suit *communi dividundo,* or between neighbours by the suit *finium regundorum,* the issue would briefly describe the circumstances and matter in question, and then instruct the judge by an adjudication clause to adjudge such part as might seem to him right to this or that litigant, *e.g. quantum adjudicari oportet, M. Titi, A. Agerio, M. Seio adjudicato,* and finally subjoin the general instruction in some such words as *quicquid ob eam rem alterum alteri praestare oportet, ejus M. Titi alterum alteri condemna, etc.*[1] (Gai. iv 42).

3. The condemnation in every issue 'sounded in damages,' *i.e.* it directed not, as under the former system, specific restoration of a thing or specific performance of a neglected duty, but the payment of money (Gai. iv 48: see above, p. 344 n. 1). The judge valued the thing or estimated the loss which had arisen from the neglect, and condemned the defendant in that amount. But specific restoration or performance might practically be obtained by the insertion of such words in the issue as *nisi restituet,* or *neque (si) ea res A. Agerio restituetur,* or by the action of the judge (Gai. iv 48; Cic. *Verr.* II 2, 12 § 31; and below, p. 411). Similarly in a noxal action the condemnation was couched in the alternative, *e.g. aut x milia sestertiûm solvere aut Stichum noxae dedere* (Gai. iv 75; Paul i 15 § 1): but in the

[1] Puchta (*Inst.* I § 167) and Lenel add *si non paret absolve* (*EP.* pp. 164, 165). No doubt if there were more than two co-holders and a payment was imposed on one for equality of distribution, the others might require an acquittal (cf. D. x 2 fr 27), but these words seem incongruous.

action *judicati* founded on this condemnation, plaintiff claims the 10000 sesterces, and defendant will be condemned to that, but has a statutable right to free himself by noxal surrender (D. xlii 1 fr 6 § 1).

The damages stated in the condemnation-clause may be either a certain or an uncertain amount. There are two cases of an uncertain amount: the damages may be put at the value of the thing or of the interest of the plaintiff, whatever that may be (1) without limit: or (2) with a superior limit. It is uncertain without limit (for instance) in a vindication or suit for production: *quanti ea res erit, tantam pecuniam, judex, N. Negidium A. Agerio condemna: si non paret, absolvito.* It is uncertain, but with a maximum limit (*cum taxatione*) when *dum taxat* appears in the formula, *e.g. N. Negidium A. Agerio dum taxat sestertiûm x milia condemna; si non paret absolve* (Gai. iv 49—51) or *dum taxat de peculio et quod in rem ejus* (*i.e. patris*) *versum est* (D. v. 1 fr 57)[1].

It may be noted here that the words *quanti ea res erit* (or *est*) sometimes denote the actual value of the thing, *verum pretium rei, vera rei aestimatio* (D. L 16 fr 179, 193: xlvii 2 fr 50 pr) more frequently were extended, or sometimes confined, by the lawyers to the plaintiff's interest, *utilitas, quanti actori interest, quod interest* (D. vi 1 68; xliii 16 fr 6; 17 fr 3 § 11; xlvi 5 fr 11; cf x 4 fr 9 § 8; Just. iv 3 § 10)[2].

4. One important difference in the frame of the issue was determined by the nature of the action, as founded on the civil law, or as granted by the praetor to meet the particular circumstances. In the former case the issue was shaped for law (*formula in jus concepta*); in the latter case it was shaped for

[1] In the case of *Tullius* v. *Fabium* the issue contained a limit. Cicero says *Judicium vestrum est, recuperatores. Quantae pecuniae paret dolo malo familiae P. Fabi vi hominibus armatis coactisve damnum datum esse M. Tullio. Ejus rei taxationem nos fecimus: aestimatio vestra est: judicium datum est in quadruplum, i.e.* the recoverers would if they found for the plaintiff fix the amount of damages at some figure not exceeding plaintiff's estimate (*taxatio*). Whatever the amount so fixed, defendant would be in this case condemned for fourfold that amount (Cic. *Tull.* 3 § 7).

[2] See Savigny *Syst.* v. *Beil.* xii; F. Mommsen *Beitr.* ii § 6; Demelius *Exhibitionspflicht* p. 10.

fact (*in factum concepta*). A formula 'shaped for law' was an issue directing a judge to inquire whether the facts that should be proved shewed a right known to the civil law, *e.g.* that a thing is ours by the law of the Quirites, or that this or that thing or sum of money should be given us, or that some damage caused to us by defendant, either as thief (*pro fure*) or as committing a wrong within the Aquilian statute (*damnum injuria*), ought to be settled for (*decidi oportere*), or the like. The amount might by the pleading be left to the judge to determine (*quidquid dare facere oportet*) or be claimed by the plaintiff definitely: that did not affect the general character of the issue, which, presuming the judge to know what was required for Quiritian ownership, and what the civil law recognised as a personal obligation from contract or from tort, gave him the task of deciding whether the plaintiff proved his ownership or contract, or established his case for compensation for neglected duty.

On the other hand a formula 'shaped for fact' limited the judge to the task of ascertaining whether the facts were really as stated in the formula hypothetically: the praetor had already determined that these facts entitled the plaintiff to redress: if therefore the facts were found to be as alleged, the judge had nothing more to do (at least at this stage) than to find for the plaintiff and condemn the defendant in an amount which would redress the wrong.

Usually one only of these two kinds of issue would be so often required for a particular class of action as to make it worth while for the praetor to publish the types of issue on his *album*. But for some reason or other in the cases of deposit and loan (*commodatum*) the edict contained both types, and these may therefore be suitably used in illustration. The *formula in jus concepta* for deposit is given by Gaius thus:

Judex esto: Quod A. Agerius apud N. Negidium mensam argenteam deposuit, qua de re agitur, quidquid ob eam rem N. Negidium A. Agerio dare facere oportet ex fide bona[1], *ejus*

[1] Cf. Cic. *Top.* 17 § 66 *in omnibus his judiciis in quibus 'ex fide bona' est additum.*

iudex N. Negidium A. Agerio condemnato N. R.[1]*: si non paret absolvito.*

The *formula in factum concepta* is given as follows:

Judex esto. Si paret A. Agerium apud N. Negidium mensam argenteam deposuisse eamque dolo malo N. Negidii A. Agerio redditam non esse, quanti ea res erit, tantam pecuniam judex N. Negidium A. Agerio condemnato: si non paret absolvito (Gai. iv 45—47: cf. 60).

The *formula in jus concepta* just mentions the general nature of the suit and then leaves free hand to the judge to determine what the equity of the case demands, the suit being *bonae fidei*. There might be claims of the plaintiff for non-return of the table or for delay in returning it, or for damage done to it, or for its having been carried off and left in a distant place, and there might be counter-claims for expenses in recovering it from robbers or repairing damage from inevitable accidents, *etc.* The judge might direct the immediate return and ascertain the balance on claims, or might direct plaintiff on receiving the value to transfer his actions to defendant, *etc.*

The *formula in factum concepta* makes it necessary for plaintiff to prove the fact of the deposit of a table, of its being silver, of its non-return, and of this non-return being due to the fraudulent (*i.e.* wrongful) conduct of defendant: if these facts are severally proved, the judge has simply to allow plaintiff to fix on oath the value of the table (D. xvi 3 fr 1 § 26), or if plaintiff does not do so, to fix the value himself and order defendant to pay the value. One may conjecture that when the facts were clear and there was no complication of counter-claims, a plaintiff might prefer this form of action to one which left more openings for chicanery and delay.

Gaius gives another instance of an action *in factum concepta* where a freedman has summoned his patron into court contrary to the edict (see p. 335) and the patron therefore sues him

[1] Supposed by some to be for *nisi restituat*, but there is no authority for such an explanation, and no other example of *nisi restituat* in the formula of an action of *dare oportere*. See Keller *Institutiones* p. 115.

for damages[1]: *L. Titius, C. Seius, M. Flavius recuperatores sunto. Si paret M. Albium Sexti filium Quirina (patronum) a M. Albio liberto suo contra edictum C. Burrieni praetoris in jus vocatum esse, L. Titi, C. Sei, M. Flavi, M. Albium libertum M. Albio Sexti filio Quirina x milia condemnate: si non paret, absolvite.* The same title of the edict (*de in jus vocando*) was filled with *formulae* of this class *e.g.* in actions against one who being summoned into court neither came nor furnished a *vindex* in his stead, or one who had forcibly carried off a person who was under summons to court; these and many others (*innumerabiles*) being cases where the praetor held that the fact once established was sufficient to constitute a claim for redress (Gai. iv 46).

5. There are some cases in which the formula contains neither demonstration nor condemnation, but only the claim or rather the point in dispute (*intentio*). Gaius gives as instances certain preliminary questions (*praejudicia*), 'whether a person is a freedman' (cf. D. xl 14 fr 6), 'how large a dowry is,' *etc.* No formula ever contained only a *demonstratio* or an *adjudicatio* or a *condemnatio*: they would have no point by themselves; the *intentio* is essential (Gai. iv 44). In the *formulae in factum conceptae* the demonstration is absorbed into the claim (cf. *ib.* 60).

B. Error in plaintiff's statement.

The importance of an error in the plaintiff's statement of claim is different according to the part of the formula in which it occurs.

1. In the clause containing the claim (*intentio*) a misstatement is fatal to the plaintiff, if in excess of his right. *Causā cadit* 'he falls from his case,' *i.e.* loses his suit (*rem perdit*)[2].

[1] I have filled up Gaius' blank form with conjectural names (cf. Cic. *Quinct.* § 24).

[2] A case in point (but *lege agendo*) is mentioned by Cicero (*Orat.* i 36 §§ 166, 167). Hypsaeus acting for a ward against his guardian urged the praetor to allow him to make his claim for more than the XII tables permitted (see vol. I p. 111) in which case he would have lost his case (*causā caderet*). Octavius for the defendant was equally stupid; he vigorously

And the praetor rarely quashed the proceedings (*in integrum restituere*), unless plaintiff was under twenty-five years of age. If he were older, it must be shewn that there was much to excuse the error (Gai. iv 53 mutilated, cf. Just. iv 6 § 3). Excess of claim (*plus petere*) might be in several ways; viz. in the thing itself, in point of time, in point of place and in the particular character (*re, tempore, loco, causa* Gaius; *loco, summa, tempore, qualitate* Paul i 10). There is excess in the thing if a man sue for 20,000 when only 10,000 is owed him, or when with an issue framed *in factum* a man states a deposit of more things than was true (Gai. iv 60), or when a part owner or co-heir sues for the whole or for a larger share than belongs to him, or when a man claims (*vindicat*) the right of raising his house without specifying any limit of height, although he has only a right of raising to a certain height (Vat. 53). There is excess in point of time, when one sues for what is not yet due; or when one who has a temporary usufruct claims it, without adding the period (Vat. 52). Excess in point of place is when what is promised to be paid in a certain place is sued for in another place, without mention of the place agreed on, as if a man has stipulated for something to be given him at Ephesus, and then at Rome sues for it to be given him without any qualification. The rates for money and the price of commodities vary in different places and hence the claim may by the change of place become more irksome. There is excess in the particular character (*causa*) of the claim, if a man sues for a thing without giving an option between that and something else in conformity with the stipulation. So if a man has promised purple generally, and you sue him for Tyrian purple; or has promised a slave generally, and you sue him expressly for a particular slave. Nor does it matter whether the thing sued for is cheaper than what was promised or not: the excess lies in taking away defendant's option, for although the claim may be for what is really less, yet it may sometimes be easier for defendant to give the other, and thus an excess of claim is the result.

urged that this should not be permitted, thereby missing his opportunity of getting a certain acquittal for his client in a suit which involved infamy to the person condemned.

And therefore in suing on a stipulation, the claim should be expressed in the precise terms of the stipulation (Gai. iv 53; cf. Just. iv 6 § 33).

If the claim is, as defined above, uncertain[1], *i.e.* if the formula runs *Quidquid N. Negidium A. Agerio dare facere oportet*, there can be no excess of claim. And the same applies when (as is however rarely allowed) an undefined part of a thing is claimed in an action *in rem*, *e.g. quantam partem paret in eo fundo de quo agitur A. Agerii esse* (Gai. iv 54).

If one claim less than is really due, his claim is good so far, but he cannot sue for the balance within the same praetorship, as the defendant could defeat him with the plea *litis dividuae*, *i.e.* that he has split his claim (Gai. iv 56, 122, see below).

If the plaintiff errs by substituting one thing for another, so that he claim the slave Eros when he ought to have claimed Stichus; or if he based his claim on a will (*ex testamento dare sibi oportere*) when the thing was due on a stipulation; or if an attorney or agent claims that a thing ought to be given *to him* (instead of to the person whom he represents); in all these cases the plaintiff's action goes for nothing, and he is not prevented from suing afresh on his real claim rightly stated (Gai. iv 55).

2. If in the condemnatory clause plaintiff puts a larger sum than he ought, he only so far injures himself that he enables the defendant to get the proceedings quashed (*in integrum restituta*) on the ground of the formula which he has accepted being unfair. If plaintiff puts a less sum than he ought, the balance is lost, for the claim puts the whole matter

[1] Cicero dwells on the difference between a suit for something certain and for something uncertain, calling the former a *judicium*, the latter an *arbitrium*. (*Rosc. Com.* 4 § 10) *Pecunia tibi debebatur certa, quae nunc petitur per judicem. Hic tu, si amplius* HS *nummo petisti quam tibi debitum est, causam perdidisti, propterea quod aliud est judicium, aliud est arbitrium. Judicium est pecuniae certae, arbitrium incertae: ad judicium hoc modo venimus, ut totam litem aut obtineamus aut amittamus; ad arbitrium hoc animo adimus, ut neque nihil neque tantum quantum postulavimus consequamur. Ei rei verba formulae testimonio sunt. Quid est in judicio? Derectum, asperum, simplex: si paret* HS ꟾↃↃ *dari; hic nisi planum facit* HS ꟾↃↃ *ad libellam sic deberi, causam perdit. Quid est in arbitrio? Mite moderatum, 'Quantum aequius et melius sit dari'*

in issue, and the judge cannot give sentence for a larger amount than is named in the condemnation. Nor will the praetor assist the plaintiff by quashing the proceedings, unless he is under 25 years of age, for in the case of minors the mistake of a plaintiff meets with as much indulgence as that of a defendant (Gai. iv 57).

3. A mistake, whether by excess or defect, in the demonstration, does no harm, the rule being *falsa demonstratio rem non perimit*. Plaintiff's real claim is not put in issue at all (*nihil in judicium deducitur*) and the proceedings go for nothing. According to some lawyers (says Gaius), including Labeo, a demonstration is not bad which states less than the real claim, so that one who has bought two slaves Stichus and Eros, can take a formula commencing 'Whereas I have bought from you the slave Eros,' and can afterwards sue for Stichus, for it is true that having bought the two, he has also bought each one. But if he has bought only one, and sets forth that he has bought two, the demonstration is false. And the same applies in suits for loan (*commodati*) and deposit. Other writers again hold that in some cases a demonstration setting forth more than is true occasions a loss of the suit altogether, these cases being actions of deposit and all others wherein condemnation was followed by infamy. For instance, one who sets forth a deposit of two or more things when he has only deposited one, or who, bringing an action for insulting conduct in consequence of a blow on his cheek with a fist, alleges a blow on another part of his body also. Gaius apparently agrees that this is so in an action for deposit where the formula was *in factum concepta* because there the demonstration is merged in the claim and the judgment made to depend on the finding of the facts; but with a formula *in jus concepta* the two are quite separate, and a misstatement does no harm, because the claim is only for what is found to be right (*quicquid ob eam rem illum illi dare facere oportet*: Gai. iv 58—60 mutilated at end).

Where the claim set forth is true in itself, but is on certain grounds of law not fully recoverable, because for instance the defendant as father or master is responsible only to the extent of the son's or slave's *peculium* and that is inadequate to the claim, or because the relation of plaintiff and defendant prevents the claim being pressed to the full (cf. p. 416), the apparent excess of demonstration or of claim or of condemnation does not injure the plaintiff's suit: the judge makes the necessary reduction (Just. iv 6 §§ 36—38: Gaius' text is lost but cf. iv 134).

C. Set off (*Compensatio*).

Other circumstances may make a practical reduction of the plaintiff's demand. In all *bonae fidei* actions, and, since M. Aurelius, in strict actions also, the judge could set off against the claim of plaintiff a debt in reference to the same matter due from him to the defendant. But this was not explicitly stated in the formula and will be better dealt with later on. 1. There are however two cases in which 'set off' or an analogous deduction found place in the formula. A banker suing his customer for money due, must set off all sums due to him; in short he can sue for the balance only. Thus if he owes Titius 10,000 sesterces and Titius owes him 20,000, the claim must be made in this fashion; 'if it appears that Titius ought to pay plaintiff '10,000 more than he himself owes to Titius, then condemn 'Titius in that amount.' 'Set off' can only be between debts actually due and of the same kind, *e.g.* money against money, wheat against wheat, wine against wine; and some lawyers held that they must be of the same quality as well as of the same kind. Account is taken of the set off in the clause containing the claim (*intentio*), so that if the banker sue for a sesterce more than the balance, he loses his case and therefore the debt is gone.

2. The purchaser of a bankrupt estate (*bonorum emptor*) is in somewhat the like position. He must sue with a deduction: *i.e.* he can sue a debtor to the estate only for what remains due, after deducting what he owes to the defendant on the defaulter's account. But the deduction is not confined to what is actually due; a debt due on a future day has also to be deducted. Nor is it necessary that the debt should be of the same kind of thing: from a money demand must be deducted the value of any corn or wine due. Account is taken in the condemnation clause, so that the rule which attends the

banker's set off does not hang over the purchaser of bankrupt estate: though his claim is for a defined amount, the condemnation clause is uncertain: *quanti id erit, deducto quod actor debet, etc.* (Gai. iv 61—68; Paul ii 5 § 3).

D. Pleas (*Exceptiones*).

1. The praetor in settling the issue is not concerned only with the plaintiff's claim, but has to regard and embody in the formula any special answer in law or equity which the defendant may put forward, and which is not regarded by the praetor as sufficient in itself or sufficiently evident to justify him in refusing the action altogether. The formula, being the instructions to the judge that he is to condemn or not, according as he finds the facts and law to support the plaintiff's or defendant's case, must embrace the salient points on which the defendant bases his refusal, as well as the plaintiff's allegation of right. Thus it may be that the plaintiff has strict law on his side, but that it would be inequitable for defendant to be condemned. Suppose for instance that I have stipulated that you should repay me so much money which I am going to count over to you as a loan and yet have never done so, you are still bound by your promise to pay it me—that is clear law; but, the equity of the case being against me, you are allowed a plea of fraud (*doli mali*), and, if this be proved, the judge will acquit you from my suit. Or suppose that I have made a bargain with you not to sue you upon your debt, the bargain does not cancel the obligation to pay in strict law, but if I sue notwithstanding, the praetor will allow you the plea of 'bargain agreed' (*pacti conventi exceptio*) and thus defeat my action. Other pleas are such as arise when an oath has been tendered and defendant has sworn that he does not owe the money, or that the land sought is his own; or when a man has been compelled by fear or induced by fraud to mancipate to another some property. If he is then sued, the plea of oath or intimidation or fraud will be fatal to plaintiff. Or if a man has knowingly bought land with disputed title (*fundum litigiosum*) from one who is not possessor, and then sues the person possessing for it,

a plea of the fact puts the suitor out of court (Gai. iv 115—117; Just. iv 13 §4; see below, p. 406).

2. Some pleas were in constant use, and were set out in the edict as standing pleas: others were granted specially by the praetor after full hearing (*causa cognita*). All rested either on statute or what is equivalent to statute, or on the praetor's jurisdiction. They were inserted in the formula in a shape which expressed the contrary of the defendant's contention[1], being in fact conditions on which the judge was not to find for the plaintiff; or, in other words, only if the fact alleged by defendant was found not to be true, was the judge to condemn the defendant. Thus, taking the first case mentioned above, the formula would run thus: *si paret N. Negidium A. Agerio x milia sestertium dare oportere*[2], *si in ea re nihil dolo malo A. Agerii factum est neque fit, judex, N. Negidium A. Agerio x milia sestertium condemna; si paret absolve.* So the plea of 'bargain agreed' would be in the form *si inter A. A. et N. N. non convenit ne ea pecunia peteretur,* and only if the judge finds there has been no fraud or no such bargain is he to condemn the defendant (Gai. iv 118).

3. Pleas are called either peremptory or dilatory. The former are those which are always in force and cannot be avoided, the latter are good only for a time. Peremptory pleas are such as intimidation, fraud, violation of a statute or senate's decree, matter already decided or brought to issue (*rei judicatae vel in judicium deductae*)[3], bargain never to sue. Dilatory pleas

[1] The words used in *formulae* for introducing a plea are *quod non, quod nec...nec* (Cic. *Fam.* vii 13; *Tull.* 19 § 44; *lex Agrar.* 18; D. xliii 24 fr 7 § 3; *etc.*); *qua de re non* (*lex Rubr.* 19); *extra quam* (Cic. *Inv.* ii 20 § 59); *extra quam si* (D. xliii 12 fr 1 § 16); *si non* (Gai. iv 119, 126); *neque*, after *si paret* (C. *Verr.* ii 12 § 31). *Nisi* appears to have been avoided, perhaps because of its use in offering the alternative of restitution (*nisi restituat*, see p. 411). *Nisi*, as well as *ni*, *si*, is common in wagers. See Keller *CP.* § 34; Schmidt *Interd.* p. 108; and on wagers the references below, p. 374 n. 1.

[2] In actions for *certa credita pecunia* the ground of debt was not stated. Lenel *EP.* p. 187; infra, p. 497.

[3] Most writers treat this as two pleas. Lenel shews that Gaius gives it apparently as one, and points out possible risks which would be avoided by the combination. It is referred to (not quoted) in Cic. *Orat.* i 37 § 168 *ne*

are such as 'bargain not to sue within (say) five years': after that time has expired, suit could be brought. So the pleas of 'split suit' (*litis dividuae*) and 'remaining matter' (*rei residuae*) are only temporary bars: the former is when a plaintiff has already sued for part of a debt and sues for remainder within the same praetorship; the latter is when a plaintiff, who has several actions with the same defendant, has sued on some and put off others with a view to getting different judges, and then sues on these remaining matters within the same praetorship: in both cases plaintiff is put out of court by the plea. Whenever there is a dilatory plea applicable, plaintiff's right course is to defer suit until the next praetorship or whatever the period may be, and thus avoid the plea; otherwise if he persists in suing, the matter having been brought to issue and destroyed by the plea, his claim is gone. If defendant omits to use a dilatory plea which he might use, it is, says Gaius, a question whether he can get the proceedings quashed: if he omits by mistake to use a peremptory plea, he can get them quashed so far as to admit of the addition of the plea (Gai. iv 120—123; 125).

Other dilatory pleas are concerned with the persons appearing as parties, such as cognitorial (or procuratorial D. xliv 1 fr 2 § 4 fr 3) pleas. If plaintiff sue by attorney (*cognitor*), when he is disabled by the edict from appointing one, or has appointed one who is disabled from acting as such (see chap. iii A, B), he is liable, if he proceeds, to have this pleaded against him and thus lose his claim. His right course, on the insertion of this plea being demanded by his opponent, is to appear in person in the former case, and in the second case either to appear in person or to appoint a duly qualified attorney. In one of these ways he can avoid the plea. Concealment of the disqualification is fatal (Gai. iv 124).

exceptione excluderetur quod ea res in judicium antea venisset (*EP.* p. 404). Observe too that *rei* is not repeated before *in judicium*, as would be natural in giving the name of a separate plea. (Eisele in *Abhandl. d. röm. C. P.* argues against Lenel, but considering how little we know of the *legis actio* procedure and how little we can trust conjectural restorations, I am surprised at the stress laid by him on them, *e.g.* pp. 20, 26. He has a further article on the subject in *ZRG.* xxxiv.)

A defendant is not limited to a single plea; and is not held by the use of a plea to admit the claim of plaintiff to be good in itself (D. xliv fr 5, 8, 9).

E. Replications, *etc.* Plaintiff will sometimes have a good answer to defendant's plea, and this also will consequently be inserted in the formula. It is called a *replicatio*[1]. For instance it may be quite true that I bargained not to sue you for a debt, but a subsequent bargain between us may have been made, which restored me my liberty. The formula should therefore contain not only the plea of bargain made not to sue (*si non convenerit, ne eam pecuniam peterem*), but also a replication subjoined *si non postea convenit ut mihi eam pecuniam petere liceret.* So a banker may have conducted an auction and given notice that payment must be made before delivery. If he sues a purchaser for the money and the purchaser pleads non-delivery of the goods bought, the plea will run *si ei res quam emerit tradita est*; the plea being as usual contradictory to the defendant's contention, *i.e.* in this case in the affirmative because defendant denies delivery. To this the replication will be appended *aut si praedictum est ne aliter emptori res traderetur quam si pretium emptor solverit.* A rejoinder to a replication may perhaps be required on the part of the defendant: this is called a *duplicatio.* Again this may lead to surrejoinder (*triplicatio*) from the plaintiff; and it is possible that the controversy may require further additions (Gai. iv 126—129; cf. D. iii 3 fr 48).

The replication is sometimes regarded as the second stage in the pleading, the exception being the first: the reply to plaintiff is then *triplicatio.* Thus if a caretaker who ought by a decree of the praetor to have given security has sold and conveyed some thing belonging to the madman and the madman's heir brings a vindication against the purchaser, he will plead (*exceptio*) that it was sold to him. The madman's heir can reply (*replicatio*) that the caretaker was bound to give security for his due administration, and that the purchaser can proceed against him, and will not therefore be damnified by giving up

[1] *I.e.* the 'undoing, because the leaf folded is folded back again,' *Quia per eam replicatur atque resolvitur vis exceptionis* (Gaius).

the thing illegally sold to the madman's heir. To this the purchaser can perhaps retort (*triplicatio*) that the purchase money has been applied to defray debts of the madman and that therefore the madman's heir, holding an estate which has been benefited by the act of the caretaker in raising money, is acting fraudulentlyin redemanding the thing sold. This pleading would be expressed: *si non curator rem de qua agitur vendiderit* (exceptio), *aut si satisdatione interposita secundum decretum vendiderit* (replicatio) *neque in ea re dolo malo Titii* (*i.e. heredis*) *quidquam factum est* (triplicatio). Cf. D. xxvii 10 fr 7 § 1; Keller *CP.* § 37; Savigny *Syst.* v p. 193. So in Vat. 259 the reply to a plea of the *lex Cincia* is called *duplicatio* (= *replicatio*).

F. Praescriptions.

1. Praescriptions[1] are limitations prefixed to the formula for the protection of plaintiff. It often happens that several claims may arise from the same obligation, part due now, part only at a future time. Thus if a person has stipulated for a certain sum of money to be paid him every year or every month, at the end of some years or months certain amounts will be due, others under the same obligation not due, and we may desire to collect what is due without impairing the obligation of future payments. Plaintiff therefore must put at the head of the issue words to limit his suit: *e.g. Ea res agatur cujus rei dies fuit*[2]. Otherwise if he sue with the regular *formula* for an uncertain amount, *quidquid paret N. Negidium A. Agerio dare facere oportere,* he puts the whole obligation in issue[3], and yet cannot get judgment for more than is actually due: and thus will lose future payments altogether.

2. Similarly if a man sue on a purchase (*ex empto*), so many matters may be the subject of this suit, that it is necessary to

[1] Cf. Cic. *Fin.* ii 1 § 3 *Omnis oratio praescribere primum debet, ut quibusdam in formulis, 'Ea res agatur,' ut inter quos disseritur conveniat quid sit id de quo disseratur.*

[2] Cicero speaks of it as an old and much used plea (*exceptio*), and says it was a plea framed on behalf of plaintiffs (*Orat.* i 37 § 168). See above, p. 179.

[3] In issues for trial *oportet* includes *oportebit* (D. xlv 1 fr 76 § 1). Cf. p. 53.

use a praescription, lest in suing on one point he may be precluded from afterwards suing on others, as occasion may arise[1]; *e.g.* if he wish to obtain mancipation of the land purchased, he should prefix *Ea res agatur de fundo mancipando,* which will prevent the whole obligation coming to issue and therefore leave it open for him afterwards to sue for delivery of vacant possession, or on a covenant for quiet enjoyment, or the like (Gai. iv 130—132). Again if a slave or other person under power has stipulated for something, and an action is necessary to enforce it, the master or father appears in the formula claiming that defendant is bound to give something to him, and yet plaintiff has himself made and can prove no such stipulation or reason for the *dare oportere.* A clause is therefore prefixed stating that he is suing on a stipulation made by his slave or son (Gai. iv 134 much mutilated, 135).

3. Where an uncertain stipulation has been made and the promiser is supported by a *sponsor* or *fidejussor*, and suit is brought only for what is due, the necessary limitation is inserted in the demonstration itself[2], in the case of suit against the principal debtor; but in the case of suit against a surety this limitation is added to the praescription which is required for shewing the character of his obligation. Thus the formula for suit against principal will be *Quod A. Agerius de L. Titio*

[1] Two passages have led to a general opinion that several claims arising from the same subject were sometimes made in one action, each with a limiting praescription: Cic. *Fin.* v 29 § 88 *Ut in actionibus praescribi solet 'de eadem re, alio modo'*; *Fam.* xiii 27 (addressed to Servius) *ut vos soletis in formulis, sic ego in epistolis, 'de eadem re alio modo'*; cf. D. xliv 2 fr 14. Modern jurists have difficulty in finding the right occasion for such a praescription. Cf. Savigny *Syst.* vi p. 425, 6; Salpius *Novation* p. 184, *etc.* I am inclined to think that Cicero has in mind not the *formula* itself, but books of precedents, so that *in actionibus, in formulis* mean 'in the case of actions' or 'in your lists of actions or formulae,' *praescribere* being used in the general sense of 'make a heading' (cf. *Fin.* ii 1 § 3) and not in the technical sense of plea or limitation. Since writing this I notice B. Kübler (*ZRG.* xxix 148) has put forth the same view, and compares Cic. *Orat.* i 57 § 245 *ad Hostilianas te actiones contulisses*; Varr. *RR.* ii 5 § 11 *qui Manili actiones sequuntur; ib.* 5 § 11 *ut in Manili actionibus sunt perscripta.*

[2] *Loco demonstrationis*, cf. Gai. iv 68 *quo loco.* It can hardly mean 'instead of' as the praescription is given as only part of the demonstration.

incertum stipulatus est, cujus rei dies fuit, quidquid ob eam rem L. Titium A. Agerio dare facere oportet, tantam pecuniam, etc.

Against a *sponsor*, as follows: *Ea res agatur, quod A. Agerius de L. Titio incertum stipulatus est, quo nomine N. Negidius sponsor est, cujus rei dies fuit.* [1]*(Quod A. Agerius de N. Negidio incertum stipulatus est, quidquid ob eam rem N. Negidium A. Agerio dare facere oportet, tantam, etc.)*

Against a *fidejussor* (who may have been surety for a verbal or non-verbal obligation of his principal) the frame is different: *Ea res agatur, quod N. Negidius pro L. Titio incertum fide sua esse jussit, cujus rei dies fuit.* [1]*(Quod A. Agerius de N. Negidio incertum stipulatus est, quidquid ob eam rem N. Negidium A. Agerio dare facere oportet, tantam, etc.)* (Gai. iv 136, 137).

4. Gaius mentions that though in his time all praescriptions were on behalf of the plaintiff, there was a time (*olim*) when some were inserted also on behalf of the defendant[2], and instances the case of a disputed inheritance, where a defendant

[1] The parts added in brackets are not given by Gaius, who simply says *deinde formula subicitur.* Keller subjoined *quidquid paret ob eam rem N. Negidium dare facere oportere, etc.*, without any demonstration (*CP.* p. 198). Lenel agrees (*EP.* p. 119). Karlowa objects that, when a *praescriptio* is put first with *ea res agatur*, there should be a demonstration. So far I am inclined to agree, but not when he (*RG.* ii 737 n.) makes the demonstration to contain not the name of the surety, but that of the principal debtor. I think the surety should be sued on his own stipulation, not on that of his principal, especially as sometimes he was obliged for a less sum than the principal (Gai. iii 126). It was important to have a praescription in order to make the accessory nature of this stipulation clear and enable surety to use pleas open to his principal. Karlowa's reason, that it was intended to prevent the consumption of the action against the principal debtor and thus to leave it open to the creditor to cede this to the surety (D. xlvi 1 fr 36, *etc.*), seems to me to tell against his bringing the principal debtor into the demonstration. (Of course in the *intentio* it would be fatal.)

If there were several sureties, would this fact appear in the formula, *e.g.* after *sponsor* add *cum duobus aliis* or *dumtaxat ex tertia parte?*

[2] Quintilian (*Inst.* vii 5 §§ 2, 3) uses *praescriptio* in this way. *Aut intentio aut praescriptio habet controversiam...cum ex praescriptione lis pendet, de ipsa re quaeri non est necesse. Ignominioso patri praescribit filius; de eo solo judicatio est, an liceat (i.e. patri agere)?* So *praescribere* in D. xlix 1 fr 3 § 1; 4 fr 1 § 10. Compare the case in D. xxvi 7 fr 37 § 2.

might fear that a decision in a suit for a particular thing, apparently belonging to the inheritance, might be held to involve a decision on the claim to the inheritance as a whole. He could then have a praescription, *ea res agatur, si in ea re praejudicium hereditati non fiat* (cf. D. v 1 fr 54). In Gaius' time this danger was met by a plea (iv 133; after which section begins a long gap in our MS. of Gaius). See below, p. 393.

G. Fictions.

1. Besides the enumeration of facts (mentioned above, A 4) the praetor had other means of framing *formulae* to give redress in cases not within the civil law. One of these was by fictitious assumptions. The judge was instructed by the formula to act on certain assumptions, which if true would put the case on the lines of the ordinary civil law. Thus the praetor could not make a man heir, but the same considerations which made the edict set forth a succession to deceased's estates different from that of the old law, made him grant to these 'possessors of the estate' analogous rights of suit to those which the statutable heir would have. They could not use the regular expressions which an heir would use; they could not say that the property of the deceased was theirs, or that debtors ought to give them (*dare oportere*) this or that thing, owed to the deceased, except by a fiction. The formula therefore was modified in this way: *M. Seius judex esto. Si A. Agerius L. Titio heres esset; tum si eum fundum de quo agitur ex jure Quiritium ejus esse oporteret, M. Sei, N. Negidium A. Agerio x milia sestertium condemna; si non oporteret absolve.* 'M. Seius shall be judge. If A. A. 'had been heir to L. Titius, and if then the farm in question 'ought to belong to him in accordance with the law of the 'Quirites,' *etc.* A like fiction would be made in case of an action for debt (*dare oportere*). Similarly if a man on the ground of purchase or other lawful cause had had delivery of something, but had not had time to gain the ownership by usucapion, and had lost possession, the praetor granted him an action (*Publiciana* vol. I p. 443) against any unlawful possessor, similar to a regular vindication, but based on the

fiction that he had possessed it for the full time requisite; *si quem hominem A. Agerius emit et is ei traditus est anno possedisset, tum si eum hominem de quo agitur ex jure Quiritium ejus esse oporteret, etc.* 'Assume that the slave in question, which 'A. Agerius bought and which was delivered to him, had been possessed by him for a year, then, if it should have been his by 'the law of the Q.,' *etc.* Again it is sometimes just that a foreigner should be enabled to sue or be sued in cases where a Roman citizen would be able and liable by the civil law, *e.g.* for theft, aiding or counselling theft, or Aquilian damage: Roman citizenship is attributed to him for the purpose of the action, and the judge is directed to condemn or acquit on that hypothesis. So also the difficulty arising from the old Roman law that *capitis deminutio* destroyed all contractual obligations of the person, as in the case of a woman who was copurchased, or a man who was arrogated, was met by the praetor's allowing any creditor, who would thus be deprived of his rights, to bring his action against them and allege that they were bound to give him his demand (*sibi dare eum eamve oportere*). For this purpose the formula contained the fictitious assumption that they had not suffered *capitis deminutionem.* (Gai. iv 34, 36—38, in some parts mutilated.)

2. So the *formulae* for 'apprehended damage' (*damni infecti*) given by the *lex Rubria* (cap. 20) for the inhabitants of Cisalpine Gaul are framed so as to make one who had failed to give due promise or security responsible just 'as if he had given it' (Bruns no. 16). The same is found in the praetor's edict on the subject (D. xxxix 2 fr 7 pr).

In the formula given to a tax farmer, a kind of fiction is introduced: the condemnation is to be made for the amount which defendant would have had in old times to pay to redeem his pledge, if a pledge had been taken (Gai. iv 32)[1].

3. The '*bonorum emptor*' 'purchaser of a bankrupt estate' required actions for recovering the debts *etc.* due and belonging to it. His case was met in two ways. There was an *actio*

[1] Gaius' appended remark that '*nulla formula ad condictionis fictionem exprimitur*' probably only means that no occasion was found under the formulary procedure for a fictitious assumption of a 30 days' notice, *etc.*

Serviana (introduced by Serv. Sulpicius ?) which was based on the fiction that the man instead of being bankrupt was dead, and the purchaser was the heir. Another way was the invention of P. Rutilius, the praetor to whom the whole law for the sale of bankrupts' estates was attributed. On this method the claim (*intentio*) ran in the name of the bankrupt; but the condemnation was couched in favour of the purchaser of the estate, viz. that the judge should condemn the defendant to pay plaintiff damages if the thing claimed was the bankrupt's, or to pay plaintiff whatever defendant was shewn to be indebted to the bankrupt (Gai. iv 35). The purchaser was in fact treated as procurator for the bankrupt.

4. A similar mode of drafting the formula to that of Rutilius was adopted whenever a suit was conducted on behalf of another (*alieno nomine*) *e.g.* by attorney, agent, guardian, or caretaker (*cognitor*, *procurator*, *tutor*, *curator*). The formula contains the name of the principal in the claim (*intentio*), and the representative's name appears in the condemnation clause. Thus if P. Mevius be plaintiff, and L. Titius be acting for him, these two clauses will run thus in a personal action: 'If it 'appears that N. Negidius ought to give P. Mevius 10000 ses- 'terces, judge, condemn N. Negidius to pay to L. Titius 10000 'sesterces: if it does not so appear, acquit him.' If defendant is represented by another, defendant's name will similarly be put in the claim and the representative's name in the condemnation clause. In an action *in rem*, where plaintiff is represented by attorney, *etc.* the form will run: 'if it appears that 'the thing in question is P. Mevius' by the law of the Quirites, 'condemn N. Negidius to pay to L. Titius, *etc.*[1]' Where defendant is represented by attorney, *etc.*, the condemnation clause will be altered in the same way, but defendant's name is not given in the claim, any more than it would be if he defended in person (Gai. iv 86, 87).

5. A similar frame will be adopted when a principal is

[1] Where the representative was a *cognitor* and consequently the principal was responsible, perhaps his description was added in the formula, *e.g.* *Lucio Titio, P. Maevi cognitori*, and the same for *tutor* and *curator*.

made responsible by the praetor for his skipper or his manager (*exercitoria, institoria actio*), the claim having the name of the subordinate as the person who made the contract, the condemnation clause having that of the principal (D. xiv 1 fr 1 § 24).

H. *Sponsiones*[1] 'judicial wagers.'

One of the methods used by the praetor to expedite a suit was to direct an issue on a particular question, whether the main question between the parties or one ancillary or preparatory to it. The parties under his instruction made a wager (*sponsio*), by single or double stipulation, with one another for a nominal sum on the truth either of the plaintiff's claim or assertion or on some counter-assertion of the defendant's. Thus a wager, that the thing in question was the plaintiff's, was one of two methods for pursuing an action *in rem*. The terms of the wager are given us by Gaius (iv 93) *Si homo quo de agitur ex jure Quiritium meus est, sestertios xxv nummos dare spondes?* The formula or issue for trial would be a claim for the payment of the 25 sesterces; and plaintiff would win only if he proved his ownership of the slave named in the wager. Cicero (*Verr.* iii 57 § 132) refers to the same method for claiming an inheritance. A wager could be used in the procedure under any interdict[2], and was always used where the interdict was prohibitory, as in the interdicts *uti possidetis* and *utrubi* for trying who is the lawful possessor (Gai iv 141). Cicero's speech for Caecina was

[1] *Sponsio.* Schmidt (*Interd. Verfahren* p. 244) raises the question whether these wagers were necessarily in the form *spondesne? spondeo* and answers in the negative, because, if so, foreigners would be excluded. He refers to D. L 16 fr 7.

See a collection of passages containing wagers in Bekker *Actionen* i 249 sq. In one which he quotes (Val. M. vi 5 § 4) *sponsio* is I think used for a surety's bond. On the grammatical form of wagers, when reported, see my Lat. Gr. §§ 1752, 1753.

[2] The wager mentioned by Cicero in Silius' case *Si bonorum Turpiliae possessionem Q. Caepio praetor ex edicto suo mihi dedit* (*Fam.* vii 21) appears to belong to the interdict *quorum bonorum* (vol. I p. 239). It would raise the issue whether a grant of possession of Turpilia's estate *secundum tabulas testamenti* had been duly made. There appears to have been a question whether Turpilia had a right to make a will at all (without the authority of her guardians?). See vol. I p. 101.

made on the trial of a wager on an interdict *de vi armata* (8 § 23). His speech *pro Quinctio* was made on the trial of a wager on defendant's denial of plaintiff's allegation (8 § 30; 9 § 32). Similar, but not strictly judicial, cases are in Liv. xxxix 43 § 5 where Cato the Censor, removing a consular from the senate for an act of atrocious cruelty offered him the chance of making a wager on the fact in order to prove his innocence: and in Val. M. vi 1 § 10 where a delinquent asks to have a trial on a wager to prove a fact which would mitigate his admitted guilt[1].

Where a wager was thus merely ancillary or preparatory to the main issue, it was called *sponsio praejudicialis*[2]. The wager was one-sided, only the one party stipulating, and the amount of the wager was not exacted. If defendant won, he could await any further action on the part of the plaintiff. If plaintiff won, he would still have to take some further step to get satisfaction of his claim on the main issue; but of this we know only what Gaius tells us in relation to interdicts (see below, p. 445). Sometimes security for this would be taken before trial of the wager (Gai. iv 94, 165).

Other wagers were called *poenales* because they were used to check litigation by imposing additional penalties on the defeated party. Their earliest form was the *sacramentum* of the *legis actio* (Gai. iv 13, 14); and they were used for this purpose

[1] Some such defensive wagers appear to be intended in Plaut. *Men.* 592.

[2] The plaintiff was said *sponsione provocare* (Gai. iv 95; 165, cf. 166) *lacessere* (Cic. *Verr.* iii 57 § 132), but the more usual phrase, applicable to both parties, was *sponsionem facere*, *e.g.* Cic. *Quinct.* 8 §§ 30, 31; 9 § 32; *Caecin.* 16 § 45; *Fam.* vii 21; Liv. xl 46 § 14; Val. M. vi 1 § 10, *etc.* According to Huschke (*Anal.* p. 146) followed by Jordan (*ad Caecin.* 31 § 91) if plaintiff won, he was said *sponsione vincere* (Gai. iv 165; Cic. *Quinct.* 27 § 84); if defendant won, he was said *sponsionem vincere* 'overcome the wager' (Cic. *Tull.* 9 § 30; *Caecin.* 31 § 91). Huschke therefore in *Caecin.* 32 § 92 alters the MS. reading *sponsione* into the accusative. The passage in *ad Heren.* iv 23 *ipse grandi sponsione victus est* proves nothing. I doubt the distinction and think the expressions are like our 'win a wager' and 'win in a wager,' the accusative being cognate. So in the fragm. of Cic. *Tull.* quoted by Victorinus p. 209 Halm we have *vici unam rem* and *vici alteram*: in *Rosc. Com.* 18 § 53 *quod vicisset judicio ferres tuum* 'what he had won'; *Verr.* ii 1 53 § 139 *judicium me uno dependente vicit.* In Liv. xxxix 43 § 5 we have *sponsione defenderet sese.*

in certain actions under the formulary system, viz. for a loan of money certain and for money 'appointed to be paid' (*certa credita pec.* and *constituta pec.:* Gai. iv 191; cf. Cic. *Rosc. Com.* 4 § 10); and also in interdict procedure (Gai. iv 166, 167). A *sponsio* is mentioned as a customary part of procedure in *Lex Rubr.* 21, 22[1].

(In the English Chancery Courts, when a trial of fact by a jury was desirable, the practice formerly prevailed to feign a wager which the parties were bound to admit, and direct it to be tried in a Court of Common Law. Such an issue is now either sent for trial in a direct form without any wager being feigned, or is tried in the Court itself (Stephen's *Comm.* iii p. 661 12th ed.).)

CHAPTER IX.

REPRESENTATION AND SECURITY.

A. Representation of parties.

1. Under the system of action by statute (*legis actiones*) representation of the parties was allowed only in a few cases (Gai. iv 82; cf. D. L 17 fr 123 pr). In Justinian's *Institutes* (iv 10

[1] Other instances of wagers are mentioned in the classical writers, which might no doubt, like any other verbal contract by stipulation, be the subject of a trial, but which are neither directed by the magistrate nor form part of legal procedure. Such was a bet between the consul and praetor as to which deserved the credit of having led the fleet to victory over the Carthaginians (Val. M. ii 8 § 2), or that which two men in succession publicly offered to make, and one made, that Verres was partner with a tax-farmer in his contract for the Sicilian tithes (Cic. *Verr.* iii 57 § 132; 58 § 135). In another case Verres retaliated for similar freedom of speech by compelling the speaker to make a wager; he had him so severely beaten that he died in consequence (*Verr.* v 54 § 141). Other cases are Piso's offer to Cicero, who had said he had entered the city by the Caelimontan gate, to bet that it was by the Esquiline gate (Cic. *Pis.* 23 § 55); or the bet made by Lutatius and brought to trial 'that he was a good man' (*quod vir bonus esset*, cf. Gell. xiv 2 § 26); or several which

pr) we are told that such cases were suits on behalf of the people, or for one claiming his freedom, or on behalf of a ward (*pro populo, pro libertate, pro tutela*). The first probably includes as well actions to assert a public right of road, as actions on behalf of a municipality or for extortion against a provincial governor. One suing *pro populo* could not appoint an agent; the person sued could (D. xlvii 23 fr 5). The agent in claiming freedom was a *vindex*. A guardian would appear for a ward, and a curator for a minor or a lunatic. Where there was no guardian ready to defend a ward and there were pressing claims against him, as heir or otherwise, the praetor would call on relatives or friends or freedmen to appear for him, and only if no one could be got to undertake the task would he allow creditors to take possession of the estate (D. xlii 4 fr 5). A *lex Hostilia* allowed a representative to bring an action for theft on behalf of one who was in the enemy's hands, or who was absent on public business, or who was their ward (Just. l.c.). Some concession appears also to have been made for persons over 60 years of age, or who were disabled by sickness or infirmity (*ad Heren.* ii 14). But both *cognitores* and *procuratores* are found in Cicero. Women were not qualified (D. L 17 fr 2).

2. Gaius mentions no restrictions on the use of representatives, but distinguishes between a *cognitor* and a *procurator*. A cognitor is appointed for a particular suit or cause of suit (*in litem*) in a set form of words in the presence of the opponent. Gaius gives two forms[1], the first apparently for a suit actually in court and ready for joinder of issue. Thus in an action *in rem* plaintiff would say 'Whereas I am suing thee for a farm' (no doubt naming it) 'I give to thee L. Titius as (my) attorney' (*Quod ego a te fundum peto, in eam rem L. Titium cognitorem do*): defendant, if appointing such an attorney, would say

appear elsewhere. Cf. Plaut. *Pseud.* 1077 (where however the bet is one-sided, *i.e.* a mere single stipulation).

The expression *ferre judicem alicui* is used in Livy iii 24, 56; cf. Plaut. *Rud.* 1380 and 713 of similar challenges to have issues tried; and *da pignus* is common in Plautus for bets of all kinds (*e.g. Epid.* 699; *Pers.* 186; *Poen.* 1242, *etc.*).

[1] See Wlassak *Gesch. der Cognitur* pp. 23, 26, *etc.*, D. xlvi 8 fr 15.

'Because[1] thou art suing me for (such and such) a farm, for that 'matter I give thee P. Mevius as (my) attorney.' The other form is apparently intended where the case has not yet come into court, or at least not yet reached the stage of trial. Thus in a personal action plaintiff says, 'Whereas I mean to sue thee '(*tecum agere volo*), for that matter I give L. Titius as (my) 'attorney.' Defendant says 'Because thou meanest to sue me, for that matter I give P. Mevius as (my) attorney.' The words are not so strictly framed as are the phrases in the *legis actiones*, and they admit of addition or omission: and even Greek words might be used. It is immaterial whether the cognitor be present or absent at the nomination, but, if he be absent, he becomes cognitor only if he is informed and accepts the duty. His appointment must however be absolute: an appointment under condition, whether express or implied, is invalid. He is put in his principal's place, with the opponent's full knowledge, and, if acting for plaintiff, binds his principal so that no second action for the same matter can be brought by the principal, any more than if he had conducted the suit himself (Gai. iv 82, 83, 97, 98; Vat. 318, 319, 329). If he act for defendant and has assented to the appointment and to the principal's giving security for him *judicatum solvi*, he will be compelled by the praetor to accept trial, except for grave reason, *e.g.* if he has received an accession of dignity, or is going to be absent on public business, or has an inheritance fallen to him, or is in bad health, or going on a necessary journey, or has a capital quarrel with the principal (D. iii 3 fr 8 § 3—fr 15). Until joinder of issue the principal (or his heir) is free to change his cognitor for another or act himself, but after joinder of issue he must show the praetor good cause for so doing, *e.g.* besides such reasons as above, that the cognitor is in captivity or imprisoned or in exile or hiding or engaged in a public or private suit or has become connected with his adversary by marriage or has become his heir or is too old. And the like applies if he is

[1] In both cases Plaintiff uses '*quod*,' Defendant '*quia*.' Any reason of substance is not apparent. Gradenwitz suggests that it is a matter of euphony, so as not to have, either hiatus (*quia-ego*) or such a combination of dentals as *quod tu* (*ZRG.* xxix 130).

cognitor for plaintiff (fr 16—25)[1]. On the way in which the formula was made to fix a representative with responsibility see above, p. 373.

3. A procurator (or agent) is on a different footing. He may be agent for the principal's business generally or for a certain department of his affairs or he may be appointed to act for a particular suit[2]. His relation to his principal is a contract of mandate, which may be made by words orally or by writing or message without any set form, and even without the knowledge or presence of the other party to the suit. The mandate is often not shewn at first but only in the course of the suit: and is liable to expire by the death of either mandator or mandatee or by revocation. Such an agent does not bind his principal, who is therefore not disabled from suing again on the same matter; the opponent must therefore protect himself against the agent's want of authority by requiring security for his principal's approval (*de rato*). Indeed some lawyers, says Gaius, were of opinion that no mandate was necessary, if the agent undertook the business in good faith and gave security. Children, parents, brothers, relatives by marriage, freedmen, may certainly sue for their relative without a mandate, provided they are not shewn to be acting against their relative's will (Gai. iv 84; Vat. 333; D. iii 3 fr 42 § 2; fr 35 pr, 40 § 4; cf. xlvi 7 fr 3 § 3). A procurator accounts to his principal for what he gets and can claim reimbursements for expenses rightfully incurred (fr 46 §§ 4, 5).

If a procurator brought an action for another person or made an application to the praetor for an interdict or for a praetorian stipulation, the edict required that he should also

[1] I have followed Lenel in considering these passages to relate originally to *cognitores*.

[2] Cf. Cic. *Caecin.* 20 § 57 *De liberis* ('freemen') *quisquis est, procuratoris nomine appellatur* (*i.e.* in the interdict *de vi*); *non quo omnes sint aut appellentur procuratores qui negotii nostri aliquid gerant....Non alia ratio juris est, utrum me tuus procurator dejecerit is qui legitime procurator dicitur, omnium rerum ejus, qui in Italia non sit absitve reipublicae causa, quasi quidam paene dominus, hoc est, alieni juris vicarius, an tuus colonus aut vicinus aut cliens aut libertus aut quivis qui illam vim dejectionemve tuo rogatu fecerit.*

accept trial in actions brought by others against such principal, should duly conduct the defence, and should give adequate security. And not only must he defend him in regular actions and interdicts but in praetorian stipulations and interrogatories, being bound to answer what his principal would be bound to answer. The like responsibility was incurred by relatives who sued on behalf of others though not requiring a mandate. But no such responsibility was incurred by undertaking the defence of another (fr 33 §§ 3, 4; 35 pr §§ 2, 3; 39 pr; Vat. 330).

4. The great distinction between a cognitor and a procurator is that the judgment in the suit is enforced in the former case by and against the principal and his heir[1], whereas a procurator has the control of the suit, is responsible on an adverse judgment, and if successful has a right to sue upon the judgment[2]. But if a cognitor is acting for his own interest (*in rem suam*), being another's representative only in form, as often occurs in the cession of actions, he is in the same position as a procurator as regards the judgment, but has no obligation to account to, and no claim against, the nominal principal (any more than a procurator *in rem suam*). On the other hand if a procurator was appointed by his principal present in person and thus is free from all suspicion of being a mere volunteer or the holder of an insufficient or expiring mandate, he is treated as a cognitor, so as if acting for the plaintiff not to be required to give security, though if acting for defendant he was still bound to give security (see below, p. 382). The praetor will however after due inquiry allow the principal to sue and be sued on the judgment. The principal need not be present in court or even in the forum: it is enough if he is in the city. The ordinary

[1] Cf. Cic. *Rosc. Com.* 18 § 53 *Qui per se litem contestatur sibi soli petit, alteri nemo potest nisi qui cognitor est factus. Cognitor si fuisset tuus, quod vicisset judicio, ferres tuum.*

[2] The passages in the Digest which appear to put a procurator into a different position (D. iii 3 fr 28; tit. 4 fr 6 § 3; xlii 1 fr 4 pr; xlvi 3 fr 86) are probably to be explained (see Lenel's *Palingenesia*) by supposing Tribonian to have put *procurator* for *cognitor*. But there was, no doubt, in the latter part of the Antonine times a tendency to give a *utilis actio* to one (*e.g.* a principal) who was directly concerned though not technically entitled.

procurator is spoken of as *procurator absentis*, in contrast to such a *procurator praesentis* (Vat. 317, 331—333; Paul i 2 § 4).

The rules respecting compelling cognitors to accept trial and changing cognitors apply also to procurators.

5. A woman can appoint a procurator without the authority of her guardian; a girl cannot. If parents are too ill or old to sue and there is no one else, the praetor will sometimes allow a woman to sue for them (Vat. 326, 327; D. iii 3 fr 41). Deaf and dumb persons are not prevented from appointing procurators (fr 43 pr). Sons and daughters under power can appoint procurators to sue, if the case be one (*e.g. injuriarum*) in which they can bring an action themselves. Slaves cannot appoint procurators to sue, except when they are engaged in a trial of their *status* (fr 8 pr, 33 pr, § 1; see Book 1 chap. v). Soldiers cannot be procurators while in service (fr 8 § 2).

A list is given in the edict of persons disqualified from appointing or being appointed cognitors or procurators (see chap. ii B). Anyone disqualified and yet suing would be met by a plea to that effect (*exceptio cognitoria, procuratoria*, fr 57 § 1, Vat. 323).

B. Security to be given by suitors.

1. If plaintiff sue either in his own name or by attorney (*cognitor*) neither he nor his attorney is required to give security, whether the suit be *in rem* or *in personam*. Defendant of a suit *in rem* always has to give security, so that, if he is defeated, and does not either restore the thing in his possession or pay the adjudged damages, plaintiff may have the power of suing his sureties as well as himself. If the action be *in personam* and an attorney accepts trial on account of a principal the principal must give security; for it is a general rule that no one is an adequate defendant of another's concern without security being given (Gai. iv 88—90, 96, 97, 100, 101). If however the principal accepts issue on a personal suit in his own name, he is still liable to give security in certain cases, specified by the praetor, on the ground partly of the nature of the action (*a, b, c*), and partly of defendant's own character (*d, e, f*). Thus he must give security, if the action be (*a*) on a judgment,

or (*b*) on money paid down by a sponsor (vol. II p. 184), or (*c*) on a woman's conduct (*de moribus mulieris* vol. I p. 157), or (*d*) if defendant have run through his property (*si decoxerit*[1]), or (*e*) had his goods seized and advertised by his creditors, or (*f*) be an heir held by the praetor to be suspect (Gai. iv 102).

2. Where an agent (*procurator*) is employed, he himself, not his principal, has to give security: viz. if plaintiff, *ratam rem dominum habiturum*; if defendant[2], either *judicatum solvi* or (if the proceeding was by wager) *pro praede litis vindiciarum.* Guardians and caretakers are as a rule in the same position, but, when they are plaintiffs, are sometimes excused (Gai. iv 91, 98—101; cf. D. xxvi 7 fr 23[3]). A procurator for defence whose appointment is recorded in court (*apud acta constitutus*) is still, by a constitution of Severus, compelled to give security *judicatum solvi* (Vat. 317). Where a procurator demands security for payment of legacies, or against anticipated damage from a building, or for double value in case of eviction, he can be called upon to give security for his principal's ratification, such securities as these being in fact preventive substitutes for suits (D. xlvi 8 fr 20; iii 3 fr 40 § 1); and by agreement this stipulation is often used when a procurator sells or lets, *etc.* (xlvi 8 fr 10).

3. Security (*satisdatio*) in all these cases means not pledges or deposit of money, but promise given in reply to stipulation and supported by like promises made by sureties (D. xlvi 5 fr 1 § 5; fr 7). These (as well as other) stipulations were required by the praetor and set out in his edict and hence called *praetoriae.*

[1] *Decoquere* did not necessarily, though it did usually, imply moral delinquency. Cf. Cic. *Phil.* ii 18 § 44 *Lege Roscia decoctoribus certus locus constitutus, quamvis quis fortunae vitio non suo decoxerit.*

[2] In Cic. *Verr.* ii 24 § 60 the practice of requiring security from defendants on others' account is recognized: *Amici, si quis quid peteret, judicio se passuros, judicatum solvi satis daturos esse dicebant.* (On *judicio pati* see p. 459 n. 5.). In Cic. *Quinct.* 7 § 28 a procurator protests against having to give security, unless his principal if present would have to give it. But the circumstances there were peculiar; see below, pp. 460, 477.

[3] D. xxvi 7 fr 23 (unless altered by Tribonian, cf. Gradenwitz *Interpol.* p. 100) shews that the ordinary practice in Ulpian's time was not to require security *ratam rem pupillum habiturum*, seeing that the guardian's suit commits his ward (*rem in judicium deducit*).

They were not subject to alteration by the parties without the praetor's approval (D. xlv 1 fr 5 pr; 52 pr; xlvi 5 fr 1 § 10). On due cause being shewn (*causa cognita*) the principal was held entitled to sue on any praetorian stipulation made on his behalf by his procurator (D. xlvi 5 fr 5).

Their contents appear to have been as follows:

4. *Ratam rem dominum habiturum, i.e.* that the procurator's action shall be held as the action of the principal. There were usually as it appears three clauses: (*a*) *amplius non peti*[1], or more fully, *amplius non petiturum eum cujus de ea re actio petitio persecutio sit*: (*b*) *ratam rem dominum habiturum* or more fully *ratum habituros omnes ad quos ea res pertinebit*; (*c*) *de dolo i.e. dolum malum abesse afuturumque esse* (D. xlvi 8 fr 14, 22, § 7, 23, *etc.*, cf. Lenel *EP.* § 289). The guaranty was therefore both negative, that no further action of any kind should be brought in the matter by anyone entitled to do so[2], and positive, that his principal, or generally, that all concerned, would ratify his suit. If the principal only were named when the intention was to include also his heir and others concerned (which term did not include creditors, D. iii 3 fr 39 § 2), the last clause would come in to justify the stipulator in suing, if necessary, on account of their action (xlvi 8 fr 22 § 7). There is no forfeit under the stipulation, if an action is brought by someone who is not a properly appointed procurator or otherwise not concerned (fr 23). Nor if the principal appealed from a decision given against the procurator; for that is in the natural course of the

[1] For *peti* see p. 402.

[2] This would apply *e.g.* where a stipulator left several heirs (D. xlv 1 fr 4 § 1); or where an Aquilian action is brought by a farmer which might also be brought by his landlord (ix 2 fr 27 § 14). Cicero refers to this clause in *Brut.* 5 §§ 17, 18 *Ego a te hujus voluntarius procurator petam. 'At vero' inquam 'tibi ego non solvam, nisi prius a te cavero amplius eo nomine neminem, cujus petitio sit, petiturum'*; *Att.* i 8; *Fam.* xiii 28 *a* § 2 *Rogo ut, si quid satis dandum erit 'amplius eo nomine non peti,' cures ut satisdetur fide mea.* The absence of such a stipulation is used as an argument in Cic. *Rosc. Com.* 12 § 35.

The clause for approval by the principal might be used separately, where (as mentioned above) an agent has sold or let property or otherwise acted for an absentee (D. xlvi 8 fr 10, 11). Cf. Lenel *EP.* § 289.

suit, and implies a ratification of the plaintiff's action. Nor, unless express words are added to the stipulation, is there a forfeit, if the suit was on behalf of a minor and the minor obtained a quash of the proceedings (fr 3, 5).

The ratification ought to be made within a reasonable time after any payment or other satisfaction made to the procurator. If the principal in any way fails to recognise the settlement, *e.g.* by setting off the original debt, the (former) debtor can sue on this stipulation (fr 12 §§ 2, 3). So also if the principal sue a surety or partner in the obligation or anyone whom he could not have sued if the ratification had been duly made (fr 1, 14). If the principal leave several heirs, and one ratify and another do not, the stipulation is good for a partial forfeit, and so also if the principal himself partially ratify (fr 17, 18). The liability under the stipulation is not affected, whether the procurator have obtained payment which was due or not due, or whether he has got it without bringing suit or by the decision in a suit, though it might be argued that, when a judge had found due what was not due, there was nothing for the principal to ratify and no interest for the unfortunate defendant in having a ratification. When defendant would have a condiction for undue payment to the procurator, the stipulation supersedes it: if the principal ratifies the procurator's action, the stipulation fails and the condiction will be against the principal (fr 22 §§ 1—3). Action could be brought on the stipulation more than once—whenever in fact the stipulator is put to expense and loss by the principal's not ratifying the procurator's action: he is not bound to wait till the whole loss is ascertained (fr 18).

The measure of damages on the stipulation is the interest of the stipulator in due ratification; *in quantum mea interfuit, id est, quantum mihi abest quantumque lucrari potui* (fr 13, 19). The words in the stipulation would be *quanti ea res erit* (D. xlvi 5 fr 2 § 2).

5. *Judicatum solvi, i.e.* for payment of the judgment. Here also were three clauses *de re judicata, de re defendenda, de dolo malo.* The second clause was necessary because judgment might be staved off or prevented by defendant's or his representative's shirking or failing to appear. In fact the stipu-

lation was intended to guaranty both an honest defence (*boni viri arbitratu*), such as might not prevent the attainment of a judgment, and the due performance of the judgment when obtained (D. v 1 fr 63). No one could be sued on the stipulation on both clauses, but of two sureties or two heirs to the promiser one might incur a forfeiture on one clause and one on the other (D. xlvi 7 fr 6, 21). If a release was given or other settlement made on the principal clause (*de re jud.*), the others fell with it (D. xlvi 4 fr 20). Any one surety could undertake the defence to the action on the stipulation. If there were more than one surety or more than one heir, the plaintiff could demand that one agent should act for all. Sureties sued on the stipulation should require security that their principal should be acquitted in the original suit, else they could not claim against him on the mandate, for their payment would not have freed him (xlvi 7 fr 5 §§ 1, 7, fr 14 § 1). The stipulation failed if the action which it guarantied was brought before a different judge, or was itself of a different kind from that contemplated, or if it was brought by one not duly authorised (fr 3 pr, 7). It is not necessary for the promiser or his sureties themselves to undertake the defence: the clause for due defence is satisfied if an outsider undertake it, provided he give proper security or be accepted by plaintiff even without security (fr 3 § 9, 5 § 3). If a slave object of the original suit dies after joinder of issue, the sureties are not freed, for it is important to have judgment in order to preserve the action against eviction and the fruits (fr 11). The measure of damages in this stipulation is the amount of the judgment (fr 9). If a suit is transferred from a defender to his principal, the defender's sureties and pledges are no longer bound (D. xx 6 fr 1 § 2).

6. *Pro praede litis vindiciarum* was the form of security required when an action *in rem* was tried by means of a wager. The wager took the place of the *sacramentum* in the old *legis actio*, and this security took the place of the sureties there given. But as the amount of the wager was only nominal, security to be effectual had to be given not for that amount (as in *judicatum solvi*) but for the restitution of the thing in dispute and the mesne profits or its equivalent in money. In other

respects probably this form of security resembled that of *judicatum solvi* (Gai. iv 91—94; cf. 16).

In all these guaranties breach of the *doli clausula* gave rise, like the other clauses, to an action on the stipulation, not to the special *doli actio* (D. xliv 4 fr 4 § 16; cf. iv 8 fr 31).

CHAPTER X.

CHECKS ON LITIGATION.

A. General.

Both plaintiff and defendant were subjected to various risks, if found to have brought or defended a suit unjustifiably.

Plaintiff may be met at the outset by a challenge of his good faith. Defendant may either call upon him to take his oath that he is suing in good faith (*non calumniae causa se agere*): or he may call for a trial of his good faith (*calumniae judicium*), the penalty to plaintiff being one-tenth of the amount of his suit. But plaintiff is not condemned unless shewn to be bringing the suit without reasonable ground and merely in order to harass his opponent, hoping to win by a blunder or partiality of the judge and not on the merits: for *calumnia* like *furtum* lies in the evil intent. One who calumniously claims another's slave as a freeman is liable to a fine of one-third instead of one-tenth.

In certain cases defendant can have instead of one of the above-named two courses a counter trial (*contrarium judicium*) with penalty attached. Three cases are named: viz. if one is sued for insulting conduct (*injuriarum*); if a woman, who has been sent into possession of an estate on account of her unborn child (*ventris nomine*), is charged with having *dolo malo* transferred the possession to another: if one is sued for refusing to admit into possession a person who has the praetor's order for entering. The penalty in the first case is one-tenth: in the other two one-fifth, and plaintiff (in the direct suit, now defendant in the *contr. jud.*) is liable to the penalty notwithstanding his having believed in the justice of his charge.

Where plaintiff has the right of challenging defendant to a penal wager (see below) defendant has sometimes the right to challenge back (*restipulari* Gai. iv 13). The penalty in these counter-wagers was consequent on defeat of the plaintiff, irrespectively of his belief in the justice of his suit.

These several checks were alternative: one only could be adopted (Gai. iv 174—181).

Defendant is liable to a penal wager in the sacramental procedure; in interdicts; and in an action on loan of money certain (*pecunia certa credita*) and money appointed to be paid (*constituta pecunia*), for one-third and one-half the value respectively in the two last named cases. Women and wards are not liable to the risk of a wager. In some other suits a defendant, who does not admit the claim, is liable to pay, if he lose the case, twice the value (*lis crescit infitiando in duplum* (see Book v chap. v)). These cases are for money due on a judgment, money paid down by a sponsor, damages under the *lex Aquilia*, and legacies left in the damnatory form. And an agreement for settling these cases is invalid (*pacto decidi non potest*). In cases of theft the damages are not increased by non-admission, but are from the first laid at four times the value for theft manifest, at thrice the value for theft non-manifest, or *corruptum* or *oblatum*. And there are, says Gaius, other cases of this kind (Gai. iv 171, 173; Paul i 19).

If none of these checks are applicable, the praetor permits plaintiff to call upon defendant to swear that it is in good faith that he disputes the claim (*non calumniae causa infitias ire*). Neither heirs, nor persons in heirs' place (*i.e.* possessors of the estate), nor women, nor wards are exempted from this: parents and patrons are (Gai. iv 172; D. xii 2 fr 34 § 4).

Besides these checks may be mentioned also the disgrace and consequent personal disqualification which was attached to condemnation in certain actions (see p. 327).

Where a suit was found by the judge to have been brought without due consideration (*temere*), he may condemn the plaintiff to pay costs and travelling expenses of defendant (D. v 1 fr 79 pr).

B. *Exceptio rei judicatae.*

A further and most important check on litigation is found in the rule that a matter once brought to trial should not be tried again, except of course by way of appeal. In one important class of cases a renewal of the claim was stopped before trial; in the rest, defendant was entitled to plead the fact of previous judgment or trial, and, this if established, was fatal to plaintiff's case (see pp. 403, 404). The discussion on this matter is in the Digest connected with this plea, which is there called *exceptio rei judicatae* (D. xliv 2) but by Gaius *exceptio rei judicatae vel in judicium deductae* (iv 106). See p. 365. The matter of the plea may also take the shape of a rejoinder (*replicatio* D. xliv 2 fr 9 § 1; 24).

The general principle was that one suit and one decision was enough for any single dispute; *singulis controversiis singulas actiones unumque judicati finem sufficere* (D. xliv 2 fr 6)[1]: and consequently whenever the same question is brought into court again between the same parties, although by a different form of suit[2], defendant has a right to be freed on shewing that the matter has been already decided or is actually before the court in another proceeding. *Exceptio obstat quotiens inter easdem personas eadem quaestio revocatur vel alio genere judicii* (Jul. *ap.* fr 7 § 4).

1. What is *eadem quaestio*? Substantial identity is required, not a precise identity of the particular quality or quantity of the land or other article claimed or of the amount of demand. The farm may have had a natural accession since the former trial; it still remains the same farm. A flock of sheep may be larger or smaller than it was, but the flock as a whole is the same. My former claim may have been to raise my house ten feet higher, notwithstanding any inconvenience to my neighbour; my present suit may be to raise it twenty

[1] See Terence and Quintilian quoted above, p. 344.

[2] Cicero speaks of a suit for freedom being the only suit in which *res judicata* was not a good plea: *Si decemviri (i.e. stlitibus judicandis) sacramentum in libertatem injustum judicassent, tamen quotiescunque vellet quis, hoc in genere solo rem judicatam referri posse voluerunt* (*Dom.* 29 § 78; cf. *Caecin.* 38 § 97).

feet, or ten feet higher than I claimed before: a decision against my former claim is fatal to my present contention (fr 14 pr, 26). And generally the greater includes the less, and a whole includes any part, so that one who has already sued for a farm cannot afterwards sue for a part of it, whether a fractional part or a particular field: one who has sued (and been defeated) for an inheritance cannot afterwards sue for a slave belonging to the inheritance or for a debt due to it; and *vice versa*, one who has sued for two things cannot afterwards sue for one of them. But this does not apply when my building materials have been used in your house or my planks in your ship. I can claim them (when separated), though defeated on a claim for the house or the ship. A claim for fruits or the offspring of slaves is not barred[1] by a decision on a claim for the land or for the mother, unless indeed they have already been included in the damages on the former trial (fr 3, 7). A legatee of all the deceased's silver, who supposed only the silver tables to have been left him and claimed only for their value, is not debarred from claiming the rest, for neither litigants nor judge could have supposed the whole to have been included in the suit: nor would a suit for all the silver preclude a suit for the wearing apparel, if that also were found later to have been bequeathed by codicils (fr 20, 21). A suit for interest does not bar a suit for the principal, nor a suit for interest now due bar a suit for future interest (fr 23): a suit for *iter* is no bar to a suit for *actus* (fr 11 § 6).

The question of pledge is distinct from that of ownership, and therefore a pledge-creditor without notice (although deriving his title from the debtor) is not affected by the decision in a suit for the ownership between the debtor and another, if the pledge was given before the suit: the ownership might have changed hands subject to the pledge (fr 11 § 10, fr 29 § 1). Nor is the assertion of a prior pledge barred by the success of a creditor in establishing a later pledge in a suit against the owner, who was not aware of his having himself also the right of a prior pledge made to his grandfather (fr 30 § 1).

[1] Many read *noceat* (fr 7) instead of *non noceat*. See *e.g.* Savigny *Syst.* vi p. 508, Windscheid *Pand.* § 130 n. 16.

In suits *in rem* a previous adverse decision is no bar to a fresh suit, if a new title be acquired in the meantime. But a mistake as to the ground of title does not prevent the effect of the decision. *Adquisitum postea dominium aliam causam facit, mutata autem opinio petitoris non facit.* Whether my title is legacy or purchase, if it exist at the time of suit it is brought to issue[1] and I am bound by the decision. But I can sue again if I subsequently obtain a fresh title and state it (*causa adjecta*) in my repeated suit (fr 11 §§ 1—5; 14 § 2; cf. fr 19). Nor is there any bar, if the former suit was decided, not on the ground of my want of title but of defendant's not being in possession and not having dishonestly lost the possession. My right to sue the possessor, whether the former defendant or not, remains unaffected by the previous decision (fr 9 pr, 17, 18). Between two claimants of an inheritance, each in possession of part of the estate, a suit is decisive if it be in favour of plaintiff and establish his ownership, thereby disproving defendant's ownership: but if it was in favour of defendant, his right is not thereby established but only plaintiff's right disproved. Still even if such plaintiff be really the true owner and afterwards happen to become possessor, he cannot resist a suit for recovery urged by the former defendant, who has thus got a decision in his favour which he can use to rebut his opponent's proof of ownership (fr 15, 24, 30). Fresh evidence gives no claim for renewal of a suit on the titles previously put forward or existing (fr 27, cf. xlii 1 fr 35).

A partial usufructuary who has been defeated in a suit for the whole is not debarred from claiming it, when the remainder has naturally accrued to him (D. xliv 2 fr 14 § 1, cf. vii 1 fr 33 § 1): nor is an unsuccessful suit for a usufruct a bar to a renewal of the suit after acquisition of the ownership, an independent usufruct being a different thing from a usufruct consequent upon the ownership (D. xliv 2 fr 21 § 3).

2. For the plea of *res judicata* to be available the parties

[1] I am inclined to take *non expressa causa* in fr 14 § 2 of the general character of *in rem actiones*, not of a power to avoid the inclusion of all grounds by expressing a particular one. Cf. Cogliolo *Cosa giudicata* p. 273; Windscheid *Pand.* § 130 note 6.

must be the same as in the former suit. *Res inter alios judicata nullum aliis praejudicium facit* (fr 1). Success in an action *in rem* does not give defendant any title against others than the plaintiff (fr 15). Action on a deposit brought against one heir of the depositary is no bar to an action against his coheirs; nor if one coheir brings a suit is the decision against him any bar to suits by other coheirs (fr 22, 29 pr). If, legacies and freedoms being left by the same will, a legatee sues and the will is alleged to be broken or invalid or not duly made, claims for freedom are not barred by a decision against the legatee; so if one coheir only is ousted by a plaint of unduteous will, or if one such plaint, out of several by different persons, succeeds, freedoms left by the will are not upset, but the judge will arrange for the victor to be compensated (fr 1, 29).

The benefit as well as the burden of a decision passes to one (*e.g.* a purchaser) who derives his title from the suitor; but a suit by a third party, whether successful or not against the purchaser, gives no right to the use of this plea in a suit between the third party and the vendor (fr 4, 9 § 2, 10, 11 §§ 3, 9, fr 28). A pledge-creditor allowing his debtor to conduct a suit concerning the ownership of the pledged property, a husband allowing his wife's or her father's suit concerning the ownership of what has been given him in dowry, a possessor allowing his vendor to defend his title, is bound by the result of the suit (D. xlii 1 fr 63). The decision in a suit by myself or by my procurator (on mandate) or guardian or caretaker against either the defendant himself or one who undertakes his defence is good against any future suit between us. For such persons are held to bring the matter to an issue (*rem in judicium deducunt*). And a suit against a son under power is a bar to a suit for the same matter against his father (D. xliv 2 fr 11 §§ 8, 9). A decision for the principal debtor may be pleaded by a surety (fr 21 § 4). On the other hand a decision against a suit by an unauthorized agent does not bind the principal unless he ratify the proceeding, and accordingly the same agent on receiving the principal's mandate to sue can renew the suit (fr 25 § 2).

3. The plea of 'matter decided' is available though the second suit be different from the first: *de eadem re agere*

videtur et qui non eadem actione agat. A plaintiff who has commenced an action for mandate cannot sue also for 'business done' or bring a condiction on the same matter. Nor, if he has failed in a suit for an inheritance, can he bring a suit for *fam. ercisc.* or *com. div.* relating to the same estate. But the decision on an interdict is no bar to a vindication, for the one relates to possession, the other to ownership. And a plaintiff defeated in a vindication is not barred from bringing a condiction, because the claim is wholly different (fr 5, 14 § 3, 18, 31).

4. In special cases a right to this plea either was not created or could be defeated, as where the judge in the former suit refrained from deciding the particular question which forms the subject of the second suit (D. iii 5 fr 7 § 2; xvi 2 fr 7 § 1; xlii 1 fr 15 § 4; see above on *in rem actiones*), or where, though the plea was founded, the circumstances were such as to justify its being rebutted by an allegation of fraud (D. xxvi 7 fr 46 § 5; Cod. iii 1 fr 2), or the documents on which the decision was made proved to be forged (D. xliv 1 fr 11); or where an action had been brought under an important misconception (D. xiv 3 fr 13 pr; xv 1 fr 30 § 4; xliv 2 fr 11 pr, but *contra* D. ix 4 fr 4 § 3; and cf. xxxviii 2 fr 12 § 3); or of course where minority justified a restoration to the former position (Cod. ii 26 fr 1). Where in an action *de peculio* full satisfaction had not been obtained, and the *peculium* was afterwards increased, a fresh action might be brought for the deficit (D. xv 1 fr 30 § 4).

On the rule in concurrent actions see below.

5. In order to make a decision *res judicata* it must be given by persons with full executive authority and jurisdiction (*qui imperium potestatemque habent*) or by persons appointed under the authority of such to judge between the parties, or (within the pecuniary limits assigned to them) by the municipal magistrates, or by judges obtained out of the regular course from the emperor. An arbitrator appointed by mere agreement between the parties does not give a binding decision; *rem judicatam non facit* (Paul v 5 *a* 1).

The decision must be within the jurisdiction of the judge[1];

[1] A judgment outside the sphere of the judge's competence is declared by Cicero to be no judgment. *Frustra judices solent cum sententiam*

and it must be given in the presence of the parties (Paul v 5 *a* 5).

It was not necessary that the bench should be composed of the same judges throughout the hearing (D. v 1 fr 76)[1].

C. A suit for a smaller matter was not allowed to be pressed if its decision involved the decision of a larger matter in dispute between the parties. Thus the claimant of an inheritance is not allowed first to sue for some object belonging to the inheritance: the claimant of a farm cannot first bring a condiction for its fruits; or first sue for an accessory right of road through another farm belonging to defendant; or bring an action for partition (*com. div.*) before he had established his joint ownership. At one time defendant applied in such cases for a praescription to the formula, *e.g. si in ea re praejudicium hereditati non fiat:* but afterwards the objection took the form of a plea, *e.g. quod praejudicium hereditati* (or *praedio*) *non fiat* (Gai. iv 133; D. v 1 fr 54; xliv 1 fr 16, 18; cf. iv 1 fr 4). The claimant of joint heirship, if actually possessing a part of the inheritance, is however allowed to sue *fam. ercisc.*, and the judge in that trial will decide also his claim to be heir (D. x 2 fr 1 § 1). A claim for civil redress was not barred by the matter being also criminal (D. xlvii 8 fr 2 § 1; xlix 1 fr 4, *etc.*)[2].

pronuntiant, addere 'si quid mei judicii est.' Si enim non fuit eorum judicii, nihilo magis, hoc non addito, illud est judicatum (*Fin.* ii 12 § 36).

[1] This extract is from Alfenus and contains a curious misapplication of philosophy and analogy in defence of what seems a dangerous proposition requiring much careful guarding.

[2] So also apparently in Cicero's time (*Inv.* ii 20 § 59) where a case is supposed of armed men going to commit an act of violence, and being met by other armed men. A Roman knight in the struggle has a hand cut off by one of them and sues him *injuriarum.* Defendant applies to the praetor to grant him the plea, *extra quam in reum capitis praejudicium fiat.* Plaintiff objects and asks for a *judicium purum, i.e.* without such a plea. Defendant argues that no question which must arise on a crime tried under the law of cut-throats (*inter sicarios*) should be tried in a suit before Recoverers. Plaintiff replies that the wrong is so great that it should be tried on the first opportunity.

CHAPTER XI.

A. Oaths.

An oath by one of the parties to a suit was sometimes the means of ascertaining a disputed point as between the parties, and thus abridging further proceedings. Such an oath might be (1) voluntary *i.e.* taken or declined at the will of the party; or (2) necessary *i.e.* not to be declined without serious risk; or (3) judicial *i.e.* suggested by the judge to assist in forming his mind. The Digest (xii 2) treats them all together with but slight distinction, but it appears probable that this assimilation is largely due to Justinian[1].

1. A voluntary oath is taken by the free consent of the parties either out of court or in the course of the proceedings before praetor or judge. But to be effectual it must not be volunteered, but taken on a precise tender made by the opponent, who by this tender (*deferre*) offers to accept the other's oath as decisive of the particular question. It is allowable in all kinds of suits and on any question. But in most cases it appears as a final settlement or compromise of the whole issue. Plaintiff for instance suing on a loan tenders to defendant an oath (*defert jusjurandum* or *condicionem jurisjurandi*) *i.e.* challenges him to swear that he does not owe the money (*se dare non oportere*). If defendant takes the oath the issue between the parties is established as sworn; defendant is thereupon not liable, and can plead this oath in any future suit between him and the plaintiff which raises this precise issue. Or, it may be, defendant when sued on the loan challenges the plaintiff in the same way to swear to the justice of his claim. If plaintiff accepts the oath and swears defendant is thereupon liable just

[1] The Antonine jurists treated of oaths in comments on two parts of the edict, viz. on procedure and on the section *de rebus creditis* (Lenel *Ed.* § 54; 95 § 3). Demelius has, partly on this ground, partly on rational considerations, endeavoured to detect the old law under Justinian's alterations (*Schiedseid* &c. 1887). See also Gradenwitz's review *ZRG.* xxi 269.

as if he had fought out the case and judgment had gone against him. And in case of any dispute on the point, plaintiff is entitled to have an action, not on the main issue, which is now held to be decided, but on the simple issue whether such an oath was duly taken. In fact the oath ranks as a judgment for and against the parties. Plaintiff with such an oath in his favour can proceed to execution. Defendant in the like case is as free as if he had paid the claim, sureties and pledges are freed also, and if money has been paid, it can be recovered. Co-stipulators and co-promisers are all bound by the tender or oath of one.

It is immaterial what the terms of the oath are, provided the object or form of adjuration does not belong to an illicit religion, but it must be taken (*datum, praestitum*) in the terms tendered (*delatum*), just as exactness is required in the answer to a stipulation. It may be offered or taken by a ward with his guardian's authority, by a procurator with adequate powers, or by a son or slave in matters relating to his *peculium*, if he have the management of it. Even on his master's concerns, a slave taking an oath tendered obtains a plea for his master. Still more a son. If a minor has been cheated into taking it, or a fraud on creditors has been thereby committed, a replication as to the circumstances under which it was taken will be allowed on defendant's pleading the oath. Any contention as to the truth of the matter sworn to was not encouraged by the praetor. In suits where non-admission (*infitiatio*) doubles the damage, if the case be established by an oath, only single damages can be recovered (D. xii 2 fr 1—9; fr 17 § 3—fr 21; fr 23, 24, 27, 28, 30 pr; xliv 1 fr 15; Quintil. *Inst.* v 6).

2. In a few suits only (as appears probable; Justinian has no restriction), plaintiff has the right of tendering before the praetor an oath to defendant on the justice of his claim, and defendant cannot put aside the tender. *Solvere aut jurare cogam* are the words preserved to us from the praetor's edict: defendant must either pay the demand or swear that he does not owe it. He can however require that plaintiff should first take the oath of good faith (*de calumnia*): from which oath however parents and patrons are exempted; and he may, instead

of taking the oath demanded by plaintiff, retort the challenge. In that case plaintiff must either at once swear to the justice of his claim or be non-suited, *i.e.* the praetor will refuse him a trial. Nor can he call upon defendant to take an oath of good faith, for by his original challenge he has shewn that he trusts defendant's honesty. If, when the party challenged is ready to take the oath offered, his opponent waives it (*remittit*), the effect is as if the oath had been taken. Paul (if the text be uncorrupted[1]) allows either party to tender an oath, with a prior claim to the plaintiff if both are desirous to tender (D. xii 2 fr 34; Paul ii 1 §§ 1—4).

The suits in which this compulsory oath was allowed appear to be *de certa credita pecunia* (D. xii 2 fr 14) and probably also the *condictio triticaria* (cf. fr 34 pr); *de pecunia constituta* (fr 14, 36); *de operis* (fr 34 pr); *rerum amotarum* (fr 16; xxv 2 fr 11); in noxal actions on the question of the slave's being in defendant's power (ix 4 fr 21 § 2); *de injuriis* under the *lex Cornelia* (xlvii 10 fr 5 § 8); and *furti* (xxv 2 fr 12; cf. xlvii 2 fr 52 § 27).

3. Judicial oaths are taken, not by agreement of the parties or at the challenge of one of them, but at the suggestion of the judge who seeks thus to inform his mind on a doubtful point, and proposes an oath to one of the parties with the promise naturally implied of deciding in his favour if he take it[2] (*solent saepe judices in dubiis causis exacto jurejurando secundum eum judicare qui juraverit*). In such a case imperial constitutions allowed a further hearing, if new documents (*nova instrumenta*) were discovered (D. xii 2 fr 31). Probably to judicial oaths refers the statement by Paul (v 32) that an appeal is allowable only at the time when the oath was tendered and not when it was actually taken.

A special occasion of judicial oaths was when, after an interlocutory decision with which defendant did not comply, the judge allowed the plaintiff to assess the damages himself on

[1] He speaks also generally '*in pecuniariis causis*' which is a phrase meaning civil, as opposed to criminal, cases. *Ad pecunias* in D. fr 34 pr refers to the *actio creditae pecuniae*.

[2] An interesting case is given by the elder Seneca (*Contr.* vii *Praef.* § 7).

oath. This was called *in litem jurare* (D. xii 3; and see below, p. 415).

B. ADMISSION (*CONFESSIO IN JURE*).

The decision of the judge, after trial had, ascertains the justice or injustice of the plaintiff's claim, and, if the claim be found to be just, defendant is then in the position of one bound to satisfy the plaintiff. If there be an appeal and the judgment appealed from is confirmed, the case is ripe for execution. But trial is required only when defendant denies the justice of the claim. If he admits it, no trial is necessary, and defendant is in the same position as one against whom final judgment is past. The XII tables put admission and judgment on the same level (see p. 423), and as a general phrase *confessus pro judicato est* is clearly true. Defendant, as Paul puts it, has passed judgment against himself (D. xlii 2 fr 1). As such it is accepted by the law as final, and, after the ordinary interval allowed to condemned defendants, may be enforced by distress under Ant. Pius' rescript (Paul v 5 *a* §§ 2—4).

An admission is good, whether oral or written or given in any other way *e.g.* by gesture, but it must be given in the presence of the opponent or at any rate of his procurator, guardian or caretaker. Such representatives are not competent to make admissions. A ward requires the authority of his guardian; and a minor can get his admission quashed (Paul *ib.*; D. xlii 2 fr 6 §§ 3—6).

Where the claim is for money certain, and an admission of debt is made by defendant, no further proceedings are necessary, but after the usual interval execution can ensue. But where the claim is for something uncertain, an admission can only prepare the way for a judgment, but cannot supersede it. A defendant against a claim under the *lex Aquilia* can admit that he killed or wounded a slave, but his obligation to compensate the owner is not thereby established. The question of *jure an injuria* remains for the judge to decide; and even if *injuria* be admitted, the amount of damages has to be determined. One who has admitted obligation should be pressed to agree to an amount of damages. So, if a person admits that he owes plaintiff a certain thing, the amount of the damages is still open to question. In such cases the admission of the fact only can at most lead only to an interlocutory finding (*pronuntiatio*) on the part of the magistrate; and the trial will then proceed; the admission will be stated in the formula, and the fact admitted be withdrawn from any dispute before the judge. This appears to be the meaning of Marcus Aurelius' declaration, that the praetor is to accept, as if decided after trial, every fact admitted by defendant[1], *praetorem debere omne omnino quod quis confessus est pro judicato habere* (D. xlii 2 fr 6 § 2). In an action *ad rem*, if defendant admits that the farm claimed is plaintiff's, plaintiff is thereby established as owner (at least as against defendant) as fully as if the judge had so pronounced (*ib.*).

An admission made in error, if an error of fact, does not bind, and consequently forms no hindrance to a *condictio indebiti* (Demelius p. 226 sq.). But an admission, in a suit under the *lex Aquilia*, of having killed a slave is good against defendant whether *he* actually killed him or not, provided only the slave was killed. An admission of owing a particular slave is likewise good, even if the slave was already dead or died during the trial: but if there was no such slave, or generally if it is even doubtful whether the thing admitted to be due ever existed, the admission is not good. On the other hand an heir, admitting that he owes a legacy certain, is bound by his admission, even if the thing never existed or has ceased to exist: he has to pay its value (D. *ib.* fr 2—5, 8; cf. xi 1 fr 20 pr). But an heir admitting that he owes something on trust, is not necessarily to be condemned to payment, if it turn out that, from some cause unknown to him, nothing is really due (xlii 2 fr 7). His admission is only an admission of the existence of such a trust in the will (Demelius *Conf.* p. 211).

Advocacy of another's claim does not preclude the advocate, on subsequent knowledge of the thing's being his own, from claiming it for himself (D. vi 1 fr 54).

Along with judgment and admission was placed in the *lex*

[1] Demelius (*Confessio* pp. 194—204) criticises the passage and regards it as partly interpolated.

Rubria (*capp.* 21, 22), and doubtless in the edict also, failure in due defence, leading in the case of a loan of money (*certa credita pecunia*) to personal arrest and in other cases to seizure and possession of the defendant's estate. A defendant who does not admit the debt or obligation charged and yet will not join in the necessary steps to secure a trial and decision, was treated as contumacious, and subjected to like execution (cf. Demelius *Conf.* pp. 127 foll., 159, 160; Lenel *EP.* p. 329).

C. *Interrogationes in jure*[1].

In some cases where the course to be taken by a plaintiff would necessarily be different according to the position taken up by defendant, plaintiff was allowed to ascertain this definitively by a question to defendant by or before the praetor. The most usual case was that of a creditor against the estate of a deceased. If an heir has entered on the inheritance, the creditor can sue for his debt: if there be no heir, he can apply to the praetor for possession of deceased's estate. He is allowed therefore to ask the supposed heir whether he is so; if he says he is, whether really heir or not, he has as it were contracted with plaintiff to accept the responsibility. If he denies that he is heir, he will not be allowed to obstruct plaintiff's application for possession of the estate. If defendant has answered under a mistake, and a subsequent will be discovered, or the will under which he was heir be upset in any other way, the praetor will grant him relief (D. xi 1 fr 4; 9 § 1; 11 §§ 8—12). Silence or indistinct answering are held equivalent to denial (fr 11 §§ 4, 7). But due time for deliberation is granted if asked *bona fide*; and if defendant's claim is contested by another, Hadrian directed that he should not be compelled to answer, and thereby either prejudge his own case or assume a responsibility which he might be deprived of the means of meeting (fr 5, 6). Defendant might also be asked his age, apparently because if under twenty-five the creditor might be exposed afterwards to have his victory cancelled (fr 11 pr). Where there is a trust, defendant might be asked whether the estate had been accordingly restored to him (fr 9 § 7).

[1] See Demelius *Confessio* §§ 18—26.

Another important question for a creditor of deceased for an amount certain, was what was defendant's share of the inheritance: else plaintiff might run the risk of an excessive claim (*plus petendi*, fr 1 pr). If defendant reply that he is universal heir, or heir to a larger extent than is true, he is still bound by his answer. If he reply less than is true, or give no reply, plaintiff can sue him, and he is liable for the whole debt (fr 11 §§ 1—5). Whether further questions could be put, such as concerning the nature of his title to the inheritance, whether in his own right or in that of persons in his power, was a matter for the praetor to decide according to circumstances (fr 9 § 6).

Again, one who is suing under the *lex Aquilia* or other noxal action will have to take a different course, according as the slave's master or child's father is ready to defend him or at once to surrender him or is not disposed to do anything. It is the owner or superior who is liable. Plaintiff was allowed to ask defendant whether he had the slave or child in his power[1]. And according to the answers to this question plaintiff's course would be clear (D. ii 9 fr 2 § 1; xi 1 fr 5). An answer admitting ownership of another's slave is good against the answerer, and, if he be sued noxally, the real owner is freed (D. xi 1 fr 20 pr, 28). But if, instead of being another's slave, it is a freeman, defendant is not bound by his answer, any more than he is if he declares one to be his son whose age makes the relationship impossible. For a confession to be accepted by the law must be consistent with the law and with nature (fr 13 pr, 14 § 1). In an action for *pauperies*, the question as to ownership is allowed (fr 7).

In two other cases questions of this binding character could be put. When possible damage was threatened by a neighbouring building, plaintiff might ask the supposed owner whether he was owner and, if a co-owner, what was his share, so that he might compel him to give the usual security (fr 10). Similarly the question whether and to what extent a defendant possessed, *i.e.* owned[2], a farm was allowed, but probably only in

[1] See Lenel *EP.* pp. xiii, 127; Demelius *Conf.* p. 310. The special meaning of *potestas* given in ix 4 fr 21 § 3 is at most only part of the meaning.

[2] See Demelius *Conf.* § 25.

the case of an action *aquae pluviae arcendae* and the like, whereas in the case of *damni infecti* the object of the suit was in effect a restoration of the old state of things (fr 20 § 1; cf. xxxix 3 fr 11 § 3).

In all these cases the gist of the question allowed to be put to defendant is not the ascertainment of a fact, but the willingness of the defendant to accept liability (cf. fr 4 pr), instead of leaving the plaintiff to the remedy of applying to the praetor to be put into possession of the inheritance or slave or animal or land concerned. The actions in which the interrogatories were put were called *interrogatoriae*, and the fact of the question having been put was named in the formula, and the claim was based on it[1]. Some questions apparently were put without leading to actions, but the answer might, if calculated to deceive, justify an action for fraud (D. xxvii 6 fr 12).

Where one was asked whether he maintained that his guardian's heirs were in debt to him and he answered no, it was held that he could not afterwards withdraw his statement, and the heirs were freed, whether the answer was in consequence of a compromise having been made or was to be taken as expressing a gift (D. xxxix 5 fr 29 § 1).

CHAPTER XII.

JOINDER OF ISSUE.

1. The settlement by the praetor of the instructions for trial, containing the appointment of a judge (or recoverers) with the issue to be tried, and its acceptance by the parties, formed the conclusion of the proceedings before the praetor, and were preparatory to the real trial of the suit. It is only now that the plaintiff's claim against the defendant is definitely

[1] Interrogatory actions ceased with the abolition of procedure *per formulas*, and the answers to questions became available only in evidence. See D. xi 1 fr 1 § 1; which fragment and fr 21 in their present form are doubtless due to Justinian.

ascertained and allowed, and the suit effectively begun. Till now he could withdraw altogether, and defendant could satisfy him without legal process. This is the time *cum petitur* in the full sense (cf. *e.g.* D. xii 1 fr 22; xxii 1 fr 2; xlvi 8 fr 15; *etc.*). In early days it is said the parties called on the bystanders to witness the acceptance of the issue by crying *testes estote* (Fest. p. 38) and hence *litis contestatio* (joinder of issue) was the name of this step in the procedure. However that may be, the name is suitable enough for a 'joint declaration of the suit.' The same was denoted (from defendant's act) *judicium acceptum* (cf. *e.g.* D. iii 3 fr 15): also *lis inchoata* (Vat. 263; *Consult.* vi 8 § 9); *res in judicium deducta* (Gai. iii 181; D. xxvi 7 fr 22, 23). The exact form of this final act before the praetor is not known. It may have consisted, as Wlassak contends with some probability, in the plaintiff's handing to the defendant a written copy of the issue made by the praetor's official and defendant's taking it[1]: or the plaintiff may have merely shewn him the issue as settled by the praetor, or read it out to him (*dictare e.g.* D. ix 4 fr 22 § 4; xlv 1 fr 112 pr), and the defendant may have declared orally his acceptance of it (cf. D. ii 13 fr 1 pr, § 1)[2].

[1] H. Erman (*ZRG.* xxx 334, cf. xxxii 270) suggests that the formula was written and sent to the judge sealed up and that this gives an explanation of a difficult passage in Hor. *Sat.* ii 1. 86. Horace is professing to consult the lawyer Trebatius in reference to the charges made against him for satirising persons. Treb. says *si mala condiderit in quem quis carmina jus est judiciumque.* Horace replies *Esto, si quis mala; sed bona si quis judice condiderit laudatus Caesare? si quis opprobriis dignum latraverit, integer ipse?* Treb. replies: *Solventur risu tabulae, tu missus abibis.* Suppose a suit for *injuriarum* with an issue, *Quod Q. Horatius Flaccus mala carmina condidit, etc.* On the tablets containing the formula (cf. *tabulas cautionis* D. xxvi 10 fr 5; *tabulas chirographi* D. xxxii fr 59) being 'opened,' the court bursts into laughter and dismisses the case. *Solventur* may also be taken as 'dissolved,' 'discharged'; cf. Cic. *Or.* ii 58 § 236; Quintil. v 10 § 67. The expression *jus judiciumque* makes a civil action most likely: in Hor. *Ep.* ii 1. 153 criminal procedure under the *lex Cornelia* seems to be meant: cf. Gai. iii 220; D. xlvii 10 fr 5 § 9, 15 § 27; criminal procedure was more advantageous when the person libelled was not named, *ib.* fr 6. Horace's justification *si quis opprobriis, etc.* finds support in *ib.* fr 18 pr. Trampedach (*ZRG.* xxxi 143) suggests the translation 'the libellous writings will be set free (acquitted) amidst laughter.'

[2] Cf. Wlassak *Litiscont.* p. 53 n.; Bekker *ZRG.* xxviii 181; Lenel *ib.* 380.

Issues for trial (*judicia*) were either statutable (*legitima, quae legitimo jure consistunt*) or imperial (*imperio continentia*[1], *quae imperio continentur*). The former were such as rested or were supposed to rest on the ancient constitutional authority of the XII tables[2] or the like; the latter are attached to the executive power of the praetor and controlled by it.

2. *Legitima judicia* are described by Gaius as those accepted in Rome or within a mile of it, between parties who were all Roman citizens, and to be tried by a single judge, also a Roman citizen. In other words they were issues in conformity with the law of Roman citizens and tried by the regular courts. With them joinder of issue works as of course (*ipso jure*) in transforming the original cause of action into a new obligation. The old lawyers said *ante litem contestatam dare debitorem oportet, post litem contestatam condemnari oportet, post condemnationem judicatum facere oportet.* Joinder of issue is a kind of contract under authority (cf. D. xv 1 fr 3 § 11; v 1 fr 61), and effects a novation in some sort[3] of the previously existing obligation, so far as is necessary to obtain a practical result. The original tie between plaintiff and defendant is loosed: it is only in the form now given to it that plaintiff can prosecute his claim against this defendant on this matter: defendant is no longer subject to an undefined possibility of suit, but is under a definite obligation to abide judgment on a precise issue (Gai. iii 180, 181).

The consequence is that, whatever be the result of the trial, plaintiff is as of course disabled from suing defendant again on the matter. But this is true only when the issue is so framed as to put the whole claim before the judge and nothing but this claim; that is, when he is directed to determine the duty of the defendant towards the plaintiff in respect of a particular

[1] Cf. *aedificia urbi continentia* in *lex Quinct.* Bruns no. 22 ed. 6.

[2] According to Wlassak *legitimum* refers to the *lex Aebutia* which authorised trials of written issues (*Pr. Gesetz.* i p. 29, 37 n., *etc.*, ii p. 83, 363, *etc.*). But see above (vol. I p. 95) on the use of *legitimus*.

[3] Gaius' treatment distinguishes *novatio* from *litis contestatio* (iii 176—180). Only one passage is found in the classical Jurists or Digest in which *novatio* is applied to joinder of issue (Vat. 263), cf. Salkowski *Novation* pp. 118, 119. Justinian so applies it in Cod. vii 54 fr 3 § 2.

matter according to the law of the citizens (*si legitimo judicio in personam actum sit ea formula, quae juris civilis habet intentionem*[1]). If the issue is one of fact, not of law (see Gai. iv 45—47), the truth of the facts as alleged, not the plaintiff's right, is before the judge, and a different statement of the facts might give a different result; defendant's conduct may have given the plaintiff a good legal claim, which has not been heard at all. Or again the issue may be general (*in rem*), and not particular to this defendant only, *e.g.* that a certain farm is the plaintiff's: if his claim is good, it concerns not only the defendant, but all the world, and is therefore too large a question to be disposed of by this contest, which strictly speaking only decides whether defendant is bound to recognize the claim.

Thus statutable trials *in rem*, and also those *in personam* with a *formula in factum concepta*, leave an opening for a fresh trial. But as the reasons for this are technical, and defendant may have a real grievance if a fresh trial be allowed, the praetor granted in these cases a plea of 'matter already brought to trial or decided' (see p. 388) which gave practical security against a rehearing of the same matter. The plaintiff was not stopped from proceeding to trial, but would lose his case if it were really a repetition of what had been already brought before a court (Gai. iii 180, 181; iv 107; cf D. L 17 fr 112).

Judicia legitima have some other peculiarities. Only in trials so conducted could a usufruct be established in suits for peti-

[1] There are three important classes of actions about which it is not clear whether they can be said for this purpose to have *juris civilis intentio*. These are (1) actions where the formula has a fiction; (2) where the condemnation clause has a different person from the clause of intention, as where a cognitor or procurator sues; and (3), with a similar frame to the last, actions against the principal on a shipmaster's or shopkeeper's contracts, or against a father or master on a son's or slave's contracts. Pokrowsky (*ZRG.* xxix p. 80 sq.) in an excellently written paper maintains that in all these cases the Digest does not allow, or at least does not require, *ipso jure* consumption, and consequently that they all belong to the large class of actions with a *formula in factum concepta*, which is not to be limited to the ordinary *actiones in factum*. H. Erman (*ZRG.* xxxii 261) in an elaborate criticism rejects Pokrowsky's theory, but he rests too much on historical hypotheses to carry conviction to my mind. Pokrowsky has replied in *ZRG.* xxxiii p. 99 sqq.

tioning an inheritance or dividing common property (Vat. 47 *a*). A woman could not proceed in a statutable trial without the authority of her guardian, just as she could do no other civil business (Ulp. xi 27). And if a paterfamilias or a woman was engaged in such a suit, when adopted or coempted respectively, the suits did not pass to the adopter or copurchaser but perished entirely (Gai. iii 83: text not certain).

The *lex Julia judiciaria* made all such issues (*judicia legitima*) to lapse if not brought to judgment within one year and six months (from joinder of issue? Gai. iv 104).

3. Imperial *judicia* were all such as had not the three characteristics named above, viz. Rome for place, Roman citizens for parties, and a single Roman judge. Consequently they included:

(*a*) Trials in the provinces or more than a mile from Rome, even though they rested on the *lex Aquilia* or *Ollinia*[1] or *Furia* or any other *lex*, whether the parties or judges were Roman citizens or foreigners:

(*b*) Trials before recoverers, even though held in Rome:

(*c*) Trials before a single judge, if one of the parties or the judge was a foreigner.

But the mere fact that the authority for granting the action was the praetor's edict did not in any way prevent the trial being statutable, if it was at Rome, between Roman citizens, and before a single judge, who also was a Roman citizen.

In no imperial trials had joinder of issue a necessary action in destroying the claim and thus preventing a second trial: the previous trial or judgment had to be pleaded. The character of the trial as dependent on the praetor's authority was thus maintained throughout.

On the same principle trials thus granted expired, if not brought to judgment within the praetor's year of office (Gai. iv 103—109).

4. Joinder of issue (in both classes of trials) has certain other effects:

(*a*) All actions run against heirs, even if, as for torts, they did not run against them at first; and an action for

[1] This *lex* is not otherwise known. For *lex Furia* see p. 30.

insulting conduct (*injuriarum*) can now be continued against heirs (D. xliv 7 fr 26, 59; xlvii 10 fr 13 pr; L 17 fr 87).

(*b*) An action which could only be brought before plaintiff's death or within a certain time from the ground of complaint is now beyond risk from these causes (D. L 17 fr 139; xii 2 fr 9 § 3). But this has nothing to do with the periods stated above for the completion of a suit. Nor is a person over 25 years of age who has once desisted from the suit, helped by the fact that issue was joined within the proper time, *i.e.* one year after 25 years of age (D. iv 4 fr 20 § 1).

(*c*) Defendant, if condemned, is answerable as from this date for whatever fruits, offspring, interest, *etc.* the plaintiff could have had, if he had then been put into possession of what he claimed (or of what was awarded). The subsequent loss of his right by usucapion, or the loss by fault of defendant of the object of suit, or of the means of satisfying the plaintiff (*i.e.* by surrender of a noxal slave) do not as a rule remove his liability (D. v 3 fr 40; vi 1 fr 15—18, 20; ix 4 fr 21 § 2; xii 1 fr 31 pr; xxii 1 fr 2).

(*d*) In strict suits the value of the thing is taken as at this time, whereas in *bonae fidei* suits it is taken as at date of judgment (D. xiii 6 fr 3 § 2).

(*e*) From this time the object of suit becomes *res litigiosa*. As such it was not alienable or pledgable voluntarily, and the acquirer would be met by a fatal plea, at least if he bought from one not in possession. Apparently alienations by the plaintiff were meant, for the defendant if he has parted with possession is in any case answerable for the value (D. x 2 fr 13; xx 3 fr 1 § 2; Gai. iv 117 *a*; Cod. iii 37 fr 1 § 1). An edict of Augustus inflicted a penalty of 50 sesterces to be paid to the fisc (*Frag. de jure fisci* § 8 mutilated; cf. D. xlix 14 fr 1 pr). The rule appears to have originally related only to suits for Italic land, but was extended to moveables (D. xx l. c. *Fragm. fisc.* l. c.). The XII tables forbad the consecration of anything in dispute under a penalty of double value; and this rule remained in the Digest (xliv 6 fr 3). See Cod. Theod. iv 5 fr 1 and Vangerow *Pand.* i 256, Lenel *EP.* p. 107.

CHAPTER XIII.

PROCEEDINGS *IN JUDICIO.*

A. The judge (or recoverers) named in the formula settled by the praetor (or proconsul, *etc.* in the provinces) was, if not present, informed of it, probably by the praetor, who might also fix the place and limit of time within which the trial should be held (cf. D. ii 1 fr 13; v 1 fr 2 § 2; fr 59 *lex Urson.* 95; Wlassak *P. G.* ii 56). Otherwise the judge would name a day[1]. The hearing was open to the public. The judge was sometimes accompanied by assessors chosen by himself, who formed his *consilium*[2]. In Cicero's speech for *Quinctius* (cf. 7 § 54) the judge C. Aquilius, able lawyer as he was, still had three assessors, men of dignified position. The different parts of a judge's duty are named in an old statute, *ad id judicium adesse, verba audeire, in consilium eire, judicare* (*lex Acilia repetundarum*, § 71).

The parties whether appearing in person or by attorney or agent had, at least in important cases, their cause pleaded by orators (*oratores, advocati, patroni*), who in early times acted gratuitously, looking to fame and influence as their reward, but in imperial times received fees (see vol. 1 p. 526). They were assisted by lawyers[2]. We hear of limitations of time for the advocates' speeches in criminal cases, *e.g.* three hours for each by Pompey's law on occasion of Milo's case 52 B.C. (Cic. *Brut.* 94 § 324; Ascon. *Milon.* § 25), of statutable (*legitimae*) hours in Cicero's impeachment of Verres (Act. ii 1, 9 § 25). Pliny complains of restrictions of time, apparently made at the discretion of the judge (*Ep.* i 20 §§ 10, 11; iv 9 § 9), six hours for accuser, nine for

[1] Cf. Cic. *Flac.* 24 § 57 *forum plenum judiciorum, plenum magistratuum.*

[2] Cf. Cic. *Top.* 17 § 65 *Privata enim judicia maximarum quidem rerum in jurisconsultorum mihi videntur esse prudentia* ('to rest on their skill'), *nam et adsunt jurisconsulti multum, et adhibentur in consilia, et patronis diligentibus ad eorum prudentiam confugientibus hastas ministrant.*

accused (vi 2 §§ 6, 7): and Cicero refers in a private suit to the natural pressure to get a case finished in the day (*Tull.* 3 § 6). Each party's advocate spoke once only, but sometimes several advocates were heard (Cic. *Quinct.* 26 § 80), and on adjourned consideration sometimes the same, sometimes different advocates spoke (*ib.* 1 § 3; *Caecin.* 2 § 6). The conclusion sometimes took the shape of a sharp short discussion and questioning of the opposing advocate, presumably to put in relief some decisive point. This was called *altercatio* (Quintil. vi 4).

B. Evidence was produced and commented on by the advocate during his speech. The witnesses appeared voluntarily; but sometimes (in criminal cases) on summons from the magistrate (*quibus denuntiatur* Quintil. v 7 § 9) or through the prosecutor (Cic. *Verr.* ii 1 19 § 51; *Flacc.* 6 § 14). The compulsory witnesses were limited to ten in some semicriminal cases (*lex Mam.* 55; *Ed. Venafr.* 68; cf. Val. Prob. 5); in the borough of Ossuna to 20 (*lex Urson.* 95). Ten witnesses only are commented on by Cicero in the speech *pro Caecin.* (10 § 28).

Witnesses gave their evidence on oath (Cic. *Rosc. Com.* 15 § 45). Declarations made in the presence of witnesses, written, and sealed up[1] were sometimes produced (Cic. *Rosc. Com.* 14 § 43; Quintil. v 7); as also notices given in the presence of witnesses (*testato e.g.* D. xlv 1 fr 122 pr and § 3): and documents of various kinds (*tabulae, codices, instrumenta*), especially copies of accounts in bankers' books. Bankers were compellable to allow a customer to have inspection and a copy made of his own account (D. ii 13 fr 4, 10).

The evidence of slaves was taken by torture, and taken only in default of other (D. xxii 5 fr 7). Paul appears to limit its use

[1] In Cic. *pro Flacco* we have several instances of sealed up documents produced in evidence on a trial against a provincial governor; a resolution in his favour from the town of Acmon, sealed with special Asiatic chalk much used by the publicans (16 § 37); some evidence against him, denounced as false by Cicero, sealed with wax (*ib.*); a decision in an arbitration suit (36 § 89); record of trials which ought by law to have been sealed by the judges in public and brought to the praetor in three days, but which had been kept back for thirty days, presumably forged (9 § 21).

in private suits to cases of guardianship and inheritance, where the judge of guardianship or the *centumviri* find no other evidence of the assets of the deceased or the connexion with the family (*de rebus hereditariis vel de fide generis* Paul v 15 §6; 16 § 2).

An oath sometimes supplied the place of evidence, but if it is to have full weight, it must not be volunteered but tendered, either by the opposite party (which was the usual case), out of court or before the praetor, or be invited by the judge in order to satisfy his own mind (see p. 394).

The burden of proof falls, as a general rule, on the party making an assertion (*ei incumbit probatio qui dicit, non qui negat* D. xxii 3 fr 2). Hence it falls usually on the plaintiff, but pleas must be proved by defendant. So anyone imputing disability to his opponent, *e.g.* that he could not be, or appoint, a procurator, must prove it, and so must one who, having promised to appear before the judge, alleges detention on public business, fraud of his opponent, ill-health or tempest (*ib.* fr 19, cf. fr 5; xliv 1 fr 1).

On points of law[1] it was the practice at one time for the parties to get and produce opinions from jurisconsults who in Augustus' time and after were specially selected and licensed. They either wrote their opinions directly to the judge or declared them in the presence of witnesses who wrote them and produced them in court. Hadrian made them binding on the judge if they were unanimous (Gai. i 7; D. i 2 fr 2 § 49). In the provinces the governors were consulted by the judges on matters of law, but left them to themselves on matters of fact (D. v 1 fr 79 § 1).

[1] An advocate was not necessarily a trained lawyer: if any special point of law had to be argued, his clients would consult lawyers and furnish him with their opinions, or he would himself consult them. See Cic. *Orat.* i 15 § 56; 58 §§ 249, 250, *etc.*; *Top.* 17 § 65. The special functions of the lawyer as distinguished from the orator are satirically described by one of Cicero's interlocutors. *Ita est tibi iurisconsultus ipse per se nihil nisi leguleius quidam cautus et acutus, praeco actionum, cantor formularum, auceps syllabarum* (*Orat.* i 55 § 236) 'You make the lawyer 'merely by himself to be only a cautious and sharp statutemonger, who 'announces his suits like a public crier, repeats his *formulae* by rote, and 'lays snares to catch only the letter of the law.'

C. The judge was left to act as he thought right in the conduct of the case subject to the instructions contained in the formula given by the praetor (or governor) and to the general law. He was not bound to exercise his full powers (D. v 1 fr 40 pr).

He formed his own judgment on the evidence. In several rescripts Hadrian dealt with this question and directed the judge not to give exclusive credence to one kind of proof. 'Sometimes the number, sometimes the dignity and authority 'of the witnesses carried most weight; oral evidence was much 'more important than affidavits (*testimonia*); the manner of the 'witnesses should be noted, whether they told a simple tale and 'answered naturally at the moment, or gave uniform evidence 'carefully prepared.' As to affidavits Hadrian declined to admit them in criminal matters, when hearing cases himself. The judge was to give credence or not *ex animi sui sententia* (D. xxii 5 fr 3 §§ 1—4). He might after hearing the case, instead of pronouncing judgment, endeavour to bring the parties to an agreement on terms; he might intervene in the conduct of the case and put questions and suggest points not adverted to by the litigants: he might make use in forming his opinion of any knowledge which he personally happened to have on disputed facts[1]. But the propriety of such action on the part of the judge seems to have been much discussed (Gell. xiv 2 §§ 14—19). He might allow adjournments (*diem diffindi*), for which in Cicero's time the phrase appears to have been '*Amplius pronuntiare*' 'to declare for further hearing' (Cic. *Brut.* 22 § 86; *Verr.* ii 1 9 § 26; 29 § 74).

D. On preliminary and collateral points he would give interlocutory findings preparatory to the final formal judgment. Some instances may be given:

[1] Demelius however thinks the two following rules, though not actually found, must be regarded as in force among the Romans. (1) The judge cannot in giving judgment pay regard to any facts which are not maintained by the parties. (2) All facts maintained by one and admitted by the other he must take as a basis for his decision without inquiring into their material truth. In short he must not be actively inquisitorial (*Confessio* p. 365).

1. In actions *in rem* the condemnation is for the value of the thing and mesne profits, deducting necessary expenses (D. v 3 fr 38), but may be averted by due restitution. If therefore the judge finds (*pronuntiat*) for the plaintiff, he will call upon defendant to restore, and, only if defendant refuses to obey the judge's direction, will he give judgment for damages[1]. The formula contains such words as *nisi restituet*, and thus invites the judge's action (Cic. *Verr.* ii 2 cap. 12 § 31; cf. Gai. iv 114). In the mortgagee's action (*Serviana*), if the mortgage is only conditional and the mortgagee sue before the condition takes effect, the judge will not require the possessor to give up the thing, but to give a bond for delivery when the condition exists, if the money is not by that time repaid (D. xx 1 fr 13 § 5). In the ancillary personal action *ad exhibendum*, if production is made, there will be no condemnation, except for the consequences of delay (cf. D. x 4 fr 9 § 8; Just. iv 17 § 3).

2. In *bonae fidei* actions, the settlement being largely dependent on the discretion (*arbitrium, arbitratus*[2]) of the judge, he may direct various duties to be performed, and security to be given (D. v 1 fr 41), *e.g.* in an action *commodati* he may simply require defendant to surrender his actions against a third party and pay costs (D. xiii 6 fr 5 § 12). In a redhibitory action by the purchaser, the judge must ascertain whether vendor is prepared to restore everything he has received as price, and, if not, the condemnation will be double instead of single (D. xxi 1 fr 45; see p. 153); *etc.*

3. In actions on torts committed by slaves defendant can avoid condemnation by surrendering the slave (*e.g.* D. iv 3 fr 9 § 4), but, if he did not, the condemnation would still contain

[1] In D. vi 1 fr 57 Alfenus tells of a case where two suits by different persons were brought before different judges at the same time for a farm. He advises that whichever judge decided first should, if he found for the plaintiff, order restitution, only if plaintiff gave security against the other's claim.

[2] Actions in which such a discretion is exercisable by the judge are called by Justinian *arbitrariae* (*Inst.* iv 6 § 31). The Antonine jurists appear to have confined the term to the *actio de eo quod certo loco dari oportet* (which see) and perhaps to *quod metus causa gestum*, but this is by Gradenwitz held to be interpolated (*Interpol.* p. 99).

the alternative of damages or surrender (D. xlii 1 fr 6 § 1; cf. Just. iv 17 § 1, and see above, p. 355).

In an action for fraud or intimidation, restitution may, if the judge think fit, avert damages (D. iv 3 fr 18 pr; cf. the case of publicans xxxix 4 fr 5 pr).

4. Where defendant has got a plea of fraud admitted in order to recover expenses (beyond necessary expenses) to which he has been put for the benefit of others' property, considerable discretion is left to the judge in dealing with the matter: that is, if defendant had by mistake bought with a bad title and had built or planted, the judge may require plaintiff to repay the cost, or at least the additional value thus given to the land: or, if plaintiff is a poor man and would thus be deprived of the home and grave of his ancestors, he may permit defendant to remove his improvements so far as it can be done without injury to the place, or reduce the demand on the plaintiff to the value of what is thus removable (D. vi 1 fr 38; v 3 fr 38; xliv 4 fr 14).

5. The judge may require, as the condition on which he would condemn the defendant, the surrender by plaintiff of the actions which he has against others, *e.g.* where a surety is sued and pays he can get the creditor's actions against the principal debtor or other sureties (D. xlvi 1 fr 13, 17, 36); or, if the creditor has also a pledge, he can get this transferred to him (Cod. viii 40 fr 2; D. xx 5 fr 2). In actions on loan and deposit, where the defendant is condemned for fraudulent loss of the thing, it was the practice for the owner to cede his actions to defendant (D. xlii 1 fr 12). See also D. xlvii 2 fr 81 §§ 5, 7.

6. Where there are concurrent actions, the judge can arrange that plaintiff release the others before condemnation be passed on the one in process; *e.g.* where a guardian is sued *tutelae*, but liable also to an action on stipulation (D. xlvi 2 fr 9 pr); or where a thief is sued by a vindication but is also liable to *condictio furtiva* (D. xlvii 2 fr 9 § 1). (If the damages would be larger in the second action, the praetor in settling the issue will arrange for the defendant's being liable in that only for the excess, D. xlvii 7 fr 1; 2 fr 89; xliv 7 fr 34 pr, fr 41 § 1.) If the duty of the judge would not of itself secure such

results, a plea of fraud would enable it to be done (D. iv 9 fr 3 § 5).

7. In an action *de peculio* the judge inquires whether any part of the debt incurred has been really for the master's or father's service, and gives judgment for that (*de in rem verso*), before he inquires into the amount of the *peculium* (Just. iv 7 § 4*b*).

8. Further, in all *bonae fidei* suits it was the duty of the judge to look at both sides of the matter and determine the reciprocal obligations of the parties. He allowed for any expenses properly incurred by defendant or counterclaims of any kind in reference to the particular subject of suit. In partnership actions he could even set off (*compensare*) the negligence of one against negligence of the other or against a gain made by the other from the common property (D. xvi 2 fr 10 pr). From this general position of the parties and the judge, a further step was taken, and a defendant was permitted to set off against the sum found to be due from him to the plaintiff the amount of any money due from plaintiff to him. The judge was free to permit it or not: there was nothing in the formula to bind him; but it was held to be more consonant with the requirements of good faith, that a man who was called on to pay should pay over only the balance of what he was entitled to receive, or if amounts were equal, should not have to pay at all (Gai. iv 61—63). A rescript of M. Aurelius admitted compensation in strict suits also, by allowing defendant a plea of fraud for this purpose (Just. iv 6 § 30). And it was admissible in a suit on tort or a noxal suit (D. xvi 2 fr 10 § 2). It had long been usual in bankers' suits (above, p. 363).

The conditions of set-off were that the debt should be of the same kind, money against money, corn against corn, *etc.*[1]; that it should be actually due, whether in suit, or already a judgment debt, or not even recoverable at all by suit (a natural debt only), but it should not be one which plaintiff can destroy by a plea (D. xvi 2 fr 6, 7 pr, 8, 14, 16 § 1). Money debts were held (by a constitution of Alexander Severus) to

[1] This is named in the case of bankers in Gai. iv 66, and appears probable for other cases of compensation.

cancel one another from the date of the counterbalance[1], and interest not to be due on the amount set off, even if one debt bore interest and the other did not, or the rates of interest were different (Cod. iv 31 fr 4; cf. D. fr 11, 12, which refers to a constitution of Sept. Severus). A surety could set off a debt due to his principal or to himself; a person sued by a guardian could not set off, against a debt due to the ward, a debt due from the guardian on his own account (fr 4, 23). A son under power could set off a debt due to his father, but had to guaranty that his father would ratify (fr 9 § 1). A creditor is not bound to accept a set-off of what he owes to a third party, even though this last consents (fr 18 § 1). If the judge rejected the set-off on the ground that there was no such debt, any suit for that debt could be met by a plea of 'matter decided'; but if he simply rejected it as not suitable or as involving controversy or for any other reason, defendant was not precluded from suing for it (fr 7 § 1; iii 5 fr 7 § 2).

E. Whether the judgment should be condemnation or acquittal, when defendant, after joinder of issue but before judgment, had satisfied the plaintiff, as required by the judge, was a matter on which the two schools of lawyers held different opinions. Sabinus and Cassius held that all kinds of trials admitted of acquittal in such a case (*omnia judicia absolutoria esse*), on the ground that defendant was now no longer liable (cf. D. xxxix 4 fr 5 pr). The opposite school appear to have held (Gaius is mutilated) the same as regards suits *in rem*, because condemnation was expressly made contingent on non-restoration (*nisi restituet, condemna*): and as regards *bonae fidei* trials, because the judge is free; but that in strict suits the condemnation depended on the position at the joinder of issue, and defendant, if in the wrong then, could not escape condemnation (Gai. iv 114).

[1] On the much disputed meaning of *ipso jure* as applied to set-off see different opinions in Windscheid *Pand.* § 349 n. 10. Dernburg (*Pand. Oblig.* § 62) and others take it to mean that since M. Aurelius' rescript it is a matter of right, and not in the discretion of the judge; cf. Paul D. xvi 2 fr 21. The expression is more probably due to Justinian; cf. *Inst.* iv 6 § 30.

F. Suit can be brought only for what is now due and unconditionally due. The judge must accordingly decide absolutely, and the condemnation in damages must be for a fixed sum (Gai. iv 51; D. v 1 fr 35). Where there was no limit, he could fix the sum as high as he pleased; where there was a maximum (*taxatio*), he must not exceed it, but may name a less sum; where the amount is fixed in the formula, he must neither exceed nor reduce it[1]. If he thus exceeded his instructions, although by mistake, he was said *litem suam facere*[2] 'to treat the suit as his own' (Gai. iv 52); as he did, when he gave a judgment not in conformity with the statute (*in fraudem legis*) from corrupt motives (favour, enmity, bribery[3]). The judge was liable to an action *in factum*, the damages to be fixed by the judge in that trial. If he was a *filius familias*, his father was liable only to the extent of his *peculium*: the heir of a judge was not liable (D. v 1 fr 15, 16; L 13 fr 6).

If the judge finds interest due as well as the principal, he must not simply add to his judgment the words 'and interest,' but should ascertain the amount (D. xlii 1 fr 59 § 2).

G. The judge had in many suits a potent means of compelling defendant's obedience to his findings by allowing the plaintiff to fix on oath the amount of the damages for defendant's failure to restore or give guaranty as required. The judge may, if he think fit, put a maximum, and may, but only for very strong reasons, not adopt the amount sworn. This mode of fixing the damages is resorted to principally

[1] Cf. Sen. *Clem.* ii 7 § 3 *Clementia liberum arbitrium habet: non sub formula sed ex aequo et bono judicat: et absolvere illi licet, et quanti vult taxare litem.*

[2] Cicero *Or.* ii 305 uses the expression metaphorically. *Quid si, cum pro altero dicas, litem tuam facias, aut laesus efferare iracundia, causam relinquas?* So Gellius (x 1 § 5) contented himself in reply to a question with quoting Varro, for *adversus eum qui doctus esse dicebatur, litem meam facere absens nolui.* The orator G. Titius (2nd cent. B.C.) speaks as if a late appearance or non-appearance in court made a judge liable; *inde ad comitium eunt ne litem suam faciant* (*ap.* Macrob. *Sat.* iii 16 § 16).

[3] A constitution of Caracalla decided that money given in any suit either to the judge or the adversary should cause plaintiff to lose his suit (Cod. vii 49 fr 1; D. iii 6 fr 1 § 3).

where there is fraud or obstinacy on the defendant's part: if there be only negligence attributable, the judge makes the estimate himself (D. xii 2 fr 2, 4 §§ 3, 4, fr 5 §§ 1—3; v 1 fr 64). 'Swearing to the claim' (*jurare in litem*)[1] was not used in strict actions, unless there was something making the value very uncertain, *e.g.* if a slave who was promised had died. Nor would it be used in a suit on the deposit of a known sum of money, unless, by the failure to restore, some special damage had been caused. But it was in use in suits *in rem, ad exhibendum, rerum amotarum* and *bonae fidei* (*ib.* fr 3, 5 pr § 4; xxv 2 fr 8 § 1), and in the interdict *quod vi aut clam* (D. xliii 24 fr 15 § 9).

This oath is good only if tendered by the judge. A ward cannot be compelled to swear, nor can guardians or caretakers; but a youth (*adulescens*) and guardians and caretakers are permitted to swear if they are willing to incur the risk. This was settled by the Antonines (*ib.* fr 4). No one could take this oath who had not joined issue in his own name (fr 7).

H. Apart from the merits of the case a reduction of damages was made in favour of a defendant standing in such a relation to the plaintiff as was held to give a claim to consideration. Such a defendant is a partner, a parent, a patron and a patron's children and parents, a husband, and, on other grounds, a soldier who has been in active service. These are to be condemned only *in id quod facere possunt, i.e.* not beyond their actual means of payment, without taking any account of what they may owe to others, the principle in this as in some other matters (see pp. 240, 255) being 'first come first served' (*occupantis melior condicio est* D. xlii 1 fr 16—fr 19 pr; xxiv 3 fr 54). In the case of a husband this limitation was originally granted only on the wife's action for repayment of the dowry, but allowed by Antoninus Pius in other suits by the wife; and the lawyers

[1] Cicero in *Rosc. Com.* i § 11 (which was a strict suit) alludes to *in litem jurare* as if applicable, and as if at that point of the trial it could take place: *Essene quemquam tanta audacia praeditum qui, quod nomen referre in tabulas timeat, id petere audeat, quod in codicem injuratus referre nolit, id jurare in litem non dubitet?* This however is probably only rhetorical.

were inclined to apply it by analogy to suits by the husband against the wife (xlii 1 fr 20). The limitation was further extended, so as to require the means of actual subsistence to be left to such a defendant (*ne egeat* D. L 17 fr 173). The limitation could not be claimed by the heirs or sureties of such a person (D. xlii 1 fr 24, 25). The time for estimating the means of defendant is the time of judgment (D. xxiv 3 fr 15 pr).

A like limitation is granted to the husband's father if he be sued on a promise of dowry, while the marriage still subsists (fr 21, 22 pr), and to anyone accepting the defence of any of the above-named persons whose means are insufficient (fr 23; xvii 2 fr 63 § 1).

A like limitation is allowed to a son emancipated or disinherited, *etc.* (see p. 244), if sued on his contracts made while he was in his father's power (D. xiv 5 fr 2; xxvi 7 fr 37 § 2; xlii 1 fr 49); and (by a rescript of Ant. Pius) to a donor sued upon his promise: in which last case other debts (not being voluntary gifts) were deducted to ascertain *quod facere potest* (D. xxxix 5 fr 12; xlii 1 fr 19 § 2). An intended donor, if delegated by the donee to a creditor, is liable to him in full (D. xlii 1 fr 41 pr).

A partner (and perhaps others) could be sued for the residue of his debt, if he subsequently acquired means, and this was secured by his own guaranty (D. xvii 2 fr 63).

If the limit has by inadvertence not been regarded in the original action, the omission can be remedied by a plea of fraud in the action on the judgment (D. xxiv 3 fr 17 § 2; xlii 1 fr 41 § 2).

J. When the cause had been fully heard it was the judge's duty *ire in consilium, i.e.* to consider his judgment with his assessors and pronounce sentence accordingly (*de consilii sententia*). And something of the kind would take place before any important pronouncement on preparatory points. He was not however bound by their opinion: he might adopt it or not as his own honest opinion inclined, and in case of complete perplexity he could declare on his oath 'the matter is not clear to me' (*non liquet*) and thereby the trial was put an end to, the judge was free, and the plaintiff must if he chose begin again (Gell. xiv 2 § 25; cf. D. xlii 1 fr 36)[1]. There was no particular form for the final judgment. It was delivered orally in the presence of all the parties (or their representatives), and apparently not accompanied by a statement of reasons. A decision given in the absence of some of the parties binds only those who were present; and does not make the matter *res judicata*, unless the absent party has been summoned by the judge by three letters or notices (*edicta*) or, if the judge see cause, by one peremptory notice in lieu of all, or by a thrice repeated notice (*denuntiatio*) given by his opponent. If he does not then appear before the judge named in the notices, he may be pronounced contumacious and judgment given against him, which then will not be subject to any appeal or revocation (Paul v 5*a* §§ 5, 6; D. xlii 1 fr 53). A bad fever or other serious disease (*morbus sonticus*) was an adequate excuse, and the proceedings were adjourned (*ib.* fr 60).

A decision once given by the judge could not be altered by him: he was *functus officio* (*ib.* fr 55). If the parties agreed

[1] Aulus Gellius (l.c.) naïvely describes his own experience when first put on the list of *judices* by the praetor. He got books in both languages (Greek and Latin) on the duty of a judge, but found they did not meet his practical difficulties. In one case plaintiff sued for money paid down, but had no evidence either oral or documentary. Defendant demanded an acquittal for himself and the condemnation of his opponent for *calumnia*. Gellius' assessors unhesitatingly recommended acquittal, but Gellius was not satisfied, because plaintiff was a man of honour and proved integrity, and defendant was a rogue and oft-convicted liar. He adjourned the case and consulted a philosophic friend who referred him to a speech of Cato (*pro L. Turio contra Cn. Gellium*) which recommended, when there was no evidence and the parties were equal in point of character, judgment to be given for defendant, but if one was of a better character than the other, judgment to follow superiority in character. Gellius however thought this too bold a course and contented himself with a *non liquet*.

Seneca *Ep.* 65 § 15 imagines his friends impatient of the length of his discussion and saying to him: *Aut fer sententiam aut, quod facilius in ejusmodi rebus est, nega tibi liquere et nos reverti jube.* So in a reproach by Cicero: *Quid dicam nisi id, venisse eum in consilium publicae quaestionis et in eo consilio, cum causam non audisset et potestas esset ampliandi, dixisse sibi liquere; cum de incognita re judicare voluisset, maluisse condemnare quam absolvere* (*Caecin.* 10 § 29).

upon the judgment to be given, it was quite in order that the judge should adopt it (*ib.* fr 26).

When there was a plurality of judges, all ought to be present to give the decision. The majority decides. If an equal number were for different opinions on a question of freedom, the opinion in favour of freedom prevailed by a constitution of Ant. Pius: in other cases, civil as well as criminal, the defendant had the benefit of the doubt. In plaint of an unduteous will, the will would be upheld unless the testator was clearly shewn to have acted with partiality. If the judges differed in the amount to which they condemned defendant, the smallest amount was taken. If two of three judges appeared and one was absent, no decision could be given, but if he was present, neither his opposition to their opinion (if agreed), nor his declaration on oath of his inability to make up his mind (*sibi non liquere*), prevented their decision being good (D. xlii 1 fr 36—39; xl 1 fr 24; v 2 fr 10).

CHAPTER XIV.

APPEALS.

A. 1. Appeals were allowed not only from the final judgment, but sometimes from interlocutory decisions, *e.g.* when in a civil matter the judge required examination of a slave by torture, or when on an application by minors for reinstatement an interlocutory decision was given on their age (D. xlix 5 fr 2; iv 4 fr 39). Notice of the intended appeal had to be given, either in court at the time by simply saying *Appello*, or by application for a dimissory letter to the judge in appeal, such application to be made in writing (*libelli appellatorii*) within a period of two or three days from the judgment, two days, if the appellant was acting in his own case, three days, if as procurator or guardian, *etc.* he was acting in another's case. Any days in which the judge was not accessible did not count. If the appellant was absent, the time ran from his getting knowledge of the decision (D. xlix 5 fr 2, 5 § 4; tit. 4 fr 1 §§ 11, 12, 15).

Five days were allowed for obtaining the dimissory letters: if, notwithstanding repeated application, he could not get them, he must protest. These letters were to state the fact of the appeal and the names of the appellant, of the parties to the case, and of the judge (D. *ib.* 6 § 2; Paul v 34). The applicant had within five days (or longer if he lived at a distance) to give a bond forfeiting in case of non-success a penalty, which in civil cases was one-third of the damages to which he was condemned. One good surety (or more) was to be given unless the money was deposited or something of equivalent value. The bond ought to fix the amount of the penalty, so that it could be sued for in case of forfeiture. If the possessor appeals, in the case of land he has to deposit the mesne profits, or, in the case of houses or slaves or ships, the rents or wages or passage moneys (Paul v 33, 36; cf. D. ii 8 fr 15).

A time for prosecuting the appeal was also fixed. Any failure to proceed within the times stated, involved defeat by a praescription (*i.e.* plea to that effect), and loss of the penalty of the bond (Paul v 34 § 2).

If the judge from whom the appeal is made refuse to receive the notice of it, appeal may be made on the refusal (D. xlix 5 fr 5).

2. The appeal judge was usually the person who appointed the judge who had given the decision. If he had been appointed by a deputy of the regular magistrate, the appeal lay to the magistrate himself. An appeal, made to a judge inferior in rank to the judge appealed from, is lost: if to a superior judge but not the right one, the appellant will be sent before the proper one. An appeal might (according to a rescript of Ant. Pius) be taken even from a judgment given in pursuance of a rescript of the emperor, if it could be shewn that the facts had been wrongly stated (D. xlix 1 fr 1; tit. 3 fr 1).

3. No one could appeal from a decision in a suit to which he was not a party, unless he was directly interested in the decision, *e.g.* as a coheir or a legatee or one entitled to freedom under the will which was assailed. If a procurator does not

appeal, his principal can; so also if vendor and purchaser acquiesce in an eviction, the guarantor of both can appeal, or a surety on behalf of his principal (D. *ib.* 1 fr 4 § 2—fr 5 § 2).

4. An appeal in civil cases may be conducted by an agent, unless it concerns a man's freedom. The decision could be appealed from as a whole, without specifying any particular part; but if the decision of one case embraced two different matters, *e.g.* principal of a loan and interest, appeal on one only implies acquiescence in the other. At least in Diocletian's time and probably always before, an appeal was a rehearing of the matter, and new facts and witnesses could be adduced (Paul v 35 § 1; D. *ib.* fr 13 pr, fr 17 pr; tit. 5 fr 1; Cod. vii 62 § 6).

5. Success in appeal benefited those concerned in the same case even if they had not appealed. Defeat made the appellant liable for fourfold the other party's cost in the appeal (D. xlix 1 fr 10 § 4; Paul v 37).

During an appeal, whether allowed or refused by the judge, all proceedings on the judgment are suspended (D. xlix 5 fr 6, 7).

B. 1. For some obvious matters an appeal was not necessary: mistakes could be corrected in the proceedings on the judgment (*actio judicati*). A sentence given when the defendant was dead, either at the time of the appointment of the judge or at the time of sentence, was invalid (D. xlix 8 fr 3). So also when defendant had been professedly summoned by peremptory edict, which in fact had neither been proposed nor come to his knowledge (*ib.* fr 1 § 3); or when the judge had declared that there were no such rights as were plainly given by imperial constitutions (*ib.* § 2); or had directed something to be done which was physically impossible (*ib.* fr 3); or had made a mere mistake in arithmetic (*ib.* fr 1 § 1; Paul v 5*a* § 11). On such points probably a replication could be made if a plaintiff was met by a plea of 'matter decided.'

2. Where fraud, intimidation, minority, absence in the public service could be proved, proceedings for reinstatement (*in integrum restitutio*) would supply effectively the place of an appeal (see pp. 226, 228, 259, 262).

C. Another proceeding is coupled with appeal in some passages of Paul under the name of *in duplum revocare*. All that we are told is that it was not applicable by a defendant to his own confession; nor (any more than an appeal) to a sentence passed against him as contumacious, nor in reference to a matter which had been decided, 'as long ago as ten years if the 'parties were present[1], twenty years if absent, and had not been 'stirred since' (Paul v 5 *a* §§6 *a*—8; cf. Cod. Greg. *ap.* Krüger *Jus antejustin.* iii p. 261)[2].

[1] *I.e.* domiciled in the same town, cf. Cod. vii 33 § 1.

[2] This proceeding is generally identified with one referred to in Cic. *Flac.* 21 § 49. Hermippus, as surety for Heraclides, both citizens of Temnos (in the province of Asia), had to pay a sum borrowed by Heraclides. He sued Heraclides, got judgment, and took defendant in execution, but settled with him by taking some slaves in payment. Heraclides waited for a new governor, and, on Q. Cicero succeeding, applied to him and complained that the Recoverers in Hermippus' suit had been intimidated by the governor at the time (Flaccus) into condemning him. Q. Cicero decreed *ut, si judicatum negaret, in duplum iret; si metu coactos diceret, haberet eosdem recuperatores, i.e.* that if he challenged the judgment as illegal and therefore no judgment, he should 'proceed for the double' (see below), and, if the special ground of his plaint was that the judgment was due to intimidation, the case should come before the same men as Recoverers, who could then give free expression to their convictions. Bethmann-Hollweg supposes that Heraclides would bring a *condictio* to recover the amount of the condemnation under a penalty of twice the amount, if he failed in his suit (*CP.* ii 726: so also Eisele *Abhandl.* p. 163). This mode of proceeding would be applicable only when a judgment had been obeyed, and therefore the opportunity of raising the point of 'no judgment' in the *actio judicati* was past. Eisele considers the proceeding mentioned by Paul to belong not to the formular procedure but to the extraordinary cognition, *ib.* p. 188. The whole matter is obscure and much debated: see references in the above.

All seem to agree in one point, viz. that *in duplum* (*ire* or *revocare*) refers to the risk of defendant, who in this as in other cases of opposing a judgment, was liable to double damages (Gai. iv 171). Probably he was; but it is difficult to see how, as a matter of language, *in duplum ire, etc.* can refer to a penalty on failure instead of the gain on success. The object or direct result or extent of the action of the verb is the invariable meaning of *in duplum, in quadruplum* (*e.g.* with *judicium dabo* Ed. *ap.* D. xvi 3 fr 1 § 1; *agentis* Gai. iv 9; *damnatur* D. iv 6 fr 9; *etc.*), cf. *in creditum ire* of plaintiff (D. xii 1 fr 2 § 1; xvi 1 fr 19 § 5); *actio in ipsum et in solidum et in duplum et in perpetuum datur* (D. xvi 3 fr 18); cf. Just. iv 6 § 21, *etc.* I believe *plaintiff sued for double damages* on the ground that defendant had enforced a judgment which was no judgment.

CHAPTER XV.

EXECUTION.

The execution of a judgment was not a matter for the judge (at least before the time of Antoninus Pius), but for the successful party. The judgment ascertained his right. But plaintiff had to sue on the judgment for execution. This could be done at any time and both by heirs and against heirs (D. xlii 1 fr 6 § 3). The defendant (if there was no appeal taken) would usually conform, but the law put great pressure to induce him to do so. Only fragments of the details are known to us. In early days imprisonment or worse was the fate of an obstinate judgment debtor: towards the end of the Republic (probably), the seizure and distribution of the debtor's property, if it was not made over voluntarily, could be obtained by application to the praetor.

Where a defendant was condemned on several suits, the earlier condemnation gave no priority in suing execution (D. xlii 1 fr 61).

A. Attachment of the person.

1. When the *legis actiones* were in use, one of them was a form of execution. It was authorized by the XII tables. The words given us are *Aeris confessi rebusque jure judicatis*[1] *triginta dies justi sunto. Post deinde manus injectio esto, in jus ducito. Ni judicatum facit aut quis endo eo in jure vindicit, secum ducito, vincito aut nervo aut compedibus: quindecim pondo ne minore aut si volet majore*[2] *vincito. Si volet, suo vivito. Ni suo vivit, qui eum vinctum habebit libras farris endo dies dato* (Sex. Caecilius *ap.* Gell. xx 1 45). 'Thirty days shall be lawful 'for those who have admitted a debt of money or in the case of 'matters lawfully judged. Thereafter shall be a "laying hand

[1] These first words are no doubt corrupt in some way: the difference of case is enough to shew that.

[2] Some reverse *minore* and *majore* (by conjecture). But cf. Liv. xxxii 26 § 18 (*Jussum*) *captivi ne minus decem pondo compedibus vincti essent* (quoted by Hertz *Gell.* xx 1 § 45).

"on"; plaintiff shall take defendant into court. If he does not 'the judgment, and no one in court makes opposing claim in his 'case, plaintiff shall take him off, fasten him either in a block 'or with fetters; he shall fasten him with a weight of 15 pounds, 'not less: if he chooses, with more. If defendant will, he 'shall live on his own[1]. If he does not live on his own, he that 'shall have him fastened shall give him pounds of corn per day[2].' Sex. Caecilius proceeds to say that this state lasted for sixty days, during which debtor had the opportunity of coming to terms with his creditor; and on three consecutive market days debtor was led forth into the comitium to the praetor, and announcement was made of the amount of the judgment debt. On the third market day he paid with his person (*capite poenas dabat*), or was sold into foreign parts beyond the Tiber. If there were more creditors than one, the XII tables said, *tertiis nundinis partis secanto: si plus minusve secuerunt, se fraude esto* (*ib.* § 50). The meaning of these words has been much disputed: Caecilius took them literally of the creditors being entitled to cut up the debtor himself, and having no need to be particular as to the precise correspondence of each man's share of the body with his share of the total debts[3]. So also Quintilian (*Inst.* iii 6 § 84) and Dio Cassius (*Fragm.* 17 § 8), but Quintilian says that such a proceeding was repudiated by custom (cf. Tertull. *Apol.* 4); and the others deny that any instance was known of its ever being done. Similar savagery

1 Cf. D. xlii 1 fr 34.

2 On the duty of feeding see S. Ambros. l.c. (p. 431).

3 Some writers have taken the words in the more humane sense of division of the estate and not the person of the debtor. If so, they may be understood to free the creditors from liability, if they sold and divided more than would cover the debts, or from loss of the remainder of their claim, if the first sale did not realize enough. Münderloh (*ZRG.* xii 202) takes the words to mean that whether the proceeds were more or less than the debts the creditors must be content. H. Nettleship says *secare partes* is not Latin for 'to cut into pieces' and suggests that *secare* is another form of *sequi* and means to claim their shares in the debtor's property (Essays p. 374). Schulin proposes *secunto* with like root and meaning (*RG.* p. 535). I see no objection in point of language to taking *secare partes* as 'to cut (off their) shares' whether in the body or in the property.

is recorded of other nations, and one cannot deny that the early Roman laws may have had it, and that it may have been retained by the *decemviri*, in order to compel the debtor to submit his property and the services of himself and family to the creditor's disposition. It could hardly have been a bit of grim inexorable logic. Be that as it may, we hear nothing of it in our legal authorities, and whatever else may have been done by the *lex Poetelia* (326 ? or 313 ? B.C.), we may conclude that it was then abolished if it ever existed. In ordinary language the sale or *sectio* of the person is sometimes spoken of in Cicero's time where the property alone is really meant[1] (see p. 435 n. 2; so in English 'A. B. is sold up').

2. Gaius (iv 21) gives the following account of *manus injectio*. The plaintiff laid hold of some part of defendant's body and said, 'Whereas thou hast been judged or condemned to me 'for 10000 sesterces, seeing thou hast not paid, therefor I lay 'hand on thee for the judgment of 10000 sesterces (*Quod tu 'mihi judicatus sive damnatus*[2] *es sestertium x milia, quandoc 'non solvisti, ob eam rem ego tibi sestertium x milium judicati*[3] *'manum inicio*).' The judgment debtor was not allowed to throw off the plaintiff's hand, and act by statute (*lege agere*) for himself, but would offer (*dabat*) some champion (*vindex*[4]) who,

[1] Something analogous is seen in the language used where the division of (the burden of) stipulations among the heirs of the stipulator or of the promiser is spoken of: *Cum species stipulamur necesse est inter dominos et inter heredes ita dividi stipulationem ut partes corporum cuique debeantur* (MS. *debebuntur*) D. xlv 1 fr 54 pr, *i.e.* each heir of the stipulator will have a right to (the conveyance of) a share in the slave or other chattel.

[2] Krüger and others take *sive dam.* as Gaius' words, not part of the formula.

[3] Sc. *nomine* or *causa*.

[4] *Vindex* appears to be from *vim dicere* 'to assert force, *i.e.* to declare a counter claim': hence *vindicare* of claiming a thing as one's own; *vindiciae* 'claims'; *vindicta* the rod used as a symbol of force (cf. vol. I 26, II 341). Livy uses these terms frequently in his account of Appius' treatment of Verginia: *M. Claudio negotium dedit, ut virginem in servitutem assereret neque cederet secundum libertatem postulantibus vindicias* (iii 44 § 5). *Me vindicantem sponsam in libertatem vita citius deseret quam fides* (45 § 11). *Postero die vindex injuriae praesto erat* (46 § 6), cf. 56 §§ 4–6; 57 §§ 4, 5. In *lex Ossun. init.* we have *vim facere* in close connexion and contrast with *vindex* (p. 426).

as the practice was, acted for him: if he got no champion he was led off home by plaintiff and fastened up. The charter of the colony of Ossuna in Spain (44 B.C.) adds a little to our information: we may presume that it followed the Roman practice. 'If anyone shall be bidden to lay hand on[1], the 'hand-laying shall be as for a judgment, and it shall be 'lawful for him to do it without risk to himself. A champion '(*vindex*) shall be substantial (*locuples*)[2] in the opinion of the 'commissioner or chief law-officer. If he shall get no champion 'and shall not do the judgment, plaintiff shall lead him off. 'He shall keep him bound in accordance with the civil law. 'If anyone shall use force therein (*i.e.* attempt a rescue ?)[3] and 'is convicted thereof, he shall be condemned in the double, and 'to colonists of that colony in the sum of 20000 sesterces: any-'one who will may sue for it and the commissioner or chief 'law-officer shall have the exaction and the judging' (cap. 61).

Sex. Caecilius (Gellius' authority) tells us of a fact not mentioned in the above accounts, viz. that in default of payment, the debtors after being summoned before the praetor were by him assigned to the persons to whom they had been judged (*nisi dissolverant ad praetorem vocabantur et ab eo quibus erant judicati addicebantur*, Gell. xx 1 § 44).

In Livy's sixth book we have frequent mention of persons being judged for money debts, assigned, and led off by private creditors into confinement (see Essay on *nexum*, above p. 297).

3. The result of the above may be briefly stated thus. *Manus injectio* in itself is simply 'bodily arrest[4].' It is used

[1] The bronze does not give the circumstances for this *manus injectio*.

[2] Cf. Cic. *Top.* 2 § 10 *Cum lex assiduo vindicem assiduum esse jubet, locupletem jubet locupleti. Assiduus* is 'settled' from *adsidēre* (not *ab asse dando*, as suggested by a writer in Gell. xvi 10 § 16). See Mommsen *Staatsr.* iii p. 237 n. The XII tables are said to have *Assiduo vindex assiduus esto: proletario jam civi cui quis volet vindex esto* (Gell. *ib.* § 5).

[3] *Si quis in eo vim faciet, ast ejus vincitur.* See Exner *ZRG.* xiii pp. 395—397. Girard objects that the penalty for such a robbery (cf. Gai. iii 199) would be not double but quadruple, and refers the words to the interference of the *vindex* (*Textes* p. 84). But the position of the sentence is against this view. See also p. 325 n. 4.

[4] It is used by Livy of Claudius' assertion of his claim to Verginia as

of a master reasserting his right over a slave, sometimes for the slave's benefit, in consequence of a breach of condition of sale (Vat. 6; D. xviii 7 fr 9; xl 1 fr 20 § 2). It was used in the XII tables of plaintiff's seizure of a defendant who declined to obey a summons into court (see above, p. 334). As the act of a creditor in execution of a judgment, it was accompanied by the formal words given by Gaius. The debtor against whom judgment had passed, by this formal act of the creditor lost his power as a free citizen of acting for himself in court[1], and had, in the course of a month, either to pay his debt, or to find someone to act for him and undertake or guaranty his liability. At the expiration of the month he had to appear before the praetor; if no payment had been made and no one appeared for him, the praetor *addixit* *i.e.* bade the creditor take him off to his own house[2]. Perhaps in Cicero's and later

a slave (iii 44 § 6) and of Manlius' interference with a creditor's leading his debtor into confinement (vi 14 § 3). There is an allusion apparently to the judicial (criminal) *manum inicere* in Plaut. *Pers.* 70 where a parasite proposes *ubi quadruplator quempiam injexit manum, tantidem illa illi rursus iniciat manum, ut aequa parte prodeant ad tres viros.*

[1] Cf. Unger *ZRG.* vii 196 foll., 203: 'It was an old Roman principle 'that the object of a suit could not also be a party. One in slavery could 'not assert his own claim to be a freeman but, until Justinian's law (Cod. 'vii 17), required an *adsertor*; and a suit whether a person was in one's 'power was conducted by the alleged father not the son himself (D. xliii 30 'fr 3 § 3). The suit in the case of the *vindex* of a judgment debtor would be 'immediately over the person of the debtor, indirectly over the existence of 'the judgment debt.'

[2] The regular phrase for committing a debtor to his creditor's prison was *Duci jubere* 'bid him to be taken off,' *e.g.* Cic. *Verr.* ii 2 26 § 63; *Cum judicatum non faceret, addictus Hermippo et ab hoc ductus est* (*Flac.* 20 § 48; also § 45), *Apud Novium quidam, judicatum duci videns percontatus ita: quanti addictus? 'Mille nummum': Nihil addo, ducas licet* (Cic. *Orat.* ii 63 § 255), where the joke lies in the use by the play-writer Novius of *addictus* both of a slave knocked down at a price by an auctioneer, and of the fate of a judgment debtor.

Some refer *addicere* and *duci jubere* to different occasions, cf. Karlowa *CP.* § 19; Wlassak *PG.* i 96. On *addicere* see my Comm. on *de Usufructu* p. 184. *Duci jussu praetoris* is used of a creditor's taking off slaves in default of noxal transfer (D. ix 4 fr 26 § 6; fr 28). It is constant in Livy of persons being ordered to prison on criminal charges (iii 49 § 2; 56 § 4, *etc.*).

times the personal confinement took place only in the case of utterly insolvent debtors, and there was no repetition of the appearance before the praetor and of the proclamation of the debt. A champion surety (*vindex*) who paid the debt had a right to the like stringent process to recover his money from the debtor (*actio depensi*). Anyone who endeavoured to rescue the debtor by force, when led off or imprisoned by his creditor, was condemned not only in twice the amount of the debt but in a fine besides. If however the *vindex* instead of paying the creditor appeared in court and disputed the judgment, he was himself responsible for the issue, and if the decision (whether by the praetor himself or by a judge appointed by him to try the case) was against the *vindex*, he would, I presume, be condemned in damages to twice the amount of the debt. The debtor would be then liable to the *vindex* only[1].

The debtor in his creditor's shackles is, in Livy's account of early Roman history, spoken of as in slavery, and Quintilian (*Inst.* vii 3 § 26) mentions as a question for discussion in the schools of rhetoric *an addictus, quem lex servire donec solverit jubet, servus sit,* but gives decisive arguments for the negative. The truth is, his legal rights were in suspense but not destroyed. No Roman could be slave of another Roman within Roman territory[2]. The judgment debtor retained his full name and tribe as any other free person: he was held under the authority of the law[3], not as a mere chattel at the caprice and disposal of his master: whether the creditor consented or not, he recovered his liberty on full discharge of his debt, and then did not, like an emancipated slave, become a *libertinus*, but remained *ingenuus* (if he had been so before). Whether he was held as a

[1] Unger (*ZRG.* vii 203) holds that the debtor, not the *vindex*, would be liable for the double.

[2] Otherwise in Gaul. *Plerique (de plebe) cum aut aere alieno aut magnitudine tributorum aut injuria potentiorum premuntur, sese in servitutem dicant nobilibus, (quibus) in hos eadem omnia sunt jura, quae dominis in servos* (Caes. *B. G.* vi 13 § 2). See Mommsen in *Festgabe für Beseler*, p. 266.

[3] A *judicatus* could be stolen but so could other free persons (Gai. iii 199; D. xlvii 2 fr 38). A free man in bodily confinement was not technically possessed (D. xli 2 fr 23 § 2).

mere pledge or was legally compellable[1] to work for his creditor is not said: he may have been willing to do so, in order to pay off his debt or to keep down interest (if that continued to run), or to obtain better treatment. Practically he would have little choice in the matter. The original purpose of the treatment was no doubt to put pressure on him, so as to induce him to give up his property and the services of his family and self for the discharge of his debts.

4. Execution on the person was allowed by the XII tables in the case of one who admitted a money debt (cf. *confessi debitores pro judicatis habentur* Paul v 50 § 2) as well as in that of a judgment. In the *lex Rubria* (42—35 B.C.) the local magistrates (in Cisalpine Gaul) can allow it (*duci jubeto*), in the case of a loan certain of coined money[2] (see p. 309) not exceeding 15000 sesterces (£120 to £150), provided defendant has admitted the debt, but not paid it or satisfied his creditor; or has given no answer at all on the matter, or has not made due defence, or after lawful trial has been condemned (cap. 21). This was no doubt following the practice at Rome but limiting the jurisdiction to small amounts. In any other case except that of loan certain as above, the praetor at Rome is to grant execution, whether by arrest or by possession and sale of defendant's estate, the occasion for one of these remedies rather than the other being not determined in the law so far as we have it (cap. 22). Nor do we know when the remedy by *manus injectio* was to be applied under the charter of Ossuna; the clause is only half preserved.

5. But it was not only in execution of a judgment that 'laying hand on' was allowed. Statutable authority was required for subjecting a debtor to such a stringent and summary

[1] The words in Quintilian's *lex servire jubet* prove nothing in a rhetorical thesis. To another question *An is, quem dum addicta est mater peperit, servus sit natus* he gives no answer (*Inst.* iii 6 § 25). See Savigny *Verm. Schr.* ii 446 sq.

[2] Demelius (*Confess.* p. 140) supposes that this procedure was applicable to all admissions of debts of money certain, not merely of loans as Savigny (*Verm. Schr.* ii 431, *etc.*) takes it. A large meaning was given to *credita pecunia* in the interpretation of the *lex Cornelia* respecting sureties, and Gaius' words may be taken as more general (Gai. iii 124).

process. Such authority was given (evidently in early times) in certain cases named by Gaius (iv 22—25). The first is the *lex Publilia* which granted it against the debtor who had not repaid his surety (*sponsor*) within six months. Then the *lex Furia* against any creditor who had exacted more than his fair share from one of several co-sureties; besides several others in many cases. The plaintiff, after naming the subject of his suit, accompanied the arrest with the words 'on that account I lay hand on thee as upon one judged (*pro judicato*),' and in consequence the defendant was not allowed to throw off the hand and plead his own case (*pro se agere*). By the *lex Vallia* however this incapacity was removed from all persons subjected to personal arrest, except judgment debtors and those who had not repaid their surety (*depensi*). The attachment of the person however remained: and it was allowed also in many other cases, distinguished from the above by the words *pro judicato* being omitted from the formal words. Thus it was allowed by the *lex Furia testamentaria* against anyone, not within the exceptions of the statute, who had taken by will or *mortis causa* more than 1000 (MS. has 100) asses; and by the *lex Marcia* against moneylenders in order to enforce repayment of interest which they had exacted[1]. Gaius notes that by a mistake the draftsman of the *lex Furia testamentaria* had inserted the words *pro judicato* in the form of words given, though the statute had not directed the treatment as of a judgment debtor. In this latter class of cases the fatal words were not used in making the arrest and the debtor was under no incapacity to maintain his own cause.

6. By Gaius' time arrest in private causes had ceased at least in this form of *manus injectio* along with the other *legis actiones*. But a reminiscence of the old stringency survived in

[1] If the moneylender had exacted (*i.e.* by process), not merely received, interest it would be double of the amount in consequence of the debtor's contesting the judgment. If the moneylender in his turn contested the suit for recovery under the *lex Marcia*, he would have to pay twice this, *i.e.* fourfold the original amount. Karlowa (*CP.* p. 197) points out that this might explain Cato's language (*RR.* 1) *Majores nostri ita in legibus posiverunt furem dupli condemnari, feneratorem quadrupli.*

the requirement that in suits *judicati* or *depensi* defendant should give security for payment of the judgment (*judicatum solvi*) (Gai. iv 22—25).

Attachment of the person still remained[1], as we see from Caecilius' words: *addici nunc et vinciri multos videmus* (Gell. xx 1 § 51); from such expressions as *vel in publica vel in privata vincula ductus* (D. iv 6 fr 23 pr); from the grant of an action against those who prevented food and bedding being brought in to one judged (D. xlii 1 fr 34) and other allusions (*e.g.* Gai. iii 199 *si judicatus subreptus est*; Cod. vii 71 fr 1). It is not likely that they are mere relics of old times: but they may be instances of imprisonment for contempt of court or for special misdemeanours (cf. Paul v 26 § 2).

7. The compatibility of a supposed abolition of imprisonment for debt with its evident continuance long afterwards is well illustrated by English experience. In 1869 the Debtors'

1 In Greek countries, especially in Egypt before and after the Empire was established, execution on the person was found, but it may have been always, as it certainly was sometimes, illegal. Papyri shew it was sometimes included in the acknowledgment of debt, and an edict (Bruns no. 69) of Tib. Alexander praefect of Egypt (68 A.D.) speaks of persons being thrown into prison nominally for debts due to the fisc, really for private debts. (This may, as Revillout and Mitteis suggest, be due to the fact that a fine to the State was sometimes made part of the penalty for non-payment of a private debt. Or may it be that the fisc-collectors were engaged to collect private debts?)

In the 4th century St Ambrose speaks of it as a fact in vivid language. *Vidi ego pauperem duci, dum cogeretur solvere quod non habebat; trahi ad carcerem, quia vinum deerat ad mensam potentis, deducere in auctionem filios suos ut ad tempus poenam differre posset* (*de Nabuth.* p. 724, ed. Ballerini): and in speaking of arrests of corpses he alludes no doubt to treatment of the living also: *Quotiens vidi teneri defunctos pro pignore et negari tumulum dum faenus exposcitur. Quibus ego acquievi libenter ut suum constringerent debitorem ut electo eo fidejussor evaderet. Hae sunt feneratoribus leges. Dixi itaque: tenete reum vestrum, et, ne possit elabi, domum ducite; claudite in cubiculo vestro....Peccatorum reos post mortem carcer emittit, vos clauditis. Nunc vero capite minutus est, vehementioribus tamen nexibus alligate, ne vincula vestra non sentiat durus et rigidus debitor et qui jam non noverit erubescere. Unum sane est quod non timere possitis, quia poscere non novit alimenta* (*de Tobia* 10). See Mitteis' *Reichsrecht, etc.* p. 445 foll.

Act (32 and 33 Vict. cap. 62) was passed, and the general impression of the public (who had not read the Act) seemed to be that imprisonment for debt (except for fraud) was gone. The Act did abolish in general terms arrest or imprisonment for default of payment of money[1]: but preserved it (with the maximum limit of one year) in certain cases of which the principal were when the money required was a penalty by law, and when it was an amount recoverable summarily by Justices *e.g.* for police offences. And it authorized any court to commit, for six weeks or less, any debtor who has been ordered to pay and has had means to pay since the order. Debtors suspected of fleeing from justice and fraudulent debtors are of course also excepted. "Yet according to the latest returns 8375 persons "were committed to prison in one year and these were not "exceptional figures. Some County Court Judges make orders "for committal freely, and they fill the local prisons with debtors "technically guilty of contempt of court[2]. Others rarely send "anyone to prison. Yet debtors who have incurred debt on "a large scale, apply to the Bankruptcy Court and are not sent "to prison unless guilty of grave fraud." (*Times*, 7 June, 1897, abridged.) I suspect some such description would not be unsuitable if applied to Rome after the Poetelian statute, though execution by seizure and sale of defendant's property had legally and usually superseded personal detention for non-payment in private actions.

B. ATTACHMENT OF THE PROPERTY.

1. The ordinary mode of executing a judgment in Gaius' time when the debtor was unwilling or unable to pay was by seizure and sale of the whole estate of the debtor. Seizure of the estate (*missio in possessionem*)[3] was ordered by the praetor in several cases in order to secure it for rightful claimants, *e.g.* for legatees or claimants under a trust when the heir did not give proper security (D. xxxvi 4); for a pregnant woman

[1] Compare the humorous account of something analogous in Scotch law in Scott's *Antiquary* ch. xxxix.

[2] *Quod jus dicenti non obtemperaverint* (Paul v 26 § 2).

[3] Equal in modern English law to 'a receiving order.'

whose child would have a prior claim to a vacant inheritance (D. xxxvii 9); for a ward who is without proper guardians to defend him against a suit (D. xlii 4 fr 3—5); for one *bona fide* absent on state service or captured by the enemy (*ib.* fr 6 §§ 1, 2); and in cases of *damni infecti* (D. xxxix 2 fr 7 pr), *etc.*

This seizure and possession does not lead to usucapion[1]; and has nothing to do with the *bonorum possessio* granted to a praetorian heir. It has for its object the protection of the estate and is of a temporary and provisional character, giving way eventually either to a definitive transference to the rightful claimant or to sale for the satisfaction of creditors (D. xlii 4 fr 12). The praetor protected those sent into possession by an interdict against disturbers (D. xliii 4).

Possession, with sale in immediate prospect (*possideri vendique*), was the Roman term for proceedings in bankruptcy against debtors deceased, or avoiding creditors, or failing to satisfy a judgment. The last is the case particularly in view now. A reasonable time, fixed partly by the XII tables, partly by the praetor's edict, was allowed to enable the debtor to find the money. If this time elapsed without payment or the creditor's being otherwise satisfied, application was made to the praetor, and he directed the petitioning creditor to take possession of the estate of the debtor. The order was apparently almost a matter of course, not one granted only after inquiry by the praetor (cf. Keller *Semestr.* p. 79 sqq.).

2. As a rule, only those debts which are absolute and actually due justify such an application by a creditor. A debt due from a *peculium* is good for this purpose, until it is ascertained that there is nothing in the *peculium*. A conditional creditor may in some cases be sent into possession *rei servandae causa*, but for bankruptcy proceedings a creditor must be one

[1] As it was not a question of exclusive possession to secure usucapion there was no necessity to turn out the owner. Cicero gives the words of the edict in his time: *Qui ex edicto meo in possessionem venerint, eos ita videtur in possessione esse oportere; quod ibidem recte custodire poterunt id ibidem custodiant; quod non poterunt, id auferre atque abducere licebit. Dominum invitum detrudere non placet* (*Quint.* 27 § 84. Cf. D. xxxix 2 fr 15 §§ 20, 23).

entitled to press for a sale (D. xlii 4 fr 6 pr; fr 14 § 2; xv 1 fr 50 pr; cf. xlii 4 fr 7 § 14)[1]. The creditor sent into possession was not regarded as an officer of the court: he was acting on his own and other creditors' behalf as a volunteer and could leave possession when he chose. But while there he was competent and was bound to manage properly, to let or sell the fruits, to let out the services of slaves or beasts, to feed the household, repair the buildings, and, if that be the best course, to defend the slaves against noxal suits. He was not responsible for mere fault (as is a creditor in possession of a pledge) but for fraud in a wide sense, and is liable to an action *in factum*. On the other hand he could recover his expenses. The persons entitled to sue him or be sued by him are the creditors or their caretaker, or, if the matter does not proceed to a sale, the debtor himself (D. xlii 5 fr 8 §§ 1—4; fr 9).

From the time of Labeo at least, other creditors were entitled to join in the possession, and to continue even if the petitioning creditor has got payment and retired. If several creditors in possession did not agree who should manage and make an inventory, *etc.* the praetor decided. For the conduct of a suit a *curator* ought to be appointed with the consent of the majority of the creditors, either from among themselves or not. When an estate was large and scattered, several caretakers would be appointed, and any persons deputed by them to conduct suits gave or took security in the name, not of the estate-owner, but of the appointing caretaker. Any actions to be brought against them might be brought *in solidum* against any one of them at the creditor's option. Such caretakers would also conduct the sale (D. xlii 5 fr 8 § 4; 14, 15 pr; tit. 7 fr 2, 3).

After possession had lasted for thirty days, further proceedings could be taken with a view to a sale[2]. The thirty days gave

[1] See Dernburg *Emt. bonor.* p. 97 sq.

[2] This was a matter which formed part of a provincial governor's edict: cf. Cic. *Att.* vi 1 § 15 *Edicendum putavi...de hereditatum possessionibus, de bonis possidendis vendendis, magistris faciendis, quae ex edicto et postulari et fieri solent.* The procedure is referred to impressively by Cicero *Quint.* 15 § 50 *Cujus bona ex edicto possidentur, hujus omnis fama et existimatio cum bonis simul possidetur; de quo libelli in celeberrimis locis proponuntur,*

an opportunity for the debtor or his friends or representatives to settle the affair or to apply to the praetor with suitable objections, and the creditors would then be better able to estimate the financial position of the estate. The creditors then met, and one of their number was elected to arrange the sale and settle its conditions. He was called *magister*. Sometimes it was a *curator* appointed by the praetor. The sale, apparently by auction, followed in ten days. Where it was a deceased's estate that was sold, the times were half those named (*i.e.* 15 and 5 days)[1], there not being in that case the same cause for indulgent consideration as there was when the debtor was alive; for the sale was followed by infamy. A necessary heir (*i.e.* a slave) was not liable to have any property of his own sold, which he had acquired independently of the inheritance after the testator's death (Gai. iii 79; ii 154, 155; *lex Agrar. i.e.* Bruns no. 11 § 56).

3. The estate (*bona*) was sold[2] as a whole (*per universitatem*). It is not definitely stated whether the biddings were for the assets only and the purchase money then distributed

huic ne perire quidem tacite obscureque conceditur; cui magistri fiunt et domini constituuntur ('for whom masters are appointed and put as owners of his property') *qui qua lege et qua conditione pereat pronuntient, de quo homine praeconis vox praedicat et pretium conficit, huic acerbissimum vivo videntique funus ducitur.*

The *magister* is also referred to in Cic. *Att.* i 1 § 3.

[1] All these figures are doubtful owing to the state of Gaius' MS.

[2] The *bonorum emptio* of private bankrupts must be distinguished from the purchase of goods or estates confiscated by the State, whether taken in war or from citizens condemned for crime. This was usually sold as a whole by the quaestors. The purchaser was called *sector* (*sectores vocantur qui publice bona mercantur* Gai. iv 146) apparently because he sold it in detail ('cut it up'). *Sector* is frequent in Cic. *Rosc. Com.* (§§ 80, 88, 94, *etc.* cf. § 21). The term *sectio* was often applied to the mass of property itself, *e.g.* Cic. *Inv.* 45 § 85 *Ex hostibus equus est captus, cujus praedae sectio non venit; Phil.* ii 26 § 64 *Hasta posita pro aede Jovis Statoris, bona Cn. Pompei voci acerbissimae subjecta praeconis. Exspectantibus omnibus quisnam ad illud scelus sectionis auderet accedere, inventus est nemo praeter Antonium qui Pompei sector...esse auderet;* Caes. *B. G.* ii 33 *Sectionem ejus oppidi universam Caesar vendidit.* The purchaser became owner *ex jure Quiritium* (Varr. *RR.* ii 10 § 4). Prisoners taken in war were generally sold separately by the quaestors.

rateably to the creditors, the surplus, if any, being given to the debtor, or were directed primarily to the liabilities, and the person who offered to pay the largest percentage of the debts was declared purchaser. The latter course is generally assumed to have been taken, and where the estate was known or supposed to be insolvent, was no doubt the most convenient[1]. If the creditors were not paid in full, after-acquired property was liable to be taken and sold for the benefit of the creditors (Gai. ii 155; D. xlii 3 fr 7)[2]. Otherwise the debtor was not liable[3] after the sale to any suit, or able to bring any suit, on matters preceding the sale (*ex ante gesto* D. xlii 7 fr 4; 8 fr 25 § 7). Among bidders preference is given to the largest creditor, then to other creditors, and then to relatives (D. xlii 5 fr 16).

The purchaser (*bonorum emptor*) acquired the equitable ownership of the things constituting the estate, without further conveyance, but needed usucapion to perfect his legal title. The praetor protected his position by granting him an interdict (sometimes called *possessorium* Gai. iv 145) against disturbers, and actions (*utiles*), framed on the analogy of the successor to a deceased's estate (*bonorum possessor*), to enable him to collect debts due to the estate. He could be sued by creditors in a like way (Gai. iii 80, 81; iv 35). If a debtor to the estate was also creditor, the *bonorum emptor* had in suing to deduct accordingly (see chap. viii C 2). As regards goods pledged, he stood in the shoes of the debtor and could claim only for the surplus (cf. Cod. vii 72 fr 6)[4].

4. In payment of debts, some were privileged and entitled to payment in full before ordinary debts were regarded. Of these the first in rank were the fisc (including anything due

[1] It is implied in Milo's goods being sold *semuncia* (Ascon. *in Milon.* p. 159 Hot.=48 Kiessling). Cf. *pro portione venire* in Gai. ii 155.

[2] In the case of *publicatio bonorum* the fisc did not take after-acquired property, unless the owner was deported (D. xvii 1 fr 22 § 5; Cod. ix 49 fr 2).

[3] But see Lenel *EP.* p. 347.

[4] The interposition of an *emptor bonorum* between debtor and creditors was given up along with the formulary procedure (Just. iii 12).

to Caesar and Augusta), and funeral expenses of the debtor himself (if deceased) or of anyone for whose funeral he was liable (Paul i 21 § 15; v 12 § 10; D. xlix 14 fr 6; xlii 5 fr 17 pr). Next came a woman's claim for her dowry by the *rei uxoriae judicium*, and some other cases where there was no legal marriage and consequently no right to that action (Cod. viii 17 fr 12 §§ 1, 5; D. xxiv 3 fr 22 § 13; xlii 5 fr 17 § 1); debts due to a ward by one who, not being a guardian, acted as his guardian or did business for him; debts due by their caretakers to spendthrifts, deaf, mutes, or idiots; debts due on loans for the repair of buildings (this was by a constitution of Marcus Aurelius); or for building or buying or fitting ships (D. xlii 5 fr 19 § 1—fr 23, 24 § 1; 34). Among these there is no preference, date of debt not being regarded. The privilege of the fisc is only for its own proper debts, not for debts of an estate which has fallen to it; and claims for penalties come after creditors (D. xlix 14 fr 6 pr; fr 17). Anyone who has supplied money to pay a privileged debtor stands in his place (D. xlii 5 fr 24 § 3; tit. 3 fr 2). Those who have deposited money with a banker at interest rank with other creditors, but if it was a mere deposit and the actual money is found, the depositor can claim it before all privileges (D. xvi 3 fr 7 § 2; xlii 5 fr 24 § 2).

5. If a debtor dies and his heir is, or is thought to be, insolvent, the creditors of the debtor can obtain separation of the two estates so that those who trusted the deceased may not be swamped by the creditors of one whom they never trusted. The separation is not granted at the request of the heir's creditors, who cannot prevent their debtor from incurring fresh debts by acceptance of another's inheritance any more than in any other way. Such a separation is not granted more than five years after the acceptance of the inheritance, nor if the estates have been inextricably confused (which can hardly take place with landed property), nor if the debtor has sold the inheritance, nor if the applying creditors have accepted the heir as their debtor (*heredis personam secuti*) by novating their debts with him or taking interest or pledges or sureties from him. Nor can they, after obtaining separation and finding the

result unsatisfactory, go back upon it, and claim for the residue of their debts upon the heir's estate. On the other hand, if the debtor's estate prove more than sufficient for its own creditors, the heir's creditors can, if not fully satisfied, come upon what is left (D. xlii 6 fr 1 §§ 1, 2, 10, 12, 15, 17; fr 5, 22). Legatees could however claim before the heir's creditors (fr 6 pr).

So if a debtor become heir to his surety, the surety's creditor (or creditors) can obtain separation of the two estates, notwithstanding that in strict law the surety's obligation is extinguished by merger. If the surety's estate is not sufficient to satisfy the creditor, he can still claim with the other creditors of the principal debtor's own estate, which was primarily responsible (*ib.* fr 3 pr, § 1).

6. The persons liable to a sale of their estates at the instance of their creditors were (see Gai. iii 78):

(*a*) Judgment-debtors. With these may be classed those who admitted (without discharging) the debt; and those who had taken no steps to meet the suit (D. xlii 2 fr 1; and *lex Rubr.* 21).

(*b*) Persons hiding from their creditors[1] without anyone to defend them in their absence. The hiding must be intentional in order to avoid their creditors; not merely momentary or occasional but persistent; the debtor may be abroad or in Rome, but dodging behind a column is enough to make latitation; it need not be against all creditors, but, in order to justify the application, it must be latitation against the applicant (D. xlii 4 fr 7 §§ 1—8, § 13 *ad fin.*; tit. 5 fr 36).

(*c*) Madmen and spendthrifts, who are not in the eye of the law properly hiding, may yet, if their debts be urgent, have their estates sold, the surplus being reserved for them (*ib.* §§ 10—12).

(*d*) Persons in exile, if not defended against their creditors (D. xlii 4 fr 13; Cic. *Quinct.* 19 § 60, see pp. 465, 470).

(*e*) Persons who under the *lex Julia* have voluntarily surrendered their estates to their creditors[2]. This might be

[1] Cf. Cic. *Verr.* ii 24 § 59 *Insimulant hominem fraudandi causa discessisse; postulant ut bona possidere jubeat* (*Verres*). On this matter see Cic. *pro Quinctio* and below, pp. 472, 480.

[2] Compare in English law, 'file petition in bankruptcy.'

done in court, or informally by letter or message, and must be preceded or accompanied by distinct acknowledgment of debt or by confession in court or by condemnation. The debtor does not lose the ownership of his goods until the sale, and can up till then recall his surrender and defend himself against actions. If his assets are not sufficient to pay his debts in full, his after-acquired property, if considerable, will be held liable, but only with the limit of *in quod facere potest* (D. xlii 2 fr 3—9). A debtor so surrendering his estate did not become infamous by its sale; and he was not liable to personal imprisonment (Cod. ii 11 fr 11; vii 71 fr 1).

(*f*) Deceased persons, when it is certain that there is no heir or possessor of the estate or other lawful successor who will defend deceased against creditors (Gai. iii 78; Cic. *Quinct.* 19 § 60; cf. D. xlii 5 fr 4 *sub fine*).

7. If possession and sale are obtained by fraud or by one who is not a creditor, they are null (D. xlii 4 fr 7 § 3; tit. 5 fr 12). A rescript of M. Aurelius directed complainants of non-legal sale to have the question tried by a *praejudicium* and not appeal to the emperor (*ib.* 5 fr 30; cf. Cic. *Quinct.* 8 § 30).

The seizure and sale of a debtor's estate rested on the *imperium*, *i.e.* executive authority of the praetor or provincial governor; and was beyond the power of municipal magistrates (*lex Rubr.* 21, 22; D. ii 1 fr 4; L 1 fr 26). It is said to have been introduced by a praetor, P. Rutilius (Gai. iv 35), who is generally supposed to have been the consul of 105 B.C. But some such arrangement may have existed before. A *bonorum emptor* is mentioned in the *lex Agrar.* 56 (B.C. 111).

8. In the case of an inheritance an heir, before entering, sometimes bargained with the creditors to accept a percentage of their debts as a due discharge. Such a bargain was good according to a rescript of M. Aurelius, only if made after a meeting of the creditors and a resolution passed by the majority. A majority for this purpose meant a majority not in number but in amount of debt; if that were equal, then a majority in number was required: and again if that was equal, then the praetor accepted the opinion of the more distinguished. If several persons were joint creditors for the same debt,

they were reckoned as one. Absent creditors, at least since M. Aurelius' rescript, if privileged, or possessing special claims by mortgage or mandate, were not bound by the decision. Such a bargain may be made by a *suus heres* or a necessary heir though a slave, if it be made before any actual meddling with the inheritance (D. ii 14 fr 7 § 17—fr 10 pr; xvii 1 fr 58 § 1; xl 4 fr 54 § 1).

C. 1. The system of possessing and selling a debtor's whole estate, however suitable when he was really insolvent, was a cumbrous mode of enforcing a judgment against a solvent but obstinate defendant. Antoninus Pius took apparently a new step in directing the magistrates of the Roman people to execute the sentences of the judges or arbitrators appointed by them. In the provinces the Governors were empowered by a rescript of Caracalla to execute the judgments given in Rome as well as those of provincial judges. The magistrate was to direct *pignora capi et distrahi*, in fact to levy a distress of so much of the debtor's property as might be sufficient to meet the judgment, or admitted debt. By preference moveables and animals were to be first taken: in default of these, land; then rights and lastly investments (*nomina*) if admitted to be due to debtor. Moneys in the hands of bankers or others, in the name of the debtor, or intended for him, was also taken. Two months was allowed to elapse before sale, which was conducted under the magistrate's authority, not left to the creditor.

If no purchaser were found, the pledges thus taken might be made over (*addici*) to the creditor in full satisfaction of the debt. If any of the things were in pledge previously, the surplus value only could be applied. If sales yielded more than was required to meet the judgment, the surplus was to be handed over to the debtor. If the ownership of something taken was disputed, the magistrate was to decide the question: if he was not satisfied, the seizure was to be dropt without prejudice to the question of title (D. xlii 1 fr 15, 31; Cod. viii 22; Paul v 5*a* § 4). This mode of execution seems to be an adaptation of the old magisterial *pignoris capio* (see p. 115). Any creditor on a written instrument (*chirographarius*), without any mortgage, forcibly seizing property of defendant was liable criminally under the *lex Julia* (Paul v 26 § 4).

2. Specific performance, *e.g.* by restoration of land or thing, was not, so far as we know, enforced in Antonine times, but the defendant had often the option (see p. 411). Such directions for transfer of possession *manu militari, i.e.* 'by actual force,' as are found *e.g.* in D. vi 1 fr 68 are probably due to Justinian[1]. Where the defendant in a suit for land or an inheritance did not appear, and had no defender, Celsus recommends the course of simply directing plaintiff to take possession of the object of suit rather than seizing the whole estate: this was directed by Ant. Pius in case of an inheritance, but the practice was not general (D. xlii 4 fr 7 §§ 16—19).

CHAPTER XVI.

INTERDICTS AND THEIR PROCEDURE.

A. Interdicts formed a special kind of legal process used principally in questions relating to possession or quasi-possession[2], *i.e.* they were used to protect persons in the enjoyment of what was or appeared to be their property or of rights over others' property. They were also applied to prevent invasion by private persons of the enjoyment of property or rights belonging to the public. In form they were directions or prohibitions from the praetor, being called *decreta* when they directed something to be done, *interdicta* when they forbad it, the latter term however being also commonly used of the whole class. A main division of them was into prohibitory, exhibitory and restitutory.

1. Prohibitory interdicts were such as protected consecrated ground: *e.g. in loco sacro facere inve eum immittere quid veto* 'I forbid doing or putting anything in a consecrated

[1] See Gradenwitz *Interp.* p. 14.

[2] *Quasi possessio* is the exercise of rights such as usufruct, predial servitudes, *etc.*; cf. D. iv 6 fr 23 § 2; viii 5 fr 10.

place' (cf. vol. I p. 412): or the interdicts which frequently prepared matters for an *actio in rem* (cf. vol. I p. 460): *Uti nunc possidetis eas aedes quibus de agitur nec vi nec clam nec precario alter ab altero possidetis, quominus ita possideatis vim fieri veto* (D. xliii 17 fr I pr) 'I forbid force to be used to prevent your 'possessing that house, as you now possess it, neither by force 'nor stealth nor request, the one from the other.' Or the like interdict for moveables, *Utrubi hic homo quo de agitur majore parte hujusce anno fuit, nec vi nec clam nec precario ab altero possessus fuit, quominus is eum ducat, vim fieri veto* (D. xliii 31: cf. Lenel *EP.* p. 392) 'I forbid force to be used to prevent that 'one of you with whom the slave in question has been for the 'greater part of the year, *etc.* from leading him off.'

2. Exhibitory interdicts were such as ordered the production of a person under our power who is detained by another, *Qui quaeve in potestate L. Titii est si is eave apud te est, dolove malo tuo factum est quo minus apud te esset, ita eum eamve exhibeas* (D. xliii 30). 'You are to produce him or her who is under 'L. Titius' power, if he or she is with you or by your fraud has 'been made not to be so.' See vol. I p. 63.

3. Restitutory interdicts are such as order the restitution of what has been wrongfully withdrawn from one's possession, as that commonly called *de vi*: viz. *Unde in hoc anno tu illum vi dejecisti aut familia tua dejecit, cum ille possideret quod nec vi nec clam nec precario a te possideret, eo illum restituas* (so Lenel *EP.* p. 373: cf. D. xliii 16 fr I pr and below, p. 521). 'You 'are to restore so and so to the place whence you or your house-'hold have forcibly turned him off, though he was in possession 'without having gained it from you by force or stealth or 'request.' (Gai. iv 139, 140.) See vol. I p. 462.

4. All exhibitory and restitutory interdicts are simple, *i.e.* one party is plaintiff, the other is defendant: plaintiff is he who applies for protection or restitution, defendant is he who is called upon to produce or restore.

Prohibitory interdicts are often simple like these, but sometimes are double, *i.e.* both litigants are in the same position, equally plaintiffs and defendants, the interdict being addressed to both as in the case quoted above of *uti possidetis*. The procedure in prohibitory interdicts is always by a wager (Gai. iv 141, 156—160; Ulp. *Inst.* in *Jus Antejust.* ii p. 159).

B. The issue of the interdict was only the first step in the procedure. Gaius tells us nothing of the procedure on application, whether or not the defendant was summoned and the application made in his presence or at least when he had had an opportunity of being present. If relevant facts were stated to the praetor and there was nothing unusual in the application, the interdict was issued, probably as a matter of course, at the risk of the applicant. There was no proper *causae cognitio* at this stage of the proceedings.

Suppose an interdict granted to order restitution of an evicted person, or production of a freedman from whom the patron desired to require promised services (*operas indicere*). The operative words are *restituas* or *exhibeas*, a definite order to the defendant to do a certain thing. If the defendant intimated his willingness to do it, the litigation would at once come to an end, or at any rate be suspended till further difficulties arose. But if he shewed fight, he had his choice of two courses[1], either to have the matter referred to arbitration or to enter into a wager on the justice of his case. The choice must however be exercised before he leaves the praetor's court. If he chooses arbitration, he accepts what is called the arbitration formula (*f. arbitraria*), and if the judge on hearing the case in his discretion orders him to restore or produce, defendant does what is bid, and is acquitted without incurring any penalty. Nor, if the judge find no restoration or production due, is plaintiff exposed to any penalty, unless he is met with a trial of good faith (*calumniae judicium*), which involves a penalty of one-tenth the value. Proculus maintained that a defendant, who requested an arbiter, had no right to call upon plaintiff to undergo a trial of good faith, because he had by such a request admitted some obligation to restore or produce (as the case might be). But the practice was the other way, and, as Gaius says, rightly, the request for an arbiter not being an admission

[1] Cf. Cic. *Tull.* 23 § 53 *Tecto illo disturbato si hodie postulem quod vi aut clam factum sit* ('if I should ask the praetor for the interdict *quod vi aut clam*') *tu aut per arbitrum restituas aut sponsione condemneris necesse est.*

of the plaintiff's case, but merely a modest way of meeting the suit (Gai. iv 161—164).

If defendant, on the interdict being granted, leaves the court without making the request for an arbitration, plaintiff challenges him to a wager (*sponsio*) that he has, contrary to the praetor's edict, failed to restore or to produce. Defendant counter-stipulates, *i.e.* demands that plaintiff should pay him a like amount, if plaintiff turns out to be wrong. Plaintiff serves defendant with the formula of the wager, and defendant replies with the formula embodying the counter-stipulation. Plaintiff demands a trial of the wager as to the fact of violation or not of the praetor's edict, and a further trial, if the wager is decided in his favour and defendant does not obey, to ascertain the damages. Gaius' MS. here becomes illegible. No doubt a judge would be appointed to try the issues raised by the wagers and according to his judgment of the facts to condemn the one party and acquit the other, the amount stated in the wager being payable by the defeated party in addition (if the defendant be found wrong) to the damages in default of restoration (or production).

C. The state of the MS. prevents our knowing the initial steps in the case of a double interdict, like the *uti possidetis.* Here the operative words do not enjoin any positive act; they are, as in all prohibitory interdicts, simply negative: *Vim fieri veto quominus etc.*, an injunction not forcibly to encroach upon a person's liberty or rights. If the use of a road or a stream is in question, probably no further steps might be taken until some fresh act of encroachment or hindrance were done. But if defendant meant to challenge plaintiff's right, there seems no reason for postponing the trial. If the interdict is resorted to, as *uti possidetis* often was, merely to determine the relative position of the parties preparatory to a suit respecting the ownership, the applicant at least, if not both parties, would desire to proceed to trial at once. If the parties agree in this desire, it may be (as some think) that to give a clear foundation for the subsequent proceedings a formal encroachment was actually made by both parties (as the interdict was double) or was agreed to be taken to be made. The act of force or presumed force would be justified if on trial the doer were found to have been the rightful possessor, and would be the technical ground for loss of his wager in the case of the one not found to be rightful possessor. What steps were adopted, if one of the parties wished to avoid or delay trial, will be better considered after the general procedure has been stated.

The first step is to settle which of the two shall be possessor during the trial of the interdict. This is done by the parties bidding against each other for the interim profits (*fructus licitando*): the highest bidder is placed (*constituitur*) in possession, but has to covenant by a stipulation, that if the decision is against him he will pay the amount of his bidding to his adversary as a fine for his attempt to occupy another's property. Each party now challenges the other to a wager, maintaining that force had been used to him contrary to the praetor's edict: each counter-stipulates (*restipulatur*) against the other. There are thus two wagers, each with its counter-stipulation; possibly they were sometimes consolidated. The matter then comes before a judge, who, in order to determine which has won his wager, tries this issue, viz. which of the two parties, during the time at which the interdict was given, possessed the land or house in question without having obtained it from his opponent by force or stealth or request. Suppose the judge after examination to decide this issue in my favour: he condemns my opponent to pay me the amounts of my wager and counter-stipulation, and acquits me from any obligation to him on his wager and counter-stipulation. Further, suppose my opponent to have won in the bidding and consequently to be holding the interim possession: he is now proved to be there without good title, and consequently has to pay me in addition the amount of his bidding for the profits, to give up to me possession of the land or house, and further to pay all the profits he has meanwhile taken, *i.e.* since the issue of the interdict (D. xliii 1 fr 4; cf. tit. 16 fr 1 § 40). On the other hand if I am unsuccessful in proving that the possession rightfully belongs to me, as I was also unsuccessful in the contest for interim possession, I have only to pay the amounts of the wager and counter-stipulation (Gai. iv 166—168).

The sums payable by the defeated party are recoverable by the judge's decision on the wagers or stipulations. But the possession and mesne profits, if not surrendered, are recovered by what was called a Cascellian or consequent trial (*secutorio judicio*). And a similar trial, but called *fructuarium*, could be resorted to for recovering the amount of the possessor's bidding, if the party defeated in the contest for interim possession prefers that course to making a stipulation for it. The plaintiff is entitled to security for the payment of the judgment (*judicatum solvi* Gai. iv 169).

All this presumes the two parties, after the interdict is granted, to be willing to further the procedure in order to get a decision of their dispute. But it may happen that one of the parties shews himself reluctant to do so and declines to take the requisite steps consequent on the interdict (*cetera ex interdicto facere*). He may decline to use force (see below), he may decline to bid for the profits, or when successful to give security for the amount of his bidding, or he may decline to make wagers or to accept trial of the wagers when made. In any of these cases the praetor provides a remedy by issuing a secondary interdict requiring the person who thus blocks the course to a decision, if possessor, to restore possession to his opponent; if not possessor, to refrain from forcibly disturbing his opponent's possession. Whatever be the real merits of his case, he is treated as one who practically concedes the ground to his opponent[1] (Gai. iv 170). The suit is therefore closed and judgment at once pronounced.

D. The account given in the last paragraph follows closely Gaius' text as given by Studemund, but the mutilation of the MS. leaves many things either uncertain or without answers to natural questions. Whether the *moribus deductio* spoken of by Cicero is connected with this interdict, whether *vim faciat* in § 170 is identical with *vis ex conventu* in Cicero, whether *vis* has the same force in *vim faciat* as it has in *vim fieri veto*, whether real or conventional force is intended, are questions much discussed. See Keller *ZGR.* xi 325 foll.; Karlowa *RG.* ii 325;

[1] Cf. *lex Rubr.* 21, 22 *si se sponsione judicioque uti oportebit non defendet, etc.*

Kappeyne van de Coppello *Abhandl.* p. 115 foll.; A. Exner *ZRG.* viii 167 foll.; and the latest (and very voluminous) writer Ubbelohde (in Glück's *Pand.* Pt. i § 1836 Nos. 39—45; Pt. ii § 1850 p. 387), who give other references. With Cicero I deal elsewhere (p. 515). I assume that *vim fieri* and *vim facere* have like meaning: nor do I see that much depends on the distinction between real and conventional force, except that the latter might take place in court and the former probably requires action on the spot: otherwise conventional force is merely force regulated by agreement or by court rules, but so that the legal consequences of real force shall follow[1]. It is to be taken as real force. It is action against the other's will. Nor indeed need force be active in order to be real. But I am inclined to think that much of the discussion and difficulty is due to a slight corruption of the text of Gaius (iv 170), a text which Studemund[2] does not give as certain but only as fairly probable. Gaius says, speaking of the secondary interdicts, *vis et potestas haec est ut qui cetera ex interdicto non faciat veluti qui vim non faciat aut fructus non liceatur aut qui fructus licitationis satis non det aut si sponsiones non faciat sponsionumve judicia non accipiat, sive possideat, restituat adversario possessionem, sive non possideat, vim illi possidenti ne faciat.* I believe we should read *qui vim faciat* for *qui vim non faciat.* First, nothing could be more likely than the insertion of *non* by a copyist in order to assimilate this clause to the four following clauses, each of which has *non,* and thus apparently make it conform to *cetera ex int. non faciat.* But, secondly, the interdict runs *vim fieri veto,* and it is not the non-use but the use of force which is not in pursuance of the interdict. Thirdly, it seems to me most improbable that the praetor should follow up an interdict forbidding force by an injunction to use force, and that the non-use of force should be the ground of the further injunction to one of the parties not to use force (*vim illi pos. ne faciat*). Fourthly, if such had been the course of the procedure, Gaius would not have mentioned so strange a requirement in this simple manner without explanation (of which I

1 Karlowa *RG.* ii 326 seems to ignore this.

2 See the Apograph.

see no sign in the fragments at the end of § 170). Fifthly, I see no necessity for acts of force, agreed or not, in order to found the subsequent proceedings. Some forcible act or contentious declaration must have already founded the proceedings, and the issue of the interdict only declares the law, as shewn in the edict, and initiates the procedure for the determination of the right. Either party can withdraw: by persistence in his contention if ultimately proved to be in the wrong, he offends against the edict[1] from the moment that the interdict is issued, and the natural course of business is at once to make the biddings for the interim possession, to challenge each other and go to trial, cf. § 141 *Nec, cum quid praetor jusserit fieri aut fieri prohibuerit, statim peractum est negotium, sed ad judicem recuperatoresve itur et ibi editis formulis quaeritur an aliquid adversus praetoris edictum factum sit, etc.* Sixthly, nothing can be more suitable than that any act of force during the procedure for peaceable determination of the parties' rights should at once bring about the condemnation of the offender. Hence *qui vim faciat* is appropriate, if not necessary.

A wrong insertion or omission of a negative is not lightly to be assumed, but is by no means uncommon[2]. I am only surprised not to have seen this suggestion made by others. But its acceptance would cut short a great deal of learned conjectural controversy.

1 The phrase throughout is (*contra*) *edictum* not *interdictum*, cf. §§ 141, 165, 166; Cic. *Caecin.* 16 § 45; D. xxxix 1 fr 5 § 4, fr 22; xliii 8 fr 7; L 17 fr 102. (Schmidt interprets *edictum* as not referring to the *Ed. Perpetuum* but to any order of the praetor (*Interdictverf.* p. 241 sqq.).)

2 *E.g.* it is inserted by the editors in Gai. iv 98 and 117: it is evidently to be struck out in D. viii 6 fr 7. It is omitted in the Florentine MS. in D. xliv 4 fr 2 § 1; but inserted by the corrector and modern editors. It appears in *Collat.* ii 4 § 1 *in hac nec mihi videri* where the Digest (ix 2 fr 27 § 17) rightly omits *nec.* Many other instances occur in the Digest. In Vat. 154 *non* is omitted, and is found in 223 of the same matter.

CHAPTER XVII.

PROCEDURE *EXTRA ORDINEM*.

There were cases in which for some reasons the praetor or provincial Governor did not send the parties before a judge or recoverers, but himself heard and decided the matter. Where personal or ethical or social considerations entered largely into the question, and the strict rights of the parties or the pecuniary importance were relatively small, the praetor reserved the case for himself. Such was compelling a guardian to act (D. xxvi 7 fr 1 pr); claims for support (*alimenta*) brought by parents and children or patrons and freedmen against each other (D. xxv 3 fr 5), and the approval of compromises of legacies or *mortis causa* gifts for this purpose (D. ii 15 fr 8); grant of access to tombs belonging to the applicants (D. xi 7 fr 12 pr); claims for remuneration of physicians, advocates, teachers, scribes, notaries, accountants. But philosophers and law-professors were deemed to have too lofty a work for their payment to be subject of ordinary legal claim: a fee (*honor* or *honorarium*) was allowed (D. L 13 fr 1). Trusts (*fidei commissa*) were at first dealt with in this way (cf. Just. ii 23 § 1; Ulp. xxv 12). Semicriminal cases are in the same position, *e.g.* where one who had commenced a suit for some one's freedom threw up the case unfinished (Paul v 1 § 5). Cases thus decided by the praetor were often called *cognitiones*, because the case was heard (*causa cognita*) by himself (cf. D. i 18 fr 8, 9).

Spendthrifts were interdicted from the management of their property by the praetor[1]. The words used in such a case are given us by Paul (iii 4 *a* § 7) *Quando tibi bona paterna avitaque*

[1] Cf. Cic. *Sen.* 7 § 22 *Sophocles a filiis in judicium vocatus est, ut, quemadmodum nostro more male rem gerentibus patribus bonis interdici solet, sic illum quasi desipientem a re familiari removerent judices.*

nequitia tua disperdis liberosque tuos ad egestatem perducis, ob eam rem tibi ea re commercioque interdico.

This procedure (without *judex*), which in the times with which I am concerned was only of special and occasional use, was gradually extended, until, probably under Diocletian, it became the regular mode for all trials, and the formulary procedure with a *judex* was discontinued.

APPENDIX TO VOL. II.

Essays on the matters of law in Cicero's speeches

A. pro P. Quinctio
B. pro Q. Roscio (comoedo)
C. pro M. Tullio
D. pro A. Caecina

Errat vehementius, si quis in orationibus nostris, quas in judicio habuimus, auctoritates nostras consignatas se habere arbitratur. Omnes enim illae causarum ac temporum sunt, non hominum ipsorum aut patronorum (Cic. *Cluent.* 50 § 139).

Cicero might now say:

'Modern critics seem sometimes to regard my speeches as 'professorial lectures or as counsel's formal opinions, and treat 'the statements and arguments in them as expositions of estab- 'lished law, and a measure of my knowledge of it. I venture 'to remind them that an advocate has to deal, as best he may, 'with the particular case in the circumstances of the time. 'I am not freely uttering either my own opinions or those 'of my client: my speeches do not treat of law or politics 'disengaged from personal interests and particular occasions.'

Mea autem ratio haec esse in dicendo solet, ut boni quod habeam id amplectar, exornem, exaggerem, ibi commorer, ibi habitem, ibi haeream, a malo autem vitioque causae ita recedam non ut me defugere adpareat sed ut totum bono illo ornando et augendo dissimulatum obruatur....Illud mihi pro meo jure sumo, ut molesto aut difficili argumento aut loco non nunquam omnino nihil respondeam. Confiteor me, si quae premat res vehementius, ita cedere solere, ut non modo non abjecto sed ne rejecto quidem scuto fugere videar, sed adhibere quandam in dicendo speciem atque pompam et pugnae similem fugam; consistere vero in meo praesidio sic, ut non fugiendi hostis sed capiendi loci causa cessisse videar (Cic. *Orat.* ii 72 §§ 292, 294).

(This is put into the mouth of the orator Antonius, but may well be applied to Cicero himself.)

APPENDIX.

A. Cicero *pro Quinctio*[1].

This speech was delivered in the year 673 U.C. = 81 B.C. when Sulla was dictator and Cicero twenty-five years of age. (Gell. xv 28). The question really raised is the due execution of an order of the praetor arising out of a partnership dispute. Recent political disturbances are several times alluded to, Cicero's client having as alleged been assisted previously by the influence of the party opposed to Sulla, and his opponent having influential friends in Sulla's party.

The speech is not quite wholly preserved, and apparently one part of Cicero's argument is lost, but the substance is given in the summary at the close of the speech, and some small fragments of it are found in a late writer on Rhetoric, Julius Severianus § 15 (Halm's *Rhet. Script.*, p. 362), which have been in Baiter's and other recent editions inserted in § 85.

The facts, as given by Cicero, were as follows:

C. Quinctius, brother of Cicero's client P. Quinctius, had a considerable grazing farm (*pecuaria res*, § 12) in Gaul, apparently near Narbo Martius[2] (now Narbonne), well cultivated and profitable. He took into partnership in his Gallic business a friend, Sex. Naevius, by trade an auctioneer, but at the time or afterwards connected with the family by marrying a first cousin of Quinctius (§ 16). Cicero speaks in very disparaging terms both of Naevius' contribution to the partnership resources

[1] The principal essay on this speech is one of the three in Keller's admirable *Semestria* (1842). See also Frei *Der Rechtstreit zwischen Q. und N.* (1852); Bethmann-Hollweg *Röm. Civ. Proc.* ii 783 sqq. (1865); Oetling *Abhandlung* (Oldenburg Progr. 1882); B. Kübler *ZRG.* xxvii p. 54 (1893). Comments on the speech are also given by De Caqueray *Passages de droit privé dans les œuvres de Cicéron* (1857); Gasquy *Cicéron Jurisconsulte* (1887); E. Costa *Le orazioni di diritto privato di M. Tullio Cicerone* (1899); Greenidge *Legal Procedure of Cicero's Time* App. I (1901).

[2] Cf. § 15. On Narbo see Cic. *Font.* § 13. The farm of Quinctius and Naevius was in the country of the *Sebagini* (§ 80), who are not known.

(§ 12) and of his character. He had some ability—at least as a buffoon; he was a man of some polish—for an auctioneer; but he was greedy, and evidently thought the duty of a partner was to study his separate interests (§§ 11—13). The partnership lasted several years, C. Quinctius having occasional doubts of Naevius' honesty, and not being able always to get a satisfactory account of his proceedings, but there was no rupture. At a time when both partners were in Gaul, C. Quinctius died suddenly, leaving a will in which he made P. Quinctius his heir (§ 14).

P. Quinctius, not long after, went to Gaul and for about a year or more[1] lived in intimacy with Naevius, often discussing the partnership business and property in Gaul. Naevius, as Cicero says, never hinted at anything being due to him from the partnership or from Quinctius on any private account. Probably accounts were periodically taken of the expenses and profits of the business, the balance was divided, and there were no outstanding claims on this head. Cicero speaks as if Publius succeeded his brother in the partnership as well as in his private property. In strict law the partnership came to an end on the death of a partner (D. xvii 2 fr 40, 59, *etc.*), and all that remained would be to take final accounts and divide the property (*ib.* fr 34, 65 § 9). We hear nothing of any fresh contract being entered into with the brother; but Publius, being sole heir to Caius, would easily glide into partnership with Naevius (*ib.* fr 37). Repeated allusion is made to their being partners (cf. §§ 23, 25—28, 48, 52—54, 74); and though the term *socius* could be used of one who was only tenant in common (cf. § 52), Cicero uses it here mainly in the sense of one standing in a relation voluntarily formed by contract, and in virtue of which he was entitled to expect, and bound to perform, mutual friendly services.

P. Quinctius as heir to his brother had to discharge some debts at Rome, and in order to raise money for this purpose, gave notice of sale by auction at Narbo of some property in Gaul which was not held in partnership. Naevius dissuades him from this course, telling him that it was a bad time to sell, and that he himself had plenty of money at Rome, which he

[1] *Annum fere* § 15; *anno et sex mensibus* § 40.

would readily put at the disposal of his partner and kinsman. Quinctius accepts the offer, gives up his proposed sale, and returns to Rome, whither Naevius also proceeds at the same time (§§ 15, 16).

Among other debts of his brother's, one at least was pressing, due originally to P. Scapula and now to Scapula's children. The amount of the debt was ascertained from the documents, but the amount now to be paid was something different. *Propter aerariam rationem non satis erat in tabulis inspexisse quantum deberetur, nisi ad Castoris quaesisses quantum solveretur* (§ 17). Castor's temple in the forum was the centre of the money-changers' and bankers' shops, and of the official testing and stamping of weights[1]. The present was a time of great disturbance in the money world from two special causes[2], in addition to the civil wars. The first was the currency: the second the *lex Valeria*. M. Drusus, in 663 U.C. = 91 B.C. by a law authorized the mint to issue one plated *denarius* in every seven. The confusion caused was great: no one knew whether his money was good or bad. At length the praetors and tribunes during Cinna's rule, probably in 670 U.C. = 84 B.C., resolved on the replacement of the plated denars by silver. M. Marius Gratidianus stole a march on his colleagues, and at once announced the resolution from the *rostra*, gaining thereby credit with the people for its authorship (Cic. *Off.* iii 20 § 80; Plin. *HN.* xxxiii 132, xxxiv 27). The denar was the ordinary coin used for payments, though the sesterce (one-fourth of the denar) was used for reckoning, as being the silver representative of the old *as* (Marquardt ii p. 16 sqq.). This state of the currency has been taken to be the meaning of the words *propter aerariam rationem*. Niebuhr (*Rhein. Mus. für Philolog.* for 1827, i 224) objected on two grounds: first that for this meaning *argentaria*, not *aeraria ratio*, would be the proper term; and secondly that the

[1] See *Corp. Inscr. Lat.* v 8119, 4 and others referred to by B. Kübler l.c. pp. 77, 78.

[2] The reduction of the coined *as* to one half of its former weight by the *lex Papiria* in 665 U.C. = 89 B.C. had no important effect, as it was only token money (Marquardt ii p. 18).

difficulty of determining the number of denars to be paid (*quid ad denarium solveretur*) could not have been great or of a nature to require the services of a jurist like Aquilius. He explains the words by a reference to the *lex Valeria* proposed by L. Valerius Flaccus, successor to Cinna in the consulate 668 U.C. = 86 B.C., which reduced all debts to one-fourth of their amount (*creditoribus quadrantem solvi jusserat*, Vell. ii 23), or, as Manlius is made by Sallust (*Catil.* 33) to express it, *propter magnitudinem aeris alieni argentum aere solutum est.* Cicero in the fragmentary commencement of the speech *pro Fonteio* apparently speaks of all debts being paid on this ratio for some time, presumably until Sulla abrogated the law. Mommsen takes the same view (*Röm. Münzw.* p. 383). *Aeraria ratio* would thus be in fact the substitution in the reckoning of a bronze *quadrans* for a silver sesterce (a sesterce, representing the *as*, being a regular symbol for a whole). Mommsen puts it as the substitution in calculation of the reduced *as* (= $\frac{1}{16}$ denar) for the libral *as* which was represented by the silver sesterce (= $\frac{1}{4}$ denar). The difficulty in calculation spoken of by Cicero, would arise, as Niebuhr supposes, from the law applying only to debts at the date of the enactment, and not to any interest accruing since or to any new debts, so that the account between the Scapulae and Quinctius would not be all on the same footing.

The notion that the difficulty arose in the exchange of foreign coins is found in several expositors, but there seems no way for foreign money to come in. Narbo was a Roman colony and had Roman money; and Naevius was expected to provide the money at Rome. The debt was contracted at Rome as likely as anywhere else. Besides Aquilius was hardly an expert in money-changing.

In these circumstances the great lawyer C. Aquilius, who was a friend[1] of the Scapulas, was called in by both parties to decide how many *denarii* should be paid to settle the debt (*quid ad denarium solveretur*, *i.e.* what debt should be discharged

[1] Kübler (l.c. p. 78) refers to Plin. *HN.* vii 183 *Obiit P. Quinctius Scapula cum apud Aquilium Gallum cenaret.*

for each denar). He does so: the amount neither of debt nor of denars is given us. But the whole arrangement was made with the knowledge and approval of Naevius, who frequently repeated his promise to find the money for Quinctius, whenever he asked him. Quinctius accordingly had no hesitation in making a binding engagement[1] with the Scapulae to pay them on some near fixed day, and applies to Naevius to find him the money. Naevius thinking that now he had Quinctius on the hip and could make his own terms, replies, that before he provides a penny, he must have a complete settlement of all partnership matters and accounts, and know that there will be no dispute with Quinctius about them in future. Quinctius replies that that matter can wait, but the money is wanted at once, and reminds Naevius of his promises, but in vain. Quinctius being bound to keep his word under a penalty of an additional 50 per cent. (Gai. iv 171) was in a fix. He gets the Scapulae to allow him a few days and sends at once to Gaul to carry out the sale of which he had given notice before. The time was unfavourable, and he was not present, so that the sale was a bad one; and he settles with the Scapulae on worse terms than he had previously arranged. The other creditors of his brother's estate do not appear to have pressed him, and he was now free to turn his attention to the partnership affairs (§§ 17—20).

He at once takes the initiative and formally calls upon Naevius (*appellat ultro Naevium*, § 20) to get the matters arranged with the least trouble. Naevius appoints a friend M. Trebellius as his representative: Quinctius appoints Sex. Alfenus, a connexion of both parties, who indeed had been brought up at Naevius' house, to act for him. Naevius was too exacting: a friendly arrangement could not be made, and the business had to come before the courts. Several appointments for appearance in court were made and adjourned. Eventually Naevius appeared, but said he had sold by auction in Gaul what he thought fit, and had taken care to satisfy

1 *Constituit Scapulis se daturum*, *i.e.* he promised payment of a definite ascertained amount on a certain day (see p. 86; D. xiii 5).

fully his claims on the partnership[1]: he had therefore no cause either to summon Quinctius to any more appearances or to accept any summons from him: but of course if Quinctius chose to bring any suit against him, he had no objection. Quinctius, thinking he had better revisit Gaul and see how matters stood there, took no formal step. The parties separate without any appointment for appearance in court being made (*sine vadimonio disceditur*, § 23).

Quinctius stays about 30 days in Rome; puts off such court engagements as he had with his other creditors, and starts on his journey on 27 January in the year 671 U.C. = 83 B.C. (*ante diem IV Kal. Febr. Scipione et Norbano coss.*)[2], with L. Albius as his companion (§ 24). He arrives in Gaul, but we hear nothing of what he did or found on his arrival, except that a few days afterwards, on the day before the intercalary Kalends, *i.e.* 23 Feb., the slaves belonging to the partners eject him from the mountain pastures and farm lands of the estate (§ 28). Quinctius applied to C. Flaccus, who was *imperator* in the province at the time, and Flaccus made some strong orders denouncing this eviction, but what they were is not told us. They were apparently produced in court (§ 29). If they were interdicts *de vi, etc.* such as are mentioned in the speeches for Tullius and Caecina one would have expected to hear more of the results.

Cicero gives the distance from Rome as 700 Roman miles (equal to 643 English statute miles)[3]. If a traveller did 50 miles (Roman) a day the journey would take (apart from stoppages) 14 days[4]. Possibly however Quinctius might go by sea from *Vada Volaterrana,* where was a roadstead with good

1 Presumably this refers only to advances he had made or expenses incurred or profits accrued: the land and slaves of the partnership remained common to N. and Q. (§ 28).

2 In § 57 he is said to have started *prid. Kal. Febr.* The editors usually alter in § 24 iv to ii but this is a very unusual way of marking *pridie.*

3 The distance by railway from the modern Narbonne appears to be kilom. 1160=725 Engl. statute miles. But the situation of the farm is uncertain and may well have been nearer than Narbonne.

4 40—50 miles a day is assumed by Friedländer as the usual rate of travelling in a hired carriage (*Sittengeschichte* ii 19 ed. 5).

anchorage for coasting vessels. At this place (according to the Antonine Itinerary p. 139 ed. Parthey) 186 or 189 m. p. on the *Via Aurelia* from Rome (now about 280 kilometres by rail) it happened that he saw L. Publicius, an intimate friend of Naevius, who was bringing him some slaves from Gaul for sale. Publicius reports to Naevius where he had met Quinctius. Naevius at once, as Cicero implies, saw his opportunity. He sends messages to his friends to meet him at the *tabula Sextia*[1] at the second hour of the day following. His friends come in good numbers. Naevius[2] calls upon them to bear witness to the fact that he has appeared and that Quinctius has not appeared[3]. A big[4] formal affidavit is drawn, and Naevius' friends of rank seal it up. They then separate. Naevius applies to the praetor on the 20th February (*ante diem V Kalendas intercalares* § 79) to allow him to proceed against Quinctius as a defaulter. The praetor Burrienus accordingly issues the usual order for him to take possession of the estate of Quinctius in accordance with the edict (*ut ex edicto bona possidere liceat*). Naevius proceeds to put it into force. He has notices affixed to Quinctius' house, and endeavours to lay hold of a slave. Alfenus at once contests these proceedings, pulls down the notices, carries off the slave, and formally notifies Naevius that he is Quinctius' agent (*procurator*), and that, if Naevius will assail in this cruel manner the civic life and fortunes of his friend, patron, and kinsman, and not await as was reasonable Quinctius' return, he (Alfenus) asks no favour but is ready to defend Quinctius at law (*judicio defendere*[5] § 27) and accept

[1] *Tabula* is often used for an auction notice, *Caecin.* § 16 *adest ad tabulam*; *Att.* xii 40 § 4; xiii 33 § 4. What 'Sextius' board' was we do not know. It was apparently near the praetor's court.

[2] In § 53 Naevius is supposed to say *Horae duae fuerunt: Quinctius ad vadimonium non venit.* It would appear that the appointment is presumed to have been for daybreak, and hence Naevius allows two hours and invites his friends to come *hora secunda* to certify Quinctius' failure.

[3] *Stetisse* (not *stitisse*) is right. See p. 337; and *Introd. Just.* p. ccxxvii.

[4] I am inclined to agree with Oetling p. 13 in retaining the old reading *maximae* (not *maxime*).

[5] *Judicio defendere, judicio pati* are used as opposites of *judicio agere.* See Müller *Adn. Crit.* on § 63; Mommsen *apud* Cic. Orell.[2] i p. 454.

issue on any suit Naevius may choose to bring. The attachment of the estate in Gaul was apparently more successful. It must have been done on instructions given by Naevius previously, either by a special messenger despatched when he heard of Quinctius' journey or even perhaps in anticipation of it[1]. Kübler (p. 69) suggests that Naevius probably acted in the belief that Quinctius was going to secure to himself the Gaulish estate.

Naevius persists, as Cicero expresses it, in aiming at the head of Quinctius, and in reply to Alfenus' declaration that he is Quinctius' agent, formally applies (*postulat*) for Alfenus to give the security (*i.e.* sureties) usually given by an agent, *judicatum solvi*, *i.e.* for due defence of Quinctius and payment of the judgment if the decision should be against him (see p. 384). Alfenus urged that it was not fair for an agent to give security, where the principal in person was not required to do so. The praetor threatened to make an order in Naevius' favour[2], when Alfenus appealed to the tribunes, one of whom, M. Brutus, said that he would interpose his veto upon the praetor's order if some arrangement were not made between Naevius and Alfenus (§ 65). Accordingly further proceedings were stayed until Quinctius could return. Alfenus promises to produce Quinctius in court (*P. Quinctium sisti promittit* § 29) on the 13th September (671 U.C. = 83 B.C.).

Quinctius returns and appears. Naevius takes no formal step for eighteen months (probably owing to the civil war in the neighbourhood of Rome and to Sulla's proscription[3]), but

[1] In § 82 '*post dies* XXX' is found and is not easy to reconcile with other dates. Mommsen (*apud* Orelli[2]) says it is a gloss. Baiter may be right in referring it to the time between Naevius' despatch of a messenger and the day of his application. Hartmann (*Contumacial-Verf.* p. 33) refers *postulaturus eras* (§ 82) to the final application for sale. (See above, p. 434.)

[2] Probably, that unless Alfenus gave the regular security he would protect Naevius' possession of Quinctius' estate, and authorise his proceeding to a sale (cf. D. xliii 4).

[3] In 672 U.C. were the fights of Sulla and Marius the younger at Signia and Praeneste, then the fight between Sulla and Carbo at Clusium, and on 1 Nov. 672 U.C. the battle at the Colline gate, which was soon followed by Sulla's dictatorship and proscription in 673 U.C.

makes illusory proposals (*condicionibus hunc quoad potest, producit*). At last he applies to the praetor Cn. Dolabella to order Quinctius to give him security for payment of the judgment (*judicatum solvi*), on the ground that Quinctius is a person whose goods have been possessed for thirty days in accordance with the praetor's edict. Quinctius made no objection to giving security, if the allegation were true, but objected to conceding the truth of the allegation by giving security on that ground. Whereupon Dolabella intimated his intention to direct an issue to try the fact[1]. Quinctius was to make a wager with Cn. Naevius, that is, to stipulate for a nominal sum to be paid by Naevius, if his goods had not been possessed for thirty days in accordance with the edict of P. Burrienus the praetor. Naevius having made this promise, Quinctius would have to bring a suit for this nominal penalty and naturally have to prove his case. Quinctius and his friends objected strongly to the proposed order, as unnecessarily risking Quinctius' civic reputation. If he failed to prove that Naevius had not been in possession as alleged, he was a ruined and disgraced man; and by such a form of issue Quinctius would have to speak first and to make out the negative, instead of Naevius, who was the real plaintiff, having to make out the affirmative. Why not have the real rights of the two parties tried in action (*pro socio*?) on the main question, and then, if desired, both parties might give security *judicatum solvi*? (In a partnership suit with counter-claims this would be a natural course.) Dolabella however adhered to his view: he probably thought that he owed it to his predecessor Burrienus and to the continuity of judicial action not to put aside his order, and treat the whole dispute between Quinctius and Naevius as *res integra*: he must regard that order as *prima facie* valid, and conduct matters on that assumption, till it was shewn either that the order was not right or that it had not been duly carried into effect. If this issue were decided in Quinctius' favour, the proceedings taken in default failed, Quinctius' goods had not been legally in alien possession for thirty days, and the partnership dispute could be gone into.

[1] A similar course was adopted in a case named in D. xlii 5 fr 30.

If the decision went against Quinctius, then he must submit to the consequences of not having duly met Naevius' claim by appearance in court. As regards the form of issue, Dolabella, I suppose, would say that, on an issue of that kind it could not much matter which party spoke first, but that there were two reasons for putting Quinctius in this position; first, because an order had been made against him and Naevius was in possession, partial or complete, regular or irregular; and secondly, because it was a simpler course, if Quinctius were right, to shew a flaw or flaws in Naevius' position and conduct, than for Naevius to go through the whole proceedings bit by bit and shew their legality. If Quinctius declined to accept this issue, Dolabella said he should grant Naevius' application and order Quinctius to give the required security. Quinctius' advocates continuing to protest, Dolabella had them sent out of court (§ 31). Cicero sarcastically observes on Dolabella's conduct that noblemen attain a height in wrong-doing as well as in right-doing which humbler persons cannot reach[1].

Quinctius came reluctantly to the conclusion that it was better to accept the issue and trust to getting an impartial judge to try it. He took[2] C. Aquilius as judge (who chose as assessors L. Lucilius, P. Quinctilius, and M. Marcellus §§ 5, 34), and then sued Naevius on the wager. M. Junius pleaded Quinctius' cause several times (§ 3). Why the case was not decided, we are not told: it is hinted that Junius spoke at too great a length[3] (§ 34). However when the case came on again, Junius was absent on public business (*nova legatione impeditus* § 3), and young Cicero had to take it up on short notice (§§ 3, 4). Hortensius made an application for Aquilius to come before the praetor on the preceding day to be made to fix a limit of time for Cicero's speech[4]. The praetor according to Cicero

[1] This Dolabella was governor of Cilicia in 80 and 79 B.C. with Verres as legate and was convicted of extortion by M. Aem. Scaurus 78 B.C. See Cic. *Verr.* ii 1 38 §§ 96, 97 (Zumpt's *Röm. Crim. Proc.* p. 484).

[2] *I.e.* he proposed Aquilius, and Naevius accepted. See above, p. 351.

[3] Similarly Cicero complains in *pro Tull.* § 6 of his opponent spinning out his speech.

[4] Pliny says (*Ep.* vi 2 § 7) *Equidem quotiens judico, quod vel saepius*

would have been ready enough to do what Hortensius asked, but Aquilius objected to any such interference with his duty and functions as *judex*, and no order was made. Cicero declares that brevity is best suited to his powers and inclination and therefore he will give no cause for delay, but will at once lay down three propositions conclusive of his case, and keep himself strictly to them (§ 35).

The three propositions which Cicero undertakes to prove are:

1. There was no ground for Naevius' applying to the praetor for any order to take possession of Quinctius' estate.

2. Naevius could not have possessed the estate in accordance with the edict.

3. Naevius did not possess the estate.

In short Cicero contests the justice of Naevius' application, the legality of the order and its execution, and lastly whether Naevius' possession, such as it was, amounted to good possession in law.

1. The first proposition is made by Cicero the text for an animated and vituperative discussion of Naevius' conduct, partly no doubt in order to create such a prejudice against Naevius as might facilitate the acceptance of Cicero's proofs of the second and third propositions. Cicero proceeds to establish his first proposition by arguing (*a*) that Naevius' conduct was wholly inconsistent with the existence of any such debt. Naevius puts the debt as a large one owed by C. Quinctius on certain specific matters. C. Quinctius dies; his brother the defendant is heir and comes to him in Gaul. Naevius never mentioned such a debt, though P. Quinctius was more than a year with him in Gaul, and on a change of debtor it would have been natural to do so: there was nothing to prevent him: he saw Quinctius continually; justice was administered in Gaul, and the courts in Rome were open also[1]; and Naevius was not of a character to waive a claim or to have any reluctance to press it (§§ 37—41). Further even now Naevius shrinks from

facio quam dico, quantum quis plurimum postulat aquae do. He evidently gave to others what he wished for himself.

[1] *In provincia jus dicebatur, et Romae judicia fiebant* (§ 41).

getting the money question tried, and prefers to force on another issue which may ruin Quinctius (§§ 43—47).

(*b*) Cicero next argues that even granting that Naevius had a well-founded claim against Quinctius, that was no reason for taking such an extreme step. Suppose Quinctius had failed to keep an appointment to appear, he was a kinsman, a partner, a friend in constant intercourse: was it reasonable to take advantage of the first slip, and resort to an act, which would have been justified only when the wrong was clear, when there was no chance of getting a trial, and when the defendant had broken his engagement over and over again? (§§ 48—53). Quinctius had a house in Rome: his wife and children were there: was there any justification for Naevius' asking the praetor to treat him as one who shirked a trial instead of seeing his friends, inquiring for his agent, or giving formal notice at his house? (§ 54).

(*c*) Finally on this head Cicero disputes altogether that the appointment for appearance which Naevius alleged Quinctius had failed to keep, had ever been made. Quinctius, as soon as he got back to Rome, asked Naevius to give him the date when the appointment was made. Naevius immediately answered 'on the nones (5th) of February.' Quinctius looks in his diary and finds that he had left Rome for Gaul on the last day of January[1] (*prid. Kal. Feb.*) and consequently was absent from Rome on the 5th February and could not have made the appointment. Albius was his fellow traveller: several friends saw them off. There is (says Cicero) therefore plenty of evidence for the date of Quinctius' departure, such as will effectually rebut any evidence which can be given by Naevius' ally[2], who is alleged to have joined in the stipulation for the appointment (§ 58).

Naevius, says Cicero, is a man of influence, especially among those who are dominant in Rome at this time. Quinctius is a plain, quiet man, in his sixtieth year, of old-fashioned habits and

[1] *I.e.* the 29th. In § 24 the 27th is named as the day. The MSS. are wrong no doubt in one or other place.

[2] The object of having an *adstipulator* may have been to act in case of Naevius' absence (cf. Gai. iii 110, 111, and above, p. 28).

sombre and reserved character, no lounger in the forum[1] or *Campus Martius*, unused to society, devoted to those old notions of thrift and duty which have in modern times become blurred and forgotten; but he has a good case, and he relies on the judge to save his reputation and fortunes from the cruelty and greed of Naevius (§§ 59, 99).

Cicero having thus made an appeal to the sympathies of the court, and shewn that Naevius had no ground for his application to the praetor (the issue of the rule if applied for was almost a matter of course: cf. pp. 349, 350), and that his action was precipitate, unnecessary, and cruel, because in fact nothing was due to him, no appointment had been made, and consequently no desertion had taken place, proceeds to his second proposition.

2. Could Naevius have possessed the estate of Quinctius in accordance with the edict? What are the terms of the edict? It lays down several cases in which the praetor promises to order possession to be taken of a defendant's estate. The first is, if a man fraudulently keeps out of the way (*latitarit*). That does not apply to Quinctius, who went away on business and left an agent to act for him. The two next cases named by the praetor have also clearly no application, 'one who is dead without an heir,' and 'one who has gone into exile.' But it is said Quinctius comes within the words of the edict 'absent without due defence[2].' When then was Quinctius absent without defence? He was absent no doubt when Naevius applied to the praetor for an order to take possession of the estate, for no one could imagine that such an application would be made. Nor indeed was it important for anyone to attend, for the praetor's order would not be absolute, but for something to be done in accordance with his edict. (That is to say, the praetor gave the order on *ex parte* information, and in case of dispute the whole matter would have to be gone into, and in some shape compensation be made, if the order was not justified and

1 *Ad solarium* is taken to mean 'at a sundial' near the Rostra in the forum (Censorin. 24 § 7) where people gathered for talk. Cf. *ad Heren.* iv 10 § 14.

2 On the text here see below, p. 471.

damage had been done.) The first opportunity that there really was for his agent to defend Quinctius, was when Naevius proceeded to put up notices of seizure on his property. Alfenus at once interfered and tore down the notices, and on Naevius attempting to seize in the streets a slave belonging to Quinctius took the man away by force, and had him taken back to Quinctius' house. Further Naevius asserts his claim of debt, Alfenus denies it; Naevius demands a formal promise to appear, Alfenus gives it; Naevius summons him into court, Alfenus obeys the summons; Naevius applies for a trial, Alfenus does not refuse it. Nor was Alfenus a man of straw or needy hack. He was a Roman knight of good means, managing well his own business, and, what is more, he was the very man whom Naevius always left as his agent whenever he went into Gaul. Can Naevius pretend that Quinctius was not duly defended in his absence? (§§ 61, 62).

To all this Naevius replied that Alfenus declined to give him security, and, when the praetor was going to make an order to that effect, appealed to the tribunes as previously mentioned. This is where, as Cicero supposes, Naevius finds Quinctius liable under the praetor's edict. 'A man who is 'absent and whose agent does not submit to a suit or defend 'him against it in a regular trial but appeals to the tribunes, is 'a man who is absent undefended.' The practical answer to Naevius is that the order of the praetor for Alfenus to give security was either not actually made (*decernebat praetor* § 63), or if made (cf. § 65 *decreto praetoris oportuisse-parere*) was rendered ineffective by the threatened interposition of the tribune M. Brutus. Alfenus made an affidavit, supported by others, in Naevius' presence, that he claimed on the ground of their relationship, that Naevius should not press serious measures against Quinctius in his absence; and further that if Naevius persisted, he himself was ready to accept process on any issue proposed by Naevius and to defend Quinctius against Naevius' claim of debt. A new start was made by the arrangement to await Quinctius' return and by his due appearance in court (§ 67). Naevius and his counsel may grumble as much as they like about Alfenus' influence with the dominant powers at that time: the real issue is not affected. Quinctius was defended, and defended by means of the law and of the lawful magistrate (§ 68).

Be that as it may, the question now at issue is whether Naevius has possessed in accordance with the edict, that is to say, whether the directions of the edict have been followed. Now (*a*) the edict requires all the sureties[1] and creditors of the defendant to meet, and the estate when possessed to be sold. Neither of these things took place. Yet there were other creditors who were entitled to take part, who however, so far from enforcing their claims, are here to assist the defendant. True, some witnesses are said to be ready to speak of other acts of *laches* or fraud on the part of Quinctius: it will be seen what they have to say. They will be wise to remember that the only way to gain or maintain credit is to support the truth (§ 75).

(*b*) It is clear from Naevius' own conduct that he did not consider effective possession had been taken of Quinctius' estate. For if it had, Quinctius was ruined in reputation and position. Yet when the estate of Alfenus was confiscated and sold by Sulla as dictator, Naevius bought it and gave the name of Quinctius as his partner in the matter—a course quite inconsistent with Naevius' present contention.

(*c*) The dates[2] shew that the edict was not followed. For the application was made to the praetor on the fifth day before the intercalary Kalends, *i.e.* on Feb. 20; and Quinctius was ejected from the Gaulish farm on the day before the Kalends, *i.e.* Feb. 23. The ejectment was therefore on the second or third day after the praetor's order. It is impossible for the

[1] *Ceteri sponsores et creditores.* The *sponsores* would be sureties who had not yet been made to pay but were liable to do so. If they had paid they would be creditors, though they may perhaps have been treated as a distinct class. They had a more summary remedy usually. See Gai. iv 22. The same expression in like connexion occurs in Cic. *Phil.* vi 4 § 11.

[2] The dates are as follows: Q. leaves Rome, Jan. 27 or 29; is at *Vada*, *cir.* Feb. 4; is at Narbonne, *cir.* Feb. 18 (?); is ejected, Feb. 23. Publicius sees Q. at *Vada* and reports to Naevius. As he was taking slaves, we do not know how long his journey required. He reports to Naevius after Feb. 8 (?); N. meets his friends, Feb. 10—20; applies to praetor, Feb. 20.

distance of 700 (Roman) miles to be covered in that time[1]. Consequently Naevius must have presumed some time before on the order being made. In a matter which concerned the very life and fortunes of another, Naevius must have boldly assumed, when he sent his messenger to Gaul, that he would persist in his purpose, that he would be alive and well and able to come before the praetor to make this application, that the praetor would be well and in court, that he would consent to make the order, and that no one would make a valid defence, give such security as might be required, accept an issue for trial, and thus prevent any decree being made for possession of Quinctius' estate as a defaulter (§§ 78—82, 88).

(*d*) Finally the praetor's edict expressly directs that in taking possession of the estate the owner should not be himself ejected against his will. This provision applies even in the case of an absconding and undefended debtor. Yet Naevius actually ejects Quinctius, who did not abscond and who was defended by a regular agent (§§ 84, 85).

It may be remarked on this part of Cicero's argument that on the first point counter evidence was to be produced, and Cicero does not attempt to deal with it in detail. Perhaps he really did not know what evidence Hortensius had. But he distinctly asserts that whatever may have been the case before, now all the creditors are on Quinctius' side (§§ 76, 88). The second point again is very briefly treated, and we know nothing of the circumstances of Sulla's putting Alfenus to death and the confiscation of his property. It was probably a mere ordinary incident in that reign of terror. Very likely Naevius and Quinctius combined to buy the estate of their old friend. Such action on the part of friends was, I expect, frequent in cases of public sales (see vol. 1 p. 482). The third point, which Roscius suggested, raises the question, whether an act was legitimate for which the instructions were given without authority at the time. Similarly on the fourth point the question is whether an expulsion of the owner himself, though contrary to edict, made the seizure bad in law.

[1] This point is said by Cicero to have been suggested to him by Roscius the actor, whose sister was Quinctius' wife.

3. The last of the three heads into which Cicero divided his defence has been lost in the MSS. But the purport is given in Cicero's summary at the end (§§ 89, 90) and accords with Severian's brief extracts. It was that due possession had not in fact been taken, because Naevius had not possessed all, but only a part of, Quinctius' estate. There were a house and slaves in Rome, there were some slaves on the Narbonne pasture and there were some farms in Gaul, belonging to Quinctius separately from Naevius, which had escaped his hands (§ 90). He had not possessed the estate (*bona*), he had only seized one piece of land. In other words Cicero maintains that Quinctius must win on the wager, because even if Naevius had ground for his hostile proceedings, even if he had in other respects followed the directions of the edict, his possession was not in fact such a possession as was intended in the edict: consequently he had not possessed (§§ 85—89).

It is clear from the language frequently used that the lawless and terrible state of Rome under Marius and Sulla had its effect even on this private suit. Probably it accounts for much of the delay which occurred; possibly it afforded occasion to Naevius and to Quinctius to take advantage of each other in a way which would not have been practicable in quiet times. Alfenus is charged with using extra-judicial means through his influence with Brutus in order to set aside or suspend the praetor's decree. He was a strong partisan and fell in Sulla's proscription with his party and for them. Naevius was quite as strong a partisan, with more craft and greater influence: he deserted his party in order to be on the winning side; and just as he is alleged to have got his first advantage from Burrienus by political influence, so he is now, says Cicero, availing himself of the triumph of Sulla's party to secure his victory over Quinctius (§§ 68—70). One cannot but admire young Cicero's courage in taking up the case and pleading it with such vigour against orators like Philippus and Hortensius and members of Sulla's faction, while Sulla was dictator[1]. But genius gives impulse and confidence; and

[1] The speech *pro Sex. Roscio* of Ameria is a still greater proof of Cicero's boldness.

genius alone could have excited the enthusiasm and won the favour which have preserved to us so many of Cicero's speeches and writings, when all the other oratory and almost all the prose writings of the Republic, except his, have been allowed to perish.

As I have said above, it does not seem to me unreasonable for the issue to have been directed by Dolabella in the form given, much as Cicero protests against it. I assume that this form really throws open the whole matter, and that Cicero is justified in discussing the validity of the praetor's first decree for taking possession as well as the subsequent proceedings[1]. The summary with which Cicero concludes his argument (§§ 85—90) is clear, precise, and effective, but, as orator, Cicero cannot leave the matter without a last appeal to the equity and compassion of the judge and his assessors. Such an appeal was a regular part of a speech (cf. Cic. *Inv.* i 55 § 106) and would be expected by any court. We should think it natural, if addressed to a popular body like an assembly of the people or even to an ordinary jury. Addressed to a lawyer like Aquilius and to his dignified and competent assessors, it may seem out of place and rather an indication that the purely legal argument was felt to be weak. But besides the general fact, on which Cicero often dwells in his *de Oratore*, that judges are men as well as lawyers, and consequently accessible to feelings of pity, we cannot assume that the separation of strict law from looser considerations of fair dealing was as complete in the time of Cicero as it may have been in later days. By Ulpian's time they had both come to be fully recognised by the courts, and assigned to their respective provinces. But the very stiffness and rigour of the early Roman forms and procedure must have continually excited a desire for larger consideration. Moreover the wholesale slaughters and confiscations, which Rome had seen in the last few years, must have had their effect in weakening the hold which pure law would have on the minds of Roman citizens. *Inter arma silent leges.* It is difficult for anyone not bound in parchment to lay great stress on technical require-

[1] Cf. D. xlii 1 fr 14 *Quod jussit vetuitve praetor contrario imperio tollere et remittere licet.*

ments, when life, liberty, and property are dealt with every day without reference to any law, at the caprice of a dominant party or of the captain of an army. If Habeas Corpus were suspended in fact, and the King's Writ ceased to run, it would be somewhat difficult even in these days for an English advocate before a fair and competent bench to lay almost exclusive stress on defects in procedure, and to argue that the court should still look to precedent or should still be guided solely by the words of a statute or a rule, if the conduct of the parties would otherwise justify a different conclusion.

We have only Cicero's eloquent speech for Quinctius: we have not Hortensius' pleading on the other side, nor the statements or affidavits of witnesses; we really do not know the merits of the two parties' conduct. Nor have we even a copy of the praetor's edict, as it was either in Cicero's or indeed at any time. But dealing with the law as best one can, I proceed first to speak of the text of § 60, which raises an important question, and then to remark on the leading points, without inferring, as some writers seem inclined to do, from the excellence of the rhetoric the badness of the cause.

Most editions contain after *solum verterit* (§ 60) some such words as *Dici id non potest. Qui absens judicio defensus non fuerit. Ne id quidem.* They are not found in any existing MS. and were first inserted, professedly on MS. authority (not an unusual way with the older editors, when introducing a mere conjecture) by Hotoman. Lambin professed also to have MS. authority for his insertion of *Dici hoc de P. Quinctio non potest. Qui absens judicio defensus non fuerit.* The variation in these supplements is not great, but it is enough to strengthen the suspicion that neither editor had manuscript authority. At the same time it must be admitted the words seem to suit the context and at first sight to be justified by *reliquum est ut eum nemo judicio defenderit* (§ 87). Short negations very similar (*ne id quidem, dici non potest*) are found in *pro Tullio* § 48, and in other speeches of Cicero[1].

[1] *E.g. Verr.* ii 43 § 106; iv 65 § 146 *Ne id quidem*; *ib.* iii 88 § 205 *ne id quidem dicet*; i 46 § 118 *non enim hoc potest hoc loco dici*; *Caecin.* 25 § 72 *illud enim potest dici, etc. hoc non potest*; *etc.*

Mommsen in an early review (dated Nov. 1843) of Keller's *Semestria* (published in *Zeitschrift für Alterth.* p. 1084 for Dec. 1845) rejected these supplements and proposed to read and punctuate thus: *Quo tempore? Existimas oportuisse, Naevi, absentem Quinctium defendi. At quo modo?* This seems to me not Ciceronian. *Quo tempore* would be a strange answer to the suggested application of the clause about exiles: the subsequent argument is not introduced by any particle or other suitable words: and the second question (*quo modo?*) is answered by reference not to manner but to time. I agree with B. Kübler in rejecting Mommsen's solution and in believing with him and others that there is some omission in the MS.

The supplements mentioned above however involve the insertion in this part of the Edict of a separate independent clause, *Qui absens judicio defensus non fuerit*, and accordingly most editors insert it here in Cicero's speech. Keller (*Sem.* p. 45), Bethmann-Hollweg (ii 560), Hartmann (*Contumacial-Verfahren* p. 24), Karlowa (*Beiträge* p. 133), Lenel (*EP.* p. 333), and Costa (pp. 13, 14), all approve (cf. Kübler *l.c.* p. 63). The contrary is maintained by Mommsen (*l.c.*), Dernburg (*Emt. bon.* p. 66), Bachhofen (*ap.* Karlowa), Oetling (p. 6), and apparently by Rudorff (Pucht. *Inst.* § 179 n. *bb*). The extracts from the edict given in the Digest do not contain such a clause.

The evidence for such an addition to the edict is very weak (see it stated in Karlowa pp. 133—139). The most important is Gai. iii 78, *Bona autem veneunt aut vivorum aut mortuorum: vivorum veluti eorum qui fraudationis causa latitant nec absentes defenduntur*. Karlowa persuades himself that the words admit of those *qui absentes defenduntur* being a different class from those *qui latitant*. I cannot agree; and I feel confident that Gaius is here shortly stating by *nec abs. def.*[1] the effect or the words of such a conditional clause (omitted by Cicero after *latitarit* § 60) as we find in the fragment of the edict given in

[1] *Absens* is somewhat superfluous, but, I think, formed with *def.* a kind of technical phrase, cf. D. iv 6 fr 1 § 1; 21 §§ 1, 2; 28 § 6; xlii 4 fr 2 § 2. In our speech Cicero often uses it, §§ 60, 61 (*bis*), 62, 65, 68 (*bis*), 74; as well as a phrase of like meaning, *judicio defendere*, §§ 62, 63, 68, 84, 87.

D. xlii 4 fr 7 § 1, *Qui fraudationis causa latitabit, si boni viri arbitratu non defendetur, ejus bona possideri vendique jubebo.* Ulpian's treatment of this fragment seems to me altogether inconsistent with the supposition, that this section of the edict contained in his time a distinct clause for undefended absentees[1] (see *ib.* §§ 9—12). And in our speech Cicero similarly connects undefended absence with fraudulent hiding (§§ 74, 75, 84, 85). Nor is the way in which the words *reliquum est, etc.* (§ 87) are appended to a positive denial of liability under the edict really such as one would expect, if a separate coordinate clause of the edict and not an appended condition were referred to.

Moreover I do not believe that mere undefended absence[2] could have been placed by the edict or by the law generally on the same footing as fraudulent keeping out of the way[3]. Only when there is fraudulent purpose does absence become penally blamable. But when an absentee however innocent has no adequate representative, a creditor may be unable to get satisfaction; and if a summons has been served, and agreement for appearance in court has been come to, a creditor has a well-founded right that undefended absence shall not for ever bar his suit or expose the property on which he relies to dissipation. The praetor therefore granted possession of the debtor's estate, but it was possession for safe keeping only. *In bona ejus qui vadimoni* (Dig. *judicio sistendi*) *causa fidejussorem dedit, si neque potestatem sui faciet neque defendetur, iri jubebo*[4] (D. xlii 4 fr 2 pr). This included both the fraudulent and the innocent absentee (*ib.* §§ 2, 3). It is *possideri*, not

[1] *Absens* is either *qui non est eo loci ubi petitur* (i.e. Rome) or *qui in jure non est* (D. L 16 fr 199; xxxix 2 fr 4 § 5).

[2] Cf. Hartmann *Contum.* §§ 8—12.

[3] The Digest is express on this point (iv 6 fr 21 § 2) *Eorum qui non defenduntur si quidem latitent, Praetor ex edicto pollicetur in bona (eorum) mittere, ut si res exegerit etiam distrahantur, si vero non latitent, licet non defendantur, in bona tantum mitti.* Karlowa and, following him, Lenel (*Paling.* ii p. 480) declare these words to be an addition of Tribonian's. I don't believe this as regards the substance. Some expressions may be due to Tribonian's abridgment.

[4] This originally referred to *in jus vocatio.* See Lenel *EP.* p. 58 and above, p. 334, but this principle applies after *vadimonium* also. The precise shape of the edict in Cicero's time is of course uncertain.

possideri vendique that is spoken of here (compare *ib.* fr 7 §§ 1, 2). The creditor was entitled to have the possession secured. Subsequent events might explain the absence, or shew that it should be treated as fraudulent latitation. No doubt a further application to the praetor would have to be made before steps were taken for a sale (cf. *ib.* fr 6 § 1, 7 § 11). If latitation or other sufficient cause[1] were found to exist, a sale would be ordered. Meantime the appearance of the defendant or of an adequate representative would put an end to the creditor's occupation, but security must be given, at least if the defendant does not appear in person (D. *ib.* fr 5 pr; tit. 5 fr 33 § 1).

Such seems to have been the position in the case of Quinctius. Some considerable time had elapsed since Naevius first got the order for possession. Had Alfenus not interfered, Naevius would probably (after thirty days?) have applied again to the praetor to order a sale on the ground that Quinctius was fraudulently keeping out of the way. Alfenus' energetic action prevented this.

I suppose that there is some part of Cicero's speech lost after the words *solum verterit* in § 60. He probably returned to the mention of latitation and took up the conditional clause (*si absens non defendetur*[2] or the like) to shew that no part of this head of the edict had any application to Quinctius. 'He 'wasn't hiding, he wasn't undefended in his absence. Hiding 'is much more than non-appearance: it is shirking appearance, 'it is fraudulent avoidance of your adversary, it is *turpis occul-* '*tatio sui*[3]. And even hiding is not enough without the 'additional fact of want of due defence. Where is there any 'basis for applying this to Quinctius? *Quo tempore existimas* '*oportuisse, etc.*' I do not pretend to suggest the words of any precise supplement, but I have put into Latin (see note 4 below) my conception of what would suit Cicero's argument.

[1] Cf. D. xlii 5 fr 5.

[2] In this suggestion I have been anticipated by B. Kübler (p. 64).

[3] Ulpian D. xlii 4 fr 7 § 4 attributes to Cicero a definition of *latitare* as *turpis occultatio sui*. It is not found in Cicero's works, and may very possibly have been given in our speech at this point.

[4] Suppose for instance Naevius interrupted him or is imagined by Cicero to interrupt him. Something of this kind might have been said:

The leading points in Cicero's defence which seem to require special notice are:

1. Had Quinctius failed to keep an appointment or appearance?

2. Was Alfenus' defence of Quinctius good without his giving security *judicatum solvi*?

3. Was Alfenus' application to the tribunes an illegal disobedience to the praetor's orders?

4. Under this decree was the concurrence of the other creditors necessary? and had it been obtained and the sale proceeded with?

5. Was it necessary for effective seizure, that all the property of the defendant, whatever and wherever it was, should be seized?

6. Must such seizure be made, as it were, with the praetor's warrant in hand?

7. Was the personal eviction of Quinctius a fatal flaw to a good execution of the order?

---

1. The first point is one of fact, on which I expect Quinctius was in the right. There may have been misunderstanding or there may have been fraudulent assumption on the part of Naevius. Keller (p. 175) supposes that Naevius made a slip of memory when he named the Nones of February (§ 57),

'At absens fuit, at non defensus est. Quid est aliud latitare nisi copiam 'sui non facere nec absentem defendi?' Primum, Naevi, velim consideres non hoc solum exegisse praetorem ut quis latitasse convinceretur, sed ut cum latitasse videretur tum idem etiam non esset defensus. Non latitavit Quinctius, sed etiamsi latitasset nihil contra edictum committebat qui absens defendebatur. Deinde aliud est, mehercule, latitare quam copiam sui non facere. Qui latitat, timet et vitat adversarium, decipere ac fraudare cupit; non modo occultat se sed turpiter occultat. Quae res a Quinctio alienissima fuit. Non evitabat te, neque cur evitare vellet ulla causa erat; sed cum velle te illum morari negavisses, in Galliam rei suae curandae causa profectus est, Romae procuratorem reliquit qui tibi praesto esse semper posset. Quo tempore, etc.

and that Cicero ought to have shewn that no appointment was made on any other day. How? surely that was for Naevius to prove; and if Naevius had really made it on some other day and said so, Cicero could not have avoided dealing with it. It does not seem likely that Quinctius should have deliberately gone to Gaul only a few days after he had made a formal appointment with Naevius, and yet it is not likely that the praetor made his order without some evidence of the appointment. But Naevius could no doubt get some affidavit of this concocted, and it might easily pass muster when no one was present on the other side to contest it.

It was the risk of such proceedings taking place, that made it usual for Romans with business affairs to have a competent agent to represent them in their absence, and led to legal recognition of the action of persons who without any commission conducted business for absentees (*negotiorum gestio*). In a case like that before us the risk was modified by the praetor's order being only what we should call a rule *nisi*, an order issued on *prima facie* evidence, and subject to be cancelled or altered on sufficient cause shewn[1]. It was good, as Cicero remarks, only if the edict had been fully observed (§ 60 *nec quemquam, etc.*). The praetor in fact would say to Naevius, 'You may take your rule, but if your statements and affidavits 'are not true, you will be liable to Quinctius for the damage you 'may cause him' (cf. § 83 *corrigeres haec scilicet tu postea*). Indeed if Naevius falsely alleged a debt, he was liable to a suit *injuriarum* in having taken possession of Quinctius' estate (Gai. iii 220). The possibility of rescission of the sale is stated in D. xlii 4 fr 7 § 3; cf. tit. 5 fr 30; tit. 1 fr 51. If however an appointment had been made and not kept and no defence put in, the order for possession was regular, however harsh.

2. There is no doubt that in the time of Gaius and later a procurator for the defendant was bound to give the security *judicatum solvi*. *Ab ejus parte cum quo agitur, siquidem alieno nomine aliquis interveniat, omni modo satisdari debet, quia nemo alienae rei sine satisdatione defensor idoneus intelligitur. Sed*

[1] So Keller *Semestr.* p. 79 sq.; Gai. iv 141 is also in point.

siquidem cum cognitore agatur, dominus satisdare jubetur, si vero cum procuratore, ipse procurator (Gai. iv 101). *Defendere est id facere, quod dominus in litem faceret et cavere idonee. Nec debebit durior conditio procuratoris fieri quam est domini praeterquam in satisdando.* (D. iii 3 fr 35 § 3 Ulp.; cf. *ib.* fr 46 § 2; 51 § 2—fr 53; xlii 4 fr 5 § 3; tit. 5 fr 33 § 1; xlvi 7 fr 10; Vat. 317, 333.) It is of course possible that the rule may not have been fixed and universal in Cicero's time, especially in the case of one who was a standing agent[1] for Quinctius' affairs and not merely appointed for a particular suit: and yet this is unlikely in the case of a rule, which though not resting on legislation was founded on clear principle: and Keller points to Cic. *Verr.* ii 24 § 60 as some evidence of its general recognition. Modern expositors are pretty well agreed that the rule did exist, and consequently that Alfenus' position was completely untenable. If so, how are we to account for its being taken? There are some considerations which seem to me to have been overlooked or at least not sufficiently regarded.

It is nowhere said that Alfenus definitely declined to give security. He said it was not fair (*aequum*: cf. Oetling p. 9) that a procurator should give security when his principal, if he had been present, would have been under no obligation to do so and appealed to the tribunes. The tenses are noticeable[2]. *Postulabam*, says Naevius, *ut satis daret. Injuria postulabas* (replies Cicero); *ita videbare; recusabat Alfenus.* Naevius replies, *Ita, verum praetor decernebat.* Says Cicero, *Tribuni igitur appellabantur* (§ 63). Again *Bruti erat* (*Alfenus*) *familiaris; itaque is intercedebat*, says Naevius; to which Cicero replies, *Tu contra Burrieni, qui injuriam decernebat* (§ 69). The imperfect is not the tense for positive final acts. What is thus described is rather a series of negotiations and proposals; perhaps threats and alternative proposals. Cicero admits that, if the tribunes had declined to interfere and the praetor had

[1] Cf. Cic. *Caecin.* 20 § 57. This suggestion is made by several writers and carefully dealt with by Keller p. 117 sqq.

[2] Comp. Cic. *Verr.* iii 22 § 55; 28 § 69. In neither of these cases, as I understand, did Verres actually send the matter to trial.

made the order, Alfenus would have had (*oportuisse*) to give security (§ 65).

Alfenus' contention was first, that the whole matter should rest until Quinctius' return: secondly, that if Naevius was determined to push things to extremities, well, he must bring his suit, and he (Alfenus) would accept process (§§ 27, 66), but in that case he ought not to be called on to give security simply as procurator. His reasons, I imagine, would be founded on the special circumstances of the case. It was not a case of a claim being pressed for the first time against an absent defendant, but of some suit to be brought against one whose estate had been already, as Naevius professed, seized. Alfenus had offered to accept any issue proposed by his opponent (§ 63); but such issue would obviously have reference to the partnership matter, no other being alluded to, and was in all probability the same as that on which Naevius asserted he had given Quinctius notice of trial, and then alleging default, had applied to the praetor Burrienus for an order for possession. What more security did he want than the possession of the whole of the defendant's estate[1] (to which alone Alfenus could look for reimbursement)? It was unreasonable to require sureties for the execution of the judgment, when he had already as it were executed it himself. Usually when sureties were given, possession of the estate would be given up (D. xlii 5 fr 33). If Naevius had offered to withdraw from possession, possibly Alfenus would have consented to give sureties, and been glad of such a solution of the difficulty. No hint is given of any such course. I cannot help thinking that in the circumstances the objections of Alfenus had reasonable ground. Moreover he was not a mere outsider meddling with another's concerns without call to do so. He was a man of character and substance well known to Naevius, who could not doubt his legitimate connexion with Quinctius, when he had already been appointed to act for the latter in trying to get a friendly settlement (§ 21). One would however like to know why the praetor did not do of his own motion what was done

[1] Cf. the language in § 98 *Cum illum (Naevium) in suis paternis bonis dominari videret.*

afterwards through the appeal to the tribunes, viz. adjourn the proceedings till Quinctius' return, and fix an early day. It looks as if Dolabella had either formed a very unfavourable opinion of Quinctius' conduct, or were far from impartial.

3. Alfenus' application to the tribunes seems to us at first sight at variance with the proper conduct of judicial procedure. But the tribunicial power of veto was not limited. The order of the praetor was a magistrate's order, just as any order of a consul in public affairs, and was liable to the interference of the tribunes, who in fact were created for the very purpose of checking the improper exercise of public authority. Alfenus claimed to be acting *more et instituto, per eum magistratum qui auxilii causa constitutus est*[1] (§ 63). Nor was his action without parallel. In the speech *pro Tullio* an appeal is made to the tribunes to alter the issue directed by the praetor (*Tull.* §§ 38, 39). The allowance of pleas by the tribunes is playfully alluded to in Cic. *Acad.* ii 30 § 97 ed. Reid *Tribunum aliquem censeo adeant: a me istam exceptionem numquam impetrabunt.* Pliny the younger in *Epist.* i 23 gives as one reason for his not acting as advocate when he was tribune, that he was liable to be appealed to by plaintiffs and defendants (Mommsen *Staatsr.* i 264; Cic. *in Vatin.* § 33; Ascon. *in orat. in toga cand.* p. 111). It can hardly however have been common for the tribunes thus to interfere on interlocutory judicial questions[2]. On this point probably Hortensius did not dispute the right of the defendant to appeal, and did not maintain that defendant was bound to accept without appeal any issue offered[3], but

[1] I am inclined to agree with most of the earlier editors in thinking that something has been lost in the MSS. just before this. See Kübler p. 68 against Keller p. 244.

[2] A courteous reviewer of this Essay (*Athenæum*, 7 June 1902) disagrees from this opinion; he emphasizes the fact that two of our four private speeches of Cicero contain instances of this interference, and refers to Tac. *An.* xiii 28 and Juv. vii 228 in proof of the tribunes' activity in judicial matters. But Tacitus tells us only of the senate's forbidding the tribunes from usurping the functions of the praetors and consuls by summoning defendants *ex Italia*, *i.e.* from outside Rome. And Juvenal refers only to tribunes being appealed to in matter of school fees. See Mommsen *Staatsr.* ii p. 298.

[3] Müller is wrong in bracketing these words (§ 64). They are the natural alternative to an appeal.

urged that an appeal to the tribunes on a matter of ordinary routine and settled practice could only be for the sake of delay (§ 65 *ad fin.*), and constituted a breach of a defendant's duty *judicio defendere* (§ 63); and he further pointed out that the tribunes though appealed to did not interpose their *veto*. Alfenus therefore had not complied with the praetor's uncancelled direction to give security, whether made into a formal order or not. To this Cicero replies, that the appeal to the tribunes was perfectly constitutional, and was practically successful in producing through Brutus' threat a stay of proceedings, until Quinctius could himself appear. So far there seems to be no doubt, but Cicero I think goes too far in asserting that the original position was thus restored; that Quinctius' goods were not to be regarded as under notice or in alien possession; that time could not run against him, and that there could be now no talk of a thirty days' possession (*Fit rebus integris neque proscriptis neque possessis bonis, ut Alfenus promittat Naevio sisti Quinctium* § 67). I take the effect to have been simply a suspension of proceedings[1]. On the fresh hearing of the case the praetor would be able to put matters right, and rescind or confirm or amend his previous order.

4. If we may assume that in this respect the rules for the possession and sale of an estate given by Gaius were the same in essentials as those in the praetor's edict in Cicero's time, it is clear that such an order as Naevius obtained was one of which he had only the carriage and in which others were interested besides him. If the estate is that of a living person, the praetor directs the effects to be possessed and advertised (*proscribi, i.e.* by notices affixed) for thirty days continuously: after that a meeting of creditors to be held, one of them appointed to conduct the sale (called *magister*), and the sale to take place only after a further period[2] (Gai. iii 79, above p. 434). This accords very well with Cicero's language in § 50 *de quo libelli in celeberrimis locis proponuntur,...cui magistri*

[1] Both Keller doubtfully (pp. 162—168) and Frei decidedly (p. 134) go further, and think the appointment made between the parties at Brutus' instance might well be regarded as a waiver of any claim based on the want of due defence of Quinctius.

[2] The times are uncertain. See Stud. and Krüg.'s edit. of Gaius.

fiunt et domini constituuntur (*i.e.* for whom masters are appointed and made owners of the property); *qui, qua lege et qua condicione pereat, pronuntient, de quo homine praeconis vox praedicat et pretium conficit*[1] (declares the bids and fixes the price), *huic acerbissimum vivo videntique funus ducitur*[2]. In the Digest we find Paul laying down the rule that one creditor obtaining an order for possession opens the door for all; the grant by the praetor is one free from limitation to particular persons (*in rem permissum videri* D. xlii 5 fr 12 pr), and Labeo's opinion is referred to as authority. This language makes one think that it was not a generally admitted rule in Labeo's, *i.e.* Augustus' time; and if so, we can hardly think that in Cicero's time it was beyond doubt. But probably the question was whether some further application to the praetor should not be required before the custody of the goods should be open to others. Clearly the other creditors' interests had to be consulted when the whole estate of a debtor was seized, unless indeed the principle of *occupantis melior condicio est* was applied at that time. So that, as far as we know, Naevius' proceeding, not in first taking possession but subsequently, was incomplete and perhaps irregular. The appeal to the tribunes however interrupted the course of events; it may have taken place before the thirty days had expired. Anyhow no hint is given of any formal meeting of the creditors, still less of any sale of Quinctius' effects. Naevius would probably say that he had been interrupted by Alfenus' interference or by the state of political affairs.

5. On the fifth point I think Cicero is mixing up two different things. His argument is good against one who is trying to get possession with a view to become owner by usucapion. An inheritance (which is not merely a collection of separate bits of property, but an ideal whole) could in olden times be acquired by usucapion, and for this purpose no doubt

[1] The *magister* only directed the terms of sale and perhaps presided. The actual bids were collected and repeated by a *praeco*.

[2] Cf. D. xvii 2 fr 65 § 12 *Publicatione distrahi societatem diximus, quod videtur spectare ad universorum bonorum publicationem si socii bona publicentur: nam cum in ejus locum alius succedat, pro mortuo habetur.*

an extensive control over the whole estate, or rather over all the different bodily components of the estate would be necessary (Gai. ii 54). But some reasonable interpretation would be put even then (cf. D. xli 2 fr 3 § 1). And the position of the purchaser of the goods of an insolvent or fugitive was much the same (cf. Gai. iii 80, 81, and iv 35). The position of Naevius was quite different. He was sent into possession *rei servandae causa*, to hold and preserve the estate until further order. He was, as the Antonine jurists sometimes distinguish, to be in possession (*in possessione esse*) but not to possess (*possidere*)[1]; *i.e.* he had no proper possession in the technical sense (cf. D. xli 2 fr 3 § 23; xliii 17 fr 3 § 8); he could not by occupation however long continued acquire the ownership; and the doctrines of the Roman lawyers on the technical sense of possession, as inchoate or presumptive ownership, do not apply. Proper notices would doubtless have to be affixed to the main items of the estate, to the house in Rome and to the lands in Gaul or elsewhere, and proper means would have to be taken to secure that the goods were not carried off and the slaves did not run away. But all that was required was honest care and maintenance of the goods (see § 84, and cf. D. xlii 5 fr 8 § 2; fr 9 § 5). Naevius was answerable for this by an action on the case (*ib.* fr 9 pr), and, if he were interfered with, the praetor would protect him with a like action (cf. D. xlii 4 fr 14 pr; xliii 4 fr 1 sqq.). So that on Cicero's third head as a technical point, I think the argument does not come to much. But practically there seems to be a good deal. The circumstances of this taking possession were not those of an insolvent debtor, hiding from, or seeking to defraud, his creditors. The possession was disputed by Alfenus on Quinctius' behalf from the first; the actual occupation of Quinctius' property by Naevius was ridiculously incomplete; no other creditor was with Naevius; the regular procedure and preliminaries for a sale

[1] The language of the edict was *possideri et proscribi* (Gai. iii 79): *bona possidere* in *Quinct.* 6 § 25; cf. 19 § 60; but it also has *in possessione esse* 27 § 84; cf. D. xlii 4 fr 2 pr; 5 § 2; 7 § 1; tit. 5 fr 9 pr. The two expressions are sharply distinguished in the edict on *damnum infectum* (xxxix 2 fr 7 pr).

had not been followed; there was really no fair ground for saying that the edict applied and that Quinctius could be regarded as a defaulting and undefended absentee. One wonders what were the facts of possession during the eighteen months after Quinctius' return from Gaul (§ 30).

It is noticeable that in the passage of Paul above referred to (D. xli 2 fr 3 § 23) we are told that Q. Mucius actually counted such an occupation (*rei servandae causa*) among the kinds (*genera*) of possession. Paul characterises Mucius' view as *ineptissimum.* But Mucius very possibly was merely making a formal enumeration of *genera possessionis,* based on the use of the word *possessio,* and may have afterwards distinguished some classes of possession as leading to usucapion and others as not doing so (cf. Pernice *Lab.* II^2 p. 427). Whether the difference of his treatment from Paul's was formal or substantial, Cicero may have been led by his classification and the actual use of *possidere* in the edict into making this point.

6. On the hasty seizure of the Gallic land Cicero's language is noticeable. He says such a thing was unheard of, it was wicked, but he hardly commits himself to the assertion that the possession was bad in law. The point was apparently a new one. It was certainly a great risk for Naevius to run, but as he actually got the praetor's order, and got it before the eviction in Gaul took place, can it be said that in this respect he did not *possidere ex edicto*[1]? I do not think so. How was the praetor, in a matter in which it was important to make the time as short as possible, to fix precisely a time for the communication of his orders to different parts of the Roman world? Nor was there any requirement or practice, so far as we know, of producing a warrant from the praetor or an attested declaration of the issue of the order when

[1] Compare Ulpian's words in another matter: *Totiens ei sua praesumptio proficit quotiens concurrit cum veritate* (D. xxix 2 fr 30 § 4; cf. xxxiv 5 fr 15). A stipulation between persons at Rome for money to be paid on the same day at Carthage was held by some lawyers to be not invalid, if previous arrangements had been made in view of this stipulation (D. xlv 1 fr 141 § 4).

it was put into execution. But such precipitate action on Naevius' part would be taken into account by the praetor in any judgment he might have to form on the merits of the two parties' conduct; and if Naevius was not justified in his action, he was, as said above, liable to a suit *injuriarum* (Gai. iii 220; cf. D. xlvii fr 10 fr 13 § 3; fr 15 § 31).

7. As to the eviction of Quinctius personally the words of the edict given by Cicero are *Dominum invitum detrudere non placet*[1]. The praetor does not say *non licebit* in correspondence with the preceding directions. Still *placet* is a usual word for expressing decisions both of the senate and of others[2]. Much might depend on the conduct of the owner at the time. If he acquiesced in the bailiff's presence and control, there would be nothing gained by turning him out. The occupation for this purpose would be valid and complete, notwithstanding his presence. But if he resisted, asserted his rights, and attempted to exercise control over the property or remove it from the place or from the control of the bailiffs, the praetor I expect would not object to his being put out. In our case it must be remembered the pasture and farm were common property of Naevius and Quinctius (*de saltu agroque communi a servis communibus vi detruditur* § 28; cf. §§ 79, 85), and any damage thereby suffered by Quinctius would be taken into account in an action *pro socio* or *com. div.* (D. x 3 fr 3), and the interdicts *de vi* and *uti possidetis* might also apply. Some injunction was probably the purport of the orders issued by C. Flaccus *imperator* to whom Quinctius appealed (§ 28). I assume that Naevius was not ejecting Quinctius in order to assert (irrespective of the insolvency proceedings) a claim to the exclusive property, for then the interdicts would clearly apply. But if Naevius proved

[1] So in the case of *damni infecti* D. xxxix 2 fr 15 § 20 *Si quis in possessionem missus nondum possidere jussus sit, an dominus decedere possessione debeat, videamus. Et ait Labeo non decedere, sicuti nec cum creditores vel legatarii mittuntur: id quod est verius*; § 23 *Ubi autem quis possidere jussus est, dominus dejiciendus erit possessione* (see *Introd. Just.* p. 56, above vol. I p. 513). Similarly one in possession *legatorum serv. causa, expellendi heredem jus non habet* (D. xxxvi 4 fr 5 pr).

[2] Keller treats this too lightly (*Sem.* p. 187).

that the slaves ejected Quinctius only in order to insure for the benefit of the creditors the control of the Gallic pasture and farm so far as Quinctius' share was concerned, then I think Cicero's argument on this head would go for nothing.

Cicero says that Quinctius was ejected by the slaves owned in common by him and Naevius. According to the law in the Digest, if a common slave remained in possession, Quinctius would retain possession through him (D. xli 2 fr 40 pr).

On the whole, if an opinion is justifiable on such one-sided and imperfect information, I am inclined to think Quinctius would win the wager, on the ground of his not having been a defaulter in the sense of the edict and having had till now no reasonable opportunity of meeting Naevius' claims on the merits. The appeal to the tribunes was justified by the result: it was plainly equitable that the whole case should be discussed in Quinctius' presence. But on some of the other points, the proceedings of Naevius might probably be found technically defensible. What answer Naevius might have had on the merits, what light he could have thrown on Quinctius' conduct as justifying his imputation of fraudulent absence, we are wholly ignorant.

B. Cicero *pro Roscio Comoedo*[1].

This speech has come down to us in a mutilated condition. Something considerable apparently has been lost both at the commencement and at the end. The speech, as we have it, contains no distribution of the matter, so that we are unable to form any trustworthy opinion as to how much has been lost, though we have no doubt lost more than a rhetorical introduction and a rhetorical peroration. We begin and end in the midst of an argument.

In these circumstances it is more than usually difficult to construct a tenable account of the case. The difficulty is increased by the frequent mention of different sums of money intimately connected with its very substance, whereon however the MSS. maintain no consistent story. I shall adhere closely to the amounts and figures given in Orelli's second edition, without professing any confidence in their correctness, but thinking this to be a safer course than to make conjectural alterations in accordance with some particular theory.

The date of this speech is uncertain. Some contend for the year 77 or 76 B.C., some for 68, others for 66. See below, p. 502.

In the first part of the speech as we have it (§§ 1—15) Cicero deals with the conditions required by the special form of action adopted by the plaintiff. In the second part (§§ 16—56) he goes into the merits of the case in order to vindicate the character and justify the conduct of the defendant, Roscius, for

[1] The most important discussion of this case is by Jul. Baron in *ZRG.* xiv 166 sqq. (1880) republished with slight alterations in *Die Condictionen* § 11 (1881). See also Bethmann-Hollweg *Röm. Civilprozesz* ii 804 sqq. (1865); P. Krüger (giving Keller's view) *ZRG.* vii 237 (1868); Ruhstrat *ZRG.* xvi 34 sqq. An earlier book is an edition by C. A. Schmidt (1839); and there is an essay by Puchta (1832) in *Rhein. Mus.* v 316=*Kleine Schriften* p. 272. Comments will be found also in the books of De Caqueray, Gasquy, Costa, and Greenidge cited above.

whom he is pleading. The facts of the case are mainly to be found in this second part, especially in § 27 foll. Saturius was advocate for the plaintiff (§§ 22, 51). Of him we know nothing. C. Piso was judge.

C. Fannius Chaerea, plaintiff, had bought a slave of the name of Panurgus ('Rascal'), and agreed with Roscius, the great actor, to train him for the stage, and to be partner with him in the slave and his earnings (§ 27)[1]. As nothing is said on the point, they would no doubt have equal shares. Cicero puts the value of the slave untrained at a maximum of 4000 sesterces, and the additional value produced by Roscius' training at 100,000 sesterces. Nor was it merely training. The knowledge that he was Roscius' pupil secured him the favour of all those who were admirers of Roscius. He began a successful career, which however was brought to an end through his being killed by Q. Flavius of Tarquinii. The partners brought an action (*damni injuria* sc. *dati*) under the Aquilian statute against Flavius for damages, which would be reckoned at the greatest value the slave had in the preceding year (§ 32; Gai. iii 210), and this amount would be doubled, if the claim were contested (Gai. iv 171). Roscius appointed his partner, Fannius, as his attorney (*cognitor*) to conduct the case for him. Issue was joined, but before judgment Roscius came to an agreement with the defendant Flavius, and accepted some land as the price of withdrawing his claim. What was the value of the land at that time we are not informed. The land-market was greatly depressed, probably on account either of the social war or of the civil war between Marius and Sulla (the time is uncertain). The farm was not cultivated and there was no homestead. By the time this speech was made, a homestead had been erected and the farm well cultivated. Fannius declared it was worth, according to most editors, 100,000 sesterces, according to Mommsen 600,000[2]. At any rate it seems clear that Roscius, as things turned out, had made a good settlement. The question

[1] Some cases more or less resembling this are discussed in D. xix 5 fr 13 § 1.

[2] Hermes xx p. 317 reading ɑcccIↃↃↃ = 600,000 (500,000 + 100,000) sesterces.

was however disputed, whether he had settled for his own share only or for both partners (§ 34). Fannius maintained the latter; Cicero declares that the former was the fact, and was the only hypothesis consistent with all the proceedings. This took place fifteen years[1] before the present speech (§ 36).

What further happened at the time or indeed for some years afterwards, we do not know. The state of tumult in Italy, and especially in Rome and the neighbourhood, may very likely account for much delay. The next thing of which we hear are some legal proceedings about three years before the present speech. Fannius appears to have brought a claim against Roscius for the same sum[2] of money that he claims now, and, though professing to rely on his books to support the claim for a sum certain, consented to go to arbitration, either under an order from the praetor or more probably by agreement. C. Piso was arbitrator, apparently at the proposal of Fannius (§§ 12, 26). We know nothing more of Fannius' suit on this occasion, than that it was not an action *pro socio* (§ 25), nor do we know any of the proceedings except the result. The matter was arranged. According to Cicero, Piso requested Roscius, in consideration of Fannius' exertions as his attorney, and his trouble in attending the trial, to pay him 100,000 sesterces[3], on condition that Fannius bound himself to give Roscius one half of anything Fannius might recover from Flavius (§ 38). Fannius' advocate appears to have put the matter as a bargain[4] which Roscius

[1] Some editors alter xv to iv; but this would scarcely agree with *re vetere* (§ 38) and *decisionem veterem* contrasted with *repromissionem recentem* (*i.e.* three years ago) in §§ 39, 41.

[2] *De hac pecunia, de his ipsis HS* ↀↀ (§ 12). It was the same amount, being half of the value of the land received from Flavius, but not the same claim which he makes now and which is for the second instalment of the amount promised by R. under the compromise.

[3] Cicero denies that there was any formal stipulation binding Roscius: on the other hand Roscius did stipulate that Fannius should give him half of his expected gain. This last is the *restipulatio* and *repromissio* in § 37 where the words of the latter are given and inaccurately called *restipulatio*. (Müller with other editors conjectures 15,000 for 100,000 sesterces.)

[4] In § 25 *cur non nominas?* is unintelligible to me and probably corrupt, as the text is two lines before. A little higher I think *non* in

entered into in order to prevent an adverse decision of the case. The two modes of viewing the matter are quite compatible with one another, if allowance be made for advocates' language. But Cicero describes the arrangement as one which was welcome to Fannius[1]. He came unasked to Roscius' house; he gave him the undertaking requested; he begged Roscius to pardon him for having been so precipitate, and to inform the judge of the acceptance of the proposal, and he promised not to appear again, as he had no further claim on the partnership. Roscius gave notice to the judge accordingly, and Piso acquitted him (§ 26).

It is the arrangement so made for settlement of the partners' disputes which is sought to be enforced by Fannius in the suit in which Cicero makes this speech. Incidental mention occurs of a first payment having been made by Roscius, and of a second payment being due (§ 51). We do not know when payment was expected or why Roscius did not pay. But in the course of his argument Cicero states that Fannius had gone on with his suit against Flavius and had recovered from him 100,000 sesterces (§ 41). According to the arrangement, Roscius was to have half of whatever Fannius obtained, and as Fannius appears now to be claiming 50,000 sesterces as the second and final instalment from Roscius, we may conjecture that Fannius' success was so soon after the arrangement with Roscius, that the latter practically set one against the other and declined to pay Fannius a sum equal to that which Fannius was also to pay him. True, the fact of Fannius' having recovered these damages from Flavius is denied by Fannius' advocate (§ 41). Flavius was dead, and Cicero offers as proof a statement made by Cluvius who was judge in the case, in the hearing of two senators whose declaration is read in court. This was a usual

proprium non erat judicium is right, though only Müller retains it. Cicero says, 'In this case it was not for an *arbiter* to give a strict verdict any more than for a *judex* to regard all the equities.'

[1] If the figures are right, Fannius had got in cash or promise everything, and Roscius was left with nothing. Roscius is represented in § 23 as not eager for money; perhaps also the land was becoming more valuable.

mode of taking evidence when the witness for some reason was unable to attend in person (cf. Quintil. v 7 § 1; *Dial. de Orat.* 36 fin.). Cluvius apparently made this statement in ordinary conversation with his friends and of course was not sworn, but Cicero argues that he was a man of integrity, selected as judge by Fannius along with Flavius, and therefore entitled to credit, with no motive for making a misstatement, and not likely to tell a lie to please Roscius, even if Roscius, whose high character was well known and was inconsistent with such an action, had used any blandishments for the purpose (§§ 42—51).

The arrangement which closed the arbitration three years before is difficult to understand. If Roscius had handed over the whole of the money suggested by Piso at once, it would have been natural for Fannius to give a binding promise (*repromissio*) to Roscius while Roscius made no such binding promise to Fannius. He did very possibly pay half at once, and both parties may have expected Fannius' suit against Flavius to follow shortly and to render further payment unnecessary. At any rate Cicero challenges any evidence of such a stipulation by Fannius, and promise by Roscius, and in fact asserts that there was none (§§ 13, 14). On the other hand he argues for some time against Fannius' assertion that he has a book entry to establish his claim. A properly made book entry would have answered Fannius' purpose as well as a stipulation, though why this method of putting Roscius under a strict obligation should have been adopted is not clear. As however Roscius' promise was absolute, a book entry was possible. Fannius' promise being practically conditional on success in his suit against Flavius, did not admit of book entry (§ 37; cf. Vat. 336). On the evidence of such a book entry against Roscius something will be said later on.

Apart from any strictly technical repulse of this action for want of legal ground, Cicero proceeds to shew that there is no claim on the merits. Roscius settled the lawsuit against Flavius only so far as his own share in the dead Panurgus was concerned. He left Fannius' claim untouched, and Fannius had as a matter of fact got full compensation in his turn from Flavius. Fannius contended that whatever Roscius got ought by partnership law to be divided between the partners. With Cicero's argument against this contention the speech is broken off. But the substance of it appears to be given.

First, Cicero argues, each partner, like each coheir, is master as regards his own share, and no one can sue for more than his share, unless duly appointed attorney (*cognitor*) for another (§§ 52, 53, 55). Secondly, Fannius was appointed by Roscius to be his attorney in the first suit against Flavius, which fact shewed that Fannius could otherwise have acted only for himself (§ 54). Thirdly, if Roscius had not settled only for himself, Flavius would have justly demanded that Roscius should give the usual security against any further claim in the matter of Panurgus (*amplius neminem petiturum*, § 35: see p. 383) Flavius was fully aware of Fannius being partner in Panurgus, as issue had been joined in the suit between them (§ 35). Fourthly, the agreement, for Roscius to have a moiety of anything Fannius might recover in the second suit from Flavius, shewed that without such agreement one partner had no right to share in the gains of the other, if he dealt with his own share only (§ 56). Lastly, the successful prosecution of his suit by Fannius shewed that Roscius had in fact left Fannius' share and claim untouched (§ 55).

It is plain that the conduct of Roscius in making a separate settlement with Flavius is at the bottom of the present dispute. Had he the right so to act? and is Cicero's comparison of the position of a coheir justifiable? Both Baron and Bethmann-Hollweg deny the latter, and are, to say the least, not satisfied on the former head. Baron however clears Roscius on the ground that the partnership was dissolved by the death of Panurgus, and that no new partnership for obtaining compensation had been formed (l.c. pp. 127, 150). Bethmann-Hollweg points out that an heir lies under no obligation to his fellow heirs, and is master of his share of the inheritance without regard to others, while a partner has to look to what good faith and mutual regard may require (*CP.* ii. pp. 825–6).

I do not think there can be any doubt that Cicero, not only as Baron admits (p. 149), calls Roscius and Fannius partners but also treats them throughout the speech as being partners, both while Panurgus was alive and after his death. It is true that *socii* is a term applied in Roman law to persons who by a will or other cause are tenants in common of the same thing, as well as to persons who have voluntarily entered into partnership relations (Cic. *Quinct.* 16 § 52, 24 § 76 contrasting *voluntaria societas* with *hereditaria societas*; D. x 3 fr 4 § 3; 6 § 12; 8 §§ 3, 4, *etc.*). But it does not seem necessary to restrict Cicero's meaning in some parts of the speech, whereas generally *socii* means partners entitled to and governed by the action *pro socio*. Baron's discussion appears to me to be somewhat affected by two mistakes. First he brings into the case the rule of the XII tables that *nomina ipso jure divisa sunt*[1] and hence infers that a partnership in a debt is inconceivable, and only a partnership in collecting a debt is possible (l.c. p. 149). But the XII tables are speaking only of inheritance, and no doubt the action *fam. ercisc.* did not, usually at least, regard debts (D. x 2 fr 2 § 5; fr 25 § 1); one pound of money owed is as good as another pound, and there is no need for a judge to make a division. But the action *pro socio* did regard debts as well as other forms of property (*actio pro socio nominum rationem habet*, D. xvii 2 fr 43). Strictly speaking, though *prima facie* each is entitled to his share of debts as of other property, the actual division of a particular debt is not a necessary consequence of the respective shares in the partnership: the debts are merely items in the general account between them. And further the partnership formed between Roscius and Fannius was a partnership in Panurgus and not merely in his professional career; and it therefore covered not only the produce of his earnings when alive, but the substituted produce arising from the mode of his death. The *actio pro socio* was certainly required to deal with the doings and negligences, the gains and expenses of partners on the subject-matter of their agreement, and was not put out of

[1] Baron elsewhere also gives an unrestricted application to this rule, *e.g. Institut.* § 117, 3; *Pand.* §§ 244, 245 (pp. 447, 448, ed. 9). Cf. Savigny *Oblig.* § 31.

court immediately on the death of a slave who was the object of the partnership (cf. D. ix 4 fr 10 arg.). That would, I think, be pressing such words as we find in D. xvii 2 fr 63 § 10 and fr 65 § 10 beyond their meaning. Such cases as the sinking of a ship by act of God, or the natural death of a slave, or the collapse of an *insula* might be in point and justify the partnership being considered at an end. The case of Panurgus is different: there was a continuing joint interest, *finis negotio non positus est* (fr 65 § 10 above). Certainly Cicero[1] presumes that an *actio pro socio* was or had been possible in our case (see § 25), and though not a jurisconsult he knew, I expect, a great deal more law than Baron credits him with, and I should readily take his word if he spoke as lawyer, not as advocate. I admit however that we cannot rely on an advocate's looking to law only or stating it impartially.

Baron's second mistake is in supposing, very naturally, the words *in societate dissoluta*, § 38, to contain an assertion by Cicero that the partnership was already dissolved at the time of the settlement proposed by Piso in the arbitration suit. But, if the passage be read carefully, it will be seen that these words are only part of an *argumentum ad hominem*. 'If,' says Cicero, 'what you say is right, that Roscius settled 'with Flavius for the whole of the partnership claim on account 'of the death of Panurgus, how could you expect to get any- 'thing from Flavius? why should Roscius make a restipulation 'for what he had long ago actually got paid? What was Flavius 'to give you when he had already paid to Roscius all he owed? 'The matter of Panurgus' death was twelve years old (*in re 'tam vetere*), the business for which the partnership existed 'was now concluded (*in negotio jam confecto*), the partnership 'was consequently dissolved (*in societate dissoluta*): there could 'remain only the division between Roscius and Fannius of the 'land which Flavius, as plaintiff contended, had conveyed to 'Roscius for the joint account.' But Cicero denies that this

[1] I am glad to see Alf. Pernice (*ZRG*. xvi p. 99; cf. *Labeo* iii 224) differs from Baron, and thinks that Cicero simply neglects the "'fine legal "distinction' between continuance of the partnership and continuance of "the partnership action." Ruhstrat *ZRG*. xvi p. 47 agrees with Baron.

was the true account of the matter, and denies that the partnership was wound up before the arbitration suit (cf. § 25, *etc.*).

As regards Bethmann-Hollweg's strictures, I doubt whether Cicero has pressed the analogy between partner and heir too far, considering the particular point in dispute. There are important differences between their positions, but there are also important resemblances. An heir has a claim only to the division of the assets and fruits and expenses thereon according to the shares of the coheirs: a partner has this and in addition is responsible for his acts and negligences so far as the interests of his partners are touched and for sharing anything which has come to him on partnership account (D. xvii 2 fr 74; fr 67 § 1). But it is true as regards both that they can bring actions separately or together against outsiders, and if they obtain each his own share only, a partner cannot claim for this to be divided any more than an heir can. As regards outsiders the partnership was *nil*: outsiders were not bound by any mutual engagements between persons who made themselves partners; and a suit by partners against outsiders is a suit by each of the partners for his share (D. ix 2 fr 19, 20, 27 § 2), and only, if duly authorised, can one partner sue for his fellows or alienate their property or claims as well as his own. *Nemo ex sociis plus parte sua potest alienare* (D. xvii 2 fr 68 pr): and fr 62 *pro socio* (xvii 2) seems expressly in point: *meae dumtaxat partis pretia perceperam, neque interesse utrum per se partes vendidissem an communiter cum eo qui reliquas partes ad se pervenire diceret. Alioquin eventurum ut etiam si duo socii rem vendiderint unus quisque (ejus) quod ad se pervenerit partem alteri societatis judicio praestare debeat, etc.* Whether other circumstances existed to give a countervailing claim to the other partners is a matter which could only be properly entertained in an *actio pro socio* (cf. D. *ib.* 63 § 9).

Some expressions at the end of 9 § 26 and beginning of 10 § 27 should here be noticed. Plaintiff talks of 'fraud and theft'; 'Roscius had made a bargain to avoid condemnation.' Why, asks Cicero, should Roscius have been afraid of being condemned? The answer given is *Res erat manifesta: furtum erat apertum.* To which Cicero pertinently replies *Cujus rei furtum factum erat?* What was the chattel he stole? Plaintiff replies with a detailed history of the partnership, but we hear no more of the 'theft': what appears to be intended is Roscius' having, as plaintiff contended, settled the whole of the partnership claims and kept the proceeds to himself. Cicero fully admits *Roscium, si quid communi nomine tetigit, praestare debere societati* (12 § 35). But for theft we require physical handling of a moveable corporal object. The damages were not paid in cash but by conveyance of a farm (12 § 33). Roscius' entry on the farm was no act of theft, for *fundi furtum non fit.* But if he took any produce from the farm beyond what was his own share, he would no doubt be chargeable with theft, provided that the farm was not his own but common to him and plaintiff, and that he took the produce with the intention of appropriating it to himself (D. xxii 1 fr 25 pr; xlvii 2 fr 25). And the action *furti* could be brought against a partner as well as the action *pro socio* (D. xvii 2 fr 45, 51 pr). It does not appear that plaintiff had as yet sued Roscius for theft, and the bargain made under Piso's advice would presumably bar it for the future. (Baron (p. 127) treats the charge of theft to be merely rhetorical vituperation of Roscius' conduct and not meant literally. Bethmann-Hollweg (p. 819) thinks it possible the *condictio* now brought by plaintiff was a *condictio furtiva*: for which view there seems to be no ground.)

If indeed it could be shewn that Roscius had purposely concealed his settlement from Fannius, or had obtained some unfair advantage over him, Fannius might reasonably have called him to account (see the general reasoning in D. xvii 2 fr 65 §§ 3—6). Ruhstrat (*ZRG.* xvi 44) supposes Flavius to have made proposals for a settlement to Fannius which Fannius rejected, on account of the land being in his opinion an inadequate compensation. It seems to me more likely that Fannius had in those stormy times been compelled to leave Rome for a period or was otherwise inaccessible to Roscius. But no such suggestions are made by Cicero, and with only this torso of

Cicero's speech left us it is useless to make conjectures. However that be, unfair separate action was a matter for an *actio pro socio*, and the present suit is certainly not that. Cicero expressly reproaches Fannius for not having brought such an action (§ 25). And this reproach appears to make it impossible to suppose that the *arbitrium* which took place three years before could have been the regular *arbitrium pro socio*. It must have been, as Baron contends[1], an informal arbitration agreed on by the parties (*ex compromisso* § 12). Nor is the fact (mentioned by Cicero) that the decision of the arbitrator was given in the absence of Fannius any objection to this view. In both kinds of arbitration the rule was that the parties should be present at the decision (cf. D. iv 8 fr 27 § 4, *etc.*; Paul v 50 § 5). In our case the absence was agreed on by the parties, and there could be little risk of objection to the arbitrator's proceeding (cf. Cod. vii 43 fr 1, 2). Had it been a formal *arbitrium pro socio*, it could not have been brought a second time, nor could a *condictio* be brought either (D. xii 2 fr 28 § 4; Pernice *Labeo* iii 225), and therefore on this ground also Cicero's reproach would have been pointless.

The present action is undoubtedly a *condictio certae pecuniae* (cf. Gai. iv 19), and it is accompanied by a wager for a third part of the damages (*Pecunia petita est certa; cum tertia parte sponsio facta est* § 14). This characteristic identifies it with the *actio pecuniae certae creditae* (described by Gaius iv 13; 171). And we know from Gaius also (iii 124) that *pecunia credita* at least in the *lex Cornelia* (and probably in other matters) was taken by the lawyers to include not only money lent, but all money which was the subject of unconditional obligation. The formula would be: *Si paret Q. Roscium C. Fannio* ↀ *HS dare oportere, Gai Piso, Q. Roscium C. Fannio quinquaginta milia sestertium condemna: si non paret, absolve.*

The amount claimed, if the MSS. are right, was 50,000 sesterces, and is said to be the same amount about which the

[1] One of Baron's arguments is based on *repromittive* in § 12. This is the conjectural reading of Orelli's first edit. The MSS. have *repromittique.*

friendly arbitration had already taken place (§ 12). That arbitration (as already mentioned p. 488) was settled by Piso's requesting Roscius to pay Fannius 100,000 sesterces, of which he actually paid one half. It looks as if we had to allocate that half to remuneration for Fannius' trouble and regard the other 50,000 as Fannius' share of what Roscius received, though why Roscius should have nothing left for himself is a problem. I don't trust the figures.

This being a *strictum judicium* would not admit of Roscius' pleading his claim against Fannius as a set off to Fannius' claim against him (Just. iv 6 § 30: Gaius iv 61 is mutilated).

Two points still await discussion: (1) the ground for action alleged by Fannius; and (2) the relation of the second part of the speech (§ 15 to end) to the first part.

(1) It appears that the formula stated only the amount due, and not the ground of obligation. It was an action for ascertained debt, and the proof of the amount of the debt and of the mode of contraction would lie together in a nutshell. There were, as Cicero says, only three grounds on which a definite sum of money could be claimed (*i.e. inter vivos*, legacy being out of the question): viz., money paid down, money promised by formal stipulation, money debited in the ledger[1]. Proof of any one of these was sufficient without discussion of the transactions which led to it. *Plus petere*, 'excessive claim,' was of course fatal, and the addition of the wager made the consequences of failure more serious (§ 10). But there were advantages in the form of action (see p. 71).

If Cicero could shew that none of the three grounds, on which this form of action rested, existed in this case, he had a complete technical answer to the action. According to him Fannius admits that he never paid down the money; he produces no evidence whatever of any stipulation (§ 13); he relies on an alleged book entry in his *adversaria* (§ 5). The *adversaria* were something in the nature of a day-book or waste-book, loose papers on which entries were made as the business was done day by day. From these the ledger would be posted up monthly or thereabouts (§ 8). It is obvious that

[1] Compare the language of the Baetic inscription given on p. 101.

such tablets might contain much that was of slight or temporary importance, and might more easily admit insertions or additions at a later time, than would a ledger with its regular order and definite headings. The custom of accepting book entries as a ground of obligation evidently sprang from regular commercial business duly recorded in a book intended for the owner's own permanent use and reference. If the entry of an agreed amount of money debited against another is found only in the loose sheets of a day-book and not in the ledger, it would naturally be supposed to be a note for temporary purposes, and not intended (unless eventually entered in the ledger) to be set up as a legitimate obligation (§§ 6, 7). We have only Cicero's argument on the matter, but reason seems to be with him. Such a ground for not entering in the ledger as that suggested by Fannius[1], viz. that Roscius did not wish the matter to be known, is hardly worth discussing. If true, it amounts probably to a statement that no legal obligation was intended and only a friendly understanding took place (§ 9).

Another essay contains a full explanation of *litterarum obligatio*. Baron seems to have no definite conception of it (see also his *Institutionen* i § 119)[2]. That Fannius could have maintained his book-entry against Roscius to have been in the books of Perperna and Saturius seems to me incredible as contrary to the usage of merchants and the nature of the contract. What was the reason for demanding production of the *tabulae* of Perperna, who was on the bench in this case (§ 22) and of Saturius, who was Fannius' advocate, I do not attempt to guess. No hint is given what the *tabulae* contained.

(2) The second part of the speech is according to Cicero intended not to defend Roscius from the technical suit (that was sufficiently done by Cicero's shewing that no ground for the action had been proved by Fannius) but to vindicate the

[1] Kappeyne van de Coppello (*Abhandl.* p. 214) takes *rogatus eras ne referrem* (§ 9) as a positive statement that Roscius was unwilling that this should be entered in the *codex* and thus become an obligatory debt. It seems to me to be merely an allegation of Fannius.

[2] I have dealt with some of the passages quoted by Baron and others on this matter at the end of the essay on *litt. oblig.*

character of Roscius from foul aspersions of fraud. In fact Cicero demurs to the action: admitting all that Fannius says to be true, he declares no cause of action had been made good: no money paid down, no stipulation, no valid book entry. But Cicero is not content that a client like Roscius should lie under the smallest suspicion of breach of faith, or that a judge like Piso should think unfavourably of his client, even though he decided for him, or that such assessors as were present on the bench[1] should hear only a bare technical defence. He volunteers to shew that Roscius is open to no charge whatever; that all suits which could be brought against him, whether strict or wide, whether statutable or praetorian, nay that all charges *in foro domestico* before a tribunal judging of good conduct and morality only are alike capable of complete defence and refutation, as much as if they were all legally involved in the present issue. And accordingly he proceeds to discuss the whole dispute and set forth its history, so as to make clear that Roscius' conduct throughout had been legal, honest, and honourable (§ 15).

Baron takes these last words *perinde ac si in hanc formulam omnia judicia legitima, omnia arbitria honoraria, omnia officia domestica conclusa et comprehensa sint* as referring to the abstract character of the *condictio certi*. According to him the basis of claim was not declared before the praetor and was not stated in the issue for trial, and any basis of obligation might on the trial be put forward by the plaintiff. 'Fannius alleged 'two such bases *pecunia credita* formed by literal contract, and 'partnership. He had entered into a *sponsio*, and if he proved 'his book entry he won his wager, if he did not prove it, he 'had the other string to rely upon, and consequently Cicero 'was bound to address himself to the obligation of partnership, 'as he does in the second part of the speech.'

The much discussed passage in the Digest xii 1 fr 9 pr[2] *Certi condictio competit ex omni causa, etc.* Baron (l.c. pp. 131—135, 145) takes to mean that, besides any special action,

[1] So rightly Schmidt *ad loc.*, comparing Cic. *Quinct.* § 5 *Quos tibi advocasti.*

[2] On its probable interpolation see Pernice *ZRG.* xxvi 252.

and concurrently therewith, a plaintiff might always bring a *condictio certi*, and that the requisite certainty might be obtained, if necessary, by an estimate made at plaintiff's risk. In the present case Fannius on the ground of partnership could only claim half the land which Roscius had got from Flavius, and consequently had to make an assessment of its value; which he put at 100,000 sesterces. But Baron admits that no such right of getting certainty by independent estimate is ever mentioned in these cases, except in the Basilica, *e.g.* ii 596 f.; and it is generally considered a post-Justinian practice. Secondly, if such were the practice in Cicero's time, would he not in some way have alluded to it in this speech, particularly in §§ 32, 33? It is I think quite inconsistent with Cicero's language in §§ 13, 14. Thirdly, I do not agree, any more than do most lawyers[1], with Baron's interpretation of fr 9 *de reb. cred.* even supposing that we have there Ulpian's words and not Tribonian's. I take the law simply to mean that any business which gives rise to one person's being bound formally to make over to another (*dare oportere*) a liquidated amount of money or a clearly ascertained thing may form a basis for *condictio certi*. Had a slave, instead of land, been delivered to Roscius, when he ought by a definite obligation to have been delivered to Fannius, and had died, a *condictio certi* would have been allowable under the law as laid down in the Digest—quite a different case from ours. The certainty must either be found in the business itself or arise from a stipulation, *etc.* made in relation to it.

I am inclined to think Cicero to have been right in saying that the issue raised by this action depended on one of the three grounds of obligation being shewn, and that in Roscius'

[1] See for instance Karlowa *RG.* ii p. 764; Pernice *Labeo* iii p. 228; Kappeyne van de Coppello *Abhandl.* p. 220. Bekker vigorously rejects the possibility of Baron's view (*ZRG.* xvii 49 sqq.; see also his *Actionen* i 136). Keller takes a similar view of this fragment to Baron's, provided the obligation was originally one for payment of money, but he holds this to be one of the latest developments of the Jurists and therefore long after Cicero (*Civ. Pro.* p. 440, n. 107). Cogliolo (Padelletti p. 330 i) accepts Baron's view. But see Girard *Manuel* p. 599 ed. 2.

case it depended on the validity of book entry in *adversaria*. If Fannius' contention were negatived, the judge ought to pronounce in Roscius' favour. But Cicero was too good an advocate to be content with arguing a dry point of law. If Fannius was substantially in the right, though mistaken in bringing this action or unfortunate in his proof, the judge might hesitate to condemn him, and a *non-liquet* might leave Roscius still exposed to suit and still under an imputation of sharp practice or dishonesty. Piso had been concerned with the case before; but would be none the worse for having his half recollection refreshed and perhaps recoloured. Besides a Roman *judex* was not a jurisconsult called to decide an abstract question, but one sworn to do justice on a particular issue between man and man, and however strict the issue might be, he would more readily form his opinion and deliver his decision, if he thought the merits as well as the law were against Fannius[1]. Cicero's treatment was calculated to secure this without throwing any legitimate doubt on his contention that the law was on Roscius' side.

We do not know what were really the respective merits of Roscius and Fannius' conduct or what was Piso's decision. Cicero's speech has at any rate had the effect of surrounding Roscius' name with eulogies which posterity will be slow to believe are due only to the boldness of the advocate or to the popular appreciation of defendant's qualities as an actor.

P.S. R. v. Mayr in a recent book (*Die Condictio, etc.* 1900) holds[2] that the arbitration mentioned in §§ 12, 26 was an *arbitrium pro socio*, and that the latter part of Cicero's speech is intended to shew that under a different *formula* Fannius is raising again a matter already decided and thereby entitling Roscius to an *exceptio rei judicatae*. Even if the former proceeding was a non-judicial arbitration, he would be entitled to an *exceptio pacti* (D. iv 8 fr 13 § 2), so that the character of the arbitration is not of great moment (Mayr p. 60). He

[1] See the passage from Quintilian quoted below, p. 530.

[2] Throughout his discussion Mayr calls the speech *pro Q. Roscio Comoeda* (sic !) *oratio*.

conjectures some (impossible) supplements in § 25, which would clearly express Cicero's object to be the establishment of such a plea. Against Bethmann-Hollweg's objection (*Röm. C. P.* ii 809) that *quantum aequius meliusve* § 85 does not suit an arbitration enforced by a *stipulatio poenae* (see above, p. 320) the answer seems ready that all arbitrations are based on the desire to get a free and equitable adjustment of the dispute, and the stipulation comes into play only on this adjustment being disobeyed. Another objection (with which Mayr agrees, pp. 59, 60), that an arrangement putting an end to the arbitration is incompatible with an acquittal by the judge (§ 26), is I think as readily answered by the simple supposition that an acquittal by the judge was part of the terms of the arrangement, or that the language is only a loose description of the result.

Prof. Morris H. Morgan (in *Harvard Studies*, vol. XII (1901), which he has kindly sent me) discusses the date of this speech, and makes out a good case for the year 66 B.C. This date accords with the depression in the land market, at the time of Roscius' settlement with Flavius, being due to Sulla's confiscations (§§ 33, 37); and the judgeship of the *eques* Cluvius would then fall after B.C. 70, when the *equites* were no longer disqualified (see above, p. 322). And a date approaching the close of Roscius' career (he died *cir.* 62 B.C.) best suits the language of § 23. There is however a difficulty in the language of § 44 (*mea adulescentia*), which is hardly met by referring, as Bethmann-Hollweg does, to the words *defendi rempublicam adulescens* in *Philipp.* ii § 118. An old man looking back on himself at 42 may naturally call himself young 20 years ago, but Cicero after a dozen years of brilliant advocacy and holding the praetorship would hardly speak of his then age of 40 as *adulescentia.*

On the other hand if the depression is referred to the Social or Marsic War (B.C. 91—88), this speech would fall in B.C. 76—73; and consequently the judgeship of Cluvius, two or three years before, would fall during the period when *equites* were disqualified. Some writers try to overcome the difficulties of the earlier date by altering XV in § 13; see above, p. 488 n. 1.

C. CICERO *pro M. Tullio*[1].

This speech is supposed to have been delivered 682 or 683 U.C. = 72 or 73 A.C. As far as we can make out the story (in the present state of the MS. which is really only a series of fragments) the facts appear to be as follows. M. Tullius, the plaintiff, had in the district of Thurii an estate, which he had inherited from his father. It was adjacent to an estate formerly belonging to M. Claudius, a senator, who had bought it in good condition at a high price, and recently sold it to P. Fabius the defendant. Fabius had made money in some way while serving under the consul in Macedonia and Asia, and now gave Claudius half as much again, though the homesteads had been burnt and the land was waste. He became dissatisfied with his purchase and advertised it for sale. Apparently Fabius had bought it in partnership with Acerronius, and now persuaded him to buy the whole. In this district and conveniently close to Fabius' land there was a plot of 200 jugera, called the Populian Century which had been in the possession of Tullius' father, and still belonged to Tullius. Fabius seems to have included this in the quantity of land advertised for sale, and, in the absence both of Tullius and of Tullius' agent and farm bailiff, pointed out the bounds of the estate to Acerronius, but did not deliver him due (*vacuam*) possession of the Populian Century. Tullius had written to his agent and bailiff on the matter, and we may conjecture that Fabius was prevented by Tullius' slaves from doing so. Fabius now brings to his estate a number of bold and strong men and arms them. They go

[1] This speech has been edited with notes and essays by P. E. Huschke in I. G. Huschke's *Analect. Litteraria*, 1826 and by F. L. Keller in his *Semestria* vol. i. Explanations are given also in the works of De Caqueray, Gasquy, Costa, and Greenidge cited above. The speech itself was a long one: cf. Tac. *Dial.* 20 *Quis de exceptione et formula perpetietur illa immensa volumina quae pro M. Tullio aut Aulo Caecina legimus?*

about armed and brawl in the neighbourhood; amongst other things kill two slaves of Q. Catius Aemilianus, and keep the farms and roads in a state of constant warfare. Soon after Tullius comes to his Thurine estate. While he is there, Fabius walking about his (or Acerronius') estate sees a building in the Populian Century, and a slave of Tullius named Philinus there. 'What's your business on my land?' says Fabius. The slave said his master was at the homestead, and referred Fabius to him. Fabius takes Acerronius with him, comes to Tullius, and formally proposes, in order that the ownership of the land might be determined, either to eject Tullius or be ejected by him. Tullius says he will eject Fabius and will, as usual in such cases, make a formal engagement to attend trial at Rome. Fabius accepts and they soon part. But the next night just before daybreak, a numerous band of Fabius' slaves come to the building in the Populian Century, break in by force, attack the slaves of Tullius who were few and unprepared, kill them nearly all, and damage the roof and homestead. Of the slaves (who were valuable) one, Philinus, escapes though severely wounded and tells Tullius, who sends for his friends to advise him.

Tullius applies to the praetor Metellus, who directs an issue under the edict first proposed by M. Lucullus five years before for damage done by armed bands[1]. The pith of the issue is given in these words: *Quantae pecuniae paret dolo malo familiae P. Fabii vi hominibus armatis coactisve damnum datum esse M. Tullio.* The damages were laid by Tullius at a sum not told us, but which would form the maximum in the praetor's *formula*; and the penalty was to be fourfold the amount at which the 'Recoverers' who were to try the issue should assess the damage. L. Quinctius (*vir primarius*, as Cicero calls him, § 1) was advocate for Fabius.

Fabius fought hard before the praetor to get him to insert the word *injuria* in the formula (before *datum*?) and even appealed, but without success, to the tribunes of the *plebs* against the praetor's refusal. (A similar appeal is mentioned

[1] See above, p. 216.

in the speech *pro Quinctio* § 63.) He now complained of the praetor's unfairness in refusing to insert the word (§ 38).

Fabius admitted (1) that Tullius had suffered damage and that men had been killed, (2) that this was done by his slaves, (3) that it was done by force and by men armed for the purpose; but denied that it was done wrongfully (*dolo malo* §§ 24, 25, 31). Evidently his contention was that these acts were only in self-defence against the conduct and assaults of Tullius' slaves. He asserted that the land, on which the building was erected, was his (Fabius') land, and further alleged various charges or suspicious facts against Tullius' slaves; viz. that one of Fabius' slaves, who had been seen in company with Tullius' slaves, had disappeared; that a cottage of his had been set fire to by Tullius' slaves; and that Fabius was in fear of an attack from them. Cicero denies the allegations of fact, and adds that even if true neither they nor Fabius' fears were any adequate ground for such a murderous attack (§§ 54, 55).

Cicero's main argument is to establish that the admitted facts were sufficient to insure condemnation. He argued that the whole intention of the edict was to put down violence by armed slaves, without inquiry whether there was any justification for their conduct.

1. This is shewn by the refusal of the praetor to insert *injuriā* in the formula. The object of obtaining the insertion was to enable the question of justification to be argued. The praetor, according to Cicero, said that there could be no justification for armed violence carried on by a band of slaves. For ordinary violence the *lex Aquilia* gave adequate remedy, and allowed a plea of justification to be raised: damage under that statute must be *injuria datum, i.e.* wrongfully caused: but under Lucullus' edict the case was different. Brigand-like violence by slaves must be suppressed: to get a prompt decision the court was to be not a single judge but *recuperatores*: the charge was laid not against specified individuals but against the whole band: the penalty was to be fourfold, not twofold, the damage; and *injuria* was left out (cf. §§ 10, 11, 38—42). (Cicero compares the two interdicts *de vi* (§ 44), and *de vi*

hominibus armatis to point out how much more severe the law was when armed men were brought to the decision of a legal question; but the MS. is mutilated (§46) and the general argument can be better dealt with in the speech *pro Caecina*.)

It is not difficult to imagine what Quinctius' answer was to this. He no doubt urged that the reason why the praetor refused to insert *injuria* in the formula, was because *dolo malo*, which was in the formula, included it: and that why he pressed the insertion of *injuria* was in order to remove all chance of cavil on Tullius' part, not because *dolo malo* did not fully permit him to plead a justification for the violence under the actual circumstances.

2. Cicero accordingly deals at length with the meaning and purpose of *dolo malo* in this formula. It was, as he contended, an addition in favour of the plaintiff, and not in favour of the defendant. It made a conviction possible where a *familia* had contrived and prepared the attack, but had not themselves borne a hand in it. It made a person liable, if it was done *consilio et opera ejus*, as well as if he had done it in person[1]. *Vis* does not include *dolus malus*: but *dolus malus* includes *vis*[2]. Every part of this proceeding was characterised by *dolus malus*, both their forming the plan, their taking arms, their selecting time and place, their breaking into the building, their killing the slaves, their pulling down the roof. And how then can it be said that the assault as a whole was not done *dolo malo*, when those words are strictly applicable to every incident separately? (§§ 26—34).

3. Quinctius here took a technical objection. He insisted that *dolus malus* cannot properly be applied to a *familia* (§ 35). Presumably his reason was that *dolus malus* implies a mind, and that a *familia* as a whole has no mind (like the old argu-

[1] Cf. D. xlvii 2 fr 50 §§ 1—3.

[2] Compare Ulpian in D. xlvii 8 fr 2 § 8 *Qui vim facit dolo malo fecit, non tamen qui dolo malo facit utique et vi facit. Ita dolus habet in se vim, et sine vi siquid callide admissum est aeque continebitur. ib.* § 2 *Dolo malo facere potest non tantum is qui rapit sed et qui praecedente consilio ad hoc ipsum homines colligit armatos ut damnum det bonave rapiat.* (But the edict there is somewhat wider than in our speech.)

ment that a corporation has no conscience[1]). To this Cicero replies that the argument would prove not merely that Fabius should be acquitted, but that no conviction against a *familia* was possible, and the edict would thus be reduced to an absurdity. What more he said the mutilation of the MS. prevents our knowing. But it may be supposed that he argued that though sometimes an expression like *familia* referred to the body of slaves as a whole, yet on other occasions it was merely a short phrase for the individuals, one or more, who composed it. Thus Ulpian says on this edict (D. xlvii 8 fr 2 § 14) *Haec actio familiae nomine competit, non imposita necessitate ostendendi qui sunt ex familia homines qui rapuerunt vel etiam damnum dederunt. Familiae autem appellatio servos continet, hoc est eos qui in ministerio sunt, etiamsi liberi esse proponantur vel alieni bona fide nobis servientes.* And again D. L 16 fr 195 § 3 (quoted by Huschke p. 151) *servitutium* (*servitium* conj. Mommsen) *solemus appellare familias, ut in edicto praetoris ostendimus sub titulo 'de furtis' ubi praetor loquitur de familia publicanorum. Sed ibi non omnes servi sed corpus quoddam servorum demonstratur huius rei causa paratum, hoc est, vectigalis causa, alia autem parte edicti omnes servi continentur, ut 'de hominibus coactis' et 'vi bonorum raptorum'; item, etc.*

4. Such a construction of the edict and formula as Cicero puts forward was based[2], Quinctius appears to have argued, on an exaggerated respect for human life, which is not in harmony with other legislation. The laws of the XII tables sanctions killing a thief at night, and, if the thief defend himself, even in the daytime. Another law allows the killing of one who has struck a tribune to go unpunished (§ 47). These laws shew that the mere fact of killing is not enough to ensure condemnation: the further question must be considered, whether the killing was justified (§ 49). Cicero replies that it was

[1] Cf. D. iv 3 fr 15 *An in municipes de dolo detur actio dubitatur. Et puto ex suo quidem dolo non posse dari, quid enim municipes dolo facere possunt?* xli 2 fr 1 § 22 *Municipes per se nihil possidere possunt quia universi consentire non possunt.*

[2] Keller (p. 643) rightly refers to Cicero's own language in the *Pro Milone* §§ 7—11 as expressing what Quinctius probably said.

necessary to secure the life of the tribunes, if magistrates were to be expected to do their duty of protecting the citizens: and that the restriction on killing a thief by day was a proof of the reluctance of the laws to sanction men's taking the law into their own hands. Even accidental injury met with no indulgence from the XII tables (§§ 49—51). Later on (some pages having been lost) Cicero appears to have contrasted Quinctius' arguments for impunity with the law on forcible or stealthy acts. Even if Fabius owned the land in dispute on which Tullius had erected the building, he could not pull it down without the knowledge or against the opposition of Tullius who claims it as his own. Fabius would come under the interdict *quod vi aut clam*, and be liable to compensate Tullius for the injury done to his building[1]. Can it be said that the law will justify the killing of the men who were in the building? (§ 53).

Keller has set out what he takes to be Quinctius' view of the facts in a speech for the defence well devised and in some parts eloquent. Quinctius is made to claim that the Populian Century was his property, that Tullius had endeavoured to seize it, and had erected a house to protect his slaves, that he kept there a band of ruffians who spread terror through the neighbourhood, and that Fabius, hearing of an intended fresh expedition of these brigands, determined to prevent it by destroying the building and crushing the resisting slaves, but took nothing away, and was then ready to have the legal ownership determined by law.

I am myself disposed to connect Fabius' assault with the arrangement made for a formal ejection. Fabius had given Tullius the choice whether he would be plaintiff or defendant. Tullius chose the position of defendant: he was possessor at the time and proposed to continue. Fabius would come with his friends to the spot and demand possession: Tullius would eject him with sufficient show of force to enable Fabius to assert that he had been *vi dejectus*, and then apply for an interdict to have the title to possession duly tried. It would appear as if Fabius repented of his offer of the option to Tullius, and thought it would be wise to get possession himself.

[1] Cf. D. xliii 24 fr 1 § 2.

Knowing that Tullius's slaves were in occupation, he collects his own followers, and on the day after the arrangement had been made, before daybreak, makes for the building, and meeting with resistance was led on into a fight. He would say that he intended nothing more than a quiet and conventional seizure (*vis quotidiana*)[1] and had brought a superior force with him in order to prevent any imprudent resistance; that Tullius' slaves however met him with violence, and in self-defence his followers killed them and damaged the building. Then he would say the law was on his side: *arma armis repellere* was allowable if done *non ex intervallo sed ex continenti* (see Ulpian's language on the Interdict *de vi* D. xliii 16 fr 3 § 9)[2].

The disregard of the arrangement which had been come to with Tullius, the deliberate use of arms (cf. *Caecin.* § 45), and the bloody result would I think be fatal to Fabius' cause, even if the terms of the issue admitted (contrary to Cicero's argument) of a justification being attempted. With *dolo malo* in the formula I do not see how a justification could be excluded on the words. At the same time Fabius' persistence in his claim for the insertion of *injuria* and his charge of unfairness against the praetor for his refusal (§ 38) certainly strengthen Cicero's position. The analogy of the interdicts and probable object of Lucullus in first framing the edict make one incline to think that in the main Cicero's argument is right.

[1] See *Caecin.* 32 § 92 and below, p. 514.

[2] In Cicero's letter to Trebatius (*Fam.* vii 14) he jokes the lawyer on his position with Caesar's army in Gaul: *Tantum metuo ne artificium tuum tibi parum prosit; nam, ut audio, istic 'non ex jure manum consertum sed magis ferro rem repetunt'; et tu soles ad vim faciundam adhiberi: neque est quod illam exceptionem in interdicto pertimescas 'quo tu prior vi hominibus armatis non veneris'; scio enim te non esse procacem in lacessendo.* I am only afraid that your professional craft is of little good to you, for I am told where you are (to quote Ennius) 'men link not hand in lawful course, but use the sword their right to enforce': and *you* are habitually called in to use violence! Nor need you much fear that plea in the interdict 'Provided that thou hast not been the first to come with 'violence and armed men; for I know that you are not very forward in 'attack.' For *manum consertum* cf. Cic. *Mur.* 12 § 26; Gell. xx 10 § 7. (Some interpreters take *soles ad v. fac. adhib.* to refer to Trebatius' usual work in advising on conventional struggles. See below, p. 514.)

D. Cicero *pro Caecina*[1].

This very brilliant speech has many points of resemblance with that *pro Tullio*, but fortunately is preserved in much better condition. We seem to have the whole with the exception of one not very large or important part of the argument. It is supposed to have been delivered in 685 U.C. = 69 B.C.

The case had been argued before Recoverers (*recuperatores*) twice already without any decision having been come to, a fact which Cicero chooses to attribute rather to the reluctance of the Recoverers to pass so severe a condemnation of Aebutius' character and conduct than to any doubt of the right verdict (§§ 6—10). Condemnation in an Interdict proceeding was not however followed by technical infamy (D. xliii 16 fr 13).

M. Fulcinius of the town of Tarquinii in Etruria had married a lady of the same place named Caesennia and was a banker at Rome. They had one son. The dowry of his wife had been paid to him in money and he invested it in some land in the Tarquinian district[2]. Soon after he gives up his bank and buys some farms adjoining this land of his wife's. He dies leaving by will his son as heir, but bequeathing a life interest (usufruct) in all his estate to his wife in common with their son. The young man soon dies, leaving P. Caesennius as his

[1] The leading treatment of this speech is by Keller *Semestr.* 273 sq. (1842). See also C. A. Jordan's edition (1848); Bethmann-Hollweg's essay in *Röm. Civilprocesz* ii 827 sqq. (1868) and various writers on Interdicts, *e.g.* Karlowa *RG.* ii 325 (who gives many references); Savigny *Besitz* § 40; Kappeyne van de Coppello *Abhandl.* p. 129 sqq.; Ubbelohde *Glück's Pand.* § 1863 *a*; and more fully §§ 1848, 1848 *a* (pub. 1896). Comments are also found in De Caqueray, Gasquy, Costa, and Greenidge's works already cited.

[2] This is spoken of as a sale by Fulcinius to his wife at a time when cash was difficult to obtain. He had the cash representing his wife's dowry employed in his business and treated it as payment for the land. Cf. D. xxiii 4 fr 21.

heir, a legacy to his wife of a large amount of money, and one to his mother of a larger share[1] of his property. In order to satisfy these legacies the young man's estate is put up for sale by auction, not as a whole but in detail. It occurs both to Caesennia and to her friends that it would be a good thing for her to buy the land (*i.e.* the reversion after her usufruct of the land) formerly her husband's, which adjoined her own land (*i.e.* the dowry land) with some of the money which was coming to her under her son's will. She had been in the habit of employing in business matters a man named Sex. Aebutius, in no way related to her, but one of whose business ability she had a high opinion. Aebutius accordingly is commissioned to attend the sale. He does so and bids for this land: it is knocked down to him, and he is debited in the banker's[2] books for the purchase money and afterwards credited for its payment, Caesennia having found the money. Caesennia took possession of the land and let it: soon after she married A. Caecĭna[3], and four years after the purchase, died. By her will she made her husband A. Caecĭna heir to 11½ shares out of 12, and of the remaining half-twelfth gives two-thirds to M. Fulcinius a freedman of her first husband, and one-third to Aebutius, who was thus

[1] This interpretation is preferable to 'the greater part,' both on other grounds and because no reference is made to the *lex Voconia* which otherwise might be a question in the case. See Jordan *ad loc.*

[2] *Argentarius.* A banker was usually the responsible person in an auction. A *praeco* called out the bids. Cf. Gai. iv 126 *a.*

[3] The family of Caecina was called on the Etruscan tombs at Volaterrae *Ceicnas,* and hence it has been supposed the vowel *i* was short (Caecĭna) as *Lekne* is supposed to be for Licĭnius. Prof. A. S. Wilkins points out that *musni* at Cortona seems to be for *Musōnius* (cf. Deecke's Müller i 488) and *meknate* of Perusia for *Maecēnatem.* If so, the elision in Etruscan of the vowel *i* in Caecina is no argument for its penultima being short. But the river (and railway station) *Cecina* (near *Vada Volaterranorum*) is pronounced with penult short in modern Italian. (So in Dante *Inferno* xiii 9.) 'There are in Italian words for a boy and girl '*cecino* and *cecina* which in living Tuscan are pronounced with accent 'on penult; but *Cecina* as name of a town, of a river and as an old Roman 'name are pronounced with accent on antepenult' (L. Barboni in *Antologia ricreativa* p. 490 Livorno 1895). On the whole I am inclined to think that the name Caecina had a short penult.

heir to one seventy-second part of the lady's estate (§§ 10—17). He soon began to make himself disagreeable. Caecina was a Volaterran: and the people of Volaterrae had taken arms against Sulla who had passed a law which reduced their civic position to that of the people of Ariminum (§ 102). Aebutius declared that this disqualified Caecina from being heir. Caecina was not frightened, but on Aebutius' claiming a larger part of Caesennia's property than he was entitled to applied to the court to appoint an arbitrator for division of Caesennia's estate among the coheirs[1]. A few days afterwards (*illis paucis diebus*) Aebutius gives him formal notice in the forum at Rome that the land which he had bid for at the sale of the younger Fulcinius's property, was not part of Caesennia's estate, but was Aebutius' own: 'He had bought it for himself.' 'What! 'that land which without dispute Caesennia held as long as she 'lived, do you assert to be yours?' says, or is supposed to say, Caecina. 'True,' Aebutius replies, 'but Caesennia occupied it by virtue of the usufruct which her first husband left her.' Caesennia being dead, the usufruct ceased, and Aebutius claimed to have bought the land (*i.e.* the ownership subject to the usufruct) for himself (§§ 18, 19).

Caecina consults his friends on this new contention of Aebutius, and determines at once to try his right to the ownership of the farm. As a usual preliminary for this purpose he makes an appointment with Aebutius to go to the spot on a certain day and there be formally turned off the land by Aebutius. Accordingly Caecina and his friends go to a place named Axia[2], not far from the land in question. They are informed that Aebutius has collected and armed a large number of persons, both free and slave. Aebutius comes himself to Axia and notifies Caecina that he has got armed men, and that if Caecina comes on to the land, he will never leave it. Caecina and his friends, disbelieving Aebutius' threats, determine to make the attempt. They find men placed at every approach, not merely to the land in dispute, but also to the adjacent farm

[1] I agree with Keller in reading *iste* for *ipse*.

[2] Identified probably with Castel d'Asso about 6 miles west of Viterbo (Bunbury in *Dict. Geog.* s.v.).

which was Caesennia's dowry. Caecina being driven off from there by armed men tries another approach. The disputed land on this side was bounded by a straight row of olive trees. As Caecina was approaching them, Aebutius met him with all his forces, summoned one of his slaves named Antiochus to him, and in a loud voice ordered him to cut down anyone who entered the row of olives. Caecina saw the armed men and heard the order, but still went nearer, and was just passing within the boundary made by the olives, when Antiochus armed, as well as others, made a rush: Caecina retreated, and his friends and advocates in fear betook themselves to flight with him (§§ 20—22). These being the facts, the praetor, P. Dolabella issued his injunction, in the ordinary way *de vi hominibus armatis* without any qualifying clause (*sine ulla exceptione*), simply directing Aebutius 'to restore whence he had ejected.' Aebutius replied that he had restored. A wager was made raising the issue, and Recoverers were appointed to try it (§ 23). This is a short statement of the facts, as told with much humour and skill by Cicero.

Aebutius' contention that Caecina was disqualified for being heir to Caesennia, because he was a Volaterran, is dealt with by Cicero at the end of the speech, and may be well deferred for the present. Caecina's application for an arbiter to divide Caesennia's estate was a direct defiance of Aebutius. The *judicium familiae erciscundae* was a suit founded on the XII tables, and lay only between heirs or others entitled to a deceased's estate. If a man's being heir was disputed, and he was not in possession of his part of the estate, he could be repelled, until he had proved his title to the inheritance. Caecina was no doubt in possession of most of Caesennia's estate, and the question, whether he was heir or not, was one cognisable by the judge in the case. Under the circumstances it was the proper suit to bring, and Caecina thus challenged a decision on his alleged disqualification (Gai. ii 219; D. x 2 fr 1, 36, 43). Had Aebutius accepted the challenge, it is possible that he would thereby have admitted Caecina to be coheir (Keller *Sem.* p. 283 sqq.; Vangerow *Pand.* § 514. 4 and others on D. x 2 fr 37). Anyhow, instead of doing so, he raised a different question, and meeting Caecina in the forum formally gave him notice, that he claimed as his own the farm which had fallen to his bidding at the sale of the younger Fulcinius' estate; 'he had bought it for himself.' Caecina of course disputed the claim, but the issue, whether a particular piece of land was parcel of the inheritance or the private property of one of the coheirs, was not determinable in a suit for dividing the inheritance (D. x 2 fr 25 § 7, 45 pr; xliv 1 fr 18). Caecina had therefore to face a suit in respect to the ownership of this particular farm. If Caecina were possessor, Aebutius would have to vindicate it as his own, and be put to the proof of his title. If Aebutius were possessor, Caecina would bring his suit as heir to eleven and a half twelfths of it (D. v 4 fr 1 § 1) and would have the burden of proving Caesennia's ownership and his own inheritance. Meantime the suit for division of her estate must either be postponed, or, if it proceeded as regards other items about which there appears to have been no dispute, the ultimate division of this farm, if proved to be part of Caesennia's estate, would be effected in default of agreement by a suit *communi dividundo* (D. v 4 fr 7; x 2 fr 20 § 4)[1].

It was important therefore to settle who was possessor. In Gaius' time (iv 148; D. vi 1 fr 24) a suit for the ownership of land was often preceded by a judicial inquiry into the possession, and this was done by the interdict *uti possidetis*. The proceedings so far as known to us are described above (Book VI chap. XVI C). It is a question what if any relation this procedure had to what we find in Cicero's time, as shewn in this speech and in that *pro Tullio*. In Gaius (iv 170) we read (if the text be right, Book VI chap. XVI D) of *vim facere* apparently as a formal method of bringing the matter to a legal issue, but it is *after* the grant of the interdict, and there is no allusion to any private arrangement between the litigants. In our speech the dispute is frequently spoken of as one relating to possession

[1] See Keller p. 359 sqq.; Ubbelohde *Glück's Pand.* § 1848 *a* p. 176.

Keller suggests a possible additional difficulty for Caecina, if the suit was brought at Tarquinii, and thus might expire with the expiration of the magistrate's *imperium* (Gai. iv 105).

(*e.g.* §§ 2, 32, 35, 41, *etc.*); and to facilitate a judicial process conventional force was to be used (*vim moribus*[1] *facere* § 2; *ex conventu vim fieri* § 22; *ut vis ac deductio moribus fieret* § 32). But this was to be done by agreement between Caecina and Aebutius, apparently *before* any application to the praetor.

Keller (in an excellently written essay in *ZRG.* xi p. 322 foll.; see also *Semestria* p. 369 sqq.) holds that the *deductio quae moribus fit* served to introduce the suit for ownership *per sponsionem*, where there was no dispute about the possession, and that the interdict *uti possidetis* was used when there was such a dispute (cf. D. xliii 17 fr 1 § 3). Karlowa (*Beiträge* p. 27; *RG.* ii 325) holds that the *deductio* introduced the interdict *uti possidetis.* Ubbelohde (to take the latest writer) holds that it was simply to establish the actual fact of possession, so that without any discussion over the right of possession, the *actio sacramento in rem* (not the *actio per sponsionem*) might proceed, and the praetor might at once require securities from the actual possessor so fixed (*Glück's Pand.* § 1852, v p. 639 sqq.). Here, as in many other cases, I think that we have not information enough to enable us to come to any decided opinion. The *deductio* could not be identical with the *vim facere,* which is found in the present text of Gaius; but there was clearly a common practice in disputes about ownership of land to prepare for the trial by having an agreed eviction peacefully carried out. Where the dispute was between occupants of contiguous tenements, such a course might be almost necessary to enable each formally to ascertain the limits of his adversary's claim and define his own (see Exner *ZRG.* xxi 190). Force (*vis*) is a term which varies in meaning. Marcus Aurelius was indignant at a creditor who had seized something belonging to his debtor and pleaded *vim nullam feci.* The Emperor replied *Tu vim putas esse solum si homines vulnerentur? vis est et tunc quotiens quis id quod deberi sibi putat non per judicem reposcit* (D. iv 2 fr 13 = xlviii 7 fr 7). In the interdict *de vi* we are told that it relates

[1] For this use of *moribus* cf. Ulp. xi 24; D. xxvii 10 fr 1, *etc.*; and for definition of *mores* D. i 3 fr 32 pr § 1; xvi 1 fr 1 § 1.

only to brutal force (*ad solam atrocem*[1] *vim pertinet hoc interdictum,* D. xliii 16 fr 1 § 3); but slight force if seriously intended may practically be brutal violence (Cic. *Caecin.* 14—16, §§ 41—47). In the interdict *quod vi aut clam,* force is any act done in defiance of a prohibition by the possessor (D. xliii 24 fr 1 § 5; cf. L 17 fr 73 § 2). In our speech what was contemplated by *vis ac deductio moribus* was for Caecina with a few friends as witnesses to come to the farm at an agreed time, to assert in some way his right to remain there as possessor, and for Aebutius, with sufficient force but without any real struggle or violence, to conduct him off the land. It was part of the arrangement that the evictor should formally promise to appear in court to answer the suit of the person evicted (see Cic. *Tull.* § 20; and above, p. 504).

This pacific course for bringing about a settlement of Caecina's and Aebutius' rival claims was rudely interrupted by the conduct of Aebutius on the eventful day. What was his motive? The notion, that Aebutius suspected Caecina of the intention of forcing an entry and holding the land, seems to be negatived by the fact declared by Aebutius' witnesses (if we so far trust Cicero's analysis, §§ 24—30), that Caecina had but few persons with him. But that the suspicion was unfounded is no proof that it was not entertained by Aebutius, who might point to Caecina's persistence in attempting an entry instead of contenting himself (as others sometimes did[2], cf. § 45) with a formal declaration of the presence of armed men. At any rate, on some ground or other, Aebutius saw his advantage in preventing Caecina's putting a foot inside the boundary of the disputed farm. If the farm was of some size, a number of people would be necessary to secure this object; and the arms and threats may have been for deterrent purposes only. We are not told by Cicero of anyone being hurt. Terror was sufficient to accomplish Aebutius' object.

Whether Aebutius or Caecina had in any legal or proper

1 *Atrox* implies desire or at least readiness to wound: 'in deadly earnest,' 'seriously meant,' cf. Cic. *Orat.* ii 200; and our speech § 9.

2 This practice is differently explained by various writers. Compare also Cic. *Inv.* ii 20 § 59.

sense possession of this farm, is not clear, but will be discussed at a later period of Cicero's speech. For the present the situation was this: Aebutius was in actual physical possession of the farm, and Caecina was not. He had attempted to enter, and had fled on a clear and threatening demonstration of armed force. He applied to the praetor and obtained as a matter of ordinary routine the issue of an interdict in peremptory language directing Aebutius 'to put him back whence he had thrown him off.' The words of the interdict would be these: *Unde tu, Sexte Aebuti, aut familia aut procurator tuus A. Caecinam vi hominibus coactis armatisve dejecisti, eo restituas* (cf. §§ 55, 59). Aebutius appears not to have urged the insertion of any plea (*e.g.* that Caecina had first used armed force, cf. Cic. *Fam.* vii 13 § 2, quoted p. 58)[1], but met the interdict directly with the technical answer 'that he had put Caecina back.' The order, being based on an alleged state of facts, was really conditional on the facts being found to be as alleged. The meaning of Aebutius' joinder of issue was that he was not in default. He had restored Caecina, so far as the praetor could be taken to have really ordered it. He would not have ordered it had he been rightly informed, and Aebutius had therefore obeyed the praetor in not restoring Caecina, where the praetor never intended him to be restored. An exact issue being thus joined, a wager is entered into, pledging the parties to their respective assertions; and the case goes at once to trial on this wager.

That the case was one admitting of much doubt is a natural inference from the fact of the Recoverers having twice heard the case and been unable to come to a decision. We do not know their number: unanimity was not apparently required (cf. D. xlii 1 fr 36). Yet the difficulty does not seem to lie in the facts. There is no dispute, so far as we can gather from Cicero, that an agreement for customary formal eviction was come to, that Aebutius had collected a number of armed men and had them at his call, that they were there to prevent Caecina's entering on the farm, that Aebutius threatened Caecina's life if he entered, that Caecina none the less

[1] The fact that Dolabella issued the interdict *sine ulla exceptione* does not at all imply that the interdict did not admit of one.

attempted it twice, and called upon Aebutius to carry out the customary ejectment (§ 27), and that he gave way and retired, only when in some danger of his life (see §§ 32, 33). What then was the defence set up by Aebutius' advocate Piso? It was as follows:

1. Caecina has not been dejected but rejected[1]. He could not be turned off a place when he was never on it. Aebutius did not evict him, he prevented him from entering (§§ 31—40; 49; 64 sqq.).

2. No force (*vis*) was used to Caecina. No one was slain, no one was wounded. Caecina and his friends took fright and fled before entering the place (§§ 41—63).

3. No one could be dejected who did not possess at the time. Caecina was not possessor (§§ 90—94).

4. Caecina was not owner and had no right to the possession. This argument seems to be hinted at in the conclusion (§ 104).

5. Caecina was under disability as a Volaterran in consequence of Sulla's law reducing the status of the people of Volaterrae[2] (§ 95 sqq.). From this Piso seems to have argued, that he had no right to the interdict or to a legal wager. His right to take as heir under Caesennia's will is not strictly relevant to this trial, but may, as Keller thinks, have been at the bottom of Piso's objection. If not heir, Caecina was the merest outsider.

But though these appear to be the arguments resulting from an examination of Cicero's references to the defence, and can be dealt with separately, they were probably combined in Piso's actual speech. He may have said: 'This interdict is not 'one to which Caecina has the smallest right. He is a Vola-'terran, and wholly disqualified from enjoying the rights of 'Roman citizens. The interdict is concerned with recovery of 'possession. Caecina was neither possessor of the estate in

[1] I accept Keller's correction of *rejeci* for *ejeci* in §§ 38 and 84, and *rejectus* for *ejectus* in § 66. See his *Sem.* p. 393 foll.

[2] Volaterrae resisted a siege by Sulla for two years and then capitulated (Strab. v 6 p. 223; *Corp. Ins. Lat.* xi p. 325).

'question, nor was he owner so as to have a right to the posses- 'sion. He was not even in actual occupation, rightly or wrongly, 'either for himself or for others: he was a mere outsider trying 'to force his way on to my property. I had a sufficient force to 'prevent him, and I made a serious demonstration, which caused 'him to run away before he put a foot on my ground. Neither 'he nor any one of his party was hurt. If Caecina is entitled 'by this interdict to be put into possession of my farm, then 'any loafers or ruffians from Gaul or Greece may collect in 'force and trespass on my land, just because they choose to call 'it theirs, and I shall have no right to arm my servants for 'their own defence while turning or keeping off intruders. Let 'him bring his suit for the ownership: I will not assist him to a 'trial, but stand on my rights.'

Cicero treats the fifth point with care: the fourth hardly at all, unless something material has been lost in the middle of §95. The third includes a question of law and a question of fact. The latter is treated very summarily (in §§94, 95), the question of law is argued in §§90—93. The great bulk of his argument on the whole case is expended on the first and second points. And here the case which Cicero puts is that of a man who has left his house for a time and on returning is prevented from entering by armed force (§34). On such a supposition we may well believe an interdict framed like this was as effectual against exclusion as against expulsion, and against a threatening display of force as against physical pressure, and against the use of arms whether they drew blood or not. Ulpian agrees, and very possibly he or his authorities had Cicero's speech in recollection when they wrote on this interdict: *Si quis de agro suo vel de domo processisset nemine suorum relicto, mox revertens prohibitus sit ingredi vel ipsum praedium, vel si quis eum in medio itinere detinuerit, et ipse possederit, vi dejectus videtur, ademisti enim ei possessionem, quam animo retinebat etsi non corpore* (D. xliii 16 fr 1 §24). *Qui armati venerunt, etsi armis non sunt usi ad deiciendum sed dejecerunt, armata vis facta esse videtur; sufficit enim terror armorum, ut videantur armis dejecisse* (*ib.* fr 3 §5). *Si, cum dominus veniret in possessionem, armati eum prohibuerunt, qui invaserant possessionem, videri eum armis dejectum* (*ib.* § 8). So far as the first two allegations are concerned, Cicero's argument, at once close and broad, logical and eloquent, was doubtless convincing if anyone required convincing on the case put.

Unfortunately for Caecina the case put was not his. The farm in question was not his home: it is doubtful whether it was his in any sense; it is even doubtful whether he ever put a foot on it except perhaps in doing his wife's business during her life. Cicero glides somewhat quickly over this part of the argument (§§ 90—93) but meets such an objection by saying that though Caecina was possessor, possession was not required for this interdict: whether Caecina was or was not possessor was therefore wholly irrelevant: possession was required in order to bring the interdict *de vi*; it was not required in order to bring the interdict *de vi hominibus armatis*.

Possession is quite different from ownership[1]. A man may own without possessing, though he might have a right to the possession: he may possess without being owner: and under Roman law possession, as such, if honest, was entitled to protection, and the ordinary form of protection was by interdict. For our purpose, possession[2] may be defined as occupation either by yourself or someone for you with the intention to hold as of right for yourself. Occupation as tenant or depositary was occupation for another, and did not as a rule entitle the tenant or depositary himself to the interdicts (D. xliii 16 fr 1 § 10): occupation as usufructuary did, though the frame of the interdict *de vi* was modified to suit the usufructuary's position.

The interdicts *de vi* and *de vi armata* are treated together (under these names) in the Digest and no express mention of possession is made in the extract from the praetor's edict there given; but we are told by Ulpian that possession was

[1] Ulpian's expression is strong: *Nihil commune habet proprietas cum possessione* (D. xli 2 fr 12 § 1).

[2] *Possidere* is used for occupation generally as well as for technical possession. Thus it is used in the edict of a seizure and occupation *rei servandae causa*. Cf. Gai. iii 79; D. xlii 4; xliii 4; and the Essay on *pro Quinctio* (above, p. 482).

required, and the only difference between the requirements, in this respect, of the two interdicts, is that in the former the possession must be free from force, stealth or request as against the opponent, but that faulty possession will do in the case of the latter (D. xlii 16 fr 14, 15). It is noticeable however that the requirement of possession is in the Digest deduced from, or at any rate specially connected with, the word *deici*. *Deicitur is qui possidet sive civiliter sive naturaliter possidet, nam et naturalis possessio ad hoc interdictum pertinet* (*ib.* fr 1 § 9). *Interdictum hoc nulli competit nisi ei qui tunc cum deiceretur possidebat; nec alius deici visus est quam qui possidet. Eum qui neque animo neque corpore possidebat, ingredi autem et incipere possidere prohibeatur, non videri dejectum verius est: deicitur enim qui amittit possessionem, non qui non accipitur* (*ib.* § 26). One might fancy this last passage was written in recollection of Piso's defence[1] in our case. Gaius (ii 155) treats the interdict *de vi armata* as only a modification of the other by the omission of the requirement that the possession should not be faulty, and says not a word of any other view.

Cicero on the contrary rests his case in this respect mainly on the difference of language between the interdict *de vi* and that *de vi hominibus armatis*. He says the former contained the words *cum ego possiderem*, the latter did not (§ 91). In the speech *pro Tullio* he gives the words of the former interdict as '*cum ille possideret*,' and in addition (*et hoc amplius*) *quod nec vi nec clam nec precario possideret*. Savigny (*Besitz* § 40 p. 426) holding that possession was necessary for both interdicts[2] suggests that Cicero has here made one clause into two, and that the interdict *de vi* really ran thus '*cum ille nec vi nec clam nec precario ab illo possideret*,' so that *cum possideret* was there only to support the three grounds of exception and, as these

[1] *Exoritur hic illa defensio eum deici posse qui tum possideat, qui non possideat nullo modo posse; itaque, si ego sim a tuis aedibus dejectus, restitui non oportere, si ipse sis, oportere* (*Caecin.* § 90).

[2] Most recent writers differ from Savigny. See Keller *Semestr.* pp. 427-8. I understand Lenel to consider that possession was necessary in the case of both interdicts, being expressed in the one (*de vi*) and deduced from *deici* in the other (*EP.* p. 372).

dropped out in the interdict *de vi armata*, the words *cum possideret* dropped out also. Keller thinks that Cicero's language is too clear and positive to be doubted: and that the frame of the interdict which Cicero appears to give and which Savigny alters is confirmed by the *lex Agraria* (Anno 643 U.C. Bruns[6] no. 11), where the affirmation of possession is a separate clause from the negation of faulty possession (§ 18): *si quis...ex possessione vi ejectus est quod ejus is quei ejectus est possederit, quod neque vi neque clam neque precario possederit, ab eo quei eum ex possessione vi ejecerit.* He holds therefore that possession was not required in the interdict *de vi armata* in Cicero's time, but admits that the generality of the interdict obviously needed some limitation, and suggests that Piso's argument was probably one of many arguments to get the courts to require some kind of occupation as necessary for this interdict; until at length, by Ulpian's time, possession was required for this as well as for the more ordinary interdict. Meantime the frame of the interdict had been so far modified, as to make no mention of possession, *deici* being understood to imply it (*Semestria*, pp. 301, 378—389). Cicero's argument (§ 86 sqq.) that *deici* and *unde* might be used as well of a place *a quo* as of a place *ex quo*, is admitted by Keller to be probably correct (*ib.* p. 422).

The most recent writer on this matter, Ubbelohde (l.c. p. 170 sqq.), holds that juristic possession was not in the general opinion necessary in Cicero's time for this interdict; else how could Cicero have addressed this argument to the judges[1]? but that there must have been required some kind of relation between the applicant for the interdict and the land, though it is difficult to say what; and hence the hesitation of the Recoverers was well grounded.

It is not easy at first to resist the force of Cicero's pleading in this matter; and it is clear that so far as the words went, there was some such difference between the two interdicts as Cicero points out. Keller pours scorn on anyone who, looking at the care with which the language of the interdicts was settled, thinks that the insertion of the words *cum ille possi-*

[1] But Piso's argument has to be considered as well as Cicero's.

deret in one and their omission in the other could be compatible with possession being a condition of both interdicts (*Semestr.* pp. 301, 339). But is the alternative offered to us by Keller easier to accept? A theory which supposes an irrational form of interdict, and an unproved series of attempts to make it rational, with the result that in Gaius and Ulpian's time we have a frame of interdict not containing these distinctive words[1] but with *deici* rationally interpreted, so as to carry the very meaning which Cicero and Keller suppose to be impossible here, may seem to justify scorn, as much as the belief that the wording of the interdict might have been in some respects verbose and ambiguous, so as to lend itself to the ingenious perversion of an advocate. Anyhow I venture to differ in this matter from Keller (much as I respect his authority), and I rest my opinion not only on the rational character of praetorian action but also on examination of the words themselves. First take the passage from the Agrarian law. The introductory words *ex possessione vi ejectus est* require an addition to shew that the ejection was from land occupied by *him*, not by someone else. That is why we have the clause *quod ejus*[2] *is qui ejectus est possederit*, 'so far as the land was possessed by the evicted person and possessed neither, *etc.*' This clause could not have been intended to lay stress on the bare fact of possession, when the eviction had been already described as *ex possessione*. Now take the interdict *de vi*, which according to Cicero ran thus: *unde tu aut familia aut procurator tuus illum aut familiam aut procuratorem illius in hoc anno vi dejecisti, cum ille possideret quod nec vi nec clam nec precario possideret, eo restituas* (*Tull.* 19 § 44; *Caecin.* 8 § 23; 19 § 55; 31 § 91). I cannot persuade myself that *cum ille possideret* was meant to be taken by itself, as a bald requirement

[1] *I.e.* according to Keller (p. 313); but I think Lenel (*EP.* p. 372, especially note 3) is right in supposing these words to have been in the edict for the interdict *de vi* in Ulpian's time and omitted only by Justinian.

[2] On this use of *quod ejus* compare the *lex Agrar.* 5, 16, 24, 33, *etc.*; Cic. *Top.* 17 § 66 *quod ejus melius aequius*; and the aedile's edict in D. xxi 1 fr 1 § 1. See my Lat. Gr. § 1297. H. Jordan (*Beiträge* p. 336) gives a full account.

of possession, without an object, without any description of the kind of possession, or any other natural and significant addition to the predicate[1]. By itself what would it add to the implication inherent in *dejecisti?* How could he have been dejected, if he had not been in possession of any sort? The real cause of this particular frame of the interdict was this. The drafter had three things to embrace, viz. (1) to make it as general as possible, hence *unde,* not *ex quo fundo, etc.*; (2) to identify the time of dejection with the time of possession[2], hence *cum...possideret*; (3) to shew that that from which he was dejected was held in lawful possession. The clause with *quod* would not follow *unde* very well, and the time-clause thus forms a convenient link. 'Although his 'possession at the time was one which was neither forcible 'nor stealthy nor by request' (literally 'whereas he was possess- 'ing what neither by force nor stealth nor prayer-wise was he 'possessing'). Then when the interdict *de vi armata* came to be framed, the omission of flawless possession carried away with it of course the link '*cum...possideret*[3],' leaving the fact of some sort of possession involved in the word *dejecisti.* Cicero adroitly in the interest of his client seized on the apparent difference between the wording of the two interdicts, and gave an independence and an importance to the clause which it was never intended to have. His argument had no doubt some effect on the minds of the Recoverers, as it has had on modern critics.

Further, there is no trace (I admit our information is meagre) of any change in the fundamental conditions of the interdict *de vi armata* having taken place between Cicero's time and that of Gaius or Ulpian; and in Gaius and Ulpian's

[1] *E.g.* in the interdict *uti possidetis* the *uti* gives the required point to *possidetis.* N.B. The repetition of *possidere* is seen in the formula of *uti possidetis* (D. xliii 17 fr 1 pr) and in this agrarian law, as well as in our interdict.

[2] Cf. Ulpian D. xliii 16 fr 1 § 23 *Interdictum hoc nulli competit nisi ei qui tunc cum deiceretur possidebat.*

[3] My view resembles Savigny's, but was taken without any recollection of his suggestion. It is always a pleasure to agree with or follow that admirable lawyer and writer.

times possession, civil or at least natural, was no doubt required. Nor is there any sense, as it seems to me, in supposing the praetors to have ever conceived, still less to have 'carefully drafted,' an interdict which should be as useful for a tramp as for a lawful, or at any rate for a settled, occupier. It is one thing to check and punish armed brigandage or armed violence of any kind: it is quite a different thing to enact such a fantastic remedy as putting (*or* restoring!) into possession any casual intruders who have been threatened with a pike or sword by the farmer or his servants on a lonely holding. Armed violence was punishable as crime under the *lex Julia* (D. xlviii 6 fr 3 § 6; Just. iv 15 § 6) and probably before: it was punishable with heavy damages under the *lex Aquilia*, or on a charge of *injuriarum* or *vi bonorum raptorum* (see *Tull.* 17, 18; *Caecin.* 12 § 35). But to say that an actual occupant, if he used arms against a mere intruder, who without any tittle of right tried to force his way into the other's land, should be bound to give him up the possession, is not at all in harmony with the good sense and practical character either of Roman legislation or of the praetor's action.

I hold with Ulpian and Piso (§ 91) that no one could be dejected who had not some kind of possession, and that this, though not set out as a distinct condition in the interdict, was implied in the very nature of the case. And it must be a possession at the time in some sense of the place or thing really in dispute (the usual *qua de agitur* is implied). Cicero himself lays no stress on the argument suggested to him by a lawyer (§§ 78, 80) that at any rate Caecina ought to be restored somewhere, if not to the farm itself. Yet if there is to be no kind of possession required, and the whole gist of the interdict is to impose a punishment for armed violence, such an interpretation seems to me bearable: 'If you turn a person off by armed violence, you shall put him back wherever it was.' But I agree with Cicero (§ 85) in thinking this was not the real meaning of the interdict. Interdicts are in fact steps or remedies for obtaining, protecting and regaining possession (Gai. iv 143 sqq.): this particular interdict is for regaining lost possession; the nature of possession may possibly vary with different interdicts, and the sufficiency of the possession asserted is a fit subject for argument; whether a *bona fide* purchaser or a usufructuary or an heir or the occupant, without title, of a vacant farm, or the holder by an illegal gift, or a tenant by agreement or on sufferance has the right for himself to this particular form of legal remedy, may be an arguable question; but a mere outsider, attempting a trespass, refusing to retire, and threatening violence, can hardly under any circumstances have a claim to be put into possession by the praetor's edict.

Cicero declares that in his argument on this matter he is defending the common interest of all: it does not concern Caecina, for Caecina had possession, and that, he says, may be shewn in a few words, although in truth it is irrelevant to the question of the interdict. He gives four arguments to prove Caecina's possession. (1) He had possession as heir through Caesennia's tenant, (2) he had personally taken possession, (3) Aebutius had recognised his position in this respect, (4) his conduct in arranging for a *moribus deductio* shews it.

(1) It was admitted that Caesennia possessed on account of the 'usufruct left her by her husband's will. Caesennia 'let the farm to a tenant. The same tenant on the same hiring 'was in the farm when she died. Can it be doubted that if 'Caesennia possessed when her tenant was in her farm, on her 'death her heir possessed by the same right?'

This is a close translation of Cicero's words, but at first sight it appears full of fallacies as an argument. It is incorrect, at least according to the post-Augustan lawyers[1], to speak of a usufructuary's possessing. He has not the necessary *animus* to hold as of right permanently, and has only a *quasi-possessio* (Gai. ii 94; iv 139; D. iv 6 fr 23 § 2; x fr 5 § 1; *naturaliter possidet* D. xli 2 fr 12; *neque usus fructus neque usus possidetur sed magis tenetur* D. xliv 3 fr 1 § 8). He occupies because occupation is the obvious and proper means of exercising his right in the thing: but this exercise of his right is quite

[1] Keller argues not improbably that this was a later subtlety and that in Cicero's time a usufructuary might have been held to possess (p. 345 sqq.).

compatible with another's having the technical possession (D. xli 2 fr 52). So that Aebutius might have been possessor all the while notwithstanding Caesennia's usufruct, and two persons (not being joint owners) could not be technically possessors of the same thing at the same time. Secondly, there is no inheritance of a usufruct. If Caesennia had only the usufruct of the farm, it died with her. No doubt her occupation as usufructuary would have entitled her to protection by this or an analogous interdict in Cicero's days. In Ulpian's time there was a special interdict for usufructuaries *qui fundo vel aedificiis uti frui prohibiti sunt* (D. xliii 16 fr 3 § 15; Vat. 90, 91). But this right was no more transmissible to her heir than the usufruct itself was; and the lease died with her right, if Caesennia held as usufructuary only. Thirdly, there is no inheritance in possession at all. It must be acquired *corpore* as well as *animo*. Paul's language in D. xli 2 fr 30 § 5 is an express negative to Cicero's confident question. *Quod per colonum possideo, heres meus, nisi ipse nactus possessionem, non poterit possidere: retinere enim animo possessionem possumus, apisci non possumus.* So also Javolen: *Cum heredes instituti sumus, adita hereditate omnia quidem jura ad nos transeunt, possessio tamen nisi naturaliter comprehensa ad nos non pertinet* (*ib.* fr 23 pr); and Ulpian D. xlvii 4 fr 1 § 15; cf. Gai. iv 153. I see no reason to doubt this being good law in Cicero's time, as applied to such a possession as led to usucapion; and Keller (*Semestr.* p. 351) points out that the doctrine of *pro herede usucapio* (Gai. ii 52), certainly an old doctrine, implies this state of the law.

It is impossible to suppose Cicero ignorant or unobservant of the general character of usufruct or of the law of usucapion. He would I think have replied (1) that the distinction between the possession of an owner and the possession (whatever it be called) of a usufructuary was not relevant to the question, for if possession was required at all, the possession of a usufructuary was sufficient for this interdict (cf. D. xliii 16 fr 1 § 9); (2) that he referred to the usufruct, only because possession so far was admitted by the other side, but that his own contention was that Caesennia had had the usufruct, but that it was now merged in the ownership, and her tenant held the possession after her death for the heirs to her ownership[1]; and (3) that the requirement of personal acquisition of possession by the heir applied only to the civil possession, which led to usucapion[2]; whereas Caecina succeeded to Caesennia's position as lessor of this farm as well as to her other obligations; and Aebutius' violent conduct was not merely an obstruction to Caecina's taking or exercising personal possession, but in effect an ejection of Caecina from the possession held for him by his tenant (D. xliii 16 fr 1 § 22; *e.g.* cf. this speech 13 § 37). Cicero's position thus appears tenable, or at least plausible.

Aebutius might be expected to retort that there were no rights at all in this farm belonging to Caesennia or her heirs after her death. He himself was owner and in possession all along[3], notwithstanding the usufruct being out in Caesennia. The lease was put an end to by the extinction of the usufruct on her death, and the tenant was responsible to him for any fruits after that time; any obligation created by the lease was personal to Caesennia's heirs and did not affect the land.

(2) Cicero's second argument brings Caecina into direct touch with the land. He says that Caecina when going round the farms came into this farm and received accounts from the tenant (§ 94). We are not told when this took place, but the presumption is that it was after Caesennia's death. Savigny (*Besitz* § 40 p. 425 note) suggests that this was only a visit to take the account of what was due to Caesennia's estate. But Cicero puts it forward as more than that. If Caecina without opposition came into the farm, took the accounts, and continued the tenant in the holding, he would presumably thereby have

[1] Where possession is acquired by an heir he can count as part of his possession for the purpose of usucapion the period from the death of testator to his own entry into possession (D. xli 3 fr 31 § 5; fr 44 § 3).

[2] Cf. D. xliii 16 fr 1 § 26 *Eum, qui neque animo neque corpore possidebat, ingredi autem et incipere possidere prohibeatur, non videri dejectum verius est*, *i.e.* there were disputes on the question, it was not settled law even in Ulpian's time. If so, Cicero might well have maintained either argument.

[3] If Aebutius took possession at first in the name of Caesennia, he could not afterwards by mere change of intention convert his possession as her agent into rightful possession for himself (cf. D. xli 2 fr 3 §§ 18, 19; fr 42 § 1).

taken possession. No mention is made of any interference by Aebutius at the time. It is noticeable that the tenant was not among Aebutius' witnesses; indeed no further reference at all is made to him. He may have been dead, he may now have left the farm, he may have been got at by Aebutius; we know nothing.

(3) Cicero next questions Aebutius how, if Caecina was not possessor, he came to give him notice (*denuntiare*) about this particular farm, rather than others which he possessed, if, adds Cicero, he had any. A notice, Cicero implies, is given to a possessor, *e.g.* D. xli 4 fr 13; and so in the case of *damni infecti* (D. xxxix 2 fr 4 § 5), or *quod vi aut clam* (D. xliv 24 fr 1 § 7). But the answer to Cicero is obvious. Notices are very common for all kinds of purposes (*e.g.* Cic. *Quint.* § 27; § 54; *Rosc. Com.* § 26; D. xiv 3 fr 17 § 4; iv 4 fr 47 pr; xxi 2 fr 55 § 1, *etc.*)[1]. Aebutius might easily know or guess that Caecina regarded this farm as part of Caesennia's estate; and seeing that a suit for the division of the estate was begun, it was natural for Aebutius to give a warning to Caecina, that the suit must be conducted without reference to this farm, and that any attempt to exercise rights over the farm would be disputed as a trespass.

(4) Cicero's last argument is imperfectly given in the MS., but appears to be that Caecina's wish to be formally evicted, expressed after consulting his legal advisers, was evidence of his possession. 'If not in possession, how could he ask to be evicted?' Cicero seems to say. One would have thought from the similar case in the *pro Tullio* (8 § 20) that a possessor would claim to evict the claimant, and that Caecina by his consent to be evicted really yielded the point, at least for the time, to Aebutius. But the *deductio moribus* is too little known to permit inferences. Possibly Cicero only meant that, if there had been any doubt on the fact of possession, Caecina would not have challenged a decision on that point[2] but brought his action for the ownership at once.

[1] See Keller *Sem.* p. 355; Kipp *Litis-denuntiation* § 26.

[2] To the expected result of such a trial on the possession I refer the

It must be admitted that Cicero's hurried argument for Caecina's possession is not such as to convince one of his having a clear case. Nor have we a particle of evidence of any rightful possession by Aebutius either.

I pass now to the fourth head of Piso's defence, which so far as our text goes is only touched in a line by Cicero, in the summary at the end of the speech: *multo minus quaeri A. Caecinae fundus sit necne, me tamen id ipsum docuisse fundum esse Caecinae* (§ 104). If the interdict required possession, it was strictly speaking of no avail to allege or prove ownership; but it was natural, especially for Cicero, who denied this requirement, to shew that Caecina had a *bona fide* interest of the strongest kind in claiming the use and protection of the interdict[1]. It was not an intruder and trespasser, but the owner of the land, who had been subjected to this unprovoked attack by Aebutius, and if Aebutius honestly disputed his ownership, why did he not let the question come in the ordinary way to trial?

As regards Caecina's claim, there is a minor difficulty in the fact that Caecina was not the universal heir of Caesennia (though very nearly so) and till the estate was divided, either by agreement or by judicial action, Caecina could not be sole owner of this farm or of any particular portion of the estate. There might no doubt have been an agreement with the freedman M. Fulcinius: there was clearly none with Aebutius, and the suit *fam. ercisc.* had been stopped by Aebutius' conduct. Nor is any mention made of any special bequest or gift of the farm to Caecina. However if the facts were at all what Cicero sets forth, Aebutius' claim to the ownership appears impudent,

words in i § 2 *Si facta vis esset moribus, superior in possessione retinenda non fuisset* (*Aebutius*). See below, p. 532. Bethmann-Hollweg (ii p. 236 and *Pref.* p. xiii) takes them differently.

[1] Quintilian actually recommends this course (*Inst.* vii 5 § 3) *Quotiens tamen poterimus, efficiendum est ut de re quoque judex bene sentiat: sic enim juri nostro libentius indulgebit; ut in sponsionibus quae ex interdictis fiunt, etiamsi non proprietatis est quaestio sed tantum possessionis, tamen non solum possedisse nos sed etiam nostrum possedisse docere oportebit.* Perhaps our passage was in his mind.

but might be difficult to disprove. The mere fact of the bidding at the auction being by Aebutius, and the payment of the purchase money being entered in Aebutius' name in the banker's books, is after all only *prima facie* evidence[1]. Aebutius is said to have made away with the accounts (§ 17), presumably the accounts between himself and Caesennia, whose business he often managed (§ 15); but still there should have been means of proving, whence the purchase money really came, and who took possession and acted as the proprietor of the farm. Cicero tells us *Caesennia fundum possedit locavitque*, but it is not unlikely that Aebutius acted as her agent in taking possession (cf. D. xli 1 fr 53), and thus appeared throughout as purchaser. Paul says (ii 17 § 14) *Fundus ejus esse videtur cujus nomine comparatus est, non a quo pecunia numerata est, si tamen fundus comparatori sit traditus.* The statement is reasonable: *cujus nomine* may mean whose name was given as the purchaser or (what would usually be the same) 'on whose account' it was purchased. And the doctrine is quite in accordance with recognised law (see Cod. iv 50) and good sense. If a man buys an estate with money borrowed from his banker, the banker has no claim thereby to the ownership of the estate.

Among the witnesses produced by Aebutius were P. Caesennius, *fundi auctor, i.e.* the vendor and guarantor of title of the farm, and Sex. Clodius Phormio the banker. Cicero dismisses them with scoffs: the former was weightier in body than in character (*auctoritate*, with a pun on *auctor*); the latter was as black (*niger* cf. Hor. *Sat.* i 4 85) and confident (Ter. *Phorm.* 123) as the Phormio in Terence, but neither said anything which could affect the judgment (10 § 27). These were the only witnesses who had nothing to say about the forcible eviction. It seems clear that they were there to depose to the entries of sale and payment in the banker's books being in Aebutius' name, and to the delivery of the price by him. So much Cicero admits: as to the mode of delivery of possession of the land, he says nothing (6 §§ 16, 17), and whatever view Caesennius and Clodius may have taken of the transaction, as

[1] Persons of position did not always like their names to occur in documents of sale (D. xxvi 8 fr 5 § 4).

the money was duly paid, they were not further concerned. If Aebutius played Caesennia false at the time, acted for himself and took delivery for himself, he would be legal owner (D. xli 2 fr 1 § 20; Cod. iv 50 fr 1, 8, *etc.*), but liable to Caesennia's heirs for theft of the money and to a condiction for the money. But it is more likely that he did not so act, and that this posing as the real purchaser and owner was an afterthought, when Caesennia was dead and Aebutius found so little left him by her will. Caecina's marriage with Caesennia had probably interfered with his employment by Caesennia, and now Caecina's heirship threatened to oust him altogether.

If he was neither owner nor possessor with a good title, but only possessor by stealth, his conduct in breaking the agreement and at all hazards preventing Caecina from getting legal foothold is more explicable. If the question of possession came to a decision under the interdict *uti possidetis*, he must expect to lose[1]: his chance seemed to be to interpose as much difficulty and delay as possible, and to rely on Caecina's being precluded from the interdict *de vi* by not being possessor, and from the interdict *de vi armata* by such a defence as Piso appears to have set up.

The fifth point of Piso's defence is one on which our information is only what is given us in this speech. We have not Sulla's law: and the question raised by Cicero (33 §§ 95, 96) whether there are not limitations on any and every law is a difficult constitutional question. If the people of Rome were really sovereign (and one can hardly deny it) their power to take away citizenship and freedom is clear. But there is a wide gulf between abstract power and those limits of legislation which are felt by practical statesmen, and which are so conformable to the habits of a people, that they cannot be overstepped without revolutionary action. Yet even if such limits were usual, would an ordinary tribunal be justified in refusing to recognise enactments not in conformity with them? In the absence of a written constitution, it is difficult to think so.

[1] Cf. § 2 *Si facta vis esset moribus, superior in possessione retinenda non fuisset* (*Aebutius*) and Gai. iv 150, 153; D. xli 2 fr 6 pr.

Cicero says that in a previous case when he was quite a young man and opposed as an advocate to Cotta, the most skilful orator in Rome, he succeeded in obtaining a decision from the Decemviri[1] in favour of the freedom of a woman of Arretium, and established the principle that citizenship could not be taken away, and *a fortiori* freedom could not[2]. This, too, was in Sulla's lifetime. Banishment was not recognised by the Roman law as a punishment. It was the refuge voluntarily sought by those to whom, by the prohibition of fire and water, the means of living in their own country were denied. They lost the Roman citizenship only when they were received into another state[3]. So with freedom: if a man declines to serve in the army or to be enrolled in the list of burgesses, the state directed him to be sold; but strictly this meant that by these refusals, he had himself declined to bear the burdens and maintain the *status* of a freeman (§§ 97—100).

Cicero challenges the production of any case in which freedom or citizenship had been taken away by statute or bill (*lege aut rogatione* § 100, *i.e.* taken by statute or proposed by bill to be taken). As regards Sulla's law in the case of Volaterrae it contained the usual clause declaring that the law did not apply in any matter which was not lawfully the subject of a bill, and this saving clause therefore protected the rights of citizens. Cicero adds further that all that Sulla proposed to do by that law was to reduce the people of Volaterrae to the position of the people of Ariminum: and the people of Ariminum were one of the twelve (Latin) colonies and were capable of taking inheritances from Romans[4]. Sulla's bill did not affect *nexa*[5] *atque hereditates, i.e.* the rights of mancipation and inheritance peculiar to Roman citizens (35 §§ 101, 102).

The meaning of the customary saving clause is pressed too

[1] *I.e. xviri stlitibus judicandis* (see p. 315).

[2] The same argument is found in Cic. *Dom.* § 77 sqq.

[3] Not necessarily 'acquired the citizenship of another state' according to Mommsen *Staatsrecht* iii 50. Cf. also Madvig *Verfassung* i 50, 51.

[4] Cf. Mommsen *Röm. Gesch.* i[7] p. 421; *Staatsrecht* iii[2] 624; Madvig *Verfassung* i 67.

[5] On *nexa* see my Essay on *nexum* above, p. 304.

far by Cicero[1]. It could hardly be held to take out of the law any matters forming part of its obvious intention and substance, but only to deal with collateral and unintended effects. Cicero's previous success, however, in a similar pleading on the general argument, forms a good precedent for him on this occasion. His express statement in reference to the terms of Sulla's law is, if accurate, decisive of the question.

As regards mancipation, Gaius speaks of it as peculiar to Roman citizens (Gai. i 119). Ulpian however speaks more exactly, when he says that mancipation was valid between Roman citizens and Latin colonists and Junian Latins and such foreigners as have rights of commerce granted them. In effect the power of conveyance of property in full ownership by properly Roman forms had been conceded to these other classes. But in our case inheritance was the important point. Gaius tells us that, while the *lex Junia* created a class of persons with rights in general the same as those belonging to Latin colonists, it expressly denied them the power to make a will or to take under a will or to be appointed guardians by will (Gai. i 22, 23; ii 275); and Ulpian confirms this as special to the Latins under Junius' law (xx 14; xxii 3; xi 16). There were obvious reasons for this restriction. Junian Latins were slaves emancipated by informal methods (Ulp. i 9; Gai. i 35; see vol. 1 p. 38), and protected in freedom by the praetor, and afterwards by Junius' statute. If they had the right of making wills and being appointed guardians, they might remove their property or that of their wards from their patron's control and reversion. And the right of taking under a will, if fully recognised, would be inconsistent with their being, as they still were in theory, slaves, whose acquisitions passed in law to their masters (Gai. iii 56). But these reasons in no way applied to the Latin colonists proper, who were freeborn citizens, voluntarily adopting another place as their residence and country.

We find it stated in other passages of Cicero, that Sulla's

[1] Mommsen (*Staatsrecht* iii p. 43 note) observes that with the help of this principle an advocate can reduce any law to nothing.

confiscation of the land of the Volaterrans and reduction of their civic status were not eventually given effect to, though Rullus and others proposed to confirm them. *Hodie non modo cives sed etiam optimi cives fruuntur nobiscum hac civitate* (*Dom.* 30 § 79). *Sullani temporis acerbitatem subterfugerunt. Cum enim tribuni plebi legem iniquissimam de eorum agris promulgavissent, facile senatui populoque Romano persuasi ut eos cives quibus fortuna pepercisset salvos esse vellent. Hanc actionem meam C. Caesar primo suo consulatu lege agraria comprobavit agrumque Volaterranum et oppidum omni periculo in perpetuum liberavit* (Cic. *Fam.* xiii 4 § 2).

On this part of the case therefore Cicero was probably successful, however fine-drawn we may think some of his arguments. Whether he won his case altogether, we do not know. The mere facts, that Cicero had the speech published, and was proud of it as a speech[1], and that he was on pleasant terms with an Aulus Caecina in the time of Caesar's dictatorship, seem to me to prove nothing to the point. There are letters to and from Aulus Caecina in Cicero's correspondence (*Fam.* vi 5—9). In 7 § 4 he speaks of himself as Cicero's *veterem clientem*, and may for aught I see be the Caecina of our speech. Recent writers treat him as the son of our defendant. Cf. Teuffel-Schwabe's *Gesch. röm. Litt.* § 199, 5; Tyrrell and Purser's edit. of Cicero's correspondence, vol. iv, p. lxxiii; Pauly-Wissowa *Realencycl.* iii 1237.

[1] Cf. *Orator* 29 § 102 *Tota mihi causa pro Caecina de verbis interdicti fuit: res involutas definiendo explicavimus, jus civile laudavimus, verba ambigua distinximus.*

I. INDEX OF WORDS AND MATTERS.

Roman figures denote volume; Arabic denote pages or (with n.) notes.

abdication of guardianship i 94
abigeatus ii 212
abjurare ii 328 n. 2
absens defined ii 473; *defendi* ii 472
absent *reipublicae causa* ii 262
abstinere se hereditate i 229
abusus 'consumption' i 488 n.
acceptilatio ii 55
accepto facere, fieri, etc. ii 56 n.
acceptum facere ii 55; *ferre, referre* ii 290; *habere* ii 61 n.
accessio, of time in usucapion i 469; in *interd. utrubi* i 462; to price ii 150
accounts, slaves to give i 321
accrescere in partem i 241
accretions go with legacy i 328; with usufruct i 489
accrual of usufruct i 494; of legacy i 296
acquisition of property; original i 415; derivative i 419; of inheritance by usucapion i 227; by transfer i 228; by entry i 229; by cretion i 232; by acting as heir i 232
through children, slaves, *etc.* i 432; through free persons i 437, 400
per universitatem i 62, 227 n. 2, 238, ii 49
acquittal on defendant's satisfaction ii 414
acta 'court proceedings' i 37, 49, ii 382
actio or *judicium*
ad exhibendum i 446
aquae pluviae arcendae i 515
arbitraria ii 86
arborum furtim caesarum ii 194
auctoritatis ii 157
bonae fidei ii 88
Calvisiana ii 277
civilis in factum ii 180
commodati ii 92
communi dividundo ii 135
conducti ii 169
confessoria i 495, 504
contraria ii 91; *etc.* See *contrarium*
damni injuria ii 186
doli ii 228
dotis i 150
de dejecto effusove ii 195
de eo quod certo loco ii 86
de in rem verso ii 245
de jurejurando ii 395
de modo agri ii 156 n.
de moribus i 157
de pastu ii 212
de pauperie ii 198
de peculio ii 238
de servo corrupto ii 218
de tigno juncto ii 212, i 421
depensi ii 184
depositi ii 94
empti ii 140, 160
ex stipulatu for dowry i 156; on purchase ii 155, 158, 160

actio (continued)
ex testamento i 296
exercitoria ii 248
Fabiana (*Faviana*) ii 220; for patron ii 276
familiae erciscundae i 287
fiduciae ii 98
finium regundorum i 449
funeraria i 431
furti ii 201; *ope consilio facti* i 203; *concepti* i 215; *manifesti* i 209; *non exhibiti* i 216; *oblati* i 215; *prohibiti* i 215
hypothecaria ii 114
in factum ii 179, 189, 197, 236, *etc.*
in personam i 3
in rem i 3, 438, 517; *Publiciana* i 443
injuriarum ii 220
institoria ii 248
interrogatoria ii 401
judicati ii 421, 423
legati i 296, ii 185
legis Aquiliae ii 186
legitima i 95 n.
locati ii 169
mandati ii 117
negatoria i 495, 504
negotiorum gestorum ii 123
noxalis ii 252
patronum in jus vocandi ii 225
Pauliana ii 273
pecuniae constitutae ii 86
pigneraticia ii 102
praescriptis verbis ii 179 n.; *aestimatoria* ii 180
pro socio ii 128
protutelae i 114
Publiciana i 443; *rescissoria* i 446 n.
quanti minoris ii 151, 154
quasi Serviana ii 114
quod jussu ii 237
quod vi metusve causa ii 226
rationibus distrahendis i 111
recepticia ii 88
redhibitoria ii 151
rei uxoriae i 153
rerum amotarum i 158
restitutoria ii 272

actio (continued)
Rutiliana i 89
sacramenti ii 340
sepulcri violati i 394
servi corrupti ii 218
Serviana ii 114; *quasi-Serviana ibid.*
stricti *judicii* ii 3 n.
subsidiaria i 114
tributoria ii 247
tutelae i 109
venditi ii 140
vi bonorum raptorum ii 216
actionem mandare, praestare ii 49; *actione cedere* ii 49, cf. ii 37, 121, *etc.*
actor 'manager' ii 113, 134
actum ne agas ii 344 n. 2
actus i 498, 505
actus legitimus i 402, 404
actus rerum ii 324
adcrescere scriptis heredibus i 241
addicere bona i 35; *debitorem* ii 427; *judicem* ii 352; *pignus* ii 440
addictio in diem ii 165
addictus ii 210, cf. 427, 428
ademption of bequest i 310
adfirmatores i 113
adhibere of witnesses i 178 n.
adigere arbitrum ii 129 n. 4
adire hereditatem i 229, 405
adjecta causa i 342
adjudication i 422, ii 355
adjudicatus ii 210
admission (*confessio*) ii 397
adoption i 58; by will i 59 n.
adpromissores ii 29
adrogatio i 60; effect of i 62; of freedman i 62; of woman i 62
adscriptum nomen i 180
adscriptus or *adscitus socius* ii 133
adserere i 47 n.
adsertor i 47
adstipulator ii 28; in *lex Aquilia* ii 193
adulescens i 123, ii 502
adventicia dos i 138
adversaria ii 497
advocatus ii 407
aediles' edict ii 149
aequitas i 89 n. 2

aequom et bonum i 89 n. 2
aequo, ex i 430 n.
aeraria ratio ii 455
aes militare, etc. ii 115
aes et libram, per in will i 179; conveyance i 424; discharge ii 185, 299; cf. *per assem et libram* i 75 n. 2
aestimata dos i 143; *aestimatum instrumentum* ii 171
aestimatoria actio ii 180
aetas i 30 n.; for marriage i 131; *legitima* i 95; *suae aetatis fieri* i 324
affection i 159, 199, 326, ii 225
affinity i 128
age of puberty i 102; for marriage i 131; for *judex* ii 323; for guardian i 117; sixteenth year, how interpreted i 323
agency ii 249; of slaves and children i 432, ii 238
agent (*procurator*), acquisition through i 437
ager limitatus i 417; *stipendiarius* i 429, 430 n.
agere lege ii 339; *in factum* ii 179
agnates i 79, 218, 222; statutable guardians i 95
agnatione, agnascendo i 189, 207; *quasi agnatione* i 207
agnationis stemma i 222
agnoscere bon. possessionem i 238
agrimensor, action against ii 236
album praetoris ii 349; *judicum* ii 322
aleatores ii 330
alere. See alimony
alienation by women and wards i 430; by non-owners i 430; by slaves i 55; *judicii mutandi causa* ii 277; of ward's land i 108
alimony i 81, 84, 266, 269; legacy of i 331
alluvion i 417
altercatio ii 408
alteri stipulari i 401, ii 14
altius tollendi servitus i 500 n.
alveus derelictus i 418
ambitus aedium i 414
amita i 263
amitini fratres i 263
amotas res, propter i 152, 158
anatocismus ii 74 n. 2
ancilla i 343
animals, wild i 416; danger from ii 199
animus in possession i 456; in novation ii 39
anniculus i 30 n., 39
annuity, bequest of i 331; valuation of i 350
antestari ii 333, 334
antestatus i 423 n. 3, 180 n.
ἀντίχρησις ii 107
apocha ii 59
appeal ii 419
appulsus pecoris ad aquam i 499
aqua aestiva, cottidiana i 506
aquae ductus, haustus i 498; *aq. pluviae arcendae* i 515; *aqua et igni interdictio* i 45; *aqua et ignis* presented to bride i 132 n. 1
arbiter=judex ii 318; *ex compromisso* ii 320; *arbitrum adigere* ii 129 n.; *arbitri* in *fin. reg. jud.* i 450
arbitraria actio ii 86, 411 n. 2
arbitrium boni viri i 144, ii 90, 131
arbor not a vine ii 346 n. 2; *arborem caedere* i 508
arcaria nomina ii 65
argentarii ii 132, 511 n. 2. See banker
argentum, bequest of i 341
Ariminum: *status* as colony ii 533
arra, arrabo ii 139 n.
as, parts of i 200; change of value ii 456
assessors ii 407, 462
assignment of patron's rights i 82, 276
atrox ii 516, 223
auction receipts ii 59
auctor, i.e. vendor ii 156, 157 n.; *secundus* ii 157 n.
auctorari ii 174
auctoritas, guaranty of title i 467 n., ii 157; of guardian i 101; *auctoritatem defugere* ii 159
auditorium ii 325
aureus ii 197

aurum, legacy of i 341
aversio 'in block' ii 142; *oneris aversi* ii 176
avitum ii 170

bail. See *vas*
bakers, guild of i 117
banker, special partnership ii 132; subject to *actio recepticia* ii 88; deposit with ii 96; *compensatio* ii 363; their books ii 280, 409
bargain ii 6; not to sue ii 61
betrothal i 132
bona=*hereditas* i 238, cf. 233 n.; *rapta* ii 216; *in bonis* i 428, ii 104; *ex bonis* i 428
Bonitarian ownership i 428
bonorum cessio ii 438; *emptio* ii 435, 372; *missio in possessionem* i 266, 354, 453, ii 432; *possessio* i 170, 236; *sectio* ii 435 n.; *separatio* ii 437; *venditio* ii 434
book-entry ii 65, 279
book-keeping terms ii 288
bottomry, loans on ii 75
buildings, *urbana praedia* i 497, 507

caduca i 382; *in causa caduci* i 383
Caecina, how pronounced ii 511 n. 3; his identity ii 535
caelibes, disability of i 379
calatis comitiis i 176
calumniae judicium ii 234; oath ii 387
cancelment of transactions ii 258
capere i 379; *mortis causa* i 532; *usu* i 467
capi of vestal virgins i 79, 174
capitis deminutio i 41; *maxima* i 41; *minor* or *media* i 45; *minima* i 80; effects cancelled ii 266
captatory appointment i 200
captivus, his *status* i 41; his will i 175, 210; his children, *etc.* ii 264
capture as title i 419
captus 'caught,' 'done' ii 259 n.
caput i 41
Carbonianum Edictum i 268
caretaker (*curator*) i 121
carmen famosum ii 220 n.
cash-loan ii 66
castellum i 507
Castor's temple ii 455
castrense peculium i 66
Catoniana regula i 306 n.
cattle-lifting ii 213
cavere i 14 n., 510, ii 477
caupona, actions for loss in ii 178, 197
causa cadere ii 359; *condictio sine causa* ii 82; *causa data, etc.* ii 77; *cognita* ii 365, 383; *cum sua causa* ii 147; *secundum suam causam* ii 341 n. 1; *omnis causa praestanda* i 441, 495
causae cognitio ii 313, 365; *conjectio* ii 243; *probatio* i 39
causae liberales i 46
cautio ii 12, 71; *Muciana* i 318; usufructuary's i 487; *rei uxoriae* i 137, 149 n.
cedere of time i 312; *actione* ii 49
cenotaph i 393
censu manumissio i 25
centesimae usurae ii 74
centumviri ii 314
cedere of time (*dies*) i 312; *in jure* i 425; *actionibus* ii 49; *bonis* ii 438; *hereditatem* i 228
cernere i 231
certa credita (*pecunia*) ii 71 n. 1
certi condicere ii 84 n., 499
cessicius tutor i 97
cessio bonorum ii 438; *in jure* i 425
chalk, Asiatic ii 408 n.
child, *status* at birth i 20; power to expose i 64 n. 2; includes grand-child i 83; number of children at a birth i 287
chirographa ii 48 n., 66, 72, i 479
chirographarius creditor ii 110
chose in action ii 45 n.
cingere of trees ii 195
circumscriptio minorum ii 259
citizenship of one State only i 18; acquisition of i 20 sqq.; loss of i 41 sqq.; Caracalla's grant i 24
civile jus i 6
codex accepti et expensi ii 280, 291
codicilli i 181; codicillar clause i 182 n. 1

coemptio matrimoni causa i 70; *tutelae evitandae causa* i 71; *test. fac. causa* i 73
coemptionales senes i 71 n. 1
cognati i 80; succession i 261; *stemma* i 263
cognatio i 23; *servilis* i 53, 129
cognitio extra ordinem ii 449
cognitor praediorum i 479, 480; attorney ii 377; *in rem suam* ii 47
cohabitation i 169; of free persons with slave i 21, 43
coire societatem ii 128
collatio bonorum i 247; *dotis* i 249
collegia ii 134
colonies, Latin i 19, 45, ii 533
colonus ii 171; *partiarius* ii 169 n.
combination i 419
commercium i 19
committere edictum i 244; *stipulationem* ii 159
commodare ii 92
commodum medii temporis ii 275
common slave i 433; tenants in common ii 133
communi dividundo ii 135
companies ii 133
compensare ii 363, 413
competere opposed to *dari* i 11, ii 332
compromise (*transactio*) ii 8
compromissum ii 9 n.
co-purchase. See *coemptio*
concepta verba ii 347
conception i 20, 22
concubinage i 168
concurrent actions ii 193, 210, 412
concursu partes fiunt i 296; *divisus est usufructus* i 494
condemnation clause *in formula* ii 354, 355; *in id quod facere potest* i 154, *etc.* ii 416
condicione tua non utor i 133; *condicio melior* in sales ii 165
condictio by *lex Silia* ii 71; *ob rem dati re non secuta* ii 77; *indebiti* ii 79; *sine causa* ii 82; *ob turpem causam* ii 82; *furtiva* ii 82; *incerti* ii 84; *triticaria* ii 76
condition, in appointment of heir i 198; in legacy i 312; implied i 313; fulfilment of i 315; conditions of freedom i 321; of sale ii 164; suspensive and resolutive ii 164; in restraint of marriage ii 317
conductor ii 169
confarreatio i 69, 134
confessio in jure ii 397
confusio 'merger' ii 34, 55; of usufruct i 492
conjunctim legacy i 296; conditions i 315
consanguinei i 220, 260
consensus in classification of contracts ii 2; as essential of contract ii 13, 65, 89, 138, *etc.*; of marriage i 131, 132
consilium in theft ii 203
consilium, ire in ii 417
consobrini i 262
consortes ii 128
constitutions imperial, form of i 6 n. 3, earlier in Digest i 9
constitutum ii 87; *possessorium* i 458
consuetudo i 1
consul's judicial power ii 313
contempt of court ii 432
contestari ii 402
continens 'pertaining' ii 403
contractus ii 6 n.
contrarium judicium, *e.g.* i 110, ii 93, 96, 102, 117, 126, 386
contubernium i 169
conubium i 20, 24, 128
conventio ii 6 n.
conventio in manum i 68, 136
convicium in suit *injuriarum* ii 221
corporation ii 133
corpore, in possession i 456
corpore corpori, in Aquilian damage ii 188
corpus of freeman ii 192, 195
correal obligation ii 26
corrumpere servum ii 219
credita pecunia ii 32, 68; *de rebus creditis* ii 3 n.
creditor, wide meaning ii 1
cretio i 231, 396 sqq.
cum moriar, *etc.* stipulation ii 16
curator i 121

Curius v. Coponium i 203
custom i 7

damnas esto ii 194; i 296
damnatio partes facit i 297; *per damnationem legatum* i 296
damni infecti i 509; *legis actio* ii 347
damni injuria ii 186
damni in turba facti ii 218
damnum dare and *facere* i 510 n.; *decidere* ii 208, 211
dare i 4, ii 20; *stipulationes dandi* ii 20; *dare damnas esto* i 296; *dare operas* i 85
datio in solutum i 51
de plano ii 313
deaf i 176
debiti legatum i 334
decemviri litibus aestimandis ii 315
deception not theft ii 203
decima, Caracalla's tax i 24
decoquere ii 382 n. 1
decretum i 8
decuriones i 23
dedere noxae ii 198, 252
dediticii i 19; slaves on same footing i 32
deductio, domum i 132; *moribus* ii 515; in case of *peculium* ii 240; of *bonorum emptio* ii 363
defence, want of due ii 398, 472
defensor ii 49
defugere auctoritatem ii 159
dejectio 'ejectment' i 463, ii 519, 521
delation of inheritance i 230
delay. See *mora*
delegatio ii 42, 45, 65
delictum ii 199
delivery i 426, 457
dementia i 124 n. 3, 131
deminutio capitis, see *capitis; hereditatis* i 233, 257
demonstratio in issues for trial ii 354, 362, 211; *falsa demonstratio* in legacies i 307
denarius ii 455
denegare actionem ii 350
denuntiatio ii 159, 343, 418, 529
depasci ii 198
dependere ii 184
deportation i 45, 133
depositum ii 94; *irregulare* ii 97; with *fiducia* i 97
derelictum i 416
despondere i 132 n.
detention i 452
dicere dotem i 139
dicis gratia 'for form's sake' i 76
dictare judicium ii 350, 402
dies cedit, venit i 312; *ex die, in diem, ad diem* i 198; *annua, etc. die* in dowry i 153 and note; in legacies i 323; in freedoms i 320; in stipulations ii 23; *repetita* i 448; *diem diffindere* ii 410
diffarreatio i 70, 134
distance, allowance for i 118
distractio bonorum ii 440
distress ii 115
divorce i 134; under *lex Julia* i 135
do, dico, addico ii 323, 352; *do lego* i 294; *do ut des* ii 181
dogs ii 168
Dolabella, Cn. ii 461, 462
—— P. Corn. (Tullia's husband) ii 35
doli or *doli mali* suit ii 228; plea, 231; *clausula* in stipulations ii 20
dolo malo ii 506
domestici testes i 179; *domesticum malum* ii 197
domicile ii 331
dominium i 414; *ex jure Quiritium* i 429
donatio i 525; *mortis causa* i 530; between husband and wife i 159
donum distinguished from *munus* i 86 n. 2
dos i 136; *adventicia, profecticia, recepticia* i 138; *dicitur* i 139, 140; given back to wife during marriage i 147; apportionment of fruits i 152; *aestimata* i 143
dowry. See *dos*
duci jubere ii 427 n. 2, 429
duoviri i 478
duplae stipulatio i 158; *in duplum actio* ii 183; *in duplum revocare* ii 421; *non ultra duplum* ii 75 n.
duplicatio ii 367

eadem quaestio ii 388
edictum of emperor i 9; of praetors i 10; *Carbonianum* i 268; *perpetuum* i 13; *tralaticium* i 12; *de alterutro* i 150; *contra edictum* ii 448 n. 1; *ex edicto* ii 465, 483, *etc.*
edere actionem ii 349; *operas* i 85
ejurare iniquum ii 351
emancipare i 77
emphyteusis ii 170
emptio ii 138; *spei* ii 141; *hereditatis* ii 162; *nominis* ii 163; *ususfructus* ii 164
endowment, how made ii 170 n.
epitome Gai, i Pref. p. xv
equity ii 89 n. 2
ercto non cito i 288 n.
ereptorium i 383
erro ii 152
erroris probatio i 39
evidence ii 408
eviction ii 156
ex ante gesto ii 436
ex asse, ex uncia heres i 201, 281; *ex bonis* i 428 n. 1; *ex liberis* i 243
exceptio ii 364
cognitoria, procuratoria ii 366
dilatoria ii 365
doli mali ii 231
legis Cinciae i 259
legis Plaetoriae i 124, 126
litis dividuae ii 366
metus causa ii 228
non numeratae pecuniae ii 71
onerandae libertatis causa i 89
pacti conventi ii 7, 364
rei cohaerens ii 36
rei judicatae vel in judicium deductae ii 365, 388
rei residuae ii 366
rei venditae et traditae ii 143
SC. Macedoniani ii 267
SC. Vellaeani ii 268
excuses from guardianship i 115
execution ii 423
exemplo ii 78 n.; *ad exemplum legis Aquiliae* ii 189
exercitor ii 249
exercitoria actio ii 248
exheres esto i 191
exhibendum, actio ad i 446; *interdictum lib. exhib.* i 63
exhibere=alere i 81
exilium i 45 n., ii 533
expenditure on dowry, classified i 150
expensum ferre ii 288
expromissio ii 46, 49
extra ordinem, procedure ii 449
extra quam ii 365 n. 1
extraneus manumissor ii 260, 264

facere in stipulations ii 20; ground of *condictio* ii 85
factum, actio in ii 179; cf. ii 404 n.
faenus ii 72
Falcidia i 345
falsa causa in legacies i 308; *demonstratio* i 307, ii 362
familia i 51, 173, 393; ii 23, 507; *patroni* i 278; of publicans ii 236; *familiae erciscundae* i 287; *paterfamilias* i 52; *materfamilias* i 52, 68 n.
family trusts i 361; tomb i 393
famosum carmen i 175, ii 221
farreo i 69
feriae denicales ii 338
ferrum, condemnatio ad i 175
ferruminatio i 420
festuca i 26
fictio in *formulae* ii 371; *legis Corneliae* i 210
fidei bonae ii 89
fidei commissum i 356
fidejussor ii 29, 31; *fidepromissor* ii 29; *fiderogare* ii 13
fidem sequi ii 121 n.
fiducia ii 97
fiduciarius heres i 358; *pater* i 75
filiusfamilias, legal position of i 64; in public office i 62; could be vindicated i 64; be surrendered noxally ii 258; emancipation i 74; his *peculium* i 65; his camp-*peculium* i 66; not allowed to borrow ii 267
filios includes daughters i 225 n.
finibus regendis arbiter i 449 n.
fiscus 'crown' i 141
flamines i 69; *flaminica Dialis* i 69

foreigners. See *peregrini*
formula ii 349 n.; procedure *per formulas* ii 349; *petitoria* i 443; *in jus* or *in factum concepta* ii 356
fornix i 514
fratres patrueles i 262
fraud. See *dolus*
freedmen: position i 82; who desert patrons i 44; should not be arrogated i 62; jurisdiction over i 84, 89
freedwoman's marriage with patron i 135
freeman's body not property ii 192
fructus=*ususfructus* i 496; *licitatio* ii 445
fruits, to whom belonging i 418; in case of vindication i 441; claim of *bonae fidei emptor* ii 161; on sale of land ii 146; sometimes include interest of money ii 73
frumentaria tessera i 327
fugitive slave ii 219; under aediles' edict ii 152; retains possession i 459; bequeathed i 326
fundus 'farm'; *instructus* i 339; *cum instrumento* i 339; *dotalis* i 141; *ut optimus maximusque* ii 147; *fundi furtum* ii 205, cf. 495; *fundi usus* i 496
funestare i 393
fungibles ii 66 n. 3; cf. 176
funus i 301
furiosus i 121, 131, 176
furtiva res i 475
furtum ii 201; *conceptum, etc.* ii 215; *manifestum* ii 209; *possessionis* ii 213; *non exhibitum* ii 216

Gabine cincture i 176 n. 3
Gaius, i Pref. p. xiv; his classification ii 2
generic thing bequeathed i 329
gens i 80, 95, 221
gentiles i 221
gentium jus i 5 n. 2, 20
gestation, period of i 22
gestio pro herede i 233
gestorum negotiorum ii 123
gifts, between husband and wife i 159; in general i 525; *mortis causa* i 530
gladiator's contract ii 174; oath ii 174 n.
glans included all fruit i 509; *de glande legenda* i 509
gods appointed heirs i 194
golden rings, right of i 92
gradus cognationis i 262 n. 1
grammarians excused from guardianship i 117
guardianship i 92. See *tutela*
guardian and ward i 92

habere licere ii 17, 143, 158
habitatio i 497
hand, see *manus*; handtake, see *mancipium*
hasta of centumviral court ii 315; in State auctions ii 341 n. 2, 435; *rectam hastam ferre* i 498 n.
heredis institutio i 187
hereditas i 170; *jacens* or *vacans* i 171; *legitima* i 95; *sine sacris* i 390; *hereditatis usucapio* i 227; *possessio* i 236 n.; *petitio* i 281; sale of ii 162; *hereditatis expilatae* ii 214
heres suus i 188; *necessarius* i 197; *suus et necessarius* i 188; *legitimus* i 219, 95; *secundus* i 203
honor or *honorarium* 'fee' ii 449
honorem habere alicui, name him as legatee i 251
honorarium jus i 13; cf. ii 320 n. 2
hostis i 468
hypotheca ii 99, 102

jettison ii 177
ignominia ii 327
Ilium, privilege of i 118
illata, inducta, etc., silently pledged ii 105
immiscere se hereditati i 229
immissum habere ii 195
impensae in dowry i 150
imperium, praetor's i 10; *imperio continens judicium* ii 403, 405
impossible conditions in heirship i

199; in legacy i 317; of freedom i 322; in stipulation ii 17
imprisonment for debt ii 431, 432
impuberes, maximum age i 102; require guardians i 93, 103; their liability i 108, ii 25, 187, 207, 230
inalienability of ward's land i 108; of Italian land in dowry without wife's consent i 141
in bonis i 428, also n.
in factum actio ii 179, 182
in rem actiones i 3, cf. i 281, 438, 443, 495; *in rem permissum* ii 481
in rem versum ii 245
incapacity for citizenship i 32; for guardianship i 100; for will-making i 175; for legacies i 305, 379; for alienation i 430 sq.; otherwise with trusts i 367, 382
incerta persona i 194, 306
incestuous marriages i 129
indefensus ii 438, 472 sqq.
indictio operarum i 87
infamy ii 326, 329
infans i 104, ii 25
infitiatio doubled damages ii 183
ingenui i 18; suit to determine i 49
in jure cessio i 425
injury under *lex Aquilia* ii 186
injuriarum actio ii 220
in integrum restitutio ii 259, 272, *etc.*
in jus vocare ii 333
inofficiosi test. querela i 211
in personam actio i 3
inquilinus ii 171, 105; special interdict ii 106
insanire distinguished from *furere* i 121 n.
instalments yearly i 153; ii 23
institor ii 249
institoria actio ii 249
institutio heredis i 187
instrumentum 'stock,' 'plant,' *etc.* i 339; 'document' i 340; ii 396; *dotale* i 37; *manumissionis* i 37
insula in a river i 418; 'a block of building' i 414; ii 249
intentio in *formula* ii 354, 359
intercessio of women ii 268; of tribunes ii 479
interdictio aqua et igni i 45
interdictum, general character ii 441; procedure ii 443
de aqua cottidiana et aestiva i 506
de aqua ex castello ducenda i 507
de arboribus caedendis i 508
de cloacis i 508
de fluminibus i 411
de fonte i 508
de glande legenda i 509
de homine libero exhibendo ii 225
de itinere actuque privato i 505
de itinere reficiendo i 506
de liberis exhibendis et ducendis i 63
de migrando ii 106
de mortuo inferendo i 392
de precario i 466
de remissionibus i 519
de rivis i 507
de superficie ii 176
de tabulis exhibendis i 185
de vi i 462
de vi armata i 465
de via publica i 411
fraudatorium ii 273
ne quid in loco publico fiat i 412
ne quid in loco sacro fiat i 412
ne vis fiat ei qui in poss. missus erit i 355
possessorium ii 436
quem fundum i 439
quam hereditatem i 287
quod legatorum i 240
quod vi aut clam i 520
quorum bonorum i 239
Salvianum i 113
uti possidetis i 460, 524
utrubi i 461
interest on loans ii 70, 72; maximum rate ii 74; in *bon. fid.* actions ii 89; maritime ii 75
interest, plaintiff's ii 209, *etc.*; must be money interest ii 14
interrogatio in jure ii 399
ex interrogatione (in Pompeian quittance) ii 61 n.
interruption of possession i 470
intestate succession statutable to freeborn i 218 sqq.; praetorian i

258 sqq.; to freedmen i 276 sqq.; *bon. poss.* on intestacy i 258
intestabiles i 175; ii 220 n. 1
intra pedes quinque i 450
invecta, illata, etc., pledged ii 145
island, new i 418
Italic land i 141, 424, 426
iter i 498
iteratio (*manumissionis*) i 39
joinder of issue ii 461
jubere ii 122
judex ii 322, cf. ii 318; *judicem ferre, sumere, accipere, recusare* ii 351; *judicis postulatio* ii 345
judicatus ii 299, 438 n. 3, 431
judicatum solvi ii 384
judicio defendere, pati ii 459, 382 n. 2
judicio sistendi put by Justinian for *vadimoni* ii 335 n.
judicium ii 349; *legitimum* ii 403; *imperio continens* ii 403; *Cascellianum vel secutorium* ii 446. See also *actio*
Juliani postumi i 193
jumenta i 498
Juniani i 38, 94
jurare in litem ii 416
jurisconsulti i 14, ii 409
jus eundi, agendi, etc. i 498
jus gentium i 5, 19
jus honorarium i 13
jus Latii i 23
jus naturale i 17
jus novum statuere ii 353
jusjurandum operarum i 86
  de calumnia ii 386
jus trium liberorum i 29, 102, 271; *quattuor* i 271; *duorum* i 272; *jus tr. lib.* granted i 381 n. 4
jussus ii 122
justae nuptiae i 127
justa possessio i 453; *servitus* i 18
Justinian's legislation i Pref. p. v

kalendarium i 340

laesio enormis i 149
land bequeathed i 344
land of ward not alienable i 108; of dowry i 141
lapilli ictus i 519
larvali habitu i 198
Latini coloniarii i 19; *Juniani* i 38, 279
latitare ii 438, 472, 474 n. 3
Latium majus, and *minus* i 23
laudare auctorem ii 157 n. 1
ledger ii 280
legare i 173 n. 2
legatum i 293—356; *sub modo* i 322
lege acquisitio i 415; *lege agere* ii 339 n.
leges Juliae on procedure ii 347
legis actio ii 339
legitimus, when technical i 95 n.; cf. ii 403 n. 2
lex 'terms,' 'condition,' *mancipii* i 426, ii 167; *commissoria* in *fiducia* ii 100; in pledge ii 110; in sales ii 165; *praediatoria* i 480
lex 'statute' i 6, 7; not accessible i 9 n.
  Aebutia ii 347
  Aelia Sentia i 30
  Appuleia ii 30
  Aquilia ii 186
  Atilia i 98
  Atinia i 475
  Calpurnia ii 71
  Cicereia ii 31
  Cincia i 526
  Claudia i 95, 474
  Cornelia, of wills, i 210; of sureties ii 33; of *injuriae* ii 224; of forgeries i 180
  Crepereia i 442
  curiata de imperio i 10
  Fabia de plagiariis ii 220; i 33
  Falcidia i 345
  Fufia Caninia i 33; cf. i 183
  Furia de sponsu ii 30; *testamentaria* i 344
  Hortensia i 6
  Julia caducaria i 223; *de adulteriis* i 34, 135, 141; *de cessione bonorum* ii 438; *de vi publica* ii 525; *repetundarum* i 474
  Julia on marriage i 130, 132, 139, 148, 379
  Julia et Plautia i 475
  Julia et Titia i 98

lex (continued)
Julia municipalis ii 327 n. 2
Julia de vicesima i 188, ii 32 n.
Junia Norbana i 38
Junia Vellaea i 191
Laetoria. See *lex Plaetoria*
Malacitana i 479
Mamilia i 450
Minicia i 21
Papia Poppaea i 130, 148, 379, 383
Papiria i 408 n. 2
Pesolania ii 198
Petronia i 54
Pinaria ii 343
Plaetoria i 123
Plautia Papiria i 23
Poetelia ii 305, 310
Publilia ii 184
Rubria i 69
Scribonia i 503
Silia ii 71
Valeria ii 456
Vallia ii 430
Visellia i 40
Voconia i 193 n. 4, 345
libellus i 215, 419
liber i 52; *liberi loco* i 48
libera peculi administratio i 55
liberalis causa i 46
liberatio legata i 333; *lib. per aes et libram* ii 185, 299
liberi i 52; wide meaning i 93 n., 251; *vulgo concepti* i 22; *patrem, matrem sequuntur* i 20; *sine liberis* i 363; *inter liberos* i 189 n.; *ex liberis* i 243; *liberorum quaerendorum causa* i 39, 127; *jus trium lib.* i 381 n.
liberi et parentes, saving of legacies to i 251
libertas not admitting valuation ii 342; favour shewn to i 49, 366
libertinus i 18, 51
libertus i 18; position i 82; assignment i 82; under praetor's protection i 89; *centenarius* i 270; *orcinus* i 28; use in notice of divorce i 135
libra ii 185
librarius i 486
libripens 'balanceholder' i 178, 423 n.
licence to jurisconsults i 14, ii 409
licitatio fructuum ii 445
ligna bequeathed i 343
lignum, bon. poss. contra i 244
linum in bequest i 343
liquet non ii 417
lis=*res* ii 342 n.; contestata, inchoata ii 402
litem suam facere ii 415; *jurare in litem* ii 416
litis contestatio ii 402
litigiosa res ii 140
litterarum obligatio ii 64, 279
litus i 410
loan (*commodatum*) ii 91; (*mutuum*) ii 66
locatio ii 169
locuples ii 336, 426
locus i 450
lucrative acquisitions i 310; ii 18
lugere ii 330
luminum servitus i 499 n. 1; *lumina recipere* i 501 n.

mad. See *furiosus*
magister in sales in bankruptcy ii 480; of tax companies ii 133; of a ship ii 249
magistrates local, limited power of i 515; liable to wards i 112
maleficium no basis for partnership ii 130
manceps i 481
Mancinus i 42
mancipation i 423, 177; carried guaranty ii 156, 157 n.; use in adoption i 75; in freeing from power i 74; by slaves i 425
mancipi res i 424
mancipium i 423, 486 n. 1; *in mancipio* i 73; position of persons in i 76
mandata, imperial i 9, 131
mandator, as guarantor ii 121
mandatum ii 116
manes i 408
Manili actiones ii 155 n.
manum conserere ii 340 n.
manu militari ii 441
manumission, formal i 25; informal

i 36; direct by will i 26, 28; indirect through heir i 27; by statute i 35; age required i 30; in fraud of creditors i 32; purchase by slave i 29; conditions i 319; by trust i 303 sqq., 368; rarely granted by Augustus i 24 n. 1; under rescript of M. Aurelius i 35; by foreigners i 38

manumission in coemption i 72; of children i 74, 77; in adoption i 75

manumissor parens, right to *bon. poss. c. tab.* i 254; *extraneus* i 264, cf. 74, 96

manumissoris cognati i 278

manus: wife *in manu* i 68, 94, 136, 189; women i 71

manus injectio ii 423, 425, 426

mare common to all i 409

marriage: conditions i 58, 127; definition i 127, 128 n.; purpose i 39, 127 n., 134; age i 131; distinctive mark i 132; with cousins i 128 n.; with wife's sister i 129 n.; with freedwoman i 135; free i 137; dissolution of i 133; gifts during i 159; penalties in default of i 379

marshalling of debts ii 54

materfamilias i 52, 68 n.

matertera i 263

matrimonium justum i 20

medical expenses, of mandatee ii 120; under *lex Aquilia* ii 192

media tempora non nocent i 193

melior condicio in sales ii 165

mente captus i 121 n., 131, 176

merces ii 169

metus ii 226; ground for reinstatement ii 262

military service, excuses from guardianship i 116

militia 'a service-post' i 327

mines, fructuary's right i 485; condemnation to i 44

minors under caretakers i 123; reinstatement ii 259

missio in possessionem, to protect *venter* i 266; legatees i 354; in general ii 432

modus, limitation of use i 322, ii 166; action *de modo agri* ii 156 n.

Mohatra ii 68 n. 2

moneylending in England ii 299 n.

morari in libertate i 37

mora as condition of interest ii 89, 94; *in rei vindicatio* i 441; *hered. petitio* i 284; on part of heir i 360

morbus, in redhibition ii 151; *sonticus* ii 338

mores 'custom' i 7, cf. 229; *jud. de moribus* i 157, cf. i 146; *vis facta moribus* ii 446, 514 sq., 532 n.

morte Cincia removetur i 529

mortgage, English ii 99

mortis causa donatio i 530; *capere* i 532

mother, inheritance from i 225, 260

mother's claim to inherit i 223; as cognate i 261; not a guardian i 100; nor defender in court ii 269

mourning ii 330

Muciana cautio i 318; *praesumptio* i 165

munus 'gift' i 86 n. 2; to wife i 164

mundus muliebris i 342

muri i 409

mutuum ii 66

Narbo ii 453, 458

natalibus restitutus i 92

nation of slave to be stated ii 152, 168

natural children opposed to adoptive i 115, 189, 270; under *lex Papia* i 90, 381; alimony for i 81

naturalis possessio i 452; *obligatio* ii 1, cf. 80

nauticum faenus ii 75

necessary, expenditure i 151; heir i 197, 198, 229

nectere ii 296

negotiorum gestio ii 123

negotium 'lawsuit' ii 234

nepos as own heir i 189

nexum ii 296; *inire* ii 301, 303; *aes* ii 306

nisi restituet ii 355, 411, cf. 358 n.
nomen in descriptions i 195, 307; heir to bear testator's i 59 n.
nomen 'a debt,' *legatum* i 332; *facere* ii 286, 291; *arcarium* ii 65; *bonum* ii 267, 292; regarded in *actio pro socio* ii 132, 492
nominatim 'expressly' i 99, 173 n., 190, cf. i 34
nominum dies i 381
non wrongly inserted or omitted ii 448 n. 2
non-feasance ii 18; cf. 189
novatio ii 38; by sons or slaves ii 41
Novels, Justinian's, vol. i Pref. p. i
novicius servus ii 150
noxa ii 252; *noxae dedere*, not *dare*, ii 252 n.; *noxam nocere* ii 252 n.; *sarcire* ii 198, 252 n.
noxa caput sequitur ii 193, 198, 208, 252
noxal surrender of children ii 258, 309
noxia ii 252 n.
nuda pactio ii 7; *ratio* ii 284 n.
nudum dominium i 428; *nudus usus* i 496
nummo uno vendere i 370; *mancipare* i 529, ii 102; *nummis colere* ii 169 n.
nuncupata pecunia ii 306
nuncupatio in wills i 178; in mancipations i 426
nuntiatio op. novi i 517
nuntium, per i 402, 405; ii 87, *etc.*
nuntium remittere of divorce i 135 n., 150 n. 3
nuptiae i 127. See marriage

oath ii 394; as condition of heirship i 199; or of legacy i 317
oats hurt barley ii 188 n.
oblatum furtum ii 215
obligation i 2; ii 1; strict ii 10; *bonae fidei* ii 88; transfer of ii 45; discharge ii 49; release ii 55; semi-delictal ii 183; *ex delicto* ii 199; noxal ii 253; natural ii 1, 80; *perpetuatur culpā* ii 18
ob rem i 530; ii 77
obsequium i 84
obsignare i 180; ii 408
occupantis melior est condicio ii 240, 255, 416
occupation as title i 415
officium judicis ii 411 sqq.
omissa causa testamenti i 302
omnis causa i 441
ope consilio furtum factum ii 203
operae liberti i 85; *servi* i 315, 319, 496; *ex operis suis vel ex re nostra* i 435
optimo jure legatum i 295
optimus maximusque fundus i 147 n.; *optimum triticum Africum* ii 24
option in legacies i 329; of guardian i 94; in stipulations ii 19
oratio of emperor i 7
orbus i 380
orcinus libertus i 28
ornamenta in legacies i 342; of horses, *etc.* ii 150
ownership, restrictions on i 414

pactum ii 6; attached to *bon. fid.* contract ii 8; to *mutuum* ii 63; to dowry i 145; to mancipation ii 101; to sale ii 139; *de non petendo* ii 61
paganorum testamenta i 218
painting as title i 421
parapherna i 148
pararii ii 293
parens manumissor i 254
pars pro indiviso ii 21
partes concursu fiunt i 296
partis et pro parte stipulationes i 325, 370
partition of inheritance i 288; by legacy i 325
passenger (*vector*), protection of ii 178, 182; in case of general average ii 177
pastu, de pecoris ii 212
pater est quem nuptiae demonstrant i 58
pater fiduciarius i 75
patria potestas i 57; removal of i 77; conferred by grant i 62; position of children i 64
patrimonium i 377, 408

patrimus i 69 n. 3
patron i 83; succession to Roman freedmen, general view i 270; possession of freedman's estate *c. tab.* i 273; intestate i 276; to estate of Latin freedmen i 279; cancelling fraudulent acts of freedman ii 276
Pauliana actio ii 273
payment, what is ii 50; to whom should be made ii 52; tender of ii 53
pecora, pecudes i 343
peculium i 54; free management of i 55; *castrense* i 66; *de peculio actio* ii 238; rustic use of term i 54 n.; could be used to gain freedom i 320; bequeathed i 337
pecunia, in early law i 174 n., ii 32
pecunia credita ii 32, 68
penalty in stipulations. See *poena*
pendere in vacuom i 480 n.
peregrini i 19; marriage with Romans i 21, 39; obtaining citizenship by grant i 23; in suretyship ii 30; whether capable of *litt. oblig.* ii 66; praetor for their suits ii 312
perhibere testimonium i 424 n.
perscribere ii 292
pertinere i 294; *ad quos pertinet* i 513
petitio hereditatis i 281
petitoria formula i 443
philosophers excused from guardianship i 117; how paid ii 449
pigneraticia actio ii 103
pignoris capio ii 115; by magistrates ii 440
pignus ii 99, 102; tacit ii 105; sale of ii 108; pledge of ii 113; *nominis* ii 103
pileati i 37
placere ii 484
plea. See *exceptio*
plebiscitum i 6, 7
pledge. See *pignus*
plurality of guardianships i 116
pluris petitio ii 360
poena in appointment of heir i 199; in bequest i 304; in stipulations ii 14, 19; in arbitrations ii 320
poenae servus i 44
pollicitatio i 533
pontifices preside over adrogations i 60; over private *sacra* i 387
ports i 409
possession i 451; civil and natural i 452; *justa* and *injusta* i 453 n.; in *damni infecti* i 454, 510, 513; leads to usucapion i 467; character of i 472; required in *int. de vi* i 463; *de vi armata* i 465, ii 523; *missio in possessionem* for legatees i 354; *vi clam, etc.* i 521; possession through others i 437, 454; *possessionis furtum* i 478; *causam possessionis mutare* i 474
possessio bonorum. See *bonorum*
possessor in vindications i 439; in servitudes i 504; of inheritance i 283
possessor=owner i 451; *pro possessore possidere* i 472
possidere distinguished from *in possessione esse* i 453, 454, 513, ii 482
possideri et proscribi ii 480, 482 n.; *poss. vendique* ii 433
postliminium as regards *status* i 42; wills i 210; property and family ii 264; of chattels ii 265
postulare ii 326
postulatio judicis ii 345
postumi, when legitimate i 22; as own heirs i 188, 190, 191 n.; *Aquiliani, Vellaeani, Juliani* i 192, 193; *alieni* i 194
potioris nominatio i 118
potestas i 52, 57; *habere in potestate* ii 255
poverty considered i 117, 442
pp., i.e. propositum i 8
praeceptio i 240, 291, 298, 372
praedes et praedia i 478; *pro praede litis vindiciarum* ii 385
praediatura i 480
praedium i 478, 498
praedo i 283, 472
praefectus vigilibus ii 210
praejudicium i 49, 92, ii 31, 359, 393
praelegare i 301

praelegata dos i 335
praescriptio i 483, ii 370
praescriptis verbis ii 179
praeses ii 313
praestare i 4; *causam* i 442; *his rebus recte praestari* i 442
praetextati i 64 n. 1
praetor i 10, ii 312, 352; *peregrinus* ii 312; *tutelaris* i 99
praetorian heir i 237; praetorian will i 256 n.; guardian i 98
precarium i 406, 506
pregnancy asserted in case of woman divorced i 166; by widow i 167
price in money, characteristic of sale ii 138, 181
prison of creditor ii 307, 427 n. 2
probare causam (under *lex Aelia Sentia*) i 38; *errorem* i 39
procinctus i 176
proconsul ii 313; Cicero as proc. i 12; jurisdiction over manumissions i 36 n. 2
Proculiani i 15. See *Sabiniani*
procurator, acquisition through i 437; *ad litem* ii 379; *omnium bonorum* ii 379; *in rem suam* ii 49
prodigus i 121, 176, ii 449
professors of law, how paid ii 449; cf. i 117
promissio ii 12, 13
promissor fide i 29, 30
pronuntiare ii 398, 411
proof, burden of ii 409
proscribere ii 459, 480, 482 n.
protutor i 114, ii 206
provincial land i 429, 430 n., ii 306
provocare sacramento ii 342; *sponsione* ii 375 n.
prudentes juris i 7, 14
pubertas i 102
publica judicia ii 328 n. 4
publicani i 478; action against ii 235
publice emere or *vēnire* i 481 n. 2
pueri i 343
pupillar wills i 203
pupillus 'ward,' guardian's administration of i 103; suits of i 109, 111, 112; definition of i 123 n. 2, 204 n. 1; cannot alienate by himself i 431
purchase. See *emptio*

quadruplex judicium ii 315
quaerere, of getting children i 127 n.
quaestor i 7
quanti res erit ii 355, 356; *quanti plurimi* ii 186
quarta divi Pii i 61; *Falcidiae* i 346; to defeat *querela inoff. test.* i 213
querela inofficiosi testamenti i 211
quidquid paret dare oportere i 354, 357
Quiritium, owner *ex jure* i 424, 428
quittance ii 59
quod ejus ii 523 n. 2
quod interest ii 356; *quod facere possunt* ii 416
quod jussu ii 237
quod vi aut clam interdict i 520

rapina i 216, 217
ratam rem habere stipulation ii 383
ratification ii 117
ratio, of accounts ii 291; *rationes reddere* i 321; *aeraria ratio* ii 455
receipt ii 59
recepticia dos i 138, cf. 136 n.; *actio* ii 88
receptum argentari ii 88; *arbitri* ii 321; *nautarum* ii 178
recipere, general use i 538; in easements i 501, 534 sqq.; *recte recipitur* i 541
recoverers. See *recuperatores*
recuperatores ii 315
redemptor 'ransomer' i 42, ii 264; 'contractor' ii 175
reditus omnibus annis i 331
referre acceptum ii 59, 288
Regulae, Ulpian's i Pref. p. viii
Regulus i 42 n., ii 265 n.
reinstatement. See *restitutio in integrum*
release ii 55
relegata dos i 335
relegatio 'banishment' i 46
religiosus i 409
remissio of a notice 'discharged' i 518

remittere nuntium in divorce i 135
renouncement of legacy i 308
repairs of dowry property i 151; by usufructuary i 485
repetition of legacies i 309
replicatio ii 367
representation, different kinds i 401; in suits ii 47
repromittere i 510, ii 29, 488 n. 8, 490
repudiatio of a legacy ii 309
repudium i 134
res=lis ii 342 n.; *furtiva* i 475; *in judicium deducta* ii 388; *judicata* ii 388; *litigiosa* ii 406; *mancipi* i 423; *religiosa* i 409; *sancta* i 410; *bon. poss. sine re* i 239
rescribere ii 293
rescriptum i 8
resolutive condition ii 164
responsa prudentium i 7, 14
restipulatio ii 387, 445, 488 n. 3
restitutio in integrum of minors ii 259; of *majores* ii 262; of creditors ii 274; of patron ii 276; of heir i 26
restitutio of profits i 441; to trust heir i 357, 370 sqq.
restrictions on amount of legacies i 344
retentiones from dowry i 150
reus stipulandi or *promittendi* ii 12; *duo rei* ii 26
reverter. See *postliminium*
revocatio, domum ii 332; *in duplum* ii 421
revoke a will i 209
risk of a thing bequeathed i 326; lent ii 92; deposited ii 94; pledged ii 106; sold ii 145; leased ii 172
rivers, public i 411; *interdictum de rivis* i 507
Roma, its practice to be followed elsewhere i 1
Roman law not territorial i 16
ruta caesa ii 146, i 448
Rutiliana constitutio i 101 n. 4
Rutilius, his *formulae* ii 373; on slave's services i 89
Sabiniani i 15; dispute on appointment of guardian before heir i 94; on age of puberty i 102; on postumous children i 188, 191; on transfer of inheritance i 229; acquisition of legacy i 294; pending condition i 295; on *praeceptum* i 299; on legacy to one *in potestate* i 306; on impossible condition i 317; case of codicils i 183; legacy of share i 325; on specification i 422; acquisition by slaves i 434; on dereliction i 416; on honest possession i 471; stipulation for another ii 15; *datio in solutum* ii 51; novation ii 39; price in money ii 138; price to be ascertained ii 142; noxal surrender ii 257, 258; satisfaction after suit accepted ii 414; mandate ii 119
sacer i 408; *sacra privata* i 387
sacramentum ii 340
sale, contract of ii 138
saltus 'mountain pastures' i 459
salvum fore recipere ii 179
sarta tecta i 485
satis dare ii 382, 476; *secundum mancipium* ii 102, 157
satisfacere ii 42 n. 2
sea-shore, definition of i 410; buildings on i 410, 422
secare partes ii 424
second will i 208
sectio bonorum ii 435 n. 2; *praedis* i 482, 426 n.
sector ii 435 n. 2, 482
secundus auctor ii 157 n. 2; *heres* i 203 n. 1
security ii 381; to be given by procurator ii 381, 476
senator forbidden to marry freedwomen, *etc.* i 130
Senatusconsultum i 7
  Afinianum i 60 n.
  Apronianum i 368
  Articuleianum i 365
  Calvisianum i 380
  Claudianum on cohabitation with slaves i 43, 21

Senatusconsultum (continued)
Dasumianum i 365
Juncianum i 365
Juventianum i 283
Largianum i 280
Libonianum i 177, 383 n. 1
Macedonianum i 267
Neronianum i 295
Orfitianum i 225
Pegasianum i 38, 39, 371, 376
Pernicianum i 380
Plancianum i 166
Sabinianum i 61 n.
Silanianum i 185
Tertullianum i 223
Trebellianum i 370
Vellaeanum / *Velleianum* ii 268
sententia judicis ii 352, 418
Sententiae Pauli vol. i Pref. p. viii
separatio bonorum ii 437
sepulcrum i 392
sequester ii 97
serviens bona fide i 436
servitus personarum i 484; *praediorum* i 497
servus i 17, 19; manumission i 24; position i 51, 53; liable to be tortured i 54; surrendered noxally i 51, ii 252; appointment as heir i 195; enters i 234; conditions of freedom by will i 319; stipulates for master i 431; takes by mancipation i 401; *morans in libertate* i 37; *hereditarius* i 170; *fugitivus* ii 152; claim of freedom i 46; subject of aediles' edict i 150; *quasi*-marriage i 169; when can bring master into court i 30, 57; *quasi*-will i 175 n. 3
servus poenae i 44; *publicus* ii 134; *recepticius* i 136 n.; *sine domino* i 28; *vicarius* i 55, ii 243
set-off ii 363
ship-building gives privilege i 40 n. 1
sinendi modo legatum i 297
sine re, bon. poss. i 239; *heres* i 241
sistere reum ii 336 n.
slaves. See *servus*
snakes ii 199
sobrinus, sobrino propior i 263; marriage of i 128 n. 1
societas, partnership ii 127, 494; company ii 133; tenancy in common ii 135; *leonina* ii 131; compared to heirship ii 491, 494
socio, actio pro ii 128, 492
solarium 'ground-rent' i 412, ii 176; 'sun-dial' ii 465 n. 1
soldiers' wills i 216, 377
solidus (coin) ii 197, 199
solutio ii 49
solvere ii 49 n.; *tabulas* ii 402 n.
sonticus morbus ii 338
sors 'principal sum' ii 72, 300
spadones i 103
species i 326
specification i 421
spondeo ii 12
sponsalia i 132
sponsio ii 374, 444; *sponsione* or *sponsionem vincere* ii 375 n. 2
sponsor ii 29
stage-players ii 329 n. 2
stare, stetisse, of appearance in court ii 337
statuliber i 27, 28; *statulibera*'s child i 22
status, trial of i 50
stellionatus ii 104
stemma agnationis i 222; *cognationis* i 263
stillicidium i 499
stipendiarii agri i 429, 430 n.
stipulatio amplius non peti ii 383; *dolum malum abesse* ii 15, 383; *duplae* ii 155, 158; *fructuaria* i 487; *habere licere* ii 158; *illum sisti* ii 337; *judicatum solvi* ii 384; *mihi et Titio* ii 14; *mihi aut Titio* ii 15; *operarum* i 86; *partis et pro parte* i 325, 370; *pridie quam moriar* ii 16; *pro praede litis, etc.* ii 385; *de rato habendo* ii 383
stipulation ii 11; certain and uncertain ii 24
stirps i 219, 221
streets, oversight of i 410
stricti juris actio a mistake ii 3 n.; *stricta judicia* ii 10

sublucare i 509
subscriptio i 181
subsignare i 479
substitutus i 202; *vulgaris, pupillaris* i 204
successio, none *in legitimis hereditatibus* i 220
sufferance, tenant on i 466
suicide i 210
suis nummis emi i 29; *suus heres* i 188; *pro suo possidere* i 472; *suae aetatis fieri* i 324
Sulla's conscription ii 468 sqq.; law about *Volaterrae* ii 532
superficies ii 176; *solo cedit* i 420
superstites ii 340 n. 2
suppellex i 341
surculo defringendo i 470 n.
suretyship ii 29
surveyors, actions against ii 236
suscipere liberos i 64 n. 2, 198
suspectum facere i 119
suspensive condition ii 164
syngraphae ii 66 and n. 2

tabulae of will i 179; of stipulation ii 12; of *formula*? ii 403; of notice-board ii 459; *b. p. contra tabulas* i 237; *secundum tabulas* i 255
taxatio ii 356, 415
tempus, mode of reckoning i 30 n. 3; *utile* i 231, ii 333
tender of payment ii 53; of oath ii 394
testamenti, factio i 193, 255 n. 1
testamentum i 173; mode of making i 176; *inofficiosum* i 211; *irritum* i 209, 210; *militare* i 216; *ruptum* i 207; *per aes et libram* i 177
testatio i 403; ii 459
testes to wills should not be *domestici* i 179; in suits ii 408, 410
tignum junctum i 421, ii 212; *immittendi jus* i 500
torture i 54, ii 408
tradere rem or *possessionem* i 457 n.
traditio i 426, 457; *brevi manu, longa manu* i 458
trajectitia pecunia ii 75
tralaticium edictum i 12
transactio ii 8, 322
transcripticiis nominibus ii 285
transcriptio ii 65, 283 n., 293
transfer of inheritance or legacy from heir, *etc.* by trust i 370
transferre judicium ii 352; *obligationem* ii 45
translatio ii 347 n. 2
Transpadani i 23
treasure-trove i 417
trespass i 416 n.
tribunes in appointment of guardians i 98; appealed to in private cases ii 479
tributaria (*praedia*) i 429
tributoria actio ii 247
trinoctium i 68
triplicatio ii 367
turba: damni in turba facti ii 219
turpis causa ii 82
tutela i 92; *mulierum* i 101; *impuberum* i 102; *judicium tutelae* i 109, 111 n. 1; *in tutelam suam pervenire* i 323
tutor Atilianus i 98; *cessicius* i 97; *dativus* i 93; *falsus* i 114; *fiduciarius* i 96; *honorarius* i 106; *legitimus* i 95; *optivus* i 94; *praetorius* i 98; *temporarius* i 98; *suspectus* i 119

uncia = $\frac{1}{12}$ of inheritance i 200
unciarium faenus ii 74
unde liberi, unde legitimi, etc. i 259 n. 1
universitas i 377; transference *per universitatem* i 68 n. 3, 227 n. 2
urbana praedia, servi, etc. i 497 n.
usu as mode of marriage i 68
usucapio i 467; *pro possessore, etc.* i 472; *pro herede* i 227
usu receptio i 477
usurae ii 74; *pupillares* i 105
usurpatio i 69
usus i 497
ususfructus i 484; of consumables i 488; granted in dowry i 142; fructuary's possession ii 454, 526
utendum dare ii 92
uti possidetis i 460, 524

uti legassit super pecunia, etc. i 93 n. 2
utilis actio ii 189, 333; *tempus utile* i 231, ii 333
utique i 540 n.
utrubi i 461
uxor i 68 n. 1, 127

vacans hereditas i 171
vacua possessio i 457; ii 144 n. 2, 503; *venditio praedis in vacuom* i 480
Vada Volaterrana ii 458
vadari ii 336 n.
vadimonium ii 336
vas 'bail' ii 336 n.
vectigal i 412, 429
venditio ii 139
ventris missio in possessionem i 266
vestal virgins i 174
vestis in legacy i 342
veterans granted citizenship and *conubium* i 24
veterator ii 150
veteres 'republican lawyers' ii 204
via i 498; *via consularis, etc.* i 411
vicarius i 55; ii 243
vicesima (hereditatum) ii 32; i 24
vigiles i 40, 217
vindex ii 335, 425, 426
vindicatio rei i 438; of children, *adjecta causa* i 64, ii 390; *legati* i 294
vindiciae ii 342; *vindicias dare* i 48 n.
vindicta, manumission by i 25, 26 n.
vis defined i 521, ii 515; *interd. de vi* i 462; *de vi armata* i 465; *quod vi aut clam* i 520; *vis quotidiana* ii 514—516; *ex conventu* ii 446, 515
vites not *arbores* ii 346
vitium, servi ii 151; of building i 514 n.
vocare in jus ii 333
Volaterrae, Sulla's law for reducing *status* ii 532
vulgo concepti i 22, 129, 224; *quaesiti* i 225

wagers ii 376 n. 1; see also *sponsio* ii 374
ward. See *pupillus*
way to a tomb i 394. See *via, iter*
will making i 176; opening i 184; breaking, *etc.* i 207; will with five or seven seals i 255 n. 2; speaks from date of making i 324. See also *testamenti factio*
wine, legacy of i 343
women after divorce not to alienate slaves i 34; cannot adopt i 58; cannot be arrogated ii 62; come into hand i 68; require guardian's authority i 101; esp. for alienation i 430; punished for drinking wine i 158 n.

II. INDEX OF PRINCIPAL PASSAGES IN LAY WRITERS REFERRED TO.

A. IN CICERO.

Acad. II 30 § 97 ii 479
Agrar. (or *Rull.*)
III 2 § 9 i 479
3 § 11 i 460
Att. (*Epist. ad Att.*)
I 1 § 3 ii 273, 435
3 *fin.* i 132
5 § 6 i 227
7 § 1 ii 86
13 § 3 i 135
IV 16 § 8 ii 8
17 ii 294
V 1 § 1 ii 157
11 § 2 i 23
21 §§ 11, 13 ii 74
IX 12 § 3 ii 293
XI 2 § 2 i 153
12 *sub fin.* i 396
XII 3 § 2 ii 42
17 § 2 ii 30
18 i 179
XIII 46 § 3 i 397
50 § 2 i 432
51 ii 292
XVI 2 § 1 ii 293
15 § 5 ii 86
Brut. 5 §§ 17, 18 ii 383
11 § 44 ii 161
22 § 86 ii 410
58 § 112 i 59
Caecin. 2 § 6 ii 320
3 § 7 i 111, ii 10
4 § 11 i 138, 146, 488
§ 12 i 325
6 § 17 ii 289
10 § 29 ii 418
13 § 36 i 464
19 § 54 i 123, 467, 499, ii 157
20 § 57 ii 379
Caecin. 25 § 72, 73 i 101, 139, 192
26 § 74 i 468
32 § 92 ii 375
34 § 99 i 43
besides Essay ii 510–535
Cael. 7 § 17 ii 238
Cluent. 7 § 21 i 325
11 § 33 i 203
15 § 45 i 261
42 § 119 ii 327
50 § 139 ii 452
60 § 165 i 261
Dom. 13 § 34 i 61
29 § 77 i 60
§ 78 i 49, ii 388
49—53 i 408
Fam. (*Epist. ad Familiares*)
VII 2 i 86
12 § 2 ii 135
14 ii 509
21 i 255, ii 374
22 ii 213
23 § 1 ii 291
29 i 72
32 i 453
XIII 7 § 2 ii 170
27 ii 369
28a § 2 ii 383
56 § 2 ii 100
§ 3 ii 54
XV 16 § 3 i 465
Fin. I 4 § 12 i 486
7 § 24 i 77
II 1 § 3 ii 368
12 § 36 ii 392
17 § 55 i 357
22 § 74 i 11
V 29 § 88 ii 369
18 § 43 i 482

Flac. 20 §§ 46, 47 ii 29
21 § 49 ii 350, 422
§ 50 ii 320
§ 51 ii 100
32 § 80 i 479
34 § 84 i 68
§ 85 i 227
35 § 87 i 136, 139
36 § 89 ii 226
Font. I § 15 ii 456
8 § 18 ii 47
Har. R. 7 § 14 ii 304
Invent.
II 11 § 57 ii 308
21 §§ 62–64 i 204
50 § 148 i 121, 173
Legg. I 21 § 55 i 450
II 19 sqq. i 387 sqq.
22 § 55 i 393
23 § 58 i 409
24 § 61 i 393
III 20 § 46 i 9
Mil. 18 § 48 i 179
Mur. I § 3 ii 304
2 § 3 ii 157
9 § 19 i 14
12 § 26 ii 340
§ 27 i 70, 71
14 § 30 ii 341
Nat. D. II 3 § 9 i 176
III 18 § 45 i 20
30 § 74 i 123, ii 89, 203, 228
Off. I 7 § 21 i 415
10 § 32 ii 226
12 § 37 i 468
13 § 43 i 174
II 8 § 27 ii 341
III 5 § 23 i 5
14 §§ 58–60 ii 228, 287
15 § 61 i 123, ii 98
16 § 65 ii 149
§ 67 i 536, ii 147
17 § 69 i 5
§ 70 ii 89, 98, 259
§ 71 ii 149
23 § 91 ii 151
Orat. (*de oratore*)
I 10 § 41 ii 341
Orat. (*de oratore*) continued
I 36 §§ 166, 167 i 111, ii 359
37 § 173 ii 314
38 § 175 i 190
39 § 176 i 221
§ 178 ii 147
§ 179 i 501, 534 sqq.
§ 180 i 203
48 § 212 i 14
53 § 228 i 176
55 § 236 ii 409
56 § 237 i 70, 288
57 § 241 i 192
II 63 § 255 ii 427
70 § 283 i 227
75 § 305 ii 415
III I § 4 ii 116
28 § 110 i 470
41 § 165 i 466
Orator 29 § 102 ii 535
Part. Orat.
28 § 98 i 237
§§ 99, 100 ii 349
31 § 107 i 342, ii 146
Philipp.
II 26 § 64 ii 435
28 § 69 i 134
VI 4 § 11 ii 467
X 5 § 11 i 382
Pison. 9 § 18 ii 28
Quint. Fr. (*Epist.*)
II 13 § 3 ii 347
III I § 3 i 498
Quinct. 2 § 5 ii 499
3 § 13 ii 128
6 § 25 ii 337
15 § 50 ii 434
16 § 52 ii 133
27 § 84 ii 435
besides Essay ii 453–485
Rosc. Am.
38 § 111 sqq. ii 117
40 § 116 ii 128
Rosc. Com.
I § 2 ii 292
§ 4 ii 416
4 § 12 i 156, ii 318
6 § 16 ii 128
9 § 25 ii 128

Rosc. Com. II § 32 ii 186
18 § 53 ii 380
besides Essay ii 486–502
R.P. (*de republica*)
I 13 § 20 i 460
II 34 § 59 ii 304
III 10 § 17 i 345
IV 10 ii 220
Senect. 7 § 22 ii 449
11 § 38 i 77
Top. 2 § 9 i 5
§ 10 i 25, ii 426
3 § 13 i 341
§ 14 i 68
§ 16 i 341
§ 17 i 488
4 § 18 i 73
§ 19 i 150
§ 20 i 150
§ 21 i 490
§ 22 i 514
§ 23 i 467
5 § 27 i 413
§ 28 i 6, 423, ii 305
6 § 29 i 174, 229
7 § 32 i 410
8 § 37 i 42
9 § 39 i 516
10 § 43 i 449, 516
Top. 10 § 45 i 426
11 § 46 i 431, ii 52
17 § 65 ii 407
§ 66 i 156, ii 117
25 § 96 ii 11
26 § 100 ii 140
Tull. 3 § 7 ii 356
7 § 17 ii 144
23 § 53 i 520, ii 443
besides Essay ii 502–509
Verr. Act. II
I 42 § 107 i 193, 211
§ 109 i 10
43 § 110 i 345
44 § 114 i 258
45 § 115 i 221, 282, 443
§ 117 i 255
48 § 125 i 275
50 § 130 i 478
2 24 § 59 ii 438
§ 60 ii 382
25, 26 §§ 62, 63 ii 258
70 § 170 ii 289
77 § 188 ii 291
3 10 § 26 ii 342
11 § 27 ii 115
15 § 38 ii 331
60 § 139 ii 56
65 § 152 ii 226

B. IN OTHER WRITERS.

Asconius Ped. *in Corn.* i 46
Bell. Alex. 39 ii 289
Caesar *B. G.*
II 33 ii 435
VI 13 § 2 ii 428
Cato, *de dote* i 157
pro lège Voconia i 136
R. R. I ii 74
5 § 3 ii 67
146 § 2 ii 106
149 ii 42, 106
Frontin.
II p. 36 *Agrimens.* i 430
ad Heren.
I 14 ii 221
II 13 § 19 ii 117, 133, 221
IV 2 § 14 ii 465
29 § 40 i 457
Horat. *Od.* III 5 41 ii 265
Carm. Sec. 17 i 379
Sat. I 1 11 ii 336
8 12 i 392
9 36 ii 336
76 i 423, ii 334
II 1 86 ii 402
3 76 i 293

Author / Work	Passage	Reference
Horat. (continued)		
Sat.	II 3 217	i 121
	284	i 151
	5 51	i 180
Epist.	I 1 101	i 121
	16 43	ii 29
	II 1 234	ii 290
	253	ii 220
	2 14	ii 152
	67	ii 29
	158	i 423
	159	i 468
Juvenal	VI 146	i 135
	IX 53	i 164
	86	i 383
	XVI 51	i 175
Liv.	I 24 § 7	ii 184
	III 13	ii 336
	VII 2 § 12	ii 329
	VIII 28	ii 302, 310
	XX *fragm.*	i 128
	XXII 60 § 3	i 481
	XXVI 15 § 9	ii 339
	XXVII 3 § 1	ii 169
	XXXII 26 § 18	ii 423
	XXXV 7	ii 283
	XXXIX 9 *sub fin.*	i 98
	19	i 130
	XLI 8 § 10	i 74
and *nexum* in Books II, VI, VII		ii 297 sqq.
Martial	I 52	i 49
Nepos, *Att.*	13 § 16	ii 289
Pers.	V 78, 175	i 26
Plaut. *Asin.*	243	ii 72
Aul.	255	i 132
Bac.	92	i 78
Capt.	78, 86	ii 324
	179	ii 165
Curcul.	5	i 27
	496	ii 328
Plaut. *Merc.*	93	ii 180
	420	ii 166
Mil.	961	i 26
Most.	647	ii 139
Pers.	70	ii 427
	478	ii 318
	524	ii 156
	669	ii 150
Poen.	1285	ii 115
Plaut. *Pseudol.*	286	ii 72
	303	i 123
Rud.	860	ii 334
Stich.	171	ii 150
Trin.	420	ii 143
	425	ii 184
Truc.	762	ii 252
Plin. *N. H.*		
	XIV § 90	i 158
	XXXIII § 28	ii 139
Plin. *Epist.*	II 4	i 525
	16 § 1	i 182
	IV 10	i 305
	V 1 § 9	i 212
	7	i 194
	9 (21) § 5	ii 315
	VI 2 § 7	ii 462
	VII 16	i 25, 175
	VIII 18 § 4	ii 128
	IX 37	ii 169
Ep. Traj.	4	i 526
	6	i 40
	11	i 63
	39 § 3	i 533
	50	i 409
	65	i 46
	75	i 298
	104	i 279
Paneg.	36	ii 352
	37	i 22, 188
Quintil. *Inst.*		
	IV 2 § 5	i 102
	§ 61	ii 71
	VII 3 § 26	ii 428, 429
	4 § 32	ii 210
	§ 35	i 105
	5 §§ 2, 3	ii 370, 530
	6 § 2	ii 210
	§ 4	ii 344
	VIII 3 § 14	ii 71
Seneca, *Rhet.*		
Contr.	VII Pref. § 7	ii 324
	X 1 30	ii 221
Seneca, *Benef.*	II 23	ii 293
	III 7 § 5	ii 318
	§ 7	ii 322
	22 § 3	i 54
	IV 26	ii 328
	32 § 4	ii 291
	VI 5 § 2	ii 42

Sen. *Clem.* I 18 i 53
II 7 § 3 ii 415
Epist. 37 *init.* ii 174
80 § 4 i 29
Sueton. *Jul.* 32 ii 134
42 ii 134
Aug. 40 i 24, 30
64 i 75
Tib. 15 i 66
Claud. 9 i 480
18, 19 i 40
24 i 18
25 i 85
Ner. 17 i 180
Sueton. *Oth.* 4 i 78
Galb. 14 i 381
Dom. 9 i 307
Tacit. *Ann.* VI 17 i 480
Tacit. *Ann.* XI 5 i 526
XII 6 i 128
XIII 4 i 10
26 i 85
27 i 36
32 i 157
Hist. I 16 i 288
Terent. *Phorm.* 403, 419 ii 344
Varro, *L.L.* V 102 ii 306
VI 60 ii 306
VII 105 ii 305
R.R. II 2 § 6 ii 143, 155
5 §§ 10, 11 ii 155
10 § 4 i 425
§ 5 i 56, ii 150, 156
Verg. *Buc.* V 37 ii 188

CAMBRIDGE: PRINTED BY J. AND C. F. CLAY, AT THE UNIVERSITY PRESS.

By the same author.

INTRODUCTION TO THE STUDY OF JUSTINIAN'S DIGEST. 8vo. (1884).

COMMENTARY ON THE TITLE *DE USUFRUCTU.* 8vo. (1884).

(These are also bound together in one vol.)

GRAMMAR OF THE LATIN LANGUAGE FROM PLAUTUS TO SUETONIUS. Crown 8vo.

PART I. SOUNDS, INFLEXIONS, WORD-FORMATION. (Last ed. 1896.)

PART II. SYNTAX. (Last ed. 1896.)

SCHOOL LATIN GRAMMAR. Crown 8vo. (Last ed. 1900.)

Reprints of Legal Classics
Published by The Lawbook Exchange, Ltd.

A'Beckett, Gilbert Abbott. *The Comic Blackstone* **[bound with] [Anstey, John].** *The Pleader's Guide, A Didactic Poem by John Surrebutter; American edition by James L. High.* With illustrations by George Cruikshank. Chicago: Callaghan & Cockcroft, 1870. xii, 376, 57, 65 pp. Reprint available December 2000 by The Lawbook Exchange, Ltd. ISBN 1-58477-104-6. Cloth. $95.

Anderson, William C. *A Dictionary of Law, Consisting of Judicial Definitions and Explanations of Words, Phrases, and Maxims, and an Exposition of the Principles of Law: Comprising a Dictionary and Compendium of American and English Jurisprudence.* Chicago: T.H. Flood and Company, 1889. viii, 1140pp. Reprinted 1996 by The Lawbook Exchange, Ltd. LCCN 96-35844. ISBN 1-886363-23-4. Cloth. $125.

Austin, John. [1790-1859]. *The Province of Jurisprudence Determined.* London: John Murray, 1832. xx, 392, lxxvi pp. Reprinted 2000 by The Lawbook Exchange, Ltd. LCCN 99-33457. ISBN 1-58477-023-6. Cloth. $75.

Baldwin, Henry. *A General View of the Origin and Nature of the Constitution and Government of the United States, Deduced from the Political History and Condition of the Colonies and States, from 1774 until 1788. And the Decisions of the Supreme Court of the United States. Together with Opinions in the Cases Decided at January Term, 1837, Arising on the Restraints on the Powers of the States.* Philadelphia, Printed by J. C. Clark, 1837. v, [1], 197 p. Reprint available August 2000 by The Lawbook Exchange, Ltd. LCCN 00-026728. ISBN 1-58477-098-8. Cloth. $60.

Bancroft, George. *History of the Formation of the Constitution of the United States of America. Second Edition.* New York: D. Appleton and Company, 1882. Two volumes. xxiv, 520; xiv, pp. Reprint available July 2000 by The Lawbook Exchange, Ltd. LCCN 99-23946. ISBN 1-58477-002-3. Cloth. $175.

Bar, Carl Ludwig von. *A History of Continental Criminal Law.* Boston: Little, Brown, and Company, 1916. lvi, 561 pp. Reprinted 1999 by The Lawbook Exchange, Ltd. LCCN 99-32341. ISBN 1-58477-013-9. Cloth. $90.

Barton, Dunbar Plunket. *Shakespeare and the Law.* With a foreword by James M. Beck. Boston: Houghton Mifflin Company, 1929. xl, 167 pp. Reprinted 1999 by The Lawbook Exchange, Ltd. LCCN 99-26602. ISBN 1-58477-000-7. Cloth. $60.

Bauer, Elizabeth Kelley. *Commentaries on the Constitution 1790-1860.* New York: Columbia University Press, 1952. 400 pp. Reprinted 1999 by The Lawbook Exchange, Ltd. LCCN 98-45409. ISBN 1-886363-66-8. Cloth. $75.

Beard, Charles Austin. *The Office of the Justice of the Peace in England, in its Origin and Development.* New York: Columbia University Press, 1904. 184, [1] pp. Reprint available November 2000 by The Lawbook Exchange, Ltd. ISBN 1-58477-102-X. Cloth. $60.

Beard, Charles. *An Economic Interpretation of the Constitution of the United States.* New York: The Macmillan Company, 1952. xxi, 330 pp. Reprint available September 2000 by The Lawbook Exchange, Ltd. LCCN 00-036834. ISBN 1-58477-111-9. Cloth. $80.

Beard, Charles A. *The Supreme Court and the Constitution.* New York: The Macmillan Company, 1912. vii, 127 pp. Reprinted 1999 by The Lawbook Exchange, Ltd. LCCN 98-50368. ISBN 1-886363-78-1. Cloth. $45.

Beck, Theodric Romeyn. *Elements of Medical Jurisprudence.* Albany: Websters and Skinners, 1823. Two volumes. xxxiv, 418; viii, [9]-471 pp. Reprinted 1997 by The Lawbook Exchange, Ltd. LCCN 96-35845. ISBN 1-886363-24-2. Cloth. $125.

Benedict, Russell. *Acts and Laws of the Thirteen Original Colonies and States: Constituting the extraordinary collection of Hon. Russell Benedict.* New York: American Art Association, 1922. [272]pp. Reprinted 1998 The Lawbook Exchange, Ltd. LC 98-20196 ISBN 1-886363-56-0. Cloth. $85.

Black, Henry Campbell. *A Dictionary of Law. Containing Definitions of the Terms and Phrases of American and English Jurisprudence, Ancient and Modern. Including the Principal Terms of International, Constitutional, and Commercial Law; with a Collection of Legal Maxims and Numerous Select Titles from the Civil Law and Other Foreign Systems.* St. Paul, Minn.: West Publishing, 1891. x, 1253 pp. Reprinted 1991 by the Lawbook Exchange, Ltd. LCCN 91-62383. ISBN 0-9630106-0-3. $125.

Black, Henry Campbell. *A Law Dictionary. Containing Definitions of the Terms and Phrases of American and English Jurisprudence, Ancient and Modern. And Including the Principal Terms of International, Constitutional, Ecclesiastical and Commercial Law, and Medical Jurisprudence, with a Collection of Legal Maxims, Numerous Select Titles from the Roman, Modern Civil, Scotch, French, Spanish, and Mexican Law, and Other Foreign Systems, and a Table of Abbreviations.* St. Paul, Minn.: West Publishing, 1910. 1314 pp. Reprinted 1995 by the Lawbook Exchange, Ltd. LCCN 97-10320. ISBN 1-886363-10-2. Cloth. $125.

[Blackstone, William]. Eller, Catherine Spicer. *The William Blackstone Collection in the Yale Law Library. A Bibliographical Catalogue.* New Haven: Yale University Press, 1938. xvii, 113 pp. Reprinted 1993 by The Lawbook Exchange, Ltd. LCCN 99-38826. ISBN 0-9630106-5-4. Cloth. $50.

Bondy, William. *Separation of Governmental Powers in History, in Theory, and in the Constitutions.* New York: Columbia College, 1896. Reprinted 1999 by The Lawbook Exchange, Ltd. vi,[7]-185, [1] pp. LCCN 98-44994. ISBN 1-886363-65-X. Cloth. $65.

Bonner, Robert J. and Gertrude Smith. *The Administration of Justice from Homer to Aristotle.* Chicago: The University of Chicago Press, [1930]. Two volumes. ix, 390; vii, [320] pp. Reprint available November 2000 by The Lawbook Exchange, Ltd. ISBN 1-58477-117-8. Cloth. $160.

Bouvier, John. [1787-1851]. *Institutes of American Law. New Edition by Daniel A. Gleason. In Two Volumes.* Boston: Little, Brown, & Company, 1880. lxviii, 651; iv, 798pp. Reprinted 1999 by The Lawbook Exchange, Ltd. LCCN 98-54288. ISBN 1-886363-80-3. Cloth. $250.

Bouvier, John. *A Law Dictionary Adapted to the Constitution and Laws of the United States of America, and of the Several States of the American Union; with References to the Civil and Other Systems of Foreign Law.* Philadelphia: T. & J.W. Johnson, 1839. Two volumes. 559; 628 pp. Reprinted 1993 by The Lawbook Exchange, Ltd. LCCN 99-047231. ISBN 0-9630106-7-0. Cloth. $130.

[Brandeis, Louis D.]. [1856-1941]. *Brandeis on Zionism. A Collection of Addresses and Statements by Louis D. Brandeis with a Foreword by Mr. Justice Felix Frankfurter.* Washington, D.C.: Zionist Organization of America, [1942]. viii, 156 pp. Reprinted 1999 by The Lawbook Exchange, Ltd. LCCN 98-49331. ISBN 1-886363-60-9. Cloth. $65.

Broom, Herbert. *A Selection of Legal Maxims, Classified and Illustrated. Eighth American, from the Fifth London Edition, with References to American Cases.* Philadelphia: T. & J.W. Johnson & Co., 1882. lxxviii, 993 [i.e. 779] pp. Reprinted 2000 by The Lawbook Exchange, Ltd. LCCN 99-049329. ISBN 1-58477-052-X. Cloth. $125.

Brown, Basil. [1860-1928]. *Law Sports at Gray's Inn (1594) Including Shakespeare's connection with the Inns of Court, the origin of the Capias Utlegatum re Coke and Bacon, Francis Bacon's connection with Warwickshire, together with a reprint of the Gesta Grayorum.* New York: [Privately Printed by the Author], 1921. xciv, 188, 88, [9] pp. LCCN 99-049829. ISBN 1-58477-056-2. Reprint available December 2000 by The Lawbook Exchange, Ltd. Cloth. $85.

Browne, Arthur. *A Compendious View of the Civil Law and of the Law of the Admiralty: being the substance of a course of lectures read in the University of Dublin.* New York: Halstead and Voorhies, 1840. Two volumes. xvi, 536; xi, 567 pp. Reprinted 2000 by The Lawbook Exchange, Ltd. LCCN 99-18284. ISBN 1-886363-88-9. Cloth. $175.

Buckland, W.W. *The Roman Law of Slavery: The Condition of the Slave in Private Law from Augustus to Justinian.* Cambridge: Cambridge University Press, 1908. xii, [2], 735 pp. Reprint available August 2000 by The Lawbook Exchange, Ltd. LCCN 99-056922. ISBN 1-58477-068-6X. Cloth. $175.

Burrill, Alexander M. *A New Law Dictionary and Glossary: Containing Full Definitions of the Principal Terms of the Common and Civil Law, Together with Translations and Explanations of the Various Technical Phrases in Different Languages, Occurring in the Ancient and Modern Reports, and Standard Treatises; Embracing Also All the Principal Common and Civil Law Maxims. Compiled on the Basis of Spelman's Glossary, and Adapted to the Jurisprudence of the United States; with Copious Illustrations, Critical and Historical.* New York: John S. Voorhies, 1850. Two volumes. xviii, 1099 pp. Reprinted 1998 by The Lawbook Exchange, Ltd. LCCN 97-38481. ISBN 1-886363-32-3. Cloth. $175.

Bussell, F.W. *The Roman Empire. Essays on the Constitutional History from the Accession of Domitian (81 A.D.) to the Retirement of Nicephorus III. (1081 A.D.)* London: Longmans, Green, and Co., 1910. Two volumes. xiv, 402; xxiii, 521 pp. Reprint available May 2000 by The Lawbook Exchange, Ltd. LCCN 99-087026. ISBN 1-58477-082-1. Cloth. $175.

Calabresi, Guido. *A Common Law for the Age of Statutes.* Cambridge: Harvard University Press, 1982. xi, 319 pp. Reprinted 2000 by The Lawbook Exchange, Ltd. LCCN 99-44889. ISBN 1-58477-040-6. Cloth. $85.

Calhoun, George M. *The Growth of Criminal Law in Ancient Greece.* Berkeley: University of California Press, 1927. x, 149 pp. LCCN 99-43192. ISBN 1-58477-037-6. Reprinted 2000 by The Lawbook Exchange, Ltd. Cloth. New. $50.

[Cardozo, Benjamin]. *Law is Justice. Notable Opinions of Mr. Justice Cardozo.* Foreword by Robert F. Wagner. Edited by A.L. Sainer. New York: Ad Press Ltd.,

[1938]. xvii, 441 pp. Frontis. Reprinted 1999 by The Lawbook Exchange, Ltd. LCCN 99-34154. ISBN 1-58477-010-4. Cloth. $75.

Cardozo, Benjamin. *The Paradoxes of Legal Science.* New York: Columbia University Press, 1928. v, 142 pp. Reprint available August 2000 by The Lawbook Exchange, Ltd. LCCN 00-024469. ISBN 1-58477-097-X. Cloth. $75.

Chafee, Zechariah. *Free Speech in the United States.* Cambridge, Massachusetts: Harvard University Press, 1967. xviii, 634 pp. Reprint available September 2000 by The Lawbook Exchange, Ltd. LCCN 99-087317. ISBN 1-58477-085-6. Cloth. $125.

[Cherokee Laws]. *Compiled Laws of the Cherokee Nation.* Tahlequah, I.T.:National Advocate Print, 1881. 370pp. Reprinted September 1998 by The Lawbook Exchange, Ltd. With a new introduction by Michael Weber. LCCN 98-12741. ISBN 1-886363-42-0. Cloth. $60.

Chipman, Nathaniel. *Principles of Government. A Treatise on Free Institutions Including the Constitution of the United States.* Burlington: Edward Smith, 1833. viii, 144, 145a-188a, [145]-330 pp. Reprint available November 2000 by The Lawbook Exchange, Ltd. LCCN 99-048863. ISBN 1-58477-046-5. Cloth. $80.

Chitwood, Oliver Perry. *Justice in Colonial Virginia.* Baltimore: Johns Hopkins Press, 1905. 123, [1] pp. Reprint available November 2000 by The Lawbook Exchange, Ltd. ISBN 1-58477-114-3. Cloth. $65.

Clark, H.B. *Biblical Law: Being a text of the statutes, ordinances, and judgments established in the Holy Bible-with many allusions to secular laws-ancient, medieval, and modern-documented to the Scriptures, judicial decisions, and legal literature.* Portland, Ore.: Binfords & Mort, [1943]. . xxiv, 304 pp. LCCN 99-053316. ISBN 1-58477-062-7. Reprint available July 2000 by The Lawbook Exchange, Ltd. Cloth. $75.

Cohn, Morris M. *An Introduction to the Study of the Constitution; A Study showing the Play of Physical and Social Factors in the Creation of Institutional Law.* Baltimore: The Johns Hopkins Press, 1892. xi, 235 pp. Reprint available December 2000 by The Lawbook Exchange, Ltd. LCCN 99-38730. ISBN 1-58477-032-5. Cloth. $50.

Coke, Edward, Sir. *The First Part of the Institutes of the Laws of England, or, A commentary upon Littleton. Not the name of the Author only, but of the Law Itself. Revised and Corrected With Additions of Notes, References, and Proper Tables, by Francis Hargrave and Charles Butler, Esqrs. Of Lincoln's Inn, Including also The Notes of Lord Chief Justice Hale and Lord Chancellor Nottingham; and An Analysis of Littleton, written by an unknown Hand in 1658-9. By Charles Butler, Esq. The Eighteenth Edition, Corrected.* London, J. & W.T. Clarke, 1823. Two volumes. ccxvi,[606]; iv, [772] pp. Reprinted 2000 by The Lawbook Exchange, Ltd. LCCN 99-41675. ISBN 1-58477-033-3. Cloth. $195.

[Continental Legal History]. *A General Survey of Events, Sources, Persons & Movements in Continental Legal History. By Various European Authors.* With an introduction by Albert Kocourek. Boston: Little, Brown, 1912. liii, 754pp. Reprinted 1998 by The Lawbook Exchange, Ltd. LCCN 98-11159. ISBN 1-886363-47-1. Cloth. $110.

Cooley, Thomas M. [1824-98]. *A Treatise on the Constitutional Limitations which Rest Upon the Legislative Power of the States of the American Union. Fifth edition.* Boston: Little, Brown, and Co., 1883. lxxxi, 886pp. Reprinted 1998 by The Lawbook Exchange, Ltd. LCCN 98-12730. ISBN 1-886363-53-6. Cloth. $120.

Cooley, Thomas McIntyre. [1824-1898]. *A Treatise on the Constitutional Limitations Which Rest Upon the Legislative Power of the States of the American Union. [1st edition].* Boston: Little, Brown, and Co., 1868. xlvii, 720pp. Reprinted 1999 by The Lawbook Exchange, Ltd. LCCN 99-20589. ISBN 1-886363-92-7. Cloth. $95.

Corwin, Edward. *The Doctrine of Judicial Review: Its Legal and Historical Basis and Other Essays.* Princeton: Princeton University Press, 1914. ix, 178 pp. Reprinted 2000 by The Lawbook Exchange, Ltd. LCCN 99-32362. ISBN 1-58477-011-2. Cloth. $60.

Darrow, Clarence and William J. Bryan. *The World's Most Famous Court Trial. Tennessee Evolution Case. A Complete Stenographic Report of the Famous Court Test of the Anti-Evolution Act, at Dayton July 10 to 21, 1925, Including Speeches and Arguments of Attorneys.* Cincinnati: National Book Company, [1925]. [4], 339 pp. Reprinted 1997 by The Lawbook Exchange, Ltd. LCCN 97-38485. ISBN 1-886363-31-5. Cloth. $65.

Darrow, Clarence. *A Persian Pearl. And Other Essays.* East Aurora, NY: The Roycroft Shop, 1899. 175 pp. Reprinted 1997 by The Lawbook Exchange, Ltd. LCCN 97-5174. ISBN 1-886363-27-7. Cloth. $50.

Darrow, Clarence S. *An Eye for an Eye.* New York: Fox Duffield & Company, 1905. 213 pp. Reprinted 1996 by The Lawbook Exchange, Ltd. LCCN 99-047232. ISBN 1-886363-07-2. Cloth. $40.

Davis, C.K. *The Law in Shakespeare.* Washington, D.C.: Washington Law Book Co., [1883]. 303 pp. Reprinted 1999 by The Lawbook Exchange, Ltd. LCCN 98-32333. ISBN 1-886363-75-7. Cloth. $60.

Dawson, John P. *A History of Lay Judges.* Cambridge, Mass.: Harvard University Press, 1960. viii, [2], 310 pp. Reprinted 1999 by The Lawbook Exchange, Ltd. LCCN 98-50812. ISBN 1-886363-69-2. Cloth. $75.

Dodd, Walter Fairleigh. *The Revision and Amendment of State Constitutions.* Baltimore: The Johns Hopkins Press, 1910. xvii, 350 pp. Reprinted 1999 by The Lawbook Exchange, Ltd. LCCN 98-50815. ISBN 1-886363-73-0. Cloth. $65.

Duer, William Alexander. *A Course of Lectures on the Constitutional Jurisprudence of the United States; Delivered Annually in Columbia College, New York. The Second Edition, Revised, Enlarged, and Adapted to Professional as well as General Use.* Boston: Little, Brown & Co., 1856. xxiv, 545 pp. Reprinted 2000 by The Lawbook Exchange, Ltd. LCCN 99-16385. ISBN 1-58477-020-1. Cloth. $85.

Esmein, A[dhemar]. *A History of Continental Criminal Procedure with Special Reference to France. Translated by John Simpson; with an editorial preface by William E. Mikell and introductions by Norman M. Trenholme and by William Renwick Riddell.* Boston: Little, Brown and Company, 1913. xlv, 640 pp. Reprint available July 2000 by The Lawbook Exchange, Ltd. LCCN 99-045906. ISBN 1-58477-042-2. Cloth. $100.

Evans, E.P. *The Criminal Prosecution and Capital Punishment of Animals.* New York: E.P. Dutton, 1906. x, 384pp. Reprinted 1998 by The Lawbook Exchange, Ltd. LCCN 98-12801. ISBN 1-886363-52-8. Cloth. $65.

Farnam, Henry W. *Chapters in the History of Social Legislation in the United States to 1860.* Washington: Carnegie Institution of Washington, 1938. xx, 496 pp. Reprint available December 2000 by The Lawbook Exchange, Ltd. LCCN 99-049362. ISBN 1-58477-054-6. Cloth. $100.

[Field Codes]. [New York 1850-1865]. New York Field Codes. 1850-1865.
Vol. I. *The Code of Civil Procedure of the State of New-York, Reported Complete by the Commissioners on Practice and Pleadings. 1850.*
Vol. II. *The Code of Criminal Procedure of the State of New York, Reported Complete by the Commissioners on Practice and Pleadings. 1850.*
Vol. III. *The Civil Code of the State of New York, Reported Complete by the Commissioners of the Code. 1865.*
Vol. IV. *The Penal Code of the State of New York, Reported Complete by the Commissioners of the Code. 1865.*
Vol. V. *The Political Code of the State of New York. 1860.*
With a new introduction by Michael Weber. Reprinted 1998 by The Lawbook Exchange, Ltd. Five volume series. [8], xcvi, 791; liii, [1], 486; cxii, 776; lxiv, 406, clxvii; xlvii, 607 pp. ISBN 1-886363-40-4 (set). Cloth. $495.

Finkelman, Paul, editor. *A Brief Narrative of the Case and Tryal of John Peter Zenger Printer of the New York Weekly Journal.* New York: Brandywine Press, [1997]. vii, 175 pp. Reprinted 2000 by The Lawbook Exchange, Ltd. LCCN 99-049431. ISBN 1-58477-051-1. Cloth. $50.

Finkelman, Paul. *An Imperfect Union: Slavery, Federalism and Comity.* Chapel Hill: The University of North Carolina Press, 1981. xii, 378 pp. Reprint available May 2000 by The Lawbook Exchange, Ltd. LCCN 00-021509. ISBN 1-58477-092-9. Cloth. $85.

Finkelman, Paul. *Slavery in the Courtroom. An Annotated Bibliography of American Cases.* Washington:Library of Congress, 1985. Illustrated. xxvii, 312pp. Reprinted 1998 by The Lawbook Exchange, Ltd. LCCN 98-11284. ISBN 1-886363-48-X. Cloth. $85.

Fisher, Sydney George. *The Evolution of the Constitution of the United States. Showing That It Is a Development of Progressive History and Not an Isolated Document Struck Off at a Given Time or an Imitation of English or Dutch Forms of Government.* Philadelphia: J.B. Lippincott, 1897. 398 pp. Reprinted 1996 by The Lawbook Exchange, Ltd. LCCN 97-41054. ISBN 1-886363-08-0. Cloth. $65.

Flanders, Henry. [1824-1911]. *A Treatise on Maritime Law.* Boston: Little, Brown and Company, 1852. xvi, 444 pp. Reprinted 1999 by The Lawbook Exchange, Ltd. ISBN 1-886363-72-2. Cloth. $75.

Flanders, Henry. *An Exposition of the Constitution of the United States. Designed as a Manual of Instruction.* Philadelphia: E.H. Butler & Co., 1860. xii, 311 pp. Reprinted 1999 by The Lawbook Exchange, Ltd. LCCN 99-31594. ISBN 1-58477-014-7. Cloth. $60.

Ford, Paul Leicester. *Pamphlets on the Constitution of the United States, Published During Its Discussion by the People 1787-1788.* Brooklyn, N.Y., 1888. viii, 451 pp. Reprint available December 2000 by The Lawbook Exchange, Ltd. LCCN 99-25089. ISBN 1-886363-95-1. Cloth. $75.

Forsyth, William. *The History of Lawyers. Ancient and Modern.* Boston: Estes & Lauriat, 1875. Illustrated. xvii, 404 pp. Reprinted 1996 by the Lawbook Exchange, Ltd. LCCN 95-51103. ISBN 1-886363-14-5. Cloth. $60.

Forsyth, William. *History of Trial by Jury* [*Second edition*]. Jersey City: Frederick D. Linn, [1875]. x, 388 pp. Reprinted 1994 by The Lawbook Exchange, Ltd. LCCN 96-14505. ISBN 0-9630106-8-9. Cloth. $65.

Fortescue, Sir John. [?1394-1476?]. *The Governance of England: Otherwise Called The Difference between an Absolute and a Limited Monarchy. A Revised Text edited with Introduction, Notes, and Appendices by Charles Plummer.* London: Oxford University Press, 1885. xxiii, 387pp. Reprinted 1999 by The Lawbook Exchange, Ltd. ISBN 1-886363-79-X. Cloth. $65.

Fortescue, Sir John. *DeLaudibus Legum Angliae. A Treatise in Commendation of the Laws of England.* With Translation by Francis Gregor. Notes by Andrew Amos and a Life of the Author by Thomas (Fortescue) Lord Clermont. Cincinnati: Robert Clarke & Co., 1874. lxiv, 302 pp. Reprinted 1999 by The Lawbook Exchange, Ltd. LCCN 99-16485. ISBN 1-58477-019-8. Cloth. $65.

Foss, Edward. *A Biographical Dictionary of the Judges of England From the Conquest to the Present Time 1066-1870.* London: John Murray, 1870. xv, 792 pp. Reprinted 2000 by The Lawbook Exchange, Ltd. LCCN 99-12577. ISBN 10886363-86-2. Cloth. $100.

Freeman, A.C. *A Treatise of the Law of Judgments. Including All Final Determinations of the Rights of Parties in Actions or Proceedings at Law or in Equity. Revised, and Greatly Enlarged by Edward W. Tuttle.*
San Francisco: Bancroft-Whitney, 1925. Three volumes. 1216; 1280; 1264 pp. Reprinted 1993 by The Lawbook Exchange, Ltd. LCCN 99-047228. ISBN 0-9630106-6-2. Cloth. $295.

Friedberg, Emil Albert [1837-1910]. Richter, Aemilius Ludwig [1808-1864]. *Corpus iuris canonici.-Editio Lipsiensis secunda / post Aemilii Ludouici Richteri curas ad librorum manu scriptorum et editionis Romanae fidem recognouit et adnotatione critica instruxit Aemilius Friedberg.* Liepzig : Tauchnitz, 1879-1881. Two volumes. civ, 1472 columns (736 pp.); lxxxii, 1340 columns (670 pp.) LCCN 99-088231. Reprint available June 2000 by The Lawbook Exchange, Ltd. ISBN 1-58477-088-0. Cloth. $300.

Friend, Willam L. *Anglo-American Legal Bibliographies. An Annotated Guide.* Washington, D.C.: United States Government Printing Office, 1944. xii, 166 pp. Reprinted 1996 by The Lawbook Exchange, Ltd. LCCN 96-11002. ISBN 1-886363-21-8. Cloth. $65.

Fuller, Lon L. *The Law in Quest of Itself.* Boston: Beacon Press, 1966. [vi], 150 pp. Reprinted 1999 by The Lawbook Exchange, Ltd. LCCN 99-32863. ISBN 1-58477-016-3. Cloth. $45.

Futrell, William H. *The History of American Customs Jurisprudence.* New York: Published privately, 1941. 314pp. Reprinted 1998 by The Lawbook Exchange, Ltd. LCCN 98-11342. ISBN 1-886363-51-X. Cloth. $60.

Gest, John Marshall. *The Lawyer in Literature.* London: Sweet & Maxwell, Limited, 1913. xii, 249 pp. Reprinted 1999 by The Lawbook Exchange, Ltd. LCCN 99-18365. ISBN 1-886363-90-0. Cloth. $60.

Gilmore, Grant. *Security Interests in Personal Property.* Boston: Little, Brown & Company, 1965. Two volumes. xxxiv, 651; xiii, 653-1508 pp. Reprinted 1999 by

The Lawbook Exchange, Ltd. LCCN 99-10258. ISBN 1-886363-81-1. Cloth. $195.

Girard, Paul F. *A Short History of Roman Law. Being the First Part of his Manuel Elementaire De Droit Romain. Translated by Augustus Henry Frazer and John Home Cameron.* Toronto: Canada Law Book Company, 1906, v, 220 pp. Reprint available June 2000 by The Lawbook Exchange, Ltd. LCCN 99-087383. ISBN 1-58477-078-3. Cloth. $55.

Goodhart, Arthur L. *Five Jewish Lawyers of the Common Law.* London: Oxford University Press, 1949. [4], 74 pp. Reprint available August 2000 by The Lawbook Exchange, Ltd. LCCN 99-049934. ISBN 1-58477-045-7. Cloth. $60.

Greenidge, A.H.J. *The Legal Procedure of Cicero's Time.* Oxford: The Clarendon Press, 1901. xiii, 599 pp. Reprint available July 2000 by The Lawbook Exchange, Ltd. LCCN 99-26771. ISBN 1-886363-99-4. Cloth. $85.

Greenleaf, Simon. *The Testimony of the Evangelists Examined by the Rules of Evidence Administered in Courts of Justice with an Appendix Containing a History of the Most Ancient Manuscript Copies of the New Testament, and a Comparison of their Text with that of the King James' Bible by Constantine Tischendorff. Also a Review of the Trial of Jesus.* New York: James Cockcroft & Company, 1874. Reprint available December 2000 by The Lawbook Exchange, Ltd.xxiii, 613 pp. LCCN 00-021510. ISBN 1-58477-020-1. Cloth. $95.

Greenleaf, Simon. *A Treatise on the Law of Evidence.* Boston: Little, Brown, and Company, 1899. Three volumes. Reprint available November 2000 by The Lawbook Exchange, Ltd. ISBN 1-58477-116-X. Cloth. $350.

Haines, Charles Grove. *The Conflict over Judicial Powers in the United States to 1870.* New York: Columbia University Press, 1909. 180 pp. Reprint available December 2000 by The Lawbook Exchange, Ltd. LCCN 99-088241. ISBN 1-58477-080-5. Cloth. $60.

Hale, Matthew. *The History and Analysis of the Common Law of England.* Stafford: J. Nutt, 1713. [x], 264, [28], 176 pp. Reprinted 2000 by The Lawbook Exchange, Ltd. LCCN 99-33739. ISBN 1-58477-024-4. Cloth. $85.

Harper, Robert Francis. *The Code of Hammurabi King of Babylon. About 2250 B.C. Autographed Text transliteration...* Chicago: The University of Chicago Press, 1904. xxviii, 194, ciii (plates) pp. London: John Murray, 1832. xx, 392, lxxvi pp. Illus. Reprinted 2000 The Lawbook Exchange, Ltd. LCCN 99-23953. ISBN 1-58477-003-1. Cloth. $75.

Harris, Virgil M. *Ancient, Curious, and Famous Wills.* Boston: Little, Brown, and Company, 1911. xiv, 472 pp. Reprinted 1999 by The Lawbook Exchange, Ltd. LCCN 99-20588. ISBN 1-886363-93-5. Cloth. $75.

Henderson, Gerard Carl. *The Position of Foreign Corporations in American Constitutional Law. A Contribution to the History and Theory of Juristic Persons in Anglo-American Law.* Cambridge: Harvard University Press, 1918. xix, 199 pp. Reprinted 1999 by The Lawbook Exchange, Ltd. LCCN 99-18233. ISBN 1-886363-89-7. Cloth. $50.

Hicks, Frederick. *Men and Books Famous in the Law. With an introduction by Harlan F. Stone.* Rochester, New York: Lawyers Co-operative Publishing, 1921. 259 pp.

Reprinted 1992 by The Lawbook Exchange, Ltd. LCCN 92-070809. ISBN 0-9630106-2-X. Cloth. $50.

Holdsworth, William S. *Charles Dickens as a Legal Historian.* New Haven: Yale University Press, 1929. 157 pp. Reprinted 1995 by The Lawbook Exchange, Ltd. LCCN 96-46579. ISBN 1-886363-06-4. Cloth. $40.

Holdsworth, William S. *Essays in Law and History.* Edited by A.L. Goodhart and H.G. Hanbury. Oxford: At the Clarendon Press, 1946. xv, 302 pp. Reprinted 1995 by The Lawbook Exchange, Ltd. LCCN 99-047234. ISBN 1-886363-13-7. Cloth. $65.

Holdsworth, W.S. *The Historians of Anglo-American Law.* New York: Columbia University Press, 1928. 175 pp. Reprinted 1994 by The Lawbook Exchange, Ltd. ISBN 0-9630106-9-7. Cloth. $50.

Holt, W. Stull. *Treaties Defeated by the Senate. A Study of the Struggle Between President and Senate Over the Conduct of Foreign Relations.* Baltimore: The Johns Hopkins Press, 1933. vi, [1],328 pp.
Reprinted 2000 by The Lawbook Exchange, Ltd. LCCN 99-39606. ISBN 1-58477-029-5. Cloth. $65.

Holthouse, Henry James. *A New Law Dictionary, Containing Explanations of Such Technical Terms and Phrases As Defined in the Works of Legal Authors, in the Practice of the Courts, and in the Parliamentary Proceedings of the Houses of Lords and Commons, To Which Is Added An Outline of An Action at Law and of A Suit in Equity. Edited, from the Second and Enlarged London Edition, With Numerous Additions, by Henry Penington.* Philadelphia: Lea and Blanchard, 1847. viii, [17]-495 pp. Reprinted 1999 by The Lawbook Exchange, Ltd. LCCN 98-49350. ISBN 1-886363-67-6. Cloth. $75.

Horton, John Theodore. *James Kent: A Study in Conservatism, 1763-1847.* New York: D. Appleton-Century Co., [1939]. xi, 354 pp. Reprint available June 2000 by The Lawbook Exchange, Ltd. LCCN 99-056927. ISBN 1-58477-069-4. Cloth. $80.

Huebner, Rudolf. *A History of Germanic Private Law.* Translated by Francis S. Philbrick; with an editorial preface by Ernest G. Lorenzen and introductions by Paul Vinogradoff and by William E. Walz. Boston: Little, Brown and Company, 1818. lix, 788 pp. Reprint available June 2000 by The Lawbook Exchange, Ltd. LCCN 99-055138. ISBN 1-58477-065-1. Cloth. $120.

Hurst, James Willard. *Law and Social Order in the United States.* Ithaca: Cornell University Press, 1977. 318 pp. Reprint available August 2000 by The Lawbook Exchange, Ltd. ISBN 1-58477-113-5. Cloth. $85.

Ilbert, Courtenay. *The Mechanics of Law Making.* New York: Columbia University Press, 1914. viii, 209 pp. Reprint available November 2000 by The Lawbook Exchange, Ltd. LCCN 99-047156. ISBN 1-58477-044-9. Cloth. $70.

Jackson, E. Hilton. *Latin for Lawyers. Containing I: A Course in Latin, with Legal Maxims and Phrases As a Basis of Instruction. II. A Collection of Over One Thousand Latin Maxims, with English Translations, Explanatory Notes, and Cross-References. III. A Vocabulary of Latin Words.* London: Sweet & Maxwell, 1915. viii, 300 pp. Reprinted 1992 by The Lawbook Exchange, Ltd. LCCN 92-074408. ISBN 0-9630106-4-6. Cloth. $50.

Jacob, Giles. [1686-1744]. *The Law-Dictionary: Explaining the Rise, Progress, and Present State of the English Law; Defining and Interpreting the Terms or Words of Art; and Comprising Copious Information on the Subjects of Law, Trade, and Government. Corrected and Greatly Enlarged by T[homas] E[dlyne] Tomlins.* New York: Printed for, and Published by I. Riley, 1811. Six volumes. viii, 531; [2], 543; [2],618; [2], 472; [2], 553; [2], 471pp. Reprinted 2000 by The Lawbook Exchange, Ltd. LCCN 98-49349. ISBN 1-886363-68-4. Cloth. $495.

Jaques,E.T. *Charles Dickens in Chancery: Being an Account of his Proceedings in Respect of the "Christmas Carol" with Some Gossip in Relation to the Old Law Courts at Westminster.* London: Longmans, Green & Company, 1914. 95 pp. Reprint available December 2000 by The Lawbook Exchange, Ltd. ISBN 1-58477-106-2. Cloth. $60.

Jhering, Rudolf Von. *Law as a Means to an End.* Translated from the German by Isaac Husik with an Editorial Preface by Joseph H. Drake and with Introductions by Henry Lamm and W.M. Geldart. Boston: The Boston Book Company, 1913. lxi, 483 pp. Reprinted 1999 by The Lawbook Exchange, Ltd. LCCN 99-23754. ISBN 1-58477-009-0. Cloth. $80.

Jhering, Rudolph von. *The Struggle for Law. Translated from the Fifth German Edition by John J. Lalor. Second Edition, with an Introduction by Albert Kocourek.* Chicago: Callaghan and Company, 1915. lii, 138 pp. Reprinted 1997 by The Lawbook Exchange, Ltd. LCCN 97-6826. ISBN 1-886363-25-0. Cloth. $60.

Johns, C.H.W. *Babylonian and Assyrian Laws, Contracts and Letters.* Edinburgh: T. & T. Clark, 1904. xxii, 424 pp. Reprinted 2000 by The Lawbook Exchange, Ltd. LCCN 99-32862. ISBN 1-58477-022-8. Cloth. $75.

Johns, C.H.W. , translator. *The Oldest Code of Laws in the World: The Code of Laws Promulgated by Hammurabi, King of Babylon, B.C. 2285-2242.* Edinburgh: T. & T. Clark, 1926. xii, 88 pp. Reprint available November 2000 by The Lawbook Exchange, Ltd. LCCN 99-053070. ISBN 1-58477-061-9. Cloth. $60.

Kames, Henry Home, Lord. [1696-1782]. *Historical Law-Tracts. The Second Edition.* Edinburgh: A. Kincaid, 1761. xv, 463 pp. LCCN 99-43133. ISBN 1-58477-038-4. Reprint available July 2000 by The Lawbook Exchange, Ltd. Cloth. $95.

Keller, Morton. *Affairs of State: Public Life in Late Nineteenth Century America.* Cambridge: Harvard University Press, 1977. ix, 631 pp. Reprinted 2000 by The Lawbook Exchange, Ltd. LCCN 99-087921. ISBN 1-58477-086-4. Cloth. $95.

Kelsen, Hans. [1881-1973]. *General Theory of Law and State.* Translated by Anders Wedberg. Cambridge: Harvard University Press, 1945. xxxiii, 516pp. Reprinted 1999 by The Lawbook Exchange, Ltd. LCCN 98-32334. ISBN 1-886363-74-9. Cloth. $75.

Kelsen, Hans. *The Law of the United Nations. A Critical Analysis of Its Fundamental Problems.* New York: Frederick A. Praeger, [1964]. xvii, 994 pp. Reprint available July 2000 by The Lawbook Exchange, Ltd. ISBN 1-58477-077-5. Cloth. $125.

Kelsen, Hans. *Peace Through Law.* Chapel Hill: The University of North Carolina Press, 1944. xii, 155 pp. Reprint available September 2000 by The Lawbook Exchange, Ltd. ISBN 1-58477-103-8. Cloth. $60.

Kelsen, Hans. *Society and Nature: A Sociological Inquiry.* London: K. Kegan Paul, Trench, Trubner & Co., Ltd., [1946]. viii, 391 pp. Reprint available September 2000 by The Lawbook Exchange, Ltd. LCCN 99-054869. ISBN 1-58477-064-3. Cloth. $85.

Kelsen, Hans. *What is Justice? Justice, Law and Politics in the Mirror of Science.*Berkeley: University of California Press, 1957. [vi], 397 pp. Reprint available August 2000 by The Lawbook Exchange, Ltd. ISBN 1-58477-101-1. Cloth. $95.

Kent, William. *Memoirs and Letters of James Kent, L.L.D.* Boston: Little, Brown, and Company, 1898. x, 341 pp. Reprint available December 2000 by The Lawbook Exchange, Ltd. ISBN 1-58477-100-3. Cloth. $75.

Kovalevsky, Maxime. *Modern Customs and Ancient Laws of Russia. Being the Ilchester Lectures for 1889-90.* London: David Nutt, 1891. x, 260 pp. Reprinted 2000 by The Lawbook Exchange, Ltd. LCCN 99-16487. ISBN 1-58477-017-1. Cloth. $65.

Kulsrud, Carl J. *Maritime Neutrality to 1780. A History of the Main Principles Governing Neutrality and Belligerency to 1780.* Boston: Little, Brown, and Company, 1936. x, 351 pp. Reprint available May 2000 by The Lawbook Exchange, Ltd. LCCN 99-38825. ISBN 1-58477-027-9. Cloth. $65.

Langdell, C.C. [1826-1906]. *A Selection of Cases on the Law of Contracts. With References and Citations. Prepared for Use as a Text-book in Harvard Law School.* Boston: Little, Brown & Co., 1871. xvi, 1022 pp. Reprinted 1999 by The Lawbook Exchange, Ltd. LCCN 99-28293. ISBN 1-58477-001-5. Cloth. $120.

Lauterpacht, H[ersch]. *The Function of Law in the International Community.* Oxford: Clarendon Press, 1933. xxvi, 470 pp. Reprint available August 2000 by The Lawbook Exchange, Ltd. LCCN 00-022124. ISBN 1-58477-090-2. Cloth. $90.

[Legal History]. *Select Essays in Anglo-American Legal History. By Maitland, Pollock, Holmes, Beale, Holdsworth and Others.* Boston: Little, Brown, and Company, 1907. Three volumes. 847; 823; 862 pp. Reprinted 1992 by The Lawbook Exchange, Ltd. LCCN 91-77977. ISBN 0-9630106-0-1. Cloth. $195.

Lieber, Francis. *On Civil Liberty and Self-government. Enlarged edition in one volume.* Philadelphia: J.B. Lippincott & Co.. 1859. xix, [15]-629 pp. Reprint available October 2000 by The Lawbook Exchange, Ltd. LCCN 99-056928. ISBN 1-58477-070-8. Cloth. $100.

Livingston, Edward. *A System of Penal Law, for the State of Louisiana: Consisting of A Code of Crimes and Punishments, A Code of Procedure, A Code of Evidence, A Code of Reform and Prison Discipline, A Book of Definitions. Prepared Under the Authority of a Law of the Said State. To Which are Prefixed a Preliminary Report on the Plan of a Penal Code, and Introductory Reports to the Several Codes Embraced in the System of Penal Law.* Philadelphia: James Kay, Jun. & Brother, 1833.v, 745 pp. Reprinted 1999 by The Lawbook Exchange, Ltd. LCCN 99-11403. ISBN 1-886363-83-8. Cloth. $95.

Llewellyn, Karl N. *Jurisprudence. Realism in Theory and Practice.* [Chicago]: The University of Chicago Press, 1962. viii, 531 pp. Reprinted 2000 by The Lawbook Exchange, Ltd. LCCN 99-056923. ISBN 1-58477-067-8. Cloth. $95.

[Macaulay, Thomas Babington]. *A Penal Code Prepared by the Indian Law Commissioners, and published by Command of the Governor General of India in Council.*

London: Pelham Richardson, Cornhill, 1838. viii, 138 pp. Reprint available December 2000 by The Lawbook Exchange, Ltd. LCCN 99-16486. ISBN 1-58477-018-X. Cloth. $65.

[MacDonell, Sir John and Edward Manson]. *Great Jurists of the World.* Edited by Sir John MacDonell and Edward Manson. With an Introduction by Van Vechten Veeder. Boston: Little, Brown, and Company, 1914. Illustrated. xxxii, 607 pp. Reprinted 1997 by The Lawbook Exchange, Ltd. LCCN 97-8298. ISBN 1-886363-28-5. Cloth. $95.

[Madison, James]. Hunt, Gaillard, Scott, James Brown. *The Debates in The Federal Convention of 1787 Which Framed the Constitution of the United States of America.* New York: Oxford University Press, 1920. xcvii, [1], 731 pp. Reprinted 1999 by The Lawbook Exchange, Ltd. LCCN 98-51911. ISBN 1-886363-77-3. Cloth. $110.

Maitland, Frederick William. *English Law and the Renaissance (The Rede Lecture for 1901) with Some Notes.* Cambridge: at the University Press, 1901. 98 pp. Reprint available July 2000 by The Lawbook Exchange, Ltd. LCCN 99-41654. ISBN 1-58477-034-1. Cloth. $60.

Maitland, Frederic William. *Roman Canon Law in the Church of England: Six Essays.* London: Methuen & Co., 1898. vii, 184 pp. Reprinted 1998 by The Lawbook Exchange, Ltd. LCCN 98-22357. ISBN 1-886363-57-9. Cloth. $65.

Maitland, Frederick W., Montague, Francis C., *A Sketch of English Legal History.* Edited with Notes and Appendices by James F. Colby. New York: G.P. Putnam's Sons, 1915. x, 234pp. Reprinted 1998 by The Lawbook Exchange, Ltd. LCCN 98-11337. ISBN 1-886363-50-1. Cloth. $50.

Mangum, Charles. *The Legal Status of the Negro.* New York: D. Appleton-Century Co., [1939]. xi, 354 pp. Reprint available October 2000 by The Lawbook Exchange, Ltd. LCCN 99-056927. ISBN 1-58477-069-4. Cloth. $80.

Marke, Julius J., editor. *A Catalogue of the Law Collection at New York University With Selected Annotations.* New York: The Law Center of New York University, 1953. xxxi, 1372 pp. Reprinted 1999 by The Lawbook Exchange, Ltd. LCCN 99-19939. ISBN 1-886363-91-9. Cloth. $185.

Marsden. R.[eginald]. G.[odfrey], ed. *Documents Relating to Law and Custom of the Sea.* [n.p.]: The Navy Record Society, 1915-6. Two volumes. xxxiii, 561; xl, 457, [5] pp. Reprinted 1999 by The Lawbook Exchange, Ltd. LCCN 99-24138. ISBN 1-886363-96-X. Cloth. $175.

Marshall, John. *The Constitutional Decisions of John Marshall,* Edited, with an introductory essay by Joseph P. Cotton, Jr. New York: G.P. Putnam, 1905. Two volumes. viii, 144, 145a-188a, [145]-330 pp. Reprint available December 2000 by The Lawbook Exchange, Ltd. LCCN 99-048862. ISBN 1-58477-050-3. Cloth. $175.

[Marshall, John]. Servies, James Albert. *A Bibliography of John Marshall.* Washington: United States Commission for the Celebration of the Two Hundredth Anniversary of the Birth of John Marshall, 1956. xix, 182 pp. Reprint available June 2000 by The Lawbook Exchange, Ltd. LCCN 99-088239. ISBN 1-58477-083-X. Cloth. $65.

Maxwell, W. Harold and C.R. Brown. *A Complete List of British and Colonial Law Reports and Legal Periodicals. Arranged in Alphabetical and in Chronological Order with Bibliographical Notes.* **[With]:** *Check List of Canadian and Newfoundland Statutes.*[Third Edition]. Toronto: The Carswell Company, Limited, 1937. viii, 141, 49 pp. Reprinted 1995 by The Lawbook Exchange, Ltd. LCCN 96-14504. ISBN 1-886363-11-0. Cloth. $70.

McCulloch, J.R. *The Works of David Ricardo, Esq., M.P. with a Notice of the Life and Writings of the Author.* London: John Murray, 1846. xxxiii, 584 pp. Reprint available December 2000 by The Lawbook Exchange, Ltd. LCCN 99-39612. ISBN 1-58477-028-7. Cloth. $90.

McKechnie, William Sharp. *Magna Carta. A Commentary on the Great Charter of King John. With an Historical Introduction. Second Edition, Revised and in part Re-written.* Glasgow: James Maclehose and Sons, 1914. xvii,530, [2] pp. Reprint available July 2000 by The Lawbook Exchange, Ltd. LCCN 99-38731. ISBN 1-58477-031-7. Cloth. $95.

McNamara, M. Frances. *Ragbag of Legal Quotations.* Albany: Matthew Bender & Company, 1960. xi, 334 pp. Reprinted 1992 by The Lawbook Exchange, Ltd. LCCN 92-074141. ISBN 0-9630106-3-8. Cloth. $50.

Meiklejohn, Alexander. *Free Speech and Its Relation to Self Government.* New York: Harper Brothers Publishers, [1948]. xiv, 107pp. Reprint available October 2000 by The Lawbook Exchange, Ltd. LCCN 99-87204. ISBN 1-58477-087-2. Cloth. $80.

Merriam, C.E., Jr. *History of the Theory of Sovereignty Since Rousseau.* New York: Columbia University Press, [1900]. x, [11]-233 pp. Reprinted 1999 by The Lawbook Exchange, Ltd. LCCN 98-32385. ISBN 1-886363-76-5. Cloth. $65.

Minor, Raleigh C. *Notes on the Science of Government and the Relations of the States to the United States.* [Charlottesville]: University of Virginia, 1913. x, 171 pp. Reprinted 1995 by The Lawbook Exchange, Ltd. LCCN 99-047233. ISBN 1-886363-09-9. Cloth. $40.

Moore, Blaine Free. *The Supreme Court and Unconstitutional Legislation.* New York: Columbia University Press, 1913. 158 pp. Reprint available August 2000 by The Lawbook Exchange, Ltd. ISBN 1-58477-099-6. Cloth. $60.

Morris, Thomas D. *Free Men All: The Personal Liberty Laws of the North 1780-1861.* Baltimore: The Johns Hopkins University Press, 1974. xii, 253 pp. Reprint available September 2000 by The Lawbook Exchange, Ltd. ISBN 1-58477-107-0. Cloth. $75.

Neely, Robert D. *The Lawyers of Dickens and Their Clerks.* Boston: The Christopher Publishing House, [1936]. 67pp. Reprint available December 2000 by The Lawbook Exchange, Ltd. LCCN 00-021520. ISBN 1-58477-091-0. Cloth. $60.

Neilson, George. *Trial by Combat.* Glasgow: William Hodge & Co., 1890. xiv, 348 pp. Reprinted 2000 by The Lawbook Exchange, Ltd. LCCN 99-059101. ISBN 1-58477-075-9. Cloth. $75.

[Nichols, J.]. *A Collection of all the Wills, Now Known to Be Extant, of the Kings and Queens of England, Princes and Princesses of Wales, and every Branch of the Blood Royal, from the Reign of William the Conqueror, to that of Henry the Seventh Exclusive: With*

Explanatory Notes and a Glossary. London: J. Nichols, 1780. x, 434 pp. Reprinted 1999 by The Lawbook Exchange, Ltd. LCCN 99-17114. ISBN 1-886363-87-0. Cloth. $75.

Ogle, Arthur. *The Canon Law in Mediaeval England. An Examination of William Lyndwood's "Provinciale," in Reply to the Late Professor F.W. Maitland.* London: John Murray, 1912. xv, 220 pp. Reprinted 2000 by The Lawbook Exchange, Ltd. LCCN 99-33827. ISBN 1-58477-026-0. Cloth. $65.

Perry, Ross R. *Common-law Pleading: Its History and Principles. Including Dicey's Rules Concerning Parties to Action and Stephen's Rules of Pleading.* Boston, Little, Brown and Company, 1897. xxvi, 494 pp. Reprint available October 2000 by The Lawbook Exchange, Ltd. ISBN 1-58477-105-4. Cloth. $95.

Pollock, Frederick and Frederic William Maitland. *The History of English Law before the Time of Edward I.* Cambridge: Cambridge University Press, 1898. Two volumes. xxxviii, 688; xiv, 691 pp. Reprinted 1996 by The Lawbook Exchange, Ltd. LCCN 96-16003. ISBN 1-886363-22-6. Cloth. $165.

Pollock, Sir Frederick. *The Genius of the Common Law.* New York: The Columbia University Press, 1912. vii, 141 pp. Reprinted 2000 by The Lawbook Exchange, Ltd. LCCN 99-047160. ISBN 1-58477-043-0-1. Cloth. $55.

Pomeroy, John N. *A Treatise on Equity Jurisprudence As Administered in the United States of America. Adapted for All the States and to the Union of Legal and Equitable Remedies under the Reformed Procedure.* San Francisco and New York: Bancroft-Whitney and Lawyers Cooperative, 1941. Five volumes. 914; 1134; 1063; 1104; 716 pp. Reprinted 1995 by The Lawbook Exchange, Ltd. ISBN 1-886363-05-6. Cloth. $450.

Pothier,R.J. (1699-1772)]. *Treatise on the Contract of Sale.* Translated from the French by L.S. Cushing. Boston: Charles C. Little and James Brown, 1889. xvi, 406 pp. Reprinted 2000 by The Lawbook Exchange, Ltd. LCCN 99-10260. ISBN 1-886363-82-X. Cloth. $70.

Pothier, Robert Joseph [1699-1772]. *A Treatise on the Law of Obligations, or Contracts. Translated from the French, with an Introduction, Appendix, and Notes, Illustrative of the English Law on the Subject. By William David Evans.* London: A. Strahan, 1802. Two volumes. [1], 578, [1]; iv, 715, [1]pp. Reprint available August 2000 by The Lawbook Exchange, Ltd. LCCN 99-26397. ISBN 1-886363-98-6. Cloth. $195.

Pothier, Robert Joseph [1699-1772]. *A Treatise on Obligations, Considered in a Moral and Legal View. Translated from the French of Pothier. Translated by Francois-Xavier Martin.* Newburn, N.C.: Martin & Ogden, 1802. 2 vols. in 1 book. Reprinted 2000 by The Lawbook Exchange, Ltd. With a new introduction by Warren M. Billings. LCCN 98-38360. ISBN 1-886363-62-5. Cloth. $75.

Powell, Chilton Latham. *English Domestic Relations 1487-1653. A Study of Matrimony and Family Life in Theory and Practice as Revealed by the Literature, Law, and History of the Period.* New York: Columbia University Press, 1917. xii, 274 pp. Reprint available October 2000 by The Lawbook Exchange, Ltd. ISBN 1-58477-096-1. Cloth. $75.

Radin, Max. *Law as Logic and Experience.* New Haven: Yale University Press, 1940. ix, [1], 171 pp. Reprinted 2000 by The Lawbook Exchange, Ltd. LCCN 99-30670. ISBN 1-58477-008-2. Cloth. $55.

Rapalje, Stewart and Lawrence, Robert L. *A Dictionary of American and English Law with Definitions of the Technical Terms of the Canon and Civil Laws. Also, Containing a Full Collection of Latin Maxims, and Citations of Upwards of Forty Thousand Reported Cases, in which Words and Phrases Have Been Judicially Defined or Construed.* Jersey City: Frederick C. Linn & Co., 1888. Two volumes. xxxviii, 1380 pp. Reprinted 1997 by The Lawbook Exchange, Ltd. LCCN 97-38484. ISBN 1-886363-33-1. Cloth. $195.

Reeve, Tapping. [1744-1823]. *The Law of Baron and Femme, of Parent and Child, Guardian and Ward, Master and Servant, and of the Powers of the Courts of Chancery; with an Essay on the Terms Heir, Heirs, Heirs of the Body. Third Edition, With Notes and References to English and American Cases by Amasa J. Parker and Charles E. Baldwin, Counselors-At-Law.* Albany: William Gould, 1862. xlvi, 677pp. Reprinted 1998 by The Lawbook Exchange, Ltd. LCCN 98-36057. ISBN 1-886363-58-7. Cloth. $75.

Richards, John T. *Abraham Lincoln The Lawyer-Statesman.* Boston: Houghton Mifflin, 1916. Frontis. Illustrated. xii, 260 pp. Reprinted 1999 by The Lawbook Exchange, Ltd. LCCN 99-20587. ISBN 1-886363-94-3. Cloth. $60.

Roby, Henry John. *An Introduction to the Study of Justinian's Digest Containing an Account of its Composition and of the Jurists Used or Referred to Therein.* Cambridge: At the University Press, 1886. cclxxix pp. Reprint available July 2000 by The Lawbook Exchange, Ltd. ISBN 1-58477-073-2. Cloth. $65.

Roby, Henry John. *Roman Private Law in the Times of Cicero and of the Antonines.* Cambridge: At the University Press, 1902. Two volumes. xxxii, 543; xiii, [1], 560 pp. Reprint available July 2000 by The Lawbook Exchange, Ltd. ISBN 1-58477-074-0. Cloth. $180.

Sandys, Sir John Edwin. *Aristotle's Constitution of Athens. A Revised Text with an Introduction Critical and Explanatory Notes Testimonia and Indices. Second edition, Revised and Enlarged.* London: Macmillan & Co., Limited, 1902. xcii, 331 pp. Frontis. Illus. Reprint available December 2000 by The Lawbook Exchange, Ltd. LCCN 99-23952. ISBN 1-58477-004-X. Cloth. $75.

Schechter, Frank I. *The Historical Foundations of the Law Relating to Trade-Marks.* New York: Columbia University Press, 1925. xxviii, 211 pp. Reprinted 2000 by The Lawbook Exchange, Ltd. LCCN 99-41673. ISBN 1-58477-035-X. Cloth. $60.

Schroeder, Theodore. *Constitutional Free Speech Defined and Defended in an Unfinished Argument in a Case of Blasphemy.* New York: Free Speech League, 1919. 456 pp. Reprint available December 2000 by The Lawbook Exchange, Ltd. LCCN 99-049361. ISBN 1-58477-053-8. Cloth. $90.

Schroeder, Theodore. *Free Speech Bibliography Including Every Discovered Attitude Toward the Problem Covering Every Method of Transmitting Ideas and Abridging Their Promulgation upon Every Subject-Matter.* New York: The H.W. Wilson Company, 1922. 456 pp. Reprint available November 2000 by The Lawbook Exchange, Ltd. LCCN 99-049361. ISBN 1-58477-053-8. Cloth. $85.

Schulte, Joh. Friedrich von. *Die Geschichte der Quellen und Literatur der canonischen Rechts.* Stuttgart: Verlag von Ferdinand Enke, 1875. Three volumes. Reprint available August 2000 by The Lawbook Exchange, Ltd. LCCN 99-087494. ISBN 1-58477-089-9. Cloth. $225.

Schwartz, Bernard, editor. *The Code Napoleon and the Common-Law World. The Sesquicentennial Lectures Delivered at The Law Center of New York University December 13-15, 1954.* New York: New York University Press, 1956. x, 438pp. Reprinted 1998 by The Lawbook Exchange, Ltd. LCCN 98-34100. ISBN 1-886363-59-5. Cloth. $65.

Schwarz, Philip J. *Twice Condemned: Slaves and the Criminal Laws of Virginia, 1705-1865.* [Baton Rouge: Louisiana State University Press]. [1988]. xvi, 354pp. Reprinted 1998 by The Lawbook Exchange, Ltd. LCCN 98-4424 ISBN 1-886363-54-4. Cloth. $75.

Scott, Henry W. *The Courts of the State of New York: Their History, Development and Jurisdiction: Embracing a complete history of all the Courts and Tribunals of Justice, both Colonial and State, established from the first settlement of Manhattan Island and including the status and jurisdiction of all the Courts of the State as now constituted.* New York: Wilson Publishing Co., 1909. Reprint available December 2000 by The Lawbook Exchange, Ltd. LCCN 99-10259. ISBN 1-886363-84-6. Cloth. $95.

Scott, James Brown. *The Spanish Origin of International Law. Francisco De Vitoria and His Law of Nations.* London: Humphrey Milford, 1934. 19a, 288, clviii pp. Frontispiece and portrait. Reprint available August 2000 by The Lawbook Exchange, Ltd. LCCN 00-036835. ISBN 1-58477-110-0. Cloth. $90.

Sears, John H. *Trust Estates as Business Companies.* [*Second Edition*]. Kansas City, Mo.: Vernon Law Book Company, 1921. xx, 782 pp. [1921]. Reprinted 1998 by The Lawbook Exchange, Ltd. LCCN 97-32423 ISBN 1-886363-41-2. Cloth. $95.

Shumaker, Walter A. *The Cyclopedic Law Dictionary Comprising the Terms and Phrases of American Jurisprudence, Including Ancient and Modern Common Law, International Law, and Numerous Select Titles from the Civil Law, the French and the Spanish Law, etc., etc. with an Exhaustive Collection of Legal Maxims. Second Edition by James C. Cahill.* Chicago: Callaghan and Company, 1922. xii, 545 pp. Reprint available October 2000 by The Lawbook Exchange, Ltd. LCCN 99-16385. ISBN 1-58477-020-1. Cloth. $150.

[St. Germain, Christopher]. [1460-1540]. *The Doctor and Student or Dialogues Between a Doctor of Divinity and a Student in the Laws of England Containing the Grounds of Those Laws Together with Questions and Cases Concerning the Equity Thereof Revised and Corrected by William Muchall, Gent. to which are added two pieces concerning Suits in Chancery by Subpoena.* Cincinnati:Robert Clarke & Co., 1874. xiv, 401pp. Reprinted 1998 by The Lawbook Exchange, Ltd. LCCN 98-11338. ISBN 1-886363-49-8. Cloth. $65.

Stammler, Rudolph. *The Theory of Justice.* Translated by Isaak Husik. New York: The Macmillan Company, 1925. xli, 591 pp. Reprinted 2000 by The Lawbook Exchange, Ltd. LCCN 99-054019. ISBN 1-58477-066-X. Cloth. $95.

Stimson, Frederic Jesup. *Glossary of Technical Terms, Phrases, and Maxims of the Common Law.* Boston: Little, Brown, and Company, 1881. iv, 305pp. Reprinted 1999 by The Lawbook Exchange, Ltd. LCCN 98-50813. ISBN 1-886363-70-6. Cloth. $60.

Stimson, Frederic Jesup. *Popular Law-Making. A Study of the Origin, History, and Present Tendencies of Law-Making by Statute.* New York: Charles Scribner's Sons, 1910. xii, 545 pp. Reprint available December 2000 by The Lawbook Exchange, Ltd. LCCN 00-022513. ISBN 1-58477-094-5. Cloth. $85.

Stokes, I.N. Phelps. *The Iconography of Manhattan Island 1498-1909.* New York: Robert H. Dodd, 1915. Six volumes. Reprinted 1998 by The Lawbook Exchange, Ltd. LCCN 97-30604. ISBN 1-886363-30-7. Cloth. $750.

Stone, Harlan F. *Law and its Administration.* New York: Columbia University Press, 1915. vii, 232 pp. Reprint available December 2000 by The Lawbook Exchange, Ltd. LCCN 00-021508. ISBN 1-58477-093-5. Cloth. $70.

Story, Joseph. [1779-1845]. *A Familiar Exposition of the Constitution of the United States:* Containing a Brief Commentary on Every Clause, Explaining the True Nature, reasons, and Objects Thereof; Designed for the Use of School, Libraries and General Readers. With an Appendix, Containing Important Public Documents, Illustrative of the Constitution. New York: Harper & Brothers: 1865. 372 pp. Reprinted 1999 by The Lawbook Exchange, Ltd. LCCN 98-50811. ISBN 1-886363-71-4. Cloth. $60.

[Story, Joseph]. [1779-1845]. Story, William. *Life and Letters of Joseph Story, Associate Justice of the Supreme Court of the United States and Dane Professor of Law at Harvard University, edited by his son, William W. Story.* Boston: Charles C. Little and James Brown, 1851. Two volumes. xii, 574; viii, 676 pp. Frontispiece. Reprint available October 2000 by The Lawbook Exchange, Ltd. LCCN 99-058777. ISBN 1-58477-071-6. Cloth. $195.

[Story, Joseph]. Story, William W., ed. *The Miscellaneous Writings of Joseph Story, Associate Justice of the Supreme Court of the United States and Dane Professor of Law at Harvard University, edited by his son, William W. Story.* Boston: C.C. Little and J. Brown , 1852. x, 828 pp. Reprint available October 2000 by The Lawbook Exchange, Ltd. LCCN 99-058559. ISBN 1-58477-072-4. Cloth. $125.

Tayler, Thomas. *The Law Glossary: Being a Selection of the Greek, Latin, Saxon, French, Norman and Italian Sentences, Phrases, and Maxims, Found in the Leading English and American Reports, and Elementary Works.* New York: Lewis & Blood, 1856. 580 pp. Reprinted 1995 by The Lawbook Exchange, Ltd. ISBN 1-886363-12-9. Cloth. $65.

[Taylor, John]. [1753-1824]. *A Defence of the Measures of the Administration of Thomas Jefferson. By Curtius.* Washington: Samuel H. Smith, 1804. 136 pp. Reprinted 1999 by The Lawbook Exchange, Ltd. LCCN 99-24139. ISBN 1-886363-97-8. Cloth. $60.

Taylor, John. *Construction Construed and Constitutions Vindicated.* Richmond: printed by Shepherd & Pollard, 1820. iv, 344pp. Reprinted 1998 by The Lawbook Exchange, Ltd. LCCN 97-49411. ISBN 1-886363-43-9. Cloth. $65.

Taylor, John. *An Inquiry into the Principles and Policy of the Government of the United States.* Fredericksburg:Green and Cady, 1814. With an introduction by Roy Franklin Nichols, Yale University Press, 1950. 562pp. Reprinted 1998 by The Lawbook Exchange, Ltd. LCCN 98-11147. ISBN 1-886363-46-3. Cloth. $75.

Taylor, John, of Caroline. *New Views of the Constitution of the United States.* Washington City: Printed for the Author, 1823. [4], 316pp. Reprint available December 2000 by The Lawbook Exchange, Ltd. ISBN 1-58477-079-1. Cloth. $70.

Thomson, Richard. *An Historical Essay on the Magna Charta of King John: to which are added, the Great Charter in Latin and English, the charters of liberties and confirmations,* *granted by Henry III and Edward I, the original Charter of the forests, and various authentic instruments connected with them: Explanatory Notes on their Several Privileges; A Descriptive Account of the Principal Originals and Editions Extant, Both in Print and Manuscript; and Other Illustrations, Derived from the Most Interesting and Authentic Sources.* London: John Major and Robert Jennings, 1829. xxxii, 612 pp. Reprint available July 2000 by The Lawbook Exchange, Ltd. LCCN 99-40987. ISBN 1-58477-030-9. Cloth. $95.

Townsend, William H. *Lincoln the Litigant.* Boston: Houghton Mifflin Company, 1925. [ix], [117] pp. Frontis. Illus. Reprinted 2000 by The Lawbook Exchange, Ltd. LCCN 99-16499. ISBN 1-58477-021-X. Cloth. $60.

[Trials]. [Witchcraft Trials]. *Curious Cases and Amusing Actions at Law Including Some Trials of Witches in the Seventeenth Century.* Toronto: The Carswell Co., Limited, 1916. vii, 234 pp. Reprint available September 2000 by The Lawbook Exchange, Ltd. LCCN 99-032361. ISBN 1-58477-012-0. Cloth. $65.

Tucker, Henry St. George. *Commentaries on the Laws of Virginia. Comprising the Substance of a Course of Lectures Delivered to the Winchester Law School. With an Introduction by David Cobin and Paul Finkelman.* Richmond: Shepherd and Colin, 1846. Two volumes. 34, 468; 24, 512 pp. Reprinted 1998 by The Lawbook Exchange, Ltd. LCCN 97-10313. ISBN 1-886363-26-9. Cloth. $175.

Tucker, Henry St. George. *Limitations on the Treaty-Making Power Under the Constitution of the United States.* Boston: Little, Brown, and Company, 1915. xxi, 444 pp. Reprinted 2000 by The Lawbook Exchange, Ltd. LCCN 99-31589. ISBN 1-58477-015-5. Cloth. $75.

Tucker, St. George. *Blackstone's Commentaries. With Notes of Reference to the Constitution and Laws, of the Federal Government of the United States, and of the Commonwealth of Virginia. In Five Volumes, with an Appendix to Each volume, Containing Short Tracts upon Such Subjects As Appeared Necessary to Form a Connected View of the Laws of Virginia As a Member of the Federal Union.* Philadelphia: William Young Birch and Abraham Small, 1803. Five volumes. Reprinted 1996 by The Lawbook Exchange, Ltd. LCCN 96-12566. ISBN 1-886363-15-3. Cloth. $450.

[Twiss, Sir Travers]. *The Black Book of the Admiralty, with an Appendix.* Monumenta Juridica. Edited by Sir Travers Twiss. Four volumes. 4, xciii, 491, [2]; 4, lxxxvii, 500, 31; 4, lxxxvi, 673, [1], 31; 4, clii, 559, 32 pp. LCCN 97-38809 ISBN 1-886363-39-0. 1871. Reprinted 1998 by The Lawbook Exchange, Ltd. Cloth. $495.

[Upshur, Abel Parker]. *A Brief Enquiry Into the True Nature and Character of Our Federal Government, being a review of Judge Story's Commentaries on the Constitution of the United States. By a Virginian.* Petersburg: Printed by Edmund and Julian C. Ruffin, 1840. 132pp. Reprinted 1998 by The Lawbook Exchange, Ltd. LCCN 97-11151. ISBN 1-886363-44-7. Cloth. $45.

Valmaer. [pseud]. [Ream, Michael]. *Lawyer's Code of Ethics. A Satire.* St. Louis: The F.H. Thomas Law Book Co., 1887. 143 pp. Reprint available December 2000 by The Lawbook Exchange, Ltd. LCCN 00-021508. ISBN 1-58477-093-5. Cloth. $65.

Vinogradoff, Paul. *Custom and Right.* Oslo: H. Aschehoug, 1925. 110 pp. Reprint available December 2000 by The Lawbook Exchange, Ltd. LCCN 99-0474851. ISBN 1-58477-048-1. Cloth. $45.

Vinogradoff, Paul. *Roman Law in Mediaeval Europe.* London: Harper & Brothers, 1909. 136 pp. Reprint available September 2000 by The Lawbook Exchange, Ltd. LCCN 00-039068. ISBN 1-58477-109-7. Cloth. $65.

Vinogradoff, Sir Paul. *Outlines of Historical Jurisprudence.* London: Oxford University Press, 1920. Two volumes. 428; x, 315 pp. Reprinted 1999 by The Lawbook Exchange, Ltd. LCCN 98-42298. ISBN 1-886363-64-1. Cloth. $150.

Walker, James. *The Theory of the Common Law.* Boston: Little, Brown and Co., 1852. xxiv, 130pp. Reprinted 1998 by The Lawbook Exchange, Ltd. LCCN 98-9522. ISBN 1-886363-45-5. Cloth. $65.

Warren, Charles. *History of the Harvard Law School and of Early Legal Conditions in America.* New York: Lewis Publishing Company, 1908. Three volumes. xiv, 543; iv, 560; 397 pp. Illustrated. Reprinted 1999 by The Lawbook Exchange, Ltd. LCCN 99-29193. ISBN 1-58477-006-6. Cloth. $275.

White, Edw. J. *The Law in Scriptures. With Explanations of the Law Terms and Legal References in Both the Old and the New Testaments.* St. Louis: Thomas Law Book Company, 1935. xxiv, 422 pp. Reprint available June 2000 by The Lawbook Exchange, Ltd. LCCN 99-059102. ISBN 1-58477-076-7. Cloth. $80.

Whiting, William. *War Powers under the Constitution of the United States. Tenth edition.* Boston: Little, Brown, and Company, 1864. xvii, 342 pp. Reprint available September 2000 by The Lawbook Exchange, Ltd. LCCN 99-049360. ISBN 1-58477-055-4. Cloth. $80.

Whitney, Henry C. *Life on the Circuit with Lincoln. With Sketches of Generals Grant, Sherman and McClellan, Judge Davis, Leonard Swett, and Other Contemporaries.* Illustrated. Boston: Estes & Lauriat, 1892. viii, 601 pp. Reprint available October 2000 by The Lawbook Exchange, Ltd. ISBN 1-58477-115-1. Cloth. $110.

Wiener, Leo. [1862-1939]. *Commentary to the Germanic Laws and Mediaeval Documents.* Cambridge: Harvard University Press, 1915. lxi, 224 pp. Reprinted 2000 by The Lawbook Exchange, Ltd. LCCN 99-23969. ISBN 1-58477-005-8. Cloth. $60.

Woodbine, George E. *Four Thirteenth Century Law Tracts. A Thesis Presented to the Faculty of the Graduate School of Yale University in Candidacy for the Degree of Doctor of Philosophy.* New Haven: Yale University Press, 1910. vi, 183 pp. Reprinted 1999 by The Lawbook Exchange, Ltd. LCCN 99-29294. ISBN 1-58477-007-4. Cloth. $50.

Woolsey, Theodore D. *Divorce and Divorce Legislation, Especially in the United States. Second Edition Revised.* New York: Charles Scribner's Sons, 1882. x, [9]-328 pp. Reprint available December 2000 by The Lawbook Exchange, Ltd. ISBN 1-58477-118-6. Cloth. $75.

[Worrall, John and Edward Brooke]. *Bibliotheca Legum Angliae. Or, a Catalogue of the Common and Statute Law Books of This Realm, and Some Others Relating Thereto: Giving an Account of Their Several Editions, Ancient Printers, Dates, and Prices, and Wherein They Differ. [With a Supplement to 1800]. Part I Compiled by John Worrall, Part II and Supplement Compiled by Edward Brooke. Parts I, II and Supplement bound in one volume.* London: Printed for Edward Brooke, 1788-1800. 316; 264; 48 pp. 1788-1800. Reprinted 1997 by The Lawbook Exchange, Ltd. LCCN 97-12962. ISBN 1-886363-29-3. Cloth. $110.

Wright, John S. *Citizenship Sovereignty.* Chicago: Published for American Citizens, the True Maintainers of State Sovereignty, 1864. Reprinted 1998 by The Lawbook Exchange, Ltd. LCCN 98-15940 ISBN 1-886363-55-2. Cloth. $65.